P9-CRF-379

H-WESTERN
GE Learning™

mination, **Fourth Edition**

Albrecht
Albrecht
Albrecht
Zimbelman

al Director: Jack W. Calhoun

Chief: Rob Dewey

itions Editor: Matt Filimonov

Developmental Editor: Julie

Assistant: Ann Mazzaro

Manager: Natalie Livingston

Coordinator: Nicole Parsons

roject Management:
Global

acturing Buyer: Doug Wilke

House/Compositor:
Global

ector: Stacy Shirley

quisition Director: Audrey

esign: PreMediaGlobal

ign: Mike Stratton

ge: iStock Photo

For product information and technology assistance, contact us at
Cengage Learning Customer & Sales Support, 1-800-354-9706.

For permission to use material from this text or product,
submit all requests online at **www.cengage.com/permissions**
Further permissions questions can be e-mailed to
permissionrequest@cengage.com

Library of Congress Control Number: 2010940986

ISBN-13: 978-0-538-47084-1

ISBN-10: 0-538-47084-4

South-Western
5191 Natorp Boulevard
Mason, OH
USA

Cengage Learning is a leading provider of customized learning solutions with office locations around the globe, including Singapore, the United Kingdom, Australia, Mexico, Brazil, and Japan. Locate your local office at: **international.cengage.com/region**

Cengage Learning products are represented in Canada by Nelson Education, Ltd.

To learn more about South-Western, visit
www.cengage.com/South-Western

Purchase any of our products at your local college store or at our preferred online store **www.cengagebrain.com**

e United States of America
7 15 14 13 12

Fraud Examination

FOURTH EDITION

W. STEVE ALBRECHT

Brigham Young University

CHAD O. ALBRECHT

Utah State University

CONAN C. ALBRECHT

Brigham Young University

MARK F. ZIMBELMAN

Brigham Young University

SOUTH-WESTERN
CENGAGE Learning™

Australia • Brazil • Japan • Korea • Mexico • Singapore • Spain • United Kingdom • United States

To LeAnn, Jenny, Laurel, and Karen

Brief Contents

Contents

PART 5   Management Fraud

About the Authors

W. Steve Albrecht is a professor of Accountancy in the Marriott School of Management and Andersen Alumni Professor at Brigham Young University. Dr. Albrecht, a certified public accountant (CPA), certified fraud examiner (CFE), and certified internal auditor (CIA), came to BYU in 1977 after teaching at Stanford and at the University of Illinois. He served as both associate dean of the Marriott School and as the director of the School of Accountancy and Information Systems at BYU.

Dr. Albrecht received a bachelor's degree in accounting from Brigham Young University and his MBA and PhD degrees from the University of Wisconsin. He is past President of the American Accounting Association, the Association of Certified Fraud Examiners (ACFE), and Beta Alpha Psi. He was a former member of the Board of Regents of the Institute of Internal Auditors and served on the task force of the AICPA that wrote SAS 82, a fraud auditing standard, and on the FASAC, an advisory committee to the FASB. He was a member of the Committee of Sponsoring Organizations (COSO) from 1997 to 2000 and the AICPA Council from 2000 to 2003 and was chair of the AICPA's Pre-Certification Executive Education Committee from 2002 to 2004. He previously served as a trustee of the Financial Accounting Foundation that oversees the FASB and GASB. Dr. Albrecht has done extensive research on business fraud. His research has resulted in the publication of over one hundred articles in professional and academic journals. He is the author or co-author of over 20 books or monographs, several of which are on fraud. His financial and principles of accounting textbooks are in their 11th editions. In 1997, 2001, 2002 and 2003, and 2004 he was chosen as one of the 100 most influential accounting professionals in the United States by *Accounting Today* magazine. Because of his extensive work with the ACFE, one of the headquarters buildings in Austin, Texas is named after him.

Dr. Albrecht has consulted with numerous organizations, including Fortune 500 companies, major financial institutions, the United Nations, FBI, and other organizations, and has been an expert witness in some of the largest fraud cases in America. He currently serves on the audit committees and boards of directors of two public companies.

Chad O. Albrecht is an assistant professor at the Jon M. Huntsman School of Business at Utah State University. Chad has taught forensic accounting and fraud investigation at various schools both in Europe and the United States.

Chad's research focuses on international fraud and corruption. This research addresses how fraud is perceived and perpetrated across cultures. Chad's research has been published in the *Journal of Business Ethics, Business and Society, Internal Auditing, Corporate Finance Review, Cross Cultural Management: An International Journal* and the *International Journal of Human Resource Management* among others. Chad's research has been reporting in various news outlets including the prestigious *Times of London*. Before pursuing doctoral studies Chad worked as a licensed stockbroker for The Harris, a subsidiary of the Bank of Montreal.

Chad received his bachelor's degree in accounting at Brigham Young University and his Ph.D. from ESADE Business School in Barcelona, Spain. *The Wall Street Journal, Business Week* and *The Financial Times* consistently rank ESADE as one of the top 20 business schools in the world.

Conan C. Albrecht is an associate professor of Information Systems at Brigham Young University. He teaches classes in enterprise development, computer-aided fraud detection, and business programming. Dr. Albrecht researches computer-based fraud detection techniques and online group dynamics. He has published articles on fraud detection and information theory in *The Journal of Forensic Accounting, The Journal of Accountancy, The Communications of the ACM, Decision Support Systems, Information and Management,* and other academic and professional outlets.

Dr. Albrecht received a bachelor's and master's degree in accounting from Brigham Young University and his Ph.D. in information systems from the University of Arizona. Dr. Albrecht is currently working on an open source framework for computer-based fraud detection. The core of this research is detectlets, which encode background and detection information for specific fraud schemes. In the next few years, he hopes the system will serve as the foundation of a large, online repository of detectlets about all types of fraud.

Mark F. Zimbelman is a professor and the Selvoy J. Boyer Fellow at Brigham Young University's (BYU) School of Accountancy. He teaches classes on auditing and fraud examination and focuses his research on auditors' detection of financial statement fraud. His research has been published in numerous academic journals including *Journal of Accounting Research, The Accounting Review, Journal of Accounting Literature, Organizational Behavior and Human Decision Processes, Auditing: A Journal of Practice and Theory, Contemporary Accounting Research* and *Accounting Horizons*.

Dr. Zimbelman received his doctorate in 1996 from the University of Arizona where he completed his dissertation on SAS 82. A paper from his dissertation was honored to be one of six that were presented at the 1997 *Journal of Accounting Research* Conference at the University of Chicago. In 1999, he returned to that conference to present another paper on fraud. In addition to his academic research on fraud, Dr. Zimbelman has worked with the American Institute of Certified Public Accountants and the Institute of Internal Auditors in writing various publications on fraud.

After graduating from BYU's accounting program in 1984, Dr. Zimbelman received his CPA license and worked for over six years as a financial statement auditor and, later, as a controller in industry. After getting his Ph.D. and working for three years at the University of Oklahoma, he returned to BYU in 1999. In 2005, he took a leave of absence to work with KPMG in their fraud and forensics practice. This opportunity gave him hands on experience investigating violations of the Foreign Corrupt Practices Act, financial statement fraud, vendor fraud and embezzlement.

Foreword

According to the Association of Certified Fraud Examiners' 2010 Report to the Nations on Occupational Fraud and Abuse, certified fraud examiners estimate that organizations lose, on average, about 5 percent of their revenues to dishonesty from within.

If multiplied by the estimated Gross World Product, the cost of occupational fraud and abuse may run a staggering $2.9 trillion annually. By the breadth of the definition, it covers all corporate dishonesty—from the mailroom to the boardroom. While executives are "cooking" the company's earnings to show better profits, purchasing agents are getting kickbacks from suppliers, and employees are embezzling money to improve their lifestyles.

Knowing how much fraud actually costs is an impossible task. The cases we know about only represent the tip of the iceberg; those discovered tend to be greedy or careless. Executives and employees who are neither may well commit fraud throughout their entire careers and get away with it.

The huge cost of occupational fraud begs an obvious question: Why does it occur? The answers aren't always easy. Although the simple explanation is greed—a natural human trait—even greedy people don't always lie, cheat, and steal. A more complete answer for corporate dishonesty involves three factors: the individual, the workplace, and society.

Individuals likely to commit occupational fraud are often on the financial ropes. This can occur when people spend more money than they make or when there is a personal financial crisis demanding immediate resolution. Although many of us have had such difficult situations, dishonest employees are more likely to salve their consciences with rationalizations that justify fraud. In short, they lack the convictions of their own ethics.

Workplace environments also contribute to occupational fraud. Organizations that are viewed by employees as uncaring, stingy, or dishonest can run a much higher risk of being victimized from within. Many workers—in an attempt to right what they consider to be corporate wrongs—may address these perceived injustices in a variety of ways: goldbricking, excessive absences, pilferage, and dishonesty.

Moreover, some entities unwittingly contribute to the problem. By failing to establish reasonable workplace conditions, safeguards, and controls, companies might make fraud too easy, and thus too tempting. Organizations have a duty to help keep the workforce honest. Societal conditions also influence the rate of occupational fraud. If dishonesty is easily accepted and goes largely unpunished, we can only expect it to thrive.

It was my own search for answers to occupational fraud twenty years ago that led me to W. Steve Albrecht. In the early 1980s, after ten years with the FBI, I practiced as a fraud examiner. Increasingly, my corporate clients were referring me cases of embezzlement, corruption, and other misdeeds.

One client, certainly on the cutting-edge at the time, wanted help in developing an antifraud program. That request led me to the vast libraries of the University of Texas at Austin, where I discovered one of Dr. Albrecht's first published works on the subject, *Deterring Fraud: The Internal Auditor's Perspective.*

After reading this seminal research by Steve and his colleagues, I sought him out personally. Even though Steve had never heard my name, he graciously invited me to Brigham Young University, where he was teaching. Dr. Albrecht answered my questions and volunteered his valuable time to aid on the topic of occupational fraud. After that, we've always stayed in touch.

Neither of us then could have imagined the paths our lives would take together. In 1988, Steve was a major influence in encouraging me to start the Association of Certified Fraud Examiners, and he served with distinction as its first president.

Since that time, the ACFE has grown to the world's largest antifraud organization with nearly 60,000 members in over 140 countries. Steve's lifetime of contributions to the field of fraud detection and deterrence simply cannot be overstated. The ACFE recognized the enormity of Dr. Albrecht's body of work in 1998 when it honored him with its most valued prize: the Cressey Award.

However, the many awards Steve has received do not capture the kind of man he is. A devoted father and husband, Steve lives his life by high example. Regardless of his many accomplishments, you won't hear about them from him; humility is one of his most endearing traits. I have had the pleasure of meeting the co-authors, Conan and Chad Albrecht, two of Dr. Albrecht's sons. There is no question that they will carry on his work. I am proud to call Steve my great friend.

Steve and I are of a common mind when it comes to fraud. First, the accounting community, which has the lion's share of responsibility to control occupational fraud, is ill-equipped for the job. Second, education is the cornerstone to preventing fraud. The more we know, the less likely we are to become victims.

The terms "fraud examination" and "forensic accounting" are often used interchangeably. However, they refer to different but overlapping concepts. The latter phrase, although highly popular as a euphemism for fraud investigation, actually refers to any kind of accounting work done for litigation purposes.

According to the *Fraud Examiners Manual*, fraud examination is a methodology for resolving allegations of fraud from inception to disposition. The process involves gathering evidence, taking statements, writing reports, and assisting in the detection and deterrence of fraud. Although many organizations employ fraud examiners, audit professionals and others also conduct fraud examinations on a limited, as-needed basis. The fraud examination field draws its common body of knowledge from four areas: accounting and auditing, fraud investigation techniques, the legal elements of fraud, and criminology and ethics. Steve's work in helping define this field was indispensable.

For accountants, antifraud education has been practically nonexistent for decades. One of the main reasons has been the lack of authoritative texts on the subject. Educators and students alike will find *Fraud Examination* to be a solution. Packed full of real examples, thought-provoking discussion issues and questions, this book is ideal for both undergraduate and graduate students.

Moreover, practitioners will find a great deal of guidance in resolving current cases. Managers and executives will benefit from understanding the myriad of issues that can assist them in deterring occupational fraud. And for all of us, *Fraud Examination* is simply a wonderfully engaging read.

Dr. Joseph T. Wells, CFE, CPA
Chairman of the Board of Directors
The Association of Certified Fraud Examiners
Austin, Texas
jwells@acfe.com
http://www.acfe.com/home.asp

Preface

Fraud examination (sometimes called forensic accounting) is one of the most exciting careers for students studying accounting and business today. The AICPA has called forensic accounting one of the hot new "sizzling" career areas in accounting. It is estimated that there will be a shortage of between 25,000 and 50,000 security professionals in the next few years in the United States. Exciting opportunities for accounting and business students who become knowledgeable in fraud prevention, detection, and investigation abound in various federal agencies, such as the FBI and Postal Inspectors, major corporations, and professional service and consulting firms. Both the size and the number of frauds are increasing, which will result in an even greater demand for fraud-fighting professionals in the future.

You've probably heard about Enron, World-Com, Madoff, and other major frauds. But, there are many other types of frauds that occur every day. Fraud is an extremely costly business problem. For example, not long ago a Fortune 500 automaker experienced a $436 million fraud. Because the fraud reduced the company's net income by $436 million from what it would have been and because the company had a profit margin (net income divided by net sales) of approximately 10 percent, the company would have to generate an additional $4.36 billion (10 times the amount lost in the fraud) in revenues to restore net income to its pre-fraud level. If you assume that an average car sells for $30,000, this company would have to make and sell over 145,000 additional cars ($4.36 billion divided by $30,000 sales price) to recover the effect on net income. In other words, this company faced a major business problem: it could either make and sell 145,000 more cars, or it could work hard to prevent these types of frauds from occurring in the future. When faced with the choice of generating that much additional revenue—which would have been difficult if not impossible—the company decided that reducing and eliminating future frauds was the more effective way to spend its money. As a result, it hired additional fraud and control experts and implemented extensive fraud prevention procedures throughout the organization. Eliminating fraud is a problem that every organization faces, and you can help them deal with this growing problem.

Even if you decide not to become a fraud expert, the topics you will study in this book will help you be a better professional in whatever career path you choose. The technology, interviewing, document examination, public records, and other tools and knowledge you will gain will make you a better consultant, auditor, tax professional, or manager, as well as a better and more astute investor.

As you will discover in this book, there is a very active professional organization that deals with fighting fraud called the Association of Certified Fraud Examiners (ACFE), which currently has over 40,000 members and is based in Austin, Texas. This organization, as well as others, can provide future fraud training. In addition, the ACFE will provide its educational materials free of charge to institutions of higher learning that agree to offer a three-hour course entitled "Fraud Examination." These materials include several original videos related to fraud detection and prevention. A complete listing of the ACFE's materials and other information can be found at the Association's Web site at www.acfe.com.

New To This Edition

For our fourth edition, we have added enhancements and updates that will help you better understand the significance of fraud in the modern business world. In this revision, there has been a significant amount of changes to each chapter:

- *In Part 1 of the textbook, we introduce students to new frauds such as the Madoff Scandal in Chapter 1. All chapters in Part 1 have introduced new references, inserted additional learning objectives, updated all statistics (including information about the COSO report in Chapter 2), added a new section on the ACFE, added additional end-of-chapter questions, and overall increased readability and layout of each chapter in the first part of the book. Also, the Red Hat section in Chapter 3 has been moved to create Appendix A.*
- *Part 2 and Part 3 of the textbook also contains new learning objectives, new references, new statistics and increased readability and layout of the chapters. Chapter 6 contains new updates to reflect the current state of technology and software packages. The technology assignments in Chapter 6 have been revised to be compatible with the student version of ACL.*
- *Chapters 7–10 in Part 4 contain information on the most recent software for detecting fraud, updates to the public record search sites, and we updated the FBI information with the most recent data available. All chapters have also undergone significant changes to certain sections to improve readability. As with the previous chapters, additional end-of-chapter questions and references have also been added.*
- *Part 5 contains new cases and has changed the main fraud case from Rite Aid to Enron in order to present students with a more widely-known financial statement fraud case. It also contains a discussion of the subprime lending crisis, Lehman Brothers and the Satyam frauds and provides more current evidence of the problem of financial statement fraud. Chapter 17 contains new examples from recent events and surveys. This chapter also discusses changes in technology which present new challenges to fraud detection and prevention. New cases help students familiar with mobile platforms and social networks see fraud from these perspectives.*

- *Overall, the textbook contains several new cases that detail recent frauds and many of the former cases were re-worked in order to make them more understandable for students.*

Featured Topics by Chapter

In this book, we cover seven different topics:

- *Part 1, comprising Chapters 1, 2, and 3, provides an introduction to fraud and an overview of the fraud problem. Chapter 1 discusses the nature of fraud, Chapter 2 describes fraud perpetrators and their motivations for being dishonest, and Chapter 3 provides an overview of the different ways to fight and, hopefully, reduce fraud.*
- *The second and third parts of the book focus on fraud prevention (Chapter 4) and fraud detection (Chapters 5 and 6.) Chapter 5 provides an overview of and discusses traditional fraud detection methods, while Chapter 6 introduces you to the use of technology to proactively detect fraud.*
- *Part 4 covers the various elements of fraud investigation. In Chapter 7, we cover theft act investigation methods; in Chapter 8, we cover concealment investigation methods; in Chapter 9, we discuss conversion investigative methods; and in Chapter 10, we cover various types of interviewing and other query approaches to investigating fraud. The interview techniques you learn in Chapter 10 will make you a more discerning husband or wife, parent, manager, employee, or friend.*
- *Parts 5 and 6 discuss the various types of fraud. In Part 5, we include three chapters on management, or financial statement, fraud. In Chapter 11, we provide an overview of financial statement fraud and introduce a proactive model for detecting fraud and errors in the financial statements. In Chapter 12, we discuss both revenue- and inventory-related frauds, the two most common ways to intentionally misstate financial statements. In Chapter 13, we discuss three other types of financial statement frauds: understating liabilities and expenses, overstating assets, and inadequate*

disclosures. These chapters will help you better understand and critique the financial statements of any organization.

- *In Part 6, we discuss four other types of fraud. Chapter 14 covers fraud committed against organizations by employees, vendors, and customers. Chapter 15 covers consumer fraud, a chapter that will have immediate relevance to you and will alert you to the fraud exposures you face every day. Chapter 16 introduces divorce, tax and bankruptcy fraud, all of which are very common because people often try to hide assets from those who want to take them away—the government in the case of taxes and others in the cases of divorce and bankruptcy. Chapter 16 also covers money laundering frauds. Chapter 17 discusses e-Business frauds, a growing type of fraud problem because of the increasing use of the Internet to conduct business.*

- *The final part in the book—Chapter 18—discusses options that victims have when deciding how to follow-up on frauds they experience. This chapter provides an overview of the criminal and civil statutes governing fraud legal proceedings and helps you understand the various ways organizations have to resolve dishonest acts.*

We realize that there are many other fraud-related topics that we could have included. We have tried to strike a balance between brevity and topics of general interest and detailed investigation and specific knowledge that experienced professional fraud examiners would need. We also realize that, for most of you, this book will be used in the only fraud-related course you will take in your college studies. We are certain, however, that studying fraud will be one of your most exciting courses and will spark an interest that will stimulate career-changing plans for many of you. At a minimum, after studying fraud examination, you should be a much more careful investor and business decision maker. You will never view business transactions or reports the same way, and you will be a much more careful and skeptical observer and participant in future endeavors.

We are excited to share this exciting topic with you. We wish you success and enthusiasm as you study this book, and we welcome suggestions for improvement.

W. Steve Albrecht, Ph.D., CFE, CPA, CIA
Chad O. Albrecht, D.E.A.[1]
Conan C. Albrecht, Ph.D.
Mark F. Zimbelman, Ph.D.

---

[1]D.E.A.—Diploma de Estudios Advanzados or First Doctoral Degree. The D.E.A. is similar to the British Master of Philosophy or the French Diploma D'etudes Approfondies.

Acknowledgements

Several reviewers and supplemental preparers provided valuable comments that aided in the development of the 4th edition of this book. They were:

Carla Allen
Northwood University

Sandra Augustine
Hilbert College

Lisa Banks
Mott Community College

Thane E. S. Butt
Champlain College

Linda Christiansen
Indiana University Southeast

Sandra S. Lang
McKendree University

Janice Lawrence
University of Nebraska-Lincoln

Erik Lindquist, CFE
Lansing Community College

Jill Christopher
Ohio Northern University

LuAnn Bean
Florida Institute of Technology

Rodney R. Michael
University of North Texas

David A. O'Dell
McPherson College

Susan E. Wright
DeKalb Technical College

We are very grateful for the help of many other individuals who made this book possible. Beyond the official reviewers mentioned above, professors and students from around the world sent us ideas, comments, and errors, and we appreciated the feedback. We appreciate the talented word processing help of many several secretaries and assistants at BYU. We appreciate the able and talented editing of Matt Filimonov, Julie Warwick, Jean Buttrom of Cengage South-Western as well as Divya Divakaran of PreMediaGlobal. We also appreciate Brigham Young University for its support and for providing an environment of stimulation and challenge. Joseph T. Wells, Chairman of the Association of Certified Fraud Examiners (ACFE), has been inspiring and helpful in many ways. In this area of fraud examination, he has been our closest and most supportive friend. He and the ACFE have made their materials available to us in writing this book and, through their generous offer to support fraud education, will make their videos and other materials available to professors. Joseph Wells, through his work with the ACFE, has done more to fight fraud in the United States and the world than any other person we know. We also appreciate the help of valuable colleagues with whom we have collaborated previously. Gerald W. Wernz and Timothy L. Williams were co-authors on a previous book and several academic articles from which many ideas for this book were taken. Joe Brazel, Gregory J. Dunn, Vicky Hoffman, Keith Jones, William Waller, and Jeff Wilks have been co-authors on journal articles from which ideas have been taken as well. We are also grateful to the many law firms, professional service firms, corporations, and government organizations that have provided us with consulting and expert witnessing opportunities to enrich our fraud experience and background.

Introduction to Fraud

CHAPTER **1**

The Nature of Fraud

LEARNING OBJECTIVES

After studying this chapter, you should be able to:

- Understand the seriousness of fraud and how fraud affects individuals, consumers, organizations, and society.

- Define fraud.

- Understand the different types of fraud.

- Understand the difference between fraud committed *against an* organization and fraud committed *on behalf* of an organization.

- Understand the difference between criminal and civil fraud laws.

- Understand the types of fraud-fighting careers available today.

TO THE STUDENT

With this chapter, you are embarking on an exciting journey of the study of fraud. Many of you will find this course more interesting than any other course you have taken before. Chapter 1 will provide an overview of fraud—what is fraud, how serious is the problem, fraud-fighting careers, criminal and civil laws, and other overview topics.

On December 11, 2008 the Federal Bureau of Investigation (FBI) arrested Bernard "Bernie" Madoff for perpetrating the single largest investment fraud in the history of the world. A day earlier, Madoff's own sons had turned him in, reporting to authorities that Madoff's wealth management business was not a legitimate business but was a shell company for a large scam. While the actual amounts of the fraud are still not known, estimates suggest that the amount missing from client accounts, including fabricated gains, may be as much as \$65 billion.[1]

Madoff was born in Queens, New York, and later graduated from Hofstra College in 1960. After college he dedicated himself to building his firm, Bernard L. Madoff Investment Securities, where he remained until his arrest in 2008. Throughout his career, Madoff became one of the most respected and trusted individuals on Wall Street, serving both as Chairman of the Board of Directors and on the Board of Governors of the NASD (National Association of Securities Dealers). Madoff was also actively engaged in creating the technology that eventually became the NASDAQ stock exchange.

Madoff perpetrated his scheme by consistently providing high returns for his investors. Madoff claimed that he was able to provide such returns by investing in what is known as a split-strike conversion strategy. A split-strike conversion strategy is a complicated investment where investors take a long position in equities together with a short call and a long put on an equity index to lower the volatility of the position.[2] While the entire split-strike conversion strategy may seem very elaborate, the strategy was nothing more than a tool employed by Madoff to attract additional investors to his large Ponzi scheme.

A Ponzi scheme is a type of fraud that lures investment funds from victims and then pays those victims a premium or interest from money that is paid by subsequent investors.[3] Without intervention, Ponzi schemes will continue to grow until new recruits become unavailable, at which time, the scam is broken down and discovered.

Individuals throughout the world lost money in Madoff's pyramid scheme.[4] While many of the victims were blue-collared workers that came from humble backgrounds, others were extremely wealthy. For example, Prince Michel of Yugoslavia traveled across Europe to raise money for Madoff. Other victims included various royal families and even London's House of Lords. Actor Kevin Bacon and producer Steven Spielberg, as well as various other Hollywood movie stars had invested with Madoff. Because Madoff had connections to the Jewish community, many Jewish charities and institutions lost a significant amount of money in the scam.[5]

Seriousness of the Fraud Problem

Bernard Madoff is an example of an individual who misrepresented himself and his company to commit fraud. Investment fraud, like the fraud committed by Bernard Madoff, is just one of the many types of frauds that present major problems for businesses and consumers throughout the world.

Although most people and even most researchers believe that fraud is increasing both in size and frequency, it is difficult to know for sure.[6] First, it is impossible to know what percentage of fraud **perpetrators** are caught. Are there perfect frauds that are never detected, or are all frauds eventually discovered? In addition, many frauds that are detected are quietly handled by the victims and never made public. In many cases of employee fraud, for example, companies merely hide the frauds and quietly terminate or transfer perpetrators rather than make the frauds public. Companies and individuals who have been defrauded are often more concerned about the embarrassment of making frauds public, and the costs of investigating fraud, than they are about seeking justice and punishing fraud perpetrators.

Statistics on how much fraud is occurring, whether it is increasing or decreasing, and how much the average fraud costs come from four basic sources.

1. Government agencies—Agencies such as the FBI, FDIC, IRS, and various health agencies publish fraud statistics from time to time, but these organizations only publish those statistics that are directly related to their **jurisdiction**. As a result, their statistics are not complete, and do not provide a total picture of fraud—even in the areas for which they have responsibility.
2. Researchers—Researchers often conduct studies about particular types of fraud within certain industries. Unfortunately, data on actual frauds are hard to obtain and, as a result, most research only provides small insights into the magnitude of the problem, even in the specific areas being studied. Comprehensive research on the occurrence of fraud is rare and is not always based on sound scientific approaches.
3. Insurance companies—Insurance companies often provide fidelity bonding or other types of coverage against employee and other fraud. When fraud occurs, they undertake investigations and, as a result, collect some fraud statistics. Generally, however, their statistics relate only to actual cases where they provided employee bonding or other insurance. At best, their analysis of the problem is incomplete.
4. Victims of fraud—Sometimes we learn about fraud from those who have been **victims**. In almost all industries, there is no organized way for victims to report fraud and, even if there were, many companies would choose not to make their fraud losses public.

The **Association of Certified Fraud Examiners (ACFE)** regularly conducts one of the most comprehensive fraud studies in the United States. First conducted in 1996 and then conducted again in 2002, 2004, 2006, and 2008, the ACFE study, also known as the *Report to the Nation on Occupational Fraud & Abuse*, is based on actual fraud cases reported by certified fraud examiners (CFEs) who investigate the frauds.

The 2008 study estimates that U.S. organizations lose roughly 7 percent of their annual revenues to fraud. Applied to the 2008 U.S. gross domestic product (GDP), this 7 percent figure would translate to approximately $994 billion in fraud losses—in the United States alone.

Even with the difficulties in measuring fraud, most people believe that fraud is a growing problem. Both the numbers of frauds committed and the total dollar amounts lost to fraud seem to be increasing.[7] In the past few years alone, we have seen huge frauds both in the form of the largest-ever investment scam committed by Bernard Madoff as well as the massive frauds in the mortgage and insurance industries that contributed to the world's economic decline.[8]

Because fraud affects how much we pay for goods and services, each of us pays not only a portion of the fraud bill but also for the detection and investigation of fraud. It is almost impossible to read a newspaper or business magazine without coming across multiple incidents of fraud.

Even more alarming than the increased number of fraud cases is the size of discovered frauds. In earlier times, if a perpetrator wanted to steal from his or her employer, he or she had to physically remove the assets from the business premise. Because of fear of being caught with the goods, frauds tended to be small. With the advent of computers, the Internet, and complex accounting systems, perpetrators now need only to make a telephone call, misdirect purchase invoices, bribe a supplier, manipulate a computer program, or simply push a key on the keyboard to misplace company assets.[9] Because physical possession of stolen property is no longer required and because it is just as easy to program a computer to embezzle $1 million as it is $1,000, the size and number of frauds have increased tremendously.

In addition, as companies have given in to the pressures to meet Wall Street's earnings expectations and as these pressures to "meet the numbers" have intensified, some very large financial statement frauds have been committed. Hundred million- or even billion-dollar frauds are not unusual and, in some cases, the decline in market value of the company's stock has been in the billions of dollars.

To understand how costly fraud is to organizations, consider what happens when fraud is committed against a company. Losses incurred from fraud reduce a firm's income on a dollar-for-dollar basis. This means that for every $1 of fraud, **net income** is reduced by $1. Since fraud reduces net income, it takes significantly more **revenue** to recover the effect of the fraud on net income. To illustrate, consider the $436 million fraud loss that a large U.S. automobile manufacturer experienced a few years ago.[10] If the automobile manufacturer's **profit margin** (net income divided by revenues) at the time was 10 percent, the company would have to generate up to $4.36 billion in additional revenue (or 10 times the amount of the fraud) to restore the effect on net income. If we assume an average selling price of $20,000 per car, the company must make and sell an additional 218,000 cars. Considered this way, fighting fraud is serious business. The automobile company can spend its efforts manufacturing and marketing additional new cars, or reducing fraud, or a combination of both.

As another example, consider the case of a large bank that was the victim of several frauds that totaled approximately $100 million in one year alone. With a profit margin of 5 percent, and assuming that the bank made $100 per checking account per year, how many new checking accounts must the bank generate to compensate for the fraud losses? The answer, of course, is up to 20 million new checking accounts ($100 million fraud loss/0.05 = $2 billion in additional revenues; $2 billion/$100 per account = 20 million new accounts).

Firms are not the only victims of fraud. In the aggregate, national economies also suffer from large-scale fraud and corruption. If we use the logic described in the case of the automobile manufacturer described earlier, we can better understand how, from a macro-level, countries suffer from fraud. Take, for example, three different economies. If Economy A, whose profit margin is 10 percent, loses $500 million to fraud, it must generate $5 billion of additional revenue to offset the loss to net income. If Economy B, whose profit margin is also 10 percent, loses $200 million to fraud, it must generate $2 billion. Finally, if Economy C, whose profit margin is 5 percent, loses $100 million to fraud, it must also generate $2 billion. The strain fraud imposes on economies throughout the world is tremendous. If just one fraud is prevented, billions of dollars can be saved—resources that can be reinvested in building the economy. Given this analysis, it is easy to see how difficult it is for countries with high amounts of corruption to ever compete with countries with low rates of corruption. High-corruption countries are constantly trying to overcome fraud losses, while low-corruption countries are growing and moving ahead. As a result, many honest economists, politicians, and regulators spend a considerable amount of time and resources trying to reduce fraud.

In addition to the actual reduction of a country's total GDP, the amount of fraud an economy suffers has a big impact on how willing investors are to invest in a given economy. When organizations commit fraud, for example, investors lose confidence in the integrity of the country and become more hesitant to invest. After the revelations of corporate wrongdoing in the early 2000s in the United States, for example, foreign investors' purchases of U.S. stocks dropped to

$49.5 billion, the lowest level since 1996. Whether these foreign investors' funds moved to stocks in other economies that were deemed safer or whether investors decided to stand on the sidelines and wait out the corporate scandals is not clear. What is clear is that the U.S. economy was significantly hurt by the fraudulent acts at Enron, WorldCom, and others.

Because of different cost/revenue structures, the amount of additional revenues a firm must generate to recover fraud losses varies from firm to firm and from industry to industry. However, it is easy to see that in order to maximize profits, eliminating fraud should be a key goal of every organization. The best way to minimize fraud is to prevent it from occurring. In this book, we will cover fraud prevention, as well as fraud detection and investigation.

> **Remember this ...**
>
> *Statistics about how much fraud is occurring are difficult to get. However, all signs indicate that fraud is increasing both in frequency and amount. Fraud is very costly to organizations and to economies. Because fraud reduces net income on a dollar-for-dollar basis, the amount of additional revenue needed to restore the stolen funds is many multiples of the amount of the fraud.*

What Is Fraud?

There are two principal methods of getting something from others illegally. Either you physically force someone to give you what you want (using a gun, knife, or other weapon), or you trick them out of their assets. The first type of theft we call robbery, and the second type we call **fraud**. Robbery is generally more violent and more traumatic than fraud and attracts much more media attention, but losses from fraud far exceed losses from robbery.

Although there are many formal definitions of fraud, probably the most common is the following:

Fraud is a generic term, and embraces all the multifarious means which human ingenuity can devise, which are resorted to by one individual, to get an advantage over another by false representations. No definite and invariable rule can be laid down as a general proposition in defining fraud, as it includes surprise, trickery, cunning and unfair ways by which another is cheated. The only boundaries defining it are those which limit human knavery.[11]

Fraud is deception that includes the following elements:

1. A *representation*
2. About a *material* point,
3. Which is *false*,
4. And *intentionally or recklessly* so,
5. Which is *believed*
6. And *acted upon* by the victim
7. To the victim's *damage*

CAUTION *Who is in the best position to "con" you right now? Who is in the best position to "con" your parents? Remember, it is always those you "trust most" who are in the best position to con you or commit fraud.*

Fraud is different from unintentional errors. If, for example, someone mistakenly enters incorrect numbers on a **financial statement**, is this fraud? No, it is not fraud because it was not done with *intent* or for the purpose of gaining advantage over another through false pretense. But, if in the same situation, someone purposely enters incorrect numbers on a financial statement to trick investors, then it *is* fraud!

As was discussed in the beginning of this chapter, one of the most common types of fraud today is a scam that lures investment funds from victims and then pays those victims a premium or interest from money that is paid by subsequent investors. This popular fraud scheme, also known as a Ponzi scheme, was named after Charles Ponzi who perpetrated a large scam in the early 1900s. To better understand fraud in general, let's take a closer look at Charles Ponzi.

Charles Ponzi and the Famous Ponzi Scheme

Carlo "Charles" Ponzi was born in Parma, Italy, in 1882 and then emigrated to the United States in November 1903. Over the next 14 years, Ponzi wandered from city to city and from job to job. He worked as a dishwasher, waiter, store clerk, and even an Italian interpreter. In 1917, he settled in Boston where he took a job typing and answering foreign mail. It was in Boston in 1919 that Ponzi discovered the mechanism that he thought would make both him and his investors very wealthy.[12]

At the time, Ponzi was considering issuing an export magazine. He had written a letter about the proposed publication to a gentleman in Spain, and when Ponzi received his reply, the man had included an international postal reply coupon. The idea behind this enclosure was quite simple. Ponzi was to take the coupon to his local post office and exchange it for American postage stamps. He would then use those American stamps to send magazines to Spain.

Ponzi noticed that the postal coupon had been purchased in Spain for about one cent in American funds. Yet, when he cashed it in, he was able to get six American one-cent stamps. Immediately, Ponzi started to consider the many possibilities to invest. Assuming this was possible, he could buy $100 worth of stamps in Spain and then cash them in for $600 worth of stamps in the United States. Then cash in or sell the stamps to a third party and Ponzi would have, well, good old cash. In the early 1900s, just like today, it was impossible to get this kind of interest in the bank.[13]

Ponzi's mind quickly went into overdrive and devised a clever scheme to capitalize on his idea. He was determined to be a rich man. His first step was to convert his American money into Italian lire (or any other currency where the exchange rate was favorable). Ponzi's foreign agents would then use these funds to purchase international postal coupons in countries with weak economies. The stamp coupons were then exchanged back into a favorable foreign currency and finally back into American funds. He claimed that his net profit on all these transactions was in excess of 400 percent.

Was he really able to do this? The answer is a definite no. The red tape of dealing with the various postal organizations, coupled with the long delays in transferring currency, ate away at all of Ponzi's imagined profits.

However, a failed scheme couldn't keep Ponzi from bragging about his great idea. As a result, friends and family members easily understood what he was saying, and they wanted in on the investment.

On December 26, 1919, Ponzi filed an application with the city clerk establishing his business as The Security Exchange Company. He promised 50 percent interest in 90 days, and the world wanted in on it. However, personally he claimed to be able to deliver on his promise in just 45 days. This, of course, translates into doubling investors' money in just 90 days.

Word spread very quickly about Ponzi's great idea, and within a few short months, the lines outside the door of his School Street office began to grow. Thousands of people purchased Ponzi promissory notes at values ranging from $10 to $50,000. The average investment was estimated to be about $300, a large sum of money in the 1920s.

Why would so many people invest in a scheme that didn't work? The real reason was that the early investors did see the great returns on their money. Ponzi used the money from later investors to pay off his earlier obligations. It was a new twist on the age-old pyramid scheme.

With an estimated income of $1,000,000 per week at the height of his scheme, his newly hired staff couldn't take in the money fast enough. They were literally filling all of the desk drawers, wastepaper baskets, and closets in the office with investors' cash. Branch offices opened, and copycat schemes popped up across New England.

By the summer of 1920, Ponzi had taken in millions and started living the life of a very rich man. Ponzi dressed in the finest suits, had dozens of gold-handled canes, showered his wife in fine jewels, and purchased a 20-room Lexington mansion.

Any get-rich scheme is certain to attract the attention of the law, and Ponzi's was no exception. From the start, federal, state, and local authorities investigated him. Yet, no one could pin Ponzi with a single charge of wrongdoing. Ponzi had managed to pay off all of his notes in the promised 45 days and, since everyone was happy to get their earnings, not a single complaint had ever been filed.

On July 26, 1920, Ponzi's house of cards began to collapse. The *Boston Post* headlined a story on the front page questioning the legitimacy of Ponzi's scheme. Later that day, the district somehow convinced Ponzi to suspend taking in new investments until an auditor examined his books. Within hours, crowds of people lined up outside Ponzi's door demanding that they get their investment back. Ponzi obliged and assured the public that his organization was financially stable and that he could meet all obligations. He returned the money to those who requested it. By the end of the first day, he had settled nearly 1,000 claims with the panicked crowd.

By continuing to meet all of his obligations, the angry masses began to dwindle and public support swelled. Crowds followed Ponzi's every move. He was urged by many to enter politics and was hailed as a hero. Loud cheers and applause were coupled with people eager to touch his hand and assure him of their confidence.

Because of the additional attention, Ponzi dreamed of opening more investments. For example, Ponzi began to make plans to establish a new type of bank where the profits would be split equally between shareholders and depositors. Ponzi also planned to reopen his company under a new name, the Charles Ponzi Company, whose main purpose was to invest in industries throughout the world.

The public continued to support Ponzi until August 10, 1920. On this date, the auditors, banks, and newspapers declared that Ponzi was indeed bankrupt. Two days later, Ponzi confessed to serving 20 months in a Canadian prison in 1908 on forgery charges related to a similar high-interest scheme followed by an additional two-year sentence in Atlanta, Georgia, for smuggling five Italians over the Canadian border into the United States.

On August 13, Ponzi was finally arrested by federal authorities and released on $25,000 bond. Just moments later, he was rearrested by Massachusetts authorities and re-released on an additional $25,000 bond.

Following his arrest, there were federal and state civil and criminal trials, bankruptcy hearings, suits against Ponzi, suits filed by Ponzi, and the ultimate closing of five different banks. An estimated 40,000 people had entrusted an estimated $15 million (about $140 million in U.S. funds today) in Ponzi's scheme. A final audit of his books concluded that he had taken in enough funds to buy approximately 180 million postal coupons, of which authorities could only actually confirm the purchase of two.

Ponzi's only legitimate source of income was $45 that he received as a dividend of five shares of telephone stock. His total assets came to $1,593,834.12, which didn't come close to paying off the outstanding debt. It took about eight years, but noteholders were able to receive an estimated 37 percent of their investment returned in installments.

Ultimately, Ponzi was sentenced to five years in federal prison. After three years in prison, Ponzi was sentenced to an additional seven to nine years by Massachusetts' authorities. However, Ponzi was released on $14,000 bond pending an appeal and disappeared the following month.

Ponzi turned up a short time later in Florida under the assumed name of Charles Borelli. Ponzi was involved in a pyramid land scheme and was purchasing land at $16 an acre, subdividing it into 23 lots, and selling each lot off at $10 a piece. He promised all investors that their initial $10 investment would translate into $5.3 million in just two years. Unfortunately, much of the land was under water and worthless.

Ponzi was indicted for fraud and sentenced to one year in a Florida prison. Once again, Ponzi jumped bail and was later found in Texas. Ponzi hopped a freighter headed for Italy but was captured on June 28 in a New Orleans port. On June 30, he sent a telegram to President Calvin Coolidge asking to be deported. Ponzi's request was denied, and he was sent back to Boston to complete his jail term. After seven years, Ponzi was released on good behavior and deported to Italy on October 7, 1934. Back in Rome, Ponzi became an English translator. Mussolini then offered Ponzi a position with Italy's new airline, and he served as the Rio de Janeiro branch manager from 1939–1942. Ponzi discovered that several airline officials were using the carrier to smuggle currency, and Ponzi wanted a cut. When they refused to include him, he tipped off the Brazilian government. World War II brought about the airline's failure, and Ponzi found himself unemployed.

Ponzi died in January 1949 in the charity ward of a Rio de Janeiro hospital. He left behind an unfinished manuscript appropriately titled "The Fall of Mister Ponzi."

Fraud, Greed, Deception, and Confidence

Ponzi's scam is extremely helpful in understanding fraud. Certainly, the scheme involved deception. It also involved greed by the *perpetrator* and—this is important—greed by the *investors*, who wanted higher-than-sensible returns. Finally, Ponzi's scheme involved the element of *confidence*. If he had not paid returns to original investors, no one would have invested additional money. By paying early "returns," Ponzi gained investors' confidence and convinced them that he had a legitimate business. In fact, confidence is the single most critical element for fraud to be successful. (The word "con," which means to deceive, comes from "confidence.") It is difficult to con anyone out of anything unless the deceived has confidence in the deceiver. We cannot be conned unless we trust the person trying to deceive us. Similarly, employers cannot con employees if they do not have their employees' trust and confidence. And, without investor confidence, fraudulent companies cannot con unsuspecting investors.

The following example illustrates the role that confidence plays in committing fraud:

> *Two men enter a bank. One is dressed in a business suit and is well groomed. The second has scraggly hair, has tattoos up and down both arms, is wearing tattered jeans, and is carrying a motorcycle helmet under his arm. Based on the probably unfounded categorization of these two individuals by most people in society, which one do you think is in the best position to successfully con a teller?*

Most of us would agree that the man in the business suit is in a better position to defraud the bank. He is, simply put, much more likely to be trusted, stereotypes being what they are. Most people would argue that the scraggly fellow is unlikely to pull off a successful fraud because the bank employees are less likely to trust him initially.

One common response of fraud victims is disbelief: "I can't believe she would do this. She was my most trusted employee … Or my best customer … Or my best friend." Someone who understands fraud will sadly tell you, "What else could they be? They wouldn't have succeeded *without* your trust!" Indeed, fraud perpetrators are often the least suspected and the most trusted of all the people with whom victims associate.

One company's research revealed that its largest group of fraud perpetrators is comprised of people between the ages of 36 and 45.[14] The statistics don't tell us *why* this is the case, but one reason may be that this age group includes managers who have worked themselves into positions of trust. In addition, they are probably the group with the highest financial pressures. When young people graduate from college, they look ahead and think, "By the time I'm 40, I'll have my house and cars paid off and have savings to pay for my children's college." But, when many people reach 40, their houses and cars are mortgaged to the hilt and they have no savings to pay for their children's college. During this same time frame (36–45), people are also better positioned in their careers to commit fraud. As we will discuss in future chapters, anytime opportunity and life pressures are present, the number of fraud cases increase.

STOP & THINK *Why is it more difficult to tell if someone can be trusted on the Internet than in person?*

Types of Fraud

While there are many ways to classify the various types of fraud, the most common way is to simply divide frauds into those that are committed *against* organizations and those that are committed *on behalf* of organizations.

In employee fraud, for example—fraud committed against an organization—the victim of the fraud is the employee's organization.[15] On the other hand, with financial statement fraud, for example, executives usually commit fraud "on behalf" of an organization,[16] usually to make its reported financial results look better than they actually are. In this case, the executives of the company benefit because a company's stock price increases or remains artificially high and the victims are investors in the company's stock. Sometimes, executives misstate earnings in order to ensure a larger year-end bonus. Financial statement fraud often occurs in companies that are experiencing net losses or have profits much less than expectations.

Another way to classify frauds is to use the ACFE's definition of "occupational fraud." The ACFE defines this type of fraud as, "The use of one's occupation for personnel enrichment through the deliberate misuse or misapplication of the employing organization's resources or assets."[17] Occupational fraud results from the misconduct of employees, managers, or executives. Occupational fraud can be anything from lunch break abuses to high-tech schemes. *The Report to the Nation on Occupational Fraud & Abuse* by the ACFE states that, "The key to occupational fraud is that the activity

Remember this …

Fraud involves all deceptive ways in which one individual obtains an advantage over another by false representations. Fraud always involves confidence and trickery. Fraud is different than robbery where force is used.

(1) is clandestine, (2) violates the employee's fiduciary duties to the organization, (3) is committed for the purpose of direct or indirect financial benefit to the employee, and (4) costs the employing organization assets, revenues, or reserves."[18]

The ACFE includes three major categories of occupational fraud: (1) asset misappropriations, which involve the theft or misuse of an organization's assets; (2) corruption, in which fraudsters wrongfully use their influence in a business transaction in order to procure some benefit for themselves or another person, contrary to their duty to their employer or the rights of another; and (3) fraudulent statements, which generally involve falsification of an organization's financial statements.

A third classification scheme divides fraud according to victims:

1. Frauds where a company or organization is the victim.
   a. Employee embezzlement—perpetrator is an employee of the organization.
   b. Vendor fraud—perpetrator is a vendor of the organization.
   c. Customer fraud—perpetrator is a customer of the organization.

2. Management fraud—victims are shareholders or debt-holders of the organization.
3. Investment scams and other consumer frauds—victims are unwary individuals.
4. Miscellaneous frauds—any other type of fraud.

Fraud that doesn't fall into one of the first three types of fraud and may have been committed for reasons other than financial gain is simply labeled **miscellaneous fraud**. The various types of fraud are summarized in Table 1.1 and are discussed in the paragraphs that follow.

Employee Embezzlement

Employee embezzlement is the most common type of occupational fraud. As stated previously, in this type of fraud, employees deceive their employers by taking company assets.[19] Embezzlement can be either direct or indirect. Direct fraud occurs when an employee steals company cash, inventory, tools, supplies, or other assets. It also occurs when employees establish dummy companies and have their employers pay for goods that are not actually delivered. With direct fraud, company assets go directly into the perpetrator's pockets without

TABLE 1.1 TYPES OF FRAUD

TYPE OF FRAUD	PERPETRATOR	VICTIM	EXPLANATION
Employee embezzlement	Employees of an organization	The employer	Employees use their positions to take or divert assets belonging to their employer. This is the most common type of fraud.
Vendor fraud	Vendors of an organization	The organization to which the vendors sell goods or services	Vendors either overbill or provide lower quality or fewer goods than agreed.
Customer fraud	Customers of an organization	The organization which sells to the customers	Customers don't pay, pay too little, or get too much from the organization through deception.
Management fraud (Financial statement fraud)	Management of a company	Shareholders and/or debt-holders and regulators (taxing authorities, etc.)	Management manipulates the financial statements to make the company look better than it is. This is the most expensive type of fraud.
Investment scams and other consumer frauds	Fraud perpetrators—all kinds	Unwary investors	These types of frauds are committed on the Internet and in person and obtain the confidence of individuals to get them to invest money in worthless schemes.
Other (Miscellaneous) types of fraud	All kinds—depends on the situation	All kinds—depends on the situation	Anytime anyone takes advantage of the confidence of another person to deceive him or her.

the involvement of third parties. Indirect employee fraud, on the other hand, occurs when employees take bribes or kickbacks from vendors, customers, or others outside the company to allow for lower sales prices, higher purchase prices, nondelivery of goods, or the delivery of inferior goods. In these cases, payment to employees is usually made by organizations that deal with the perpetrator's employer, not the employer itself.

The case of CVC Construction provides an example of direct employee fraud:

CVC Construction specializes in building new homes as well as remodeling older homes. While CVC Construction has a large market share they, unfortunately, have a hard time making a profit. An investigation into the matter revealed that several of CVC's employees were using company supplies and equipment to do their own remodeling jobs on the side and pocketing the profits. One employee alone had stolen more than $25,000 worth of company assets.

To highlight indirect fraud, consider the case of Mark who committed fraud against his employer "Big D" Advertising:

In his role as purchase agent, Mark paid a company in New York City nearly $100,000 for contracted work that should have cost about $50,000. The contractor then paid Mark a kickback of nearly $30,000. Only after someone noticed that the quality of work performed by the New York contractor decreased substantially was the fraud suspected and eventually detected.

Vendor Fraud

Vendor fraud has been in the news time and again over the years because of significant overcharges by major vendors on defense and other government contracts. Vendor fraud, which is extremely common in the United States, comes in two common forms: (1) fraud perpetrated by vendors acting alone, and (2) fraud perpetrated through collusion between buyers and vendors. Vendor fraud usually results in either an overcharge for purchased goods, the shipment of inferior goods, or the nonshipment of goods even though payment was made.[20]

A recent Department of Defense case highlights the typical vendor fraud. As a result of a joint FBI/Department of Defense investigation, an Illinois-based corporation pleaded guilty to false claims and conspiracy charges pertaining to cost overruns and executive personnel expenses charged to the Department of Defense. The corporation agreed to make restitution of $115 million to the government. The corporation later agreed to an additional payment of $71.3 million to resolve pending administrative and noncriminal issues and to dismiss certain officers proven criminally culpable through investigation.[21]

Over the last several years, Halliburton—a large defense contractor—has been accused of bribery, bid rigging, defrauding the military, and various other fraud claims as it has secured contracts to help rebuild Iraq. In one case alone, it was alleged that the Pentagon secretly awarded billions of dollars of Iraqi oil field work to Halliburton without giving any other contractors a chance to bid on the work. The claims against Halliburton are considered a type of vendor fraud, as the claims have included multiple vendors and parties.

Customer Fraud

When **customer fraud** takes place, customers either do not pay for goods purchased or they get something for nothing.[22] For example, consider the bank customer who walked into a branch of a large bank one Saturday morning and convinced the branch manager to give her a $525,000 cashier's check, even though she had only $13,000 in her bank account. The manager believed she was a very wealthy customer and didn't want to lose her business. Unfortunately for the bank, she was a white-collar thief, and she proceeded to defraud the bank of over $500,000. In another customer fraud, six individuals sitting in a downtown Chicago hotel room pretended to be representatives of large corporate customers, made three calls to a Chicago bank, and had the bank transfer nearly $70 million to their accounts in another financial institution in New Jersey. Once the money was transferred to New Jersey, it was quickly transferred to Switzerland, withdrawn, and used to purchase Russian diamonds.

Management Fraud

As stated previously, **management fraud**, often called *financial statement fraud*, is distinguished from other types of fraud both by the nature of the perpetrators and by the method of deception. In its most common form, management fraud involves top management's deceptive manipulation of financial statements.[23] Well-known examples of alleged management fraud in recent years include WorldCom, Enron, Waste Management, Sunbeam, Rite-Aid, Phar-Mor, Parmalat,

ZZZZ Best, ESM Government Securities, Regina Vacuum Company, and MiniScribe Corporation, among others.

To illustrate management fraud, consider John Blue, the CEO for a fast-growing music store chain. The company was opening new stores almost monthly. The company had loyal customers and was famous for its low prices. When the company went public, shares of the stock soared. Unfortunately, the new shareholders didn't know that the chain was selling the music below cost and was actually losing money on each item it sold. John and the other executives hid the losses by inflating inventories and recording fictitious revenues. The scam eventually unraveled when a top accountant reported the fraud. When word leaked out, shares of the company's stock became worthless overnight.

STOP & THINK *Why do you think it is easier for top management to manipulate financial statements than for other individuals in the organization?*

Investment Scams and Other Consumer Frauds

Closely related to management fraud are **investment scams**. In these scams, fraudulent and usually worthless investments are sold to unsuspecting investors.[24] Telemarketing fraud falls into this category, as does the selling of worthless partnership interests and other investment opportunities. As discussed earlier, Charles Ponzi is regarded as the father of investment scams. Unfortunately, he has not lacked imitators. His form of deception is extremely common today. In fact, research suggests that one of every three Americans will fall prey to this type of fraud during his or her lifetime.

The FBI has suggested that the following are some of the most common consumer fraud schemes:[25]

1. **Ponzi schemes**. As discussed earlier in the chapter, these schemes are named after Charles Ponzi and are quite simple: Lure investment funds from victims and then pay those victims a premium or interest from money that is paid by subsequent investors.

2. **Telemarketing fraud**. When telemarketing fraud takes place, victims send money to people they do not know personally or give personal financial information to unknown callers. Typically, these callers put pressure on potential victims to "act now because the offer won't last" or somehow convince the victim that he or she has won a free gift such as a cruise, trip, or vacation. In order to redeem the prize, the victim must pay for postage and/or handling by providing their credit card number and personal information to the perpetrator.

3. **Nigerian letter or money scams**. This type of fraud typically occurs when a potential victim receives an e-mail or other form of communication promising the victim a large financial payout in exchange for help in transporting large sums of money from one country to another. The author of the letter usually states that an up-front cost is needed in order to pay taxes, bribe government officials, or pay other legal fees.

4. **Identity theft**. Identity theft occurs when someone assumes the identity of another person to purchase goods, engage in criminal activity, or perpetrate fraud. Perpetrators steal a person's identity by accessing personal financial information such as information that is found on credit statements, credit cards, bank statements, social security, and other personal documents such as a driver's license. Perpetrators will also gain this information by going through a victim's mailbox or trashcan.

5. **Advance fee scams**. An advance fee scam occurs when a victim pays an up-front cost for a good or service that is never delivered. In the scam, the victim pays up-front cost to secure a payment, loan, contract, investment, or gift. In the end, once the perpetrator receives the money, the victim will be unable to contact the perpetrator and the victim loses the original payment that was made.

6. **Redemption/strawman/bond fraud**. In this scam, perpetrators claim that the U.S. government controls certain bank accounts that can be accessed by submitting paperwork with government officials. In order to gain access to this paperwork, victims must buy expensive training kits that teach individuals how to access the funds. When the victim is unable to access the government funds, the perpetrator will indicate that the paperwork was not filled out correctly and will often charge additional fees for more training.

7. **Letter of credit fraud**. A letter of credit is a legitimate document that is issued by banks to guarantee payment for goods that are shipped in international trade. In order to scam victims, fraud perpetrators will often create bogus letters of credit and then sell them to unsuspecting victims. The victims are told that they can use these letters as

investments that will pay unrealistic returns. In order to avoid this type of scam, consumers should be aware that legitimate letters of credit are never sold or offered as investments.

8. **Internet fraud**. According to the North American Securities Administrators Association (NASAA), Internet fraud has become a booming business. Recently, federal, state, local, and foreign law enforcement officials targeted Internet fraudsters during Operation Cyber Sweep. In the raid, law enforcement identified more than 125,000 victims with estimated losses of more than $100 million and made 125 arrests. Many of the online scams that are perpetrated today are simply new versions of schemes that have been perpetrated offline for years.

As an example of how consumer frauds can occur, consider Brian, a hard-working college student, who was victimized by an investment scam.

During the day, Brian attended school, and at night, to support himself, he worked as a server at a downtown diner. On a good night, Brian brought home about $100 in tips. During a period of three years, Brian saved almost $1,200. One day at lunch, Brian's friend, Lance, told him about a startup company in Canada. "If you get in now," Lance said, "you'll be in on the bottom. You'll make at least three times your money in only a couple of weeks." That same night, Brian accompanied Lance to a meeting describing the investment opportunity. The following day, they each invested $1,000. Lance and Brian had never been so excited. They thought the opportunity was almost too good to be true—and unfortunately, they were right. The investment was a scam, and Brian and Lance never saw their $1,000 again, let alone any of the exorbitant earnings they were promised.

CAUTION You recently received the following e-mail: *Please be so kind as to contact me at your earliest convenience for a possible business deal involving a money transfer of about $22,000,000.*

In conducting an audit of a financial institution, I discovered a dormant account with a balance of $22,000,000 which has not been accessed for the past three years. From my investigations and confirmations, the owner of this account is a foreigner by the name of John Doe who died without a will. I am presently in London working as an investment consultant with the above bank at their London office, and I am poised to work this deal out if we can do business. At the moment, I am constrained to

issue more details about this business until your response is received. As we have not met before, I will give you every detail you need to know regarding the business and about me as we progress with the business.

At the conclusion of this business, you will be given 35 percent of the total amount, 60 percent will be for me, and 5 percent will be for expenses.

You should send me your bank account information as indicated below where you would like the money to be transferred so that I can send an application for the release of the funds immediately with your account information.

Beneficiary Name _____

Bank Name _____

Bank Address _____

Account Number _____

Swift Code _____

Routing Number _____

State & Country _____

Your Mobile Telephone Number/Fax Number _____

I look forward to hearing from you as soon as possible. Obviously, this e-mail, which was actually received by one of the authors, is an attempt to fraudulently steal your money. What in this e-mail suggests that you should never participate in this scheme?

Remember this ...

Frauds can be classified in several ways: by victim, by perpetrator, or by scheme. Frauds against organizations are most common, but financial statement frauds are usually most expensive.

Criminal and Civil Prosecution of Fraud

When people commit fraud, they can be prosecuted criminally and/or civilly. To succeed in a criminal or civil prosecution, it is usually necessary to show that the perpetrator acted with *intent* to defraud the victim. This is best accomplished by gathering evidential matter. **Evidential matter** consists of the underlying data and all corroborating information available. In a later chapter, we will discuss types of evidence and the role evidence plays in successful prosecution and/or litigation of fraud.

Criminal Law

Criminal law is that branch of law that deals with offenses of a public nature. Criminal laws generally deal with offenses against society as a whole. They are prosecuted either federally or by a state for violating a **statute** that prohibits some type of activity.

Every state and the federal government have statutes prohibiting a wide variety of fraudulent and corrupt practices. Some of the principal federal statutes are listed in Table 1.2.

A variety of statutes cover fraudulent activity. Usually, when perpetrators are convicted, they serve jail

TABLE 1.2 PRINCIPAL FEDERAL FRAUD STATUTES

STATUTE	TITLE AND CODE	DESCRIPTION
Bribery of Public Officials and Witnesses	Title 18, U.S. Code § 201	Bribery is punishable by up to 15 years in prison, a fine of up to three times the thing of value given or received, and disqualification of officer.
Anti-Kickback Act of 1986	Title 41, U.S. Code § 51 to 58	This act outlaws the giving or receiving of any thing of value by a subcontractor to a prime contractor in U.S. government contracts. Willful violations are punished by a fine and up to 10 years in prison.
Mail Fraud	Title 18, U.S. Code §1341	"Whoever, having devised or intending to devise any scheme or artifice to defraud, or for obtaining money or property by means of false or fraudulent pretenses, representations, or promises, for the purpose of executing such scheme or artifice or attempting so to do, places in any post office or authorized deposits or causes to be deposited any matter or thing whatever to be sent or delivered by any private or commercial interstate carrier, … shall be fined under this title … or imprisoned."
Bank Fraud	Title 18, U.S. Code §1344	Any scheme to defraud federally insured financial institutions by customers, officers, employees, and owners. Covers banks, savings and loans, credit unions, and other financial institutions insured by government agencies.
Racketeer Influenced and Corrupt Organizations (RICO) Statute	Title 18, U.S. Code §1961	This statute makes it an offense for any person associated with an "enterprise" engaged in interstate commerce to conduct the affairs of the enterprise through a "pattern of racketeering activity." A pattern is defined as two or more enumerated criminal violations.
Computer Fraud	Title 18, U.S. Code §1030	Section 1030 punishes any intentional, unauthorized access to a "protected computer" for the purpose of obtaining restricted data regarding national security, obtaining confidential financial information, using a computer which is intended for use by the U.S. government, committing a fraud, or damaging or destroying information contained in the computer.
Securities Fraud	Rule10(b)5 Securities Act of 1934, $17(a)	It is unlawful for an insider who has material inside information to purchase or sell the company's securities, irrespective of whether the insider deals directly or through an exchange. The antifraud provisions impose civil liability on those who perpetrate or who aid and abet any fraud in connection with any offer and sale of securities.
Foreign Corrupt Practices Act (FCPA)	Title 15, U.S. Code §78m, 78a(b), 78dd-1, 78dd-2, 78ff	This law outlaws bribery of foreign officials by U.S. companies for business purposes. The FCPA also requires that SEC-regulated companies keep accurate books and records, and have sufficient internal controls to assure that "access to assets is permitted only in accordance with management's … authorization," to prevent slush funds and bribe payments.
Tax Evasion	Title 26, U.S. Code §7201	Failure to report income from fraud or bribes may be prosecuted as tax evasion, or for filing a false return. Also, bribes may not lawfully be deducted as business expenses.

sentences and/or pay fines. Before perpetrators are convicted, they must be proven guilty "beyond a reasonable doubt." Juries must rule unanimously on guilt for the perpetrator to be convicted. Recent cases of people who were prosecuted criminally include Bernard Madoff; Ken Lay; Jeff Skilling of Enron; the CEO of Financial News Network (FNN), who was sentenced to five years in prison for spinning companies he controlled into a plot that inflated FNN's sales; the CEO of Towers Financial,[26] who was sentenced to 20 years for a Ponzi-like scheme that defrauded investors of $450 million; and Donald Ferrarini, who was sentenced to 12 years in prison for reporting nonexistent revenues that made his income-losing company look like a profit maker.[27]

Sometimes fraud perpetrators and other criminals plead guilty without being tried in order to seek more lenient sentences. These guilty pleas are usually accompanied by a willingness to help prosecutors in their investigations of other perpetrators. For example, in the Enron case, former Enron executive Michael Kopper pleaded guilty to charges of money laundering and wire fraud. The guilty pleas were the first criminal charges brought against a former Enron employee and represented significant progress in the U.S. government investigation into the scandal. As part of the plea deal, Mr. Kopper agreed to cooperate with prosecutors and paid back $12 million of assets.

Civil Law

Civil law is the body of law that provides remedies for violations of private rights. Civil law deals with rights of individuals. Civil claims begin when one party files a complaint against another, usually for the purpose of gaining financial restitution. The purpose of a civil lawsuit is to compensate for harm done to another individual. Unlike criminal cases, juries in civil cases need not consist of 12 jurors but may have as few as six jurors. The verdict of the jury need not be unanimous. Civil cases are often heard by judges instead of juries. To be successful, plaintiffs in civil cases must only prove their case by the "preponderance of the evidence." In other words, there need only be slightly more evidence supporting the plaintiff than supporting the defendant. In both civil and criminal proceedings, the parties often call expert witnesses to give their opinion on matters thought to be too technical for the jurors or judge to understand. Fraud examiners and accountants are often used as experts in fraud cases to compute and testify to the amount of damages. When fraud is committed, criminal prosecution usually proceeds first.

STOP & THINK *O. J. Simpson was tried for murder both criminally and civilly. He was found innocent in the criminal trial but guilty in the civil trial. Why do you think that was the case?*

Table 1.3 identifies the major differences between a civil and criminal case.

As an example of civil litigation, consider the case of WorldCom. After the WorldCom fraud was discovered, investors sued various organizations that the investors claimed help perpetrate the fraud. In 2004, one of those organizations, Citigroup, agreed to settle investors' civil claims by agreeing to pay $2.65 billion to investors. These kinds of out-of-court settlements often occur before civil cases actually go to trial.

TABLE 1.3 DISTINCTIONS BETWEEN CIVIL AND CRIMINAL CASES

	CRIMINAL CASE	CIVIL CASE
Purpose	To right a wrong	To obtain a remedy
Consequences	Jail and/or fines	Restitution and damage payments
Burden of Proof	"Beyond a reasonable doubt"	"Preponderance of evidence"
Jury	Jury must have 12 people	May consist of fewer than 12 persons
Initiation	Determination by a grand jury that sufficient evidence exists to indict	Filing of a claim by a plaintiff
Verdict	Unanimous verdict	Parties may stipulate to a less than unanimous verdict
Claims	Only one claim at a time	Various claims may be joined in one action

> **Remember this …**
>
> *The purpose of a criminal case is to right a wrong, whereas the purpose of a civil case is to obtain a remedy. Criminal cases result in jail and/or fines, while civil cases result in restitution and damage payments. Juries must reach unanimous verdicts in criminal cases; only a majority is necessary to convict someone in a civil case.*

How to Prepare to Be a Fraud-Fighting Professional

At most universities, there is not a major called "Fraud Prevention, Detection and Investigation." Rather, students who want to prepare for fraud-fighting careers must usually choose majors and courses that will provide the skills that will make them a successful fraud fighter. The following are some of the most important skills for a fraud-fighting professional to have:

- **Analytical skills:** Fraud detection and investigation are analytical processes where investigators identify the kinds of fraud that could occur, the kinds of symptoms and indicators those frauds would generate, and ways in which to examine and follow up on symptoms that are discovered. Being a fraud investigator is very much like being a physician: it requires significant amounts of diagnostic and exploratory work to discover what is really happening. It is impossible to be a good fraud examiner without having great analytical skills.
- **Communication skills:** Fraud examiners spend considerable amounts of time interviewing witnesses and suspects and communicating those findings to witnesses, courts, and others. A good communicator will know how to push for evidence and confessions, how to structure questions and interviews, and how to write reports that are valued by courts, lawyers, and others. It is impossible to be a good fraud examiner without refined communication skills.
- **Technological skills:** In the past, fraud detection and investigation involved more luck than anything else. However, with the technological advances of the last two decades, we can now proactively search for fraud symptoms and fraud perpetrators and build both fraud-free and fraudulent profiles. Technology allows fraud examiners to analyze huge databases very efficiently.

Computers and other forms of technology provide some of the best evidence to determine if someone is guilty of fraud. Real-time and even post-hoc fraud detection and investigation in the future will involve the use of technology.

While the three skills addressed here are critical and most important, other skills that will be extremely useful for future fraud examiners are as follows:

- **Some understanding of accounting and business.** One of the major differences between fraud and other types of crime is the always present concealment attempts to hide the fraud. Usually, concealment attempts involve altering accounting records and documents. Fraud examiners who understand accounting and business will be highly valued in the future. For example, the FBI has a large number of agents who are CPAs. The expertise of these agents is highly valued by the FBI.
- **A knowledge of civil and criminal laws, criminology, privacy issues, employee rights, fraud statutes, and other legal fraud-related issues.** Investigating and resolving frauds always involves legal questions such as "should this case be pursued in the criminal or civil courts, are certain evidence-gathering techniques legal, and when should law enforcement be involved?"
- **The ability to speak and write in a foreign language.** With developments in travel, communication, and technology, many frauds today involve individuals in multiple countries. Cross-border investigations are not uncommon, and the ability to speak and write a foreign language, such as Spanish, or Chinese, will be highly valued.
- **A knowledge of human behavior, including why and how people rationalize dishonesty, how they react when caught, and what is the most effective way(s) to deter individuals from committing fraud.** These kinds of skills are usually learned in behavioral courses such as psychology, social psychology, or sociology.

Many readers are probably wondering which major on campus will provide them with all of these skills. The answer is probably none.[28] But, majors such as information systems, accounting, and law can provide a basic understanding that is extremely helpful. Regardless of the major one chooses, it would be beneficial to fulfill elective requirements with courses in the above-mentioned topics. For example, if you are an accounting major, you should probably take as many technology and behavioral type classes as you can. While no candidate will possess all of the skills identified earlier, the more of these skills an individual possesses, the better qualified he or she will be to find success as a fraud examiner.

Certified Fraud Examiners

The ACFE provides the opportunity for an individual to become a "CFE." CFEs are considered to be leaders in the antifraud community and have recognition as such throughout the world. They represent the highest standards held by the ACFE and possess expertise in all aspects of the antifraud profession. The CFE designation is acknowledged globally and preferred by many employers. The ACFE states that becoming a CFE immediately sets an individual apart and launches an individual to the top of their profession.

When an individual becomes a CFE he or she automatically becomes a member of the ACFE. The ACFE is the world's largest antifraud organization and the premier provider of antifraud training and education. With more than 50,000 members throughout the world, the ACFE reduces fraud and corruption around the globe.

The ACFE has the following requirements for an individual to become a certified fraud examiner:

- Be an associate member of the ACFE in good standing.
- Meet minimum *academic* and *professional* requirements.
- Be of high moral character.
- Agree to abide by the Bylaws and Code of Professional Ethics of the ACFE.

Academic Requirements

Generally, applicants for CFE certification have a minimum of a bachelor's degree (or equivalent) from an institution of higher learning. No specific field of study is required. If you do not have a bachelor's degree, you may substitute two years of fraud-related professional experience for each year of academic study. For example, if you successfully attended college full time for only two years, you would need an additional four years of professional experience to satisfy the education requirements.

Professional Requirements

When an individual becomes a CFE, he or she must have at least two years of professional experience in a field either directly or indirectly related to the detection or deterrence of fraud. The following categories are deemed acceptable as fraud-related experience:

- **Accounting and Auditing:** A candidate may qualify to become a CFE if he or she has experience as an accountant or auditor (e.g., internal or external auditor) and has had certain responsibilities for the detection and deterrence of fraud by evaluating accounting systems for weaknesses, designing internal controls, determining the degree of organizational fraud risk, interpreting financial data for unusual trends, and following up on fraud indicators.
- **Criminology and Sociology**: Only those professionals with education or research in the fraud and white-collar crime dimensions of sociology or criminology may claim experience under this category. An experienced background in general sociological fields is insufficient.
- **Fraud Investigation:** Experience in the investigation of civil or criminal fraud, or of white-collar crime for law enforcement agencies or in the private sector, qualifies an individual to become a CFE. Examples include federal, state, or local law enforcement (e.g., IRS, inspectors general, and district attorney investigators) as well as insurance fraud investigators and fraud examiners working for corporations, businesses, or other associations.
- **Loss Prevention:** Security directors for corporations or other organizations who deal directly with issues of loss prevention may claim this experience as credit to become a CFE. Security consultants dealing with fraud-related issues are also eligible. Experience as a security guard or equivalent is not acceptable.
- **Law:** Candidates with experience in the legal field might qualify, provided the experience deals with some consideration of fraud. Examples include prosecuting lawyers, fraud litigators, and others with an antifraud specialization.

If an individual's experience does not fall into one of these categories, but their responsibilities include the detection, investigation, or deterrence of fraud, they must make a case why their experience is relevant.

Fraud-Related Careers

As the number of frauds and the amounts of fraud losses increase, so do the opportunities for successful careers in fraud fighting. *U.S. News and World Report* identified fraud examination as one of the fastest growing and most financially rewarding careers.[29] The American Institute of Certified Public Accountants (AICPA) touted fraud examination/fraud auditing as one of the six fastest growing and most profitable opportunities for accountants. Although there are numerous opportunities for fraud-fighting professionals, careers in forensic work can be broadly classified according to employer, as shown in Table 1.4.

Taken together, the cost of fighting fraud is very high. In high-profile civil cases, it is not uncommon for defendants and plaintiffs to spend tens of millions of dollars defending and prosecuting alleged frauds. Many large fraud cases involve multiple law firms, multiple lawyers from each firm, multiple investigators, expert witnesses, and large support staff. Often, after spending large sums of money defending or prosecuting a fraud case, a pretrial settlement is reached, with no public announcement of the terms of the settlement.

One author of this textbook has, throughout his career, been retained as an expert witness in various fraud cases. To illustrate the many kinds of fraud, Table 1.5 lists some of these cases.

Throughout the next few months, you will find your study of fraud examination to be very interesting and helpful—whether or not you become a professional fraud fighter. As a businessperson, understanding the tremendous costs of fraud and learning to recognize fraud may someday mean the difference between your business surviving or failing. If you become a financial consultant, you will be better equipped to help your clients avoid high-risk and fraudulent investments. As an investor, you will learn skills that help you distinguish between fraudulent and profitable investments. If you become an auditor, you will find the document examination and evidence-gathering skills you learn here invaluable. If you work with taxes, you will be alert to when information from clients is questionable. Finally, the interviewing skills you learn will be helpful in nearly every possible profession you may choose.

You may find, to your surprise, that fraud examination and forensic accounting are not only rewarding and challenging, but they are also intriguing and endlessly interesting (what good mystery isn't?). We hope you enjoy the adventure.

Remember this …

Very few fraud-fighting specialties are offered at U.S. universities. Instead, a person should choose a path of study that will result in obtaining those skills that are most helpful for fraud fighters. The Association of Certified Fraud Examiners is a professional organization comprised of fraud-fighting professionals that certifies individuals as certified fraud examiners. There are many different fraud-fighting careers, including auditing, consulting, law, investigation, and law enforcement.

TABLE 1.4 FRAUD-RELATED CAREERS

TYPES OF EMPLOYERS	TYPE OF CAREER
Government and law enforcement	FBI, postal inspectors, Criminal Investigation Division of the IRS, U.S. marshals, inspector generals of various governmental agencies, state investigators, and local law enforcement officials.
CPA firms	Conduct investigations, support firms in litigation, do bankruptcy-related accounting work, provide internal audit and internal control consulting work.
Corporations	Prevent, detect, and investigate fraud within a company. Includes internal auditors, corporate security officers, and in-house legal counsels.
Consulting	Serve as an independent consultant in litigation fraud work, serve as expert witness, consult in fraud prevention and detection, and provide other fee-based work.
Law firms	Lawyers provide litigation and defense work for companies and individuals being sued for fraud and provide special investigation services when fraud is suspected.

TABLE 1.5 AUTHOR'S EXPERT WITNESSING EXPERIENCES

CASE	NATURE	RETAINED BY	CITY
Bank	Fraud by a customer	Plaintiff's attorneys	Philadelphia, PA
Large industrial company	Financial statement fraud	Defendant's attorneys	Chicago, IL
Financial services firm	Financial statement fraud by Hedge fund	Plaintiff's attorneys	Miami, FL
Financial services firm	Financial statement fraud	Plaintiff's attorneys	Miami, FL
Large industrial company	Financial statement fraud	CPA firm's attorneys	Chicago, IL
EDS Corporation	Fraud by vendor	Defendant' attorneys	Dallas, TX
Financial institution	Derivatives fraud	Defendant's attorneys	New York, NY
Large insurance company	Fraud by executives	Defendant's attorneys	West Palm Beach, FL
Wealthy individual	Fraud by major stockholders	Plaintiff's attorneys	Salt Lake City, UT
Large industrial company	Financial statement fraud	CPA firm's attorneys	Chicago, IL
Large industrial company	Financial statement fraud	CPA firm's attorneys	Chicago, IL
Large credit union	Fraud by customer	Plaintiff's attorneys	Salt Lake City, UT
Large industrial company	Financial statement fraud	CPA firm's attorneys	Atlanta, GA
Large industrial company	Financial statement fraud	CPA firm's attorneys	Chicago, IL
Large medical company	Financial statement fraud	CPA firm's attorneys	Chicago, IL
Large oil and gas company	Financial statement fraud	CPA firm's attorneys	New York, NY
Large retailer	Financial statement fraud	CPA firm's attorneys Thomas et al.	Houston, TX
Large financial institution	Financial statement fraud	CPA firm's attorneys	Cincinnati, OH
Large bank	Fraud by executives	CPA firm's attorneys	Philadelphia, PA
Savings and loan institution	Fraud by executives	CPA firm's attorneys	Chicago, IL
Limited real estate company	Financial statement fraud by partners	CPA firm's attorneys	Chicago, IL
Large financial institution	Fraud by employee	CPA firm's attorneys	Cleveland, OH
Large industrial company	Fraud by vendor	Plaintiff's attorneys	Los Angeles, CA
Large savings and loan	Financial statement fraud	U.S. government	Los Angeles, CA
Limited partnership	Financial statement fraud	Plaintiff's attorneys	Salt Lake City, UT
Wealthy taxpayer	Tax fraud	Defendant's attorney	Boise, ID

Review of the Learning Objectives

- **Understand the seriousness of the fraud problem and how it affects individuals, consumers, and organizations**. While it is difficult to get accurate fraud statistics, the statistics and studies that are available suggest that fraud is increasing in both amount and frequency. Fraud is extremely costly to organizations and economies, often resulting in the bankruptcy of companies. When someone embezzles from an organization, that organization must generate many times the amount embezzled in additional revenues to recover the effect on net income.

- **Define fraud.** Fraud is theft by deception. There are two ways to get something from someone illegally—through force or by trickery. Fraud involves all the different ways of using trickery to get another person's or organization's assets.
- **Understand the different types of fraud.** Frauds can be classified by type of victim, type of perpetrator, or type of scheme. The most common victims of frauds are organizations, in the case of employee, vendor, and customer fraud; stockholders and debtholders, in the case of management fraud; and individuals, in the case of investment scams and other types of consumer frauds.
- **Understand the difference between fraud committed *against* an organization and fraud committed *on behalf* of an organization.** The most common way to classify fraud is to simply divide frauds into those that are committed *against* an organization and those that are committed *on behalf* of an organization. Fraud that is committed against an organization is typically a form of employee (occupational), vendor, or customer fraud. Fraud that is committed on behalf of an organization is a form of management fraud or financial statement fraud.
- **Understand the difference between criminal and civil fraud laws and how these laws relate to fraud.** Criminal laws are used to right a wrong—to send someone to jail or to have the government invoke fines and penalties. Civil cases are used to seek remedies—usually in the form of financial restitution.
- **Understand the types of fraud-fighting careers available today.** Fraud-fighting professionals today include lawyers, auditors, accountants, consultants, and government employees. Fraud-ighting professionals can best prepare for their careers by studying those skills useful in fighting fraud. The ACFE certifies individuals as certified fraud examiners.

KEY TERMS

perpetrators, p. 4
jurisdiction, p. 5
victims, p. 5
Association of Certified
   Fraud Examiners
   (ACFE), p. 5
net income, p. 5

revenue, p. 5
profit margin, p. 5
fraud, p. 6
financial statement,
   p. 7
miscellaneous fraud,
   p. 10

employee
   embezzlement, p. 10
vendor fraud, p. 11
customer fraud, p. 11
management fraud,
   p. 11

investment scams,
   p. 12
evidential matter, p. 13
criminal law, p. 14
statute, p. 14
civil law, p. 15

QUESTIONS
Discussion Questions

1. What is fraud?
2. How does fraud affect individuals, consumers, and organizations?
3. List and describe the five different types of frauds.
4. What is the difference between civil and criminal laws?
5. For each of the following, indicate whether it is a characteristic of a civil or a criminal case:
   a. Jury may consist of fewer than 12 jurors.
   b. Verdict must be unanimous.
   c. Multiple claims may be joined in one action.
   d. "Beyond a reasonable doubt."
   e. Purpose is to right a public wrong.
   f. Purpose is to obtain remedy.
   g. Consequences of jail and/or fines.
   h. Juries may have a less-than-unanimous verdict.
6. Why was Charles Ponzi so successful with his fraud scheme?
7. What are some of the different types of fraud-fighting careers?
8. How do employee fraud and management fraud differ?
9. Do you think the demand for careers in fraud prevention and detection is increasing or decreasing? Why?
10. Why are accurate fraud statistics hard to find?
11. Describe the relationship between fraud, net income, profit margin, and the revenue required to make up for fraud losses.
12. Why does it usually require trust for someone to be able to commit a fraud?
13. In what ways is the Ponzi scam similar to other frauds?
14. In your own words describe a CFE.
15. In your own words describe the purpose of the ACFE.

True/False

1. All frauds that are detected are made public.
2. Perpetrators use trickery, confidence, and deception to commit fraud.
3. One of the most common responses to fraud is disbelief.
4. Manufacturing companies with a profit margin of 10 percent must usually generate about 10 times as much revenue as the dollar amount from the fraud in order to restore net income to its pre-fraud level.
5. Fraud involves using physical force to take something from someone.
6. Telemarketing fraud is an example of employee embezzlement.
7. When perpetrators are convicted of fraud, they often serve jail sentences and/or pay fines.
8. Management fraud is deception perpetrated by an organization's top management.
9. A Ponzi Scheme is considered to be a type of investment scam.
10. Most people agree that fraud-related careers will be in demand in the future.
11. In civil cases, fraud experts are rarely used as expert witnesses.
12. Many companies hide their losses from fraud rather than make them public.
13. The only group/business that must report employee embezzlement is the federal government.
14. Advances in technology have had no effect on the size or frequency of fraud.
15. Fraud losses generally reduce a firm's income on a dollar-for-dollar basis.
16. The single most critical element for a fraud to be successful is opportunity.
17. Fraud perpetrators are often those who are least suspected and most trusted.
18. Unintentional errors in financial statements are a form of fraud.
19. Occupational fraud is fraud committed on behalf of an organization.
20. Companies that commit financial statement fraud are often experiencing net losses or have profits less than expectations.
21. Indirect fraud occurs when a company's assets go directly into the perpetrator's pockets without the involvement of third parties.
22. In vendor fraud, customers don't pay for goods purchased.
23. A negative outcome in a civil lawsuit usually results in jail time for the perpetrator.
24. When fraud is committed, criminal prosecution usually proceeds first.
25. A fraud may be perpetrated through an unintentional mistake.
26. It is most often people who are not trusted that commit fraud.
27. Management fraud is when managers intentionally deceive their employees about the potential of raises, vacations, and other perks.
28. Despite intense measures meant to impede it, fraud appears to be one of the fastest growing crimes in the United States.
29. The ACFE is a nonprofit organization dedicated to the prevention and dedication of fraud throughout the world.
30. There is no difference between a Certified Fraud Examiner (CFE) and a Certified Public Accountant (CPA).

Multiple Choice

1. Why does fraud seem to be increasing at such an alarming rate?
   a. Computers, the Internet, and technology make fraud easier to commit.
   b. Most frauds today are detected, whereas in the past many were not.
   c. A new law requires that fraud be reported within 24 hours.
   d. People understand the consequences of fraud to organizations.
2. Which of the following is *not* an important element of fraud?
   a. Confidence.
   b. Deception.
   c. Trickery.
   d. Intelligence.
3. Fraud is considered to be:
   a. A serious problem that continues to grow.
   b. A problem that affects very few individuals.
   c. A mild problem that most businesses need not worry about.
   d. A problem under control.
4. People who commit fraud are usually:
   a. New employees.
   b. Not well groomed and have long hair and tattoos.
   c. People with strong personalities.
   d. Trusted individuals.
5. "The use of one's occupation for personal enrichment through the deliberate misuse or

misapplication of the employing organization's resources or assets" is the definition of which of the following types of fraud?
   a. Employee embezzlement or occupational fraud.
   b. Investment scams.
   c. Management fraud.
   d. Vendor fraud.

6. Corporate employee fraud fighters:
   a. Work as postal inspectors and law enforcement officials.
   b. Prevent, detect, and investigate fraud within a company.
   c. Are lawyers that defend and/or prosecute fraud cases.
   d. None of the above.

7. Investment scams most often include:
   a. An action by top management against employees.
   b. Worthless investments or assets sold to unsuspecting investors.
   c. An overcharge for purchased goods.
   d. Nonpayment of invoices for goods purchased by customers.

8. Which of the following is *not* true of civil fraud?
   a. It usually begins when one party files a complaint.
   b. The purpose is to compensate for harm done to another.
   c. It must be heard by 12 jurors.
   d. Only "the preponderance of the evidence" is needed for the plaintiff to be successful.

9. Future careers in fraud will most likely be:
   a. In low demand.
   b. In moderate demand.
   c. Low paying.
   d. In high demand and financially rewarding.

10. Studying fraud will help you:
   a. Learn evidence-gathering skills.
   b. Avoid high-risk and fraudulent activities.
   c. Learn valuable interviewing skills.
   d. All of the above.

11. Which of the following is *not* a reliable resource for fraud statistics?
   a. FBI agencies.
   b. Health agencies.
   c. Insurance organizations.
   d. Fraud perpetrators.

12. Which of the following statements is true?
   a. Bank robberies are more costly than frauds.
   b. Fraud is often labeled the fastest growing crime.

   c. FBI agencies are currently spending approximately 35 percent of their time on fraudulent activities.
   d. None of the above statements are true.

13. Which of the following is *not* an element of fraud?
   a. False representation.
   b. Accidental behavior.
   c. Damage to a victim.
   d. Intentional or reckless behavior.

14. What is the best way to minimize fraud within an organization?
   a. Detection of fraud.
   b. Investigation of fraudulent behavior.
   c. Prevention activities.
   d. Research company activities.

15. What is the most important element in successful fraud schemes?
   a. Promised benefits.
   b. Confidence in the perpetrator.
   c. Profitable activities.
   d. Complexity.

16. Which of the following characters is least likely to be involved in a fraud?
   a. A middle-aged person with a middle management position.
   b. A long-haired teenager wearing leather pants.
   c. A recent college graduate.
   d. A senior executive who has significant stock options.

17. Which of the following is *not* a fraud type?
   a. Direct employee embezzlement.
   b. Indirect employee embezzlement.
   c. Supervisor fraud.
   d. Investment scams.

18. Which of the following is *not* a form of vendor fraud?
   a. Overcharge for purchased goods.
   b. Shipment of inferior goods.
   c. Nonshipment of goods even though payment has been made.
   d. Not paying for goods purchased.

19. Civil law performs which of the following functions?
   a. Remedy for violation of private rights.
   b. Remedy for violations against society as a whole.
   c. Punishment for guilt "beyond reasonable doubt."
   d. Monetary reimbursement for federal damages.

20. Fraud fighting includes what type of careers?
    a. Professors.
    b. Lawyers.
    c. CPA firms.
    d. All of the above.
21. Which of the following is *not* an example of employee embezzlement?
    a. Land conservation employees stealing equipment.
    b. Cashiers stealing money from the cash register.
    c. Angry employees vandalizing the building with spray paint.
    d. Salespeople overcharging for products and pocketing the excess cash.
22. Which of the following is *not* an example of vendor fraud?
    a. A vendor overcharges a contracting job that it completed on time.
    b. A vendor bills for services not performed.
    c. A vendor bills for goods not provided.
    d. A vendor has much higher prices than its competitors.
23. "Deceptive manipulation of financial statements" describes which kind of fraud?
    a. Management fraud.
    b. Criminal fraud.
    c. Stock market fraud.
    d. Bookkeeping fraud.
24. Which of the following is required to become a CFE?
    a. An individual must commit to abide by a strict code of professional conduct and ethics.
    b. Be an associate member, in good standing, of the ACFE.
    c. Be of high moral character.
    d. All of the above.
25. Which of the following is *not* true regarding the ACFE.
    a. It is the largest antifraud organization in the world.
    b. It has roughly 12,000 members throughout the world.
    c. The entire organization is dedicated to the prevention of fraud.
    d. It is the premier provider of antifraud training.

SHORT CASES

Case 1

Clever, Inc., is a car manufacturer. Its 2011 income statement is as follows:

Clever, Inc. Income Statement For the Year Ended December 31, 2011	
Sales revenue	$20,000
Less cost of goods sold	10,000
Gross margin	$10,000
Expenses	8,000
Net income	$ 2,000

Alexander, Inc., is a car rental agency based in Florida. Its 2011 income statement is as follows:

Alexander, Inc. Income Statement For the Year Ended December 31, 2011	
Sales revenue	$20,000
Expenses	15,000
Net income	$ 5,000

During 2011, both Clever, Inc., and Alexander, Inc., incurred a $1,000 fraud loss.

1. How much additional revenue must each company generate to recover the losses from the fraud?
2. Why are these amounts different?
3. Which company will probably have to generate less revenue to recover the losses?

Case 2

You are having lunch with another graduate student. During the course of your conversation, you tell your friend about your new fraud examination class. After you explain the devastating impact of fraud on businesses today, she asks you the following questions:

1. What is the difference between fraud and error?
2. With all the advances in technology, why is fraud a growing problem?

Case 3

For each of the following examples, identify whether the fraud is employee embezzlement, management fraud, investment scam, vendor fraud, customer fraud, or miscellaneous fraud.

1. Marcus bought a $70 basketball for only $30, simply by exchanging the price tags before purchasing the ball.
2. Craig lost $500 by investing in a multilevel marketing scam.
3. The Bank of San Felipe lost over $20,000 in 2011. One of its employees took money from a wealthy customer's account and put it into his own account. By the time the fraud was detected, the employee had spent the money and the bank was held responsible.
4. The CEO of Los Andes Real Estate was fined and sentenced to six months in prison for deceiving investors into believing that the company made a profit in 2011, when it actually lost over $150 million.
5. The government lost over $50 million in 2011 because many of its contractors and subcontractors charged for fictitious hours and equipment on a project in the Middle East.
6. A student broke into the school's computer system and changed her grade in order to be accepted into graduate school.

Case 4

Fellow students in your fraud examination class are having a hard time understanding why statistics on fraud are so difficult to obtain. What would you say to enlighten them?

Case 5

You're telling your boyfriend about your classes for the new semester. He is very interested and intrigued by the idea of becoming a fraud detective, but wants to know whether fraud detectives will have job security and the type of work that is available. How would you respond to his questions?

Case 6

A bookkeeper in a $3 million retail company had earned the trust of her supervisor, so various functions normally reserved for management were assigned to her, including the authority to issue and authorize customer refunds. She proceeded to issue refunds to nonexistent customers and created documents with false names and addresses. She adjusted the accounting records and stole about $15,000 cash. She was caught when an internal audit sent routine confirmations to customers on a mailing list and received excessive "return-to-sender" replies. The investigation disclosed a telling pattern. The bookkeeper initially denied accusations but admitted the crime upon presentation of the evidence.

You are a lawyer for the retail company. Now that the fraud has been detected, would you prosecute her criminally, civilly, or both? What process would you use to try to recover the $15,000?

Case 7

You are a new summer intern working for a major professional services firm. During your lunch break each day, you and a fellow intern, Bob, eat at a local sandwich shop. One day, Bob's girlfriend joins you for lunch. When the bill arrives, Bob pays with a company credit card and writes the meal off as a business expense. Bob and his girlfriend continue to be "treated" to lunch for a number of days. You know Bob is well aware of a recent memo that came down from management stating casual lunches are not valid business expenses. When you ask Bob about the charges, he replies, "Hey, we're interns. Those memos don't apply to us. We can expense anything we want."

1. Is fraud being committed against the firm?
2. What responsibility, if any, do you have to report the activity?

Case 8

After receiving an anonymous note indicating fraudulent activities in the company, XYZ Company officials discover that an employee has embezzled a total of $50,000 over the past year. Unfortunately, this employee used an assumed identity and has suddenly disappeared. The CFO at XYZ wants to know how badly this fraud has hurt the company. If XYZ has a profit margin of 7 percent, how much additional revenue will XYZ have to generate to cover the loss?

Case 9

Your friend John works for an insurance company. John holds a business degree and has been involved in the insurance business for many years. In a recent conversation, John shares some company information with you. He has heard that the internal auditors estimate that the company has lost about $2.5 million over the last year as a result of fraud. Because you are a certified fraud examiner, John asks you how this will affect the company's profitability. John doesn't have access to the company's financial information.

1. Compute the additional revenues needed to make up for the lost money, assuming that the company has profit margins of 5, 10, and 15 percent.
2. Give examples of three types of fraud that could affect the insurance company.
3. In the case, who are the victims and who are the perpetrators?

Case 10

You are an accounting student at the local university pursuing your master's degree. One of your friends has been intrigued by the numerous frauds that have recently been reported in the news. This friend knows you are going to pursue a job as an auditor with a large public accounting firm, but your friend does not understand the difference between what you will be doing and what fraud examiners do. Write a paragraph that explains the difference between auditing and fraud examination.

Case 11

You own a local pizza delivery store. Cesar Rodriquez has been working for you as a manager for two years and has been a close friend of yours. Cesar has the reputation of being a hard worker and has not taken vacation for the entire time he has worked for you. Last week, Cesar left town to attend a family funeral. While he was gone, you received several phone calls that seemed suspicious. During these suspicious calls, a potential customer would call and ask for the manager. When you answered the phone (representing the manager), the customer would ask for the "manager's special." When informed that there was not a "manager's special" offered this weekend, the caller would quickly hang up. This occurred several times. When Cesar returned, you decided to spend an evening observing the order-taking process. It became apparent that Cesar was skimming cash from the business. Cesar would take the order for the "manager's special" without entering the sale into the computer. Cesar would then deliver the pizza and pocket the money.

1. Write a paragraph explaining why Cesar should be terminated from employment.
2. Write a paragraph explaining why it is important that Cesar is prosecuted for his crime.

Case 12

Bob, who works as a credit manager for a large bank, has a reputation for being a very hard worker. His convenient downtown apartment is located near the bank, which allows him to work undisturbed late into the night. Everyone knows that Bob loves his job because he has been with the bank for many years and hardly ever takes a vacation. He is a very strict credit manager and has the reputation for asking very difficult questions to loan applicants before approving any credit.

Nancy, Bob's director, noticed that Bob had not taken a mandatory weeklong vacation for a number of years. Given Bob's history of being tough on approving credit for the bank, should Nancy be concerned?

Case 13

Upon hearing that you are enrolled in a fraud class, a manager of a local business asks, "I don't understand what is happening with all these major scandals such as the Bernie Madoff scandal, the Goldman Sachs accusations, and the Enron fraud. There are billions of dollars being stolen and manipulated. How can any good auditor not notice when billions of dollars are missing?" How would you respond?

Case 14

While discussing your class schedule with a friend who is an accounting major, your friend describes why she decided not to take the fraud class you are enrolled in: "With advances in audit technology and the increased digitalization of business records, fraud detection is a dying part of a financial statement audit." How would you respond?

Case 15

After telling one of your parents that you want to be a fraud examiner after graduation, your parent expresses concerns about your career choice. How would you explain to your father the kind of career opportunities you will have as a fraud examiner, the types of organizations that will hire you, and the kind of work you will be doing?

CASE STUDIES

Case Study 1[30]

Gus Jackson was hired from a Big Four public accounting firm to start a new internal audit function for ABC Company, a newly acquired subsidiary of a large organization. His first task involved getting to know ABC management and supporting the public accountants in their year-end audit work.

Once the year-end work was finished, Gus started an audit of the accounts payable function. Jane Ramon, who had worked on the parent company's internal audit staff for about four years, supported him in this activity.

The accounts payable audit went smoothly, although many employees made no effort to conceal their hostility and resentment toward anyone associated with the new parent company. One exception was Hank Duckworth, the accounts payable manager. Hank was extremely helpful and complimentary of the professional approach used by the auditors. Gus had actually met Hank four years earlier, when Hank had been an accounting supervisor for an audit client where Gus was the junior accountant.

As the audit neared completion, Gus reviewed an audit comment Jane had written—a statement concerning some accounts payable checks that lacked complete endorsement by the payees. Both Gus and Jane recognized that in some situations and in some organizations less-than-perfect endorsements were not a critical concern; but these checks were payable to dual payees, and the endorsement of each payee was required. Gus asked Jane to make some photocopies of the examples so the evidence would be available for the audit close-out meeting with the management.

Jane returned 20 minutes later with a puzzled expression. "I pulled the examples," she said, "but look at these!" Jane placed five checks on the desk in front of Gus. "What do you make of these?" she asked.

"Make of what?" asked Gus.

"Don't you see it? The handwriting on all the endorsements looks the same, even though the names are different! And these are manual checks, which in this system usually means they were pushed through the system as rush payments."

"They do look similar," Gus replied, "but a lot of people have similar handwriting."

It hit Jane and Gus at the same time. All five checks had been cashed at the same convenience store less than five miles from the home office, even though the mailing address of the payee on one of the checks was over 200 miles away!

Jane decided to pull the supporting documentation for the payments but found there was none! She then identified other payments to the same payees and retrieved the paid checks. The endorsements did not look at all like the endorsements on the suspicious checks. To determine which of the endorsements were authentic, Jane located other examples of the payees' signatures in the lease, correspondence, and personnel files. The checks with supporting documentation matched other signatures on file for the payees.

Gus and Jane decided to assess the extent of the problem while investigating quietly. They wanted to avoid prematurely alerting perpetrators or management that an investigation was underway. With the help of other internal auditors from the parent company, they worked after normal business hours and reviewed endorsements on 60,000 paid checks in three nights. Ninety-five checks that had been cashed at the convenience store were identified.

Still, all Gus and Jane had were suspicions—no proof. They decided to alert executive management at the subsidiary and get their help for their next step.

The Follow-Through   Since the subsidiary had little experience with dishonest and fraudulent activity, it had no formalized approach or written fraud policy. Gus and Jane, therefore, maintained control of the investigation all the way to conclusion. With the help of operating management, the auditors contacted carefully selected payees. As is often the case involving fictitious payments to real payees, the real payees had no knowledge of the payments and had no money due to them. The auditors obtained affidavits of forgery.

In order to identify the perpetrator, the auditors documented the processing in more detail than had been done in the original preliminary survey for the routine audit. There were seven people who had access, opportunity, and knowledge to commit the fraud. The auditors then prepared a personnel spreadsheet detailing information about every employee in the department. The spreadsheet revealed that one employee had evidence of severe financial problems in his personnel file. It also showed that Hank Duckworth's former residence was three blocks from the convenience store.

Armed with the affidavits of forgery, the auditors advised management that the case was no longer merely based on suspicions. Along with members of operating management, the auditors confronted the convenience store owners to learn why they had cashed the checks, and who had cashed them.

The convenience store manager had a ready answer. "We cash those for Hank Duckworth. He brings in several checks a month to be cashed. He used to live down the street. Never had one of those checks come back!"

The rest is history. Hank was confronted, and confessed. The fully documented case was turned over to law enforcement. Hank pled guilty and received a probated sentence in return for full restitution, which he paid.

Questions

1. What clues caused Jane to suspect that fraud was involved?
2. Why is it important for fraud examiners to follow up on even the smallest inconsistencies?
3. In an attempt to identify possible suspects, the auditors researched the personal files of every employee in the department. What things might they have been looking for to help them identify possible suspects?

Case Study 2: Sweepstakes-legitimate or deceptive?

Sweepstakes Company Agrees to Pay Up[31]
A recent newspaper contained the following story:

Publishers Clearing House agreed to pay $34 million in a deal with 26 states to settle allegations the sweepstakes company employed deceptive marketing practices. The $34 million will cover customer refunds, legal expenses, and administrative cost to the states. Each state's share has yet to be determined. In the lawsuits, state attorney generals accused Publishers Clearing House of deceptive marketing for its sweepstakes promotions. The suit alleged that the company was misleading consumers by making them believe they had won prizes or would win if they bought magazines from Publishers Clearing House.

As part of the settlement, the company will no longer use phrases like "guaranteed winner." "This will in fact revolutionize the sweepstakes industry," Michigan Attorney General Jennifer Granholm stated. "We listened to the states' concerns and have agreed to responsive and significant changes that will make our promotions the clearest, most reliable and trustworthy in the industry," said Robin Smith, chairman and CEO of the Port Washington, N.Y.–based company.

Publishers Clearing House reached an $18 million settlement last August with 24 states and the District of Columbia. The states involved in the latest settlement are: Arizona, Arkansas, Colorado, Connecticut, Delaware, Florida, Indiana, Iowa, Kansas, Kentucky, Maine, Maryland, Massachusetts, Michigan, Minnesota, Missouri, New Jersey, North Carolina, Oregon, Pennsylvania, Rhode Island, Tennessee, Texas, Vermont, West Virginia, and Wisconsin.

Questions

1. Based on this information, do you believe Publishers Clearing House has committed fraud?
2. Why or why not?

Case Study 3: Trading After Hours

Several years ago, Prudential Securities was charged with fraud for late trading. This was the first major brokerage house to be charged with the illegal practice of buying mutual funds after hours.

The regulators who accused Prudential Securities charged them with carrying out a large-scale, late-trading scheme that involved more than 1,212 trades that were valued at a remarkable $162.4 million. These trades were placed after hours in order to benefit favored hedge funds. The complaint did not contain information regarding any profits that were protected by the scandal.

The regulators who accused Prudential stated that Prudential should have noticed the considerable number of trades that were being placed after 4 p.m. and should have begun an internal inquiry. However, the complaint stated that Prudential possessed "no internal supervisory procedures" to detect trades placed after hours.

Market timing, often done in conjunction with late trading, involves rapid in and out trading of a mutual fund designed to take advantage of delays in marking up prices of securities in the funds. By buying before the markups and selling quickly after them, Prudential traders realized quick profits for the firm's clients at the expense of others. A group of managers and top-producing brokers were charged last month by the SEC and/or state in separate civil actions related to market timing. The firm denies all wrongdoing.

Normally, orders to buy funds after 4 p.m. should be filled at the price set the next day. In late trading, which is illegal, orders instead get the same day's 4 p.m. price, enabling investors to react to news a day ahead of other investors.

In order to accomplish late trading, the complaint stated that Prudential clients would engage in the following activities: Prudential clients would submit a list of potential trades to brokers before the 4 p.m. deadline by fax, e-mail, or telephone. After 4 p.m., clients notified Prudential which of the long list of trades it wished to execute. Prudential brokers would take the original order, cross out the trades the client didn't want to execute, and then forward the order to the firm's New York trading desk. The time stamp on the fax would often deceptively reflect the time it was received originally, not the time that the client confirmed the order. For example, in just one afternoon, at 4:58 p.m., Prudential's New York office executed more than 65 mutual fund trades, for a total of $12.98 million.

According to the complaint, Prudential did nothing to substantiate the orders that were received before 4 p.m. In early 2003, the brokerage firm issued a policy change requiring branch managers to initial a cover sheet for trades before faxing them to New York. Lists of trades could be received at Prudential's New York trading desk as late as 4:45 p.m. Accusations against the firm state that, "The orders were never rejected and were always executed at same-day prices."

The complaint further states that Prudential also allowed the brokers involved in the market-timing and late-trading scheme to have dedicated wire-room personnel to execute trades. It has been suggested that the brokers compensated the wire-room employees for their efforts, by sharing year-end bonuses. The state alleges that Prudential also authorized one broker to obtain special software that gave the employee "electronic capacity to enter bulk mutual fund exchanges after 4 p.m."[32]

Questions

1. Determine whether this case would be prosecuted as a criminal or civil offense, and state reasons to support your conclusion.
2. Who are the victims of this late-trading scheme, and what losses do they incur?

INTERNET ASSIGNMENTS

Your best friend wants to know why "on earth" you are taking a fraud examination class. He is curious about what careers this class prepares you for. Go to the Internet and find information about two different careers that you could pursue in the field of fraud examination.

Write two or three brief paragraphs about what you found. Remember to include the Web sites where your information came from so that your friend can do some investigating of his or her own.

DEBATES

For the past year, you have been working as a secretary/processor for a local construction company, XYZ Homes, which specializes in the building of low-cost, limited-option homes. You left a comfortable, good-paying job to work for XYZ because it was family-owned and operated by long-time friends.

Soon after you began working for XYZ, you noticed questionable behavior on the part of Mr. and Mrs. XYZ's two sons, who are company salesmen. In fact, you are positive that they are falsifying documents to increase their commissions and to trick local banks into approving mortgages to customers who don't meet credit standards.

You are trying to decide how to handle the situation when one of the sons approaches you and asks you to produce and sign a memo to a bank, falsely stating that a certain potential home buyer is creditworthy. You refuse to do so and, after much consideration, approach Mr. XYZ about the situation. To your surprise, he simply brushes off your comments as unimportant and laughingly states that "boys will be boys."

What would you do in this situation? Is the fact that you correctly refused to produce and sign a false memo enough, or are you obligated to report these crimes to the banks and proper authorities? Discuss the options, responsibilities, and implications you are facing.

END NOTES

1. D. Teather, 2009, "Bernard Madoff Receives Maximum 150-Year Sentence," *The Guardian*, available at: www.guardian.co.uk/business/bernard-madoff.

2. G. Gregoriou and F. Lhabitant, 2009, "Madoff: A Riot of Red Flags," available at: http://papers.ssrn.com/sol3/papers.cfm?abstract_id=1335639.

3. U. Bhattacharya, The Optimal Design of Ponzi Schemes in Finite Economies, *Journal of Financial Intermediation*, Vol. 12 (2003): 1.

4. E. Arvedlund, *Madoff—The Man Who Stole $65 Billion* (London, England: Penguin Books, 2009).

5. D. Hart and G. Strober, *Catastrophe: The Story of Bernard L. Madoff, the Man Who Swindled the World* (Beverly Hills, California: Phoenix Books, Inc., 2009).

6. R. Bolton and D. Hand, Statistical Fraud Detection: A Review, *Statistical Science*, Vol. 17 (2002): 3.

7. S. Zahra, R. Priem, and A. Rasheed, Understanding the Causes and Effects of Top Management Fraud, *Organizational Dynamics*, Vol. 36 (2007): 2.

8. G. Sadka, The Economic Consequences of Accounting Fraud in Product Markets: Theory and a Case from the U.S. Telecommunications Industry (WorldCom), *American Law and Economics Review*, Vol. 8 (2006): 3.

9. H. Tan, E-Fraud: Current Trends and International Developments, *Journal of Financial Crime*, Vol. 9 (2002): 4.

10. "McNamara's Money Game," *Newsday: The Long Island Newspaper* (April 16, 1992).

11. *Webster's New World Dictionary, College Edition* (Cleveland and New York: World Publishing, 1964): 380.

12. I. Hamilton and I. Francis, *The Enron Collapse, IMD Case Study* (Wellesley, Massachusetts: ECCH, 2003).

13. Galbraith, J. K., *A Short History of Financial Euphoria* (London, England: Penguin Books, 1994).

14. This statistics is the proprietary information of a major financial institution for which two of the authors were consultants.

15. W. S. Albrecht and D. Schmoldt, "Employee Fraud," *Business Horizons*, Vol. 31: 4.

16. C. Hogan, R. Zabihollah, R. Riley, and U. Velury, Financial Statement Fraud: Insights from the Academic Literature, *Auditing: A Journal of Practice & Auditing*, Vol. 27 (2008): 2.

17. The Association of Certified Fraud Examiners (ACFE), *The Report to the Nation on Occupational Fraud and Abuse* (Austin, Texas: ACFE, 2008).

18. The Association of Certified Fraud Examiners (ACFE), *The Report to the Nation on Occupational Fraud and Abuse* (Austin, Texas: ACFE, 2008).

19. J. Bologna, *Handbook on Corporate Fraud* (Woburn, Massachusetts: Butterworth-Heinemann, 1993).

20. J. Tackett, "Bribery and Corruption," *Journal of Corporate Accounting & Finance*, Vol. 21 (2010): 4.

21. Federal Bureau of Investigation (FBI), *White Collar Crime: A Report to the Nation* (Washington, D.C.: Department of Justice, 1989).

22. T. King, C. Dennis, and L. Wright, "Myoptia, Customer Returns and the Theory of Planned Behavior," *Journal of Marketing Management*, Vol. 24 (2008): 1, 2.

23. J. Efendi, A. Srivastava, and E. Swanson, "Why Do Corporate Managers Misstate Financial Statements? The Role of Option Compensation and Other Factors," *Journal of Financial Economics*, Vol. 85 (2007): 3.

24. E. Rice, and B. Shah, "He's Madoff with My Money!," *Trust & Trustees*, Vol. 16 (2010): 4.

25. Federal Bureau of Investigation, *Common Fraud Schemes*, available at: www.fbi.gov/majcases/fraud/fraudschemes.htm, accessed April 14, 2010.

26. Securities and Exchange Commission (SEC), 2000, *Litigation Release No. 16489*.

27. Securities and Exchange Commission (SEC), 1997, *Litigation Release No. 38765*.

28. A few business schools have recently started offering fraud-related majors with as many as 10 to 12 different fraud-related courses.

29. "Careers to Count On," *U.S. News and World Report* (February 18, 2002), p. 46–48.

30. C. Thompson, "The First Audit," *The Internal Auditor*, Vol. 52 (1995): 4.

31. T. Miller, 2001, *Iowa Department of Justice PCH Settlement Release*, News Release: June 26, 2001.

32. "Fraud Charges Widen Scope of Scandal Facing Mutual Funds," *The Wall Street Journal* (December 12, 2003).

CHAPTER **2**

Why People Commit Fraud

LEARNING OBJECTIVES

After studying this chapter, you should be able to:

- Know the types of people who commit fraud.
- Explain why people commit fraud.
- Describe the fraud triangle.
- Explain the fraud scale.
- Understand how pressure contributes to fraud.
- Understand why opportunity must be present for fraud to occur.
- Understand why people rationalize.
- Understand how people are recruited to participate in fraud schemes.

TO THE STUDENT

This chapter covers some of the basic principles of fraud. It begins with a description of the types of people who perpetrate fraud. We then discuss why people commit fraud, including the fraud triangle. Finally, we examine how honest individuals are recruited to participate in fraud schemes. By understanding these basic principles, you will see fraud perpetrators in a different light and begin to understand how a trusted friend or colleague could, unfortunately, become involved in fraud.

I, Dennis Greer, am making this statement on my own, without threat or promises, as to my activities in regard to the activity of kiting between Bank A and Bank B. As of May 20XX, I was having extreme emotional and financial difficulties. For religious reasons, I was required without notice to move out of where I was living, and I had no place to go. Also, my grandmother—the only family member I was close to—was dying. I had to live out of my car for three weeks. At the end of this time, my grandmother died. She lived in Ohio; I went to the funeral and returned with a $1,000 inheritance. I used this money to secure an apartment. The entire sum was used up for the first month's rent, deposit, and application fee. From that time, mid-June, until the first part of August, I was supporting myself on my minimum-wage job at the nursery. I had no furniture or a bed. I was barely making it. I was feeling very distraught over the loss of my grandmother and problems my parents and brother were having. I felt all alone. The first part of August arrived, and my rent was due. I did not have the full amount to pay it. This same week, I opened a checking account at Bank B. I intended to close my Bank A account because of a lack of ATMs, branches, and misunderstanding. As I said, my rent was due, and I did not know how to meet it. On an impulse, I wrote the apartment manager a check for the amount due. I did not have the funds to cover it. I thought I could borrow it, but I could not. During the time I was trying to come up with the money, I wrote a check from my Bank B account to cover the rent check and put it into Bank A. I did not know it was illegal. I knew it was unethical, but I thought since the checks were made out to me that it wasn't illegal. This went on for about a week—back and forth between banks. I thought I could get the money to cover this debt, but I never did. My grandmother's estate had been quite large, and I expected more money, but it was not to happen. After a week of nothing being said to me by the banks, I began to make other purchases via this method. I needed something to sleep on and a blanket and other items for the apartment. I bought a sleeper sofa, a desk, a modular shelf/bookcase, and dishes and also paid off my other outstanding debts—college loans, dentist bill, and credit. I was acting foolishly. No one had questioned me at the banks about any of this. I usually made deposits at different branches to try to avoid suspicion, but when I was in my own branches, no one said a thing. I thought maybe what I was doing wasn't wrong after all. So I decided to purchase a new car, stereo, and a new computer to use at home for work. Still, I did not have a problem making deposits at the banks. But, I was feeling very guilty. I knew I needed to start downsizing the "debt" and clear it up. I began to look for a better-paying job. Finally, last week I got a call from Bank B while I was at work. They had discovered a problem with my account. I realized then that the banks had found out. Later that day, I got another call from Bank A. They told me that what I had been doing was illegal and a felony. I was in shock. I didn't know it was that bad. I realize now how wrong what I did was. From the start, I knew it was unethical, but I didn't know it was indeed a crime until now. I have had to do a lot of thinking, praying, and talking to those close to me about this. I am truly sorry for what I have done, and I don't EVER plan to do it again. All I want now is to make amends with the banks. I do not have the money to pay back either bank right now. I realize this hurts them. I want to try to set this right, whether I go to prison or not. I am prepared to work however long it takes to pay the banks back in full with reasonable interest from a garnishment of my wages from now until the full amount is paid and settled. I committed this act because I was feeling desperate. I was emotionally a wreck and physically tired. I felt I didn't have a choice but to do what I did or return to living in my car. I know now that what I did was wrong, and I am very sorry for it. I am attempting to seek psychological counseling to help me deal with and resolve why I did this. I feel I have a lot to offer society, once I am able to clean up my own life and get it straightened out. I pray the bank employees and officers will forgive me on a personal level for the hardship my actions have caused them, and I want to make full restitution. I have done wrong, and I must now face the consequences. This statement has been made in my own words, by myself, without threat or promise, and written by my own hand.

Dennis Greer

Obviously, the name of the perpetrator in the case shown here has been changed. However, this is a true confession written by a person who was involved in the fraud of kiting[1]—using the float time between banks to give the impression that he had money in his accounts. The case includes many of the common pressures and rationalizations that a person goes through when faced with an opportunity to commit fraud. Pressure, rationalization, and opportunity will become a central theme in this chapter as we discuss the fraud triangle[2] and the various reasons why people commit fraud.

In Chapter 1, we talked about what fraud is, the seriousness of the fraud problem, many of the different types of frauds, how much fraud costs organizations, and the difference between civil and criminal law. In this chapter, we will discuss who commits frauds and why individuals commit fraud. We will also discuss how a person, once he or she has become involved in fraud, will then use various types of power to recruit others to participate in fraud. To prevent, detect, and investigate fraud, you must understand what motivates fraudulent behavior and why otherwise honest people behave unethically.

Who Commits Fraud

Research shows that anyone can commit fraud. Fraud perpetrators usually can't be distinguished from other people on the basis of demographic or psychological characteristics. Most fraud perpetrators have profiles that look like those of other honest people.[3]

Several years ago, a study was conducted to determine the physical and behavioral characteristics of fraud perpetrators. In this study, fraud perpetrators were compared with (1) prisoners incarcerated for property offenses and (2) a sample of noncriminal, college students. The personal backgrounds and psychological profiles of the three groups were compared. The results indicated that incarcerated fraud perpetrators were very different from other incarcerated prisoners. When compared to other criminals, they were less likely to be caught, turned in, arrested, convicted, and incarcerated. They were also less likely to serve long sentences. In addition, fraud perpetrators were considerably older. While only 2 percent of the property offenders were female, 30 percent of fraud perpetrators were women. Fraud perpetrators were better educated, more religious, less likely to have criminal records, less likely to have abused alcohol, and considerably less likely to have used drugs. They were also in better psychological health. They enjoyed more optimism, self-esteem, self-sufficiency, achievement, motivation, and family harmony than other property offenders. Fraud perpetrators also seemed to express more social conformity, self-control, kindness, and empathy than other property offenders.[4]

> **Remember this ...**
>
> *Individuals involved in fraud are typically people just like you and me, but have compromised their integrity and become entangled in fraud. When doing business in the future, remember that fraud perpetrators will, unfortunately, often be those colleagues in whom you place a great amount of trust.*

When fraud perpetrators were compared with college students, they differed only slightly. Fraud perpetrators suffered more psychic pain and were more dishonest, more independent, more sexually mature, more socially deviant, and more empathetic than college students. However, fraud perpetrators were much more similar to college students than they were to property offenders. Figure 2.1 illustrates the differences among the three groups.

It is important to understand the characteristics of fraud perpetrators because they appear to be very much

FIGURE 2.1   PROFILES OF FRAUD PERPETRATORS

College Students   Fraud Perpetrators   Other Property Offenders

like people who have traits that organizations look for in hiring employees, seeking out customers and clients, and selecting vendors. This knowledge helps us to understand that (1) most employees, customers, vendors, and business associates and partners fit the profile of fraud perpetrators and are capable of committing fraud and (2) it is impossible to predict in advance which employees, vendors, clients, customers, and others will become dishonest. In fact, when fraud does occur, the most common reaction by those around the fraud is denial. Victims cannot believe that trusted colleagues or friends have behaved dishonestly.

The Fraud Triangle

While there are thousands of ways to perpetrate fraud, Dennis Greer's example (in the opening case of the chapter) illustrates the three key elements common to all of them. His fraud included: (1) a perceived pressure, (2) a perceived opportunity, and (3) some way to rationalize the fraud as acceptable. These three elements make up what we call the fraud triangle,[5] as shown in Figure 2.2.[a]

After moving into an apartment, Dennis Greer could not pay the second month's rent. Faced with the choice between being dishonest or going back to living in his car, Dennis chose to be dishonest. Every fraud perpetrator faces some kind of **perceived pressure**. Most pressures involve a financial need, although nonfinancial pressures, such as the need to report financial results better than actual performance, frustration with work, or even a challenge to beat the system, can also motivate fraud. In Dennis Greer's case, he had an actual pressure. You may look at a fraud perpetrator and think "but he

or she didn't have a real pressure." However, it doesn't matter what you think—what matters is the perception of the perpetrator at the time of the fraud. Later in this chapter, we will discuss the different kinds of pressures experienced by fraud perpetrators.

Dennis found a way to commit fraud by repeatedly writing bad checks to give the impression that he was depositing real money in his accounts. He didn't need access to cash, to use force, or to even confront his victims physically. Rather, he simply wrote checks to himself in the privacy of his own apartment and deposited them in two different banks. His weapons of crime were a pen and checks from the financial institutions. Whether or not Dennis could actually get away with his crime didn't matter. What mattered was that Dennis believed he could conceal the fraud—in other words, he had a **perceived opportunity**.

Fraud perpetrators need a way to **rationalize** their actions as acceptable. Dennis's rationalizations were twofold: (1) he didn't believe what he was doing was "illegal," although he recognized it might be unethical; and (2) he believed he would get an inheritance and be

FIGURE 2.2   THE FRAUD TRIANGLE

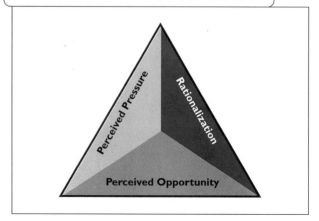

---

[a] In recent years, some researchers have added "capability" as a fourth element of the fraud triangle, suggesting that an individual's personal traits and abilities play a major role in the perpetration of fraud. As a result, in some circumstances, the fraud triangle may be referred to as *The Fraud Diamond*.

FIGURE 2.3   THE FIRE TRIANGLE

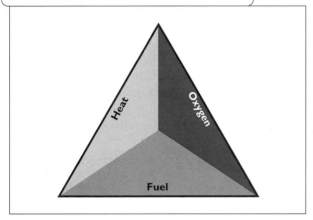

able to pay the money back. In his mind, he was only *borrowing,* and, while his method of borrowing was perhaps unethical, he would repay the debt. After all, almost everyone borrows money.

Perceived pressure, perceived opportunity, and rationalization are common to every fraud. Whether the fraud is one that benefits the perpetrator directly, such as employee fraud, or one that benefits the perpetrator's organization, such as management fraud, the three elements are always present. In the case of management fraud, for example, the pressure could be the need to make earnings look better or to meet debt covenants, the opportunity could be a weak audit committee and the rationalization could be "we'll only 'cook the books' until we can get over this temporary hump."

In many ways, fraud is like fire. In order for a fire to occur, three elements are necessary: (1) oxygen, (2) fuel, and (3) heat. These three elements make up the

"fire triangle," as shown in Figure 2.3. When all three elements come together, there is fire.

Firefighters know that a fire can be extinguished by eliminating any one of the three elements. Oxygen is often eliminated by smothering, by using chemicals, or by causing explosions, as is the case in oil well fires. Heat is most commonly eliminated by pouring water on fires. Fuel is removed by building fire lines or fire breaks or by shutting off the source of the fuel.

As with the elements in the fire triangle, the three elements in the fraud triangle are interactive. With fire, the more flammable the fuel, the less oxygen and heat it takes to ignite. Similarly, the purer the oxygen, the less flammable the fuel needs to be to ignite. With fraud, the greater the perceived opportunity or the more intense the pressure, the less rationalization it takes to motivate someone to commit fraud. Likewise, the more dishonest a perpetrator is, the less opportunity and/or pressure it takes to motivate fraud. The scale in Figure 2.4 illustrates the relationship between the three elements.[6]

As we will show in later chapters, people who try to prevent fraud usually work on only one of the three elements of the fraud triangle: opportunity. Because fraud-fighters generally believe that having good internal controls can eliminate opportunities, they focus all or most of their preventive efforts on implementing controls and ensuring adherence to them.[7] Rarely do they focus on the pressures motivating fraud or on the rationalizations of perpetrators.

It is interesting to note that almost every study that has been done on honesty in advanced countries reveals that levels of honesty are decreasing. Given

FIGURE 2.4   THE FRAUD SCALE

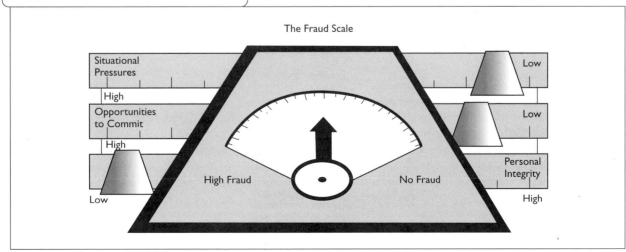

the interactive nature of the elements in the fraud triangle, the decreasing levels of honesty present a scary future concerning fraud. Less honesty makes it easier to rationalize, thus requiring less perceived opportunity and/or pressure for fraud to occur.

Rationalizations and related honesty levels, as well as fraud opportunities, will be discussed later in this chapter. We now turn our attention to a discussion of the pressures motivating individuals to commit fraud.

The Element of Pressure

Fraud can be perpetrated to benefit oneself or an organization. Employee fraud, in which an individual embezzles from his or her employer, usually benefits the perpetrator. Management fraud, in which an organization's officers deceive investors and creditors by manipulating financial statements, is most often perpetrated to benefit an organization and its officers. In this section, we will discuss the different pressures that motivate individuals to perpetrate fraud on their own behalf. Most fraud experts believe that the pressures can be divided into four main groups: (1) financial pressures, (2) vices, (3) work-related pressures, and (4) other pressures.

Financial Pressures

Studies suggest that approximately 95 percent of all frauds involve either financial or vice-related pressures. Dennis Greer's financial pressures were that he was living in his car, didn't have furniture or other living necessities, and was broke. Common financial pressures associated with fraud that benefits perpetrators directly include the following:

1. Greed
2. Living beyond one's means
3. High bills or personal debt
4. Poor credit
5. Personal financial losses
6. Unexpected financial needs

This list is not exhaustive, and these pressures are not mutually exclusive. However, each pressure in this list has been associated with numerous frauds.[8] Many individuals have committed fraud because they were destitute. Other frauds include perpetrators who were living lifestyles far beyond that of their peers. When one perpetrator was caught embezzling over $1.3 million from his employer, for example, it was discovered that he had spent the money on monogrammed shirts and gold cuff links, two Mercedes-Benz cars, an expensive suburban home, a beachfront condominium, furs, rings and other jewelry for his wife, a new car for his father-in-law, and

a country club membership. Most people would say that this person didn't truly have financial pressures. But to him, the pressures of these luxuries were enough to motivate him to commit fraud.

Financial pressures can occur suddenly or be long term. Unfortunately, very few fraud perpetrators inform others when they are having financial problems. As an example, consider Susan Jones. She had worked at the same company for over 32 years. Her integrity had never been questioned. At age 63, she became a grandmother. Immediately, she became a "spendaholic." She bought everything she could get her hands on for her two grandchildren. She even became addicted to the Home Shopping Network. During the three years prior to her retirement, Susan stole over $650,000 from her employer. When caught, she was sentenced and served one year in prison. She also deeded everything she and her husband owned to her former employer in an attempt to repay the employer. By giving her employer her home, her retirement account, and her cars, she repaid approximately $400,000 of the $650,000 she stole. She also entered into a restitution agreement to pay back the remaining $250,000 she still owed. And, because she had not paid income taxes on the $250,000 of fraudulent "income," the IRS required her to make monthly tax payments after she got out of prison.

The fact that someone has been an "honest" employee for a long time (32 years in this example) seems to make no difference when severe financial pressures occur or an individual perceives that such pressures exist. Recent studies have found that while approximately 30 percent of employee frauds are perpetrated by employees during their first three years of employment, 70 percent are committed by employees with four to 35 years of experience, and the age group with the highest evidence of fraud involves individuals between the ages of 35 and 44 years old.

Financial pressure is the most common type of pressure to commit fraud. Usually, when management fraud occurs, companies overstate assets on the balance sheet and net income on the income statement. They usually have pressure to do so because of a poor cash position, receivables that aren't collectible, a loss of customers, obsolete inventory, a declining market, or restrictive loan covenants that are being violated. For example, Regina Vacuum was a company whose management committed massive financial statement fraud. Their major pressure was that the vacuum cleaners they were selling were defective and had melting parts, and thousands were being returned. The large number of sales returns reduced revenues significantly and created such income pressures that management intentionally understated sales returns and significantly overstated actual sales.

Vice Pressures

Closely related to financial pressures are motivations created by vices such as gambling, drugs, alcohol, and expensive extramarital relationships. As an example of these vices motivating a person to commit fraud, consider one individual's confession of how gambling led to his dishonest acts.

As I sat on the stool in front of the blackjack table, I knew I was in trouble. I had just gambled away my children's college fund. I stumbled to my hotel room, hoping to wake up and realize this evening was nothing more than a nightmare. While driving back to San Jose from Reno Sunday morning, I could not face the embarrassment of telling my wife. I had to come up with the money. I was sure that if I had only $500, I could win the money back. But how could I get $500? A short time later at work, an accounts payable clerk came to my office seeking assistance with a problem. The clerk was matching invoices with purchase orders. He had found an invoice for $3,200 that did not match the purchase order. Immediately, I realized how I could get the $500 "loan." My company was a fast-growing microchip producer whose internal controls were quite good on paper but were often not followed. The company had a policy of paying, without secondary approval, any invoice of $500 or less. I decided to set up a dummy company that would issue invoices to my employer for amounts up to $500. I was confident my winnings from these "borrowings" would not only allow me to replace the college fund, but would also allow repayment of the "loan." I couldn't believe how easy it was to "borrow" the money. The first check showed up in a PO box I had opened a few days earlier. I called my wife with the bad news. Together with the controller, I would have to fly to Los Angeles over the weekend to meet with lawyers over a company matter. Within minutes, I was on my way to Reno. Upon arrival, I went straight to the craps tables. By 4:00 a.m. I was not only out of money but was in the hole over $600. I was concerned about the losses, but not as worried as before. I would just submit more fictitious bills to the company. Over the next few months, my fraud progressed to the point where I had set up two more dummy companies and insisted that accounts payable clerks not verify any invoice of less than $750. No one questioned my changing the policy because I had worked for the company for over 14 years and was a "trusted" employee. After one year, I had replaced the college fund and purchased a new automobile; I had stolen over $75,000. I was caught when the internal auditors matched addresses of vendors and found that my three dummy vendors all had the same PO box.

Vices are the worst kind of pressures to commit fraud. Examples include female employees who embezzled because their children were on drugs and they couldn't stand to see them go through withdrawal pains. Other examples involve "successful" managers who, in addition to embezzling from their companies, burglarized homes and engaged in other types of theft to support their drug habits. To understand how addictive vices can be, consider the following confessions from reformed gamblers:

- *"Gambling was the ultimate experience for me—better than sex, better than any drug. I had withdrawal tortures just like a heroin junkie."*
- *"I degraded myself in every way possible. I embezzled from my own company; I conned my 6-year-old out of his allowance."*
- *"Once I was hooked, any wager would do. I would take odds on how many cars would pass over a bridge in the space of 10 minutes."*
- *"I stole vacation money from the family sugar jar. I spent every waking hour thinking about getting to the track."*
- *"After I woke up from an appendectomy, I sneaked out of the hospital, cashed a bogus check, and headed for my bookie. I was still bleeding from the operation."*
- *"I'll never forget coming home from work at night, looking through the window at my family waiting for me, and then leaving to place a couple more bets. I was crying the whole time, but I had simply lost all control."*

If someone will steal from his 6-year-old child or sneak out of a hospital still bleeding from an operation, he or she will certainly steal from his or her employer or commit other types of fraud. The number of embezzlers who trace their motivation for embezzlement to alcohol, gambling, and expensive extramarital relationships is high. However, the motivation to steal for drugs may even be higher. Consider these confessions of former addicted drug users:

- *"I began living with a man who was a heavy drug user. We had a child, but the relationship didn't last. By the time it ended, I was high on drugs and alcohol so much of the time I could barely manage to make it to work every day."*
- *"I was the branch manager of a large bank. But secretly I was shooting up in my office all day and stealing money from my employer to finance it."*
- *"One day my daughter stretched out her little arms in front of me. She had made dots with a red pen on each of the creases in her arms. 'I want to be just like my Daddy,' she said proudly."*

- *"My wife and I literally whooped for joy at the sight of our newborn son: a 7-pound baby with big eyes and rosy cheeks—normal and healthy looking. But we both knew the moment we had been dreading was now just hours away. The baby would be going through withdrawal. We didn't want him to suffer because of our awful habit. And we had to keep the doctors from finding out he had drugs in his system, or he would be taken from us and placed in foster care. We felt we had no choice. When the nurses left the room, I cradled our baby in my arms and clipped a thin piece of heroin under his tongue."*
- *"I lost my job. I was robbing and stealing every day to support my habit, which cost $500 per day."*

Someone who will clip a piece of heroin under a newborn baby's tongue or burglarize homes to support his or her habit will surely look for ways to embezzle from employers or commit other types of fraud.

Work-Related Pressures

While financial pressures and vices motivate most frauds, some people commit fraud to get even with their employer or others. Factors such as getting little recognition for job performance, having a feeling of job dissatisfaction, fearing losing one's job, being overlooked for a promotion, and feeling underpaid have motivated many frauds. Here is an example.

I began my career at XYZ Company as a staff accountant. I am a religious person. In fact, I spent a year volunteering with a nonprofit agency that provided relief to people in need of food and shelter. Because of this experience and because of my six years with the company, I was considered a person of impeccable character and a very trusted employee. The president of XYZ is a workaholic and considers an eight-hour day to be something a part-time employee works. As a result, I spent six years working in my finance position, putting in between 12 and 14 hours per day. During this period, I was paid a salary, with no overtime compensation. Early in my career, the extra hours didn't bother me; I considered them an investment in my future. Soon, I was named manager of the purchasing department. After two years in that position, I realized that the 12- to 14-hour days were still an expected way of life at the company. I was becoming bitter about the expectation of overtime and felt that the company "owed me" for the time I had worked for "nothing." I decided to get my "pay" from the company. Working with a favored vendor, I accepted kickbacks to allow over $1.5 million in overcharges to the company. I figured the $80,000 I received in kickbacks was compensation that I deserved.[9]

Other Pressures

Once in a while, fraud is motivated by other pressures, such as a spouse who insists on an improved lifestyle or a challenge to beat the system. In the famous Bernie Madoff Scandal discussed in Chapter 1, for example, experts believe that one of the pressures that led Madoff to commit fraud was the need to appear successful. When investments were not performing well, in order to save face, Madoff would simply make up fictitious returns. In another situation, the perpetrator embezzled over $450,000 so her husband could drive a new car, enjoy a higher lifestyle, and eat steak instead of hamburger. One famous computer consultant, who is now retained by major companies to help them deter and detect computer fraud, once felt personally challenged to "commit the perfect crime." After purchasing and taking delivery of over $1.5 million in inventory that was paid for by accessing a large company's computer records, he was caught when one of his inventory managers turned him in.

Most of us face pressures in our lives. We have legitimate financial needs, we make foolish or speculative investments, we are possessed by addictive vices, we feel overworked and/or underpaid, or we are greedy and want more. We sometimes have a difficult time distinguishing between wants and needs. Indeed, the objective of most people in a capitalistic society is to obtain wealth. We often measure success by how much money or wealth a person has. If you say you have a very successful relative, you probably mean that he or she lives in a big house, has a cabin or a condominium, drives expensive automobiles, and has money to do whatever he or she wants.

To some people, being successful is more important than being honest. If they were to rank the personal characteristics they value most in their lives, being successful would rank higher than having integrity. Psychologists tell us that most people have a price at which they will be dishonest. Individuals with high integrity and low opportunity need high pressure to be dishonest.

Most of us can think of scenarios in which we, too, might commit fraud. If, for example, we were starving, we worked in an environment where cash was abundant and not accounted for, and we really believed that we would repay the money taken to feed ourselves, we might commit fraud. The U.S. president most famous for his honesty, Abraham Lincoln, once threw a man out of his office, angrily turning down a substantial bribe. When someone asked why he was so angry, he said, "Every man has his price, and he was getting close to mine." One thing is for certain—eliminating pressures in the fraud triangle has an effect similar to the removal of heat from the fire triangle. Without some kind of pressure, fraud rarely occurs.

The Element of Opportunity

A perceived opportunity to commit fraud, conceal it, or avoid being punished is the second element of the fraud triangle. In this section, we will discuss fraud opportunities. At least six major factors increase opportunities for individuals to commit fraud within an organization. The following list of these factors is not exhaustive, but it does provide a sufficient number of settings to illustrate the role of opportunities in the fraud triangle.

1. Lack of controls that prevent and/or detect fraudulent behavior
2. Inability to judge quality of performance
3. Failure to discipline fraud perpetrators
4. Lack of access to information
5. Ignorance, apathy, and incapacity
6. Lack of an audit trail

Controls That Prevent and/or Detect Fraudulent Behavior

Having an effective control framework is probably the most important step an organization can take to prevent and detect employee fraud. The organization that established the common internal control framework that most businesses subscribe to is the Committee of Sponsoring Organizations (COSO). While COSO[10] identifies five elements of an organization's internal control framework, we will discuss three of them including the control environment, the accounting function, and control activities.

The Control Environment

The **control environment** is the work atmosphere that an organization establishes for its employees. The control environment includes management's role and example, management communication, appropriate hiring, clear organizational structure, and an effective internal audit department.

Management's Role and Example The most important element in establishing an appropriate environment is *management's role and example*. In numerous instances, management's dishonest or inappropriate behavior has been learned and modeled by employees.

In the famous Equity Funding case, management was writing insurance policies on individuals who didn't exist and selling them to other insurance companies. Seeing this dishonest behavior, one employee said to himself, "It doesn't make sense to have all these fictitious people live forever. I'll knock a few of them off and collect death proceeds. My actions won't be any different from those of the management of this company." In another case, employees realized top management was overstating revenues. In response, the employees began overstating expenses on their travel reimbursement forms, billing for hours not worked, and perpetrating other types of fraud.

———

Proper **modeling** (being an example) and proper **labeling** (communication) are some of the most important elements in the control environment. When management models unacceptable behavior, the control environment is contaminated. Similarly, if management models a behavior that is inconsistent with good control procedures, the effectiveness of the control system is eroded. When a manager says, "Don't loan keys or share passwords with others," and then shares his or her password or keys, he or she is sending mixed signals and the inappropriate behavior will be followed by other employees. In other words, "actions speak louder than words." Management's example or model is the most critical element of the control environment when it comes to preventing fraud. Inappropriate behavior by management allows others to justify overriding and ignoring control procedures. As an example of how a manager's lack of proper modeling can lead to fraud, consider the following case: A branch manager stole $36,357 from the bank by cashing in seven customer CDs. She used the passwords of two other employees to execute six of the transactions and her own password to execute the seventh. She was caught when a customer complained. Why would this manager have the other employees' passwords? Most likely, she had set a tone through her modeling that the security of passwords was not important.

———

The importance of tone at the top was emphasized in the Sarbanes-Oxley legislation that was passed in 2002. It requires every public company to have a code of ethics or conduct to help deter wrongdoing and to promote the following:

- *Honest and ethical conduct, including the ethical handling of actual or apparent conflicts of interest between personal and professional relationships*
- *Avoidance of conflicts of interest, including disclosure to an appropriate person or persons identified in the code of any material transaction or*

relationship that reasonably could be expected to give rise to such a conflict

- *Full, fair, accurate, timely, and understandable disclosure in reports and documents that a company files with, or submits to, the Securities and Exchange Commission (SEC) and in other public communications made by the company*
- *Compliance with applicable governmental laws, rules, and regulations*
- *The prompt internal reporting of code violations to an appropriate person or persons identified in the code*
- *Accountability for adherence to the code*

Under this new requirement, a company must disclose in its annual report whether or not it has a code of ethics. Companies are also required to disclose, either on Form 8-K or on their Web sites, any changes to, or waivers of, such codes of ethics.

Management Communication   The second critical element in the control environment is *management's communication*. Communicating what is and is not appropriate is critical. Just as parents who are trying to teach their children to be honest must communicate often and openly with them, organizations that want employees to behave in a certain way must clearly label what is and is not acceptable. Codes of conduct, orientation meetings, training, supervisor/employee discussions, and other types of communication that distinguish between acceptable and unacceptable behavior are critical.

To be an effective deterrent to fraud, communication must be consistent. Messages that change based on circumstances and situations serve not only to confuse employees but also to encourage rationalizations. One of the reasons that so many frauds occur in crash or rush projects is that typical control procedures are not followed. Inconsistent messages relating to procedures and controls are often conveyed. Strikes, mergers, bankruptcies, and other dramatic events usually result in inconsistent communication and allow for increased fraud.

Just as good communication between managers and employees is critical, accurate and consistent communication between organizations and their customers, vendors, and shareholders is also critical. Consider the following example of a fraud and lawsuit that occurred between a bank and its customer because of failed communication.

A financial institution was sending out new credit cards to customers whose credit cards were about to expire. However, the financial institution sent a credit card belonging to one customer to a different customer with the same name but with a different address and Social Security number. The unintended recipient, a person of unsavory character, immediately used the card to withdraw a cash advance of approximately $1,300. He then used the credit card to buy several items, totaling approximately $5,000. The bank sent him the credit card bill (because it now had the incorrect address for the card). The man, however, didn't pay the bill. After several months of nonpayment, the financial institution called the true owner of the card. When the owner insisted that he had never received the card, the bank researched the problem and discovered that the person using the card was someone different than the owner. The financial institution turned this information over to law enforcement who put out an "all points bulletin (APB)" on the thief. The man was caught and arrested in a nearby state. He spent three days in jail before being deported back to the state where the financial institution was located. Because he had been incarcerated, he sued the financial institution for $3 million for unlawful imprisonment. Before the case was settled, the financial institution had spent nearly $300,000 defending itself. Making sure it was communicating with the proper customer would have prevented the entire mess.

Appropriate Hiring   The third critical element in creating the proper control structure is *appropriate hiring*. Research has shown that nearly 30 percent of all people in the United States are dishonest, another 40 percent are situationally honest (honest where it pays to be honest and dishonest where it pays to be dishonest), and 30 percent are honest all the time.[11] While most organizations are convinced that their employees, customers, and vendors are among the 30 percent who are honest, this usually isn't the case.

When dishonest individuals are hired, even the best controls will not prevent fraud. For example, a bank has tellers, managers, loan officers, and others who have daily access to cash and can steal. Because it is impossible to deter all bank fraud, banks hope that personal integrity, together with preventive and detective controls and the fear of punishment, will deter theft.

As an example of the consequences of poor hiring, consider the case of a famous person who was raped a few years ago. The singer checked into a well-known hotel. A few hours after her arrival, there was a knock on her door, accompanied by the words "Room Service." She hadn't ordered anything but thought that maybe, because she was famous, the hotel was bringing her a basket of fruit or some complimentary wine. When she opened the door, three hotel custodians burst into her room and raped her. She later sued the hotel for $4 million and won. The basis of her lawsuit was that the hotel had inadequate hiring procedures because all three custodians had previous arrest records and had been fired from previous jobs because of rape. The person then donated the $4 million to a charity for abused women.

If an organization does not carefully screen job applicants and hires dishonest individuals, it will suffer from fraud, regardless of how good its other controls are. To understand how good hiring practices can help prevent fraud and other problems, consider a company that decided to take extra precautions in its hiring practices. Its approach was first to train all persons associated with hiring decisions to be expert interviewers and, second, to check three background references for each prospective employee thoroughly. Because of these extra precautions, over 800 applicants (13 percent of all individuals) who would have been hired were disqualified. These applicants had undisclosed problems, such as falsified employment information, previous arrest records, uncontrollable tempers, alcoholism, drug addition, and a pattern of being fired from previous jobs.

The effects of poor hiring practices are illustrated in the following excerpt from an article in *Business Week Online*:

> *These days, it's tempting to hire the first person who seems capable of doing a job. But do you know what lurks behind that spiffy résumé? The Association of Certified Fraud Examiners estimates that employee fraud costs small companies an average of $120,000 per incident. It's a good idea to check the backgrounds of all applicants. At the very least, you'll be certain the person has the credentials they claim.... Three years ago, managers hired a security expert to conduct background checks on employees and potential hires, examining credit and criminal backgrounds and verifying education and experience. Good thing they did—the company was on the verge of hiring a director of finance who turned out to have neither the MBA nor any of the experience he said he had.*[12]

Clear Organizational Structure   The fourth fraud-deterring element of the control environment is a *clear organizational structure*. When everyone in an organization knows exactly who has responsibility for each business activity, fraud is less likely to be committed. In such situations, it is easier to track missing assets and harder to embezzle without being caught. Strict accountability for job performance is critical for a good control environment.

As an example of how failure to assign proper custody resulted in a fraud, consider the case of Jane D.

I was one of eight tellers in a medium-sized bank. Because we all had access to money orders and bank checks, I stole 16 money orders. I didn't use them for two weeks to see if anyone would notice them missing. Then, I used one for $300. After nothing being said during the next two weeks, I used seven more.

In this case, someone independent from the teller should have had the organizational responsibility to reconcile money orders on a daily basis.

Effective Internal Audit Department   The fifth element of the control environment is *an effective internal audit department*,[13] combined with security or loss prevention programs. While most studies have found that internal auditors detect only about 20 percent of all employee frauds (others are detected through tips, by alert employees, or accidentally), the mere presence of internal auditors provides a significant deterrent effect. Internal auditors provide independent checks and cause perpetrators to question whether or not they can commit fraud and not be caught. A visible and effective security function, in conjunction with an appropriate loss prevention program, can help ensure that fraud is properly investigated and that control weaknesses and violations are appropriately handled and punished.

Taken together, the five control environment elements—(1) management's role and example, (2) management communication, (3) appropriate hiring, (4) clear organizational structure, and (5) an effective internal audit department—can create an atmosphere in which fraud opportunities are decreased because employees see that fraud is not acceptable and not tolerated. Relaxing any one of these five elements increases fraud opportunities.

The Accounting System

The second component of the control structure is a good **accounting system**. Every fraud is comprised of three elements: (1) the theft act, in which assets are taken, (2) concealment, which is the attempt to hide the fraud from others, and (3) conversion, in which the perpetrator spends the money or converts the stolen assets to cash and then spends the money. An effective accounting system provides an **audit trail** that allows frauds to be discovered and makes concealment difficult. Unlike bank robbery, in which there is usually no effort to conceal the theft act, concealment is one of the major distinguishing elements of fraud.

Frauds are often concealed in accounting records. Accounting records are based on transaction documents, either paper or electronic. To cover up a fraud, paper or electronic documentation must be altered, misplaced, or made fraudulent. Frauds can be discovered in accounting records by examining transaction entries that have no support or by probing financial statement amounts that are not reasonable. Without a good accounting system, distinguishing between actual fraud and unintentional errors is often difficult. A good accounting system should ensure that recorded transactions are (1) valid, (2) properly authorized, (3) complete, (4) properly classified, (5) reported in the proper period, (6) properly valued, and (7) summarized correctly.

Control Activities (Procedures)

The third component of the control structure is good **control activities** (or **procedures**). An individual who owns his or her own business and is the sole employee probably does not need many control procedures. While such people may have ample opportunity to defraud their companies, they have no incentive to do so. They wouldn't steal from themselves, and they would never want to treat customers poorly. However, organizations that involve many employees must have control procedures so that the actions of employees will be congruent with the goals of management or the owners. In addition, with control procedures, opportunities to commit and/or conceal frauds are eliminated or minimized. No matter what the business is, whether it is the business of raising children; the business of operating a financial institution, a grocery store, or a *Fortune* 500 company; or the business of investing personal assets, the following five primary control procedures are necessary:

1. Segregation of duties, or dual custody
2. System of authorizations
3. Independent checks
4. Physical safeguards
5. Documents and records

While thousands of control procedures are followed by businesses, they are all variations of each of these five basic procedures. Good fraud detection and prevention efforts involve matching the most effective control procedures with the various risks of fraud. As an illustration of how control procedures can be used to achieve goal congruence and prevent fraud, consider the following situation:

Mark was a seventh grader. At the annual parent-teacher conferences, Mark's parents discovered that he was getting straight As in all of his classes except one—a German class in which he was getting an F. When Mark's parents later asked him about the class, he said, "I hate the teacher. She is a jerk and I refuse to work for her." After discussions with the teacher and Mark, Mark's parents decided to implement three controls so that his actions would be consistent with the desires of his parents. First, Mark's parents printed up some simple forms (documents) for the teacher to check off each day. These pieces of paper contained two simple statements: (1) Mark (was) (was not) prepared for class today, and (2) Mark (was) (was not) responsible in class today. The teacher would circle the appropriate response to each phrase, initial the paper, and send it home with Mark. By insisting on reading the note each night, Mark's parents were performing an independent check on his performance. In addition, his in-line skates were taken away until his grade improved. Taking away his right to play street hockey was a variation of an authorization control. (He lost his authorized use.) When Mark's parents invoked the three controls of (1) documents, (2) independent checks, and (3) taking away an authorized activity, his behavior performance in German changed to become more in line with the goals of his parents. By the end of the term, his grade in German changed from an F to a B.

Segregation of Duties and Dual Custody
Segregation of duties involves dividing a task into two parts so that one person does not have complete control of the task. Dual custody requires two individuals to work together at the same task. Either way, it takes two people to do one job. This form of control, like most preventive controls, is most often used when cash is involved. For example, the opening of incoming cash receipts in a business is usually done by two people or by segregating duties. The accounting for and the handling of cash receipts are separated so that one person does not have access to both. The case of Fred R. is

a good example of the ease with which fraud can be perpetrated when there is no separation of duties.

Fred R. worked for a medium-size homebuilder. He was in charge of writing checks as well as reconciling bank statements. Over a period of time, Fred stole over $400,000 by manipulating the check register and forcing the bank reconciliation to balance. If, for example, his employer owed a subcontractor $15,000, Fred would write the check for $15,000 and write $20,000 on the check stub. Then, using the next check, he would write himself a check for $5,000 and mark the check stub "voided." When the bank statement was returned, he would destroy the checks written to himself and force the reconciliation.

Fred's fraud could easily have been caught, if not prevented, if someone besides Fred had either reconciled the bank statements or written checks. There are at least three critical functions that even small business owners should either set up as segregated duties or always do themselves. These include: (1) writing checks, (2) making bank deposits, and (3) reconciling bank statements.

Because two individuals are involved, dual custody or segregation of duties is usually the most expensive of all controls. Labor costs are high, and hiring two people to complete one job is a luxury that most businesses don't believe they can afford. This control always involves a tradeoff between higher labor cost and less opportunity for error and fraud. Besides being expensive, good dual custody is often difficult to enforce. When two individuals are working on the same task, they should both focus on the assignment and not be distracted by conversation, phone calls, or other interruptions. An example of a fraud that was perpetrated in a supposed "dual-custody environment" is the case of Roger M., who made the following confession:

In January 20XX, I took the amount of $3,062 in cash, which was contained in a disposable night drop bag. I concealed my actions by putting it inside a night drop envelope that I processed on the same day. I have no real excuse for taking the money. I saw an easy way of getting money, and I took advantage of it. Circumstances that made it seem easy to take the money without being caught or observed were that I was situated on the customer side of the merchant vault, which obscured the view of my dual-custody partner. I have reimbursed the bank today (January 27, 20XX) the amount of $3,062.

System of Authorizations The second internal control procedure is a proper **system of authorizations**. Authorization control procedures take many forms. Passwords authorize individuals to use computers and to access certain databases. Signature cards authorize individuals to enter safe deposit boxes, to cash checks, and to perform other functions at financial institutions. Spending limits authorize individuals to spend only what is in their budget or approved level.

When people are not authorized to perform an activity, the opportunity to commit fraud is reduced. For example, when individuals are not authorized to enter safe deposit boxes, they cannot enter and steal someone else's contents. When individuals are not authorized to approve purchases, they cannot order items for personal use and have their companies pay for the goods. As the following fraud case shows, the failure to enforce authorization controls makes the perpetration of fraud quite simple.

Mary and Ron had been customers of a certain bank for many years. Because Ron owned a jewelry store, they maintained a safe deposit box at the bank to store certain inventory. Most employees of the bank knew them well because of their frequent visits to make deposits and conduct other business. What was unknown to the bank employees was that Mary and Ron were having marital difficulties, which ended in a bitter divorce. After the divorce, they canceled their joint safe deposit box. Ron came in to the bank a short time later and opened a new safe deposit box, with his daughter as cosigner. Because Mary was bitter about the divorce settlement, she entered the bank one day and told the safe deposit custodian (who had been away on vacation when she and Ron closed their box) that she had lost her key and needed to have the box drilled. Because the custodian knew Mary and didn't know the old box had been closed and a new one opened, Mary arranged to force open the box. Without any problems, the box was drilled, and Mary emptied the contents. When Ron tried to open the box a few days later, he discovered what had happened. Because Mary was not a signer on the account at the time the box was forced open, the bank was completely liable and settled out of court with the jeweler for $200,000. This fraud was allowed to be perpetrated because the authorization control of matching signatures to a signature card was not performed.

Independent Checks The theory behind **independent checks** is that if people know that their work or activities will be monitored by others, the opportunity to commit and conceal a fraud will be reduced. There are many varieties of independent checks. The Office of the Controller of the Currency (OCC) requires that every bank employee in the United States take one week's vacation (five consecutive days) each year. While employees are gone, others are supposed to perform their work. If an employee's work piles up while he or she is out for the week, this "mandatory vacation" control is not working as it should and the opportunity to commit fraud is not eliminated.

Periodic job rotations, cash counts or certifications, supervisor reviews, employee hot lines, and the use of auditors are other forms of independent checks. One large department store in Europe has a complete extra staff of employees for its chain of department stores. This staff goes to a store and works while everyone who is employed there goes on vacation for a month. While they are gone, the transient staff operates the store. One of the purposes of this program is to provide complete, independent checks on the activities of store employees. If someone who is committing fraud is forced to leave for a month, the illegal activity is often discovered.

As an illustration of the creative use of independent checks, consider the case of a Baskin-Robbins ice cream store in Washington, DC.

Upon entering this 31-flavors establishment, the customer is greeted by a smiling cashier. Two large signs hang on the wall behind the cashier. One sign reads, "If you have problems with service, please call the manager at this telephone number." The other reads, "If you get a star on your sales receipt, you receive a free sundae."

In an ice cream store or any other retail establishment, one of the easiest ways to perpetrate fraud is to accept cash from customers and either not ring it into the cash register or ring it in as a lesser amount. If the store happens to sell ice cream, cones can be made a little smaller during the day so that the extra ice cream used in cones not entered into the cash register is not noticeable. The purpose of the Baskin-Robbins signs is to encourage customers to receive and examine their sales receipts. In order for customers to be able to look for a star, sales receipts must be issued. If the cashier charges $2 for an ice cream cone and rings only $1 into the cash register, sooner or later a customer will report the embezzlement.

Physical Safeguards   **Physical safeguards** are often used to protect assets from theft by fraud or other means. Physical safeguards, such as vaults, safes, fences, locks, and keys, take away opportunities to commit fraud by making it difficult for people to access assets. Money locked in a vault, for example, cannot be stolen unless someone gains unauthorized access or unless someone who has access violates the trust. Physical controls are often used to protect inventory by storing it in locked cages or warehouses, small assets such as tools or supplies by locking them in cabinets, and cash by locking it in vaults or safes.

Documents and Records   The fifth control procedure involves using **documents and records** to create a record of transactions and an audit trail. Documents rarely serve as preventive controls but provide excellent detective controls. Banks, for example, prepare kiting suspect reports as well as reports of employee bank account activity to detect abuse by employees or customers. Most companies require a customer order to initiate a sales transaction. In a sense, the entire accounting system serves as a documentary control. Without documents, no accountability exists. Without accountability, it is much easier to perpetrate fraud and not get caught.

Sometimes an organization can have good documents and records but not use them appropriately. For example, most banks maintain safe deposit boxes for their customers. To enter the safe deposit box area, banks require customers to sign a signature card and provide proof of box ownership. In one case, however, the bank employee looked at the signature and document but opened the wrong box for a customer. Instead of opening the customer's box, he mistakenly opened a box in which the bank was storing its excess cash. Once the teller had left the room, the customer put the bank's excess cash (approximately $110,000) in his briefcase and exited the bank. He hadn't entered the bank intending to steal, but the bank teller, by not examining the document containing his box number carefully, had made it too easy for him not to take the money.

Summary of the Controls that Prevent or Detect Fraud

The control environment, the accounting system, and the many variations of the five control activities or

TABLE 2.1 INTERNAL CONTROL STRUCTURE

CONTROL ENVIRONMENT	ACCOUNTING SYSTEM	CONTROL ACTIVITIES OR PROCEDURES
1. Management philosophy and operating style, modeling	1. Valid transactions	1. Segregation of duties
2. Effective hiring procedures	2. Properly authorized	2. Proper procedures for authorization
3. Clear organizational structure of proper modeling and labeling	3. Completeness	3. Adequate documents and records
4. Effective internal audit department	4. Proper classification	4. Physical control over assets and records
	5. Proper timing	5. Independent checks on performance
	6. Proper valuation	
	7. Correct summarization	

procedures work together to eliminate or reduce the opportunity for employees and others to commit fraud. A good control environment establishes an atmosphere in which proper behavior is modeled and labeled, honest employees are hired, and all employees understand their job responsibilities. The accounting system provides records that make it difficult for perpetrators to gain access to assets, to conceal frauds, and to convert stolen assets without being discovered. Together, these three components make up the control structure of an organization. Table 2.1 summarizes these components and their elements.

Unfortunately, many frauds are perpetrated in environments in which controls are supposed to be in place but are not being followed. Indeed, it is the overriding and ignoring of existing controls—not the lack of controls—that allow most frauds to be perpetrated. However, many other factors allow fraud to be perpetrated. We will now discuss some of these common factors that allow frauds to take place within organizations. These include the inability to judge the quality of performance; the failure to discipline fraud perpetrators; a lack of access to information; ignorance, apathy, and incapacity; and lack of an audit trail.

Inability to Judge the Quality of Performance

If you pay someone to construct a fence, you can probably examine the completed job and determine whether or not the quality of work meets your specifications and is consistent with the agreed contract. If, however, you hire a lawyer, a doctor, a dentist, an accountant, an engineer, or an auto mechanic, it is often difficult to know whether you are paying an excessive amount or receiving inferior service or products. With these kinds of contracts, it is easy to overcharge, perform work not needed, provide inferior service, or charge for work not performed. The *Los Angeles Times* recently reported on a California dermatologist who was accused of saving skin samples from patients with skin cancer and then using those cancerous tissues to diagnose healthy patients with skin cancer. The doctor did this to increase his pay from roughly $50 for removing noncancerous skin tissue to the more than $150 he was paid for removing cancerous tissues. Unfortunately, once a search warrant was issued on his behalf, the pressure and associated guilt was too much and contributed to his apparent suicide. Reports to the highway patrol stated that the doctor basically parked his car and walked in front of traffic on a California freeway. Employees of the doctor stated that hundreds of patience diagnoses had been faked.[14]

Another example of the inability to judge the quality of performance was the case of Sears Automotive in California:

Prompted by an increasing number of consumer complaints, the California Department of Consumer Affairs completed a one-year investigation into allegations that Sears Tire and Auto Centers overcharged their customers for auto repair services. The undercover investigation was conducted in two phases. In the first phase, agents took 38 cars known to have defects in the brakes and no other mechanical faults to 27 different Sears Automotive Centers in California. In 34 of the 38 cases, or 89 percent of the time, agents were told that additional work was necessary, involving additional costs. The average amount of the over-charge was $223, but in the worst case, which occurred in San Francisco, agents were overcharged $585 to have the front brake pads, front and rear springs, and control-arm bushings replaced. Although a spokesman for Sears denies the allegations and says that Sears will fight any attempt to deprive it of its license to do auto repair work in California, the evidence of fraud is substantial. In one case, Ruth Hernandez, a citizen of Stockton, California, went to Sears to have new tires put on her car. While she was there, the mechanic informed her that she also needed new struts, which would cost an additional $419.95. When Mrs. Hernandez sought a second opinion, she was told her struts were fine. The Sears mechanic later admitted to having made an incorrect diagnosis.[15]

In trying to understand why a well-established, well-reputed company such as Sears might commit such a fraud, it is important to know that Sears had established a quota for parts, services, and repair sales for each eight-hour shift. Allegedly, mechanics who consistently did not meet their quotas either had their hours reduced or were transferred out of the parts and services department. Apparently when faced with the pressure to cheat or fail, and believing that customers would not know for themselves whether or not the parts and services were actually needed, many service center employees decided to commit fraud.

Failure to Discipline Fraud Perpetrators

Criminologists generally agree that rapists have the highest rate of repeat offenses (recidivism) of all criminals. The next highest rate of repeat offenders is probably fraud perpetrators who are not prosecuted or disciplined. An individual who commits fraud and is not punished or is merely terminated suffers no significant penalty and often resumes the fraudulent behavior.

Fraud perpetrators are usually individuals who command respect in their jobs, communities, churches, and families. If they are marginally sanctioned or terminated, they rarely inform their families and others of the real reason for their termination or punishment. On the other hand, if they are prosecuted, they usually suffer significant embarrassment from having family, friends, and business associates know about their offenses. Indeed, suffering humiliation, more than any other factor, deters future fraud activity by fraud perpetrators.

Because of the expense and time involved in prosecuting, many organizations merely dismiss dishonest employees, hoping to rid themselves of the problem. What these organizations fail to realize is that such action is rather shortsighted. While they may rid themselves of one fraud perpetrator, they have sent a signal to others in the organization that fraud perpetrators do not suffer significant consequences for their actions. Indeed, lack of prosecution can give others a "perceived opportunity" that, when combined with pressure and rationalization, can result in additional frauds in the organization. Perceived opportunity is removed when there is a high probability that perpetrators will be punished, not just discovered.

In a society in which workers are mobile and often move from job to job, mere termination often helps perpetrators build an attractive résumé but does not eliminate fraud opportunities. A man we'll call John Doe is a classic example of someone whose termination without being punished for fraud allowed him to get increasingly attractive jobs at increased salary levels. His employment and fraud history for 14 years are outlined in Table 2.2.

According to one reference who described the fraud, this man was never prosecuted. His victim organizations either felt sorry for him, thought prosecution would be too time consuming and too expensive, or merely chose to pass the problem on to others. As a result, every succeeding job this perpetrator obtained was better than his previous one until he became a controller and chief financial officer (CFO) making $130,000 a year. By merely terminating the perpetrator, his victims helped him build a résumé and secure increasingly attractive jobs.

TABLE 2.2 JOHN DOE'S EMPLOYMENT AND FRAUD HISTORY

OCCUPATION	JOB LENGTH	AMOUNT EMBEZZLED
Insurance sales	10 months	$200
Office manager	2 years	1,000
Bookkeeper	1 year	30,000
Accountant	2 years	20,000
Accountant	2 years	30,000
Controller & CFO	6 years	1,363,700
Manager	Still employed	?

Lack of Access to Information

Many frauds are allowed to be perpetrated because victims don't have access to information possessed by the perpetrators. This is especially prevalent in many of the large management frauds that have been perpetrated against stockholders, investors, and debt holders. In the famous ESM fraud case, for example, the same securities had been sold to investors several times. Yet, because those investment records were only in the possession of ESM, victims didn't know of the fraudulent sales.

A classic example of a fraud in which lack of information allowed the fraud to be perpetrated is the Lincoln Savings and Loan case. On January 6, 1992, Charles Keating and his son, Charles Keating III, were convicted on 73 and 64 counts, respectively, of racketeering and fraud. Charles Keating had created sham transactions to make Lincoln Savings look more profitable than it really was in order to please auditors and regulators. He was able to perpetrate the fraudulent schemes because auditors and regulators were not given complete access to transactions. For example, one transaction, known as the RA *Homes sale*, was structured as follows:

On September 30, 1986, defendants Keating and others caused a subsidiary of Lincoln Savings to engage in a fraudulent sale of approximately 1,300 acres of undeveloped land northwest of Tucson, Arizona, to RA Homes, Inc., at a price of approximately $25 million, consisting of a $5 million cash down payment and a $20 million promissory note, secured only by the undeveloped land. Defendants Keating and others caused Lincoln to record a sham profit of approximately $8.4 million on the sale. RA Homes agreed to purchase the land only after Keating orally (1) promised that Lincoln would reimburse RA Homes for the down payment on the purchase, (2) agreed that the Lincoln subsidiary would retain responsibility for developing and marketing the property, and (3) guaranteed that RA Homes would be able to sell the land at a profit within a year following the purchase.[16]

Auditors didn't know about any of the oral commitments, all of which violated accounting standards for recording a real estate sale. Subsequent to these oral agreements, in supposedly separate transactions, Keating loaned RA Homes $5 million (to cover the down payment) and then continued to manage, market, and develop the "sold" property. When the real estate agent, who supposedly had an exclusive selling arrangement, discovered that the 1,300 acres had supposedly been sold by Charles Keating himself, he contacted Charles Keating for a commission on the sale and was told that no real estate commission was due because the land had just been "parked" with RA Homes. With the higher reported profits of his company, Lincoln Savings and Loan was able to appear profitable and further perpetrate its fraud on investors and others.[17]

Most investment scams and management frauds are dependent on the ability to withhold information from victims. Individuals can attempt to protect themselves against such scams by insisting on full disclosure, including audited financial statements, a business history, and other information that could reveal the fraudulent nature of such organizations.

Certain employee frauds are also allowed to be perpetrated because only offenders have access to information. One small business employee, for example, stole $452,000 from her employer by writing checks to herself. Because she both wrote checks and reconciled the bank statement, no one caught her illegal activity. If, for example, a vendor was owed $10,000, she would write a check to that vendor for $10,000 but enter $20,000 in the check register. Then, after writing a $10,000 check to herself, she would write the word "VOID" in the check register next to the $10,000 check number. Her very simple fraud continued undetected because she was the only employee who had access to the checking account, the check register, and the bank statement.

Asymmetrical information, where one party has more or better information than another party, has in several cases led to lawsuits. For example, a company had a controller who embezzled over $5 million. He committed the fraud by writing company checks to himself. While the company had poor internal controls, especially a lack of segregation of duties, it sued its financial institution for negligence to recover the stolen funds. The basis of its lawsuit was that the organization's bank had superior information to detect the fraud because both the perpetrator and the company had accounts at the same bank. And, since the perpetrator embezzled money by writing company checks from an account in the bank and depositing the checks in his personal account at the bank, the plaintiff company believed the bank had the best information to detect the fraud.

Ignorance, Apathy, and Incapacity

Older people, individuals with language difficulty, and other "vulnerable" citizens are often fraud victims because perpetrators know that such individuals may not have the capacity or the knowledge to detect their illegal acts. For example, consider the following case:

A nurse with purple hands was charged with embezzling money from patients' rooms at a local hospital. The nurse's hands were purple because invisible dye had been put on money planted in a purse used to trap the embezzler. The nurse was on loan from a temporary-help agency. After money was reported missing from a patient's room, management checked the staff roster that indicated this nurse had recently been alone in the room just before the money was discovered missing. In order to gather additional evidence, hospital security put a purse containing dye-covered bills in a room. Later that day, a supervisor reported that the nurse had dye on her hands. When confronted, the nurse first said she had accidentally knocked the purse to the floor and her hands had been stained while she was replacing the items. However, after further questioning, the nurse admitted to taking the money from patients' rooms.

The nurse had found that hospital patients were an easy target for theft. In a hospital room, where patients are often under the influence of sedating drugs, victims may not have the ability to recognize that they have been robbed.

Frauds called *pigeon drops* are specifically designed to take advantage of elderly victims. In such thefts, perpetrators often pose as bank examiners trying to catch dishonest bankers, or they may use some other scheme to get elderly or non-English-speaking customers to withdraw money from banks. When these customers leave the bank with their money, the perpetrators grab the money and flee instead of examining it as promised, knowing the elderly person has no chance to catch them.

Many investment scams are also designed to take advantage of elderly victims. In the AFCO fraud case, a real estate investment scam, elderly victims were convinced to take out mortgages on their homes. These elderly victims were persuaded by questions and statements such as the following:

- *Do you know you have a sleeping giant in your home that you are not using?*
- *Your home is worth $100,000, is completely paid off, and you could get $80,000 out of it with no debt to you.*
- *If you are willing to borrow and invest $80,000, we'll make the mortgage payments, pay you interest of 10 percent on the money you're earning nothing on now, and buy you a new luxury car to drive.*

A financially prudent person would recognize that the perpetrators could not possibly pay the mortgage payment and pay 10 percent interest plus a brand new car. However, many elderly victims found the offer too good to refuse. As a result, several hundred elderly, retired citizens invested a total of over $39 million in the AFCO scam.

Many scams prey on elderly or uneducated victims. Various consumer frauds such as prime bank fraud, pyramid scams, Internet fraud, phone scams, chain letters, modeling agencies, telemarketing fraud, and Nigerian scams are all crimes of persuasion that try to get victims to unknowingly invest money.

Consider Nigerian investment scams, for example. Very few of us have not received a letter inviting us to share in huge wealth if only we will make a small investment or share bank account information. Estimates put the losses from these "Nigerian Advance Fee" operations at over $1 million "every single day" in the United States alone. The multistage fraud starts when you receive a scam fax, e-mail, or letter such as the one shown in Figure 2.5.

Lack of an Audit Trail

Organizations go to great lengths to create documents that will provide an audit trail so that transactions can be reconstructed and understood. Many frauds, however, involve cash payments or manipulation of records that cannot be followed. Smart fraud perpetrators understand that their frauds must be concealed. They also know that such concealment must usually involve manipulation of financial records. When faced with a decision about which financial record to manipulate, perpetrators almost always manipulate the income statement, because they understand that the audit trail will quickly be erased. Here is an example.

Joan Rivera was the controller for a small bank. Over a period of four years, she stole more than $100,000 by having an upstream bank pay her credit card bills. She covered her fraud by creating an accounting entry like the following:

Advertising Expense.........................1,000
    Cash...1,000

Joan used this approach because she knew that at year-end all expense accounts, including advertising expense, would be closed and brought to zero balances. If bank auditors and officials didn't catch the fraud before year-end, the audit trail would be erased and the fraud would be difficult to detect. On the other hand, she knew that if she covered the cash shortage by overstating outstanding checks on the

FIGURE 2.5   NIGERIAN SCAM LETTER

Lagos, Nigeria.

Dear Sir,

Confidential Business Proposal

Having consulted with my colleagues and based on the information gathered from the Nigerian Chambers Of Commerce And Industry, I have the privilege to request your assistance to transfer the sum of $47,500,000.00 (forty seven million, five hundred thousand United States dollars) into your accounts. The above sum resulted from an over-invoiced contract, executed, commissioned and paid for about five years (5) ago by a foreign contractor. This action was however intentional and since then the fund has been in a suspense account at The Central Bank Of Nigeria Apex Bank.

We are now ready to transfer the fund overseas and that is where you come in. It is important to inform you that as civil servants, we are forbidden to operate a foreign account; that is why we require your assistance. The total sum will be shared as follows: 70 for us, 25 for you and 5 for local and international expenses incidental to the transfer.

The transfer is risk free on both sides. I am an accountant with the Nigerian National Petroleum Corporation (NNPC). If you find this proposal acceptable, we shall require the following documents:

a. your bankers name, telephone, account and fax numbers.
b. your private telephone and fax numbers for confidentiality and easy communication.
c. your letter-headed paper stamped and signed.

Alternatively we will furnish you with the text of what to type into your letter-headed paper, along with a breakdown explaining, comprehensively what we require of you. The business will take us thirty (30) working days to accomplish.

Please reply urgently.

Best regards

---

bank reconciliation, the cash shortage would be carried from month to month, creating a "permanent" concealment problem. She also knew, for example, that if she manipulated the inventory, an asset, that inventory shortage would carry over into the next period.

In the earlier example, Joan was not caught until she got greedy and started using other fraud methods that were not as easily concealed.

The Element of Rationalization

So far, we have discussed the first two elements of the fraud triangle: perceived pressure and perceived opportunity. The third element is *rationalization*. An example of how rationalization contributes to fraud is the case of Jim Bakker and Richard Dortch. These men were convicted on 23 counts of wire and mail fraud and one count of conspiracy to commit wire and mail

fraud. As a result of their conviction, the perpetrators of one of the largest and most bizarre frauds in U.S. history were sent to jail. In his remarks to the court prior to Jim Bakker's sentencing, prosecutor Jerry Miller summarized this PTL (Praise-the-Lord) fraud with the following comments:

The biggest con man to come through this courtroom, a man corrupted by power and money and the man who would be God at PTL, is a common criminal. The only thing uncommon about him was the method he chose and the vehicle he used to perpetrate his fraud. He was motivated by greed, selfishness, and a lust for power. He is going to be right back at it as soon as he gets the chance. Mr. Bakker was a con man who in the beginning loved people and used things, but he evolved into a man, a ruthless man, who loved things and used people.

How did Jim Bakker, the beloved TV minister of the PTL network, rationalize the committing of such a massive fraud? Here is his story.

PTL had a modest beginning in 1973 when it began operating out of a furniture showroom in Charlotte, North Carolina. By October 1975, it had purchased a 25-acre estate in Charlotte, North Carolina, and had constructed Heritage Village, a broadcast network of approximately 70 television stations in the United States, Canada, and Mexico on which the PTL ministry's show was aired. PTL's corporate charter stated that the religious purposes of the organization were: (1) establishing and maintaining a church and engaging in all types of religious activity, including evangelism, religious instruction, and publishing and distributing Bibles; (2) engaging in other religious publication; (3) missionary work, both domestic and foreign; and (4) establishing and operating Bible schools and Bible training centers. Over the following 11 years, PTL built a multimillion-dollar empire that consisted of PTL and a 2,300-acre Heritage USA tourist center valued at $172 million. Specific activities of the organization included Heritage Church with a weekly attendance of over 3,000; Upper Room prayer services where counselors ministered to people; Prison Ministry, with a volunteer staff of over 4,000; Fort Hope, a missionary outreach house for homeless men; Passion Play, a portrayal of the life of Christ in an outdoor amphitheater; a dinner theater; a day care center; Heritage Academy; a summer day camp; the Billy Graham Home; workshops; and a Christmas nativity scene that had been visited by over 500,000 people.

PTL also had a wide range of activities that were ultimately deemed by the IRS to be commercial. In one such venture, PTL viewers were given an opportunity to become lifetime partners in a hotel for $1,000 each. Bakker promised that only 25,000 lifetime partnership interests would be sold and that partners could use the hotel free each year for four days and three nights. In the end, however, 68,412 such partnerships were sold. Through this and similar solicitations, Jim Bakker's PTL had amassed gross receipts of over $600 million, much of which had been used to support the extravagant lifestyle of Bakker and other officers of PTL. Time and time again, Bakker mislead worshippers, investors, and his faithful followers by misusing contributions, overselling investments, evading taxes, and living an extravagant lifestyle.[18]

How could a minister perpetrate such a large and vicious fraud in the name of religion? Most people believe that Jim Bakker's ministry was initially sincere, inspired by a real desire to help others and to teach the word of God. He believed that what he was doing was for a good purpose and rationalized that any money he received would directly or indirectly help others. He even recognized at one time that money might be corrupting him and his empire. In 1985 he said, "I was going to say to listeners, 'Please stop giving.' But, I just couldn't say that." What started out as a sincere ministry was corrupted by money until Jim Bakker rationalized on a television program, "I have never asked for a penny for myself. ... God has always taken care of me."[19] His rationalizations increased to the point that one of the trial attorneys, in her closing argument, stated, "You can't lie to people to send you money—it's that simple. What unfolded before you over the past month was a tale of corruption— immense corruption. ... What was revealed here was that Mr. Bakker was a world-class master of lies and half-truths." Jim Bakker rationalized his dishonest acts by convincing himself that the PTL network had a good purpose and that he was helping others.

Nearly every fraud involves the element of rationalization. Most fraud perpetrators are first-time offenders who would not commit other crimes. In some way, they must rationalize away the dishonesty of their acts. Common rationalizations used by fraud perpetrators include the following:

- *The organization owes it to me.*
- *I am only borrowing the money and will pay it back.*
- *Nobody will get hurt.*
- *I deserve more.*
- *It's for a good purpose.*
- *We'll fix the books as soon as we get over this financial difficulty.*
- *Something has to be sacrificed—my integrity or my reputation. (If I don't embezzle to cover my inability to pay, people will know I can't meet my obligations and that will be embarrassing because I'm a professional.)*

Certainly, there are countless other rationalizations. These, however, are representative and serve as an adequate basis to discuss the role of rationalization in the perpetration of fraud.

It is important to recognize that there are very few, if any, people who do not rationalize. We rationalize being overweight. We rationalize not exercising enough. We rationalize spending more than we should. And unfortunately, many of us rationalize being dishonest. We rationalize our dishonest acts in order to not feel guilty. This same sort of rationalization often allows the perpetration of fraud. Usually, fraud involves lying to someone else. However, fraud always involves the fraud perpetrator lying to him- or herself that what they are doing is justifiable.

As an example of rationalization, let's take a look at the issue of income tax evasion. Many people rationalize underpaying taxes by using the following rationalizations:

- *I pay more than my fair share of taxes.*
- *The rich don't pay enough taxes.*
- *The government wastes money.*
- *I "work" for my money.*

To understand the extent of income tax fraud, consider that, in 1988, for the first time, the IRS required taxpayers who claimed dependents to list the Social Security numbers for their dependents. In 1987, 77 million dependents were claimed on federal tax returns. In 1988, the number of dependents claimed dropped to 70 million. Fully one-tenth of the dependents claimed, or 7 million dependents, disappeared. Where did they go? Had they never existed? The IRS determined that in 1987 and probably in previous years, over 60,000 households had claimed four or more dependents who didn't exist, and several million had claimed one or more who didn't exist. Claiming dependents who don't exist is one of the most blatant and easiest-to-catch income tax frauds. Yet, millions of U.S. citizens rationalized and then blatantly cheated on their tax returns.

When interviewed, most fraud perpetrators say things like, "I intended to pay the money back. I really did." They are sincere. In their minds, they intended to (or rationalized that they would) repay the money, and since they judge themselves by their intentions, they do not see themselves as criminals. On the other hand, victims judge perpetrators by their actions and say, "You dirty rotten crook! You stole money from me and my organization."

One of the first white-collar criminals to be convicted and incarcerated during the major fraud scandals of 2002–2003 was Dr. Sam Waksal, CEO of ImClone.[20] Waksal was convicted in the same insider trading scandal involving Martha Stewart. In 2000, Waksal was one of Wall Street's men of the moment. As the CEO of ImClone, he had just sold an interest in a new cancer drug called Erbitux to Bristol-Myers for $2 billion. Everyone expected that the Food and Drug Administration would soon approve the drug. Shortly thereafter, however, Waksal learned from a Bristol-Myers executive that the drug wouldn't be approved. The FDA was refusing to consider the Erbitux application—not because the drug didn't work, but because the data were insufficient. New clinical trials would

have to be conducted, and the price of ImClone stock was going to plummet. Based on this insider information, Sam Waskal told his daughter to sell her shares, thinking that the price was about to go down. He also tried to sell 79,000 of his own shares (he owned millions of shares)—about $5 million worth. He transferred the 79,000 shares to his daughter thinking that if she sold them that was okay. He rationalized that he wasn't doing the selling.

Remember this …

We have now learned that people commit fraud as a result of pressure, opportunity, and rationalization. However, most companies today try to combat fraud only by decreasing opportunities for fraud to occur. While this is a good option, most companies overlook the elements of pressure and rationalization. By implementing programs that focus on eliminating employee pressure and decreasing the likelihood of employee rationalization, organizations will have an effective tool to deter fraud.

Later on, when explaining his actions, Waksal said the following: "I could sit there at the same time thinking I was the most honest CEO that ever lived. And, at the same time, I could glibly do something and rationalize it because I cut a corner, because I didn't think I was going to get caught. And who cared? Look at me. I'm doing 'X,' so what difference does it make that I do a couple of things that aren't exactly kosher?" In fact, Waksal's rationalization had allowed him to have a long history of ethical lapses, reckless behavior, and embellishing the truth. He had been dismissed from a number of academic and research positions for questionable conduct. One former colleague said, "Cutting corners for Sam was like substance abuse. He did it in every aspect of his life, throughout his entire life."[21]

Summary of the Fraud Triangle

As we conclude our discussion of the fraud triangle, consider one last example of fraud. Jerry Schneider, at age 21, was the model West Coast Business executive, bright and well educated. He was different from others in only one respect. He embezzled over $1 million from Pacific Telephone Company. Here is the story of his fraud.

———

Jerry Schneider's fraud had its genesis at a warm, open-air evening party where he and some friends had gathered for drinks, socializing, and small talk. Schneider was the young president of his own electronics corporation. This night, the talk was of organized crime and whether or not it could be profitable. "All these press stories of the big-time killings, and the crooks who build palaces down in Florida and out here on the coast, aagh …" said a cynical male voice, "they're cooked up for the movies."

Schneider recognized the speaker as a young script-writer whose last outline—a crime story set among the Jewish mafia—had been turned down. "Not so," he said. "Some of them clean up. Some of them walk away clean, with a huge pot. You only hear of the ones that don't. The others become respectable millionaires."

A lawyer asked, "You believe in the perfect crime, do you?"

"Yes, if what you mean is the crime that doesn't get detected. I'm sure there are crooks clever enough to figure ways to beat the system."

Long after everyone had left the party, Jerry Schneider was still thinking about whether or not there was a perfect crime. He had a great knowledge of computers and he thought maybe he could use his knowledge to perpetrate the perfect crime. Finally, about 2 a.m. he felt sick about the whole idea.

No one knows why Schneider later changed his mind. An investigator with the district attorney's office in Los Angeles believes it was because Jerry got possession of a stolen computer code book from Pacific Telephone Company. Schneider accessed the company's computer from the outside. Exactly how he did it was not fully revealed at his trial. He used a touch-tone telephone to place large orders with Pacific's supply division, inserting the orders into the company's computer. He then programmed Pacific Telephone's computers to pay for the merchandise. After he received the merchandise, he sold it on the open market.

Schneider was caught when an embittered employee noticed that much of the stuff Schneider was selling was Pacific's. The employee leaked to the police a hint about how Schneider had acquired the material. An investigation revealed that huge amounts of equipment were missing from Pacific's dispatch warehouse. Invoices showed that the equipment had been ordered and authorized for dispatch. The goods had then been packaged and put out on the loading bays ready for collection. Schneider had collected the goods himself, always early in the morning. To avoid the scrutiny of a gate guard and a tally clerk, who

would have required bills of lading, Schneider left home at two and three in the morning night after night, in a pickup truck painted to look like a company transport.

Schneider merely drove in among the assorted wagons and freight piles. He had somehow acquired keys, and documents issued by the computer gave him access to the yard. The inexperienced night security guards not only let him through but even offered him cups of coffee and cigarettes as he and his men loaded the equipment.

Schneider started to have fears about what he was doing: the morality of it and the cheating it involved. He had intended the theft to be just a brilliant near-scientific feat. Jerry began to realize that the effort of the crime was greater than the reward. In Schneider's words, "It got so that I was afraid of my ex-employees, men I knew were aware of what I was up to because they'd seen the stuff come in, day after day, and go out again as our stuff. I began to feel hunted. Scared." The crime left him short of sleep, exhausted, and feeling guilty. In addition, the value of the stolen material passing into his possession was rising dramatically.[22]

———

STOP & THINK *Think about a time in your life when you compromised your own ethical standards. How did the elements of pressure, rationalization, and opportunity affect your decision making? Were the three elements interactive—in other words, did it take less opportunity to make the decision when you were under tremendous pressures?*

Schneider claims to have "robbed" the company of nearly $1 million worth of equipment. His crime is interesting because his rationalization was "to see if the perfect crime could be committed." In fact, he probably couldn't have rationalized committing a crime for any other reason. When he was asked whether he considered himself an honest man, Schneider responded with a firm "yes." When he was asked whether, if he saw a wallet on the sidewalk, he would pocket it or try to return it to the owner, his answer was that he was like everyone else—he'd try to return it if it was at all possible. However, when he was asked whether, if he saw $10,000 lying in an open cash box in a supermarket and nobody was watching him, if he would take the money, he answered, "Sure, I would. If the company was careless enough to leave the money there, it deserved to have the money taken."

Schneider's pressures were greed, retaliation (it was revealed at his trial that he hated Pacific Telephone Company), and a compulsion to prove his superiority.

Schneider is a man of inner disciplines. He is a strict vegetarian who does a lot of physical exercise to keep fit. He works hard, brilliantly, and successfully at whatever he undertakes. There is little doubt that he could be a valued and even trusted executive at most corporations. Schneider's opportunity was his tremendous knowledge of computers and ability to get keys and passwords.

Jerry Schneider's "perfect crime" failed. It would have never happened, however, if he hadn't acted on a personal challenge and rationalized that he was only playing a game—a game of intellectual chess with a faceless company.

Fraud Recruitment

The fraud triangle is extremely useful in that it helps us to understand how one person becomes involved in fraud. Unfortunately, many frauds today are perpetrated by more than one person.[23] In fact, the majority of frauds—especially financial statement frauds—are collusive, meaning that the act involves more than one perpetrator. At a *Business Week* forum for chief financial officers, the following was stated:

At that forum, participants were queried about whether or not they had ever been asked to "misrepresent corporate results." Of the attendees, 67 percent of all CFO respondents said they had fought off other executives' requests to misrepresent corporate results. Of those who had been asked, 12 percent admitted they had "yielded to the requests," while 55 percent said they had "fought off the requests."[24]

In the following section, we will discuss how one person, after he or she has become involved in fraud as a result of the fraud triangle, influences another individual to participate in the fraud.[25] We will begin our discussion with the different ways that people use power to recruit others to participate in fraud.

Power

In 1947, Max Weber[26] introduced **power** as the probability that a person can carry out his or her own will despite resistance. When a fraud takes place, the conspirator has the desire to carry out his or her own will—influence another person to act and do as the perpetrator wishes—regardless of resistance. In 1959, two researchers[27] by the names of French and Raven classified power into five separate variables, each stemming from the different aspects of the relationship between an

actor and his or her target of influence. Specifically, French and Raven showed that A's power over B is determined by (1) A's ability to provide benefits to B (reward power), (2) A's ability to punish B if B does not comply with A's wishes (coercive power), (3) A's possession of special knowledge or expertise (expert power), (4) A's legitimate right to prescribe behavior for B (legitimate power), and (5) the extent to which B identifies with A (referent power). Recent research has shown that it is perceived power, rather than actual power, that affects the desired outcome in any given situation. Therefore, if B perceives A to have power over B, then it is as if A truly has power over B. The five types of power are shown in Figure 2.6.

Reward power is the ability of a fraud perpetrator to convince a potential victim that he or she will receive a certain benefit through participation in the fraud scheme. Examples of such benefits include the promise of a large bonus, stock option rewards, other equity payments, and job promotions.

Coercive power is the ability of the fraud perpetrator to make an individual perceive punishment if he or she does not participate in the fraud. This punishment is typically based on fear. For example, individuals often participate in fraud because they believe that by not participating in the fraud they may lose their job, receive public humiliation, be discriminated against as a whistle-blower, or be punished in another way.

Perceived **expert power** is the ability of the fraud perpetrator to influence another person because of expertise or knowledge. In the case of Enron, for example, management claimed to have expert knowledge

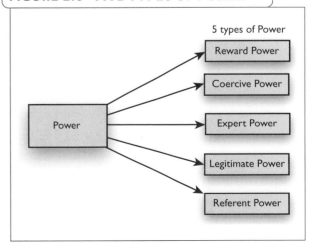

FIGURE 2.6   FIVE TYPES OF POWER

regarding complicated business models and arrangements.[28] This caused individuals, who would have otherwise refused to participate in the fraud scheme based on personal ethical standards, to participate in the scheme. These individuals convinced themselves that others knew more about the complex transactions than they did and that those knowledgeable individuals must understand what they were doing.

Legitimate power refers to the ability of the fraud perpetrator to convince a potential perpetrator that he or she truly has power over him or her. For example, within an organization, the chief executive officer and other members of management may claim to have legitimate power to make decisions and direct the organization—even if that direction is unethical. In this way, conspirators assume authoritative roles and convince potential co-conspirators that their authority is legitimate. Potential conspirators in this situation often feel tension between loyalty and ethics. Legitimate power can be an extremely powerful tool in recruiting individuals to participate in fraud in authoritarian cultures.

Referent power is the ability of the perpetrator to relate to the potential co-conspirator. Perpetrators will often use perceived referent power to gain confidence and participation from potential co-conspirators when performing unethical acts. Many individuals, when

Remember this …

By understanding the five types of power we can better protect ourselves from becoming involved in a fraudulent or other illegal act in the future. This knowledge will also aid in understanding how people become involved in a fraud, and as fraud examiners, help us to better detect fraud. For example, if someone asks us to do something that we may not fully understand (expert power), and we question the validity of doing such a thing, we should try to understand exactly what it is we are doing. We can also become more aware of our actions instead of focusing only on the rewards (reward power) of our actions. Remember, if something sounds too good to be true, it probably is!

persuaded by a trusted friend to participate in fraud, will rationalize the actions as being justifiable.

By looking at the schemes that individuals use to recruit others to participate in fraud from a power-based perspective, it is possible to understand how some frauds can become large and involve many people. Figure 2.7 explains the process of recruitment in greater detail.

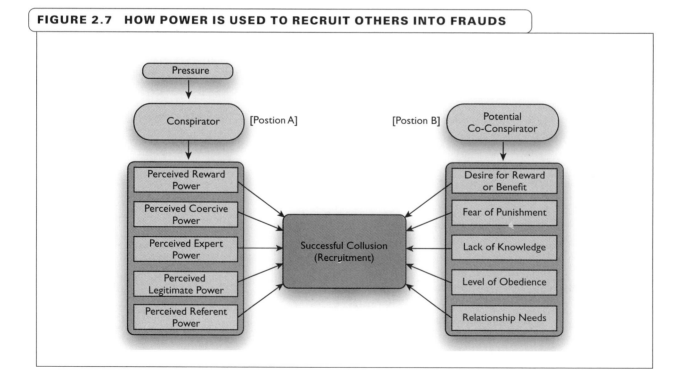

FIGURE 2.7 HOW POWER IS USED TO RECRUIT OTHERS INTO FRAUDS

FIGURE 2.8 HOW OTHERS ARE RECRUITED INTO FRAUD SCHEMES

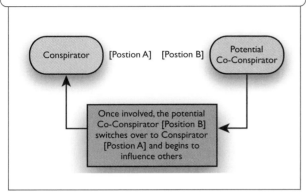

The effectiveness of the perpetrator to influence the potential recruit depends upon the susceptibility of the victim as well as the perpetrator's ability to manipulate the various types of power. Figure 2.7, much like the fraud triangle in Figure 2.2, is interactive, meaning that the more susceptible a victim is to the various types of power, the less effective the perpetrator has to be for recruitment to occur. Often, after the initial victim is recruited into the fraud scheme, that individual will then become a conspirator (in position A) and begin to influence other individuals to participate in the fraud. This process is shown in Figure 2.8.

STOP & THINK   *How have individuals you know used power to influence your actions? Have you done something simply because a person(s) had legitimate authority (such as a boss or teacher) over you? Have you ever done anything because a person offered you a reward or benefit for your actions? Have you ever been influenced to participate in something simply because you were asked by a close friend or colleague? Perhaps, in a group project at school you have agreed to do an assignment a certain way because you felt a classmate knew more about the subject matter than you did. Have you ever done anything because you feared possible punishment for not doing it? Chances are that all of us have been influenced to do something based upon power that was exerted by others. These five types of power influence all of our actions everyday.*

Review of the Learning Objectives

- **Know the types of people who commit fraud**. Research shows that anyone can commit fraud. Fraud perpetrators usually cannot be distinguished from other people on the basis of demographic or psychological characteristics. People that commit fraud are usually good people who consider themselves to be honest—they just get caught up in a bad situation as a result of pressure, opportunity, and rationalization.

- **Explain why people commit fraud**. As has been shown in the chapter, people commit fraud because of a combination of perceived pressure, rationalization, and opportunity. The majority of frauds start small as the result of an immediate financial need. Once individuals gain confidence in their fraudulent scheme, the fraud continues to get larger and larger until it is discovered.

- **Describe the fraud triangle**. The fraud triangle is comprised of a perceived pressure, a perceived opportunity, and rationalization. The fraud triangle provides a lens from which to analyze any fraud. Fraud will only occur if all three elements of the triangle are present.

- **Explain the fraud scale**. The fraud scale simply depicts the relationship between the three elements of the fraud triangle. For example, with fraud, the greater the perceived opportunity or the more intense the pressure, the less rationalization it takes to motivate someone to commit fraud. Likewise, the more dishonest a perpetrator is, the less opportunity and/or pressure it takes to motivate fraud.

- **Understand how pressure contributes to fraud**. Pressure is one of the three elements of the fraud triangle. Pressure is especially important because it is typically an immediate financial pressure that leads people to engage in fraud.

- **Understand why opportunity must be present for fraud to occur**. A perceived opportunity to commit fraud, conceal it, and avoid being punished is the second element of the fraud triangle. Opportunity is an essential part of every fraud because if perpetrators don't have the opportunity to commit fraud then fraud becomes impossible to commit. While eliminating all fraud opportunities may be impossible, reducing or minimizing the opportunity for fraud to occur can pay big dividends for organizations.

- **Understand why people rationalize**. Rationalization is one of the three elements of the fraud triangle. Rationalization is important because it is the mechanism that allows otherwise ethical individuals to justify unethical behavior. People rationalize to eliminate the inconsistency between what they do and what they know they should do.
- **Understand how people are recruited to participate in fraud schemes**. People typically become involved in already existing fraud schemes as a result of power that is exercised on them by another individual. The five separate types of power include reward, coercive, expert, legitimate, and referent. It is through either one or a combination of several types of power that a potential perpetrator is influenced to become involved in a fraudulent scheme.

KEY TERMS

perceived pressure, p. 34	system of authorizations, p. 43
perceived opportunity, p. 34	independent checks, p. 43
rationalize, p. 34	physical safeguards, p. 44
control environment, p. 39	documents and records, p. 44
modeling, p. 39	power, p. 53
labeling, p. 39	reward power, p. 53
accounting system, p. 42	coercive power, p. 53
audit trail, p. 42	expert power, p. 53
control activities, p. 42	legitimate power, p. 54
procedures, p. 42	referent power, p. 54
segregation of duties, p. 42	

QUESTIONS

Discussion Questions

1. What types of people commit fraud?
2. What motivates people to commit fraud?
3. What is the fraud triangle, and why is it important?
4. What is the fraud scale, and how does it relate to pressure, opportunity, and integrity?
5. What are some different types of pressures?
6. What are some of the controls that prevent and/or detect fraudulent behavior?
7. What are some common factors that provide opportunities for fraud?

8. How does rationalization contribute to fraud?
9. What were Jim Bakker's pressures, opportunities, and rationalizations to commit fraud?
10. In what ways did Dr. Sam Waksal rationalize his illegal and unethical actions?
11. What is power?
12. How is power used to influence another person to participate in an already existing fraud scheme?

True/False

1. When hiring, it is usually difficult to know which employees are capable of committing fraud, especially without performing background checks.
2. The three elements of the fraud triangle are a perceived pressure, a perceived opportunity, and rationalization.
3. Management's example or modeling is of little importance to the control environment.
4. Good controls will often increase opportunities for individuals to commit fraud within an organization.
5. Effective fraud-fighters usually put most of their time and effort into minimizing the pressures for fraud perpetrators to commit fraud.
6. The greater the perceived opportunity or more intense the pressure, the less rationalization it takes for someone to commit fraud.
7. Fraud can be perpetrated to benefit oneself or to benefit one's organization.
8. Fraud perpetrators who are prosecuted, incarcerated, or severely punished usually commit fraud again.
9. Many organizations merely dismiss dishonest employees because of the expense and time involved in prosecuting them.
10. Appropriate hiring will not decrease an organization's risk of fraud.
11. An individual who owns his or her own business and is the sole employee needs many control procedures.
12. A proper system of authorization will help ensure good internal controls.
13. Good documents and records are some of the best preventive controls.
14. Many frauds are allowed to be perpetrated because victims don't have access to information possessed by the perpetrators.
15. Power is rarely used to influence another person to participate in an already existing fraud scheme.

Multiple Choice

1. Fraud perpetrators:
   a. Look like other criminals.
   b. Have profiles that look like most honest people.
   c. Are usually very young.
   d. Are none of the above.
2. Which of the following is *not* one of the three elements of fraud?
   a. Perceived pressure.
   b. Perceived opportunity.
   c. Rationalization.
   d. Intelligence.
3. Which of the following is a common perceived pressure?
   a. The ability to outsmart others.
   b. Opportunity to cheat others.
   c. A financial need.
   d. The ability to "borrow" money by committing fraud.
4. If pressures and opportunities are high and personal integrity is low, the chance of fraud is:
   a. High.
   b. Medium.
   c. Low.
   d. Very low.
5. Which of the following is *not* a common type of fraud pressure?
   a. Vices.
   b. Work-related pressures.
   c. Financial pressures.
   d. Pressure to outsmart peers.
6. Opportunity involves:
   a. Opportunity to conceal fraud.
   b. Opportunity to avoid being punished for fraud.
   c. Opportunity to commit fraud.
   d. All of the above.
   e. None of the above.
7. Which of the following is *not* one of the three elements of the control system of an organization?
   a. The control environment.
   b. The accounting system.
   c. Management.
   d. Control activities or procedures.
8. Which of the following noncontrol factors provides opportunities for fraud?
   a. Inability to judge the quality of performance.
   b. Lack of access to information.
   c. Failure to discipline fraud perpetrators.
   d. Lack of an audit trail.
   e. All of the above.

9. Who generally has the highest risk of becoming a fraud victim?
   a. Businessperson.
   b. Older, less educated people.
   c. College students.
   d. None of the above.
10. How frequently do most people rationalize?
    a. Often.
    b. Sometimes.
    c. Rarely.
    d. Never.
11. Which of the following kinds of pressure is most often associated with fraud?
    a. Work-related pressure.
    b. Financial pressure.
    c. Vice pressure.
    d. All of the above.
12. Which of the following is *not* a primary control procedure?
    a. Use of documents and records to create an audit trail.
    b. Independent checks.
    c. Decreasing work-related pressure.
    d. Physical safeguards.
13. It is the __ and __ of existing controls, not the __ of controls, that allows most frauds to be perpetrated.
    a. Existence, use, lack.
    b. Lack, ignoring, existence.
    c. Overriding, ignoring, lack.
    d. Overriding, lack, use.
14. On what element of the fraud triangle do most fraud-fighters usually focus all or most of their preventive efforts?
    a. Perceived pressure.
    b. Perceived opportunity.
    c. Perceived weak internal controls.
    d. Rationalization.
15. Which of the following is *not* a control activity (procedure)?
    a. System of authorizations.
    b. Appropriate hiring procedures.
    c. Independent checks.
    d. Documents and records.
    e. All of the above are control activities.
16. Which of the following is *not* a common vice that motivates people to commit fraud?
    a. Gambling.
    b. Drugs.
    c. Expensive extramarital relationships.
    d. Alcohol.
    e. All of the above are vices that motivate people to commit fraud.

17. Which of the following is *not* a way that management can establish a good control environment?
    a. Having a clear organizational structure.
    b. Proper training.
    c. Communicating openly.
    d. Appropriate hiring procedures.
    e. All of the above are ways that management can establish a good control environment.
18. Which of the following is *not* an element of most frauds?
    a. Taking the assets.
    b. Concealment.
    c. Breaking and entering.
    d. Conversion.
19. Which of the following is an example of legitimate power?
    a. The offer of valuable stock options.
    b. A decision to participate in fraud based upon fear.
    c. Your boss tells you to do something.
    d. You do something because your colleague is more knowledgeable than you are in that particular subject matter.
20. Which of the following is an example of referent power?
    a. Fear that you may lose your job.
    b. Your friend asks you to do a special favor for him or her.
    c. The offer of a job promotion.
    d. Your teacher asks you to do an assignment.

SHORT CASES

Case 1

As an auditor, you have discovered the following problems with the accounting system of Jefferson Retailers. For each of the following occurrences, tell which of the five internal control activities or procedures was lacking. Also, recommend how the company should change its procedures to avoid the problem in the future.

1. Jefferson Retailers' losses due to bad debts have increased dramatically over the past year. In an effort to increase sales, the managers of certain stores have allowed large credit sales to occur without review or approval of the customers.
2. An accountant hid his theft of $200 from the company's bank account by overstating outstanding checks on monthly reconciliation. He believed the manipulation would not be discovered.
3. Michael Meyer works in a storeroom. He maintains the inventory records, counts the inventory, and has unlimited access to the storeroom. He occasionally steals items of inventory and hides his thefts by overstating the physical inventory accounts.
4. Receiving reports are sometimes filled out days after shipments have arrived.

Case 2

A few years ago, there was a large oil refining company (based in New York) whose top executive was convicted of financial statement fraud. One of the issues in the case involved the way the company accounted for its oil inventories. In particular, the company would purchase crude oil from exploration companies and then process the oil into finished oil products, such as jet fuel, diesel fuel, and so forth. Because there was a ready market for these finished products, as soon as the company would purchase the crude oil, it would record its oil inventory at the selling prices of the finished products less the cost to refine the oil (instead of at cost). While there was fraud in the case, this type of accounting was also questioned because it allowed the company to recognize profit before the actual sale (and even refining) of the oil. This method was even attested to by a large CPA firm. If you were the judge in this case, would you be critical of this accounting practice? Do you believe this "aggressive" accounting was a warning signal that fraud might be occurring?

Case 3

Helen Weeks has worked for Bonne Consulting Group (BCG) as the executive secretary in the administrative department for nearly 10 years. Her apparent integrity and dedication to her work has quickly earned her a reputation as an outstanding employee and has resulted in increased responsibilities. Her present responsibilities include making arrangements for outside feasibility studies, maintaining client files, working with outside marketing consultants, initiating the payment process, and notifying the accounting department of all openings or closings of vendor accounts.

During Helen's first five years of employment, BCG subcontracted all of its feasibility and marketing studies through Jackson & Co. This relationship was subsequently terminated because Jackson & Co. merged with a larger, more expensive consulting group. At the time of termination, Helen and her supervisor were forced to select a new firm to conduct BCG's market research. However, Helen never informed the accounting department that the Jackson & Co. account had been closed.

Since her supervisor allowed Helen to sign the payment voucher for services rendered, Helen was able to continue to process checks made payable to Jackson's account. Because her supervisor completely trusted her, he allowed her to sign for all voucher payments less than $10,000. The accounting department continued to process the payments, and Helen would take responsibility for distributing the payments. Helen opened a bank account in a nearby city under the name of Jackson & Co., where she would make the deposit. She paid all of her personal expenses out of this account.

Assume that you have recently been hired by Bonne Consulting Group to help detect and prevent fraud.

1. What internal controls are missing in Helen's company?
2. What gave Helen the opportunity to perpetrate the fraud?
3. How could this fraud have been detected?

Case 4

The following actual fraud occurred in a communications company.

What Ruth Mishkin did in her spare time didn't concern the Boca Raton, Florida, public relations firm where she worked very much. "We thought she was just playing cards with the girls," says Ray Biagiotti, president of Communications Group, the firm that had employed her for nine years.

She had become such a trusted employee that her bosses had put her in charge of paying bills, balancing bank accounts, and handling other cash management chores. They didn't realize their mistake until Ruth took a sick leave, and they discovered she had been pocketing company funds for years. The money had helped stoke a gambling habit that took the 60-year-old widow on junkets to casinos in the Bahamas, Monte Carlo, and Las Vegas. In all, the company claims she stole about $320,000.

Ruth pleaded guilty to one count of grand theft and four counts of check forgery. She was placed on 10 years' probation and ordered to attend meetings of a chapter of Gamblers Anonymous, the national self-help group.

1. What were Ruth's perceived opportunities?
2. What pressure did Ruth have to commit fraud?

3. How did the fact that Ruth was a trusted employee give her more opportunity to commit fraud?
4. How do vices such as gambling motivate people to commit fraud?

Case 5

Full-of-Nature is a vitamin supplement company in New York that makes different herbal pills for gaining muscular strength, losing weight, and living a healthier life. You have been hired to audit Full-of-Nature and soon realize that the company has many problems. You notice the following frauds being committed and are writing a report to the board of directors about what should be done to fix the problems. For each fraud, list one control procedure that was not followed and suggest how the company should eliminate the fraud and deal with the perpetrator.

1. There are journal entries for consulting expenses that, when traced back, show five companies using the same post office box for receiving consulting fees from Full-of-Nature. You discover that the accountant has been embezzling money and listing it as consulting expenses.
2. The warehouse manager has been stealing pills to help his son get stronger (he wants his son to play football). To cover the losses, he issued credit memos to customers, showing that they returned bad goods that were replaced with new pills.
3. The CEO decided he did not like paying payroll taxes anymore, so he fired all of his employees and rehired them as contractors. However, he still withholds payroll taxes and keeps the money for himself.
4. The accounts payable clerk likes to go shopping with the company checkbook and always buys herself a little something when she orders office supplies. However, since she is the one who handles office supplies, no one knows what was purchased for the company and what was ordered for her living room.

Case 6

Alexia Jones is a worker at a local 24-hour pharmacy. Alexia works the night shift and is the only worker. Because management is cost-conscious and business is slow at night, Alexia has been given the responsibility to do the accounting from the previous day. Alexia has two children, and her husband does not work. Alexia has strong pressure to provide well for her family.

1. Is the pharmacy at risk for fraud? Why or why not?
2. How does the fraud scale help us to determine if risk for fraud is high or low in this situation?

3. Assuming that you were recently hired by the pharmacy as a business consultant, what information would you provide to the owner of the pharmacy concerning fraud?

Case 7

Bob's Country Kitchen, a small family-owned restaurant in northern New York, has seen a drop in profitability over the past three years and the owners want to know why. Bob's has been a local favorite for the past 20 years. Two brothers opened it in the early 1980s because they couldn't find a burger they liked. Bob's initially served only hamburgers, but has rapidly expanded to almost all types of American food. Bob's became so popular in the late 1980s that Tom and Bob (the owners) had to hire several people to help manage the day-to-day activities of the restaurant. Until this point, Tom and Bob had managed the place themselves.

Bob and Tom felt that their new management was doing a good job and so they gradually became less and less involved. In 2005, Bob and Tom gave up all management duties to Joel, a friend of the family who had been employed by Bob's for 15 years. Bob's has no computer system in place for customer orders— each order is written on a pad with a duplicate carbon, one copy is taken to the kitchen, and the other is given to the customer. All customers pay at the old cash register at the front of the restaurant, after which their receipts are pegged on a tack and are totaled at day's end to determine total sales. Bob and Tom have noticed a gradual decline in profits over the past three years and, up until now, figured it was just because of increased restaurant competition in the area.

However, it seemed odd to Bob and Tom that revenues had increased substantially but profits had not. When asked about the change in relationships between revenues and profits, Joel said it was because of a large increase in the cost of food and that he had to pay his employees more with the increased competition. Bob and Tom have no reason to disbelieve Joel, since he is a trusted family friend. Joel's responsibilities at Bob's include preparing the nightly deposits, managing accounts payable, handling payroll, and performing the bank reconciliations. He also has the power to write and sign checks. No one checks his work.

1. What possible opportunities does Joel have to commit fraud?
2. What signs could signal a possible fraud?

3. How likely is it that a few internal controls could reduce the opportunities for fraud?
4. Which internal controls would you suggest be implemented?

Case 8

In October 2001, the following case was heard in New Jersey.

A former optometrist was sentenced to seven years in state prison for conspiracy, theft by deception, falsifying records, and falsification of records relating to medical care, as part of a massive health insurance fraud. In addition to his prison sentence, the optometrist was ordered to pay a criminal insurance fraud fine of $100,000 and restitution of $97,975. The state is also in the process of seeking an additional $810,000 in civil insurance fraud penalties.

The optometrist was found guilty of false insurance billing for providing eyeglasses and routine eye exams at no cost or at reduced cost, and making up the difference by billing insurance carriers for services not rendered to patients. The optometrist also had his office staff create approximately 997 false patient records and charts and falsely bill insurance carriers for prescribed optometric services that were not rendered to his patients. He would also bill insurance companies for optometric treatments and tests for ocular conditions that patients did not actually suffer. The optometrist was also charged with falsifying patient records and charts. What factors provided the optometrist with an opportunity to commit fraud?

Case 9

FCS Fund Management is an investment marketing business with sales of over $10 million and with offices in Norwich, Connecticut, Dubai, and Hong Kong. It sold high-yield investment schemes, offering returns of up to 20 percent. FCS has clients in the United Kingdom, Europe, and the Middle East, many of whom are U.S. expatriates. FCS sold its investment products through salesmen operating in these locations. The CEO of FCS Fund Management, James Hammond, knew that many of the accounts were, or might be, misleading, false, or deceptive in that they purported to confirm the existence of genuine investments. Describe how the rationalization element of the fraud triangle is present in this case.

Case 10

Len Haxton is the owner of a local CPA firm with four separate offices in a medium-size town. He and his wife started the firm 20 years ago, and they now have over 50 full-time employees. Recently, he discovered that one of his employees had stolen over $20,000 from the business during the past six months because of lax internal controls. Len was furious about the situation, but was uncertain about whether he should initiate a criminal investigation or just fire the employee.

1. List four reasons why Len should have the employee prosecuted.
2. List three reasons why Len might not want to seek prosecution of his employee.
3. If you were Len, what would you do?

Case 11

As a new staff member in a large, national company, you are excited about your career opportunities. You hope senior employees in the company will perceive you as being one of the "rising stars." During your first week of training, you are assigned a mentor. The mentor's role is to help you learn your way around the company and to answer questions you may have about the work you are expected to complete. As it turns out, your mentor is another "rising star" whom you respect. One day, she takes you out to lunch. While you are eating, you begin discussing company policies. She explains to you the expense reimbursement policy. Company policy dictates that expenses such as lunch are the responsibility of the employee and are not reimbursable. The exception to this policy is for lunches with clients and potential recruits, or for other work-related circumstances. She tells you "off the record" that nobody really follows this policy, and that you can always find a "business purpose" to justify your lunch expenses with fellow employees, as long as you don't do it every day. Besides, your supervisor won't really scrutinize any expense reimbursement requests that are below $25, so why worry about it?

1. Is it a fraud to charge the company for personal lunches that you submit as business expenses?
2. What elements of fraud, if any, are present in this situation?
3. How would you respond to your mentor, or to other employees that may encourage you to pick up the tab for lunch with the understanding that you will charge the company for the lunch?

Case 12

You are the owner of a local department store in a small town. Many of your employees have worked for your company for years, and you know them and their families very well. Because your business is relatively small, and because you know your employees so well, you haven't worried about establishing many internal controls. You do set a good example for how you wish your employees to work, you are actively involved in the business, and you provide adequate training to new employees. One day, you become suspicious about an employee at a checkout desk. You fear that he may be stealing from the company by altering the day's totals at his register. He has worked for you for 15 years, and he has always been honest and reliable. After several weeks of investigation, you discover that your fears are correct—he is stealing from the company. You confront him with the evidence, and he admits to stealing $25,000 over several years. He explains that, at first, he stole mainly to pay for small gifts for his wife and young children. But then last year, his wife lost her job, they had another child, and he wasn't sure how to pay all of the bills.

1. What elements of fraud are present in this case?
2. How might you have detected this fraud earlier, or prevented it from happening?
3. How will you approach your employee interaction and relationships in the future?
4. Do you feel a better system of internal controls, such as surveillance cameras and an improved computer system, is necessary or justified to prevent future frauds?

Case 13

A prominent New York fertility doctor was recently sentenced to more than 7 years in prison for his insurance fraud conviction. Dr. Niels Lauersen received the 73-month sentence and was ordered to pay $3.2 million in restitution and an additional $17,500 in fines.

Niels was convicted of pocketing $2.5 million during a 10-year period. Prosecutors say he stole from insurance companies by falsely billing fertility surgeries that were not covered by insurance as gynecological surgeries. Tearful former patients called out to Niels and wished him well as he was led away. He is now in prison.

At his sentencing, the judge said, "You were a medical doctor at the top of your profession and a public figure at the apex of New York society. Your fall from prestige has been Faustian in its dimensions." A probation report recommended that Niels be sentenced to 14 years imprisonment. Niels, 64, has lived in the United States since 1967, when he left Denmark. His lawyer,

Gerald Shargel, argued for leniency, saying Niels had an honorable purpose: to make it affordable for women with fertility problems to have children.

"This is a very tough sentence. This is a very unusual case," Gerald said. His client had treated 14,000 women, delivering 3,000 children in a single year.

1. What pressure might have motivated Niels to commit fraud?
2. What opportunity might have allowed Niels to commit fraud?
3. How did Niels rationalize his fraudulent activities?
4. How could Niels have both helped his patients and not lied or stolen from the insurance company?

Case 14

Nancy is the receptionist and office manager at a local doctor's office where you are working as a doctor's assistant. The doctor leaves Nancy to handle all office duties including collecting cash receipts, billing patients, depositing checks, and the monthly bank reconciliation. The doctor doesn't have any training in accounting or collecting insurance payments and wants to be able to focus on treating his patients. Since the work in the office doesn't require an additional employee, Nancy has been given all office managing responsibility. The receptionist could share the office managing duties, but she is too busy greeting patients, pulling charts, and answering phone calls. Nancy is also a single mother of four. She likes to give her children the best possible care and enjoys having the finer things of life to the extent that she can afford them. Nancy also works a second job because her job as office manager "just never seems to pay the bills."

Most patients visiting the doctor have insurance and are only required to pay a co-payment for the services that they receive. As you are filling out some patient information during a routine visit, you overhear the patient say to her husband. "Honey, do you have any cash with you today? This office prefers the co-payment to be paid in cash and I have forgotten to stop by the ATM this morning." You thought that this was an interesting comment since you had never heard of the office having a cash co-payment preference. In addition, you haven't seen a written sign or ever heard that the doctor prefers cash co-payments. You are aware that in addition to a co-payment, Nancy bills the entire remaining cost of service. The remaining amount is then billed directly to the patient. As you have been filing patient records, you have often heard

Nancy complain that "full payment cannot be collected from yet another patient." You are aware that several accounts are written off each month due to the high amount of uncollectible accounts. A high percentage of bad debts seems to be a common and expected occurrence in the physician/patient business. You are currently taking a fraud class and realize that several opportunities for fraud exist.

1. Consider the fraud triangle. What opportunities and motivation exist for Nancy to commit fraud?
2. What should be done to improve internal controls and reduce the risk of fraud as it relates to the segregation of duties?

Case 15

"But I intended to pay it all back, I really did," Joseph Swankie said as he talked to his manager. How did I ever get into this situation, he thought.

Two years ago, Joe received the promotion for which he had been working so hard for. In addition, Joe's new manager told him that Joe had a very promising future at the company. Joe and his wife Janae quickly purchased a new home. Not long after, Joe and Janae had their fourth child, and life was great. After having their fourth child, Janae quit work to spend more time with her kids.

Suddenly, things started to turn upside down. The economy took a downturn and had a negative impact on Joe's company. His pay, which was based on commission, was reduced nearly 50 percent. Joe still worked hard but thought he should be paid more. Unable to find another job, Joe resentfully decided he would stay with the company even with the lower pay.

Not long after he started receiving lower commissions, Joe noticed that the controls over the petty cash fund weren't very strong. The records were not reviewed very often, and small shortages were usually written off. One week, Joe took $50. When questioned by his wife, Joe said he had found a few odd jobs after work. Joe continued this habit of taking small amounts for a couple of weeks. After realizing that no one had noticed the shortage, he started to take up to $100 a week.

One day, another employee noticed Joe taking some cash from the fund and putting it in his wallet. When questioned, he simply stated that it was a reimbursement the company owed him for supplies. An investigation began, and Joe's fraud was discovered.

1. Identify the opportunities, pressures, and rationalizations that led Joe to commit this fraud.
2. What simple procedures could the company have implemented to prevent the fraud from occurring?

CASE STUDIES

Case Study 1

Green Grass is a small, family-operated company whose core service is in horticultural care and lawn care for customers in the local city. The owner of the company is the father of the family. He has used the company to cover the costs of his children's college education. At the same time, he has been able to give his children some work experience and an opportunity to earn their own money to pay for school. The company has grown steadily over the last few years, and the owner has hired many employees outside of the family to be able to keep up with the demand of the increasing number of customers. The company is run from a small office building, and there is only one employee running the operations in the company office. The father had usually been in charge of this aspect of the company, but now leaves the responsibility to his trusted friend, who has experience in accounting and information systems. This employee is in charge of scheduling the routes of all the employees and is responsible for payments, receipts, and balancing the books.

The company performs two major operations. First, it provides lawn care using insecticides, fertilizer, and weed killers. Eight employees are responsible for this activity. They each drive a truck and are responsible for collecting money from the customers they serve. They are also responsible for loading and mixing chemicals in the tanks they use during the day. The second part of the operation is the lawn mowing care. Usually, a four-man crew is responsible for all the machines they use, and they are responsible for taking care of the lawns on their daily schedule. This is where the owner has hired his children to work, and the whole team is usually made up of younger workers than the team that works with the chemicals.

Over the years, Green Grass has experienced small growth and success. Profits have increased steadily as the company has picked up new clients. However, the owner noticed that last year's accounts were different. The revenues increased a marginal amount, while the expenses for the company increased more than they should have. The owner has noticed that his interactions with his friend in the office have been fewer. Also, his employees have been finishing their routes later in the day than they had in previous years.

Questions

1. What are some of the fraud opportunities within Green Grass?
2. What symptoms of fraud exist, and what symptoms should the owner look for if he believes fraud may be occurring?
3. What steps should be taken to make sure fraud does not occur, and what are the costs associated with these steps?

Case Study 2

James Watkins, an ambitious 22-year-old, started an entertainment business called Best Club after he graduated from California State University. Best Club initially was a business failure because James ignored day-to-day operations and cost controls. One year later, James was heavily in debt. Despite his debt, James decided to open another location of Best Club. He was confident that Best Club would bring him financial success.

However, as his expenses increased, James could not meet his debts. He turned to insurance fraud to save his business. He would stage a break-in at a Best Club location and then claim a loss. In addition, he reported fictitious equipment to secure loans, falsified work order contracts to secure loans, stole money orders for cash, and added zeros to customers' bills who paid with credit cards. James was living the "good life," with an expensive house and a new sports car.

Two years later, James decided to make Best Club a public corporation. He falsified financial statements to greatly improve the reported financial position of Best Club. In order to avoid the SEC's scrutiny of his financial statements, he merged Best Club with Red House, an inactive New York computer firm, and acquired Red House's publicly owned shares in exchange for stock in the newly formed corporation. The firm became known as Red House, and the Best Club name was dropped. James personally received 79 percent of the shares. He was now worth $24 million on paper. James was continually raising money from new investors to pay off debts. A few months later, Red House's stock was selling for $21 a share, and the company's book value was $310 million. James was worth $190 million on paper. A short time later, he met John Gagne, president of AM Firm, an advertising service. Gagne agreed to raise $100 million, via junk bonds, for Red House to buy out Sun Society, a travel service.

Afterward, with television appearances, James became a "hot figure" and developed a reputation as an entrepreneurial genius. However, this reputation changed after an investigative report was published in a major newspaper. The report chronicled some of his early credit card frauds. Within two weeks, Red House's stock plummeted from $21 to $5.

After an investigation, James was charged with insurance, bank, stock, and mail fraud; money laundering; and tax evasion; and Red House's shares were selling for just pennies. A company once supposedly worth hundreds of millions of dollars dropped in value to only $48,000.

Questions

From this case, identify:
1. The pressures, opportunities, and rationalizations that led James to commit his fraud.
2. The signs that could signal a possible fraud.
3. Controls or actions that could have detected James's behavior.

Case Study 3

Johnson Manufacturing, a diversified manufacturer, has seven divisions that operate in the United States, Mexico, and Canada. Johnson Manufacturing has historically allowed its divisions to operate independently. Corporate intervention occurs only when planned results are not obtained. Corporate management has high integrity, although the board of directors is not very active. Johnson has a policy of performing employee screenings on all employees before hiring them. Johnson feels its employees are all well educated and honest.

The company has a code of conduct, but there is little monitoring of employees. Employee compensation is highly dependent on the performance of the company.

During the past year, a new competitor has entered one of Johnson's highly successful markets. This new competitor has undercut Johnson's prices. Johnson's manager of this unit, Debbie Harris, has responded by matching price cuts in hopes of maintaining market share. Debbie is very concerned because she cannot see any other areas where costs can be reduced so that the division's growth and profitability can be maintained. If profitability is not maintained, the division managers' salaries and bonuses will be reduced.

Debbie has decided that one way to make the division appear more profitable is to overstate inventory, since it represents a large amount of the division's balance sheet. She also knows that controls over inventory are weak. She views this overstatement as a short-run solution to the profit decline due to the competitor's price cutting. The manager is certain that once the competitor stops cutting prices or goes bankrupt, the misstatements in inventory can be corrected with little impact on the bottom line.

Questions

1. What factors in Johnson's control environment have led to and facilitated the manager's manipulation of inventory?
2. What pressures did Debbie have to overstate inventory?
3. What rationalization did Debbie use to justify her fraud?

Case Study 4

The following describes an actual investment fraud that occurred:

Mr. Armstrong stands accused in a federal indictment for committing one of the most common frauds in the history of finance: making big promises to investors that he couldn't deliver. Mr. Armstrong is accused of securities fraud after allegedly trying to cover up millions of dollars in bets on the yen and other markets that went horribly wrong.

It is probably not the ending that the 49-year-old Mr. Armstrong envisioned when he fell in love with business as a boy. It was a love that turned him into an active stamp dealer at just 13 years old, only to be kicked out of the stamp world's most elite fraternity as a young man in 1972, amid accusations of selling extremely rare stamps that he didn't own and couldn't deliver.

Undaunted, he fought back and became a stamp authority—and eventually an authority on the far more sophisticated financial markets on which he was widely quoted. His self-confident forecasting style made him a hit in Japan, where Mr. Armstrong is now accused of bilking investors out of $950 million.

Documents he used to sell his investments show that he promised buyers of his securities that a yield of 4 percent was guaranteed on the fixed-rate instrument, a strong selling point in a country where interest rates on government bonds are less than half that. Moreover, the securities were designed to offer further returns as high as 25 percent, depending on market conditions.

Mr. Armstrong's bets on the markets increasingly began turning against him. The Securities and Exchange Commission says that from late 1997, Mr. Armstrong began to rack up increasingly big losses on large investments he made in currencies and options. Between November 1997 and August 1999, for example, SEC officials say Mr. Armstrong lost $295 million in trading the yen alone—all money that belonged to clients. "In the wake of the discovery of the fraud," the SEC said in its civil complaint that was filed, "Armstrong has transferred millions of dollars from Princeton Global accounts into foreign-bank accounts he controls." SEC officials declined to disclose how much money Mr. Armstrong allegedly transferred overseas, or to what countries.

On two previous instances, Mr. Armstrong did face commodities trading scrutiny. In 1985, the agency overseeing commodities trading in the United States lodged a complaint against him for allegedly not registering and maintaining proper investment records. Then in June 1987, the same agency fined Mr. Armstrong $10,000 and suspended his trading privileges for a year for improper risk disclosure and misrepresentation of his trading returns. Part of the complaint was related to advertising in a Princeton newsletter.

Questions

1. How did trust contribute to Mr. Armstrong's fraud?
2. In the chapter, lack of access to information was discussed as one of the factors that provide opportunities for fraud. If investors would have known Mr. Armstrong's background and had access to other information about him, how would it have affected the fraud? Why?

INTERNET ASSIGNMENT

1. Visit the Association of Certified Fraud Examiners (ACFE) Web site at www.acfe.com. Once you have logged on, explore the pages of the site and then answer the following questions:
   a. How many professionals make up the (ACFE)?
   b. What are the requirements to become a certified fraud examiner (CFE)?
   c. What is the overall mission of the ACFE?
   d. What does a CFE do? What are some of the professions from which they originate?
   e. Take the CFE Practice Quiz. Do you have what it takes to be a CFE?
   f. List a few of the products offered on the Web site for educating those interested in fraud examination. Which materials would be most beneficial to you in your profession? Why?
   g. What service does the association provide to allow individuals to anonymously report allegations of ethical violations, fraud, waste, and abuse? How does this service work?

DEBATE

The introduction to this chapter discusses the case of Dennis Greer, an individual who became involved in a large-scale kiting scheme. The fraud literature suggests that when an individual becomes involved in fraud (such as Dennis), he or she should get the maximum punishment available. By doing so, other individuals who may consider committing fraud would be deterred from doing so. After reading Dennis's situation do you believe that he should receive the maximum punishment available? Or do you believe that his honesty (once the fraud was discovered), his unusually difficult circumstances, and repentant attitude should allow him to receive some leniency? Why or why not?

END NOTES

1. For more information about kiting and bank fraud see McCurnin, T. E. and Frandsen, P. A. 2008, Grounding Check Kiting With Check 21: The Civil and Criminal Ramifications of check Kiting in the 21st Century, *The Banking Law Journal*, April, 2008.

2. LaSalle, R. E., 2007, Effects of the Fraud Triangle on Students' Risk Assessments, *Journal of Accounting Education*, Vol. 25: 1–2.

3. Greenlee, J., Fischer, M., Gordon, T., and E. Keating, 2007, An Investigation of Fraud in Nonprofit Organizations: Occurrences and Deterrents, *Nonprofit and Voluntary Sector Quarterly*, Vol. 36: 4.

4. See Marshall B. Romney, W. Steve Albrecht, and David J. Cherrington, "Red-Flagging the

White-Collar Criminal," *Management Accounting* (March 1980): 51–57.

5. Ramos, M., 2003, Auditor's Responsibility for Fraud Detection, *Journal of Accountancy*, Vol. 195: 1.

6. Albrecht, C., 2007, A Comment on Koerber and Neck's (2006), "Religion in the Workplace: Implications for Financial Fraud and Organizational Decision Making", *Journal of Management, Spirituality & Religion*, Vol. 4: 1.

7. Caplan, D., 1999, Internal Controls and the Detection of Management Fraud, *Journal of Accounting Research*, Vol. 37: 1.

8. Wilks, J. T., and Zimbelman, M. F., 2004, Decomposition of Fraud-Risk Assessments and Auditors' Sensitivity to Fraud Cues, *Contemporary Accounting Research*, Vol. 21: 3.

9. This case was relayed to us by a former student who asked that we not identify the source.

10. One of the authors of this book used to be a member of COSO. COSO has defined an organization's internal control framework as consisting of five interrelated components. These five components are derived from the way management runs a business, and are integrated with the management process. The components are as follows:

Control Environment

The control environment sets the tone of an organization, influencing the control consciousness of its people. It is the foundation for all other components of internal control, providing discipline and structure. Control environment factors include the integrity, ethical values, and competence of the entity's people; management's philosophy and operating style; the way management assigns authority and responsibility and organizes and develops its people; and the attention and direction provided by the board of directors.

Risk Assessment

Every entity faces a variety of risks from external and internal sources that must be assessed. A precondition to risk assessment is establishment of objectives, linked at different levels and internally consistent. Risk assessment is the identification and analysis of relevant risks to achievement of the objectives, forming a basis for determining how the risks should be managed. Because economic, industry, regulatory, and operating conditions will continue to change, mechanisms are needed to identify and deal with the special risks associated with change.

Control Activities

Control activities are the policies and procedures that help ensure management directives are carried out. They help ensure that necessary actions are taken to address risks to achievement of the entity's objectives. Control activities occur throughout the organization, at all levels and in all functions. They include a range of activities as diverse as approvals, authorizations, verifications, reconciliations, reviews of operating performance, security of assets, and segregation of duties.

Information and Communication

Pertinent information must be identified, captured, and communicated in a form and timeframe that enables people to carry out their responsibilities. Information systems produce reports containing operational, financial, and compliance-related information that make it possible to run and control the business. They deal not only with internally generated data, but also with information about external events, activities, and conditions necessary to informed business decision making, and external reporting. Effective communication also must occur in a broader sense, flowing down, across, and up the organization. All personnel must receive a clear message from top management that control responsibilities must be taken seriously. They must understand their own role in the internal control system, as well as how individual activities relate to the work of others. They must have a means of communicating significant information upstream. There also needs to be effective communication with external parties, such as customers, suppliers, regulators, and shareholders.

Monitoring

Internal control systems need to be monitored—a process that assesses the quality of the system's performance over time. This is accomplished through ongoing monitoring activities, separate evaluations, or a combination of the two. Ongoing monitoring occurs in the course of operations. It includes regular management and supervisory activities and other actions personnel take in performing their duties. The scope and frequency of separate evaluations will depend primarily on an assessment of risks and the effectiveness of ongoing monitoring procedures. Internal control deficiencies should be reported upstream, with serious matters reported to top management and the board.

11. Richard C. Hollinger, *Dishonesty in the Workplace: A Manager's Guide to Preventing Employee Theft* (Park Ridge, IL.: London House Press, 1989): 1–5.

12. Alison Stein Wellner, "Background Checks," *Business Week Online* (August 14, 2000).

13. James, K. L., 2003, The Effects of Internal Audit Structure on Perceived Financial Statement Fraud Prevention, *Accounting Horizons*, Vol. 17: 4.

14. "Doctor Listed as Suicide Was Target of Fraud Investigation," *Los Angeles Times* (December 10, 1992): A3.

15. Kevin Kelly, "How Did Sears Blow the Gasket? Some Say the Retailer's Push for Profits Sparked Its Auto-Repair Woes," *Business Week* (June 29, 1992): 38 and Tung Yin, "Sears Is Accused of Billing Fraud at Auto Centers," *The Wall Street Journal* (June 12, 1992, Western ed.): B1.

16. Expert witness testimony, June 1990 grand jury indictment, U.S. District Court for the Central District of California.

17. The information on Lincoln Savings and Loan was taken from the June 1990 grand jury indictment, U.S. District Court for the Central District of California.

18. Facts about the PTL case were taken from "PTL: Where Were the Auditors?" a working paper by Gary L. Tidwell, Associate Professor of Business Administration, School of Business and Economics, College of Charleston, Charleston, South Carolina.

19. Albert, J. A., 1998, *Jim Bakker: Miscarriage of Justice?*, Peru, Illinois: Carus Publishing Company.

20. Gilpin, K. N., 2003, ImClone Founder Pleads Guilty to Avoiding Sales Tax on Art, *The New York Times*, March 3, 2003.

21. News story adapted from CBSNews.com, "Sam Waksal: I Was Arrogant" (October 6, 2003).

22. Information about this fraud was acquired from Donn Parker's computer fraud files at the Stanford Research Institute. Donn Parker personally interviewed Jerry Schneider.

23. Association of Certified Fraud Examiners (ACFE), 2006. ACFE Report to the Nation on Occupational Fraud & Abuse. Austin, Texas. Association of Certified Fraud Examiners.

24. W. P. Schuetze, 1998. *Enforcement Issues: Good News, Bad News, Brillo Pads, Miracle-Gro, and Roundup*. Paper presented at the twenty-sixth annual AICPA national conference on SEC developments, Washington, DC.

25. Much of the information on the recruitment of individuals into fraud schemes has been adapted from a paper by Chad Albrecht and Simon Dolan, entitled "Exploring the Recruitment of Individuals into Financial Statement Fraud Schemes," presented at the 2007 European Academy of Management Conference in Paris, France.

26. See M. Weber, *The Theory of Social and Economic Organization* (New York, NY: Free Press, 1947).

27. J. R. P. French, Jr., and B. Raven, "The Basis of Social Power," in D. Cartwright, ed., *Studies in Social Power* (Ann Arbor, MI: University of Michigan Press, 1959).

28. While some financial statement frauds involve easily understood transactions (e.g., WorldCom), Enron was a very complicated fraud that involved off-balance-sheet special purpose entities (SPEs, now called variable interest entities, VIEs) and transactions that occurred between Enron and these various off-balance-sheet entities.

CHAPTER **3**

Fighting Fraud: *An Overview*

LEARNING OBJECTIVES

After studying this chapter, you should be able to:

- Become familiar with the different ways that organizations fight fraud.
- Understand the importance of fraud prevention.
- Understand how to create a culture of honesty and high ethics.
- Understand why hiring the right kind of employees can greatly reduce the risk of fraud.
- Understand how to assess and mitigate the risk of fraud.
- Understand the importance of early fraud detection.
- Understand different approaches to fraud investigation.
- Be familiar with the different options for legal action that can be taken once fraud has occurred.

TO THE STUDENT

You should now understand the various types of fraud and fraud-fighting careers as well as those who commit fraud and why they do it. This chapter is a transition chapter to introduce you to the various ways in which organizations deal with fraud. The most cost-effective fraud-fighting activities involve preventing fraud from occurring. The second most cost-effective fraud-fighting activities involve implementing proactive approaches to detect fraud early, before it has a chance to grow. Once fraud has been detected (or there is *predication* that fraud might be occurring), organizations undertake various types of fraud investigation methods. After fraud has been investigated and the perpetrators are known, various types of legal action are possible. This chapter provides an overview of each of these activities. We then provide detailed coverage of these topics in the later chapters of this book. Fraud prevention is covered in Chapter 4; proactive fraud detection is the topic of Chapters 5 and 6; and fraud investigation is the focus of Chapters 7 through 10. Then, after discussing specific types of fraud in Chapters 11–17, we conclude the book with Chapter 18, which discusses legal actions that organizations can take against perpetrators. Essentially, this chapter provides an overview of the remainder of the book.

During the past two years, Mark-X Corporation has had three major frauds. The first involved a division manager overstating division profits by reporting fictitious revenues. Faced with declining sales and fearful of not meeting the level of sales to qualify for the company's bonus plan at the expense of being terminated, the manager inflated the amounts of service contracts to overstate revenues by $22 million. The second fraud was committed by the manager of the purchasing department. In his responsibility to secure uniforms for company employees, the manager gave favored treatment to a certain vendor. In return for allowing the vendor to charge higher prices and provide inferior goods, the vendor hired the purchasing manager's daughter as an "employee" and paid her over $400,000 for rendering no service. In fact, when investigated, the daughter didn't even know the location of the vendor's offices or telephone number (for whom she supposedly worked). As an "employee" the daughter funneled bribes to her father, the purchasing agent. As a result of this kickback scheme, Mark-X purchased $11 million of uniforms at inflated prices. The third fraud involved two warehouse managers stealing approximately $300,000 in inventory. This fraud was perpetrated by issuing credit memos to customers who supposedly returned defective merchandise and were given product replacements. In fact, the merchandise was never returned. The credit memos were used to conceal the theft of "high value" merchandise from the warehouse.

All three of these frauds were uncovered and brought significant embarrassment to the company's management and board of directors. The three frauds also cost the company a tremendous amount of money to investigate. In a board of directors meeting, the chairman of the board made the following comment to the CEO: "I am sick and tired of these fraud surprises hitting the newspapers. If there is one more high-profile fraud in this company, I will be resigning from the board and recommending that you be replaced as CEO."

Following the board meeting, the CEO called an emergency meeting with the CFO, the internal audit director, in-house legal counsel, and the director of corporate security. In the meeting, he told them that unless the company successfully developed a proactive fraud prevention and detection program, all of them would lose their jobs. He reviewed the three major frauds and told them what the chairman of the board had said. His final words were, "I don't care how much you spend, I want the best proactive, fraud-mitigating program possible. Hire whatever consultants you need, but get me a proactive fraud program that I can report to the board, and do it quickly."

Knowing Different Ways That Organizations Fight Fraud

Assume that you are the fraud-fighting consultant hired by the company. What advice would you give this company? What kind of fraud prevention, detection, and investigation programs would you recommend be implemented? What kind of ethics programs would you put in place? What kind of prosecution policies would you establish? A consultant would probably start by telling the management of the company that there are four activities on which money can be spent to mitigate the occurrence of fraud. These four activities are (1) fraud prevention, (2) early fraud detection, (3) fraud investigation, and (4) follow-up legal action and/or resolution. The consultant would inform the company representatives that there is no such thing as a small fraud—just large frauds that are caught early. The consultant would most likely tell the company that frauds grow geometrically and that, if frauds are allowed to continue unchecked, perpetrators get braver and braver and the amounts stolen or manipulated in the final weeks of the fraud usually dwarf the amounts taken in the early periods of the fraud. The advice would include a combination of fraud training, ethics programs, better controls, reviewing incentive programs, and harsher treatment of perpetrators. Indeed, a comprehensive fraud program would focus on all four elements of fraud: prevention, proactive detection, investigation, and legal follow-up. Like many organizations, Mark-X has probably been concentrating its fraud-fighting efforts on only the last two: fraud investigation (once the frauds had become so large and egregious that they could no longer be ignored) and follow-up legal action. These are probably the least effective and most expensive fraud-fighting efforts.

An overview of all four elements of a comprehensive fraud program provided in this chapter will help you understand the various fraud-fighting efforts.

> **Remember this ...**
>
> *There are four fraud-fighting activities that organizations can use: (1) fraud prevention, (2) proactive fraud detection methods, (3) fraud investigation once fraud is suspected, and (4) legal follow-up of fraud perpetrators. Many organizations focus on the last two, which are the most costly and least effective. An overview of these four fraud-fighting activities is given in this chapter.*

Fraud Prevention

Preventing fraud is generally the most cost-effective way to reduce losses from fraud.[1] Once a fraud has been committed, there are no winners. Perpetrators lose because they are usually first-time offenders who suffer humiliation and embarrassment as well as legal consequences. They usually must make tax and restitution payments, and there are often financial penalties and other consequences. Victims lose because not only are assets stolen but they also incur legal fees, lost time, negative publicity, and other adverse consequences. Further, if organizations don't deal harshly with the perpetrators, a signal is sent to others in the organization that nothing serious happens to fraud perpetrators, making fraud by others more likely. Organizations and individuals that have proactive fraud prevention measures usually find that their prevention efforts pay big dividends. On the other hand, the investigation of fraud can be very expensive.

STOP & THINK *Why do you think a fraud perpetrator who is caught would suffer more humiliation and embarrassment than a bank robber or other property offender?*

As we explained in Chapter 2, people commit fraud because of a combination of three factors: (1) perceived pressure, (2) perceived opportunity, and (3) some way to rationalize the fraud as acceptable. In Chapter 2, we introduced a scale showing that these factors differ in intensity from fraud to fraud. When perceived pressures and/or opportunities are high, a person needs less rationalization to commit fraud. When perceived pressures and/or opportunities are low, a person needs more rationalization to commit fraud. Unfortunately, sometimes pressures and/or the ability to rationalize are so high that no matter how hard an organization tries to prevent fraud, theft still occurs. Indeed, fraud is generally impossible to prevent completely, especially in a cost-effective way.[2] The best an organization can hope for is to manage the costs of fraud effectively.

Organizations that explicitly consider fraud risks and take proactive steps to create the right kind of environment and reduce its occurrence are successful in preventing most frauds.

Effective **fraud prevention** involves two fundamental activities: (1) taking steps to create and maintain a culture of honesty and high ethics and (2) assessing the risks for fraud and developing concrete responses to mitigate the risks and eliminate the opportunities for fraud. We discuss these activities in the following paragraphs.

Creating a Culture of Honesty and High Ethics

Organizations use several approaches to create a culture of honesty and high ethics. Five of the most critical and common elements are (1) making sure that top management models appropriate behavior, (2) hiring the right kind of employees, (3) communicating expectations throughout the organization and requiring periodic written confirmation of acceptance of those expectations, (4) creating a positive work environment, and (5) developing and maintaining an effective policy for handling fraud when it does occur.

Tone at the Top (Proper Modeling)

Research in moral development strongly suggests that honesty can be best reinforced when a proper example (model) is set—sometimes referred to as the *tone at the top.* Management of an organization cannot act one way and expect others in the organization to behave differently. Management must reinforce to its employees through its actions that dishonest, questionable, or unethical behavior will not be tolerated.[3]

Research into why people lie (or are dishonest) indicates that there are four major reasons why people lie. The first is fear of punishment or adverse consequences. The fear may be because they know they have done something wrong or their performance hasn't met expectations. Individuals who are constantly in fear of being punished develop a habit of lying, which is a second reason for lying. Even when confronted by the truth, once they are conditioned to lie, they usually insist the lie is the truth. A third reason for lying is because they have learned to lie by watching others lie or through negative modeling. When people see others lie, especially when those others get away with their lies, people may become more prone to lying. Finally, people lie because they feel if they tell the truth they won't get what they want.[4]

Unfortunately, bad modeling is everywhere today. And, with increased accessibility to information (blogs, Web sites, PDAs, cable, podcasts, etc.), news about bad modeling is more detailed and more accessible than ever before. So, when someone like Bernie Madoff is alleged to have committed a fraud, his bad modeling is not only known in detail throughout his firm and among his close associates but it is also broadcast through numerous media around the world.

Hiring the Right Kind of Employees

The second key element in creating a culture of honesty and high ethics is hiring the right employees. Not all people are equally honest or have equally well-developed personal codes of ethics. In fact, research results indicate that many people, when faced with significant pressure and opportunity, will behave dishonestly rather than face the "negative consequences" of honest behavior (e.g., losing reputation or esteem, failing to meet quotas

or expectations, having inadequate performance exposed, inability to pay debts, etc.). If an organization is to be successful in preventing fraud, it must have effective hiring policies that discriminate between marginal and highly ethical individuals, especially when recruiting for high-risk positions. Proactive hiring procedures include such things as conducting background investigations on prospective employees, thoroughly checking references and learning how to interpret responses to inquiries asked about candidates, and testing for honesty and other attributes.[5]

Recent research[6] has suggested an **ethical maturity model (EMM)** (shown in Figure 3.1) that explains why people make unethical decisions.

The foundation of ethics, *Personal Ethical Understanding,* represents the most basic ethical boundaries of personal actions. It involves learning the difference between right and wrong, developing a sense of fair play, learning to care for and empathize with others, developing respect for others, learning basic principles of integrity and reality, and acting in a consistent manner with the values a person knows to be right.

The second level of the EMM, *Application of Ethics to Business Situations,* is being able to translate one's ethical understanding to the business world or to other settings in which people earn a living (e.g., the medical profession, engineering profession, etc.). Such translation is not always easy. For example, a person may have very strong ethics in the way he or she treats family and friends, but may not understand how cooking the books or failing to submit tax withholdings to the government affects peoples' lives or constitutes unethical or fraudulent behavior.

Most of the people involved in the financial shenanigans of the past few years considered themselves

FIGURE 3.1　ETHICS DEVELOPMENT MODEL

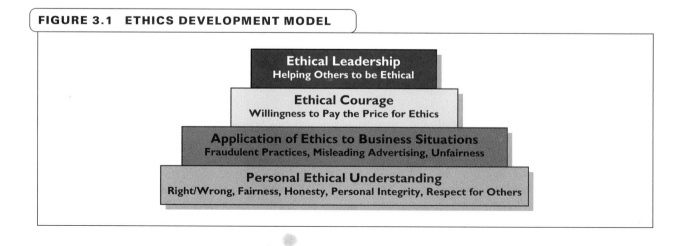

to be honest, ethical people. Yet, when faced with decisions about whether to go along with requests to "cook the books" or to reveal observed inappropriate behavior, they made the wrong choices. They did not know how or were afraid to translate their personal ethical values to the business world.

The third level of the EMM is *Ethical Courage.* Ethical courage is the strength and conviction to act appropriately in difficult or questionable situations. A person can have a personal ethical understanding and be able to translate that understanding to business settings but may not have the courage to take a stand when necessary. In one recent fraud, for example, more than 20 people falsified financial statements. All testified they were aware that their actions were unethical, but none had the courage to stand for their beliefs.

The highest level, *Ethical Leadership,* is instilling in others a desire to develop ethical awareness and courage. This higher form of ethical behavior requires a person to inspire others through word, example, persuasion, and good management.[7] We believe the employees in most organizations look something like those shown in Figure 3.2.

In most organizations, there is a small group of employees who have well-defined personal codes of conduct and who have learned how to translate those ethical values to business settings. They also have the courage to do what is right. These employees will almost always do the right thing. There is another small group that lacks strong personal codes of conduct. This group will be dishonest anytime it benefits them. The largest group, however, is the "swing group" comprised of individuals with situational ethics. This group knows what is right and wrong, knows how to translate their ethical values to the business world, and at times even have the courage to do what is right. Yet, because of inconsistent modeling and labeling, their ethics depend upon the situation they are placed in. Generally, this group will follow their leaders and can be influenced by organizational structure and culture. When there is a strong, positive tone at the top and strong ethical leadership in the company, this large group will usually make the right decisions. The labeling and modeling of the leaders sends a powerful message that keeps employees honest and making the right decisions.

Companies should do their best to both hire ethical individuals and then make sure that the right tone at the top is set by executives. Consider the following case of how poor hiring allowed fraud to occur in an organization:

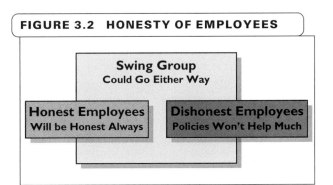

FIGURE 3.2   HONESTY OF EMPLOYEES

Swing Group
Could Go Either Way

Honest Employees
Will be Honest Always

Dishonest Employees
Policies Won't Help Much

Philip Crosby was a former president of ITT. While president, he wrote a book advocating that producing error-free products was possible and could be very profitable. He left ITT to form Philip Crosby Associates, Inc. (PCA), a consulting firm based on his own book's principles. The new company became so successful that it began to attract Fortune 500 executives, who paid large fees to spend a few days at PCA with Philip. PCA was a unique reflection of its founder's values. Crosby argued that to produce error-free products, you have to have an environment of mutual respect. If employees have pride in working for their company, and feel that their company is open and honest, they will perform to the best of their abilities and will not steal from the company. PCA had an international division, created in 1984, that posted $2 million in sales in its first year and had expectations to double that figure in the second year. In February of the second year, PCA opened an office in Brussels and had more offices in the planning stages. PCA decided it needed a director of finance who could work with each new country's reporting rules and translate foreign currencies into their U.S. equivalents. After a reasonable search, the eight senior PCA executives agreed to hire John C. Nelson. John had an M.B.A. and seemed to have an impressive understanding of the technical aspects of the international marketplace. He also had an impressive reference provided to PCA by his previous company. Steve Balash, vice president of human resources, said, "He seemed like the kind of honest individual we'd want to hire." Unfortunately, John C. Nelson was not an honest individual. In fact, he wasn't even John C. Nelson. Rather, his real name was Robert W. Liszewski. When hired, Robert decorated his office with an Illinois CPA license; the CPA certificate had been created on his home computer. The background reference that was provided to PCA had been written by Robert's wife, who was a part-time worker with "John's former employer." Robert's job at PCA was to develop financial information for PCA's fast-growing international operations. Robert's work did not go very smoothly, even from the start. He was terribly slow at converting numbers from foreign currencies to U.S. dollars, which should not have been a tough task for a CPA. In addition, his monthly reports were always late. After about a year on the job, Robert faced his first big test. The company's third-quarter report deadline had passed, and Robert was far from completing it. His excuses ranged from "The outside bookkeepers ... haven't yet computed the final receipts" to "the computer crashed." PCA executives decided to let Robert continue because he seemed to be catching on and was doing better on other projects. In December of the third year, Robert's bookkeeper quit, leaving him completely in charge of all the money that flowed through that division (approximately $12 million that year). Robert quickly became hopelessly behind in keeping the books and was finally called in to explain his problems to the chief financial officer. In the interview, Robert started crying, saying that he had cancer and had only three months to live. The chief financial officer believed Robert's lie, and he was allowed to keep his job. PCA's business began to get worse. In the third year, the company's stock fell to $12 per share from $20 the year before. On March 12 of that year, the chief financial officer tried to move $500,000 from one bank account to another. He was informed by the controller that the account did not have a sufficient balance for the transfer. The CFO knew that the account was supposed to have at least $1 million in it. To see where the money went, the controller scanned the ledgers of wire transfers from the questionable account. She found an unposted transfer that did not appear to be legitimate. The amount of $82,353 had been transferred to a U.S. company called Allied Exports, supposedly to pay for shipping products to Brussels. The materials were being sent from South Bend, Indiana, to Brussels. The controller knew that South Bend was Robert's hometown, but did not think anything of it. Subsequent searches found several more wire transfers to South Bend totaling more than $425,000. The company called the Indiana secretary of state's office to check on Allied Export's incorporation records. They were informed that the president of Allied Export was a woman named Patricia Fox. Management recognized Patricia as Robert's wife. With help from his wife, Robert had created a dummy company in South Bend, Indiana. In over eight months, Robert funneled over $961,000 to the dummy company by charging the expenditures to a number of different expense accounts. Robert's wife was arrested in South Bend when she tried to withdraw $230,000 from the account. In their home, detectives found PCA's ledgers that Robert had stolen and a lockbox that contained all of Allied Export's monthly statements, canceled checks, and incorporation papers. While searching the house, the police spotted Robert driving by in a white Porsche, but they were unable to catch him. Two weeks later, police computers showed a new driver's license had been issued to a John C. Nelson. When they checked out the address, police found an elderly man. The man was the real John C. Nelson, who identified Robert's picture as his old boss,

Bruce Fox, who had been fired from a bank in Indiana when the bank discovered that he had previously served an 18-month sentence for embezzling $400,000.

———

Research on honesty shows that individuals fall into three groups: (1) those who will almost always be honest (approximately 30 percent of the population); (2) those who are situationally honest,[8] who will be honest when it pays to be honest but dishonest when it pays to be dishonest (approximately 40 percent of the population); and (3) those who will always be dishonest (approximately 30 percent of the population). Good modeling and other good fraud prevention measures will usually keep the second group from being dishonest; there is usually not much that can be done to prevent the third group from being dishonest. As a result, having good screening policies in place to eliminate the hiring of dishonest individuals and having positive modeling for situationally honest individuals can prevent most frauds from occurring in an organization. In Chapter 4, we discuss various ways to hire honest employees.

Communicating Expectations of Honesty and Integrity

The third critical element in creating a culture of honesty and high ethics—communicating expectations of honesty and integrity—includes (1) identifying and codifying appropriate values and ethics, (2) fraud awareness training that helps employees understand potential fraud problems they may encounter and how to resolve or report them, and (3) communicating consistent expectations about punishment of violators. For **codes of conduct** to be effective, they must be written and communicated to employees, vendors, and customers.[9] They must also be developed in a manner that will encourage management and employees to take ownership of them.[10] Requiring employees to confirm in writing that they understand the organization's ethics expectations is an effective element of communication in creating a culture of honesty. In fact, many successful organizations have found that annual written confirmation is very effective in both preventing and detecting frauds before they become large.

Red Hat, Inc., a provider of open source software solutions to businesses, has an extensive code of conduct. That code, which is publicly available on Red Hat's website[11] and included in Appendix A of this chapter, shows that all Red Hat employees are required to certify that they will abide by the company's code of conduct.

In addition to expectations about ethical behavior, expectations about punishment of those who commit fraud must also be clearly communicated from top management to everyone in the organization. For example, a clear statement from management that dishonest actions will not be tolerated and that violators will be terminated and prosecuted to the fullest extent of the law is helpful as part of a fraud prevention program. Obviously, such a statement must be followed up with real discipline when fraudulent acts occur.

Codes of conduct (like Red Hat's) are required under the Sarbanes-Oxley Act of 2002 to convey expectations about what is and is not appropriate in an organization. Every public company today must have such a code for its directors and officers.

STOP & THINK *Do you really believe that having a written code of conduct will reduce fraud and other dishonest acts in an organization? Why or why not?*

Creating a Positive Work Environment

The fourth element in creating a culture of honesty and high ethics involves developing a positive work environment. Research results indicate that fraud occurs less frequently when employees have positive feelings about an organization, and have a feeling of ownership in that organization, than when they feel abused, threatened, or ignored. Factors that have been associated with high levels of fraud and that detract from a positive work environment include the following:

1. Top management that does not care about or pay attention to the behavior of employees,
2. Negative feedback or lack of recognition of job performance,
3. Perceived inequities in an organization,
4. Autocratic rather than participative management,
5. Low organizational loyalty,
6. Unreasonable budget expectations,
7. Unrealistically low pay,
8. Poor training and promotion opportunities,
9. High turnover and/or absenteeism,
10. Lack of clear organizational responsibilities, and
11. Poor communication within the organization.

As an indication of the changing nature of companies and how they treat their employees, consider the case of IBM. From the time IBM was organized as Computing Tabulating Recording Company in 1911 until the 1980s, IBM's job security was legendary. It wasn't unusual to find two generations of the same family working for the company. There were never any layoffs or unions. This loyalty to employees buttressed the promise to customers: A happy and motivated workforce meant good service.

However, the bond between the company and its workers began to fray with massive reorganizations in the 1980s, followed by huge layoffs of employees. Like many other companies, IBM's employees felt less job security and ownership in the company.

With today's focus on short-term results, particularly quarterly earnings per share, and the effect those results have on stock prices, many companies have started to treat their employees more like assets that can be bought and sold rather than individuals who need to be nurtured and invested in. With increased layoffs and re-hires, comes less security, commitment, and perceived ownership in companies. And, less perceived ownership and commitment to a company often results in an increase in frauds against those companies.

Proper Handling of Fraud and Fraud Perpetrators When Fraud Occurs

The fifth and final element in creating a culture of honesty and high ethics is having appropriate policies in place for handling fraud if it occurs. No matter how good an organization's fraud prevention activities are, as stated previously, fraud can still occur. The way an organization reacts to fraud incidents sends a strong signal that affects the number of future incidents. An effective policy for handling fraud should ensure that the facts are investigated thoroughly, firm and consistent actions are taken against perpetrators, risks and controls are assessed and improved, and communication and training are ongoing. Every organization should have a fraud policy that determines whose responsibility fraud prevention, detection, and investigation are, how incidents of fraud will be handled legally, and what kind of remediation and education efforts will take place when fraud does occur.

Assessing and Mitigating the Risk of Fraud

In addition to creating a culture of honesty and high ethics, effective fraud prevention involves eliminating opportunities for fraud to occur. Neither fraud committed by top management on behalf of an organization, nor fraud committed against an organization can occur without perceived fraud opportunity. Organizations can proactively eliminate fraud opportunities by (1) accurately identifying sources and measuring risks, (2) implementing appropriate preventative and detective controls to mitigate those risks, (3) creating widespread monitoring by employees, and (4) having internal and external auditors who provide independent checks on performance.

Identifying, sourcing, and measuring the risk of fraud means that an organization should have a process in place that both defines where the greatest fraud risks are and evaluates and tests controls that mitigate those risks. In identifying fraud risks, organizations should consider organizational, industry, and country-specific characteristics that influence the risk of fraud. One organization that effectively prevented most frauds held brainstorming sessions with members of management, internal audit, corporate security, and legal counsel and focused on the following questions:

- *If fraud were to occur in our organization, where would it most likely happen? The types of fraud that were perceived as most likely were cataloged, and the organization paid special attention to these types of fraud.*
- *Which of our employees are in the best positions to commit fraud against our company? The organization then made sure that appropriate preventive and detective controls were in place around those employees.*
- *If each of these possible frauds were to occur in our organization, what kinds of symptoms would they generate?*

Once fraud risk assessment has taken place, the organization can identify the processes, controls, and other procedures that are needed to mitigate the identified risks. An appropriate internal control system will include a well-developed control environment, an effective accounting system, and appropriate control activities. Risks, control environments, and control activities are discussed in Chapter 4.

Research has shown that it is employees and managers, not auditors, who detect most frauds. They are the ones who work side by side with perpetrators and can most easily recognize changes in behavior, lifestyle, financial records, and other things that would indicate that fraud might be occurring. Because coworkers can more easily detect fraud than can auditors and others who provide only episodic reviews, to effectively prevent and detect fraud, employees and managers must be taught how to watch for and recognize fraud. The most effective way to involve employees in the monitoring process is to provide a protocol for communication that informs employees and others to whom they should report suspected fraud and what form that communication should take. The protocol should assure confidentiality

> **Remember this ...**
>
> *Fraud prevention involves two elements: (1) creating and maintaining a culture of honesty and high ethics and (2) assessing the risks for fraud and developing concrete responses to mitigate the risks and eliminate the opportunities for fraud. Five of the most critical and common elements in creating a culture of honesty and ethics are (1) making sure top management models appropriate behavior, (2) hiring the right kind of employees, (3) communicating expectations throughout the organization and requiring periodic written confirmation of acceptance of those expectations, (4) creating a positive work environment, and (5) developing and maintaining an effective policy for handling fraud. Organizations can proactively mitigate risks and eliminate fraud opportunities by (1) accurately identifying sources of and measuring risks, (2) implementing appropriate preventative and detective controls to mitigate those risks, (3) creating widespread monitoring by employees, and (4) having internal and external auditors who provide independent checks on performance.*

and stress that retribution will not be tolerated. Organizations that are serious about fraud prevention must make it easy for employees and others to come forward and must reward and not punish them for doing so.

The **Sarbanes-Oxley Act of 2002** recognized the value of having a system for employees and others to report wrongdoing, including fraud. Section 307 of that law requires every public company to both have a whistle-blower system in place and prohibit retaliation against any employee or other person who reports questionable activities using the whistle-blower system. One of the events that prompted this legislation was a letter that former Enron chairman Kenneth Lay received from a senior executive in August 2001 warning that the company—once a pillar of the U.S. energy industry—could "implode in a wave of financial scandals." Apparently, the letter pointed out the questionable nature of some partnerships involving company executives.

The letter was unsigned, but its author was later identified as Sherron Watkins, a vice president for corporate development at Enron. If Enron directors had seen Sherron Watkins's whistle-blowing letter, Enron might still be a going concern, but, unfortunately, she sent her letter to the CEO, not to members of the board or anyone else. The rest is now history. Congress's response to Enron and other corporate scandals was to place responsibility on a company's audit committee (a subcommittee of the board of directors) to implement and oversee a whistle-blowing process for soliciting, evaluating, and acting on complaints about how the company handles financial reporting and securities law compliance.

The final element in eliminating fraud opportunities is having internal and external auditors who provide periodic audits of financial statements and accounting records. While neither internal auditors nor external auditors are usually specifically trained to detect fraud, their presence provides a major deterrent effect and their audits of books and records often discover frauds, especially when they are large. Research has shown that approximately 20 percent of all frauds are detected by auditors.

Fraud Detection

In a fraud perpetrated by a bank teller, the amounts in the Table 3.1 were taken on the dates noted.

When caught, the teller made the following statement: "I can't believe this fraud went on this long without anyone ever suspecting a thing, especially given the larger and larger amounts."

As you can see, this fraud started very small, with the perpetrator stealing larger and larger amounts as it continued. Not being caught, the perpetrator's confidence in his fraud scheme increased, and he became greedier and greedier. In fact, you will note that, on 7-23, there is a two-week period where fraudulent behavior stopped. The reason for this pause in the perpetrator's dishonest behavior was that auditors came to the branch where he worked. You will also notice that once the auditors left, the perpetrator resumed his fraudulent behavior but only stole small amounts. For a short time, he was testing the system to make sure the auditors hadn't detected him or put processes in place that would reveal his dishonest activity. Once he again had confidence that he wouldn't be caught, he quickly escalated the amounts stolen into hundreds of dollars per day.

While the amounts involved in this fraud are small, the pattern is very typical. Like the one described

TABLE 3.1

DATE	AMOUNT STOLEN						
4-1	$10	5-8	$20	6-5	$50	7-16	$600
4-4	$20	5-9	$30	6-9	$30	7-23	$600
4-7	$20	5-12	$30	6-10	$40	8-4	$20
4-9	$20	5-13	$30	6-11	$30	8-8	$20
4-10	$20	5-14	$30	6-12	$50	8-11	$30
4-14	$40	5-15	$30	6-13	$50	8-14	$30
4-16	$30	5-16	$40	6-16	$50	8-19	$20
4-22	$30	5-19	$40	6-17	$50	8-22	$40
4-23	$30	5-20	$40	6-18	$30	8-26	$400
4-24	$30	5-21	$40	6-20	$70	8-27	$600
4-25	$30	5-22	$20	6-23	$100	8-28	$400
4-28	$30	5-27	$30	6-24	$200	9-2	$400
4-29	$30	5-28	$40	6-25	$400	9-5	$100
4-30	$30	5-29	$40	6-26	$600	9-12	$100
5-1	$20	5-30	$50	7-8	$400	9-15	$200
5-5	$30	6-2	$40	7-9	$700	9-16	$400
5-6	$30	6-3	$50	7-14	$400		
5-7	$20	6-4	$50	7-15	$600		

previously, most frauds start small and, if not detected, continue to get larger and larger. Events that scare or threaten the perpetrator result in discontinuance of the fraud, only to be resumed when threats pass. Because perpetrators increase the amounts they steal, in most cases, amounts taken during the last few days or months of a fraud far exceed those taken during earlier periods. In one case, for example, the amounts taken quadrupled every month during the period the fraud continued. As stated previously, there are no small frauds—just large ones that are detected early. And, in cases where it is top management or business owners who are perpetrating the fraud, fraud prevention is difficult and early detection is critical. Consider the following fraud:

The president of a New Hampshire temporary service company intentionally misclassified employees as independent contractors rather than as employees of his company. The misclassification allowed him to avoid paying $211,201 in payroll taxes over a three-year period. In addition, he provided an insurance company with false information on the number of people he actually employed, thereby avoiding $426,463 in workers' compensation premiums.

When fraud is committed by the president or owner of an organization, as it was in this case, prevention is very difficult. Maybe the president's company could have had a higher code of ethics, but if the president wants to commit fraud, there is probably nothing anyone can do to stop him. Rather, the emphasis on these types of fraud must be on fraud detection. Because all frauds cannot be prevented, organizations should have both preventive and detective controls in place. Preventive controls are aimed at keeping fraud from happening, while the goal of detective controls is to catch frauds early before they have a chance to get very large.

As a third example of how frauds increase over time, consider the case of a Japanese copper trader who was making rogue trades. Over a period of nine years, his fraudulent trading resulted in a fraud totaling $2.6 billion. The following theft amounts show how much the fraud grew by not being detected early:

YEAR OF FRAUD	CUMULATIVE AMOUNT OF THE FRAUD
Year 1	$600,000
Year 3	$4 million
Year 5	$80 million
Year 7	$600 million
Year 9	$2.6 billion

In years 8 and 9, four of the world's largest banks became involved and lost over $500 million.

The detection of fraud includes steps or actions taken to discover a fraud that has been or is being committed. Detection does not include investigative procedures taken to determine motives, extent, method of embezzlement, or other elements of the dishonest act. As you will discover in subsequent chapters, fraud is unlike other crimes that are easily recognized. Because fraud is rarely obvious, one of the most difficult tasks is determining whether or not a fraud has actually occurred.

Detection of fraud usually begins by identifying symptoms, indicators, or red flags[12] that tend to be associated with fraud. Unfortunately, these "red flags" can often be associated with nonfraud factors as well. There are three primary ways to detect fraud: (1) by chance, (2) by providing ways for people to report suspicions of fraud, and (3) by examining transaction records and documents to determine if there are anomalies that could represent fraud. In the past, most frauds were detected by accident. Unfortunately, by the time detection occurred, the frauds were usually large and had been going on for some time. In most cases, there were even individuals in the victim organizations who suspected that fraud was occurring but did not come forward, either because they weren't sure it was fraud, didn't want to wrongly accuse someone, didn't know how to report the fraud, or were fearful of the consequences of becoming a whistle-blower.

In recent years, organizations have implemented a number of initiatives to detect fraud more proactively. The first and most common proactive fraud detection approach has been to install reporting hotlines (**whistle-blowing systems**) as described earlier whereby employees, coworkers, and others can call in using a telephone or submit (using a Web page) an anonymous tip of a suspicion of fraud. Some of these hotlines are maintained within the company, and others are outsourced to independent organizations to provide hotline services for them. (The Association of Certified Fraud Examiners and a company called Allegience [formerly Silent Whistle], for example, provide fee-based hotline service.) Organizations that have installed hotlines have detected many frauds that would have remained undetected, but they have often paid a fairly high price for doing so. Not surprisingly, many of the calls made through hotlines do not involve fraud at all. Some represent nonfraud issues such as employee work-related concerns; some represent hoaxes; some are motivated by grudges, anger, or a desire to do harm to an organization or an individual; and some represent honest recognition of fraud symptoms that are caused by nonfraud factors.

CAUTION *It is very important that fraud fighters exercise care when proactively detecting fraud. First, there are almost always alternative explanations for what looks like fraud symptoms. For example, a person whose lifestyle suddenly changes could have inherited money from a deceased relative. Second, it is important that proactive fraud detection does not get in the way of effective business. As an example, one of the authors of this book trained several internal auditors of a large corporation how to proactively detect fraud. After a few months, however, those trained auditors had succeeded in upsetting nearly all managers in the company because of their egregious and sometimes disruptive fraud detection techniques. Fraud detection efforts are best when they are invisible to employees and managers of an organization.*

The second proactive fraud detection approach is to analyze data and transactions to look for suspicious trends, numbers, and other anomalies. Recent developments in technology have allowed organizations to comprehensively analyze and mine databases to proactively look for fraud symptoms. Banks, for example, have installed programs to identify suspected kiting. These programs draw the bank's attention to customers who have a high volume of bank transactions within a short period of time. Insurance companies have implemented programs that examine claims within a short time after purchasing insurance. Some organizations have even implemented comprehensive fraud detection programs by systematically identifying the kinds of frauds that could be occurring, cataloging the various symptoms those frauds would generate, and then building real-time queries into their computer systems to search for these symptoms. Fraud detection research, mostly using technology-based search techniques, is now being conducted by academics and other investigators. Anyone who is seriously interested in understanding and fighting fraud should be following this research. In the next two chapters, we will discuss proactive fraud detection.

As an example of proactive **fraud detection**, a large U.S. bank installed a back-room function that used computer programs to scan customer transactions looking for unusual activity. Customers who make rapid deposit and withdrawal transactions, especially depositing checks written on the same account, for example, are often committing the fraud of kiting. Once kiting is suspected, the branch where the suspect's

account is domiciled is contacted and told to look into possible fraud. In one instance, the branch was warned that a particular three-year customer had account activity that looked as if he were kiting. Unfortunately, the branch manager knew the customer and felt that he was trustworthy. A few days later, the branch was again notified that this same customer's deposit and withdrawal activity looked very suspicious. Finally, after the third warning, the branch manager decided to investigate. In the meantime, the other bank the dishonest customer was using had discovered the kiting and this bank was left to cover the loss which had grown from $70,000 to over $600,000 between the first and third notification by those doing the data mining. As this real account illustrates, proactive fraud detection can be very valuable, but only when the symptoms generated are not ignored.

Remember this ...

Fraud detection involves activities to determine whether or not it is likely that fraud is occurring. Fraud detection allows companies to identify suspicions or predications of fraud. Historically, most frauds were caught by chance. In recent years, two major proactive fraud detection developments have occurred: (1) installing hotlines or whistle-blower systems and encouraging employees and others to report any suspicious activity they see and (2) mining various databases looking for unusual trends, numbers, relationships, or other anomalies that could indicate fraud.

Fraud Investigation

Mark and Jane were husband and wife. Mark was the CEO of McDonald's Incorporated, and Jane was a partner in the CPA firm of Watkiss[13] and McCloy. After a hard day at work, they met at a local restaurant for dinner. Mark told Jane about an incident that happened at work. He showed her an anonymous note that stated: "You had better look into the relationship between John Beasley (the manager of the purchasing department) and the Brigadeer Company (a supplier) because something fishy is going on." He told Jane that he had no idea who sent him the note and that he wasn't even sure what to do about it. He told her that he was concerned about possible collusion and should probably pursue the "lead." Jane couldn't believe what she was hearing. "What a coincidence," she stated. "Today, something very similar happened to me." She said that a junior auditor had approached her, confiding in her that he was concerned that the client's sales were overstated. He said that he had found some sales contracts without support (there was usually significant documentation supporting the contracts), all signed at the end of the accounting period. He told Jane that he was concerned that the client was artificially inflating revenues to improve the company's financial performance.

———

Both of these situations involve matters that need to be investigated. If Mark does not investigate the anonymous tip, he may never uncover a possible kickback fraud and inflated purchasing costs for the company. Likewise, Jane needs to perform some follow-up investigation on the revenue problem brought to her attention by the junior auditor.

There are at least three reasons why the auditors in this case must investigate to determine whether or not the client is really overstating revenues. First, the company's shareholders could face significant losses. Second, the auditors' failure to discover the overstatement could expose them to legal action (and consequent losses). Finally, and perhaps most important, an overstatement of revenues may expose management's integrity to such serious doubt as to make the firm "unauditable."

Both of these situations have created a "predication of fraud." **Predication** refers to the circumstances, taken as a whole, that would lead a reasonable, prudent professional to believe a fraud has occurred, is occurring, or will occur. Fraud investigations should not be conducted without predication. A specific allegation of fraud against another party is not necessary, but there must be some reasonable basis for concern that fraud may be occurring. Once predication is present, as in these cases, an investigation is usually undertaken to determine whether or not fraud is actually occurring, as well as the who, why, how, when, and where elements of the fraud. The purpose of an investigation is to find the truth—to determine whether the symptoms observed actually represent fraud or whether they represent unintentional errors or other factors. Fraud investigation is a complex and sensitive matter. If investigations are not properly conducted, the reputations of innocent individuals can be irreparably injured, guilty parties can go undetected and be free to repeat the act, and the offended entity may not have information to use in preventing and detecting similar incidents or in recovering damages.

Approaches to Fraud Investigation

The investigation of fraud symptoms within an organization must have management's approval. Investigations can be quite expensive and should be pursued only when there is reason to believe that fraud has occurred (when predication is present).

———

CAUTION   *Fraud investigations must be undertaken with extreme care. It is important not to alert potential perpetrators about the investigation, or they can hide or destroy evidence. In addition, since most fraud perpetrators are first-time offenders, the thought of being caught is a traumatic experience for them and there have been many cases where perpetrators have become aware that they were targets of investigation and have committed suicide or taken other drastic actions.*

———

The approaches to fraud investigation vary, although most investigators rely heavily on interviews. Fraud investigations can be classified according to the types of evidence produced or according to the elements of fraud. Using the first approach, the evidence square in Figure 3.3 shows the four classifications of investigation techniques.

The four types of evidence that can be accumulated in a fraud investigation are as follows:

1. **Testimonial evidence**, which is gathered from individuals. Specific investigative techniques used to gather testimonial evidence are interviewing, interrogation, and honesty tests.
2. **Documentary evidence**, which is gathered from paper, computers, and other written or printed sources. Some of the most common investigative techniques for gathering this evidence include document examination, data mining, public records searches, audits, computer searches, net worth calculations, and financial statement analysis. Recently, corporate databases and e-mail servers have been very useful sources of documentary evidence.
3. **Physical evidence** includes fingerprints, tire marks, weapons, stolen property, identification numbers or marks on stolen objects, and other tangible evidence that can be associated with dishonest acts. The gathering of physical evidence often involves forensic analysis by experts.
4. **Personal observation** involves evidence that is sensed (seen, heard, felt, etc.) by the investigators themselves. Personal observation investigative techniques involve invigilation, surveillance, and covert operations, among others.

FIGURE 3.3   EVIDENCE SQUARE

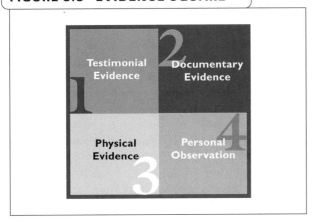

A second approach to fraud investigation is to focus on the two different fraud triangles: (1) the fraud motivation triangle and (2) the fraud element triangle. These triangles are shown in Figure 3.4.

Investigation involves investigating the various elements of each of these triangles. In focusing on the fraud motivation triangle, investigators search for perceived pressures, perceived opportunities, or rationalizations that others have observed or heard. Focusing on the fraud element triangle is a little more complicated. **Theft act** investigative methods involve efforts to catch the perpetrator(s) in the embezzlement act or to gather information about the actual theft acts. **Concealment** investigative methods involve focusing on records, documents, computer programs and servers, and other places where perpetrators might try to conceal or hide their dishonest acts. **Conversion**

investigative methods involve searching for ways in which perpetrators have spent or used their stolen assets.

Conducting a Fraud Investigation

For now, it is important to know that a fraud investigator needs some way to coordinate the fraud investigation. Some investigations are extremely large, and conducting the various investigative steps in the wrong order or doing them inappropriately can lead to a failed investigation as well as other problems. As a result, it is very important to understand the significant risks that investigators face.

And, as stated in the previous caution box, you must also remember that investigating a fraud is a traumatic experience for everyone involved, including the perpetrators. Most fraud perpetrators have positive reputations in their work, community, family, and church environments. Sometimes, admitting that they are being investigated for fraud or have committed fraud is more than they can take. Consider the following obituary, for example:

> *Memorial services for John Jones will be held Thursday, May 5, 2001, at the Springer-Wilson Funeral Home. John was 35 at the time of his death. He was preceded in death by his mother, Jane Jones, and a younger brother, Tom Jones. John is survived by his wife, Rebecca, and four children ages 9, 7, 6, and 4. He is also survived by three brothers, a sister, and his father. In lieu of flowers, please make contributions to the Improvement Memorial Fund for Children.*

This obituary, which is real but has been modified slightly, is for a person who embezzled $650,000 from

FIGURE 3.4   ELEMENTS OF FRAUD

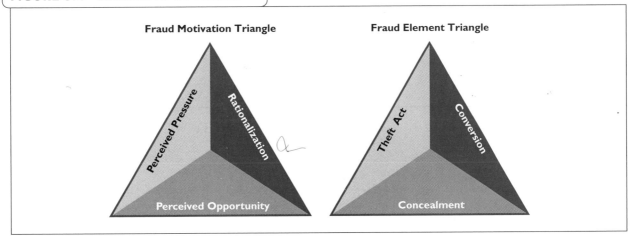

his employer's company. Over a seven-year period, he embezzled nearly half of all cash received from customers. He did not steal when customers used checks or credit cards to pay their bills—only when payment was with cash. When the company finally determined that he was stealing, they called him on the telephone at night and asked him to meet with the company's lawyers the next morning. John did two things that night after receiving the telephone call. First, he called an attorney and told her that he had been stealing from his employer for seven years and would like her to represent him at a meeting with the company's attorneys the next morning. Then, a couple of hours later, he changed his mind, drove into some nearby mountains, and committed suicide.

This actual case illustrates one reason why investigations must be conducted carefully. Maintaining high ethics in conducting investigations is also very important. At a minimum, investigations of fraud must proceed as follows:

1. They must be undertaken only to "establish the truth of a matter under question."
2. The individuals charged with the responsibility for conducting the investigation must be experienced and objective. If individuals conducting investigations do not exercise care in choosing words describing the incident or maintaining a neutral perspective, their objectivity can immediately become suspect in the eyes of management and employees. Investigators should never jump to conclusions.
3. Any hypothesis investigators have about whether or not someone committed fraud should be closely guarded when discussing the progress of an investigation with others. While good investigators often form preliminary opinions or impressions at the start of an investigation, they must objectively weigh every bit of information against known facts and evidence and must always protect the confidentiality of the investigation.
4. Investigators must ensure that only those who have a need to know (e.g., management) are kept apprised of investigation activities and agree to the investigation and techniques employed.
5. Good investigators must ensure that all information collected during an inquiry is independently corroborated and determined to be factually correct. Failure to corroborate evidence is often a key mistake made by inexperienced investigators.
6. Investigators must exercise care to avoid questionable investigative techniques. Experienced investigators

make sure that any technique used is scientifically and legally sound and fair. Usually, thoroughness and dogged tenacity rather than questionable techniques lead to a successful investigation.

7. Investigators must report all facts fairly and objectively. Communications throughout the term of an investigation, from its preliminary stage to the final report, should be carefully controlled to avoid obscuring facts and opinions. Communication, including investigative reports, must not only include information obtained that points to guilt, but must also include facts and information that may exonerate. Ignoring and failing to document information is a serious investigative flaw, with potential for serious consequences.

Remember this ...

Fraud investigation should only occur when fraud predication exists. The purpose of an investigation is to find the truth—to determine whether the symptoms observed actually represent fraud or whether they represent unintentional errors or other phenomena. There are many different ways to organize and think about fraud investigations including focusing on the types of evidence gathered and the fraud motivation and fraud element triangles. Because of the sensitive nature of fraud investigations, fraud investigators must exercise extreme care in how investigations are conducted, who knows about the investigations, and the way investigations are described.

Follow-Up Legal Action

One of the major decisions a company, stockholders, or others must make when fraud is committed is what kind of follow-up legal and other actions should be taken. Why the fraud occurred should always be determined, and controls or other measures to prevent or deter its reoccurrence should be implemented. Training of appropriate people so that similar frauds won't reoccur is also required. The bigger question that must be addressed, however, is what, if any, legal action should be taken with respect to the perpetrators.

Most organizations and other fraud victims usually make one of three choices: (1) take no legal action, (2) pursue civil remedies, and/or (3) pursue criminal action against the perpetrators, which is sometimes done for them by law enforcement agencies. While we have already addressed civil and criminal law in Chapter 1 and will discuss follow-up action in future chapters, we will briefly review some of the pros and cons of each alternative here.

Descriptive fraud research has consistently shown that legal action is taken against perpetrators who commit fraud against organizations in less than half of fraud cases. Management often only wants to get the fraud behind it as quickly as possible. It understands that pursuing legal action is expensive, time consuming, sometimes embarrassing, and often considered an unproductive use of time. Most often, management terminates fraud perpetrators, but sometimes it does not even do that. Unfortunately, when organizations do not pursue legal action, the word usually spreads quickly throughout the organization that "nothing serious will happen if you steal from the company." Employees who understand this message are more likely to steal than are employees of organizations who understand that there is an expectation of strict and universal punishment for dishonest acts. When one Fortune 500 company changed its stance on fraud from "the CEO is to be informed when someone is prosecuted for fraud" to "the CEO is to be informed when someone who commits fraud is not prosecuted," the number of frauds in the company decreased significantly.

Civil Action

As you learned in Chapter 1, the purpose of a civil action is to recover money or other assets from the fraud perpetrators and others associated with the fraud. Unless perpetrators have considerable assets (e.g., homes, expensive cars, and other assets), civil actions are quite rare in cases of employee fraud because perpetrators have usually spent the money they stole. However, civil action is much more common when frauds involve other organizations. Vendors who pay kickbacks to company employees are often the target of civil actions by victim companies, especially if the losses to the company are high. Consider the example in the following real case where the names have been changed.

Mark L. was the purchasing agent for a company that purchased large amounts of uniforms for its employees. Mark typically used three different vendors but started accepting bribes from a particular vendor from Korea. Once the bribes were being paid, the control of purchasing transactions shifted from the buyer to the supplier, with the supplier demanding that Mark's company purchase more uniforms at higher prices and even at lower quality. Once the quality deteriorated, the uniforms starting falling apart, changing colors when being washed, and buttons started falling off. In the meantime, the Korean company shifted manufacturing to a lower-cost country and demanded that the purchasing company buy increasing numbers of uniforms. Because of the decreased quality, Mark's company sued the supplier for failing to meet contract specifications. After subpoenaing purchasing records, Mark's company found a 1099 (tax form indicating payment) to Mark. Seeing the red flag that their own purchasing agent was being paid by a supplier, Mark's company hired a fraud examiner who detected and investigated the fraud. Mark's company sued the Korean manufacturer civilly for triple damages according to RICO statues. Just before the trial started, the Korean company settled with Mark's company by paying it $46 million to cover the triple damages and legal fees incurred.

Similarly, stockholders and creditors who suffer losses when management fraud occurs almost always sue not only the perpetrators but also usually the auditors and any others associated with the company who may have "deep pockets." The plaintiff's lawyers are usually more than willing to represent shareholders in class action, contingent fee lawsuits.[14]

Criminal Action

Criminal action can only be brought by law enforcement or statutory agencies. Organizations that want to pursue criminal action against perpetrators must work with local, state, or federal agencies to get their employees or other perpetrators prosecuted. As you learned in Chapter 1, criminal penalties usually involve fines, prison terms, or both. They can also involve the perpetrators entering into restitution agreements to pay back stolen funds over a period of time. Pursuing criminal penalties is becoming more and more common in fraud cases. Corporate executives who commit fraud are often sentenced for up to 10 years in jail and ordered to pay fines equal to the amounts they embezzled.

As an example of criminal penalties that can be imposed, consider the case of Bernie Ebbers, the former CEO of WorldCom.

One of the largest criminal sentences ever handed to a fraud perpetrator was given to ex-WorldCom chief executive Bernie Ebbers in 2005. The 63-year-old Mr. Ebbers was sentenced to 25 years in prison for his role in orchestrating the biggest corporate fraud in U.S. history.

Mr. Ebbers was convicted in March 2005 for his part in the $11 billion accounting fraud at WorldCom that was the biggest in a wave of corporate scandals at Enron, Adelphia, and other companies.

WorldCom, now known as MCI, filed the largest bankruptcy in U.S. history in 2002. The company's collapse led to billions of dollars in losses for shareholders and employees.

Mr. Ebbers had previously agreed to forfeit the bulk of his assets—including a Mississippi mansion and other holdings estimated to be worth as much as $45 million—to burned WorldCom investors and MCI. His wife did keep a modest home in Jackson, Mississippi, and about $50,000.

Mr. Ebbers appealed the verdict, but it was reaffirmed by a higher court in September 2006.

Remember, however, that it is much more difficult to get a criminal conviction than it is to get a judgment in a civil case. Whereas only a preponderance of the evidence (more than 50 percent) is necessary to win a civil case, convictions are only successful if there is proof "beyond a reasonable doubt" that the perpetrator "intentionally" stole money or other assets.

Remember this ...

Once a fraud has been investigated, victim organizations must decide what legal and other actions to pursue. At a minimum, they should make sure that controls are implemented and training takes place to prevent similar occurrences in the future. In addition, the company must decide whether to sue civilly (to try to recover stolen funds) or to pursue criminal prosecution or both. Guilty verdicts in criminal cases can result in prison sentences and/or restitution.

Review of the Learning Objectives

- **Become familiar with the different ways that organizations fight fraud.** Organizations generally fight fraud in four ways: (1) by trying to prevent frauds from occurring, (2) by using proactive detection methods for frauds that do occur, (3) by investigating fraud once there is suspicion (predication) that a fraud is or has occurred, and (4) by following up legally and in other ways.
- **Understand the importance of fraud prevention.** Fraud prevention is the most cost-effective fraud-fighting activity. Once fraud occurs, everyone

loses. Fraud prevention involves (1) taking steps to create and maintain a culture of honesty and high ethics and (2) assessing the risks for fraud and developing concrete responses to mitigate the risks and eliminate the opportunities for fraud.

- **Understand how to create a culture of honesty and high ethics.** Organizations that take proactive steps to create a culture of honesty and high ethics can successfully eliminate much fraud. Creating a culture of honesty and high ethics includes (1) making sure that top management models appropriate behavior, (2) hiring the right kind of employees, (3) communicating expectations throughout the organization, (4) creating a positive work environment, and (5) developing and maintaining an effective policy for handling fraud when it does occur.
- **Understand why hiring the right kind of employees can greatly reduce the risk of fraud.** Unfortunately, not all people are equally honest or have equally well-developed personal codes of ethics. If an organization is to be successful in preventing fraud, it must have effective hiring policies that discriminate between marginal and highly ethical individuals, especially when recruiting for high-risk positions. Proactive hiring procedures include such things as conducting background investigations on prospective employees, thoroughly checking references and learning how to interpret responses to inquiries asked about candidates, and testing for honesty and other attributes.
- **Understand how to assess and mitigate the risk of fraud.** Assessing and mitigating the risk of fraud means that an organization should have a process in place that both defines where the greatest fraud risks are and evaluates and tests controls that mitigate those risks. In identifying fraud risks, organizations should consider organizational, industry, and country-specific characteristics that influence the risk of fraud.
- **Understand the importance of early fraud detection.** No matter how good a company's fraud prevention activities are, some frauds will still occur. Companies should use proactive fraud detection techniques, such as whistle-blower systems and data mining tools, to detect frauds before they become large.
- **Understand different approaches to fraud investigation.** Fraud investigation involves the steps taken, once fraud is detected or suspected, to determine the who, why, when, and how much of the fraud. Fraud investigation identifies perpetrators,

amounts taken, and breakdowns in controls or other elements that allowed the fraud to occur. Fraud investigation is expensive and time consuming.

- **Be familiar with the different options for legal action that can be taken once fraud has occurred.** Once frauds occur, companies should take both internal and external actions. Internal actions involve making sure controls and training are in place to prevent future occurrences of similar frauds. External actions include civil suits and/or criminal prosecution.

KEY TERMS

fraud prevention, p. 71
ethical maturity model
  (EMM), p. 72
codes of conduct, p. 74
Sarbanes-Oxley Act
  of 2002, p. 76
whistle-blowing
  systems, p. 78
fraud detection,
  p. 79
predication, p. 80

testimonial evidence,
  p. 80
documentary evidence,
  p. 80
physical evidence, p. 80
personal observation,
  p. 80
investigation, p. 81
theft act, p. 81
concealment, p. 81
conversion, p. 81

QUESTIONS

Discussion Questions

1. Why is fraud prevention so important?
2. How does building a culture of honesty and high ethics help to reduce the possibility of fraud?
3. How does a company assess and mitigate the risk of fraud within an organization?
4. Why is it important to detect fraud early?
5. Why is it important to conduct a thorough fraud investigation when fraud is suspected?
6. Describe the evidence square.
7. How is the evidence square useful in thinking about fraud investigation?
8. For each of the following, identify whether the evidence would be classified as testimonial evidence, documentary evidence, physical evidence, or personal observation.
   a. Surveillance
   b. Tire marks
   c. Honesty test

   d. Interview
   e. A computer hard drive
   f. A financial statement analysis
   g. A paper report
   h. Identification numbers on vehicles
   i. Audit of financial statements
   j. Check stubs
   k. Fingerprints
   l. Background checks
   m. Interview
9. What are some of the legal actions that can be taken after a fraud has occurred?
10. Why might civil proceeding be ineffective against employee fraud? When might they be more useful?
11. Why might management avoid taking legal action against fraud perpetrators? What are the perceived benefits of inaction? What are the costs?

True/False

1. Once fraud has been committed, there are no winners.
2. Fraud prevention involves two fundamental activities: (1) a hotline for tips and (2) assessing the risk of fraud and developing concrete responses to mitigate the risks and eliminate opportunities for fraud.
3. Developing a positive work environment is of little importance when creating a culture of honesty.
4. No matter how well an organization has developed a culture of honesty and high ethics, most organizations will still have some fraud.
5. Research has shown that it is employees and managers, not auditors, who detect most frauds.
6. Organizations that want to prevent fraud must make it easy for employees and others to report suspicious activities.
7. If a perpetrator is not caught, his confidence in the scheme will decrease, and he will become less and less greedy.
8. Once predication is present, an investigation is usually undertaken to determine whether or not fraud is actually occurring.
9. Most investigators rely heavily on interviews to obtain the truth.
10. Physical evidence includes evidence gathered from paper, computers, and other written documents.
11. Legal action taken by an organization can affect the probability of whether fraud will reoccur.
12. Investigating fraud is the most cost-effective way to reduce losses from fraud.

13. Fraud prevention includes taking steps to create and maintain a culture of honesty and high ethics.
14. Effective hiring policies that discriminate between marginal and highly ethical individuals contribute to an organization's success in preventing fraud.
15. Expectations about punishment must be communicated randomly among work groups if fraud is to be prevented.
16. Frauds typically start large and get smaller as the perpetrator tries to conceal his dishonest acts.
17. Fraud is difficult to detect because some fraud symptoms often cannot be differentiated from nonfraud factors that appear to be symptoms.
18. The three elements of the fraud triangle by which the investigative techniques are often classified are (1) the theft act, (2) concealment efforts, and (3) conversion methods.
19. Organizations often want to avoid embarrassment and expense, so they terminate fraudulent employees without having them prosecuted further.
20. Criminal conviction is much more difficult to achieve than a civil judgment because there must be proof "beyond a reasonable doubt" that the perpetrator intentionally stole assets.
21. In order to create a culture of honesty and confidentiality, persons aware of fraudulent activity should be encouraged to tell only the CEO.
22. Since complete fraud prevention is impossible because it requires changing actual human behavior, successful companies should forgo fraud prevention and instead focus on strong fraud detection programs.
23. Since fraud prevention programs are so costly, despite being ethically superior, they almost always result in higher costs and thus lower net income than using only a strong system of fraud detection.
24. Most fraud perpetrators have a long history of dishonesty and deceit.

Multiple Choice

1. The most effective way to reduce losses from fraud is:
   a. Detecting fraud early.
   b. Implementing proactive fraud detection programs.
   c. Preventing fraud from occurring.
   d. Severely punishing fraud perpetrators.

2. To successfully prevent fraud, an organization must:
   a. Identify internal control weaknesses.
   b. Explicitly consider fraud risks.
   c. Take proactive steps to create the right kind of environment.
   d. All of the above.
3. The best way for management to model appropriate behavior is to:
   a. Enforce a strict code of ethics.
   b. Set an example of appropriate behavior.
   c. Train employees about appropriate behavior.
   d. Make employees read and sign a code of conduct.
4. Which of the following is *not* a proactive way for a company to eliminate fraud opportunities?
   a. Severely punishing fraud perpetrators.
   b. Assessing risks.
   c. Implementing appropriate preventive and detective controls.
   d. Creating widespread monitoring of employees.
5. Most frauds start small and:
   a. If not detected, continue to get larger.
   b. Usually decrease in amount.
   c. Remain steady and consistent.
   d. None of the above.
6. It is most difficult to prevent which type of fraud?
   a. Investment scams.
   b. Fraud committed by a company president.
   c. Employee fraud.
   d. Customer fraud.
7. Which of the following refers to the circumstances, taken as a whole, that would lead a reasonable prudent professional to believe fraud has occurred, is occurring, or will occur?
   a. Evidential circumstance.
   b. Investigation.
   c. Service of process.
   d. Predication.
8. An investigative approach that includes testimonial evidence, documentary evidence, physical evidence, and personal observations is referred to as the:
   a. Investigative square of evidence.
   b. Investigation square.
   c. Evidence square.
   d. Fraud triangle plus.
9. Usually, for everyone involved—especially victims—the investigation of fraud is very:
   a. Pleasant and relaxing.
   b. Educational.
   c. Exciting.
   d. Traumatic and difficult.

10. To prevent fraud from reoccurring, most organizations and other fraud victims should:
    a. Take no legal action.
    b. Pursue civil remedies.
    c. Pursue criminal remedies.
    d. Pursue either civil or criminal action.
11. All of the following are ways to create a culture of honesty and high ethics except:
    a. Creating a positive work environment.
    b. Hiring the right kind of employees.
    c. Having top management model appropriate behavior.
    d. Eliminating opportunities for fraud.
12. The *tone at the top* when related to fraud usually refers to management's attitude about:
    a. Office parties.
    b. Fraud prosecution.
    c. Employee absenteeism.
    d. How it models and labels appropriate behavior.
13. Research shows that fraud occurs less frequently when employees feel:
    a. Abused by management.
    b. Threatened.
    c. Challenged with unreasonable performance goals.
    d. Ownership in the organization.
14. Opportunities to commit fraud can be eliminated by identifying sources of fraud, by implementing controls, and through independent checks. One other effective way of eliminating opportunities is:
    a. Teaching employees to monitor and report fraud.
    b. Terminating and punishing employees who commit fraud.
    c. Failing to terminate or punish employees who commit fraud.
    d. Identifying indicators of fraud or red flags.
15. Drawbacks to establishing a hotline for employees to report fraud include all of the following except:
    a. Expense.
    b. Many incidents reported are hoaxes motivated by grudges.
    c. Fraud symptoms reported are caused by nonfraud factors.
    d. This method for finding fraud is outdated.
16. "Predication of fraud" is defined as:
    a. Reasonable belief that fraud has occurred.
    b. Irrefutable evidence that fraud has been committed.

c. Motivation for committing fraud.
    d. Punishment of fraud perpetrators.
17. Which of the four types of evidence includes interrogation and honesty testing?
    a. Testimonial.
    b. Documentary.
    c. Physical.
    d. Personal observation.
18. The three elements of fraud are:
    a. Theft act, rationalization, and opportunity.
    b. Pressure, opportunity, and conversion.
    c. Theft act, concealment, and conversion.
    d. Theft act, pressure, and opportunity.
19. Most often, victims of fraud do not take legal action against perpetrators. This is because legal action can be:
    a. Unproductive.
    b. Embarrassing.
    c. Expensive.
    d. All of the above.
20. Arguments for taking legal action against perpetrators of fraud include:
    a. Huge cash settlements from prosecuting fraud are an excellent source of revenue.
    b. Legal action usually results in positive publicity for the company.
    c. Prosecution keeps lawyers busy.
    d. Prosecution discourages reoccurrence of fraud.
21. Factors that are usually associated with high levels of employee fraud include all of the following except:
    a. Negative feedback and lack of recognition of job performance.
    b. Perceived inequalities in an organization.
    c. Long and difficult hours shared equally by everyone in the organization.
    d. High turnover and absenteeism.
22. Which of the following is true regarding the Sarbanes-Oxley Act of 2002:
    a. Companies with revenues exceeding $10 million must have a whistle-blower system in place.
    b. Public companies must have a whistle-blower system in place.
    c. Public companies with revenues exceeding $10 million must have a whistle-blower system in place.
    d. All companies must have a whistle-blower system in place.

SHORT CASES

Case 1

Assume that you are a consultant for Long Range Builders, a company that specializes in the mass production of wood trusses. The trusses are used in the building of houses throughout the United States, Canada, and Mexico. While implementing a fraud prevention program, you realize the importance of creating a culture of honesty and high ethics within the company.

1. What critical elements are key factors in creating an atmosphere of honesty and high ethics?
2. How would you implement these elements in your company?

Case 2

The chapter stressed that preventing fraud is the most cost-effective way to reduce losses from fraud. Why is fraud prevention more cost-effective than fraud detection or investigation?

Case 3

Fraud detection is an important element of minimizing losses to fraud, especially if frauds can be detected early. Explain why it is important that frauds be detected early.

Case 4

Assume that you are the fraud expert for a large Fortune 500 company located in Miami, Florida. In a recent meeting with the executive committee, one of the officers explains that the fraud prevention program, which teaches managers and employees how to detect and report fraud, costs the company $150,000 a year. The officer then explains that it is a waste of time and money for the company to educate employees and managers about fraud. "Is it not the responsibility of the auditors to detect fraud?" he questions. As the fraud expert of the company, the president asks you to explain why managers and employees should be educated in the detection of fraud.

1. What would you tell the committee about why it is important to train managers and employees in fraud detection?
2. After explaining to the committee why it is important to train management and employees, the president asks you about effective ways to involve employees and managers in the prevention and detection of fraud. What would you tell the president?

Case 5

You have recently graduated from college with an MBA. Upon graduation, you start working for Roosevelt Power Plant. The boss, Mr. Jones, invites you into his office. Mr. Jones describes to you a large fraud that has recently taken place in the company. He asks you what actions should be taken to ensure that fraud does not occur again. After analyzing the company, you compile a list of actions that will be needed to prevent fraud from occurring again. Upon presenting the necessary steps and controls to be taken, Mr. Jones notices your suggestion: "Create a culture of honesty and create a positive work environment for employees." Mr. Jones is enraged and wants to know what a positive work environment has to do with the prevention and detection of fraud.

1. What would you tell Mr. Jones about why a positive work environment will help prevent fraud?
2. What factors would you tell Mr. Jones contribute to a negative work environment?

Case 6

The text pointed out that it is important to hire employees who are honest and have a well-developed personal code of ethics. Derek Bok, former law professor and president of Harvard University, has suggested that colleges and universities have a special obligation to train students to be more thoughtful and perceptive about moral and ethical issues. Other individuals have concluded that it is not possible to "teach" ethics. What do you think? Can ethics be taught? If you agree that colleges and universities can teach ethics, how might the ethical dimensions of business be taught to students?

Case 7

Predication refers to circumstances that would lead a reasonable professional to believe that fraud has occurred. Why should you not conduct a fraud investigation without predication?

Case 8

When a fraud has occurred within an organization, management must decide what follow-up action to take. Briefly describe the three follow-up alternatives available to organizations.

Case 9

In 2001, the country of Peru was thrown into political turmoil as its president, Alberto Fujimori, was accused of conspiring with the head of the national army to accept bribes and steal money from the government. As a result, Fujimori fled the country to avoid impeachment and prosecution. Fujimori was elected 10 years earlier based on his promises to lower inflation and combat terrorism. He was not, however, elected for his honesty. At the time he was elected, many people expressed the thought, "All of our presidents steal from us, but he steals the least." Although he was successful as a president, what could the Peruvian people have done to avoid the frauds committed by President Fujimori?

Case 10

You are the controller at a start-up company named HyperGlobal created by your friend, Kevin. Your company is growing quickly, and you and Kevin are finding it difficult to hire qualified people fast enough. Kevin suggests over lunch that you should expedite the process by skipping the sometimes time-consuming chore of running background checks. He notes, "I interview them anyway, and I can tell if they are honest just by talking to them. We should do away with this silly background checking business." Do you agree? How would you respond to Kevin? What is at stake if hiring mistakes are made?

Case 11

Business 2.0 recently reported on Men's Warehouse's CEO George Zimmer's policy "that no employee or interviewee will ever undergo a criminal background check."[15] The company, however, loses an average of 0.4 percent of revenues to theft, compared to a typical 1.5 percent faced by most large retailers. What things might create this low rate of theft despite not performing criminal background checks?

Case 12

According to the text, when one Fortune 500 company changed its stance on fraud from "the CEO is to be informed when someone is prosecuted for fraud" to "the CEO is to be informed when someone who commits fraud is not prosecuted," the number of frauds in the company decreased significantly. Why might that be?

Case 13

As a fraud expert asked to investigate possible fraud at a local nonprofit organization, you suspect that one of the workers, Stacey, has been embezzling money. After securing enough evidence to be very confident of Stacey's guilt, you speak with the president of the organization, Jamie. Jamie assures you that Stacey could be doing nothing wrong, that she has known Stacey for years, and that Stacey is a good person. Further, she indicates that because of her relationship with Stacey, even if something were going wrong, no action would be taken with respect to the potential fraud. How do you respond to Jamie? How do you explain to her what is at stake?

Case 14

Peter Jones, a senior accountant, and Mary Miller, a junior accountant, were the only accountants for XYZ Company, a medium-size business. Peter had been with the company for over four years and was responsible for the Purchasing Department. Mary had been working at the company for a little over five years, and she had neither applied for a vacation nor taken any days off in the last three years. She was responsible for cash receipts and disbursements. She also collected the cash from the cash register, counted it and matched it with cash register receipts, made a record of daily receipts, and then put the money in the safe. Once a week, she would take the paperwork to her supervisor, Susan Lowe, one of the managers, who would check it. Mary later resigned from the company. At the time of her resignation, Peter was asked to handle Mary's responsibilities while the company looked for a person to replace her. Peter soon realized that there had been some manipulation of accounting records and embezzlement of funds. Investigations revealed that approximately $30,000 had been stolen.

1. What do you think might have allowed this fraud?
2. How could this fraud have been avoided?

CASE STUDIES

Case Study 1

Plutonium was an Internet start-up company founded in 1988 at the beginning of the technology boom. One of the largest problems for Plutonium was developing the technological systems necessary to support the rapidly expanding user base. Furthermore, due to the rapid expansion in recent years, many of its systems had been added hastily, resulting in poor integration and eroding data integrity. As a result, the CEO of Plutonium announced an initiative to integrate all systems and increase the quality of internal data. In compliance with this initiative, Plutonium purchased an expensive and complex billing system called Gateway, which would automate the billing for thousands of Internet accounts via credit cards. During the integration, Gateway, in collaboration with Visa, created a phony credit card number that could be used by developers and programmers to test the functionality and integration of the Gateway system. Moreover, this credit card number was fully functional in "live" environments so testers and developers could ensure functionality without being required to use actual personal or company credit card numbers (the activity on this card was not monitored). The integration went smoothly; however, it created thousands of corrupt accounts that required fixing.

Jonathan, the manager of the Operations Department, was responsible for the resolution of all data integrity issues. His team was tasked with fixing all corrupt accounts created by the launch and integration of the Gateway system. As a result, Jonathan was given the phony credit card number, which was kept on a Post-it Note in his drawer.

One of the top performers on the Operations team was a 29-year-old male named Chris. Chris had worked in Operations for over a year and was making $15 per hour, the same salary at which he was hired. He was an introvert working to support a family and put himself through school. Chris was the most technologically savvy individual on the team, and his overall systems knowledge even exceeded that of his manager, Jonathon. Chris was very brilliant in creating more efficient tools and methods to repair corrupted accounts. Therefore, Chris was tasked with conducting training for new employees and updating team members on new processes and tools that he had created. As a result, Chris quickly became a trusted and valuable team member; thus, Jonathon gave him and other team members the phony credit card number in order to further increase the productivity of the team.

However, after six months of working at Plutonium, Chris received an official reprimand from the company for using the company system to access Web sites containing pirated software and music. The FBI attended the investigation and determined that Chris had not been a major player in the piracy. Therefore, Chris was quietly warned and placed on a short-term probation. Jonathon was asked to write a warning letter for the action; however, after a brief conversation with Chris, Jonathon determined that Chris's intentions were good and never officially submitted the letter because Chris was a trusted employee and elevated the overall performance of the team. A few months after the piracy incident, Jonathon noticed some changes in Chris's behavior such as (a) his computer monitor was repositioned so that his screen was not visible to other coworkers, (b) he had almost all the latest technological innovations (new Palm Pilot, MP3 player, Play Station, new laptop, and a new car stereo system), (c) he was going out to lunch more frequently, and (d) he frequently used multiple fake usernames and passwords for testing purposes.

Questions

1. Evaluate this case using the three elements of the fraud triangle to identify the following:
   a. Potential pressures for Chris to commit fraud.
   b. Potential opportunities for Chris to commit fraud.
   c. Potential rationalizations that Chris could use to commit fraud.
2. What are some of the symptoms that fraud potentially exists in this situation?
3. What could Jonathon have done to eliminate some of the opportunities for fraud?

Case Study 2

Derek worked for a reputable global consulting firm. His firm specialized in helping companies analyze their people, processes, systems, and strategy. Derek was hired into the San Francisco office and put through weeks of training to help him understand the firm methodology, technology, and culture. The firm looked for people with the right aptitude who had demonstrated a record of success in previous school, work, or extracurricular activities. They found that this type of person worked out best for the type of work the firm was paid to do.

Derek was flattered to be considered the right type of person for this company. He was excited to be assigned to a project and begin work. Even though Derek was trained in certain technologies, he was assigned a project for which he had no training. The project was implementing SAP—a multimillion-dollar enterprise resource planning software package. The client was a mid-sized manufacturer with revenues of approximately $100 million located in Topeka, Kansas.

Derek was not trained in SAP and found out that he was replacing two managers who were just removed from the project. The project was running over budget so the firm looked for ways to get the work done less expensively. Derek, who billed out at the lower "consultant's" rate (instead of the "manager" rate), was a cheap solution, although it would be a tough sell to the client. They liked the previous managers and felt comfortable with their skill level. Because of the demand for the SAP experts, Derek's firm could charge Derek's time at a billing rate of $200/hour—expensive, but less than the client was paying for the managers.

During the first day on the job, Derek's manager took him out to lunch to give him "the scoop" on what was happening on the project and what he would be expecting from Derek. "Derek, this is going to be a very difficult assignment. You've replaced two skilled managers who the client liked. I know you haven't been trained on, or actually even seen SAP before, but you're smart and can come up to speed quickly. I had to tell the client you were an expert in the software in order for them to agree to bring you on. If you have any questions, don't hesitate to ask me but definitely don't look stupid or seem like you don't know what you're doing in front of the client. The client will be skeptical of you at first, but be confident and you'll win them over. I think the transition will smooth out quickly. See me if you have any questions."

Derek was scared to death—but what was he to do? Was this standard procedure to throw employees into this kind of situation? Regardless, he had to get to work. His immediate tasks were to map out the processes for the client's order-to-cash, purchase-to-pay, and capital acquisition business scenarios. This involved interviewing managers and looking around most of the functional departments in the company. Here are some interesting things he found as he did his work.

PURCHASING DEPARTMENT: The head of purchasing was a handsome gentleman named Mike. Mike was very different from any other employee who Derek encountered while at the client. He wore expensive suits to work and liked to talk about his clothes with colleagues. He also drove the latest model BMW and would take the other consultants on the project for rides during lunch. Derek thought this odd because he didn't think a purchasing manger at this company made enough money to have these luxuries. Mike also took his relationships with "his" vendors very seriously. He would spend lots of time "understanding who they were." Some days, Mike was very supportive of Derek and other days seemed completely different and almost hostile and combative. When Derek informally inquired about the purchasing manager's clothes and car and his Dr. Jekyll and Mr. Hyde syndrome, he heard the following justification, "He probably has a lot of money because he's worked here for over 20 years. Plus, he never takes vacations. Come to think of it, the vacation part probably explains why he seems hostile to you some of the time." Derek couldn't figure this guy out but proceeded to do his work with the Purchasing Department.

INTERNAL SALES AND SHIPPING DEPARTMENT: Internal Sales was run by a stressed out single mom named Kathy. You could tell at first glance that she had probably lived a rough life. Kathy was probably not college educated but had a lot of "street smarts." Kathy was cooperative with Derek. During the course of their interaction, Derek noticed how periodically there would be huge returns that were stacked nearly to the ceiling in the Shipping Department. When Derek inquired about these periodic huge returns, Kathy told him that sometimes they would ship orders to customers based on past purchasing habits even though the customer had not recently placed an order. As it turns out, when the customers saw a delivery at their door someone would just assume they had placed an order and would keep it. However, other customers would quickly return the supplies. "Was that a good business practice?" Derek inquired. "Well, we have to make our numbers at quarter's end—you have to do what you have to do," Kathy replied. On one of Derek's weekly flights home, he picked up a newspaper and began to read about all the current frauds. Man, it seems like every company is committing fraud these days, Derek thought to himself after seeing multiple fraud-related articles. Derek hadn't had any fraud training but began to wonder if his firm or the client he was working for could be committing fraud.

Questions

Based on the case data, comment on the following issues as they relate to possible fraud:

1. Derek's firm "selling" Derek to the client as an "SAP expert" though he hadn't even seen the software before
2. The unpredictable well-dressed purchasing manager.
3. The sales practices revealed in the Internal Sales Department.

INTERNET ASSIGNMENTS

1. Visit the Web site of the National White Collar Crime Center at www.nw3c.org. This site is funded through a grant from the Department of Justice. Its purpose is to assist federal law enforcement agencies in the investigation and prevention of white-collar crime. The center also has a college internship program. Click on the "Research" link, select "Papers, publications and reports," select "Papers," and then read the study on Embezzlement/Employee Theft from October 2009 and answer the following questions:

a. Research suggests that embezzlement accounts for approximately what percentage of all business failures[16]?

b. According to the study what percentage of employees steal from their employers?[17]

2. Go to www.fraud.org and learn about the National Fraud Information Center (NFIC). What does it do, and specifically, how does it make it easy for people to report fraud?

DEBATES

Fred is a friend of yours and works with you at the same company. He is a well-respected and trusted employee. He has two young children and is a leader in his community. You have discovered that Fred has embezzled $3,000 over a period of several years. While this is not much money for such a large company, you suspect that if you don't report him, the problem may get worse. On the other hand, he has young children, and he has done so much good in the company and the community. If you report him, he may go to prison because your company has an aggressive fraud prosecution policy. Should you report him or are there any other alternatives available?

END NOTES

1. Wells, J. T., 2007, *Corporate Fraud Handbook*, Hoboken, New Jersey: John Wiley & Sons, Inc.

2. Biegelman, M. T., Bartow, J. T., 2006, *Executive Roadmap to Fraud Prevention and Internal Control*, New Jersey: John Wiley & Sons, Inc.

3. Schwartz, M. S., Dunfee, T. W., and M. J. Kline, 2005, Tone at the Top: An Ethics Code for Directors, *Journal of Business Ethics*, Vol. 58: 1–3.

4. www.mental-health-matters.com/articles/article.php?artID=153, accessed May 22, 2004.

5. Wang, J.-M. and B. H. Kleiner, Effective Employment Screening Practices, *Management Research News*, Vol. 27: 4–5.

6. See, for example, W. Steve Albrecht, Conan C. Albrecht, and Ned C. Hill, "The Ethics Development Model Applied to Declining Ethics in Accounting," *Australian Accounting Review*, Issue 38, Vol. 16, No. 1 (March 2006): 30–40.

7. Trevino, L. K., Hartman, L. P. and M. Brown, 2000, Moral Person and Moral Manager: How Executives Develop a Reputation for Ethical Leadership, *California Management Review*, Vol. 42: 4.

8. For more information about situational honesty see Scott, E. D., 2000, Moral Values: Situationally Defined Individual Differences, *Business Ethics Quarterly*, Vol. 10: 2.

9. Stevens, B., 1999, Communicating Ethical Values: A Study of Employee Perceptions, *Journal of Business Ethics*, Vol. 20: 2.

10. Kaptein, M. and M. S. Schwartz, 2008, The Effectiveness of Business Codes: A Critical Examination of Existing Studies and the Development of an Integrated Research Model, *Journal of Business Ethics*, Vol. 77: 2.

11. Red Hat's Code of Business Conduct and Ethics can be found at http://investors.redhat.com/governance.cfm, accessed May 23, 2010.

12. Cottrell, D. M. and W. S. Albrecht, 1994, Recognizing the Symptoms of Employee Fraud, *Healthcare Financial Management*, Vol. 48: 5.

13. The names and setting in this case are fictitious.

14. Class-action lawsuits are permitted under federal and some state rules of court procedure in the United States. In a class-action suit, a relatively small number of aggrieved plaintiffs with small individual claims can bring suit for large damages in the name of an extended class. After a fraud, for example, 40 bondholders who lost $40,000 might decide to sue, and they can sue on behalf of the entire class of bondholders for all their alleged losses (say, $50 million). Lawyers are more than happy to take such suits on a contingency fee basis (a percentage of the judgment, if any).

15. http://money.cnn.com/galleries/2007/biz2/0705/gallery.contrarians.biz2/10.html

16. Bullard, P. and A. Resnick, 1983, SMR Forum: Too many hands in the corporate cookie jar, *Sloan Management Review*, Vol. 24: 3.

17. McGurn, J., 1988, Spotting the Thieves Who Work Among Us, *Wall Street Journal*, p. 16, March 7.

Red Hat Code of Business Conduct and Ethics

As Amended and Restated As of February 28, 2009

This Code of Business Conduct and Ethics (the "Code") sets forth legal and ethical standards of conduct for directors, officers and employees of Red Hat, Inc. and its subsidiaries (the "Company"). This Code is intended to deter wrongdoing and to promote the conduct of all Company business in accordance with high standards of integrity and in compliance with all applicable laws and regulations. This Code applies to the Company and all of its subsidiaries and other business entities controlled by it worldwide.

If you have any questions regarding this Code or its application to you in any situation, you should contact your supervisor or Red Hat's General Counsel.

Compliance with Laws, Rules and Regulations

The Company requires that all employees, officers and directors comply with all laws, rules and regulations applicable to the Company wherever it does business, including with respect to the conduct of business with governments and the protection of classified information. You are expected to be familiar with the laws, rules and regulations applicable to your place of work, and such additional laws, rules and regulations which may apply and of which the Company gives you written notice. With respect to conducting business with governments and associated governmental entities in the United States, please also consult Red Hat's Policy on Business Conduct for the United States Government Marketplace, which is available in the Legal section of the Company's Intranet.

You are expected to use good judgment and common sense in seeking to comply with all applicable laws, rules and regulations and to ask for advice when you are uncertain about them.

If you become aware of the violation of any law, rule or regulation by the Company, whether by its officers, employees or directors, it is your responsibility to promptly report the matter to your supervisor, the Red Hat General Counsel, or the Chairman of the Audit Committee of the Red Hat Board of Directors. While it is the Company's desire to address matters internally, nothing in this Code should discourage you from reporting any illegal activity, including any violation of the securities laws, antitrust laws, environmental laws or any other federal, state or foreign law, rule or regulation, to the appropriate regulatory authority. Employees, officers and directors shall not discharge, demote, suspend, threaten, harass or in any other manner discriminate against an employee because he or she in good faith reports any such violation. This Code should not be construed to prohibit you from testifying, participating or otherwise assisting in any state or federal administrative, judicial or legislative proceeding or investigation.

Conflicts of Interest

Employees, officers and directors must act in the best interests of the Company. You must refrain from engaging in any activity or having a personal interest that presents a "conflict of interest." A conflict of interest occurs when your personal interest interferes, or appears to interfere, with the interests of the Company. A conflict of interest can arise whenever you, as an officer, director or employee, take action or have an interest that prevents you from performing your Company duties and responsibilities honestly, objectively and effectively.

Employees and Officers. In the following instances a conflict of interest is deemed to exist absent mitigating facts and circumstances:

1. where the officer or employee performs services as a consultant, employee, officer, director, advisor or in any other capacity for, or has a financial interest in, a Direct Competitor of the Company, other than services performed in the context of the officer's or employee's job with the Company or at the request of the Company and other than a financial interest representing less than one percent (1%) of the outstanding shares of a publicly-held company;

2. where the officer or employee uses his or her position with the Company to influence a transaction with a Significant Supplier or Significant Customer in which such person has any personal interest, other than a financial interest representing less than one percent (1%) of the outstanding shares of a publiclyheld company;

3. where the officer or employee has any Close Relative who holds a financial interest in a Direct Competitor of the Company, other than an investment representing less than one percent (1%) of the outstanding shares of a publicly-held company;

4. where the officer or employee supervises, reviews or influences the performance evaluation or compensation of a member of his or her Immediate Family who is an employee of the Company; or

5. where the officer or employee engages in any other activity or has any other interest that the Board of Directors of the Company may reasonably determine to constitute a conflict of interest.

Directors. Directors must not:

1. perform services as a consultant, employee, officer, director, advisor or in any other capacity for, or have a financial interest in, a Direct Competitor of the Company, other than services performed at the request of the Company and other than a financial interest representing less than one percent (1%) of the outstanding shares of a publicly-held company;

2. have, or permit any Close Relative to have, a financial interest in a Direct Competitor of the Company, other than an investment representing less than one percent (1%) of the outstanding shares of a publicly-held company;

3. use his or her position with the Company to influence any decision of the Company relating to a contract or transaction with a Significant Supplier or Significant Customer of the Company if the director or a Close Relative of the director:
   - performs services as a consultant, employee, officer, director, advisor or in any other capacity for such Significant Supplier or Significant Customer; or
   - has a financial interest in such Significant Supplier or Significant Customer, other than an investment representing less than one percent (1%) of the outstanding shares of a publicly-held company.

4. directly supervise, review or influence the performance evaluation or compensation of a member of his or her Immediate Family; or

5. engage in any other activity or have any other interest that the Board of Directors of the Company may reasonably determine to constitute a conflict of interest.

For purposes of this Code, the following definitions apply:

"Close Relative" means a spouse, domestic partner, dependent child (including step-child) or any other person (other than a tenant or employee) sharing the person's household.

"Direct Competitor" means any commercial business entity which directly competes with one or more of the Company's product or service lines of business representing at least five percent (5%) of the Company's gross annual revenues.

"Immediate Family Member" of a person means that person's Close Relative and that person's child (including step-child), parent, stepparent, sibling, mother-in-law, father-in-law, son-in-law, daughter-in-law, brother-in-law, or sister-in-law and anyone else (other than a tenant or employee) sharing the person's household.

"Significant Customer" means a customer that has made during the Company's last full fiscal year, or proposes to make during the Company's current fiscal year, payments to the Company for property or services in excess of one percent (1%) of (i) the Company's consolidated gross revenues for its last full fiscal year or (ii) the customer's consolidated gross revenues for its last full fiscal year.

"Significant Supplier" means a supplier to which the Company has made during the Company's last full fiscal year, or proposes to make during the Company's current fiscal year, payments for property or services in excess of one percent (1%) of (i) the Company's consolidated gross revenues for its last full fiscal year or (ii) the supplier's consolidated gross revenues for its last full fiscal year.

Participation in an open source project, whether maintained by the Company or by another commercial or non-commercial entity or organization does not constitute a conflict of interest even where such participant makes a determination in the interest of the project that is adverse to the Company's interests.

The rules set forth above are threshold rules. It is your responsibility to disclose to the General Counsel any transaction or relationship that reasonably could be expected to give rise to a conflict of interest, or, if you are an officer or director, to the Chairman of the Audit Committee of the Board of Directors (or in the case of such Chairman, to the Board of Directors), who shall be responsible for determining, based on all of the facts and circumstances, whether such transaction or relationship constitutes a conflict of interest. Determinations by the General Counsel of a conflict of interest may be appealed to the Audit Committee, and determinations by the Audit Committee of a conflict of interest, whether sustaining the General Counsel or made independently, may be appealed to the Board of Directors, which determination shall be final.

Upon a determination that a conflict exists, the finding party (General Counsel, Audit Committee or Board of Directors) must make an independent finding as to how the conflict of interest is to be mitigated. Mitigating actions include such measures as are reasonably certain to eliminate the conflict of interest, including, but not limited to reassignment of job duties, transfer of job assignment, termination of employment, or removal from office. All such mitigating actions are to be taken in accordance with the laws pertaining to the place of employment of the subject party, including laws governing due process and employment, and such other agreements of employment as may exist between the Company and the subject employee.

Insider Trading

Employees, officers and directors who have material non-public information about the Company or other companies, including our suppliers and customers, as a result of their relationship with the Company are prohibited by law and Company policy from trading in securities of the Company or such other companies, as well as from communicating such information to others who might trade on the basis of that information. To help ensure that you do not engage in prohibited insider trading and avoid even the appearance of an improper transaction, the Company has adopted an Insider Trading Policy, which is available in the Legal section of the Company's Intranet.

If you are uncertain about the constraints on your purchase or sale of any Company securities or the securities of any other company that you are familiar with by virtue of your relationship with the Company, you should consult with Red Hat's General Counsel before making any such purchase or sale.

Confidentiality

Employees, officers and directors must maintain the confidentiality of confidential information entrusted to them by the Company or other companies, including our suppliers and customers, except when disclosure is authorized by a supervisor or legally mandated. Unauthorized disclosure of any confidential information is prohibited. Additionally, employees should take appropriate precautions to ensure that confidential or sensitive business information, whether it is proprietary to the Company or another company, is not communicated within the Company except to employees who have a need to know such information to perform their responsibilities for the Company.

Third parties may ask you for information concerning the Company. Employees, officers and directors (other than the Company's authorized spokespersons) must not discuss internal Company matters with, or disseminate internal Company information to, anyone outside the Company, except as required in the performance of their Company duties and after an appropriate confidentiality agreement is in place. This prohibition applies particularly to inquiries concerning the Company from the media, market professionals (such as securities analysts, institutional investors, investment advisers, brokers and dealers) and security holders. All responses to inquiries on behalf of the Company must be made only by the Company's authorized spokespersons. If you receive any inquiries of this nature, you must decline to comment and refer the inquirer to your supervisor or one of the Company's authorized spokespersons. The Company's policies with respect to public disclosure of internal matters are described more fully in the Noncompetition, Confidentiality and Assignment of Inventions Agreement which you signed at the time you joined the Company.

You also must abide by any lawful obligations that you have to your former employer. These obligations may include restrictions on the use and disclosure of confidential information, restrictions on the solicitation of former colleagues to work at the Company and non-competition obligations.

Finally, if you are involved in conducting business in the federal, state or local government marketplace(s), you may be subject to other obligations regarding the use, disclosure, safeguarding or receipt of particular types of information, including restrictions regarding competition-sensitive information such as government "source selection" or contractor bid and proposal information.

Honest and Ethical Conduct and Fair Dealing

Employees, officers and directors should endeavor to deal honestly, ethically and fairly with the Company's suppliers, customers, competitors and employees. Statements regarding the Company's products and services must not be untrue, misleading, deceptive or fraudulent. You must not take unfair advantage of anyone through manipulation, concealment, abuse of privileged information, misrepresentation of material facts or any other unfair-dealing practice.

Protection and Proper Use of Corporate Assets

Employees, officers and directors should seek to protect the Company's assets. Theft, carelessness and waste have a direct impact on the Company's financial performance. Employees, officers and directors must use the Company's assets and services solely for legitimate business purposes of the Company and not for any personal benefit or the personal benefit of anyone else.

Employees, officers and directors must advance the Company's legitimate interests when the opportunity to do so arises. You must not take advantage of opportunities for yourself or another person that are discovered through your position with the Company or the use of property or information of, or entrusted to, the Company.

Gifts and Gratuities

Employees, officers and directors must not accept, or permit any member of his or her Immediate Family to accept, any gifts, gratuities or other favors from any customer, supplier or other person doing or seeking to do business with the Company, other than items of nominal value. Any gifts that are not of nominal value should be returned immediately and reported to your supervisor. If immediate return is not practical, they should be given to the Company for charitable disposition or such other disposition as the Company believes appropriate in its sole discretion. For purposes of this policy, nominal value is considered $100 or less.

Common sense and moderation should prevail in the acceptance or provision of business entertainment for the Company. Employees, officers and directors should provide, or accept, business entertainment to or from anyone doing business with the Company only if the entertainment is infrequent, modest in light of the circumstances and intended to serve legitimate business goals.

It is not unusual for software and hardware companies in the Company's industry to offer free software and/or hardware to employees for testing purposes. If you are offered such equipment, you may accept it on behalf of the Company provided the equipment is necessary to your performance of your job or an open source project in which you participate and you notify the Company's General Counsel of the hardware or software contributed. All such donated hardware and software shall be the property of the Company.

Bribes and kickbacks are criminal acts, strictly prohibited by law. You must not offer, give, solicit or receive any form of bribe or kickback anywhere in the world.

You must also abide by the often stringent laws regulating gifts and gratuities to government officials and employees.

Accuracy of Books and Records and Public Reports

Employees, officers and directors must honestly and accurately report all business transactions. You are responsible for the material accuracy of your records and reports. Accurate record keeping and reporting are essential to the Company's ability to meet legal and regulatory obligations, including specific obligations relating to the Company's transactions with governments and governmental entities.

All Company books, records and accounts shall be maintained in accordance with all applicable regulations and standards and accurately reflect the true nature of the transactions they record in all material respects. The financial statements of the Company shall conform in all material respects to generally accepted accounting rules and the Company's accounting policies. No undisclosed or unrecorded account or fund shall be established for any purpose. No false or misleading entries shall be made in the Company's books or records for any reason, and no disbursement of corporate funds or other corporate property shall be made without adequate supporting documentation.

It is the policy of the Company to provide full, fair, accurate, timely and understandable disclosure in reports and documents filed with, or submitted to, the Securities and Exchange Commission and in other public communications.

Concerns Regarding Accounting or Auditing Matters

Employees with concerns regarding questionable accounting or auditing matters or complaints regarding accounting, internal accounting controls or auditing matters may confidentially, and anonymously if they wish, submit such concerns or complaints in writing to the Chairman of the Audit Committee of the Board of Directors at the address listed below. See "Reporting and Compliance Procedures." A complete record of all complaints will be prepared by the Audit Committee each fiscal quarter and reported to the Board of Directors.

The Audit Committee will evaluate the merits of any concerns or complaints received by it and authorize such follow-up actions, if any, as it deems necessary or appropriate to address the substance of the concern or complaint.

The Company will not discipline, discriminate against or retaliate against any employee who reports a complaint or concern (unless the employee is found to have knowingly and willfully made a false report).

Waivers of this Code of Business Conduct and Ethics

While some of the policies contained in this Code must be strictly adhered to and no exceptions can be allowed, in other cases exceptions may be possible. Any employee or officer who believes that an exception to any of these policies is appropriate in his or her case should first contact his or her immediate supervisor. If the supervisor agrees that an exception is appropriate, the approval of the General Counsel must be obtained. The General Counsel shall be responsible for maintaining a complete record of all requests for exceptions to any of these policies and the disposition of such requests and report such record to the Audit Committee each fiscal quarter.

Any executive officer or director who seeks an exception to any of these policies should contact the Chairman of the Audit Committee of the Board of Directors. Any waiver of this Code for executive officers or directors or any change to this Code that applies to executive officers or directors may be made only by the Board of Directors of the Company and will be disclosed as required by law or stock market regulation.

Reporting and Compliance Procedures

Every employee, officer and director has the responsibility to ask questions, seek guidance, report suspected violations and express concerns regarding compliance with this Code. Any employee, officer or director who knows or believes that any other employee or representative of the Company has engaged or is engaging in Company-related conduct that violates applicable law or this Code should report such information to his or her supervisor, the Red Hat General Counsel, or to the Chairman of the Audit Committee of the Red Hat Board of Directors, as described below. You may report such conduct openly or anonymously without fear of retaliation. The Company will not discipline, discriminate against or retaliate against any employee who reports such conduct in good faith, whether or not such information is ultimately proven to be correct, or who cooperates in any investigation or inquiry regarding such conduct. Any supervisor who receives a report of a violation of this Code must immediately inform the General Counsel.

You may report violations of this Code on a confidential or anonymous basis by calling Red Hat's Corporate Governance Hotline. Depending on the nature of the information you are providing, your message will be directed to either the Chairman of the Audit Committee or the General Counsel. Instructions are provided on the Hotline. While we prefer that you identify yourself when reporting violations so we may follow up with you as necessary for additional information, you may leave messages anonymously if you wish.

If either the General Counsel or the Chairman of the Audit Committee receives information regarding an alleged violation of this Code, he or she shall, as appropriate, (a) evaluate such information, (b) if the alleged violation involves an executive officer or a director, inform the Chief Executive Officer and Board of Directors of the alleged violation, (c) determine whether it is necessary to conduct an informal inquiry or a formal investigation and, if so, initiate such inquiry or investigation and (d) report the results of any such inquiry or investigation, together with a recommendation as to disposition of the matter, to the Board of Directors or a committee thereof. Employees, officers and directors are expected to cooperate fully with any inquiry or investigation by the Company regarding an alleged violation of this Code. Failure to cooperate with any such inquiry or investigation may result in disciplinary action, up to and including discharge.

The Company shall determine whether violations of this Code have occurred and, if so, shall determine the disciplinary measures to be taken against any employee who has violated this Code. In the event that the alleged violation involves an executive officer or a director, the Chief Executive Officer and the Board of Directors, respectively, shall determine whether a violation of this Code has occurred and, if so, shall determine the disciplinary measures to be taken against such executive officer or director.

Failure to comply with the standards outlined in this Code will result in disciplinary action including, but not limited to, reprimands, warnings, probation or suspension without pay, demotions, reductions in salary, discharge and restitution. Certain violations of this Code may require the Company to refer the matter to the appropriate governmental or regulating authorities for investigation or prosecution. Moreover, any supervisor who directs or approves of any conduct in violation of this Code, or who has knowledge of such conduct and does not immediately report it, also will be subject to disciplinary action, up to and including discharge. All such disciplinary actions are to be taken in accordance with the laws pertaining to the place of employment of the subject party, including laws governing due process and employment, and such other agreements of employment as may exist between the Company and the subject employee.

Dissemination and Amendment

This Code shall be distributed annually to each employee, officer and director of the Company, and each employee, officer and director shall certify that he or she has received, read and understood the Code and has complied with its terms.

The Company reserves the right to amend, alter or terminate this Code at any time for any reason. The most current version of this Code can be found in the Legal section of the Company's Intranet.

This document is not an employment contract between the Company and any of its employees, officers or directors and does not alter any existing employment contract, if any, or, where no such employment contracts exists, the Company's at-will employment policy.

Certification

I, _____ do hereby certify that:
(Print Name Above)

1. I have received and carefully read the Code of Business Conduct and Ethics of Red Hat, Inc., as amended and restated on February 28, 2009, and the Red Hat Insider Trading Policy.
2. I understand the Code of Business Conduct and Ethics and the Red Hat Insider Trading Policy.
3. I will comply with the terms of the Code of Business Conduct and Ethics and the Red Hat Insider Trading Policy.

Date: _____

(Signature)

EACH EMPLOYEE, OFFICER AND DIRECTOR IS REQUIRED TO RETURN THIS CERTIFICATION TO THE HUMAN CAPITAL DEPARTMENT WITHIN 14 DAYS OF REQUEST. FAILURE TO DO SO MAY RESULT IN DISCIPLINARY ACTION UP TO AND INCLUDING TERMINATION.

PART 2

Fraud Prevention

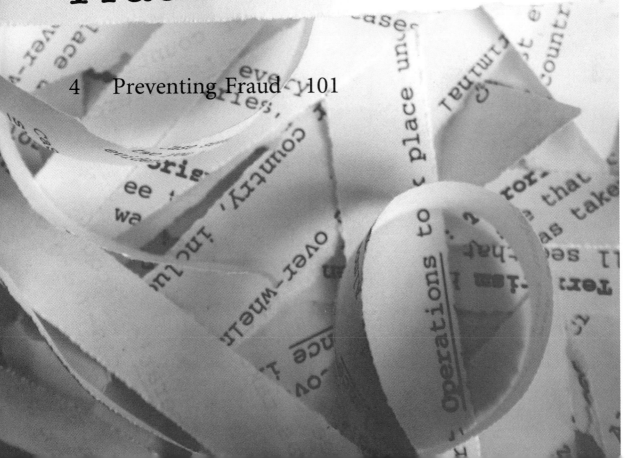

4   Preventing Fraud 101

CHAPTER **4**

Preventing Fraud

LEARNING OBJECTIVES

After studying this chapter, you should be able to:

- Understand how to create a culture of honesty, openness, and assistance.
- Know how to eliminate opportunities for fraud.
- Understand how to create an effective organization to minimize fraud.
- Understand the importance of proactive fraud auditing.
- Understand the importance of creating a comprehensive approach to fighting fraud.

TO THE STUDENT

The past three chapters were introductory. Chapter 4 is the first chapter that deals with fighting fraud, in this case, preventing fraud. The chapter identifies two major ways that organizations can work to prevent fraud: (1) create a culture of honesty, openness, and assistance; and (2) eliminate opportunities for fraud. There are several ways to do each of these which are covered in the chapter. You should realize, however, that no matter how good an organization's fraud prevention efforts are, an organization will never prevent all fraud using cost-effective techniques.

Margaret worked for First National Bank. For 34 years, she was an honest and trusted employee. In the three years prior to her retirement, she embezzled over $600,000. The fraud was discovered after she retired. Once the fraud was known, Margaret and the bank suffered tremendous adverse consequences. The bank lost several customers and was the subject of numerous negative articles about the fraud. The bank also spent significant amounts of time investigating the fraud and dealing with the negative effect on other employees. As for Margaret, the bank took possession of her home and her retirement account. Her husband, who supposedly had no knowledge of the fraud, voluntarily contributed the proceeds of his retirement account from another company to the bank. The bank took possession of virtually every asset the couple owned. In addition, Margaret still owes the bank over $200,000 and has entered into a restitution agreement to make regular payments toward meeting the agreement. Margaret was prosecuted and incarcerated for one year. All of her friends and family members, including her children and grandchildren, know that she is a convicted felon. When Margaret was released from prison, she was ordered by the judge to seek active employment so she could start making restitution payments. If she fails to make regular payments, she violates her parole agreement and must return to jail. Margaret and her husband suffered tremendous embarrassment from the fraud. When Margaret's fraud was written up in local newspapers, many of her long-time friends called her and the bank to learn more about the fraud. The bank was required to submit a criminal referral form to the Office of the Controller of the Currency (OCC). By law, the OCC was required to submit a copy of the referral form to the FBI and the IRS. The FBI investigated Margaret, and the IRS came after her. The IRS levied fines, penalties, interest, and back taxes on Margaret because she had over $600,000 in income that she had failed to report on her tax returns. (Although in subsequent negotiations, the portion she paid back by giving the bank her assets was determined to be a nontaxable loan.) Margaret will probably always have difficulty getting a job, buying life or car insurance, or doing many other things without informing people that she is a convicted felon. In many ways, Margaret's life and reputation have been ruined.

As you can see from this example, there are no winners when fraud occurs. The results are the same in management fraud cases as well. Take the case of Adelphia, for example, where John Rigas and his son, Timothy, were convicted of orchestrating a massive management fraud on investors in Adelphia Communications Corp. As for the perpetrators, John Rigas, the 80-year-old founder of the cable company, was given a 15-year prison sentence. The judge who passed sentence said that he would have jailed Rigas for much longer if not for his age and poor health. John's son, Timothy, who was the company's former chief financial officer, was sentenced to 20 years. The perpetrators weren't the only losers. Adelphia declared bankruptcy following the frauds costing shareholders of the company approximately $25 billion, making it one of the largest bankruptcies in U.S. history. Hundreds of fraud investigators, lawyers, accountants, and others spent years trying to determine exactly what happened. Civil cases surrounding the fraud—against banks, accountants, and others related to their work with Adelphia—will continue for years.

At best, a person who commits fraud may enjoy a higher lifestyle or keep a company from failing for a while.[1] Organizations or individuals from whom funds are stolen are also losers. In Margaret's case, the bank's name was splashed across the front pages of the local newspapers. Some customers terminated business relationships with the bank for fear that "if the bank can't safeguard funds, then my money is not safe there." The bank also lost the money that Margaret hasn't yet paid (over $200,000), plus interest on the $600,000 that she embezzled. Margaret will probably never be able to pay back the entire sum she stole, because the kinds of jobs that were available to her upon release from prison don't pay much. In addition, bank employees spent hundreds of hours investigating, preparing legal defenses, and testifying in the case. In the end, dishonesty cost both the victims and the perpetrators much more than they embezzled.

Clearly, fraud prevention is where the big savings occur. When fraud is prevented, there are no detection or investigation costs. There are no bad apples—no examples of fraud in the organization. The organization doesn't have to make tough termination and prosecution decisions. Valuable work time is not lost to unproductive activities and dealing with crises.

Just About Everyone Can Be Dishonest

It would be nice to believe that most individuals and most employees are so honest that they would never commit fraud and, therefore, the kind of culture an organization creates and the fraud opportunities that exist aren't important. Unfortunately, that is not the case. Most people are capable of committing fraud, and most people adapt to their environments. When placed in an environment of low integrity, poor controls, loose accountability, or high pressure, people tend to become increasingly dishonest. There are numerous examples of companies where top management's dishonest practices were adopted by workers after seeing the bad modeling by top executives. In the famous Equity Funding case, for example, management created fictitious policyholders and wrote insurance policies on them. The fraudulent policies were then sold to other insurance companies or reinsurers. An employee of the company, who observed the dishonest behavior, thought to himself, "I might as well get in on the action. It doesn't make sense that all these fake insurance policies are written and no one ever dies." Therefore, he started causing a few

of the fictitious people to "die" and personally collected the death proceeds.

STOP & THINK *Do you agree with the statement that most people are capable of committing fraud? Do you believe that you could ever commit fraud?*

Organizations can create either a low-fraud or a high-fraud environment. In this chapter, we identify two essential factors involved in a low-fraud environment that are important in preventing fraud. The first involves creating a culture of honesty, openness, and assistance—attributes of a low-fraud environment. The second involves eliminating opportunities to commit fraud and creating expectations that fraud will be punished. At the end of the chapter, we show how fraud prevention, detection, and investigation efforts should be combined to provide a comprehensive fraud-fighting program for a company.

Creating a Culture of Honesty, Openness, and Assistance

Three major factors in fraud prevention relate to creating a culture of honesty, openness, and assistance. These three factors are (1) hiring honest people and providing fraud awareness training; (2) creating a positive work environment, which means having a well-defined code of conduct, having an open-door policy, not operating on a crisis basis, and having a low-fraud atmosphere; and (3) providing an employee assistance program (EAP) that helps employees deal with personal pressures.

Hiring Honest People and Providing Fraud Awareness Training

Effectively screening applicants so that only "honest" employees are hired is very important. As stated earlier in this book, studies have indicated that nearly 30 percent of Americans are dishonest, 40 percent are situationally honest, and only about 30 percent are honest all the time. Nonpublic studies conducted at firms with which we have consulted have also shown that 25 percent of all frauds are committed by employees who have worked three years or less. Individuals with gambling, financial, drug, or past criminal problems should not be hired, or, at least, if they are hired, the adverse information about their backgrounds or characters should be known.

As an example of how prevalent lying is by potential recruits, consider the following excerpts from an online article about lying on résumés by Andrea Kay.[2]

Lying on résumés is apparently on the rise, according to several surveys. A Knight-Ridder-Tribune Business News article reported that an online survey conducted by the Society for Human Resource Management determined that more than 60 percent of the 373 human resource professionals who responded found inaccuracies on résumés. Nearly half the respondents to a Korn/Ferry online survey said 44.7 percent of their 300 respondents said they believed résumé fraud among executives is increasing.

What do they lie about? "About 71 percent of the résumés misrepresent the number of years they've worked on a job," said Jeff Christian, chairman of the search firm Christian & Timbers in an interview on NPR's program, Talk of the Nation.

"Next, they exaggerate accomplishments such as taking credit for something they didn't do or misrepresent the size of an organization they managed," he said. Most often people fabricate reasons for leaving a previous job, according to the Korn/Ferry survey.

In 2003, an employee screening firm in London reported that its research suggests lying on résumés is growing around the world, with the number of people who falsify information jumping 15 percent between 2001 and 2002, according to the Institute of Management & Administration.

With today's stringent privacy laws, it is essential that companies have good employee screening policies. Even in a highly controlled environment, dishonest employees with severe pressures often commit fraud. Résumé verification and certification are two tactics that organizations should use to prevent fraud. One of the most important responsibilities of an employer is the hiring and retention of its employees. In today's market, turnover tends to be high and employee loyalty may be low.

Poor hiring decisions may not only lead to hiring employees who are dishonest but also under a negligent hiring and/or retention claim, an employer may be liable for acts or omissions of the employee, either within or outside the scope of the employee's employment, as long as the injured party can show specific negligent acts of the employer itself. An example of

negligent hiring and/or retention claims includes a trucking company liable for a wrongful death resulting from one of its truckers driving drunk on the wrong side of the road and colliding with an oncoming car, killing the driver. The trucking company failed to verify the trucker's claimed perfect driving record, which would have shown numerous prior DUI violations.

Another example is a church member who was raped during counseling sessions with a church employee. In his lawsuit, the church member claims that the church should not have had the church employee in a counseling position, especially in light of his prior record of sexual offenses during such sessions.

No employer can totally immunize itself from hiring fraudulent employees or from liability for claims asserting negligent hiring and/or negligent retention. However, the employer that follows the following recommendations as part of its hiring and retention policies and practices will be as successful as possible in avoiding frauds and negligent hiring claims.

First, before hiring an applicant for any position, especially key management positions, the employer should verify all information on the applicant's résumé and/or application. The verification should be complete and conducted by an employee who is thorough and persistent in this important procedure. There is no question that verifying an applicant's résumé and/or application is a resource-consuming process. (In the case of a top executive, you should make sure that a search firm that is hired verifies all information on candidates' résumés.) The benefits of such precautions include increased knowledge of the applicant and his or her propensity to be truthful as well as significant reduction in hiring and retaining dangerous, unfit, or dishonest employees. As an example of a CEO who lied on his résumé, consider the case of RadioShack's CEO David Edmondson.[3] Edmondson resigned after the *Star-Telegram* of Fort Worth, Texas, reported he had lied on his résumé.

Edmondson claimed degrees in both theology and psychology from Pacific Coast Baptist College in California. The school's registrar told the *Star-Telegram* that records showed Edmondson had completed two semesters and that the school had never offered degrees in psychology.

Other prominent people who have recently lied on their résumés include the mayor of Rancho Mirage, California, who admitted he didn't hold degrees that he'd claimed, a former football coach at Notre Dame, and a former spokesman for NASA. A recent congressional investigation uncovered 463 federal employees who had credentials from unaccredited schools giving bogus degrees. A recent example of resume embellishment is Gregory Probert, COO of Herbalife who stated that he obtained an M.B.A. from UCLA. After a report by the Fraud Discovery Institute, Probert admitted that he faked his degree and resigned in May, 2008.

An important part of the employer's verification of all information on the applicant's résumé and/or application is verification of the applicant's references. Due to statutory restrictions on the dissemination of such information and the applicant's reasonable expectation of privacy, employers should always obtain a written authorization and/or a "hold harmless agreement" from the applicant to obtain information from references.

CAUTION   *When conducting job-seeking interviews, the interviewer must be very careful not to ask discriminatory questions, or base an evaluation of the applicant on criteria that are of a discriminatory nature. Many discrimination complaints and lawsuits are filed against employers from job-seeking interviews. Many government and state laws must be followed when conducting interviews, including the Federal Equal Employment Opportunity Commission (EEOC) which enforces EEO laws such as Title VII of the Civil Rights Act of 1964, the Age Discrimination in Employment Act (ADEA), and the Americans with Disabilities Act (ADA). Most states have their own Human Rights Acts as well that must be complied with. Questions that deal with an applicant's race, sex, age, religion, color, national origin, or disability are usually prohibited unless the criterion is a bona fide occupational qualification. Whether asked on an application form or in an interview, the federal and state agencies mentioned above will consider questions on the subjects listed below as evidence of discrimination, unless the employer is able to show that the inquiries are job-related or that there is a business necessity for asking the question.*

1. *Arrest records*
2. *Garnishment records*
3. *Marital status*
4. *Child-care provisions*
5. *Contraceptive practices—questions such as "What kind of birth control method do you use?"*
6. *Pregnancy and future childbearing plans*
7. *Physical or mental disabilities*
8. *Height and weight*
9. *Nationality, race, or ancestry*

Second, the employer should require all applicants to certify that all information on their application and/or résumé is accurate. A requirement that all applicants must affirm the truth of the matters set forth in their application and/or résumé will act as a deterrent against false or misleading statements or omissions. The application should provide, in writing acknowledged and agreed to by the applicant, that, in the event false information in the form of statement or omission is discovered on the application and/or résumé, then such discovery is grounds for immediate termination.

Third, the employer should train those involved in the hiring process to conduct thorough and skillful interviews. Interviewing prospective employees is one of the most important activities employers do. The employer's objective of an interview is to determine whether an applicant is suitable for an available position. The interview provides the employer an opportunity to obtain in-depth information about a job applicant's skills, work history, and employment background.

Many prudent employers require interviewers to ask a standard set of questions designed to obtain certain information from the application. The interviewer is then left to her own discretion to follow up and/or ask additional questions during the course of the interview. Numerous companies specialize in helping companies hire the right employees, ask the right hiring questions, and avoid legal traps by asking illegal questions.

There are also other ways to be creative in hiring processes. Many financial institutions, for example, now use systems to determine whether prospective employees and customers have had past credit problems. Banks are also fingerprinting new employees and customers and comparing the fingerprints with law enforcement records. Other organizations are hiring private investigators or using publicly available databases to search information about people's backgrounds. Some organizations are administering drug tests. Pen-and-pencil honesty tests are also being used as a screening tool.

One company, for example, extensively trained several interviewers to know which questions were legal to ask and which were illegal, to recognize deception and lying, and to probe legally into applicants' backgrounds. It also adopted a policy of calling three previous references instead of one. It developed a rule that if no gratuitously positive information was received in any of the three background checks, these checks would be viewed as negative. (The interviewers tried to call references who personally knew the applicants, rather than personnel officers who didn't know them.) Over a three-year period, this company found that 851 prospective employees, or

14 percent of all applicants, had undisclosed problems, such as previous unsatisfactory employment, false education or military information, criminal records, poor credit ratings, alcoholism, or uncontrolled tempers. People with these types of problems generally find it easier to rationalize dishonest acts, and preventing such people from being hired can reduce fraud.

> ### Remember this ...
>
> *Verify all information on the applicant's résumé and/or application using the following suggestions:*
>
> 1. *Require all applicants to certify that all information on their application and/or résumé is accurate.*
> 2. *Train those involved in the hiring process to conduct thorough and skillful interviews.*
> 3. *Use industry-specific or other approaches as deemed necessary (credit checks, fingerprinting, drug tests, public record searches, honesty tests, etc.).*

As an example of poor screening, consider the following actual fraud:

> *A controller defrauded his company of several million dollars. When the fraud was investigated, it was discovered that he had been fired from three of his previous five jobs, all in the last eight years. He was discovered when the CEO came to the office one night and found a stranger working in the accounting area. The nocturnal stranger was a phantom controller who was actually doing the work of the hired "corporate controller," who wasn't even trained in accounting.*

Once people have been hired, it is important to have them participate in an employee awareness program that educates them about what is acceptable and unacceptable, how all parties, including them, are hurt when someone is dishonest, and what actions they should take if they see someone doing something improper. A comprehensive awareness program should educate employees about how costly fraud and other types of business abuses are. Employees must know that fraud takes a bite out of their pay and benefits, as well as corporate profits and returns to shareholders, and that no dishonest acts of any kind will be tolerated. Most companies with successful fraud awareness programs have packaged fraud training with other sensitive issues important to employees, such as employee safety, discrimination, substance abuse, and the availability of EAPs.

One company, for example, educates all employees about abuses and gives them small cards to carry in their purses or wallets. The cards list four possible actions employees can take if they suspect abuses are taking place. They can (1) talk to their immediate supervisor or management, (2) call corporate security, (3) call internal audit, or (4) call an 800 hotline number. Employees are told that they can either provide hotline information anonymously or disclose their identities. This company has also made several videos about company abuses, including frauds, which are shown to all new employees. New posters relating to the awareness program are posted conspicuously throughout the organization on a regular basis. Because of these awareness programs, fraud and other abuses have decreased substantially.

Creating a Positive Work Environment

The second factor important in a culture of honesty, openness, and assistance is creating a positive work environment. Positive work environments do not happen automatically; rather, they must be cultivated. It is a fact that employee fraud and other dishonest acts are more prevalent in some organizations than in others.

Organizations that are highly vulnerable to fraud can be distinguished from those that are less vulnerable by comparing their corporate climates. Three elements that contribute to the creation of a positive work environment, thus making the organization less vulnerable to fraud, are (1) creating expectations about honesty through having a good corporate code of conduct and conveying those expectations throughout the organization, (2) having open-door or easy access policies, and (3) having positive personnel and operating procedures.

Setting proper expectations is a powerful tool in motivating employees to behave honestly. Consider the following story about expectations:

> *Imagine Miss Periwinkle, a fourth-grade teacher, arriving for class on the first day of school. Before she enters her classroom, the principal stops her in the hall.*
>
> *"Miss Periwinkle, there's something you should know about this class. We've placed all the bright and talented children on the right side of the room. On the left, we've seated the ones we know are slower and lack motivation. We thought the seating arrangement would help you in your teaching."*
>
> *Armed with this information, she begins a semester of instruction. But there's a catch. There are no divisions of intelligence or motivation in this classroom; those on both sides of the room were randomly*

selected from a group of equally able and motivated students. They are part of an experiment to determine if the teacher's expectations will affect the children's learning and testing.

This is a hypothetical recasting of various psychological experiments done many times over the last 30 years. The results are invariably the same. Students the teacher thinks are "smart" score well on tests; the "dull" ones don't do as well. The difference is not a result of biased grading; the "dull" ones really have learned less. Why?

The explanation is often described as the Pygmalion effect. Sterling Livingston, writing in the *Harvard Business Review* (September 1988), extended this phenomenon into management with a simple thesis: People generally perform according to a leader's expectations. If expectations are low, actual performance is likely to be "substandard." If, however, expectations are high, performance is usually high as well. "It is as though there were a law that caused subordinates' performance to rise or fall to meet management's expectations," Livingston wrote.

Livingston and others have also found that expectations must be genuine and accepted by leaders. The studies have concluded that people know when they are being conned. If expectations are unrealistically high or if they are not being taken seriously by leaders, people know it. Conversely, if a manager pretends that he has confidence and high expectations when he really has doubts, people will know that, too.

The lesson about expectations is clear: People have keen senses about expectations. You can't fool them; expectations must be genuine. Trying to create expectations, especially about integrity and ethics, when top management isn't serious about the expectations, only erodes their credibility.

According to the researchers, a good axiom to remember is, "What you expect is what you'll get."[4] As an example of the power of expectations, consider the following true story.

A wife told her husband that she had accepted an invitation for the two of them to be chaperons at a high school dance where their daughter attended. The husband wasn't excited about the assignment but agreed to go. At the dance, his wife seemed very unhappy and at one point ran out of the building crying. Following her out, the husband asked, "Why are you so unhappy? I came to this dance with you even though I really didn't want to. I thought I was being a good husband." Still crying, she said "Can't you see

it? Every other husband who is here as a chaperon bought his wife a corsage but you didn't." The wife's expectation was not only that the husband would attend the dance but that he would also get her a corsage like other chaperoning husbands.

One way to create and communicate clear expectations about what is and is not acceptable in an organization is to have an articulated code of conduct. Section 406 of the Sarbanes-Oxley Act of 2002, "Code of Ethics for Senior Financial Officers," requires that every public company have a code of ethics for management and its board of directors. Shortly after Congress passed the Sarbanes-Oxley Act, the Securities and Exchange Commission (SEC) revised its listing standards to require public companies to create and distribute a code of conduct to all employees. Merely having a code of conduct, however, is not sufficient. It must be visible and communicated frequently. Some companies have found it helpful to even have employees read and sign their code annually and certify that they have not violated the code or seen others who have. In Chapter 3, we included the code of conduct for Red Hat, Inc. As another example of a good code of ethics for all employees, consider the code of Hormel Foods shown in Figure 4.1.

Hormel's code not only clarifies what is and is not acceptable, but it also specifies the disciplinary action that will be applied to violators and provides contact (whistle-blower) information for reporting violations. If Hormel is successful in keeping this code in front of its employees, just the mere fact that everyone knows that others know what is expected, what expected punishments are, and how to escalate information about violations should reduce the number of dishonest incidents in the company.

Literature on moral development suggests that if you want someone to behave honestly, you must both label and model honest behavior. As we have discussed, a clearly defined code of conduct labels for employees what is acceptable and unacceptable. Having employees periodically read and sign a company code of ethics reinforces their understanding of what constitutes appropriate and inappropriate behavior. A clearly specified code inhibits rationalizations, such as "It's really not that serious," "You would understand if you knew how badly I needed it," "I'm really not hurting anyone," "Everyone is a little dishonest," or "I'm only temporarily borrowing it." When a company specifies what is acceptable and what is unacceptable and requires employees to acknowledge that they understand the

FIGURE 4.1   HORMEL FOODS CODE OF CONDUCT

Code of Ethical Business Conduct

Introduction

This Code of Ethical Business Conduct ("Code") covers a wide range of business practices and procedures. It does not cover every issue that may arise, but it sets out basic principles to guide all employees, officers and directors of the Company. Obeying the law, both in letter and in spirit, is the foundation on which this Company's ethical standards are built. All of the Company's employees and directors must conduct themselves accordingly and seek to avoid even the appearance of improper behavior. All employees, officers and directors must respect and obey the laws of the cities, states and countries in which they operate.

Conflict of Interest

A "conflict of interest" exists when a person's private interests interfere in any way with the interests of the Company. All employees, officers and directors should avoid any personal activity or participation in any venture which may create a conflict with their responsibility to protect and promote the best interests of the Company. Employees, officers and directors should assure that their spouses and dependents avoid any activity which would constitute a conflict of interest if engaged in by the employee, officer or director. For example, any activity which would allow you, or a member of your immediate family, to enjoy personal gain or benefit as a result of your employment relationship with the Company would be considered a conflict of interest.

Gifts

No gift, loan or favor should be made to or accepted by employees, officers, directors or their immediate families involving any supplier, customer, or others with whom the Company does business if it is intended to influence a business decision. This does not prohibit casual entertainment, business entertainment consistent with the Company's usual practices, or gifts which are reasonably viewed under the circumstances in which they are given or received to be of nominal value. For this purpose, any gift in kind of less than $100 would be considered of nominal value. Acceptance of cash or cash equivalents is not acceptable under any circumstances. By way of example, attendance at a professional sporting event as a guest of a supplier or customer would constitute business entertainment consistent with the Company's usual practices; however, the receipt of tickets to the same event from a supplier or customer without the attendance of the supplier or customer would be viewed as a gift which must be of nominal value.

Corporate Opportunities

Employees, officers and directors are prohibited from taking for themselves personally opportunities that are discovered through the use of corporate property, information or position without the consent of the Board of Directors. No employee, officer or director may use corporate property, information, or position for improper personal gain, and no employee may compete with the Company directly or indirectly. Employees, officers and directors owe a duty to the Company to advance the Company's legitimate interests when the opportunity to do so arises.

Illegal Payments

Any payments by the Company to the United States or foreign persons or companies are prohibited if the payments would be illegal under the Foreign Corrupt Practices Act of 1977 or other United States or foreign laws. This prohibition includes any payments to government officials or their agents, domestic or foreign, unless Company counsel has advised the payment is legal and acceptable. It is never acceptable to pay any third party anywhere an undisclosed commission, kickback or bribe to obtain business.

Illegal Political Contributions

Corporate funds and other assets shall not be used for any illegal political contribution. This prohibition includes any political contribution unless otherwise advised by Company counsel. Employees are encouraged to make personal contributions to candidates and political parties of their choice.

Protection and Proper Use of Company Assets

All employees, officers and directors should endeavor to protect the Company's assets and ensure their efficient use. The use of any funds or other assets of, or the providing of any services by, the Company for any purpose which is unlawful under applicable laws of the United States, any state thereof, or any foreign jurisdiction, is prohibited. Employees, officers and directors may not use employees, materials, equipment or other assets of the Company for any unauthorized purpose.

(continued)

FIGURE 4.1   CONTINUED

Proper Accounting

Employees, officers and directors must comply with prescribed accounting, internal accounting, and auditing procedures and controls at all times. All records must accurately reflect and properly describe the transactions they record. All assets, liabilities, revenues and expenses shall be properly recorded on a timely basis in the books of the Company.

Insider Trading

Employees, officers and directors shall not buy or sell Company stock or make recommendations regarding it based upon insider information. Insider information is material information that is not generally known by those outside the Company that could affect the value of the Company's stock.

Confidential Information

Employees, officers and directors may not directly or indirectly use or disclose any secret or confidential knowledge or data of the Company, except as authorized in their ordinary course of employment or as required by law. Any notes, memoranda, notebooks, drawings or other documents made, compiled or delivered to employees during the period of their employment are the exclusive property of the Company and must be turned over to it at the time of termination of their employment or at any other time upon the Company's request. Additionally, while it is appropriate to gather information about the Company's markets, including publicly available information regarding competitors, employees and officers should not seek to acquire proprietary and confidential information of competitors by unlawful or unethical means, including information resulting in the breach of nondisclosure obligations by competitors' employees or other third parties.

Inventions, Developments, Improvements

Any inventions, developments or improvements which are conceived by employees during their period of employment by the Company must be promptly disclosed to the Company in writing, and will in most cases be the Company's exclusive property. Inventions which were developed on an employee's own time and are not related to the Company's business or research would not be the Company's property.

Antitrust Compliance

Activity which violates the antitrust laws of the United States, any state thereof, or comparable laws of foreign jurisdictions, is prohibited. Employees, officers and directors must comply with all antitrust compliance policies adopted by the Company. Areas in which employees, officers and directors must be sensitive to antitrust problems include pricing, termination of existing relationships with customers or suppliers, the establishment of either exclusive customers or suppliers, tie-in sales, boycotts and reciprocity.

Fair Dealing

Employees, officers and directors must observe the highest ethical standards in relationships with competitors, suppliers and customers. Each employee, officer and director should endeavor to respect the rights of, and deal fairly with, the Company's customers, suppliers, competitors and employees. No employee, officer or director should take unfair advantage of anyone through manipulation, concealment, abuse of privileged information, misrepresentation of material facts, or any other intentional unfair-dealing practice.

Harassment

All employees have a right to work in an environment free of harassment, and the Company prohibits harassment of its employees in any form—by supervisors, co-workers, customers, or suppliers.

Safety

All employees have a right to work in a safe environment, and all safety rules as well as common safety practices must be followed. Conduct which is unsafe, including possession or being under the influence of a controlled substance on Company premises or Company time, is prohibited.

Government Reporting

Employees, officers and directors must assure that any reports to any listing agency, or any governmental unit or agency in the United States or abroad, including the Securities and Exchange Commission, and the Internal Revenue Service, made by them or under their supervision, are honest, accurate and complete.

The Chief Executive Officer and the Chief Financial Officer of the Company are responsible for full, fair, accurate, timely and understandable disclosure in the periodic reports required to be filed by the Company

(continued)

FIGURE 4.1 CONTINUED

with the Securities and Exchange Commission. As a result, the Chief Executive Officer and Chief Financial Officer of the Company shall promptly bring to the attention of the Director of Internal Audit any material information of which they become aware that could affect the disclosures made by the Company in its public filings.

Environmental Responsibility

All employees, officers and directors are required to comply with all applicable federal, state and local laws and regulations relating to the protection of the environment, as well as any requirements which pertain to the Company's operations outside the United States. Additionally, employees, officers and directors must comply with all environmental policies adopted by the Company.

Product Integrity

The Company's products and their labeling must reflect the integrity of the Company and its employees. All Company products must be produced, labeled and handled in keeping with the Company's high standards of sanitation, and in compliance with all Company specifications and governmental requirements for content and process, to produce safe and wholesome, high quality and accurately labeled products.

Diversity

The Company welcomes diversity in its employees, suppliers, customers, and others with whom the Company does business. The Company is affirmatively committed to providing the same opportunities for success to all individuals, regardless of race, religion, national origin, age, sex, or disability. All employees are expected to share in and support that commitment.

Fair Employment Practices

In addition to prohibiting harassment and providing a safe workplace, the Company and its employees, officers and directors must comply with all applicable laws governing employment. Discrimination on account of race, religion, national origin, sex, age, disability, or status as a veteran will not be tolerated.

Foreign Trade

Employees involved in foreign trade operations are expected to maintain an awareness of, and comply with,

the requirements of the U.S. Antiboycott Laws, the U.S. Trade Embargo Regulations, and any other U.S. or foreign laws applicable to the Company's foreign trading operations. The U.S. Antiboycott Laws prohibit U.S. companies and their foreign subsidiaries from entering into agreements in support of any foreign boycott which has not been sanctioned by the U.S. government. The U.S. Trade Embargo Regulations prohibit U.S. companies and their foreign subsidiaries from entering into transactions with countries with whom the U.S. government maintains a trade embargo, as well as with entities that are owned or controlled by those countries.

Responsible Delegation

Discretionary authority must not be delegated to anyone, within or on behalf of the Company, where there is reason to believe that individual might engage in illegal activities.

Disciplinary Action

While the Company relies on the voluntary compliance with this Code by each employee, officer and director as a matter of personal integrity, disciplinary action will be taken in appropriate instances. Such instances include: actions which violate this Code; withholding information regarding violations; supervision which is inadequate to the point of evidencing a negligent or willful disregard for this Code in connection with a violation; and any form of retaliation against an employee reporting a violation. Disciplinary action may include suspension, termination, recovery of damages, or criminal prosecution.

Reporting Illegal, Unethical Behavior, or Violations of the Code

With the exception of concerns or complaints regarding questionable accounting or auditing matters, or internal accounting controls which must be promptly forwarded directly to the Audit Committee of the Board of Directors, any employee, officer or director who observes or otherwise becomes aware of any illegal, unethical behavior, or any violation of the Code shall report the violation to a supervisor, the General Counsel, or the Director of Internal Audit, or he or she may report the matter to any member of the Audit Committee of the Board of Directors. Additionally, employees, officers and directors may report any violation, or suspected violation, of the Code, including concerns regarding questionable accounting or auditing matters, by using the anonymous "Hot Line"

(continued)

FIGURE 4.1 CONTINUED

established for this purpose. The telephone number for this Hot Line is: 1-800-750-4972.

Employees and officers are encouraged to talk to supervisors, managers or other appropriate personnel when in doubt about the best course of action to take in a particular situation. It is the policy of the Company not to allow retaliation for reports of misconduct by others made in good faith by employees. Employees are expected to cooperate in internal investigations of misconduct.

Waivers of the Code

Every effort will be made to resolve potential conflicts of interest or other ethics code situations when these are disclosed promptly to management, and the parties involved have acted in good faith. In the unlikely event that potential conflicts cannot be resolved, waivers will only be given for matters where appropriate. Any waivers for executive officers and directors must be approved, in advance, by the Board of Directors, and will be promptly disclosed as required by law or stock exchange regulation.

SOURCE: www.hormel.com/templates/corporate.asp?catitemid=71&id=634, accessed June 14, 2007.

---

organization's expectations, they realize that fraud hurts the organization, that not everyone is a little dishonest, that the organization won't tolerate dishonest acts, that dishonest behavior is serious, and that unauthorized borrowing is not acceptable.

A second way to create a positive work environment, thus making the organization less vulnerable to fraud, is having open-door or easy access policies. Open-door policies prevent fraud in two ways. First, many people commit fraud because they feel they have no one to talk to. Sometimes, when people keep their problems to themselves, they lose their perspectives about the appropriateness of actions and about the consequences of wrongdoing. This loss of perspective can lead to making decisions to be dishonest. Second, open-door policies allow managers and others to become aware of employees' pressures, problems, and rationalizations. This awareness enables managers to take fraud prevention steps. Studies have shown that most frauds (71 percent in one study) are committed by someone acting alone. Having people to talk to can prevent this type of fraud. One person who had embezzled said, in retrospect, "Talk to someone. Tell someone what you are thinking and what your pressures are. It's definitely not worth it…. It's not worth the consequences."

As an example of a person who committed fraud that probably could have been prevented had the organization had an open-door policy, consider Micky:

Micky was the controller for a small fruit-packing company. In that position, he embezzled over $212,000 from the company. When asked why, he said, "Nobody at the company, especially the owners,

ever talked to me. They treated me unfairly. They talked down to me. They were rude to me. They deserve everything they got."

A third way to create a positive work environment, thus making the organization less vulnerable to fraud, is having positive personnel and operating policies. Research has shown that positive personnel and operating policies are important factors in contributing to high- or low-fraud environments. Uncertainty about job security, for example, has been associated with high-fraud environments. Other personnel and operating conditions and procedures that appear to contribute to high-fraud environments include the following:

- *Managers who don't care about or pay attention to honesty (who model apathetic or inappropriate behavior)*
- *Inadequate pay*
- *Lack of recognition for job performance*
- *Imposition of unreasonable budget expectations*
- *Expectations that employees live a certain lifestyle (e.g., belong to a country club)*
- *Perceived inequalities in the organization*
- *Inadequate expense accounts*
- *Autocratic or dictatorial management*
- *Low company loyalty*
- *Short-term business focus*
- *Management by crisis*
- *Rigid rules*
- *Negative feedback and reinforcement*
- *Repression of differences*
- *Poor promotion opportunities*

- *Hostile work environments*
- *High turnover and absenteeism*
- *Cash flow or other financial problems*
- *Reactive rather than proactive management*
- *Managers who model wheeler-dealer, impulsive, insensitive, emotional, or dominant personalities*
- *Rivalrous rather than supportive relationships*
- *Poor training*
- *Lack of clear organizational responsibilities*
- *Poor communication practices*

Each of these conditions or procedures contributes to creating a high-fraud environment. For example, during crisis or rush jobs, there are additional opportunities to commit fraud. When a special project is being hurried toward completion, for example, the normal controls are often set aside or ignored. Signatures are obtained to authorize uncertain purchases. Reimbursements are made rapidly, with little documentation. Record keeping falls behind and cannot be reconstructed. Inventory and supplies come and go rapidly and can easily be manipulated or misplaced. Job lines and responsibilities are not as well defined.

> *In a recent interview, the controller of a Fortune 500 company indicated that his company had experienced three large frauds in the past year. Two of them, both totaling millions of dollars, had occurred while the company was rushing to complete crash projects.*

It would be easy to include many examples of fraud that have been facilitated by each of these high-fraud environmental factors, but we include only two. The first is an example of fraud associated with inadequate pay. The second is an example of fraud associated with the imposition of unreasonable expectations.

> *A long-time employee of a company believed that he had performed well, but was passed over for a raise he felt he had earned. He was earning $30,000 a year and decided that he was entitled to a 10 percent raise. He stole $250 a month, which was exactly 10 percent of his salary. His moral standards permitted him to steal that much because he felt it was "owed to him," but he could not embezzle one cent more, since that would have been "dishonest."*

> *A division manager of a large conglomerate was told by the company's CEO that he "would" increase his division's segment margin by 20 percent during the coming year. When he realized he could not meet the imposed budget, he overstated revenues. He feared losing his job if he didn't meet his assigned budget.*

Implementing Employee Assistance Programs (EAPs)

The third factor in creating a culture of honesty, openness, and assistance is having formal **employee assistance programs (EAPs)**. One of the three elements of the fraud triangle is perceived pressure. Often, fraud-motivating pressures are what perpetrators consider to be unsharable or what they believe have no possible legal solutions. Companies that provide employees with effective ways to deal with personal pressures eliminate many potential frauds. The most common method of assisting employees with pressures is by implementing formal EAPs. EAPs help employees deal with substance abuse (alcohol and drugs); gambling; money management; and health, family, and personal problems.

An EAP that is successfully integrated into an organization's other employee support systems with programs and services that include wellness, team building, coaching, conflict resolution, critical incident response, assessment, counseling, and referral can and does help reduce fraud and other forms of dishonesty. Employees welcome this benefit, they use it, and they report consistently in impact surveys that the EAP made a difference in their lives, and in the quality of their work.

Most successful organizations view EAPs as important contributors to the success of their businesses and as valuable benefits for their employees. Employers are convinced that EAP programs make a difference. Why? Organizations recognize that having the ability to provide a troubled employee with timely and appropriate help results in reducing the financial and human costs associated with an employee who is not fully functioning. Valuable employees have been assisted in dealing successfully with issues that threatened their health, finances, relationships, energy, and ability to contribute strongly in the workplace.[5]

Return on investment (ROI) for EAPs has been studied repeatedly, yet definitive proof of their benefits remains difficult to demonstrate.

As examples of frauds that might have been prevented with EAPs, consider the following two real cases:

> *An unmarried woman became pregnant. She didn't want her parents or anyone else to know. Needing money desperately, she stole $300 from her company. Then, realizing how easy the theft had been, she stole another $16,000 before being detected.*

> *An employee of a large bank embezzled over $35,000. When she was caught and asked why, she stated that her son was "hooked on heroin at a cost of*

nearly $500 per day." Because she could not stand to see him go through withdrawal pains, she had embezzled to support his habit.

Remember this …

In preventing fraud, it is important to create a culture of honesty, openness, and assistance. Table 4.1 summarizes how to create such a culture.

Eliminating Opportunities for Fraud to Occur

Earlier in this text, the fraud motivation triangle—perceived pressure, perceived opportunity, and rationalization—was introduced to explain why fraud occurs. When pressure, opportunity, and rationalization combine, the likelihood of a fraud being perpetrated increases dramatically. If one of the three elements is missing, fraud is less likely. In this section, we discuss the second major element in fraud prevention—eliminating opportunities to commit dishonest acts.

In this section, we will cover five methods of eliminating fraud opportunities: (1) having good internal controls, (2) discouraging collusion between employees and customers or vendors and clearly informing vendors and other outside contacts of the company's policies against fraud, (3) monitoring employees and providing a hotline (whistle-blowing system) for anonymous tips, (4) creating an expectation of punishment,

and (5) conducting proactive auditing. Each of these methods reduces either the actual or the perceived opportunity to commit fraud, and all of them together combine with the culture factors described earlier to provide a comprehensive fraud prevention program.

Having a Good System of Internal Controls

The most widely recognized way to deter or prevent fraud is by having a good system of controls. The Institute of Internal Auditors' Web site contains the following statement, for example:[6]

Internal auditors support management's efforts to establish a culture that embraces ethics, honesty, and integrity. They assist management with the evaluation of internal controls used to detect or mitigate fraud.

Figure 4.2 shows how organizations assess risks and then implement various controls to minimize those risks.

As stated previously in this text, the Committee of Sponsoring Organizations' (COSO) definition of an *internal control framework* for an organization should include (1) a good control environment, (2) a good accounting system, (3) good control activities, (4) monitoring, and (5) good communication and information. The *control environment* is the overall tone of the organization that management establishes through its modeling and labeling, organization, communication, and other activities. As stated in COSO's report, the control environment sets the tone of an organization,

TABLE 4.1 CREATING A CULTURE OF HONESTY, OPENNESS, AND ASSISTANCE

WAY TO CREATE A CULTURE OF HONESTY, OPENNESS, AND ASSISTANCE	HOW THIS STEP IS ACCOMPLISHED
1. Hire honest people and provide fraud awareness training.	1. Verify all information on the applicant's résumé and application. 2. Require all applicants to affirm the truth of the matters set forth in their application and résumé. 3. Train management to conduct thorough and skillful interviews.
2. Create a positive work environment.	1. Create expectations about honesty by having a good corporate code of conduct and conveying those expectations throughout the organization. 2. Have open-door or easy access policies. 3. Have positive personnel and operating procedures.
3. Provide an employee assistance program (EAP).	1. Implement an EAP that helps employees deal with personal and nonsharable pressures in their lives.

influencing the control consciousness of its people.[7] It is the foundation for all other components of internal control, providing discipline and structure. Control environment factors include the integrity, ethical values, and competence of the entity's people, management's philosophy and operating style, the way management assigns authority and responsibility and organizes and develops its people, and the attention and direction provided by the board of directors. The control environment also includes well-defined hiring practices, clear organization, and a good internal audit department.

The second element—having a good accounting system—is important so that the information used for decision making and provided to stakeholders is valid, complete, and timely. The system should also provide information that is properly valued, classified, authorized, and summarized.

Good control activities involve policies and practices that provide physical control of assets, proper authorizations, segregation of duties, independent checks, and proper documentation. (Physical control, proper authorization, and segregation of duties are controls that usually prevent fraud, thus called preventive controls, while independent checks and documents and records are usually detective controls that provide early fraud detection opportunities.) A control system that meets these requirements provides reasonable assurance that the goals and objectives of the organization will be met and that fraud will be reduced.

Obviously, if a person owns a company and is that company's only employee, not many controls are needed. The owner would not likely steal from the company or serve customers poorly. In organizations with hundreds or thousands of employees or even two or three, controls are needed to ensure that employees behave according to the owner's expectations.

STOP & THINK   *It is obvious that controls are important in a business organization to get employees and others to act in a manner consistent with management or the owner's desires. In what other settings would controls be important?*

No internal control structure can ever be completely effective, regardless of the care followed in its design and implementation. Even when an ideal control system is designed, its effectiveness depends on the competency and dependability of the people enforcing it. Consider, for example, an organization that has a policy requiring the dual counting of all incoming

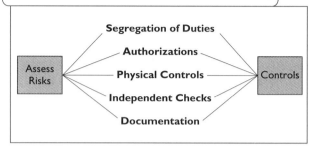

FIGURE 4.2   ASSESSING RISK AND IMPLEMENTING APPROPRIATE CONTROLS

cash receipts. If either of the two employees involved in the task fails to understand the instructions, is careless in opening and counting incoming cash, or fails to pay attention to the task at hand, money can easily be stolen or miscounted. One of the employees might decide to understate the count intentionally to cover up a theft of cash. Dual custody can be maintained only if both employees pay full attention to the task and completely understand how it is to be performed.

Because of the inherent limitations of controls, a control system by itself can never provide absolute assurance that all fraud will be prevented. Trying to prevent fraud by having only a good control system is like fighting a skyscraper fire with a garden hose. In combination with the other methods described in the following, however, having a good control framework is an extremely important part of any fraud prevention program.

In determining what kind of control activities an organization should have, it is important to identify the nature of risks involved and the types of abuses that could result from these risks. There are only five types of control activities: (1) segregation of duties—having two people do a task together or splitting the task into parts so that no one person handles the complete assignment; (2) having a system of proper authorizations so that only authorized or designated individuals have permissions to complete certain tasks; (3) implementing physical safeguards such as locks, keys, safes, fences, and so on, to prohibit access to assets and records; (4) implementing a system of independent checks such as job rotations, mandatory vacations, audits, and so on; and (5) having a system of documents and records that provide an audit trail that can be followed to check on suspicious activity and to document transactions. As shown in Table 4.2, the first three are preventive controls, and the last two are detective controls.

TABLE 4.2 TYPES OF CONTROL ACTIVITIES

TYPE OF CONTROL	CONTROL ACTIVITIES
Preventive controls	1. Segregation of duties
	2. System of authorizations
	3. Physical safeguards
Detective controls	1. Independent checks
	2. Documents and records

Once identified and put into place, controls need to be monitored and tested to ensure that they are effective and are being followed. In fact, Section 404 of the Sarbanes-Oxley Act requires all public companies to have their external auditors test their system of internal controls and attest that there are no material weaknesses in the controls.

In determining what kinds of control activities to implement, it is important to assess their costs and benefits. For example, while the most appropriate control from a risk perspective might involve segregation of duties, this control is usually quite expensive. In small businesses with only a few employees, segregation of duties may be too expensive or even impossible. In such cases, it is important to identify less expensive or "compensating" controls that can provide some fraud prevention assurance. For example, in a small service business with eight employees, the owner might personally sign all checks and reconcile all bank statements to control cash.

Often, the problem when fraud is committed is not a lack of controls, but the overriding of existing controls by management or others. Consider the role of controls in the theft of $3.2 million from a small bank—a case that we have discussed previously.

———

Marjorie, head of accounting and bookkeeping in a small bank, was responsible for all proof reconciliations and activities. Over a seven-year period, she embezzled $3.2 million, or approximately 10 percent of the bank's assets. Auditors and management recognized the lack of segregation of duties in her department, but believed they had compensating controls in place that would prohibit such a theft—that would provide "reasonable assurance" that no fraud was possible in the bank. Some of the compensating controls and the ways they were overridden to allow her fraud were as follows:

1. All deposits and transfers of funds were to be made through tellers. Yet, proof employees were making transfers for bank officers and for themselves. Most people in the bank were aware of this practice, but because it was being done at their boss's request, they didn't think it was wrong.

2. All documents were to be accessible to external auditors. Yet, Marjorie kept a locked cabinet next to her desk, and only she had a key. At one point, a customer whose statement had been altered by Marjorie complained, but was told that he would have to wait until Marjorie returned from vacation because the documentation relating to his account was in Marjorie's locked cabinet.

3. Auditors were supposed to have access to all employees, but Marjorie told her employees not to talk to auditors. Thus, all questions were referred to her during audits.

4. Every employee and every officer of the bank was required to take a two-week consecutive vacation. At Marjorie's request, management allowed this control to be overridden. Based on her memos, that "proof would get behind if she took a two-week vacation," Marjorie was allowed to take her vacation one day at a time. In addition, no one was allowed to perform Marjorie's most sensitive duties while she was away.

5. General ledger tickets were supposed to be approved by an individual other than the person who completed the ticket. To override this control, Marjorie had her employees pre-sign 10 or 12 general ledger tickets, so she wouldn't have to "bother" them when they were busy.

6. There were supposed to be opening and closing procedures of the bank in place to protect the bank, but many employees had all the necessary keys and could enter the bank at will.

7. An effective internal audit function was supposed to be in place. For a period of two years, however, no internal audit reports were issued. Even when the reports were issued, internal audit did not check employee accounts or perform critical control tests, such as surprise openings of the bank's incoming and outgoing cash letters to and from the Federal Reserve.

8. Incoming and outgoing cash letters were supposed to be microfilmed immediately. This compensating control was violated in three ways. First, letters were not usually filmed immediately. Second, for a time, letters were not filmed at all. Third, Marjorie regularly removed items from the cash letters before they were filmed.

9. Employees' accounts were not regularly reviewed by internal audit or by management. On the rare occasions when accounts were reviewed, numerous deposits to and checks drawn on Marjorie's account that exceeded her annual salary were not questioned.

10. Loans were supposed to be made only to employees who met all lending requirements, as if they were

normal customers. At one point, a $170,000 mortgage loan was made by the bank to Marjorie, without any explanation as to how the loan would be repaid or how she could afford such a house.

11. Employees in proof and bookkeeping were not supposed to handle their own bank statements. Yet, employees regularly pulled out their own checks and deposit slips before the statements were mailed.

12. Managers were supposed to be reviewing key daily documents, such as the daily statement of condition, the significant items and major fluctuation report, and the overdraft report. Either managers didn't review these reports, or they didn't pay close attention to them when they did review them. There were daily fluctuations in the statements of condition of over $3 million. The significant items and major fluctuation reports revealed huge deposits to and checks drawn on Marjorie's account. In addition, Marjorie appeared on the overdraft reports 97 times during the first four years she was employed by the bank she defrauded.

If these controls that were supposedly in place had been effective, Marjorie's fraud would have been prevented or at least detected in its early stages. Because management and internal auditors were overriding controls, the bank's "reasonable assurance" provided by internal controls became "no assurance" at all.

Having a good system of internal control is the single most effective tool in preventing and detecting fraud. Unfortunately, sometimes in practice, control procedures are rarely followed the way they are designed or intended. Sometimes, a lack of compliance occurs because employees emulate management's apathetic attitude toward controls. Other times, managers properly model and label good control procedures, but employees do not comply because of disinterest, lack of reward for following or punishment for not following controls, lack of focus, or other reasons. Because control procedures can provide only "reasonable assurance" at best, controls are only one element of a comprehensive fraud prevention plan.

Discouraging Collusion between Employees and Others and Alerting Vendors and Contractors to Company Policies

As stated previously, empirical research has shown that approximately 71 percent of all frauds are committed by individuals acting alone. The remaining 29 percent of frauds—those involving collusion—are usually the most difficult to detect and often involve the largest amounts. Collusive fraud is usually slower to develop (it takes time to get to know others well enough to collude and to "trust" that they will cooperate rather than blow the whistle) than frauds committed by one individual.

Unfortunately, two recent trends in business have probably increased the number of collusive frauds. The first is the increasingly complex nature of business. In complex environments, trusted employees are more likely to operate in isolated or specialized surroundings in which they are separated from other individuals. The second is the increasing frequency of supplier alliances, where oral agreements replace paper trails and closer relationships exist between buyers and suppliers. Certainly, there are increased cost savings and increased productivity from using supplier alliances. How much increased complexity and supplier alliances will cause fraud to increase is still unknown, although most fraud studies show that fraud is increasing every year. Generally, it is the people we "trust" and "have confidence in" who can and do commit most frauds. The reaction of one manager to a recent fraud involving a trusted vendor was, "I just couldn't believe he would do it. It's like realizing your brother is a murderer."

The problem with trusting people—through supplier alliances, and so on—too much is that opportunity and temptation increase. A helpful analogy is that of a company nearly a century ago that was looking for someone to drive its wagons over a rugged mountain.

In interviewing prospective drivers, the interviewer asked the first applicant, "How close to the edge of the cliff can you get without going over?" "Why, I can maneuver within six inches without any problems," was the response. When asked the same question, the second interviewee responded, "I can drive within three inches of the edge without going over the cliff." When the third and final applicant was asked, he responded, "I will keep the wagon as far away from the edge as I possibly can, because it is foolish to place yourself in a risky position." Guess which one got the job!

Fraud is similar to driving wagons over a treacherous road. When risks are higher, there will be more problems. When employees are solely responsible for securing large contracts with vendors, bribes and kickbacks often occur. In some cases, purchasing employees can double or triple their salaries by allowing very small increases in the costs of purchased goods. Purchase and sales frauds are the most common types of collusive frauds. When the opportunity is too high, even individuals whose professional lives are guided by professional codes of conduct will sometimes commit fraud. Consider the ESM fraud as an example.

In the ESM fraud case, the CPA firm partner accepted under-the-table bribes from his client, in return for staying quiet about fraudulent financial transactions. The fraud being perpetrated by the client exceeded $300 million. The CPA had been the partner-in-charge of the engagement for over eight years. For not disclosing the fraud, the client paid him $150,000. If the CPA firm had not allowed him to be managing partner of the job for such a long time, his participation in the fraud and erosion of integrity would probably have been impossible.

Sometimes otherwise innocent vendors and customers are drawn into frauds by an organization's employees because they fear that if they don't participate, the business relationship will be lost. In most cases, such customers or vendors have only one or two contacts with the firm. They are often intimidated by the person who requests illegal gratuities or suggests other types of inappropriate behavior. A periodic letter to vendors that explains an organization's policy of not allowing employees to accept gifts or gratuities helps vendors understand whether buyers and sellers are acting in accordance with the organization's rules. Such letters clarify expectations, which is very important in preventing fraud. Many frauds have been uncovered when, after such a letter was sent, vendors expressed concern about their buying or selling relationships.

A large chicken fast-food restaurant discovered a $200,000 fraud involving kickbacks from suppliers. After investigating the fraud, the restaurant management decided to write letters to all vendors explaining that it was against company policy for buyers to accept any form of gratuities from suppliers. The result of the letters was the discovery of two additional buyer-related frauds.

A related precaution that is often effective in discouraging collusive-type frauds is printing a "right-to-audit" clause on the back of all purchase invoices. Such a clause alerts vendors that the company reserves the right to audit their books any time. Vendors who know that their records are subject to audit are generally more reluctant to make improper payments than those who believe their records are confidential and will never be examined. A right-to-audit clause is also a valuable tool when conducting fraud investigations.

Monitoring Employees and Having a Whistle-Blowing System

Individuals who commit fraud and hoard stolen proceeds are virtually nonexistent. Almost always, perpetrators use their stolen money to support habits, increase their lifestyle, or pay for expenses already incurred. When managers and their colleagues pay close attention to lifestyle symptoms resulting from these expenditures, fraud can often be detected early. Most stolen funds are spent in conspicuous ways. Fraud perpetrators usually buy automobiles, expensive clothes, or new homes; take extravagant vacations; purchase expensive recreational toys, such as boats, condominiums, motor homes, or airplanes; support extramarital relationships or outside business interests. Consider again the case of Marjorie, our previously discussed bank proof operator:

Marjorie first started working for the bank in 1980. During her first four years of employment, she took out a debt consolidation loan of approximately $12,000 and had 97 personal overdrafts. During the next seven years, while committing fraud, her salary never exceeded $22,000 per year. Yet, colleagues and officers of the bank knew that she had done the following:

- Taken several expensive cruises
- Built a home on a golf course, costing over $600,000
- Purchased and was currently driving the following cars:
  Rolls Royce
  Jeep Cherokee
  Audi
  Maserati
- Purchased the following personal items:
  Expensive jewelry, including 16 diamonds and sapphires
  Computers
  Stereos
  VCRs
  Electronic gear
  Snowmobiles
  Golf cart
  Expensive gifts for colleagues and relatives
  Fur coat
  Tanning bed
  Expensive clothes

- Taken limousines several events
- Held extravagant parties for employees and others at her home
- Bought a condominium for her mother-in-law
- Purchased a glass art collection costing over $1.5 million
- Taken domestic trips to buy glass art
- Had her home extravagantly remodeled

Anyone paying attention would have realized that Marjorie's lifestyle was inconsistent with her level of earnings. When a coworker finally asked her how she could afford everything, she explained that her husband had received a one-third inheritance of $250,000. The story wasn't true, but even if it had been, the $83,333 that her husband had supposedly inherited wouldn't have paid for the Maserati, let alone all the other luxuries that managers knew she had purchased.

Close monitoring facilitates early detection. It also deters frauds because potential perpetrators realize that "others are watching." It is because monitoring by colleagues is such an effective way to catch dishonest acts that Section 307 of the Sarbanes-Oxley Act of 2002 requires all public companies to have a whistleblower system that makes it easy for employees and others to report suspicious activities.

In most cases of fraud we have studied, individuals suspected or knew that fraud was occurring but were either afraid to come forward with information or didn't know how to reveal the information. The new whistle-blowing laws should help in these cases.

Even with advances in technology, the most common way in which fraud is detected is through tips. In one empirical study, for example, the authors found that 33 percent of all frauds were detected through tips, while only 18 percent were detected by auditors. A company that experienced over 1,000 frauds in one year determined that 42 percent were discovered through tips and complaints from employees and customers. A good whistle-blowing program is one of the most effective fraud prevention tools. When employees know that colleagues have an easy, nonobligatory way to monitor each other and report suspected fraud, they are more reluctant to become involved in dishonest acts.

Deloitte, one of the Big 4 CPA firms, in a worldwide study it conducted, concluded that there were four reasons why some whistle-blowing systems fail in their attempts to detect misconduct.[8]

1. **Lack of anonymity**—One of the biggest impediments for whistle-blowers to report misconduct is the fear of retribution. If employees have to report misconduct through an internal channel that doesn't guarantee anonymity, they are less likely to "blow the whistle." They want to alert their organization to misconduct but not at a personal expense.
2. **Culture**—An organization's culture is set by the tone at the top. If management sets a poor example regarding misconduct, employees are less likely to speak out for two reasons: first they fear being chastised by management; and second, they believe that management is unlikely to act on a whistleblower's report, especially if it relates to the management team.
3. **Policies**—If policies in relation to acceptable behavior and ethics are not abundantly clear within an organization, employees will be uncertain about what constitutes misconduct and whether or not to report suspicious activity.
4. **Lack of awareness**—If the existence of the whistleblowing system is not communicated effectively or continually reinforced, employees are less likely to use it or know how to access it.

Consistent with these findings, research has shown that for a whistle-blowing system to work effectively, it must have the following elements:

1. **Anonymity**—Employees must be assured that they can report suspected incidents of misconduct without fear of retribution. An effective system must conceal the identity of a whistle-blower. While this may lead to a proportion of mischievous reports, these can be easily verified through a follow-up investigation of reported incidents.
2. **Independence**—Employees feel more comfortable about reporting misconduct to an independent party that is not in any way related to the organization or the party or parties involved in the misconduct.
3. **Accessibility**—Employees must have several different channels through which they can report misconduct, that is, via the telephone, e-mail, online, or mail. This ensures that all employees—entry-level, managers on-site, off-site—can anonymously make a report using the channel that suits them.
4. **Follow up**—Incidents reported through the whistleblowing system must be followed up and corrective action must be taken where necessary. This will demonstrate the benefit of the system and encourage further reporting of misconduct.

It is not only companies in the United States that have whistle-blowing systems but also government agencies and foreign companies in major countries including Korea. The following was taken from the Web site of Toshiba, a Japanese company:

Toshiba introduced the Risk Hotline, a whistleblower system, in January 2000. Using the system, employees can report their concerns or seek advice via the intranet so that Toshiba can find risks in advance and preclude breach of compliance. Further improvements have been made to the whistle-blower system. Since January 2005, it has been possible to contact an outside attorney in addition to the Legal Affairs Division, thereby strengthening the reliability and the transparency of the system and its convenience for whistle-blowers.

In response to the Whistle-Blower Protection Act of Japan which came into force in April 2006, all Toshiba Group companies in Japan have implemented whistle-blower systems and a growing number of Group companies overseas have adopted such systems. Similar to Toshiba Corporation, major Group companies in Japan have enhanced their whistle-blower systems by setting up direct links to outside attorneys.

Pursuant to the Whistle-Blower Protection Act of Japan, whistle-blowers among employees of suppliers/ partners who report concerns about a company are also granted protection from disadvantageous treatment. Therefore, Toshiba introduced the Clean Partner Line in Japan, a whistle-blower system for suppliers/partners.[9]

Creating an Expectation of Punishment

The fourth factor in eliminating fraud opportunities is creating an expectation that dishonesty will be punished. As stated several times, one of the greatest deterrents to dishonesty is fear of punishment. In today's business and social environment, merely being terminated is not meaningful punishment. Real punishment involves having to tell family members and friends about the dishonest behavior. Fraud perpetrators are usually first-time offenders who suffer tremendous embarrassment when they are forced to inform their loved ones that they have committed fraud and been caught. When fraud perpetrators are merely terminated, they usually give those close to them a morally acceptable, but false, reason for the termination, such as, "the company laid me off," "the company is downsizing," or "I just can't stand working there any more."

A strong prosecution policy that is well publicized lets employees know that dishonest acts will be harshly punished, that not everyone is dishonest, and that unauthorized borrowing from the company will not be tolerated. While investigation and prosecution are often expensive and time consuming, and while pursuing legal action stimulates concerns about unfavorable press coverage, not prosecuting is a cost-effective strategy only in the short run. In the long run, failure to take legal action sends a message to other employees that fraud is tolerated and that the worst thing that happens to

perpetrators is termination. Because of today's privacy laws and high job turnover rates, termination alone is not a strong fraud deterrent. Like a good code of ethics that conveys expectations, a strong policy of punishment helps eliminate rationalizations. Some people believe the reason there is so much fraud and white-collar crime is that perpetrators are not usually punished and, when they are, the punishments are light.

Conducting Proactive Fraud Auditing

Very few organizations actively audit for fraud. Rather, their auditors are content to conduct financial, operational, and compliance audits and to investigate fraud only when symptoms are so egregious that fraud is suspected. Organizations that proactively audit for fraud create awareness among employees that employees' actions are subject to review at any time. By increasing the fear of getting caught, proactive auditing reduces fraudulent behavior.

As will be discussed in Chapter 5, good fraud auditing involves four steps: (1) identifying fraud risk exposures, (2) identifying the fraud symptoms of each exposure, (3) building audit programs to proactively look for symptoms and exposures, and (4) investigating fraud symptoms identified. One company, for example, decided to use proactive computer auditing techniques to compare employees' telephone numbers with vendors' telephone numbers. The search revealed 1,117 instances in which telephone numbers matched, indicating that the company was purchasing goods and services from employees—a direct conflict of interest.

Even CPA firms have become very serious about proactively auditing for fraud. Part of this motivation comes from Statement on Auditing Standards (SAS) No. 99, *Consideration of Fraud in a Financial Statement Audit.* SAS No. 99 includes sections dealing with brainstorming the risks of fraud while emphasizing increased professional skepticism; discussions with management and others as to whether or not they are aware of fraud or fraud symptoms; the use of unpredictable audit tests; and responding to management override of controls by requiring on every audit certain procedures responsive to detecting management override.

SAS No. 99 was issued because the Auditing Standards Board [which has now been replaced by the Public Company Accounting Oversight Board (PCAOB)] believes that by forcing auditors to explicitly consider and brainstorm about fraud, the likelihood that auditors will detect material misstatements due to fraud in a financial statement audit will be increased.

In addition to being more skeptical in their auditing of financial statements, large CPA and other firms have developed dedicated units that specialize in pro-actively detecting fraud. With advances in technology, the proactive detection of fraud is now possible more than ever before. The use of technology to proactively detect fraud will be addressed in Chapter 6. For now, you only need to know that proactive fraud detection cannot only catch frauds that are occurring early, but it can also serve as a powerful deterrent when employees and others know that an organization is always search-ing for fraud that may be occurring.

Remember this ...

The five methods of eliminating fraud opportu-nities are (1) having good internal controls, (2) discouraging collusion between employees and customers or vendors and clearly informing ven-dors and other outside contacts of the company's policies against fraud, (3) monitoring employees and providing a hotline (whistle-blowing system) for anonymous tips, (4) creating an expectation of punishment, and (5) conducting proactive auditing. When fraud opportunities are elimi-nated or seriously curtailed, it takes more pres-sure and rationalization for fraud to be committed.

Preventing Fraud — A Summary

Thus far in this chapter, we have stated that fraud is reduced and prevented by (1) creating a culture of honesty, openness, and assistance and (2) eliminating fraud opportunities. These two fraud prevention activi-ties, together with their sub-elements, are shown in Figure 4.3.

Organizations that employ these steps and techni-ques have significantly fewer fraud problems than those that don't. One company that worked hard at imple-menting these steps reduced known fraud from an average of more than $20 million per year to less than $1 million per year.

A Comprehensive Approach to Fighting Fraud

Until now, this chapter has focused only on preventing fraud. We will also combine prevention with detection, investigation, and follow-up to consider a comprehen-sive approach to fighting fraud. As mentioned earlier, the authors conducted a study that involved surveying Fortune 500 companies about fraud. Questionnaires were sent to each of the 500 companies, with instruc-tions that the individual in the company who was most responsible for fraud prevention should respond. Of the 242 responses, 62 percent (150 responses) came from directors of internal audit, 28 percent (67

FIGURE 4.3 FRAUD PREVENTION

responses) from directors of corporate security, and 10 percent (25 responses) from personnel or human resource directors. Many respondents wrote that their organization had no one person who was "most responsible for fraud prevention," but that they personally were taking responsibility for completing the questionnaire.

The diversity in the job titles of respondents, combined with comments that no one in the organization was primarily responsible for preventing fraud, is a discouraging commentary on the status of fraud prevention in the United States. Fraud is an extremely costly problem for organizations. Yet, responsibility for fraud in an organization is often seen as belonging to "someone else." Independent auditors maintain they can't detect fraud because it isn't their responsibility and because their materiality levels are too high.[10] Internal auditors usually stress that their functions are to evaluate controls and to improve operational efficiency. If they happen to find fraud, they'll pursue or report it, but fraud prevention and detection isn't their primary responsibility. Corporate security officers, in most organizations, believe that theirs is an investigative role and that they will pursue reported frauds. They don't envision their role as including prevention or detection. Managers usually perceive running the business as their responsibility and seldom even acknowledge the possibility that fraud could occur in their organization. Fraud, to them, is something that happens in "other organizations." Further, they don't know how to handle fraud situations that do occur. Employees who are usually in the best position to prevent and detect fraud often don't know what to do or whom to talk to when they have suspicions, and they also often feel that it is unethical or unwise to blow the whistle or report colleagues.

Because this "non-ownership" attitude regarding fraud is prevalent in most businesses, frauds like the one described below will continue to occur.

Jerry Watkins had been working for Ackroyd Airlines for 17 years. During this time, he held several positions in accounting, finance, and purchasing. Jerry was the father of three children, two boys and one girl. Over the years, Jerry and his family had been active in the community and in their church. Jerry coached both Little League baseball and football. He and his wife, Jill, both had college degrees, both worked full time, and both had a long-term goal of sending their children to college. Despite their plans for college, each year the Watkins spent most of what they made and saved very little for college tuition and other expenses.

After Jerry had been working at Ackroyd for 15 years, Steve (Jerry and Jill's oldest son) attended college at a well-known Ivy League university. He performed well, and both Jerry and Jill were proud of Steve's and their other children's accomplishments. Approximately a year later, Jerry, who handled all the family finances, realized they could no longer pay Steve's college expenses, let alone pay future college expenses for their other two children. Jerry, a proud man, could not bring himself to admit his financial inadequacy to his family. He already had a large mortgage and several credit card and other debts, and he knew he could not borrow the money needed for college.

Because of his financial predicament, Jerry decided to embezzle money from Ackroyd Airlines. He had heard of several other thefts in the company, and none of the perpetrators had been prosecuted. In fact, the frauds that he knew about had resulted in the company merely transferring the employees. In addition, Jerry rationalized that he would pay the money back in the future. In his current position as purchasing manager, he found it easy to take kickbacks from a vendor who had previously approached him with favors to get business. At first, Jerry took only small amounts. As the kickbacks proceeded, however, he found that he increasingly relied on the extra money to meet all kinds of financial "needs" in addition to college expenses. He felt guilty about the kickbacks but knew that the company auditors never thought about fraud as a possibility. Anyway, he felt the company would understand if they knew how badly he needed the money. Significant good was coming from his "borrowing." His children were getting an education they could otherwise not have afforded, and Ackroyd didn't really miss the money. Because of his pressure, his opportunity, his rationalization, and Ackroyd's inattention to fraud prevention and detection, the company's honest employee of 17 years stole several hundred thousand dollars.

What is alarming is that Jerry's case is not unusual. Jerry had never signed a code of conduct. Ackroyd's auditors had never proactively searched for fraud. The company didn't have an EAP to help employees with financial and other needs. Furthermore, as Jerry was well aware, the company had never taken actions harsher than terminating previous fraud offenders.

Organizations and Fraud—The Current Model

Like Ackroyd Airlines, many organizations do not have a proactive approach to dealing with fraud and reducing fraudulent behavior. Since fraud prevention is not emphasized in many companies, there is significant confusion about who has responsibility for the

FIGURE 4.4 DEALING WITH FRAUD: THE CURRENT (DEFAULT) MODEL

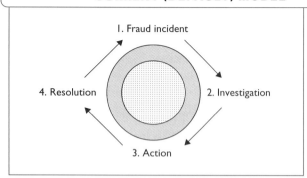

detection, prevention, and investigation of fraud. The current model that most organizations typically use for dealing with fraud, often by default, is shown in Figure 4.4.[11]

This model is characterized by four stages. In Stage 1, a fraud incident occurs in an organization. This fraud incident is not preceded by formal awareness training or other prevention measures. Once the incident occurs, the firm shifts into a crisis mode, because it (a) needs to identify the perpetrator, (b) wants to avoid publicity, (c) wants to attempt to recover the losses, (d) wants to minimize the overall impact of the occurrence on the organization, and (e) is caught up in the emotion of the crisis.

Stage 2 is investigation. Here security and internal audit usually become involved. Most of the investigative work involves interviewing and document examination. Investigation may or may not lead to resolution, can take extensive time, and may be relatively costly.

In Stage 3, after the investigation has been completed, the company must decide what actions to take regarding the perpetrator(s). The choices are (a) take no action, (b) terminate or transfer only, or (c) terminate and seek prosecution.

Stage 4 involves closing the file, tying together loose ends, replacing the employee (obviously incurring additional costs), perhaps implementing some new controls, and otherwise resolving the problem. Once these four stages are completed, no further action is taken—until another fraud occurs. Unfortunately, with this model, fraud will never decrease. Instead, it will become a recurring problem. A much better approach to fighting fraud is the one depicted in Figure 4.5.

As you can see, there are six elements included in the fraud-fighting model. First and probably most important is having management, the board of directors, and others at the top of an organization set a positive "tone at the top." Creating a positive tone involves two steps: (1) caring enough about having a positive organization that effective fraud teaching and training is conducted throughout the organization and a well-defined corporate code of conduct is promoted and (2) setting a proper example or modeling appropriate management behavior.

When the management of one company changed its attitude from "we want to know when someone who commits fraud is prosecuted" to "we want to know

FIGURE 4.5 SOUND ORGANIZATIONS—MINIMAL FRAUD

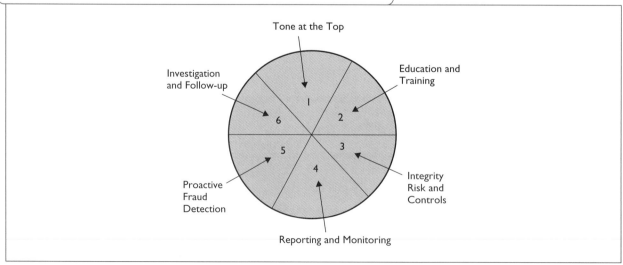

when someone who commits fraud *isn't* prosecuted" and made fraud against the company, along with safety, discrimination, and substance abuse, significant issues in the organization, the number and size of frauds decreased substantially. Likewise, top management cannot accept expensive perks and gifts from vendors and others and not expect employees to do the same.

The second element in this fraud-fighting model is educating employees and others about the seriousness of fraud and informing them what to do if fraud is suspected. As we have repeatedly said, it is fraud prevention, not detection or investigation, that results in big savings. Therefore, significant attention should be given to instituting proactive fraud education initiatives, rather than to dealing with losses that have already occurred.

Fraud awareness training helps to prevent fraud and ensure that frauds that do occur are detected at early stages, thus limiting financial exposure to the corporation and minimizing the negative impact on the work environment. Education includes instructing vendors and other outsiders, not just employees, about the organization's expectations.

The third fraud-fighting element involves integrity risk assessment and having a good internal control system. We have already discussed internal controls in this chapter. It is important to note that having a good system of controls means that there will be an explicit study of all frauds and why they occurred, together with implementation of control activities necessary to prevent future occurrences of the same types of frauds in the future.

Analysis of frauds involves determinations by people in management, audit, security, human resources, control, and finance of why and how the fraud occurred. The focus is on the individuals who were involved, the controls that were compromised or absent, the environment that facilitated the fraud, and related factors. This step is important in understanding the kinds of preventive measures that are needed within the environment in which the fraud occurred. An appropriate preventive solution does not take long to be developed, once all the parties work together to resolve the problems. Obviously, additional or new controls must meet the cost-effectiveness test and may not be implemented. The decision not to implement, however, should be based on an analysis of costs and benefits. They should not be made by default because the proper analysis was not conducted.

The fourth element includes having a system of reporting and monitoring. Fraud reporting must be facilitated. With murder, bank robbery, or assault, there is usually no question about whether a crime has been committed. Fraud, however, is a subtle crime, for which there are usually no obvious signs. Only fraud symptoms or red flags are observed. Because hotlines or other reporting systems often don't exist, employees rarely volunteer information about possible fraud symptoms. This lack of reporting is unfortunate, because employees are in the best position to recognize dishonest behavior or to question red flags with which they are more familiar than anyone else. Monitoring involves having internal auditors, external auditors, and even management performing audits and reviews. Employees and vendors who know that an effective monitoring and reporting system is in place are much less likely to commit fraud than are individuals who work in high fraud environments. Effective prevention of fraud usually involves efforts to create in the minds of potential perpetrators that their activities will be uncovered. For prevention purposes, it doesn't really matter whether a perpetrator actually will be caught, but rather only whether he or she thinks they will.

Reporting also involves publishing facts about the fraud to those who can benefit from the information. Publication does not mean making sure the case and all its accompanying details are in local newspapers. Indeed, until there is a conviction, such publication is ill-advised, because it can lead to slander or libel suits. Rather, what "publication" means in this context is depersonalizing the case (that is, disguising the identities of the perpetrators and other people involved) and publishing it internally in a security newsletter or a memo that is distributed to auditors, security personnel, and appropriate management and employees. Even generic publication of fraud has a tremendous impact, because it helps readers understand that fraud happens in their own organization and is not just a horrible nightmare that occurs elsewhere.

The fifth element of a good fraud-fighting system involves having proactive fraud detection methods in place. No matter how good fraud prevention efforts are, some frauds will still be committed. And, since frauds grow geometrically over time, it is important to detect frauds early. Proactive fraud detection methods, such as those discussed in Chapter 5, are not only effective in detecting fraud, but knowledge of their use is a good fraud deterrent.

The final element involves having effective investigation and follow-up when fraud occurs. Effective investigation means an organization will have pre-specified formal fraud policies stating who will carry out all elements of an investigation. The investigation procedures must be well established, including (a) who will conduct the investigation; (b) how the matter will be communicated to management; (c) whether and when law enforcement officials will be contacted; (d) who will determine the scope of investigation; (e) who will determine the investigation methods; (f) who will follow up on tips of suspected fraud; (g) who will conduct interviews, review documents, and perform other investigation steps; and (h) who will ultimately determine the corporate response to fraud, disciplines, control, and so on. This stage also involves having preset policies regarding follow-up actions against perpetrators.

Taking no action should not even be a possibility; rather, whenever possible, fraud perpetrators should be prosecuted. A strong prosecution policy must have the support of top managers, and they must be informed if someone commits fraud and is not prosecuted. Gone are the days when prosecution resulted in bad publicity. Most people now realize that fraud exists in every organization. They also realize that organizations that take a tough prosecution stance will reduce the number of future frauds significantly and will ultimately be more profitable because of the deterrent effect of prosecution.

As stated previously, the single greatest factor in deterring dishonest acts is the fear of punishment. Companies with successful prosecution policies have developed their own internal investigation experts. They recognize that in order to obtain cooperation from law enforcement officers and the justice system, it is almost always necessary to conduct a thorough and complete investigation (usually including obtaining a signed confession) before the overworked law enforcement agencies and criminal justice systems can accommodate the prosecution.

Remember this ...

Every organization will have some fraud. The amount of fraud different organizations have will depend on what kind of training and education they provide, the tone at the top of the organization, how good their risk assessment and internal controls are, what kind of proactive fraud detection programs they have in place, and how they investigate and follow up on frauds that do occur.

Review of the Learning Objectives

- **Understand how to create a culture of honesty, openness, and assistance**. Creating a culture of honesty, openness, and assistance includes three factors: (1) hiring honest people and providing fraud awareness training; (2) creating a positive work environment, which means having a well-defined code of conduct, having an open-door policy, not operating on a crisis basis, and having a low-fraud atmosphere; and (3) providing an employee assistance program that helps employees deal with personal pressures.

- **Know how to eliminate opportunities for fraud**. The five ways to eliminate fraud opportunities are (1) having good internal controls, (2) discouraging collusion between employees and customers or vendors and clearly informing vendors and other outside contacts of the company's policies against fraud, (3) monitoring employees and providing a hotline (whistle-blowing system) for anonymous tips, (4) creating an expectation of punishment, and (5) conducting proactive auditing. Most organizations try to eliminate fraud opportunities by having a good system of internal controls.

- **Understand how to create an effective organization to minimize fraud**. Most organizations do not have a comprehensive approach to preventing and deterring fraud. In fact, most companies don't think about fraud until they experience one. When fraud occurs, they go into crisis mode, investigate and try to resolve the fraud, and then wait until another fraud occurs. A much more comprehensive fraud-fighting approach would involve (1) creating the right kind of modeling and tone at the top, (2) educating and training employees about fraud, (3) assessing risks and putting proper controls in place, (4) having reporting and monitoring systems in place, (5) proactively auditing for fraud and then, when fraud does occur, (6) investigating and following up on the fraud.

- **Understand the importance of proactive fraud auditing.** Very few organizations actively audit for fraud. Rather, their auditors are content to conduct financial, operational, and compliance audits and to investigate fraud only when symptoms are so egregious that fraud is suspected. Organizations that proactively audit for fraud create awareness among employees that their actions are subject to review at any time. By increasing the fear of getting caught, proactive auditing reduces fraudulent behavior.

- **Understand the importance of creating a comprehensive approach to fighting fraud.** In order to minimize fraud, organizations should combine fraud prevention with fraud detection efforts as well as investigation and follow-up efforts to create a comprehensive approach to fighting fraud. By doing so, organizations can create a synergistic approach that reduces fraud and creates a positive work environment.

KEY TERMS

Employee Assistance Programs (EAPs), p. 112

QUESTIONS

Discussion Questions

1. How do organizations create a culture of honesty, openness, and assistance?
2. What are different ways in which companies can eliminate opportunities for fraud?
3. What is the purpose of adopting a code of ethics throughout a company?
4. Why are good internal controls important?
5. In what ways can organizations discourage collusive fraud?
6. Why is it important to inform outside vendors of company policies concerning payments to buyers?
7. How can organizations monitor their employees?
8. In what ways can organizations conduct proactive fraud auditing?
9. How does a response hotline for anonymous tips help to prevent fraud?
10. What is implied by the phrase "just about everyone can be dishonest"?
11. What are some nonstandard ways of trying to detect dishonest employees in the employee hiring process?
12. How does the Pygmalion effect relate to fraud prevention?

True/False

1. Even with the right opportunity or significant pressure, most people would probably not steal or embezzle.

2. Studies show that a positive and honest work culture in a company does little to prevent fraud.
3. An important factor in creating a culture of honesty, openness, and assistance in the workplace is maintaining an employee assistance program.
4. A good internal control system within a company can ensure the absence of fraud.
5. When fraud is committed, the problem is often not a lack of controls, but the overriding of existing controls by management and others.
6. The two elements in creating a positive work environment are (1) having an open-door policy and (2) having positive personnel and operating procedures.
7. Not prosecuting fraud perpetrators is cost effective both in the short run and the long run.
8. Even a good system of internal controls will often not be completely effective because of fallibilities of the people applying and enforcing the controls.
9. The increasingly complex nature of business helps to decrease the number of collusive frauds.
10. Tips and complaints are the most common way fraud is detected.
11. The major role of employee assistance programs is to help employees recover from the damaging psychological effects of fraud.
12. Not all possible controls should be implemented; rather, one must assess a control's cost and benefits before implementation.
13. Creating an expectation of punishment causes firm morale to deteriorate and often results in lower productivity.

Multiple Choice

1. People will often be dishonest if they are placed in an environment of:
   a. Poor controls.
   b. High pressure.
   c. Low integrity.
   d. Loose accountability.
   e. All of the above.
2. Which of the following factors contribute to creating a corporate culture of honesty and openness?
   a. Hiring honest people.
   b. Performing criminal background checks.
   c. Not having an open-door policy.
   d. Having a well-understood and respected code of ethics.
   e. Both a and d.
   f. All of the above.

3. Which of the following personnel and operating policies contribute to high-fraud environments?
   a. Management by crisis.
   b. Rigid rules.
   c. High employee lifestyle expectations.
   d. Poor promotion opportunities.
   e. All of the above.

4. The single most effective tool in preventing and detecting fraud is usually:
   a. Monitoring employees.
   b. Having a good system of internal controls.
   c. Having a well-written company code of ethics.
   d. Following strict hiring procedures.

5. A company's control environment includes:
   a. The tone that management establishes toward what is honest and acceptable behavior.
   b. Corporate hiring practices.
   c. Having an internal audit department.
   d. All of the above.

6. Which of the following factors generally results in a high-fraud environment?
   a. Hiring honest people.
   b. Providing an EAP.
   c. Autocratic management.
   d. Both a and b.

7. Which of the following aspects of fraud usually results in the largest savings?
   a. Fraud prevention.
   b. Fraud detection.
   c. Fraud investigation.
   d. It is impossible to tell.

8. Which of the following is usually the most effective tool in preventing and detecting fraud?
   a. Discouraging collusion between employees and customers or vendors.
   b. Effective investigations of fraud symptoms.
   c. Having a good system of internal controls.
   d. Creating an expectation of punishment in the company.

9. Which of the following is the typical fraud model that describes most firms?
   a. Fraud incident, assessing risk, investigation, reporting.
   b. Fraud incident, investigation, action, resolution.
   c. Assessing risk, fraud incident, investigation, resolution.
   d. Assessing risk, investigation, implementing a fraud program, reporting.

10. The "tone at the top" is an important element in fighting fraud which involves:
    a. Doing a good job of integrity risk assessment.
    b. Having a positive organization where effective fraud teaching and training is conducted.
    c. Setting a proper example or modeling appropriate management behavior.
    d. Both b and c.

11. Which of the following is *not* a recognized method of eliminating fraud opportunities?
    a. Having good internal controls.
    b. Monitoring employees.
    c. Creating an expectation of punishment.
    d. Engendering employee goodwill by having lax rules.

12. Which of the following is *not* a reason identified by Deloitte why whistle-blowing systems fail?
    a. Lack of anonymity.
    b. Pressure to comply.
    c. Culture.
    d. Lack of awareness.

13. Alerting vendors and contractors to company policies often results in:
    a. Loss of interest in the organization by vendors.
    b. Discovery of current frauds and the prevention of future frauds.
    c. Strained vendor/purchaser relationships.
    d. Heightened incidence of recurrent reverse-vendor fraud.

SHORT CASES

Case 1

Karen, a friend of yours, recently started her own business, The Bike and Boulder Company (B&B). B&B specializes in the sales of mountain bikes and rock-climbing equipment. Karen is putting the finishing touches on her company policies and procedures. She knows you are taking a fraud class and asks you to review what she has completed thus far. You quickly notice that Karen has neglected to address fraud and fraud prevention in her policies and procedures. What policies and procedures would you suggest Karen implement to prevent and detect fraud at B&B?

Case 2

Because ABC Company suffered large losses from fraud last year, senior management has decided to be more proactive in implementing a fraud prevention environment. In interviewing employees, they found that many employees were unclear about which behaviors were ethical and which were not. What could management do to better educate employees about ethical behavior?

Case 3

Jason works at a new software development company. The company has been in existence for only two years. Since the company is new, everybody is working extra hours and spending all of their time developing new products that can be sold to customers. Everybody is busy, and there is very little time for manager–employee interviews. The culture of the company is trusting and fun. When Jason started with the company, the only agreement he had to sign was an agreement to not transfer company software secrets to other organizations. Earlier in the year, Jason learned of an instance where another employee in accounting was fired. The reason was rumored to be fraudulent behavior, but nobody really knew the reason. Do the company's operating procedures encourage fraudulent behavior? In what ways?

Case 4

Nellie works for a large Fortune 500 company. She heads the information systems department and works closely with the accounting department. The company works with many associates. They have many buyer and supplier companies they work with. Nellie knows a lot about the database systems and accounting practices in the company. She even works closely with buyers and suppliers to create data communication lines. Recently, Nellie has become concerned about the integrity and reliability of the accounting and information systems. The company has grown to a point where she cannot manage or supervise all the activities performed in these areas. What proactive steps can Nellie take to ensure systems and accounting integrity and prevent fraudulent behavior?

Case 5

While performing an audit of TCC Corporation, the audit team noticed something that didn't look right. The company's receivables aging report showed that bank loan eligible receivables were approximately $91 million. The audit team calculated the bank loan eligible receivables to be approximately $50 million. The client didn't identify specific accounts in writing off bad debts, there was extremely slow credit memo processing, and items that management had not focused on remained uncollectible and ineligible for financing. In addition, over the last two years, the company's credit department has had unusually high turnover—four different people had held the credit manager

position under an intimidating CFO. The current credit manager was a friend of the CFO and had worked with him at a previous company. After looking at some invoices and asking about customer information to confirm, the credit manager admitted to creating false documents and arranging fictitious sales with clients—all with the knowledge of the CFO.

1. What are some of the red flags that point to the possibility of fraud?
2. What would you say was the main problem in this case that allowed the fraud to occur?

Case 6

Joseph Gonzales recently bought a new business that included a small 20-room motel and coffee shop. He hired a young couple to run the business and plans to pay them a monthly salary. The couple will live for free in a small apartment behind the motel office and will be in charge of the daily operations of the motel and coffee shop. They will also be responsible for hiring and supervising the four or five part-time employees who will help with cleaning the rooms, cooking, and waiting on customers in the restaurant. The couple will also maintain records of rooms rented, meals served, and payments received (which can be in the form of cash, checks, or credit cards). They will make weekly deposits of the business's proceeds at the local bank. Joseph lives about six hours away and will only be able to visit periodically.

1. What are your two biggest concerns about possible fraud on the part of the couple?
2. For each concern, identify a possible control that could reduce the risk of fraud.

Case 7

Danny has been working at Gant Automobile for two years. He feels fortunate to have held his job for so long, considering his past, which involved being fired for fraudulent activities in two different cases. His boss, Mr. Gant, is generally a pretty cold person and only says hello to Danny upon arriving and leaving work each day. All of the guys at work tend to slack a little here and there. They don't mind eating lunch at the company's expense, and there is a general lack of order about the place. Danny has been feeling tight on cash lately, having just moved into a home that is perhaps a little too expensive. With this internal pressure and no one on whom to unload his troubles or with whom to talk, Danny decides to steal parts from the parts garage and sell them on the street for cash. What could Gant Automobile have done to prevent Danny's fraud?

Case 8

Mary is the owner of a small flower shop. With only 12 employees, the environment is one of trust. Mary personally knows each employee, and most have worked at the shop since its opening. Although few controls exist, Mary is the only person allowed to sign checks. Mary's good friend, Steve, is very important to the business. Not only is he the head accountant, but he also helps maintain relationships with vendors. Steve is the proud father of three children, two sons and one daughter. Steve's son was soon to start college at an Ivy League school. Although immensely proud, Steve was worried about making tuition payments as well as providing for the rest of his family. After his son's freshman year, things began to get really tight. Not wanting his son to know that the family was hurting financially, he decided to talk to a vendor who was interested in doing business with the company. After accepting the first kickback, the second was easier. Soon Steve was able to pay for his son's tuition and more. He began buying expensive jewelry for his wife and taking extravagant trips. Because Mary was a personal friend, she inquired where the money was coming from. Steve told Mary that his wife had received an inheritance from an aunt. Because Mary trusted him, she believed his story. She did not become suspicious until one day she tried to contact a vendor directly. Steve would not allow her to do so and insisted that she talk to the vendor through him. Soon Mary discovered that Steve had taken a substantial amount of money and had taken advantage of their trusting relationship. How could this fraud have been prevented?

Case 9

Robert was the chief teller in a large New York bank. Over a period of three years, he embezzled $1.5 million. He took the money by manipulating dormant accounts. Unfortunately, Robert was both responsible for handling dormant accounts and for dealing with complaints from customers. When a customer would complain about his account, Robert was always the one to explain the discrepancy. He usually used the excuse that "it's a computer error." What internal control weaknesses allowed this fraud to occur?

Case 10

A controller of a small fruit-packing company in California stole $212,000 from the company. When asked why, he said, "Nobody at the company (especially the owners) ever talked to me. They treated me unfairly, they talked down to me, and they were rude to me. They deserve everything they got." What could the company have done to prevent this fraud?

Case 11

Jorge recently graduated with his MBA from a prestigious Ivy League school. Lacking external financial support, Jorge was forced to finance his MBA with a significant amount of student debt. Unfortunately, he also developed a love of eating out and golfing that exacerbated his debt problem, as he financed his expensive outings with credit cards. Jorge was not as successful as he had hoped and secured a job that paid substantially less than what he had anticipated making when he took out his student loans. After graduation, his monthly loan payments were a significant financial burden. Further, soon after starting work, Jorge's mother died, and Jorge became clinically depressed which engendered even more poor financial management. About this time, Jorge also started drinking. Is Jorge at a higher risk for fraud than a normal person? Why? How might an employee assistance program help Jorge?

Case 12

MegaGlobular is a large, private international corporation that has been experiencing problems with fraud. Management has heard of the success other companies have had with whistle-blowing programs mandated by the Sarbanes-Oxley Act and decides to implement a formal whistle-blower system and other fraud prevention programs. In every office, they assign an employee to be the fraud liaison, usually someone in middle management. They hang signs in all break rooms alerting employees about the liaisons. The signs instruct employees to call the liaisons and report any observed fraud. After a year, MegaGlobular realized it was having minimal success with its whistle-blowing program, no one had called liaisons, and the number of frauds was unchanged. What went wrong? How could Mega-Globular change its program to get a better response?

Case 13

Your friend Mark Ambrose runs a small convenience store. He recently fired an employee who had repeatedly stolen merchandise when closing the store alone. Mark is now looking for a replacement and asks for your advice on how he can make sure he hires someone that will be honest. Given the small scale of his operation, he needs someone he can trust, as they will often be working alone with the merchandise and the cash register. What would you advise Mark to do?

Case 14

You are the owner of a privately owned, moderate-sized company. The business was founded over 20 years ago and has experienced impressive growth and profitability. The only frustrating thing, however, is that you know the company's profits would be significantly higher if you could rid it of its problems with fraud. Your accountants estimate that the company has lost approximately 7 percent of its earnings to fraud over the past five years. The company has adequate controls in place, and you try to ensure that people don't override them. Since you are the owner, however, you often bypass some controls. You know that you aren't out to rob the company, so you believe that the controls aren't applicable to you. You try to keep a close eye on most aspects of the business, but with about 500 employees, it's difficult to know about everything that is going on. Employees have been caught in fraudulent activities in the past, but you have never bothered prosecuting them. You wish to avoid the negative publicity that would result, and you see no valid reason to publicly humiliate former employees—their shame won't bring back the money they've stolen. Questions: What aspects of the company can you change in order to reduce the amount of fraud that is occurring? Use the five factors described in the chapter relating to creating a culture of honesty, openness, and assistance to explain your answer.

CASE STUDIES

Case Study 1

May 13, 1988, a Friday incidentally, will be remembered by a major Chicago bank. Embezzlers nearly escaped with $69 million! Arnand Moore, who was released after serving four years of his 11-year sentence for a $180,000 fraud, decided it was time to put his fingers in something a little bigger and better. He instigated a $68.7 million fraud plan. Naming himself as "Chairman," he assembled Herschel Bailey, Otis Wilson, Neal Jackson, Leonard Strickland, and Ronald Carson to complete the formation of his "Board." Most importantly, the "Board" was able to convince an employee of the Chicago bank to provide their "in." The caper required one month of planning in a small hotel in Chicago and took all of 64 minutes to complete.

The bank employee had worked for the Chicago bank for eight years, and he was employed in the bank's wire-transfer section, which dispatches multimillion-dollar sums around the world via computers and phone lines. Some of the bank's largest customers send funds from their accounts directly to creditors and suppliers. For electronic transfers, most banks require that a bank employee call back another executive at the customer's offices to reconfirm the order, using various code numbers. All such calls are automatically taped. The crooked employee participated in these deposits and confirmations, and he had access to all the code numbers and names of appropriate executives with whom to communicate.

The "Board's" targets were Merrill Lynch, United Airlines, and Brown-Forman Distillers. A few members of the gang set up phony bank accounts in Vienna under the false names of "Lord Investments," "Walter Newman," and "GTL Industries." At 8:30 a.m., a gang member posing as a Merrill Lynch executive called the bank to arrange a transfer of $24 million to the account of "Lord Investments," and was assisted by one of the crooked employee's unsuspecting coworkers. In accordance with the bank's practice of confirming the transfers with a second executive of the company, the employee stepped in and called another supposed "Merrill Lynch" executive who was actually Bailey, his partner in crime. Bailey's unfaltering, convincing voice was recorded automatically on the tape machine, and the crooked employee wired the funds to Vienna via the New York City bank. The same procedure followed at 9:02 and 9:34 a.m. with phony calls on behalf of United Airlines and Brown-Forman. The funds were initially sent to Citibank and Chase Manhattan Bank, respectively.

On Monday, May 16, the plot was uncovered. The "Chairman" and his "Board" were discovered due to no effort on the part of the Chicago bank nor any investigative authority. Although bank leaders do not like to admit just how close the culprits came to "getting away with it," investigators were amazed at how far the scheme proceeded before being exposed. Had the men been a little less greedy, say possibly $40 million, or if they had chosen accounts that were a little less active, they may have been touring the world to this day! The plot was discovered because the transfers overdrew the balances in two of the accounts, and when the companies were contacted to explain the NSF transactions, they knew nothing about the transfers.

Questions

1. How could this fraud have been prevented? Why is this a difficult fraud to prevent?

Case Study 2

Code of Ethics   ABC Enterprises has developed the following code of ethics:

Corporate Governance Code of Ethics for Financial Professionals

This Code of Ethics for Financial Professionals (the "Code of Ethics") applies to the Chief Executive Officer, Chief Financial Officer and all professionals worldwide serving in a finance, accounting, treasury, tax or investor relations role at ABC Enterprises, Inc. ("ABC"). ABC expects all of its employees to act in accordance with the highest standards of personal and professional integrity in all aspects of their activities. ABC therefore has existing Codes of Ethics and Business Conduct applicable to all directors, officers and employees of ABC. In addition to the Codes of Ethics and Business Conduct, the CEO, CFO and all other financial professionals are subject to the following additional specific policies: As the Chief Executive Officer, Chief Financial Officer, or other financial professional, I agree to:

a.   *Engage in and promote honest and ethical conduct, including the ethical handling of actual or apparent conflicts of interest between personal and professional relationships;*

b.   *Avoid conflicts of interest and to disclose to the General Counsel any material transaction or relationship that reasonably could be expected to give rise to such a conflict;*

c.   *Take all reasonable measures to protect the confidentiality of non-public information about ABC or its subsidiaries and their customers obtained or created in connection with my activities and to prevent the unauthorized disclosure of such information unless required by applicable law or regulation or legal or regulatory process;*

d.   *Produce full, fair, accurate, timely, and understandable disclosure in reports and documents that ABC or its subsidiaries files with, or submits to, the Securities and Exchange Commission and other regulators and in other public communications made by ABC or its subsidiaries;*

e.   *Comply in all material respects with applicable governmental laws, rules and regulations, as well as the rules and regulations of the New York Stock Exchange and other appropriate private and public regulatory agencies; and*

f.   *Promptly report any possible violation of this Code of Ethics to the General Counsel or any*

of the parties or through any of the channels described in ABC's Whistleblower Policy.

I understand that I am prohibited from directly or indirectly taking any action to fraudulently influence, coerce, manipulate or mislead ABC or its subsidiaries' independent public auditors for the purpose of rendering the financial statements of ABC or its subsidiaries misleading.

I understand that I will be held accountable for my adherence to this Code of Ethics. My failure to observe the terms of this Code of Ethics may result in disciplinary action, including termination of employment. Violations of this Code of Ethics may also constitute violations of law and may result in civil and criminal penalties against me, my supervisors and/or ABC.

Any questions regarding the best course of action on a particular situation should be directed to the General Counsel. Please be aware that ABC's Whistleblower Policy provides the option to remain anonymous in reporting any possible violation of the Code of Ethics.

Questions

1. ABC Enterprises has created multiple codes of conduct applicable to different groups of employees. Why wouldn't they create just one code of conduct, applicable to everyone in the company?
2. Who, specifically, has agreed to follow the "Code of Ethics for Financial Professionals"?
3. How is ABC helping to prevent white-collar crime within its company by defining and clarifying appropriate and inappropriate behavior in its codes of conduct?

INTERNET ASSIGNMENTS

1.   As mentioned in the chapter, the Committee of Sponsoring Organizations produced several reports on internal control. One of these relates to internal controls over financial reporting for smaller companies.

Visit the Web site at red hat code of business conduct and ethics www.coso.org and read how the commission defines "smaller companies." What is their definition?

2.   Go to www.insurancefraud.org and read the information about insurance fraud for consumers.

Insurance fraud is a problem that has become increasingly costly for the insurance industry. The Coalition

Against Insurance Fraud estimates that insurance losses are at least $90 billion per year or $950 per family. Besides the dollar costs of insurance fraud, what are the other ways discussed in the article that Americans are hurt by insurance fraud?

DEBATES

1. You work for a small manufacturing firm, where it is clearly too expensive to have proper segregation of duties. Because of this lack of control, management knows that opportunities exist to perpetrate fraud within the company. Management is particularly concerned with possible collusion between purchasing agents and vendors because of the relatively small size of the company and the fact that a single purchasing agent is often solely responsible for a vendor's account. Management knows now that a lot of money can be saved by proactively preventing fraud and not just acting on a reactionary or crisis basis. They have started to establish an open-door policy where all employees are encouraged to talk about pressures and opportunities faced while on the job. Management also wants to establish a hotline where employees can report suspicious activity.

   a. Is an employee hotline necessary?
   b. Is this sort of whistle-blowing ethical?
   c. What can management do as they establish this hotline to encourage employees to actually use it?

2. During the past year, your company has discovered three major frauds. The first was a $3.9 million theft of inventory that had been going on for six years. The second was a $2.8 million kickback scheme involving the most senior purchasing agent. She had been allowing certain customers to overcharge for products in return for personal payments and other financial favors. The third was an overstatement of receivables and inventories by a subsidiary manager to enhance reported earnings. Without the overstatement, his unit's profit would have fallen far short of budget. The amount of overstatement has yet to be determined. All three of these frauds have been reported in the financial newspapers and have been embarrassing to the company.

   In response to these incidents, the board of directors has demanded that management take "positive steps to eliminate future fraud occurrences." In their words, they are "sick and tired of significant hits to the bottom line and negative exposure in the press." The responsibility to develop a program to eradicate fraud has fallen on your shoulders. You are to outline a comprehensive plan to prevent future frauds. In devising your strategy, outline the roles the following groups will play in preventing fraud:

   - Top Management
   - Middle Management
   - Internal Audit
   - Corporate Security
   - Audit Committee
   - Legal Counsel

   Why are each of the groups above reluctant to take the responsibility for detecting and preventing fraud? Who should be responsible? Debate the issues.

END NOTES

1. Albrecht, C., 2007, "A Comment on Koerber and Neck's (2007) 'Religion in the Workplace: Implications for Financial Fraud and Organizational Decision Making,'" *Journal of Management, Spirituality, and Religion*, 4:1.

2. Job Hunting, http://andreakay.com/articles/job-hunting/lying-on-resumes/, accessed June 13, 2007.

3. www.abcnews.go.com/GMA/story?id=1643683, accessed June 13, 2007.

4. www.pnafoundation.org/Training/ColumsBy EdMiller/Power.htm, accessed May 25, 2004.

5. E. Thomas Garman, Irene E. Leech, and John E. Grable, 1996, "The Negative Impact of Employee Poor Personal Financial Behaviors on Employers," *Financial Counseling and Planning*, 7.

6. http://stage.theiia.org/theiia/about-the-profession/internal-audit-faqs/?i=3087, accessed June 14, 2007.

7. Committee of Sponsoring Organizations, 1992, *Internal Control—Integrated Framework*, Treadway Commission.

8. www.deloitte.com/dtt/alert/0,2296,sid% 253D5628%2526cid%253D42825,00.html, accessed May 26, 2004.

9. www.toshiba.co.jp/csr/en/compliance/index.htm, accessed June 14, 2007.

10. Independent auditors are examining the consolidated financial statements of an organization. In that role, they are primarily concerned only with amounts significantly large enough to effect the financial statements. In some cases, amounts of several million dollars are considered "immaterial."

11. Part of the material that follows has been previously published in W. S. Albrecht, E. McDermott, and T. Williams, (February 1994), "Reducing the Cost of Fraud," *The Internal Auditor*, 28–35.

PART **3**

Fraud Detection

5   Recognizing the Symptoms of Fraud   135
6   Data-Driven Fraud Detection   167

CHAPTER **5**

Recognizing the Symptoms of Fraud

LEARNING OBJECTIVES

After studying this chapter, you should be able to:

- Understand how symptoms help in the detection of fraud.
- Identify and understand accounting symptoms of fraud.
- Describe internal controls that help detect fraud.
- Identify and understand analytical symptoms of fraud.
- Explain how lifestyle changes help detect fraud.
- Discuss how behavioral symptoms help detect fraud.
- Recognize the importance of tips and complaints as fraud symptoms.

TO THE STUDENT

Chapter 5 is the first of two chapters that deal with fraud detection. Although the act of fraud itself is seldom observed, symptoms and indicators of fraud are often observable. In this chapter, we discuss several fraud symptoms in an attempt to help you recognize when fraud is occurring. If these fraud symptoms are recognized, many frauds can be detected at an early stage. We share many examples of various real-life frauds and how they could have been detected if the fraud symptoms had led someone to investigate.

Elgin Aircraft had claims processing and claims payment departments to administer its health care plans. The company was self-insured for claims under $50,000. Claims above this amount were forwarded to an independent insurance company. The claims processing department's responsibility was to verify the necessary documentation for payment and then to forward the documentation to the claims payment department. The claims payment department approved and signed the payment.

Elgin employees had a choice between two different types of insurance plans. The first was a health maintenance organization (HMO) plan in which employees went to an approved doctor. Elgin had a contract with a group of medical doctors who treated the employees for a set fee. The second plan allowed employees to go to doctors of their own choice rather than to the HMO, but only 80 percent of their medical bills were paid by Elgin.

Management believed that the company had an excellent internal control system. In addition, the company continually had various auditors on its premises: government contract auditors, defense auditors, outside auditors, and internal auditors. Health claims were processed from an extensive form filled out by the attending physician and a statement from his or her office verifying the nature of the dollar amount of the treatment. This form was given to the claims processing department, which would verify the following:

- *The patient was an employee of Elgin Aircraft.*
- *Treatments were covered by the plan.*
- *Amounts charged were within approved guidelines.*
- *Amount of the claims per individual for the year were not over $50,000; if they were, a claim was submitted to the insurance company.*
- *Which plan the employee was on, and that the calculation for payment was correct.*

After verification of the above facts, the claims were forwarded to the claims payment department, which paid the doctor directly. No payments ever went to employees.

One day, a defense auditor observed the manager of the claims payment department taking her department employees to lunch in a chauffeured limousine. The auditor was curious about how the manager could afford such expensive occasions and was concerned that the cost of the lunch and the limousine were being paid for by the government. In speaking with the vice president of finance, he learned that the manager was "one of the company's best employees." He also learned that she had never missed a day of work in the last 10 years. She was indeed a very conscientious employee, and her department had one of the best efficiency ratings in the entire company.

Concerned about the limousine and other indicators of fraud, the auditor began an investigation that revealed that the claims payment department manager had embezzled over $12 million from Elgin Aircraft in four years. Her scheme involved setting up 22 dummy "doctors" who would submit medical bills for employees who had not had much medical work during the year. Her fictitious doctors would create claims forms and submit them to the claims processing department. The claims processing department would send the approved forms to the claims payment department, which would then send payment to the dummy doctors.

Fraud is a crime that is seldom observed. If a body is discovered and the person has obviously been murdered, there is no question whether or not a crime has been committed. The dead body can be touched and seen. Likewise, if a bank is robbed, there is no question whether or not a crime has been committed. Everyone in the bank, including customers and employees, witnessed the robbery. In most cases, the entire episode is captured on video and can be replayed. But with fraud, it is not usually obvious that a crime has been committed. Only fraud symptoms, red flags, or indicators are observed.

Symptoms of Fraud

A person's lifestyle may change, a document may be missing, a general ledger may be out of balance, someone may act suspiciously, a change in an analytical relationship may not make sense, or someone may provide a tip that fraud is occurring. Unlike videos in robbery or bodies in a murder, however, these factors are only symptoms rather than conclusive proof of fraud. There may be other explanations for the existence of these symptoms. Lifestyle changes may have occurred because of inherited money. Documents may have been legitimately lost. The general ledger may be out of balance because of an unintentional accounting error. Suspicious actions may be caused by family dissension or personal problems. Unexplained analytical relationships may be the result of unrecognized changes in underlying economic factors. A tip may be motivated by an envious or disgruntled employee's grudge or by someone outside the company desiring to settle a score.

To detect fraud, managers, auditors, employees, and examiners must recognize these fraud indicators or symptoms (sometimes called *red flags*) and investigate whether the symptoms resulted from actual fraud or were caused by other factors. Unfortunately, many fraud symptoms go unnoticed, and even symptoms that are recognized are often not vigorously pursued. Many frauds could be detected earlier if fraud symptoms were investigated.

Symptoms of fraud can be separated into six groups: (1) accounting anomalies, (2) internal control weaknesses, (3) analytical anomalies, (4) extravagant lifestyle, (5) unusual behavior, and (6) tips and complaints. In this chapter, we discuss these six types of symptoms in

detail. But first, we illustrate how these symptoms could have revealed the fraud at Elgin Aircraft.

Accounting anomalies result from unusual processes or procedures in the accounting system. Several accounting anomalies resulted from the Elgin Aircraft fraud. The fraudulent claims forms from the 22 phony doctors originated from two locations. One was a post office box, and the other was a business located in a nearby city that was owned by the manager's husband. The checks being paid to the 22 doctors were sent to the same two common addresses. Checks were deposited in the same two bank accounts and contained handwritten rather than stamped endorsements.

The likely reasons that none of these anomalies were recognized are that managers trusted the perpetrator completely and auditors merely matched claim forms with canceled checks. The auditors did not ask questions such as the following:

- *Are the payments reasonable?*
- *Do the endorsements make sense?*
- *Why are the checks going to and the bills coming from the same two addresses?*

A major difference between financial statement auditors and fraud examiners is that most financial statement auditors merely match documents to see whether support exists and is adequate. Auditors and examiners who detect fraud go beyond ascertaining the mere existence of documents to determine whether the documents are authentic or fraudulent, whether the expenditures make sense, and whether all aspects of the documentation are in order.

Significant **internal control weaknesses** were ignored by the Elgin Aircraft auditors. First, the claims payment department manager had not taken a vacation in 10 years. Second, employees of Elgin Aircraft never received payment confirmation so they could determine whether the medical claims being paid on their behalf were incurred by them. Third, payments to new doctors were never investigated or cleared by the company.

Allowing employees—especially those in accounting—to forfeit use of their vacation time is a control weakness that must always be questioned. Implementing a system of independent checks is one of the most effective ways to deter fraud. Employee transfers, audits, and mandatory vacations are various ways of providing independent checks on employees. The Office of the Controller of the Currency requires all bank employees in the United States to take at least one week of consecutive vacation days each year. Many frauds come to light when employees are on vacation and cannot cover their tracks. In Elgin's case, if another employee had made payments during the manager's absence, the common addresses or the payments being made to a business may have been recognized.

Not confirming payments made to employees is also a serious control weakness. In Elgin's case, doctors were paid for hysterectomies, tonsillectomies, gallbladder surgeries, and other procedures that were never performed. If employees were aware that payments were made for these fabricated services, they probably would have complained and the fraud scheme would have been discovered much sooner.

Unfortunately, even if an auditor or manager discovered the internal control weaknesses, they may still not have uncovered the fraud. Most likely, they would have recommended that the weaknesses be fixed without giving thought to the possibility that the weaknesses might have been exploited. A major difference between an auditor who uncovers fraud and one who does not is that the first auditor not only fixes a control weakness, but he or she also immediately enlists procedures to determine whether the weakness has been exploited. The second auditor merely fixes the control weakness without investigating possible exploitation of the weakness.

Before doctors were cleared for payment, some form of background check should have been conducted to determine whether the doctors were legitimate. Just as Dun & Bradstreet checks should be performed on companies with which business is conducted, the validity of a doctor who is requesting payment should be verified by checking resources such as state licensing boards, medical groups, or phone listings.

Analytical anomalies are relationships in financial or nonfinancial data that do not make sense, such as an unreasonable change in a volume, mix, or price. In the Elgin Aircraft case, several analytical symptoms should have alerted others to the fraud. The sheer volume of insurance work performed by the 22 fictitious doctors was very high. Why would $12 million be paid to only 22 doctors over a period of four years? None of the phony doctors were licensed by the state, yet payments to them exceeded payments to almost all other doctors. Another analytical symptom was that there were no other payments to any of the dummy doctors by outside insurance companies. In other words, none of the payments to these doctors were for employees who incurred over $50,000 of medical expenses in any year. Finally, the company's medical costs increased significantly (29 percent) during the four years of the fraud.

CAUTION *Analytical anomalies involve unusual relationships in data such as accounting information. Be careful not to confuse these with accounting anomalies which involve unusual processes or procedures in the accounting system.*

Several **lifestyle symptoms** at Elgin Aircraft, such as taking the employees to lunch in a limousine, should have been recognized. The Defense Department auditor was told that the manager paid for the limousine from personal funds and that she was independently wealthy. She claimed that she had inherited a large sum of money from her husband's parents. Those who worked with her knew that she lived in a very expensive house, drove luxury cars, and wore expensive clothes and jewelry. However, apparently nobody wondered why she worked and never took a vacation. While wealthy people may be employed because they love their work, rarely is their love so great that they never take a vacation.

Several **behavioral symptoms** also should have alerted others that something was wrong. Employees in the department regularly joked that their manager had a "Dr. Jekyll and Mrs. Hyde" personality. Sometimes she was the nicest person to be around, and other times she would have periods of unexplained anger. Interviews with employees revealed that her highs and lows had become more intense and more frequent in recent months.

With the Elgin Aircraft fraud, there were no tips or complaints. No employees who felt that something was wrong came forward, and other doctors were still getting all the legitimate business. They had no reason to complain. Indeed, the only party really being hurt was Elgin Aircraft.

The Elgin Aircraft fraud was discovered because an observant auditor noticed a fraud symptom. In this chapter, we will discuss how understanding fraud symptoms helps us detect fraud much more effectively. We will now discuss in detail the six groups of fraud symptoms.

Remember this …

Symptoms of fraud can be separated into six main groups: (1) accounting anomalies, (2) internal control weaknesses, (3) analytical anomalies, (4) extravagant lifestyle, (5) unusual behavior, and (6) tips and complaints.

Accounting Anomalies

Common accounting anomaly fraud symptoms involve problems with source documents, faulty journal entries, and inaccuracies in ledgers. We discuss each of them in the following section.

Irregularities in Source Documents

Common fraud symptoms involving source documents (either electronic or paper)—such as checks, sales invoices, purchase orders, purchase requisitions, and receiving reports—include the following:

- *Missing documents*
- *Stale items on bank reconciliations*
- *Excessive voids or credits*
- *Common names or addresses of payees or customers*
- *Increased past-due accounts*
- *Increased reconciling items*
- *Alterations on documents*
- *Duplicate payments*
- *Second endorsements on checks*
- *Document sequences that do not make sense*
- *Questionable handwriting on documents*
- *Photocopied documents*

We describe three actual frauds that illustrate how document symptoms can signal that embezzlement is taking place. The first involves the use of photocopied documents; the second, the recognition of increased past-due accounts receivable; and the third, excessive voids or credits. While we discuss only three frauds, many frauds have been detected by using source documents.

In the first case, an alert internal auditor detected a fraud while examining the purchase of new equipment. Further investigation revealed a large, collusive fraud. A thin line running through a photocopied letter in a vendor invoice file alerted the auditor to probe further. The photocopied letter was from a manufacturer who suggested the repair of machinery parts as a less costly alternative to replacement, which was also set forth in the letter. By cutting out the paragraph pertaining to the repair, the purchase of new machinery appeared justified.

A second fraud was detected by recognizing an increase in past-due accounts from customers. This fraud was committed against one of the largest Fortune 500 companies in the United States. Mark Rogers was the accounts receivable department manager at XYZ Foods. In his position, he developed a close relationship with one of the company's largest customers and used the relationship to defraud his employer. In return for a kickback, he offered to

"manage" his company's receivable from the customer. In doing so, Mark permitted the customer to pay later than would otherwise have been required. The customer's payable was not recognized as delinquent or past due. Because the receivable involved millions of dollars, paying 30 to 60 days later than was required cost Mark's employer $3 million in lost interest. Mark received kickbacks totaling $350,000 from the customer. Mark's fraud was discovered when an alert coworker realized that the company's accounts receivable turnover ratio was decreasing substantially. The coworker prepared an aging schedule of individual accounts receivable balances that identified the customer as the source of the problem. A subsequent investigation revealed the kickback scheme.

A third fraud was discovered because of excessive credit memos. The case involved a fraud of over $5,000 by a supervisor in the shipping department of a wholesale-retail distribution center warehouse facility. The supervisor was responsible for the overall operations of the warehouse and had individual accountability for a cash fund that was used for collecting money (usually under $500) from customers who came to the warehouse to pick up cash-on-delivery orders. The established procedures called for the supervisor to issue the customer a cash receipt, which was recorded in a will-call delivery logbook. The file containing details on the customer order would eventually be matched with cash receipts by accounting personnel, and the transaction would be closed.

Over approximately one year, the supervisor defrauded the company by stealing small amounts of money. He attempted to conceal the fraud by submitting credit memos (with statements such as "billed to the wrong account," "to correct billing adjustment," or "miscellaneous") to clear the accounts receivable file. The accounts would be matched with the credit memo, and the transaction would be closed. A second signature was not needed on the credit memos, and accounting personnel asked no questions about credit memos originated by the supervisor of the warehouse.

At first, the supervisor submitted only two to three fraudulent credit memos a week, totaling approximately $100. After a few months, however, he increased the amount of his theft to about $300 per week. To give the appearance of randomness, so as to keep the accounting personnel from becoming suspicious, the supervisor intermixed small credit memo amounts with large ones.

The fraud surfaced when the supervisor accidentally credited the wrong customer's account for a cash transaction. By coincidence, the supervisor was on vacation when the customer complained and was not available to cover his tracks when accounting personnel investigated the transaction. Because of his absence, the accounts receivable clerk questioned the manager of the warehouse who investigated the problem. The manager examined the cash receipts and determined that fraud had occurred.

Faulty Journal Entries

Accounting is a language, just as English and Japanese are languages. For example, consider the following journal entry:

Legal Expense 5,000

Cash 5,000

In the English language, this entry says, "An attorney was paid $5,000 in cash." In the language of accounting, this entry says, "Debit Legal Expense; credit Cash." A person who speaks both accounting and English will realize that these statements say exactly the same thing.

The problem with the language of accounting is that it can be manipulated to tell a lie, just as can English or Japanese or any other language. For example, with the above entry, how do you know that an attorney was actually paid $5,000? Instead, maybe an employee embezzled $5,000 in cash and attempted to conceal the fraud by labeling the theft as a legal expense. Smart embezzlers sometimes conceal their actions in exactly this way, realizing that the fraudulent legal expense will be closed to Retained Earnings at the end of the accounting period, making the audit trail difficult to follow. And, if the fraudulent employer routinely pays large amounts of legal expenses, this small fraud could easily go unnoticed. To understand whether journal entries represent truth or are fictitious, one must learn to recognize journal entry fraud symptoms.

An embezzler usually steals assets, such as cash or inventory. (No one steals liabilities!) To conceal the theft, the embezzler must find a way to decrease either the liabilities or the equities of the victim organization. Otherwise, the accounting records will not balance, and the embezzler will be quickly detected. Smart embezzlers understand that decreasing liabilities is not a good concealment method. In reducing payables, amounts owed are eliminated from the books. This manipulation of the accounting records will be recognized when vendors do not receive payments for amounts owed to them. When the liability becomes delinquent, they will notify the company. Subsequent investigation will usually reveal the fraud.

Smart embezzlers also realize that most equity accounts should not be altered. The owners' equity balance is decreased by the payment of dividends and expenses and is increased by sales of stock and by revenues. Embezzlers rarely conceal their frauds by manipulating either dividends or stock accounts because these accounts have relatively few transactions and alterations can be quickly noticed. In addition, transactions involving stocks or dividends usually require board of director approval, go through a transfer agent, and are monitored closely.

Thus, income statement accounts such as revenues and expenses remain as possible accounts for decreasing the right side of the accounting equation and making the accounting records balance when stealing an asset. Balancing the equation by manipulating revenues would require that individual revenue accounts be reduced. However, since revenues rarely decrease (except through adjusting entries at the end of an accounting period), a decrease in a revenue account would draw attention. Therefore, embezzlers who manipulate accounting records to conceal their frauds usually attempt to balance the accounting equation by increasing expenses. Increasing expenses decreases net income, which decreases retained earnings and owners' equity, thus leaving the accounting equation in balance, as illustrated in Figure 5.1.

Recording an expense to conceal fraud involves making a fictitious journal entry. Fraud examiners must be able to recognize signals that a journal entry may have been manufactured to conceal a fraud. Manipulating expense accounts also has the advantage that expenses are closed or brought to zero balances at

FIGURE 5.1 ACCOUNTING EQUATION EXAMPLE

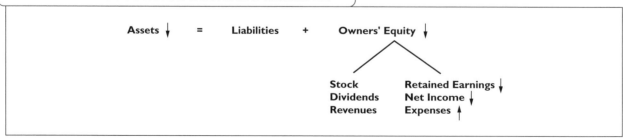

year-end, thus obscuring the audit trail. The following are common journal entry fraud symptoms:

- *Journal entries without documentary support*
- *Unexplained adjustments to receivables, payables, revenues, or expenses*
- *Journal entries that do not balance*
- *Journal entries made by individuals who would not normally make such entries*
- *Journal entries made near the end of an accounting period*

To illustrate journal entry fraud symptoms, we describe three actual embezzlements. In the first, a $150,000 embezzlement was concealed by creating journal entries without support.

John Doe was the controller of a small bank. Over a period of several years, he embezzled approximately $150,000 from his employer by telephoning larger banks and having them pay his personal credit card bills. He concealed his fraud by creating fictitious journal entries to recognize the shortages as advertising expense. Because the total advertising expense was large and the increase in expense resulting from his fraud was relatively small, no one ever questioned his journal entries. Because he was the bank's controller and in charge of accounting, he did not even forge fictitious documentation to support the entries. He was caught when he deposited a duplicate $10,000 payment from one of the bank's customers in his personal bank account. When the customer realized he paid twice, he asked for a refund, and the deposit was traced to John's account.

If anyone had questioned the journal entries that were being made without documentary support, John's fraud would have been quickly discovered. In this case, however, if John had not been so greedy, his fraud might have continued indefinitely.

The manipulation of income at Lincoln Savings and Loan illustrates how fraud perpetrators make journal entries at the end of accounting periods to artificially inflate reported net income. For many successive quarters, large journal entries recorded fictitious revenues that took Lincoln Savings and Loan from a loss to a profit position.

The accounting firm that reviewed Lincoln's transactions (after the fraud was discovered) concluded that 13 transactions overstated income by more than $100 million. The investigative auditors called the transactions the most egregious misapplication of accounting they had ever seen. If Lincoln's auditors and regulators had recognized the pattern of successive last-minute

entries, Lincoln's massive fraud might have ended much earlier and investors would have been spared losing millions of dollars.

At Waste Management Corporation, the chief financial officer realized that their outside auditors only performed audits on the annual financial statements and that only a cursory review was performed at the end of each quarter. Therefore, to overstate net income at the end of each quarter, he made a simple "topside" journal entry that debited or increased Accounts Receivable and credited or increased Revenue. These entries, which cumulatively got larger each quarter during the year, were reversed at the start of each successive quarter. Then, at the end of the year, the fraud that had been committed with the topside entries was buried in complex merger reserve accounts. This type of fraud, where topside entries are made without any support, is quite egregious and was part of the financial statement fraud committed at several other companies in the late 1990s.

Inaccuracies in Ledgers

The definition of a ledger is "a book of accounts." In other words, all transactions related to specific accounts, such as cash or inventory, are summarized in the ledger. The accuracy of account balances in the ledger is often proved by ensuring that the total of all asset accounts equals the total of all liability and equity accounts or, if revenues and expenses have not yet been closed out, that the total of all debit balances equals the total of all credit balances. Many frauds involve manipulating receivables from customers or payables to vendors. Most companies have master (control) receivable and payable accounts, the total of which should equal the sum of all the individual customer and vendor account balances. Two common fraud symptoms relating to ledgers are as follows:

1. A ledger that does not balance; that is, the total of all debit balances does not equal the total of all credit balances.
2. Master (control) account balances that do not equal the sum of the individual customer or vendor balances.

The first symptom is indicative of a fraud in which cover-up in the accounting records is incomplete. For example, a perpetrator may embezzle inventory (an asset) but not reflect the reduction of inventory in the accounting records. In this case, the actual inventory balance, as determined by a physical count, is lower than the recorded amount of inventory, and the ledger does not balance. Another example of a ledger out of balance is the theft of cash accompanied by the failure to record an expense. In this case, total assets would be less than total liabilities plus owners' equity.

The second ledger symptom is indicative of manipulation of an individual customer's or vendor's balance without altering the master receivable or payable account in the ledger. In this case, the sum of the individual customer or vendor balances does not agree with the master account balance.

The following example shows how this second ledger symptom revealed a fraud that was perpetrated by the bookkeeper of a small bank.

Using the following schemes, she embezzled over $3 million from the bank, which had only $30 million in assets. (Note: The Federal Reserve is the "bankers' bank"; that is, every bank has one or more accounts at the Federal Reserve. When a check drawn on one bank is sent to the Federal Reserve by a different bank, the Federal Reserve increases the account of the depositing bank and decreases the account of the bank on which the check was drawn. The Federal Reserve then accumulates all checks drawn on a given bank and sends them back to that bank in what's called the incoming cash letter. All checks are drawn on different banks and sent to the Federal Reserve for credit in what is called the outgoing cash letter.)

Using two different schemes, Marjorie defrauded First National Bank of Atlanta of over $3 million. Her first scheme involved writing personal checks on her bank account at First National to pay for art, jewelry, automobiles, home furnishings, and other expensive acquisitions. Then, when her check was sent from the Federal Reserve to the bank (in the incoming cash letter), she would allow the overall demand deposit account balance to be reduced but would pull her checks before they could be processed and deducted from her personal account.

The result of this scheme was that the master demand deposit account balance was lower than the sum of the bank's individual customers' demand deposits. The second scheme involved making deposits into her account by using checks drawn on other banks and then pulling the checks before they were sent in the outgoing cash letter to the Federal Reserve. Thus, her checks were never deducted from her accounts at the other banks. In fact, her accounts at the banks did not contain sufficient funds to cover the checks if they had been processed. The result of this scheme was that the individual demand deposit balances increased, but the master demand deposit account balance did not.

Both of these schemes had the effect of making the master demand deposit account balances lower than the sum of the individual account balances. Over time, as Marjorie wrote checks and made fictitious deposits, the difference between the sum of the individual accounts and the master account balances became larger and larger. At the end of each accounting period, to cover her tracks and

prevent the auditors from discovering the fraud, Marjorie would pull some official bank checks (cashier's checks) that had previously been used and send them in the outgoing cash letter to the Federal Reserve.

Because the Federal Reserve procedures were automated, no one ever personally examined the checks or noticed that they had already been processed several times. In fact, some of the checks were totally black from being processed so many times. Her fraud was assisted by the Federal Reserve's policy of giving immediate credit to First National for the total amount supposedly contained in the outgoing cash letter. The next day, as the checks were processed using bank routing numbers, the Federal Reserve would realize that the official checks were not drawn on other banks but were really First National's own checks and would reverse the credit previously given to First National. The reduction would again throw First National's ledger accounts out of balance. But, for one day—the day the auditors examined the records—the bank's books would be balanced and the shortage would be "parked" at the Federal Reserve. Because the financial statements were prepared for that one day, the bank records balanced for the auditors and the Federal Reserve confirmed the misstated receivable from them as being correct.

This fraud could easily have been discovered if someone had noticed that, although the books balanced at month-end, they were out of balance during the rest of the month. Bank managers received daily reports that showed balances significantly different from the balances on the financial statements. They never questioned these unusual balances. This fraud could also have been uncovered if someone had recognized many other control weaknesses and other symptoms. For example, Marjorie had significant personality conflicts with other employees, and she lived a lifestyle far beyond what her income would support. In addition, individual accounting records had been altered, and a previous fraud at the same bank had indicated a need for reports and procedures that, if implemented, would have made the fraud impossible. Surprisingly, the fraud was not discovered until a cashier's check that Marjorie had reused several times was kicked out of a Federal Reserve sorter because it could not be read.

Remember this ...

The three main areas of accounting anomalies include irregularities in source documentation, faulty journal entries, and inaccuracies in the ledger.

Internal Control Weaknesses

As discussed previously, fraud occurs when perceived pressure, perceived opportunity, and rationalization combine. Many individuals and organizations have pressures. Everyone rationalizes. When internal controls are absent or overridden, the risk of fraud is great.

As discussed in Chapter 2, internal control is comprised of the control environment, the accounting system, and control procedures. Common internal control fraud symptoms include the following:

- *Lack of segregation of duties*
- *Lack of physical safeguards*
- *Lack of independent checks*
- *Lack of proper authorization*
- *Lack of proper documents and records*
- *Overriding of existing controls*
- *Inadequate accounting system*

Many studies have found that the element most common in frauds is the overriding of existing internal controls.

Three examples of control weaknesses that allowed fraud to occur are discussed in the following text. In the first, a control weakness allowed a customer to defraud a bank of over $500,000. In the second, a significant internal control weakness allowed a fraud to continue over several years.

Lorraine was a customer of Second National Bank. She opened her account 16 months previously, and she often made deposits and withdrawals in the hundreds of thousands of dollars. She claimed to be a member of a well-known, wealthy family. She drove a Porsche, dressed very nicely, and was able to earn the trust and confidence of the bank's branch manager. One day, she approached the manager and said that she needed a cashier's check for $525,000. The manager, realizing that Lorraine had only $13,000 in her account, denied the request. Then, deciding that Lorraine was a valued customer, and based on Lorraine's promise to cover the shortage the next day, the manager gave Lorraine the cashier's check. It turned out that Lorraine was not who she claimed to be. In fact, she was an embezzler who had stolen over $5 million from her employer; all the funds that had gone through her bank account were stolen. Her employer had caught her and promised not to seek prosecution if she would repay the company. She was stealing from Second National to repay the money.

As it turned out, Second National had a control requiring two signatures on all cashier's checks exceeding $500,000. However, the bank manager, who was an imposing figure, had "ordered" his assistant to sign the cashier's check. Without making an independent decision and

because the manager told him to sign, the assistant had merely followed the manager's order without questioning the appropriateness of the request. As a result, the control requiring two independent signatures was compromised. There were two signatures, but they were not independent. Both the assistant and the manager were quickly terminated, and the assistant wished he had made an independent, informed decision.

The second example of an internal control weakness fraud is the famous Hochfelder case. This fraud went to the U.S. Supreme Court before it was decided that Ernst & Ernst (now Ernst & Young), a large public accounting firm, had not been negligent in performing an audit.

Leston Nay, the president of First Securities Co. of Chicago, fraudulently convinced certain customers to invest funds in escrow accounts that he represented would yield a high return. There were no escrow accounts. Nay converted the customers' funds to his own use.

The transactions were not in the usual form of dealings between First Securities and its customers. First, all correspondence with customers was done solely by Nay. Because of a "mail rule" that Nay imposed, such mail was opened only by him. Second, checks of the customers were made payable to Nay. Third, the escrow accounts were not reflected on the books of First Securities, nor in filings with the SEC, nor in connection with customers' other investment accounts. The fraud was uncovered only after Nay's suicide.

Respondent customers sued in district court for damages against Ernst & Ernst as assisting in the fraud under Section 10b-5 of the 1933 SEC Act. They alleged that Ernst & Ernst had failed to conduct a proper audit, which would have led them to discover the mail rule and the fraud. The court reasoned that Ernst & Ernst had a common-law and statutory duty of inquiry into the adequacy of First Securities' internal control system, because the firm had contracted to audit First Securities and to review the annual report filings with the SEC.

The U.S. Supreme Court reversed the decision of the court of appeals, concluding that the interpretation of Section 10b-5 required the "intent to deceive, manipulate or defraud." Justice Powell wrote, in the Supreme Court's opinion: "When a statute speaks so specifically in terms of manipulation and deception, and of implementing devices and contrivances—the commonly understood terminology of intentional wrongdoing—and when its history reflects no more expansive intent, we are quite unwilling to extend the scope of the statute to negligent conduct." The Supreme Court pointed out that in certain areas of the law, recklessness is considered to be a form of intentional conduct for purposes of imposing liability.

In this case, the mail rule that required that no one except Leston Nay open the mail was an internal control weakness. Had this weakness not been allowed, Nay's fraud would probably have been revealed much earlier and investors would not have lost so much money.

The third case is a very simple one. A few years ago, one of the authors of this text had a new home built by a building contractor. Shortly after the home was finished, the author received a call from the builder whom he had now come to know quite well. The building contractor told the author that his secretary/bookkeeper had stolen over $10,000 and he had caught her. When asked how she did it, the builder replied that "she both wrote checks and reconciled the bank statement." To steal the money, she had simply written checks to herself and then listed the checks as "outstanding" on the bank reconciliation. The builder had caught her when he had to submit bank statements to a lender for a loan and the amount shown on the bank statements was significantly different than what he had been told it was. After he discovered the theft, he called one of the authors of this book and asked what he should do. The author told him that people who embezzle and are not prosecuted have a high likelihood of committing fraud again and that he should probably fire her and have her prosecuted. He didn't follow this advice. Unfortunately, later the secretary/bookkeeper stole over $25,000.

There are three simple procedures that small business owners should do personally when they can't afford sufficient employees to guarantee effective segregation of duties. The first is that they should always open the bank statement themselves and, if possible, *reconcile the bank statement.* Second, they should *pay everything by check* so there is a record. Third, they should *sign every check* themselves and not delegate the signing to anyone else. These simple procedures, if done on a timely basis, will prevent many frauds.

Remember this ...

The fraud triangle includes pressure, opportunity, and rationalization. Nearly all individuals and organizations are subject to pressures and can rationalize. A common element in most frauds is the overriding of existing internal controls. When internal controls are absent or overridden, this provides for the opportunity of fraud, thus increasing the risk of fraud.

Analytical Fraud Symptoms

Analytical fraud symptoms are procedures or relationships that are unusual or too unrealistic to be believable. They include transactions or events that happen at odd times or places; that are performed by or involve people who would not normally participate; or that include odd procedures, policies, or practices. They also include transactions and amounts that are too large or too small, that are performed or occur too often or too rarely, that are too high or too low, or that result in too much or too little of something. Basically, analytical symptoms represent anything out of the ordinary. They are the unexpected. Common examples of analytical symptoms include the following:

- *Unexplained inventory shortages or adjustments*
- *Deviations from specifications*
- *Increased scrap*
- *Excess purchases*
- *Too many debit or credit memos*
- *Significant increases or decreases in account balances, ratios, or relationships*
- *Physical abnormalities*
- *Cash shortages or overages*
- *Excessive late charges*
- *Unreasonable expenses or reimbursements*
- *Excessive turnover of executives*
- *Strange financial statement relationships, such as:*
  - *Increased revenues with decreased inventory*
  - *Increased revenues with decreased receivables*
  - *Increased revenues with decreased cash flows*
  - *Increased inventory with decreased payables*
  - *Increased volume with increased cost per unit*
  - *Increased volume with decreased scrap*
  - *Increased inventory with decreased warehousing costs*

An example of fraud detected by considering analytical relationships was the Mayberry fraud.

The internal auditors for Mayberry Corporation, a conglomerate with about $1 billion in sales, were auditing the company's sheet metal division. Every past audit had resulted in favorable outcomes with few audit findings. This year, however, something did not seem right. Their observation of inventory had revealed no serious shortages, and yet inventory seemed dramatically overstated. Why would inventory increase fivefold in one year? Suspecting that something was wrong, the auditors performed some "midnight auditing" and found that the company's sheet metal inventory was grossly overstated. The auditors had almost been deceived. Local management had falsified the *inventory by preparing fictitious records. The auditors had verified the amount of inventory shown during the year-end count and had deposited their verifications in a box in the conference room they were using. A manager at Mayberry added fake inventory records to the box at night with some of the records showing unreasonably large amounts of sheet metal. The manager had also substituted new inventory reconciliation lists to agree with the total of the valid and fictitious records.*

The magnitude of the Mayberry fraud was discovered when the auditors performed analytical tests. First, they converted the purported $30 million of sheet metal inventory into cubic feet. Second, they determined the volume of the warehouse that was supposed to contain the inventory. At most, it could have contained only one-half the reported amounts; it was far too small to house the total amount. Third, they examined the inventory tags and found that some rolls of sheet metal would weigh 50,000 pounds. However, none of the forklifts that were used to move the inventory could possibly lift over 3,000 pounds. Finally, the auditors verified the reported inventory purchases and found purchase orders supporting an inventory of about 30 million pounds. Yet, the reported amount was 60 million pounds.

Faced with this evidence, the company's managers admitted that they had grossly overstated the value of the inventory to show increased profits. The budget for the sheet metal division called for increased earnings, and without the overstatement, the earnings would have fallen far short of target.

In this case, it was the relationship between amounts recorded and the weight and volume that the recorded amounts represented that did not make sense. Unfortunately, few managers or auditors ever think of examining physical characteristics of inventory.

STOP & THINK *What other unusual financial statement relationships may exist in the presence of a fraud?*

Sometimes, it is not unusual relationships that signal fraud but transactions or events that do not make sense. Such was the case with the following fraud:

Don was the business manager of Regal Industries. In his position, he often arranged and paid for services performed by various vendors. An alert accountant caught Don committing a fraud. The first symptom observed by the accountant was payments made to an Oldsmobile dealership, though the company only had a few company cars and all were Cadillacs. The accountant thought it strange that the company cars were being serviced at an Oldsmobile dealership rather than a Cadillac dealership. He knew that both cars were made by General Motors,

but he still wondered about the transactions. Maybe the Oldsmobile dealership was closer, he reasoned. Upon checking, he discovered that it was not. Further investigation by the accountant revealed that, although payments had also been made to the Oldsmobile dealership for body damage on company cars, no claims had been filed with insurance companies. The accountant also noticed that payments of exactly the same amount were being made to the Oldsmobile dealer every month. The combination of Oldsmobile dealer, body damage without corresponding insurance claims, expenditures every month, and expenditures of the same amount raised his suspicion. He concluded that the only legitimate explanation for these anomalies would be a fixed-fee maintenance contract with the Oldsmobile dealer to service the company's Cadillacs. An investigation revealed that no such contract existed. Further investigation revealed that Don had a girlfriend who worked at the Oldsmobile dealership and that he was buying her a car by having the company make the monthly payments.

In this case, an alert accountant saved his company approximately $15,000. Unfortunately, many accountants and auditors would have missed this fraud. They would probably have seen the check being paid to the Oldsmobile dealer, matched it with the invoice that Don's girlfriend supplied each month, and been satisfied. They would not have asked whether the expenditure made sense or why Cadillacs were being serviced at an Oldsmobile dealership.

Recognizing analytical symptoms has always been an excellent method of detecting fraud. A successful fraud investigator became interested in investigation when he discovered his first fraud. This discovery, which determined his lifelong career, is one of the best examples of the use of analytical symptoms. Here is the career-changing experience.

It was the summer of 1956. That's what I remember, at least, though it was a long time ago and things get distorted when you look back. And, I have looked back quite a bit since then, for the entire episode was quite an eye-opener for an 18-year-old kid. I was a "numbers man" then and still am. Mathematics is an art to me. I find a beauty in pure numbers that I never see in the vulgar excesses that most of society chases after. You might wonder, then, what I was doing working in a movie theater that summer—the summer that Grace Kelly became a princess and the whole country seemed to worship the cardboard stars on the silver screens. Well, the truth is, I spent the summer in a movie theater because I needed employment. I'd just graduated from South High and was waiting to begin college. To earn money, I took a job as a ticket taker at the Classic Theater. As movie theaters go, the Classic was considered one of the best. Not in terms of elegance: it wasn't one of those gild and velvet-lined monstrosities with fat plaster babies and faux chandeliers. No! What the Classic had was a certain charm in the same way that drive-in hamburger joints of the decade did. I think the style was called deco-modern and it made me feel a bit like I was rushing toward the 21st century. So the place wasn't all bad, though it was not the kind of job that a dedicated numbers man usually sought. But as it turned out, my numbers did come in useful. For that's how I caught on to him, you see; it was because of the numbers.

Ticket taking is not the most exciting job there is, and I didn't find it a real intellectual challenge. My mind was free to wander, and I got in the habit of noting the number of each ticket that I tore: 57, 58, 59, 60. The numbers would march to me in a more or less consecutive order as they came off the roll that the ticket seller sold from: 61, 62, 63, 64. But sometimes, I noticed, the sequence would be off. A whole chunk of numbers would appear that should have come through earlier: 65, 66, 40, 41, 42. It would happen almost every time I worked. I thought it was odd and was curious about what could be disturbing the symmetry of my numbers. The world of numbers is orderly and logical; for every apparent irrationality, there is an explanation. I began to use the puzzle as a mental game to occupy my working hours. Noting each time the sequence was off, I came to realize that it always happened after my daily break. The manager, Mr. Smith, would relieve me while I was on break. I watched closer and noticed another fact: the numbers would always be off while the ticket seller, who had the break after mine, was being relieved. Mr. Smith filled in for the ticket seller, too.

Until this point, the amateur detective work had been merely a way to pass the time. I began to suspect that something wrong was going on, and it made me uncomfortable. After more observation and thought, I solved Mr. Smith's scheme. When he relieved me as ticket taker during my break, he would pocket the tickets instead of tearing them in two. Then, when he relieved the ticket seller, he would resell the tickets he had just pocketed and keep the cash. Thus, the ticket numbers that I saw coming through out of sequence were really coming through for the second time.

Although this was a small fraud that took place in a little theater, it illustrates that when things do not look right, they probably are not right. If the ticket taker had not been fascinated with numbers, the manager probably would not have been detected. The manager was trusted more than other workers. The number of tickets he pocketed was small in relation to the total number of tickets sold in a day, and so management did not see a large drop in profits. Every night, the bookkeeper computed the total number of tickets sold, using the beginning and ending ticket numbers, and compared the total to the cash taken in. Unfortunately, the balance was not wrong. The theater hired separate people to sell and take tickets specifically to avoid this type of fraud. But Mr. Smith was the manager, and no one perceived a problem with letting him do both jobs while others were on break. There is

probably no way Mr. Smith's fraud would have been caught if it had not been for a "numbers man" who saw relationships in the numbers that did not make sense.

Relationships between financial statement numbers are also predictable. To individuals who really understand accounting, financial statements tell a story. The elements of the story must be internally consistent. Many large financial statement frauds could have been discovered much earlier if financial statement preparers, auditors, analysts, and others had understood numbers in the financial statements the way the ticket taker understood his numbers.

One of the best examples of financial statement numbers that did not make sense was in MiniScribe Corporation's financial statements. MiniScribe was a Denver-based producer of computer disk drives. Here is a description of the MiniScribe fraud and an analysis of the numbers in the firm's financial statements that did not make sense.

On May 18, 1989, MiniScribe Corporation announced that the financial statements that had been issued for 1986, 1987, and the first three quarters of 1988 could not be relied upon because sales and net income had been grossly overstated. In 1988, Mini Scribe was voted the most "well-managed" personal computer disk drive company in the industry. The company experienced an increase in sales from $113.9 million in 1985 (the year it lost its largest customer, IBM) to a reported $603 million in 1988. In April 1985, Quentin Thomas Wiles was appointed CEO and director of the company, with the hope that he might lead the company out of financial trouble. Under his management, the company's sales and profits seemed to increase, even though downturns in the market and severe price cutting were taking place within the industry. Unfortunately, the financial statement numbers were fraudulent. Wiles had a reputation for using a strict, overbearing management style to reach his goal of turning failing companies into successes. At MiniScribe, he set stringent goals for each manager to increase sales and income and did not tolerate failure to reach these goals. In an effort to please Wiles, reports were forged and manipulated throughout the company. One marketing manager revealed that division managers were told to "force the numbers" if they needed to. Thus, the fraud began with managers simply touching up internal documents as they moved up the line. Wiles continued, however, to push for increases in sales, even during times of recession and price cutting within the industry. This pressure led managers to invent various schemes *to make the company look better than it really was. Some of the schemes used were as follows:*

- *Packaging bricks, shipping them, and recording them as sales of hard drives*
- *Dramatically increasing shipments to warehouses and booking them as sales*
- *Shipping defective merchandise repeatedly and booking the shipments as sales*
- *Shipping excess merchandise that was not returned until after the financial statements had been released*
- *Understating bad debt expense and the allowance for doubtful accounts*
- *Changing shipping dates on shipments to overseas customers so that revenues were recognized before sales were made*
- *Changing auditors' working papers*

The result of these and other schemes was a significant overstatement of net income and sales. Inventory records as of the end of 1987 revealed $12 million on hand; in reality, it was around $4 million. In 1989, the company booked a $40 million charge to income to offset these overstatements. On January 1, 1990, the company filed for bankruptcy, listing liabilities of $257.7 million and only $86.1 million in assets.

Several analytical symptoms indicated that things were not right at MiniScribe. First, MiniScribe's results were not consistent with industry performance. During the period of the fraud, severe price cutting was going on, sales were declining, and competition was stiff. MiniScribe reported increases in sales and profits, while other companies were reporting losses. MiniScribe had very few large customers and had lost several major customers, including Apple Computer, IBM, and Digital Equipment Corporation. MiniScribe was also falling behind on its payments to suppliers. Returns to suppliers forced the bankruptcy of MiniScribe's major supplier of aluminum disks, Domain Technologies.

In addition, numbers that were reported at the end of each quarter were amazingly close to the projections made by Wiles. Financial results were the sole basis for management bonuses. There were significant increases in receivables, and yet the allowance for doubtful accounts was far less than the industry average. An aging of receivables revealed that many accounts were old and probably not collectible. A simple correlation of inventory with sales would have revealed that while reported sales were increasing, inventory was not increasing proportionately. Indeed, the financial statement numbers did not make sense. Relationships within the statements,

relationships with industry trends, and an examination of MiniScribe's customers provided analytical symptoms suggesting that something was seriously wrong. Unfortunately, by the time these symptoms were recognized, investors, auditors, lawyers, and others had been fooled, and many people lost money.

Several research papers have studied different analytical "symptoms" to determine if they can be used to predict fraud. For example, one study examined the relationship between high management turnover and financial distress and accounting fraud. This paper, based on an analysis of SEC Accounting and Auditing Enforcement Releases between 1990 and 2000 found that fraud firms are more likely to be financially distressed and have higher management turnover (both analytical symptoms) than are nonfraud firms.[1]

Auditors often use **analytical procedures** to look for fraud symptoms. Unfortunately, analytical procedures are not always effective because sometimes analytical relationships stay the same even when fraud is being perpetrated. Such was the case at WorldCom.

In the WorldCom case, significant decreases in the purchase of fixed assets were offset by improper capitalization of expenses, thus leaving the relative amount of increases in assets about the same from period to period. Here is a summary of the WorldCom fraud:

On July 8, 2002, Melvin Dick, Arthur Andersen's former senior global managing partner for Andersen's technology, media, and communications practice, testified before the House Committee on Financial Services and stated:

> *"We performed numerous analytical procedures ... in order to determine if there were significant variations that required additional work. We also utilized sophisticated auditing software to study WorldCom's financial statement line items, which did not trigger any indication that there was a need for additional work."*

This statement is an acknowledgment that analytical procedures failed to detect the greatest management fraud in history. Why?

While the details of Andersen's analytical procedures have not been disclosed, it would not be unreasonable to assume that Andersen used sophisticated procedures. The nature of the problem the firm faced may be illustrated by comparing key financial statement ratios for WorldCom with those of seven other publicly held communications companies: Sprint, AT&T, Nextel, Castle Crown, AmTelSat, U.S. Cellular, and Western Wireless. Five ratios, all related to revenues, expenses, and (gross) plant and equipment are ... taken from the company's SEC filings.

We now know that WorldCom's revenues, expenses, and property and equipment were materially misstated in

2000 and 2001. The first two ratios—cost of revenues to revenues and the change in cost of revenues to the change in revenues—showed declining trends for WorldCom, but nothing that would be characterized as unusual. By 2001, WorldCom was in the middle of the pack.

The property, plant, and equipment ratios revealed greater volatility in the WorldCom values, but normal values for the critical years 2000 and 2001. If anything, these ratios showed unusual changes in the years preceding the fraud (1996–1998).

Each of these ratios, or some variation, might have been considered by Andersen. Because the ratios are presented at high levels of aggregation, they may not be sufficiently sensitive to display unusual behavior. One can only assume that Andersen's "sophisticated auditing software" disaggregated the data and analyzed them at a more refined level. Nevertheless, these ratios suggest why no unusual behavior was revealed to Andersen: management had manipulated the data to conform to expectations. Writing in the Mississippi Business Journal *(July 22, 2002), James R. Crockett, an accounting professor at the University of Southern Mississippi, noted that "WorldCom had previously invested heavily in capital equipment and had quit making as much investment. By shifting expenses to plant and equipment accounts, WorldCom was able to disguise the changing conditions by meeting expectations." In other words, the historical trend no longer applied, but management manipulated the data to make it appear as though that trend continued to be valid.*[2]

Remember this ...

Analytical fraud symptoms are anything out of the ordinary. When using analytical procedures to look for signs of fraud, make sure you develop an independent expectation of what the analytical relationships should be, based on your understanding of the economics affecting the company.

Extravagant Lifestyles

Most people who commit fraud are under financial pressure. Sometimes the pressures are real; sometimes they merely represent greed. Once perpetrators meet their financial needs, they usually continue to steal, using the embezzled funds to improve their lifestyles. Often, they buy new cars. They sometimes buy other expensive toys, take vacations, remodel their homes or move into more expensive houses, buy expensive jewelry or clothes, or just start spending more money on food and other day-to-day living expenses. Very few perpetrators save what they steal. Indeed, most immediately spend everything they steal. As they become more and more confident in their fraud schemes, they steal and spend larger amounts. Soon they are living lifestyles far beyond what they can afford.

To illustrate how people's lifestyles change when they embezzle, consider the following two examples.

Kay embezzled nearly $3 million from her employer. She and her husband worked together to perfect the scheme over a period of seven years. Because they knew they might someday get caught, they explicitly decided not to have children. With their stolen funds, they purchased a new, expensive home (supposedly worth $500,000) and five luxury cars—a Maserati, a Rolls-Royce, a Jeep Cherokee, and two Audis. They filled their home with expensive artwork and glass collections. They bought a boat and several expensive computers, and they paid cash to have their yard extensively landscaped. They frequently invited Kay's coworkers to parties at their home and served expensive foods, including lobster flown in from the east coast. Yet none of the employees noticed the change in lifestyle. They did not note, for example, that Kay drove a different car to work every day of the week and that all her cars were extremely expensive.

In the second case, Randy stole over $600,000 from his friend's small company, for which he worked. The business constantly had cash flow problems, but Randy drove a Porsche, bought a cabin in the mountains, and took expensive vacations. At one point, he even loaned his friend $16,000 to keep the business going. Never once did the owner question where the money was coming from, even though Randy was being paid less than $25,000 per year.

Embezzlers are people who take shortcuts to appear successful. Very few crooks, at least those who are caught, save embezzled money. The same motivation for stealing seems to also compel them to seek immediate gratification. People who can delay gratification and spending are much less likely to possess the motivation to be dishonest.

Lifestyle changes are often the easiest of all symptoms to detect. They are often very helpful in detecting fraud against organizations by employees and others but not as helpful in detecting fraud on behalf of a corporation, such as management fraud. If managers, coworkers, and others pay attention, they notice embezzlers living lifestyles that their incomes do not support. While lifestyle symptoms provide only circumstantial evidence of fraud, such evidence is easy to corroborate. Bank records, investment records, and tax return information are difficult to access; but property records, Uniform Commercial Code (UCC) filings, and other records are easy to check to determine whether assets have been purchased or liens have been removed.

FIGURE 5.2 BEHAVIOR SIGNALS OF FRAUD PERPETRATORS

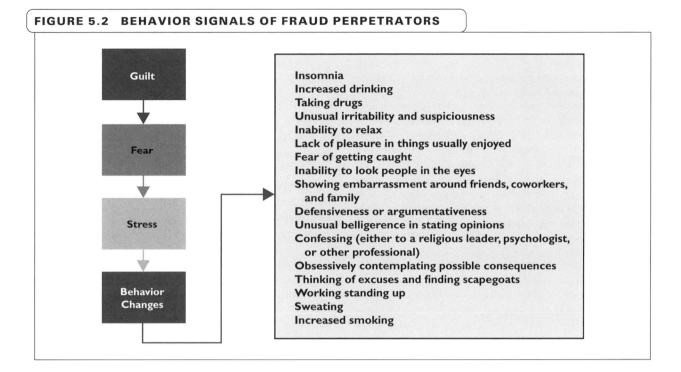

Remember this ...

Fraud perpetrators often live beyond their means since their income does not support their lifestyle. Lifestyle changes are often easy fraud symptoms for coworkers, managers, and other employees to observe.

Unusual Behaviors

Research in psychology reveals that when a person (especially a first-time fraud perpetrator) commits a crime, he or she becomes engulfed by emotions of fear and guilt. These emotions express themselves as stress. The individual often exhibits unusual and recognizable behavior patterns to cope with the stress, as shown in Figure 5.2.

No particular behavior signals fraud; rather, changes in behavior are signals. People who are normally nice may become intimidating and belligerent. People who are normally belligerent may suddenly become nice.

Even perpetrators recognize their behavioral changes. A woman who stole over $400,000 said, "I had to be giving off signals. I could not look anyone in the eye." A man who embezzled over $150,000 said, "Sometimes I would be so wound up I would work 12 or 14 hours a day, often standing up. Other times I would be so despondent I could not get off the couch for over a week at a time."

Eddie Antar, mastermind of the Crazy Eddie fraud described in the following text, became very intimidating and then finally vanished.

Crazy Eddie, Inc., a 42-store retail company located in New York, New Jersey, Connecticut, and Pennsylvania, sold entertainment and consumer electronic products. Eddie hired his father, brother, uncle, cousin, and father's cousin as officers of the company. Allegedly, he overstated inventory by over $65 million. As the fraud progressed, he was said to have become increasingly overbearing. Finally, overwhelmed by fears that he would be caught and prosecuted, he skipped the country and ended up in Israel. He has since been extradited back to the United States and sent to prison for his fraud.

Two other examples of changes in behavior motivated by the stress caused by committing fraud were the behaviors of Donald Sheelen, CEO of Regina Vacuum Company, and Leston Nay, CEO of First National of Chicago. Although their actions were different, neither was able to cope with the stress. Before his fraud was discovered, Sheelen went to his priest and confessed his entire scheme. Nay's actions were even more dramatic. After penning a suicide note detailing how he defrauded investors of millions of dollars, he took his life. However a fraud perpetrator copes with the stress caused by guilt—by being intimidating, by confessing, or by committing suicide—stress always seems to be present.

The following fraud illustrates how stress can change the behavior of a perpetrator.

Johnson Marine is an industrial diving company that services marine-related problems all over the eastern United States. The firm salvages downed aircraft in oceans, lays submarine pipelines, inspects dams, conducts insurance recoveries, and performs search-and-rescue missions. Johnson's part-time accountant, Rick Smith, uncovered a serious fraud perpetrated by Joseph Simons, vice president of the company. After Rick was hired by the office manager, Joseph told Rick that he was to report only to him, to pay bills only when he asked, and to ask only him whenever he had a question. It was apparent to Rick that the office manager was intimidated by Joseph. Joseph not only treated the office manager like a slave but also continually reminded him that if he did not mind his own business, he would no longer be with the company.

Rick's first job was to update all the accounts payable balances. Upon close inspection, he found that very few of the 120 balances were correct. He spent a week fixing them on the computer, only to be criticized by Joseph. Joseph said that Rick should spend his time on more productive work and not worry about trivial things. When Rick opened the petty cash box and tried to identify the petty cash system, he found none. He found that no petty cash reconciliation had been done in over five months and that a negative difference of $13,600 existed between checks written to replenish the cash box and total receipts in the cash box. Rick immediately went to Joseph to tell him what he had found and was told to make an adjusting entry on the computer to fix the problem.

Rick's next discovery came when he reviewed the company's life insurance policies, two of which were for over $1 million. Joseph was listed as the beneficiary. Next, Rick noticed that large balances were being accrued on the company's American Express card. Although overdue notices were being received, Joseph forbade Rick to pay the bill. When Rick asked the president about it, the president informed Rick that the company did not have an American Express card. Yet, the balance was over $5,500. A similar problem was occurring with the Phillips 66 bill. Again, Joseph told Rick not to pay the bill, even though final notices were being sent. Rick later learned that the company used only Chevron cards.

Looking back over the accounts payable balances, Rick noticed an account with TMC Consulting that had an outstanding balance over 90 days old. He tried to find out more about the account, but there was nothing on file. By coincidence, Rick noticed that the address was 10 Windsor Circle, the same address to which Rick had sent a diving catalog that was addressed to Joseph two weeks previously. Upon printing out a history of the company's transactions with TMC Consulting, Rick found a series of five $2,000 payments on the account spread over a period of several months. He

presented this information to the president, who confronted Joseph. Joseph stalled the president until the next day but never came back. An investigation revealed that Joseph moved to California, leaving no forwarding address.

In this case, Joseph's intimidating personality had kept the office manager and others at a distance. Although the office manager seemed to know something was wrong, he had never been given the chance to find out. The office manager had always been blamed by Joseph when petty cash was out of balance, yet he had never been allowed to balance it. In fact, Joseph had constantly blamed others for problems. In retrospect, employees understood that Joseph's intimidating behavior was his way of keeping the fraud from being discovered and of dealing with the stress he felt from committing the crime.

The largest fraud ever to be perpetrated in Australia was HIH, a fraud that was discovered in 2002. The HIH fraud was concealed for years by an executive who changed his behavior to intimidate others so that they did exactly what he wanted. By becoming almost totalitarian, he was able to do anything he wanted. Here is the story.

HIH was one of Australia's biggest home-building market insurers. HIH was the underwriter for thousands of professional indemnity, public liability, home warranty, and travel insurance policies.[3] HIH was started in 1968 by Raymond Williams and Michael Payne. Michael Payne was chief executive of the UK operations until 1997, when health problems forced him to limit his activities in the company. He became chairman of the main UK entity in 1999. He was an executive director of the holding company from 1992 until June 1998 and a nonexecutive director from July 1998 until September 2000.

Raymond Williams was the CEO for HIH from its inception in 1968 until October 2000. Other key employees were George Sturesteps and Terrence Cassidy, who became members of senior management in 1969 and 1970, respectively. They both held their positions until September 2000 and March 2001, respectively.

Williams was the dominant member of management at HIH. Although many close members of upper management had been with him for over 25 years, they were reluctant to tell him how to run the business, give suggestions, or question Williams' motives and business decisions. The Royal Commission report, which summarizes the Australian government's investigation of HIH, suggested that a lack of strategic direction and of questioning authority set the stage for the eventual downfall of the

HIH Insurance group. If asked about the strategic goals or mission of HIH, the report states that neither Williams nor the board of directors would have been able to explain them. Although HIH was a public company that had grown quickly, the report states that Williams continued to run HIH much like the small company it had been when it first started. That is, he made most of the decisions, used business accounts as personal accounts, overrode internal controls, and so forth.

Within an environment dominated by a larger-than-life CEO, Ray Williams, the board presided over a string of ill-fated expansions—costing HIH more than $3 billion—without ever analyzing the group's strategy or assessing its risks. Although the Royal Commission report points to many different ancillary reasons for the HIH downfall, they summed up the main problem as follows: HIH did not provide properly for future claims and the failure of all involved to understand the degree of the shortfall. Apparently, HIH's financial statements were misstated because of inflated profits, overstated accounts, and understated liabilities. According to the report, all other problems were supportive in nature and helped to promote HIH's downfall.

It has been argued that HIH didn't fail because of any systemic fraud but because of two influences. First, HIH had a flawed business model which consistently underprovided for its claims. Second, HIH's governance structures, including the board and senior management, were ineffective since they allowed Williams to dominate their decisions.

HIH's dysfunctional governance structures led to several factors that are common in organizations that are perpetrating massive fraud. First, an insufficient independence of mind to see what had to be done and what had to be stopped or avoided. Also, risks were not properly identified and managed. Unpleasant information was hidden, filtered, or sanitized. Finally, there was a lack of skeptical questioning and analysis when and where it mattered.

This case brought the effectiveness of regulatory organizations into serious questioning. Virtually no one who had any involvement with HIH escaped unscathed. HIH experienced a near-total breakdown of governance and supervisory structures. None of the checks and balances within the systems functioned. The people involved failed to meet their responsibilities.

Once in a while, someone commits a fraud or another crime and does not feel stress. Such people are called sociopaths or **psychopaths**. They feel no guilt because they have no conscience. The following is an example of a psychopathic individual.

Confessed killer Marvin Harris's ability to pass a lie detector test left two nationally known polygraph experts baffled and anxious to question the dealer in bogus documents on how he passed the test. Harris pled guilty to the bombing deaths of two people, which he said he carried out to avoid exposure of his fraudulent documents dealings. He had been judged truthful during an earlier polygraph test and had denied his involvement with the slayings.

What was most puzzling to the polygraph experts was that Harris did not just sneak by on the tests. On the plus–minus scale used to gauge truthfulness, a score of plus 6 would have been considered a clear indication that the subject was not lying; but Harris had scored twice that—plus 12. The experts were simply wrong. Apparently, Marvin Harris had no conscience and thus felt no guilt about creating bogus documents or killing people.

Remember this ...

No particular behavior signals fraud, but changes in behavior do. Perpetrating a fraud will often be accompanied by stress brought on by fear and guilt. This stress will often cause perpetrators to act in abnormal ways.

Tips and Complaints

Auditors are often criticized for not detecting more frauds. Yet, because of the nature of fraud, auditors are often in the worst position to detect its occurrence. As we covered previously, the factors that lead to fraud are depicted in the fraud triangle. These factors consist of pressure, opportunity, and rationalization. As you may recall, the **elements of fraud** can be illustrated as shown in Figure 5.3.

FIGURE 5.3 ELEMENTS OF FRAUD

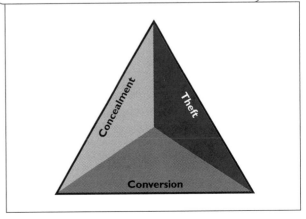

The *theft act* involves the actual taking of cash, inventory, information, or other assets. Theft can occur manually, by computer, or by telephone. *Concealment* involves the steps taken by the perpetrator to hide the fraud from others. Concealment can involve altering financial records, miscounting cash or inventory, or destroying evidence. *Conversion* involves selling stolen assets or transferring them into cash and then spending the cash. If the asset taken is cash, conversion means merely spending the stolen funds. As we have noted previously, virtually all perpetrators spend their stolen funds.

Fraud can be detected in all three elements. First, in the theft act, someone can witness the perpetrator taking cash or other assets. Second, in concealment, altered records or miscounts of cash or inventory can be recognized. Third, in conversion, the lifestyle changes that perpetrators almost inevitably make when they convert their embezzled funds are visible.

Company Employees Are in the Best Position to Detect Fraud

Who in an organization is in the best position to recognize fraud in each of these elements? Certainly, for the theft act, it is not the auditors. Auditors are rarely present when funds are stolen or fraud is committed. Rather, they spend a few weeks on periodic audits, and thefts usually stop during the audit periods. Instead, coworkers, managers, and other employees are usually in the best position to detect fraud in the theft act stage.

In concealment, auditors do have a chance to detect fraud. If audit samples include altered documents, miscounts, or other concealment efforts, auditors may detect fraud. Similarly, they may see internal control weaknesses or analytical relationships that don't make sense. However, company accountants and even coworkers are probably in a better position to detect fraud in concealment since they are exposed to the concealment on a regular basis while auditors see only a sample of the activity involving the concealment.

At the conversion stage, auditors are definitely not in the best position to detect fraud. There is no way, for example, that auditors could recognize certain changes, such as an employee who used to drive a used Ford and now drives a new BMW or Lexus. Likewise, auditors will not recognize a perpetrator's unusual activities, such as wearing designer socks or suits, taking expensive vacations, buying expensive jewelry, or buying a new home with stolen funds. Auditors do not have a reference point from which to see these changes in lifestyle. Again, it is coworkers, friends, and managers who should detect fraud in conversion.

Although coworkers and managers are in the best position to detect fraud, they are usually the least trained to recognize fraud or even be aware that it can exist. Even so, many frauds are detected when an employee, a friend, a manager, a customer, or another untrained person provides a tip or complaint that something is wrong. One large company, for example, which uncovered over 1,500 individual frauds, discovered 43 percent of the frauds on the basis of customer complaints or employee tips.

Tips and Complaints Are Fraud Symptoms

Complaints and tips are categorized as fraud symptoms rather than actual evidence of fraud because many tips and complaints turn out to be unjustified. It is often difficult to know what motivates a person to complain or provide a tip. Customers, for example, may complain because they feel they are being taken advantage of. Employee tips may be motivated by malice, personal problems, or jealousy. Tips from spouses and friends may be motivated by anger, divorce, or blackmail. Whenever tips or complaints are received, they must be treated with care and considered only as fraud symptoms. Individuals should always be considered innocent until proved guilty and should not be unjustly suspected or indicted. The following example illustrates how tips can be spurious.

―――――

Joan worked in a bank. One day, Joan approached the bank branch's operations manager and informed her that two weeks ago she had seen Julie, a coworker, place a bundle of bills (currency) in her blouse. She said that for two weeks she had not been able to sleep, so she had finally decided to inform the bank. For several days, auditors and security people scoured the bank's records and cash vault. Employees cried, and suspicion and distrust abounded. Finally, the fraud investigators discovered that Julie had been sleeping with Joan's boyfriend, and Joan's tip was false and motivated by jealousy. Joan then resigned. Because of the nature of the event that aroused the jealousy, branch management could not inform all employees about what had happened.

―――――

Several reasons exist why people are hesitant to come forward with knowledge or suspicions of fraud. These reasons are as follows:

1. It is usually impossible to know for sure that a fraud is taking place.
2. They fear reprisal for being a whistle-blower.

3. They are often intimidated by the perpetrator.
4. They often think that squealing on someone is wrong.
5. It is not easy to come forward within many organizations.

In most organizations, coworkers and others have knowledge or suspicions that fraud is occurring but do not come forward with their information. There are several reasons for this hesitancy. First, knowing for sure that fraud is taking place is usually impossible. Since there are no dead bodies or videotapes of the crime, all that potential informants see are symptoms. They may see someone experiencing a changed lifestyle, behaving strangely, or stashing company inventory in a garage. Because they recognize that they are seeing only symptoms, they do not want to wrongly accuse someone. Even when their suspicions are strong, the possibility exists that there is a legitimate reason for the symptom.

Second, informants may be hesitant to come forward because they have often read or heard horror stories about what happens to whistle-blowers. Even though such reports are usually anomalies and are often exaggerated, people often fear that they will suffer or undergo some reprisal if they become informants. The new whistle-blower protection laws that were mandated by the Sarbanes-Oxley Act, and were discussed earlier, are attempts to eliminate this fear and provide protection for whistle-blowers.

Third, employees and others are often intimidated by perpetrators. Especially when perpetrators are superiors, subordinates are afraid to come forward with their suspicions. For example, one fraud continued for six years, even though seven coworkers knew about it. The perpetrator had such a dominant personality that he made others afraid of him, and he quickly fired people who questioned his integrity.

Fourth, many of us have been conditioned from a young age to believe that it is not good to squeal on others, even when they are doing something wrong. Technically, one who will not tell on another is an ethnological liar. Not squealing is the creed of the Mafia. As an illustration of people's general reluctance to become an informant, consider the following actual event.

———

Scott, a junior in high school, was enrolled in a word processing class. He was informed that students' grades for the class would be mostly determined by how many processed projects they completed. The teacher informed the students that they must work alone, and, in fact, that working together constituted cheating and would result in an F for the course. One night, Scott informed his dad that the best grade he could get in word processing was a B unless he cheated, and then he could probably get an A.

"What do you mean?" Scott's dad asked.

"Well," said Scott, "our grades are mostly based on the number of jobs we complete. And while we have been told we must work alone, a number of student groups have formed in the class. Within these groups, each member completes a certain number of projects and then they all copy each other's disks as though they had completed the projects themselves. There is no way I can complete as many projects alone as a group of three or four students can. I have been invited to work in a group, but I do not know whether I should. What do you want me to do, Dad? Should I cheat and get an A or settle for a B?"

Needless to say, Scott's dad was very frustrated. While he did not want Scott to cheat, he did not want him to be disadvantaged and earn a B either. His counsel to Scott was to do neither but to go to the teacher and tell her what was happening. Scott's quick reply was "I cannot." When asked why, Scott said, "These are my friends, and it would not be right to squeal on them."

———

A fifth reason most employees and others have not historically come forward with their suspicions or knowledge of fraud is that organizations have not made it easy for them to do so. In most organizations, employees do not know to whom they should talk if they suspect fraud, how the information should be conveyed, or what the consequences would be if they did come forward. In addition, they do not know whether their tips would remain anonymous or whether their squealing would be exposed.

New Laws Protect Whistle-Blowers and Promote Fraud Detection

The new whistle-blowing laws have helped make tips and complaints more effective, especially for public companies, by mandating that every public company have a whistle-blower system in place and that it be promoted among employees and others. These new whistle-blowing laws should help reveal many frauds that would not have been discovered otherwise.

Even before these laws passed, some organizations found that encouraging and dealing with tips could make a difference. They found that by giving employees easy avenues for whistle-blowing, they did discover frauds and other problems in the organization. For example, for years, Domino's Pizza has had a hotline that drivers can use when managers are sending them out with so little time that they must speed to deliver a pizza within the allotted 30 minutes. Complete anonymity is guaranteed. Another company included fraud in a list of such undesirable actions as drug use, safety violations, discrimination, and harassment. It trained all employees what to do if they saw any of these activities. In this company, the training took the form of seminars for new hires, posters and other periodic reminders, a billfold card that listed alternative actions employees could take if they witnessed violations, and videos that were periodically shown. Employees were told, and the information was reinforced on the billfold card, that they had five options if they suspected problems in any of these areas: (1) they could talk to their manager or to their manager's manager; (2) they could call corporate security at a specified number; (3) they could call internal audit at a specified number; (4) they could call a company-wide ombudsman, who forwarded the complaint or tip; or (5) they could call an 800-number hotline, which connected them to an independent monitoring service that screened the calls, guaranteed anonymity, and forwarded the information to relevant company individuals who dealt with the problem.

Whistle-blowing systems should not be considered substitutes for maintaining an open environment in which employees feel comfortable about reporting known or suspected fraudulent activities. Employees should be encouraged to first consider reporting such activities to someone in their management chain, to an internal auditor, to corporate security, or to legal counsel. They should, however, be kept aware of the hotline option and encouraged to use it if they are not comfortable with other options.

Companies that provide hotlines have detected numerous frauds that would not otherwise have been detected. These companies have also reported that the hotline use is somewhat erratic, with periods of considerable use and periods of very little use. What is important is to create a reporting option for employees who would not otherwise reveal suspected activities.

Many organizations have adopted whistle-blowing systems that are managed by third parties. Some organizations have even gone so far as to reward employees for legitimate tips. While research evidence suggests that hotlines are an excellent fraud detection tool, the evidence about rewarding employees for tips is mixed at best.

Three frauds that were detected by tips and complaints or that involved whistle-blowers are the GE fraud, the Revere Armored Car Company fraud, and the fraud at Enron. A description of GE's fraud follows.

A few years ago, John Michael Gravitt, a machine foreman at GE, stood up at an assertiveness training session and told the class that GE was ripping off the government. He told approximately 30 colleagues that the time cards going into supervisors' offices were not the same ones coming out. Within a few minutes, several other foremen stood up to confirm Gravitt's story. Even after his outburst in the assertiveness class, Gravitt's superiors still pressured him to coax his subordinates to cheat on their time cards. Gravitt was told that if his subordinates would not alter their own time cards, he was to do so. When Gravitt refused, his supervisors altered the cards for him. According to Gravitt, the process was hardly subtle. "With black or blue felt-tipped pens, they (the supervisors) altered the billing vouchers. Usually, they scrawled the number of a project safely within cost constraints over the number of a job that was already running over budget." Foremen who refused to falsify vouchers had their vouchers sent to the unit manager, Robert Kelly. Kelly would then complete the blank vouchers himself. When Kelly died, his successor, Bill Wiggins, continued the falsification of time cards and billing vouchers. At one time, Wiggins told Gravitt that GE was like a great big pie and that everyone who participated (in cheating) got a piece; those who did not participate did not get a slice.

Falsifying at GE had become a way of life. One foreman confessed to personally altering 50 to 60 percent of his subordinates' time cards during an eight-month period. Once, when Gravitt told his foreman that he could go to jail for altering cards, the foreman replied that he was only carrying out orders and that there was not any chance of getting caught. Finally, Gravitt decided he needed to alert someone who could do something about the problem. One weekend, he slipped into a secretary's office and photocopied about 150 altered time cards and billing vouchers. He wrote an eight-page letter explaining what had been going on. The next week, he delivered the letter and the photocopies to Brian H. Rowe, the senior vice president in charge of the engine plant. The same day, Gravitt was dismissed from GE. A subsequent investigation by the FBI and the Defense Contract Audit Agency revealed that $7.2 million of idle time had been falsely billed to the U.S. government. They also found that 27 percent of the time-sheet vouchers in the shop where Gravitt worked had been falsified during the three years Gravitt worked at GE.

In this case, John Gravitt's tips were the sole reason fraud was detected. Certainly, GE did not make it easy for Gravitt to come forward. GE's fraud highlights many of the mistakes that companies make regarding informants. Even though Gravitt knew fraud was occurring, the firm's punishment and intimidation of whistle-blowers and its not making it easy to come forward allowed the fraud to be concealed for a long time.

A second fraud revealed by tips was the Revere Armored Car case, in which the informants were competitors.

The revelation of fraud at Revere Armored Car began when some competitors, tired of losing customers to Revere's cutthroat prices, employed a video camera. In December 1992, the competitors taped a Revere delivery of $100 million to the New York Federal Reserve Bank's Buffalo branch. They were hoping for evidence of shoddy security. They got it. In the parking lot of a highway restaurant, the tape showed the driver and a guard leaving the truck locked but unguarded, its engine running, while they went inside to eat. The competitors presented their tape to Lloyds of London, the underwriting group that had insured Revere for $100 million. The tape was aimed at demonstrating to Lloyds the "ease with which someone could whack 'em." The video prompted Lloyds to hire an investigator to check out Revere. Among other things, the investigation turned up evidence of past wrongdoings. Based on the evidence, federal authorities launched a predawn raid on Revere headquarters and found what could be the biggest scandal ever in the armored-truck industry: millions of dollars missing, allegedly pilfered by Revere owners Robert and Susanna Scaretta. Of the $84.6 million that banks said they had in storage at Revere, only $45 million was discovered. Apparently, the Scarettas had run up significant gambling debts. They may have been using Revere Armored Car as a money-laundering operation for illegal gambling proceeds. Several banks lost considerable amounts of money in this fraud. Citicorp's Citibank lost more than $11 million, and Marine Midland Bank lost nearly $34.8 million.

This fraud was allowed to continue because banks and Lloyds of London did not perform adequate due diligence. Neither the banks nor Lloyds were regularly monitoring Revere's operations. If it had not been for the tip from competitors, this fraud might still be going on today. Revere had been commingling funds of different banks rather than keeping each bank's funds separate. Even though large amounts had been stolen, Revere was always able to have enough money on hand to satisfy auditors of any one bank at a given time.

Enron is probably the most famous fraud in the history of the United States. While it is famous for many reasons, one reason for which it will be forever known is the anonymous whistle-blower letter that was sent to its CEO, Kenneth Lay, by Sherron Watkins. Sensing that something was seriously wrong at Enron, Sherron wrote the letter shown in Figure 5.4.

**FIGURE 5.4   WATKINS' WHISTLE-BLOWER LETTER
TO ENRON CHAIRMAN**

Has Enron become a risky place to work? For those of us who didn't get rich over the last few years, can we afford to stay? Skilling's abrupt departure will raise suspicions of accounting improprieties and valuation issues. Enron has been very aggressive in its accounting—most notably the Raptor transactions and the Condor vehicle. We do have valuation issues with our international assets and possibly some of our EES MTM positions.

The spotlight will be on us, the market just can't accept that Skilling is leaving his dream job. I think that the valuation issues can be fixed and reported with other good will write-downs to occur in 2002. How do we fix the Raptor and Condor deals? They unwind in 2002 and 2003, we will have to pony up Enron stock and that won't go unnoticed.

To the layman on the street, it will look like we recognized funds flow of $800 million from merchant asset sales in 1999 by selling to a vehicle (Condor) that we capitalized with a promise of Enron stock in later years. Is that really funds flow or is it cash from equity issuance?

We have recognized over $550 million of fair value gains on stocks via our swaps with Raptor. Much of that stock has declined significantly—Avici by 98 percent from $178 million, to $5 million; the New Power Company by 80 percent from $40 a share, to $6 a share. The value in the swaps won't be there for Raptor, so once again Enron will issue stock to offset these losses. Raptor is an LJM entity. It sure looks to the layman on the street that we are hiding losses in a related company and will compensate that company with Enron stock in the future. I am incredibly nervous that we will implode in a wave of accounting scandals. My eight years of Enron work history will be worth nothing on my résumé, the business world will consider the past successes as nothing but an elaborate accounting hoax. Skilling is resigning now for "personal reasons" but I would think he wasn't having fun, looked down the road and knew this stuff was unfixable and would rather abandon ship now than resign in shame in two years.

Is there a way our accounting gurus can unwind these deals now? I have thought and thought about a way to do this, but I keep bumping into one big problem—we booked the Condor and Raptor deals in 1999 and 2000, we enjoyed wonderfully high stock price, many executives sold stock, we then try and reverse or fix the deals in 2001, and it's a bit like robbing the bank in one year and

(continued)

FIGURE 5.4   CONTINUED

trying to pay it back two years later. Nice try, but investors were hurt, they bought at $70 and $80 a share looking for $120 a share and now they're at $38 or worse. We are under too much scrutiny and there are probably one or two disgruntled "redeployed" employees who know enough about the "funny" accounting to get us in trouble.

What do we do? I know this question cannot be addressed in the all-employee meeting, but can you give some assurances that you and Causey will sit down and take a good hard objective look at what is going to happen to Condor and Raptor in 2002 and 2003?

Summary of Alleged Issues:

RAPTOR Entity was capitalized with LJM equity. That equity is at risk; however, the investment was completely offset by a cash fee paid to LJM. If the Raptor entities go bankrupt LJM is not affected, there is no commitment to contribute more equity.

The majority of the capitalization of the Raptor entities is some form of Enron N/P, restricted stock and stock rights.

Enron entered into several equity derivative transactions with the Raptor entities locking in our values for various equity investments we hold.

As disclosed in 2000, we recognized $500 million of revenue from the equity derivatives offset by market value changes in the underlying securities.

This year, with the value of our stock declining, the underlying capitalization of the Raptor entities is declining and credit is pushing for reserves against our MTM positions.

To avoid such a write-down or reserve in quarter one 2001, we "enhanced" the capital structure of the Raptor vehicles, committing more ENE shares.

My understanding of the third-quarter problem is that we must "enhance" the vehicles by $250 million.

I realize that we have had a lot of smart people looking at this and a lot of accountants including AA & Co. have blessed the accounting treatment. None of that will protect Enron if these transactions are ever disclosed in the bright light of day. (Please review the late 90's problems of Waste Management (news/quote)—where AA paid $130 million plus in litigation re questionable accounting practices.)

The overriding basic principle of accounting is that if you explain the "accounting treatment" to a man in the street, would you influence his investing decisions? Would he sell or buy the stock based on a thorough understanding of the facts? If so, you best present it correctly and/or change the accounting.

My concern is that the footnotes don't adequately explain the transactions. If adequately explained, the investor would know that the "entities" described in our related party footnote are thinly capitalized, the equity holders have no skin in the game, and all the value in the entities comes from the underlying value of the derivatives (unfortunately in this case, a big loss) AND Enron stock and N/P. Looking at the stock we swapped, I also don't believe any other company would have entered into the equity derivative transactions with us at the same prices or without substantial premiums from Enron. In other words, the $500 million in revenue in 2000 would have been much lower. How much lower?

Raptor looks to be a big bet if the underlying stocks did well, then no one would be the wiser. If Enron stock did well, the stock issuance to these entities would decline and the transactions would be less noticeable. All has gone against us. The stocks, most notably Hanover, the New Power Company and Avici are underwater to great or lesser degrees.

I firmly believe that executive management of the company must have a clear and precise knowledge of these transactions and they must have the transactions reviewed by objective experts in the fields of securities law and accounting. I believe Ken Lay deserves the right to judge for himself what he believes the probabilities of discovery to be and the estimated damages to the company from those discoveries and decide one of two courses of action:

1. The probability of discovery is low enough and the estimated damage too great; therefore we find a way to quietly and quickly reverse, unwind, write down these positions/ transactions.
2. The probability of discovery is too great, the estimated damages to the company too great; therefore, we must quantify, develop damage containment plans and disclose.

I firmly believe that the probability of discovery significantly increased with Skilling's shocking departure. Too many people are looking for a smoking gun.

Summary of Raptor Oddities:

1. The accounting treatment looks questionable.
   a. Enron booked a $500 million gain from equity derivatives from a related party.
   b. That related party is thinly capitalized with no party at risk except Enron.
   c. It appears Enron has supported an income statement gain by a contribution of its own shares.

(continued)

FIGURE 5.4 CONTINUED

One basic question: The related party entity has lost $500 million in its equity derivative transactions with Enron. Who bears that loss? I can't find an equity or debt holder that bears that loss. Find out who will lose this money. Who will pay for this loss at the related party entity?

If it's Enron, from our shares, then I think we do not have a fact pattern that would look good to the S.E.C. or investors.

2. The equity derivative transactions do not appear to be at arms length.
   a. Enron hedged New Power, Hanover and Avici with the related party at what now appears to be the peak of the market. New Power and Avici have fallen away significantly since. The related party was unable to lay off this risk. This fact pattern is once again very negative for Enron.
   b. I don't think any other unrelated company would have entered into these transactions at these prices. What else is going on here? What was the compensation to the related party to induce it to enter into such transactions?
3. There is a veil of secrecy around LJM and Raptor. Employees question our accounting propriety consistently and constantly. This alone is cause for concern.
   a. Jeff McMahon was highly vexed over the inherent conflicts of LJM. He complained mightily to Jeff Skilling and laid out five steps he thought should be taken if he was to remain as treasurer. Three days later, Skilling offered him the C.E.O. spot at Enron Industrial Markets and never addressed the five steps with him.
   b. Cliff Baxter complained mightily to Skilling and all who would listen about the inappropriateness of our transactions with LJM.
   c. I have heard one manager-level employee from the principal investments group say, "I know it would be devastating to all of us, but I wish we would get caught. We're such a crooked company." The principal investments group hedged a large number of their investments with Raptor. These people know and see a lot. Many similar comments are made when you ask about these deals. Employees quote our C.F.O. as saying that he has a handshake deal with Skilling that LJM will never lose money.
4. Can the general counsel of Enron audit the deal trail and the money trail between Enron and LJM/Raptor and its principals? Can he look at LJM? At Raptor? If the C.F.O. says no, isn't that a problem?

Condor and Raptor Work:

1. Postpone decision on filling office of the chair, if the current decision includes C.F.O. and/or C.A.O.
2. Involve Jim Derrick and Rex Rogers to hire a law firm to investigate the Condor and Raptor transactions to give Enron attorney-client privilege on the work product. (Can't use V & E due to conflict—they provided some true sale opinions on some of the deals.)
3. Law firm to hire one of the big 6, but not Arthur Andersen or PricewaterhouseCoopers due to their conflicts of interest: AA & Co. (Enron); PWC (LJM).
4. Investigate the transactions, our accounting treatment and our future commitments to these vehicles in the form of stock, NP, etc., For instance: In the third quarter we have a $250 million problem with Raptor 3 (NPW) if we don't "enhance" the capital structure of Raptor 3 to commit more ENE shares. By the way: in Q. 1 we enhanced the Raptor 3 deal, committing more ENE shares to avoid a write-down.
5. Develop cleanup plan:
   a. Best case: Clean up quietly if possible.
   b. Worst case: Quantify, develop P.R. and I.R. campaigns, customer assurance plans (don't want to go the way of Salomon's trading shop), legal actions, severance actions, disclosure.
6. Personnel to quiz confidentially to determine if I'm all wet:
   a. Jeff McMahon
   b. Mark Koenig
   c. Rick Buy
   d. Greg Walley

To put the accounting treatment in perspective I offer the following:

1. We've contributed contingent Enron equity to the Raptor entities. Since it's contingent, we have the consideration given and received at zero. We do, as Causey points out, include the shares in our fully diluted computations of shares outstanding if the current economics of the deal imply that Enron will have to issue the shares in the future. This impacts 2002–2004 earnings-per-share projections only.
2. We lost value in several equity investments in 2000, $500 million of lost value. These were fair-value investments; we wrote them down. However, we also booked gains from our price risk management

(continued)

FIGURE 5.4　CONTINUED

transactions with Raptor, recording a corresponding PRM account receivable from the Raptor entities. That's a $500 million related party transaction—it's 20 percent of 2000 IBIT, 51 percent of NI pretax, 33 percent of NI after tax.

3. Credit reviews the underlying capitalization of Raptor, reviews the contingent shares and determines whether the Raptor entities will have enough capital to pay Enron its $500 million when the equity derivatives expire.

4. The Raptor entities are technically bankrupt; the value of the contingent Enron shares equals or is just below the PRM account payable that Raptor owes Enron. Raptor's inception-to-date income statement is a $500 million loss.

5. Where are the equity and debt investors that lost out? LJM is whole on a cash-on-cash basis. Where did the $500 million in value come from? It came from Enron shares. Why haven't we booked the transaction as $500 million in a promise of shares to the Raptor entity and $500 million of value in our "economic interests" in these entities? Then we would have a write-down of our value in the Raptor entities. We have not booked the latter,

because we do not have to yet. Technically we can wait and face the music in 2002–2004.

6. The related party footnote tries to explain these transactions. Don't you think that several interested companies, be they stock analysts, journalists, hedge fund managers, etc., are busy trying to discover the reason Skilling left? Don't you think their smartest people are poring over that footnote disclosure right now? I can just hear the discussions—"it looks like they booked a $500 million gain from this related party company and I think, from all the undecipherable half-page on Enron's contingent contributions to this related party entity, I think the related party entity is capitalized with Enron stock." … "No, no, no, you must have it all wrong, it can't be that, that's just too bad, too fraudulent, surely AA & Co. wouldn't let them get away with that?" "Go back to the drawing board, it's got to be something else. But find it!" …"Hey, just in case you might be right, try and find some insiders or 'redeployed' former employees to validate your theory."

SOURCE: http://news.bbc.co.uk/1/hi/business/1764308.stm, accessed June 1, 2004.

This letter, together with whistle-blowing acts by Colleen Rowley of the FBI and Cynthia Cooper of WorldCom, resulted in the three of them being named *TIME* magazine's 2002 "Persons of the Year." As *TIME* magazine stated, "These three did the right thing by just doing their jobs rightly."

Remember this …

Employees other than auditors (such as coworkers or managers) are usually in the best position to detect fraud. Unfortunately, these individuals often lack training in this area. Many reasons exist why people do not report fraud, but companies need to set up methods to encourage employees to report suspicious behavior or other potential signs of fraud.

Review of the Learning Objectives

- **Understand how symptoms help in the detection of fraud.** When unusual symptoms of fraud become apparent, a more focused, directed search of where the fraud is originating from should be conducted.

- **Identify and understand accounting symptoms of fraud.** Knowing how certain accounts interrelate is important and can help in determining the possibility for fraud.

- **Describe internal controls that help detect fraud.** Segregation of duties is a key element in reducing the potential for fraud.

- **Identify and understand analytical symptoms of fraud.** Knowing relationships within the financial statements regarding separate accounts as well as logically thinking through the implications of the reported financials will assist in detecting fraud.

- **Explain how lifestyle changes help detect fraud.** One strong indicator of the occurrence of fraud is if an employee lives well beyond his or her means. If employees suddenly have more extravagant lifestyles, auditors may want to assess the source of the money.
- **Discuss how behavioral symptoms help detect fraud.** People who commit fraud usually display unusual changes in behavior.
- **Recognize the importance of tips and complaints as fraud symptoms.** Most frauds are not detected by auditors. Rather, most are detected by coworkers, managers, or other employees. Tips and complaints are main sources of investigating fraud.

KEY TERMS

accounting anomalies, p. 137

behavioral symptoms, p. 138

internal control weaknesses, p. 137

analytical procedures, p. 147

analytical anomalies, p. 138

psychopaths, p. 151

lifestyle symptoms, p. 138

elements of fraud, p. 151

QUESTIONS

Discussion Questions

1. How do fraud symptoms help in detecting fraud?
2. Why do internal control weaknesses help detect fraud?
3. What are accounting symptoms?
4. What are analytical symptoms?
5. How can lifestyle changes help in detecting fraud?
6. How can behavioral symptoms help in detecting fraud?
7. How can tips and complaints help in detecting fraud?
8. What is the theft act of a fraud?
9. What is conversion?
10. What is concealment?
11. How would you react in the following situations?
    a. You discover an internal control weakness in the company you are auditing.
    b. You notice your coworker has recently been coming to work in a new car and more expensive clothes and jewelry.
    c. You are the assistant controller and you notice a control weakness that would allow you to embezzle funds from the company.

True/False

1. Analytical anomalies are present in every fraud.
2. Recording an expense is a possible way to conceal the theft of cash.
3. A check is an example of a source document.
4. Internal control weaknesses give employees opportunities to commit fraud.
5. Internal control is composed of the control environment, the accounting system, and control procedures (activities).
6. Analytical fraud symptoms are the least effective way to detect fraud.
7. Most people who commit fraud use the embezzled funds to save for retirement.
8. As fraud perpetrators become more confident in their fraud schemes, they steal and spend increasingly larger amounts.
9. First-time offenders usually exhibit no psychological changes.
10. Psychopaths feel no guilt because they have no conscience.
11. It is safe to assume that fraud has not occurred if one or more elements of the fraud triangle cannot be observed.
12. The fraud elements consist of concealment, conversion, and completion.
13. Auditors can best help detect fraud in conversion.
14. Some complaints and tips turn out to be unjustified.
15. Fraud is a crime that is seldom observed.
16. Because of the nature of fraud, auditors are often in the best position to detect its occurrence.
17. Most people who commit fraud are under financial pressure.
18. Studies have found that the most common internal control problem when frauds occur is having a lack of proper authorizations.
19. Fraud perpetrators who manipulate accounting records to conceal embezzlements often attempt to balance the accounting equation by recording expenses.

20. Employee transfers, audits, and mandatory vacations are all ways to provide independent checks on employees.
21. New whistle-blowing laws have helped make tips and complaints more effective.
22. Coworkers are usually in the best position to detect fraud.
23. Fraud perpetrators often live beyond their means since their income does not support their lifestyle.
24. Nearly all individuals and organizations are subject to pressures and can rationalize.

Multiple Choice

1. Which of the following is true regarding fraud?
   a. It is easily identified.
   b. It is seldom observed.
   c. When a fraud occurs, there is no question whether or not a crime has been committed.
   d. Many witnesses are usually available when fraud occurs.
2. Which of the following is *not* a fraud symptom related to source documents?
   a. Duplicate payments.
   b. Missing documents.
   c. A tip from an employee.
   d. Photocopied documents.
3. Which of the following is a fraud symptom related to an internal control weakness?
   a. Lack of proper authorization.
   b. Lack of independent checks.
   c. Inadequate accounting system.
   d. Lack of physical safeguards.
   e. All of the above.
4. In the three elements of fraud (theft act, concealment, conversion), who is usually in the best position to detect the fraud?
   a. Coworkers and managers.
   b. Customers.
   c. Owners.
   d. Vendors.
5. When a person commits a crime:
   a. He or she usually becomes engulfed by emotions of fear and guilt.
   b. He or she will experience no changes in behavior.
   c. He or she usually becomes friendly and nice.
   d. He or she experiences a lower stress level.
6. Most people who commit fraud:
   a. Use the embezzled funds to build a savings account..

   b. Give the embezzled funds to charity.
   c. Experience no change in their lifestyle.
   d. Use the embezzled funds to improve their lifestyle.
7. Which of the following is *not* a reason people are hesitant to come forward with knowledge or suspicions of fraud?
   a. They often think that squealing on someone is wrong.
   b. They fear reprisal for being a whistle-blower.
   c. It is usually impossible to know for sure that a fraud is taking place.
   d. People who report fraud are often rewarded monetarily.
8. Which of the following is *not* one of the categories of employee fraud symptoms?
   a. Accounting anomalies.
   b. Analytical anomalies.
   c. Tips and complaints.
   d. Firm structure.
9. Embezzlement of assets reduces the left side of the accounting equation. To conceal the theft, the embezzler must find a way to reduce the right side of the accounting equation. A perpetrator would most likely reduce the right side of the equation by:
   a. Reducing accounts payable.
   b. Paying dividends.
   c. Increasing expenses.
   d. Altering stock accounts.
10. Which of the following is *not* a fraud symptom related to journal entries?
    a. Unexplained adjustments to receivables, payables, revenues, or expenses.
    b. Journal entries that do not balance.
    c. Journal entries without documentary support.
    d. Journal entries made near the beginning of accounting periods.
11. Which of the following is *not* a common internal control fraud symptom or problem?
    a. Lack of segregation of duties.
    b. Unexplained adjustments to receivables, payables, revenues, or expenses.
    c. Lack of independent checks.
    d. Overriding of existing controls.
12. Once in a while, someone commits fraud or another crime and does not feel stress. Such people are referred to as:
    a. Psychopathic.
    b. Altruistic.
    c. Philanthropic.
    d. Magnanimous.

13. Fraud is usually detected by recognizing and pursuing:
    a. Synonyms.
    b. Symptoms.
    c. Equity.
    d. Legends.
14. A letter is most likely to be fraudulent if:
    a. It is signed by only one person.
    b. It is addressed to an individual, rather than a department.
    c. It is a photocopy of an original letter.
    d. It is written on outdated company letterhead.
15. If a perpetrator has stolen assets, which of the following is the easiest method for concealing the theft?
    a. Reduce liabilities (such as payables).
    b. Manipulate dividend or stock accounts.
    c. Increase other assets (such as receivables).
    d. Increase expenses.
16. Which of the following is a common fraud symptom relating to ledgers?
    a. A ledger that does not balance.
    b. A ledger that balances too perfectly.
    c. Master account balances that do not equal the sum of the individual customer or vendor balances.
    d. Both a and c.
17. Which element is *not* a common element of fraud?
    a. Concealment.
    b. Coercion.
    c. Conversion.
    d. Theft act.
    e. None of the above.

SHORT CASES

Case 1

Cal Smith Jr. is the night manager at a local doughnut shop that is doing very well. The shop sells doughnuts 7 days a week, 24 hours a day. Cal runs the graveyard shift by himself, since none of the other employees want to work at night. Since opening six months ago, Cal has not been able to find anyone to work for him and therefore has never missed one day of work. Cal makes his deposit every morning before going home.

Cal feels that he is overworked and underpaid. The franchise owner, Kenny Jones, has praised Cal for his hard work and dedication to the company. Kenny's only concern is that, once or twice a week, an entire batch of traditional glazed doughnuts has been thrown away because of over-baking. Despite these problems, Cal maintains a clean work environment and is considered a valuable employee.

Recently, Cal has yelled at people on shifts before and after him for seemingly insignificant reasons. He was hired as manager because he gets along with everyone and is usually easygoing. His recent irritability could stem from the fact that business is slowing down and he does not have much interaction with anyone at night. He also has been complaining that he has not been getting very much sleep. One day, Cal came to work in a new BMW M3, the car of his dreams. Cal said that his dad helped him buy the car.

1. What areas of the business are most at risk for fraud?
2. Identify any symptoms of fraud that appear to exist at the doughnut shop.
3. What steps could be taken to reduce opportunities for fraud?

Case 2

James Davis owns a small Internet service provider business. Recently, customers have been complaining that they are overcharged and are not receiving timely customer service. Billing rates seem to increase without notice.

Five years ago, James used funding from several different investors in order to start his Internet service. Currently, he has 17 outstanding bills to be paid, all with late charges. Five of the bills include notices stating that lawsuits are pending. Also, he has not paid dividends to investors in two years.

Every day, James drives either his Mercedes Benz or his new Lexus to work. Before starting the business, James drove only one car, a Suzuki Samurai. James now lives in a palatial home and owns very expensive furniture. Employees constantly ask James for new equipment, but the "boss" refuses to update the old equipment. Two weeks ago, James was irate and fired one of his accounting clerks for not depositing some checks on time. James is known for losing his temper.

1. Discuss any fraud symptoms that are present in this case.
2. Why would complaints from customers be a fraud symptom?

Case 3

Joan Longhurst, along with three of her best friends, started her own ranching operation in Hawaii. The business began with two bulls and 20 heifers. After their first year, the partners were turning profits, and everything seemed to be going well. The heifers were bred each year by using a patented new technique, and the steer population grew to 100 in two years. Most heifers would produce twins, and 90 percent were male. This allowed for future breeding of the remaining 10 percent.

New investment was needed, so limited partners were invited to join the partnership with an initial investment of $20,000 each. The partnership interests were advertised as "hot in the hands" and "very exclusive." In interviews, Joan described the investments as a "double-your-money, sure thing." She stated that the best way to get in was to act within 10 days of the initial offering of the investment. The annual report of the company showed enormous growth, with the pro forma statements predicting phenomenal success. Because of the exorbitant food prices in Hawaii, Joan says she can demand a premium for all cattle sold. Based on this scenario, what symptoms of fraud exist?

Case 4

The text states that tips and complaints are not evidence of fraud but instead are fraud symptoms. Do you agree with this statement? Why?

Case 5

You are a staff auditor on a very important audit engagement. You are assigned to audit two parts of your client's purchasing department. After several days of studying purchase orders and sales invoices, you notice that three vendors have identical addresses. After further examination, you notice that the documents only have one of the two required signatures for purchases of those accounts. You decided to interview the purchasing manager in charge of those accounts, but you discover that he is "out to lunch." While you are waiting for him, you notice through his office window a very nice Bose™ stereo system. It's the same system you have been wanting, but will only be able to afford after you make partner. What symptoms of fraud exist?

Case 6

You have been hired by a small firm to analyze its accounts receivable department and assess how susceptible it is to fraud. The company operates a table manufacturing facility. The only employee in accounts receivable is Joanne, an employee of 10 years. Joanne opens all cash receipts, credits the clients' accounts, and deposits the money at the bank. What fraud-related

risks does this company face? What changes, if any, should be made?

Case 7

Many people feel that it is the job of auditors to detect fraud. What circumstances make it difficult for auditors to detect fraud? Who is more likely to be in a better position to detect fraud?

Case 8

1. According to the chapter, which groups (auditors, managers, coworkers, company accountants, or friends) are in the best position to observe fraud symptoms in each of the three elements of fraud?
2. Which group is surprisingly absent in each element?

Case 9

Sally was aware of a fraud being committed by one of her coworkers, but she never reported it. What are some possible reasons for her hesitancy to come forward?

Case 10

John Adams is the manager at a local store. The store opened four years ago and has been doing very well. With current business growing, John decided to hire Peter O'Riley to work as an accountant. When Peter started working at the store, he found several things that appeared unusual. For example, six receiving documents have been lost, the general ledger is out of balance, one customer has complained that he is continually overcharged, and another customer complains that he does not receive timely service. John lives in an expensive house and has several beautiful sports cars.

Discuss whether fraud could be occurring. Does evidence of fraud exist, or are only fraud symptoms present?

Case 11

Consider the three aspects of the fraud triangle. If you were hired by the board of directors to tell them what they could do to prevent fraud, what general activities would you tell them to engage in? List four or more activities for each of the three dimensions of the fraud triangle listed here.

- Attitude/Rationalization
- Motivation/Pressure
- Opportunity

CASE STUDIES

Case Study 1

The balance sheet and income statement for ABC Company for the years 2011 and 2012 are as follows:

CASE STUDY 1

BALANCE SHEET	2011	2012
Cash	$ 460	$ 300
Accounts receivable	620	480
Inventory	1,000	730
Total assets	$2,080	$1,510
Accounts payable	$580	$ 310
Notes payable	500	100
Common stock	400	400
Retained earnings	600	700
Total liabilities and stockholders' equity	$2,080	$1,510
Income Statement		
Net sales	$ 550	$ 840
Cost of goods sold	120	160
Gross margin	$ 430	$ 680
Expenses:		
Salaries	$ 100	$ 150
Warehousing costs	80	120
Advertising	60	90
Taxes	45	75
Total expenses	$ 285	$ 435
Net income	$ 145	$ 245

Questions

1. Perform vertical and/or horizontal analysis of the statements and identify two things that appear to be unusual and could be possible symptoms of fraud.

Case Study 2

In his own words, Daniel Jones was "The Dude." With his waist-long dreadlocks, part-time rock band, and well-paid job managing a company's online search directory—he seemed to have it all. Originally from Germany, Jones, now age 32, earned his doctorate and taught at the University of Munich before coming to the United States, where he started his career in computers. In 1996, Jones started working with the company as a director of operations for U.S.-Speech Engineering Service and Retrieval Technology—working on a new, closely guarded search engine tied to the company's .net concept.

The company allows employees to order an unlimited amount of software and hardware, at no cost, for business purposes. Between December 2001 and November 2002, Jones ordered or used his assistant and other employees (including a high school intern) to order nearly 1,700 pieces of software which had very low cost but were worth a lot on the street. He then resold them for reduced prices—reaping millions. When items with a cost of goods sold of more than $1,000 are ordered, an e-mail is sent to the employee's direct supervisor, who must click on an "Approve" button before the order is filled. In no individual order was the cost of goods more than $1,000—he made sure none of the orders required a supervisor's approval. The loosely controlled internal ordering system reflects the trust the company puts in its employees.

In June, FBI agents said they saw Jones exchanging a large box of software for cash in a department store parking lot. The FBI contacted the company's security and began monitoring Jones' bank accounts. Previously, one account with his bank had an average balance of $2,159. In a short time, however, the average balance ballooned to $129,775. Another account at another bank showed irregular deposits totaling $500,000—none of which appeared to be from any legitimate income or other source.

Investigators also noted that Jones purchased a Ferrari F355 Berlinetta, a Jaguar XJ6, and traded in lesser vehicles for a Hummer, a Mercedes 500SEL, and a Harley-Davidson motorcycle. He also bought an $8,000 platinum diamond ring, a $2,230 wristwatch, and a $4,000 bracelet. "You figured that I like big boy's toys by looking at some of my pictures," Jones wrote on his personal Web page. "I just can't resist." The Dude's Web page includes a camera for monitoring his cat and photos of his yacht, cars, and other treasures. For a relatively low-level manager, it was an impressive collection. But at his company, where teenage software engineers can earn more than company directors, no one batted an eyelid.

A neighbor across the street from Jones said that he was clearly wealthy, but not flamboyant with his money. He described Jones as an intelligent man who didn't flaunt his education, would loan neighbors tools, and was always friendly. The neighbor was surprised to hear the accusations against someone he called his friend. All he knew about Jones was that he was a good neighbor who loved cars. "He was very, very helpful. The few times I had problems with my PC, he'd come and help straighten them out," the neighbor said. "They are just ideal neighbors. I feel terrible for him and his wife." Jones and his wife lived in a modest 1960s split-level home.

In 2001, he joined the city's Rotary Club, "where he seemed more outgoing and personable than the stereotype techie," said a local jeweler and immediate past president of the club. "He seemed like what I would expect a genius software developer to be."

The Dude was fired from the company in December 2002, shortly after the fraud was discovered. He has been charged with 15 counts of wire, mail, and computer fraud—with each count carrying a maximum of fives years in prison. He is expected to remain in custody until his preliminary hearing.

Questions

1. Describe the symptoms of fraud that might be evident to a fellow employee.
2. Recently, his employer has been putting more emphasis on controlling cost. With the slowing of overall technology spending, executives have ordered managers to closely monitor expenses and have given vice presidents greater responsibility for balance sheets. What positive or negative consequences might this pose to the company in future fraud prevention?
3. As discussed previously, all frauds involve the following key elements: perceived pressure, perceived opportunity, and rationalization. Describe two of the key elements of the Jones fraud— pressure and opportunity.
4. From the scenario, what measures has the company taken to prevent fraud? In what ways could the company improve?

Case Study 3

In June of a recent year, allegations of fraud regarding repair contracts for work on board U.S. Naval Ships (USNS) were reported to law enforcement agents. The allegations indicated that fraud was rampant and could possibly impact the seaworthiness of these vessels. Employees from ABC Construction, Inc. (ABC), the entity in charge of getting contracts for USNS, were demanding that a high volume of contracts be processed, and they were also demanding faster processing time for these contracts. When some employees started quitting because of increased pressure, ABC made sure it did not get attention from the federal government. ABC had close relationships with some of the subcontractors, but had always kept totally independent from these subcontractors. A task force of agents from the FBI, Defense Criminal Investigative Service, and the

Naval Criminal Investigative Service was quickly formed to investigate. The task force agreed that the most effective approach to investigating possible fraud was the use of an undercover operation utilizing a covert contracting business.

Questions

1. What are some of the symptoms of fraud in this case?
2. What questions would you ask yourself about fraud symptoms that might help you investigate this fraud?
3. Why would an undercover operation be the most effective approach to investigate?

Case Study 4

MHZ, Inc., is a high-tech company that produces miniature computer processor chips. The company is one of the most successful companies in its industry because it is always developing faster and more efficient processors in order to maintain a competitive advantage. Sales and earnings have increased significantly in recent quarters causing the company's stock price to rise.

Hal Smith was recently appointed to be the new chief financial officer (CFO) of MHZ. Hal is 45 years old and has worked at MHZ for over 15 years. Hal was promoted to CFO because he has an excellent understanding of MHZ and the high-tech industry. Hal is well respected and knows everyone very well. At the close of the third quarter, Mark Jones, CEO of MHZ, asked Hal and management to meet with him to discuss year-end projections. During the meeting, Hal noticed that Mark and other members appeared to be stressed and nervous that the company might not meet analysts' expectations because it had lost a contract with one of its major vendors. In the following weeks, Hal noticed Mark and other key employees began to appear more stressed and worried than normal. In addition, Hal recognized that Mark and one of his internal auditors would work continually into the night. At the close of the fourth quarter, everyone cheered when the company managed to meet its earnings expectations. Hal was relieved to see that the company had achieved its goal, but he couldn't help wondering if something suspicious was going on.

Questions

1. List and briefly describe the six different types of fraud symptoms.
2. Describe the different fraud symptoms present at MHZ, Inc.
3. Assume that Hal has access to the company's income statement and balance sheet. What types of

analysis can Hal perform to determine whether fraud may be occurring at MHZ?

INTERNET ASSIGNMENTS

1. How many different Web sites can you find dealing with fraud auditing and detection? Try a few different search strings in Google or another search engine and see what sites are available.
2. Locate the Web site of the American Society of Questioned Document Examiners (ASQDE) at www.asqde.org. What is the ASQDE? What is its purpose?

END NOTES

1. http://207.36.165.114/NewOrleans/Papers/1401559.pdf.

2. www.nysscpa.org/cpajournal/2004/204/essentials/p32.htm, accessed June 1, 2004.

3. Much of this discussion came from the HIH Royal Commission report and from articles that have been written about the report such as those found at the following Web site: www.smh.com.au/articles/2003/04/16/1050172655327.html.

CHAPTER **6**

Data-Driven Fraud Detection

LEARNING OBJECTIVES

After studying this chapter, you should be able to:

- **Describe the importance of data-driven fraud detection, including the difference between accounting anomalies and fraud.**

- **Explain the steps in the data analysis process.**

- **Be familiar with common data analysis packages.**

- **Understand the principles of data access, including Open Database Connectivity (ODBC), text import, and data warehousing.**

- **Perform basic data analysis procedures for fraud detection.**

- **Read and analyze a Matosas matrix.**

- **Understand how fraud is detected by analyzing financial statements.**

TO THE STUDENT

This chapter describes one of the most exciting developments in fraud investigation: data-driven fraud analysis. This emerging field is a synthesis of many different knowledge areas, including fraud, audit, investigation, database theory, and analysis techniques. Because it requires more skills than traditional fraud investigation, data-driven fraud analysis provides a new opportunity for those willing to learn concepts from these various fields. As you read the chapter, consider your own skill set and what other classes you might take to best prepare yourself for these new fraud detection methods.

On April 26, 2007, the *Daily Tar Heel*, a newspaper at the University of North Carolina at Chapel Hill, published the following story:

> *A recently retired University employee of 30 years was discovered to have provided the Social Security number (SSN) of a dead person, a state auditor's report revealed. ...*
>
> *... In January an audit of UNC-CH Hospitals revealed that 17 of its employees had provided false SSNs. Eight were fired, and nine others resigned. ... The auditor's office also has investigated the Department of Motor Vehicles, N.C. Central University and the Department of Justice. At the DMV, it was found that about 27,000 fraudulent SSNs had been provided to obtain driver's licenses, Mears said. The office takes SSNs from the payroll office of the agency being audited and cross references them with valid numbers in the Social Security Administration's database.*

This example shows the application of a very simple **data-driven fraud detection** method: comparing SSNs with a list of valid numbers or with a list of known invalid numbers.

A common **scheme** is for people to purchase illegal SSNs "on the street" that they use in obtaining drivers' licenses and employment. Street dealers either use identity theft or SSNs of people who have recently passed away when they create illegal Social Security cards.

The U.S. Social Security Administration (SSA) publishes a monthly list of SSNs that are no longer in use—normally because of the death of their owners. It also hosts a service to validate lists of active SSNs submitted to it. The North Carolina state auditor's office, like many other organizations nationwide, subscribes to this monthly download and validation service.

Even though the organizations in this example used internal checks for SSN validity, perpetrators were able to use fraudulent SSNs in gaining employment and drivers' licenses. By using a simple database comparison, the auditor's office found thousands of cases of fraudulent use.

The example highlights the trend toward data-driven, full-population fraud detection that has become popular in recent years. For many, including the authors of this textbook, these methods represent state-of-the-art fraud detection today. Students who learn and understand the application of these methods will be well prepared for the future as the field transitions into these approaches.

Anomalies and Frauds

Auditors have analyzed data to detect fraud and anomalies for many decades. In particular, the advent of the personal computer, with applications like VisiCalc, Lotus 1-2-3, Excel, dBASE, and Access, provided auditors with user-oriented and accessible tools to analyze large and small data sets.

However, it is important to realize that the methods auditors used (and still often use) were based on traditional audit procedures like statistical sampling, spot checking, and control totals. While the tools became electronic, many auditors still performed analysis techniques tailored to manual checking methods. Unfortunately, these traditional methods were more suited to finding anomalies than fraud.

Accounting anomalies are primarily caused by control weaknesses. They are not intentional mistakes; they are simply problems in the system caused by failures in systems, procedures, and policies. For example, a typical anomaly might be double payment of invoices because of printer errors. If a system often has printer errors (such as running out of paper or ink) and does not correctly respond to these errors, employees may simply reenter the invoices and cause two credits to Cash in the journal entry table. This is a simple error, but it illustrates several attributes of control and system weaknesses.

First, anomalies are not intentional. They do not represent fraud and normally do not result in legal action being taken. There is no "criminal" other than a weak system or an employee that needs to be censured or reprimanded.

Second, anomalies will be found throughout a data set. For example, the double-payment-of-invoices anomaly would likely occur every time a printer failure happens. If paper or ink problems occur every two weeks, the problem will be found in the journal entry table at the corresponding intervals. An auditor simply needs to take a statistical sample of the data set to discover the anomaly because the anomaly is *spread throughout the data set*. If you look at the entire data set as a haystack, the anomaly will be spread fairly evenly throughout the haystack. Taking a handful of hay brings about good chances that you'll catch the anomaly.

Fraud is different: it is the intentional subvertion of controls by intelligent human beings. Perpetrators cover their tracks by creating false documents or changing records in database systems. Evidence of fraud may be found in very few transactions—sometimes only one or two. Rather than being spread throughout the data set, fraudulent symptoms are found in single cases or limited areas of the data set. Detecting a fraud is like finding the proverbial "needle in the haystack."

Audit Sampling and Fraud

Because discovery of anomalies has been a very important part of financial statement, control, and compliance audits in recent decades, it is not surprising that statistical sampling has become a standard auditing procedure. Sampling is often the subject of entire chapters and sections of auditing textbooks. It is an effective analysis procedure for finding routine anomalies spread throughout a data set.

In contrast, sampling is usually a poor analysis technique when looking for a needle in a haystack. If you sample at a 5 percent rate, you effectively take a 95 percent chance that you will miss the few fraudulent transactions! Fraud examiners must take a different approach; they should normally complete full-population analysis to ensure that the "needles" are found.

CAUTION *Because of the nature of fraud, sampling can undermine an otherwise well-planned fraud investigation.*

Fortunately, almost all data in today's audits and fraud investigations are electronic. Computers can often analyze full populations almost as fast as they can analyze samples. Certainly, some tasks will always require sampling. But the majority of tasks can be analyzed at a full-population level without significant increases in cost or time.

When given a task to complete—whether as part of an audit or a full fraud investigation—the benefits and costs of full-population analysis should be considered. Given the right tools and techniques, full-population analysis is often an attractive option.

The Data Analysis Process

Data analysis for fraud detection requires reengineered methods to be effective. Simply applying yesterday's sampling-based techniques to full populations should be considered a less effective method. Fraud investigators must be prepared to learn new methodologies, software tools, and analysis techniques to successfully take advantage of data-oriented methods.

Consider the traditional approach to fraud detection: it is usually a reactive approach that starts when an anonymous tip is received or when a symptom is detected. It is considered a reactive approach because the investigator waits for a reason (predication of fraud) to investigate.

Data-driven fraud detection is proactive in nature. The investigator no longer has to wait for a tip to be received; instead, he or she brainstorms the schemes and symptoms that might be found and looks for them. It should be considered a hypothesis-testing approach: the investigator makes hypotheses and tests to see if each one holds true.

The proactive (data-driven) method of fraud detection is shown in Figure 6.1. These steps are described in the next sections.

STOP & THINK *How are the six steps in the data-driven approach to fraud detection different from the traditional reactive approach?*

Step 1: Understand the Business

The proactive detection process starts with an understanding of the business or unit being examined. Since each business environment is different—even within the same industry or firm—fraud detection is largely an analytical process. Since examiners are going to make hypotheses about the schemes that could exist, they must have a good understanding of the business processes and procedures.

The same fraud detection procedures cannot be applied generically to all businesses or even to different units of the same organization. The proactive method is an analytical approach that takes analytical thinking on

FIGURE 6.1   THE PROACTIVE METHOD OF FRAUD DETECTION

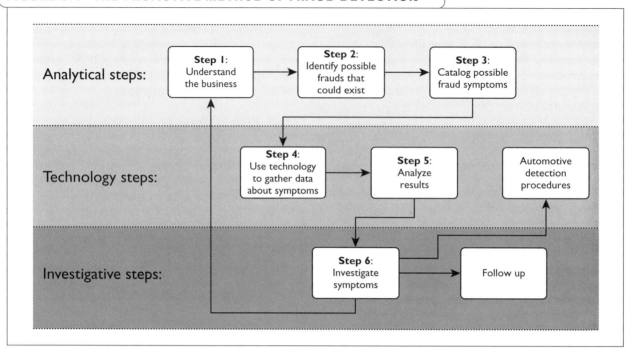

the part of the investigator. Rather than rely on generic fraud detection methods or generic queries, examiners must gain intimate knowledge of each specific organization and its processes. Having a detailed understanding underlies the entire strategic fraud detection process.

It is often useful to create a team of individuals to perform proactive detection. This ensures that the effort contains expertise from many backgrounds, including business experts, fraud detectors, database programmers, auditors, and other interested parties.

Several potential methods to gather information about a business are as follows:

- *Tour the business, department, or plant*
- *Become familiar with competitor processes*
- *Interview key personnel (ask them where fraud might be found)*
- *Analyze financial statements and other accounting information*
- *Review process documentation*
- *Work with auditors and security personnel*
- *Observe employees performing their duties*

Step 2: Identify Possible Frauds That Could Exist

Once the team members are confident in their understanding of the business, the next step is to identify what possible frauds might exist or could occur in the operation being examined. This **risk assessment** step requires an understanding of the nature of different frauds, how they occur, and what symptoms they exhibit. The fraud identification process begins by conceptually dividing the business unit into its individual functions or cycles.

Most businesses or even subunits are simply too large and diverse for examiners to consider simultaneously. Dividing the business into its individual functions or cycles helps focus the detection process. For example, an examiner might decide to focus directly on the manufacturing plant, the collections department, or the purchasing function.

In this step, people involved in the business functions are interviewed. Fraud examiners should ask questions such as the following:

- *Who are the key players in the business?*
- *What types of employees, vendors, or contractors are involved in business transactions?*
- *How do insiders and outsiders interact with each other?*
- *What types of fraud have occurred or been suspected in the past?*
- *What types of fraud could be committed against the company or on behalf of the company?*

- *How could employees or management acting alone commit fraud?*
- *How could vendors or customers acting alone commit fraud?*
- *How could vendors or customers working in collusion with employees commit fraud?*

Also during this stage, the fraud detection team should brainstorm potential frauds by type and player. The likely occurrence of the various frauds should be considered, and in the end, a laundry list of frauds that will be studied should be developed.

Step 3: Catalog Possible Fraud Symptoms

As you learned previously, fraud itself is rarely seen; only its symptoms are usually observed. What may appear to be a fraud symptom often ends up being explained by nonfraud factors, which creates confusion, delay, and additional expense for the fraud team. For example, a company's accounts receivable balance might be increasing at a rate that appears to be unrealistically high. The increasing receivable balance could be the result of fraud, the result of major customers having financial difficulties, or a change in credit terms. In addition, no empirical evidence suggests that the presence of more apparent red flags increases the probability of fraud (although the more confirmed red flags there are, the higher the probability of fraud), or that certain red flags have greater predictive ability than other red flags.

Even with these weaknesses, however, identifying red flags or fraud symptoms is often the best—and sometimes the only—practical method of proactive fraud detection. All auditing fraud standards, for example, recommend the red flag approach for detecting fraud. Although tips and reports account for the detection of most serious frauds, they usually occur too late, after the fraud has grown to the stage that the tipster overcomes his or her natural reluctance to report it.

Types of Fraud Symptoms

As discussed in Chapter 5, fraud symptoms can be divided into the following groups:

- *Accounting anomalies*
- *Internal control weaknesses*
- *Analytical anomalies*
- *Extravagant lifestyles*
- *Unusual behaviors*
- *Tips and complaints*

Note that up to and including Step 3, the data-driven approach is purely analytical. No data have been collected, and results have not been analyzed.

FIGURE 6.2 RED FLAGS OF KICKBACKS

Analytical Symptoms
- Increasing prices
- Larger order quantities
- Increasing purchases from favored vendor
- Decreasing purchases from other vendors
- Decreasing quality

Behavioral Symptoms
- Buyer doesn't relate well to other buyers and vendors
- Buyer's work habits change unexpectedly

Lifestyle Symptoms
- Buyer lives beyond known salary
- Buyer purchases more expensive automobile
- Buyer builds more expensive home

Control Symptoms
- All transactions with one buyer and one vendor
- Use of unapproved vendors

Document Symptoms
- 1099s from vendor to buyer's relative

Tips and Complaints
- Anonymous complaints about buyer or vendor
- Unsuccessful vendor complaints
- Quality complaints about purchased products

The first three steps are generic and can be applied in any type of organization or subunit. This strategic approach produces a comprehensive and zero-based analysis of the specific types of fraud that might be found in various business entities.

In Step 3, the fraud examiner should carefully consider what type of symptoms (red flags), described previously, could be present in the potential frauds identified in Step 2. A matrix, tree diagram, or brainstorming map can be created to correlate specific symptoms with specific possible frauds.

For example, kickbacks from vendors to buyers might generate the symptoms shown in Figure 6.2. In a real case, the list of symptoms would be more specific to the business being investigated.

Step 4: Use Technology to Gather Data about Symptoms

Once symptoms are defined and correlated (catalogued) with specific frauds, supporting data are extracted from corporate databases, online Web sites, and other sources. While the previous steps were general, analytical exercises, searching for symptoms is specific to each company and even each unit or cycle in a company. Searching and analysis are normally done with data analysis applications (discussed later in this chapter) or with custom **structured query language (SQL)** queries and scripts that are specific to the client.

The deliverable of this step is a set of data that matches the symptoms identified in the previous step. Since real-world data sources are noisy (meaning they contain errors from a variety of sources), searching for symptoms is often an iterative process. For example, the first run of queries and algorithms usually generates thousands of hits. Since most businesses do not have thousands of frauds occurring, it is almost always necessary to analyze the results to find trends and other cases that do not constitute fraud. After inspection, the fraud examiner usually modifies and reruns the analysis to filter out the nonfraud results. A second run might produce a few hundred results. Subsequent filtering and runs will continue to hone the results until a manageable set of indicators is found.

Step 5: Analyze Results

Once anomalies are refined and determined by the examiners to be likely indications of fraud, they are analyzed using either traditional or technology-based methods. Since computer-based analysis is often the most efficient method of investigation, every effort should be made to screen results using computer algorithms. Investigation of leads should only be done on anomalies that cannot be explained through continued analysis. Examiners normally work with auditors and security personnel to identify reasons for anomalies. They talk with coworkers, investigate paper documents, and contact outside individuals.

Several fraud analysis techniques are presented later in this chapter. These include discovery of outliers, digital analysis, stratification and summarization, trending, and text matching.

One advantage of the deductive approach is its potential reuse. Analyses can often be automated and integrated directly into corporate systems in a way that provides real-time analysis and detection of fraud as well as prevention of known fraud types. Subsequent runs through the deductive steps reach economies of scale because many of the steps can be reused.

Step 6: Investigate Symptoms

The final step of the data-driven approach is investigation into the most promising indicators. Investigators should continue to use computer analyses to provide support and detail. Investigation of fraud is the subject of the next section of this book.

The primary advantage of the data-driven approach is the investigator takes charge of the fraud investigation process. Instead of merely waiting for tips or other indicators to become egregious enough to show on their own, the data-driven approach can highlight frauds while they are still small. Instead of simply throwing a "fishing line" into the water and waiting for a bite, this approach allows the investigator to dive in and directly target potential frauds.

The primary drawback to the data-driven approach is that it can be more expensive and time intensive than the traditional approach. Since the brainstorming process in Steps 2 and 3 usually results in hundreds of potential indicators, it can take a significant amount of time to complete Steps 4 and 5.

Appendix A at the end of this chapter presents two examples of the data-driven approach.

Data Analysis Software

In recent years, many **data analysis software** packages have been developed to aid investigators. As data analysis is a large field with many uses, it is not possible to list all the available software in this chapter. However, several software packages are widely used by auditors and investigators for data analysis. These include the following:

- *ACL Audit Analytics is the data application used most widely by auditors worldwide. It has been adopted by most major accounting firms and is a stable, powerful platform for data analysis. While its primary focus is auditing (including techniques like sampling), a fraud module is also available. ACL also includes a programming language called ACLScript that makes automation of procedures possible. A limited academic version of ACL for Windows is included with this book.*

- *CaseWare's IDEA is ACL technology's primary competitor. Feature for feature, it is very similar to ACL, but the interface is slightly different. Some users prefer ACL; others prefer IDEA. As with ACL, IDEA's primary focus is auditing, but recent versions include an increasing number of fraud techniques. IDEA's programming language is similar to Visual Basic and makes automation of procedures possible.*

- *Picalo is an open source data analysis toolkit written by one of the authors of this book. It is similar in features to ACL and IDEA, but it adds the concept of detectlets, which are small plug-ins* *that discover specific indicators such as the matching of vendor addresses with employee addresses or comparisons of invoice amounts with **Benford's Law**. Detectlets present a wizard-based interface for context-specific fraud detection. End users can write detectlets, and they can contribute them to a shared online repository. Picalo can be downloaded for free at www.picalo.org.*

- ***Microsoft Office + ActiveData** is a plug-in for Microsoft Office that provides enhanced data analysis procedures. Since it is based in Excel and Access, it inherits the native capabilities of Office, such as queries, reports, numerical analysis, and Visual Basic. This product is a good option for users who want a familiar interface and less expensive alternative to ACL and IDEA.*

Other software that should be noted includes SAS and SPSS (**statistical analysis** programs with available fraud modules); traditional programming languages like Java, Perl, Python, Ruby, Visual Basic, and others; and a host of specialized data mining packages available.

Data Access

The most important (and often most difficult) step in data analysis is gathering the right data in the right format during the right time period. Often, just getting an understanding of the available data can be a daunting task for investigators who are under time and cost constraints. For example, at one organization, the IT department identified over 400 potential databases in the company that might be useful for data-driven fraud detection. It took many days for the investigator to narrow the list down to two primary databases the team would search.

During the last few decades, most businesses have standardized on *relational* databases, especially for financial, payroll, and purchasing systems. This standardization is a significant benefit to investigators—if they can learn the basics of table structure, field types, primary and foreign key relationships, and query syntax, they can access data in almost any company. A discussion of relational databases is beyond the scope of this book; however, it is a must for any investigator who wants to do data analysis. Even though Microsoft Access is often not considered a "professional" database (like Oracle, MySQL, or SQL Server), it is an excellent way to learn relational database principles. Those wanting to perform quality data analysis are encouraged to learn the Microsoft Access platform by reading online

tutorials, taking an entry-level database class, or purchasing a help book.

Open Database Connectivity

Open Database Connectivity (ODBC) is a standard method of querying data from corporate relational databases. It is a connector between analysis applications like ACL, IDEA, and Picalo and databases like Oracle, SQL Server, and MySQL. It is usually the best way to retrieve data for analysis because (1) it can retrieve data in real time, (2) it allows use of the powerful SQL language for searching and filtering, (3) it allows repeated pulls for iterative analysis, and (4) it retrieves metadata like column types and relationships directly.

ODBC is already included with most operating systems. It is a system-wide setting rather than an application-level setting. Once a connection is created on a computer, it is available in all data analysis applications installed on that computer. For example, Windows users set up ODBC connections in the control panel under "Data Sources (ODBC)."

Each database vendor publishes ODBC drivers for its products. These drivers can be downloaded for free from vendor Web sites. For example, a Web search of "Oracle ODBC drivers" finds Oracle's download page with drivers for most versions of its products. Once a driver is installed, it shows up in the control panel.

Many IT departments are not comfortable giving out ODBC connections because of security and privacy issues. One way to compromise with these real concerns is to ask the IT department for a *read-only* connection to a *limited number* of tables in the database. This ensures that data are not modified and allows efficient use of system resources. As an alternative to extracting data from databases using ODBC, ACL has server-based technology that enables auditors and fraud examiners to analyze data directly from Oracle, DB2, and Microsoft SQL Server databases.

Suppose Mark is asked to investigate a large chain of ice cream shops for fraud. Since he has no idea where frauds might be occurring in the company, he decides to use the data-driven approach to fraud investigation. He works with the company to create a list of fraud schemes and indicators for which he will search. The following describes the process he goes through to set up an ODBC connection:

1. Mark contacts the IT department and asks for a description of the databases at the company. He determines that the *genjournal* database holds much of the information he needs to search for the indicators.

2. Mark asks the IT department what kind of database the *genjournal* is running on. He is told it is PostgreSQL version 8.1.9. He asks for a read-only ODBC connection to the database, and after some discussion, is given access.
3. The IT department gives Mark the server IP address, a username and password, and other technical information required to set up the connection.
4. Mark searches www.postgresql.org for the appropriate driver and installs it to his computer. He sets up a connection in the control panel using the user information provided by the IT department.
5. Mark opens Picalo (or ACL, IDEA, MS Access, etc.) and selects *File | New* Database Connection. He configures his connection and finishes the connection wizard. He now has access to all the tables in *genjournal* as if they were regular Picalo tables.

Text Import

Several text formats exist for manually transferring data from one application (i.e., a database) to another (i.e., an analysis application). The most common of these, is a plain text file that contains one row per database record. Columns are separated by a delimiting character like a comma, a tab, or another character. Specific implementations of **delimited text** are called **comma separated values (CSV)** and **tab separated values (TSV)**. The actual delimited text format used is merely a preference of the person exporting the data.

Another common text format for transfer of data is **fixed-width format**, which again uses one row in the file per record in the database. However, rather than using a delimiting character like a comma to denote columns, spaces are used to pad each field value to a standard position. For example, Column 1 may be assigned positions 1–10, Column 2 may be assigned positions 11–17, and so forth. If the value in Column 1 is "Abcorp," four extra spaces are added to the end of the name to take the entire first 10 positions. Fixed-width format is usually easier for human readers to understand than delimited text, but it requires more work to import (because exact column positions must be described to the software). It is most common in older software packages and mainframe applications.

Many other text-based formats exist, such as extensible markup language (XML) (used in many new applications) and EBCDIC (used primarily on IBM mainframes).

ODBC is generally faster and more robust than text file import. Since text files only include plain text,

investigators must assign column types and relationships during import. Different methods of encoding text files, like CSV, TSV, and EBCDIC, also cause problems when applications use different standards or are simply programmed less correctly than they should be. However, since ODBC connections are often unavailable, text import is a common task.

STOP & THINK *What are the relative advantages and disadvantages of ODBC compared with text file import?*

Hosting a Data Warehouse

Many investigators simply import data directly into their analysis application, effectively creating a **data warehouse**. For example, data are imported, stored, and analyzed within ACL. This provides an all-in-one solution for the investigator.

However, while most programs are capable of storing millions of records in multiple tables, most analysis applications are relatively poor data repositories. It should not be surprising that databases are the optimal method of storing data—this is what databases were created to do. This approach allows each application to do what it does best.

A best practices model for data storage and analysis is a two-stage import. This includes hosting a data warehouse on the investigator's computer, or even better, on an inexpensive server controlled by the investigator. Instead of data being directly imported from the corporate database into an analysis application, a set of pre-analysis queries transfers data from the corporate database into the data warehouse. These queries can summarize data, convert data types and scales, and perform other modifications to make later analysis more efficient and effective.

Once the data are in the data warehouse, the investigator connects (via ODBC) his or her analysis application to the data warehouse for primary analysis procedures. Since the warehouse is within the investigator's direct control, it can be continually improved to provide better and better results over time.

Any database, including Microsoft Access, can be used to host a data warehouse. The following are notable options for many investigators that are inexpensive but scalable to large amounts of data:

- *MySQL is a powerful, free database available at www.mysql.com. MySQL runs many of the largest sites on the Internet and handles the capacity well.*

- *PostgreSQL is a standards-based, free database available at www.postgresql.org. It can be fine-tuned to handle almost any load.*
- *SQL Server is a Microsoft product to which many investigators may have site licenses or other legal but inexpensive access. SQL Server is a great option for those wanting a familiar Windows interface.*

ACL offers server editions upon which investors can create a centralized, secure and managed environment where all pertinent data (in flat files, PDF, print files or in databases) can be stored and accessed using the ACL desktop product. It is through this mechanism that a collaborative analytical environment can be established to address the challenges of distributed, PC-based analytics.

Data Analysis Techniques

Once data are retrieved and stored in a data warehouse, analysis application, or text file, they need to be analyzed to identify transactions that match the indicators identified earlier in the process. As with the discussion of relational databases, a full treatment of data analysis techniques would take an entire course and textbook. However, this section will go over a few analysis techniques that are most commonly used by fraud investigators. Readers are encouraged to use this discussion as a jumping point to more powerful analysis techniques found in the statistics, finance, data mining, computer science, and other related fields.

When performing data analysis, it is important to consider the need for multiple indicators of a scheme. Suppose an individual goes to the hospital with a severe headache; after listening to this single symptom and before any additional tests, the doctor immediately declares that the individual has a severe brain tumor and must start radiation therapy. Few would call this doctor a competent medical professional. Fraud investigation is similar: investigators start by discovering one red flag in their analyses. They then follow up by running related analyses to better understand what type of scheme might be occurring. While some indicators (like an employee/vendor address match) are alone quite telling, most schemes require multiple indicators before traditional investigation should commence.

Data Preparation

One of the most important tasks in data analysis is proper preparation of data. This includes type conversion and ensuring consistency of values. Investigators should ensure that number columns are correctly typed as numbers and that text columns are correctly typed as text. For example, the text "1" added to the text "1" yields the text "11" because the two values are concatenated. In addition, if an analysis includes ratio comparisons, division by zero and denominators very close to zero can be a significant concern.

Most software packages have functions for generating **descriptives** about a table. Descriptives include statistical summaries of each column that include control totals, mean, maximum, minimum, standard deviation, number of zero values, number of empty records, and so on. Histograms and other graphs can give further insight into the data being analyzed. Trusting that data are correctly retrieved by IT staff or even directly via ODBC is a common mistake. During each phase of import and preparation, the investigator should print control totals and verify a few cases manually.

One of the most common errors investigators make when analyzing time trends is not standardizing for time (the x-axis if graphed). Production software generally makes an entry each time something happens, such as when a sale is made, a product is ordered, or a timecard is swiped. For example, a table may contain four purchases on Day 1, none on Day 2, and five on Day 3. If these transactions are being analyzed over time, the natural scale is not 1, 2, 3, and so on, as might be expected, but it is actually 1.00, 1.25, 1.50, 1.75, 3.00, 3.20, 3.40, 3.60, and 3.80.

To correctly prepare data for time trend analysis, the time scale must be standardized per some value of time, such as sales *per day*, hours worked *per week*, and so forth. In the previous example, the data should be converted to three records: total purchases for Day 1, for Day 2 (which will be 0.0), and for Day 3. This type of summarization can be difficult with standard database queries, but data analysis applications usually contain functions that summarize over time.

CAUTION *Incorrect data preparation is the most common cause of problems in data-driven fraud investigations. Use control totals, individual case checks, and other methods to ensure that the data are prepared correctly for analysis.*

Digital Analysis

In 1881, the American astronomer Simon Newcomb noticed that the first pages of books of logarithms were much more soiled than the remaining pages. In 1938, Frank Benford applied Newcomb's observation to various types of data sets. According to "Benford's Law," the first digit of random data sets will begin with a 1 more often than with a 2, a 2 more often than with a 3, and so on. In fact, Benford's Law accurately predicts for many kinds of financial data that the first digits of each group of numbers in a set of random numbers will conform to the predicted distribution pattern.

Digital analysis is the art of analyzing the digits that make up numbers like invoice amounts, reported hours, and costs. For example, the numbers 987.59 and 9,811.02 both have a 9 in the first position and an 8 in the second position. People usually assume that the digits 1–9 have an equal chance of appearing in the first position, but reality is very different. The distribution of digits actually follows Benford's Law, which is the primary method of digital analysis in fraud investigations.

Table 6.1 shows the probabilities for Benford's Law on the first two digits. Using this table, a set of invoices from a vendor should have a 1 in the first position 30 percent of the time, a 2 in the first position 18 percent of the time, and so forth, in the invoice total field. Benford's Law applies to *naturally occurring* numbers, such as invoice totals and product costs. It does not apply to assigned or generated numbers, like sequential invoice numbers and SSNs. The numbers must occur naturally in the real world. Benford's Law has been shown to effectively model lake sizes, stock prices, and accounting numbers.

Generally, the distribution is run on only the first position or first and second positions; calculating the probabilities on the third and fourth positions generally produces results so close to zero that conclusions cannot be drawn. To calculate the probability of a number being in the first position, simply use the probabilities in Table 6.1. To calculate the probabilities of two numbers in the first and second positions, multiply the two probabilities from Table 6.1.

Digital analysis is useful for fraud detection because human-generated numbers are usually randomly distributed—they *do not* match Benford's Law. Suppose an employee has set up a phantom vendor and is sending invoices to his company. Unless the employee is wise to digital analysis, the total amounts of the invoices will not match the Benford's Law distribution. This type of analysis is useful in identifying invoices that are not real.

STOP & THINK   *Ask a friend (who isn't biased by reading this) to generate 25 numbers between 0 and 100 on a scratch piece of paper. Calculate the distribution of digits in the first position: how many 1s, how many 2s, and so forth? Do the numbers match Benford's Law? They are likely evenly distributed rather than skewed toward the lower numbers like Benford's Law.*

It is important to realize that a real vendor usually submits some invoices that do not match Benford's Law. The distribution only holds true *across many cases or invoices*. The best method to perform digital analysis is to calculate the average probability for each grouping of data. One way of performing digital analysis is described as follows:

1. Add a new column to the data set that calculates the probability for each row's number digit in the first position. For example, if a set of invoices is being analyzed, look up the probability for the first digit of the invoice price column. If analyzing the first two digits, multiply the probabilities for each row's first and second digits.
2. Summarize the data by vendor, employee, product, or other column that denotes a logical group. In the calculation of each summary, calculate the average and standard deviation of the new Benford's probability column. This step can be accomplished with a summarization procedure described later in this chapter.
3. Sort the results by average probability. Those cases with the lowest probabilities do not match Benford's Law and may need further investigation. Note that the highest probability any case can have is 30 percent (1's in the first digit of all cases), not 100 percent.

TABLE 6.1 BENFORD'S LAW PROBABILITY VALUES

DIGIT	POSITION 1	POSITION 2
0	n/a	0.12
1	0.30	0.11
2	0.18	0.11
3	0.12	0.10
4	0.10	0.10
5	0.08	0.10
6	0.07	0.09
7	0.06	0.09
8	0.05	0.09
9	0.05	0.09

FIGURE 6.3   DIGITAL ANALYSIS—SUPPLY MANAGEMENT

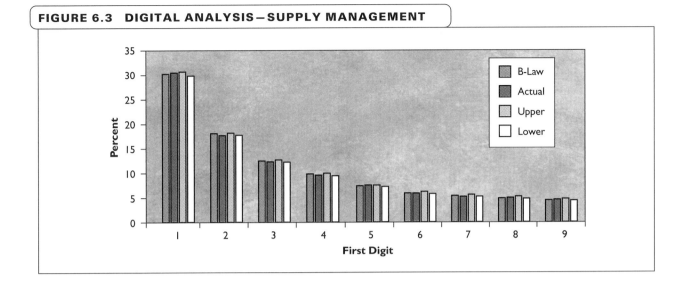

One company, a multibillion-dollar organization we will call Company X, decided to test its data from supplier invoices against Benford's Law. First, Company X analyzed the first digits of dollar amounts on its total population of 820,651 supplier invoices and plotted the results against the expectations of Benford's Law and an upper and lower bound. The graph in Figure 6.3 shows the results.

The company's results for its entire population of supplier invoices tracked Benford's predicted results closely. In fact, for all digits except 2, the actual results fell within Benford's upper and lower bounds. Such close tracking might cause many managers to decide that all is well in supply management and move on to other business. Fortunately, those in charge of this analysis knew that just because the entire population looked good did not rule out the possibility that specific populations would still deviate and thereby indicate fraud. In a follow-up analysis, Company X compared the first digits of dollar amounts on invoices from each supplier with Benford's distribution. The four graphs in Figure 6.4 show the results for four suppliers.

Supplier 1 appears to be in good shape. Its actuals conform closely to Benford's predictions. Although no upper and lower bounds are shown, the actual distribution is obviously within bounds at all points.

Supplier 2 also follows the general slope, but the results are not so precise. Even though the results conform to the general shape of the distribution, the variances are still enough to convince most fraud examiners that a follow-up is in order.

Suppliers 3 and 4 have several major problems. Random distributions of first digits simply do not follow the predicted patterns. Fraud examiners should be highly suspicious of these results. Supplier 4 looks particularly rigged; it appears that someone has attempted to use numbers that would look random. In other words, someone tried to use every digit approximately the same number of times as every other digit.

Using Benford's Law to detect fraud has the major advantage of being the least expensive method to implement and use. And, since you apply it to the company's own databases (that is, you don't query data that are then analyzed by consultants or others), potential suspects are less likely to know you are trying to detect fraud. Fraud perpetrators are certainly easier to catch if they have not ceased their activities because they believe someone suspects them.

The disadvantage of using Benford's Law is that it is tantamount to hunting fraud with a shotgun—you pull the trigger and hope that a few pellets hit something important. To understand what this means, consider Company X again. What would have happened if the analysts had stopped after seeing that all vendor invoices taken together tracked Benford's predictions so closely? They might very well have concluded that their organization was free from fraud.

Another shortfall in relying solely on Benford's Law is that it only broadly identifies the possible existence of fraud; it fails to narrow possibilities to a manageable field of promising leads. Once anomalies are identified by Benford's Law, the fraud examiner must still

FIGURE 6.4   SUPPLIER GRAPHS

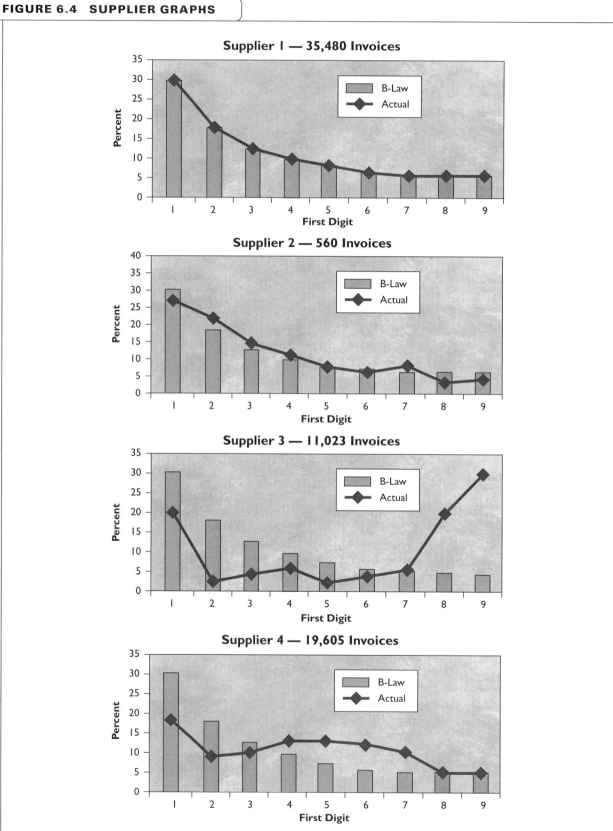

determine the nature of the fraud being perpetrated and the identity of the perpetrator.

Outlier Investigation

One of the most common analyses that fraud investigators perform is identification of outliers. By focusing on outliers, investigators can easily identify cases that do not match the norm. This section shows a statistically sound method of identifying outliers and of knowing how egregious each outlier is.

To illustrate the need for statistics, consider a janitorial company that purchases push brooms. What price point for these brooms would warrant further investigation? Few investigators would start an investigation if brooms were being purchased for $10. But what if the brooms were $25 or $100? Most investigators would begin to feel less comfortable with the purchases, but there may be disagreement on whether to start an investigation. What about $1,500 per broom? Almost all investigators (assuming these were regular brooms) would want to investigate at this point.

The point is that there are definite amounts that do and do not warrant investigation. The difficulty comes in drawing the line between the two. Additionally, the distribution of purchases also makes a difference in the decision; if brooms from one vendor were $25 and similar brooms from all other vendors were $10, investigation would be much more warranted than if brooms from all vendors were $25.

The statistical **z-score** calculation is one of the most powerful and yet simple methods for identifying outliers. It converts data to a standard scale and distribution, regardless of the amounts and variances in the data.[1] The calculation for a z-score is as follows:

$$Z-score = \frac{(Value - Mean)}{Starndard\ Deviation}$$

The numerator pulls each data point to the center (on 0 rather than on the true average). The denominator standardizes the result to a standard deviation of 1. Statistical theory predicts that 68 percent of the data have scores between -1 and 1, 95 percent will have scores between -2 and 2, and 99.7 percent will have scores between -3 and 3. With real-world data, cases sometimes have z-scores of 7, 9, or even 12. As a general rule, values greater than 2 or 3 should be investigated.

You may wonder why the z-score is useful when a data set can simply be sorted to highlight the outliers. For example, a set of invoices sorted by total price will have the same order as the same invoices sorted by the z-score of total price. The reason the z-score is so useful is that it gives the analyst *a sense of how far outside the norm a case is.* While a good understanding of a data set's descriptives will also provide this information, the z-score is a fast, reliable, and standardized way to look at a data set. The values of 1, 2, and 3 essentially mean the same thing across all data sets, even when one data set has dollar ranges in the millions and another has dollar ranges in the hundreds.

The z-score analysis for outliers is often done by adding a new column with the calculation to a data table. This provides the investigator with the original and the z-score side by side for easier analysis. This technique is a good first step when analyzing a new data set.

Stratification and Summarization

Stratification is the splitting of complex data sets into case-specific tables. Most database tables contain cases from a number of vendors, employees, companies, or customers. When cases are analyzed together, the meaning of the data can be impossible to see. For example, consider the janitorial example discussed previously. The purchasing data set will contain purchases not only for push brooms but also for cleaning supplies, uniforms, and many other items. If brooms usually cost $15 and uniforms cost $85, calculating a z-score or even a simple average across both sets of purchases makes little sense. The data set must be stratified into a number of subtables before analysis can be done. In this example, stratification separates the data into a table for push brooms, a table for uniforms, and so forth.

For many data sets, stratification can result in thousands of subtables. While basic programs like spreadsheets make working with this many tables difficult and time consuming, analysis applications like ACL, IDEA, and Picalo make working with lists of tables much easier.

Stratification is one of Picalo's most useful functions. Stratification of a table (by value, formula, or time range) results in a Table List containing a subtable for each case value. Techniques like z-scores, sorts, and digital analysis can be performed once on the Table List, and Picalo will automatically perform the actions individually and correctly on each subtable.

Summarization is an extension of stratification. Instead of producing a number of subtables (one for each case value), summarization runs one or more calculations on the subtables to produce a single record summarizing each case value. Continuing the janitorial example, suppose the investigator wanted to know the average price of each product in the purchasing table.

A summarization function would first stratify the data set by product; it would then calculate the average price for each subtable and return a single table containing two columns: the product name and the average price.

Summarization takes different forms in different applications. Basic summarization usually produces a single results table with one record per case value. **Pivot tables** (also called *cross tables*) are two-dimensional views with cases in one dimension and the calculations in the other. Databases perform basic summarization via the SQL *GROUP BY* command, although the available calculations are limited to basic statistics like means, counts, and standard deviations.

> ### Remember this ...
>
> *Stratification and summarization are similar analysis methods. The difference is that stratification provides the record detail for each group, while summarization provides summary calculations only.*

Time Trend Analysis

Many frauds can be found through analysis of prices, quantities, costs, or other values over time. Kickbacks are a classic case of increasing prices because parties in these schemes usually get greedy: the more product purchased and the higher the prices, the more money made in the scam. One classic kickback scheme resulted in a warehouse full of uniforms that were either too small or too damaged to be used. Despite the oversupply of uniforms, the purchaser kept buying more and more uniforms to increase the kickback earnings. **Time trend analysis** of quantity and price (measured by purchases) or quality (measured by returns and complaints) would have revealed the fraud.

Before time trend analysis can be performed, data must be standardized for time. This data preparation technique was described earlier in the chapter.

The most basic technique for time trend analysis is easy: simply graph each case. For example, a graph of the price of each product over time will reveal the products that are increasing abnormally. This can be done in a spreadsheet program or in a more advanced analysis application.

More advanced techniques are required when the number of cases is large. Suppose the janitorial purchasing data set used earlier contained the purchase of 3,000 products. Few investigators have the time or capability to manually create and look at this many

graphs! Time trend analysis is a summarization technique that produces a single number describing each graph in a regular data table. By sorting the results table appropriately, the investigator immediately knows which graphs need further manual investigation.

While methods like high-low slope, average slope, handshaking, and Box-Jenkins exist (these can be researched elsewhere), one of the most popular techniques for summarizing the slope of a graph is statistical regression. In regression for time trend analysis, the dependent variable is a column in the data set, and the independent variable is time (generally totals per day, per week, or per month). The regression calculation is included in many analysis applications, and it provides the slope and goodness-of-fit figures. While each regression on individual cases may not be statistically significant, it is generally close enough to guide investigators to the cases that need further investigation.

Figure 6.5 contains a time trend graph from a real fraud case. Each point represents total purchases by an employee for a week of time. Even without the full case context, many useful principles can be seen in the graph. First, note the increasing trend. This may be caused by the perpetrator's greediness, increasing need or addiction, or comfort with the scheme.

Second, many weeks have no purchases. This may be caused by the perpetrator testing the system, spending monthly limits, waiting for balances to clear through the system, or needing supervisor approvals. It may even be caused by guilt on the part of the perpetrator; each time the perpetrator steals money, he or she feels guilt and vows never to do it again. However, as the pressure builds during each downtime, a new, increased purchase is made. When running time trend calculations, zero or low values are generally ignored and not used in the calculation.

Third, the fraud occurs from December to March. Months on either side of this period are relatively stable. The principle is that frauds rarely start at the beginning of an investigative period and finish at the end. In other words, investigators employing the data-driven approach must choose a period to audit: six months, one year, and so on. What fraud perpetrator, when planning his or her fraud, wants to make things easy on the investigator by starting and ending during the exact period chosen for investigation? Frauds start when perceived pressure, perceived opportunity, and rationalization come together; frauds end when the person is caught or moved to another position.

Investigators must consider that frauds may be two years long, even though an audit may only look at a

FIGURE 6.5   TIME TREND GRAPH

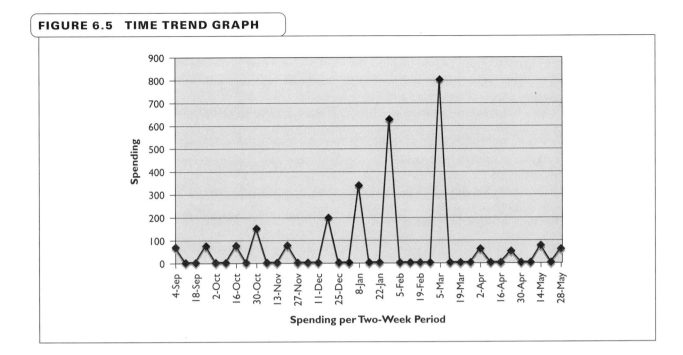

single period. In like manner, frauds may last only a few months, as shown in Figure 6.5. In this example, a regression run on the entire year would not result in a correct slope for the fraudulent period because the normal values on each side would bias the calculation. Investigators must take care when analyzing time trends to account for these situations.

Fuzzy Matching

A common technique in fraud investigation is **fuzzy matching** of textual values. The classic use of this technique is matching of employee and vendor addresses, ZIP Codes, phone numbers, or other personal information. Many employees who set up dummy companies use their home address as the company address. Another common scam is to set up a dummy company using a name similar to an existing company. If ABC Inc. is a real vendor, invoices from the fake ABC Corp. will raise little suspicion. These scams may seem obviously simplistic, but they are quite common; sometimes the simplest analyses produce the most useful results.

While cross-correlations such as these might seem simple, they are actually complicated to perform correctly. The major problem is that personal data contain so many inconsistencies. For example, assume that a perpetrator's address is 925 South 700 East, Jackson, New Jersey, 00035-4658. The following are ways in which the address might be written:

925 S. 700 East, Jackson, New Jersey 00035-4658

925 So. 700 East, Jackson, New Jersey 00035-4658

925 So. 700 E., Jackson, New Jersey 00035-4658

925 S. 700 E., Jackson, New Jersey 00035-4658

925 South 700 E., Jackson, New Jersey 00035-4658

All of these combinations with N.J. instead of New Jersey

All of these combinations with NJ instead of New Jersey

All of these combinations with 00035 instead of 00035-4658

Matching these addresses requires the use of a fuzzy text matching algorithm. The first and most common method of fuzzy matching is use of the **Soundex** algorithm. Soundex is a phonetic algorithm that assigns a numerical score based on the sounds of the letters in text. For example, both "Maple" and "Mable" have Soundex values of "M140," indicating they sound very similar. The actual Soundex score (like M140) is unimportant—the focus is on words that result in the same score. By calculating and then matching Soundex values for addresses or names, tables can be joined in a fuzzy way.

Soundex has several limitations. First, the traditional scoring for each letter of the alphabet is geared toward the English language; many applications do not allow resetting of these scorings for Spanish, Chinese, or other languages. Second, the Soundex algorithm ignores vowels, and scores only the consonants. Third, numbers (such as those in addresses) play havoc with the scorings.

A more powerful technique for fuzzy matching uses **n-grams**. This technique compares runs of letters in two values to get a match score from 0 to 100 percent. For example, "Maple" has three n-grams of size three (called a trigram): "Map," "apl," and "ple." This technique is done by splitting each value into its component n-grams and comparing the number of matching n-grams. If two words have three matching n-grams out of a possible 12 matches, the match score is 25 percent.

N-grams generally work best with larger sequences (usually more than 20 characters). Because the number of matches is exponential with the size of each value, n-gram matching can take significant amounts of time. While intermediate database tables can speed the process up considerably, this technique can be more complex than simpler methods like Soundex. Despite these limitations, the n-gram technique is often preferred because the scoring is intuitive and usually generates worthy results. A match percentage of 20 percent or greater generally indicates very similar values.

Consider the use of fuzzy matches by Systems Research & Development Corporation (SRD) of Las Vegas. The company's technology identifies alarming nonobvious relationships between individuals and companies. For example, employee data provide information on residence, banking, phone number, and affiliations. These records can be cross-referenced to identify criminal activity or to highlight questionable relationships, such as supervisors and their direct subordinates having the same addresses.

Approaches like SRD's can quickly search through vast sources of data to identify relationships within an organization to (1) detect potential collusion between employees and vendors, (2) identify suspect relationships between employees and customers, (3) locate repeat risk management claims across a corporation, and (4) find employees or clients who are "in cahoots" with lists of known criminals. Even more impressive, these technologies are very fast and can be used in almost any setting. For example, in just a few seconds, someone at an airline counter checking in for a flight or purchasing a ticket can be identified as someone appearing on a terrorist list, someone shopping at a store can be identified as a person who passes bad checks, someone betting at a blackjack table at a casino can be identified as a person who has previously been caught cheating, someone applying for a driver's license can be recognized as a person owing back child support, or someone proposing to your daughter can be identified as having a criminal record.

Three case studies recently conducted by SRD, for example, found the following:

- *Case 1.* *Data from a large consumer products distributor with more than 800,000 employees were analyzed. The analysis revealed 564 employees who had vendor or criminal relationships and 26 employees who were, in fact, vendors.*
- *Case 2.* *In collusion testing at a major Las Vegas resort, an analysis of more than 20,000 employees (current and terminated), all vendors, customers, in-house arrests and incidents, and its known list of problem people, found 24 active players who were known criminals, 192 employees who had possible vendor relationships, and seven employees who were, in fact, vendors.*
- *Case 3.* *A government organization's 10,000 employees, 75,000 vendors, and more than 50,000 known problem people were analyzed. The analysis found 140 employee relationships with vendors, 1,451 vendor relationships to security concerns, 253 employee relationships to security concerns, two vendors who constituted a security concern, and some employees who were either a security concern or vendor.*

Real-Time Analysis

Data-driven investigation is one of the most powerful methods of discovering fraud. It is usually performed during investigation (i.e., during periodic audits), but it can be integrated directly into existing systems to perform real-time analysis on transactions.

While real-time analysis is similar to traditional accounting controls because it works at transaction time, it is a distinct technique because it specifically analyzes each transaction for fraud (rather than for correctness). One result of this distinction is the need for continual improvement and updating of indicators. If indicators are hard-coded into existing systems, they quickly become outdated or circumvented. Systems that allow real-time modification of indicators, deletion of less effective indicators, and addition of new indicators

FIGURE 6.6   EXAMPLE MATOSAS MATRIX FOR CONTRACT BIDDING

CONTRACT	WINNING VENDOR	NUMBER OF RED FLAGS	LOST BIDS	BRAND NAMES	LAST BIDDER WINNER	SEQUENTIAL BID SECURITY NUMBER
100221	Direct Corp.	1	0%	70%	0%	0%
523332	Satyoo	2	0%	68%	0%	100%
351223	Danicorp	1	0%	72%	0%	0%
387543	Under Inc.	3	0%	70%	100%	100%

without reprogramming of the greater system have the greatest chance of success.

As an example of a compromise between periodic and real-time analysis, one corporation created a number of indicators that ran each weekend on the previous week's data. A scheduler in the fraud system automatically ran each indicator, compiled the results into PDF documents, and e-mailed the results to the security director by Monday morning. When the security director arrived at work, he was able to quickly scan the documents for transactions that needed investigation.

One way to view the results of multiple indicators is to use a chart called a **Matosas matrix**, as shown in Figure 6.6. This matrix lists one record per contract for which vendors bid. Each column in the table represents an indicator run by the system. The Matosas matrix is a high-level view of which contracts have indicator hits that need to be investigated. It allows the investigator to mentally combine different indicators to different schemes. While the matrix shown in Figure 6.6 contains only four indicators, a matrix in the real world might contain 50 or 100 indicator columns.

For example, the Brand Names column calculates what percentage of the items of each contract uses brand names rather than generic descriptions. Using brand names in a contract is a common procurement scam: a procurement officer ensures that a specific vendor wins the procurement process by writing the contract with brand name items that are so specific that all other vendors are unable to meet the request. All vendors but the targeted one decline to bid or are deemed unresponsive in their bids.

Looking vertically at the Matosas matrix helps investigators continually improve the set of indicators. Indicators that never achieve hits, such as the Lost Bids column in the example, may need refinement to produce better results. Indicators that achieve hits on every contract, such as the Brand Names column, may need to be dropped or modified because they are too

general. Columns like Last Bidder Winner seem to be performing well because they discriminate well between contracts.

Analyzing Financial Statement Reports

The previous section discussed analysis methods that can be used with many different databases, including purchasing, invoice, procurement, timecard, equipment use, and other operations data sets. These methods allow full-population analysis and allow the investigator to analyze detailed records. Data-driven analysis at the highly summarized financial statement level is also useful and important, especially in external audits. This section presents a specialized type of data- driven analysis that targets fraud and corruption in financial statements.

Financial statements are the end product of the **accounting cycle**. They can be viewed as summaries of all the transactions that occurred during a specific period of time. Fraud can be detected anywhere along the way—through transaction source documents, journal entries of the transactions based on those documents, ledger balances (which are summaries of journal entries)—and finally in the resulting financial statements (which summarize the ledger totals in prescribed formats). Unless a fraud is large, however, it may not affect summarized financial statements significantly enough to be detected. Large frauds, however, are a different "animal" and can often be detected through financial statements. Small frauds are usually detected by focusing on source documents or other symptoms.

To detect fraud through financial statements, investigators focus on unexplained changes. For example, in most companies, very few customers pay cash at the time of purchase. Rather, their payments are made by check based on monthly bills. As a result, revenues normally do not increase without a corresponding increase in accounts receivable. Similarly, an increase in revenues should be accompanied by an increase in cost of goods sold and in inventory purchased and accounts payable balances. Also, inventory levels don't usually increase while purchases and accounts payable remain constant. In all cases, unexplained changes must be the focus of attention.

To understand how financial statement changes can signal fraud, one must be familiar with the nature of the three primary financial statements. Most organizations publish periodic **balance sheets, income statements**, and **statements of cash flows**. The balance sheet is a position statement. It shows what an organization's asset, liability, and equity balances are at a *specific* point in time (like a snapshot). A balance sheet prepared as of December 31, 2011, for example, reveals what the organization owns and owes on that date only. A balance sheet prepared on January 3, 2012 (three days later), may show drastically different numbers. Because a balance sheet is a position statement as of a specific date, it must be converted to a change statement before it can be used to detect fraud. The changes can then be analyzed to determine whether they make sense or represent symptoms that should be investigated.

An income statement shows what an organization's revenues, expenses, and income were for a period of time. An income statement prepared for the year ending December 31, 2011, for example, would reveal revenues, expenses, and income for the 12 months January through December 2011. Although an income statement is for a period of time rather than as of a specific date, it is not a change statement. Like a balance sheet, it must also be converted to a change statement before it can be used effectively as a fraud detection tool.

Balance sheets and income statements are converted from position and period statements to change statements in four ways: (1) comparing account balances in the statements from one period to the next, (2) calculating key ratios and comparing them from period to period, (3) performing **vertical analysis**, and (4) performing **horizontal analysis**. The first approach compares numbers in the statement from one period to the next. For example, the accounts receivable balance of one period is compared to the balance in a subsequent period to see whether the change is in the expected direction and whether the magnitude of change is reasonable, given changes in other numbers. Unfortunately, because financial statement numbers are often large and difficult to compare, assessing levels of change can be difficult.

In the second approach—converting balance sheets and income statements to change statements—key financial statement ratios are calculated and changes in these ratios from period to period are compared. The **quick ratio** (also called the **acid-test ratio**) and the **current ratio** assess a company's liquidity. **Accounts receivable turnover** and **inventory turnover ratios** assess a company's operational efficiency. **Debt-to-equity** and **times-interest-earned ratios** assess a company's solvency. **Profit margin, return on assets, return on equity**, and **earnings per share** ratios assess profitability. By examining ratios, it is possible to see whether resulting changes in liquidity, efficiency, solvency, and profitability are as expected. Changes in ratios that do not make sense are often the result of fraudulent activity by managers.

Detecting fraud through financial statement ratios is much easier than assessing changes in the financial statement numbers themselves. Ratios usually involve small, easily understood numbers that are sensitive to changes in key variables. In addition, benchmarks for most ratios are well known. Common ratios that can be used to detect fraud are shown in Table 6.2.

The third approach—converting balance sheets and income statements to change statements—uses vertical analysis, which converts financial statement numbers to percentages. For a balance sheet, total assets are set at 100 percent, and all other balances are a percentage of total assets. A simple example of vertical analysis of a balance sheet is shown in Figure 6.7.

Vertical analysis is a very useful fraud detection technique, because percentages are easily understood. When we spend $1 or part of $1, we know what it means. If we spend it all, we know we have spent 100 percent. Similarly, all through school, we scored 70 or 80 or 90 percent on examinations. Everyone understands which of these scores is good, which is bad, and what the percentage represents. Changes in cumbersome financial statement balances can be readily assessed by converting the numbers to percentages. Understanding that sales increased 20 percent, for example, is much easier than understanding that sales increased from $862,000 to $1,034,400.

When vertical analysis is used to analyze changes in income statement balances, gross sales are set at 100 percent, and all other amounts are converted to a percentage of sales. A simple example of an income statement converted to percentages by using vertical analysis is shown in Figure 6.8.

In this example, the cost of goods sold increased from 50 percent of sales in Year 1 to 60 percent of sales in Year 2. Does this change make sense? Why would the cost of sales increase twice as much as sales? Possible explanations include: (1) inventory costs rose faster

TABLE 6.2 COMMON RATIOS

1. Current Ratio	=	$\dfrac{\text{Current Assets}}{\text{Current Liabilities}}$
2. Quick Ratio (Acid-test)	=	$\dfrac{\text{Cash + Accounts Receivable}}{\text{Current Liabilities}}$
3. Accounts Receivable Turnover	=	$\dfrac{\text{Sales}}{\text{Average Accounts Receivable}}$
4. Days in Receivable	=	$\dfrac{365}{\text{Receivable Turnover}}$
5. Receivable Percentage	=	$\dfrac{\text{Accounts Receivable}}{\text{Total Assets}}$
6. Bad Debt Percentage	=	$\dfrac{\text{Bad Debt Expense}}{\text{Average Accounts Receivable}}$
	=	$\dfrac{\text{Bad Debt Expense}}{\text{Total Sales}}$
7. Inventory Turnover	=	$\dfrac{\text{Cost of Goods Sold}}{\text{Average Inventory}}$
8. Days in Inventory	=	$\dfrac{365}{\text{Inventory Turnover}}$
9. Cost of Goods Sold Percentage	=	$\dfrac{\text{Cost of Goods Sold}}{\text{Sales}}$
10. Inventory Percentage	=	$\dfrac{\text{Inventory}}{\text{Total Assets}}$
11. Property, Plant, and Equipment (PPE) Turnover	=	$\dfrac{\text{Sales}}{\text{Average PPE}}$
12. PPE percentage	=	$\dfrac{\text{PPE}}{\text{Total Assets}}$
13. Sales Return Percentage	=	$\dfrac{\text{Sales Returns}}{\text{Total Sales}}$
14. Debt to Equity (Leverage)	=	$\dfrac{\text{Total Liabilities}}{\text{Stockholders' Equity}}$
15. Debt Percentage	=	$\dfrac{\text{Total Liabilities}}{\text{Total Assets}}$
16. Profit Margin	=	$\dfrac{\text{Net Income}}{\text{Net Sales}}$
17. Earnings per Share	=	$\dfrac{\text{Net Income}}{\text{Number of Shares of Stock}}$

than sales prices, (2) inventory is being stolen, and (3) the accounting records are not accurate. An analyst can easily determine which of these (or other) factors caused the unusual changes.

The fourth approach—converting balance sheets and income statements to change statements—uses horizontal analysis. Horizontal analysis resembles vertical analysis in that it converts financial statement balances to percentages. However, instead of computing financial statement amounts as percentages of total assets or gross sales, it converts the percentage change in balance sheet and income statement numbers from one period to the next. Simple examples of horizontal

analysis of a balance sheet and horizontal analysis of an income statement are shown in Figure 6.9.

Horizontal analysis is the most direct method of focusing on changes. With ratios and vertical analysis, statements are converted to numbers that are easier to understand, and then the numbers are compared from period to period. With horizontal analysis, the changes in amounts from period to period are converted to percentages (Change/Year 1 Amount = % Change).

As an example of the usefulness of vertical and horizontal analyses, consider the ESM fraud described in the following by an expert witness in the case.

I received a call from an attorney asking me to be an expert witness in a major fraud case. The case was ESM Government, a securities dealer that had been in the news recently. The attorney indicated that the large accounting firm he was defending was being sued for some $300 million by the insurance commission for negligent auditing. The suit related to the firm's audit of a savings and loan that had invested in ESM. To defend the firm, the attorney was trying to understand the nature and extent of the fraud as well as to obtain an independent opinion on whether his client was negligent in performing the audit.

The attorney requested that I analyze the financial statements to determine whether fraud existed and, if so, in which accounts. I used both horizontal and vertical analyses. My converted financial statements are shown in Figures 6.10 and 6.11.

Based on my analysis, I drew three conclusions. First, if there were fraud, it had to be in either the "securities sold under agreement to repurchase (repo) account" or in the "securities purchased under agreement to resell (reverse repo)" account. I was not familiar with either of these accounts, but recognized them as being the only accounts large enough to hide massive fraud. Second, I wondered

FIGURE 6.7   VERTICAL ANALYSIS OF A BALANCE SHEET

JOHN DOE COMPANY Vertical Analysis of Balance Sheet December 31, 2008 and 2007

	2008		2007	
Cash	$ 64,000	8%	$ 50,000	5%
Accounts receivable	96,000	12	100,000	10
Inventory	160,000	20	200,000	20
Fixed assets	480,000	60	650,000	65
Total assets	$800,000	100%	$1,000,000	100%
Accounts payable	$ 16,000	2%	$ 70,000	7%
Mortgage payable	80,000	10	120,000	12
Bonds payable	160,000	20	200,000	20
Common stock	400,000	50	400,000	40
Retained earnings	144,000	18	210,000	21
Total liabilities and equity	$800,000	100%	$1,000,000	100%

FIGURE 6.8   VERTICAL ANALYSIS OF AN INCOME STATEMENT

JOHN DOE COMPANY Vertical Analysis of Income Statement for the Period Ending December 31, 2008 and 2007

	2008		2007	
Sales	$1,000,000	100%	$800,000	100%
Cost of goods sold	600,000	60	400,000	50
Gross margin	$ 400,000	40%	$400,000	50
Expenses:				
Selling expenses	$ 150,000	15%	$120,000	15%
Administrative expenses	100,000	10	88,000	11
	$ 250,000	25%	$208,000	26
Income before taxes	$ 150,000	15%	$192,000	24%
Income taxes	60,000	6	80,000	10
Net income	$ 90,000	9%	$112,000	14%

why these two accounts would have identical balances in three of the four years. After I realized that these accounts were really only payables and receivables for the company, my concern heightened. It did not make sense that a company's receivable balance should exactly equal its payable balance in even one year, let alone three in a row. Third, the numbers in the financial statements jumped around randomly. There were large changes from year to year, and often these changes were in opposite directions. In a stable company, only small, consistent changes from year to year are the norm.

I called the attorney with my conclusions and stated that I wasn't sure whether the financial statements were fraudulent but that there were three very significant red flags.

I also stated that if fraud were present, it would have to be in the repo and reverse repo accounts.

Based on this analysis, I was retained as an expert witness in the case. I did not testify, however, because the case was settled out of court for less than $5 million.

―――

Examples of financial statement fraud abound. Some of these frauds are missed by auditors, but they could be easily detected using horizontal or vertical analysis. In many cases, the unexplained changes are obvious; in other cases, they are subtle. Unfortunately, however, managers and even auditors generally use

---

FIGURE 6.9 HORIZONTAL ANALYSIS OF A BALANCE SHEET AND AN INCOME STATEMENT

JOHN DOE COMPANY Horizontal Analysis of Balance Sheet December 31, 2008 and 2007

	2008	2007	Change	% Change
Cash	$ 64,000	$ 50,000	$ 14,000	22%
Accounts receivable	96,000	100,000	(4,000)	(4)
Inventory	160,000	200,000	(40,000)	(25)
Fixed assets	480,000	650,000	(170,000)	(35)
Total assets	$800,000	$1,000,000	($200,000)	(25)
Accounts payable	$ 16,000	$ 70,000	($ 54,000)	(338)
Mortgage payable	80,000	120,000	(40,000)	(50)
Bonds payable	160,000	200,000	(40,000)	(25)
Common stock	400,000	400,000	0	0
Retained earnings	144,000	210,000	(66,000)	(46)
Total liabilities and equity	$800,000	$1,000,000	($200,000)	(25)

JOHN DOE COMPANY Horizontal Analysis of Income Statements for the Period Ending December 31, 2008 and 2007

	2008	2007	Change	% Change
Net sales	$1,000,000	$800,000	$200,000	25%
Cost of goods sold	600,000	400,000	200,000	50
Gross margin	$ 400,000	$400,000	0	0
Expenses:				
Selling expenses	$ 150,000	$120,000	$ 30,000	25
Administrative expenses	100,000	88,000	12,000	14
	$ 250,000	$208,000	$ 42,000	20
Income before taxes	$ 150,000	$192,000	$ (42,000)	22
Income taxes	60,000	80,000	(20,000)	25
Net income	$ 90,000	$112,000	$ 22,000	(20)

ratios, horizontal analysis, and vertical analysis only as tools for assessing an organization's performance. Rarely do they use these measures to detect fraud.

The third financial statement—the statement of cash flows—is already a change statement and doesn't need to be converted. The statement of cash flows shows the cash inflows and cash outflows during a period. A graphic description of this statement is shown in Figure 6.12.

Increases or decreases that do not make sense serve as red flags and should be investigated. Because the statement of cash flows focuses on changes, it can be used to answer questions such as the following:

- *Is the increase in cash flow as expected?*
- *Why did receivables go up (down)?*
- *Why did inventory increase (decrease)?*
- *Why did payables increase (decrease)?*
- *Why was there an increase in payables when inventory decreased?*
- *Why were assets sold (bought)?*
- *Where did the cash come from to pay dividends?*

FIGURE 6.10 ESM GOVERNMENT-HORIZONTAL ANALYSIS

	Horizontal Analysis[†]		
	Year 1 to Year 2	Year 2 to Year 3	Year 3 to Year 4
Assets			
Cash	1,684%	(40%)	(67%)
Deposits	0	0	0
Receivables from brokers and dealers	(91)	1,706	102
Receivables from customers	19.5	(48)	(23)
	Horizontal Analysis		
	Year 1 to Year 2	Year 2 to Year 3	Year 3 to Year 4
Securities purchased under agreement to resell	(3)	(44)	205
Accrued interest	0	190	487
Securities purchased not sold at market	829	13	120
Total assets	7.5	(38)	183
Liabilities and Shareholders' Equity			
Short-term bank loans	898	40	14
Payable to brokers and dealers	(72)	658	33
Payable to customer	50	(64)	158
Securities sold under agreement to repurchase	(3)	(44)	232
Accounts payable and accrued expenses	192	(100)	55
Accounts payable—parent and affiliates	279	(25)	(4)
Common stock	0	0	0
Additional contributed capital	0	0	0
Retained earnings	127	113	21

† Dollar amounts are omitted to simplify the presentation.

Note: This horizontal analysis, based on ESM's actual financial statements, was prepared by Steve Albrecht.

FIGURE 6.11 ESM GOVERNMENT-VERTICAL ANALYSIS

Vertical Analysis

	$ (Year 1)	%	$ (Year 2)	%	$ (Year 3)	%	$ (Year 4)	%
Assets								
Cash	$ 99,000	0.000	$ 1,767,000	0.001	$ 1,046,000	0.001	$ 339,000	0.000
Deposits	25,000	0.000	25,000	0.000	25,000	0.000	25,000	0.000
Receivables from brokers and dealers	725,000	0.000	60,000	0.000	1,084,000	0.001	2,192,000	0.001
Receivables from customers	33,883,000	0.024	40,523,000	0.027	21,073,000	0.022	16,163,000	0.006
Securities purchased under agreement to resell	1,367,986,000	0.963	1,323,340,000	0.867	738,924,000	0.781	2,252,555,000	0.840
Accrued interest	433,000	0.000	433,000	0.000	1,257,000	0.001	7,375,000	0.003
Securities purchased not sold at market	17,380,000	0.010	161,484,000	0.106	182,674,000	0.193	402,004,000	0.150
Total assets	$1,420,531,000		$1,527,632,000		$946,083,000		$2,680,653,000	
Liabilities and equity								
Short-term bank loans	$ 5,734,000	0.005	$ 57,282,000	0.037	$ 80,350,000	0.085	$ 91,382,000	0.034
Payable to brokers and dealers	1,721,000	0.001	478,000	0.000	3,624,000	0.004	5,815,000	0.000
Payable to customers	2,703,000	0.002	4,047,000	0.003	1,426,000	0.002	3,683,000	0.000
Securities sold under agreement to repurchase	1,367,986,000	0.963	1,323,340,000	0.867	738,924,000	0.781	2,457,555,000	0.917
Accounts payable and accrued expenses	272,000	0.000	796,000	0.000	591,000	0.001	1,377,000	0.000
Accounts payable—parent and affiliates	33,588,000	0.020	127,604,000	0.084	95,861,000	0.101	92,183,000	0.014
Common stock	1,000	0.000	1,000	0.000	1,000	0.000	1,000	0.000
Additional contributed capital	4,160,000	0.040	4,160,000	0.003	4,160,000	0.004	4,160,000	0.000
Retained earnings	4,366,000	0.040	9,924,000	0.006	21,146,000	0.022	24,497,000	0.010
Total liabilities and equity	$1,420,531,000		$1,527,632,000		$946,083,000		$2,680,653,000	

Note: This vertical analysis, based on ESM's actual journal, was prepared by Steve Albrecht.

FIGURE 6.12   STATEMENT OF CASH FLOWS

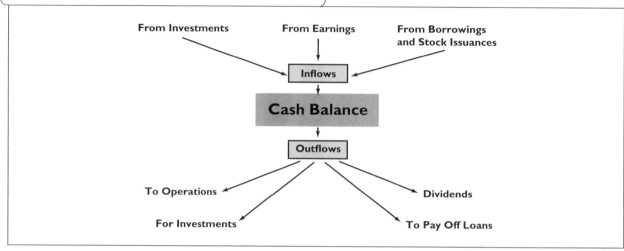

Review of the Learning Objectives

- **Describe the importance of data-driven fraud detection, including the difference between accounting anomalies and fraud.** Sampling is an effective method for discovering routine anomalies that occur throughout an audit period, but it is risky when used for fraud detection.
- **Explain the steps in the data analysis process.** The steps in the data-driven process are (1) understand the business, (2) identify the potential schemes, (3) determine the symptoms of the schemes, (4) search for symptoms, (5) analyze the search results, and (6) investigate.
- **Be familiar with common data analysis packages.** Data analysis packages like ACL, IDEA, Picalo, and ActiveData provide tools and techniques for the data-driven approach.
- **Understand the principles of data access, including Open Database Connectivity (ODBC), text import, and data warehousing.** Most businesses have a large set of electronic data in databases that can be accessed and analyzed via ODBC and text import. Data warehouses provide an efficient and effective intermediate storage location for data used in fraud analyses.
- **Perform basic data analysis procedures for fraud detection.** Basic fraud analysis techniques include digital analysis, discovery of outliers, stratification and summarization, time trending, and fuzzy matching.

- **Read and analyze a Matosas matrix.** A Matosas matrix provides a comprehensive view of the results of fraud indicator analysis as well as a view of indicator effectiveness.
- **Understand how fraud is detected by analyzing financial statements.** Horizontal and vertical financial statement analyses using different financial ratios can detect problems and anomalies in financial data.

KEY TERMS

data-driven fraud detection, p. 168
scheme, p. 168
accounting anomalies, p. 168
risk assessment, p. 170
structured query language (SQL), p. 172
data analysis software, p. 172
Benford's Law, p. 173
statistical analysis, p. 173
Open Database Connectivity (ODBC), p. 173
delimited text, p. 174
comma separated values (CSV), p. 174
tab separated values (TSV), p. 174

fixed-width format, p. 174
data warehouse, p. 174
descriptives, p. 175
digital analysis, p. 176
z-score, p. 179
stratification, p. 179
summarization, p. 179
pivot tables, p. 180
time trend analysis, p. 180
fuzzy matching, p. 181
soundex, p. 181
n-grams, p. 182
Matosas matrix, p. 183
accounting cycle, p. 183
balance sheets, p. 184
income statements, p. 184

statements of cash flows, p. 184
vertical analysis, p. 184
horizontal analysis, p. 184
quick ratio, p. 184
acid-test ratio, p. 184
current ratio, p. 184
accounts receivable turnover, p. 184

inventory turnover ratios, p. 184
debt-to-equity, p. 184
times-interest-earned ratios, p. 184
profit margin, p. 184
return on assets, p. 184
return on equity, p. 184
earnings per share, p. 184

QUESTIONS

Discussion Questions

1. Why is it important to proactively detect fraud?
2. What are the differences between anomalies and fraud?
3. What are the risks of sampling when searching for fraud?
4. What are the advantages of using data analysis software to detect fraud in a data-driven approach?
5. What are the advantages of using statistical analysis to detect fraud?
6. What are the disadvantages of statistical analysis?
7. What is Benford's Law?
8. List and describe the steps of the data-driven fraud-detection approach.
9. How can fraud be detected by analyzing financial statements?
10. What is the significance of unexplained changes in financial statements in detecting fraud?
11. What are some of the difficulties in trying to correlate customers, vendors, or employees with known problem people?
12. What are the benefits of using a two-stage import that utilizes a data warehouse?
13. What is ODBC? How does it compare with text file import?
14. What are the benefits and drawbacks of the Soundex and n-gram methods of fuzzy matching text?

True/False

1. Unusual patterns always indicate the existence of fraud.
2. ODBC is the best approach to import because it achieves a direct, rich connection to the source database.

3. Data-driven analysis uses the company's database to search for normal relationships between numbers.
4. According to Benford's Law, the first digit of natural sets of numbers will begin with a 9 more often than with an 8.
5. When using Benford's Law, potential suspects are less likely to know you are trying to detect fraud than if you use more direct detection techniques.
6. Understanding the kinds of frauds that can occur is not important when using a data-driven detection method.
7. Digital analysis using Benford's Law can be performed on databases of any size.
8. Data-driven fraud detection can pay large dividends and is an effective way to reduce the cost of fraud in any organization.
9. Unexplained changes are common in financial statements.
10. Balance sheets must be converted to change statements before they can be used in detecting fraud.
11. Vertical analysis is a more direct method than horizontal analysis in focusing on changes in financial statements from one period to another.
12. Vertical analysis is a useful detection technique because percentages are easily understood.
13. The z-score calculation is the best way to stratify data.
14. A single symptom (red flag) is almost always enough information to identify the type of fraud scheme occurring.

Multiple Choice

1. When detecting fraud, it is important that fraud investigators:
   a. Remain objective and neutral.
   b. Assume guilt.
   c. Assume innocence.
   d. None of the above.
2. Data-driven fraud detection:
   a. Determines the cost of fraud.
   b. Identifies possible fraud suspects.
   c. Looks for anomalies in databases.
   d. All of the above.
3. Once a buyer starts accepting kickbacks from a supplier:
   a. Prices often increase.
   b. Purchases from other vendors often decrease.
   c. The supplier usually takes control of the purchasing relationship.
   d. All of the above.

4. The most obvious disadvantage of the data- driven approach is:
   a. Databases are very large and often cannot be analyzed using analysis packages like ACL, IDEA, or Picalo.
   b. High cost.
   c. The decrease in employee morale.
   d. None of the above.

5. Benford's Law:
   a. Is usually unsuccessful as a fraud detection tool.
   b. Predicts that the first digit of random number sets will begin with a 1 more often than a 2, a 2 more often than a 3, and so on.
   c. Applies to personal ID numbers.
   d. All of the above.

6. A detection method that focuses on the kinds of frauds that can occur and then uses technology to determine whether those frauds actually exist is called:
   a. Fishing fraud detection.
   b. Data mining.
   c. Data-driven fraud detection.
   d. Benford's Law.

7. When deciding which detection method to use, it is important to:
   a. Determine the advantages and disadvantages of each approach.
   b. Identify the costs involved.
   c. Determine which method will meet the client's objectives.
   d. All of the above.

8. Fraud is best detected through financial statements by focusing on:
   a. Unexplained changes in financial statement balances.
   b. Consistencies.
   c. Intuition.
   d. Management's behavior when financial statements are released.

9. The most effective way to convert balance sheets and income statements from position and period statements to change statements is to:
   a. Compare balances in the statements from one period to the next.
   b. Calculate key ratios and compare them from period to period.
   c. Perform horizontal and vertical analyses.
   d. All of the above.

10. Profit margin, return on assets, and return on equity are all examples of:
    a. Vertical analysis.
    b. Key financial statement ratios.
    c. Horizontal analysis.
    d. None of the above.

11. When vertical analysis is performed:
    a. Ratios are used to detect fraud.
    b. Changes in significant balance totals are examined.
    c. Financial statement balances are converted to percentages.
    d. Total revenues are compared to total expenses.

12. Horizontal analysis is different from vertical analysis in that:
    a. There is no difference between horizontal and vertical analysis.
    b. Horizontal analysis calculates the percentage change in balance sheet and income statement numbers from one period to the next, while vertical analysis converts balances in a single period to percentages.
    c. Horizontal analysis converts balances in a single period to percentages, while vertical analysis calculates the percentage change in balance sheet and income statement numbers from one period to the next.
    d. Key ratios are compared from one period to the next.

13. Which of the following is an advantage of using data analysis software to detect fraud?
    a. It is a static approach, and results cannot be recombined in different ways.
    b. Data analysis software can only be used to analyze small data sets.
    c. Data analysis software can analyze entire populations rather than just samples.
    d. Significant numbers of hits can occur, requiring iterative refinement of analyses.

14. Benford's Law is:
    a. The most expensive of all the digital analysis methods to implement and use.
    b. The most effective way to identify actual frauds.
    c. A method that uses vertical financial statement analysis.
    d. An effective way to identify anomalies in data sets.

15. If a search reveals that an employee and a vendor have the same telephone number, this result may indicate that:
    a. Vendors are overcharging for goods purchased.
    b. Employees may be establishing dummy vendors.
    c. Contractors are billing at the wrong rates.
    d. A vendor is receiving kickbacks or other favors.

16. When conducting financial statement analysis, which ratio will be the most useful in determining whether a company has erroneously inflated accounts receivable?
    a. Current ratio.
    b. Profit margin.
    c. Accounts receivable turnover.
    d. Debt percentage.
17. When trying to identify outliers, what is one of the best statistical approaches?
    a. A pie graph indicating the relative amounts.
    b. Stratification of cases by value.
    c. Time trending using the high-low slope method.
    d. The z-score calculation.
18. An advantage of using ODBC to import data into a data warehouse is that:
    a. ODBC doesn't require the use of corporate database servers.
    b. ODBC compresses data when stored on a CD or DVD.
    c. ODBC automatically retrieves column names and types from the database.
    d. ODBC keeps the investigator from dealing with the difficult SQL language.
19. The Soundex algorithm:
    a. Uses consonants but ignores vowels.
    b. Creates a numerical score representing how a word sounds.
    c. Is useful when fuzzy matching values.
    d. All of the above.

SHORT CASES

Case 1
Boxer Incorporated has hired you as a consultant to implement a data-driven fraud detection program in the company. One of the owners, Priscilla Boxer, asks you to give a presentation to several executives on the data-driven approach.

1. What are the primary advantages and disadvantages of this approach?
2. How does this approach compare to the traditional, reactive approach to detecting fraud?

Case 2
A large manufacturing business has hired you as a fraud detection specialist. The first day on the job your boss asks you the following questions:

1. What is Benford's Law?
2. In what situations is it appropriate to use Benford's Law, and in what situations is Benford's Law inappropriate?

Case 3
Dennis Jones, an old college friend, contacted you last week. Dennis owns several car washes, and he believes that financial statement fraud may be occurring. (He pays each car wash manager a bonus if a certain level of profits is earned and is worried that some managers are overstating profits to earn a higher bonus.) Dennis is coming over today to see whether you can help him determine if his suspicions are valid. He is bringing along the financial statements for each car wash (income statements, balance sheets, and cash flow statements) for the last five years.

1. What kind of financial statement analysis could you perform to help Dennis detect possible fraud?

Case 4
Your boss knows that you are taking a fraud examination course at a local university. He is interested in learning more about data-driven fraud detection and asks you to prepare a short memo briefly explaining data-driven fraud detection methods and techniques.

1. List three data analysis methods and techniques and briefly explain them.

Case 5
There once was a corporation from Nantucket,
Its controls leaked like holes in a bucket.
Smelling trouble with the buyer,
And with the supplier,
They determined to fix it or chuck it.

This limerick accurately depicts Bucket Corp., which manufactures wood furniture. Bucket has enjoyed several years of good profits but has recently seen some alarming trends in its bottom line. Although not drastic, Bucket's profits first stagnated and are now beginning to decline. After some cost analysis and investigation of financial records, the company has determined that the problem may be coming from the procurement division of operations. On the following page is a small random sample of invoices from various vendors:

CASE 5

SUPPLIER	PRODUCT	PRICE/TON	QUANTITY	TOTAL
Woods 'R' Us	Oak	$ 157.00	2	$ 314.00
	Cherry	75.00	3	225.00
	Cedar	125.00	1.5	187.50
	Spruce	42.00	3	126.00
Harris Lumber	Oak	215.00	4	860.00
	Cherry	115.00	8	920.00
	Cedar	140.00	6	840.00
	Spruce	80.00	9	720.00
Lumber Jack's	Oak	158.00	1	158.00
	Cherry	74.00	2	148.00
	Cedar	124.00	2	248.00
	Spruce	43.00	3	129.00
Small's Lumber	Oak	156.00	3	468.00
	Cherry	76.00	3	228.00
	Cedar	127.00	1	127.00
	Spruce	41.00	4	164.00

1. What could the CFO do to investigate the potential problems in the procurement department of Bucket Corp.?
2. Do you think it is possible there is fraud involved? Why?

Case 6

By ordering unnecessary products at inflated prices, the purchasing manager of XYZ Company defrauded his employer of over $40,000 over a two-year period.

1. How could you have detected this fraud?

Case 7

As CEO of your company, you've been going over your financial statements and have noticed something disturbing. You perform a horizontal analysis and find that sales have been increasing at a rate of 3 percent per year, while inventory has risen at a rate of 29 percent per year.

1. Could fraud be occurring? Why or why not?
2. Assuming that fraud is being committed, how would you investigate?

Case 8

1. Compare the first-digit frequency in the transactions in this table below with Benford's Law. What are the results?

2. Could fraud be occurring in this organization?

CASE 8

AMOUNT	DESCRIPTION	CHECK NO.
$235.65	Payment to U.S. West for phone bill	2001
$654.36	John's Heating and Cooling for fixing A/C in December	2002
$4,987.36	Sharky's Used Car Dealership for Yugo truck	2003
$339.13	Salt River Project for power in December	2004
$475.98	Arizona Department of Internal Revenue for taxes	2005
$254.14	Grainger Corp. for power tools	2006
$504.17	Home Depot for outdoor carport	2007
$171.54	Steelin's Consulting for help with computer network	2008
$326.45	Payment to U.S. West for phone bill in January	2009
$477.67	Bank of America for loan payment	2010

CASE 10

KELLY ENTERPRISES, INC.
STATEMENT OF CASH FLOWS
FOR THE PERIOD ENDED DECEMBER 31, 2012

IN MILLIONS	2012	2011	2010
Cash from Operations			
Net income	$ 900	$ 800	$ 450
Change in accounts receivable	(706)	(230)	25
Change in accounts payable	150	45	90
Change in inventory	(50)	15	25
Depreciation	105	90	65
Net cash from operations	$ 499	$ 690	$ 655
Cash from Investing			
Additions to property, plant, and equipment	$ (950)	$ (690)	$(790)
Proceeds from sale of securities	25	56	15
Net cash from investing	$ (925)	$ (634)	$(775)
Cash from Financing			
Borrowings of long-term debt	$ 250	$ (150)	$ 34
Cash dividends	(140)	(85)	(45)
Net cash from financing	$ 110	$ 65	$ (11)
Increase (decrease) in cash	$ (316)	$ 121	$(131)

Case 9

As an internal auditor for CRA, Inc., you are assigned to a team working on an ongoing project to identify possible fraud. The project started with time trend analysis of purchase prices of all items in the company. The project was started last year, but because of budget problems, it was delayed until this year. Most of the data mining is complete, but the team is having problems understanding how to continue the approach.

1. Describe the steps in time trend analysis, including correct data preparation.
2. What types of fraud can be identified with time trend analysis?

Case 10

Large frauds can often be detected by performing financial statement analysis. Although such analysis can raise areas of concern, not all red flags are the result of fraudulent activities. Reasonable explanations often exist for anomalies in financial statements.

The statement of cash flows is one financial statement that is analyzed in order to identify possible fraud. This statement for Kelly Enterprises, Inc., for a three-year period is shown in the table on this page.

1. Identify possible red flags.
2. Indicate if reasonable explanations exist for the areas of concern.

Case 11

By examining first digits, Company XXX suspects fraud. You are asked to review the sample of invoices

CASE 11

INVOICE AMOUNTS		
$ 149,200.00	$ 19,489.00	$ 1,134.00
1,444.00	12,485.00	446.00
1,756.00	26,995.00	678.00
91.59	235,535.00	456.00
2,250.00	59,155.00	341.00
38,005.00	109,995.00	890.00
45,465.00	212,536.00	402.00
112,495.00	685.00	467.00
137,500.00	765.00	465.00
37,300.00	234.00	1,516.00
36,231.00	435.00	375.00
26,695.00	1,045.00	679.00

shown on the previous page to see if they make sense. You are familiar with several fraud detection methods and are eager to try out Benford's Law.

1. Do you suspect possible fraud? Why?

Case 12

You are hired as a consultant to determine if fraud is occurring at Startis Company, a manufacturer of designer makeup. An initial search of the company reveals there are three modern, relational databases and a 30-year-old time card system that can be searched for fraud. The databases support ODBC, but the time card system exports data in fixed-width files only.

1. What are the advantages and disadvantages of ODBC?
2. What precautions should be taken when importing the time card data?

CASE STUDIES

Case Study 1

You are in your first month as an internal auditor in the corporate offices of Cover-Up Fraud-Mart, a large regional variety store chain based in Los Angeles. Your manager has just given you a general overview of the company's problems with fraud. In fact, losses from fraud exceed losses from shoplifting by tenfold, and management wants your perspective on what it can do to proactively detect fraud. From your fraud auditing class, you know that the data-driven approach is one of the most effective detection methods.

Questions

1. Prepare a project plan for implementing the six- step data-driven approach. List the types of team members who should be involved in each step, how long each step will take, and cost estimates for each step.
2. What software package will you need to purchase to complete the process? Provide arguments for your decision.
3. What techniques should be run in Steps 4 and 5?

Case Study 2

You have recently joined the internal audit team at a large company responsible for janitorial work at many different local businesses. Because of the significant number of consumables used in janitorial work, your company has a large purchasing department. You have been asked to analyze the purchases data set for potential frauds. Download the ch06_janitorial_purchases. csv data set from the book's Web site and import it into an analysis software package.

Questions

1. The Vendor column contains the names of the vendors from which the purchases were made. Use a fuzzy matching algorithm to find any vendors with similar names. Do you suspect any purchases were made from phantom vendors?
2. Find any vendors who are charging too much for their product compared with other vendors. In addition to average prices for each product and vendor, do you see any increasing trends that might indicate kickbacks?
3. Calculate the average product price paid by purchaser. For example, calculate the average price paid for "All Purpose Wipers" when Jose, Sally, and Daniel are purchasing. Compare these average prices. Do you see any issues to search further?
4. Verify that all purchases are included in the data set. If a purchase was left out, its ID would be removed from the sequential list of IDs. Compare each ID and ensure the column increases by one in each record.
5. Verify the values in the Quantity and Total columns. Are any missing or abnormal values present?
6. Analyze the Product Price column from each company using Benford's Law. Analyze only the first digit of the column. On average, do any of the vendors stand out? In other words, are the transactions from any vendor not matching Benford's Law?

Case Study 3

Import the ch06_charges.tsv and ch06_approved_vendors.tsv data sets into your analysis software. These files give a list of purchases and vendors that are approved for use, respectively.

Questions

1. Are any vendors used that are not approved vendors? If so, list the vendor names and the employees who used these vendors. What follow-up steps should be taken on these vendors?
2. Were any vendors unused by the purchasing department? What does this fact tell us about these vendors?

Case Study 4
Using the financial information in the following tables, compute the required ratios list on the ratio analysis sheet and then complete the horizontal and vertical analyses worksheets.

ABC COMPANY BALANCE SHEET AS OF DECEMBER 31, 2012			
ASSETS	**2012**	**2011**	**2010**
Current assets			
Cash	$ 501,992	$ 434,215	$ 375,141
Accounts receivable	335,272	302,514	241,764
Inventory	515,174	505,321	310,885
Prepaid expenses	251,874	231,100	136,388
Total current assets	$1,604,312	$ 1,473,150	$ 1,064,178
Property, plant, and equipment	765,215	735,531	705,132
Accumulated depreciation	(218,284)	(196,842)	(175,400)
TOTAL ASSETS	$2,151,243	$ 2,011,839	$ 1,593,910
LIABILITIES			
Current liabilities			
Accounts payable	$248,494	$ 366,864	$ 322,156
Accrued liabilities	122,192	216,533	215,474
Income taxes payable	10,645	25,698	22,349
Current portion of long-term debt	42,200	42,200	42,200
Total current liabilities	$423,531	$ 651,295	$ 602,179
Long-term liabilities			
Long-term debt	425,311	400,311	375,100
TOTAL LIABILITIES	$848,842	$ 1,051,606	$ 977,279
STOCKHOLDERS' EQUITY			
Common stock	$370,124	$ 356,758	$ 320,841
Additional paid-in capital	29,546	24,881	21,910
Retained earnings	902,731	578,594	273,880
Total stockholders' equity	$1,302,401	$960,233	$ 616,631
TOTAL LIABILITIES AND STOCKHOLDERS' EQUITY	$2,151,243	$ 2,011,839	$ 1,593,910

ABC COMPANY
INCOME STATEMENT
FOR THE PERIOD ENDED DECEMBER 31, 2012

	2012	2011	2010
Sales	$1,572,134	$1,413,581	$1,158,417
Cost of goods sold	$601,215	556,721	500,702
Gross profit	$970,919	$856,860	$657,715
EXPENSES			
Advertising	$555,153	$50,531	$42,150
Depreciation	21,442	21,442	21,442
Bad debts	20,151	18,934	17,943
Legal	17,261	10,207	9,701
Miscellaneous	91,014	31,214	29,104
Rent	148,321	142,078	141,143
Repairs and maintenance	14,315	13,642	11,932
Salaries and wages	47,121	45,312	39,142
Utilities	15,912	15,643	14,217
Total expenses	$ 430,690	$349,003	$326,774
Net income before income tax	$ 540,229	$507,857	$330,941
Income tax expense	216,092	203,143	132,376
NET INCOME	$ 324,137	$304,714	$198,565
Number of shares of stock outstanding	35,913	26,786	23,712

ABC COMPANY
RATIO ANALYSIS
DECEMBER 31, 2012

LIQUIDITY RATIOS:	12/31/12	12/31/11	Change	% Change
Current ratio				
Current assets/Current liabilities	———	———	———	———
Quick ratio				
(Current assets – Inventory)/Current liabilities	———	———	———	———
Accounts receivable turnover				
Sales/Average accounts receivable	———	———	———	———
Days' sales in accounts receivable				
365/Accounts receivable turnover	———	———	———	———
Inventory turnover				
Cost of goods sold/Average inventory	———	———	———	———
PROFITABILITY/PERFORMANCE RATIOS:				
Profit margin				
Net income/Net sales	———	———	———	———
Gross profit margin (%)				
Gross profit/Sales	———	———	———	———
Earnings per share				
Net income/Number of shares of stock	———	———	———	———
Sales/Total assets				
Sales/Total assets	———	———	———	———
Sales/Working capital				
Sales/(Current assets – Current liabilities)	———	———	———	———
EQUITY POSITION RATIOS:				
Owners' equity/Total assets				
Total stockholders' equity/Total assets	———	———	———	———
Current liabilities/Owners' equity				
Current liabilities/Total stockholders' equity	———	———	———	———
Total liabilities/Owners' equity				
Total liabilities/Total stockholders' equity	———	———	———	———

ABC COMPANY
INCOME STATEMENT
FOR THE PERIOD ENDED DECEMBER 31, 2012

	2012	2011	$ CHANGE	% CHANGE
Sales	$1,572,134	$1,413,581		
Cost of goods sold	601,215	556,721	———	———
Gross profit	$970,919	$856,860	———	———
EXPENSES				
Advertising	$55,153	$50,531		
Depreciation	21,442	21,442		
Bad debts	20,151	18,934		
Legal	17,261	10,207		
Miscellaneous	91,014	31,214		
Rent	148,321	142,078		
Repairs and maintenance	14,315	13,642		
Salaries and wages	47,121	45,312		
Utilities	15,912	15,643	———	———
Total expenses	$430,690	$349,003	———	———
Net income before income tax	$540,229	$507,857		
Income tax expense	216,092	203,143	———	———
NET INCOME	$324,137	$304,714	———	———

ABC COMPANY
BALANCE SHEET
AS OF DECEMBER 31, 2012

ASSETS	2012	% TOTAL ASSETS	2011	% TOTAL ASSETS	2010	% TOTAL ASSETS
Current assets						
Cash	$ 501,992		$434,215		$375,141	
Accounts receivable	335,272		302,514		241,764	
Inventory	515,174		505,321		310,885	
Prepaid expenses	251,874		231,100		136,388	
Total current assets	$ 1,604,312		$1,473,150		$1,064,178	
Property, plant, and equipment	765,215		735,531		705,132	
Accumulated depreciation	(218,284)		(196,842)		(175,400)	
TOTAL ASSETS	$ 2,151,243		$2,011,839		$1,593,910	
LIABILITIES						
Current liabilities						
Accounts payable	$ 248,494		$ 366,864		$322,156	
Accrued liabilities	122,192		216,533		215,474	
Income taxes payable	10,645		25,698		22,349	
Current portion of long-term debt	42,200		42,200		42,200	
Total current liabilities	$423,531		$ 651,295		$602,179	
Long-term liabilities						
Long-term debt	425,311		400,311		375,100	
TOTAL LIABILITIES	$ 848,842		$1,051,606		$977,279	
STOCKHOLDERS' EQUITY						
Common stock	$ 370,124		$ 356,758		$320,841	
Additional paid-in capital	29,546		24,881		21,910	
Retained earnings	902,731		578,594		273,880	
Total stockholders' equity	$1,302,401		$ 960,233		$616,631	
TOTAL LIABILITIES AND STOCK-HOLDERS' EQUITY	$2,151,243		$2,011,839		$1,593,910	

INTERNET ASSIGNMENTS

1. Read the article entitled "Following Benford's Law, or Looking Out for No. 1" found at www.rexswain.com/benford.html. The article mentions that a statistics professor can easily discern if students flipped a coin 200 times or if they merely faked it. Of this exercise, the professor stated, "Most people do not know the real odds of such an exercise, so they cannot fake data convincingly." How does that exercise relate to Benford's Law and detecting fraud?

2. Search an Internet search engine for "neural network fraud." Answer the following questions:
   a. What is a neural network?
   b. How can neural networks be used to detect fraud?
   c. Which industries will benefit most from neural network technology?
   d. Name a couple of firms that are developing this technology.
   e. Credit card companies are very concerned with the growing problem of credit card fraud. They spend enormous amounts of money each year on detection. Go to the Web site of a large credit card company such as Visa, MasterCard, or American Express. What are some of the proactive measures these institutions are taking to control fraud and to persuade the public that it is safe to use credit cards?

DEBATES

1. You are the new controller of a major U.S. manufacturing firm. In your previous employment, you detected multiple varieties of fraud. The CFO of your new company informs you that top management is concerned about possible fraud in the organization and is interested in taking a proactive approach both to detecting and deterring fraud. After noting that he has recommended you for the fraud detection assignment, the CFO tells you that he is a little nervous about how much this investigative approach will cost and asks you to keep your choices simple and inexpensive. You and the CFO are good friends, and you've never had a problem suggesting ideas about upcoming projects in the past. You know that to be most effective in completing your new assignment, you should do some extensive data analysis because of the large size of the company and its databases.

   Have one person take the position of the CFO who wants to keep analyses simple and another the position of the controller who believes more expensive, data-driven approaches are necessary. Debate the appropriateness of the various detec tion approaches, including the deductive approach, for your company. Explain why traditional approaches may not be sufficient.

2. Sampling is the bread and butter of a significant portion of audit work. As a team (or as a class), list several of the most common audit techniques as well as fraud investigation methods. For example, searching for missing invoice numbers or sending accounts receivable confirmation letters are two common techniques. Comparing employee addresses with vendor addresses and establishing an anonymous tip line are common fraud investigation techniques. For each technique, have one side argue why sampling is the best option for analysis and have the other side argue why full-population analysis must be done. At the end, determine what percentage of audit techniques are best performed with full-population analysis.

END NOTES

1. While a normal distribution (bell curve) is required for most statistical calculations, z-scores are useful on nonnormal distributions too. Remember that fraud investigation is only looking for indicators, not for statistical significance upon which predictions can be made. With any indicator, further investigation will reveal whether fraud is actually occurring or not.

Examples of the Data-Driven Approach

The data-driven approach to fraud detection has been used in many cases. This appendix presents two examples: a small bank case and a large oil case.

Example 1: The Banking Industry

The first example of this detection approach involves a small bank with five branches. Realizing that controls were quite loose, especially those involving top management, the board of directors decided that a risk analysis would be cost-effective. The risk assessment would determine major management fraud exposures, identify symptoms those frauds would generate, and then search 16 years of bank data for the symptoms. The tests revealed the following symptoms:

- Exception reports, reflecting fraudulent transactions, which exhibited unusual, atypical, and otherwise questionable patterns of supervisory overrides; transactions with no apparent business purpose; and transactions involving unusually large amounts. This symptom occurred at least 211 times.
- Journal vouchers containing only one signature, containing incorrect information, and/or reflecting transfers between different customers' accounts. This symptom occurred at least 20 times on exception reports.
- Deposit slips with missing information, incomplete names, or where the name of the depositor did not match the name on the passbook and/or the account name in the bank's records. This symptom occurred in at least 41 of 56 exception reports.
- Deposits and withdrawals exceeding $1,000 in one executive's passbook account. This symptom occurred in 39 of 85 exception reports.
- Deposits and withdrawals from the same account made on the same day or within a short period of time and appearing on the exception reports. This symptom occurred on every exception report.
- Bank checks reflecting transfers between different customers' accounts or checks with altered dates. All 11 exception reports contained this symptom.
- Withdrawal vouchers and checks containing purported customer signatures readily distinguishable upon comparison with the customers' signatures. This symptom occurred at least 73 times.
- Large negative available balances in slush accounts and other customer accounts. This symptom appeared 15 times.
- Deposit slips of customer funds between accounts of different customers and/or deposits of customer checks where cash was received. This symptom occurred in eight of nine exception reports.
- CDs closed prematurely, with proceeds placed in lower interest-bearing passbook accounts, sometimes with large penalties. This symptom occurred in 36 of 42 exception reports.
- Customers not present when accounts were opened and closed or when transactions were effected in the account. This symptom occurred numerous times.
- Large withdrawals of cash by executives from customers' accounts. Out of 234 exception reports, withdrawals happened in 129 of them.
- The mailing of customer account statements to executives instead of to the customer, without written authorization. This happened with at least 40 accounts.

Follow-up investigation of the "symptoms" found that one executive vice president had embezzled several million dollars through various schemes over several years.

Example 2: The Oil Industry

A second case involves a search for fraud in one of the world's largest oil refineries. This refinery's situation provided an excellent search laboratory because it involved tens of thousands of vendor and employee transactions. Its two databases gave the investigators a data-rich environment to explore. The databases contained detailed information on material acquisitions, project status, and vendor labor billings showing hours worked by individuals. A total of 1,983 vendors were analyzed, with 41 vendors having transactions with the refinery totaling over $1 million each, 242 vendors having transactions totaling over $100,000 each, and 497 vendors having transactions totaling over $25,000 each. The period studied produced over 47,000 vendor invoices, and at least that many expense reimbursement, payroll, and other employee-driven transactions. In addition, because the refinery was heavily unionized and employed many second- and third-generation employees, the company believed that there might be employees who knew about frauds but were reticent to come forward with information.

As part of the database search, the investigators developed customized queries that combined data in new and different ways. In addition, a "time engine" was developed that analyzed fraud symptoms by time period as well as by individual, invoice, product, purchase order, and other factors under consideration. Using this approach, a number of possible fraud symptoms were observed. Because of management's interest and the availability of data, detection efforts focused primarily on various types of vendor and contractor fraud. Table 6.1A identifies the types of possible fraud identified, the symptoms associated with the various frauds, and some of the searches that were performed.

Although the actual instances of fraud at the oil refinery are still being investigated (or litigated), the detection effort led to both discoveries of fraud and data errors. In addition, several of the findings that did not involve fraud resulted in valuable information for management. Some of the red flags identified are as follows:

- The search for the dollar amount, number, and percentage of returned items by vendor uncovered three suspicious vendors. The refinery was rejecting over 50 percent of goods received from these vendors, due to poor quality. Two of these were

TABLE 6.1A DATABASE SEARCH FOR FRAUD

TYPE OF FRAUD	RED FLAGS IDENTIFIED	RED-FLAG SEARCHES
Vendor(s) committing fraud	Overcharging for goods	Price increases greater than 30% for four consecutive years.
	Providing poor-quality goods	Work orders with cost overruns exceeding 50%. Dollar amount, number, and percentage of goods returned to vendor.
	Billing more than once for the same purchase	Duplicate invoice numbers. Vendors with invoices for the same amount on the same day. Multiple invoices for the same item description by vendor.
	Short shipping	Quantity paid for exceeds quantity received, ranked by dollar differences.
	Billing for goods not ordered or shipped	Vendors with sequential invoices.
Employee(s) committing purchasing fraud	Establishing dummy vendors	Two or more suppliers with same telephone number and/or address. Matching of vendors paid with company's master vendor list and with Dun & Bradstreet listings. Contractors with common names, first two letters match exactly, and 90% of the name is the same. Employee and vendor telephone numbers are the same. Contractors with only one buyer for all contracts.
	Purchasing goods for personal use	Purchase orders with zero dollar amounts by buyer. Invoices exceeding purchase order dollar amount ranked by dollar difference. Invoices without valid purchase order.

TABLE 6.1A (Continued)

TYPE OF FRAUD	RED FLAGS IDENTIFIED	RED-FLAG SEARCHES
Vendor and company employee(s) committing fraud in collusion	Receiving kickbacks or other favors	Price increases greater than 30% for four consecutive years. Dollar amount, number, and percentage of items returned by vendor and buyer. Payments without receiving reports. Increased volume of purchases by vendor and buyer. Combination of increased prices and increased purchases from specific vendors.
Contractor(s) committing fraud	Charging more hours than actually worked	Ranking of hours worked by contractor employee.
	Working excessive overtime for higher per-hour rate	Ranking of overtime hours worked per two-week pay periods by contractor and contractor employee. Ranking of contractors with rising overtime charges.
	Overbilling for equipment used	Trends in equipment rental rates by type of equipment by contractor. Differences between standard (allowed) rates and actual rates by contractor over time.
	Billing for equipment not used	Equipment charges when no labor is charged.
	Billing at the wrong rates	Licenses of workers for various crafts vs. licenses issued by states. Changes in craft designation for employees by contractor.
	Charging higher labor rates than allowed	Contractor employees with significant jumps in labor rates. Ranking of labor rates by craft by contractor. Contractors with outrageous rates per hour.
	Charging for fake employees	Contractor employee SSN's arranged by ascending numbers.
Company employee(s) committing contractor-related fraud	Charging for more hours than contractor actually worked and paying fictitious employees	Employees ranked by hours worked per pay period.
	Working excessive overtime for higher rates	Employees with rising overtime charges. Employees with high overtime per time card.
Contractor and company employee(s) committing fraud in collusion	Receiving kickbacks for favors	Increased volume of work by vendor by buyer employee(s) committing: Higher than normal rates for services. Excessive charges for equipment use. Contractors with rapidly rising invoice amounts. Increasing trend of equipment rental rates by contracting employee. Amounts contracted by contractor by buyer. Invoices with outrageous costs per hour.
All types of fraud	Nonrandomness in invoice numbers and amounts	Benford's digits tests.

small suppliers, but one represented a relationship with one of the refinery's largest vendors.

- The search for multiple invoices for the same item description by vendor uncovered six invoices for the same amount from the same vendor on the same day, all for $1,044,000. Three invoices from the same vendor, on the same day, for the same items, each for $900,000, were also found.
- Using various combinations of red flags, four companies that appeared to be committing large-scale contractor fraud were identified. The refinery no longer conducts business with two of these vendors and is pursuing recovery.
- The search for price increases greater than 30 percent per year for four consecutive years uncovered one company that had increased prices 581,700 percent and another that had increased prices by 331,879 percent. In total, 35 companies had raised prices over 1,000 percent, and 202 companies had raised prices over 100 percent.
- No incidences were found where employee and vendor telephone numbers were the same, but six employees had the same addresses as vendors.
- Of the 319 vendors with common names and addresses, all but two of these had reasonable explanations for the coincidence.
- The search for vendors not listed in the master file uncovered one unapproved vendor from whom the company had purchased $791,268 of services. Purchases from all other unapproved vendors totaled less than $10,000.
- In 20 purchases over $100,000, the quantity paid for was greater than the quantity received.
- The search for high-volume purchases by vendor uncovered only one vendor with unusually high transactions. The company paid $56,201 for items

with unit prices of 19¢ and 12¢ each. The volume on these items far exceeded the refinery's needs.

- The search for contractor employees with excessive overtime was one of the most useful analyses. Four companies had employees who reported working 150+ hours over 20 consecutive two-week pay periods. Employees of one company submitted time cards from different locations for the same period. Another company's employees averaged 2,046 hours of overtime for the year. In one year, 10 companies had averages of over 200 overtime hours per two-week period, 388 had some overtime, and hundreds had no overtime.
- Per-hour charges by craft and by company and employee ranged from $56.11 per hour to $15.43 for the same craft. Also, 40 companies had standard deviations for rates billed that were over 40 percent of the average rates billed for the same craft.
- Invoices from seven companies exceeded purchase order amounts by over $100,000. The largest difference was $713,791 on an original invoice of $21,621.
- The search for vendors with sequential invoices revealed 19 vendors that submitted sequentially numbered invoices in over 50 percent of all invoices. With one vendor, over 83 percent of the invoices submitted were sequential.
- The search uncovered three companies with over 100 zero-amount purchase orders.
- Nine contractors had cost overruns exceeding 50 percent and $100,000. The highest percentage overrun was 2,431 percent.
- Finally, only 65 companies could not be matched with Dun & Bradstreet listings. Except in a few instances, purchases from nonlisted companies were small.

PART **4**

Fraud Investigation

CHAPTER 7

Investigating Theft Acts

LEARNING OBJECTIVES

After studying this chapter, you should be able to:

- Discuss theft investigation methods and how they are used to investigate suspected fraud.

- Understand how to coordinate an investigation, using a vulnerability chart.

- Describe the nature of surveillance and covert operations.

- Understand the effectiveness of invigilation to investigate fraud.

- Explain how to obtain physical evidence and how it can be used in a fraud investigation.

- Understand how to seize and analyze electronic information from cell phones, hard drives, e-mail, and other sources.

TO THE STUDENT

Investigation is one of the most interesting facets of being a fraud investigator. This chapter introduces you to the different methods used for investigation, from surveillance to invigilation to electronic and computer searches. As you read the chapter, think of where each method would be most useful, and consider the skills you need to master each one.

No single promotion lured more people to McDonald's than its popular Monopoly game—until August 2001, when it was discovered that the Monopoly game was a large fraud. Simon Marketing, which ran the Monopoly game on behalf of McDonald's, was responsible for the fraud. Simon Marketing allegedly defrauded McDonald's out of $13 million worth of game prizes over the promotion period.[1]

In a quiet, upper-class subdivision of brick-and-stucco mansions in Lawrenceville, Georgia, Jerome Jacobson spent the past six years masterminding one of the largest promotional contests ever held. As Simon's longtime manager of game security, Jacobson, 58, traveled the country and randomly placed winning peel-off contest stickers on things like soft-drink cups and French fry boxes in McDonald's restaurants and inserted instant-winner tickets in magazines and Sunday newspaper circulars. However, the FBI says that Jacobson devised his own cash-in scheme—embezzling winning game pieces and instant tickets. In turn, he sold them to prearranged winners for kickbacks of $50,000 or more.

Jacobson pocketed at least $50,000 each from up to 13 separate $1 million prizewinners. The government's lengthy complaint described Jacobson as a savvy manipulator and crime ringleader, willing to double-cross those who dared to hold back payments. Jacobson recruited at least two accomplices who acted as recruiters themselves.

In exchange for negotiated payments, the "winners" were provided winning game pieces and instant-prize tickets. They were also instructed at length on how to disguise their actual residences and what to tell McDonald's about where and how they had picked up game pieces and instant-winner tickets.

According to federal prosecutors, at least 17 recruits won ill-gotten prizes. Besides the 13 winners of the $1 million game, one recipient won a 1996 Dodge Viper valued at about $60,000 and others won cash prizes of $100,000 and $200,000.

Without the informant who contacted the Jacksonville FBI office, the contest rip-offs allegedly orchestrated by Jacobson would likely have continued unabated. FBI agents obtained court permission for several telephone wiretaps, and they began tailing Jacobson and others. The FBI also received McDonald's cooperation in delaying the issuing of checks to winners, which helped the FBI secure evidence from wiretaps.

In previous chapters, we discussed fraud prevention and detection. In this chapter, we will discuss different methods of investigating a theft act once predication is found. Figure 7.1 shows the fraud triangle plus inquiry approach to investigations, a comprehensive model for investigations. It includes four different investigative methods: theft, concealment, conversion, and inquiry. While fraud investigations progress in unique ways to meet their specific needs, most investigations contain elements of the four methods. These methods are discussed in this and the following chapters.

When to Investigate

Before we discuss specific types of evidence that should be gathered in a case, you should understand the considerations involved in deciding whether to investigate or not. As we have discussed previously, investigation of a fraud only follows when there is predication, meaning that there are symptoms or indications (red flags) that a fraud may be occurring. That predication may have arisen because someone provided an indication that fraud may be occurring (such as providing a tip or complaint) or it may have come from proactively searching for fraud. Once there is predication, those involved must decide whether or not to investigate. That decision is often made by auditors, security personnel, human resource personnel, attorneys, or even law enforcement officials. You will likely be a key person in this decision. Some of the factors that are

FIGURE 7.1 FRAUD TRIANGLE PLUS INQUIRY APPROACH TO INVESTIGATIONS

considered in deciding whether or not to investigate are the following:

- *Perceived strength of the predication*
- *Perceived cost of the investigation*
- *Exposure or amount that could have been taken*
- *The signal that investigation or noninvestigation will send to others in the organization*
- *Risks of investigating and not investigating*
- *Public exposure or loss of reputation from investigating and not investigating*
- *Nature of the possible fraud.*

For example, under recent changes in the laws, the risks would be much higher for not fully investigating a potential fraud perpetrated by the CEO of an organization than it would be to not investigate a fraud perpetrated by a line employee.

Generally, once there is predication, the best policy is to investigate the potential fraud to determine the *who, why, how,* and *how much* questions of the fraud. Sometimes what is observed or what resulted in predication is only the tip of the iceberg. Other times, the investigation of predication may exonerate those who were suspected of wrongdoing. And, as we have already discussed, since most frauds grow geometrically over time, it is better to investigate them while they are still relatively small than to wait until they bankrupt a division or cause extreme embarrassment for an organization.

Once the decision has been made to investigate, investigators must decide what methods to use to gather evidence. In deciding which methods to use, investigators should focus on the strongest type of evidence for the specific fraud. For example, because inventory frauds involve the transporting of stolen goods, such frauds are often investigated by using theft investigative techniques to gather physical evidence. On the other hand, payroll frauds, such as charging excess overtime or adding ghost employees to the payroll, can usually be most easily investigated by focusing on concealment efforts. Such frauds must be concealed in the records of an organization, and it is usually easiest to gather documentary evidence. With collusive or kickback-type frauds, however, there is usually no direct documentary evidence (although there might be indirect documentary evidence such as purchasing records that show increasing prices or increasing work by a particular vendor). As a result, concealment investigative techniques usually do not work well in kickback situations. With such frauds, investigators often use theft act investigative methods, such as tailing or wiretaps, which were used in the McDonald's case, or gather circumstantial conversion evidence from public records and other sources showing a lifestyle beyond what the perpetrator's known income could support. Inquiry investigative methods are usually helpful in investigating all types of frauds, but they are most useful after you have gathered other types of evidence and know who to interview and what questions to ask.

As you investigate, it is important to remember to remain objective. You want to be smart and informed so you do not miss potential indicators. Look at people and evidence in a case with professional skepticism. Do not take things you see or read at face value. Try to read between the lines to see what others might have missed. On the other hand, it is not wise to think of everyone you meet as a criminal. During your career, you may meet investigators who have become somewhat callused toward people and evidence because of past investigation experiences with less-than-honest people. Instead, try to find a balance where you can exercise good judgment as a professional fraud investigator.

Theft Act Investigative Methods

Theft act investigations are those activities which directly investigate the fraud act, such as **surveillance** and covert operations, invigilation, obtaining physical evidence, and gathering electronic evidence. These investigations should usually begin by using techniques that will not arouse suspicion and, most importantly, will not wrongly incriminate innocent people. Therefore, initially, as few people as possible should be involved, words such as "investigation" should be avoided ("audit" and "inquiry" are more appropriate), and the investigation should be started by using techniques that will not likely be recognized. As the inquiry proceeds, investigative methods will work inward toward the prime suspect, until finally he or she is confronted in an interview. By waiting to interview the primary suspect, you can gather sufficient evidence to conduct a powerful, directed interview without giving your case away prematurely. Figure 7.2 provides an illustration of this pattern.

To illustrate, suppose a purchasing employee is suspected of taking kickbacks. The investigation might proceed through the following steps:

1. Check the employee's personnel records for evidence of liens, other financial difficulties, or previous problems.
2. Perform a "special audit" of the purchasing function in order to examine trends and changes in prices and purchasing volume from various vendors.
3. Search the suspect's e-mail and other electronic records for communication with outside vendors, spreadsheets, or other records related to the kickback.
4. Search public records and other sources to gather evidence about the suspect's lifestyle.
5. Perform surveillance or other covert operations.
6. Interview former buyers and unsuccessful vendors.
7. Interview current buyers, and, if no collusion with management is suspected, interview the suspect's manager.
8. Simultaneously interview the suspected buyer and the suspected vendor.

Several of these steps can be performed without arousing suspicion or without anyone who does not have the need to know being aware that an investigation is being

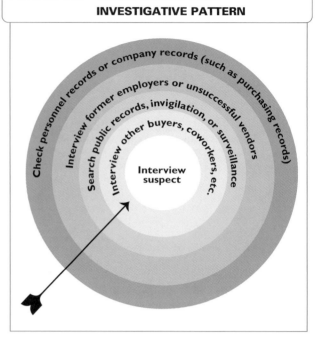

FIGURE 7.2   EXAMPLE THEFT ACT INVESTIGATIVE PATTERN

conducted. For example, security personnel, auditors, and fraud examiners commonly examine personnel records during normal audits. Similarly, purchasing records and public records searches usually do not create suspicion, because they are normal audit procedures or because they can be performed offsite. Searching of e-mail files can be done on the corporate server rather than on the suspect's computer, and hard drive information can be searched from centralized backups.

Surveillance, when properly performed, is done without the perpetrator's knowledge. Only when interviews begin is the suspect likely to become aware of the investigation. Even then, interviews should normally be conducted first with individuals who are objective and not currently associated with the suspect and should work inward until the suspect is finally interviewed. The purposes of starting tangentially and working inward are to avoid alerting suspects too early that they are under investigation and to avoid creating undue stress or suspicion among other employees. Once a case is revealed, evidence and people often have a way of "disappearing." In addition, this process best protects the target of the investigation—especially if evidence later reveals that the individual was not, in fact, involved.

STOP & THINK   *Why is it important to conduct activities that do not arouse suspicion first and interview the primary subject near the end of your investigation? What could occur if you fail to do this?*

Developing a Vulnerability Chart

When beginning a fraud investigation, it is often useful to develop theories about what kind of fraud could have occurred, who the possible perpetrators could have been, what their motivations might have been, and how much might have been taken. One way to develop such theories is to use a **vulnerability chart** as a tool for explicitly considering all aspects of the fraud and for establishing fraud theories. A vulnerability chart coordinates the various elements of the possible fraud, including (1) assets that were taken or are missing, (2) individuals who have theft opportunities, (3) theft investigative methods, (4) concealment possibilities, (5) conversion possibilities, (6) symptoms observed, (7) pressures of possible perpetrators, (8) rationalization of perpetrators, and (9) key internal controls that had to be compromised for the theft to occur. For example, assume that a bank customer complained that a deposit she made last month was not credited to her account. A vulnerability chart similar to the one in Table 7.1 would identify all the factors involved in the fraud.

As shown in the top section of this vulnerability chart, the assets that may have been taken included the customer's deposit. Theft opportunities may have been available to the teller who processed the transaction, to an operations officer who supervised the teller, or to the proof operator who processed the credit

TABLE 7.1 EXAMPLE VULNERABILITY CHART

| | | | | | VULNERABILITY CHART | | | |
| | | | | | POSSIBLE MOTIVE(S) | | | |
What was taken?	Who had opportunity?	How were assets moved?	How was theft concealed?	How are assets converted?	Red flag symptoms?	Pressures	Rationalizations	Key Internal Controls
Computer deposit	Teller operations officer Proof operator	Entering verified credits Stealing check; endorsing it	Destroying old or creating a new deposit slip Forged signature Entering credit in own account	Unlimited	Changed behavior Changed lifestyle Customer complaint	Tax lien New home Divorce	Feels underpaid or poorly treated	Use processing jacket Certification Teller counts customer receipts Restrict computer access Not allowing employees to credit their own account
Goods delivered	Receiving trucker	Not received Truck	Night Included with trash	Fenced Used personally	Control not followed Goods not counted	New car Spouse laid off	Passed over for promotion	Receiving report
Overcharged for goods	Purchasing agent	N/A	Kickback	Cash Hire spouse	Extravagant lifestyle Assets sold inexpensively	Maintain lifestyle	Greed	Bids

to the customer's account. Movement of the assets was easy and could have occurred by entering a credit in the wrong account, placing the checks (if the deposit involved checks) in the cash drawer and withdrawing cash, stealing cash, or falsely endorsing checks. Concealment was possible by destroying the customer's deposit slip, creating a new deposit slip, or forging a signature. Since the stolen funds involved cash, conversion opportunities were unlimited. Symptoms observed might include changed behavior, an improved lifestyle, or another customer complaint. Pressures motivating the fraud could have involved a tax lien against the teller's property, an expensive new home purchased by the proof operator, or a recent divorce by the operations officer. Rationalizations could have involved the perpetrator's feelings of being underpaid or treated poorly. Key internal controls that would have had to be overridden could have involved not allowing an employee to enter credits into his or her own account, use of processing jackets in the proof department, the teller omitting certification, or restricted access to the computer system.

Similar vulnerability charts can be prepared for any potential fraud. For example, frauds involving stolen inventory and overcharged goods are also shown in the vulnerability chart in Table 7.1. The advantage of using a vulnerability chart is that it forces investigators to explicitly consider all aspects of a fraud.

Remember this ...

A vulnerability chart is a tool that coordinates the assets that were taken, individuals who had theft opportunities, investigation methods, concealment and conversion possibilities, symptoms observed, pressures, rationalizations, and key controls that had to be compromised.

Surveillance and Covert Operations

Surveillance and covert or undercover operations are theft investigation techniques that rely on the senses, especially hearing and seeing. Surveillance or observation means watching and recording (on paper, film, or magnetic tape) the physical facts, acts, and movements, which form part of a fraud. The three types of surveillance are: (1) stationary or fixed point, (2) moving or tailing, and (3) electronic surveillance. Some form of surveillance is used in investigating most frauds, including even financial statement frauds.

Simple fixed-point or stationary observations can be conducted by anyone. In conducting these observations, the investigator should locate the scene that should be observed, anticipate the action that is most likely to occur at the scene, and either keep detailed notes on all activities involving the suspect or record them on film or tape. The detailed records should include the date and day of observation, the name of the observer, the names of corroborating witnesses, the position from which the observation was made, its distance from the scene, and the time the observation began and ended, along with a detailed time log of all the movements and activities of the suspect. An example of a surveillance log is shown in Table 7.2. The person under surveillance was suspected of taking kickbacks from a vendor.

Mobile observation, or tailing, as was used in the McDonald's fraud, is much more risky than stationary surveillance. In one case, an internal auditor was shot at while tailing a suspect. While the potential rewards for this type of surveillance are high and may include identifying the receiver of stolen goods or the payer of bribes or kickbacks, the chances of failure are high. Tailing should only be done by professionals.

Electronic surveillance of employees, using video cameras, is frequently used. Wiretapping, another form of surveillance, is usually only available to law enforcement officers. Electronic surveillance may have limited value in the investigation of employee frauds and many other white-collar crimes because of concerns regarding employees' privacy in the workplace. However, it is useful in kickback-type schemes, such as the McDonald's case, where law enforcement is involved. Many corporations have instituted strict controls over all forms of electronic surveillance, including video and wiretapping. However, most have policies that state that all data on corporate computers, including personal e-mail and documents, are property of the corporation and can be used in investigations. Be sure to check with legal counsel before proceeding with any of these methods.

Surveillance and covert operations are normally legal as long as they do not invade a person's reasonable expectation of privacy under the Fourth Amendment to the Constitution, which protects the right of a person against unreasonable searches. Again, legal counsel and human resource personnel should always be consulted before any form of surveillance takes place. In addition, all corporations and institutions should implement strict protocols regarding the use of any form of surveillance in order to ensure that controls are in place and that a

TABLE 7.2 SURVEILLANCE LOG

JANUARY 29, 2010 DATE/TIME	EVENT
6:30 p.m.	Instituted surveillance at Flatirons Country Club, 457 W. Arapahoe, Boulder, CO.
6:40 p.m.	Alex Tong and unidentified white male seen leaving racquetball courts and entering locker rooms.
7:00 p.m.	Both men seen leaving locker room.
7:05 p.m.	Tong and white male enter club restaurant and order drinks. White male orders beer; Tong orders orange liquid drink.
7:10 p.m.	Both men order dinner.
7:25 p.m.	Dinner arrives. Tong has white, cream-based soup and club sandwich. White male has steak and potatoes.
7:30 p.m.	Break: Surveillance terminated.
7:36 p.m.	Surveillance reinstituted. Both men still eating at table.
7:55 p.m.	Tong goes to restroom. White male remains at table.
8:00 p.m.	Tong returns to table.
8:15 p.m.	Both men order a drink each.
8:25 p.m.	White male requests check.
8:30 p.m.	Check arrives and is presented to white male. White male hands credit card to waitress without examining check.
8:35 p.m.	Waitress returns, gives bill to white male, who signs bill. Waitress gives yellow slip to white male. No indication of Tong attempting to pay check.
8:40 p.m.	White male removes envelope from portfolio and gives it to Tong. Tong looks pleased and places envelope in his pocket. Twosome leaves and is seen getting into a Mercedes Benz and a 2008 Lexus, respectively, and driving away.
8:45 p.m.	Waitress is interviewed. She displays a copy of a Citibank Gold MasterCard charge slip in the name of Christopher D. Ballard, account number 5424-1803-1930-1493. Card expires 03/2009. The amount of the check is $78.65. Waitress is given $20 cash tip for information.
9:00 p.m.	Surveillance terminated.

"reasonable person" test is given to any application. The value of surveillance can be more than offset by employee problems caused by inappropriate or improper application of the techniques.

Undercover operations are both legal and valid, provided they are not used as fishing expeditions. Undercover operations are extremely costly and time consuming and should be used with extreme care. Undercover investigations should be used only when (1) large-scale collusive fraud or crime is likely, (2) other methods of fraud investigation fail, (3) the investigation can be closely monitored, (4) there is significant reason to believe that the fraud is occurring or reoccurring, (5) the investigation is in strict compliance with the laws and ethics of the organization, (6) the investigation can remain secretive, and (7) law enforcement authorities are informed when appropriate evidence has been accumulated.

CAUTION   *Surveillance and covert activities can be dangerous to you and your case when used incorrectly or without the proper training.*

Three illustrations of actual undercover operations highlight some of the risks involved. In the first instance, which was successful, collusive fraud was suspected. The undercover agent was able to get valuable evidence that led to the conviction of several individuals. The other two undercover operations, which were unsuccessful, concerned suspected drug dealing at manufacturing facilities. Drug dealing is an activity that no organization can tolerate, because if an employee purchases and uses drugs on the job and then is involved in an automobile accident on the way home from work, for example, the organization may be legally liable for damages. In the second operation, the agent became fearful and quit. In the third operation, the agent became sympathetic to the suspects and was not helpful.

With developments in technology, many companies are using database searches and artificial intelligence systems to provide surveillance or filter huge amounts of data and identify suspicious transactions. These methods were discussed in Chapter 6 and are part of the proactive method of fraud detection. Instead of tailing or following individuals, programs using artificial intelligence now tail or monitor transactions to find transactions that are unusual or look suspicious. For example, it has been estimated that credit card fraud costs the industry about $1 billion a year, or 7 cents out of every $100 spent on plastic. But the estimate is down significantly from its peak about a decade ago. This decrease is due, in large part, to the use of powerful technology that works like a surveillance camera and can recognize unusual spending patterns. Many of us have been participants in this credit card surveillance activity. Have you ever made a large or unusual charge purchase and had the credit card company contact you to make sure the purchase was made by you? Its surveillance tracking system likely recognized the transaction that appeared unusual given your typical spending habits.

Driven by needs ranging from security to fraud protection to quality of service, applications for monitoring, surveillance, and recording are growing in importance and sophistication. In telecommunications systems, for example, signaling protocols provide access to databases and real-time call establishment requests containing highly detailed and useful information regarding locations, calling patterns, destinations, duration, and call frequency. These data are often mined for a variety of functions from traditional call-setup to billing, while signaling traffic can also be monitored for quality of service, fraud prevention, legal intercept, and billing. These capabilities can greatly enhance service providers' efforts to reduce expenses, preserve capital, and retain customers. They can also provide telecommunications vendors with a vast source of information from which they can build new applications and revenues.

As a final example of electronic surveillance, consider the tracking system used by the Financial Industry Regulatory Authority, Inc. (FINRA). FINRA is the largest securities industry self-regulatory organization in the United States. FINRA develops rules and regulations, conducts regulatory reviews of members' activities and designs, and operates and regulates securities markets all for the benefit and protection of investors.

FINRA is contracted to oversee security firms, professional training, testing, and licensing on all the major U.S. stock markets. The market regulation department is responsible for monitoring all activity to ensure compliance with market rules in order to provide a level playing field for all market participants and investors. An automated system screens all trades and quotes according to approved, standardized criteria to identify potential violations for review and, if appropriate, regulatory action.

Fraud detection capabilities are provided through rule and sequence-matching algorithms, which are used to detect instances in the database that match patterns that could indicate fraud. The surveillance techniques provide customized visualizations for depicting the relevant relationships in the data, as well as capabilities

for multiple users to review and manage the alerts that are generated and the patterns that are used.

Whether the surveillance is manual or electronic, observing someone's activities is a fraud detection tool that attempts to catch fraud and other types of crime at the theft act stage. Those who use such methods are not trying to understand the cover-up or concealment of fraud or even how the money is being spent, unless, of course, the spending of the money is the actual theft act as it would be with credit card fraud.

Invigilation

Invigilation (in-vij-uh-ley-shun) is a theft act investigative technique that involves close supervision of suspects during an examination period. Such strict temporary controls are imposed on an activity that, during the period of invigilation, makes fraud virtually impossible to commit. As we have already indicated, opportunity is one of the three conditions that must exist before fraud can occur. When controls are made so strict that opportunities to commit fraud are nonexistent, a fraud-free profile can be established. Companies normally do not implement controls at this level because their detail is cost prohibitive. However, during a fraud investigation, changes seen between the control periods highlight where fraud may be occurring. The use of detail record keeping before, during, and after invigilation is key to this method. The diagram in Figure 7.3 outlines invigilation.

The following is an example of invigilation to detect a fraud involving inventory losses:

An oil distributor was experiencing inventory losses of 0.23 percent of the inventory. The manager suspected that fraud was taking place but was not sure how or when. Observation and other investigative methods failed to produce evidence. For a 30-day period, the installation was saturated with security guards and auditors. Every movement of goods both in and out was checked, all documents were verified, and inventory and equipment were regularly reviewed. During the period of invigilation, losses ceased. After the invigilation, records kept at the plant were examined for absolute, proportional, and reasonableness changes during the invigilation period. Two service stations—which before the exercise had bought an average of only 2,000 gallons of gasoline a week—suddenly doubled their orders. During the 30 days, in fact, each received more than 19,000 gallons. In addition, a shift foreman, who in 23 years of service had taken no sick leave, was away from work on 19 of the 30 days. Two or three months were allowed to elapse, and during this time, covert observation was maintained on the service stations, whose

FIGURE 7.3   INVIGILATION DIAGRAM

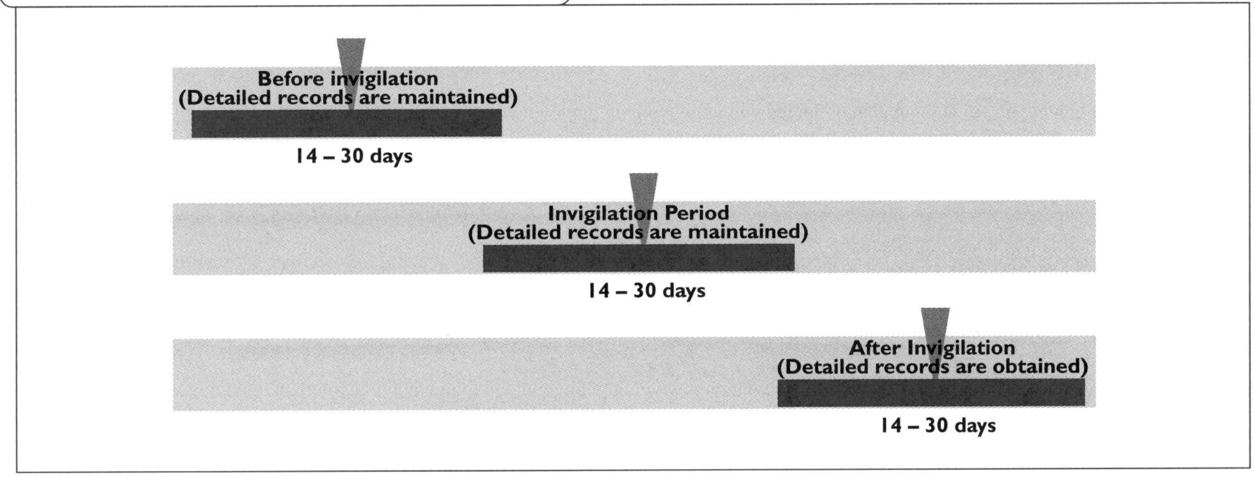

Before invigilation
(Detailed records are maintained)

14 – 30 days

Invigilation Period
(Detailed records are maintained)

14 – 30 days

After Invigilation
(Detailed records are obtained)

14 – 30 days

orders by this time had reverted to 2,000 gallons per week. Using night vision equipment and cameras, unrecorded deliveries to the service stations were detected. The owners were interviewed, and their books were examined. They were subsequently charged with fraud extending back two years and involving 62,000 gallons of gasoline.

This example of invigilation took place in a large company and involved losses in inventory. Invigilation can also be used as a fraud investigation tool in smaller organizations. The following example illustrates such a scenario:

Mark owned an auto tune-up shop. The company had 12 bays, 12 mechanics, and 1 accountant, John, who Mark completely trusted with all accounting duties, including cash receipts, bank deposits, the writing of checks, payroll, and taxes. Each year, Mark's business serviced more cars, but each year cash flows became worse. Not knowing what to do, Mark consulted a friend, who was a CPA. The friend performed various cost, volume, and profit analyses and informed Mark that he should be profitable. He suggested to Mark that maybe someone was embezzling money. Mark's reply was that the only one that was in a position to embezzle was John. The CPA friend encouraged Mark to try an experiment. He suggested that Mark first make copies of all bank statements and other cash records for one month. Next, Mark should tell all employees, including John, that he was thinking about selling the shop and that the prospective buyer insisted on daily audited records for one month. During this month, an outside CPA would come daily to count cash receipts, make bank deposits, write all checks, and check on parts and inventory. After

one month, Mark was to inform all employees that the sale had fallen through and that he was not going to sell the shop. Following the invigilation period, Mark was again to copy bank statements and other cash records for one month. To Mark's surprise, cash paid by customers as a percentage of total receipts (customers either paid by check, credit card, or cash) was 7 percent before the invigilation period, 15 percent during the one-month invigilation period, and again approximately 7 percent in the month following the invigilation period. Faced with the evidence, John admitted that he had been embezzling cash from Mark's business. A subsequent analysis revealed that the total amount he had stolen exceeded $600,000.

Invigilation is an investigative technique that can be expensive. It should be used only with management's approval, and it should be restricted to a discrete and self-contained area of business. Most commonly, it is used in such high-risk areas as expensive inventory, areas with poor controls over the receipt and loading of goods, and areas with poor controls over accounting records.

When using invigilation, management must decide on the precise nature of the increased temporary controls necessary to remove fraud opportunities. Past records should be analyzed in order to establish an operating profile for the unit under review. This profile must include such things as normal losses, the number and nature of transactions per day, the number and type of exceptional transactions, and the number of vehicle movements in and out of the facility. To get an accurate reading, it is generally agreed that the invigilation period must be at least 14 days in length. In individual cases, however, the optimal duration will depend on the frequency and nature of transactions.

Invigilation should be used wisely and with caution because it can backfire in some cases. One company, for example, was suffering significant small tool losses from its manufacturing plant. To determine who was taking the tools, the company decided to inspect all workers' lunch boxes as they exited the facility. The practice so upset employees that it caused a work slowdown that was more expensive than the fraud losses.

Remember this …

Invigilation is a technique that imposes significant controls to make fraud impossible to commit for a period of time. Profiles and trends can be found by analyzing the differences in the before, during, and after invigilation periods.

Physical Evidence

Physical evidence can be useful in some cases, especially those involving inventory where physical stock can be counted and missing inventory can be searched for. However, in most cases, physical evidence, like a fired bullet or a dead body, is more associated with nonfraud types of crimes, such as property crimes, murder, rape, and robbery. Because fraud is rarely seen and has few physical symptoms, physical evidence can often be difficult to find.

Gathering physical evidence involves analyzing objects such as inventory, assets, and broken locks; substances such as grease and fluids; traces such as paints and stains; and impressions such as cutting marks, tire tracks, and fingerprints. Physical evidence also involves searching computers. For example, physical evidence was used to discover who was involved in the 1993 bombing of the World Trade Center in New York City. The vehicle identification number engraved on the axle of the rented van that contained the explosives made it possible to trace the van to a rental agency. When the perpetrator came back to the rental agency to recover his deposit and make a claim that the van had been stolen, the FBI arrested him.

Another example of the use of physical evidence involved the famed detective, William J. Burns, who once solved a counterfeit currency conspiracy by tracking down a single clue to its source. Here is how he used the clue to solve the case.

Burns used a four-digit number preceded by "xx," which was imprinted on the burlap covering of a sofa shipped from the United States to Costa Rica. In the sofa were hidden nearly 1 million counterfeit pesos. By tracing the clue to its source, Burns gained a great deal of evidence, blew the case wide open, and was instrumental in sending the counterfeiters to Sing Sing State Prison. The steps that Burns took in making the investigation are as follows:

1. *Located and called on burlap manufacturers.*
2. *Learned the significance of the imprinted number on the burlap covering and how it might help in tracing the specific piece of burlap to its purchaser.*
3. *Dug for the precise four-digit order number in a pile of old, discarded order forms.*
4. *Located the retail dry goods store that had sold the particular piece of burlap.*
5. *Asked a retail clerk about the specific purchase and obtained a description of the person who had purchased the burlap: a little old lady dressed in black and wearing a shawl.*
6. *Located the purchaser. (Burns later learned that she had bought the burlap for her son-in-law.)*
7. *Invented a pretense to take the young retail clerk with him to call on the lady, so that the clerk would later be able to identify her.*
8. *Checked out a number of furniture moving companies to locate the one that had moved the old couch containing the pesos to the docks.*
9. *Questioned a succession of dockhands until he found one who remembered loading the sofa. The dockhand also remembered the undue concern of a dark, handsome man, who constantly urged the dockhands to handle the sofa with care. The dockhand said he was sure he could identify the man.*
10. *Located the man who had been so concerned for the safe shipment of the sofa.*
11. *Discovered that the man, whose name he now knew, had made a trip to Costa Rica shortly before the shipment of the peso-packed sofa. He had been accompanied by a beautiful woman who traveled under her real name.*
12. *Learned who had engraved the counterfeit plates used to print the pesos. The engraver turned out to be the son of a lithographer in a plant owned by the two people who had traveled to Costa Rica. The chief product of the plant was revolutionary literature that tied in with the plot to overthrow the Costa Rican government.*

Electronic Evidence

One type of physical evidence that has seen a significant increase in use in recent years is electronic evidence. The gathering of electronic evidence is usually termed **computer forensics**. Today, it is rare that the confiscating and searching of computers is not associated with a fraud investigation. The following case illustrates where electronic evidence can be the smoking gun in a case:

The management of a company suspected that kickbacks were occurring between an employee, Mary, and an external vendor, ABC, Inc. In the evidence-gathering stage of the case, Mary's e-mail was searched by going through back e-mails on the corporate server. Investigators found an e-mail that became the basis for the entire case against Mary.

Allegedly, the kickback relationship between Mary and ABC had deteriorated over time to the point where ABC had quit giving Mary her kickbacks. Since Mary had been keeping detailed records of all purchases from ABC, she prepared a spreadsheet that listed each transaction, her appropriate percentage, and the side payments from ABC to her. The result at the bottom of the spreadsheet showed a large amount owed to Mary.

Mary then proceeded to write a flaming e-mail to ABC regarding its negligence in paying her, and she attached the spreadsheet to her e-mail. When investigators found this e-mail in her sent mailbox, they retrieved a foundation piece of evidence.

Another example shows where an employee was exonerated through electronic evidence.

Jack was a computer programmer at a small startup company in Atlanta. His behavior became more erratic as the weeks went on, and finally management looked into his phone records. The phone records showed many calls that were out of the ordinary. For example, on a holiday when Jack was the only person in the office, management found that he called a hotel room in Puerto Rico several times, and each call was several hours in length. One call in particular was over 10 hours long.

The company held several patents and suspected that Jack might be selling company secrets. They surmised that the long calls might have been modem connections to Puerto Rico through which he transferred data to an outside source. The hotel room might have been used because it provided a level of anonymity for the receiver.

Management hired a fraud investigator to analyze Jack's computer after work one night. The fraud investigator started Jack's computer with a self-booting CD to bypass his passwords so his operating system log files would not show the activity. As the night continued, it became increasingly obvious from digital photos at the beach, e-mail communications, and letters on his computer that Jack was *having an affair with someone in Puerto Rico. While management didn't approve of the activity or the use of corporate resources for personal calls, the executives were relieved that Jack's behavior did not involve company patents or other work-related issues. Management dropped the case, and Jack was exonerated as a fraud suspect.*

Because of the wide variety of electronic media available today, the process for gathering electronic evidence may vary from device to device. For example, cell phones and PDAs have limited solid state memory, while computers have significant amounts of both memory and hard drives. For this discussion, we'll assume you are investigating data on a computer hard drive and give the general process for obtaining electronic evidence from hard drives. In practice, you can modify this process for each specific device.

You should normally work with IT support personnel and legal counsel to gather electronic evidence because of the significant amount of technical knowledge it takes to perform the tasks correctly. For example, if you incorrectly seize a hard drive, you may damage its data or make it inadmissible in court. This chapter gives an overview of the steps that should be performed so you can work effectively with these people.

CAUTION *The gathering of electronic evidence is a highly technical task that must be performed correctly. You may want to include a computer forensics specialist on your team.*

The general process for gathering electronic evidence is given in Figure 7.4. These steps are explained next.

Step 1: Secure the Device and Perform Initial Tasks

The first step in any electronic evidence collection is the seizure of the device. Be sure that you have the legal right to seize the hardware by checking with the corporation's policies and legal counsel. When you seize the hard drive, exercise care with respect to chain of custody, evidence marking, and so forth. Take pictures of the seizure site and have neutral witnesses on the scene. These topics are discussed at length in Chapter 9.

Recently, it has become common to get a snapshot of active memory before turning the computer off. The computer programs described later in this chapter are capable of taking a snapshot of memory. Be careful because every action you take on the computer potentially overwrites "empty" space and could invalidate the hard drive's admissibility in court. Your IT staff may

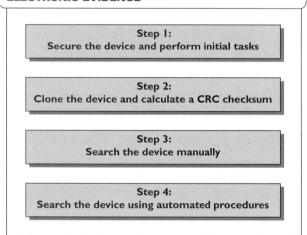

FIGURE 7.4   PROCESS FOR GATHERING ELECTRONIC EVIDENCE

Step 1:
Secure the device and perform initial tasks

Step 2:
Clone the device and calculate a CRC checksum

Step 3:
Search the device manually

Step 4:
Search the device using automated procedures

recommend or counsel against this action, depending upon the case and technology being investigated.

After these preliminary steps, turn the computer off by cutting power to the machine (or removing the battery on laptops). Do not turn the computer off normally because doing so will overwrite important parts of the disk. When most operating systems shut down, they clear important disk caches that might contain evidence. Cutting power to a computer ensures that the operating system does not have the opportunity to modify the disk further. Note that this is a general rule; some modern devices can become unstable if they are not properly shut down. As with cloning a device's running memory, recommendation of cutting power is device and case specific.

Step 2: Clone the Device and Calculate a CRC Checksum

Once the disk is in your custody, clone the entire hard drive to a separate copy and calculate a checksum to validate its authenticity. Seal away the original disk as you would any other type of physical evidence. All further investigation is done on the cloned copy. This step is important so you keep the original disk in its seized state. If you accidentally modify data or ruin the disk during analysis, you can create a new clone and continue analysis. It is also important to show in court that you have not modified the original hard drive.

When cloning the hard drive, use software that copies bit for bit. A typical hard drive contains a significant amount of "empty" space that may contain valuable evidence. When a file is deleted on a disk, its space is marked as empty in the disk's index. *The data are not actually removed from the disk* because removal

would take additional, unneeded time. The data remains accessible in special recovery utilities until another program writes to that location of the disk. This fact is extremely important for fraud examiners because subjects may delete important files in an attempt to hide their frauds.

A **cyclic redundancy check (CRC) number** is a calculation (using encryption algorithms) based on the contents of a disk or file. CRC numbers are engineered so that even small changes in the source data will produce significantly different checksum results. Checksums have been used in court cases to prove that data have not been adversely affected during analysis. By calculating the checksum number immediately, you can prove later (1) that your cloned hard drive exactly matched the original drive (by running the checksum on both drives and comparing) and (2) that you have not modified data since the hard drive was seized. Checksums have a wide variety of uses; for example, they are integral to the Internet because they ensure that packets of data are not modified during transit from one computer to another. The checksum is calculated and sent with the packet. The receiving device recalculates the CRC and compares it with the sent number. If the two are different, the data were likely damaged in transit, and the receiving side automatically requests the packet to be sent.

The two primary checksum methods used today are the MD5 and SHA-1 algorithms. MD5 is an older algorithm; SHA-1 was developed to replace it, and it is often considered more advanced and secure. Both are commonly used in forensics. Table 7.3 shows the SHA-1 result for two sentences. Note that a change in only two letters produces a significantly different result. The SHA-1 result is always the same length regardless of the length of the input data. The result is a number that is normally shown in base-16 (hexadecimal).

Step 3: Search the Device Manually

Because software packages make it so easy to run automated searches, many investigators skip the most obvious and often most fruitful step in analysis: searching the hard drive manually. Each operating system has a common directory layout that helps in investigation.

TABLE 7.3 SECURE HASH ALGORITHM

DATA	SHA-1 HEXADECIMAL RESULT
The fat cat sat	919d1cb454e3225455fd41c402b9f89ba5a0b8c8
The fat cat met	4458151a5f69f0911c2bb745b98eb843db12481e

For example, all modern operating systems generally save documents in the "Documents" directory by default. Graphics and pictures are saved in the "Pictures" directory, and movies are saved in the "Videos" directory. Manually searching these common locations allows an investigator to use human intuition while searching. Automated searches, while also useful, sometimes overlook near matches that are obvious hits to a human searcher.

Common areas of the disk to search include the following:

- *Computer logs such as Web activity, recent files on the Start menu, Web favorites, and the browser history. The browser history can often highlight the existence of online e-mail account, online data storage, common searches, or other useful locations.*
- *The Documents, Videos, Pictures, and related folders since most applications save data to these locations.*
- *The trash can or recycle bin.*
- *USB keys, CDs, or other media found around the computer.*
- *Recently loaded files listed in the "File" menu of many applications (such as Microsoft Word or Excel).*
- *Chat logs and e-mail client caches. For example, most Instant Messenger clients save conversations in the background.*

Step 4: Search the Device Using Automated Procedures

After manual search methods are exhausted, investigators should search the entire hard drive (including "empty" space) using keyword and other automated searches. For example, in a case involving interactions between Dave Smith and Jan Johansen, keyword searches for these names in the same document are useful. Because modern investigative software packages index the entire hard drive for keywords, these searches can be done quickly and easily. Some packages support the use of powerful pattern matching languages, keyword proximity searches, or even sentence comprehension using natural language processing (such as finding instances of the word "purchase" only when used as a noun).

Additionally, the software packages usually present summary statistics about the hard drive (number of documents, spreadsheets, most recently opened files, etc.). They find and show common files in areas like a picture gallery of every graphic file on the hard drive. See the documentation for your software for its searching capabilities.

Forensic Software Packages

Computer forensics is a fast-growing field with many software vendors. Many universities now have degrees or specialties in computer forensics. While new software is constantly being developed for forensics, Guidance Software's *EnCase Forensic Edition* and AccessData's *The Forensic Toolkit (FTK)* are in common use today. These software packages lead the investigator through the entire process described earlier and ensure that important steps are followed correctly. They support the tasks of cloning, CRC calculations, and searching using a variety of methods.

Many open source packages are also available for computer forensics. Some of these, such as e-fense Inc.'s Helix or Remote-Exploit.org's BackTrack, come as bootable CDs that support the investigation and searching of computers. For example, Helix was used to investigate the phone calls made to Puerto Rico in the case described earlier in this chapter. Since management was not ready to start a case (i.e., seize the computer, clone the data, etc.), the investigator used a bootable CD to boot the computer, bypass passwords, and search the drive without ever starting the normal operating system. These CDs generally have very advanced tools for password cracking, searching using a method called *regular expressions,* and network analysis programs. The open source solutions are generally not as easy to use as EnCase or FTK, and they do not have the same precedence in court. However, they are extremely useful in the right hands and in the right circumstances.

E-mail Systems

E-mail systems often prove to be an incredible repository of communications between suspects and other people. It is surprising how many people still believe e-mail to be a secure method of communicating. A single e-mail can become a smoking gun on which an entire case is based. In today's world of electronic media, e-mail should nearly always be considered during investigation.

Today, many different communication methods beyond traditional e-mail—such as text messages—are being analyzed during investigations. For example, in some countries, more people have cell phones than have computers. Consequently, text messaging is used much more than traditional e-mail and provides a better information source for investigations. Regardless of the media being investigated, the process is generally the same.

E-mail is given special consideration because copies often exist in many places: on the sending computer, on the two (or more) e-mail servers involved in transmission, and on the receiving computer. With some e-mail servers, messages only reside on the server; seizing the client laptop will not allow you to search e-mail. Talk with your IT support personnel to understand the type of e-mail used in each case and how it can be searched.

One type of e-mail, Web-based e-mail within a user's browser, is especially difficult to search. Hotmail, Yahoo! Mail, and Gmail are examples of this type of e-mail. In these cases, all e-mail is stored at the provider's site, and you will likely need a warrant to access it. However, some information may still be on the hard drive in the form of cached Web pages and can be found with keyword searches. In fact, the user may have even saved his or her Webmail password—taking the user's Web browser to his or her Webmail site may autofill the username and password fields. The legality of this and all approaches discussed in this chapter varies based on your country and situation. Always check with legal counsel to ensure that your planned methods are both legal and ethical.

A Comprehensive Example of Using Theft Act Investigation Methods

To conclude this chapter and illustrate the value of theft act investigation methods, let's review excerpts from an article written by Thomas Buckhoff and James Clifton that appeared in *The CPA Journal* entitled "Exotic Embezzling: Investigating Off-Book Fraud Schemes." The investigators in this fraud case made extensive use of both surveillance and invigilation.

Northern Exposure (case names changed) was a gentleman's club featuring exotic dancers. Its primary revenue sources were cover charges and food, beer, and liquor sales. A recent local ordinance outlawed the type of entertainment offered by Northern Exposure. The club's manager, however, successfully petitioned the city council to obtain an exemption, and Northern Exposure was allowed to continue operations in a competition-free environment. The substantial effort by the manager on the club's behalf earned her the owner's trust and loyalty. In the initial fraud investigation interview, the owner said that anyone could be a suspect—except the manager.

Because of the exemption, the club's profit potential was enormous. Northern Exposure generated huge amounts of incoming cash because no credit cards or checks were accepted. However, a huge risk existed that employees would figure out a way to divert incoming cash into their own pockets.

Larry Swenson, Northern Exposure's owner, was not satisfied with the 10 percent margins being realized. He engaged two fraud examiners to determine why the club was not generating the 35 percent margins he had expected. They embarked upon a typical fraud examination, whose steps include understanding cash controls, generating fraud theories, collecting and evaluating evidence, estimating losses, assisting in filing claims or bringing charges, and making recommendations.

By interviewing Swenson and other personnel, the fraud investigators learned that cash flowed into the business as follows: Customers paid a $6 cover charge to enter the club. No receipt was given, nor was a head count made. Customers placed orders for food or beverages with the servers. The servers started out with $40 in a cash pouch. They paid the bartenders for their orders from this pouch and then collected payment from the customer. At their shift's end, the server gave the initial $40 back to the manager and kept the difference as tips. At the end of the night, the manager counted the cash and closed out the cash registers; the cash was deposited by the manager the next morning. Changes in beer and liquor inventory were not reconciled to the drinks rung into the cash register, nor were the register tapes reconciled to deposits listed on the bank statements.

The fraud examiners determined that it would be relatively easy for employees to steal and not be caught, based on the control levels they discovered. They developed the following fraud theories:

- *Employees collecting the $6 cover charge could pocket some of the money or allow free admission to friends.*
- *Servers and bartenders could get drinks for customers, not ring them into the registers, and pocket the cash received from the customers.*
- *Anyone with access to the cash registers (i.e., servers, bartenders, and the manager) could simply take cash directly from the registers.*
- *The manager could perpetrate any of the schemes available to the employees and could steal part of the deposit.*

Off-book frauds such as the first two are called skimming and are essentially unrecorded sales. The second two would be considered on-book frauds. Because there was a transaction record, the fraud could be detected by reconciling the cash register tapes to the deposits. In Northern Exposure's case, however, cash register printing ribbons were not replaced on a timely basis, resulting in illegible tapes.

Collecting and Evaluating Evidence

Indirect investigative methods were used to test the four possible fraud theories. Financial statement analysis is one such method that can be used to test all four fraud theories presented. If employees are indeed stealing cash from the club, then the actual sales markup-over-cost ratios are expected to be less than the budgeted ratios. Accordingly, the fraud investigators determined the actual markup-cost ratios for beer and food sales. Beer was purchased for $0.60 per bottle and then sold to customers for $3 each, a markup of 500 percent. Food items costing $5 were sold to customers for $12.50, a 250 percent markup. One year's budgeted revenue was calculated, based on cost of sales and expected markup ratios, and then compared to one year's actual revenue. The significant differences in ratios clearly supported the fraud theories—in fact, food sales were less than their cost of sales! Using this indirect investigative method, the total estimated annual fraud loss due to skimming or cash larceny was $379,974.

The investigators now knew that the club had a big problem with fraud; determining which employees were responsible came next. Undercover surveillance can be used effectively for identifying dishonest employees. Posing as customers, a team of six trained fraud investigators (with experience as bartenders and servers) spent a collective 40-hour week at the club observing the employees' activities and behavior. This surveillance revealed that 90 percent of them, including the manager, regularly stole cash from the club, with little regard to subtlety. The reason that employees never complained about salary levels, despite low base wages and a lack of raises, became clear. In fact, several servers and bartenders had been there for years, which is highly unusual for this type of club. The lead investigators communicated their findings to Swenson, who, though concerned, was reluctant to take action without more substantive evidence of employee theft.

To more firmly establish the fraud losses and estimate their amount, the fraud investigators conducted a week-long invigilation. As discussed, in invigilation, the cash received and deposited during the invigilation period is compared to the periods before and after. As an indirect investigative method, invigilation can be very effective in estimating fraud losses. The key to invigilation success is making the employees think that any theft during that period will be detected. Instilling the perception of detection in this case was accomplished by sending in the same team of six investigators to watch the employees for one week. The club's employees and manager were informed that the investigators were there to make sure that every dollar collected from customers made it into the bank at the end of the day and that changes in consumable inventories were properly accounted for. During the invigilation, the investigators conspicuously watched employees handling cash, conducted surprise cash counts, reconciled changes in inventory to cash register tapes, monitored end-of-night cash counts, and witnessed the daily cash deposits.

The first day brought an incident that greatly heightened the perception of detection. Meals were served downstairs, away from the live entertainment area. Suspecting the single server working downstairs of skimming money from food sales, one of the investigators conducted a surprise cash count and reconciled cash rung into the register to meals prepared by the cooks. The server had skimmed $25 in the first hour she worked. When confronted with the evidence, the server confessed and was immediately terminated. News quickly spread to the other employees, who realized that their activities were indeed under close surveillance. No other employees were caught skimming during the remainder of the invigilation.

During the invigilation's first night, a Friday, $8,300 in cash was deposited into the bank—the largest sum for one night in the entire 15-year history of the club. This occurred on what was considered a "slow" night—unlike the previous week, which had seen near-record attendance. The manager and employees all soon realized that setting such a record on a slow night reflected poorly on them. This convinced Swenson that his employees were stealing from him, and he wanted to fire everyone on the spot. The investigators persuaded him to allow the invigilation to continue for the entire week as planned. The results of the week-long invigilation are summarized as follows:

Gross cash receipts during the invigilation were $30,960, compared with $25,775 the previous week and $22,006 for the annual weekly average. The revenue during the week of invigilation exceeded the average weekly revenue by $8,954 and the previous week's revenue by $5,185, despite being a slow week. The above differences implied that at least $259,250 and as much as $447,700 was skimmed per year. (After changes were implemented following the investigation, the remaining nine months' sales were $300,000 higher than for the same period in the prior year.)

Swenson no longer doubted that his employees were stealing from him. As noted earlier, Swenson had had difficulty believing his manager was stealing because of her efforts to exempt the club from the city ordinance. It became apparent that these efforts were motivated by a desire to protect her illicit cash flow.

Employee interviews were held during the week of the invigilation. Their purpose was twofold: to further enhance the perception of detection during the invigilation period and to provide employees with an opportunity to report any fraudulent activities. Very specific questions were asked during the interviews, based upon information from the prior undercover surveillance and the ongoing invigilation. While no one admitted to stealing, they did implicate fellow employees; many claimed that manager Betsy Smith was the primary thief.

During her interview, Betsy Smith was confronted with the evidence from the undercover surveillance, invigilation, and employee interviews. After two hours, she admitted to stealing almost $100,000 over three years. Her admission *was converted to a written statement, which she ultimately signed. The statement detailed the amounts she had skimmed, when she had done so, and the various techniques (skimming from liquor sales, bank deposits, video sales, and food deliveries) she had used. An attached summary totaled the funds skimmed by source. Since evidence collected in resolving off-book fraud schemes is mostly indirect and circumstantial, obtaining a signed admission statement greatly facilitates the filing of employee dishonesty insurance claims or criminal charges. In this case, such a claim was filed by the fraud investigators on behalf of Northern Exposure.*

The insurance company restituted Northern Exposure for the maximum coverage amount provided by its policy, $50,000. Clearly, the coverage amount was inadequate given the exposure to risk for such a cash-intensive business. As required by the insurance provider, evidence collected during the fraud examination was turned over to local law enforcement for prosecution.

Review of the Learning Objectives

- **Discuss theft investigation methods and how they are used to investigate suspected fraud.** Theft act investigation methods include activities that directly investigate the theft act (not concealment or conversion) element of fraud. Their purpose is to catch perpetrators "in the act" of committing fraud and include such investigative methods as surveillance, invigilation, obtaining physical evidence (e.g., tire tracks, broken locks, etc.), and gathering electronic evidence (e.g., e-mails, text messages, etc.)

- **Understand how to coordinate an investigation, using a vulnerability chart.** When beginning a fraud investigation, an investigator usually tries to develop theories about who committed the fraud, how the fraud was committed, etc. One way to do this is to prepare a vulnerability chart which coordinates all the elements of the fraud: which assets were taken, who had theft opportunities, possible theft methods, concealment possibilities, conversion possibilities, symptoms observed, pressures on various individuals, rationalizations that were heard or could have justified someone to commit the act, and key internal controls that were missing or could have been overridden. Often, tying these elements together provides initial indications of who could have committed the fraud.

- **Describe the nature of surveillance and covert operations.** Surveillance and covert operations are theft act investigative methods that usually involve observing or listening to potential perpetrators. Possible surveillance and covert operation methods include recording conversations, tailing, using cameras, using undercover agents, or observing individuals in various settings.

- **Understand the effectiveness of invigilation to investigate fraud.** For fraud to occur, three elements are necessary: pressure, opportunity, and rationalization. Invigilation involves implementing such strong control procedures or observations that fraud is impossible to perpetrate or is obvious when it is perpetrated. Invigilation allows investigators to compare results prior to implementing the controls, while implementing the fraud-eliminating controls, and the post period when fraud-constraining controls are lifted. Invigilation allows investigators to compare results (profits, inventory movements, revenues, etc.) when fraud is and is not occurring. In addition to helping investigators understand if fraud is occurring, invigilation can also help estimate the amount of the fraud.

- **Explain how to obtain physical evidence and how it can be used in a fraud investigation.** Typical fraud investigators are usually not very familiar with gathering physical evidence such as tire tracks, broken locks, stains, fingerprints, etc. As a result, most often, fraud investigators use law enforcement officials or consultants to obtain physical evidence.

- **Understand how to seize and analyze electronic information from cell phones, hard drives, e-mail, and other sources.** Electronic evidence is extremely useful evidence that, because of its technical nature, usually involves IT support personnel and legal counsel in gathering. There are several steps in gathering electronic evidence: (1) secure the device, (2) clone the device (cell phone, computer, etc.) and calculate a CRC checksum, (3) search the device manually, and (4) search the device using automated procedures.

KEY TERMS

theft act investigations, p. 212

surveillance, p. 212

vulnerability chart, p. 213

invigilation, p. 216

computer forensics, p. 219

cyclic redundancy check (CRC) number, p. 220

QUESTIONS

Discussion Questions

1. How are theft investigative methods used to investigate suspected fraud?
2. What factors should be considered when deciding whether or not to investigate a case of fraud?
3. How does a vulnerability chart help coordinate an investigation of suspected fraud?
4. What is a surveillance log?
5. What is invigilation?
6. How is physical evidence used to investigate fraud?
7. What are the steps to collecting electronic evidence?
8. Why is it important to use investigation techniques that will not arouse suspicion among possible perpetrators?
9. Why is it important to consult legal counsel and human resources before any form of surveillance takes place?
10. What role does the Fourth Amendment to the Constitution play in cases of fraud investigation?
11. What four methods of investigation constitute the fraud triangle plus inquiry approach to investigations?
12. What are the potential benefits and drawbacks of using open source, self-booting CDs for computer forensics?

True/False

1. The fraud triangle plus inquiry paradigm is an effective way to understand the various types of investigative methods.
2. One advantage of using a vulnerability chart is that it forces investigators to consider all aspects of a fraud.
3. Electronic surveillance is often of limited value in the investigation of employee fraud because of concerns regarding employees' privacy rights.
4. Surveillance is a theft investigation technique that relies on the examination of documents.
5. Mobile observation is usually much more risky than stationary surveillance.
6. During invigilation, no controls are imposed on any activities.
7. Surveillance logs should always be drafted before an investigation begins.
8. Not only are undercover operations both legal and valid, but they are also inexpensive.

9. Investigation of fraud should only take place when predication has first been established.
10. If possible, when using theft act investigation methods, interviewing the prime suspects should happen last.
11. Tailing includes the use of video, e-mail, wiretapping, and access to PCs.
12. Invigilation is a theft act investigative technique that involves close supervision of suspects during an examination period.
13. To get an accurate reading, it is generally agreed that the invigilation period should be at least four days in length.
14. In determining which investigative method to use, it is most important that investigators focus on the costs of each possible method.
15. Seizing and searching computers is illegal because it infringes on the rights guaranteed by the Fourth Amendment to the Constitution.
16. It is impossible to retrieve the data from a file that has been deleted on a computer.
17. The SHA-1 checksum method is more advanced and is considered more robust than the MD5 method.

Multiple Choice

1. Which of the following is *not* a category used in the fraud triangle plus inquiry paradigm?
   a. Theft investigative techniques.
   b. Concealment investigative techniques.
   c. Action investigative techniques.
   d. Conversion investigative techniques.
2. When beginning an investigation, fraud examiners should use techniques that will:
   a. Not arouse suspicion.
   b. Identify the perpetrator.
   c. Determine the amount of the fraud.
   d. Identify when the fraud occurred.
3. When conducting interviews during an investigation, which of the following words should usually be avoided?
   a. Audit.
   b. Inquiry.
   c. Investigation.
   d. Record examination.
4. When beginning a fraud investigation, which of the following methods is most useful in identifying possible suspects?
   a. Preparing an identification chart.
   b. Preparing a vulnerability chart.

c. Preparing a surveillance log.

d. None of the above.

5. Invigilation:

   a. Is most commonly associated with crimes such as robbery, murder, and property offenses.

   b. Can create tremendous amounts of documentary evidence.

   c. Provides evidence to help determine whether fraud is occurring.

   d. All of the above are true.

6. Which of the following is *not* a theft investigative method?

   a. Invigilation.

   b. Honesty testing.

   c. Seizing and searching computers.

   d. Surveillance and covert operations.

7. When deciding whether or not to investigate, which of the following factors should an organization *not* consider?

   a. Possible cost of the investigation.

   b. Perceived strength of the predication.

   c. Possible public exposure resulting because of the investigation.

   d. All of the above should be considered.

8. Surveillance, when properly performed, is done:

   a. Without the perpetrator's knowledge.

   b. During nonworking hours.

   c. Only by law enforcement agents.

   d. None of the above.

9. Which of the following is *not* included in a vulnerability chart?

   a. Explanations of the fraud triangle in relation to suspects of fraud.

   b. Breakdowns in key internal controls that may have created fraud opportunities.

   c. Internal controls that a company plans to institute in the future.

   d. Theft investigation methods.

10. A vulnerability chart:

   a. Forces investigators to explicitly consider all aspects of a fraud.

   b. Shows the history of fraud in a company.

   c. Identifies weaknesses in every aspect of a company's internal control.

   d. Gives a detailed record of all the movements and activities of the suspect.

11. Fixed-point, or stationary, observations can be conducted by:

   a. Certified fraud examiners.

   b. Company personnel.

   c. Private investigators.

   d. Anyone.

12. Surveillance logs should include all of the following except:

   a. Time the observation began and ended.

   b. Cost of the surveillance equipment used.

   c. Movements and activities of the suspect.

   d. Distance the observation was from the scene.

13. Wiretapping, a form of electronic surveillance, can be used by:

   a. Internal auditors.

   b. Company controllers.

   c. CPAs.

   d. All of the above.

   e. None of the above.

14. Which theft investigative method is most limited in value during employee fraud investigations because of concerns regarding employees' privacy at work?

   a. Electronic surveillance.

   b. Invigilation.

   c. Forensic accounting.

   d. Interviewing and interrogation.

15. Who should be consulted before any form of surveillance takes place?

   a. Public investors and the company's board of directors.

   b. State attorney general.

   c. Legal counsel and human resources.

   d. All company executives.

16. When seizing computers, a calculation (also called a hash) that ensures you have an exact clone and have not changed data is called a(n):

   a. NIST number.

   b. ODBC connection.

   c. Internet packet calculation.

   d. CRC checksum number.

17. A snapshot of active memory should be done:

   a. Before seizure of the computer.

   b. After seizure of the computer but before turning off the computer.

   c. After turning off the computer but before calculation of the checksum number.

   d. After calculation of the checksum number but before searching.

SHORT CASES

Case 1

ABC Company is a relatively small dry-cleaning operation that has a very steady level of business. Since the company hired a new employee, however, cash inflows have decreased and the amount of promotional coupon redemptions have increased dramatically. The owner of the company has been very impressed with this new employee, but has suspicions regarding her cashiering practices. When comparing cash sales to check and credit card sales, the owner noted that the coupon redemption rate was dramatically higher for cash sales. The owner does not want to wrongly accuse the employee if she is innocent, but does want to find out if fraud is occurring. The owner calls you as an expert on fraud and asks you to recommend a reliable way to gather evidence that could determine if fraud is occurring.

1. What are some possible investigative methods you could suggest?

Case 2

You are a fraud examiner who has been hired by Bellevue Company to carry out an investigation. Bellevue is a beverage company that has experienced increased shipments of beverages but no increase in revenue. Management suspects that inventory is being shipped to unknown places or is being stolen.

1. How could you use invigilation to help you determine if inventory is being stolen or shipped to unknown locations? Briefly explain how you would carry out this investigative procedure.

Case 3

A man in San Rafael County was discovered committing workers' compensation fraud. He had been observed working while at the same time receiving disability benefits. Surveillance showed the man working at an automobile auction. The investigator interviewed the owner of the auction and found that the claimant was being paid $200 per week in cash for washing vehicles and performing other shop tasks. Surveillance video showed the man carrying 25-pound bags of pet food, loading boxes, and rummaging through a trash dumpster. Obviously, he was not hurt very badly.

1. Was surveillance the proper method to use in this case? Why?
2. What are some restrictions to be careful about in conducting surveillance?

Case 4

This chapter included an example of a manufacturing firm that had problems with employee theft of tools. The company decided that it would search every employee's lunch box at the end of each shift. The employees were enraged and caused a work slowdown.

Give three alternative suggestions for how the company could have investigated or prevented this theft effectively without causing morale problems with employees.

Case 5

Assume that someone in your company is taking money from the petty cash fund. Complete a vulnerability chart similar to the one in the chapter in order to coordinate the various aspects of the fraud.

Case 6

Craig Ferguson, an internal auditor for HHG Online Booksellers, had been investigating a case of embezzlement fraud for nearly two months. After searching personnel and company records, visiting with former employees, employing invigilation tactics, and finally interviewing with several coworkers, Craig concluded that Lane Flemming, head of the shipping and receiving department, was involved in a large kickback scheme, costing the company hundreds of thousands of dollars. Finally, with evidence in hand, Craig met with Lane, presented his evidence, and steered Lane to confess that he was indeed the perpetrator.

1. Was the order of events in which Craig conducted his investigation in accordance with appropriate theft act investigative methods? Explain.
2. When investigating a case of fraud, why is it important to work inward toward the prime suspect, saving a confronting interview until the end of the investigation?

Case 7

A group of fraud examiners is coordinating an investigation at a local law firm. Several lawyers at the firm are suspected of overbilling clients, possibly creating fake client accounts, and then charging the firm for services "performed" for these fake clients. The fraud examiners begin preparing for the investigation by creating a vulnerability chart. Explain what a vulnerability chart is and how it can direct the fraud examiners in their investigation.

Case 8

ABC Company has instituted good internal controls and has never, until last month, had a problem with fraud. But, several weeks ago, someone with access to keys entered the controller's office and took two company checkbooks. Since then, several checks have been forged totaling an amount of $5,670. You are a certified fraud examiner and have been recruited to investigate the case.

1. Which theft act investigative method(s) should you use in this investigation?

Case 9

In the oil theft case discussed in this chapter, the fraud investigators conducted a week-long invigilation. The results from this period were compared to the results taken during the weeks immediately before and immediately after the invigilation.

1. Was invigilation an effective method to use in this case? Why?

Case 10

As the lead accountant for a small company, you notice that inventory purchases from a certain vendor have increased dramatically over the past few months, while purchases from all other vendors have decreased. You suspect that something may not be right.

1. Which method(s) would you use to investigate your suspicions?

Case 11

While auditing a client, the CEO asks you to look carefully at the cash flow. You notice that cash flows have decreased every year. Upon learning of your findings, the CEO remarks, "I seem to bring in more customers every year, but the cash is not there." You tell him that fraud may be occurring, and he asks you to investigate. You agree that the most likely place for a fraud to be occurring is cash collections.

1. Which investigative method(s) would be best for finding the fraud?

Case 12

Jim is the owner and president of ZZZ Company. He and his close friend, Dan, graduated with MBAs. They always dreamed about being successful and making lots of money. They have worked in the same company for years, working their way up to senior management and eventually senior executive roles. ZZZ Company has been a success the entire time that Jim and Dan have worked for the company. Stock prices have increased every year, and revenues have grown by a compounded rate of 20 percent per year. Jim is becoming a little suspicious of the company's results because the earnings per share are always equal to Wall Street's projections. In the past couple of years, Jim has noticed that his friend's personal life has become troubled. Dan has gotten a divorce and is continually struggling financially, even though Jim knows that Dan is making plenty of money to cover his bills. One night, Jim stopped by the office to respond to some e-mails he could not get to during the day. He noticed that Dan was working late as well. Dan was the CEO, and Jim just assumed that he was working late because it was close to the end of the quarter. However, after reviewing the quarter's results, Jim is suspicious again because the results are exactly equal to Wall Street's forecasts. Jim decides he needs to begin an investigation into financial reporting practices.

1. What issues must Jim consider in deciding how to investigate the financial results of the company?

Case 13

Your small company produces and sells holsters for cell phones. During the past year, monthly inventory counts have shown about 100 holsters missing. Furthermore, a customer report gives you reason to believe that one of your employees, Jackson McKnight, might be stealing the missing holsters and selling them on eBay. Since the holsters are manufactured by a separate supplier (i.e., they are not custom holsters), you cannot know whether holsters being posted to eBay are from your company or from one of your competitors. However, because eBay's selling etiquette requires that sellers respond promptly to customer questions, you think that McKnight may be accessing the account periodically from his work computer.

1. What considerations should you take into account when investigating McKnight's work computer? What legal, strategic, and other concerns should you be aware of?
2. What software would you suggest to investigate whether any information might be available on McKnight's work computer? What steps would you take with this software?
3. Do you think it would be possible to successfully approach eBay for information on this case? Why or why not?

Case 14

As a recent graduate with a bachelor's degree, you land a job with a local accounting firm. The firm hired you because of your expertise in computer forensics (a skill you gained during school). Up to this point, the firm has had no internal knowledge of forensics, and your first assignment at work is to create a 15-page slide show and presentation on the subject. You will give the presentation at the next firm-wide meeting.

Prepare a slide show detailing the background on forensics, what can be found using forensics, the steps to seizing a computer, the considerations you should have when doing forensics, and the major software packages available for this type of work.

CASE STUDIES

Case Study 1

By the time the New York identity theft fraud case was solved, over 30,000 people had suffered a total combined loss of over $2.7 million. This money had been stolen by a ring of New York residents who had accessed the victims' credit information and exploited that information to steal the victims' identity.

The fraud began when Linus Baptiste approached Philip Cummings about a plan to steal and sell people's personal information. Philip Cummings had begun to work at Teledata Communications, Inc., a third-party credit-reporting agency that facilitates the retrieval of credit history data. Teledata had outstanding contracts with over 25,000 companies, allowing these companies to check on the creditworthiness of potential customers, thus creating a direct line past the three main credit bureaus. As a customer service representative, Cummings had obtained access to many confidential access codes. These access codes were used by the clients of Teledata to gain approval on credit requests. With access to these codes, Cummings had the opportunity to commit fraud.

In early 2000, Cummings and Baptiste began to steal credit reports. The two fraudsters sold this information to a group of Nigerian nationalists. The Nigerian nationalists would pay up to $60 for one person's information. After some time, the Nigerian nationalists began to provide the two fraudsters with names and Social Security numbers to help facilitate the process even further.

To convert the information into money, the Nigerian nationalists would use the information to gain access to the victim's bank accounts and other financial information. The group of Nigerian nationalists would then take the following steps:

- Deplete the bank accounts of the victims through wire transfers.
- Change the addresses of the accounts so the current information was not sent to the victim.
- Order new checks to be written off of the victim's bank accounts.
- Order new ATM cards so the money could be taken out in cash.
- Order new credit cards under the victim's name.
- Establish new lines of credit under the victim's name.

By using these techniques, the fraud ring was able to steal over $2.7 million from consumers. This money was stolen over a period of about three years from late 1999 to late 2002. The most intriguing aspect of the fraud was that Cummings quit working at Teledata in early 2000, but was able to continue to steal the information for an additional two years. Cummings claimed that most of the access codes he had stolen while working at Teledata remained unchanged for the full two years after he left the company.

Finally, in early 2002, Cummings began to get greedy and his greed led to the detection of fraud. Perceiving that he needed to make more money, Cummings stole around 15,000 credit reports from Teledata by using the access codes of Ford Motor Company. Then from February 2002 to May 2002, Cummings again stole a large number of names. This time, Cummings used the access codes of Washington Mutual Bank to steal 6,000 credit reports. Finally, in September 2002, Cummings made what would be his last big credit report theft. Using the access codes of Central Texas Energy Supply, Cummings was able to steal 4,500 credit reports.

After the theft using Ford's access codes, Equifax, one of the three large credit bureaus in the United States, began to see the request spikes in Ford's account. After the next two large batches of requests, Equifax decided to investigate further. Equifax found that almost all of the credit report requests came from one phone number, and that the requests were done in large batches of about 100. The location of the phone number was found, and a search by federal authorities turned up a computer and other equipment that were used in the fraud.[2]

As of today, Cummings is facing a possible 30 years in prison and large fines. The victims are facing the dreadful task of restoring their credit, a process that can take years to complete.

Questions

Assuming you are an agent with the Federal Bureau of Investigation, do the following:

1. Coordinate an investigation in a manner that would not arouse suspicion from Cummings and Baptiste.
2. Create a vulnerability chart to coordinate the various elements of the possible fraud.

3. Assuming your investigation used surveillance and/or covert investigation techniques, what types of surveillance and/or covert operations would you use? How would technology play a role in this part of the investigation?
4. Finally, how would analysis of physical evidence help in this investigation? What types of physical evidence would be especially helpful?

Case Study 2

The following surveillance log was taken during two fixed-point surveillances of an employee suspected of stealing cash from the company while making nightly bank deposits.

CASE STUDY 2-SURVEILLANCE LOG	
10:47 p.m.	John Doe exits car carrying black deposit bag. Shuts car door and looks around him in every direction.
10:49 p.m.	John approaches ATM, unzips deposit bag, and pulls out a white envelope. John places white envelope in coat pocket.
10:50 p.m.	John deposits cash into ATM.
11:34 p.m.	John enters bar and sits at table with a white male. The two order drinks from waitress.
11:37 p.m.	Waitress returns with drinks and bill.

Questions

1. What is wrong with this surveillance log?
2. Why is it important to take detailed notes during surveillance and covert operations?

INTERNET ASSIGNMENTS

1. In August 2001, it was discovered that the McDonald's Monopoly game was a fraud. Simon Marketing, which ran the game on behalf of McDonald's, was responsible for the fraud. During the investigation to uncover the fraud, the FBI used several different forms of surveillance. Using the Internet, find newspapers and other sources of information that describe these forms of surveillance and then answer the following questions:

   a. How did the FBI use surveillance to gather evidence regarding Simon Marketing's illegal activities?

   b. Were the surveillance methods used by the FBI effective?
   c. If you were in charge of the McDonald's investigation, what other methods of surveillance might you have used?

2. Computer forensics is a rapidly expanding field with new software packages appearing all the time. Beyond the two largest players right now, search the Internet to find an open source or proprietary forensic application (or full application suite). For your application, search for the following information:

   a. Publisher (company or person information, including URL).
   b. Cost of software.
   c. Estimated learning curve (based on your reading of the site and external reviews, provide some indication of how easy the software would be to use).
   d. Specific functions of this software.

DEBATES

Discount Plus Company has been concerned for some time about its cash flows. Since the company began five years ago, Discount's business has increased steadily, yet cash flows have remained virtually the same every year. You have been hired by Discount Plus to detect possible fraud within the company. Discount's management is almost certain that one of its accountants is embezzling cash and has informed you that it has already begun installing surveillance cameras in possible "problem areas." In addition, management is considering some form of covert operation to detect the fraud.

a. What problems or dilemmas is Discount's management facing by installing cameras and implementing a covert (undercover) operation?
b. What privacy issues are there to consider?

END NOTES

1. Gary Strauss, "Informant Key to Unlocking Scam Behind Golden Arches," *USA Today* (August 24, 2001).

CHAPTER **8**

Investigating Concealment

LEARNING OBJECTIVES

After studying this chapter, you should be able to:

- **Describe concealment investigation methods and how they relate to fraud.**
- **Understand the value of documents and electronic records in a fraud investigation.**
- **List the different methods of obtaining documentary evidence.**
- **Understand how to perform discovery sampling to obtain documentary evidence.**
- **Explain how to obtain hard-to-get documentary evidence.**

TO THE STUDENT

Concealment investigation concerns discovering the ways perpetrators *conceal* their frauds. It is the third side of the fraud triangle plus inquiry approach to investigations. As you read the chapter, think of ways in which different types of frauds are concealed and how they might be investigated.

A number of years ago, the general partners in some limited real estate partnerships committed significant fraud by using millions of dollars of investments for their personal benefit. Their own private real estate investments were losing money, and rather than lose those investments, they siphoned money from the partnerships for personal use. The limited partnerships used money from investors to purchase buildings for use by fast-food chains such as Denny's, Kentucky Fried Chicken, and Sizzler Steak Houses. The buildings, which were fully paid for by limited partner investments, were then leased to owner-operators on a triple-net lease basis, which meant that the lessees were responsible for maintenance and for paying property taxes. To steal money from the limited partnerships, the general partners found banks in distant states that were willing to loan money against the equity in the properties and use the loan proceeds to support their personal investments.

As part of their audit procedures, the external auditors realized that lessees might not be paying the property taxes on a timely basis, thus putting the properties at risk. Therefore, the auditors performed a lien search in each of the counties where the properties were located. To their surprise, they discovered that there were liens on some properties located in Arizona and Texas that had been placed by banks in Kansas and Nebraska, two states where the partnerships didn't own any properties. The auditors then did what all good auditors would do—they sent confirmations to the banks to determine the nature and amounts of any loans on the properties. Their confirmations revealed loans totaling several million dollars on the properties. Follow-up investigation revealed the fraud by the general partners.

Interestingly, one of the specific frauds that the auditors discovered was stolen money that was supposedly being held in an escrow account by a title company in Alaska to build a new Sizzler restaurant. The general partners had told the auditors that $3.2 million was being held by the title company and gave the auditors the address where they could send the confirmation. Before giving the auditors the address, however, one of the general partners had flown to Alaska and rented a mailbox from Mail Boxes Etc. that used a street number rather than a post office box as the address (these were legally available at the time of the fraud). When the confirmation had been sent, the general partner again flew to Alaska, completed the confirmation with no exceptions by signing a fictitious name, and then sent it back to the auditors. The $3.2 million escrow and confirmation fraud would not have been discovered if the lien search and follow-up investigation hadn't taken place. Today, the auditors could perform an additional check by looking up the address in Alaska in a mapping program like Google Maps. With a few clicks of the mouse in the street view mode, the auditors would have been able to see pictures of the Mail Boxes Etc. building where the title company should have been.

In this case, the lien searches, the bank confirmations that revealed the loans, and the fictitious confirmation from the escrow company were all forms of documentary evidence. Once the fictitious confirmation from the escrow company and the bank loan documents were in hand, it was very easy to obtain a confession from the perpetrators. Unfortunately, the CPA firm that audited the partnerships was sued by the limited partners who tried to recover the losses they had incurred. Because the auditors had performed an excellent GAAS audit and because they were the ones who had actually detected the fraud, they were able to settle the case for a relatively small amount of money.

Concealment Investigative Methods

In other chapters, we discuss surveillance and covert operations, invigilation, and physical evidence, including the searching of computers and social engineering—all of which are theft investigation methods. After committing a theft, perpetrators must *conceal* their fraud by covering their tracks, obscuring evidence, and removing red flags where possible. Concealment is generally accomplished by manipulating documentary evidence, such as purchase invoices, sales invoices, credit memos, deposit slips, checks, receiving reports, bills of lading, leases, titles, sales receipts, money orders, cashier's checks, or insurance policies. From an electronic perspective, concealment can also be accomplished by modifying or deleting records in corporate databases.

Aspects of Documentary Evidence

Most concealment-based investigative techniques involve ways to discover physical documents or computer records that have been manipulated or altered. When faced with a choice between an eyewitness and a good document as evidence, most fraud experts would choose the document. Unlike witnesses, documents do not forget, they cannot be cross-examined or confused by attorneys, they cannot commit perjury, and they never tell inconsistent stories on two different occasions. Documents contain extremely valuable information for conducting fraud examinations. For example, in addition to possible fingerprints, the information on the front and back of a cancelled check (which is a document) is shown and listed in Figure 8.1.

If you were investigating a kickback or a forgery scheme, a check would direct you to the teller who processed the transaction and who may remember valuable information about the suspect. In addition, a check would allow you to complete a paper trail of the entire transaction.

Since documents make up a significant amount of the evidence in most fraud cases, investigators must understand the legal and administrative aspects of handling them. Specifically, investigators must understand the following aspects of documentary evidence:

- *Chain of custody of documents*
- *Marking of evidence*
- *Organization of documentary evidence*
- *Coordination of evidence*
- *Rules concerning original versus copies of documents*

STOP & THINK   *Does concealment investigation change when electronic transactions are involved?*

Chain of Custody

From the time documentary evidence is received, its **chain of custody** must be maintained in order for it to be accepted by the courts. Basically, the chain of custody means that a record must be kept of when a document is received and what has happened to it since its receipt. Careful records must be maintained anytime the document leaves the care, custody, or control of the examiner. Contesting attorneys will make every attempt to introduce the possibility that the document has been altered or tampered with. A memorandum should be written that describes when the document came into the hands of the examiner, and subsequent memoranda should be written whenever there is a change in the status of the document.

For computer-based evidence, professional programs like EnCase and The Forensic Toolkit calculate checksums that support the chain of evidence. We discussed these and other forensic programs in Chapter 7. But even with electronic evidence, the traditional chain of evidence must be maintained with seized computers, cellular phones, and other devices.

CAUTION   *Failing to keep a proper chain of evidence is one of the most common ways to ruin evidence or even entire cases.*

Marking the Evidence

When documentary evidence is received, it should be uniquely marked so that it can be identified later. A transparent envelope should be used to store it, with the date received and the initials of the examiner written on the outside. A copy of the document should be made, and the original document should be stored in the envelope in a secure place. Copies of the document should be used during the investigation and trial and should be kept in the same file where the original is kept. During the trial, the original can be removed from safekeeping and used.

Organization of the Evidence

Fraud cases can create tremendous amounts of documentary evidence. For example, in one case, 100 people

FIGURE 8.1   INFORMATION ON A CHECK

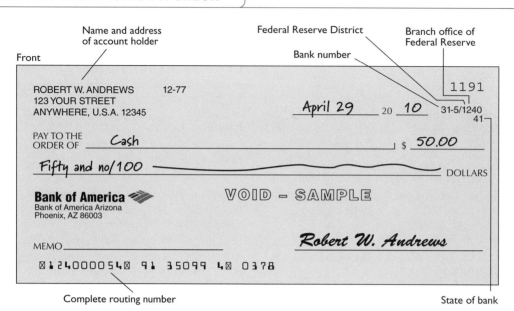

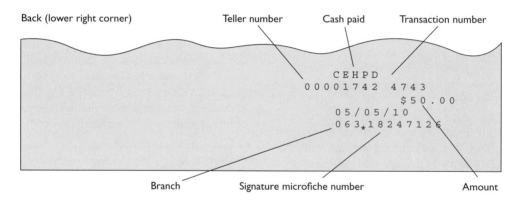

Information about the Maker and the Maker's Bank	*Information about the Bank That Processes the Check*
1. Name and address of the account holder	1. Branch number where processed
2. Bank number of the maker's bank, including: a. City and state of bank b. Bank name	2. Teller who processed the transaction
	3. Sequence number of the transaction
3. Bank routing number of the maker's bank including: a. Federal Reserve District b. Branch office of Federal Reserve c. State of the maker's bank	4. Information about the nature of the transaction, including: a. Whether the check was cashed b. Whether the check was deposited c. Whether the check represented a payment.
4. Maker's account number	5. Account number of the person who presented the check
5. Check number	6. Date of transaction
6. Amount processed	7. Amount of transaction

worked full time for over a year to input key words into a computer so that the documents could be called up on demand during the trial. In this case, there were literally millions of documents. In the Lincoln Savings and Loan Association case, the judge created a document depository containing millions of documents, from which attorneys, FBI agents, and others were able to access evidence while preparing for trial. It is not uncommon today, especially in large cases, to have electronic files of all depositions and other testimony of all exhibits coordinated electronically with the testimony. These kinds of databases are searchable by key word, by witness, by topic, and by other means. While hard copies of documents and records are still used, they are rarely used without having electronic copies as well.

The FBI has one of the most sophisticated and advanced document examination laboratories in the world. The following is an example of the kind of work they can do:

Recently, FBI headquarters got a call from a field case agent who said he'd seized a warehouse with thousands of boxes of financial records related to a criminal investigation. He said, "We need to analyze the material for prosecution, but it will take years to go through it all. Any ideas how to speed up the process?"

Absolutely! This is a job for the FBI's Document Conversion Lab, or DocLab, started in 2002 as part of a new Records Management Division.

Just exactly what is the DocLab? It is a team of FBI technicians, based in Washington, who scan and digitize hard copy files and photographs using state-of-the-art technology. So far, DocLab has scanned more than 9.5 million images (single pieces of paper), formatting many of those images into readable text and uploading them into an FBI electronic application. Once digitized, the information is easily and rapidly exchanged between bureau field offices, joint task forces, and FBI headquarters.

Is the DocLab really such a big deal? Yes, more than you might think because it:

- *Saves incredible amounts of time and space. In the above case, FBI agents walked away with a warehouse full of records—on seven CDs.*
- *Increases search capabilities exponentially. Those millions of pieces of paper can now be searched electronically in seconds, drawing connections between people, places, and events—within and across cases—in new and important ways.*
- *Enables information sharing far and wide. The CDs from the warehouse of financial records, for*

example, were copied and shared with the FBI case agent on the spot. And once uploaded into the electronic application, the files were instantaneously key word searchable throughout the FBI.

While the FBI has been digitizing records for years, the importance of digitization became very important after 9/11. Investigative priorities in the post-9/11 world of complex, voluminous, and international evidence call for focus and absolute efficiency. DocLab now has dedicated trained professionals, working around the clock, who can respond quickly to urgent needs and major cases around the world.

Here are just a few examples of what DocLab has done.

- *Traveled to Afghanistan and Iraq to help scan critical counterterrorism documents.*
- *Digitized more than 20,000 pages of records from the DC sniper case, enabling investigators to farm out leads quickly and prepare for the massive court cases.*
- *Took more than 3 million paper records in poor condition and quickly scanned them for a significant counterintelligence case.*
- *Helped Indianapolis prosecutors meet an urgent court deadline in a major health care fraud investigation.[1]*

In 2006, the FBI reported to Congress that DocLab had "scanned and converted more than 38 million pages in support of various investigative and intelligence gathering efforts of the FBI. DocLab also supports the FBI worldwide with "fly teams" consisting of trained personnel and a portable scanning capability through the deployment of scanning teams and portable scanning equipment."[2]

This kind of digitization has become quite common in both civil and criminal cases. There are literally hundreds of organizations whose major business purpose is to digitize and make searchable documentary evidence. Some of the more popular programs used to index and store evidence are CaseMap, CaseCentral, ZANTAZ, Ringtail, and DatiCon. Web searches for "case management archive" and "litigation support" will reveal further products with many different features.

Regardless of the technology or system utilized, a consistent organization scheme must be used to manage the large volume of documents in a typical case. Fraud experts use a variety of organization schemes for their document management. Some organize documents by witness, some use chronological organization, and others prefer organization by transaction. Whichever method is used, a database should be maintained that includes the following:

- *Dates of documents*
- *Sources of documents*
- *The dates on which documents were obtained*
- *Brief descriptions of document contents*
- *Subjects of documents*
- *Identifying or Bates number*

Bates numbers are used by attorneys involved in litigation to track all documents. To illustrate how Bates numbering works, assume that XYZ auditors are being sued by ABC Corporation's shareholders. Further assume that the XYZ auditors from two different offices—New York and New Jersey—worked on the case. Most likely, the 5,000 documents provided (by subpoena, court order, or voluntarily) by XYZ in the New York office will be numbered XYZ-NY 1000001–1005000. The documents provided by ABC Corporation will be labeled ABC 0000001–00100000, etc. This way, the source of the document is known, and the number provides a unique identifier that can always be tracked.

> **Remember this …**
>
> *Regardless of the organization method used, an evidence database should contain basic information about documents like dates, sources, descriptions, subjects, and identifying numbers.*

Coordination of Evidence

Some investigations are simple and involve only a few people. Coordination of evidence in these circumstances is straightforward. Investigators may decide to share evidence and plan activities through a series of meetings, and they may use a shared network drive for coordination.

In large cases that involve investigators, legal counsel, accountants, expert witnesses, and management representatives, coordination can be more difficult. Investigation analysis software can be useful in these circumstances. Two popular products in this space are the Analyst's Notebook from i2, Inc., and Xanalys Link Explorer. These products allow investigators to quickly understand complex scenarios and volumes of information in a visual, intuitive way using **link analysis**. Once investigators enter their indicators into the centralized database, the software performs link analysis to find links between people, places, and events. Automatically generated charts showing links between people, places, and documents make it easy for investigators to know

what objects are most central in a case. These software packages can do many other types of analyses—from time line analysis to graph analysis.

STOP & THINK *What types of cases should use link analysis software? Is the cost justified in these cases?*

Original Documents versus Photocopies

Original documents are always preferable to photocopies as evidence. In fact, depending on the jurisdiction, only four situations usually permit the introduction of photocopies, which are considered secondary evidence, in a court of law. In the four situations listed below, the court must have proof that an original document existed and that the secondary evidence is a genuine copy of the original.

1. The original document has been lost or destroyed without the intent or fault of the party seeking to introduce the secondary evidence.
2. The original document is in the possession of an adverse party who fails to produce it after a written notice to do so, or when the party in possession is outside the jurisdiction of the subpoena power of the court.
3. The document or record is in the custody of a public office.
4. The original documents are too voluminous to permit careful examination, and a summary of their contents is acceptable.

CAUTION *Photocopies of documents can only be used in certain limited circumstances.*

Many frauds have been allowed to be perpetrated and to go undetected because auditors and others were satisfied with photocopies rather than original documents. Perhaps one of the best examples of the use of photocopies is the ZZZZ Best case. In the case, one of the principals was a master of the copy machine. According to one source, "He could play the copy machine as well as Horowitz could play the piano." Any time photocopies are used, especially when originals would be the norm, investigators must be suspicious.

> **Remember this …**
>
> *Documents and electronic records are the backbone of concealment investigation because most concealment methods involve altering or manipulating physical documents or computer records.*

Obtaining Documentary Evidence

Most concealment investigative procedures involve accessing and accumulating documentary evidence. In the remainder of this chapter, we identify several ways to obtain such evidence. Examiners who have computer, statistics, and accounting backgrounds usually have an advantage in investigating documentary evidence. You may want to consider taking further classes in databases, statistics and/or sampling, and accounting documents.

The best way to obtain documentary evidence is through computer-based queries of accounting and other databases. As discussed in Chapter 6, these methods allow full-population analysis and are able to pinpoint evidential records within huge populations of millions of total records. When these methods are used during concealment investigation, the potential scheme has already been identified. Investigators can focus specifically on Steps 4 (query databases) and 5 (analyze results) of the data-driven approach to highlight changed or fraudulent records.

Another useful method of obtaining documentary evidence is through traditional audits, including discovery sampling. These methods are especially appropriate with nonelectronic evidence like canceled checks or confirmation letters. These methods are described in the next section.

The least reliable method of obtaining documentary evidence is by chance, accident, or tips. Once in a while, auditors and others come across documents that provide evidence of fraudulent activities. Sometimes these documents are recognized by blatant alterations or forgeries. At other times, informants bring them to an organization's attention. In either case, such instances should be considered luck; while chance evidence often occurs, it should not be seen as a routine method of discovering documentary evidence.

STOP & THINK *What are the best methods of obtaining documentary evidence? Why?*

Audits

In general, auditors conduct seven types of tests, each of which yields a form of evidence. The tests are (1) tests of mechanical accuracy (recalculations), (2) analytical tests (tests of reasonableness), (3) documentation, (4) confirmations, (5) observations, (6) physical examinations, and (7) inquiries. Because gathering documentation is a normal part of their work, auditors can often gather documentary evidence as part of an investigation without arousing suspicion. Auditors can use manual or computer procedures to gather documentary evidence.

The limited partnerships case at the beginning of the chapter illustrates how audit procedures can provide documentary evidence. In this case, auditors sent confirmations to banks that had placed liens on property the partnerships owned. The return confirmations contained the amounts of the loans, the dates they were taken out, and the remaining unpaid balance. Further inquiry of the financial institutions, with the aid of subpoenas, revealed copies of the loan origination documents with signatures of the borrowers and other information. Once these original loan documents were available, it was relatively easy to prove fraud and get a confession.

As another example of how documentary evidence can be helpful, consider again the fraud at Elgin Aircraft from Chapter 5. The defense auditor recognized several symptoms at Elgin, including (1) the limousine (a lifestyle symptom), (2) never missing a day's work (a behavioral symptom), and (3) not verifying claims with employees (a control weakness). He decided to investigate, suspecting that the manager of the claims department was committing some kind of fraud. Reasoning that the easiest way for her to be committing fraud was by setting up phony doctors and billing the company for fictitious claims, the auditor decided to gather documentary evidence in the form of checks paid to various doctors to ascertain whether the doctors and claims were legitimate.

The auditor knew it would be impossible to determine conclusively whether fraud was being perpetrated without looking at every check. He also realized that since there was no proof of fraud, his suspicions did not justify personally examining the total population of all 6,000 checks, which were numbered 2000 through 8000. Faced with the desire to examine the checks but with limited time, the auditor realized he had three alternatives. He could audit the checks by selecting a few of them to look at, he could draw a random sample and use statistical sampling techniques to examine the checks, or he could use a computer and examine certain attributes of all checks.

If the auditor chose the first alternative and analyzed in detail 40 of the checks, he could conclude that the manager was committing fraud if one or more of the selected checks had been made out to a fictitious doctor or doctors. However, if his sample of 40 checks did not include payments to fictitious doctors, the only conclusion he could draw was that there was no fraud in his sample of 40. Without drawing a random sample and using proper sampling procedures, no conclusions could be made about the total population. If he happened to find fraud, he would have succeeded. If he did not find fraud, either he was looking at the wrong sample or there was no fraud.

C A U T I O N   *Sampling can be risky when fraud may exist in only a few records. Use full-population analysis when possible to avoid these risks.*

Discovery Sampling

A better approach to auditing documentary evidence in some situations is to use a form of statistical sampling called **discovery sampling**. Using discovery (statistical) sampling allows an auditor to generalize and make inferences from the sample to the population, as shown in Figure 8.2.

Discovery sampling is the easiest of all statistical sampling variations to understand. Basically, if an auditor can read a table, he or she can conduct discovery sampling. In addition, audit applications like ACL and IDEA make discovery sampling easy. Discovery sampling deals with the probability of discovering at least one error in a given sample size if the population error rate is a certain percentage. A type of attribute sampling, which is based on normal probability theory, discovery sampling is sometimes referred to as stop-and-go sampling. Its use involves two steps: (1) drawing a random sample and (2) using a table to draw inferences about the population from the sample. To illustrate, assume that the defense auditor wanted to use discovery sampling to examine checks payable to doctors. First, he would use a random number generator or a random number table to select the checks

to be examined. A sample list of random numbers is shown in Table 8.1.

In using a random number table to select the checks to examine, an auditor must make the following four decisions:

1. Where to start in the table when selecting check numbers
2. The direction in which to move through the table
3. What to do with numbers that are outside the range, in this case, that do not fall between 2000 and 8000
4. Which four of the five digits to use, since the checks are all four-digit numbers

Assume, for example, that the auditor decided to start with the top-left number (37039), to move through the table from left to right and from top to bottom, to skip numbers that fell outside the relevant range, and to use the first four digits of each number. The checks selected for examination would be checks 3703, 6467, 3154, 6685, 2514, 2300, and so forth. (How many to select is discussed below.) Randomly choosing the checks to be examined allows the auditor to make inferences about the population, not just about the sample.

Once the checks have been selected, the next step is to use a discovery sampling table, such as the one in Table 8.2, to draw conclusions about the checks. When examining the checks in the sample, if the auditor finds a check to a fictitious doctor, he would be 100 percent certain that fraud exists. If he does not find such a check, he would still have to examine all 6,000 checks to be absolutely certain that there is no fraud. If he samples anything less than 100 percent of the checks and does not find fraud, discovery sampling allows him to decide how much risk he is willing to assume. In other words, discovery sampling

FIGURE 8.2   DISCOVERY SAMPLING

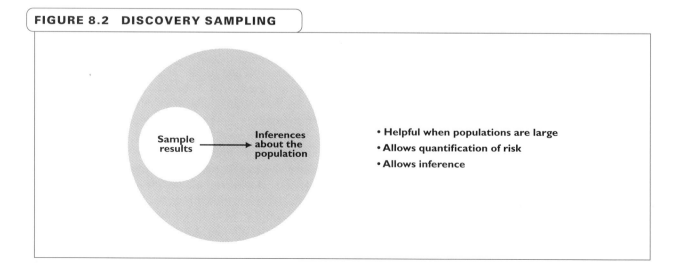

allows the auditor to quantify risk. Using Table 8.2, if the auditor samples 300 checks and finds none made out to fictitious doctors, he would be 95 percent confident that the true population fraud rate did not exceed 1 percent, 78 percent confident that no more than 0.5 percent of the checks were fraudulent, and so forth. The entire table is based on the assumption that no fictitious checks are

found. (Again, if the auditor finds even one fictitious doctor, he would be 100 percent certain that fraud exists.)

The more confident the auditor wants to be and the less risk of not identifying fraudulent checks the auditor wants to assume, the larger the sample size that must be examined. Population size seems to make little difference in sample size, unless the sample becomes a

TABLE 8.1 PARTIAL TABLE OF RANDOM NUMBERS

ITEM	(1)	(2)	(3)	(4)	(5)	(6)	(7)	(8)
1000	37039	97547	64673	31546	99314	66854	97855	99965
1001	25145	84834	23009	51584	66754	77785	52357	25532
1002	98433	54725	18864	65866	76918	78825	58210	76835
1003	97965	68548	81545	82933	93545	85959	63282	61454
1004	78049	67830	14624	17563	25697	07734	48243	94318
1005	50203	25658	91478	08509	23308	48130	65047	77873
1006	40059	67825	18934	64998	49807	71126	77818	56893
1007	84350	67241	54031	34535	04093	35062	58163	14205
1008	30954	51637	91500	48722	60988	60029	60873	37423
1009	86723	36464	98305	08009	00666	29255	18514	49158
1010	50188	22554	86160	92250	14021	65859	16237	72296
1011	50014	00463	13906	35936	71761	95755	87002	71667
1012	66023	21428	14742	94874	23308	58533	26507	11208
1013	04458	61862	63119	09541	01715	87901	91260	03079
1014	57510	36314	30452	09712	37714	95482	30507	68475
1015	43373	58939	95848	28288	60341	52174	11879	18115
1016	61500	12763	64433	02268	57905	72347	49498	21871
1017	78938	71312	99705	71546	42274	23915	38405	18779
1018	64257	93218	35793	43671	64055	88729	11168	60260
1019	56864	21554	70445	24841	04779	56774	96129	73594
1020	35314	29631	06937	54545	04470	75463	77112	77126
1021	40704	48823	65963	39659	12717	56201	22811	24863
1022	07318	44623	02843	33299	59872	86774	06926	12672
1023	94550	23299	45557	07923	75126	00808	01312	46689
1024	34348	81191	21027	77087	10909	03676	97723	34469
1025	92277	57115	50789	68111	75305	53289	39751	45760
1026	56093	58302	52236	64756	50273	61566	61962	93280
1027	16623	17849	96701	94971	94758	08845	32260	59823
1028	50848	93982	66451	32143	05441	10399	17775	74169
1029	48006	58200	58367	66577	68583	21108	41361	20732
1030	56640	27890	28825	96509	21363	53657	60119	75385

TABLE 8.2 DISCOVERY SAMPLING TABLE

	PROBABILITY (PERCENTAGE) OF INCLUDING AT LEAST ONE ERROR IN THE SAMPLE							
	RATE OF OCCURRENCE IN THE POPULATION (PERCENT)							
SAMPLE SIZE	0.01	0.05	0.1	0.2	0.3	0.5	1	2
50		2	5	9	14	22	39	64
60	1	3	6	11	16	26	45	70
70	1	3	7	13	19	30	51	76
80	1	4	8	15	21	33	55	80
90	1	4	9	16	24	36	60	84
100	1	5	10	18	26	39	63	87
120	1	6	11	21	30	45	70	91
140	1	7	13	24	34	50	76	94
160	2	8	15	27	38	55	80	96
200	2	10	18	33	45	63	87	98
240	2	11	21	38	51	70	91	99
300	3	14	26	45	59	78	95	99+
340	3	16	29	49	64	82	97	99+
400	4	18	33	55	70	87	98	99+
460	5	21	37	60	75	90	99	99+
500	5	22	39	63	78	92	99	99+
800	8	33	55	80	91	98	99+	99+
1,000	10	39	63	86	95	99	99+	99+
1,500	14	53	78	95	99	99+	99+	99+
2,500	22	71	92	99	99+	99+	99+	99+

significant part of the population (usually greater than 10 percent), and then the confidence level is higher and the risk lower than indicated in the table.

Even with discovery sampling, auditors can never be certain that fraud does not exist in a population of checks. While discovery sampling does allow inferences to be made about the problem, there is still the possibility that the sample will not be representative of the population (**sampling risk**) and that the auditor will examine a fraudulent check and not recognize it (**nonsampling risk**). Using discovery sampling, auditors can quantify both risk and samples until they have sufficient evidence that fraud does not likely exist.

Because of sampling risks involved in discovery sampling, full population analysis is necessary to discover many frauds. Indeed, frauds such as a single adjusting entry at the end of a period result in only a few journal entries. If the sample rate was determined to be 5 percent, there would be a 95 percent probability that the

sample would not include the fraudulent transaction(s). The use of computers to automate full population testing is a primary method of mitigating sampling risk. While some tests—such as verifying company loans by sending letters to banks—will always require sampling, many tests can be done on full populations. Discovery sampling is an important method in the investigator's toolkit, but be sure to evaluate when and where it is most appropriate and useful.

Documentation of Discovery Sampling The investigator should document the method used for determining sample size (that is, document the specified population error rate and confidence level) and the method used for selecting the sample. For instance, the source of the random number table should be documented by recording the name of the book or computer program from which the table was taken and the rules used for determining the starting point and moving through the table. Such documentation may be important if the investigator expands the sample later, if another person later reviews the sampling plan, or if the procedure later becomes evidence in court.

> **Remember this …**
>
> *Discovery sampling is a simple, statistically based method of analyzing a subset of transactions from a larger pool. It allows the investigator to decide on an acceptable risk level for sampling. As with all sampling, discovery sampling should only be used when full-population analysis using a computer is not possible.*

Evaluation of Errors If the investigator finds errors using discovery sampling, he or she must determine whether the errors were unintentional or are indicative of fraud. For example, in the preceding paragraphs, finding pay merits to fictitious vendors was predetermined to be indicative of fraud. However, errors in amounts of checks might be due to unintentional mathematical or typing errors or could be intentional overpayments in a fraud kickback scheme. Such evaluation can be aided if the definition of what will constitute an error indicative of fraud is made beforehand.

Consideration of Sampling Risk The investigator should be aware of the sampling and nonsampling risks associated with discovery sampling. Sampling risk is the risk that the sample was not representative of the population. To reduce sampling risk, the investigator can increase the sample size or use a random number table or generator to select the items to be examined. As stated earlier in this chapter, sampling risk can be significant when looking for fraud because fraud is not generally indicative of the general population of records.

Consideration of Nonsampling Risk The investigator should also consider nonsampling risk, which is the risk that a finding will be misinterpreted. For instance, the investigator might not recognize that an examined item contained an error, misjudge an error as unintentional instead of intentional, or fail to recognize that a document had been forged. Nonsampling risk cannot be quantified but can be reduced by careful planning, performance, and evaluation of the sampling procedure.

Hard-to-Get Documentary Evidence

Some documentary evidence, while valuable, is extremely difficult to obtain. The three most common examples of difficult evidence are Web-based e-mail accounts, private bank records, tax returns, and brokerage records. While post-9/11 legislation has made it easier to access these records, sometimes there are only three ways to obtain such documentary evidence: (1) by subpoena, (2) by search warrant, or (3) by voluntary consent. **Subpoenas** (*subpoena duces tecum*) are orders issued by a court or a grand jury to produce documents. Failure to honor such a subpoena is punishable by law. Because only agents of the grand jury or the court (usually law enforcement officers) can obtain documents by subpoena, a need to obtain a subpoena is one reason to coordinate fraud investigations with law enforcement officials.

Figure 8.3 contains an example of a subpoena. As you can see, this is a subpoena issued jointly in a civil action by two companies to provide information regarding every person who produced, received, viewed, downloaded, or accessed a certain software called "Run, Walk and Jump" or "runjump.zip" or any derivative thereof from a Web site or Web site hosting service. Other subpoenas would look about the same; that is, they would identify who is making the request for documents or information, who the request is being made of, and what exactly is being asked for. Every subpoena must be signed by a judge or court commissioner; then it is served, meaning it is delivered to the recipients, often by law enforcement officials.

A second way to obtain hard-to-get documentary evidence is to use a search warrant. A judge issues a search warrant when there is probable cause to believe that documents have been used in committing a crime. Search warrants are executed only by law enforcement officials and are generally used only in criminal cases.

The third and most common way to obtain private documents is by voluntary consent, which can be either oral or written. Often, an initial interview with a fraud suspect is for the purpose of obtaining permission to access bank or brokerage records, rather than to obtain a confession. An example of a consent, which allows a fraud examiner to access private bank records, is shown in Figure 8.4.

> **Remember this …**
>
> *Some hard-to-get evidence requires the use of subpoenas, search warrants, or voluntary consents. Examples of this type of evidence include Web-based e-mail accounts, private bank records, tax returns, and brokerage records.*

Document Experts

Sometimes it is necessary to determine whether a document is authentic. Questioned documents can be genuine, counterfeit, fraudulent, or forged. A specialized form of investigation that applies forensic chemistry, microscopy, light, and photography in making determinations about documents is known as **document examination**. **Document experts** can determine whether a document was written by the person whose signature it bears; whether a document has been forged; whether a document has been altered by additives,

deletions, obliterations, erasures, or photocopying; whether the handwriting is genuine; whether the entire document was printed on the same machine; whether a document was printed on the date it bears or before or after; whether two or more documents are significantly different or substantially the same; and whether pages have been substituted in a document.

Table 8.3 lists the most commonly encountered questions related to disputed documents or documents of unknown origin. Document experts can usually answer all these questions. For example, in answering

FIGURE 8.3   SUBPOENA FOR DOCUMENTS

United States District Court
District of New York

ABC Software, Inc., a New York Corporation

Plaintiffs,

vs.

WXYZ Software, Inc., a Delaware Corporation

Defendants.

Civil Action No.   8462359

Subpoena

        You are commanded to produce and permit inspection and copying at the place, date, and time specified below all documents in your possession, custody, or control concern:

DOCUMENTS REQUESTS

Each and every person who produced, received, viewed, downloaded or accessed the "Run, Walk and Jump" software or any derivative thereof.

PLACE
DATE AND TIME

I.M. Smarter than U. Attorneys
October 11, 2007
2250 Skyline Road
New York, New York 12121

ISSUING OFFICER SIGNATURE AND TITLE

                Attorney for Plaintiff
October 5, 2007

ISSUING OFFICER'S NAME, ADDRESS AND PHONE NUMBER

A.B. Money
I.M. Smarter than U Attorneys
2250 Skyline Road
New York, New York 12121

FIGURE 8.4   CONSENT FORM

<u>**XYZ CORPORATION**</u>
CUSTOMER CONSENT AND AUTHORIZATION
FOR ACCESS TO FINANCIAL RECORDS

I, _____Arnold Fox McCune_____ , having read the explanation of my rights which is
(Name of Customer)
attached to this form hereby authorize the _____XYZ Corporation Credit Union,_____
(Name and Address of Financial Ins.)
to disclose these financial records: All Bank Account Records, including checking

accounts, savings accounts, and loans from 1/1/2001 to present

to Michael R. Blair and Robert W. Jacobs._____ for the following purpose(s) :

_____Administrative Purposes_____

I understand that this authorization may be revoked by me in writing at any time before my records, as
described above, are disclosed, and this authorization is valid for no more than three months from the
date of my signature.

_____August 16, 2006_____   *Arnold F. McCune*
                                         (signature of customer)
                                         318 E. Birch Street

                                         Ann Harbor, MI 48159
                                         (Address of Customer)
                                         Michael R. Blair

---

questions about handwriting, examiners might look at
the characteristics listed in Table 8.3.

STOP & THINK   *When is it appropriate to hire a
document expert? When is it not required?*

To become a skilled examiner of questioned documents, one must acquire extensive and specialized
training. Though most fraud investigators are not
trained document examiners, it is important that they
understand two important elements relating to document examination: (1) when to have a document examined by an expert and (2) what the responsibility of the
investigator is with respect to questioned documents. If
one or more of the following warning signs exist, a
document should be submitted for examination:

1. Abrasions or chemical pen or pencil erasures
2. Alterations or substitutions
3. Disguised or unnatural writings
4. Use of two or more different colors of ink
5. Charred, mutilated, or torn pages
6. Pencil or carbon marks along the writing lines
7. Existence of lines made during photocopying
8. Signs of inconsistency or disruption in the continu-
   ity of the content
9. Any suspicious appearance or unusual form

In dealing with questioned documents, the fraud
investigator is responsible for taking the following
steps:

- *Collecting, protecting, identifying, and preserving
  the questioned document in as good a condition as
  possible.*
- *Collecting and being able to prove to the document
  examiner the origins of adequate comparison
  specimens.*
- *Submitting both the questioned and the comparison
  documents to the examiner.*

Two well-known organizations of document experts
can offer help in fraud investigations. The first is
the Questioned Documents Section of the Forensic
Analysis Section of the FBI. This group provides forensic support to the FBI and to law enforcement agencies
at all levels by conducting forensic examinations of
documents. The second organization of document
experts is a private group, the American Board of
Forensic Document Examiners, Inc. (ABFDE).[3] A description of the ABFDE's background, functions, and
purpose follows:

*The need to identify forensic scientists qualified to
provide essential professional services for the nation's
judicial and executive branches of government as well*

TABLE 8.3 QUESTIONS ABOUT DISPUTED DOCUMENTS

Handwriting:

1. Is the signature genuine?
2. Is the continued writing genuine?
3. Was the writing disguised?
4. Who did any unknown writing?
5. Can any hand printing that exists be identified?
6. Can any handwritten numerals be identified?
7. Which was written first, the signature or the writing above it?
8. Can the forger be identified?
9. Is the handwriting or signature consistent with the date of the document?

Printing:

1. What make and model of printer was used? During what years was the particular make and model used?
2. Can the individual printer that was used be identified?
3. Was the printing done before or after any handwriting and/or signatures?
4. Was the printing done on the date of the document or later?
5. Who did the actual printing?
6. Was the printing on the document all done at one time, or was some of it added at a later time? How much was added later?
7. Were copies made using the original document?
8. Are the copies genuine?
9. Can the printer or the document be identified from a carbon tape?

Alterations and additions:

1. Was the document altered in any way or added to at a later time? Were pages added, parts torn or cut off, pages purposely wrinkled or stained, etc.?
2. What original date or matter was altered or added to?
3. When was the alteration or addition made?
4. Who made the alteration or addition?
5. Has the photograph on an ID card or other ID document been removed and replaced with another?

Age:

1. Is the age of the document in accordance with its date?
2. How old are the paper, the printing, the ink, the seal, etc.?
3. Is there evidence of the manner or location in which the document was kept?

Copies:

1. Are the photocopies or photostatic reproductions copies of other documents?
2. What type of copy machine was used? What brand?
3. Can the individual copier be identified?
4. In what year was the particular make and model used? Produced?
5. Was any portion of the copy not on the original document? Was it pasted up?
6. Is there any indication that pages are missing on the copies that were part of the original?
7. Can the copy be traced to and identified as the particular original document that was its source?

Other:

1. Can machine-printed matter be identified?
2. Can the check writer, the adding machine, the addressograph machine, or other machine be identified?
3. Was the envelope resealed?
4. Can the stapler, glue, pin, clip, or other fastener be identified?
5. Is the printed document genuine or counterfeit? If counterfeit, can the original document used as a reproduction source be determined?
6. What processes were used to print the counterfeit document?
7. Could the printing source or counterfeiter be identified if located?

Characteristics of handwriting:

1. The basic movement of the handwriting—clockwise, counterclockwise, and straight-line—indicating direction, curvature, shapes, and slopes of the writing motions.
2. Slant—forward, backward, or in between.
3. The manner in which letters with loops are curved, and the size, shape, and proportion of the loops.
4. Peculiarities in the approach strokes and the upward strokes in the first letter of a word and in capital letters.

(continued)

TABLE 8.3 QUESTIONS ABOUT DISPUTED DOCUMENTS *(CONTINUED)*

5. Characteristic initial and terminal strokes; their length and their angle in relation to letters and words.

6. Gaps between letters in specific letter combinations.

7. The manner in which the capital letters are formed, and the additional hooks or flourishes some writers place at the start or end of these letters.

8. Relative smoothness, tremor, or hesitation in the writing. Some writing flows smoothly and is free of hesitation. Other writing shows hesitation in the formation of some letters or defective line quality in the writing as a whole.

9. The manner in which the writer varies pressure in certain pen strokes, and variations in the weight and width of stroke lines.

10. The proportion and alignment of letters; the length or height and size of capital letters compared with lowercase letters.

11. The manner in which the letter t is crossed, and the height and slant of the crossing—near the top of the t or lower down, straight or at an angle, with a flourish or plain; whether words ending in t are crossed.

12. The location of the dot over the letter i and its relationship to the location of the letter itself.

13. Types of ending strokes in words ending in the letters y, g, and s.

14. Open or closed letter style, as seen in such letters as a and o, and in letters that combine upward or downward strokes with loops, such as b, d, o, and g. Are the circles in these letters open or closed, broad or narrow?

15. Separation of letters within a word (for example, separating a t from the remainder of the word, or separating a whole syllable from the rest of the word).

16. Characteristics of the portions that appear above and/or below the line in such letters as f, g, and y.

17. Relative alignment of all letters; the uniformity and spacing of letters, words, and lines.

18. Alignment of lines.

19. Use and positioning of punctuation.

20. Indications that the writing instrument was lifted off the writing material between words and sentences.

as the community in general has been long recognized. In response to this professional mandate, the American Board of Forensic Document Examiners, Inc., (ABFDE) was organized in 1977 to provide, in the interest of the public and the advancement of the science, a program of certification in forensic document examination. In purpose, function, and organization, the ABFDE is thus analogous to the certifying board(s) in various other scientific fields.

The objective of the board is to establish, enhance, and maintain, as necessary, standards of qualification for those who practice forensic document examination and to certify as qualified specialists those voluntary applicants who comply with the requirements of the board. In this way, the board aims to make available to the judicial system, and other public, a practical and equitable system for readily identifying those persons professing to be specialists in forensic document examination who possess the requisite qualifications and competence.

Certification is based on the candidate's personal and professional record of education and training, experience, and achievement, as well as on the results of a formal examination.

The board is a nonprofit organization in the District of Columbia. Its initial sponsors are the American Academy of Forensic Sciences and the American Society of Questioned Document Examiners. The board is composed of officers and other directors who serve staggered terms and are elected from among nominees of designated nominating organizations or serve at large.

Internet searches can quickly identify qualified question document examiners. Searching such key words as "question document examiner" or "questioned document examination" will reveal numerous Web sites of question document examiners. Experienced investigators discount questionable or scientifically unproven methods and use what they know works best: thoroughness and dogged tenacity in pursuit of the truth. They also make sure that any technique they use is sound and fair. For example, if there is a question regarding the authenticity of a document or handwriting sample, they seek out a qualified documents examiner who holds a degree in the physical sciences and has undergone many years of laboratory experience under the supervision of an experienced examiner. The authors recommend always using a qualified document examiner as opposed to a graphologist. Graphologists usually obtain their designation through a home study course, whereas a qualified document examiner will hold a degree and has undergone many years of laboratory experience.

Review of the Learning Objectives

- **Describe concealment investigation methods and how they relate to fraud.** Concealment investigation methods include discovering physical documents or computer records that have been manipulated to conceal a fraud.
- **Understand the value of documents and electronic records in a fraud investigation.** Documents and electronic records are the backbone of concealment investigation because most concealment methods involve altering or manipulating physical documents or computer records. Most fraud experts prefer physical evidence to other types of evidence, such as eyewitnesses, because documents are reliable and consistent.
- **List the different methods of obtaining documentary evidence.** Documentary evidence can be obtained by searching through physical or electronic records. Proper chain of evidence, marking of evidence, organization of documentary evidence, coordination of evidence, and rules of originals versus copies of documents must be observed.
- **Understand how to perform discovery sampling to obtain documentary evidence.** Discovery sampling is a simple, statistically based method of analyzing a subset of transactions from a larger pool. It allows the investigator to decide on an acceptable risk level for sampling. As with all sampling, discovery sampling should be used only when full-population analysis using a computer is not possible.
- **Explain how to obtain hard-to-get documentary evidence.** Some hard-to-get evidence requires the use of subpoenas, search warrants, or voluntary consents. Examples of this type of evidence include Web-based e-mail accounts, private bank records, tax returns, and brokerage records.

KEY TERMS

chain of custody, p. 233
bates numbers, p. 236
link analysis, p. 236
discovery sampling, p. 238
sampling risk, p. 240

nonsampling risk, p. 240
subpoenas, p. 241
document examination, p. 242
document experts, p. 242

QUESTIONS

Discussion Questions

1. What are the most common ways perpetrators conceal their frauds?
2. What are the primary aspects of documentary evidence?
3. Why is it important to maintain a chain of custody for documentary evidence?
4. What programs can help with evidence coordination?
5. Why is it important to gather documentary evidence?
6. What is the value of documents when conducting a fraud investigation?
7. Why is it important to obtain documentary evidence?
8. How can discovery sampling help in obtaining documentary evidence?
9. What are different ways in which investigators can obtain hard-to-get documentary evidence?

True/False

1. Concealment is the covering of tracks, obscuring of evidence, and removal of red flags to hide a perpetrator's fraud.
2. Checks are excellent sources of physical evidence.
3. Traditional chain of custody evidence procedures are not appropriate when used with electronic evidence.
4. Photocopies are always preferable to original documents as evidence.
5. There is no difference between forensic document experts and graphologists.
6. Evidence should be uniquely marked so it can be easily identified later.
7. Concealment investigative methods sometimes involve the study of documents that have been manipulated.
8. Discovery sampling is probably the most difficult of all statistical sampling variations to understand.
9. As long as a sample is selected randomly, it will always be representative of the population as a whole.
10. Even if photocopies of original documents are allowed to be introduced as evidence in a court of law, they are still considered secondary evidence.
11. A canceled check typically shows the account number of the person who presented the check, the teller who processed the check, and the sequence number of the transaction.

12. Random number tables are ineffective and should not be used when selecting random samples from a population.
13. Using a computer to access records (data mining) can be a very effective approach for determining if fraud exists because the auditor can look at entire populations.
14. Bates numbers are identifying numbers used by attorneys involved in litigation to track all documents.
15. Programs like i2's Analyst's Notebook and Xanalys Link Explorer perform link analysis.
16. The best way to obtain documentary evidence in a computer database is to use discovery sampling to find the appropriate records.

Multiple Choice

1. In a fraud investigation, documents:
   a. Usually contain extremely valuable information.
   b. Are rarely used in court.
   c. Are not reliable sources of information.
   d. Are only valuable in obtaining a confession.
2. Chain of custody refers to:
   a. Marking on a document so it can be identified later.
   b. A record of when a document is received and what has happened to it since its receipt.
   c. Databases used in trials to assist lawyers.
   d. The way in which courts are organized.
3. Marking documentary evidence is important to ensure that:
   a. Documents are legal.
   b. Databases can be created with valuable information.
   c. Documents can be identified later.
   d. Marking documentary evidence is not important.
4. Discovery sampling:
   a. Is a type of variables sampling.
   b. Is one of the more difficult statistical sampling methods to understand.
   c. Is never used in conducting a fraud examination.
   d. Deals with the probability of discovering at least one error in a given sample size if the population error is a certain percentage.
5. Documentary evidence such as private tax returns can usually be obtained only by:

a. Subpoena.
b. Search warrant.
c. Voluntary consent.
d. All of the above.

6. Which of the following is *not* true regarding document experts?
   a. They can usually determine whether a document was written by the person whose signature the document bears.
   b. They can usually determine whether a document has been forged.
   c. They can usually determine whether the date the document bears is the date the document was written.
   d. All of the above are true statements.
7. Which of the following is *not* a benefit of statistical sampling?
   a. It allows auditors to be certain that fraud does not exist in a population.
   b. It is helpful when populations are large.
   c. It allows quantification of risk.
   d. It allows inference about a population.
8. Which of the following methods of gathering documents is based primarily on luck?
   a. Documents discovered during audits.
   b. Hard-to-get private documents that are subpoenaed.
   c. Documents discovered through searching public sources.
   d. Documents provided by tipsters.
9. Which of the following is true of graphologists?
   a. They can only perform their work in laboratory settings.
   b. They perform the same type of work as forensic document experts.
   c. They study handwriting as a way to interpret and identify personalities.
   d. They are required to be members of the ABFDE organization.
10. What can a fraud examiner conclude if one or more instances of fraud are found in a sample taken from a population?
    a. There is a slight risk that fraud exists in the population.
    b. The population contains fraud.
    c. The sample may not have been randomly selected, and thus no conclusions can be drawn.
    d. The sample is most likely not representative of the population as a whole.

11. What can a fraud examiner conclude if his or her tests confirm that no instances of fraud are present in a sample taken from a population?
    a. There is virtually no risk that fraud exists in the population.
    b. The population contains no fraud.
    c. Only that no fraud is present in that particular sample.
    d. The sample is most likely not representative of the population as a whole.

12. How are most frauds concealed?
    a. By shredding source documents.
    b. By converting to a paperless office without paper transactions.
    c. By creating fictitious documents or altering source documents.
    d. By firing employees who will not go along with the fraud.

13. Which of the following is usually the best way to obtain documentary evidence?
    a. Computer-based queries of full-population accounting and other databases.
    b. A statistically sound sampling approach like discovery sampling.
    c. Chance, accident, or tip discovery.
    d. None of the above are effective methods of discovering evidence.

14. Programs like CaseMap, CaseCentral, ZANTAZ, Ringtail, and DatiCon are examples of:
    a. Software that implements discovery sampling techniques.
    b. Link analysis software.
    c. Software packages used to index and store evidence.
    d. Forensic software used to investigate hard drives and other digital devices.

SHORT CASES

Case 1

The management of AAAA Company has observed that the company's cash outflows have been increasing much more rapidly than its inflows. Management cannot understand the change; from its perspective, it has been "business as usual." Management has asked you, a fraud expert, to help them understand what is going on.

You have decided that the best place to start your investigation is to take a sample of canceled checks and verify that both the controller and another manager signed them—a procedure required by company policy. Check numbers for the period range from 100 to 800.

Using Table 8.1, follow the instructions below to select a random sample of 15 checks to examine.

- *Start from the bottom left of the table.*
- *Move through the table from left to right and from bottom to top.*
- *Skip the numbers outside the relevant range.*
- *Use the middle three digits of each number.*

Case 2

Assume that you have selected a random sample of 15 checks from a population of 800 checks. The checks you have selected are the following numbers: 664, 789, 650, 136, 365, 538, 800, 657, 110, 136, 398, 645, 214, 544, and 777. Based on this sample, evaluate the truth of the following statements regarding your findings. Describe why you feel each statement is true or false.

1. You have determined that Check No. 365 was not properly signed and was paid to a fictitious vendor. You conclude that fraud exists in the population.
2. You have determined that no fraud exists in the sample of 15 checks you evaluated. You conclude that no fraud exists in the population.

Case 3

Enron, one of the largest corporations to ever file for (Chapter 11) bankruptcy protection, was number 7 on the *Fortune* 500 list of the largest companies in America as ranked by revenues at the time of its bankruptcy. It was alleged that Enron executives were involved in questionable accounting and financial statement fraud, the disclosure of which led to the downward spiral in Enron's stock price and the financial ruin of thousands of employees and investors. In addition to Enron's internal accounting problems, it is alleged that its auditor, one of the large accounting firms, instructed employees to destroy documents related to its work for Enron.

1. Based on your understanding of a fraud examiner's responsibilities regarding documents, what should the audit firm personnel have done with their documents if they had suspected that fraud had occurred?

Case 4

Marlin Company has suspected something "fishy" for several months. It has noticed that its profits have been slowly decreasing, while revenues have been increasing. After consulting with you, a fraud expert, the company has decided to investigate the purchasing patterns of its three purchasing agents—Curly, Larry, and Moe. You decide that a good method for investigation into the matter is examining a random sample of purchase invoices and verifying their accuracy and validity. Curly's invoices are numbered 0001 through 1000, Larry's are 1000 through 1999, and Moe's are 2000 through 2999.

When you approach Curly, Larry, and Moe, they seem somewhat defensive. They begin to harass one another, blaming each other for the mess in which they are involved. Moe even twitches their noses and slaps their heads. Curly attempts to retaliate by poking Moe in the eye, but misses and hits Larry instead.

When the three were done, the CFO, Mr. Rutin-Tutin, exclaimed, "Would you three stooges quit fooling around and produce the invoices immediately?"

The three shuffled off to their offices, grumbling all the way. They returned a couple of hours later with photocopies of their invoices. When Mr. Rutin-Tutin asked where the original invoices were, they explained that they always copy and destroy the originals for easier storing purposes. Rather annoyed and fed up with the three morons, Mr. Rutin-Tutin hands you the stacks of photocopied invoices and tells you to do your thing.

1. What is wrong with this picture?
2. Are you suspicious that fraud is present?
3. What is a possible first step in verifying the invoices?

CASE STUDIES

Case Study 1
John Doe, a fraud examiner, has been hired by ABC Corporation to investigate a shortage of cash, which management thinks is being caused by fraudulent behavior. John Doe could spend his time and money pursuing witnesses to the crime or collecting documents that would confirm fraudulent activities. As with most fraud examiners, he chooses to collect supporting documents instead of pursuing witnesses.

Explain why John and most other fraud examiners prefer documents over witnesses; then describe elements of good document care.

Case Study 2
You landed a summer internship with a company that processes dental insurance claims for insurance companies. The company receives the insurance claims from dental offices, achieves authorization from the correct insurance company, and sends payment checks. You do not deal with dental customers directly; instead, you work with insurance companies on one side and dental offices on the other.

After two months with the company, you think a number of frauds may be occurring, and you feel the best way to search for these frauds is to investigate documentary evidence. Because hundreds of dental offices send insurance claims to your office, some may not be real dental offices. You contact the IT department and receive a set of files that represent the documents involved in transactions for the past three months.

Download the following files from the textbook's Web site:

- *ch08_dentists.csv*
- *ch08_claims.csv*
- *ch08_patients.csv*

Go to cengagebrain.com and search for this book by title or ISBN number. Then click 'Access Now' to download the data files. To ensure that the example data set does not inadvertently refer to real dental offices or patients, each office and patient is referred to by ID rather than by name.

Questions

1. Some dental offices may not employ real dentists and may be front companies that are sending claims out for work not performed. A real dental office should have a real office address with dental chairs, reception areas, etc. Are any dental offices instead using post office boxes in their payment addresses?

2. Real dentists should be sending claims to many different insurance companies. Since your company only represents a few of these companies, the sequential numbers on the claim sheets from a given dentist will rotate through all the companies that dentist is working with. If the numbers sent to you from a given dentist are sequential, you know that the dentist is only sending claims to you. Search the claims file for sequential numbers from any given dental office. Are any sending you sequential claims?

3. A human adult has 32 permanent teeth. Your company requires that each claim list the patient seen (identified by "patient id"), the tooth worked on, and the type of work done. Because of the natural limitation on the amount of cavities that could be filled on any one person, it is rare that a person would have more than a few cavities in the

three months of your audit (it is possible for a tooth to have more than one cavity). Using this field, calculate the total number of cavities submitted for each patient. Do any patients seem to be visiting the dentist too often?

4. Patients normally need to live close to their dentists because receiving service requires a visit to the office. A good fraud search is to calculate the distance from each customer's address to his or her dentist's office address using a geographic information system like Google Maps or MapQuest. For this question, simply determine if any patients live in different states than their dentists. Do any patients seem to have a long drive to their dentists' offices?

INTERNET ASSIGNMENTS

Today, many data analysis tools are available to provide assistance to fraud examiners when searching for possible fraudulent activities within a company. Visit the Association of Certified Fraud Examiners' Web site (www.acfe.com) and list some of the computer-aided data analysis tools and services available to fraud examiners.

DEBATES

An excerpt from the Fourth Amendment reads: "The right of the people to be secure in their persons, houses, papers, and effects, against unreasonable searches and seizures, shall not be violated, and no Warrants shall issue, but upon probable cause, supported by Oath or affirmation, and particularly describing the place to be searched, and the persons or things to be seized."

Suspecting a Mr. Dayley of running an illegal gambling and loan sharking operation, the FBI obtained a federal search warrant. The FBI entered the residence of Mr. Dayley and searched through various records. Suspecting most of the records were contained on a personal computer, the FBI began attempting to access the computer's various files.

Unable to access the needed files because of password barriers, the FBI installed a system known as a key logger system (KLS). This system was able to determine the keystrokes made on a computer and thus allowed the FBI to discover the password needed to enter the incriminating files. The discovery led to the gathering of evidence linking Mr. Dayley to the suspected illegal operation.[4]

Were Mr. Dayley's Fourth Amendment rights violated?

END NOTES

1. www.fbi.gov/page2/march04/doclab033004.htm

2. www.fbi.gov/congress/congress06/mueller120606.htm

3. The authors wish to point out the difference between forensic document experts and graphologists, as commonly practiced in North America. Forensic document experts are typically required to actually practice in a laboratory setting, applying such techniques as examining documents for fingerprints, indented writing, handwriting or typewriting, similarities, etc. They generally possess accredited degrees in areas of applied science. Graphology (a term used in conjunction with some forensic document experts in Europe) is practiced in North America by individuals (graphologists) who generally undertake home study courses in handwriting and its application to personalities. We strongly urge caution in differentiating between forensic document experts and graphologists when seeking the truth in any investigation involving the need for expert review of questioned documents.

4. Based on a true case. See www.wired.com/print/politics/security/news/2002/01/49455

CHAPTER **9**

Conversion Investigation Methods

LEARNING OBJECTIVES

After studying this chapter, you should be able to:

- Explain why it is important to find out how perpetrators convert and spend their stolen funds.

- Understand how federal, state, and local public records can assist in following the financial "tracks" of suspected perpetrators.

- Access information via the Internet to assist in the investigation of a suspected fraud perpetrator.

- Perform net worth calculations on suspected fraud perpetrators and understand how net worth calculations are effective in court and in obtaining confessions.

TO THE STUDENT

The Phar-Mor case at the beginning of this chapter is a classic fraud case. As you read this case and the rest of the chapter, consider ways in which fraudsters spend the money they embezzle. If you had a seemingly easy source of money, where would you spend it? Where would those you know spend it? How would you as an investigator discover these purchases?

Phar-Mor, a dry goods retailer based in Youngstown, Ohio, was founded in 1982 by Mickey Monus.[1] Within 10 years, Phar-Mor was operating in nearly every state, with over 300 stores. The retailer's business strategy was to sell household products and prescription drugs at prices lower than other discount stores. Phar-Mor's prices were so low and expanded so rapidly that even Wal-Mart, the king of discount prices, was nervous.

Unfortunately, what appeared to be one of the fastest-growing companies in the United States was actually a massive fraud; the company never made a legitimate profit during the fraud years. Investigators eventually determined that Phar-Mor overstated revenues and profits by over $500 million. Mickey Monus personally pocketed more than $500,000.

Monus loved the good life and was often found in the middle of the action. For example, he diverted $10 million from revenues to prop a now-defunct minor league basketball venture. He also provided a portion of the original funds for the Colorado Rockies baseball team, and he personally assembled the All-American Girls, a professional cheerleading squad. His stolen money was spent drinking at expensive bars, playing golf at exclusive country clubs, paying off credit card balances, and adding additions to his house. Monus purchased a lavish engagement ring for his fiancée, and at their poolside wedding at a Ritz-Carlton hotel, his bride wore an 18-karat gold mesh dress worth $500,000. Monus's spendaholic personality exhibited itself in countless ways. Many times he would walk into the office at 3 p.m. and say, "Let's go to Vegas"—and he meant right then! Once there, a limo would whisk him to Caesars Palace, where a suite awaited him seven days a week, 24 hours a day.

Monus routinely gave employees around $4,000 to gamble with. As one employee said, "He was at home in the 'world of big bets and make-believe.'" To Monus, life was truly a game.[2]

The Phar-Mor fraud is not the only one where the perpetrators enjoyed "the good life." In another case, a perpetrator who confessed to embezzling $3.2 million was asked in her deposition the following question:

How would you describe your lifestyle during the period when the fraud was being perpetrated?

Her response was:

Extravagant. I drove expensive, very nice cars. We had an Audi 5000 Quattro, a Maserati Spider convertible, a Jeep Cherokee, and a Rolls-Royce. We bought expensive paintings, art, and glasswork. We held expensive parties, serving steak and lobster. We bought a condominium for my parents. We took cruises and other expensive vacations. And I wore expensive clothes, fur coats, diamonds, and gold jewelry.

The lifestyles of Mickey Monus and this embezzler were extreme, but they demonstrate a common theme: rarely do perpetrators save what they steal.

> **Remember this …**
>
> *With few exceptions, perpetrators spend what they steal. Because of this, looking at spending patterns is a primary investigation technique.*

Although most perpetrators begin their thefts because of a perceived critical need (the perpetrator initially stole the $3.2 million to repay a debt consolidation loan), they frequently continue to embezzle after their immediate need is met. Rather than saving or investing their stolen money, perpetrators almost always spend it to improve their lifestyles. An important focus in investigations, therefore, involves determining how perpetrators "convert" or spend the stolen funds. As we discussed previously, conversion is the third element of the fraud triangle plus inquiry approach to investigations (see Figure 7.1). Certain frauds, such as kickback schemes, do not generate fraudulent company records; investigating the theft and concealment elements of some frauds is, for practical purposes, impossible. Accordingly, these frauds are most easily detected and investigated by focusing on lifestyle changes and other conversion attempts. Even when other theft investigation techniques yield fruitful results, conversion investigation should be done to strengthen the case.

Most investigations of conversion involve searching public records and other sources to trace purchases of assets, payments of liabilities, and changes in lifestyle and net worth. When people enter into financial transactions, such as buying assets, they leave tracks or "financial footprints." Even in the so-called secrecy districts, like some island-based countries, financial footprints can be found because transactions involve many parties, countries, and financial institutions. Cash transactions can limit a person's financial tracks, but it is usually difficult to use cash for purchase transactions—especially for those involving large sums of money. Further, the popularity of the Internet has made searching much easier than it was in the past. Trained investigators who know how to follow, study, and interpret these tracks, often find valuable evidence that supports allegations of fraud.

Conversion Searches

Conversion searches are performed for two reasons: (1) to determine the extent of embezzlement and (2) to gather evidence that can be used in interrogations to obtain a confession. The most common technique used to investigate and resolve fraud is by interviewing. An **interview** is a question-and-answer session designed to elicit information. Early in an interview, effective interviewers can often get suspects to admit that their only income is earned income (in other words, a statement by the suspect that he or she has no inherited

or non-earned income). Then, by introducing evidence of a lifestyle and associated expenditures that cannot be supported by the suspect's earned income, interviewers make it difficult for the suspect to explain the source of the unknown income. Cornered suspects sometimes break down and confess. Interviewing will be discussed in further detail in Chapter 10.

To become proficient at conversion investigations, fraud examiners need to understand that information can be gleaned from (1) federal, state, and local agencies and other organizations that maintain information that can be accessed in searches; (2) private sources of information; (3) online sources of information; and (4) using the net worth method of analyzing spending information, which is especially helpful in determining probable amounts of embezzled funds. Figure 9.1 provides a breakdown of the information sources relevant to investigators.

The advent of a large number of online resources has made conversion investigation activities much more efficient than they used to be. However, the large number of resources now available can be daunting and even overwhelming. Keeping up to date on the resources available, paired with careful planning and execution of investigative tasks, is key to an efficient, effective search. The following Web sites provide overview information on how to investigate and conduct searches:

1. *HowToInvestigate.com: www.howtoinvestigate.com* This site gives information on how to conduct an investigation.
2. *Investigative Resources International: www.factfind. com* Investigative Resources International gives information on public and open source records and corporate records.

FIGURE 9.1   INFORMATION SOURCES FOR CONVERSION SEARCHES

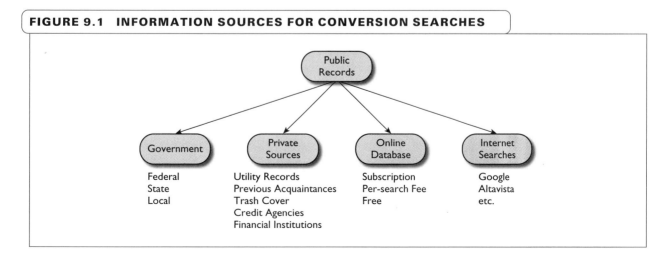

3. *Legal Resource Center: www.crimelynx.com* The Legal Resource Center gives numerous government links, criminal justice statistics, record searches, and other valuable information.

> **Remember this ...**
>
> *Conversion searches are performed for two reasons: (1) to determine the extent of embezzlement and (2) to gather evidence that can be used in interrogations to obtain a confession.*

Government Sources of Information

Many federal, state, and local agencies maintain public records in accordance with various laws. Much of this information can be accessed by anyone who requests it, but some of it is protected under privacy laws that prevent disclosure to the public. Federal records are generally not as useful as state and local records in fraud investigations, but they are helpful in certain situations. Because of the bureaucracies involved, accessing federal records can be time-consuming and costly.

Federal Sources

Most federal agencies maintain information that can be helpful in fraud investigations. Several, but not all, of these agencies are described in this section.

STOP & THINK *Why are state and local sources of information generally more useful than federal sources of information?*

Department of Defense

The Department of Defense maintains records on all military personnel, both active and inactive. Military information is maintained by branch of service. This department also contains information on individuals who may be a threat to national security. The department regularly shares information with other federal agencies, such as the Federal Bureau of Investigation (FBI) and the Central Intelligence Agency (CIA).

Military records are not confidential and provide valuable information that can help you trace a person's whereabouts through changing addresses. Military records are also helpful in searching for hidden assets, because individuals often buy property and other assets using previous addresses. The Web site of the U.S. Department of Defense is www.defense.gov.

Department of Justice

The Department of Justice is the federal agency charged with enforcing federal criminal and civil laws. It maintains records related to the detection, prosecution, and rehabilitation of offenders. The Department of Justice includes U.S. attorneys, U.S. marshals, and the FBI. The Drug Enforcement Administration (DEA) is a component of the Department of Justice and is responsible for enforcing the controlled substances laws and regulations, including drug trafficking.

The FBI is the principal investigative agency of the Department of Justice. Criminal matters not assigned to other U.S. agencies are assigned to the FBI. For example, the FBI normally investigates bank fraud, organized crime, terrorism, and illegal drug trade. The FBI is responsible for national security within U.S. borders.

The FBI maintains several databases and other records that can be accessed by state and local law enforcement agencies. The major database maintained by the FBI is the **National Crime Information Center (NCIC)**. The NCIC contains information on stolen vehicles, license plates, securities, boats, and planes; stolen and missing firearms; missing persons; and individuals who are wanted on outstanding warrants. The FBI also maintains the **Interstate Identification Index (III)**, which is an outgrowth of the NCIC and benefits state and local law enforcement agencies. The III retains arrest and criminal records on a nationwide basis.

Some states maintain databases for their states similar to the one maintained by the NCIC. To gain access to all databases, you must present identifying information, such as your birth date or Social Security number (SSN). These databases are not generally available to private investigators. Involving local law enforcement in a fraud investigation is one way to obtain access to these databases. The Web site for the U.S. Department of Justice is www.justice.gov.

Federal Bureau of Prisons

This agency operates the nationwide system of federal prisons, correctional institutions, and community treatment facilities. The Bureau is responsible for maintaining records on those who have been detained in various facilities. Since fraud perpetrators are often repeat offenders, information on previous incarcerations can often provide important evidence. The Web site of the Federal Bureau of Prisons is www.bop.gov.

Internal Revenue Service

The Internal Revenue Service (IRS) enforces all internal revenue laws, except those dealing with alcohol, firearms, tobacco, and explosives, which are handled by the Bureau of Alcohol, Tobacco, and Firearms. IRS records are not available to the public, so access to its databases normally requires the involvement of law enforcement officials. The Web site of the Internal Revenue Service is www.irs.gov.

Secret Service

The Secret Service is part of the Department of Homeland Security and is responsible for protecting the president of the United States and other federal dignitaries. However, many investigators do not know that the Secret Service also investigates counterfeiting, theft of government checks, interstate credit card violations, and some computer crimes. The Web site of the Secret Service is www.secretservice.gov.

U.S. Postal Service

The U.S. Postal Service is a quasi-governmental organization that is responsible for U.S. mail and for protecting citizens from loss through mail. **Postal inspectors** are some of the best and most helpful federal investigators. They handle major fraud cases involving the use of mail, and they work for the prosecution of offenders who violate postal laws. Postal inspectors share jurisdiction with other federal, state, and local agencies.

Postal inspectors can be very helpful in investigations of employee fraud, investment scams, or management frauds. Perpetrating a fraud in the United States is difficult without using the mail system. For example, bribes and kickbacks and false advertisements are often made through the mail, and stolen checks and funds are often deposited into banks by sending them through the mail. Because the use of mail is so common in frauds, the federal mail statutes are the workhorse statutes in federal crimes. You should become familiar with mail fraud statutes and your local postal inspectors as these sources are often very helpful in all kinds of fraud investigations. The Web site of the U.S. Postal Inspection Service is https://postalinspectors.uspis.gov/.

Central Intelligence Agency

The CIA is accountable to the president of the United States. It investigates security matters outside the United States, whereas the FBI has jurisdiction for security within the United States. The CIA can provide useful information when cases involve international issues like money laundering in the Cayman Islands or other secrecy jurisdictions. The Web site of the CIA is www.cia.gov.

Social Security Administration

The Social Security Administration (SSA) has information about individuals' SSNs. This agency can be helpful in identifying the area where a perpetrator was residing when a SSN was issued. Because every SSN contains information about the area (first three digits), the group (middle two digits), and the person's serial number (last four digits), Social Security information is extremely useful in fraud investigations. Once an individual's unique SSN is known, numerous federal, state, local, and private records can be accessed. In addition, many private sources, like credit agencies or "people finder" Web sites, are significantly more useful when searched with SSNs.

The government publishes lists of "dead" SSNs each month. The lists include SSNs for individuals who have died; these numbers are sometimes used by spouses, family, or illegal aliens to continue to receive benefits or to create bogus Social Security cards. For a small fee, companies can subscribe to this list and get the monthly updates. The Web site of the SSA is www.ssa.gov.

Other Federal Sources of Information

Many other federal sources of information are available. The ones discussed previously indicate the range and variety in the types of records available. For additional federal sources, see the U.S. Federal Government Agencies Directory at www.lib.lsu.edu/gov/ or www.usa.gov.

State Sources of Information

State resources are often very helpful in fraud investigations. Several, but not all, of these are listed in the following section.

State Attorney General

The attorney general for each state enforces all state, civil, and criminal laws in cooperation with local law enforcement agencies. Most state attorneys generally have investigative arms (similar to the FBI for the Department of Justice), such as the State Bureau of Investigation. This agency contains records relating to individuals who have been convicted of a breach of state civil and criminal laws. Visit the National Association of Attorneys General's (NAAG) Web site at www.naag.org.

State Prisons

The Federal Bureau of Prisons also maintains the network of state prisons and administers state corrections departments. It maintains records on all individuals who have been incarcerated in state prison systems, as well as on individuals who are on probation or parole. State prison records are available on the Federal Bureau of Prison's Web site by searching using the Facility Locator at www.bop.gov/DataSource/execute/dsFacilityLoc?fl_StartSearch=reset.

Secretary of State

The Secretary of State maintains all types of records relating to businesses and Uniform Commercial Code (UCC) filings. Every corporation must file documents in the state in which it was chartered. These documents, which are usually maintained by the office of the Secretary of State, reveal incorporators, bylaws, articles of incorporation, the registered agent, and the initial board of directors and officers. These records are public information and can be beneficial in gathering information about organizations that are perpetrating fraud. They can confirm whether an organization is legally conducting business and whether its taxes have been paid. They can also provide names of partners, principal shareholders, board members, and business affiliations. This information allows for the tracing of assets, establishing conflicts of interest, identifying dummy companies, and determining changes in financial status.

Secretary of State offices usually maintain UCC filings. These filings contain information about chattel mortgages (non-real estate transactions) and loans to individuals or businesses on equipment, furniture, automobiles, and other personal property. UCC records can identify collateral on purchased and leased assets, the nature of the lending company, where a person banks, and whether the person has a need for money. UCC records are sometimes available in a county clerk's office (depending on the state). Much of the information maintained by a Secretary of State's office concerning businesses and UCC filings is online at the National Association of Secretaries of State (NASS) at www.nass.org.

Department of Motor Vehicles

Driver's license records are maintained by the Department of Motor Vehicles (DMV) and are publicly available in most states. These records enable you to access a person's driving history, address, convictions for traffic violations, name, date of birth, address of birth, and photograph. Driver's license records may be a source of a person's SSN. In addition, driver's license numbers are used for identification in many transactions, such as those involving written checks. Every state has its own unique Web site. For example, view the state of California's DMV site at www.dmv.ca.gov/.

Department of Vital Statistics

This department maintains birth records. These records, although quite difficult to obtain and often for a fee, contain information about a person's birth date, place of birth, and biological parents. Since many people have an affinity for the places in which they grew up, local records in these areas may provide useful information. For example, a perpetrator might convert stolen money by purchasing private land or funding public projects in the area in which they grew up. In addition, individuals who know important information about a perpetrator may live near the person's birthplace. Many states have a Web site to locate vital records. See the state of Ohio's vital records at www.odh.ohio.gov/vitalstatistics/vitalstats.aspx.

Department of Business Regulation

Most states have a department of business regulation or a similar agency that maintains licensing information about various professionals. Licensing information is generally maintained on accountants, attorneys, bankers, doctors, electricians, plumbers, contractors, engineers, nurses, police officers, firefighters, insurance agents, bail bondsmen, real estate agents, security guards, stockbrokers, investment bankers, teachers, servers (food handler's permit), and travel agents, among others.

Licensing information that helps you access industry guidelines also leads you to an individual's memberships, specializations, current business addresses, history of business complaints, grievances, charges, investigations, and professional credentials.

As an example of how helpful this information can be, suppose you are investigating a fraud similar to the Elgin Aircraft example in Chapter 5, in which dummy doctors are set up. A quick check with the Department of Business Regulation in the relevant state will disclose whether the doctors being paid are legitimate.

County and Local Records

Counties and other local agencies maintain records that are especially useful in fraud investigations. The detailed nature of these records makes them very valuable; however, the availability of these records varies from state to state and from county to county. Below are some examples of county records that are kept.

County Clerk

County clerks maintain numerous records on local citizens, including voter registration records and marriage licenses. Marriage and voting records are always useful in fraud investigations. Voter registration records, for example, list a person's name, current address, past addresses, age, date of birth, SSN, signature, and telephone number, whether listed or unlisted. Even if a person has not voted, his or her family members (such as son, daughter, and spouse) may have voted; thus, voter registration records still provide valuable information.

Marriage records are maintained in the county clerk's office in the county of residence at the time of marriage. They often list the full legal names of the couple, their dates of birth, their SSNs, their addresses at the time of marriage (and sometimes their parents' addresses as well), driver's license numbers, passport numbers, prior marriages, and the witnesses to those marriages. Once this information has been obtained, further searches in online and other databases are much more productive.

County Land Office and Tax Assessor's Office

These offices contain real estate records for land located in the county. There are two common ways to trace real estate records. First, land ownership is normally found in the county land office or in the office of the recorder of deeds. County land office records identify owned assets, indebtedness, mortgage holders, trustees or straw buyers, and people who knew a person before and after a sale. Second, property tax records, maintained by the county assessor's office, also contain property records. Property records may be indexed by address or legal description or by the owner's name, or they may be indexed by the name of the seller or the buyer. Property tax records contain information about a property's legal description and current assessed value and the taxpayer's current status. These records are helpful in identifying assets purchased and liens removed by a perpetrator.

County Sheriff and Other Officers

Offices such as that of the city police, the county constable, probation officers, and bail bondsmen contain information about criminal charges, indictment statements, pretrial information reports, conviction statements, incarceration information, and probation information. Since many fraud perpetrators are repeat offenders, these sources may have information on past embezzlements.

Local Courts

Various local courts maintain records on past law violators, including pretrial information like personal history, employment history, personal and physical information, prior charges, divorces and property settlement agreements, personal injury lawsuits, financial claims and litigation, fraud claims and co-conspirators, bankruptcies, wills, and probates. Bankruptcy information, which can also be found at various online Web sites such as www.bankruptcyinformation.com, includes the current status of bankruptcy cases, creditor lists, debts, assets, and information on character. These records can show how assets might be hidden. Information about wills and probates helps identify the assets (and sources of the assets) of perpetrators. Many perpetrators often justify their extravagant lifestyles by claiming to have inherited money. Such claims can be validated or dismissed from information contained in wills and probate.

Permit Departments

Permit departments supply information on fire permits (hazardous chemicals), health permits (pollutants), elevator permits, and building permits. Permit-issuing departments can be helpful in identifying the nature and location of businesses, new leases, and recent construction.

Private Sources of Information

Hundreds of sources of private information are available to those willing to search for them. Utility records (gas, electric, water, garbage, and sewer), for example, supply the names of people billed, show whether or not a person lives or owns property in the service area, and identify the types of utilities a business uses.

Another way to gain financial information is through previous acquaintances. For example, a former spouse of a suspected fraud perpetrator may have documents—including bank documents—that turn out to be key in investigations.

A surprising source of valuable financial information is trash cover. **Trashing** a suspect involves looking through a person's trash for possible evidence. Note that searching trash while it is in the possession of a person is against the law. However, once the trash leaves the suspect's home, sidewalk, or fenced area, investigators can usually freely and legally search the trash. The U.S. Supreme Court case of *California vs. Greenwood* in 1988 stated that the Fourth Amendment does not prohibit the warrantless search and seizure of garbage left for collection outside the curtilage of a home. In the first months of the year, these searches can uncover valuable tax information. During all times of the year, it is possible to find credit card information, bank statements, and other valuable information.

Even shredded documents are not as safe as they were once assumed to be. A cursory search of the Internet reveals a number of software products that specialize in piecing shredded documents back together. After scanning in the remains of the documents, the user simply waits for the software to fit the puzzle back together. Some law enforcement agencies even employ specialists in manually reassembling shredded documents.

Finally, since most documents are now stored on computers, original files are often found on one's personal computer. While users might religiously destroy hard copies of documents, they often fail to do the same on their computers. Investigators often find significant sources of evidence in e-mail and other files on seized computers. See Chapter 7 for more information on these types of computer forensics.

CAUTION   *Even though information may be available, be sure you have the legal rights to gather and use the information. Laws, especially those dealing with the Internet, are still changing and evolving. Going into legal gray areas may jeopardize your case.*

Various credit-reporting companies maintain private credit records on both individuals and organizations. Reporting agencies are of two types: (1) file-based credit-reporting agencies, which develop information from their credit files, and (2) public records and investigative agencies, which gather most of their information through interviews. Credit bureaus are used primarily by retail organizations.

Credit-reporting companies typically maintain the following information:

- *Consumer information, such as addresses, ages, family members, and incomes*
- *Account information, such as payment schedules, items purchased, and buying habits*
- *Marketing information, such as customer breakdowns by age, sex, and income levels*
- *Information on current and former employees*

Information maintained by credit-reporting agencies is governed by the Fair Credit Reporting Act (FCRA) of 1971. This act regulates activities of credit, insurance, and employment investigations. Under the law, a consumer-reporting agency must, on request, furnish information to an individual that is also furnished to a third party. If adverse action is to be taken against an employee as a result of third-party information, the employee must be given advance notice. The three major credit-reporting agencies are as follows:

- *Experian, www.experian.com*
- *Equifax, www.equifax.com*
- *TransUnion, www.transunion.com*

In 2003, the Fair and Accurate Credit Transactions Act added new sections to the FCRA regarding information sharing and privacy and new consumer rights to disclosure. It also restricted individual states from adopting stronger laws than the Federal acts.

Financial institution records (including banks, brokerage, and insurance companies) are essential elements of investigations. Bank records can be obtained through a court subpoena, search warrants, a civil summons, or civil discovery. Financial institutions often sell the rights to search and retrieve records from their databases.

Until 1999, when the **Gramm-Leach-Bliley Act** was passed, investigators could only gain information from a financial institution by using false pretenses. Using false pretenses is illegal under the new act, but it does allow banks and other financial institutions to share customer information with anyone they want, including selling it to database companies. Before financial institutions can sell or disclose confidential customer information, they must provide customers the opportunity to "opt out" of information sharing; that keeps their information private. However, most people do not provide written notice to the bank denying the bank the right to sell their personal bank information (**opting out**), so bank information is more readily available than ever before. Many Internet sites, for a fee, provide information such as bank account number, bank name, bank address, approximate account balance, city and state of the bank, withdrawals, deposits, savings, wire transfers, full transactions of the bank accounts, credits, collateral records, debits, transactions of loans, bankruptcies, transaction details, and outstanding loans.

STOP & THINK   *The Gramm-Leach-Bliley Act protects against the use of false pretenses. In what ways did this act have positive investigative consequences?*

Online Databases

An increasing number of online, commercial databases provide helpful information. Databases may be subscription-based, have a per-use fee, or allow unlimited free searching. Some databases overlap one another, but most contain unique information that may be useful to a case. For example, most investigators consider searching through Accurint, AutoTrackXP (ChoicePoint), and other record Web sites to be standard practice in cases. In recent years, a significant amount of consolidation among the largest players has occurred (such as LexisNexis' parent company purchasing ChoicePoint and many related products in 2008). Despite single players gaining more information through this consolidation, it is wise to search multiple sources. Information on one person may be in one database, while information on another person may be in other databases. Many of these databases contain information on bankruptcy, court records, real estate, tax lien, UCC filing, and other important financial information. Some of the most valuable Web sites of commercial and/or public databases, along with a brief description of the type of information available on each, are listed here in alphabetical order.

Please note that due to the dynamic nature of the Internet, while these sites are current at publication time they may change over time.

STOP & THINK *This book lists only a few of the many resources available online. What other sources do you know about or can you find through searching?*

Accurint: www.accurint.com Accurint contains information about individuals from banking, human resources, government, law enforcement, legal, and media sources.

AutoTrackXP: atxp.choicepoint.com AutoTrackXP, now owned by ChoicePoint, contains billions of records about individuals, including property records, bankruptcies, links to other people, and so forth.

Black Book Online: www.blackbookonline.com Black Book Online provides searches on bankruptcies, mail drops, corporations, real estate, businesses, death records, state records, federal records, and other valuable information.

BRB Publications, Inc.: www.brbpub.com BRB Publications is a public records research library that offers access to records of over 26,000 government agencies. It also has links to 3,500 record vendors.

ChoicePoint: www.lexisnexis.com/risk/ ChoicePoint, now part of LexisNexis' risk group, contains billions of records about individuals and businesses.

Confi-Chek Online Public Records: www.confi-chek. com For a fee, Confi-Chek conducts background checks and asset identifications and searches for criminal records. Information on personal real property, bankruptcy, tax liens, civil judgments, and criminal records can be obtained here.

Data Quick: www.dataquick.com These databases contain property profiles, mortgage information, asset ownership information, and other valuable information.

Dialog: www.dialog.com Dialog's databases contain over 15 terabytes of content from the world's major publishers. Content areas include business, science, technology, media, news, property, law, government, and more. Dialog is now owned by ProQuest.

Discreet Research: www.discreetresearch.com Discreet Research offers an extensive line of public records, including business reports, telephone searches, pre-employment information, motor vehicle records, license verifications, county criminal records, metro criminal records, state criminal records, outstanding warrants, prison records, civil records, and other valuable information.

Dun & Bradstreet: www.dnb.com (also see *www. zapdata.com*) The Dun & Bradstreet databases contain information on over 140 million business records. Dun & Bradstreet also publishes several directories that provide background and financial information on businesses.

EBSCO Publishing: www.ebscohost.com This site contains many large databases that include full-text periodicals, scholarly journals, U.S. and international newspapers, reference books, and even detailed pamphlets.

Harte-Hanks: www.hartehanksmi.com Harte-Hanks's databases track technology installations, business demographics, and key decision makers at more than 4 million locations.

IRBsearch LLC: www.irbsearch.com IRBsearch is a database that helps researchers connect individuals. It allows searching by name, address, SSN, or phone number. Results include current and past addresses with links to possible relatives, possible associates, and neighbors along with their addresses and phone numbers.

KnowX: www.knowx.com One of the most comprehensive databases available, KnowX can help users find out where a former tenant lives, what business name is being used, whether a potential employer is involved in any lawsuits, and what assets an employee has. KnowX is now a LexisNexis company.

LexisNexis: www.lexisnexis.com LexisNexis provides access to thousands of worldwide newspapers, magazines, trade journals, industry newsletters, tax and accounting information, financial data, public records, legislation records, and data on companies and executives. Through a series of purchases by both LexisNexis and its parent company, it has become one of the definitive sources of information available.

Merlin Information Services: www.merlin data.com Merlin includes public record and skiptracing databases.

National Driver Register: www.nhtsa.gov The National Driver Register is a computerized database of information on drivers who have had their licenses revoked or suspended, or who have been convicted of serious traffic violations, such as driving while impaired by alcohol or drugs.

NETROnline: www.netronline.com NETROnline is an information portal to official state Web sites and tax assessors' and recorders' offices that have developed Web sites for retrieving public records. The public records include copies of deeds, parcel maps, GIS maps, tax data, ownership information and indexes, and other information.

ProQuest: www.proquest.com ProQuest provides access to thousands of current periodicals, as well as out-of-print and rare books, dissertations, newspapers, and other valuable information.

PublicData: www.publicdata.com PublicData is an online database containing criminal, sex offender, driver's license, license plate, civil court, and voter information from most states.

Public Record Finder: www.publicrecord finder.com This Web site lists over 6,000 links to government sites that offer free searches of public records.

Public Records: www.docusearch.com/free.html Public Records is a detailed collection of 300 links to databases containing public information.

SearchSystems: http://publicrecords.searchsystems.net SearchSystems claims to be the largest collection of free public records databases on the Internet.

SEC's EDGAR Database: www.sec.gov/edgar.shtml This database is useful for investigating companies.

The Web site offers free access to financial information on all public companies.

Social Security Death Index: www.ancestry.com/ search/db.aspx?dbid=3693 Go to this site to access information provided by the SSA from 1875 to the most previous year. With a fee-based subscription, more current lists (as of last month) can also be downloaded directly from the government.

TransUnion Background Data Solutions: www. transunion.com Instant online reports, including credit reports, Social Security checks, criminal investigations, and eviction and rental histories.

US Search: www.ussearch.com US Search offers instant people searches, background checks, and instant civil and criminal court record searches. A free online credit report is available.

USA Records Search: www.usarecordsearch.com This site offers background searches on people, including background checks, VIN car searches, employment screening, business credit reports, and more.

Web Detective: www.freeality.com/webdetective.htm Public record checks for people and business for both U.S. and Canadian residents.

Internet Search

The publicly available Internet is an increasingly valuable source of information. While search engines like Google, AltaVista, and Yahoo! do not search internal databases like AutoTrackXP or LexisNexis, they index a significant amount of the public Web. Results usually include media hits, corporate Web sites, and other public sites. The fact that public search results usually contain a surprising amount of information about an individual is evidenced by the increasing use of phrases such as "I *googled* Joe Brown on the 'Net' and found ..." As an example of the depth a search engine can provide, we discuss several advanced techniques available on Google; many of these techniques are available on other search engines as well.

- *Search by phrase: Including words in quotation marks (e.g.,* "Bill Clinton" *rather than* Bill Clinton) *forces results to have an exact phrase. An exact phrase is made up of words immediately next to each other rather than simply on the page together. This can be extremely useful when searching for the exact name of a perpetrator. One technique that generally provides effective results is to include the person's name in quotes followed by something specific about the person, such as a business name, city, or other information that limits results to your subject.*

- *Minus search terms: If your initial search contains a significant amount of unwanted results, filter out pages you don't want by placing a minus sign before unique terms found on the unwanted pages. For example, a search for* "Paul Allen" *alone yields many hits for the Microsoft cofounder. A search for* "Paul Allen" –microsoft *shows results for other Paul Allens on the Internet.*

- *Domain restrictions: Google allows a search to be targeted at a specific domain ending. For example, if your subject is likely to be found on German Web sites, searching for* "Subject Name" site:de *will limit results to those with domain names ending in ".de" (Germany). A full listing of country codes can be found at www.iana.org/cctld/cctld-whois.htm. Domain restrictions can also limit results to a single Web site, such as* Windows Update site: microsoft.com, *to search for information on Windows Update only within Microsoft's Web site.*

- *Google groups: Google has indexed the last 20 years of the Usenet archives, a group discussion forum that predates the World Wide Web by many years. This repository is entirely separate from the regular Google search engine and the Web. If a subject has been involved in online discussions (or has been the subject of online discussions), Google Groups is the best place to search. The URL for this service is groups.google.com. As a side note, Google Groups can be an extremely useful source of solutions to both technical and nontechnical topics.*

- *Cached results: Google provides a "cached" link following most search results that links to a cached version of the result page on Google's site. In effect, Google has cached much of the publicly accessible Web! The cached versions of pages are useful when sites are temporarily inaccessible or no longer available. A similar service, the Internet Archive (www.archive.org), provides saved copies of previous versions of Web sites.*

- *Google News: The Google News service is limited in its usefulness because it indexes only the last 30 days of news articles available on the Web. This is a significant difference from LexisNexis, which provides a historical repository of news articles found both on and off the Web.*

- *Google Images: This service provides a search of images published on the Internet. These images can be useful when looking for pictures of a suspect with other individuals or activities in which the suspect might be involved.*

- *Google Earth: This and other services like it have become increasingly useful in investigations. Because Google Earth shows satellite pictures of most of the Earth, it is useful to quickly learn about businesses and homes in a case. In one case, for example, Google Earth revealed pictures of a home (with a pool and large yard) built on a location where a public building was supposed to be built using public funds.*

To become fully conversant with the methods of your favorite search engine, pick up a book like *Google Hacks* from O'Reilly Publishers.

The Net Worth Method

Once investigators compile information about spending and lifestyle from public records and other sources, they usually want to determine the extent of the stolen funds. The most common way to make such determinations is through net worth calculations. Essentially, the **net worth method** uses the following formula, which is based on a person's assets (things owned), liabilities (debts), living expenses, and income.

The Net Worth Calculation

1. Assets − Liabilities = Net Worth
2. Net Worth − Prior Year's Net Worth = Net Worth Increase
3. Net Worth Increase + Living Expenses = Income
4. Income − Funds from Known Sources = Funds from Unknown Sources

From public records and other sources, investigators determine an individual's purchases of real estate, automobiles, and other assets. Such records also state whether liens have been removed, thus identifying whether loans have been paid. Combining public sources information with information collected from interviews of landscapers, furniture and automobile dealers, and other relevant parties, and with information gathered through subpoenas provides a reasonably accurate accounting of assets and liabilities.

When people have income, they either purchase additional assets, pay off liabilities, or improve their lifestyles, thus increasing living expenses. Known income subtracted from unknown income gives a reasonable estimate of unknown funds. Verifying or eliminating other sources of funds (such as inheritances, gambling winnings, and gifts) gives a good estimate of the amount of stolen funds.

STOP & THINK *What is the best time during an investigation to calculate the net worth method on a subject?*

The net worth method for determining amounts embezzled has gained favor among fraud investigators in recent years. The FBI regularly uses this method, as does the DEA, which uses it to determine whether suspected narcotics traffickers have income from illegal drug sales. The IRS uses it to estimate unreported income in tax fraud cases. Because only assets and reductions in liabilities that can be discovered enter into the calculation, net worth calculations tend to give a conservative estimate of stolen funds. Unfortunately, embezzlers typically spend increasing amounts on food, jewelry, vacations, and other luxuries that are difficult to track and cannot be factored into net worth calculations. However, because these calculations are conservative, the amounts determined to be stolen are usually readily accepted as evidence by courts. They also often facilitate obtaining confessions from suspects. An effective and often fruitful way to interrogate suspects is to present accurate information regarding their expenditures and lifestyle that they cannot justify from their income. When asked where the additional income came from, suspects often cannot quickly think of explanations that account for the large amounts of money; cornered without excuses, they often confess.

To illustrate the net worth method, reconsider the following example that was described in a case at the end of Chapter 2:

Helen Weeks has worked for Bonne Consulting Group (BCG) as the executive secretary in the administrative department for nearly 10 years. Her apparent integrity and dedication to her work has quickly earned her a reputation as an outstanding employee and has resulted in increased responsibilities. Her present responsibilities include making arrangements for outside feasibility studies, maintaining client files, working with outside marketing consultants, initiating the payment process, and notifying the accounting department of all openings or closings of vendor accounts.

During Helen's first five years of employment, BCG subcontracted all of its feasibility and marketing studies through Jackson & Co. This relationship was subsequently terminated because Jackson & Co. merged with a larger,

more expensive consulting group. At the time of termination, Helen and her supervisor were forced to select a new firm to conduct BCG's market research. However, Helen never informed the accounting department that the Jackson & Co. account had been closed.

Since her supervisor allowed Helen to sign the payment voucher for services rendered, Helen was able to continue to process checks made payable to Jackson's account. Because her supervisor completely trusted her, he allowed her to sign for all voucher payments less than $10,000. The accounting department continued to process the payments, and Helen would take responsibility for distributing the payments. Helen opened a bank account in a nearby city under the name of Jackson & Co., where she would make the deposit. She paid all of her personal expenses out of this account.

Suppose we are investigating Helen's fraud. As part of our investigation, we have searched public records and other sources and have accumulated the financial information on Helen in Table 9.1.

With this information, we can use the net worth method to estimate how much Helen may have embezzled. These calculations are shown in Table 9.2.

Based on this calculation, we determine that Helen had at least $46,800 of unknown income in Year 2 and

TABLE 9.1 FINANCIAL DATA FOR HELEN WEEKS

	YEAR 1	YEAR 2	YEAR 3
Assets:			
Residence	$100,000	$100,000	$100,000
Stocks and bonds	30,000	30,000	42,000
Automobiles	20,000	20,000	40,000
CD	50,000	50,000	50,000
Cash	6,000	12,000	14,000
Liabilities:			
Mortgage balance	90,000	50,000	0
Auto loan	10,000	0	0
Income:			
Salary		34,000	36,000
Other		6,000	6,000
Expenses:			
Mortgage payments		6,000	6,000
Auto loan payments		4,800	4,800
Other living expenses		20,000	22,000

TABLE 9.2 COMPARATIVE NET WORTH—ASSET METHOD

	END YEAR 1	END YEAR 2	END YEAR 3
Assets:			
Residence	$100,000	$100,000	$100,000
Stocks and bonds	30,000	30,000	42,000
Auto	20,000	20,000	40,000
CD	50,000	50,000	50,000
Cash	6,000	12,000	14,000
Total assets	$206,000	$212,000	$246,000
Liabilities:			
Mortgage balance	$90,000	$50,000	$ —
Auto loan	10,000	—	—
Total liabilities	$100,000	$50,000	$ —
Net worth	$106,000	$162,000	$246,000
Change in net worth		$56,000	$84,000
Plus living expenses		30,800	32,800
Total Income		$86,800	$116,800
Less known income		40,000	42,000
Income from unknown sources		$46,800	$74,800

$74,800 of unknown income in Year 3. This information can be used in court to obtain a criminal conviction, civil judgment, or even an order against Helen, and it can also be used to obtain a confession. A good investigator, armed with these data, may get a confession from Helen. She would first be asked to state her income and other sources of funds. The investigator would then show that she cannot maintain her lifestyle and pay her debts without additional income. Seeing that her story and reality conflict, Helen might confess.

Review of the Learning Objectives

- **Explain why it is important to find out how perpetrators convert and spend their stolen funds.** Conversion, or discovering how perpetrators convert and spend their stolen funds, is an important investigative technique. Individuals rarely steal and save; rather, they spend. Often, tracking or investigating how they spend their ill-gotten gains is the best way to catch perpetrators. When people spend money, they create financial footprints that can be examined to help detect fraud.

- **Understand how federal, state, and local public records can assist in following the financial "tracks" of suspected perpetrators.** Federal, state, and local public records are important sources of information about the financial "tracks" of suspected perpetrators. There are many federal, state, and local public records, such as voting records, driver's license records, real estate and property tax records, incorporation records, UCC records, and others, that provide information about how, where, and when people spend money. The information from these records is extremely useful in investigation fraud.

- **Access information via the Internet to assist in the investigation of a suspected fraud perpetrator.** Private and online sources of information are important sources of information during an investigation. Today, information about almost everyone is on the Internet, including boards on which people have served on, where people have lived, property tax records, employment, marriages, etc. These records can be a very helpful, almost instantaneous source of information about individuals. To see how helpful this information is, go to Google and type in the name of someone you know. You will be amazed at how many references there are to most people.

- **Perform net worth calculations on suspected fraud perpetrators and understand how net worth calculations are effective in court and in obtaining confessions.** Net worth calculations on suspected fraud perpetrators are effective in court and in obtaining confessions. Net worth calculations can provide evidence that someone is spending significantly more money than he or she can account for from known sources (wages, inheritance, etc.). Net worth calculations provide great background information for investigators before potential perpetrators are interviewed, provide evidence that can be used in court to support the fact that an individual spent more money than he or she reported for tax purposes, and are very helpful in getting people to admit that they embezzled funds.

KEY TERMS

interview, p. 253

national crime information center (NCIC), p. 254

interstate identification index (III), p. 254

postal inspectors, p. 255

trashing, p. 257

Gramm-Leach-Bliley Act, p. 258

opting out, p. 258

net worth method, p. 261

QUESTIONS

Discussion Questions

1. What are common ways to investigate conversion of stolen assets?
2. What are "financial footprints"?
3. Why is it important to know how perpetrators convert and spend their stolen funds?
4. What are the differences between public and private sources of information?
5. How do state, federal, and local public records assist fraud investigations?
6. How does the Internet assist in determining the net worth of suspected perpetrators?
7. Why are net worth calculations so valuable?
8. What are some of the advanced techniques available when searching for information on Google (or other search engines)?
9. How do these advanced techniques aid in the information-gathering process?

10. When searching public records, what are the four different types of information sources available to investigators?
11. What is the Gramm-Leach-Bliley Act? How does it apply to investigators?
12. What is "trashing"? In what ways can it (and the electronic form of it) help an investigation?

True/False

1. Perpetrators usually save what they steal.
2. One common investigation procedure determines how perpetrators convert or spend their time.
3. Investigations of perpetrators' net worth and lifestyles help investigators know what class of society the perpetrators are from.
4. It is always necessary to involve a federal law enforcement agent when accessing federal databases.
5. The secretary of state maintains many types of records relating to business and Uniform Commercial Code (UCC) filings.
6. Counties and other local agencies that contain records are usually not very useful in fraud investigation.
7. Private credit records are maintained on both individuals and organizations by various credit-reporting companies.
8. Several publicly available databases provide information that can be helpful in investigations.
9. The net worth method is rarely, if ever, helpful in actual fraud investigations.
10. For various reasons, the net worth method tends to be a conservative estimate of amounts stolen.
11. Conversion is the third element of the fraud investigation triangle.
12. The Gramm-Leach-Bliley Act of 1999 made it more difficult for officials and private citizens to access information from financial institutions.
13. Before financial institutions can sell or disclose confidential customer information, they must provide customers with the opportunity to "opt out" from information sharing.
14. Federal agencies provide better records than state or county agencies for conversion investigations.
15. When people convert stolen cash by entering into financial transactions, such as buying assets, they usually leave tracks that investigators can follow.
16. Private financial institutions can usually sell confidential customer information.

17. The net worth method cannot help in determining the extent of stolen funds.
18. An increase in a person's net worth plus living expenses equals the person's total income.

Multiple Choice

1. Although most perpetrators begin their thefts because of a perceived critical need, they usually continue to embezzle in order to:
   a. Beat the system.
   b. Fulfill an inner desire to commit fraud.
   c. Improve their lifestyle.
   d. Achieve a higher self-esteem.
2. Evidence gathered from public records can be useful in:
   a. Identifying with the suspect.
   b. Obtaining a confession.
   c. Making the suspect feel at ease.
   d. None of the above.
3. The net worth method of analyzing financial information can help to determine:
   a. The suspect's feelings about the organization.
   b. Possible perpetrators of the fraud.
   c. The suspect's personality characteristics.
   d. The amount of embezzled funds.
4. Which of the following organizations maintain public information that can be accessed in record searches?
   a. Local agencies.
   b. State agencies.
   c. Federal agencies.
   d. All of the above.
5. How useful are local and county records in fraud investigations?
   a. Very useful.
   b. Not useful.
   c. Somewhat useful.
   d. Aren't allowed in the investigation of fraud.
6. Which of the following laws regulates activities of credit, insurance, and employment investigations?
   a. Fair Investigation Act of 1980.
   b. Fair Credit Reporting Act of 1971 and Fair and Accurate Credit Transactions Act of 2003.
   c. Credit, Insurance, and Employment Investigation Act.
   d. There is no governing law.
7. The net worth method is effective:
   a. As evidence in court.
   b. To help obtain a confession.
   c. To conduct an interview of suspects.
   d. All of the above.
8. Conversion investigations focus on how suspects:
   a. Had opportunities to steal.
   b. Had motives to commit fraud.
   c. Spent stolen money.
   d. Committed the actual theft.
9. Which of the following is a possible use of conversion-based investigation techniques?
   a. Searching public records to trace purchases of assets and payments of liabilities.
   b. Attempting to locate previous spouses' bank account records.
   c. Locating significant amounts of money held by related parties.
   d. All of the above.
10. Most conversion investigations involve searching public records and other sources to trace:
    a. Purchases of assets.
    b. Payments of liabilities.
    c. Changes in lifestyle.
    d. Net worth.
    e. All of the above.
11. A database of criminal records maintained by the FBI is:
    a. The CIA.
    b. The III.
    c. The NCIC.
    d. Both a and c.
    e. Both b and c.
12. Who among the following are usually some of the best and most helpful federal fraud investigators?
    a. Officers of the Secret Service.
    b. Employees of the Federal Bureau of Prisons.
    c. Officers of the Department of Vital Statistics.
    d. Postal inspectors.
13. Which source could be used to access valuable financial information in a fraud investigation?
    a. Financial institutions.
    b. Internet sites.
    c. The former spouse of a suspected fraud perpetrator.
    d. Trash.
    e. All of the above.
14. The net worth method is a calculation based on a person's:
    a. Assets, liabilities, equity, and living expenses.
    b. Assets, liabilities, equity, and income.
    c. Assets, liabilities, income, and living expenses.
    d. Assets, income, and living expenses.

15. The formula to calculate funds from unknown sources is:
    a. Assets − Liabilities − Prior Year's Net Worth + Living Expenses − Funds from Known Sources.
    b. Assets − Liabilities − Prior Year's Net Worth − Living Expenses − Funds from Unknown Sources.
    c. Assets − Liabilities − Prior Year's Net Worth + Living Expenses + Funds from Unknown Sources.
    d. Assets − Liabilities − Prior Year's Net Worth − Living Expenses + Funds from Unknown Sources.

16. The Gramm-Leach-Bliley Act allows:
    a. Banks to sell customer information.
    b. Financial institutions to share information.
    c. Customers to "opt out" and ask that their information not be shared.
    d. All of the above.

17. Each of these agencies is correctly matched with the type of information the agency provides except:
    a. Department of Justice: Maintains records relating to the detection, prosecution, and rehabilitation of offenders.
    b. The Secret Service: Deals with counterfeiting, theft of government checks, interstate credit card violations, and some computer crimes.
    c. State Attorney General: Maintains birth records and information about people's SSNs.
    d. CIA: Investigates security matters outside the United States.
    e. Department of Business Regulation: Maintains licensing information about various professionals.

18. Each of these statements is true about the net worth method for determining embezzled amounts except:
    a. The net worth method generally understates amounts stolen.
    b. Much of the information necessary for determining an individual's assets, liabilities, living expenses, and income is available through public searches.
    c. Courts are generally suspicious of dollar amounts determined by the net worth method because courts realize that the net worth method can only provide approximations of the amount stolen.
    d. The net worth method is useful for obtaining confessions from suspects during interviews or interrogations.

19. Under the net worth method, a person who has an increase in net worth of $100,000, known expenses of $80,000, and a salary of $60,000 would have an unknown income of:
    a. $0.
    b. $110,000.
    c. $120,000.
    d. $140,000.

20. Known income subtracted from total income gives a reasonable estimate of:
    a. Unknown funds.
    b. Liabilities.
    c. Living expenses.
    d. Net worth.

SHORT CASES

Case 1

Given the following information about a potential suspect, determine whether there is a likelihood of illegal income. If so, determine the amount of unknown income.

CASE 1

FINANCIAL DATA	YEAR 1	YEAR 2	YEAR 3
Assets:			
Residence	$100,000	$100,000	$100,000
Baseball cards	15,000	15,000	25,000
Automobiles	0	30,000	50,000
Paintings	50,000	150,000	250,000
Cash	6,000	12,000	14,000
Liabilities:			
Mortgage balance	100,000	50,000	0
Auto loan	0	30,000	0
Income:			
Salary		34,000	36,000
Other		6,000	6,000
Expenses:			
Mortgage payments		6,000	6,000
Auto loan payments		4,800	4,800
Other living expenses		20,000	20,000

Case 2

You are auditing a bank, and someone provides you with an anonymous tip that an employee is embezzling money from the bank. You decide to investigate the allegation.

Your interviews with other bank employees confirm that the suspected embezzler has been acting very strange lately. Some employees have seen the employee crying in the bathroom and acting strange in other ways. The bank recently downsized due to poor economic growth, yet the suspect recently bought a new Lexus.

Based on some "helpful" hints from bank employees and through your own investigation, you discover that the mortgage taken out by the suspect three years ago for his personal home has recently been paid in full.

After calculating the suspect's net worth, you determine that he has about $249,000 in income from unknown sources this year alone.

1. What are possible explanations for why the suspect (1) is experiencing emotional changes and (2) has had an increase in unknown income?
2. Can you conclude from these facts that the suspect has indeed been committing fraud?

Case 3

You receive an anonymous tip that your controller is embezzling assets from your company. You begin your investigation by interviewing several employees in the accounting department, who report no unusual behavior or sudden changes in the suspect's standard of living. One interviewee does report that the controller has gone on a number of extravagant vacations.

You perform a net worth analysis, based on a search of public records, and find the following information:

CASE 3	YEAR 1	YEAR 2	YEAR 3
Total assets	$80,000	$82,000	$85,000
Total liabilities	$40,000	$41,000	$41,000
Net worth	$40,000	$41,000	$44,000
Change in net worth		$1,000	$3,000
Living expenses		$36,000	$36,000
Total income		$37,000	$39,000
Less known income	$35,000	$35,000	$36,000
Unknown income		$2,000	$3,000

1. Based on the evidence gathered in your search, what conclusions can you make about the controller?
2. Would you feel comfortable using the evidence above in an interview to obtain a confession? Why or why not?
3. What additional investigating could you pursue to obtain more evidence?

Case 4

Bill James is being investigated for embezzling over $700,000 from ABC Capital Management, for whom Bill has worked for nearly 10 years. When coworkers noticed the new "toys" Bill was buying, they jokingly asked him to tell them his stock picks as they wanted in too! Bill told them that they better adopt some rich relatives. "My Uncle Eddie didn't have any kids, so he left a chunk of his money to each of his nephews."

Explain how you might go about checking the validity of Bill's claim to a recent inheritance. Include in your discussion the relevant information you need about Uncle Eddie and where you could find that information.

Case 5

You manage a car dealership in a large city. Many of your sales employees are very successful and have purchased their own vehicles from your dealership. Your dealership finances the sale of some of these vehicles. One employee recently paid off the balances on a couple of new vehicles purchased from your dealership. You discover this information after investigating complaints from customers about this particular employee's actions. His sales are down, and customer complaints about his attitude abound. He previously worked for two other car dealers, both of which were satisfied with his performance. This employee is in charge of having used cars reconditioned by various automobile repair shops.

1. What signs of unusual behavior and lifestyle symptoms are present in this case? What are some possible causes for them?
2. How might this employee be defrauding the company?

Case 6

Janet Moody is one of XZY Company's most trusted employees. She never complains about her work and rarely misses work due to illness or vacation. The company has been successful over the years, but is now having cash flow problems. Because of the recent downturn in the company, you take a closer look at all the company's financial records. When you ask Janet about the recent cash flow problems, she responds, "I don't know what is going on. I only do the reporting. Ask those who manage the company." This behavior differs from Janet's normal pleasant deportment. As you continue your investigation, you discover that the reported financial results do not match what the company is doing, but you can't determine why. You decide to investigate Janet further.

1. What are some behavior and lifestyle changes that you should look for?
2. What resources can you use to conduct your research?

Case 7

Using the net worth method, analyze the financial data at the bottom of this page for potential signs of fraud or embezzlement:

1. Do your results indicate that this person could be committing some type of fraud? If so, why do you think so?
2. What other factors might you consider to determine whether fraud has been committed, other than the final total income from other sources (if any)?
3. Is this scenario realistic?

Case 8

The financial data for this case was collected during a fraud investigation:

1. Without calculating the amount of unknown income, indicate possible red flags or trends you notice in the numbers above.
2. Now calculate the amount of income and unknown income using the numbers given. Does it appear that a possible fraud exists? Could there be other explanations for the unknown income?

CASE 8

	YEAR 1	YEAR 2	YEAR 3
Assets:			
Residence	$280,000	$280,000	$280,000
Automobile	18,000	45,000	45,000
CD	5,000	15,000	15,000
Cash	8,000	8,000	2,000
Stock portfolio	3,500	15,000	15,000
Boat		15,000	15,000
Liabilities:			
Mortgage	200,000	180,000	100,000
Auto loan	12,000	30,000	
Other loan		18,000	
Income:			
Salary	55,000	90,000	130,000
Investment	800	800	800
Expenses:			
Mortgage expense	18,000	18,000	18,000
Auto expense	5,000	9,000	9,000
Living expenses	20,000	20,000	20,000

Case 9

Mr. I. M. Bezzle works in the purchasing department for Big Time Inc. During the 12 years that he has worked there, he has been a trusted employee and has sole responsibility for the company's purchasing

CASE 7

	YEAR 1	YEAR 2	YEAR 3	YEAR 4	YEAR 5
Assets:					
Residence	$200,000	$200,000	$275,000	$275,000	$275,000
Automobile	50,000	50,000	75,000	75,000	90,000
Stocks and bonds	75,000	75,000	100,000	100,000	125,000
Cash	15,000	16,500	18,150	19,965	21,962
Liabilities:					
Mortgage balance	175,000	50,000	125,000	107,000	40,000
Auto loan balance	40,000	20,000	35,000	25,000	10,000
Income:					
Salary		100,000	107,000	125,000	133,750
Other		10,000	10,000	10,000	10,000
Expenses:					
Mortgage loan payments		12,000	18,000	18,000	18,000
Auto loan payments		7,000	10,000	10,000	13,000
Other living expenses		30,000	33,000	36,300	39,930

function. He started working for the company in 1990 for $30,000 a year and now makes $100,000 a year. Fellow employees and friends have noticed that his lifestyle has improved substantially since his recent promotion to purchasing manager. Based on an anonymous tip, the CEO asks you to look into the situation. What steps would you take to investigate the possibility of fraud here?

Case 10

Tom works for ZYX Company and is suspected of embezzling funds from the company. By searching databases on the Internet, talking with his ex-wife, and searching through his trash, you gather the following information:

CASE 10

Assets	$120,000
Liabilities	70,000
Living expenses	50,000
Known income	60,000
Prior year's net worth	10,000

1. Use these data to figure out Tom's income from unknown sources by performing a net worth calculation.
2. How can this information be used to motivate Tom to confess that he has stolen from ZYX Company?

Case 11

Sarah Welch was hired 15 years ago by Produce-R-Us, an importer of rare and exotic fruits. Produce-R-Us was started by an immigrant family 20 years ago and has grown to a national company with sales of $10 million annually. Although the business has grown, the family-owned business strives to maintain a "family atmosphere" and stresses trust. Because of Sarah's honesty and hard work, the manager quickly promoted her, and she now signs checks for amounts under $5,000 and also has responsibilities for Accounts Payable. Now, however, the owners are suspicious of Sarah's recent lifestyle changes and have hired you to determine whether Sarah is embezzling from the company. Public records reveal the following:

CASE 11

	YEAR 1	YEAR 2	YEAR 3
Assets:			
Personal residence	$100,000	$100,000	$100,000
Automobiles	20,000	40,000	90,000
Stocks and bonds	30,000	30,000	30,000
Boat		30,000	30,000
CDs	25,000	25,000	50,000
Liabilities:			
Mortgage balance	90,000	40,000	
Auto loan	10,000	5,000	
Income:			
Salary	37,000	40,000	42,000
Other	4,000	4,000	4,000
Expenses:			
Mortgage payments	6,000	6,000	6,000
Auto loan payments	2,000	2,500	2,500
Other living expenses	15,000	15,000	20,000

Perform a net worth calculation using the data above. (Ignore interest in your calculations.)

Case 12

After searching public records and other sources, you accumulate the following financial information for John Dough:

CASE 12

	YEAR 1	YEAR 2	YEAR 3
Assets:			
Residence #1	$150,000	$150,000	$150,000
Residence #2			85,000
Stocks and bonds	10,000	20,000	35,000
Automobiles	18,000	35,000	35,000
Boat		22,000	22,000
CD	8,000	27,000	50,000
Cash	3,500	7,500	18,000
Liabilities:			
Mortgage balance #1	84,000	42,000	15,000

(continued on next page)

CASE 12 CONTINUED

	YEAR 1	YEAR 2	YEAR 3
Mortgage balance #2			85,000
Auto loans	12,000	38,000	
Boat loan		22,000	5,000
Income:			
Salary		49,000	55,000
Interest/other		5,000	7,000
Expenses:			
Mortgage payments		15,000	26,000
Auto loan payments		6,000	6,000
Boat loan payments		3,500	5,000
Other living expenses		22,000	31,000

Given the financial information, determine whether there is a likelihood of fraudulent income. If so, determine the amount.

Case 13

A bank manager's responsibility was making loans. Auditors discovered that several loans he made over a five-year period had not been repaid. A fraud investigation revealed that the manager had been receiving kickbacks from risky clients in exchange for extending them loans. His loans had cost the bank millions of dollars in uncollectible loans. You have been asked to determine the amount of kickbacks your loan officer has taken.

1. What type of records would you search to find information about the manager's assets?
2. Which records would be the most helpful in this case? Why?

CASE STUDIES

Case Study 1

Mark is a young business student at the University of Georgia, who works part time as a financial adviser at a local credit union. Mark has been married a little over two years. Mark's wife is currently taking care of their newborn son, while Mark finishes up school. Mark is well liked by all those who know him. In fact, those who know Mark would describe him as outgoing, funny, and very intelligent.

At the credit union, Mark's primary responsibilities are to set up new accounts, make initial loan interviews,

and work as a teller. While at work, Mark always appears to be working hard and rarely misses work (even for vacations). Often times, Mark is the first one to volunteer to stay late and look over accounts or help clean up.

Over the last four months, Mark's credit union supervisor has noticed that Mark has been making some interesting purchases. Four months ago, Mark purchased a big-screen television and has frequently invited other coworkers to watch movies at his home. One month ago, Mark bought three new wool suits, which he frequently wears to work. Two months ago, Mark traded in his old Geo Prism for a new Jeep Grand Cherokee (with many expensive features). When asked where he was getting the money for these purchases, Mark humorously responded, "I guess people are right—when you die, you can't take it all with you. However, it sure was nice they left it with me." This was an allusion to the fact that a wealthy grandmother had recently passed away and left Mark (her favorite grandson) a significant inheritance.

Also, the supervisor has recently heard some of the new customers complaining that their balances are off by $20, $30, and even $50.

CASE STUDY 1

	MONTH 1	MONTH 2	MONTH 3
Assets:			
1996 Geo Prism	$1,000		
2008 Jeep Grand Cherokee		$45,000	$45,000
Savings account	3,000	6,000	7,000
Checking account	600	800	500
CD	2,000	2,000	2,000
Laptop	2,500	2,500	2,500
Television			1,000
Liabilities:			
Auto loan		45,000	45,000
Income:			
Salary	1,000	1,000	1,000
Other	300	300	300
Expenses:			
Rent payments	700	700	700
Small expenditures	130	130	130
Auto loan payments		600	600
Other living expenses	400	700	800

Questions

1. What fraud symptoms are present in this scenario?
2. Is it possible to know from the information above that Mark is committing fraud at the credit union?
3. What is one reasonable action the supervisor could do if he or she suspected Mark was committing fraud?
4. Assuming that the credit union decides to investigate further, calculate Mark's net worth and income from other sources.

Case Study 2

Use the following financial data to prepare a comparative net worth assessment:

CASE STUDY 2

	YEAR 1	YEAR 2	YEAR 3
Assets:			
Residence	$50,000	$50,000	$200,000
Stocks and bonds	10,000	10,000	10,000
Automobiles	15,000	15,000	40,000
Cash	5,000	8,000	20,000
Liabilities:			
Mortgage balance	40,000	30,000	0
Auto loan	8,000	5,000	0
Student loans	10,000	8,000	0
Income:			
Salary	30,000	35,000	40,000
Other	0	1,000	1,000
Expenses:			
Mortgage payments	$5,000	$5,000	$0
Car payments	1,000	5,000	2,500
Student loan payments	1,000	1,000	500
Other living expenses	15,000	15,000	20,000
Total living expenses	$22,000	$26,000	$23,000

Case Study 3

Steve (Slick) Willy, 45, just got out of jail. As a reformed citizen on parole, Slick decides to go into business for himself. He starts a collections company to help companies collect debts. The terms of his parole stipulate that he pay restitution payments to the federal government of $400 a month, or 10 percent of his income, whichever is greater. As his parole officer, you notice that after a year out of jail, Slick makes some interesting purchases. First, he buys a new Jaguar, which he drives to parole meetings.

Second, he moves into an expensive neighborhood on the north side of town and takes a cruise to Jamaica with his 19-year-old girlfriend. Yet, he has never been late making his $400 monthly payments to the federal government. After obtaining a subpoena for his bank records, you notice that he has only $1,000 in his account. About this time, you receive a call from a man who is making payments to Slick's collection company. He states that Slick is threatening to break his legs and hurt his family if he doesn't pay Slick's company. The man says Slick demands the checks be made out to a woman, not a company.

This complaint convinces you to investigate Mr. Willy and his girlfriend. A search of UCC filings in the county shows that Slick's girlfriend owns three cars costing a total of $90,000, a $250,000 house, and a company called Tak'It From You. You check her bank account and see that more than $50,000 is moving through the account each month. You decide to dig through Slick and his girlfriend's trash a few times each month. In these searches, you find evidence that supports the following: three car payments totaling $1,000 per month; a $1,500 monthly mortgage payment; a credit card balance of $6,000, with $100 monthly payments; a balance of $12,000 owed to Home Shopping Network, with $500 monthly payments; $400 food payments during the past two weeks; and a $3,500 payment to Jamaican Cruise Lines. After searching the girlfriend's trash, you talk to her neighbors, friends, and coworkers and determine that she and Slick spend between $1,500 and $2,000 a month on miscellaneous items and trips. One neighbor tells you that Slick just gave his girlfriend a diamond ring that cost $3,000. Slick's girlfriend works as a waitress at a small restaurant and makes only $15,000 a year. (*Note:* Assume that both Slick and his girlfriend's net worth last year were zero.)

Questions

1. Use this information to prepare a net worth analysis of Slick's girlfriend. (Ignore interest in your calculations.)

Case Study 4

Homegrown Gardens, LLP, is a $10 million nursery and garden retailer in Florida. Homegrown employs about 20 full-time and seasonal employees. The majority of the plants and nursery stock that Homegrown sells comes from Monromio Nurseries, a wholesaler based in Alabama. Monromio is recognized throughout the South for the quality of the plants it grows and sells. Homegrown is generally happy to pay the premium prices that Monromio's plants command, because it passes the extra costs on to its customers, who value the high-quality plants it sells. However, Barry Greenstem, one of Homegrown's managing partners, is visibly upset after speaking with the owners of other nurseries at a recent trade show in Atlanta. Although Monromio has increased its prices across the board, Monromio's price hike to Homegrown is larger than the average. Barry suspects that Betty Stevenson, Homegrown's assistant manager in charge of purchasing nursery stock, may be accepting kickbacks from Monromio in return for allowing higher purchase prices. Betty and her husband, Mike, purchased a new SUV, a houseboat, and several ATVs last year and moved into a new, larger house this year. Barry knows that Betty's salary isn't high enough to support the new lifestyle, and he doubts that Mike's job as a city employee would provide large enough raises to justify the new "toys." Barry hires you to perform a net worth investigation of Betty and Mike to determine the amount of any unknown income. Your search of public and private records reveals the following information:

CASE STUDY 4

	YEAR BEFORE LAST	LAST YEAR	THIS YEAR
Assets:			
Personal residence	$70,000	$70,000	$200,000
Automobiles	15,000	45,000	45,000
Houseboat		30,000	30,000
ATVs		12,000	12,000
Liabilities:			
Mortgage balance	35,000	30,500	100,000
Auto loan	2,500		
Loan on houseboat		15,000	11,000
Income:			
Betty's salary	25,000	25,500	26,000
Mike's salary	35,000	36,000	37,000
Expenses:			
Mortgage payments	4,500	4,500	13,000
Auto payments		1,800	1,800
Houseboat payments		2,400	2,400
Other living expenses	15,000	17,000	15,000

Questions

1. Using this information, calculate the amount of income from unknown sources, if any, using the net worth method. (Ignore interest in your calculations.)

INTERNET ASSIGNMENTS

1. The Postal Service site contains a great deal of information on the detection of mail fraud and the investigation efforts of the Postal Service.
   a. Access the U.S. Postal Service Web site at www.usps.gov. Enter into the search box the words "postal inspectors." Review and become familiar with the fraud services provided by the Postal Inspection Service.
   b. Give a brief overview of the Postal Inspection Service.
   c. What does the Postal Inspection Service recommend in order to protect you against phony "one-shot" credit card offers?
   d. Name five characteristics of telemarketing fraud schemes.

2. An increasingly common way to commit fraud is to use the Internet. The Department of Justice now devotes an entire page on its Web site to Internet fraud. Visit its site at www.justice.gov/criminal/fraud/ and identify three types of Internet fraud.

3. Go to www.howtoinvestigate.com.
   a. Identify the different kinds of background checks that investigative professionals provide.
   b. What information does a basic background investigation provide?
   c. Credit bureaus gather credit data about individuals from a vast network of retailers, businesses, and financial institutions. In exchange for these data, they provide credit information to all their members. List three giant commercial credit bureaus. (*Hint:* Do an Internet search on credit bureaus.)

4. Return to www.howtoinvestigate.com. Read the section entitled "Business Background Checks."
   a. What does a complete business investigation include?
   b. Suppose you hire someone to perform some work on your house. Who do you call to find out if the contractor is licensed to conduct business in your area?

DEBATES

1. You are performing an audit of a small Internet start-up company that recently went public. During the audit, you frequently converse with the employees, with whom you have a comfortable relationship. In one conversation, an employee mentions the strange behavior of a coworker.

Apparently, this suspect employee comes to work very early and stays late. He is stressed at work and rather irritable. Although many of the company's founders are enjoying the economic fruits of the initial public offering (IPO), this person did not own any stock in the company at the time of the IPO and thus did not earn much money when the company went public. Nevertheless, this person drives a new Porsche Boxter. Is there sufficient evidence to determine whether this employee appears to be committing fraud?

2. This chapter discussed techniques for conversion investigations that involve searching public records to identify changes in lifestyle and the net worth of alleged fraud perpetrators. You recently became a certified fraud examiner (CFE) and have joined a local fraud examination firm. Your manager explains how he prefers to work with private sources of information and not involve local law enforcement agencies in the conversion investigation stage of his cases. You disagree and feel that local law enforcement can be an excellent resource.

Pair up with someone in your class. One of you take the position of the manager, and the other take the position of the new CFE. Discuss the advantages and disadvantages of involving law enforcement agencies in your fraud investigations.

END NOTES

1. Most of the facts for this Phar-Mor vignette were taken from the video "How to Steal 500 Million," *Frontline* by PBS Video. PBS 1992. Some facts were taken from an article in *The Wall Street Journal*. [See Gabriela Stern, "Chicanery at Phar-Mor Ran Deep, Close Look at Discounter Shows," *The Wall Street Journal* (January 20, 1994): 1.]

2. Mark F. Murray, "When a Client Is a Liability," *Journal of Accountancy* (September 1992): 54–58.

CHAPTER **10**

Inquiry Methods and Fraud Reports[1]

LEARNING OBJECTIVES

After studying this chapter, you should be able to:

- Understand the interviewing process.
- Plan and conduct an interview.
- Understand the nature of admission-seeking interviews.
- Describe the different deceptions and lies used by perpetrators.
- Describe the different types of honesty testing.
- Prepare a fraud report.

TO THE STUDENT

This is one of the longest chapters in the textbook, but it deals with an extremely important subject: interviewing. Be sure to take the time—breaking the reading into several sections if necessary—to understand the concepts presented here. Great interviews are a telltale sign of great investigators.

Don Restiman was the purchasing manager for Emerald Enterprises. During a four-year period, he accepted over $400,000 in bribes from one of Emerald's suppliers by having the supplier hire and pay his daughter, Jane, as a supposed "salesperson." Jane deposited her "paycheck" into an account she shared with her father. They used the money to buy real estate, automobiles, and other valuables. Fraud was suspected in the purchasing department for several reasons, which included increased amounts of purchases from the vendor, unnecessary purchases, purchases of goods at increased prices, and prices significantly higher than those of competitors.

Two skilled investigators interrogated Jane. They asked her about the specifics of her "job." As the interview proceeded, it became obvious from her responses that she was lying. She was unable to answer simple questions as: "Where are the company's headquarters located?" "What is the address and telephone number of your office?" "What companies do you sell the product to?" and "Who are your closest coworkers?"

After several obvious lies, her attorney asked the investigators if he and his client could step outside the room for a few moments. Her attorney convinced Jane that she was perjuring herself. When they returned, Jane confessed that she was lying about being employed at Emerald. In the presence of her attorney, she signed a prepared written confession that made the prosecution of her father easier.

In this chapter, we conclude our discussion of investigation methods by discussing how to query people (witnesses or suspects) through interviews and various types of honesty testing.

Interviewing—An Overview

Interviewing is by far the most common technique used to investigate and resolve fraud. An **interview** is a question-and-answer session designed to elicit information. It differs from ordinary conversation in that it is structured (not free-form) and it has a purpose. Interviewing is the systematic questioning of individuals who have knowledge of events, people, and evidence of a case under investigation. Good interviewers quickly zero in on suspects and elicit admissions from guilty parties. Interviews also help obtain (1) information that establishes the essential elements of the crime, (2) leads for developing cases and gathering other evidence, (3) the cooperation of victims and witnesses, and (4) information on the personal backgrounds and motives of witnesses. Interviews are conducted with victims, complainants, contacts, informants, clients or customers, suspects, expert witnesses, police officers, clerks, janitors, coworkers, supervisors, disgruntled spouses or friends, current and former vendors, and anyone who might be helpful in the investigation. There are three types of interviewees: (1) friendly, (2) neutral, and (3) hostile. Each type is handled differently.

STOP & THINK *What are the differences between the three types of interviewees: friendly, neutral, and hostile?*

The friendly interviewee goes above and beyond what is normally expected in order to be (or at least appear to be) helpful. Although friendly witnesses can be helpful, experienced investigators take care to determine their motives. In some cases, the motive is truly a sincere desire to help. However, possible motives also include a desire to get even with the suspect or to direct attention away from the interviewee as a suspect.

Neutral interviewees have nothing to gain or lose from the interview. They have no hidden motives or agendas, and they are usually the most objective and helpful of all interviewees.

Hostile interviewees are the most difficult to interview. They are often associated in some way with the suspect or the crime. Friendly and neutral interviewees can be questioned at any time, and appointments can be made in advance; but hostile interviewees should generally be questioned without prior notice. Surprise interviews provide hostile interviewees with less time to prepare defenses.

Characteristics of a Good Interview

Good interviews share common characteristics. Interviews should be of sufficient length and depth to uncover relevant facts. Most interviewers tend to get too little, rather than too much, information. A good interview focuses on pertinent information and quickly steers talk away from irrelevant information. Extraneous or useless facts unnecessarily complicate the gathering and analysis of information. Interviews should end on a positive note.

Interviews should be conducted as closely as possible to the time of the event in question. With the passage of time, memories of potential witnesses and respondents become faulty, and critical details can be lost or forgotten. Good interviews are objective. They endeavor to gather information in a fair and impartial manner.

Characteristics of a Good Interviewer

Good interviewers share certain characteristics. Above all, they have outgoing personalities, and they interact well with others. They are comfortable around people, and they help others feel at ease around them. Successful interviewers are people with whom others are willing to share information. Good interviewers do not interrupt respondents unnecessarily. Volunteered information, as opposed to responses to specific questions, is often pertinent information. Good interviewers display interest in the subject and in what is being said.

The person being interviewed (also called the respondent, interviewee, witness, suspect, or target) must understand that interviewers are attempting to obtain only the relevant facts and are not "out to get" them or anyone else. This is best done by phrasing questions in a nonaccusatory manner. Little is accomplished when interviewers are formal, ostentatious, or attempt to impress respondents with their authority. Information gathering is best accomplished by interviewing in an informal and low-key manner.

If respondents perceive that interviewers are biased, or are attempting to confirm foregone conclusions, respondents are less likely to cooperate. Accordingly, interviewers should make every effort to demonstrate a lack of bias.

Professionalism in the interview often involves a state of mind and a commitment to excellence. Interviewers should be on time, professionally attired, and fair in all dealings with respondents. It is vital that interviewers not appear to be a threat, but rather as people who put others at ease. If respondents perceive that they are the target of an inquiry, they will be less likely to cooperate.

Understanding Reaction to Crisis

Fraud, like death or serious injury, is a crisis. People in crisis have a predictable sequence of reactions. Interviewers who understand these reactions are much more effective than interviewers who do not. Figure 10.1 shows a classic model for understanding an individual's reaction to crisis. This model is useful when interviewing people in a case.

The first stage, denial, functions as a buffer after people receive unexpected or shocking news. It allows people who are affected by or connected with the fraud to collect themselves and to mobilize less radical defenses. Denial screens out the reality of the situation. Some studies show that carefully balanced psychological and physiological systems must be maintained for people to function normally.[2] To avoid sudden and severe disruption of this psychological equilibrium, which can destroy or incapacitate a person, the most immediate recourse is denial, which is a strategy to maintain the status quo. Because people in denial refuse to acknowledge the stress at either the cognitive or the emotional level, they do not initiate behavioral changes that help them adjust to the new reality.

FIGURE 10.1   REACTION TO CRISES

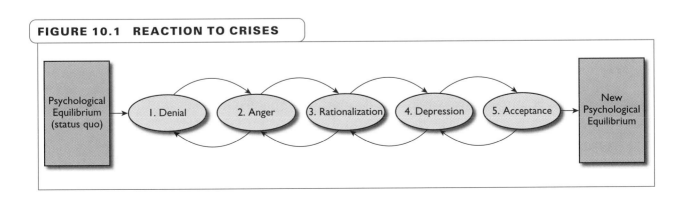

Denial takes many forms: People appear temporarily stunned or dazed, refuse to accept the information given, insist that there is some mistake, or fail to comprehend what has been said. Denial acts as a "shock absorber" to reduce the impact of sudden trauma. Denial of fraud by managers and others gives perpetrators time to alter, destroy, or conceal valuable documents and records. It also creates delays, which can mean that witnesses disappear or become confused and that valuable documentary evidence is lost. When denial cannot be maintained any longer, feelings of anger, rage, and resentment follow.

The anger stage is difficult to cope with, because anger is usually directed in every direction and it is also projected onto the environment—at times, even randomly. Anger arises because attempts to return to the old psychological status quo fail and are met with frustration. Suspects direct their anger at friends, relatives, and coworkers. Sometimes suspects direct their anger inward; this can result in feelings of guilt, but not always. Suspects are not the only ones to feel anger, however. Managers and other employees become hostile to auditors and investigators and perceive them to be cruel or unfeeling—a reaction not unlike that of the ancient Greeks who were reported to murder messengers bearing evil tidings.

The anger stage is a dangerous time to resolve frauds. While angry, managers and others can insult, harm, slander, or libel suspects and may terminate them without due cause. The result can be lawsuits—for slander, libel, assault, battery, or wrongful termination. An angry manager of a fast-food restaurant who believed that an employee was stealing, had the police handcuff the employee and drag him out of the store in front of customers. The employee, who was later found innocent, sued and won $250,000 in damages. In other situations, victims' angry reactions allowed criminals to get legal settlements larger than the amounts they stole.

People in the rationalization stage attempt to justify the dishonest act and/or to minimize the crime. During this stage, managers believe they understand why the crime was committed and often feel that the perpetrator's motivation was almost justifiable.

During this period, managers may feel that the perpetrator is not really a bad person, that a mistake was made, and that perhaps he or she should be given one more chance. Interviews during this stage are often not objective and can be detrimental to attempts to uncover the truth, or harmful to future prosecution efforts. Rationalization leads to failure to prosecute, easy penalties, and weak testimonies. Rationalization is the last

attempt of the affected group to return to the status quo (e.g., previous psychological equilibrium).

As attempts to resolve the problem and return to the status quo fail, hope diminishes. Managers are faced with the emotional burden of the truth. As trauma emerges, symptoms of depression appear; many withdraw or lose interest in the environment. Like the stages of denial, anger, and rationalization, depression is a normal part of the coping process necessary for eventual psychological readjustment. In this stage, managers no longer deny or rationalize the dishonest act. Their anger is replaced by a sense of loss and disappointment—or sometimes embarrassment that the fraud happened on "their watch." During this stage, managers and others often become withdrawn and uncooperative. They may be unwilling to volunteer information or to assist with the investigation. Interviews conducted during this stage are often less useful than those held later. Thus, it is crucial to take the state of mind of potential witnesses into consideration during interviews.

Individuals go through the five stages differently as they attempt to adjust to the crisis of fraud. A small fraud with minimal impact may only have a small psychological impact on individuals. They may go from denial to acceptance very quickly. Larger frauds with significant ramifications (such as embarrassment, loss of client, public exposure, or job jeopardy) often have larger psychological impacts. Individuals can cycle through the emotions of denial, anger, rationalization, and depression a number of times. Some people fluctuate between two phases as they strive to reach a new psychological equilibrium.

Eventually, people reach a state in which they no longer experience depression or anger; rather, they have a realistic understanding of what happened. Acceptance is not necessarily a happy or sad state; it is an acknowledgement of what happened and a desire to resolve the issue and move on. This phase is often precipitated by a knowledge of the facts surrounding the fraud, including a knowledge of the motivations of the perpetrator. It is during this phase that interviews are most useful and witnesses are most cooperative. Good interviewers know how to recognize the stage interviewees are in and, if necessary, help the interviewee move on to acceptance so that a productive interview can be conducted.

To demonstrate how these reactions play out during fraud investigations, consider one of the frauds discussed in Chapter 5. The case involved a supervisor in the shipping department of a wholesale-retail distribution center warehouse facility stealing over $5,000. The supervisor was responsible for overall operations of the warehouse and was also accountable for a cash fund used to give change (usually amounts between $25 and $500) to customers who came to the warehouse to pick up cash-on-delivery (COD) orders. The established procedures called for the supervisor to issue the customer a cash receipt, which was recorded in a will-call delivery logbook. Accounting personnel eventually matched the file containing details on the customer order with cash receipts and closed the transaction.

Over approximately one year, the supervisor stole small amounts of money. He concealed the fraud by submitting credit memos (with statements such as "billed to the wrong account," "to correct billing adjustment," and "miscellaneous") to clear the accounts receivable file. Consistent with the procedures, the accounts were matched with the credit memo, and the transactions were closed. A second signature was not needed on credit memos, and accounting personnel didn't asked questions about the supervisor's credit memos. At first, the supervisor submitted only two or three fraudulent credit memos totaling about $100 per week. After a few months, however, the amount increased to approximately $300 per week. To give the appearance of randomness, and to keep the accounting personnel from becoming suspicious, the supervisor intermixed comparatively large credit memo amounts with smaller ones.

The fraud surfaced when the supervisor accidentally credited the wrong customer's account for a cash transaction. By coincidence, the supervisor was on vacation when the error surfaced and was thus unable to cover his tracks when accounting personnel queried the transaction. Because of his absence, the accounts receivable clerk questioned the manager of the warehouse, who investigated the problem. The manager scrutinized cash receipts and determined that the potential for fraud existed.

Stage 1. Denial

Because of the possibility of fraud, the general manager and the warehouse manager started their own investigation of the warehouse cash fund. Sensing a serious problem, they decided to wait until the supervisor returned from vacation before taking further action. Both managers were anxious and somewhat irritable as they waited for the supervisor to return. Each manager later said that his work performance was adversely affected by the shock and their preoccupation with the problem. Both managers rationalized that the supervisor could

probably explain the error; after all, he had been with the firm for three years and they considered him a model employee.

Later, after the close of the investigation, both managers admitted that they tried to deny that the falsified credit memos represented intentional fraud. Because of their denial, they didn't take advantage of readily available evidence during the suspected employee's absence.

Company procedure required managers to contact either corporate security or the internal audit department if a fraud was suspected. However, because they trusted the supervisor, both managers convinced themselves that there was no possibility of fraud—that the whole thing was a mistake. When the supervisor returned from vacation, the managers asked him to discuss the situation. Still in the denial stage, the managers simply asked the supervisor to explain his handling of the cash fund. The supervisor—now thrown into his own first stage of crisis, denial—told them that he didn't know what they were talking about. Had he offered some explanation, the managers, who were still denying fraud, probably would have been satisfied and terminated their investigation.

But the supervisor denied the existence of the credit memos, and the managers knew this to be untrue, so they sent the supervisor back to work and decided to investigate further. From an investigative standpoint, sending the supervisor back to his job was a risky action. He was again in control of the original credit memos and cash transaction logs and could have easily destroyed evidence. Simply "losing" the records would have concealed the fraud and jeopardized the investigation. At this point, the warehouse managers requested the assistance of internal audit to review the matter further. A full week passed before assistance was made available.

Stage 2. Anger

While they were waiting for assistance from internal audit, both managers decided that fraud had indeed been committed. After much thought, they decided to confront the employee. This time, they vowed they would get answers. Clearly, both managers had progressed from denial to anger. Without additional information that a full investigation could have provided, the managers confronted the supervisor and demanded an explanation. This time, the supervisor said nothing. Irate, the managers fired him on the spot, without additional explanation. Firings like this jeopardize investigations and companies in several ways. First, if fraud has not been committed, the company may be subjected to litigation and sued for wrongful dismissal, slander, or libel. Second, harsh treatment jeopardizes further cooperation by the perpetrator. In this case, the basis for the termination was the several falsified credit memorandums located by the managers, totaling between $300 and $400.

The audit that followed revealed over 100 falsified credit memos and losses totaling more than $5,000. The managers were surprised at the extent of the fraud. Accusing the supervisor of fraud well before they could clearly demonstrate his guilt made the corporation vulnerable to litigation and potential liability.

CAUTION *When conducting interviews, you must try very hard to determine the crisis stage of your interviewees. Ignoring this information can significantly affect the success of your interviews.*

Stage 3. Bargaining and Rationalization

After the supervisor was summarily terminated, the general manager worried that both he and the warehouse manager had acted too quickly; perhaps they should have given the supervisor one more chance. They soon realized their actions exposed the company to liability. Although rehiring the supervisor was contrary to company policy, the general manager still felt he could "save" this "valued" employee.

Through these rationalizations, the general manager was trying to come to terms with the fact that a trusted friend and employee committed a fraud against the firm. He was "bargaining"—that is, trying to change the facts in some way that gave an acceptable explanation, although none existed.

Stage 4. Depression

Depression came after bargaining. Both the general manager and the warehouse manager grew less irritated and became much more withdrawn. Feelings of depression engulfed both individuals as they realized the scope of the situation. Their depression was reinforced by comments and reactions from other warehouse employees as details of the fraud emerged. Interestingly enough, during this period, neither manager discussed his feelings with the other. Rather, they kept their feelings to themselves, apparently because they felt that the employee had suffered enough and that the case should be closed.

Stage 5. Acceptance

The investigation conducted by corporate security and internal audit revealed the following facts:

- *The supervisor had a substance abuse problem involving cocaine and alcohol. As a result of his confrontation with management, he was considering rehabilitation.*
- *The supervisor convinced himself that he was simply borrowing the money. He rationalized that he had every intention of repaying the money borrowed, but he was also caught up in the machinations of the fraud and was shocked that in less than one year he defrauded the company of over $5,000.*
- *The supervisor informed security personnel that he had spent almost his entire life savings on cocaine and had lost his family in the process. Losing his job was the last straw.*
- *After discussions with local management, investigators learned that several managers and employees had noticed a change in the supervisor's behavior over the previous several months. The changes, which no one acted on, included frequent mood swings; frequent tardiness and absenteeism; and a preoccupation with impressing other employees by taking them out to lunch, during which the supervisor chattered relentlessly.*

Once these facts were known, both managers accepted the fraud as a reality and reached a new psychological equilibrium. Their desire at that point was to resolve the situation and move on with business.

This fraud is typical of the reactions of innocent bystanders in a fraud. Interviewers who recognize and understand these reactions, who tailor their questions and interview approaches to the reaction stages their interviewees are in, and who can nudge interviewees to the acceptance stage will have much more successful interviews.

Planning an Interview

When you conduct interviews, follow a plan or outline to make sure that you meet your objectives. Proper planning allows you to get the most from the interview and to minimize the time spent. Such planning involves ascertaining in advance as many facts as possible about the offense and the interviewee and establishing a location and time for the interview that are conducive to success.

To obtain facts about the offense and the interviewee, review relevant documents to gather as much other information as possible about the following factors:

The offense

- *Legal nature of the offense*
- *Date, time, and place of occurrence*
- *Manner in which the crime appears to have been committed*
- *Possible motives*
- *All available evidence*

The interviewee

- *Personal background information—age, education, marital status, and so on*
- *Attitude toward investigation*
- *Any physical or mental conditions, such as alcohol or drug use*

It is usually best (except with hostile interviewees) to conduct interviews at the interviewee's office or workplace, so that interviewees can access necessary papers, books, and other evidence. In addition, such locations are generally more convenient and comfortable for interviewees. The interview room should be one where distractions from colleagues and telephones are nonexistent or minimal. For example, you may want to ask those in the room to turn off their cell phones and other potential distractions.

With friendly or neutral interviewees, set up an appointment and allow sufficient (even excess) time for the interview. When you set up the appointment, identify information that the interviewee will need. Wherever possible, interview only one person at a time.

The Interviewer's Demeanor

Take special pains to be efficient, courteous, polite, and careful with the language you use during interviews. Here are some suggestions:

- *Sit fairly close to the interviewee without a desk or furniture between you. Don't walk around the room; stay seated.*
- *Do not talk down to the person. (Don't assume the person is less intelligent than you.)*
- *Be sensitive to the personal concerns of the witness, especially with regard to such matters as sex, race, religion, and ethnic background.*
- *Be businesslike. Conduct the interview in a professional manner. Be friendly but not social. Remember that you seek the truth; you are not trying to get a confession or a conviction.*

- *Avoid being authoritarian; do not dominate the interview.*
- *Be sympathetic and respectful. (If appropriate, tell the witness that anyone under similar conditions or circumstances might do the same thing.)*
- *Give careful thought to your language. Don't use technical jargon.*
- *Thank the witness for taking the time and effort to cooperate.*
- *Keep pencil and paper out of sight during the interview.*
- *End every cooperative interview by expressing your sincere appreciation.*

The Language of Interviews

Language is very important in interviews. Successful interviewers adhere to specific guidelines such as the following:

- *Use short questions, confined to one topic, which can be clearly and easily understood.*
- *Ask questions that require narrative answers; whenever possible, avoid eliciting "yes" and "no" answers.*
- *Avoid questions that suggest part of the answer, often called leading questions.*
- *Require witnesses to give the factual basis for any conclusions they state.*
- *Prevent witnesses from wandering aimlessly. Require direct responses.*
- *Don't let witnesses lead you away from the topic. Don't let them confuse the issue or leave basic questions unanswered.*
- *At all times, concentrate more on the answer you are hearing than on the next question you plan to ask.*
- *Clearly understand each answer before you continue.*
- *Maintain full control of the interview.*
- *Point out some, but not all, of the circumstantial evidence.*

STOP & THINK   *Why is it important to disclose only a portion of the circumstantial evidence you have collected?*

Question Typology

Interviewers ask five types of questions: introductory, informational, assessment, closing, and admission-seeking. In routine interviews, where your objective is to gather information from neutral or friendly witnesses, only three of the five types are normally asked: introductory, informational, and closing questions. If you have reasonable cause to believe the respondent is not being truthful, then ask assessment questions. Finally, if you decide with reasonable cause that the respondent is responsible for misdeeds, admission-seeking questions can be posed.

Introductory Questions

Interviewers use introductory questions for two purposes: to start the interview and to get the respondent to verbally agree to cooperate. This is done in a step-by-step procedure in which you briefly state the purpose for the contact and then pose a question designed to get the respondent to agree to talk.

Informational Questions

Once the proper format for the interview is set, interviewers turn to the fact-gathering portion. Three types of questions are asked: open, closed, and leading. (We discuss these in more detail later in the chapter.) Each question type is used in a logical sequence in order to maximize the information obtained. If you have reason to believe that the respondent is being untruthful, then pose assessment questions. Otherwise, bring the interview to a logical close.

Assessment Questions

If interviewers have reason to believe the respondent is being deceptive, certain types of hypothetical, nonaccusatory questions are posed. By observing the interviewee's verbal and nonverbal responses to these questions, you can assess the respondent's credibility. Your assessment will form the basis of your decision about whether to pose admission-seeking questions in order to obtain a legal admission of wrongdoing.

Closing Questions

In routine interviews, certain questions are asked at closing in order to reconfirm the facts, obtain previously undiscovered information, seek new evidence, and maintain goodwill. These three questions should always be asked in closing: (1) Do you know anyone else to whom I should talk? (2) Is there anything I have forgotten to ask that you believe is relevant? (3) Can I talk to you again if the need arises?

Admission-Seeking Questions

Admission-seeking interviews are reserved for individuals whose culpability is reasonably certain. Admission-seeking questions are posed in an exact order designed to (1) clear an innocent person or (2) encourage a culpable person to confess. These questions must not violate the rights and privileges of the person being interviewed.

Elements of Conversation

Since interviews are essentially structured conversations, it is helpful to understand the basic elements of effective communication. Whenever two or more human beings converse with one another, they engage in several types of communication—either one at a time or in combination.

Expression

A common function of conversation is self-expression in which one or more of the conversationalists expresses ideas, feelings, attitudes, or moods. The urge for spontaneous expression can be a vital asset in interviewing, and it should be encouraged in respondents. Interviewers can encourage self-expression to meet information-gathering objectives. A common error made by novice interviewers is attempting to impress respondents with their knowledge of the subject. In doing so, interviewers risk making respondents feel threatened, resulting in respondents giving guarded responses rather than expressing their feelings frankly. Experienced interviewers have the discipline to control their own responses.

Persuasion

Persuasion and expression differ in that persuasion endeavors to convince the other person. Persuasion can be effective at times in interviews; it is used mostly to convince respondents of the legitimacy of the interview.

Therapy

Making people feel good about themselves is often a function of effective communication. In our conversations with friends, we frequently express ideas and feelings to relieve emotional tension. This release, called **catharsis**, is encouraged in psychiatric interviews. Many times the information sought in an interview is closely related to the respondent's inner conflicts and tensions. For example, people embezzling money typically feel guilty. Skillful interviewers know the therapeutic implication of releasing such feelings in their attempts to gain information.

Ritual

Some aspects of conversation are ritualistic; that is, they are cultural expressions that have no significance other than to provide security in interpersonal relations. Examples include "Good morning!" and "How are you today?" These types of questions and answers can be useful at the beginning of your interview because they are considered polite in many societies, but you should generally avoid them. Learn to detect ritualistic answers by respondents and to avoid giving them yourself. Be aware of the danger of engaging in ritualistic conversation; don't confuse the results with valid information.

Information Exchange

Information exchange is the central purpose of interviews. The word *exchange* reminds us that the flow of information in interviews goes both ways. Interviewers are often so focused on the information they wish to obtain that they fail to properly exchange information with respondents. Although you should measure the details carefully, don't be "cagey." This tactic rarely works. Two basic problems occur in the exchange of information: (1) the information sought by interviewers is not of equal importance to respondents and (2) communication barriers often exist between people of diverse backgrounds. These barriers are also common between strangers.

Inhibitors of Communication

To be an effective interviewer, you must understand that certain matters inhibit communication and others facilitate it. It is your task to minimize inhibitors and maximize facilitators. An **inhibitor** is any sociopsychological barrier that impedes the flow of relevant information by making respondents unable or unwilling to provide information. Carefully examine the eight inhibitors to communication listed below. The first four make respondents unwilling to cooperate; the last four make the respondents unable to give information, even though they may be willing to do so.

Competing Demands for Time

Respondents may hesitate to begin an interview because of other demands on their time. They are not necessarily placing a negative value on being interviewed, but are instead weighing the value of being interviewed against doing something else. Successful interviewers convince respondents that the interview is a good use of their time.

Threatened Egos

Respondents in some cases withhold information because of a perceived threat to their self-esteem. Three broad responses to ego threats are repression, disapproval, and loss of status.

- *Repression. The strongest response to a threatened ego is repression. Respondents not only refuse to admit the information but also refuse to admit it inwardly. They are being honest when they answer that they don't know or they have truly "forgotten" (repressed) it.*
- *Disapproval. A less intense but more common response to threatened egos is found when respondents possess information but hesitate to admit it because they anticipate disapproval from the interviewer. If respondents are made to feel that the interviewer will not condemn them, they may welcome the opportunity to divulge information. A generally accepting and sympathetic attitude toward respondents goes a long way toward eliciting candid responses.*
- *Loss of status. Sometimes respondents fear losing status if the information provided becomes public. This can sometimes be overcome by assuring them that the information will be handled confidentially.*

Etiquette

The etiquette barrier operates when an answer to a question contains information that the respondent perceives as inappropriate. Answering candidly would be considered in poor taste or a lack of proper etiquette. For example, there are certain things that men do not discuss comfortably in front of women and vice versa, that students do not tell teachers, and that doctors do not tell patients. The desire to avoid embarrassing, shocking, or threatening answers is distinct from the fear of exposing oneself. Often, the negative effects of the etiquette barrier can be forestalled by selecting the appropriate interviewer and setting for the interview.

Trauma

Trauma denotes an acutely unpleasant feeling associated with crisis experiences. The unpleasant feeling is often brought to the surface when the respondent is reporting the experience. Trauma is common when talking to victims and can usually be overcome by sensitive handling of the issue.

Forgetting

A frequent inhibitor to communication is the respondent's inability to recall certain types of information. This is not a problem if the objectives of the interview deal only with current attitudes, beliefs, or expectations.

The natural fading of memory over time makes it easier for the ego-defense system to reconstruct its own image of the past by omission, addition, or distortion.

The memory problem is a much more frequent obstacle than interviewers generally expect. Even the most simple and obvious facts cannot always be elicited. Three factors contribute to our recollection of an event.

First, the vividness of our recall relates to the event's original emotional impact, its meaningfulness at the time, and the degree to which our ego is involved. A second factor is the amount of time that has elapsed since the event. Third is the nature of the interview situation, including the interviewer's techniques and tactics. Knowledge of these factors will help you anticipate where problems may arise.

Chronological Confusion

Chronological confusion is commonly encountered in interviews that seek case history information. This term refers to the respondent's tendency to confuse the order of events. This occurs in two ways: First, two or more events are correctly recalled, but the respondent is unsure of the sequence. Or, only one event is recalled, and it is incorrectly assumed to have been true at an earlier point.

Inferential Confusion

Inferential Confusion denotes confusion and inaccuracies that result from errors of inference. These errors fall into two categories: induction and deduction. In **induction**, the respondent is asked to convert concrete experiences into a higher level of generalization. In **deduction**, the respondent is asked to give concrete examples of certain categories of experience.

Unconscious Behavior

Often, interview objectives call for information about a person's unconscious behavior. The three types of *unconscious behavior* are **custom** or **habit**, **circular reaction** (the immediate, unwitting response of one person to the subliminal, nonverbal cues of another, which arises under special circumstances), and **acute emotional crisis** (where the behavior does not follow a habitual pattern and does not result from a reaction to others).

Facilitators of Communication

Facilitators of communication are those sociopsychological forces that make conversations, including interviews, easier to accomplish. Facilitators require a basic understanding of what motivates people.

Fulfilling Expectations

An important force in social interaction is our tendency to communicate, verbally or nonverbally, our expectations to the other person. The other person then tends to respond, consciously or unconsciously, to our expectations. This is one manifestation of the human tendency to conform to the group and to the anticipations of higher-status persons. It is in this conformity to group norms that security is sought.

In the interview setting, interviewers routinely communicate expectations to respondents. Strive to transmit both your general expectation of cooperation, as well as a more specific expectation that the respondent will answer the questions truthfully. Clearly distinguish between asking for information and expecting it. The former is mainly verbal communication; the latter is accomplished through nonverbal behavior.

Recognition

We all need the recognition and esteem of others. Social interaction often depends on an exchange of social goods. People "perform" in exchange for recognition and other social rewards. The need for recognition can be fulfilled by attention from people outside a person's social circle. Skillful and insightful interviewers take advantage of every opportunity to give respondents sincere recognition.

Altruistic Appeals

Some people need to identify with a "higher" value or cause beyond their immediate self-interest. This sometimes takes the form of identifying with the objectives of the larger group. Altruistic deeds usually increase self-esteem whether or not the deeds are made public. This distinguishes altruism from publicity. Altruism is of major importance in motivating many respondents. Interviewers who understand their respondent's value system can use strategy and techniques that appeal to altruism.

Sympathetic Understanding

We all need the sympathetic response of others. We like to share our joys, fears, successes, and failures. Our need for understanding differs from our need for recognition, which requires success and increased status. Interviewers who reflect a sympathetic attitude and who know how to direct that attitude toward the objectives of their interview find their percentages of success much higher than those who lack such abilities.

New Experience

Some people welcome new experiences. Although variety is not everybody's spice of life, escape from dreary routine is sought by almost everyone. Sometimes respondents are motivated by curiosity regarding the interviewer. Experienced interviewers consider this when deciding what to say about themselves. Do not assume that just because an interview is a new experience it will satisfy the respondent's needs. Aspects of the respondent's perception of the new experience can also be ego-threatening. Respondents may be anxious about the impression they leave with interviewers. This apprehensiveness can often be detected at the beginning of the interview. Once these fears are dispelled, respondents frequently find interviews a new and interesting experience.

Catharsis

Catharsis is the process by which we obtain release from unpleasant emotional tensions by talking about the source of these tensions. We often feel better after we talk about something that upsets us. Although we are all familiar with our own experiences with catharsis, we don't always perceive this need in others. After respondents confess, they may indicate that they feel much better about themselves. The need for sympathetic understanding and the need for catharsis are related, but they are not the same thing. Interviewers who do not have time to listen to what they consider inconsequential egocentric talk often find respondents unwilling to share important information.

Need for Meaning

Another trait common to all of us is our need for meaning. Every society has a set of assumptions, values, explanations, and myths that serves to create order in the society. Our need for meaning is related to cognitive dissonance, the psychological tension we feel when we are aware of inconsistent facts, assumptions, and interpretations. This tension is painful, and reducing it is rewarding. In cases where the interview topic deals directly with information that disturbs a person's need for meaning, respondents are often strongly motivated to talk it through, if they are convinced of the interviewer's interest.

Extrinsic Rewards

This term refers to rewards that motivate the respondent (other than those gained directly from being involved in the interview). Extrinsic rewards are helpful insofar as respondents see the interview as a means to an end. Various extrinsic rewards can come into play in interview situations, including money, job advancement, and retention of privileges. Remember that what is extrinsic to you as an interviewer may not be extrinsic to respondents. Sensitive interviewers recognize what extrinsic rewards, if any, respondents receive from being interviewed.

STOP & THINK　*Paying for information is one type of extrinsic reward. Some professionals may require that you pay them for their interview time or information. What concerns does this raise? How might it jeopardize your case? When might it be appropriate or not appropriate?*

Mechanics of the Interview
Introductory Questions

One of the most difficult aspects of interviews is getting started. Indeed, the introduction is often the hardest part. In many instances, interviewers and respondents have not met before. Interviewers have a tall order: meet the person, state a reason for the interview, establish necessary rapport, and get the information. The introduction is accomplished through questions as opposed to statements. Questions allow you to assess the respondent's feedback. This is an important aspect of the introduction. If the respondent is reluctant to be interviewed, that fact will come out through the introductory questions. They are designed to meet the objectives below.

Provide the Introduction

Obviously, you must introduce yourself as the interview commences. You should generally indicate your name and company. Normally you should avoid titles, especially if the interview is informal.

Establish Rapport

Webster's defines **rapport** as a "relation marked by harmony, conformity, accord, or affinity." In other words, establish some common ground before you begin your questioning. This is usually accomplished by spending a few minutes in "small talk." This aspect, however, should not be overdone. Most people are aware that the interviewer is not there to chitchat.

Establish the Interview Theme

State the purpose of your interview in some way prior to the commencement of serious questioning. Otherwise, the respondent may be confused, threatened, or overly cautious. Stating the purpose of the interview is known as "establishing the interview theme."

Observe Reactions

You need to become skilled in interpreting the respondent's reactions to questions. Social scientists say that more than half the communication between individuals is nonverbal. You must, therefore, observe systematically (though in an offhand, unobtrusive manner) the interviewee's responses.

There are systematic ways to observe reactions. First, pose nonsensitive questions as you establish rapport. During this phase, find some common ground so that you can "connect" with the respondent. As you establish rapport through normal conversation, observe the respondent's reactions. This is your baseline for observing later behavior, when you ask more sensitive questions. (We discuss this baseline observation or **calibration** in more detail later in the chapter.) If the respondent's verbal and nonverbal behavior is inconsistent from one type of question to another, you can then attempt to determine why.

Develop the Interview Theme

The interview theme may relate only indirectly to the actual purpose of the interview. The goal of the theme is to get the respondent to "buy in" to assisting in the interview. Generally, the most effective interview theme is that help is being sought. Nearly all of us get satisfaction from helping others.

In most interviews, it is best to treat respondents in such a manner that they feel important about helping. During this phase of the interview, respondents must not feel threatened in any way. An effective approach is to help those you interview feel that you are no threat to them and that you need their help. In the following examples, assume you are introducing yourself.

Wrong

Interviewer: "I am _____, a certified fraud examiner with the store's fraud examination unit. I am investigating a case of suspected fraud, and you may know something about it. How long have you worked here at the company?"

Right

Interviewer: "I'm _____. I work here at the company. Have we met before?"

Respondent: "I don't think so."

Interviewer: "I am working on an assignment, and I need your help. Do you have a few minutes I can spend with you now?"

Methodology

Help respondents perceive that they have something in common with you as the interviewer; they should be made to feel good about the situation. This is best accomplished when respondents perceive you as open and friendly.

Make Physical Contact

One way to promote respondents' perception of your being open and friendly is to shake hands at the beginning of the interview. Making physical contact helps break down psychological barriers to communication. However, do not invade the respondent's personal space; doing so makes people uncomfortable.

Use body language to create the impression of trust during the interview: gesture openly with your arms, clasp your hands together, and lean forward to indicate interest. You can also establish rapport verbally by using soft words, agreeing with the respondent, and avoiding negative terms.

Establish the Purpose of the Interview

The purpose of your interview must be established. Obviously, when you make official contact with respondents, a reason must be given. The reason or purpose of your interview should be general and not specific. The specific purpose will be stated later. The general purpose for the interview should be one that is logical for respondents to accept and easy for you to explain. Usually, the more general, the better.

Example

Interviewer: "I'm working on a matter, and I need your help."

|or|

"I'm reviewing procedures here at the company."

|or|

"I'm gathering information on our purchasing procedures."

Don't Interview More Than One Person at a Time

One basic rule is to question only one person at a time. The testimony of one respondent will invariably influence the testimony of another. This is one of the few hard-and-fast rules when interviewing.

Conduct the Interview in Private

Another basic rule is to conduct interviews under conditions of privacy. Interviews are best conducted out of the sight and sound of friends, relatives, or colleagues. People are reluctant to furnish information within the hearing of others.

Ask Nonsensitive Questions

Sensitive questions should be avoided until well into the interview. Such questions should be asked *only* after careful deliberation and planning. During the introductory phase, avoid emotionally charged words of all types. Such words often cause people to become defensive, reluctant to answer questions and ultimately less likely to cooperate.

NONSENSITIVE WORDS	
INSTEAD OF	USE
Investigation	*Inquiry*
Audit	*Review*
Interview	*Ask a few questions*
Embezzle/steal/theft	*Shortage or paperwork problems*

Get a Commitment for Assistance

Failure to get a commitment from the respondent to assist you is a common mistake made even by experienced interviewers. This is a critical step and sets the tone of the entire interview. A commitment of assistance requires positive action on the part of the respondent. Remaining silent or simply nodding the head is generally not sufficient.

Ask for the commitment before the interview commences, and encourage respondents to voice "yes" or "no" out loud . If you encounter silence the first time, repeat the question in a slightly different way until the respondent verbalizes an answer.

Example

Interviewer: "I'm _____, with the company. I'm reviewing our sales returns and allowances. Do you have a few minutes?"

Respondent: "Yes."

Interviewer: "I'm gathering some information on certain company procedures. Maybe you can help me?"

Respondent: (No response.)

Interviewer: "Could I get your help with me on this project?"

Respondent: "Yes. What's this about?"

Establish a Transitional Statement

At this point, you have a commitment for assistance and must describe in more detail the purpose of the interview. This is done with a transitional statement that provides a legitimate basis for your inquiry and explains to respondents how they fit into the inquiry. You can usually accomplish this using a broad, rather than a narrow, description. Note that employees in the same company will frequently assume that your request for assistance is legitimate. After describing the basic nature of the inquiry with the transitional statement, seek a second commitment for assistance.

Example

Interviewer: "I'm gathering information about the sales return function and how it's supposed to work. It would be very helpful if I could start by asking you to basically tell me about your job. Okay?"

When interviewing complete strangers, you may have to give particulars about how the respondent's assistance is needed. This can be accomplished by one or more of the methods illustrated as follows.

Example

Interviewer: "It's fairly routine, really. As I say, I work for _____ and I've been asked to gather information about the sales procedures. I thought it might be helpful to talk to you. Do you have some time to talk?"

|or|

"It's fairly routine. I've been asked by the company to gather information on some of its procedures. I thought you might be able to help by answering a few questions. Okay?"

Seek Continuous Agreement

Throughout the process—from the introduction to the close—attempt to phrase questions that can be answered with a simple "yes." People find it easier to reply in the affirmative than the negative.

Example

Interviewer: "Okay?"

"Can you help me?"

"That's okay, isn't it?"

Do Not Invade Body Space

During the introductory part of the interview, you should generally remain at a distance of 4 to 6 feet.

Do not invade the respondent's personal zone (closer than about 3 feet), as doing so will make many respondents uncomfortable.

Set up the interview in such a way that the respondent is free and clear—where you can see that person's movement from head to toe. Try not to interview someone who is sitting behind his or her desk.

Informational Questions

Informational questions are nonconfrontational, nonthreatening, and used for information-gathering purposes. Most questions fall into this category. Applications include:

- *Interviews to gain an understanding of accounting control systems.*
- *Interviews concerning documents.*
- *Gathering information regarding business operations or systems.*
- *Pre-employment interviews.*

Informational questions seek to elicit unbiased factual information. Good interviewers are alert to inconsistencies in facts or behavior. Informational questions—as well as others—fall into several general categories: open, closed, leading, double-negative, complex, and attitude.

Open Questions

Open questions are worded in a way that makes it difficult to answer "yes" or "no." Typical open questions call for a monologue response and can be answered in several different ways. During the informational phase of the interview, you should endeavor to ask primarily open questions. This stimulates conversation. Informational questions are open-ended questions and force more lengthy responses. Here is an open-ended question:

Example

"Can you explain the purpose for a sales receipt including who completes them, where copies are kept, etc.?"

Here are a few other examples:

Example

Interviewer: "Please tell me about your job."

"Please tell me about the operation of your department."

"What do you think about this problem?"

"Please describe the procedures to me."

Closed Questions

Closed questions require a precise answer—usually "yes" or "no." Closed questions also deal with specifics, such as amounts, dates, and times. As much as possible, avoid closed questions in the informational part of the interview. They are used extensively in closing questions, which will be described later in this chapter. Examples include the following:

Interviewer: "Do you work here?"

"What day of the week did it happen?"

Leading Questions

Leading questions contain the answer as a part of the question. Most commonly, they are used to confirm already known facts. Although leading questions are usually discouraged in court proceedings, they can be effective in interviews. Here is a leading question.

"I understand that you started here in November 1988 —after working for Panasonic—is that correct?"

Double-Negative Questions

Questions or statements that contain double negatives are confusing and often suggest an answer opposite to the correct one. Do not use them. Here is an example.

Interviewer: "Didn't you suspect that something wasn't right?"

Complex Questions

Complex questions and statements are not easily understood, cover more than one subject or topic, require more than one answer, and/or require a complicated answer. Simply put, avoid them—here is an example.

Interviewer: "What are your duties here, and how long have you been employed?"

Attitude Questions

Your attitude is conveyed not only by the structure of your questions and statements but also by the manner in which you ask them. When you wish to establish a friendly mood, employ questions such as the following:

Interviewer: "How are you doing this morning?"

"Have you been following the Olympic games?"

It is always a good idea, however, to ask a question to which you know beforehand that the answer will be "yes."

Question Sequence

As a general rule, questioning should proceed from the general to the specific; that is, seek general information before you seek details. A variation is to "reach backward" with questions by beginning with known information and working toward unknown areas. An efficient way to do this is to recount the known information and then frame the next question as a logical continuation of the facts previously related. Figures and numbers are critical in accounting and fraud-related matters; unfortunately, witnesses aren't always able to recall specific amounts. You can jog the respondent's memory by comparing unknown items with items of known quantity.

Interviewer: "Was the amount of money involved more than last year's figure?"

Controlled-Answer Techniques

Controlled-answer techniques or statements are used to stimulate a desired answer or impression. These techniques direct the interview toward a specific point. For example, it may be possible to get a person to admit knowledge of a matter by phrasing the question thus: *"I understand you were present when the internal controls were developed; would you please describe how they were constructed?"* This phrasing provides a stronger incentive for the respondent to admit knowledge than does: *"Were you present when the internal controls were developed?"*

To stimulate the person to agree to talk or to provide information, you can use an example such as: *"Because you're not involved in this matter, I'm sure you wouldn't mind discussing it with me."* This provides a stronger incentive to cooperate than: *"Do you have any objections to telling me what you know?"*

Free Narratives

The **free narrative** is an orderly, continuous account of an event or incident, given with or without prompting. It is used to quickly summarize what is known about a matter. Try to designate explicitly the occurrence that you wish to discuss. Sometimes respondents must be controlled to prevent unnecessary digression. Otherwise, use a minimum of interruptions and do not stop the narrative without good reason. Respondents will sometimes provide valuable clues when talking about things that are only partially related to the matter under inquiry.

Informational Question Techniques

The following suggestions improve the quality of interviews during the information-gathering phase:

- *Begin by asking questions that are unlikely to cause respondents to become defensive or hostile.*
- *Ask questions in a manner that develops the facts in the order of their occurrence or in some other systematic order.*
- *Ask only one question at a time, and frame the question so that only one answer is required.*
- *Ask straightforward and frank questions; generally avoid shrewd approaches.*
- *Give respondents ample time to answer; do not rush.*
- *Try to help respondents remember, but do not suggest answers; be careful not to imply any particular answer by facial expressions, gestures, methods of asking questions, or types of questions asked.*
- *Repeat or rephrase questions, if necessary, to get the desired facts.*
- *Be sure you understand the answers. If they are not perfectly clear, have respondents interpret them at that time instead of saving this for later.*
- *Give respondents an opportunity to qualify their answers.*
- *Separate facts from inferences.*
- *Have respondents give comparisons by percentages, fractions, estimates of time and distance, and other such comparisons to ascertain accuracy.*
- *Get all of the facts; almost every respondent can give you information beyond what was initially provided.*
- *After respondents give a narrative account, ask questions about the items discussed.*
- *Upon concluding the direct questioning, summarize the facts and have respondents verify that your summary is correct.*

Note-Taking

As stated previously, note-taking is considered problematic during interviews. That said, interviewers frequently need to take some notes. If this need arises, start each interview on a separate sheet of paper. This procedure is especially helpful should documents from a particular interview be subpoenaed. Do not try to write down all the information you are given during an interview, only the pertinent facts. Taking too many notes makes the interview process cumbersome and can inhibit respondents. If a quote is particularly relevant, try to write it down verbatim. Enclose all direct quotes in quotation marks. Do not slow down the interview process for note-taking. Instead, jot down key words or phrases, and then go back over the details at the end of the interview.

If a record of an interview is necessary, taping the interview is a desirable alternative to taking extensive notes. While permission to record an interview must usually be received from the interviewee, the recording device does not normally distract, once the interview begins.

C A U T I O N *As with any technology used during an interview, be sure to practice beforehand to ensure it will work as planned. Broken or complex technology can jeopardize an interview if it gets in the way of conversation and questioning.*

Maintain Eye Contact
Maintain eye contact with respondents in a normal way during note-taking. Just as eye contact personalizes other human communication, it also creates a more comfortable environment and facilitates the flow of information during interviews.

Opinions
Avoid making notes regarding your overall opinions or impressions of a witness. Such notes can cause problems with your credibility if they are later produced in court. Be careful not to show excitement when note-taking. During interviews of targets and adverse witnesses, take notes in a manner that does not indicate the significance of the information; that is, never allow note-taking to "telegraph" your emotions.

Writing Down Questions
Whenever possible, do not write down a list of interview questions. Let the interview flow freely. Inadvertently allowing respondents to read a written list of questions gives them an opportunity to fabricate answers. Writing down key points you want to discuss is appropriate, however.

Documenting Results
Document the results of the interview as soon as possible after its conclusion—preferably immediately afterward. If this procedure is followed, you will not have to take copious notes during the interview. Law enforcement officials are generally required to maintain notes. In the private sector, the notes can usually be destroyed once a memorandum has been prepared summarizing the interview. Check with legal counsel when in doubt.

Observing Respondent Reactions
Interviewers must be knowledgeable about respondents' behavior during interviews. Most nonverbal cues fall within one of four categories: proxemics, chronemics, kinetics, or paralinguistics.

Proxemics
Proxemic communication is the use of interpersonal space to convey meaning. The relationship between interviewer and respondent is both a cause and an effect of proxemic behavior. If the distance between interviewer and respondent is greater, they both tend to watch each other's eyes for clues to meaning.

Therefore, it is important that the conversation occur at an acceptable distance. Correct conversational distances vary from one culture to another. In the Middle East, the distance is quite short; in Latin America, equals of the same sex carry on a conversation at a much closer distance than in North America. Often, as the subject matter of the interview changes, interviewers can note the changes in the proxemic behavior of respondents. If respondents are free to back away, they might do so when the topic becomes unpleasant or sensitive.

Chronemics
Chronemic communication refers to the use of time in interpersonal relationships to convey meaning, attitudes, and desires. For example, respondents who are late in keeping appointments may convey a lack of interest in the interview or may wish to avoid it.

The most important chronemic technique used by interviewers is in their timing of questions. Effective interviewers control the length of pauses and the rate of their speech. This is called **pacing**. Interviewers can also control the length of time after respondents finish a sentence before they pose another question. This is called the **silent probe**.

Pacing is one of the principal nonverbal ways to set an appropriate mood. Tense interviewers often communicate anxiety by a rapid-fire rate of speech, which in turn can increase anxiety in respondents. To establish the more thoughtful, deliberative mood that stimulates free association, interviewers should strive to set a relaxed, deliberate pace.

Kinetics

Kinetic communication has to do with how body movements convey meaning. Even though posture, hands, and feet all communicate meaning, interviewers tend to focus their attention on the face and are more accurate in their judgments of others if they can see facial movements and expressions. When you concentrate on facial expressions, your primary interest is eye contact. Eye contact primarily communicates the desire to make or avoid communication. People who feel shame normally drop their eyes to avoid returning glances. This not only avoids seeing the disapproval but also conceals personal shame and confusion.

Paralinguistics

Paralinguistic communication involves the use of volume, pitch, and voice quality to convey meaning. One basic difference between written and verbal communication is that oral speech gives the full range of nonverbal cues. For example, a "no" answer may have different meanings depending on how the person says "no."

Theme Development

All questions should be nonaccusatory during the information-seeking phase. Nothing closes up the lines of communication in interviews like accusatory questions. Therefore, be sure to formulate your questions in a way that does not elicit strong emotional reactions. *Move from nonsensitive to sensitive.* If respondents start to become uncomfortable with the questioning, move on to a different area and return to the sensitive question later, but from a different vantage point.

Some people do not volunteer information; they must be asked. Do not be reluctant to ask sensitive questions after you have established the proper basis. If you pose the question with confidence and show that you expect an answer, respondents are much more likely to furnish the requested information. If you are apologetic or lack confidence in the question, respondents are much less likely to answer.

Transition Methodology

Once the introduction has been completed, you need a transition into the body of the interview. This is usually accomplished by asking respondents an easy question about themselves or their duties—for example:

"Can you tell me what it is that you do as far as quality control?"

Begin with Background Questions

Assuming that respondents do not have a problem answering the transitional question, you should then ask a series of easy, open questions designed to get them to talk about themselves.

Example

Interviewer: "What is your exact title?"

"What do your responsibilities involve?"

"How long have you been assigned here?"

"What do you like best about your job?"

"What do you like least about your job?"

"What would you eventually like to do for the company?"

Observe Verbal and Nonverbal Behavior

During the period when respondents talk about themselves, discreetly observe their verbal and nonverbal behavior. This allows you to establish a baseline for their behavior under little stress and will be discussed later in the chapter under the topic of **norming or calibrating**.

Ask Nonleading (Open) Questions

Open questioning techniques are used almost exclusively in the informational phase of interviews. The questions should seek information in a nonaccusatory way. Remember, the most effective questions are constructed as a subtle command.

Example

Interviewer: "Please tell me about _____."

"Please tell me about your current job procedures."

"Please tell me what paperwork you are responsible for."

"Please explain the chain of command in your department."

"Please tell me what procedures are in effect to prevent errors in the paperwork."

"Please explain what you understand to be the system of checks and balances (or internal controls) in your department."

"Please explain where you see areas that need to be improved in the system of checks and balances in your department."

Once respondents answer open questions, you can go back and review the facts in greater detail. If the answers are inconsistent, try to clarify them. But do not challenge the honesty or integrity of respondents at this point.

Approach Sensitive Questions Carefully

Words such as "routine questions" play down the significance of the inquiry. It is important for information-gathering purposes that you do not react excessively to respondents' statements. In the following example, the interviewer is talking to a potential witness and has decided to bring up the sensitive topic of a possible defalcation within the company. Several initial approaches could be used.

Example

Interviewer: "Part of my job is to prevent and uncover waste, fraud, and abuse. You understand that, don't you?"

|or|

"Please tell me where you think the company is wasting assets or money."

|or|

"Where do you think the company is vulnerable to someone here abusing his or her position?"

Dealing with Resistance

There is always the possibility that respondents will refuse a request for an interview. When the respondent and interviewer have no connection, studies show that as many as 65 percent of respondents will refuse an interview if contacted first by telephone. In contrast, one study concluded that only 33 percent of respondents are reluctant to be interviewed when contacted in person.[3] The more unpleasant the topic, the more likely respondents are to refuse.

Inexperienced interviewers sometimes perceive resistance when there is none. As a result, interviewers frequently become defensive. You must overcome such feelings to complete the interview. Here are some examples of resistance you may encounter and how to try to overcome them.

"I'm Too Busy"

When you contact a respondent without a previous appointment, the respondent may be too busy at the moment to cooperate. "I'm too busy" is also used to disguise the real source of the person's resistance, which may be lethargy, ego threat, or dislike of talking to strangers. Such objections can often be overcome by stressing the following:

- *The interview will be short.*
- *You are already there.*
- *The project is important.*

- *The interview will not be difficult.*
- *You need help.*

"I Don't Know Anything About It"

You will sometimes get this response immediately after stating the purpose of the interview. This resistance is typically softened by accepting the statement and then returning with a question. For example, if the respondent says, "I don't know anything," a potential response is:

Example

Interviewer: "I see. What do your duties involve, then?"

|or|

"Well, that was one of the things I wanted to find out. Do you know about internal controls, then?"

"I Don't Remember"

This is not always an expression of resistance. Instead, it can also express modesty, tentativeness, or caution. One of the best ways to respond here is to simply remain silent while the person deliberates. He or she is saying, in effect, "Give me a moment to think." If this is not successful, you can then counter by posing a narrower question.

Example

Interviewer: "I understand you may not remember the entire transaction. Do you remember if it was over $10,000?"

|or|

"It's okay if you don't remember the details. Do you remember how it made you react at the time?"

"What Do You Mean by That?"

When respondents ask this question, they may be signaling mild resistance. That is, they are attempting to shift the attention from themselves to you. They may also be stalling for time while they deliberate. Alternatively, they really may not understand your question. The best approach here is to treat the question as a simple request for clarification. Do not become defensive; doing so generally escalates the resistance.

Difficult People

Interviewers invariably encounter a few difficult people. Here are five commonsense steps to take with such individuals.

Don't React

Sometimes respondents give interviewers a "hard time" for no apparent reason. In reality, people refuse to cooperate for a multitude of reasons. The three natural reactions for interviewers who are verbally assailed by respondents are to strike back, give in, or terminate the interview. *Resist these reactions!* These tactics are not satisfactory; they do not lead to productive interviews. Instead, you should consciously ensure that you do not react to respondents' anger with hostility.

Disarm the Person

A common mistake is to try to reason with unreceptive people. Don't! Try instead to disarm them. Your best tactic is surprise. Stonewalling respondents *expect* you to apply pressure; attacking respondents *expect* you to resist. Disarming them surprises them—so simply listen, acknowledge the point, and agree wherever you can.

Change Tactics

In some situations, changing tactics is the only viable option to reduce hostility. This means recasting what respondents say in a form that directs attention back to the problem and to both your interests. This normally means that you ask respondents what they would do to solve the problem.

Make It Easy to Say "Yes"

In negotiating with difficult people, interviewers usually make a statement and attempt to get respondents to agree with it. A better choice is to agree with one of the respondent's statements and go from there. It is also better to break statements into smaller ones that are harder to disagree with. This helps the difficult person save face.

Volatile Interviews

Volatile interviews have the potential to elicit strong emotional reactions in respondents. Volatile interviews typically involve close friends and relatives of suspects, co-conspirators, and similar individuals.

The personalities of those involved in volatile interviews vary. Some individuals resent *all* authority figures; fraud examiners and law enforcement officers are authority figures.

Physical Symptoms

In volatile interviews, respondents typically react first—they don't think first. Additionally, they are often openly hostile to interviewers. People with high emotions often have dry mouths. Throat clearing is another sign of emotion. Restlessness may lead to fidgeting, shifting in the chair, and foot-tapping. People under emotional stress may perspire more heavily.

Other Considerations

It is best to use two interviewers in potentially volatile situations—there is strength in numbers. Additionally, two interviewers serve as corroborating witnesses in the event the interview takes a turn for the worse. Although information regarding who, what, why, when, where, and how still needs to be obtained, the order of the questioning varies from other types of interviews.

Use surprise in potentially volatile interviews. In many instances, volatile respondents are unaware that they are going to be questioned and will therefore be off guard. If you don't use surprise, you run the risk of the respondent not showing up, bringing a witness, or being present with coworkers or even counsel. In these interviews, ask questions out of sequence. This keeps volatile respondents from knowing exactly the nature of the inquiry and where it is leading. Although you will endeavor to obtain information regarding who, what, why, when, where, and how, ask your questions out of order. This technique is especially important in situations where respondents are attempting to protect themselves.

Hypothetical questions are less threatening; therefore, they are ideally suited for potentially volatile interviews. For example, suppose you are interviewing a suspect's boyfriend about his knowledge of her activities. Asking *"Did she do it?"* is a direct question. Instead, pose it as a hypothetical: *"Is there any reason why she would have done it?"*

Overcoming Objections

Volatile witnesses voice numerous objections to being interviewed. Here are some of the most common objections (along with suggested responses).

Example

Respondent: "Why should I talk to you?"

Interviewer: Say that you are trying to clear up a problem and that the respondent's assistance is important.

Respondent: "You can't prove that!"

Interviewer: Tell the person that you are not trying to prove or disprove; you are simply gathering information.

Respondent: "You can't make me talk!"

Interviewer: Tell the person that you are not trying to make him or her do anything; you are trying to resolve a problem and would deeply appreciate help.

Assessment Questions

Assessment questions seek to establish the credibility of the respondent. They are used only when interviewers decide that previous statements by respondents are inconsistent because of possible deception.

Once respondents answer all relevant questions about the event, and you have reason to believe they are being deceptive, establish a theme to justify additional questions. This theme can ordinarily be put forth by saying, "*I have a few additional questions.*" Do not indicate in any way that these questions are for a purpose other than seeking information.

Norming or Calibrating

Norming or **calibrating** is the process of observing behavior before critical questions are asked, as opposed to doing so during the questioning. Norming should be a routine part of all interviews. People with truthful attitudes answer questions one way; people with untruthful attitudes generally answer questions differently. Assessment questions ask for agreement on matters that are against the principles of most honest people. In other words, dishonest people are likely to agree with many of the statements, while honest people won't.

Assessment questions are designed primarily to get verbal or nonverbal reactions from respondents. Interviewers then carefully assess their reactions. Suggestions for observing the verbal and physical behavior of respondents include the following:

- *Use your senses of touch, sight, and hearing to establish a norm.*
- *Do not stare or call attention to the person's behavior.*
- *Be aware of the respondent's entire body.*
- *Observe the timing and consistency of behavior.*
- *Note clusters of behavior.*

On the basis of respondents' reactions to the assessment questions, interviewers then consider all the verbal and nonverbal responses together (not in isolation) to decide whether to proceed to the admission-seeking phase of the interview. Don't rely too heavily on the results of the assessment questioning.

Detecting Deception

It is said that everyone lies and that we do so for one of two reasons: to receive rewards or to avoid punishment. For most people, lying produces stress. When stress from lying occurs, the body attempts to relieve it through verbal and nonverbal reactions which can be used as cues that the individual is lying.

Unfortunately, cues to deception are not as reliable as Pinocchio's nose which grew every time he told a lie. If the cues were that reliable, detecting deception would be simple. Instead, cues to deception require points of comparison in order to detect them—thus the need for calibration. Also, both liars and truth tellers exhibit the cues used to detect deception but liars may exhibit a given cue more (or less) than they would if they were telling the truth (depending on the cue). Because of these facts, experts at detecting deception look for patterns in cues and notice changes in cue patterns under times of stressful questioning.

In some cases, cues for deception cannot be relied on. For example, someone who is mentally unstable or who is under the influence of drugs will usually be unsuitable to interview. Also, pathological liars may not exhibit stress as they lie. Some professional liars become familiar with interview techniques and are less likely to exhibit observable cues as they lie. Behavioral cues of juveniles are also unreliable. In many academic studies, the stakes for lying have been low and the cues were not found. Other studies show that under high motivation and in cases of transgressions, both of which are found in fraud interviews, the cues are more pronounced and reliable. Finally, it's important to note cultural factors. Some cultures, for example, discourage eye contact; while reduced eye contact is a reliable cue for many individuals, it won't be for those who have cultural backgrounds that discourage it.

Unfortunately, academic research has shown that most people, even those who purport to be experts at detecting deception (e.g., police officers) are only a little better than chance at using verbal and nonverbal cues for detecting deception. This should not be interpreted to mean that the cues are not useful. As it turns out, many cues have been found in research to be reliable; also, there are some real experts who have learned to use the cues reliably. However, many times either our intuition or our training on how to detect deception run counter to what research has found. Interestingly, those who study the real "wizards of deception detection" believe that the experts are highly motivated to improve and are constantly learning through practice and feedback.[4] They do not believe that there are any quick and easy techniques for detecting deception that can be learned in a one-day seminar; instead, careful practice and learning to look for patterns and comparisons lead to expertise in this skill. Next, we review many of the verbal and nonverbal cues for detecting deception with an emphasis on those that have been validated through academic research as referenced in the following sources.

Verbal and Nonverbal Cues

Verbal cues are those relating to wordings, expressions, and responses to specific questions whereas nonverbal cues include various body movements and postures accompanying the verbal reply. Extensive academic research suggests that verbal cues are more reliable predictors of deception than nonverbal cues. For example, in a comprehensive review of psychology research on cues to detection, the results showed that many cues have not been shown to be reliable; more importantly, of those that do appear reliable, about two-thirds are verbal.[5] Also, studies of people who are most effective at detecting deception show that they tend to rely on verbal cues more than nonverbal cues.

The basic premise that seems to best explain which cues are most reliable for detecting deception is that all people want to appear to be honest, whether they are telling the truth or lying. However, liars attempts to convey their honesty tend to be predictably different than those who are not under the stress of lying. For example, one reliable verbal cue is that a liar's story tends to be too good to be true whereas a truthteller's story will be told in such a manner that it will have normal imperfections. Even this cue is subject to the caveat that when the truthteller is under a fear that he or she will not be believed then he or she will exhibit the same cues as the deceiver.

The theory that best explains the research on cues to deception suggests that liars' attempts to appear honest will lead them to exhibit behaviors in five areas: (1) increased tension, (2) less positive and pleasant interactions, (3) less forthcoming responses, (4) less compelling tales and, as already mentioned, (5) fewer ordinary imperfections. Next, we discuss the cues to deception that have been found reliable.

Increased Tension Several verbal and nonverbal cues have been studied to determine if the stress of lying leads to noticeable increases in tension. The most reliable cues in this area are that liars' pupils tend to dilate more as they lie, they show increased overall nervousness or tension, their vocal tension increases, and the pitch of a liar's voice will increase compared to truthtellers. Also, liars who are discussing transgressions, such as an act of fraud, have been found to increase their rate of speech and to blink their eyes more often. Importantly, as mentioned in the following, liars may have longer pauses as they think through their story—assuming they haven't had time to construct a tale or borrow it from another experience; when they are talking they will tend to increase their rate of speaking—perhaps in an effort to catch up for their pauses.

Less Positive and Pleasant It turns out that those who are lying tend to become less cooperative; make more negative statements or complain more, saying things such as *"It's cold in here"*; and their facial expressions show more unpleasantness.

Less Forthcoming Responses Deceptive people often have a fine memory for insignificant events, but when it comes to the important facts, they "just can't seem to remember." In addition, liars often spend less time talking, and the amount of detail in their responses decreases. Interestingly, dishonest people are more likely to be very specific in their denials. For example, an honest person will offer a resounding "no—absolutely not" in reply to a question of whether they committed a fraud. In contrast, a dishonest person is more likely to "qualify" his or her denial such as *"No, I did not steal $15,000 from the company on June 27."* Other qualified denial phrases include *"To the best of my memory,"* and *"As far as I recall,"* or similar language. Interestingly, liars have also been found to press their lips more than those who are telling the truth.

Less Compelling Tales This area has the greatest number of cues that have been shown to be reliable for detecting deception. It turns out that dishonest people have more discrepancies in their tales; the logic in their stories is often flawed and the stories they tell are simply less plausible than those that are truthful. In short, they often sound too good to be true. Sometimes liars try to compensate for the flaws in their tales by adding what are known as "oaths" in an attempt to increase their credibility; for example, oaths such as *"I swear to God,"* *"Honestly,"* or *"To tell you the truth"* are believed to be used more frequently when lying. Liars may also attempt to provide character witnesses by saying things such as *"You can ask my wife if I'm honest."* They may also increase their use of respect by saying "*Sir*" or "*Ma'am*" more frequently.

Interestingly, people who are lying tend to be less engaging in their verbal and vocal emphasis as they relay their story. Similarly, their use of illustrators or hand movements decreases. Additionally, both their eye contact and foot and leg movements tend to decrease as well. They also tend to leave an impression that they are not certain of all the details and they seem more distant, impersonal, evasive or unclear in their descriptions. As such, the impression they convey is vague and they often speak more in a passive voice rather than an active voice.

Another way that liars' stories are less compelling shows up when they are accused of an act that they participated in. In responding, liars will be more likely to deny their participation in a weak manner. This is in contrast to when honest persons are accused of something they haven't done; they often become angry or forceful in their denial. The more they are accused, the more forceful is their denial. Upon repeated accusations, a liar's denials become weaker, even sometimes to the point where he or she becomes silent.

One interesting nonverbal cue that is also associated with this area is that liars tend to raise their chin more than truthtellers, perhaps in an effort to display confidence. They also tend to repeat words and phrases more frequently and even ask you to repeat your questions in order to have time to think of how to tell their tales.

Fewer Ordinary Imperfections In ordinary conversations, individuals often relay their stories in a way that is not perfect. For example, they may forget details and admit this in their discussion. They may also need to go back and correct something they said earlier. People who are concerned that someone may catch them lying have been shown to be less likely to exhibit these ordinary imperfections.

Methodology of Assessment Questions

If, based on all factors, you doubt the honesty of a respondent you can ask the following assessment questions. Note that these questions build from least sensitive to most sensitive. The initial questions seek agreement. Obviously, not all questions are asked in every situation.

In the following example, an interviewer is investigating missing funds. During a routine interview of one employee, the respondent makes several factually incorrect statements and his logic has flaws. The examiner then decides to ask a series of assessment questions

and observe the answers. Here is how the interviewer starts the questioning.

Assessment

Question 1

Interviewer: "Congress recently passed a law that allows for the levy of fines against companies that don't try to clean their own houses. Besides, when people take things from the company, it can cost a lot of money; so you can understand why the company's concerned, can't you?"

Explanation: The majority of people will say "yes" to this question. In the event of a "no" answer, you should explain the issue fully and, thereafter, attempt to get the respondent's agreement. If that agreement is not forthcoming, you should assess why not.

Question 2

Interviewer: "Of course, they are not talking about a loyal employee who gets in a bind. They're talking more about someone who is dishonest. But a lot of times, it's average people who get involved in taking something from the company. Do you know the kind of person we're talking about?"

Explanation: Most people read the newspapers and are at least generally familiar with the problem of fraud and abuse. Agreement by the respondent is expected to this question.

Question 3

Interviewer: "Most of these people aren't criminals at all. A lot of times, they're just trying to save their jobs or just trying to get by because the company is so cheap that it won't pay people what they're worth. Do you know what I mean?"

Explanation: Although both honest and dishonest people will probably answer "yes" to this question, honest people are less likely to accept the premise that these people are not wrongdoers. Many honest people will reply, "*Yes, I understand, but that doesn't justify stealing.*"

Question 4

Interviewer: "Who works here that would almost definitely not steal funds from the company?"

Explanation: Most individuals know of people who would be unlikely to commit a fraud. It may be the owner or an upper management person. However, those involved in a fraud will be less likely to want to eliminate others in an attempt to keep the circle of suspicion as large as possible.

Question 5

Interviewer: "Why do you think someone around here might be justified in taking company funds?"

Explanation: Because fraud perpetrators frequently justify their acts, dishonest people are more likely than honest people to attempt a justification such as, *"Everyone does it,"* or *"The company should treat people better if they don't want them to steal."* Honest people, on the other hand, are much more likely to say, *"There is no justification for stealing from the company. It is dishonest."*

Question 6

Interviewer: "How do you think we should deal with someone who got in a bind and did something wrong in the eyes of the company?"

Explanation: Similar to other questions in this series, honest people want to "throw the book" at the miscreant. They may say something like: *"They should be fired and prosecuted"* whereas guilty individuals are more likely to say, *"How should I know? It's not up to me."* Alternatively, those involved may say something that suggests an attitude of leniency such as: *"If they were a good employee, maybe we should give them another chance."*

Question 7

Interviewer: "Do you think someone in your department might have taken something from the company because the person thought he or she was justified?"

Explanation: Most people—honest and dishonest—answer "no" to this question. However, the culpable person will more likely say "yes" without elaborating—again in an effort to keep the circle of suspicion large. Honest people, if answering "yes," usually provide details.

Question 8

Interviewer: "Have you ever felt justified—even though you didn't go through with it—in taking advantage of your position?"

Explanation: Again, most people, both honest and dishonest, will answer "no." However, dishonest people are more likely to acknowledge having at least "thought" of doing it.

Question 9

Interviewer: "Who in your department do you believe would think they were justified in doing something against the company?"

Explanation: Dishonest people usually don't answer this question, saying instead, *"I guess anyone could have a justification if he or she wanted one."* Honest people may name names—albeit reluctantly.

Question 10

Interviewer: "Do you believe that most people will tell their manager if they believed a colleague was doing something wrong, like committing fraud against the company?"

Explanation: Honest people have a sense of integrity and are much more likely to report misdeeds. Dishonest people are more likely to say "no." When pressed for an explanation, they typically say, *"No, nothing would be done about it, and they wouldn't believe me anyway."*

Question 11

Interviewer: "Is there any reason why someone who works with you would say they thought you might feel justified in doing something wrong?"

Explanation: This question is designed to place the thought in the mind of a wrongdoer that someone has named him or her as a suspect. Honest people typically say "no." Dishonest people are more likely to try to explain by saying something like, *"I know there are people around here who don't like me."*

Question 12

Interviewer: "What would concern you most if you did something wrong and it was found out?"

Explanation: Dishonest people are likely to say something like, *"I wouldn't want to go to jail."* Honest people often reject the notion by saying, *"I'm not concerned at all, because I haven't done anything."* If an honest person does explain, it is usually along the lines of disappointing friends or family; dishonest people often mention punitive measures.

Closing Questions

Closing the interview on a positive note is a must in informational interviews. Closings serve several purposes. First, it is not unusual for interviewers to misunderstand or misinterpret statements of respondents. Therefore, interviewers should go over key facts to make certain they are accurate. The closing questions phase also seeks to obtain facts previously unknown. It provides respondents further opportunity to say whatever they want about the matter at hand. When you wind down an interview, make sure you do so positively. Then if you need to call the person back for another interview, he or she will not feel that you represent a threat.

If appropriate, ask if there are other documents or witnesses that would be helpful to the case. Do not promise confidentiality; instead, say, *"I'll keep your name as quiet as possible."*

People being interviewed often do not volunteer additional information regarding other witnesses or evidence. Therefore, the theme is to provide respondents opportunities to furnish further relevant facts or opinions. At the conclusion, attempt to determine which facts provided by the respondent are the most relevant. Do not go over all the information a second time.

Closing

Question 1

Interviewer: "I want to make sure I have my information straight. Let me take a minute and summarize what we've discussed."

Tip: Go over each key fact in summary form. The questions should be closed, so that the witness can respond either "yes" or "no."

Question 2

Interviewer: "You have known her eight years, correct?"

|or|

"You knew she had some financial problems, is that right?"

|or|

"You suspect—but don't know for sure—that she paid a lot of past due bills recently. Is that correct?"

Tip: On absolutely vital facts provided by the respondent, add "Are you sure?"

Question 3

Interviewer: "Are you sure?"

Tip: To obtain additional facts, ask respondents if there is something else they would like to say. This gives the correct impression that you are interested in all relevant information, regardless of which side it favors. Try to actively involve respondents in helping solve the case—*"If you were trying to resolve this issue, what would you do?"* This technique is sometimes called "playing detective." Another excellent closing question is: *"Is there anything that I haven't asked you that you think would be worthwhile for me to ask of you?"*

Tip: Ask respondents if they have been treated fairly. It is especially helpful to ask this question when respondents have not been cooperative or at the conclusion of an admission-seeking interview. Ask the question as if it were perfunctory. Ask if the respondent has anything else to say. This gives the respondent one final time to make a statement. Also, ask if you can call with any additional questions. It leaves the door open to further cooperation.

Tip: Leave the respondent a business card or telephone number. Invite the respondent to call about anything relevant. In some cases, try to obtain a commitment that the respondent will not discuss the matter. This step is not recommended with adverse or hostile respondents—it gives them ideas. Here is an example of the proper approach.

Question 4

Interviewer: "In situations like this one, people's reputations can suffer because of rumor and innuendo. We don't want that to happen, and neither do you. Therefore, I'd like your cooperation. Can I count on you not to discuss this until after all the facts are out?"

Tip: Shake hands with respondents, and thank them for their time and information.

Admission-Seeking Questions

Interviewers should ask accusatory or **admission-seeking questions** only when a reasonable probability exists that the respondent has committed the act in question. An assessment of culpability can be based on verbal and nonverbal responses to interview questions, as well as documents, physical evidence, and other interviews and evidence.

A transitional theme is necessary when you proceed from assessment to admission-seeking questions. The purpose of this theme is to suggest to miscreants that they have been caught. Some investigators recommend leaving the room for a few minutes, to "check on something." Then, if you have incriminating documents, place copies of them in a folder and bring them back to the room. When you return to the room, place the file folder on the desk, and ask the following question:

Example

Interviewer: "Is there something that you would like to tell me about _____?"

|or|

"Is there any reason why someone would say that you _____?"

Hand one or two of the documents to the respondent and ask for "comments." Do not introduce the evidence or explain it. In many cases, the miscreant will admit to incriminating conduct on the spot. If not, proceed.

Purpose of Questions

Admission-seeking questions have at least two purposes. The first is to distinguish innocent people from guilty ones. Culpable individuals frequently confess during the admission-seeking phase of interviews, while innocent people do not do so unless threats or coercion are used. In some instances, the only way to differentiate the culpable from the innocent is to seek an admission of guilt.

The second purpose is to obtain a valid confession. Confessions, under the law, must be voluntarily obtained. The importance of a valid and binding confession to wrongdoing cannot be overstated. Finally, the confessor should be asked to sign a written statement acknowledging the facts. Although oral confessions are as legally binding as written ones, written statements have greater credibility. They also discourage miscreants from later recanting.

Preparation

Schedule interviews when you can control the situation. Normally, do not conduct them on the suspect's "turf"; they are also best conducted by surprise.

Interview Room The location should establish a sense of privacy. The door should be closed but not locked, and there should be no physical barriers preventing the target from leaving. This avoids allegations of "custodial interrogation"—that you held someone against his or her will.

Keep distractions to a minimum. Ideally, there should be no photographs, windows, or other objects to distract attention. Place chairs about 4 to 6 feet apart, and do not permit the accused to sit behind a desk. Notes taken during the interview should be done in a way that does not reveal their significance.

Presence of Outsiders Do not suggest to the accused that he or she should have counsel present. Of course, this right cannot be denied. If counsel is present, you should have an understanding that he or she is an observer only; attorneys should not ask questions or object. Other than the accused and two examiners, no other observers are usually permitted in admission-seeking interviews. If the accused is a union member, a union representative may have the right to attend. However, this can present legal problems because it "broadcasts" the allegation to a third party. It is very difficult to obtain a confession with witnesses present. Examiners should therefore consider whether the case can be proven without a confession. If so, they may choose to omit the admission-seeking interview altogether.

Miranda Warnings Private investigators are not required to give Miranda warnings. Police are required to use them only if an arrest is imminent following the interview. Confessions are generally admissible in court if (1) they are obtained voluntarily and (2) interviewers have a reasonable belief that the confession is true. Always check with legal counsel.

Theme Development

People rarely confess voluntarily. However, they tend to confess when they perceive that the benefits of confession outweigh the penalties. Good interviewers, through the application of sophisticated techniques, can often convince respondents that a confession is in their best interest.

People generally will not confess if they believe that there is doubt in the mind of the accuser as to their guilt. Thus, you must convey absolute confidence in the admission-seeking accusation. This suggests that you should have removed most doubt in your own mind before attempting to obtain a confession. Make the accusation as a statement of fact. Accusatory questions do not ask: *"Did you do it?"* They ask: *"Why did you do it?"* Here is an example of an accusatory question:

"Is this the first time that you have taken from the company? Is this the first time you have created an overdraft?"

Innocent people generally do not accept this question's premise. People confessing need adequate time to come to terms with their guilt; obtaining admissions and confessions takes patience. Therefore, admission-seeking interviews should be done only when there is sufficient privacy and time is not a factor. Do not express disgust, outrage, or moral condemnation about the confessor's actions. Doing so goes against the basic strategy in obtaining confessions, which can be summed up as *maximize sympathy and minimize the perception judging the individual's morality.*

As this phase progresses, you should develop a theory as to how the perpetrator justified or rationalized the behavior. This justification is a morally acceptable reason for the confessor's behavior. Do not convey to the accused that he or she is a "bad person." Guilty people rarely confess under such conditions. Be firm, but also project compassion, understanding, and sympathy. Endeavor to keep the confessor from voicing a denial. Once the accused denies the act, overcoming that position will be very difficult.

It is generally considered legal to accuse innocent people of misdeeds they did not commit *as long as* the following holds:

- *The accuser has reasonable suspicion or predication to believe the accused has committed an offense.*
- *The accusation is made under conditions of privacy.*
- *The accuser does not take any action likely to make an innocent person confess.*
- *The accusation is conducted under reasonable conditions.*

But ALWAYS check with counsel.

Steps in the Admission-Seeking Interview

Effective admission-seeking interviews proceed in an orderly fashion. What follows is generally accepted as most likely to succeed in obtaining confessions. That said, the order always depends on the circumstances.

Accuse Directly

The accusation should not be a question, but a statement. Avoid emotionally charged words such as "steal," "fraud," and "crime" in your accusations. Phrase the accusation so that the accused is psychologically "trapped," with no way out.

Direct Accusations

Wrong

"We have reason to believe that you ..."

|or|

"We think (suspect) you may have ..."

Right

"Our investigation has clearly established that you:

- made a false entry (*avoid* "fraud").
- took company assets without permission (*avoid using* "theft," "embezzlement," or "stealing").
- took money from a vendor (*avoid* "bribe" *or* "kickback").
- have not told the complete truth (*avoid* "lie" *or* "fraud").

|or|

"We have been conducting an investigation into _____, and you are clearly the only person we have not been able to eliminate as being responsible."

Observe Reaction

When accused of wrongdoing, some miscreants react with silence. If the accused does deny culpability, these denials are often weak. He or she may almost mumble the denial. It is common for culpable individuals to avoid outright denials. Rather, they give reasons why they could not have committed the act in question. Innocent people will sometimes react with genuine shock at being accused. It is not at all unusual for an innocent person, wrongfully accused, to react with anger. As opposed to guilty people, innocent people strongly deny carrying out the act or acts in question.

Repeat Accusation

If the accused does not strenuously object to the accusation, repeat it with the same degree of conviction and strength.

Interrupt Denials

Both truthful and untruthful people will normally object to the accusation and attempt denial. It is very important in instances where you are convinced of the individual's guilt that the denial be interrupted. Innocent people are unlikely to allow you to succeed in stopping their denial.

It is important to emphasize that both the innocent and culpable will make outright denials if forced to do so. Accordingly, interviewers should not solicit a denial at this stage of the admission-seeking interview.

Interrupting Denials

Wrong

"Did you do this?"

|or|

"Are you the responsible person?"

Right

"Why did you do this?"

Delays

Delaying tactics are effective ways to stop or interrupt denials. Do not argue with the accused, but rather attempt to delay the outright denial. Innocent people will usually not "hold on" or let you continue to develop this theme.

Example

Interviewer: "I hear what you are saying, but let me finish first. Then you can talk."

Interruptions

Occasionally, you may have to repeatedly interrupt the accused's attempted denials. Because this stage is crucial, be prepared to increase the tone of your interruptions.

Reasoning

If the techniques discussed here are unsuccessful, you may attempt to reason with the accused and employ some of the tactics normally used for refuting alibis (see page XXX). In this situation, you present the accused with some of the evidence that implicates them. Do not disclose *all* the facts, but rather only small portions here and there.

Establish Rationalization

Once the accusation has been made and repeated and the denials have stopped, it is time to establish a morally acceptable rationalization that allows suspects to square their misdeeds with their conscience. This theme need not be related to the underlying causes of the misconduct. It is common and acceptable for suspects to explain away the moral consequences of the action by seizing on any plausible explanation other than being a "bad person."

If the accused does not seem to relate to one theme, continue with others until one seems to fit. Then develop that theme fully. Note that the theme explains away the moral—but not the legal—consequences of the misdeed. Interviewers are cautioned *not* to make any statements that would lead suspects to believe they will be excused from legal liability by cooperating. Interviewers must strike a balance between being in control of the interview and appearing compassionate and understanding. Again, regardless of the conduct the accused has committed, never express shock, outrage, or condemnation.

Unfair Treatment

Probably the most common rationalization for criminal activity in general (and fraud in particular) is in fraudsters' attempts to achieve equity. Studies show that counterproductive employee behavior—including stealing—is motivated primarily by job dissatisfaction. Employees and others feel that "striking back" is important to their self-esteem. Sensitive interviewers capitalize on these feelings by suggesting to suspects that they feel they are victims.

Example

Interviewer: "I know it isn't like you to do something like this without a reason. You've worked hard here to get a good reputation. I don't think the company has paid you what you're really worth. That's the way you feel, too, isn't it?"

|or|

"I've seen situations like this before. I think the company brought this on themselves. If you had been fairly treated, this wouldn't have happened, don't you agree?"

Inadequate Recognition

Some employees feel that their efforts have gone completely without notice. As with similar themes, interviewers strive to be empathetic.

Example

Interviewer: "I've found out a few things about you. It looks to me that you've given a lot more to this company than they recognize. Isn't that right?"

Financial Problems

Internal criminals, especially executives and upper management, frequently engage in fraud to conceal their true financial condition—either personal or business.

Aberration of Conduct

Many miscreants believe their conduct constitutes an aberration in their lives, and that it does not represent their true character. You can establish this theme using the following statements:

Example

Interviewer: "I know this is totally out of character for you. I know that this would never have happened if something unusual wasn't going on in your life. Isn't that right?"

|or|

"You've worked hard all your life to get a good reputation. I don't believe you would normally do something like this; it just doesn't fit. You must have felt forced into it. Is that how you felt?"

Family Problems

Some people commit fraud because of family problems—financial woes caused by divorce, an unfaithful spouse, or demanding children. Men in particular—who may be socially conditioned to tie their masculinity to earning power—may hold the notion that wealth garners respect. For their part, women often commit white-collar crime in response to the needs of their husbands and children. Skillful interviewers convert this motive to their advantage using one of the following approaches:

Example

Interviewer: "I know you've had family problems and your recent divorce has been difficult for you. I know how it is when these problems occur. You would have never done this if it hadn't been for family problems, isn't that right?"

|or|

"Someone in your position and with your ethics just doesn't do things like this without a reason. I think that reason has to do with trying to make the best possible life for your family. I know it would be difficult for me to admit to my family that we're not as well off as we were last year. That's why you did this, isn't it?"

Accuser's Actions

Don't disclose the accuser's identity if it is not already known. But in cases where the accuser's identity is known to the suspects, it is sometimes helpful to blame the accuser for the problem. The accuser can be a colleague, manager, auditor, fraud examiner, or any similar person, or the problem can be blamed on the company.

Example

Interviewer: "I really blame a large part of this on the company. If some of the things that went on around this company were known, it would make what you've done seem pretty small in comparison, wouldn't it?"

Stress, Drugs, Alcohol

Employees sometimes turn to drugs or alcohol to reduce stress. In some instances, the stress itself leads to aberrant behavior. The following rationalizations can work in these situations:

Example

Interviewer: "I know what you've done isn't really you. Inside, you've been in a lot of turmoil. A lot of people drink too much when they have problems When things build up inside, it sometimes makes all of us do something we shouldn't. That's what happened here, isn't it?"

|or|

"You're one of the most respected men in this company. I know you have been under tremendous pressure to succeed. Too much pressure, really. There is only so much any of us can take. That's behind what has happened here, isn't it?"

Revenge

Similar to other themes, revenge can also be effectively developed as a motive. In this technique, you attempt to blame the offense on suspects' feelings that they must "get back" at someone or something.

Example

Interviewer: "What has happened is out of character for you. I think you were trying to get back at your supervisor for the time he passed you over for a raise. I would probably feel the same. That's what happened, isn't it?"

|or|

"Everyone around here knows that the board has not supported you in your efforts to turn this company around. I would understand if you said to yourself, 'I'll show them.' Is that what happened?"

Depersonalizing the Victim

In cases involving employee theft, an effective technique is to depersonalize the victim. Suspects are better able to cope with the moral dilemma of their actions if the victim is a faceless corporation or agency.

Example

Interviewer: "It isn't like you took something from a friend or neighbor. I can see how you could say, 'This is okay to do since it's against the company, and not my coworkers.' Is that right?"

Minor Moral Infraction

In many cases, interviewers can reduce the accused's perception of the moral seriousness of the matter. To state again for emphasis, this is *not* to be confused with the legal seriousness of the act. Instead, play down the moral side. One effective way is through comparisons, such as the following.

Example

Interviewer: "This problem we have doesn't mean you're 'Jack the Ripper.' When you compare what you've done to things other people do, this situation seems pretty insignificant, doesn't it?"

|or|

"Everything is relative. What you've done doesn't even come close to some of the other things that have happened. You're not Ivan Boesky, right?"

Altruism

The moral seriousness of the matter can, in many cases, be deflected by claiming that the action was for the benefit of others. This is especially true if the accused views himself or herself as a caring person.

Example

Interviewer: "I know you didn't do this for yourself. I have looked into this matter carefully, and I think you did this to help someone, didn't you?"

|or|

"You have a big responsibility in this company. A lot of people depend on you for their jobs. I just know you did this because you thought you were doing the right thing for the company, didn't you?"

Genuine Need

In a very small number of cases, fraud is predicated by genuine need. For example, the accused may be paying for the medical care of sick parents or a child. Or some other financial disaster has befallen the miscreant. In these situations, the following statements can be effective:

Example

Interviewer: "I don't know many people who've had so many bad things happen all at once. I can see why you thought this was pretty much a matter of life or death, right?"

|or|

"You're like everyone else: you have to put food on the table. But in your position, it is very difficult to ask for help. You felt you needed to do this to survive, didn't you?"

Refute Alibis

Even when suspects are presented with an appropriate rationalization, they often continue to deny culpability. When interviewers succeed in stopping the denials, the accused will then normally turn to various reasons why they could not have committed the act in question. When this occurs, you should try to convince the accused of the weight of the evidence against him or her. Miscreants usually have a keen interest in material that implicates them. Alibis can be generally refuted using one of the methods listed here.

Display Physical Evidence

Guilty people frequently overestimate the amount of physical evidence in the interviewer's possession. You want to reinforce this notion in the way you lay out the evidence. Therefore, display the physical evidence—usually documents in fraud matters—one piece at a time, in reverse order of importance. In this way, suspects do not immediately comprehend the full extent of the evidence. When they no longer deny culpability, stop displaying evidence.

Each time a document or piece of evidence is presented, you should note its significance. During this phase, the accused is still trying to come to grips with being caught. Therefore, interviewers expect that suspects will attempt to explain their way out of the situation. Like denials, it's best to stop the alibis and other falsehoods before they are fully articulated. Once alibis are shown to be false, you can return to the theme being developed.

Discuss Witnesses

Discussing the testimony of witnesses is another way to refute alibis. The objective here is to give enough information about what other people will say without providing too much information. Ideally, your statement creates the impression in suspects' minds that many people are in a position to contradict their story.

Again, it's important not to furnish information that will allow a suspect to identify any of the witnesses. This places witnesses in a difficult position, and suspects may contact witnesses in an effort to influence testimony. Suspects sometimes take reprisals against potential witnesses, although this is rare.

Example

Respondent: "I couldn't possibly have done this. It would require the approval of a supervisor."

Interviewer: "In normal situations, it would. However, there are several people who will tell a completely different story. I can understand how you would want me to believe that. But you're only worsening the situation by making these statements. If you will help me on this, you'll also be helping yourself."

Present Alternatives

After suspects' alibis have been refuted, they normally become quiet and withdrawn. Some people in this situation may cry. If so, comfort them. Do not discourage them from showing emotion. At this stage, suspects are deliberating about confessing. Interviewers at this point should present an alternative question to the accused. This question forces suspects to make one of two choices. One alternative allows the accused a morally acceptable reason for the misdeed; the other paints the accused in a negative light. Regardless of which answer the suspect chooses, they are acknowledging guilt.

Example

Interviewer: "Did you just want extra money, or did you do this because you had financial problems?"

|or|

"Did you just get greedy, or did you do this because of the way the company has treated you?"

Benchmark Admission

Either way suspects answer the alternative question—"yes" or "no"—they have made a culpable statement, or **benchmark admission**. Once the benchmark admission is made, miscreants have made a subconscious decision to confess. The preceding questions are structured so that the negative alternative is presented first, followed by the positive one. In this way, suspects only have to nod or say "yes" for the benchmark admission to be made. They commonly answer in the negative.

Example

Respondent: "I didn't do it just because I wanted extra money."

|or|

"No, I'm not greedy."

In the cases where suspects answer the alternative question in the negative, you should press further for a positive admission.

Example

Interviewer: "Then you did it to take care of your financial problems?"

|or|

"Then you did it because of the way you've been treated here?"

Should the accused still not respond to the alternative question with the benchmark admission, repeat the questions, or variations thereof, until the benchmark admission is made. It is important that you get a response that is tantamount to a commitment to confess. Because only a commitment is sought at this point, the questions for the benchmark admission are constructed as leading questions. These questions can be answered "yes" or "no"; they do not require explanation. Explanations will come later.

Reinforce Rationalization

Once the benchmark admission is made, it is time to reinforce the confessor's decision. Then you can make the transition to the verbal confession, where the details of the offense are obtained. Reinforcing the rationalization developed earlier helps confessors feel comfortable, believing that you do not look down on them.

Verbal Confession

The transition to the verbal confession is made when suspects furnish the first detailed information about the offense. Thereafter, it is your job to probe gently for additional details—preferably including those that would be known only to the miscreant. As with any interview, there are three general approaches to obtaining the details: (1) chronologically, (2) by transaction, (3) or by event. The approach you take is governed by the circumstances of the case.

We recommend you first confirm the general details of the offense. For example, you will want the accused's estimates of the amounts involved, other parties to the offense, and the location of physical evidence. After these basic facts are confirmed, you can return to the specifics, in chronological order. It is imperative that you obtain an early admission that the accused knew that the conduct in question was wrong. This confirms the essential element of intent.

Because of the psychology underlying confessions, most confessors lie about one or more aspects of the offense, even as they confirm their overall guilt. When this happens during the verbal confession, make a mental note of the discrepancy and proceed as if you have accepted the falsehood as truthful. That is, save such discrepancies until the accused provides all other relevant facts. If the discrepancies are material to the offense, then you should either resolve them at the end of the verbal confession or wait and correct them in the written confession. If not material, such information can be omitted from the written confession.

The following items of information should be obtained during the verbal confession:

The Accused Knew the Conduct Was Wrong

As stated, intent is required in all matters involving fraud. Not only must confessors have committed the act but they may also have *intended* to commit it. This information can be developed as follows:

Example

Interviewer: "Now that you've decided to help yourself, I can help you, too. I need to ask you some questions to get this cleared up. As I understand it, you did this, and you knew it was wrong; but you didn't really mean to hurt the company, is that right?"

Facts Known Only to Confessor

Once intent is confirmed, questioning turns to those facts known only to the confessors. These facts include—at a minimum—their estimates of the number of instances of wrongful conduct as well as the total amount of money involved. The questions should not be phrased so that they can answer "yes" or "no."

Estimate of Number of Instances/Amounts

In fraud matters especially, it is common for suspects to underestimate the amount of funds involved, as well as the number of instances. This is probably because of our natural tendency to block out unpleasant matters. Take their figures with a grain of salt. If their response is *"I don't know,"* start high with the amounts and gradually come down.

Example

Interviewer: "How many times do you think this happened?"

Respondent: "I don't have any idea."

Interviewer: "Was it as many as 100 times?"

Respondent: "No way!"

Interviewer: "How about 75 times?"

Respondent: "That's still too high. Probably not more than two or three times."

Interviewer: "Are you sure?" (If respondents' estimates are too low, gently get them to acknowledge a higher figure. But do not challenge the accused by calling them liars.)

Respondent: "Maybe three times, but certainly not more than that."

Motive for the Fraud

Motive is an important element in establishing the crime. The motive may be the same as the theme you developed earlier—or it may not. The most common response is *"I don't know."* You should probe for additional information, but, if it is not forthcoming, then attribute the motive to the theme you developed earlier. The motive should be established along these lines:

Example

Interviewer: "We have discussed what led you to do this. But I need to hear it in your words. Why do you think you did this?"

When the Fraud Commenced

Interviewers need to find the approximate date and time that the fraud started. This information is usually developed by questions similar to the following:

Example

Interviewer: "I am sure you remember the first time this happened."

Respondent: "Yes."

Interviewer: "Tell me about it."

Respondent: "Around the middle of January of last year."

Interviewer: "I admire you for having the courage to talk about this. You're doing the right thing. Tell me in detail about the first time."

When/If Fraud Was Terminated

When the crime is fraud, especially internal fraud, the offenses are usually continuous. That is, miscreants seldom stop before they are discovered. If appropriate, interviewers should seek the date the offense terminated. The question is typically phrased as follows:

Example

Interviewer: "When was the last time you did this?"

Others Involved

Most frauds are solo ventures—committed without accomplices. Rather than ask if anyone else was "involved," phrase the question something like this.

Example

Interviewer: "Who else knew about this besides you?"

By asking who else "knew," you are in effect not only asking for the names of possible conspirators but also about others who knew what was going on but failed to report it. This question asks for specifics—not "Did someone else know?" but rather "Who else knew?"

Physical Evidence

Physical evidence—regardless of how limited it may be—should be obtained from perpetrators/confessors. In many instances, illicit income from fraud is deposited directly in their bank accounts. Interviewers typically want to ask confessors to voluntarily surrender

their banking records for review. Ask for either (1) a separate written authorization or (2) language to be added to the confession noting the voluntary surrender of banking information. The first evidence is preferable.

If other relevant records can be obtained only with the confessor's consent, seek permission to review them during the oral confession. In some instances, it may be advisable to delay this step until you obtain the written confession. The request for physical evidence from confessors can be set up as follows:

Example

Interviewer: "As part of wrapping up the details, I will need your banking records (or other physical evidence). You understand that, don't you?"

Respondent: "No, I don't."

Interviewer: "Well, I just need to document the facts and clear up any remaining questions. You have decided to tell the complete story, including your side of it. I just want to make sure the facts are accurate and you're not blamed for something someone else did. I want to report that you cooperated fully and wanted to do the right thing, okay?" (Avoid use of the word "evidence" or references to higher tribunals, for example, "courts" or "prosecutors.")

Respondent: "Okay."

Interviewer: "Where do you keep your bank accounts?" (If the interviewer knows of at least one bank where the confessor does business, the question should be phrased: "Where do you do business besides First National Bank?")

Respondent: "Just First National."

Interviewer: "I'll need to get your okay to get the records from the bank if we need them. Where do you keep the original records?" (Do not ask their permission to look at the records; simply tell them the records are needed. Let them object if they have a problem with this request.)

Disposition of Proceeds

If it has not come out earlier, find out what happened to any illicit income derived from the misdeeds. Typically, the money has long since been used for frivolous or ostentatious purposes. It is important, however, that confessors see their actions in a more positive light; you should therefore avoid comments or questions relating to "high living."

Example

Interviewer: "What happened to the money?" (Let the accused explain; do not suggest an answer unless they do not respond.)

Location of Assets

In appropriate situations, you will want to find out if there are residual assets that confessors can use to reduce losses. Rather than ask them: *"Is there anything left?"* the question should be phrased as: *"What's left?"*

Example

Interviewer: "What do you have left from all of this?"

Respondent: "Not much. I used most of the money to cover my bills and financial obligations. A little money and a car that is paid for is all I have."

Interviewer: "Well, whatever you have, you will look a lot better if you volunteer to return what you can. Does that make sense?"

Specifics of Each Offense

Once the major hurdles are overcome, interviewers then return to the specifics of each offense. Generally, you start with the first instance and work through chronologically in a logical fashion. Because these questions are information-seeking, they should be openly phrased so that the answer is independent of the question. It is best to seek the independent recollections of confessors first before you display physical evidence. If they cannot independently recall, use the documents to refresh their memory. It is generally best to resolve all issues on each instance before proceeding to the next. To determine the specifics of the offense, you can usually ask some of the following questions:

Example

Interviewer: "Who has knowledge of this transaction?"

"What does this document mean?"

"When did this transaction occur?"

"Where did the proceeds of the transaction go?"

"What was the purpose of the transaction?"

"How was the transaction covered up?"

Never promise immunity from prosecution. Confessors cannot be given immunity from prosecution by interviewers. There is a simple reason for this: Such promises can be interpreted as a way to unfairly extract statements that perpetrators would not have otherwise given.

Signed Statements

Verbal confessions should be reduced to short and concise written statements. Rarely should they exceed two or three handwritten pages. Interviewers prepare the statements (often in advance of the admission-seeking interview) and present them to the confessors for signature. Any necessary changes can be made in ink, with everyone present initialing the changes. Such endorsed changes often lend credibility that the signed statements are legitimate and were voluntarily given.

The following points should be covered in every signed statement:

Voluntariness of Confessions

Getting written admissions is difficult. Law that governs confessions requires that they be completely voluntary. This should be set forth specifically in the statement.

Intent

There is no such thing as an accidental fraud or crime. Both require, as key elements of proof, that fraudsters knew the conduct was wrong and intended to commit the act. This is best accomplished using precise language. The statement should clearly and explicitly describe the act—for example, *"I wrongfully took assets from the company that weren't mine,"* versus *"I borrowed money from the company without telling anyone."*

As a general rule, emotionally charged words, such as "lie" and "steal," should be avoided, because confessors often balk at signing statements that use these words. Here are some suggested wordings.

INSTEAD OF	USE
Lie	I knew the statement/action was untrue.
Steal	Wrongfully took the property of _____ for my own benefit.
Embezzle	Wrongfully took _____'s property, which had been entrusted to me, and used it for my own benefit.
Fraud	I knowingly told _____ an untrue statement and he/she/they relied on it.

Approximate Dates of Offense

Unless the exact dates of the offense are known, the words "approximately" or "about" must precede any stated dates. If confessors are unsure about the dates, include language to that effect.

Approximate Amounts of Losses

Include the approximate losses, making sure they are labeled as such. It is satisfactory to state a range (*"probably not less than $_____ or more than $_____"*).

Approximate Number of Instances

Ranges are also satisfactory for the number of instances. This number is important because it helps establish intent by showing a pattern of activity.

Willingness to Cooperate

When confessors perceive that the statement's language portrays them in a more favorable light, they have an easier time signing the statement. Confessors also convert this natural tendency to be seen favorably into cooperation and a willingness to make amends.

Example

"I am willing to cooperate in helping undo what I have done. I promise that I will try to repay whatever damages I caused by my actions."

Excuse Clause

Mention the confessor's moral excuse in the statement. This helps the accused believe he or she is being portrayed in the most favorable light. Make sure that the excuse clause wording does not diminish legal responsibility.

Example

Wrong

"I didn't mean to do this." (implies lack of intent)

Right

"I wouldn't have done this if it had not been for pressing financial problems. I didn't mean to hurt anyone."

Confessor Must Read Statement

Confessors must acknowledge that they read the statement; they should then initial every page in the statement. Some investigators show that the confessor read the entire statement by inserting intentional errors in the statement so that confessors will notice them as they read. The errors are then crossed out, the correct information inserted, and the confessor is asked to initial the changes. Whether this step is advisable depends on the likelihood that the confessor will attempt to claim the statement was not read.

Truthfulness of Statement

The written statement should state specifically that it is true. This gives it added weight in ensuing litigation. However, the language should also allow for mistakes.

Example

"This statement is true and complete to the best of my current recollection."

Key Points in Signed Statements

There is no legal requirement that statements must be in the handwriting or wording of declarants. Because examiners usually know how to draft valid statements, letting confessors draft the statement is generally not a good idea. A statement's wording should be precise. Declarants should read and sign the statement without undue delay. Do not ask confessors to sign the statement; instead, direct them—*"Please sign here."* Although there is no legal requirement, it is a good idea to have two people witness the signing of a statement.

There should be no more than one written statement for each offense. If facts are inadvertently omitted, they can later be added to the original statement as an addendum. For legal purposes, prepare separate statements for unrelated offenses. This rule applies because the target may be tried more than once (once for each offense). Preserve all notes taken during admission-seeking interviews, especially those concerning confessions. Access to pertinent notes aids in cross-examinations regarding the validity of signed statements. Stenographic notes, if any, should also be preserved. Once a confession is obtained, substantiate it through additional investigation, if necessary. A sample signed statement is included in Appendix 10 at the end of this chapter.

Honesty Testing

The most common inquiry method (and the most common of all investigation techniques) is the interview.

However, at least three other methods can also solicit information about a person's honesty: (1) pencil-and-paper tests, (2) graphology, and (3) voice stress analysis and polygraphs.

Pencil-and-Paper Test

Pencil-and-paper honesty tests are objective tests that elicit information about a person's honesty and personal code of ethics. They are used more frequently as employee screening devices than as tools to determine whether someone has committed a crime. Pencil-and-paper tests are considered to be between 50 and 90 percent accurate. Some of the more common ones are the Reid Report, the Personnel Selection Inventory, and the Stanton Survey. They use questions such as the following:

True/False 1. It is natural for most people to be a little dishonest.

True/False 2. People who are dishonest should be sent to prison.

Answers to these and similar questions create a profile of a person's personal code of conduct on which his or her risk to a business can be assessed. According to the developers of these tests, one of their advantages is that the results can be tabulated by a computer in a matter of minutes, making them ideal for applicant screening or initial identification of possible suspects. These kinds of tests are now used by a large number of retailers in the United States.

Graphology

Graphology is the study of handwriting for the purpose of character analysis. The use of graphology has increased substantially in recent years. Graphology is used in fields in which employee integrity is important, such as banking, manufacturing, and insurance. About 350 graphologists currently work as consultants to U.S. businesses. Note, however, that many fraud investigators are skeptical about the reliability of graphology.

Voice Stress Analysis and Polygraphs

Voice stress analysis determines whether a person is lying or telling the truth by using a mechanical device connected to the person. **Polygraphs** are more complicated than voice stress analyzers in that they attempt to assess stress, and hence lying, by measuring key physical responses. The theory is that people feel guilty when they lie or are dishonest. The guilt feelings produce stress, which results in changes in behavior. Polygraphs

measure pulse rate, blood pressure, galvanic skin response, and respiration. Like voice stress analyzers, polygraphs sometimes lead to incorrect decisions because they frighten innocent people. In addition, polygraphs rarely detect psychopathic liars. Why? These people feel no stress when they lie as they have suppressed their conscience to the point that they no longer feel stress.

The Employee Polygraph Protection Act passed a number of years ago has made the use of polygraphs more difficult. Although polygraphs are still legal, investigators must meet 11 conditions in order to use them—one of which is that investigators must inform suspects that they don't have to take the test if they don't want to do so.

Polygraphs and voice stress analyzers are only as good as the experts who administer them. In the hands of inexperienced administrators, they can be dangerous. Most experts agree that individuals who pass polygraph examinations are probably innocent, but that failure does not necessarily imply certain guilt.

STOP & THINK *How do you choose between traditional tests, graphology, voice stress analysis, and polygraphs? When is each method best used?*

The Fraud Report

Interrogation of suspect(s) is usually the final stage of an investigation. Once the investigation is completed, a fraud report is prepared. This report includes all findings, conclusions, recommendations, and corrective actions taken. The report indicates all pertinent facts uncovered relative to the who, what, where, when, how, and why of the fraud. It also includes recommendations for control improvements that will minimize exposure to similar occurrences in the future. It should not contain recommendations for disciplinary or legal action against anyone suspected of fraudulent or illegal activity, even when the investigation provides tenable evidence of probable culpability and/or complicity.

Particular care should be exercised to ensure that the general tone of the fraud report is neither accusatory nor conclusive as to guilt. Even when a confession of culpability or complicity is obtained during a fraud investigation, such confessions may not be considered valid or consequential evidence of guilt of fraud until a court of law decides. This is true even when management has already taken disciplinary action on the basis of the confession. Reports that refer to a confession obtained in the course of the investigation should state merely that admission of the alleged or suspected events was obtained—not that guilt was acknowledged. Attention to language is crucial here to ensure that subjective, inflammatory, libelous, or other prejudicial connotations are absent. To be objective, factual, unbiased, and free from distortion, reports should refer to "alleged" irregularities, activity, conduct, and so forth. Accordingly, the activities investigated and reported should be described as "purported" or "alleged" to have occurred. When findings support the allegations, couch reports in language such as the following:

- *The investigation disclosed the existence of reasonably credible evidence to support the allegation.*
- *The investigation concludes with a rebuttal presumption that the allegations or suspicions are tenable.*
- *The investigation concludes with plausible evidence in support of the allegation.*

Appendix 10 at the end of this chapter details an investigation of an employee fraud and an appropriate fraud report. This completed report covers the investigation of "Ivan Ben Steelin," a real estate purchasing representative who worked for "Silver Summit Real Estate." Ivan accepted kickbacks from a company called "Red Hot Real Estate"; he also inflated real estate prices as part of the scheme.

The fraud investigation documented by the report involved all four types of investigation procedures. The investigation was predicated on an anonymous tip received in a letter addressed to the company president. The investigation began with a review of the suspect's personnel records. It included one procedure to investigate the theft (surveillance of the suspects at a local restaurant) and several procedures to investigate the concealment (including computer searches of company databases, calculations of total purchase transactions by each real estate buyer, and determinations of the number of real estate agencies used, average price per acre paid, and the number of purchase transactions made with each vendor). The report documents the public records searches and net worth conversion. Searches were made of voter registration and marriage records, the secretary of state's records, as well as the real estate and contracting office records at the county level. Query procedures involved neutral interviews with the company's personnel manager, a home builder, and a company secretary, as well as a friendly interview with another real estate buyer and a hostile interview with the real estate agent who was suspected

of making illegal payments to Ivan Ben Steelin. The interrogation of Ivan (in order to gain access to his bank records) led to a signed confession. The investigation concluded with a signed confession statement and calculation of real estate overpayments (losses) by the company.

The report exemplifies the types of procedures and documentation that fraud investigations often include. We encourage you to read it carefully.

Review of the Learning Objectives

- **Understand the interviewing process.** You will conduct three types of interviews: (1) friendly, (2) neutral, (3) and hostile. Interviews help obtain information to establish elements of the fraud, develop leads for other evidence, gain cooperation of victims and witnesses, and determine backgrounds and motives of witnesses.

- **Plan and conduct an interview.** Interviews should be pointed, planned conversations to reach certain goals. Plan your demeanor, the language of the interview, the question typology, the elements of the conversation, and the questions to ask. Be aware of the inhibitors and facilitators of communication.

- **Understand the nature of admission-seeking interviews.** Use this type of interview only when you are confident that the respondent has committed the act in question. These interviews make statements and accuse directly. The goal is to elicit confessions from perpetrators.

- **Describe the different deceptions and lies used by perpetrators.** Good interviewers watch for indications that respondents are not answering truthfully. They look for patterns of verbal and nonverbal cues that have been found in research to be valid indicators that a person is lying.

- **Describe the different types of honesty testing.** Honesty testing can help identify when some respondents are lying. Become familiar with the advantages and disadvantages of pencil-and-paper tests, graphology, voice stress analysis, and polygraphs.

- **Prepare a fraud report.** The final report includes all findings, conclusions, recommendations, and correct actions to be taken. Wherever possible, fraud investigations should conclude with a signed confession of guilt from the perpetrator(s) and an accurate calculation of the extent of the theft and losses. The confession and the loss calculation, as well as the fraud investigation techniques used, must be carefully documented so that civil, criminal, and other actions can be supported. See the appendices to this chapter for example statements and fraud reports.

KEY TERMS

interview, p. 276
catharsis, p. 282
inhibitor, p. 283
induction, p. 284
deduction, p. 284
custom, p. 284
habit, p. 284
circular reaction, p. 284
acute emotional crisis,
   p. 284
facilitators of
   communication, p. 284
rapport, p. 285
informational
   questions, p. 288
controlled-answer
   techniques, p. 289
free narrative, p. 289
proxemic
   communication, p. 290
chronemic
   communication, p. 290

pacing, p. 290
silent probe, p. 290
kinetic communication,
   p. 291
paralinguistic
   communication,
   p. 291
volatile interviews, p. 293
assessment questions,
   p. 294
norming, p. 294
calibrating, p. 294
admission-seeking
   questions, p. 299
benchmark admission,
   p. 304
Pencil-and-paper
   honesty tests, p. 309
graphology, p. 309
voice stress analysis,
   p. 309
polygraphs, p. 309

QUESTIONS

Discussion Questions

1. What is an interview?
2. What are the five reactions of interviewees?
3. What are the five general types of questions that an interviewer can ask?
4. What are some of the different elements of communication?
5. What is an inhibitor of communication?
6. What are facilitators of communication?
7. What are informational questions?
8. What is meant by the "question sequence"?
9. What is a volatile interview?
10. What is the purpose of assessment questions?

11. What is norming or calibrating?
12. What are the three types of honesty testing?

True/False

1. Paper-and-pencil honesty tests are most frequently used to determine whether someone has committed a crime.
2. Failure to pass a polygraph test means certain guilt.
3. Interviews during the rationalization stage are often not objective and can be harmful to the potential prosecution efforts.
4. The general tone of a fraud report should be neither accusatory nor conclusive as to guilt, even if the suspect has confessed his or her involvement in the crime.
5. An interviewer should always be sympathetic and respectful during an interview.
6. Confrontational interviews should always be conducted even if there is no evidence that can be obtained from the suspect.
7. Telling a significant lie and getting away with it during an interview is usually very difficult if the interviewer is well trained.
8. If a suspect continually repeats phrases, words, or your questions, it could be a verbal cue that he or she is lying.
9. The fraud report should include recommendations for disciplinary action.
10. The interview should always take place at the interviewee's place of work.
11. Fraud reports should only list findings that do not negatively impact the company.
12. The first reaction to crisis is denial.

Multiple Choice

1. Which of the following is *not* a method of honesty testing?
   a. Graphology.
   b. Voice stress analysis.
   c. Body language test.
   d. Pencil-and-paper test.
2. Interviews should *not* be conducted with:
   a. Suspects.
   b. Coworkers.
   c. Clients.
   d. Interviews can be conducted with all of the above.

3. People in the rationalization stage of reaction to a fraud:
   a. Make great interviewees because they want to punish the suspect.
   b. Want to give the suspect one more chance.
   c. Believe without a doubt that the suspect is guilty.
   d. Have no sympathy for the suspect.

4. Planning for interviews should *not* involve:
   a. Judging the guilt of the suspect based on available documents.
   b. Establishing a location and time for the interview.
   c. Ascertaining in advance as many facts as possible about the offense.
   d. Understanding the attitude of the interviewee.

5. Confrontational interviews should usually be conducted when:
   a. Police decide that the suspect is guilty.
   b. The examiner is starting the investigation.
   c. All other investigative procedures have been completed.
   d. The investigation is taking too long.

6. Which of the following is *not* an inquiry technique that should be used by interviewers?
   a. Use short questions, confined to one topic.
   b. Maintain full control of the interview.
   c. Point out some, but not all, of the circumstantial evidence.
   d. All of the above are good inquiry techniques in an interview.

7. Which of the following honesty testing techniques deals with the study of handwriting for the purpose of character analysis?
   a. Polygraph.
   b. Graphology.
   c. Pencil-and-paper test.
   d. Voice stress.
   e. None of the above.

8. Which of the following traits do polygraphs *not* measure when testing for stress?
   a. Pulse rate.
   b. Blood pressure.
   c. Galvanic skin response.
   d. Respiration.
   e. All of the above are traits measured during a polygraph test.

9. Interviewing is:
   a. The systematic questioning of individuals who have knowledge of events, people, and evidence involved in a case under investigation.
   b. The process of answering questions from an interviewer for the purpose of finding a job.
   c. By far the most common technique used in investigating and resolving fraud.
   d. Both a and c.
   e. None of the above.

10. Which of the following is the typical sequence of reactions to a crisis?
    a. Anger, denial, rationalization, depression, acceptance.
    b. Rationalization, denial, anger, depression, acceptance.
    c. Denial, anger, rationalization, depression, acceptance.
    d. Depression, denial, anger, rationalization, acceptance.
    e. None of the above.

11. Which of the following reactions frequently involves appearing temporarily stunned, insisting there is some mistake, or not comprehending what has been said?
    a. Anger.
    b. Denial.
    c. Rationalization.
    d. Depression.
    e. Acceptance.

12. Which of the following is a characteristic of a good interview?
    a. Make the interview as concise as possible.
    b. The interviewer should announce his or her bias at the outset, because the interviewee will cooperate better when the interviewee knows the type of information the interviewer is seeking.
    c. Friendly interviewees appear very helpful, but they may have hidden motives and may provide bad information.
    d. It is important to schedule interviews ahead of time, especially if you are planning to interview a potentially hostile interviewee.

13. Each of the following is a clue that an interviewee is dishonest except:
    a. Upon repeated accusations, a dishonest person's denials become more vehement.
    b. In order to add credibility to false statements, liars request that the interviewer obtain character testimony from other people.
    c. Liars often refuse to implicate possible suspects—or, in other words, honest people are more willing to name others involved in misdeeds.
    d. Dishonest people frequently cover their mouths with their hands or fingers during deception.

14. Which of the following is something that an interviewee might do or feel while in the denial phase?
    a. Insult, harm, or slander.
    b. Attempt to justify the act.
    c. Become sad, withdraw, or lose interest.
    d. Not comprehend what has been said.
15. Which of the following is *not* a good thing to do during an interview?
    a. Conduct the interview in private.
    b. Establish the purpose of the interview.
    c. Interview more than one person at once.
    d. Do not invade body space.
16. A signed statement should include all of the following except:
    a. A statement that the fraudster knew the conduct was wrong and intended to commit the act.
    b. The date the fraudster was hired by the company.
    c. Approximate amount of losses.
    d. Approximate date of the offense.
17. Nonverbal cues of deception include all of the following except:
    a. Repetition of the question.
    b. Dilated pupils.
    c. Raised chin.
    d. Decreased foot and leg movements.

SHORT CASES

Case 1

Jim has been a faithful employee of Daddy's Denture, Inc. (DD) for four years. He has held various positions where he handles receipts, credit memos, and other accounting records. Along with recently added responsibilities, Jim has discovered more opportunity to commit fraud.

Over the past three months, Jim figured out that he can create fictitious vendors and write checks from DD to these fictitious vendors and deposit the checks in a new bank account he opened under a false name. Jim put this plan into action and has so far stolen $7,000 from DD.

One day, Jim had to call in sick. A coworker, Judd, assumed Jim's responsibilities for the day. As Judd reconciled cashed checks, he noticed that Jim endorsed many of them himself. Judd doesn't believe what he sees. In fact, he leaves the reconciling for Jim to finish when he returns to work.

When Jim returns to work, everything seems normal at first. However, it eventually dawns on Judd that he caught Jim in the act of stealing. Judd becomes angry and confronts Jim. When Judd mentions the endorsements, Jim is dumbfounded and denies being dishonest. After Judd leaves, Jim gets angry, thinking, "What right did he have to take over my duties?" and "I'll be fired for sure!"

Back in his office, Judd continues to think about Jim's dishonesty. He decides that Jim is just human, and that he let himself slip this once. Judd decides he should let the issue pass and just hope that Jim realizes his gig is up. Judd believes that Jim is a basically good guy and will probably reconcile his misdoings and return to honest ways. Later that night, Judd feels sad knowing that his good friend, Jim, has done such a bad thing.

Meanwhile, Jim decides he shouldn't be angry with Judd. Judd is, after all, only doing what he's been told to do by his superiors. Jim feels horrible about what he has done, not to mention the fact that he got caught. He decides to fess up and let his boss know what he has been doing before he gets into any more trouble.

Name the five reactions to crises and briefly describe how both Jim and Judd proceeded through each phase.

Case 2

Your father-in-law owns a medium-sized air conditioning company in Meza, Arizona. Because of the heat in Arizona, the company has done rather well and the business is continually growing. Your father-in-law has received tips from other employees that one of the technicians, Damon, is disgruntled and has been padding his paycheck through different internal frauds against the company. Your father-in-law noticed that while things seem to be running more efficiently, the company has not been more profitable and so you have been helping him for the last month run secret audits as part of the internal investigation. Through your investigation, you have discovered that Damon has stolen $50,000 over the last three years through the following methods:

1. Damon regularly uses the company gas card to fill up his personal pickup truck and his family's minivan.
2. Damon takes A/C units from inventory and sells them to people he knows at cost.
3. Damon sells auxiliary A/C parts, but pockets the money from the sale without including the sale on the invoice.
4. Damon often goes home from a job on Fridays after lunch, but claims on his weekly report that he worked until 5 p.m.

Think of how you would confront Damon; you have known him for two years and already have a working relationship. Specifically, what types of questions would you ask while you are talking with him? The evidence you have gathered in your investigation would support your decision to fire Damon; however, a written confession would help your court case if you decided to charge Damon for damages.

Case 3

Adam Jones, the purchasing manager for ACME Corporation, is under suspicion for committing fraud. His superiors believe he is accepting kickbacks and bribes from various vendors. As the company's fraud expert, you are investigating this possible fraud and are preparing to interview Adam. You suspect that Adam will be defensive and possibly hostile when interviewed.

1. What investigation procedures should be completed before your admission-seeking interview with Adam?
2. If you find evidence that proves Adam is committing fraud at ACME, what might his initial reaction be when he is confronted? What other emotions and/or reactions might you expect from Adam? How do you know this?

Case 4

An accountant for a small business is suspected of writing checks to "dummy" vendors and collecting the money himself. After a thorough investigation of the company, you determine that the company does not require authorization for vendor payments. In an interview with the suspect, you ask him if any controls are in place that could prevent someone from writing fraudulent checks. He quickly responds in the affirmative.

1. What type of questions could you ask next?

Case 5

Mike Trujillo has been involved in a serious relationship with his high school sweetheart, Bonny, for five years; they have even discussed marriage. One day, Bonny told Mike that she was seeing another man. Obviously, this was very difficult for Mike.

Over the course of the next few months, Mike had a bumpy ride emotionally. Initially, he simply couldn't believe it. He frequently caught himself thinking about Bonny as if they were still together. After a few days, Mike became bitter. He cut up all her pictures except for one. He hung that one on a dartboard and threw darts at it for hours. As his bitterness subsided, he looked for reasons why the breakup was actually beneficial. He told himself it was a blessing that he wouldn't have to support Bonny's rich tastes anymore and that things were turning out for the best. However, during the next six months, Mike just couldn't get excited about dating other girls. He made himself go on dates, but he never really liked any of the girls he dated. He felt empty and didn't know how to fill the void in his heart. But after a few months, Mike bounced back and started to take an interest in other women. Within four months, he found Amy, the girl of his dreams, and they got married about a year later.

1. What reactions do most people have to crises? How did Mike display these reactions?
2. How does Mike's experience relate to fraud examination?

Case 6

You manage a division that recently discovered a suspected fraud involving accounts receivable. For the past week, you and the internal auditors have been collecting documents, gathering information, and quietly interviewing personnel. It is now time to interview the suspect, who is your accounts receivable manager. She has access to cash receipts and the accounts receivable ledger and has allegedly stolen $4,000 over the last year by writing off small accounts as uncollectible.

Pair up with another student in your class. One of you should take the part of the interviewer; the other, the role of the suspect. Develop a brief outline on how you will conduct your interview. Remember that your task as the interviewer is to remain in control of the interview, but at the same time be sympathetic and understanding. If deemed appropriate, prepare a short written confession statement like the example given in the chapter. Swap roles after the first interview and apply what you learned in a second interview.

Case 7

You are an internal auditor at Dunder Company. An employee of Dunder has phoned in an anonymous tip that a fellow worker, Jane, might be embezzling money. Jane has been a trusted employee of the company for 13 years; she quickly moved through the ranks of the company because of her exemplary record, and she is now vice president in charge of treasury. Your internal audit team has conducted thorough audits of her department for years and found its control environment to be exceptional. In addition, she is a good friend of the CEO and CFO. They have tremendous confidence in her abilities and honesty, and she is being groomed to succeed the current CFO when he retires.

The person making the anonymous tip claims to have noticed large fluctuations in certain financial statement accounts. Accompanying these fluctuations are unexplainable debits and credits that were all entered by Jane. The person also alleges that Jane's behavior has been erratic. She is usually kind and patient, but recently, she has flown off the handle for no explainable reason. She insists on balancing certain accounts herself because she claims that they are too critical to trust with anyone else. Finally, the informant believes that Jane's lifestyle as a single mother is well above what her salary can support.

Investigating allegations against such a trusted person in the company will cause considerable disruption. If you investigate, you will have to proceed very carefully, especially since you have only the word of one employee who could have ulterior motives.

1. Describe the steps you would take to investigate this suspected embezzlement.
2. As a first step in your investigation, would you interview Jane about the problem? Why or why not?
3. How would you conduct Jane's admission-seeking interview in order to be most effective?

Case 8

You have been talking with your best friend, John, for the past couple of weeks about a crisis in his company. He has just learned that his boss has been embezzling money for the past six months. The day he learns about the alleged fraud, he calls to tell you the news. In the telephone conversation, John tells you how much he respects his boss and that his boss is his mentor. You note that his voice seems distant, and he doesn't respond well to your questions. Later that week, you meet John for lunch. His demeanor is completely changed since you last spoke with him. After a few drinks, John can't stop bad-mouthing his boss. John also makes a few insulting comments about you. You decide to leave him alone for a few days until he feels better.

A week later, you again meet John for lunch. The subject of the fraud comes up, and John's attitude is again considerably changed. Instead of being angry, he compares his boss's life to his own. You think it a bit odd when John says, "I completely understand why he did it. His family life was suffering, his job was in jeopardy, and his mom just died. Given the same circumstances, I might have done the same thing." You finish lunch and go your separate ways. Later that week, John

calls you again. This time, he tells you that he could have prevented the fraud. He feels embarrassed that it happened right before his eyes.

A week later, you ask John if there are any new developments in the investigation. He tells you that he is helping with the investigation by providing all the facts he knows and his observations over the last few months. Now all John wants is to move on.

1. Identify John's reactions to the fraud, and explain each stage in detail.

Case 9

As a result of the system audit performed by one of the Big 4 accounting firms at Deming Medical corporate offices, it was discovered that Paula, one of the payroll supervisors, had system access rights to transaction codes used by the HR staff. Consequently, it was determined that Paula took advantage of the situation and created a fake employee to whom she was issuing a paycheck every two weeks; only the checks went to Paula's banking account. Andrew Jacobsen, an investigator working on the case, did extensive research, details of which led him to believe that Paula was embezzling. Andrew is about to go in for a final interview with Paula. Paula had been interviewed before and denied she was involved in the embezzling scheme.

1. What interviewing tactics should Andrew use to get Paula to admit she was stealing from Deming?
2. How would he know whether she tells him the truth?

Case 10

While auditing the accounts payable of a large clothing manufacturer, you discover that four of the company's vendors have checks sent to a post office (PO) box. After further investigation, you discover that one box is registered under the same name as the CFO's son, and another is registered under the same name as his daughter—aged 3 and 5, respectively. Finding this highly suspicious, you begin questioning the employees who work directly with the CFO to determine if fraud is occurring in this case. After searching through the documentation of vendor transactions, the investigation leads you to suspect that the CFO is sending checks to the PO box of fictitious vendors to be collected and then deposited in his own account.

Over two weeks, you and your engagement team compile a large body of evidence implicating the CFO in the fraud. After this evidence has been gathered, you ask him to come to your office for questioning.

Upon his arrival, and without wasting any time, you present all the evidence against him and ask him about his involvement in stealing money from the company. The responses you receive are defensive and antagonistic. The CFO says that he has heard that you and your engagement team have been "snooping" around the office, protests his innocence, and threatens to file suit against you for slander and libel if you pursue this absurd investigation that is trying to label him a criminal. Not expecting this reaction, and being frustrated that the interview is not going as you intended, you say that you have had enough for one day and cut the interview short.

1. What steps need to be taken before interviewing a person you suspect of committing fraud in a company?
2. What are some effective methods that could have helped in dealing with an interview subject from whom you are seeking an admission?

CASE STUDIES

Case Study 1

A small group of dockworkers in California, working for Topside Industries, an international shipping company, was being investigated concerning its involvement in a theft. The theft itself was a rather simple operation. The dock hands unloading foreign-made products acted in collusion with their supervisors in order to steal certain items, which they marked on official invoices as "missing" or "damaged" due to shipping. They later sold the items on the black market and split the money between the conspirators. The fraud was discovered when Longstreet Enterprises' Asian subsidiary contacted Meade about an unusual number of microwaves that were lost during shipment from Korea to Long Beach.

Young Mr. Sherman, the newest member of Meade's security team, decided to simultaneously interview Mr. Lee and Mr. Jackson, two dockworkers, concerning their involvement in the fraud.

Never having actually met Sherman, Lee and Jackson were simply instructed to wait in the "interrogation" room in the security shop. Lee and Jackson arrived promptly at 8 a.m., dressed in their work clothes, and were seated. Via the intercom, they were told not to leave until Sherman gave them explicit permission to do so. Sherman did not enter the room until 9:30 a.m. He was escorted into the room by a burly security guard carrying a nightstick.

Lee, annoyed at Sherman's tardiness, blurted out, "Hey, man, we have to get back to work. I'm not getting paid for time off the dock!"

Sherman made no reply. He only paced the room for what seemed an eternity to Jackson. Finally, Sherman moved deliberately and directly over to a chair on Lee and Jackson's side of the table. Sherman pulled his chair within inches of the two men being interrogated and straddled the chair so that the back of the chair supported his arms.

"Lee, do you know what they did with pirates in pre-colonial Virginia?" asked Sherman. Lee shrugged a little bit and was struggling for an answer when Sherman interrupted. "They were executed in the gallows, and then their bodies were hung in iron cages on the shores of the bay as an example to would-be thieves and pirates. Not a pretty picture, is it, Lee?" Lee was at a visible loss for words.

Pulling two pens and two pieces of paper from his coat pocket and slamming them onto the table, Sherman raised his voice and said, "Now let's cut through the crap. You dockies are guilty as hell. We've got a paper trail a mile long to prove it along with surveillance tapes and written confessions from Hill and Grant. Do yourselves a favor and write out your confessions. If you don't, I might just have to leave you here with Bruno. And if you physically assault him and he beats you silly, well then it'll be your word against his, comprende? Oh, yeah, you'll still be under investigation for grand theft."

Questions

1. Name at least three mistakes that Sherman made in interviewing Lee and Jackson.
2. The chapter identifies some of the characteristics of a good interview. In what ways could Sherman have changed the interview?
3. What were some of the threats and claims made that Sherman could not prove? Is it ever acceptable to make a threat that involves physical violence?
4. The book identifies specific locations where interviews should take place. Is the "interrogation room" one of those places? Where should Sherman have met with Lee and Jackson?

Case Study 2

It is early Monday morning, and Brian is preparing to conduct his first interview as a fraud examiner. He is to meet with Sue, a laborer in the factory his firm is investigating. She is neither a suspect nor thought to be connected with the fraud. Her name simply came up in another investigator's interviews as someone who might be able to provide additional insight. They have arranged to meet at Brian's office, so he is simply awaiting her arrival.

"Hello," he hears someone say through his partially open door. "I'm Sue."

"Come in," he replies, remaining seated behind his large, oak desk. She enters and takes the empty seat across the desk from Brian. "Let me get right to the point," are his next words. "Are you aware of any reasonably credible or plausible evidence that the allegations of embezzlement at your place of employment are tenable?"

After a brief pause and a look of concern on Sue's face, Brian asks, "Do you know what embezzlement means?"

"Yes," replies Sue.

"Okay, then, do you know anyone who has embezzled from your employer?"

"No."

Sue becomes nervous as she sees Brian begin to take notes on a pad. He continues, "Specifically, have you seen Ralph perpetrating fraud?"

"No."

"Are you sure? You know that this is a big deal," he says as he stands and begins to pace around the room. "I can't imagine why anyone would steal from his own company, but he deserves to be caught if he has. It's wrong and bad, and only a horrible person would do something like this."

"I'm sure."

"Have you embezzled?"

"No," Sue states again.

"Well, then, I don't see any reason to continue. Goodbye."

Sue stands, excuses herself, and leaves the room.

Questions

1. What are some of the things Brian did wrong during this interview?

Case Study 3

James began working for NewCo nearly 20 years ago, where he has been working as the facility and maintenance supervisor. During the past 20 years, NewCo has experienced significant growth, and James has played a major part in helping move along the expansion plans. Because of his great service and abilities, James is greatly respected in the company. Although he has been very helpful to the company, he was forced to leave due to severe health problems.

Earl was called in to replace James after he was released. James's sudden departure prevented Earl from working with James and learning the proper policies and procedures James had put into place before he left. The lack of training created a problem for Earl, who was faced with finishing the projects James had started. The major project James left was a construction project where the price had already been determined but no work had begun. Unfortunately, Earl could not find any contractor information, nor could he find any of James's contacts.

As Earl continued to search, he realized that he was in more trouble than he thought because there were no records available for any of the work that James had performed. The lack of information forced Earl to bid the contract out to a new contractor. When Earl received the new bid and presented it to management, they were surprised to find that the new price was 30 percent less than the original bid.

Management believed the new bid price was wrong and questioned Earl to ensure that he had included all of the requirements for the project. Once management determined he had, it began to ask more questions. In looking around and reviewing some of his previous activities, management realized that he was no longer bidding out projects but rather giving them to specific contractors. When reviewing these contractors, management found that it had no information for the contractors on file—no addresses, phone numbers, or even tax ID numbers. All management had was a name, and from that information, accounts payable cut a check and James delivered the checks personally.

Based on this new information, management began to question other employees about James's activities. It found that others considered him very secretive and that he refused to allow anyone to work with him on his projects. Others told management that James had also recently become very violent and erratic with many of the employees. Because of the number of red flags, management has called you in to investigate James's previous activities.

Questions

1. Which people would you interview first and why?
2. What type of information would you seek?
3. How would you approach each of the different individuals?
4. Due to James's frail condition, how would you approach the interview process and investigation?

INTERNET ASSIGNMENTS

1. Go to the site www2.fbi.gov/publications/leb/1996/oct964.txt and read the article about statement analysis, which discusses interviewing and how to know whether a person is lying or not. This article examines the case of Susan Smith, who killed her two sons by strapping them into a car and pushing the car into the river. The article uses Susan's statements to discuss four components of statement analysis that can help investigators known when a person is lying. Outline the four components of statement analysis and give a short definition of each.

2. Using a search engine, find four Web sites that identify different techniques for interviewing. What characteristics or elements are the most recognizable or most distinctive? What are the most common techniques discussed across the Web sites?

3. Many universities and private companies offer courses in interviewing techniques. Find an online advertisement for one of these courses. What primary techniques does the course teach?

4. Many Internet sites contain honesty tests for screening applicants or existing employees. Most of these sites charge a fee for their services, but they do provide an easy, quick way to test employees. A Web site with a free employment honesty test is http://testyourself.psychtests.com/testid/2100. This honesty test will give you an idea of the kinds of questions asked on employment honesty tests and what information can be derived from the answers. Take the test and obtain the results. Analyze the questions and try to determine why they are being asked. Do you think this is an accurate test? Why or why not?

DEBATES

1. The Employee Polygraph Protection Act passed by Congress made it difficult to use polygraphs in fraud investigations. Currently, 11 conditions must be met in order for polygraph tests to be used.

Assume you are a member of Congress debating the use of polygraphs. Discuss both sides of the issue and make *your* recommendation. Would you make it easier or harder to obtain permission to use a polygraph?

2. You and another fraud examiner are debating whether it is ethical to "lie" during an admission-seeking interview (such as claiming to have compelling evidence of guilt when you don't) to get a confession. You believe it is okay to lie. Your co-worker believes it is unethical and even illegal to be deceptive. Who is correct?

END NOTES

1. We would like to thank the Association of Certified Fraud Examiners and Chairman Joseph Wells, in particular, for allowing us to use their interview material in this book. Much of the initial text in this chapter was taken from their self-study course on interviewing, *Beyond the Numbers: Professional Interview Techniques* (Austin, TX), 1998.

2. See, for example, the works of Elizabeth Kübler Ross, such as *On Death and Dying*, which stresses that we are all operating at a psychological steady state and that crises knock us off that equilibrium (www.elisabethkublerross.com).

3. *Beyond the Numbers: Professional Interview Techniques* (Austin, TX), 1998: 38.

4. See, for example, M. O'Sullivan and P. Ekman, "The Wizards of Deception Detection." in *The Detection of Deception in Forensic Contexts*, edited by P. A. Granhag and L. A. Stromwall, Cambridge University Press, 2004.

5. See, for example, B. M. DePaulo, J. Lindsay, B. E. Malone, L. Muhlenbruck, K. Charlton, and H. Cooper, "Cues to Deception," in *Psychological Bulletin*, 2003, Vol. 129, No. 1, pp. 74–118 and the chapter by B. M. DePaulo and W. L. Morris in the book referenced in Endnote 4.

APPENDIX A

Sample Signed Statement

Sample Signed Statement

December 14, 20XX
Edison, New Jersey

I, Dominique Santana, furnish the following free and voluntary statement to Scott Barefoot of Major Electronics, Inc. No threats or promises of any kind have been used to induce this statement.

I am a cashier at Major Electronics, Inc. Part of my duties include processing and posting cash payments, sales, returns, and allowances, as well as handling cash. Commencing in early 2007 and continuing through the current time, I have taken about $7,000 in cash from the company, knowing the cash was not mine.

I took the company's money by creating fictitious merchandise returns, forging the signature of my manager, and posting the fictitious return to the computer. I then took out the resulting cash from the register. Later, I split the money with my boyfriend, Jerry Garza, who works here in the store. He knew what I was doing and helped me several times by signing a three-part return slip as if the merchandise had been returned when it had not. Most of the time, this scheme involved my own account. I bought televisions and other merchandise using my employee discount. I then sold them to outsiders for cash. Afterward, I prepared a document showing the television was returned when it was not.

Other than my boyfriend, Jerry, no one in the store knew what I was doing. I am aware my conduct is illegal and violates the policies of Major Electronics, Inc. I participated in this scheme because I have had severe financial problems and my mother has been ill. I am truly sorry for my conduct and promise to repay all losses. Some of the company's cash was deposited in my personal account, number 436-9241-7881 at the First National Bank, Edison, New Jersey. I hereby grant Scott Barefoot or representatives from Major Electronics permission to examine the account and to obtain copies of statements, checks, and deposits from First National Bank for the period January 1, 1999, to the present.

I have read this statement consisting of this page. I now sign my name below because this statement is true and correct to the best of my knowledge.

_____   _____
Signature: Witness:

_____   _____
Date   Date

An Example Fraud Report

INVESTIGATIVE REPORT
ON IVAN BEN STEELIN

Silver Summit Real Estate

Internal Audit (or Corporate Security)
Special Cases File
030369

Silver Summit Real Estate
Internal Audit Special Cases File
(IASCF) 030369

Regarding
Ivan Ben Steelin

FILE INDEX

Silver Summit Real Estate

To: IASCF 030369
From: Scott R. Bulloch
Date: January 2, 2008
Re: Ivan Ben Steelin
Subject: Unsigned letter regarding Ivan Ben Steelin

On December 28, 2007, Vic Tumms, president and CEO of Silver Summit Real Estate, received an unsigned letter. The letter, dated December 27, 2007, referred to Ivan Ben Steelin. The letter, presented on page 2, is self-explanatory.

On December 30, 2007, the letter and its contents were discussed in a meeting at which Scott R. Bulloch (Silver Summit Real Estate's internal auditor), Vic Tumms, and Sue U. Buttz (Silver Summit Real Estate's legal counsel) were present.

Predicated on the contents of the letter, an investigation was commissioned by Sue U. Buttz, and was set to commence on January 1, 2008.

The original letter was initialed by Scott R. Bulloch and is maintained as evidence in IASCF 030369.

1

Silver Summit Real Estate

December 27, 2007

Mr. Vic Tumms
President
Silver Summit Real Estate
5511 Vero Beach Road
Denver, Colorado 84057

Dear Mr. Tumms:

I believe you should investigate the relationship between Ivan Ben Steelin, the real estate acquisition manager, and Red Hot Real Estate. I believe we paid significantly more than fair market value for the 200 acres we purchased in the river bottom, as well as for several other properties.

Sincerely,

A Concerned Associate

_____

1-1-2007

2

Silver Summit Real Estate

To: IASCF 030369
From: Scott R. Bulloch
Date: January 3, 2008
Re: Ivan Ben Steelin
Subject: Interview with Rebecca Monson

Synopsis

Rebecca Monson, personnel manager of Silver Summit Real Estate, advised on January 2, 2008, that Ivan Ben Steelin had been employed at Silver Summit Real Estate since January 7, 2000. Steelin's salary in 2007 was $45,000, and his supervisor was RaNae Workman, vice president of external affairs.

Details

Rebecca Monson, personnel manager of Silver Summit Real Estate, was interviewed at her office, 5511 Vero Beach Road, Denver, Colorado, telephone (999) 555-3463, on January 2, 2008. Rebecca was advised of the identity of the interviewers, Scott R. Bulloch and Sue U. Buttz, and provided the following information. Rebecca was advised that the nature of the inquiry was an "internal query of misconduct," as per the company's code of conduct.

The personnel records reflect that Ivan Ben Steelin, white male, date of birth August 5, 1970, social security 999-06-2828, residing at 1156 North Ocean Boulevard, Denver, Colorado, telephone (999) 225-1161, had been employed at Silver Summit Real Estate since January 7, 2000. According to the records, Steelin was married and had four children.

Steelin's initial salary was $38,000 per year, and he was an investment analyst in the external affairs department. Steelin was enlisted in the management training program on his hire date. His supervisor after he became an investment analyst was Mickey Sheraton, vice president of external affairs.

On January 1, 2002, Steelin was promoted to a purchasing representative position, still in the external affairs department. Steelin's salary was $45,000 per year, as reflected by the 2007 salary file.

RaNae Workman became vice president of external affairs in August of 2003 and was Ivan's immediate supervisor.

3

According to the records, prior to his employment with Silver Summit Real Estate, Ivan Ben Steelin was employed by Rockwell Laboratories in St. Louis, Missouri. His reason for leaving Rockwell Laboratories, as stated on the personnel information card, was that he wanted to be closer to his family in Colorado.

No background investigation was conducted by the company prior to hiring Steelin at Silver Summit Real Estate.

First National, Second National, Third National, and Fourth National Banks called in February 2003 to confirm Steelin's employment with Silver Summit Real Estate. The personnel department enters the nature of the inquiry in the personnel database each time an outside party asks about employees. No other parties have requested information about Steelin since February 2003.

The original personnel information card and a copy of outside party inquiries (consisting of two pages), were obtained from Rebecca Monson and initialed and dated by Scott R. Bulloch. They are maintained in IASCF 030369. Copies were left with Rebecca Monson.

Rebecca Monson was advised to keep the interview and its issues confidential.

4

Personnel Information Card

Hire date: January 7, 2000   Social Security Number: 999-06-2828
Name: Steelin, Ivan Ben   Birth date: August 5, 1970

Address at time of hire:
   1156 North Ocean Boulevard
   Denver, CO 80234

Emergency Contact:
   James Clintock   Relation: Father-in-law
   1145 North 8000 West   (999) 555-7974
   Denver, CO 80231

Previous Employers

Rockwell Laboratories   Position: Sales agent
66 Market Street   Supervisor: Jeff Cole, Sales Manager
St. Louis, MO 63101   Dates: 1994-2000

Reason for leaving: Would like to be closer to family in Colorado.

Ethics University   Position: Mail courier
Denver, CO 80223   Supervisor: Joseph Starks, Mail Manager
                               Dates: 1991-1994

Reason for leaving: Graduated from Ethics University and accepted a position in
St. Louis.

Ivan Ben Steelin   *1-7-2000*
Signature   Date

Administrative Use Only
Background Check: No
Other: None

sb
1-2-2008

5

Outside Party Inquiries
Print date: January 3, 2008
Employee: Ivan Ben Steelin
File: 528062828

Date	Party	Contact	Purpose
2/2/03	First National Bank	Loan department	Confirm employment
2/4/03	Second National Bank	None given	Confirm employment
2/12/03	Third National Bank	Loan department	Confirm employment
2/16/03	Fourth National Bank	Credit department	Confirm employment

sb
1-2-2008

6

Silver Summit Real Estate

To: IASCF 030369
From: Scott R. Bulloch
Date: January 4, 2008
Re: Ivan Ben Steelin
Subject: Search of voter registration and marriage license records

Voter Registration

Voter registration records were examined on January 4, 2008, to confirm the information about Ivan Ben Steelin maintained by Silver Summit Real Estate's personnel department. The registration records substantiated that Steelin's address was 1156 North Ocean Boulevard, Denver, Colorado, 80234. Social security number, phone number, and date of birth were the same as maintained by the personnel department at Silver Summit Real Estate.

Marriage License

The marriage license of Mr. Steelin was inspected on January 4, 2008, at the Moore County Clerk's office. Ivan Ben Steelin was married to Clara Clintock on July 1, 1991. The records indicated that no previous marriages existed for either Mr. or Mrs. Steelin. The marriage license of Steelin revealed that his wife's parents, James and Jennifer Clintock, live at 1145 North 8000 West, Denver, Colorado, 80231—the address of Ivan Steelin at the time he was hired by Silver Summit Real Estate.

7

Silver Summit Real Estate

To: IASCF 030369
From: Scott R. Bulloch
Date: January 5, 2008
Re: Ivan Ben Steelin
Subject: Search of records at the Colorado secretary of state's office

The office of the secretary of state was visited on January 5, 2008, to survey:

- Business license records
- The UCC Records

Business License Records

It could not be determined whether Steelin had ever sought a business license in the state of Colorado. A computer search on Prentice Hall's national database did not provide information that would substantiate that Steelin had held a business license in any other state in the United States.

Uniform Commercial Code Records

The UCC records for Ivan Ben Steelin, 999-06-2828, 1156 North Ocean Boulevard, Denver, Colorado, reported the following information:

- Steelin made an acquisition of a boat at Ron's Boats, 25000 North State Street, Denver, Colorado, on November 12, 2004. The record reflected that a loan was not secured against the acquisition, though the cost of the boat was $23,000.
- On May 1, 2004, a purchase was made at Lund Furniture, 1400 West 1200 North, Denver, Colorado. The record reflects that the purchase, secured on store credit, cost a total of $9,425, with the acquisition items being the collateral for the credit. The purchase items consisted of:
  One (1) 44-inch Mitsubishi television set.
  One (1) Samsung home entertainment center.
  One (1) Broyhill bedroom set.
- On July 1, 2005, two automobiles were leased from Quickie Auto Imports, 1400 South State Street, Denver, Colorado, 80233.
  Auto 1: Audi 100, four-wheel-drive, VIN AUDI1234567891014.
  Auto 2: Subaru Legacy wagon, VIN SUBA1234567892024.
  The bargain purchase price, pending the end of the lease, was $45,000 less the cumulative lease payments of $1,150 per month.

8

- Cellular Three Telephone, 2200 Martin Parkway, Denver, Colorado, sold merchandise to Ivan Steelin on July 13, 2005. The record does not reflect that the acquisition was collateralized, though the cost was $2,000.
- Roger Tones Motors, 1275 South University Avenue, Denver, Colorado, sold one automobile to Ivan Ben Steelin on December 19, 2006. The automobile was partially paid for through a dealer loan, with the automobile being the collateral. The auto was a 2006 Volkswagen Passat Turbo touring sedan, VIN VW987654321123459. The purchase price was $26,497, and the amount of the loan was $10,000.
- On June 28, 2007, Bullard Jewelers Company, 1100 North University Avenue, sold merchandise on credit to Ivan Ben Steelin. The collateral to the purchase was the acquired merchandise, with the credit being extended by US Jewelers Credit Corporation of Denver, Colorado. The total cost of the acquisition was $8,200, with $4,000 being the credit amount. The description of the items identified:
    One (1) ring with 1.24 carat diamonds.
    Two (2) earrings, each with a 1.5 carat diamond.

9

Silver Summit Real Estate

To: IASCF 030369
From: Scott R. Bulloch
Date: January 7, 2008
Re: Ivan Ben Steelin
Subject: Search of real estate records

On January 7, 2008, the Moore County Land Office and the Moore County Tax Assessor's Office were visited to determine Ivan Ben Steelin's real estate holdings and their respective values.

County Land Office

The property records of Moore County, Colorado, indicate that Ivan Ben Steelin's real estate holdings consist of:

- 1.1 acres of improved property located at 1156 North Ocean Boulevard, Denver, Colorado, 80234.

As cited by the County Land Office records, Steelin acquired the property on April 4, 2003, from Red Hot Real Estate. The records maintain that the property, consisting of 1.1 acres of land and one single-family dwelling, is indebted to Fourth National Bank. The amount of the indebtedness was not available from these records.

County Tax Assessor's Office

The Moore County Tax Assessor's office records show a total tax base on the improved property, 1156 North Ocean Boulevard, Denver, Colorado, held by Ivan Ben Steelin, to be $275,000. The legal description of the property is as follows:

- 1.1 acres of property, with sewer and water.
- 4,100-square-foot single-family dwelling, built from building permit 19883000, issued on May 1, 2003.

The status of the tax payments, as reflected in the records, is that Steelin is current for his annual assessment.

10

Silver Summit Real Estate

To: IASCF 030369
From: Scott R. Bulloch
Date: January 8, 2008
Re: Ivan Ben Steelin
Subject: Search of records at the Moore County Contracting Office

On January 8, 2008, building permit 19883000 was examined at the Moore County Contracting Office.

The permit revealed the following information:

- The permit was issued to Ivan Ben Steelin on May 1, 2003.
- The designated licensed contractor on the building permit was Well's Custom Homes.
- The permit was for a single-family dwelling to be constructed at 1156 North Ocean Boulevard, Denver, Colorado, 80234.

The records accompanying the permit revealed that the dwelling passed code requirements and was available to be occupied on October 28, 2003.

11

Silver Summit Real Estate

To: IASCF 030369
From: Scott R. Bulloch
Date: January 8, 2008
Re: Ivan Ben Steelin
Subject: Interview with Jack Wells, owner of Wells Custom Homes

Synopsis
Jack Wells, owner of Wells Custom Homes, telephone (999) 222-1212, was interviewed over the phone on January 8, 2008. Wells revealed that the charge for building Ivan Ben Steelin's home at 1156 North Ocean Boulevard, Denver, Colorado, was $240,000.

Details
Jack Wells, owner of Wells Custom Homes, was interviewed over the phone on January 8, 2008. Wells was advised of the identity of the caller, Scott R. Bulloch, but not of the nature of the inquiry or of Scott R. Bulloch's position.

Wells stated that custom home construction is charged to clients on a square-foot basis. He stated that the average charge is $60 to $75 per square foot.

Wells remembered building a home for Ivan Ben Steelin. He stated that Steelin's home had been one of the first built by Wells Custom Homes. He revealed that the charge to Ivan Ben Steelin was $240,000.

Wells stated that payment had been received through a construction loan at Fourth National Bank, and that full payment had been received upon the house's passing the code requirements.

12

Silver Summit Real Estate

To: IASCF 030369
From: Scott R. Bulloch
Date: January 9, 2008
Re: Ivan Ben Steelin
Subject: Net worth analysis of Ivan Ben Steelin

Synopsis
On January 9, 2008, Scott R. Bulloch and Sue U. Buttz performed a net worth analysis of Ivan Ben Steelin. The analysis revealed, conservatively, that Mr. Steelin may have had estimated income from unknown sources of $17,000, $22,000, $34,000, and $23,000 in the years 2004, 2005, 2006, and 2007, respectively.

Details
On January 9, 2008, Scott R. Bulloch and Sue U. Buttz performed a net worth analysis of Ivan Ben Steelin. Conservative estimates and interpolations were made with regard to Mr. Steelin's assets and liabilities. The estimates and interpolations were derived from information acquired through public records, interviews, and personnel records maintained by Silver Summit Real Estate.

The net worth analysis indicated that Mr. Steelin may have had unknown sources of income in the amounts of $17,000, $22,000, $34,000, and $23,000, in the years, 2004, 2005, 2006, and 2007, respectively.

Attached is the worksheet that details the process of determining the above-stated figures. The worksheet consists of one page; it was initialed by Scott R. Bulloch and is maintained in IASCF 030369.

13

Net Worth Analysis

	2004	2005	2006	2007
Assets:				
Home	$275,000	$275,000	$275,000	$275,000
Cars	5,000	45,000	70,000	70,000
Boats	23,000	23,000	23,000	23,000
Furniture and other	10,000	20,000	20,000	28,000
Total assets	$313,000	$363,000	$388,000	$396,000
Liabilities:				
Home	$240,000	$240,000	$240,000	$240,000
Cars	0	45,000	55,000	55,000
Boats	0	0	0	0
Furniture and other	10,000*	10,000	10,000	14,000
Total liabilities	$250,000	$295,000	$305,000	$309,000
Net worth	$ 63,000	$ 68,000	$ 83,000	$ 87,000
Net worth increase	$ 10,000*	$ 5,000	$ 15,000	$ 4,000
Living expenses:				
Mortgage	$ 24,000	$ 24,000	$ 24,000	$ 24,000
Food, etc.	15,000	15,000	15,000	15,000
Cars	0	12,000	15,000	15,000
Total living expenses	$ 39,000	$ 51,000	$ 54,000	$ 54,000
Income	$ 49,000	$ 56,000	$ 69,000	$ 58,000
Known sources of income (net of taxes)	32,000	34,000	35,000	35,000
Funds from unknown sources	$ 17,000	$ 22,000	$ 34,000	$ 23,000

*Determined from 2003 figures, which are not provided.

sb
1-9-2008

14

Silver Summit Real Estate

To: IASCF 030369
From: Scott R. Bulloch
Date: January 11, 2008
Re: Ivan Ben Steelin
Subject: Average prices per acre paid by Silver Summit Real Estate

Synopsis
The records of the external affairs department were analyzed to track the average prices that each of the purchasing representatives has negotiated per acre of real estate purchased. Ivan Ben Steelin's average price is 23 to 42 percent higher than the average prices of the other three purchasing representatives.

Details
Four real estate purchasing representatives are employed by Silver Summit Real Estate. Each of the representatives is assigned purchasing tasks by the vice president of external affairs. The purchasing representative then initiates contacts and proceeds to fulfill his or her respective purchasing assignments.

The assignments are distributed equally among the four representatives. The records show that each representative executed the same number of real estate transactions as his or her counterpart representatives in the years 2004, 2005, 2006, and 2007.

A real estate purchasing project, for example (project 033189), to acquire 55 acres at 2000 North 8000 West, Boulder, Colorado, in 1995, revealed the following information:

- The 55-acre lot was owned by three different parties.
- Each of the three properties was listed by three different agencies, Red Hot Real Estate, Johnson Real Estate, and Monarch Real Estate, respectively.
- Steelin negotiated with Red Hot Real Estate, Peter Principle with Johnson Real Estate, and B.J. Integrity with Monarch Real Estate.
- Peter Principle's purchase of 21 acres cost $12,000, B.J. Integrity's purchase of 20.5 acres cost $10,500, and Steelin's purchase of 13.5 acres cost $10,000.

Data were gathered from purchase agreements, according to the purchasing representative, to determine the average price per acre of the real estate purchased. The data compilations revealed that Steelin's purchases were 23 to 42 percent higher than the purchases of the other purchasing representatives.

Attached (one page) are the data compilations extracted from the records of the external affairs department, as they pertain to the average prices per acre of real estate purchased. Scott R. Bulloch initialed and dated the document, and it is maintained in IASCF 030369.

15

Average Prices Paid per Acre of Real Estate Purchased by
Silver Summit Real Estate

Purchasing Representative	2004	2005	2006	2007
Abraham Honest	515	535	543	576
B.J. Integrity	507	532	571	561
Peter Principle	555	567	581	592
Ivan Ben Steelin	678	775	898	988

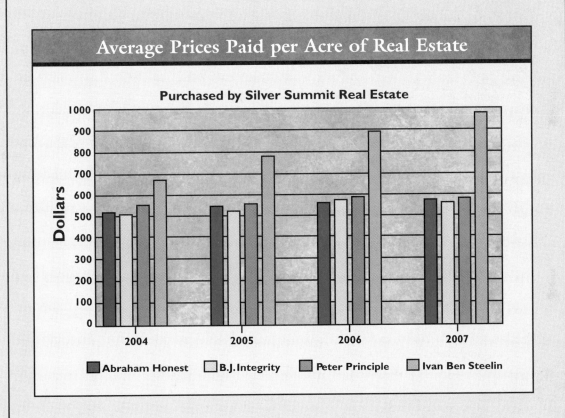

Average Prices Paid per Acre of Real Estate

Purchased by Silver Summit Real Estate

sb
1-11-2008

16

Silver Summit Real Estate

To: IASCF 030369
From: Scott R. Bulloch
Date: January 13, 2008
Re: Ivan Ben Steelin
Subject: Computer queries on Steelin's transactions with real estate agencies

Synopsis

Silver Summit Real Estate conducts real estate transactions through approved agencies that have listed the desired acquisition properties. Steelin has executed over 50 percent of his purchase transactions since January 1, 2004, through Red Hot Real Estate.

Details

Computer queries on the external affairs database were executed on January 13, 2008, to determine the extent of Steelin's relations with Red Hot Real Estate.

First, the number of total transactions per purchasing representative was queried. It was revealed that each purchasing representative has performed 165 purchasing arrangements since January 1, 2004.

Eleven real estate agencies have been utilized since January 1, 2004. The agencies, all located in Moore County, Colorado, are employed based on their listing of properties, which Silver Summer Real Estate seeks to acquire. If a property is not listed, the purchasing representatives are instructed, as per external affairs department policy, to rotate their dealings among the eleven agencies. The policy states "that by rotating among the approved agencies, equity is cultivated, which will encourage the agencies to offer competitive prices."

Since January 1, 2004, each of the four purchasing representatives has dealt with all the approved agencies. Steelin put 86 transactions through Red Hot Real Estate during the period in question, January 1, 2004, through December 31, 2007. Fifty-two percent of Steelin's transactions were made through Red Hot Real Estate.

The query regarding the distribution of purchasing transactions (one page) and charts extracted (two pages) were printed, initialed, and dated by Scott R. Bulloch. The three pages are maintained in IASCF 030369.

17

External Affairs Database
Distribution of Purchasing Transactions

January 13, 2008
User: Scott R. Bulloch
Dates searched: January 1, 2004, to December 31, 2007

Real Estate Agency	Abraham Honest	B.J. Integrity	Peter Principle	Ivan Ben Steelin
Red Hot	17	10	17	86
Johnson	16	11	12	8
Monarch	19	18	13	9
Rich	10	15	17	7
Martin	7	15	18	8
Labrum	21	19	11	7
Peterson	16	10	20	7
Century 46	22	20	14	9
Littleton	15	13	16	6
Selberg	10	15	16	6
Baker	12	19	9	8
Total	165	165	165	165

sb
1-13-2008

18

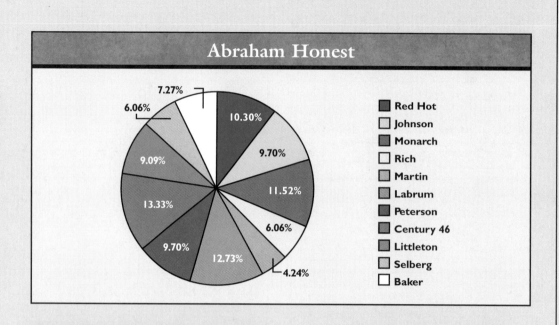

Abraham Honest

■	Red Hot
□	Johnson
■	Monarch
□	Rich
▨	Martin
▨	Labrum
■	Peterson
▨	Century 46
▨	Littleton
□	Selberg
□	Baker

Percentages: 10.30%, 9.70%, 11.52%, 6.06%, 4.24%, 12.73%, 9.70%, 13.33%, 9.09%, 6.06%, 7.27%

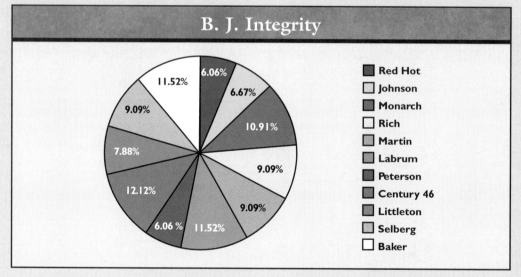

B. J. Integrity

■	Red Hot
□	Johnson
■	Monarch
□	Rich
▨	Martin
▨	Labrum
■	Peterson
▨	Century 46
▨	Littleton
□	Selberg
□	Baker

Percentages: 6.06%, 6.67%, 10.91%, 9.09%, 9.09%, 11.52%, 6.06%, 12.12%, 7.88%, 9.09%, 11.52%

sb
1-13-2008

19

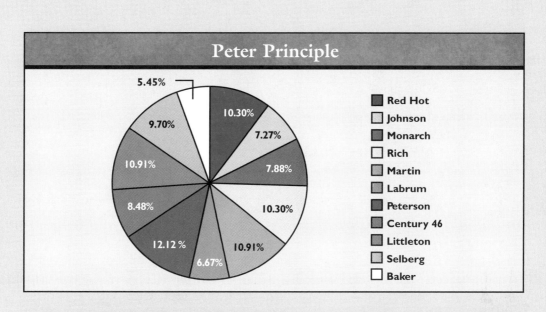

Peter Principle

Legend: Red Hot, Johnson, Monarch, Rich, Martin, Labrum, Peterson, Century 46, Littleton, Selberg, Baker

Values: 5.45%, 10.30%, 7.27%, 7.88%, 9.70%, 10.91%, 10.30%, 10.91%, 8.48%, 12.12%, 6.67%

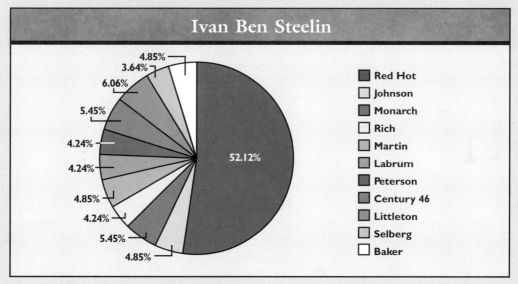

Ivan Ben Steelin

Legend: Red Hot, Johnson, Monarch, Rich, Martin, Labrum, Peterson, Century 46, Littleton, Selberg, Baker

Values: 4.85%, 3.64%, 6.06%, 5.45%, 4.24%, 4.24%, 4.85%, 4.24%, 5.45%, 4.85%, 52.12%

sb
1-13-2008

20

Silver Summit Real Estate

To: IASCF 030369
From: Scott R. Bulloch
Date: January 20, 2008
Re: Ivan Ben Steelin
Subject: Interview with Peter Principle

Synopsis
Peter Principle, a purchasing representative at Silver Summit Real Estate, stated that he believes that Ivan Ben Steelin conducts his Red Hot Real Estate transactions through Richey Rich, a broker at Red Hot Real Estate.

Details
Peter Principle, a purchasing representative at Silver Summit Real Estate, was interviewed in his office, 5511 Vero Beach Road, Denver, Colorado, telephone (999) 555-3463, on January 20, 2008. After being advised of the interviewer, Scott R. Bulloch, and the nature of the inquiry as an investigation of misconduct, Mr. Principle provided the following information regarding Ivan Ben Steelin:

Mr. Principle stated that Red Hot Real Estate is a very aggressive agency. In particular, Mr. Principle believed that one broker, Richey Rich, was the most aggressive broker that he had dealt with.

Mr. Principle stated that Richey Rich used to call him (Principle) to solicit deals. Principle became a purchasing representative in January of 2000. Mr. Principle cited that Rich became a bother at first, but after Mr. Principle worked for six months as a purchasing representative, Mr. Rich quit calling him (Principle).

Mr. Principle believes that Ivan Ben Steelin works very closely with Richey Rich. He stated that he overheard a conversation between Rich and Steelin, in Steelin's office, in which Steelin conveyed that he'd "send business his [Rich's] way."

Mr. Principle does not know of another broker at Red Hot Real Estate whom Ivan Ben Steelin has dealt with.

21

Silver Summit Real Estate

To: IASCF 030369
From: Scott R. Bulloch
Date: January 22, 2008
Re: Ivan Ben Steelin
Subject: Interview with Michelle Wang

Synopsis
Michelle Wang, a secretary at Silver Summit Real Estate in the external affairs department, advised that Ivan Ben Steelin had an appointment scheduled for 3:30 PM with Richey Rich on January 22, 2008, at the Burnt Oven Pizza Restaurant.

Details
Michelle Wang, a secretary at Silver Summit Real Estate in the external affairs department, was interviewed at her office, 5511 Vero Beach Road, Denver, Colorado, telephone (999)-555-3463, on the morning of January 22, 2008. Ms. Wang was informed of the nature of the inquiry and of the identity of the interviewer, Scott R. Bulloch. Ms. Wang provided the following information:

Ms. Wang is responsible for answering all incoming calls at the external affairs department. If the desired party is out or unavailable, Ms. Wang records a message on carbon-copied message slips.

Ms. Wang stated that she answered several calls a week from Richey Rich for Ivan Ben Steelin. On January 21, 2008, Ms. Wang documented a message telling Mr. Steelin to meet Richey Rich at the Burnt Oven Pizza Restaurant at 3:30 PM on January 22, 2008.

The duplicate copy of the message (one page) was obtained from Ms. Wang, was initialed and dated by Scott R. Bulloch, and is maintained in IASCF 030369.

22

External Affairs Department

To: Ivan   Date: 1/21/2008
From: Richey Rich   Time: 10:15 AM
Of: Red Hot Real Estate

__X__ Called   _____ Call Back at _____

_____ Stopped by

Message: Meet me at 3:30 PM on January 22—Burnt Oven Pizza Restaurant.

sb
1-22-2008

23

Silver Summit Real Estate

To: IASCF 030369
From: Scott R. Bulloch
Date: January 22, 2008
Re: Ivan Ben Steelin
Subject: Surveillance at Burnt Oven Pizza Restaurant

Synopsis
Ivan Ben Steelin had pizza and drinks with Richey Rich at the Burnt Oven Pizza Restaurant, 2750 East 1800 South, Denver, Colorado, on January 22, 2008. Steelin and Rich met from 3:30 PM to 4:45 PM. Steelin picked up the ticket of $14.50 and tipped the waiter a balance of a $20 bill. Rich gave Steelin a piece of paper before they left.

Details
During an interview, Michelle Wang, a secretary at Silver Summit Real Estate, advised of an appointment between Ivan Ben Steelin and Richey Rich. Ms. Wang provided a duplicate of a phone message slip regarding the appointment scheduled for 3:30 PM on January 22, 2008, at the Burnt Oven Pizza Restaurant.

According to the information provided, physical surveillance was established at the Burnt Oven Pizza Restaurant at 3:15 PM on January 22, and was terminated at 4:53 PM on the same date.

During the surveillance, Steelin and a white male, later identified as Richey Rich, had pizza and drinks. Steelin and Rich were observed writing in leather-like ring binders as they carried on a discussion.

After they consumed their provisions, Steelin put a $20 bill on the collection plate. As Steelin and Rich stood to leave, Rich was observed giving a piece of paper to Steelin, which Steelin placed in his left outside coat pocket.

The attached surveillance log furnished additional details. The surveillance log (one page) was initialed and dated by Scott R. Bulloch and is maintained in IASCF 030369.

24

January 22, 2008
Surveillance at the Burnt Oven Pizza Restaurant
Surveillance conducted by Scott R. Bulloch

3:15 PM   Established surveillance at the Burnt Oven Pizza Restaurant.

3:25 PM   Ivan Ben Steelin arrives at the restaurant.

3:33 PM   White male arrives and sits with Steelin.

3:40 PM   Steelin and white male place orders with waiter.

3:45 PM   Steelin and white male remove zipper ring binders from their briefcases, open them, and are observed writing in them as discussion takes place.

3:48 PM   Waiter refills glasses with clear fluid.

4:05 PM   Two pizzas are delivered to the table of Steelin and white male, and glasses are refilled with clear fluid.

4:30 PM   Waiter takes plates and tableware from table of Steelin and white male, refills glasses, and leaves a collection plate.

4:40 PM   Steelin and white male replace their zipper binders in their respective briefcases.

4:42 PM   Steelin places a form of currency on the collection plate.

4:45 PM   Steelin and white male stand up, white male hands Steelin a paper, and Steelin places the paper in his left outside coat pocket.

4:45 PM   Steelin and white male shake hands and leave the restaurant.

4:49 PM   Waiter, identified as Martin Lucky, states that the currency was a $20 bill and that the charge for the meal was $14.50. Lucky intends to keep the change as a tip. He advises that the white male is Richey Rich and that Rich is a frequent customer of the restaurant.

4:53 PM   Surveillance terminated.

sb
1-22-2008

25

Silver Summit Real Estate

To: IASCF 030369
From: Scott R. Bulloch
Date: January 28, 2008
Re: Ivan Ben Steelin
Subject: Interview with Richey Rich

Synopsis
Richey Rich, a real estate broker with Red Hot Real Estate, advised that he has conducted a few transactions with Ivan Ben Steelin. Rich denied having had any inappropriate relations with Ivan Ben Steelin. Rich denied having ever had meals with Ivan Ben Steelin at the Burnt Oven Pizza Restaurant.

Details
Richey Rich, a real estate broker with Red Hot Real Estate, was interviewed at his office, 3000 South Canyon Road, Denver, Colorado, on January 28, 2008. After being advised of the identity of the interviewer (Scott R. Bulloch) and the nature of the inquiry as an investigation of misconduct, Rich provided the following information:

"Red Hot Real Estate has done business with Silver Summit Real Estate for more than five years. I have conducted real estate transactions through all four of the purchasing representatives at Silver Summit Real Estate: Steelin, Honest, Integrity, and Principle."

Rich stated that he has conducted only a few transactions through Ivan Ben Steelin, because Steelin is "too demanding."

Richey Rich advised that not at any time have he and Steelin met for lunch at the Burnt Oven Pizza Restaurant, nor at any other restaurant.

Rich flatly denied furnishing bribes, kickbacks, or any other form of gratuities to Ivan Ben Steelin, or to any other purchasing representative at Silver Summit Real Estate. Rich stated that he suspects that other, unnamed agencies are furnishing gratuities to the purchasing representatives of Silver Summit Real Estate.

Silver Summit Real Estate

To: IASCF 030369
From: Scott R. Bulloch
Date: January 28, 2008
Re: Ivan Ben Steelin
Subject: Interview with Ivan Ben Steelin

Ivan Ben Steelin was interviewed at his office, 5511 Vero Beach Road, Denver, Colorado, telephone (999)-425-3463, on January 28, 2008. Steelin was advised that the interviewers were Scott R. Bulloch and Sue U. Buttz, and that an investigation was under way concerning an improper broker relationship.

Steelin was informed that the intent of the inquiry was to obtain a voluntary consent to examine his bank account records. Steelin stated that such a consent agreement was not necessary, and that he wished to meet in private at that time to discuss his predicament.

Ivan Ben Steelin was advised of his rights in regard to self-incrimination, and he executed an advice-of-rights form, a copy of which is attached. Steelin agreed to a videotaping of the interview that followed.

Steelin stated that family pressure to succeed and to measure up to his in-laws' expectations had led to his accepting payments from Richey Rich of Red Hot Real Estate. Steelin provided the attached free and voluntarily signed statement (three pages) regarding his association with Richey Rich, following the interview.

27

Silver Summit Real Estate

ADVICE OF RIGHTS*

Place: Silver Summit Real Estate, 5511 Vero Beach Road, Denver, Colorado
Date: January 28, 2008
Time: 11:30 AM

Before we ask you any questions, you must understand your rights.

You have the right to remain silent.

Anything you say can be used against you in court.

You have the right to talk to a lawyer for advice before we ask you any questions and to have a lawyer with you during questioning.

If you cannot afford a lawyer, one will be appointed for you before any questioning, if you wish.

If you decide to answer questions now without a lawyer present, you will still have the right to stop answering at any time. You also have the right to stop answering at any time until you talk to a lawyer.

WAIVER OF RIGHTS

I have read this statement of my rights and I understand what my rights are. I am willing to make a statement and answer questions. I do not want a lawyer at this time. I understand and know what I am doing. No promises or threats have been made to me and no pressure or coercion of any kind has been used against me.

Signed: *Ivan Ben Steelin* 1-28-2008

Witness: *Scott R. Bulloch*

Witness: *Sue U. Buttz*

Time: 11:30 AM

*Private citizens are not required to give Miranda warnings. However, many prosecutors prefer that they be given.

28

Silver Summit Real Estate

Denver, Colorado
January 28, 2008

I, Ivan Ben Steelin, furnish the following free and voluntary statement to Scott R. Bulloch and Sue U. Buttz, who have identified themselves to me as internal auditor and legal counsel, respectively, for Silver Summit Real Estate. No threats or promises of any kind have been used to induce this statement.

I have been advised that an internal inquiry has been and is being conducted to determine whether or not I have accepted any unlawful gratuities and violated the Silver Summit Real Estate code of conduct in my position as a purchasing representative for Silver Summit Real Estate. I have also been advised that I am the sole target of this internal inquiry; that the allegations could constitute a criminal act; and that I have a right to an attorney, should I choose.

I have been employed at Silver Summit Real Estate since January 7, 2000, and since January 1, 2002, have been a purchasing representative in the external affairs department, in Denver, Colorado.

I freely admit that I have accepted gratuities and other considerations from Richey Rich, real estate broker at Red Hot Real Estate, Denver, Colorado. The total amount of monies I have received is approximately $115,000 since January 2003. I have also received property, valued at approximately $35,000, from Richey Rich, on which property my personal residence was constructed.

Rich paid me the monies and provided the properties to ensure that I would continue to purchase real estate from Red Hot Real Estate. I was aware at the time I began taking money from Rich that such conduct was illegal and violated the Silver Summit Real Estate code of conduct. I committed these acts because of the financial pressure I felt to live up to others' expectations. I am sorry for my conduct, and I would like to begin to make reparations.

No one else at Silver Summit Real Estate was involved, nor did anyone else have knowledge of my activities.

29

I have read the above statement, consisting of this typewritten page and one other typewritten page. I have initialed the other page and now sign my name because this statement is true and correct to the best of my knowledge and belief.

Ivan Ben Steelin   1-28-2008
_____
Ivan Ben Steelin

Scott R. Bulloch
_____
Scott R. Bulloch   January 28, 2008

Sue U. Buttz
_____
Sue U. Buttz   January 28, 2008

30

Silver Summit Real Estate

To: IASCF 030369
From: Scott R. Bulloch
Date: February 13, 2008
Re: Ivan Ben Steelin
Subject: Estimated overpayment to Red Hot Real Estate

Synopsis
Computations indicate that the estimated loss to Silver Summit Real Estate for the years 2003 through 2007 due to overpayment to Red Hot Real Estate is approximately $436,568.

Details
On February 13, 2008, estimates were prepared concerning possible overpayment to Red Hot Real Estate as a result of activities conducted between Ivan Ben Steelin and Richey Rich.

Data on four of the eleven agencies that Silver Summit Real Estate conducts transactions with were extracted from the external affairs database. The data were extrapolated to determine the average prices paid per acre of real estate purchased through each of the four agencies.

The average cost computation was then applied to the acreage purchased from Red Hot Real Estate to determine an approximate overpayment to that agency over the last five years.

The total of the losses, as reflected on the attached one-page worksheet, is approximately $436,568 for the years 2003 through 2007.

31

Average Cost per Acre

	2003	2004	2005	2006	2007
Johnson	$505.00	$525.00	$545.00	$565.00	$576.00
Labrum	508.00	520.00	541.00	560.00	573.00
Century 46	503.00	530.00	548.00	568.00	581.00
Monarch	510.00	524.00	545.00	567.00	575.00
Average cost	$506.50	$524.75	$544.75	$565.00	$576.25

Ivan Ben Steelin's Transactions with Red Hot Real Estate

	2003	2004	2005	2006	2007
Cost paid to Red Hot	$130,500.00	$176,280.00	$240,250.00	$332,260.00	$414,960.00
Acreage received	200	260	310	370	420
Average cost	$652.50	$678.00	$775.00	$898.00	$988.00
Expected cost for acreage	$101,200.00	$136,435.00	$168,872.50	$209,050.00	$242,025.00
Estimated overpayment	$29,200.00	$39,845.00	$71,377.50	$123,210.00	$172,935.00

Total loss = approximately $436,568

32

Management Fraud

CHAPTER **11**

Financial Statement Fraud

LEARNING OBJECTIVES

- After studying this chapter, you should be able to:
- Discuss the role that financial statements play in capital markets.
- Understand the nature of financial statement fraud.
- Become familiar with financial statement fraud statistics.
- See how financial statement frauds occur and are concealed.
- Outline the framework for detecting financial statement fraud.
- Identify financial statement fraud exposures.
- Explain how information regarding a company's management and directors, nature of organization, operating characteristics, relationship with others, and financial results can help assess the likelihood of financial statement fraud.

TO THE STUDENT

Chapter 11 is the first of three chapters on financial statement fraud, also known as management fraud. This chapter discusses some of the numerous financial statement frauds discovered in corporate America in the last decade. We discuss the common elements of these frauds and the conditions that led to the rash of financial statement fraud around the turn of the new millenium. Financial statement frauds almost always involve company management and are the result of pressures to meet internal or external expectations. This chapter provides a framework for detecting financial statement fraud, which emphasizes the need to consider the context in which management is operating and being motivated.

357

Enron was a multinational company that specialized in marketing electricity, natural gas, energy, and other physical commodities. Enron initiated the wholesale natural gas and electricity markets in the United States. It was officially formed in 1985 as a result of the merger of Houston Natural Gas and InterNorth of Omaha, Nebraska. In 2000, Enron reported revenues of $101 billion, supposedly making it the seventh largest U.S. company in terms of revenue. In 2000, Enron employed 21,000 employees and operated in over 40 countries.

In October 2001, it was determined that a large financial statement fraud had been occurring at Enron and that revenues, income, and assets had been significantly overstated. Enron's stock price, which reached a high of $90 earlier in the year, dropped to less than $1 in a matter of days. In December 2001, Enron declared one of the largest corporate bankruptcies in U.S. history. Once the scandal was discovered, numerous Enron officers either plea bargained or pleaded guilty, and indictments were handed out against other corporate officers. The **Securities and Exchange Commission (SEC)** charged the former Chief Executive Officer (CEO), Jeffrey Skilling, and the current CEO, Ken Lay, with numerous incidences of fraud. Numerous other individuals were also charged with fraud, including Chief Financial Officer (CFO) Andy Fastow and Chief Accounting Officer Rick Causey. After being found guilty but before his sentencing, Lay died of heart disease. Skilling was found guilty and sentenced to 24 years in prison. Fastow and Causey also served prison terms. Arthur Andersen, Enron's auditor, was convicted of obstruction of justice, largely because of "destruction of evidence" charges brought against it by the U.S. government. Later, in

May 2005, the U.S. Supreme Court overturned these charges against Andersen but the firm was essentially dissolved because it had lost its reputation as a provider of independent audits of financial statements.

Enron, citing accounting errors, had to restate its financial statements, cutting profits for the three years (1999–2001) by about 20 percent, or around $586 million. Many of the lawsuits that were filed against Enron and related parties alleged that executives reaped personal gains from "off-the-book" partnerships, while the energy giant violated basic rules of accounting and ethics. As the accounting discrepancies became public knowledge, Enron investors lost billions of dollars, shattering their retirement plans.

Only a few months later, and about the time that the dust from the Enron fraud was settling down, another massive fraud came to light at a firm that was also audited by Andersen. This firm was a star performer in the telecom industry: WorldCom. The WorldCom fraud turned out to be much more massive than the Enron fraud, resulting in the company's total assets being inflated by approximately $11 billion. In addition, the fraud at WorldCom was much less clever than that at Enron, as WorldCom's executives, under the direction of CFO Scott Sullivan, were essentially creating assets out of expenses. Likewise, at Enron, several people were convicted of fraud at WorldCom, including the CEO, Bernie Ebbers, CFO, Scott Sullivan, and Controller, David Myers. Also, like Enron, WorldCom filed for bankruptcy soon after the fraud came to light. In combination, these two frauds at Enron and WorldCom were the main impetus for Congress passing the Sarbanes-Oxley Corporate Governance Act in 2002 and are, without doubt, the two most well-known frauds in the history of the United States.

The Problem of Financial Statement Fraud

The stock and bond markets are critical components of a capitalist economy. The efficiency, liquidity, and resiliency of these markets depend on the ability of investors, lenders, and regulators to assess the financial performance of businesses that raise capital. **Financial statements** prepared by such organizations play a very important role in keeping capital markets efficient. They provide meaningful disclosures of where a company has been, where it is currently, and where it is going. Most financial statements are prepared with integrity and present a fair representation of the financial position of the organization issuing them. These financial statements are based on generally accepted accounting principles (GAAP), which guide the accounting for transactions.

Unfortunately, financial statements are sometimes prepared in ways that intentionally misstate the financial position and performance of an organization. Such misstatements can result from manipulating, falsifying, or altering accounting records. Misleading financial statements cause serious problems in the market and the economy. They often result in large losses for investors, lack of trust in the market and accounting systems, and litigation and embarrassment for individuals and organizations associated with **financial statement fraud.**

Financial Statement Fraud in Recent Years

During the years 2000–2002, numerous revelations of corporate wrongdoing, including financial statement fraud, in the United States created a crisis of confidence in the capital markets. The crisis led to a $15 trillion decline in the market value of all public company stock. Before focusing on financial statement fraud, we include an overview of several abuses that occurred during this time period to paint a more complete picture of why corporate America experienced such a severe crisis. Some of the most notable abuses include the following:

- *Misstated financial statements or "cooking the books": Examples include Qwest, Enron, Global Crossing, WorldCom, and Xerox. Some of these frauds involved 20 or more people helping to create fictitious financial results.*
- *Inappropriate executive loans and corporate looting: Examples include John Rigas (Adelphia), Dennis Kozlowski (Tyco), and Bernie Ebbers (WorldCom).*

- *Insider trading scandals: The most notable examples are Martha Stewart and Sam Waksal, both of whom were convicted for using insider information to profit from trading ImClone stock.*
- *Initial public offering (IPO) favoritism, including spinning and laddering (spinning involves giving IPO opportunities to those who arrange quid pro quo opportunities, and laddering involves giving IPO opportunities to those who promise to buy additional shares as prices increase): Examples include Bernie Ebbers of WorldCom and Jeff Skilling of Enron.*
- *Excessive CEO retirement perks: Delta, PepsiCo, AOL Time Warner, Ford, GE, and IBM were highly criticized for endowing huge, costly perks and benefits, such as expensive consulting contracts, use of corporate planes, executive apartments, and maids to retiring executives.*
- *Exorbitant compensation (both cash and stock) for executives: Many executives, including Bernie Ebbers of WorldCom and Richard Grasso of the NYSE, received huge cash and equity-based compensation that has since been determined to have been excessive.*
- *Loans for trading fees and other quid pro quo transactions: Financial institutions such as Citibank and JPMorgan Chase provided favorable loans to companies and executives at companies such as Enron and WorldCom in return for the opportunity to make hundreds of millions of dollars in derivative transactions and other fees.*
- *Bankruptcies and excessive debt: Because of the abuses described here and similar problems, seven of the ten largest corporate bankruptcies in U.S. history up to 2002 occurred in 2001 and 2002. These seven bankruptcies were WorldCom (largest, at $101.9 billion), Enron (second, at $63.4 billion), Global Crossing (fifth, at $25.5 billion), Adelphia (sixth, at $24.4 billion), United Airlines (seventh, at $22.7 billion), PG&E (eighth, at $21.5 billion), and Kmart (tenth, at $17 billion). Four of these seven involved financial statement fraud.*
- *Massive fraud by employees: While not in the news nearly as much as financial statement frauds, there has been a large increase in fraud against organizations, with some of these frauds being as high as $2 to $3 billion.*

In 2006, many companies were investigated by the SEC for backdating stock options. Stock options are a common method of providing executive compensation by allowing top management to purchase stock at a fixed share price. If the stock rises above that price, then holders of the options can use them to profit from the increased stock price. **Backdating** is a practice where the effective dates on stock options are deliberately changed for the purpose of securing extra compensation for management. By backdating option agreements, management of several companies received stock grants at the lowest prices of the year. Then, management was able to sell the stock at a higher price and profit by the difference in price.

Academic researchers became aware of backdating as they observed that the statistical probability of granting an option at the lowest price of the year was much lower than the frequency of such occurrences. This apparently extraordinary timing by numerous companies granting options, dated at times when share prices hit yearly lows (for some companies, this occurred year after year), led the SEC to investigate the issue.

Approximately 270 companies admitted to backdating their options agreements. Backdating options led to millions of dollars in increased compensation for company executives at the expense of shareholders, and also resulted in misstated financial statements, which were subsequently restated. Companies that provided executives with backdated stock options also violated income tax rules because the difference in the grant price on the backdated dates and the market prices on the date the options were actually granted should have been taxable income to the executives.

Even more recently, the subprime lending crisis that led to the "great recession" was accompanied by a massive financial statement fraud at Satyam Computer Services in India. In January 2009, Satyam chairman, Ramalinga Raju, confessed to having falsified billions of dollars of assets on Satyam's books. Although the details of how this fraud was carried out have not been made public, we do know that a cash balance was inflated by over one billion dollars! In addition to Satyam, the collapse of Lehman Brothers Holdings, Inc. in 2008 has also been associated with financial statement manipulation that allegedly involved financial statement fraud. Lehman's bankruptcy was the largest bankruptcy in the history of the United States, with roughly $691 billion in assets. Although financial statement fraud appears to have been rampant around the turn of the millennium, this devastating problem has not gone away.

Why These Problems Occurred

Each of the problems discussed earlier represents an ethical compromise. The explanations covered previously about why people commit other frauds apply to financial statement fraud as well. Recall that three elements come

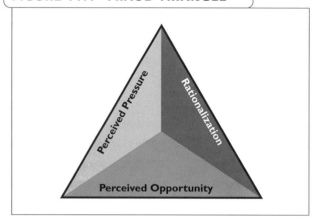

FIGURE 11.1   FRAUD TRIANGLE

together to motivate all frauds: (1) a perceived pressure, (2) a perceived opportunity, and (3) the ability to rationalize the fraud as acceptable. Whether the dishonest act involves fraud against a company, such as employee embezzlement, as we have already discussed, or fraud on behalf of a company, such as financial statement fraud that we will now discuss, these three elements are always present. Figure 11.1 shows a review of the fraud triangle, which we discussed earlier in the book.

Every fraud perpetrator faces some kind of *perceived pressure*. Examples of perceived pressures that can motivate financial statement fraud are financial losses, failure to meet Wall Street's earnings expectations, or the inability to compete with other companies. Also, executive compensation in the form of stock options is often much higher than any other form of compensation and can be in the tens of millions of dollars. As such, executives had enormous pressure to boost their stock value since a small increase in the stock price could mean millions of dollars of compensation for management.

Fraud perpetrators must also have a *perceived opportunity* or they will not commit fraud. Even with intense perceived pressures, executives who believe they will be caught and punished rarely commit fraud. On the other hand, executives who believe they have an opportunity (to commit and/or conceal fraud) often give in to perceived pressures. Perceived opportunities to commit management fraud include such factors as a weak board of directors or inadequate internal controls and the ability to obfuscate the fraud behind complex transactions or related-party structures. Some of the main controls that could eliminate the perceived opportunity for financial statement fraud include the independent audit and the board of directors. Because management can override most internal controls, the audit committee of the board of directors and the independent auditor often provide final checks to prevent financial statement fraud.

Finally, fraud perpetrators must have some way to *rationalize* their actions as acceptable. For corporate executives, rationalizations to commit fraud might include thoughts such as "we need to protect our shareholders and keep the stock price high," "all companies use aggressive accounting practices," "it is for the good of the company," or "the problem is temporary and will be offset by future positive results."

The fraud triangle provides insights into why recent ethical compromises occurred. We believe there were nine factors that came together to create what we call the *perfect fraud storm*. In explaining this "perfect storm," we will use examples from recent frauds.

Element 1: A Booming Economy

The first element of the perfect storm was the masking of many existing problems and unethical actions by the booming economy of the 1990s and early 2000s. During this time, most businesses appeared to be highly profitable, including many new "dot-com" companies, which were testing new (and many times unprofitable) business models. These booming economic conditions allowed fraud perpetrators to conceal their actions for longer time periods. Additionally, the advent of "investing over the Internet" for a few dollars per trade brought many new inexperienced people to the stock market, and many investors made nonsensical investment decisions. History has now shown that several of the frauds that came to light around the turn of the millennium were being committed during the boom years while the economy hid the fraudulent behavior.

The booming economy also caused executives to believe their companies were more successful than they actually were and that their companies' success was primarily a result of good management. Academic researchers have found that extended periods of prosperity can reduce a firm's motivation to comprehend the causes of success, raising the likelihood of faulty attributions. In other words, during boom periods, many firms do not correctly ascribe the reasons behind their successes. Management usually takes credit for good company performance. When company performance degrades, boards often expect results similar to those in the past without new management styles or actions. Since management did not correctly understand past reasons for success, it incorrectly thinks past methods will continue to be successful. Once methods that may have worked in the past because of external factors fail, some CEOs may feel increased pressure. In some cases,

this pressure contributed to fraudulent financial reporting and other dishonest acts.

Element 2: Decay of Moral Values

The second element of the perfect fraud storm was the moral decay that has been occurring in recent years. Whatever measure of integrity one uses, dishonesty appears to be increasing. For example, numerous researchers have found that cheating in school, one measure of dishonesty, has increased substantially in recent years. Whether it is letting someone copy work, using a cheat sheet on an exam, or lying to obtain a job, studies show that these numbers have drastically increased over the years. While cheating in school is not necessarily directly tied to management fraud, it does reflect the general decay of moral values in society at large.

Element 3: Misplaced Incentives

The third element of the perfect fraud storm was misplaced executive incentives. Executives of most fraudulent companies were endowed with hundreds of millions of dollars in stock options and/or restricted stock that put tremendous pressure on management to keep the stock price rising, even at the expense of reporting accurate financial results. In many cases, this stock-based compensation far exceeded executives' salary-based compensation. For example, in 1997, Bernie Ebbers, the CEO of WorldCom, had a cash-based salary of $935,000. Yet during that same period, he was able to exercise hundreds of thousands of stock options, making millions in profits, and received corporate loans totaling $409 million.[1] These incentive packages caused the attention of many CEOs to shift from managing the firm to managing the stock price, which, all too often, resulted in fraudulent financial statements. As mentioned earlier, in addition to managing stock prices, executives also defrauded shareholders by backdating options so as to maximize their compensation.

Element 4: High Analysts' Expectations

The fourth element of the perfect storm, and one closely related to the last, was the often unachievable expectations of Wall Street analysts that targeted short-term behavior. Company boards and management, generally lacking alternative performance metrics, used comparisons with the stock price of "similar" firms and attainment of analysts' expectations as important de facto performance measures. These stock-based incentives compounded the pressure induced by the analysts' expectations. Each quarter, the analysts, often coached by companies themselves, forecasted what each company's earnings per share (EPS) would be. Executives knew that the penalty for missing Wall Street's forecast was severe—even falling short of expectations by a small amount would drop the company's stock price by a considerable amount.

Consider the following example of a fraud that occurred around the turn of the millennium. For this company, the "street" made the following EPS estimates for three consecutive quarters:

FIRM	1ST QUARTER	2ND QUARTER	3RD QUARTER
Morgan Stanley	$0.17	$0.23	
Smith Barney	0.17	0.21	0.23
Robertson Stephens	0.17	0.25	0.24
Cowen & Co.	0.18	0.21	
Alex Brown	0.18	0.25	
Paine Webber	0.21	0.28	
Goldman Sachs	0.17		
Furman Selz	0.17	0.21	0.23
Hambrecht & Quist	0.17	0.21	0.23

Based on these estimates, the consensus estimate was that the company would have EPS of $0.17 in the first quarter, $0.22 in the second quarter, and $0.23 in the third quarter. The company's actual earnings per share during the three quarters were $0.08, $0.13, and $0.16, respectively. In order to not miss Wall Street's estimates, management committed a fraud of $62 million or $0.09 per share in the first quarter, a fraud of $0.09 per share in the second quarter, and a fraud of $0.07 per share in the third quarter.

The complaint in this case read (in part) as follows:

"The goal of this scheme was to ensure that [the company] always met Wall Street's growing earnings expectations for the company. [The company's] management knew that meeting or exceeding these estimates was a key factor for the stock price of all publicly traded companies and therefore set out to ensure that the company met Wall Street's targets every quarter regardless of the company's actual earnings. During the period 1998 to 1999 alone, management improperly inflated the company's operating income by more than $500 million before taxes, which represents more than one-third of the total operating income reported by [the company]."

Element 5: High Debt Levels

The fifth element in the perfect storm was the large amounts of debt each of these fraudulent companies

had. This debt placed tremendous pressure on executives to have high earnings to offset high interest costs and to meet debt covenants and other lender requirements. For example, during 2000, Enron's derivates-related liabilities increased from $1.8 billion to $10.5 billion. Similarly, WorldCom had over $100 billion in debt when it filed history's largest bankruptcy. During 2002 alone, 186 public companies, including World-Com, Enron, Adelphia, and Global Crossing, with $368 billion in debt, filed for bankruptcy in the United States.[2]

Element 6: Focus on Accounting Rules Rather Than Principles

Some believe that another element of the perfect storm was the nature of U.S. accounting rules. In contrast to accounting practices in many countries such as the United Kingdom and Australia, generally accepted accounting principles (GAAP) in the United States are more rule based than principles based.[3] One potential result of having rule-based standards is that if a client can find a loophole in the rules and account for a transaction in a way that is not specifically prohibited by GAAP, then auditors may find it hard to prohibit the client from using that method of accounting. Unfortunately, in some cases, the auditors helped their clients find the loopholes or gave them permission to account for transactions in ways that violated the principle of an accounting method but was within the rules. The result was that *specific* rules (or the lack of *specific* rules) were exploited for new, often complex financial arrangements, as justification to decide what was or was not an acceptable accounting practice.

As an example, consider the case of Enron. Even if Arthur Andersen had argued that Enron's special purpose entities weren't appropriate, it would have been impossible for the accounting firm to make the case that Enron violated any *specific* rules. Some have suggested that one of the reasons it took so long to get plea bargains or indictments in the Enron case was because it was not immediately clear whether GAAP or any laws had actually been broken.

Element 7: Lack of Auditor Independence

A seventh element of the perfect fraud storm was the opportunistic behavior of some CPA firms. In some cases, accounting firms used audits as loss leaders to establish relationships with companies so they could sell more lucrative consulting services. In many cases, audit fees were much smaller than consulting fees for the same clients, and accounting firms felt little conflict between independence and opportunities for increased profits. In particular, these alternative services allowed some auditors to lose their focus and become business advisors rather than auditors. This is especially true of Arthur Andersen, which had spent considerable energy building its consulting practice, only to see that practice split off into a separate firm. Privately, several Andersen partners have admitted that the surviving Andersen firm and some of its partners had vowed to "out consult" the firm that separated from it and they became preoccupied with that goal.

Element 8: Greed

The eighth element of the perfect storm was greed by executives, investment banks, commercial banks, and investors. Each of these groups benefited from the strong economy, the many lucrative transactions, and the apparently high profits of companies. None of them wanted to accept bad news. As a result, they sometimes ignored negative news and entered into bad transactions.[4] For example, in the Enron case, various commercial and investment banks made hundreds of millions of dollars from Enron's lucrative investment banking transactions, on top of the tens of millions of dollars in loan interest and fees. None of these firms alerted investors about derivative or other underwriting problems at Enron. A Forbes article noted that "even as late as Nov. 8, the date of Enron's disclosure that nearly five years of earnings would have to be recalculated, 11 of the 15 [stock analysts covering Enron] recommended buying the stock."[5] Enron's outside law firms were also making high profits from Enron's transactions. These firms also failed to correct or disclose any problems related to the derivatives and special purpose entities, but in fact helped draft the requisite associated legal documentation. Finally, the three major credit rating agencies, Moody's, Standard & Poor's, and Fitch/IBC—who all received substantial fees from Enron—also failed to alert investors of pending problems. Amazingly, just weeks prior to Enron's bankruptcy filing—after most of the negative news was out and Enron's stock was trading for $3 per share—all three agencies still gave investment grade ratings to Enron's debt.

Element 9: Educator Failures

Finally, the ninth element of the perfect storm involved several educator failures. First, educators had not provided sufficient ethics training to students. By not forcing students to face realistic ethical dilemmas in the classroom, graduates were ill equipped to deal with the real ethical dilemmas they faced in the business

world. In one allegedly fraudulent scheme, for example, participants included virtually the entire senior management of the company, including but not limited to its former chairman and chief executive officer, its former president, two former chief financial officers, and various other senior accounting and business personnel. In total, it is likely that more than 20 individuals were involved in the schemes. Such a large number of participants points to a generally failed ethical compass for this group.

Consider another case of a chief accountant. A CFO instructed the chief accountant to increase earnings by an amount somewhat over $100 million. The chief accountant was skeptical about the purpose of these instructions but did not challenge them. Instead, the chief accountant followed directions and allegedly created a spreadsheet containing seven pages of improper journal entries—105 in total—that he determined were necessary to carry out the CFO's instructions. Such fraud was not unusual. In many of these cases, the individuals involved had no prior records of dishonesty—and yet when they were asked to participate in fraudulent accounting, they did so quietly and of their free will.

A second educator failure was not teaching students about fraud. One author of this book has taught a fraud course to business students for several years. It is his experience that most business school graduates would not recognize a fraud if it hit them between the eyes. The large majority of business students do not understand the elements of fraud, perceived pressures and opportunities, the process of rationalization, or red flags that indicate the possible presence of dishonest behavior. And, when they see something that doesn't look right, their first reaction is to deny that a colleague could be committing dishonest acts.

A third educator failure is the way we have taught accountants and business students in the past. Effective accounting education must focus less on teaching content as an end unto itself and instead use content as a context for helping students develop analytical skills. As an expert witness, one of the authors has seen too many cases where accountants applied what they thought was appropriate content knowledge to unstructured or different situations, only to find out later that the underlying issues were different than they had thought and that they totally missed the major risks inherent in the circumstances.

Because these financial statement frauds and other problems caused such a decline in the market value of stocks and a loss of investor confidence, a number of new laws and corporate governance changes have been implemented by organizations such as the SEC, PCAOB,

NYSE, NASDAQ, and FASB. We review these changes in Appendix A to this chapter.

Nature of Financial Statement Fraud

Financial statement fraud, like other frauds, involves intentional deceit and attempted concealment. Financial statement fraud may be concealed through falsified documentation, including forgery. Financial statement fraud may also be concealed through collusion among management, employees, or third parties. Unfortunately, like other fraud, financial statement fraud is rarely seen. Rather, fraud symptoms, indicators, or red flags are usually observed. Because what appear to be symptoms can be caused by other legitimate factors, the presence of fraud symptoms does not always indicate the existence of fraud. For example, a document may be missing, a general ledger may be out of balance, or an analytical relationship may not make sense. However, these conditions may be the result of circumstances other than fraud. Documents may have been legitimately lost, the general ledger may be out of balance because of an unintentional accounting error, and unexpected analytical relationships may be the result of unrecognized changes in underlying economic factors. Caution should be used even when reports of alleged fraud are received, because the person providing the tip or complaint may be mistaken or may be motivated to make false allegations.

Fraud symptoms cannot easily be ranked in order of importance or combined into effective predictive models. The significance of red flags varies widely. Some factors will be present when no fraud exists; alternatively, a smaller number of symptoms may exist when fraud is occurring. Many times, even when fraud is suspected, it can be difficult to prove. Without a confession, obviously forged documents, or a number of repeated, similar fraudulent acts (so fraud can be inferred from a pattern), convicting someone of financial statement fraud can be very difficult. Because of the difficulty of detecting and proving fraud, investigators must exercise extreme care when performing fraud examinations, quantifying fraud, or performing other types of fraud-related engagements.

Financial Statement Fraud Statistics

How often financial statement fraud occurs is difficult to know since some frauds have not been detected. One way to measure it is to look at some of the SEC's Accounting and Auditing Enforcement Releases (AAERs). One or more enforcement releases are usually issued when financial statement fraud occurs at a company that has publicly traded stock.

Several studies have examined AAERs. One of the first and most comprehensive was the Report of the National Commission on Fraudulent Financial Reporting, issued by the National Commission on Fraudulent Financial Reporting (**Treadway Commission**). The Treadway Commission report found that while financial statement frauds occur infrequently, they are extremely costly. The Treadway Commission studied frauds that occurred during a 10-year period ending in 1987.[6] This study examined 119 SEC enforcement actions that occurred during the period 1981 through 1986.

In 1999, the **Committee of Sponsoring Organizations (COSO)** released the first of two studies they sponsored on fraudulent financial statement frauds investigated by the SEC that occurred during the period 1987–1997.[7] This study found that approximately 300 financial statement frauds were the subject of **SEC enforcement releases** during the period. A random sample of 204 of these financial statement frauds revealed the following:

1. The average fraud lasts about two years.
2. Improper revenue recognition, overstatement of assets, and understatement of expenses were the most common fraudulent methods used. These and other fraud methods are covered in more detail in the following chapters.
3. Cumulative average magnitude of fraud was $25 million ($4.1 million median).
4. The CEO perpetrated the fraud in 72 percent of the cases.
5. Fraudulent companies' average size assets were $532 million ($16 million median) and average revenues $232 million ($13 million median).
6. Severe consequences were usually associated with companies having fraudulent financial statements. For example, 36 percent of the companies filed for Chapter 11 bankruptcy, were described as "defunct" in the AAERs, or were taken over by a state or federal regulator after the fraud occurred.
7. Most of these firms had no audit committee, or one that met only once per year. Seats on the board of directors for these companies were often filled with "insiders" rather than independent directors.
8. Boards of directors were dominated by insiders and "grey" directors (i.e., outsiders with special ties to the company or management) with significant equity ownership and apparently little experience serving as directors of other companies. Family relationships between directors or officers were fairly common,

as were individuals who apparently had significant power.

9. Some companies committing financial statement fraud were experiencing net losses or were close to break-even positions in periods prior to the fraud.

10. Just over 25 percent of the companies changed auditors during the fraud period. Fraudulent companies had all different sizes of audit firms as their external auditors. Auditors were named in over 25 percent of the AAERs that explicitly named individuals. Most of the auditors named were not from the largest (i.e., Big Eight or Big Six) auditing firms.

Shortly after the 1999 COSO study there was another study performed by the Securities and Exchange Commission directed by Section 704 of the Sarbanes-Oxley Act.[8] The requirement was that the SEC study all of its enforcement actions filed during the period July 31, 1997 through July 30, 2002 that were based on improper financial reporting, fraud, audit failure, or auditor independence violations. Over the study period, the SEC filed 515 enforcement actions for financial reporting and disclosure violation involving 164 different entities. The number of actions in the five-year study was as follows:

Year 1	91
Year 2	60
Year 3	110
Year 4	105
Year 5	149

Like the previous studies, this study found that the SEC brought the greatest number of actions in the area of improper revenue recognition, including fraudulent reporting of fictitious sales, improper timing of revenue recognition, and improper valuation of revenue. The second highest category involved improper expense recognition, including improper capitalization or deferral of expenses, improper use of reserves, and other expense understatements. Other categories were improper accounting for business combinations, inadequate Management's Discussion and Analysis disclosure, and improper use of off-balance-sheet arrangements.

Like the previous studies, this study also found that CEOs, presidents, and CFOs were the members of management most often implicated in the frauds, followed by board chairs, chief operating officers, chief accounting officers, and vice presidents of finance. In 18 of the cases, the SEC also brought charges against auditing firms and individual auditors.

These findings are consistent with a study conducted in the United Kingdom by the Auditing Practices Board (APB) of England. This study found that the majority of financial statement frauds are committed by company management and that financial statement frauds do not involve actual theft and are unlikely to be detected by statutory auditors. Sixty-five percent of the cases involved misstatement of financial data to boost share prices or disguise losses.[9]

The most recent study of financial statement fraud AAERs was released in May 2010 by COSO.[10] This study updates the prior COSO study and covers the period 1998–2007. Major findings reported by this study include the following:

1. Approximately 18 percent more frauds were investigated by the SEC during this 10-year period relative to the prior 10-year period, with the average fraud increasing dramatically from $25 million (median = $4.1 million) to approximately $400 million ($12 million).

2. Median assets for the companies involved in this study increased from approximately $16 million to nearly $100 million.

3. The CFO and/or CEO were named in over 89 percent of the cases and about 20 percent of these individuals were indicted within two years of the SEC's investigation.

4. Improper revenue recognition continues to be the most common fraud method and accounted for over 60 percent of the cases.

5. In contrast to the prior study, the characteristics of board of directors for these firms were not noticeably different than those of similar firms that were not charged with fraud.

6. Twenty-six percent of the firms changed auditors around the time of the fraud; 60 percent of those that changed did so while the fraud was taking place while the other 40 percent did so just before the fraud started.

7. Press coverage of a company's alleged fraud led to a 16.7 percent abnormal decline in the company's stock price and news of a government investigation of the fraud led to a 7.3 percent abnormal stock price decline.

In addition to these dramatic declines in stock prices, both COSO studies showed that firms that engaged in fraud incurred serious long-term negative consequences soon after the fraud came to light, including bankruptcy and delisting from a stock exchange. While the percentage of fraudulent financial statements that come to light is relatively small, the damage caused by even one set of such statements is often devastating to employees, shareholders, auditors, bankers, and business partners of all kinds. Consider, for example, the Phar-Mor fraud. In this case, the COO, Michael "Mickey" Monus, was sentenced to nearly 20 years in prison. The fraud resulted in more than $1 billion in losses and the bankruptcy of the 28th largest private company in the United States. Phar-Mor's former auditor, a Big 5 firm, faced claims of more than $1 billion, but it ultimately settled for a significantly lower amount.

Phar-Mor: An Example of Financial Statement Fraud

The Phar-Mor fraud is a good example of how financial statement fraud occurs.

Mickey Monus opened the first Phar-Mor store in 1982. Phar-Mor sold a variety of household products and prescription drugs at prices substantially lower than other discount stores. The key to the low prices was claimed to be "power buying," a phrase Monus used to describe his strategy of loading up on products when suppliers were offering rock-bottom prices. When he started Phar-Mor, Monus was president of Tamco, a family-held distributing company that had recently been acquired by the Pittsburgh-based Giant Eagle grocery store chain. In 1984, David Shapira, president of Giant Eagle, funded the expansion of Phar-Mor with $4 million from Giant Eagle. Shapira then became the CEO of Phar-Mor, and Monus was named president and COO. By the end of 1985, Phar-Mor had 15 stores. By 1992, a decade after the first store opened, 310 stores had been opened in 32 states, posting sales of more than $3 billion.

Phar-Mor's prices were so low that competitors wondered how it could sell products so cheap and still make a profit, and it appeared that Phar-Mor was on its way to becoming the next Wal-Mart. In fact, Sam Walton once stated that the only company he feared in the expansion of Wal-Mart was Phar-Mor.

After five or six years, however, Phar-Mor began losing money. Unwilling to allow these shortfalls to damage Phar-Mor's appearance of success, Monus and his team began to engage in creative accounting, which resulted in Phar-Mor meeting the high expectations of those watching the company. Federal fraud examiners discerned five years later that the reported pretax income for fiscal 1989 was overstated by $350,000 and that the year 1987 was the last year that Phar-Mor actually made a profit.

Relying on these erroneous financial statements, investors saw Phar-Mor as an opportunity to cash in on the retailing craze. Among the big investors were Westinghouse Credit Corp., Sears Roebuck & Co., mall developer Edward J. de Bartolo, and the prestigious Lazard Freres & Co. Prosecutors stated that banks and investors put $1.14 billion into the company, based on its fictitious financial statements.

To hide Phar-Mor's cash flow problems, attract investors, and make the company look profitable, Michael Monus and his subordinate, Patrick Finn, altered the inventory accounts to understate the cost of goods sold and overstate income. Monus and Finn used three different methods: account manipulation, overstatement of inventory, and accounting rules manipulation. In addition to the financial statement fraud, internal investigations by the company estimated that management embezzled more than $10 million. Most of the stolen funds were used to support Monus's now-defunct World Basketball League.

In 1985 and 1986, well before the large fraud began, Monus was directing Finn to understate certain expenses that came in over budget and to overstate those expenses that came in under budget, making operations look efficient. Although the net effect of these first manipulations evened out, the accounting information was not accurate. Finn later suggested that this seemingly harmless request by Monus was an important precursor to the later extensive fraud.

STOP & THINK *Had Finn not complied with Monus's expense manipulation requests early on, would the Phar-Mor fraud have progressed to the extent it did? Also, how would Finn's career have been different?*

Finn also increased Phar-Mor's actual gross profit margin of 14.2 percent to around 16.5 percent by inflating inventory accounts. The company hired an independent firm to count inventory in its stores. After the third-party inventory counters submitted a report detailing the amount and retail value for a store's inventory, Phar-Mor's accountants would prepare what they called a "compilation packet." The packet calculated the amount of inventory at cost, and journal entries were then prepared. Based on the compilation, the accountants would credit inventory to properly report the sales activity, but rather than record a debit to Cost of Goods Sold, they debited so-called "bucket" accounts. To avoid auditor scrutiny, the bucket accounts were emptied at the end of each fiscal year by allocating the balance to individual stores as inventory. Because the related cost of goods sold was understated, Phar-Mor made it appear as if it were selling merchandise at higher margins. As the cost of sales was understated, net income was overstated.

Phar-Mor would regularly pressure vendors for large, up-front payments in exchange for not selling competitors' products. These payments were called "exclusivity payments," and some vendors paid up to $25 million for these rights. Monus would use this money to cover the hidden losses and pay suppliers. Instead of deferring revenue from these exclusivity payments over the life of the vendors' contracts—consistent with generally accepted accounting *principles—Monus and Finn would recognize all the revenue up front. As a result of this practice, Phar-Mor was able to report impressive results in the short run.*

Cases of financial statement fraud often have elements that are similar to the Phar-Mor fraud. First, the company appears to outperform others in the industry, and investors, analysts, or owners expect the company to perform at a very high level. At some point, the expectations of investors, analysts, or others will not be met, so pressure builds to do something to meet the high expectations. This is a turning point where fraud perpetrators step on to a slippery slope and slide down a mountain of deceit that is very difficult to reverse. When the CEO of Satyam Computer Services confessed his fraud he said "It was like riding a tiger, not knowing how to get off without being eaten."

The person stepping on to the slippery slope is the manager or officer over financial reporting who agrees to violate an accounting principle and/or rule. The initial violation is often small compared to the fraud that is eventually detected. Sometimes the individual is able to rationalize that he or she is simply using his or her knowledge of accounting to "manage earnings" in a way that is beneficial for the company and investors. Almost always, the initial violation is viewed as aggressive but not fraudulent and is accompanied with an expectation that it will be a "one-time" event that will be corrected when operating performance improves in the future.

At this point, the officer over financial reporting has gained a reputation as the source of earnings when operations fall short. Because of the difficulty to resist this tremendous pressure when operations fall short in the future, the manager who committed a small, one-time fraud becomes the main source of earnings—fraudulent accounting practices. At this point, the fraud grows into a monster that needs constant care and attention. This growth process has been referred to as "a trickle to a waterfall," and it is often only a few short years before this seemingly innocent case of "earnings management" grows into a flood that ends up causing a financial and economic disaster by the time it is detected.

Motivations for Financial Statement Fraud

Motivations to issue fraudulent financial statements vary. As indicated previously in the perfect storm analysis, sometimes the motivation is to support a high

stock price or a bond or stock offering. At other times, the motivation is to increase the company's stock price or for management to maximize a bonus. In some companies that issued fraudulent financial statements, top executives owned large amounts of company stock or stock options, and a change in the stock price would have enormous effects on their personal net worth.

Sometimes, division managers overstate financial results to meet company expectations. Many times, pressure on management is high, and when faced with failure or cheating, some managers will turn to cheating. In the Phar-Mor case, Mickey Monus wanted his company to grow quickly, so he lowered prices on 300 "price-sensitive" items. Prices were cut so much that items were sold below cost, making each sale result in a loss. The strategy helped Phar-Mor win new customers and open dozens of new stores each year. However, the strategy resulted in huge losses for the company, and rather than admitting that the company was facing losses, Mickey Monus hid the losses and made Phar-Mor appear profitable. While the motivations for financial statement fraud differ, the results are always the same—adverse consequences for the company, its principals, and its investors.

> ### Remember this …
>
> *During 2000–2002, numerous financial statement frauds were discovered in corporate America. Like most fraud, these frauds were perpetrated in the presence of the three elements of fraud: perceived pressure, perceived opportunity, and rationalization. The perfect fraud storm consists of the following nine factors that led to many of the more recent frauds: (1) a booming economy, (2) overall decay of moral values, (3) misplaced executive incentives, (4) high analysts' expectations, (5) high debt and leverage, (6) focus on accounting rules rather than principles, (7) lack of auditor independence, (8) greed, and (9) educator failures. Each case of financial statement fraud involves upper management, amounts to millions of dollars lost by investors, and can span many years. Management fraud is often the result of pressures to meet internal or external expectations and starts small with the expectation that it will be corrected. However, once a compromise is made to allow fraud to begin, it is very hard to reverse.*

A Framework for Detecting Financial Statement Fraud

Identifying fraud exposures is one of the most difficult steps in detecting financial statement fraud. Correctly identifying exposures means that you must clearly understand the operations and nature of the organization you are studying as well as the nature of the industry and its competitors. Investigators must have a good understanding of the organization's management and what motivates them. Investigators must understand how the company is organized and be aware of relationships the company has with other parties and the influence that each of those parties has on management. In addition, investigators and auditors should use strategic reasoning when attempting to detect fraud.

Strategic reasoning refers to the ability to anticipate a fraud perpetrator's likely method of concealing a fraud. Because external auditors are charged with the responsibility for detecting material financial statement fraud, we take the perspective of how an external auditor should engage in strategic reasoning. However, this reasoning process can also occur when internal auditors, the audit committee, fraud investigators, or others are considering efforts to detect management fraud.

Knowing that an auditor's duty is to assess the fairness of the financial statements, a fraud perpetrator will attempt to conceal his or her fraud from the auditors. Thus, fraud is *strategic* in nature such that management's propensity to commit fraud is affected by the anticipated audit, and the auditor's approach to detecting fraud is affected by the potential for management to commit fraud. Similar to a chess match where one must consider the potential moves of his or her opponent while the opponent is doing likewise, an auditor seeking to detect fraud is most effective when he or she considers how management is viewing the potential audit approach.

This type of audit planning is different from that required to discover unintentional errors in financial statements. The thinking involved in a strategic setting such as the detection of financial statement fraud is based on game theory. Game theory seeks to predict behavior based on an individual's best response given that individual's motivations and the individual's beliefs regarding the likely behavior of his or her opponent(s). The auditor's consideration of an auditee's response to auditor choices is referred to as "strategic reasoning." Academic research suggests that effective auditors need to engage in strategic reasoning to predict an auditee's response but that doing so becomes progressively more difficult as the auditor considers more levels of potential strategic behavior.

Several levels of strategic reasoning exist in the audit setting. These levels are zero-order reasoning, first-order reasoning, and higher-order reasoning. **Zero-order reasoning** occurs when an auditor and auditee consider only conditions that *directly* affect themselves but not the other party. When engaged in zero-order reasoning, the auditor simply considers his or her own incentives, such as audit fees, sampling costs, and penalties. **First-order reasoning** means that the auditor considers conditions that directly affect the auditee. In this case, auditors assume auditees use zero-order reasoning and develop audit plans that consider the auditee's incentives. For example, if the auditor expects the concealment of fraud, he or she will modify the audit plan accordingly to uncover this concealment of fraud. In this approach, the auditor does not consider whether the auditee has anticipated the auditor's behavior. **Higher-order reasoning** occurs when the auditor considers additional layers of complexity, including how management may anticipate the auditor's behavior. For example, an auditor using higher-order reasoning may adjust the audit plan by introducing unexpected audit procedures in response to what the auditor believes management may be doing to conceal a fraud based on management's strategic reasoning.

Given the difficulty of engaging in high levels of strategic reasoning, it is fortunate that auditors probably can make significant improvements in their audit approach by engaging in first- or second-order strategic reasoning. Currently, management can often accurately predict what procedures will be performed in an independent audit because they are often aware of what the auditor has done in prior audits. When this happens, financial statement fraud schemes are developed so that the auditor's typical audit approach will fail to detect the scheme. An effective auditor will use strategic reasoning —specifically high-order reasoning or, at a minimum, first-order reasoning—to effectively detect this fraudulent activity. This will lead the auditor to perform unexpected procedures and use tests that management has not seen before. Academic research suggests that engaging in such reasoning leads auditors to perform more rigorous procedures when comparing audit plans with expert fraud examiners' recommended procedures.[11]

When engaged in strategic reasoning, an auditor will consider several questions, including the following:

1. What types of *fraud schemes* is management likely to use to commit financial statement fraud? For

example, is management likely to improperly record sales before goods have been shipped to customers?

2. What *typical tests* are used to detect these schemes? For example, auditors often examine shipping documents to validate shipments to customers.

3. How could management *conceal the scheme* of interest from the typical test? For example, management may ship goods to an off-site warehouse so as to be able to provide evidence of shipment to an auditor.

4. How could the *typical test be modified* so as to detect the concealed scheme? For example, the auditor may gather information about the shipping location to ensure that it is owned or leased by the customer or interview shipping personnel to determine if sold goods are always shipped to the customer.

STOP & THINK *If auditors and investigators modified their typical procedures and regularly used a few unexpected procedures to look for fraud, how would this affect a potential perpetrator's opportunity to conceal a fraud?*

Fraudulent financial statements are rarely detected by analyzing the financial statements alone. Rather, financial statement fraud is usually detected when the information in the financial statements is compared with the real-world referents those numbers are supposed to represent, and the context in which management is operating and being motivated. Fraud is often detected by focusing on the changes in reported assets, liabilities, revenues, and expenses from period to period or by comparing company performance to industry norms. In the ZZZZ Best fraud case, for example, each period's financial statements looked correct. Only when the change in assets and revenues from period to period were examined and when assets and revenues reported in the financial statements were compared with actual building restoration projects was it determined that the financial statements were incorrect.

In addition to the typical analyses of financial statements (e.g., ratio, horizontal, and vertical analyses), research suggests that auditors, investors, regulators, or fraud examiners can benefit by using **nonfinancial performance measures** to assess the likelihood of fraud. This was illustrated in former HealthSouth CEO Richard Scrushy's trial, when prosecutors argued that Scrushy knew something was amiss with HealthSouth's financial statements because there was a discrepancy between the company's financial and nonfinancial performance. The prosecutor noted that revenues and assets were increasing while the number of HealthSouth facilities decreased. "And that's not a red flag to you?" asked prosecutor Colleen Conry during the trial. Conry pointed out that financial statement fraud risk was high at HealthSouth because the company's financial statement data were inconsistent with its nonfinancial measures. The use of financial and nonfinancial data for detecting fraud is one of four key considerations in a framework for detecting fraud. We label this framework the "fraud exposure rectangle."

Academic research on nonfinancial performance measures has shown that companies engaging in revenue fraud will have increases in revenues that are not consistent with their nonfinancial performance measures.[12] This research shows that even basic nonfinancial performance measures, such as the number of employees, can signal that a company's revenues are fraudulent. Because these basic nonfinancial performance measures are publicly available, investors, auditors, and others can use them to identify fraud risk. This makes it more difficult for fraud perpetrators to conceal their fraud since they now have additional data to manipulate. Often individuals who are not working with management on the financial fraud report the nonfinancial measures. This compounds management's challenges in concealing a revenue fraud since they may need to expand the pool of individuals who are reporting fictitious data. For these and other reasons, nonfinancial performance measures hold significant potential as a red flag for fraud.

In addition to considering financial and nonfinancial data to assess fraud risk, auditors can identify fraud risk exposures by examining four groups of fraud exposures. The fraud exposure rectangle shown in Figure 11.2 is a useful tool for identifying management fraud exposures. On the first corner of the rectangle are the management and directors of the company. On the second corner are relationships the company has with other entities. On the third corner are the nature of the organization being examined and the industry in which the organization operates. On the fourth corner are the financial results and operating characteristics of the organization.

Although CPAs and others have traditionally focused almost entirely on financial statements to detect financial statement fraud, each of these four areas should be considered to effectively assess the likelihood of fraud. We now examine each of these four areas individually.

FIGURE 11.2 FRAUD EXPOSURE RECTANGLE

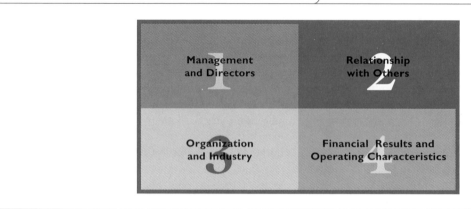

Management and the Board of Directors

As shown in the statistics presented previously, top management is almost always involved when financial statement fraud occurs. Unlike embezzlement and misappropriation, financial statement fraud is usually committed by the highest individuals in an organization, and often on behalf of the organization as opposed to against the organization. Because management is usually involved, management and the directors must be investigated to determine their involvement in and motivation for committing fraud. In detecting financial statement fraud, gaining an understanding of management and what motivates them is at least as important as understanding the financial statements. In particular, three aspects of management should be investigated:

1. Managements' backgrounds.
2. Managements' motivations.
3. Managements' influence in making decisions for the organization.

Managements' Backgrounds

With respect to backgrounds, fraud investigators should understand what kinds of organizations and activities management and directors have been associated with in the past. With the Internet today, it is very easy to conduct simple searches on individuals. One very easy way is to type the individual's name in Google or another search engine. The search engine will quickly list all the references to the person's name, including past proxy statements and any **10-Ks** (the corporate reports filed with the SEC) of companies the person has been affiliated with, newspaper articles about the person, and so forth. Also, if this simple search is not sufficient, it doesn't cost very much to hire a private investigator or to use investigative services on the Web to do a search. (Search techniques discussed in Chapter 9.)

An example of the importance of understanding management's background is the Lincoln Savings and Loan fraud. Before perpetrating the Lincoln Savings and Loan fraud, Charles Keating was sanctioned by the SEC for his involvement in a financial institution fraud in Cincinnati, Ohio, and, in fact, had signed a consent decree with the SEC that he would never again be involved in the management of another financial institution.

Another example where knowledge of management's background would have been helpful was Comparator Systems, a Los Angeles–based fingerprinting equipment company accused of securities fraud in 1996. CEO Robert Reed Rogers grew up in Chicago, majored in chemistry in college, and became a college lecturer in business and economics. He worked short stints at the consulting firm of McKinsey & Co. and Litton Industries. In information sent to investors, he boasted of many accomplishments, describing himself as founder and president of various companies developing products or processes. Missing from Rogers' biographical sketches is the fact that, in the mid-70s, he was president of Newport International Metals. Newport was involved in the speculative rage of the period—precious metals. The company claimed to have the "exclusive right" to a certain mining process for producing jewelry. The company received $50,000 in securities from investors John and Herta Minar of New York to serve as collateral to secure start-up funds. In 1976, Newport was cited by the state of California for unlawful sale of securities and was ordered to stop. The Minars sued and won a judgment for $50,000. In 1977, a warrant was issued for Rogers' arrest for failure to appear in court in connection with a lawsuit filed by investors in another company managed by Rogers. Certainly, Rogers had a tainted background that would have been of critical interest to anyone investing in or doing business with Comparator Systems.

Managements' Motivations

What motivates directors and management is also important to know. Is their personal worth tied up in the organization? Are they under pressure to deliver unrealistic results? Is their compensation primarily performance-based? Do they have a history of guiding Wall Street to higher and higher expectations? Have they grown through acquisitions or through internal means? Does the company have debt covenants or other financial measures that must be met? Is management's job at risk? These questions are examples of what must be answered in order to properly understand management's motivations. Many financial statement frauds have been perpetrated because management needed to report positive or high income to support stock prices, show positive earnings for a public stock or debt offering, or report profits to meet regulatory or loan restrictions.

Managements' Influence in Making Decisions for the Organization

Finally, management's ability to influence decisions for the organization is important to understand because perpetrating fraud is much easier when one or two individuals have primary decision-making power than when an organization has a more democratic leadership. Most people who commit management fraud are first-time offenders, and being dishonest the first time is difficult for them. For two individuals to simultaneously be dishonest is more difficult, and for three people to simultaneously be dishonest is even more difficult. When decision-making ability is spread among several individuals, or when the board of directors takes an active role in the organization, fraud is much more difficult to perpetrate. Most financial statement frauds do not occur in large, historically profitable organizations. Rather, they occur in smaller organizations where one or two individuals have almost total decision-making ability, in companies that experience unbelievably rapid growth, or where the board of directors and audit committee do not take an active role (something that is much harder to do now with the new corporate governance standards

described in Appendix A of this chapter). An active board of directors and/or audit committee that gets involved in the major decisions of the organization can do much to deter management fraud. In fact, it is for this reason that NASDAQ and NYSE corporate governance standards require that the majority of board members be independent and that some of the key committees, such as audit and compensation, be comprised entirely of independent directors.

Once management decides that it will commit fraud, the particular schemes used are often determined by the nature of the business's operations. While we usually focus on the schemes and the financial results of those schemes, remember that the decision to commit fraud in the first place was made by management or other officers. Some of the key questions that must be asked about management and the directors are as follows:

Understanding Management and Director Backgrounds

1. Have any of the key executives or board members been associated with other organizations in the past? If so, what was the nature of those organizations and relationships?
2. Were key members of management promoted from within the organization or recruited from the outside?
3. Have any key members of management had past regulatory or legal problems, either personally or in organizations with which they have been associated?
4. Have there been significant changes in the makeup of management or the board of directors?
5. Has there been a high turnover of management and/or board members?
6. Do any members of management or the board have criminal backgrounds?
7. Are there any other issues related to the backgrounds of key members of management and the board of directors?
8. Are most board members independent?
9. Is the chairperson of the board separate from the CEO?
10. Does the company have independent audit, compensation, and nominating committees?

Understanding What Motivates Management and the Board of Directors

1. Is the personal worth of any of the key executives tied up in the organization?
2. Is management under pressure to meet earnings or other financial expectations, or does management

commit to analysts, creditors, and others to achieve what appear to be unduly aggressive forecasts?

3. Is management's compensation primarily performance-based (bonuses, stock options, etc.)?

4. Are there significant debt covenants or other financial restrictions that management must meet?

5. Is the job security of any key members of management at serious risk?

6. Is the organization's reported financial performance decreasing?

7. Is there an excessive interest by management in maintaining or increasing the entity's stock price?

8. Does management have an incentive to use inappropriate means to minimize reported earnings for tax reasons?

9. Are there any other significant issues related to the motivations of management and board members?

Understanding the Degree of Influence of Key Members of Management and/or the Board of Directors

1. Who are the key members of management and the board of directors who have the most influence?

2. Do one or two key people have dominant influence in the organization?

3. Is the management style of the organization more autocratic or more democratic?

4. Is the organization's management centralized or decentralized?

5. Does management use ineffective means of communicating and supporting the entity's values or ethics, or do they communicate inappropriate values or ethics?

6. Does management fail to correct known reportable conditions in internal control on a timely basis?

7. Does management set unduly aggressive financial targets and expenditures for operating personnel?

8. Does management have too much involvement in or influence over the selection of accounting principles or the determination of significant estimates?

9. Are there any other significant issues related to the degree of influence of key members of management and the board of directors?

Relationships with Others

Financial statement fraud is often perpetrated with the help of other real or fictitious organizations. Enron's fraud was primarily conducted through what are known as special purpose entities (SPEs), which are business interests formed solely in order to accomplish some specific task or tasks. SPEs were not illegal, but were subject to accounting standards that designated which SPEs were to be reported as part of the larger, parent, company instead of being reported as independent entities and not consolidated with the parent. At the time of the Enron fraud, an SPE was considered independent if it met the following two criteria: (1) independent third-party investors made a substantive capital investment, generally at least 3 percent of the SPE's assets and (2) the third-party investment is genuinely at risk. Enron was obligated to consolidate the assets and liabilities of entities not meeting these requirements. The SEC's complaint alleges that certain SPEs of Enron should have been consolidated onto Enron's balance sheet. Further, Fastow, Kopper, and others used their simultaneous influence over Enron's business operations and the SPEs as a means to secretly and unlawfully generate millions of dollars for themselves and others. In particular, Fastow profited immensely by making tens of millions of dollars designing Enron's SPEs in his favor.

In the following examples, we review several different schemes that involved relationships with others in order to commit financial statement fraud.

First, in 1997, Enron decided to sell its interest in a California windmill farm. In order for the farm to qualify for beneficial regulatory treatment, Enron, as an electric utilities holding company, had to decrease its ownership to below 50 percent. However, Enron did not want to lose control of the profitable wind farm. Instead, Fastow created a special purpose entity (known as RADR) and recruited "Friends of Enron" (actually friends of Kopper) as outside investors. However, because these investors lacked sufficient funds, Fastow made a personal loan of $419,000 to fund the purchase of the wind farm. RADR became immensely profitable. Fastow's loan was repaid with $62,000 interest, and Kopper arranged for yearly "gifts" of $10,000 (keeping the gifts beneath the limit of taxable income) to each member of Fastow's family. Because the RADR third-party investment was funded by Fastow, and because Fastow and Kopper clearly controlled RADR's operations, the entity should have been consolidated with Enron's financial statements.

As a second example, in 1993, Enron created an entity called JEDI (named after the Star Wars characters). Because of a substantial contribution by an independent investor, the California Public Employees' Retirement System (CalPERS), Enron was justified in not consolidating JEDI onto its books. However, in 1997, as CalPERS wanted to sell its portion of JEDI, rather than consider other independent investors, Fastow arranged for the creation of Chewco (also named after a Star Wars character), an SPE *that would buy out CalPERS. Chewco, and thus JEDI, was not eligible for the off-the-book status it was given. First, Chewco was not independent. Although Fastow abandoned the idea to be Chewco's independent investor (on Jeff Skilling's advice that Enron would be forced to disclose Fastow's participation), he substituted Kopper, himself an Enron executive who was essentially controlled by Fastow. Second, Chewco's investment in JEDI was not "genuinely at risk." It was funded through two $190 million bank loans, both of which were guaranteed by Enron. As with RADR, Fastow directed Kopper to continue to make payments benefiting Fastow, including a $54,000 payment to Fastow's wife for performing administrative duties for Chewco.*

In a different scheme, Lincoln Savings and Loan used relationships to commit fraud. In Lincoln's case, it structured sham transactions with certain straw buyers to make its negative performance appear profitable. A real estate limited partnership that committed financial statement fraud structured fraudulent transactions with bankers to hide mortgages on many of its real estate properties. Relationships with related parties are problematic because they often allow for other than arm's length transactions. For example, the management of ESM Government Securities used related parties to hide a $400 million financial statement fraud by creating a large receivable from a nonconsolidated related entity.

Although relationships with all parties should be examined to determine if they present management fraud opportunities or exposures, relationships with related organizations and individuals, external auditors, lawyers, investors, and regulators should always be carefully considered. Relationships with financial institutions and bondholders are also important because they provide an indication of the extent to which the company is leveraged. Examples of the kinds of questions that should be asked about debt relationships include the following:

- *Is the company highly leveraged, and with which financial institutions?*
- *What assets of the organization are pledged as collateral?*
- *Is there debt or other restrictive covenants that must be met?*
- *Do the banking relationships appear normal, or are there strange relationships with financial institutions, such as using institutions in unusual geographical locations?*
- *Are there relationships between the officers of the financial institutions and the client organization?*

Relationship with Financial Institutions

The real estate partnership referred to earlier involved a Wisconsin company taking out unauthorized loans from a bank located in another state, where it had no business purpose. The bank was used because the CEO of the client company had a relationship with the bank president, who later falsified an audit confirmation sent by the bank to the auditors. The loans were discovered when the auditors performed a lien search on properties owned. Because the bank president denied the existence of the loans, liabilities were significantly understated on the balance sheet.

Relationship with Related Organizations and Individuals

Related parties, which include related organizations and individuals such as family members, should be examined because structuring "non–arm's length" and often unrealistic transactions with related parties is one of the easiest ways to perpetrate financial statement fraud. These kinds of relationships are usually identified by examining large and/or unusual transactions, often occurring at strategic times (such as at the end of a period) to make the financial statements look better. The kinds of relationships and events that should be examined include the following:

- *Large transactions that result in revenues or income for the organization.*
- *Sales or purchases of assets between related entities.*
- *Transactions that result in goodwill or other intangible assets being recognized in the financial statements.*
- *Transactions that generate nonoperating, rather than operating, income.*
- *Loans or other financing transactions between related entities.*
- *Any transaction that appears to be unusual or questionable for the organization, especially transactions that are unrealistically large.*

Relationship with Auditors

The relationship between a company and its auditors is important to analyze for several reasons. If there has been an auditor change, there is probably a good reason for the change. Auditing firms do not easily give up clients, and the termination of an auditor–auditee relationship is most often caused by failure of the client to pay, an auditor–auditee disagreement, suspected fraud or other problems by the auditor, or the auditee believing the auditor's fees are too high. While some of these reasons, such as high fees, may not signal a potential fraud problem, auditor–auditee disagreements, failure to pay an audit fee, and suspected problems can all be reasons that suggest a financial statement fraud problem. The fact that an auditor was dismissed or resigned, together with the difficulty of a first-year auditor to discover financial statement fraud, creates a double cause for concern when there is an auditor change. Publicly traded companies are required to publicly disclose any changes in their audit firm and the reason for the change on SEC Form 8-K.

On occasion, one auditing firm decides to accept more risk or handles risks differently than other auditing firms. Many have argued that one such firm was Laventhol & Horwath, which failed in the late 1980s. Others have argued that Arthur Andersen's failure can be attributed to the risk posture it took with its audit clients and its preoccupation with cross-selling consulting services to audit clients. Certainly, Andersen had its share of high-profile audit failures, including Sunbeam, Waste Management, Enron, WorldCom, Qwest, and others. In examining a company for possible financial statement fraud, it is important to know who its auditor is and how long that relationship has existed.

Relationship with Lawyers

Relationships with lawyers pose even greater risks than relationships with auditors. While auditors are supposed to be independent and must resign if they suspect that financial results may not be appropriate, lawyers are usually advocates for their clients and will often follow and support their clients until it is obvious that fraud has occurred. In addition, lawyers usually have information about a client's legal difficulties, regulatory problems, and other significant occurrences. Like auditors, lawyers rarely give up a profitable client unless there is something seriously wrong. Thus, a change in legal firms without an obvious reason is often a cause for concern. Unfortunately, unlike changing auditors, where an 8-K must be filed for public companies, there is no such reporting requirement for changing lawyers.

Relationship with Investors

Relationships with investors are important because financial statement fraud is often motivated by a debt or an equity offering to investors. In addition, knowledge of the number and kinds of investors (public vs. private, major exchange vs. small exchange, institutional vs. individual, etc.) can often provide an indication of the degree of pressure and public scrutiny upon management of the company and its financial performance.

If an organization is publicly held, investor groups or investment analysts usually follow the company very closely and can often provide information or indications that something is wrong. For example, some investors sell a company's stock "short," meaning they borrow shares from a brokerage and sell the shares at today's price with the intention to repay the borrowed stock they sold at some future time when the stock is trading for a lower price. These "short" sellers are always looking for bad news about an organization that will make its stock go down. If they suspect that something is not right, they will often publicly vent their concerns.

Investor groups often focus on information that is very different from that used by auditors, and sometimes the fraud symptoms are more obvious to the investor groups than to auditors, especially auditors who focus only on financial statements. Short sellers have sometimes been first to determine that financial statement fraud was occurring and then they revealed the fraud to the market. With Enron, for example, the first person to come forward with negative information about the company was Jim Chanos, who operated a highly regarded firm specializing in short selling named Kynikos Associates (Kynikos is based on the Greek word for *cynic*). Chanos stated publicly in early 2001 that "no one could explain how Enron actually made money." He noted that Enron had completed transactions with related parties that "were run by a senior officer of Enron" and assumed it was a conflict of interest. When asked, Enron wouldn't answer questions about LJM Partners and other partnerships. Then in its March 5, 2001 issue, *Fortune* magazine ran a story about Enron that stated, "To skeptics, the lack of clarity raises a red flag about Enron's pricey stock … the inability to get behind the numbers combined with ever higher expectations for the company may increase the chance of a nasty surprise. Enron is an earnings-at-risk story." Unfortunately, investors kept ignoring this bad news for over six months until late 2001, when skeptics started selling the stock. Enron declared bankruptcy in late 2001.

Relationship with Regulatory Bodies

Finally, understanding the client's relationship with regulators is important. If the company you are examining is a publicly held client, you need to know whether the SEC has ever issued an enforcement release against it. For example, in its report pursuant to Section 704 of the Sarbanes-Oxley Act, the SEC stated that during the five-year period from July 31, 1997 to July 30, 2002 it had filed 515 enforcement actions involving 869 named parties, 164 entities, and 705 individuals. You also need to know if all annual, quarterly, and other reports have been filed on a timely basis. If the company is in a regulated industry, such as banking, you need to know what its relationship is with appropriate regulatory bodies such as the Federal Deposit Insurance Corporation, the Federal Reserve, and the Office of the Comptroller of the Currency. Are there any problematic issues related to those bodies? Whether the organization owes any back taxes to the federal or state government or to other taxing districts is also important to know. Because of the recourse and sanctions available to taxing authorities, organizations usually do not fall behind on their payments unless something is wrong or the organization is having serious cash flow problems. The following questions should be asked about a company's relationships with others.

Relationships with Financial Institutions

1. With what financial institutions does the organization have significant relationships?
2. Is the organization highly leveraged through bank or other loans?
3. Do any loan or debt covenants or restrictions pose significant problems for the organization?
4. Do the banking relationships appear normal, or are there unusual attributes present with the relationships (strange geographical locations, too many banks, etc.)?
5. Do members of management or the board have personal or other close relationships with officers of any of the major banks used by the company?
6. Have any significant changes occurred in the financial institutions used by the company? If so, why?
7. Are any significant bank accounts or subsidiary or branch operations located in tax-haven jurisdictions for which business justification is not apparent?
8. Have critical assets of the company been pledged as collateral on risky loans?
9. Are there any other questionable financial institution relationships?

Relationships with Related Parties

1. Are any significant related-party transactions not in the ordinary course of business or with related entities not audited or audited by another firm?

2. Are large or unusual transactions made at or near the end of a period that significantly improve the reported financial performance of the company?
3. Are significant receivables or payables occurring between related entities?
4. Has a significant amount of the organization's revenues or income been derived from related-party transactions?
5. Is a significant part of the company's income or revenues derived from one or two large transactions?
6. Are any other related-party relationships questionable?
7. Have relationships with other entities resulted in the reporting of significant amounts of nonoperating income?

Relationships with Auditors

1. Have frequent disputes occurred with the current or predecessor auditors on accounting, auditing, or reporting matters?
2. Has management placed unreasonable demands on the auditor, including unreasonable time constraints?
3. Has the company placed formal or informal restrictions on the auditor that inappropriately limit his or her access to people or information or his or her ability to communicate effectively with the board of directors or the audit committee?
4. Does domineering management behavior characterize the dealings with the auditor, especially any attempts to influence the scope of the auditor's work?
5. Has an auditor change occurred? If so, for what reason?
6. Are any other relationships with the auditor questionable?

Relationships with Lawyers

1. Has the company been involved in significant litigation concerning matters that could severely and adversely affect the company's financial results?
2. Has any attempt been made to hide litigation from the auditors or others?
3. Has any change occurred in outside counsels? If so, for what reasons?
4. Are any other lawyer relationships questionable?

Relationships with Investors

1. Is the organization in the process of issuing an initial or secondary public debt or equity offering?
2. Are any investor-related lawsuits pending or ongoing?
3. Are any relationships with investment bankers, stock analysts, or others problematic or questionable?

4. Has significant "short selling" of the company's stock occurred? If so, for what reasons?
5. Are any investor relationships questionable?

Relationships with Regulatory Bodies

1. Does management display a significant disregard for regulatory authorities?
2. Has there been a history of securities law violations or claims against the entity or its senior management alleging fraud or violations of securities laws?
3. Have any 8-Ks been filed with the SEC? If so, for what reasons?
4. Could any new accounting, statutory, or regulatory requirements impair the financial stability or profitability of the entity?
5. Are significant tax disputes with the IRS or other taxing authorities pending?
6. Is the company current on paying its payroll taxes and other payroll-related expenses? Is the company current on paying other liabilities?
7. Are any other relationships with regulatory bodies questionable?
8. Are there SEC investigations of any of the company's 10-K, **10-Q**, or other filings?

Organization and Industry

Financial statement fraud is sometimes masked by creating an organizational structure that makes it easy to hide fraud. This was certainly the case with Enron and all of its nonconsolidated SPEs (now called variable interest entities by the FASB). Another example was Lincoln Savings and Loan, which was a subsidiary of American National, a holding company that had over 50 other subsidiaries and related companies. Lincoln Savings and Loan had several subsidiaries, some with no apparent business purpose. A significant part of the Lincoln Savings and Loan fraud was to structure supposedly "profitable" transactions near the end of each quarter by selling land to straw buyers. To entice the buyers to participate, the perpetrators often made the down payment themselves by having Lincoln Savings and Loan simultaneously loan the straw buyers the same amount (or more) of money that they needed to make the down payments on the land. The simultaneous loan and purchase transactions were not easily identifiable because Lincoln Savings and Loan would sell the land and have another related entity make the loan. In reality, a complex organizational structure was

being created that had no apparent business purpose. The complexity of the organization was being used as a smoke screen to conceal the illicit transactions.

In one transaction known as the RA Homes transaction, for example, on September 30, 2008 Lincoln Savings and Loan supposedly sold 1,300 acres known as the Continental Ranch to RA Homes for $25 million, receiving a down payment of $5 million and a note receivable for $20 million (in real estate transactions such as this, FAS No. 66 requires at least a 20 percent down payment in order to record the transaction on an accrual basis, thus recognizing profit). On the transaction, Lincoln recognized a gain on the sale of several million dollars. However, on September 25, five days before the supposed sale, another subsidiary of Lincoln loaned RA Homes $3 million; on November 12, a different subsidiary loaned RA Homes another $2 million. Given these transactions, who made the down payment? It was obvious to the jury that Lincoln Savings and Loan, itself, made the down payment and that the complicated organizational structure was used to hide the real nature of the transaction. The same was true of ESM, where related organizations were established to make it look like receivables were due to the company. However, in fact, the related organizations were not audited and could not have paid even a small portion of the amount they supposedly owed.

The attributes of an organization that suggest potential fraud exposures include such things as an unduly complex organizational structure, an organization without an internal audit department, a board of directors with no or few outsiders on the board or audit committee, an organization in which one person or a small group of individuals controls related entities, an organization that has offshore affiliates with no apparent business purpose, an organization that has made numerous acquisitions and has recognized large merger-related charges, or an organization that is new. Investigators must understand who the owners of an organization are. Sometimes silent or hidden owners use the organization for illegal or other questionable activities.

The industry of the organization must also be carefully examined. Some industries are much more risky than others. For example, in the 80s, the savings and loan (S&L) industry was extremely risky, to the extent that some auditing firms would not audit an S&L. Recently, technology companies, especially dot-com and Internet companies with new and unproven business models, have been extremely risky and represent the most frauds revealed in SEC AAERs. With any company, however, the organization's performance relative to that of similar organizations in the same industry should be examined. The kinds of questions that should be asked in order to understand the exposure to management fraud are as follows:

1. Does the company have an overly complex organizational structure involving numerous or unusual legal entities, managerial lines of authority, or contractual arrangements without apparent business purpose?
2. Is a legitimate business purpose apparent for each separate entity of the business?
3. Is the board of directors comprised primarily of officers of the company or other related individuals?
4. Is the board of directors passive or active and independent?
5. Is the audit committee comprised primarily of insiders or outsiders?
6. Is the audit committee passive or active and independent?
7. Does the organization have an independent or active internal audit department?
8. Does the organization have offshore activities without any apparent business purpose?
9. Is the organization a new entity without a proven history?
10. Have significant recent changes occurred in the nature of the organization?
11. Is monitoring of significant controls adequate?
12. Are the accounting and information technology staff and organization effective?
13. Is the degree of competition or market saturation high, accompanied by declining margins?
14. Is the client in a declining industry with increasing business failures and significant declines in customer demand?
15. Are changes in the industry rapid, such as high vulnerability to quickly changing technology or rapid product obsolescence?
16. Is the performance of the company similar or contrary to other firms in the industry?
17. Are there any other significant issues related to organization and industry?

Financial Results and Operating Characteristics

Much can be learned about exposure to financial statement fraud by closely examining management and the board of directors, relationships with others, and the nature of the organization. Looking at those three elements usually involves the same procedures for all kinds of financial statement frauds, whether the accounts manipulated are revenues, assets, liabilities, expenses, or equities. The kinds of exposures identified by the financial statements and operating characteristics of the organization differ from fraud scheme to fraud scheme.

Fraud symptoms most often exhibit themselves through changes in the financial statements. For example, financial statements that contain large changes in account balances from period to period are more likely to contain fraud than financial statements that exhibit only small, incremental changes in account balances. A sudden, dramatic increase in receivables, for example, is often a signal that something is wrong. In addition to changes in financial statement balances and amounts, understanding what the footnotes are really saying is very important. Many times, the footnotes strongly hint that fraud is occurring; but what is contained in the footnotes is not clearly understood by auditors and others.

In assessing fraud exposure through financial statements and operating characteristics, the balances and amounts must be compared with those of similar organizations in the same industry, and the real-world referents to the financial statement amounts must be determined. If, for example, an organization's financial statements report that the company has $2 million of inventory, then the inventory has to be located somewhere, and, depending on the type of inventory it is, it should require a certain amount of space to store it, lift forks and other equipment to move and ship it, and people to manage it. An examiner should ask whether the financial statement numbers are realistically given the actual inventory that is observable.

Using financial relationships to assess fraud exposures requires that you know the nature of the client's business, the kinds of accounts that should be included, the kinds of fraud that could occur in the organization, and the kinds of symptoms those frauds would generate. For example, the major activities of a manufacturing company can be subdivided into sales and collections, acquisition and payment, financing, payroll, and inventory and warehousing. Breaking an organization down into various activities or cycles such as these and then, for each cycle, identifying the major functions performed, the major risks inherent in each function, the potential abuse and fraud that can occur, and the symptoms those frauds will generate may be helpful. An examiner can then use proactive detection techniques to determine the likelihood of fraud in those cycles.

As we mentioned earlier, in addition to considering the pattern of financial relationships, nonfinancial performance measures are also valuable for detecting unusual financial results. Nonfinancial performance has been discussed in management accounting circles as a best practice for managing a business. For example, the "balanced scorecard" is a performance evaluation method that focuses on both financial and nonfinancial indicators of performance such as customer satisfaction. Academic research on using nonfinancial performance measures to assess fraud risk shows that even simple nonfinancial indicators, such as the number of employees, can help determine when financial statement fraud exists. For example, if a company's revenues are growing while employees are decreasing, then that company is more likely to be committing fraud compared to a company in which employee and revenue trends appear consistent. The value of using nonfinancial indicators for assessing fraud risk is thought to rest on the assumption that management can more easily manipulate financial numbers but finds it harder to keep all the nonfinancial information consistent with the financial information. In some industries, such as airlines, nonfinancial performance indicators are collected and independently verified. This increases the effectiveness of comparing financial and nonfinancial performance measures to look for fraud.

Some of the critical questions that must be asked about financial statement relationships and operating results are as follows:

1. Are unrealistic changes or increases present in financial statement account balances?
2. Are the account balances realistic given the nature, age, and size of the company?
3. Do actual physical assets exist in the amounts and values indicated on the financial statements?
4. Have there been significant changes in the nature of the organization's revenues or expenses?
5. Do one or a few large transactions account for a significant portion of any account balance or amount?
6. Are significant transactions made near the end of the period that positively impact results of operations, especially transactions that are unusual or highly complex or that pose "substance over form" questions?

7. Do financial results appear consistent on a quarter-by-quarter or month-by-month basis, or are unrealistic amounts occurring in a subperiod?
8. Does the entity show an inability to generate cash flows from operations while reporting earnings and earnings growth?
9. Is significant pressure felt to obtain additional capital necessary to stay competitive, considering the financial position of the entity—including the need for funds to finance major research and development or capital expenditures?
10. Are reported assets, liabilities, revenues, or expenses based on significant estimates that involve unusually subjective judgments or uncertainties or that are subject to potential significant change in the near term?
11. Does growth or profitability appear rapid, especially compared with that of other companies in the same industry?
12. Is the organization highly vulnerable to changes in interest rates?
13. Are unrealistically aggressive sales or profitability incentive programs in place?
14. Is a threat of imminent bankruptcy, foreclosure, or hostile takeover pertinent?
15. Are adverse consequences on significant pending transactions possible, such as a business combination or contract award, if poor financial results are reported?
16. Has management personally guaranteed significant debts of the entity when its financial position is poor or deteriorating?
17. Does the firm continuously operate on a "crisis" basis or without a careful budgeting and planning process?
18. Does the organization have difficulty collecting receivables or have other cash flow problems?
19. Is the organization dependent on one or two key products or services, especially products or services that can become quickly obsolete or where other organizations have the ability to adapt more quickly to market swings?
20. Do the footnotes contain information about difficult-to-understand issues?
21. Are adequate disclosures made in the footnotes?
22. Are financial results or operating characteristics accompanied by questionable or suspicious factors?
23. Are financial results consistent with nonfinancial performance indicators?

> **Remember this …**
>
> *Financial statement fraud is usually detected when information in the financial statements is compared with the real-world characteristics of the firm and the context in which management is operating and being motivated. The four elements of the exposure rectangle help in identifying management fraud exposures and understanding the various contexts in which the business operates. The four elements are (1) management and directors, (2) relationship with others, (3) organization and industry, and (4) financial results and operating characteristics.*

Review of the Learning Objectives

- **Discuss the role that financial statements play in capital markets.** Financial statements are the backbone of capitalism and allow investors, lenders, and regulators to measure the performance of a business.
- **Understand the nature of financial statement fraud.** Financial statement fraud usually involves upper management, which is motivated with enormous incentives to meet expectations of the capital markets so as to keep the company's stock price high. Financial statement fraud is often carefully crafted so as to conceal it from auditors and others. Several factors led to a perfect storm of financial statement fraud around the end of the 20th century. These factors included a booming economy, allowing fraud to be concealed; a general decay of moral values; misplaced executive incentives; analysts' high expectations; high debt levels; a focus on accounting rules rather than principles; a lack of auditor independence; greed by executives, banks, and investors; and educator failures.
- **Become familiar with financial statement fraud statistics.** Several studies have shown similarities between detected cases of financial statement fraud. For example, financial statement fraud often goes on for several years before being detected; revenue recognition, overstatement of assets, and understatement of expenses are the most common methods used; top management is usually involved in the fraud; most firms involved in financial statement fraud had weak oversight by the board of directors and audit

committee; and fraudulent companies had all different sizes of audit firms as their external auditors.

- **See how financial statement frauds occur and are concealed.** Financial statement fraud often starts when the high expectations of a company will not be met without some form of earnings manipulation. The initial act is often considered a one-time event but grows in the future as pressure builds and operations fail to produce the required results.
- **Outline the framework for detecting financial statement fraud.** Fraud is most likely to be detected when auditors or investigators use strategic reasoning to design their procedures in ways that will be most likely to detect a concealment from typical procedures.
- **Identify financial statement fraud exposures.** We covered an overall approach for detecting financial statement fraud and identified four different fraud exposure areas, including management and directors, relationships with others, organization and industry, and financial results and operating characteristics. We also emphasized the need to use nonfinancial performance measures to help detect unusual financial results.
- **Explain how information regarding a company's management and directors, nature of organization, operating characteristics, relationship with others, and financial results can help assess the likelihood of financial statement fraud.** Because financial statement fraud is seldom observed, examiners must look for red flags that indicate such fraud is occurring. We covered general conditions and characteristics of management, the organizational form, its operations and relationships with others, and patterns in the financial results that can be used as red flags to alert auditors, investors, or regulators to financial statement fraud.

KEY TERMS

Securities and Exchange Commission (SEC), p. 358

financial statements, p. 359

financial statement fraud, p. 359

backdating, p. 360

Treadway Commission, p. 364

Committee of Sponsoring Organizations (COSO), p. 364

SEC enforcement releases, p. 364

strategic reasoning, p. 368

nonfinancial performance measures, p. 369

zero-order reasoning, p. 368

first-order reasoning, p. 368

higher-order reasoning, p. 369

10-Ks, p. 370

10-Q, p. 376

QUESTIONS

Discussion Questions

1. What were some of the most notable abuses that occurred between 2000 and 2002?
2. The chapter identifies nine factors that led to the "perfect fraud storm." Explain how these factors helped create and foster the ethical compromises that occurred between 2000 and 2002.
3. Why are financial statements important to the effective operation of capital markets?
4. What is financial statement fraud?
5. Who usually commits financial statement fraud?
6. Why are CEOs perpetrators of financial statement fraud?
7. What are common ways in which financial statement frauds are concealed?
8. How can an active audit committee help to deter financial statement fraud in an organization?
9. What are some common motivations of financial statement fraud?
10. What are the four different exposure areas that must be examined while detecting financial statement fraud?
11. What are some of the ways that financial statement fraud exposures can be identified?
12. Why must members of management and the board of directors be examined when searching for financial statement fraud exposures?
13. Why must relationships with others be examined when searching for financial statement fraud exposures?
14. When looking for financial statement fraud, why is it important to analyze the relationship between a company and its auditors?

True/False

1. Unlike other types of fraud, financial statement fraud is usually not concealed and is therefore relatively easy to spot.
2. Fraud indicators, or red flags, can be caused by fraud or by legitimate, non-fraud, factors.
3. Without a confession, forged documents, or repeated fraudulent acts that establish a pattern of dishonesty, convicting someone of fraud is often difficult.
4. According to the 1999 and 2010 COSO studies of fraudulent financial reporting, the most common method used to perpetrate financial statement fraud includes overstating liabilities.
5. According to the 1999 COSO study, most companies that committed financial statement fraud had no audit committee or had an audit committee that met less than twice a year.
6. Michael "Mickey" Monus and Patrick Finn of Phar-Mor used three methods of income statement fraud: account manipulation, overstatement of inventory, and accounting rules manipulations.
7. In identifying management fraud exposures, it is useful to think of the fraud exposure triangle, which includes (1) management and directors, (2) organizations and industry, and (3) relationships with others.
8. Financial statement fraud is usually committed by entry-level accountants against an organization.
9. In searching for financial statement fraud, the three aspects of directors and members of management that should be known are (1) their backgrounds, (2) their motivations, and (3) their influence in making decisions for the organization.
10. An organization's relationship with other organizations and individuals is of no interest to a fraud examiner.
11. Recording fictitious revenues is one of the most common ways of perpetrating financial statement fraud.
12. Most often, the controller or chief financial officer (CFO) of a corporation is the perpetrator of financial statement fraud because of his or her knowledge of accounting and unlimited access to accounts.
13. Financial statement fraud, like other types of fraud, is most often committed against an organization instead of on behalf of the organization.
14. Most people who commit management fraud are repeat offenders.
15. Most financial statement frauds occur in large, historically profitable organizations.
16. Zero-order strategic reasoning takes into account the potential actions of others before one decides to act.

17. Backdating is a method of dating stock options so that stock option holders can maximize their payout.
18. Identifying fraud exposures is one of the most difficult steps in detecting financial statement fraud.
19. Higher-order reasoning is the most challenging of the types of strategic reasoning, but can potentially be the most effective in detecting financial statement fraud.

Multiple Choice

1. Financial statement fraud is usually committed by:
   a. Executives.
   b. Managers.
   c. Stockholders.
   d. Outsiders.
   e. Both a and b.
2. Which officer in a company is most likely to be the perpetrator of financial statement fraud?
   a. Chief financial officer (CFO).
   b. Controller.
   c. Chief operating officer (COO).
   d. Chief executive officer (CEO).
3. When looking for financial statement fraud, auditors should look for indicators of fraud by:
   a. Examining financial statements.
   b. Evaluating changes in financial statements.
   c. Examining relationships the company has with other parties.
   d. Examining operating characteristics of the company.
   e. All of the above.
   f. None of the above because auditors don't have a responsibly to find financial statement fraud.
4. The three aspects of management that a fraud examiner needs to be aware of include all of the following except:
   a. Their backgrounds.
   b. Their motivations.
   c. Their religious convictions.
   d. Their influence in making decisions for the organization.
5. Which of the following is least likely to be considered a financial reporting fraud symptom, or red flag?
   a. Grey directors.
   b. Family relationships between directors or officers.
   c. Large increases in accounts receivable with no increase in sales.
   d. Size of the firm.

6. Many indicators of fraud are circumstantial; that is, they can be caused by nonfraud factors. This fact can make convicting someone of fraud difficult. Which of the following types of evidence would be most helpful in proving that someone committed fraud?
   a. Missing documentation.
   b. A general ledger that is out of balance.
   c. Analytical relationships that don't make sense.
   d. A repeated pattern of similar fraudulent acts.
7. In the Phar-Mor fraud case, several different methods were used for manipulating the financial statements. These included all of the following except:
   a. Funneling losses into unaudited subsidiaries.
   b. Overstating inventory.
   c. Recognizing revenue that should have been deferred.
   d. Manipulating accounts.
8. Most financial statement frauds occur in smaller organizations with simple management structures, rather than in large, historically profitable organizations. This is because:
   a. It is easier to implement good internal controls in a small organization.
   b. Smaller organizations do not have investors.
   c. Management fraud is more difficult to commit when there is a more formal organizational structure of management.
   d. People in large organizations are more honest.
9. Management fraud is usually committed on behalf of the organization rather than against it. Which of the following would *not* be a motivation of fraud on behalf of an organization?
   a. CEO needs a new car.
   b. A highly competitive industry.
   c. Pressure to meet expected earnings.
   d. Restructure debt covenants that can't be met.
10. All of the following are indicators of financial statement fraud except:
    a. Unusually rapid growth of profitability.
    b. Threat of a hostile takeover.
    c. Dependence on one or two products.
    d. Large amounts of available cash.
11. During an audit, an auditor considers the conditions of the auditee and plans the audit accordingly. This is an example of which of the following?
    a. Zero-order reasoning.
    b. High-order reasoning.
    c. First-order reasoning.
    d. Fraudulent reasoning.

12. In the context of strategic reasoning, if an auditor only follows the established audit plan and does not consider other factors relating to the auditee, then this is an example of which of the following?
    a. Zero-order reasoning.
    b. Higher-order reasoning.
    c. First-order reasoning.
    d. Fraudulent reasoning.

13. In recent years, many SEC investigations have taken place on the improper issuance of stock options to corporate executives. These practices increase executive compensation at the expense of shareholders. This practice is known as:
    a. Backdrafting stock options.
    b. Backdating stock options.
    c. Stock option reversals.
    d. Stock option extensions.

SHORT CASES

Case 1

An electronics company that produced circuit boards for personal computers was formed in a small southern town. The three founders had previously worked together for another electronics company and decided to start this new company. They ended up as senior officers and members of the board of directors in the newly formed company. One became the chairman and CEO, the second became the company's president and COO, and the third became the controller and treasurer. Two of the three founders together owned approximately 10.7 percent of the company's common stock. The board of directors had a total of seven members, and they met about four times a year, receiving an annual retainer of $4,500 plus a fee of $800 for each meeting attended. Their new company was well received by the townspeople, who were excited about attracting the new start-up company. The city showed its enthusiasm by providing the new company with an empty building, and the local bank provided a very attractive credit arrangement for the company. In return, the company appointed the bank's president to serve as a member of its board of directors. Two years later, the company began committing financial statement fraud, which went on for about three years. The three founders were the fraud perpetrators. Their fraud involved overstating inventory, understating the cost of goods sold, overstating the gross margin, and overstating net income. Identify the fraud exposures present in this case.

Case 2

After Enron, WorldCom, and other major corporate scandals that rocked America in the recent past, it seemed that nothing would surprise investors or regulators. However, almost everyone was shocked by revelations that as many as 20 percent of all public corporations may have allowed their officers and directors to "backdate" their stock option awards and account for the awards improperly. Hardly a day goes by without another public company's fraudulent stock option practices being revealed.

A stock option is an award granted under which key employees and directors may buy shares of the company's stock at the market price of the stock at the date of the award. As an example, assume that Company A's stock price is $15 per share on January 1, 2007. Further assume that the company's CEO is awarded 200,000 stock options on that date. This means that after a certain holding (vesting) period, the CEO can buy 200,000 shares of the company's stock at $15 per share, regardless of what the stock price is on the day he or she buys the stock. If the stock price has risen to, say $35 per share, then the CEO can simultaneously buy the 200,000 shares at a total price of $3 million (200,000 times $15 per share) and sell them for $7 million ($35 per share times 200,000 shares), pocketing $4 million. Stock options are a way to provide incentives to executives to work as hard as they can to make their companies profitable and, therefore, have their stock price increase.

Until 2006, if the option granting price ($15 in this case) were the same as the market price on the date the option was granted, the company reported no compensation expense on its income statement. (Under new accounting rule FAS 123R, effective in 2006, the required accounting changed.) However, if the options were granted at a price lower than the market share price (referred to as "in-the-money" options) on the day the options were granted, say $10 in this example, then the $5 difference between the option granting price and the market price had to be reported as compensation expense by the company and represented taxable income to the recipient.

The fraudulent stock option backdating practices involved corporations, by authority of their executives and/or boards of directors, awarding stock options to their officers and directors and dating those options as of a past date on which the share price of the company's stock was unusually low. Dating the options in this post hoc manner ensures that the exercise price will be set well below market, thereby nearly guaranteeing that these options will be "in the money" when they vest and thus will provide the recipients with windfall profits. In doing so, many companies violated accounting rules, tax laws, and SEC disclosure rules. Almost all companies being investigated "backdated" their options so that they would appear to have been awarded on the low price date despite having actually been authorized months later.

1. Would a good system of internal controls have prevented these fraudulent backdating practices?
2. Why would executives and directors of so many companies have allowed this dishonest practice in their companies?
3. Would a whistle-blower system have helped to prevent or reveal these dishonest practices?

Case 3

ABC Company manufactures and sells software packages to small businesses. The company has enjoyed great success since it began business in 1998. Last year, the firm doubled its revenues, and its management is now looking closely at going public by making an initial public offering (IPO) next September. Senior management has been putting a lot of effort into further increasing sales by offering the company's sales representatives a generous commission as an incentive to increase their selling efforts.

The CEO, CFO, and COO of the company have been in business together for 20 years. Two of them were high school "buddies," and the other joined the group in college. They still interact socially with one another, and their respective wives are also very close.

In completing a background check on the company, you find that it has a positive relationship with private investors, who are excited about the proposed IPO next September. One of the investors did inform you, however, that the company changed auditors last year because of a dispute the CEO had with the audit partner regarding some "strict revenue recognition rule."

The company has a board of directors and audit committee that meets twice a year to discuss how the business is doing. The board has decided to meet four times over the next year, since it may be necessary to discuss issues regarding the upcoming IPO. The board seems to speak highly of management and compensates them generously with stock options for their "good work." What are some red flags that indicate that financial statement fraud may be occurring?

Case 4

Compare and contrast financial statement fraud with embezzlement and misappropriation, especially with respect to who usually commits the fraud. Also contrast the different kinds of fraud with respect to who benefits from the fraud.

Case 5

For each of the following red flags, identify which fraud exposure the risk falls under: management and directors, relationships with others, organization and industry, or financial results and operating characteristics.

1. The personal worth of directors is tied up in the organization.
2. The company has a complex organizational structure.
3. The audit committee rarely holds a meeting.
4. The company has recently switched to a new law firm.
5. Although sales appear to be increasing, the cost of goods sold and inventory levels remain constant.
6. The company is about to go through a debt offering.
7. A background check indicates that the new controller has been fired from five previous jobs.

CASE STUDIES

Case Study 1

You are a fraud investigator who has been hired to detect financial statement fraud for the Chipmunk Company. You have been provided with the financial statements on the following pages and are now beginning your analysis of those financial statements.

CASE STUDY 1

CHIPMUNK COMPANY
BALANCE SHEET
DECEMBER 31, 2010 AND 2009

Assets	2010	2009
Current assets		
Cash	$ 1,320,096	$ 1,089,978
Accounts receivable: net (Notes 2 and 5)	1,646,046	1,285,593
Inventories [Notes 1(a), 3, and 5]	13,524,349	12,356,400
Prepaid expenses	17,720	15,826
Deposits	7,916	5,484
Total current assets	$16,516,127	$14,753,281
Property, plant, and equipment [Notes 1(b) and 4] at cost, less accumulated depreciation	596,517	612,480
Total Assets	$17,112,644	$15,365,761
Liabilities		
Current liabilities		
Notes payable—Bank (Note 5)	$5,100,000	$ 4,250,000
Accounts payable	1,750,831	1,403,247
Accrued liabilities	257,800	217,003
Federal income taxes payable	35,284	45,990
Current portion of long-term debt (Note 6)	5,642	5,642
Total current liabilities	$ 7,149,557	$ 5,921,882
Long-term liabilities		
Long-term debt (Note 6)	409,824	415,466
Total Liabilities	$ 7,559,381	$ 6,337,348
Stockholders' Equity		
Common stock (Note 7)	$10,000	$10,000
Additional paid-in capital	2,500,000	2,500,000
Retained earnings	7,043,263	6,518,413
Total stockholders' equity	$ 9,553,263	$ 9,028,413
Total Liabilities and Stockholders' Equity	$17,112,644	$15,365,761

CASE STUDY 1

CHIPMUNK COMPANY
STATEMENT OF INCOME AND RETAINED EARNINGS FOR THE YEARS ENDED
DECEMBER 31, 2010 AND 2009

	2010	2009
Sales	$26,456,647	$22,889,060
Sales returns and allowances	37,557	27,740
Net sales	$26,419,090	$22,861,320
Cost of sales	19,133,299	16,530,114
Gross profit	$7,285,791	$6,331,206
Expenses		
Accounting	$ 48,253	$ 46,750
Advertising	28,624	27,947
Depreciation	46,415	46,578
Bad debts	148,252	162,344
Business publications	1,231	872
Cleaning services	15,817	12,809
Fuel	64,161	53,566
Garbage collection	4,870	4,674
Insurance	16,415	16,303
Interest	427,362	364,312
Legal	69,752	29,914
Licensing and certification fees	33,580	27,142
Linen service	3,044	1,939
Medical benefits	4,178	4,624
Miscellaneous	47,739	16,631
Office supplies	26,390	23,289
Payroll benefits	569,110	461,214
Pension expense	40,770	37,263
Postage and courier	8,623	20,962
Property taxes	3,978	27,947
Rent	158,526	120,000
Repairs and maintenance	51,316	26,439
Salaries and wages	4,310,281	3,970,092
Security	96,980	100,098
Telephone	5,707	7,092
Travel and entertainment	21,633	16,303
Utilities	63,329	41,919
Total expenses	$ 6,316,336	$ 5,669,023
Net income before income tax	$ 969,455	$ 662,183
Income tax expense	344,605	239,406
Net Income	$ 624,850	$ 422,777
Retained earnings at beginning of year	6,518,413	6,195,636
Less: Dividends	100,000	100,000
Retained earnings at end of year	$ 7,043,263	$ 6,518,413

Note: Inventories balance on January 1, 2009, was $11,427,937.

CASE STUDY 2

Ratio Analysis 12/31/2010

LIQUIDITY RATIOS	12/31/10	12/31/09	CHANGE	PERCENT CHANGE	INDUSTRY AVERAGE
Current ratio (current assets/current liabilities)	_____	_____	_____	_____	1.21
Quick ratio [(current assets − inventory − prepaid expenses)/current liabilities]	_____	_____	_____	_____	0.35
Sales/Receivables [net sales/net ending receivables]	_____	_____	_____	_____	23.42
Number of days sales in A/R [(net ending receivables/(net sales/365)]	_____	_____	_____	_____	15.58
Inventory turnover (cost of sales/average inventory)	_____	_____	_____	_____	1.29

Questions

1. Calculate the 2010 and 2009 liquidity ratios identified using the Ratio Analysis table above. Also calculate the change and the percentage change for the ratios and complete the table. (Formulas are given to shorten the time spent on the assignment.)
2. Analyze the Chipmunk Company's ratios for both years and compare the figures with the given industry ratios. Based on the ratios identified, where do you think fraud may have occurred?

Case Study 2

In April 1997, Bre-X Minerals, a Canadian company, was supposedly one of the most valuable companies in the world. Bre-X had convinced numerous mining experts that they had rights to one of the largest gold deposits ever discovered. It was hailed as the mining find of the century. The gold mine, located on a remote island in the East Kalimantan Province of Indonesia, supposedly had so much gold that the actual price of gold on the open market dropped significantly due to the anticipation of an increased gold supply. Within a few months, thousands of Canadians—big-time investors, pension and mutual fund, managers and many small investors, including factory workers—got caught up in "Bre-X fever." The company's stock price shot from pennies to more than $250 per share before a

10-for-1 stock split was announced. Thousands of investors believed they were on the verge of becoming millionaires.

The story took a sudden turn for the worse when Michael de Guzman, Bre-X's chief geologist and one of only a handful of company insiders entrusted with the mine's core samples, apparently committed suicide by jumping out the back of a helicopter. Guzman's suicide was reported around the time that an independent consulting firm reported that samples from the mine had been tampered with. The firm concluded that the core samples were made to appear to be rich in gold by adding a relatively small amount of gold to the samples. In essence, the firm concluded that Bre-X was a scam of epic proportions!

As the scam came to light, it was unclear who was behind the tampering. While fingers were pointed at senior Bre-X personnel, others blamed geologists in the field. Bre-X's President, David Walsh, was shocked at the news of the tampering and vowed to conduct an investigation. As is the case with many frauds of this type, numerous class-action lawsuits were filed against Walsh and other Bre-X executives, alleging that they misled shareholders. Walsh and other company officials received profits of over $50 million from selling some of their Bre-X stock the year before the tampering came to light. In the end, many people lost money as the gold find of the century turned out to be a massive hoax.

Questions

1. Assume you are a financial analyst who works for a major brokerage company that is heavily invested in Bre-X Minerals.
   a. In what ways would investigating *management and directors* help determine the value of Bre-X's gold prospects?
   b. In what ways would investigating the *company's relationships with other entities* help determine the value of Bre-X's gold prospects?
   c. In what ways would investigating *the organization and its industry* help determine the value of Bre-X's gold prospects?
   d. In what ways would investigating the *financial results and operating characteristics* help determine the value of Bre-X's gold prospects?
2. How were the gold industry and Canadian stock markets affected by this fraud?
3. Some of the aspects of the perfect fraud storm that were discussed in the chapter were also present in the Bre-X scandal. Which elements were common to both the perfect fraud storm and the Bre-X scandal?
4. What were some of the perpetrators' motivations to commit fraud?

Case Study 3

The SEC charged Midisoft Corporation with overstating revenue in the amount of $458,000. The overstatement occurred because the company recorded sales for products that had been shipped but, at the time of shipment, the company had no reasonable expectation that they would be paid for the products. In the end, the company accepted most of the shipped product as sales returns.

Apparently, Midisoft's distribution agreements allowed the distributor the opportunity to return product to Midisoft for credit whenever the distributor believed the product was unable to be sold. In FY 1994, the accounting personnel submitted a proposed allowance for future returns that was too low given the returns Midisoft received in early 1995. Furthermore, management knew the exact amount of returns affecting FY 1994 prior to the time when the independent auditors finished their 1994 audit. If Midisoft had accurately revised the allowance for sales returns, the amount of net revenue reported for FY 1994 would have been significantly reduced. Instead, management devised schemes to conceal the true amount of the returns, including preventing the auditors from examining the location where the returned goods were stored. Additionally, accounting personnel altered computer records to support a reduced level of returns.[13]

Questions

1. Imagine that you are the independent auditor of Midisoft. The audit plan specifies specific testing procedures to assess the fair representation of the "Sales and Allowances" and "Accounts Receivable" accounts. In terms of strategic reasoning and the details provided in the case, what would be your actions in the following situations?
   a. You only employ zero-order reasoning.
   b. You employ first-order reasoning.
   c. You employ higher-order reasoning.

INTERNET ASSIGNMENTS

1. The Internet is a great place to find additional information about financial statement fraud. Using your favorite Internet search engine, try various word combinations to see what you can find about financial statement fraud. For example, type in the search window "financial statement fraud" and check out some of the results. What did you find that interested you? Now go to the following Web address: www.cfo.com/article.cfm/14490470. Here you will find an article from *CFO* magazine about the auditor's role in detecting financial statement fraud.
   a. What are some of the key points of the article?
   b. What did you learn after reading this article?

DEBATES

1. Some people believe that the audit industry has fallen out of touch with the realities of business. They believe that accounting standards were developed for a manufacturing environment and are not fitted for our modern needs. As a result, they contend that financial statements have turned into a game in which all companies try to match earnings forecasts set by financial analysts. Are these statements true, or do you think that they are too cynical?
2. One of the most controversial topics to affect the accounting profession has been that of earnings management. Companies have been trying to manage their earnings to match analysts' projections.

While the accounting literature doesn't give accounting professionals a clear definition of earnings management, many people have been critical of companies for trying to manage earnings, saying that most managed financial statements are fraudulent. As a class or individually, analyze the pros and cons of earnings management and try to decide whether earnings management is the same as financial statement fraud.

END NOTES

1. www.usatoday.com/money/companies/management/2002-12-23-ceo-loans_x.htm, accessed on April 22, 2010.

2. www.bizjournals.com/portland/stories/2002/12/30/daily17.html, accessed on April 22, 2010.

3. In 2003, the SEC acknowledged that U.S. GAAP may be too "rule-based" and wrote a position paper arguing for more "principles-" or "objectives-based" accounting standards.

4. A March 5, 2001, *Fortune* article included the following warning about Enron: "To skeptics, the lack of clarity raises a red flag about Enron's pricey stock…. the inability to get behind the numbers combined with ever higher expectations for the company may increase the chance of a nasty surprise. Enron is an earnings-at-risk story…." Even with this bad news, firms kept investing heavily in Enron and partnering or facilitating Enron's risky transactions.

5. www.forbes.com/2002/02/27/0227analysts.html, accessed on April 22, 2010.

6. "Report of the National Commission on Fraudulent Financial Reporting," 1987.

7. "Fraudulent Financial Reporting: 1987–1997, An Analysis of U.S. Public Companies" Research Commissioned by the Committee of Sponsoring Organization of the Treadway Commission.

8. www.sec.gov/news/studies/sox704report.pdf, accessed on April 22, 2010.

9. *Internal Auditor* (February 1999): 15.

10. "Fraudulent Financial Reporting: 1998–2007, An Analysis of U.S. Public Companies" Research Commissioned by the Committee of Sponsoring Organization of the Treadway Commission, May 2010.

11. For example, see "Do Strategic Reasoning and Brainstorming Help Auditors Change Their Standard Audit Procedures in Response to Fraud Risk?" by V.B. Hoffman and M.F. Zimbelman in *The Accounting Review*, 2009, May: 811–837.

12. See Brazel, J.F., K.L.Jones and M. F. Zimbelman, "Using Nonfinancial Measures to Assess Fraud Risk," in *Journal of Accounting Research*, Vol. 47 No. 5 December 2009, pp. 1135–1166.

13. SEA Rel. No. 37847; AAE Rel. No. 846 (October 22, 1996).

Recent Laws and Corporate Governance Changes Following the Sarbanes-Oxley Act

As described in the chapter, the period 2001–2003 marked the discovery of some of the largest financial statement frauds in U.S. history and some of the most significant legislation regarding the auditing profession and corporate governance since the 1933–1934 SEC acts. These events followed a very prosperous decade that saw the NASDAQ grow 10 percent per year from 1987–1995 and then from an index of 1,291 on January 1, 1997 to 5,049 on March 10, 2000 for a 391 percent increase in three years. The Dow Jones Industrial Average, while not quite so dramatic, rose from 6,448 on January 1, 1997 to a high of 11,723 on January 14, 2000 for an increase of 81 percent in three years. Much of this growth came from individual investors who found they could invest on the Internet by paying only small fees ($8 to $10 per trade).

When the first financial statement frauds, including Enron and WorldCom, were revealed, there was near panic in the market. The NASDAQ fell from its high of 5,049 on March 10 to 1,114 on October 9, 2002, leaving it at only 22 percent of its peak value. Similarly, the Dow Jones Industrial Average (NYSE) fell from its high of 11,723 on January 15, 2000 to a low of 7,286 on October 9, 2002, leaving it at only 62 percent of its previous value. The total decline in worldwide stock markets was $15 trillion. These sharp declines meant that nearly everyone's 401(k) and other retirement plans and personal wealth suffered tremendous losses. Worse yet, several well-known companies that were involved in financial statement fraud declared bankruptcy. At the time when the Sarbanes-Oxley Act was passed in July of 2002, many of the companies that were found to have committed fraud around this time

period were among the largest bankruptcies in U.S. history, including WorldCom (largest), Enron (second largest), Global Crossing (fifth largest), and Adelphia (seventh largest).

The Sarbanes-Oxley Act

Because of the pressure brought by constituents, Congress was quick to act. On July 30, 2002, President Bush signed into law the Sarbanes-Oxley Act, which had been quickly passed by both the House and the Senate. The law was intended to bolster public confidence in U.S. capital markets and impose new duties and significant penalties for noncompliance on public companies and their executives, directors, auditors, attorneys, and securities analysts.

The Sarbanes-Oxley Act is comprised of 11 separate sections or titles. You can read the full text of the act on several Web sites, but the highlights of each section are discussed here.

Title I: Public Company Accounting Oversight Board

One of the concerns of legislators was that the auditing profession was self-regulating and set its own standards and that this regulation had fallen short of what it should have been. As a result, this part of the act established a five-member Public Company Accounting Oversight Board (PCAOB), with general oversight by the SEC, to:

- Oversee the audit of public companies;
- Establish audit reporting standards and rules; and
- Inspect, investigate, and enforce compliance on the part of registered public accounting firms and those associated with the firms.

Title I requires public accounting firms that participate in any audit report with respect to any public company to register with the PCAOB. It also directs the PCAOB to establish (or modify) the auditing and related attestation standards, quality control, and ethics standards used by registered public accounting firms to prepare and issue audit reports. It requires auditing standards to include (among other things): (1) a seven-year retention period for audit work papers, (2) a second-partner review and approval of audit opinions, (3) an evaluation of whether internal control structure and procedures include records that accurately reflect transactions and disposition of assets, (4) that receipts and expenditures of public companies are made only with authorization of senior management and directors, and (5) that auditors provide a description of both material weaknesses in internal controls and of material noncompliance.

Title I also mandated continuing inspections of public accounting firms for compliance on an annual basis for firms that provide audit reports for more than 100 issuers and at least every three years for firms that provide audit reports for 100 or fewer issuers. Based on these inspections, it empowered the board to impose disciplinary or remedial sanctions upon registered accounting firms and their associates for intentional conduct or repeated instances of negligent conduct. It also directed the SEC to report to Congress on adoption of a principles-based accounting system by the U.S. financial reporting system and funded the board through fees collected from issuers.

With the passing of this act, control over auditing firms and auditing standards shifted from the Auditing Standards Board of the American Institute of Certified Public Accountants (AICPA) to this new quasi-governmental organization called the PCAOB. Some people have argued that this part of the law relegated the AICPA to a trade organization.

Title II: Auditor Independence

Another concern of legislators was that the work of independent auditors of public companies had been compromised by some of the other types of consulting they had been doing for their audit clients. As a result, the next section of the Sarbanes-Oxley Act prohibits an auditor from performing specified nonaudit services contemporaneously with an audit. In addition, it specifies that public company audit committees must approve allowed activities for nonaudit services that are not expressly forbidden by the act. The prohibited activities include the following:

- Bookkeeping services.
- Financial information systems design and implementation.
- Appraisal or valuation services.
- Actuarial services.
- Internal audit outsourcing.
- Management functions or human resources.
- Broker or dealer, investment advisor, or investment banking.
- Legal services and expert services.
- Any other service that the board determines is impermissible.

In addition, this section of the act prohibits an audit partner from being the lead or reviewing auditor on the same public company for more than five consecutive years (auditor rotation). It requires that auditors report to the audit committee each of the following:

- Critical accounting policies and practices used in the audit.
- Alternative treatments and their ramifications within GAAP.
- Material written communications between the auditor and senior management of the issuer.
- Activities prohibited under Sarbanes-Oxley.

Title II places a one-year prohibition on auditors performing audit services if the issuer's senior executives had been employed by that auditor and had participated in the audit of the issuer during the one-year period preceding the audit initiation date and encourages state regulatory authorities to make independent determinations on the standards for supervising nonregistered public accounting firms and to consider the size and nature of their clients' businesses audit.

Title III: Corporate Responsibility

The first two titles of the act were directed at auditors of public companies, but the next section targeted public companies, especially their board of directors and its committees. Specifically, this part of the act involves the following provisions:

- Requires each member of a public company's audit committee to be a member of the board of directors and be independent (no other compensatory fees or affiliations with the issuer).
- Confers upon the audit committee responsibility for appointment, compensation, and oversight of any registered public accounting firm employed to perform audit services.

- Gives audit committees authority to hire independent counsel and other advisors and requires issuers to fund them.
- Instructs the SEC to promulgate rules requiring the CEO and CFO to certify that the financial statements provided in periodic financial reports:
  - Do not contain untrue statements or material omissions.
  - Present fairly in all material respects the financial conditions and results of operations.
- Establishes that the CEO and CFO are responsible for internal controls designed to ensure that they receive material information regarding the issuer and consolidated subsidiaries and that the internal controls have been reviewed for their effectiveness within 90 days prior to the report and makes them identify any significant changes to the internal controls.

Title III also deals with abuses and penalties for abuses for executives who violate the Sarbanes-Oxley Act. Specifically, it makes it unlawful for corporate personnel to exert improper influence upon an audit for the purpose of rendering financial statements materially misleading. It requires that the CEO and CFO forfeit certain bonuses and compensation received if the company is required to make an accounting restatement due to the material noncompliance of an issuer. It amends the Securities and Exchange Act of 1933 to prohibit a violator of certain SEC rules from serving as an officer or director if the person's conduct demonstrates unfitness to serve (the previous rule required "substantial unfitness"). It provides a ban on trading by directors and executive officers in a public company's stock during pension fund blackout periods. Title III also imposes obligations on attorneys appearing before the SEC to report violations of securities laws and breaches of fiduciary duty by a public company or its agents to the chief legal counsel or CEO of the company, and it allows civil penalties to be added to a disgorgement fund for the benefit of victims of securities violations.

Title IV: Enhanced Financial Disclosures

Another concern addressed by the act was that public company financial statements did not disclose certain kinds of problematic transactions properly and management and directors didn't act as ethically as they should have. As a result, Title IV:

- Requires financial reports filed with the SEC to reflect all material correcting adjustments that have been identified.

- Requires disclosure of all material off-balance-sheet transactions and relationships that may have a material effect upon the financial status of an issue.
- Prohibits personal loans extended by a corporation to its executives and directors, with some exceptions.
- Requires senior management, directors, and principal stockholders to disclose changes in securities ownership or securities-based swap agreements within two business days (formerly 10 days after the close of the calendar month).
- Requires annual reports to include an internal control report stating that management is responsible for the internal control structure and procedures for financial reporting and that they have assessed the effectiveness of the internal controls for the previous fiscal year. This Section 404 request is probably the most expensive and debated part of the act. As a result of this requirement, most companies have spent millions of dollars documenting and testing their controls.
- Requires issuers to disclose whether they have adopted a code of ethics for their senior financial officers and whether their audit committees consist of at least one member who is a financial expert.
- Mandates regular, systematic SEC review of periodic disclosures by issuers, including review of an issuer's financial statement.

Title V: Analyst Conflicts of Interest

In addition to concern over auditors, board members, management, and financial statements, legislators were also concerned that others (investment bankers and financial institution executives) also contributed to the problems. Accordingly, this section of the act:

- Restricts the ability of investment bankers to pre-approve research reports.
- Ensures that research analysts in investment banking firms are not supervised by persons involved in investment banking activities.
- Prevents retaliation against analysts by employers in return for writing negative reports. Establishes blackout periods for brokers or dealers participating in a public offering during which they may not distribute reports related to such offering.
- Enhances structural separation in registered brokers or dealers between analyst and investment banking activities.

- Requires specific conflict of interest disclosures by research analysts making public appearances and by brokers or dealers in research reports including:

  - Whether the analyst holds securities in the public company that is the subject of the appearance or report.
  - Whether any compensation was received by the analyst, broker, or dealer from the company that was the subject of the appearance or report.
  - Whether a public company that is the subject of an appearance or report is, or during the prior one-year period was, a client of the broker or dealer.
  - Whether the analyst received compensation with respect to a research report, based upon banking revenues of the registered broker or dealer.

Title VI: Commission Resources and Authority

Title VI of the act gave the SEC more budget and more power to be effective in its role of overseeing public companies in the United States. Specifically, this part:

- Authorized a 77.21 percent increase over the appropriations for FY 2002 including money for pay parity, information and technology, security enhancements, and recovery and mitigation activities related to the September 11 terrorist attacks.
- Provided $98 million to hire no less than 200 additional qualified professionals to provide improved oversight of auditors and audit services.
- Authorized the SEC to censure persons appearing or practicing before the commission if it finds, among other things, a person to have engaged in unethical or improper professional conduct.
- Authorized federal courts to prohibit persons from participating in penny stock offerings if the persons are the subject of proceedings instituted for alleged violations of securities laws.
- Expanded the scope of the SEC's disciplinary authority by allowing it to consider orders of state securities commissions when deciding whether to limit the activities, functions, or operations of brokers or dealers.

Title VII: Studies and Reports

This section of the Sarbanes-Oxley Act specified that certain reports and studies should be made, including the following:

- A study of the factors leading to the consolidation of public accounting firms and its impact on capital formation and securities markets.

- A study of the role of credit rating agencies in the securities markets.
- A study of the number of securities professionals practicing before the commission who have aided and abetted federal securities violations but have not been penalized as a primary violator.
- A study of SEC enforcement actions it has taken regarding violations of reporting requirements and restatements of financial statements (as referred to earlier in the chapter).
- A study by the Government Accountability Office (GAO) on whether investment banks and financial advisers assisted public companies in earnings manipulation and obfuscation of financial conditions.

Title VIII: Corporate and Criminal Fraud Accountability

Title VIII was the part of the Sarbanes-Oxley Act that imposed criminal penalties upon violators, extended the statute of limitations for financial crimes, and provided protection for whistle-blowers in fraud cases. Specifically, this part of the act:

- Imposed criminal penalties for knowingly destroying, altering, concealing, or falsifying records with intent to obstruct or influence either a federal investigation or a matter in bankruptcy and for failure of an auditor to maintain for a five-year period all audit or review work papers pertaining to an issuer of securities (penalty: 10 years in prison).
- Made nondischargeable in bankruptcy certain debts incurred in violation of securities fraud laws.
- Extended the statute of limitations to permit a private right of action for a securities fraud violation to no later than two years after its discovery or five years after the date of the violation.
- Provided whistle-blower protection to prohibit a publicly traded company from retaliating against an employee because of any lawful act by the employee to assist in an investigation of fraud or other conduct by federal regulators, Congress, or supervisors, or to file or participate in a proceeding relating to fraud against shareholders.
- Subjected to fine or imprisonment (up to 25 years) any person who knowingly defrauds shareholders of publicly traded companies.

Title IX: White-Collar Crime Penalty Enhancements

Because of concern that corporate executives and directors who engage in unlawful conduct were not being penalized sufficiently, this part of the act increased penalties for mail and wire fraud from 5 to 20 years in prison. It also increased penalties for violations of the Employee Retirement Income Security Act of 1974 (up to $500,000 and 10 years in prison) and established criminal liability for failure of corporate officers to certify financial reports, including maximum imprisonment of 10 years for knowing that the periodic report does not comply with the act or 20 years for willfully certifying a statement knowing it does not comply with this act.

Title X: Corporate Tax Returns

This title expressed the sense of the Senate that the federal income tax return of a corporation should be signed by its chief executive officer.

Title XI: Corporate Fraud Accountability

This final title of the act amended federal criminal law to establish a maximum 20-year prison term for tampering with a record or otherwise impeding an official proceeding. It authorized the SEC to seek a temporary injunction to freeze extraordinary payments earmarked for designated persons or corporate staff under investigation for possible violations of federal securities law. It also authorized the SEC to prohibit a violator of rules governing manipulative, deceptive devices, and fraudulent interstate transactions, from serving as officer or director of a publicly traded corporation if the person's conduct demonstrates unfitness to serve; and it increased penalties for violations of the Securities Exchange Act of 1934 up to $25 million and 20 years in prison.

The Public Company Accounting Oversight Board (PCAOB)

Once the PCAOB was up and running, it wasted no time in carrying out its mandate. With its authorized budget of $68 million per year, within weeks, it required that auditing firms of public companies register with the board. It hired inspectors to carry out inspections of the audits of public companies. It hired a new audit director (Douglas Carmichael) and created a board to issue auditing standards. It established offices in several cities around the United States.

It established its mission to oversee the auditors of public companies in order to protect the interests of investors and further the public interest in the preparation of informative, fair, and independent audit reports. It issued its first auditing standard that articulates management's responsibilities for evaluating and documenting the effectiveness of internal controls over financial reporting, identifies the kinds of deficiencies that can exist, states the consequences of having deficiencies, and identifies how deficiencies must be communicated.

Subsequent Changes Made by the Stock Exchanges

In response to the high-profile corporate failures, the SEC requested that the NYSE and NASDAQ review their listing standards with an emphasis on all matters of corporate governance. Based on that request, both the NYSE and NASDAQ conducted extensive reviews of their listing standards for corporate governance and filed corporate governance reform proposals with the SEC in 2002. In April 2003, the SEC issued Rule 10A-3, which directed all stock exchanges to prohibit the listing of any security of an issuer that is not in compliance with the audit committee requirements specified in Rule 10A-3. On November 4, 2003, the SEC approved, with certain modifications, the corporate governance reforms proposed by the NYSE and NASDAQ. Here is an overview of the changes that they made.

Nasdaq Corporate Governance Changes

NASDAQ focused almost entirely upon boards of directors and executives in making governance reforms. Specifically, NASDAQ addressed the following issues:

- Independence of majority of board members.
- Separate meetings of independent board members.
- Compensation of officers.
- Nomination of directors.
- Audit committee charter and responsibilities.
- Audit committee composition.
- Code of business conduct and ethics.
- Public announcement of going-concern qualifications.
- Related-party transactions.
- Notification of noncompliance.

NASDAQ corporate governance reforms mandate that a majority of the board of director members are required to be independent along with a disclosure in annual proxy (or in the 10-K if proxy is not filed) about the directors, which the board has determined to be independent under NASD (formerly known as the National Association of Securities Dealers) rules. In defining what constitutes an independent director, NASDAQ's rules state that a director is not independent under the following circumstances:

- The director is an officer or employee of the company or its subsidiaries.
- The director has a relationship, which in the opinion of the company's board would interfere with the director.
- Any director who is or has at any time in the last three years been employed by the company or by any parent or subsidiary of the company.
- The director accepts or has a family member who accepts any payments from the company in excess of $60,000 during the current fiscal year or any of the past three fiscal years. Payments made directly to or for the benefit of the director or a family member of the director or political contributions to the campaign of a director or a family member of the director would be covered by this provision.
- The director is a family member of an individual who is or at any time during the past three years was employed by the company or its parent or any subsidiaries of the company as an executive officer.
- The director is or has a family member who is employed as an executive officer of another entity at any time during the past three years where any of the executive officers of the listed company serve on the compensation committee of such entity.
- The director is or has a family member who is a partner in or is a controlling shareholder or an executive officer of any organization in which the company or from which the company received payments for property or services in the current year or any of the past three fiscal years that exceed 5 percent of the recipient's consolidated gross revenues for that year or $200,000, whichever is more.
- The director is or has a family member who is an executive officer of a charitable organization, if the company makes payments to the charity in excess of the greater of 5 percent of the charity's revenues or $200,000.
- The director is or has a family member who is a current partner of the company's outside auditor.
- The director was a partner or employee of the company's outside auditor and worked on the company's audit at any time in the past three years.

Under new governance standards, independent directors are required to have regularly scheduled meetings at which only independent directors are present (thus excluding all members of management). To eliminate sweetheart deals, the compensation of the CEO and all other officers must be determined or recommended to the full board for determination by a majority of the independent directors or a compensation committee comprised solely of independent directors.

In addition, director nominees should be either selected or nominated for selection by a majority of independent directors or by a nominations committee comprised solely of independent directors. NASDAQ changes also require each issuer to certify in writing that it has adopted a formal written charter or board resolution addressing the nomination process.

A written charter for the audit committee of the issuer must provide the following:

- The committee's purpose of overseeing the accounting and financial reporting processes and audits of the financial statements.
- Specific audit committee responsibilities and authority including the means by which the audit committee carries out those responsibilities.
- Outside auditor's accountability to the committee.
- The committee's responsibility to ensure the independence of the outside auditor.
- Audit committee consists of at least three members.
- Each audit committee member is required to be:
  - Independent under the NASD rules.
  - Independent under Rule 10A-3 issued by the SEC.
  - Someone who has not participated in the preparation of the financial statements of the company or any current subsidiary of the company at any time during the last three years.

Existing NASD rules already required that each audit committee member should be able to read and understand fundamental financial statements. This requirement did not change. However, under the new NASDAQ governance rules, one audit committee member must have past employment experience in finance and accounting, requisite professional certification in accounting, or any other comparable experience or background that results in the individual's financial sophistication, including being or having been a CEO, CFO, or other senior officer with financial oversight responsibilities. Audit committee members are also prohibited from receiving any payment from the company other than the payment for board or committee services and are also prohibited from serving the audit committee in the event they are deemed to be an affiliated person of the company or any subsidiary.

Under the new NASDAQ requirements, each listed company must have a publicly available code of conduct that is applicable to all directors, officers, and employees. The code of conduct must comply with the "code of ethics" as set forth in Section 406(c) of the Sarbanes-Oxley Act and must provide for an enforcement mechanism that ensures the following:

- Prompt and consistent enforcement of the code.
- Protection for persons reporting questionable behavior.
- Clear and objective standards for compliance.

Finally, each listed company that receives an audit opinion that contains a going-concern qualification must make a public announcement through the news media disclosing the receipt of such qualification within seven calendar days following the filing with the SEC of the documents that contained such an audit opinion. In addition, the audit committee of each issuer must conduct an appropriate review of all related-party transactions for potential conflicts of interest on an ongoing basis and make sure that all such transactions have been approved.

Nyse Corporate Governance Changes

Changes made by the NYSE were quite similar to those made by the NASDAQ. Specifically, the NYSE addressed the following broad categories of the proposed standards:

- Independence of majority of board members.
- Separate meetings of independent board members.
- Nomination/corporate governance committee.
- Corporate governance guidelines.
- Compensation committee.
- Audit committee charter and responsibilities.
- Audit committee composition.
- Internal audit function.
- Code of business conduct and ethics.
- CEO certification.
- Public reprimand letter.

Like the NASDAQ, the NYSE governance changes require that a majority of the directors be independent. Under the NYSE standards, no director qualifies as an independent director unless the board affirmatively determines that the director has no material relationships with the company. Like the NASDAQ, the NYSE now

requires disclosure in annual proxy (or in the 10-K if a proxy is not filed), the basis of the conclusion that the particular directors have been deemed to be independent. If an issuer fails to meet this requirement due to vacancy or due to any director ceasing to be independent due to circumstances beyond his or her reasonable control, the issuer must regain compliance by the earlier of the next annual meeting or one year from the date of occurrence.

Under NYSE guidelines, the independence of a director is impaired under the following circumstances:

- The director is an employee or whose immediate family member is an executive officer of the company would not be independent until three years after the termination of that employment.
- The director receives or whose immediate family member receives more than $100,000 per year in direct compensation from the listed company would not be independent until three years after he or she ceases to receive more than $100,000 per year.
- The director is affiliated or employed by, or whose immediate family member is employed in any professional capacity by a present or former internal or external auditor of the company would not be independent until three years after the end of the affiliation or the employment or auditing relationship.
- The director is affiliated with or employed or whose immediate family member is affiliated or employed as an executive officer of another company where any of the listed company's present executives serve on that company's compensation committee would not be independent until three years after the end of such service or employment relationship.
- The director is an executive officer or an employee or whose immediate family member is an executive officer of a company that makes payments to or receives payments from the listed company for property or services in an amount which, in any single fiscal year, exceeds the greater of $1 million or 2 percent of such other company's consolidated gross revenues would not be independent until three years after falling below that threshold.
- Immediate family member includes a person's spouse, parents, children, siblings, mothers-and fathers-in-law, sons-and daughters-in-law, brothers-and sisters-in-law, and anyone (other than domestic employees) who shares such person's home.

- Nonmanagement directors are required to have regularly scheduled executive meetings at which only nonmanagement directors would be present.

NYSE-listed companies are required to disclose a method to interested parties to communicate directly with the presiding director of such executive sessions or with the nonmanagement directors as a group. Each listed company must have a nominating/ corporate governance committee comprising solely of independent directors.

Like NASDAQ-listed companies, audit committees must have written charters that should address at a minimum the following:

- The committee's purpose and responsibilities.
- An annual performance evaluation of the nominating/governance committee.
- The committee would be required to identify members qualified to become board members consistent with the criteria approved by the board.

Each NYSE-listed company must adopt and disclose corporate governance guidelines that specify director qualification standards, director responsibilities, director access to management and as necessary and appropriate to independent advisors, director compensation, director orientation and continuing education, management succession, and annual performance evaluation of the board. These corporate governance guidelines and charters of the most important board committees must be disclosed on the company's Web site.

With respect to committees, each listed company must have a compensation committee comprised solely of independent directors and a written charter that addresses at least the following issues:

- The committee's purpose and responsibilities.
- An annual performance evaluation of the compensation committee.

The committee would be required to produce a compensation report on executive compensation for inclusion in the company's annual proxy. In addition, the committee, together with the other independent directors, would determine and approve the CEO's compensation.

Listed companies must also have an audit committee and a written charter that provides the following:

- The committee's purpose.
- Annual performance evaluation of the audit committee.

- Duties and responsibilities of the audit committee.
- Duties and responsibilities of the audit committee as defined in the charter should include at a minimum:
  - Those provisions set out in Rule 10A-3 of SEC.
  - Responsibility to annually obtain and review a report by the independent auditor.
  - Discussion of the company's annual audited financial statements and quarterly financial statements with management and the independent auditor.
  - Discussion of the company's earnings press releases, as well as financial information and earnings guidance provided to analysts and rating agencies.
  - Discussion of policies with respect to risk assessment and risk management.
  - Meet separately, periodically with management, with internal auditors, and with independent auditors.
  - Review with independent auditors any audit problems or difficulties and management's response.
  - Set clear hiring policies for employees or former employees of independent auditors.

The audit committee, which must have at least three members, must report regularly to the full board. In addition, each audit committee member is required to be:

- Independent under the NYSE rules.
- Independent under Rule 10A-3 issued by the SEC.
- Someone who has not participated in the preparation of the financial statements of the company or any current subsidiary of the company at any time during the last three years.
- Financially literate, as such qualification is interpreted by the board in its business judgment, or must become financially literate within a reasonable period of time after his or her appointment to the committee.

At least one member of the committee would be required to have accounting or related financial management expertise, as the company's board interprets such qualification in its business judgment. One of the biggest differences between audit committees of NYSE-listed companies and NASDAQ-listed companies is that if an audit committee member simultaneously serves on the audit committee of more than three public companies, and the listed company does not limit the number of audit committees on which its audit committee members may serve, each board is required to determine whether such simultaneous service would impair the ability of such a member to effectively serve on the listed company's audit committee. Additionally, any such determination must be disclosed in an annual proxy statement or in the annual report on Form 10-K in case the company does not file a proxy statement.

Another major difference is that NYSE governance requirements require each listed company to have an internal audit function to provide management and the audit committee with ongoing assessments of the company's risk management processes and system of internal control. Under the guidelines, companies may choose to outsource this function to a third-party service provider other than its independent auditor, but it must at least have this function.

Like NASDAQ, each listed company must adopt and disclose a code of business conduct and ethics that is applicable to all directors, officers, and employees. The code of conduct must be available on the company's Web site, and any waiver of the code of conduct for officers and directors must be promptly disclosed. The code of conduct must provide the following elements:

- Conflicts of interest.
- Corporate opportunities.
- Confidentiality of information.
- Fair dealing.
- Protection and proper use of company assets.
- Compliance with laws, rules, and regulations.
- Encouraging the reporting of any illegal or unethical behavior.
- Compliance standards.
- Procedures to facilitate effective operation of the code.

The CEO of each listed company must certify to the NYSE each year that he or she is not aware of any violation by the company of the NYSE's corporate listing standards. This certification would be required to be disclosed in the company's annual report on Form 10-K. Additionally, the CEO of each listed company would be required to promptly notify the NYSE in writing after any executive officer becomes aware of any material noncompliance with the applicable provisions of the new requirements.

The governance changes authorize the NYSE to issue a public reprimand letter to any listed company that violates NYSE governance requirements.

Has Recent Legislation Fixed the Problem?

To determine whether recent legislation has remedied the problem and will prevent future frauds, it is important to align the three elements of the fraud triangle with remedies that have been instituted. Table 11.1 attempts to do that.

As we described earlier in the book, fraud is like fire in that there are three elements that come together to create fire: (1) heat, (2) fuel, and (3) oxygen. The more intense or pure one element, say oxygen, the less heat and fuel are required. The same is true with fraud. The more of one element you have, say pressures, the less of the other elements (i.e., opportunities and rationalizations) it takes to commit fraud. To the extent that recent legislative and governance actions have reduced fraud opportunities, the more perceived pressure and rationalization it will take to commit financial statement fraud in the future. Eliminating opportunities will make it much more difficult for executives to argue that their personal interests will be best served by fraudulent reporting. For example, with increased independence of board members, CEOs whose performance is questionable are more likely to be dismissed. This is different than it was in the past. Boeker (1992)[1], for example, found that, historically, organizations with below-average performance and powerful chief executives failed to dismiss the chief executive. In the majority of cases, the boards were willing to take other actions to improve success but were not willing to dismiss the CEO. Legislative and governance changes make it harder to commit fraud, make it harder to conceal fraud, and impose greater penalties for those who behave dishonestly. Only when perceived pressures and the ability to rationalize increase to the point where they more than offset the decreased opportunities will future frauds occur. Our prediction, therefore, is that less corporate fraud will occur in the United States in the future, but not all of it will be eliminated. The increased pressures and rationalizations that will now be necessary will generate fraud symptoms that are more egregious than those of the past. For individuals who understand fraud, these egregious fraud symptoms will be more observable than ever before, which should make fraud easier to detect.

TABLE 11A REMEDIES ENACTED THROUGH RECENT LEGISLATION

ELEMENT OF THE FRAUD TRIANGLE	ELEMENT OF THE PERFECT FRAUD STORM	REMEDY THAT ADDRESSES THIS FACTOR
Perceived Pressures	1. Misplaced executive incentives 2. Unrealistic Wall Street expectations 3. Large amounts of debt 4. Greed	Recent legislation and corporate governance changes have not addressed perceived pressures. Significant stock-based compensation is still being given to executives. No decrease has occurred in EPS forecasts and the size of penalties when those forecasts are not met. Companies have taken on more, not less, debt.*+ And, no evidence indicates that executives are less motivated by greed than before the frauds.
Perceived Opportunities	1. Good economy was masking many problems 2. Behavior of CPA firms 3. Rules-based accounting standards 4. Educator failures	Most of the legislative and governance changes have been targeted at reducing opportunities to commit fraud. The requirement that board members be more independent from management is intended to eliminate or decrease the opportunities of management to commit fraud. Other actions that are intended to decrease opportunities+ are minimum sentencing guidelines, requiring executives to sign off on the accuracy of financial statements, holding management responsible for good controls, installing a whistle-blower system, inspecting auditors so that they increase the thoroughness of their audits, etc.
Rationalization	1. Moral decay in society	The one legislative action that addresses this fraud element is requiring all companies to have an executive code of conduct. However, with decreasing integrity in society, it is doubtful that requiring a code of conduct will eliminate rationalizations.

*One of the most common activities on Wall Street since the discovery of the corporate frauds has been the issuance of convertible debt by corporations. The convertibles market has been extremely hot and has resulted in significantly more debt for many companies. Unfortunately, convertible debt creates the same kinds of stock manipulation pressures (to have the stock price increase to the premium amount at which the debt can be called and converted to equity).

+Opportunity encompasses not only the ability to commit a fraud but also the opportunity to conceal the fraud (and not be caught) and to experience no serious punishment if caught.

END NOTE

1. For example, with increased independence of board members, CEO's whose performance is questionable are more likely to be dismissed. This is different than it was in the past. Boeker (1992), for example, found that, historically, organizations with below-average performance and powerful chief executives failed to dismiss the chief executive. In the majority of cases, the boards were willing to take other actions to improve success but were not willing to dismiss the CEO.

CHAPTER **12**

Revenue- and Inventory-Related Financial Statement Frauds

LEARNING OBJECTIVES

After studying this chapter, you should be able to:

- Identify revenue-related financial statement fraud schemes.
- List ways to search for symptoms of revenue-related financial statement fraud.
- Understand the importance of, and ways to follow up on, revenue-related fraud symptoms.
- Discuss inventory-related financial statement fraud schemes.
- Identify ways to search for inventory-related financial statement fraud symptoms.
- Explain the importance of, and ways to follow up on, inventory-related fraud symptoms.

TO THE STUDENT

The Sarbanes-Oxley Act required that the Securities and Exchange Commission (SEC) study enforcement actions over the five years (July 31, 1997 to July 30, 2002) preceding its enactment in order to identify areas of issuer financial reporting that are most susceptible to fraud, inappropriate manipulation, or inappropriate earnings management. This study provided many examples of financial statement fraud used in this chapter and Chapter 13.

This chapter focuses on revenue- and inventory-related financial statement frauds. Specifically, it focuses on identifying financial statement fraud exposures. While doing this, it is important to focus on transactions and accounts that are affected by and correspond with the potential frauds. This chapter also discusses fraud symptoms that may exist and how to actively search for these fraud symptoms. Finally, the chapter addresses ways to follow up on symptoms observed that pertain to both revenue- and inventory-related financial statement frauds.

You've probably never heard of Cendant Corporation, but you are probably familiar with some of the companies it owned before breaking up in 2006. The list includes Days Inn, Ramada Inn, Avis Car Rental, and real estate brokerage Century 21. Cendant Corporation was formed in 1997 when CUC International Inc. merged with HFS Inc. Combining the resources of both companies was intended to create one of the world's largest and most powerful hotel, car rental, reservation, and real estate companies. But Cendant's hopes for a successful company quickly turned upside down when HFS Inc. learned that CUC International had inflated its income and earnings to make it appear to be a growing, highly profitable, and successful enterprise. What started as a small fraud in 1983 quickly grew to a large fraud. From 1995 to 1997, the pretax operating income of CUC International was inflated by more than $500 million. Many executives of CUC International were fired and prosecuted.

In 1999, Cendant Corporation agreed to pay $2.8 billion to settle a shareholder lawsuit. The attorneys for the plaintiffs were awarded $262 million in fees. On April 16, 1998, when the fraud was publicly announced, Cendant's stock dropped 46 percent, making the paper value of the company drop by $14.4 billion in one day. Today, Cendant is a diversified global provider of business consumer services. It has largely overcome the fraud that cost it time, negative public exposure, and more than $2.8 billion. With headquarters in New York City, the company has approximately 60,000 employees and operates in over 100 countries.

You've probably heard of Sunbeam Corporation, the maker of home appliances. Sunbeam began developing home appliances in 1910. Over the years, Sunbeam made some of the nation's best home appliances, such as the electric iron and the pop-up toaster. In July 1996, Chainsaw Al Dunlap (given the nickname because of his reputation as a ruthless executive who employed massive layoffs to turn around troubled companies) became CEO and chairman of Sunbeam. Chainsaw Al repeatedly promised to produce a rapid turnaround in Sunbeam's financial performance. At the end of 1996, Chainsaw Al was unable to deliver on his promise. Desperate, he turned to a laundry list of fraud schemes to improve the company's financial performance. He began creating "cookie jar" reserves. These reserves were used to paint a picture of a rapid turnaround by initially increasing Sunbeam's loss for 1996 while later being reversed so as to inflate income in 1997. In 1997, Chainsaw Al caused the company to recognize revenues for sales that did not meet applicable accounting rules. As a result, at least $60 million of Sunbeam's record-setting $189 million reported earnings in 1997 came from accounting fraud. In early 1998, Chainsaw Al took even more desperate measures to conceal the company's mounting financial problems. He again recognized revenue for sales that did not meet accounting rules. He also caused Sunbeam to engage in the acceleration of sales revenue from a later period and deleted certain corporate records to conceal pending returns of merchandise.[1]

Revenue-Related Fraud

By far, the most common accounts manipulated when perpetrating financial statement fraud are revenues and/or receivables. The Committee of Sponsoring Organizations (COSO)-sponsored studies discussed in Chapter 11 found that over half of all financial statement frauds involved revenues and/or accounts receivable accounts. These studies also found that recording fictitious revenues was the most common way to manipulate revenue accounts and that recording revenues prematurely was the second most common type of revenue-related financial statement fraud. Other studies have found similar results. In fact, because of the frequency of revenue-related financial statement frauds, the American Institute of Certified Public Accountants (AICPA) published "Audit Issues in Revenue Recognition" on its Web site (www.aicpa.org) in January 1999. This publication contained authoritative and nonauthoritative auditing guidance to help financial statement auditors identify and respond to warning signals of improper revenue-recognition. It focuses on issues related to the sale of goods and services in the ordinary course of business. The publication also discusses management's responsibility to report revenues accurately and follow appropriate **revenue-recognition** policies. There are two reasons for the prevalence of revenue-related financial statement fraud. One is the availability of acceptable alternatives for recognizing revenue, and the other is the ease of manipulating net income using revenue and receivable accounts.

Acceptable Alternatives

Just as organizations are different, the kinds of revenues they generate are different, and these different types of revenues need different recognition and reporting methods and criteria. A company that collects cash before delivering goods or performing a service, such as a franchiser, needs to recognize revenue differently than a company that collects cash after the delivery of goods or the performance of a service, such as a manufacturer. A company that has long-term construction contracts needs different revenue-recognition criteria than a company whose revenue is based on small, discrete performance acts. Numerous questions arise about when to record revenue, such as whether the company has shipped a product, completed a service, collected payment, fulfilled service obligations, and so forth. In many cases, it is difficult to identify one event that should trigger the recording of revenue.

Consider, for example, a company that explores, refines, and distributes oil. When should revenue be recognized for this company—when it discovers the oil in the ground (for which there is a ready market and a determinable price), when it refines the crude oil or condensate into products such as jet and diesel fuel, when it distributes the oil to its service stations for resale, or when it actually sells the refined oil to customers? Similarly, consider a company that performs clinical trials on new drugs produced by pharmaceutical companies to determine whether the drugs should be approved for sale and distribution to the public by the Food and Drug Administration. Suppose a contract with a pharmaceutical firm states that the drug will be tested on 100 patients over a period of six months, and each patient will be observed and tested weekly. Further assume that the testing company is to be paid $100 per patient visit for a total of $2,600 (26 visits) per patient and a total contract amount of $260,000 ($2,600 per patient × 100 patients). Because the pharmaceutical company does not want to be

billed every time a patient is tested, it specifies that the testing company can submit bills for payment only when certain "billing milestones" have been reached, such as 25 patient visits, 50 patient visits, 75 patient visits, and 100 patient visits. In this case, when should the revenues be recognized—at the time the patient visits take place, at the time bills can be submitted to the pharmaceutical company, when all visits have taken place, or at some other time?

These are difficult issues that require significant judgment. In these and many other settings, both conservative and liberal methods of recognizing revenue can be applied. Even financial reporting experts do not always agree when an organization has had sufficient performance to recognize revenue and what the major revenue-recognition criteria should be. In numerous cases, these and other difficult revenue-recognition issues have been debated and have been the focus of financial statement fraud lawsuits. Specifically, the companies started out using liberal ways of recognizing revenues and when those weren't sufficient, management started committing fraud. In the oil company case mentioned earlier, the company fraudulently recognized sales on fictitious ships that were supposedly sailing the oceans. In the medical testing case, contracts with drug companies that were shown to the auditors were altered to inflate the amount of revenue per patient.

These differences in revenue-recognition and performance criteria across organizations make it very difficult to develop revenue-recognition rules for the numerous business models in today's economy. Indeed, in many situations, significant judgment must be exercised to determine when and how much revenue to recognize. This provides opportunities for managers who want to commit financial statement fraud.

Ease of Manipulating Net Income Using Revenues and Receivables

The second reason why revenue-related frauds are so common is because it is so easy to manipulate net income using revenues and receivables accounts. In the video *Cooking the Books,* produced by the Association of Certified Fraud Examiners, Barry Minkow, mastermind of the ZZZZ Best fraud, states, "Receivables are a wonderful thing. You create a receivable and you have revenue." When you have revenue, you have income. An easy way to inflate net income is to create revenue and some corresponding receivables. Additionally, revenues and receivables can be manipulated in several other ways. For example, an organization can inflate its revenues by including revenues in the current period that should be recognized in the next period. This scheme is often referred to as *early or premature revenue-recognition* or *abusing the cutoff.*

Revenues can also be recognized early by misstating the work completed in a company with long-term construction contracts where revenue depends on a project's percentage of completion. Companies can also create fictitious documents, sales, or customers to make it appear that actual sales were higher than they really were for the period. Alternatively, contracts upon which revenue is based can be altered or forged. Or, in the most egregious cases, **topside journal entries** that create revenues and receivables without underlying documentation can be created.

———

One of the most egregious revenue-related frauds in recent years was that committed by Qwest International. Qwest, a Denver-based company, is the dominant local telephone company in numerous states. It was founded in 1995 and became a public company in 1997. Qwest had 57,000 employees and reported revenues of $18 billion in 2001. It also had 30 million customers who sent 600 million e-mails and made 240 million telephone calls per day on its 190,000 miles of telephone network. During 1999, 2000, and 2001, Qwest overstated revenues by $2 to $4 billion. In 2000 and 2001 alone, it wrote off revenue of $2.2 billion. When the fraud was discovered, the price of the company's stock dropped 89 percent. Four former executives were indicted on 12 charges related to financial statement fraud: Grant Graham, the former chief financial officer; Thomas Hall and John Walker, both former vice presidents; and Bryan Treadway, a former assistant controller. Qwest's revenue fraud schemes included the following:

- Swapping with other telecom firms the rights to use fiber-optic strands for no legitimate business reason, and immediately booking revenues to meet earnings expectations. Using this method, known as "round-tripping," the company recognized gains of $3 billion. Many of these swap deals were with other telecom firms that also revealed major revenue-related frauds, including Global Crossing ($720 million in swap revenues from deals with Qwest), Enron, Flag, and Cable & Wireless.
- Improperly recognizing revenue from "bill and hold" transactions and falsifying documents to hide the fraud. One notable "bill and hold" transaction was with the Arizona School Facilities Board in the third quarter of 2000.
- Selling equipment at twice the normal price and then discounting service contracts. Because the profit on the sales could be recognized earlier than the revenue on the service contracts, the company booked more than $100 million in revenues at an 80 percent profit margin. This method became known as illegally "splitting transactions."
- Changing the publication dates on telephone directories to inflate revenue in 2000 and 2001, a practice that became known as "Dex shuffling."

The round-tripping, or swapping, scheme was the biggest revenue scheme used by Qwest. Roughly $1.5 billion of $2.2 billion in revenue written off in 2000 and 2001 came from swaps or sales of fiber-optic rights, while equipment sales accounted for only several hundred million dollars. This fraud was discovered through several sources, including telecom analysts, employees of Global Crossing and Qwest, SEC investigations, the U.S. Department of Justice, a Qwest audit committee internal probe, and an internal investigation ordered by Qwest's new CEO.

———

Identifying Revenue-Related Fraud Exposures

Revenue-related fraud exposures should be considered in every business. The exposures involve any schemes that can be used to misstate revenue and often misstate receivables, too. One of the best ways to understand how revenue frauds could be perpetrated is to understand the various revenue transactions in the company. One of the first tasks in this regard is to analyze and diagram the various transactions between an organization and its customers. Then, by analyzing the accounts involved in each transaction, an investigator or auditor can determine how each transaction could be misstated. In this regard, revenue transactions for a typical company might be diagrammed as shown in Figure 12.1.

Once the revenue transactions are diagrammed, a good way to understand the various financial statement fraud schemes is to relate the accounts involved in each transaction with the potential manipulations. The numbers provided in the diagram to identify the transactions can be used to prepare a table such as the one shown in Table 12.1. However, before we discuss the various revenue-related fraud schemes, we would like to list and briefly explain some of the more common ones.

The following is a list of common revenue-related fraud schemes:

- *Related-party transactions* are business deals or arrangements that are made by two parties who have a relationship (e.g., familial, business-related, or other) that creates conflicts of interest in a business setting. When related-party transactions are not disclosed, then fraud occurs.
- *Sham sales* is a phrase used for various types of fictitious sales.
- *Bill-and-hold sales* are orders for goods that are stored by the seller, often because the buyer is not ready or able to receive the goods at the time of the order. Fraud occurs when these sales are recognized even though the

FIGURE 12.1   BASIC REVENUE TRANSACTIONS

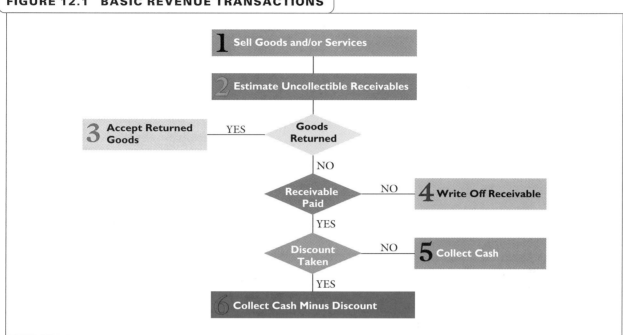

- many requirements for their recognition (e.g., risk of loss must transfer to the buyer) are not.
- **Side agreements** are sales terms and arrangements (e.g., a liberal return policy) that are made outside normal reporting channels. These agreements lead to fraud when they involve amending the terms and conditions of existing sales contracts so that they violate revenue-recognition requirements.
- **Consignment sales** are transactions where one company holds and sells goods that are owned by another company. Improperly recording consignment sales leads to inflated revenues and corresponding costs.
- **Channel stuffing** is a practice that suppliers use to encourage customers to buy extra inventory so as to increase current-year sales. This practice can inflate sales when stated or implied side agreements (e.g., allowing customers to return the goods) are not properly disclosed or accounted for. Also, channel stuffing can be deemed fraudulent when sufficient reserves are not established (e.g., for sales expected to be returned).
- **Lapping or kiting** is a practice where cash receipts are misapplied to hide fictitious receivables. For example, if a fictitious receivable is recorded for Customer X, a payment received from Customer A will be used to show that the receivable was valid. A later payment received from another customer may be used to write off the receivable recorded by Customer A, etc.

- **Redating or refreshing transactions** involve changing sale dates to more current time periods to prevent them from being deemed uncollectible or bad debts.
- **Liberal return policies** allow customers to return products and cancel sales in future periods. These policies make it difficult to estimate the amount of revenue that should be recorded in the current period.
- **Partial shipment** schemes involve recording the full amount of a sale when only part of the sale was shipped.
- **Improper cutoff** occurs when transactions are recorded in the wrong time period. This occurs when a company keeps the accounting books open for a particular period and records future-period transactions as if they occurred in the current period (also referred to as improperly holding the books open).
- **Round-tripping** involves selling unused assets for a promise to buy them or similar assets back at roughly the same price. In the end, no economic benefit exists for either company.

All of these fraud schemes result in overstated revenues and overstated net income. Of course, it would also be possible to understate revenues and net income by committing fraud in the opposite direction. Such frauds are extremely rare and usually only occur when a company wants to manage or smooth income or understate net income in order to pay lower income taxes.

TABLE 12.1 TRANSACTION TYPES USED IN VARIOUS FRAUD SCHEMES

TRANSACTION	ACCOUNTS INVOLVED	FRAUD SCHEMES
1. Sell goods and/or services to customers	Accounts Receivable and Revenues (e.g., Sales Revenue)	1. Record fictitious sales (e.g., related parties, sham sales, bill-and-hold sales, sales with side agreements, consignment sales, round-tripping, etc.). 2. Recognize revenues too early (e.g., improper cutoff, holding books open after the close of a reporting period, percentage of completion, etc.). 3. Overstate real sales (e.g., use improper valuation of revenue, alter contracts, inflate amounts, etc.).
2. Estimate uncollectible receivables	Bad Debt Expense and Allowance for Doubtful Accounts	4. Understate allowance for doubtful accounts, thus overstating receivables.
3. Accept returned goods from customers	Sales Returns and Accounts Receivable	5. Not record returned goods from customers. 6. Record returned goods after the end of the period.
4. Write off receivables as uncollectible	Allowance for Doubtful Accounts and Accounts Receivable	7. Don't write off uncollectible receivables (e.g., redating or refreshing transactions). 8. Write off uncollectible receivables in a later period.
5. Collect cash after discount period	Cash and Accounts Receivable	9. Record bank transfers as cash is received from customers. 10. Manipulate cash received from related parties (e.g., lapping). 11. Record fictitious cash entries such as debiting Cash and crediting Accounts Receivable.
6. Collect cash within discount period	Cash, Sales Discounts, and Accounts Receivable	12. Not record discounts given to customers.

Once the various fraud schemes (or exposures) have been considered, scheme-specific symptoms can be searched for proactively. Any observed symptoms can be investigated to determine if fraud exists.

Identifying Revenue-Related Fraud Symptoms

Unlike murder or bank robbery, fraud is rarely observed. Instead, only symptoms, indicators, or red flags are observed. To detect fraud, you must be able to identify something as being a symptom or red flag.

As you learned earlier in this book, fraud symptoms (for all types of fraud) can be divided into six categories as follows:

1. **Analytical symptoms.** These economic events, accounting transactions, or financial and nonfinancial relationships are unusual. For example, sales may be too big, a reserve may be too small, transactions may be recorded at the wrong time or by the wrong person, and so forth. They are the unexpected or unexplained—things out of the ordinary or the unpredictable. Sometimes they are too good to be true. One particularly promising method to find analytical symptoms of revenue fraud is to compare changes in revenue with changes in nonfinancial performance measures. For example, companies that report revenues that are increasing faster than their store space or the number of employees in the company have been found to be more likely to be recording fraudulent revenues than competitors that are increasing the number of stores and employees in ways that are consistent with the revenue growth.[2]

2. **Accounting or documentary symptoms.** These discrepancies in the accounting records or system involve such things as missing documents, photocopies where originals should exist, ledgers that don't balance, unusual journal entries, or similar events.

3. **Lifestyle symptoms.** When people steal, they spend their ill-gotten gains. Perpetrators rarely save what they steal. Once the critical need is met that motivated the fraud, perpetrators start to improve their lifestyle. Although management fraud in smaller companies and other types of misappropriation are often motivated by lifestyle symptoms, these types of symptoms are usually not as apparent in financial statement fraud in large organizations since management is usually very well compensated by legitimate means.

4. **Control symptoms.** These breakdowns in the control environment, accounting system, or internal

control activities or procedures are often so egregious that they hint that a management override is taking place. Examples are an override or lack of segregation of duties when segregation should exist, a weak or missing audit committee, etc.

5. **Behavioral and verbal symptoms.** Most fraud perpetrators are first-time offenders. When they commit fraud, they feel guilty, which creates stress. Fraud perpetrators change their behavior to cope with this stress or to hide fraud symptoms. These changes in behavior, together with verbal responses, are often excellent fraud symptoms.

6. **Tips and complaints.** The last category of fraud symptoms is tips and complaints from employees, spouses, vendors, customers, and others. Although no tip should be ignored, many tips and complaints are motivated by nonfactors, such as revenge, attention seeking, or other reasons.

It is important to know that in detecting fraud, symptoms or red flags should only be considered in context. For example, management and the external auditor could see the same thing and, because of their background, it could legitimately be a symptom to one party but not the other. Take, for example, the case where management knows from other transactions that they cannot trust the CFO because he has lied to them about various issues but the auditor is not aware of the CFO's dishonesty. Thus, if both the auditor and management see revenue that should be recognized in a later year recognized in an earlier year, for example, it could very well represent a red flag for management but not for the auditor. The auditor, whose standards tell him or her to assume neither guilt nor innocence of the CFO, could interpret the problem as an unintentional error, while management, who question the integrity of the CFO, would more likely suspect that fraud has occurred.

With revenue-related financial statement frauds, some of the most common symptoms in these six categories are as follows:

Analytical Symptoms

1. Revenue or sales that appear too high, especially relative to nonfinancial performance measures. See Table 12.2 for a list of potential nonfinancial performance measures that are publicly available.
2. Sales discounts that appear too low.
3. Sales returns that appear too low.
4. Bad debt expense that appears too low.
5. Accounts receivable that appear too high or are increasing too fast.

TABLE 12.2

NONFINANCIAL PERFORMANCE MEASURE
Amount of Annual Capacity
Amount of Developed or Undeveloped Gas Reserves
Amount of Electricity Sales
Amount of Export Volume
Amount of Gas Sales
Amount of Gas Transported
Amount of Gross Energy Producing Capacity
Number of Business Segments
Number of Customers or Customer Accounts
Number of Distribution Dealers
Number of Government Contracts Awarded
Number of Locations
Number of Manufacturing/Research Facilities
Number of New Leases
Number of New Products Introduced
Number of Outpatient Visits
Number of Plants or Warehouses
Number of Product Lines or Types
Number of Production Facilities
Number of Products
Number of R&D Technicians
Number of Retail Outlets
Number of Sales Representatives
Number of Service Facilities
Number of Stores
Number of Subsidiaries
Number or Square Feet of Leased Facilities
Population Served
Square Feet of Manufacturing Space
Square Feet of Office or Warehousing Space
Square Feet of Operating Space
Square Feet of Owned Distribution Centers
Square Feet of Property Owned
Square Feet of Space Leased

6. The allowance for doubtful accounts appears too low.
7. Too little cash collected relative to reported revenues.
8. Unusual entries made at the end of the accounting period that increase revenues.
9. Rapid changes in the mix or types of revenues.
10. Unusual relationships between costs and revenues.
11. Unexpected relationships between cash and receivables.
12. Unusual relationships between two revenue-related accounts.
13. Significant new, unknown customers.
14. Revenue-related transactions not recorded in a complete or timely manner or improperly recorded as to amount, accounting period, classification, or entity policy.
15. Last-minute revenue adjustments by the entity that significantly improve financial results.
16. A large and growing receivable balance with little or no cash received from the customer.
17. Sales of assets that are very similar to subsequent purchases at similar amounts.

Accounting or Documentary Symptoms

1. Unsupported or unauthorized revenue-related balances or transactions.
2. Missing documents in the revenue cycle.
3. Only photocopies of documents exist to support revenue transactions, when documents in original form should exist.
4. Significant unexplained items on bank and other reconciliations.
5. Revenue-related ledgers (sales, cash receipts, etc.) that do not balance.
6. Unusual discrepancies between the entity's revenue-related records and corroborating evidence (such as accounts receivable confirmation replies).
7. Nonstandard journal entries posted by top management.
8. Nonstandard journal entries posted near the end of the accounting period.
9. Nonstandard journal entries posted at unusual times, such as on weekends, late at night, or on holidays.
10. Nonstandard journal entries for round dollar amounts or for amounts that do not comply with Benford's law.

Control Symptoms

1. Management override of significant internal control activities related to the revenue cycle.
2. New, unusual, or large customers that appear not to have gone through the customer-approval process.

3. Weaknesses in the cutoff processes or other key accounting processes.

Behavioral or Verbal Symptoms

1. Inconsistent, vague, or implausible responses from management or employees arising from revenue inquiries or analytical procedures.
2. Denied access to facilities, employees, records, customers, vendors, or others from whom revenue-related audit evidence might be sought.
3. Undue time pressures imposed by management to resolve contentious or complex revenue-related issues.
4. Unusual delays by the entity in providing revenue-related, requested information.
5. Untrue responses by management to queries about revenue-related accounts.
6. Suspicious behavior from management when asked about revenue-related transactions or accounts.

Lifestyle Symptoms

1. Major sales of company stock around earnings releases or other unusual dates.
2. Significant bonuses tied to meeting earnings forecasts.
3. Executives' personal net worth tied up in company stock.

Tips and Complaints

1. Tips or complaints that revenue-related fraud (any of the schemes discussed earlier in this chapter) might be occurring, either from the company whistle-blower system or in other ways.
2. Revenue frauds disclosed at companies with which this company does significant amounts of business.

This list is not exhaustive but provides examples of the kinds of revenue-related symptoms that can be observed.

Actively Searching for Revenue-Related Fraud Symptoms

For financial statement fraud to be detected, fraud symptoms must be observed and recognized. In some of the most famous financial statement fraud cases, symptoms should have been readily observed, but were not recognized by auditors and others. In some cases, symptoms are observed and even inquired about, but alternative explanations from management are accepted. For example, in the HealthSouth financial statement fraud case that was discovered in 2003, a congressional committee now says regulators and auditors received red flags of the accounting problems at HealthSouth as early as

1998. A May 2003 article on TheStreet.com discussed the HealthSouth fraud and stated the following:

> Some critics hold E&Y at least partially accountable for the disaster. They say that E&Y ignored warnings more than once about HealthSouth's accounting. On Wednesday, the House committee investigating the scandal released a new memo, sent to E&Y nearly five years ago, that "provides a road map leading to possible fraud."
>
> The unsigned memo, faxed to E&Y by a concerned HealthSouth shareholder, states in part: "How can the company carry tens of millions of dollars in accounts receivable that are well over 360 days? How can some hospitals have NO bad debt reserves? How did the E&Y auditors in Alabama miss this stuff?"
>
> The House committee, chaired by Tauzin, collected the memo after demanding extensive access to E&Y's HealthSouth documents. In a prepared statement, E&Y attempted to explain away the memo by saying the issues raised by the shareholder "did not affect the presentation of HealthSouth's financial statements."
>
> But government officials remain skeptical. In a joint statement with the chairman of an investigations subcommittee, Tauzin said: "We now have evidence that five years ago warnings were given to HealthSouth's corporate watchdogs—their outside auditor, Ernst & Young, and perhaps even the Securities and Exchange Commission—about the accounting shenanigans at the company. Yet, no one appears to have listened."
>
> More recently, a former HealthSouth bookkeeper warned E&Y about potential accounting fraud at the company last summer. But the auditors apparently found no signs of wrongdoing.[3]

Interested parties, such as auditors, can find fraud symptoms in two ways: either they wait until they "likely discover symptoms by chance," or they "proactively search for symptoms." For years, auditors and accountants have relied primarily on chance (a tip, anomalies from a sample taken, stumbling on fraud evidence, etc.) to discover symptoms. Because of developments in technology and lessons learned from fraud research, we now have tools and knowledge available to proactively search for fraud symptoms. The specific search performed depends on the kinds of symptoms that you expect for a given fraud.

Actively Searching for Revenue-Related Analytical Symptoms

In a previous chapter, we discussed using technology to proactively search for financial statement fraud. Analytical symptoms relating to revenue accounts involve those accounts being too high or too low, increasing too fast or not fast enough, or other abnormal relationships. When searching for analytical symptoms, the question that needs answering is "too high, too low, or unusual relative to what?" To determine whether analytical symptoms exist, a point of reference, an expectation, or some reasonable balance or relationship to which recorded amounts can be compared is necessary. A practical way to begin looking for analytical symptoms is to focus on changes and comparisons within the financial statements. The specific analyses that are conducted usually include the following:

1. Analyzing financial balances and relationships within financial statements.
2. Comparing financial statement amounts or relationships with information outside the financial statements.

Two common ways for performing a within-statement analysis include looking for unusual changes in revenue-related (1) account *balances* from period to period (looking at trends) and (2) *relationships* from period to period. Two types of analyses can also be performed where financial statement amounts and relationships are compared to other information. These include the following:

1. Comparing financial results and trends of the company with those of similar firms in the same industry or with industry averages.
2. Comparing recorded revenue in the financial statements with assets or other financial or nonfinancial information.

Table 12.3 summarizes these approaches.

Focusing on Changes in Recorded Account Balances (Amounts) from Period to Period

Recorded amounts from one period can be compared to recorded amounts in another period in three ways. The first and least effective method is to focus on and calculate changes in the actual financial statement *numbers* themselves. It is often difficult, however, to assess the magnitude or significance of changes in account balances looking only at raw data, especially when the numbers are large.

The second method, and one where it is much easier to recognize analytical symptoms, is to use a process described earlier in Chapter 6, called *horizontal analysis*. Horizontal analysis is a method involving examining percentage changes in account balances

TABLE 12.3 TYPES OF FINANCIAL STATEMENT ANALYSIS

Analyzing financial balances and relationships *within* financial statements	Look for unusual changes in revenues and accounts receivable *balances* from period to period (trends).	Look for unusual changes in revenue-cycle-account *relationships* from period to period.
Comparing financial statement amounts or relationships with related information	Compare financial results and trends of the company with those of *similar firms* in the same industry.	Compare recorded amounts in the financial statements with financial or nonfinancial amounts.

from period to period. The calculation of percentage change is made by dividing the difference between the balances for period 2 and period 1 by period 1's account balances. Thus, for example, if an organization had an accounts receivable balance of $100,000 in period 1 and $130,000 in period 2, horizontal analysis would reveal a percentage change of 30 percent, calculated as follows:

$$(\$130{,}000 - \$100{,}000 / \$100{,}000 = 30\%)$$

The third way to examine changes from period to period is to study the statement of cash flows. Perhaps you are wondering why we perform horizontal analysis only on the income statement and balance sheet, but not on the statement of cash flows. The reason is because horizontal analysis converts income statements and balance sheets to "change" statements, and the statement of cash flows is already a "change statement." Every number on the statement of cash flows represents the change in account balances from one period to the next. On the statement of cash flows, the changes in Accounts Receivable, Inventory, Accounts Payable, and other accounts appear on the statement itself. Studying the statement of cash flows is like looking at the differences in raw numbers on the balance sheet and income statement from one period to the next, except that the calculations have already been made for you. When searching for fraud, examining the statement of cash flows is as effective as comparing actual changes in account balances. It is probably easier than recalculating the differences between two successive financial statements for selected accounts, but it is usually much less effective than using horizontal analysis.

Focusing on Changes in Revenue-Related Relationships

Examining changes in financial statement relationships from period to period is one of the best ways to discover analytical fraud symptoms. Changes in relationships from period to period can be examined in at least two ways. The first is to focus on changes in

various revenue-related ratios from period to period. (Ratios, as you will recall, are summary calculations of significant relationships in the financial statements.) Examining revenue-related ratios provides an efficient method of focusing on relationship symptoms within the financial statements. The most common ratios used to discover revenue-related analytical fraud symptoms are the following:

Gross profit (margin) ratio is calculated by dividing gross profit (also referred to as *gross margin*) by net sales. Gross profit, which is calculated by subtracting **cost of goods sold (COGS)** from net sales, is a function of the markup percentage. The gross profit ratio provides a measure of the markup as a percentage of sales. If someone is perpetrating revenue-related fraud by using a scheme that overstates sales or by understating sales discounts or **sales returns**, this ratio will increase. (*Note*: The ratio will also increase if management understates the cost of goods sold by overstating inventory, understating purchases, or by using other means. We will cover schemes that affect cost of goods sold later in this chapter.) When a company's gross profit percentage increases dramatically, something inappropriate, such as fraud, may be going on.

Sales return percentage ratio provides a measure of the percentage of sales that are returned by customers. It is calculated by dividing sales returns by total sales. When the sales return percentage ratio gets too high, it is a signal that too many goods are being returned. When the ratio becomes unexpectedly low, it is a signal that fraud or other problems could be occurring. One of the main methods perpetrators used to commit the MiniScribe fraud was to understate sales returns. In fact, the fraud became so egregious that at one time bricks were being boxed and shipped as software, with revenues being recognized at the time of shipment. When the bricks were returned by customers, they were stored in a separate location and not recorded as sales returns, allowing revenues and income to be overstated.

Sales discount percentage ratio is similar to the sales return percentage and is calculated by dividing sales discounts by gross sales. It provides a measure of the percentage of sales discounts taken by customers. A ratio that suddenly decreases may mean that customers are taking longer to pay (and not taking the discounts), or, in the case of fraud, it may mean that the discounts are not being recorded in the accounting records.

Accounts receivable turnover is one of the most widely used ratios to analyze revenues and receivables and is calculated by dividing sales by accounts receivable. Historically, this ratio has been used to examine the efficiency with which receivables are being collected. This ratio is also an excellent analytical tool for identifying fraud symptoms. One of the easiest ways to perpetrate revenue-related frauds is to record fictitious receivables and revenues. Unless the ratio is equal to 1, adding the same amount to the numerator (net sales) and denominator (accounts receivable) will change the ratio. If the ratio generally exceeds 1, recording fictitious sales will decrease the ratio. If the ratio is generally less than 1, recording fictitious sales will increase the ratio. Only in rare cases will the recording of significant amounts of fictitious revenues and receivables not affect this ratio. Sudden, unexpected changes in this ratio are a strong signal that fraud may be occurring.

Number of days in receivables ratio provides the same information as the accounts receivable turnover ratio. It is calculated by dividing 365 by the accounts receivable turnover. The advantage of the number of days in receivables ratio is that it identifies how quickly receivables are being collected in number of days, which is easy to understand. Adding fictitious receivables will generally increase the number of days it takes to collect receivables, because none of the fictitious receivables will be collected.

Allowance for uncollectible accounts as a percentage of receivables is calculated by dividing the allowance for uncollectible accounts by total accounts receivable. This ratio provides a measure of the percentage of receivables that are expected to be uncollectible. A common way to overstate receivables (and hence net income) is to not record bad accounts receivable as uncollectible. In one famous

fraud, for example, this percentage decreased from 4 percent to less than 0.5 percent before the fraud was discovered.

Asset turnover ratio is calculated by dividing total sales by average total assets. This ratio provides a measure of how many times an organization "turned over" its assets or the amount of sales revenue generated with each dollar of assets owned by the company. When a company records fictitious revenues, this ratio increases. As is the case with the other ratios covered in this chapter, unusually large increases in this ratio might indicate that some kind of revenue-related fraud is occurring. You should recognize, however, that this ratio is usually not as sensitive to receivable and revenue frauds as are the ratios already discussed.

Working capital turnover ratio is calculated by dividing sales by average working capital (current assets – current liabilities) for a period. This ratio indicates the amount of working capital used in generating sales for the period. Significant increases in this ratio could be a symptom of revenue fraud. As with asset turnover, this ratio is not as sensitive as the previous ratios in highlighting revenue-related frauds.

Operating performance margin ratio is calculated by dividing net income by total sales. It provides a measure of the profit margin of a company. Often, when revenue-related frauds occur, fictitious revenues are added without adding any additional expenses. These fictitious entries have the effect of increasing revenues and net income by the same or similar amounts (except for the tax effect). The result of adding fictitious revenues without additional expenses is a dramatic increase in this ratio.

Earnings per share is a very commonly used ratio that measures the profitability of an organization. It is calculated by dividing net income by the number of shares of stock outstanding. A dramatic increase in this ratio could be a signal that fraud is occurring, but is not necessarily indicative of revenue-related fraud. Again, this is one of the least sensitive ratios in helping to detect revenue-related financial statement fraud.

When using ratios to discover financial statement fraud symptoms, remember that the size or direction of the ratio is usually not important; rather, the changes (and speed of changes) in the ratios are what signal possible fraud—especially when the change is unexpected or unexplained.

CAUTION *Remember when analyzing ratios that changes in the ratios are more important than the actual sizes of the ratios.*

The second way to focus on financial statement relationships as fraud symptoms is to convert the financial statements to **percentages**[4] and perform vertical analysis, a method that was also discussed in Chapter 5. Just as horizontal analysis is a very effective way to search for analytical fraud symptoms relating to changes in account *balances,* vertical analysis is effective for identifying changes in financial statement *relationships* that must be investigated. With ratios, you generally focus on only one or two financial statement relationships at a time. If that relationship turns out to be the best indicator of fraud, you may identify a fraud symptom. On the other hand, with vertical analysis, you can simultaneously view the relationships between all numbers on the balance sheet or income statement.

The difficulty in using horizontal, vertical, or ratio analysis is knowing when a change in account balance or relationship is significant enough to signal possible fraud. Developing a reliable expectation or prediction regarding what the ratio or relationship should look like is the most important step in this process. Experience with and knowledge about a company are necessary for developing a reliable expectation. For example, knowing about the company's operations, its industry competitors, the economic conditions affecting the industry, and so forth, are critical for developing a reliable expectation. Generally, the more dramatic the change—especially if it runs counter to expectations—the higher the likelihood that something unusual (possibly fraud) is occurring. Even so, you should never conclude on the basis of analytical evidence alone that management is perpetrating fraud. At best, analytical tools merely identify potential problem areas or "circumstantial evidence" that need further analysis and investigation.

Comparing Financial Statement Information Between Companies

One of the best ways to detect financial statement fraud is to compare the performance of the company you are examining with the performance of other similar companies in the industry. Performance that runs counter to the performance of other firms in the same industry often signals fraud. For example, in the Equity Funding fraud, the financial statements showed a highly profitable and growing insurance company at a time when the rest of the insurance industry was struggling and significantly less profitable. WorldCom also showed unusually strong performance in the telecom industry when it was committing fraud. Economic and industry-wide factors usually affect similar firms in similar ways. Comparisons with other firms can be made using horizontal or vertical analysis, ratio analysis, changes reported in the statement of cash flows, or changes in the financial statement numbers themselves. Common-sizing financial statements is usually helpful when making interfirm comparisons. Common-size comparisons between companies in the same industry can quickly draw attention to, and thus encourage the investigation of, variations in financial performance. Working with percentages is usually much easier than comparing raw financial statement data.

Comparing Financial Statement Amounts with the Assets They Represent

Comparing recorded amounts in the financial statements with real-world assets is often an excellent way to detect fraud. However, this approach is not as useful for detecting revenue-related frauds as it is for detecting cash, inventory, and physical asset frauds. Generally, revenues do not correspond to physical assets that can be examined. The exception is when a company earns revenue constructing assets that involve long-term construction projects such as a building, bridge, or highway and recognizes revenue on the percentage-of-completion method. In these cases, the constructed assets should be examined to determine if the revenue recognized is reasonable, given the degree of completion of the projects.

Actively Searching for Accounting or Documentary Symptoms

One of the common ways for management to commit fraud is through posting one or more journal entries directly to the accounting records. These entries often bypass the normal process for posting journal entries and therefore involve the overriding of internal controls. These entries, are often referred to as *topside* journal entries, meaning the entries are posted directly to the summary journal or general ledger instead of a subsidiary ledger where supporting information is maintained. For example, in a sales-related fraud scheme, management might post a topside journal entry to increase both sales and accounts receivable. Normally, when sales and accounts receivable increase, entries are made to subsidiary journals showing who purchased the goods or services, the date of the purchase, when it was shipped, and so forth. With a topside journal entry, this supporting information is not recorded, and the entry increases the accounts but not the supporting ledgers such as the sales journal or the accounts receivable ledger.

A large corporation may have millions of journal entries each year. As such, searching for the few fraudulent entries is very challenging. However, computer software and hardware can be used to effectively search for these fraudulent entries. As discussed earlier, one approach is to use either inductive or deductive methods to look for these entries. Since a deductive method requires specific business and fraud exposures on which to focus, we will discuss some common inductive approaches.

Using software such as Picalo, ACL© or IDEA©, a fraud examiner can easily sift through millions of journal entries to find the potentially fraudulent few. For example, digital analysis can be used to find entries that don't conform to Benford's law. In addition, the entries should be analyzed to determine if they are unusual in terms of the five *W*s: (1) *who* posted the entry, (2) *what* the entry was for, (3) *when* the entry was posted, (4) *where* the entry was posted in the accounting system, and (5) *why* the entry was posted. Because journal entries in large companies include information about the entry (including who, when, where, and why), we can use technology to explore these questions. For example, if the CFO posted a large, round-dollar journal entry on a Sunday night near year-end, then we would be suspicious of the entry. Why? Because most CFOs have one or more staff employees who post journal entries, and they generally do their work during normal business hours. Furthermore, the amounts are not frequently large, round dollars.

One of the challenges in analyzing millions of journal entries using an inductive method is that you will end up with hundreds, even thousands, of false positives (entries that look unusual but are not). Even so, this sort of analysis was the breakthrough that allowed the WorldCom internal auditors to detect the company's massive financial statement fraud. Gene Morse was an internal auditor at WorldCom who used technology to search through the company's journal entries for unusual items. When he found a $500 million debit to a fixed asset account, he was very suspicious. After following up on this entry, Morse discovered that the

amount was part of a $1.7 billion entry at the heart of the WorldCom fraud in 2001. In the end, when the full impact of the WorldCom fraud was revealed, the company was required to restate its financial statements by $9 billion!

Actively Searching for Control Symptoms

The importance of identifying control weaknesses as possible fraud symptoms has already been discussed. However, two control-related points need mentioning with respect to revenue-related frauds. First, accountants and financial statement auditors are accustomed to accepting a limited number of control exceptions when assessing the adequacy of a system of internal controls. This approach is used because they view control breakdowns or weaknesses as something that needs to be fixed "in the future." As a fraud examiner, you must remember that most frauds are motivated by something called the *fraud triangle* as discussed previously and shown in Figure 12.2.

When an organization is experiencing pressures and management rationalizes that the pressures are only short term and will correct themselves in the future, all that is needed to commit financial statement fraud is some kind of perceived opportunity. Usually, these perceived opportunities exhibit themselves in the form of a control weakness, a control breakdown, or the ability to override key controls. For that reason, fraud examiners and investigators usually consider a control breakdown not only as something that must be fixed "in the future," but something that must be examined to see if it has been "abused in the past." In fact, one of the most common ways to detect fraud is to investigate control weaknesses or overrides to see if abuses occurred.

The second control factor that deserves special attention in considering financial statement fraud is the control environment. In many cases of financial statement fraud, the audit committee or board of directors is weak or inactive, and one or two executives have controlling power in the organization. A weak audit committee or board can lead to a control environment that does not value ethical behavior. For example, at WorldCom, upper management was known to project the message to those below them that controls were a bother and were not important. Recent legislation such as the Sarbanes-Oxley Act of 2002, described in Appendix A in Chapter 11, should help eliminate these situations for public companies. Even so, there are

FIGURE 12.2 FRAUD TRIANGLE

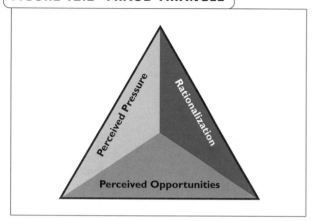

many nonpublic companies that may commit financial statement fraud and there are still instances where boards, audit committees, and executives do not operate as they are designed on organizational charts. External auditors are now supposed to assess the effectiveness of an auditee's control environment. This is something that is critical but very difficult since management may appear to have a strong control environment while concealing the fact that they override controls.

Actively Searching for Behavioral or Verbal and Lifestyle Symptoms

Lifestyle symptoms are much more helpful when trying to detect employee fraud than financial statement fraud because many financial statement frauds do not immediately benefit the perpetrators directly. Also, because upper management may already be wealthy, observing a lavish lifestyle may not mean fraud is taking place. When financial statement fraud occurs, the perpetrators benefit indirectly as the company has a higher stock price, doesn't default on a restrictive debt agreement, and so on. They may also benefit indirectly by, for example, being able to exercise stock options at a higher price because the financial results were overstated or by receiving an inflated bonus based on fictitious financial results. The same is not true of behavioral and verbal symptoms, however. In fact, one fraud detection tool that is often underused by fraud examiners and financial statement auditors is making verbal inquiries and personal observations. SAS 99 requires that external auditors make inquiries of management and others regarding fraud. Those who wrote SAS 99 believe that these inquiries should be

required since fraudulent activity can often be identified through this process. Under SAS 99, financial statement auditors are now required to make inquiries of the following individuals or groups about possible fraudulent activity or red flags: (1) management, (2) audit committee members, (3) internal audit personnel, and (4) other employees. Many times, the lower-level employees may be the most valuable sources for obtaining information that may reveal a financial statement fraud. This is true because management is likely to conceal the fraud from the audit committee, the internal auditor, and the external auditor, whereas lower-level employees may have knowledge of the scheme(s) used by management since they are required to be involved in many of them.

CAUTION *When compared to employee fraud, lifestyle symptoms are generally not as helpful for detecting financial statement fraud. However, behavioral or verbal symptoms are often very useful in detecting financial statement fraud.*

Fraud perpetrators usually have difficulty committing fraud without feeling guilty and without others knowing about the fraud. In fact, to perpetrate financial statement fraud, it is usually necessary to involve other people such as accountants and subsidiary personnel. Fraud examiners and auditors should learn to ask key fraud-related questions, such as the following:

- *Have you seen anything that resembles that something isn't right or that could be considered a red flag of fraud?*
- *Have you been asked to make any accounting entries that you consider to be unusual or about which you had questions regarding their propriety?*
- *Is there anything suspicious I should be aware of in this company?*
- *Have there been any attempts to manage earnings?*
- *Do any unusual operating or nonoperating income items concern you?*
- *Why did revenues (or returns, discounts, bad debts, allowances, etc.) change so dramatically?*
- *Should I pay particular attention to any specific individuals or units in the organization?*
- *What part of this organization, or which individuals, keep you awake worrying at night?*
- *Are there any accountants or executives in the company whose integrity and/or motivation you question?*

- *Is any executive or top-level accountant in the organization ever referred to by a name that implies he or she is unethical (e.g., "slick," "Teflon," "conniving," etc.)?*
- *Have you ever been asked or do you know of others who were asked by management to circumvent internal controls?*
- *Are you aware of any unusual sales transactions near year-end?*
- *Have you been asked to do something that would be hard to explain to a news reporter?*

With many frauds, individuals with questions about propriety of transactions or activities may be looking for a way out of the fraud or for someone with whom to talk. Once they are approached, they may open up with valuable information. You would think these individuals would voice their concerns through a company whistle-blowing system. However, until they are asked specifically about something they don't want to lie about, they often won't come forward.

Financial statement auditors and fraud examiners who can effectively communicate with management and other company personnel can often detect fraud. Effective communication with a manager who is committing financial statement fraud will often reveal inconsistencies in responses that can point to a fraud. Lying consistently takes significant effort and a good memory, so a good auditor or fraud examiner can often detect inconsistencies. While financial statement auditors and fraud examiners cannot be expected to catch all lying that takes place, the likelihood of catching a lie is much greater when examiners communicate directly and frequently with their clients while utilizing many of the interviewing principles discussed previously.

Finally, with respect to behavioral symptoms, remember that committing fraud, especially for first-time offenders, creates stress. Perpetrators must find a way to cope with that stress, and they usually do so by changing their behavior. Although financial statement auditors and fraud examiners may not be familiar enough with the management of a company to recognize changes in behavior, others within the organization are. In these situations, asking questions of lots of people will often reveal that something is not right.

Actively Searching for Tips and Complaints

The best way to search for tips and complaints for any fraud is to institute an ombudsman, hotline, or other system whereby people can anonymously call with tips

and complaints. As described earlier in this book, having a whistle-blower system and not retaliating against whistle-blowers is now a requirement in the United States for all public companies. Certainly, instituting whistle-blowing systems to gather information about clients is difficult for financial statement auditors and fraud examiners. However, even if not a public company, they should strongly encourage their clients to implement such a system. In most organizations, some individuals have knowledge or suspicions that fraud is occurring but are afraid to come forward. Some believe that the hesitancy to come forward with information about a fraud may stem back to socialization that began in grade school when children were taught by their peers that "tattletales" are looked down on. Other reasons that individuals are hesitant to come forward include the following:

- *They don't know who to tell or how to come forward.*
- *They don't want to wrongly accuse someone.*
- *They are afraid of "whistle-blower" repercussions.*
- *They only have suspicions rather than actual knowledge.*

Whistle-blowing systems are often effective in obtaining information from these individuals. If a company already has a hotline, financial statement auditors and fraud examiners can review hotline records and transcripts to see what kind of information has been collected and to review the company's process for following up on tips and complaints. Any tips or complaints about top management or other key personnel or about fraud related to the financial statements, controls, legal requirements, or fraud should be pursued vigorously. In addition, other complaints should also be reviewed from the perspective that whistle-blowers don't want to inform directly about a suspected fraud, but rather about tangential activities of the suspect, so he or she will be scrutinized carefully.

STOP & THINK *What are some potential problems with using anonymous whistle-blowing systems?*

Following Up on Revenue-Related Fraud Symptoms

As a fraud examiner, the presence of fraud symptoms provides predication or reason to believe that fraud may be occurring. When predication exists, and if conditions warrant, an investigation should take place.

In this case, various investigative procedures help to determine whether fraud is actually occurring and, if so, the extent of the fraud. The specific procedures used, and the order in which they are used, depends on the kind of fraud you suspect and the ease of collecting evidence. The fraud investigation chapters of this book (i.e., Chapters 7–10) provided information about how to investigate all types of fraud, including revenue-related frauds.

> **Remember this …**
>
> *When assessing fraud risk relating to revenue or any other account or process, it is important to identify related exposures and symptoms, actively search for those fraud symptoms, and follow up. Symptoms can be found in the following six areas: (1) analytical symptoms, (2) accounting or documentary symptoms, (3) lifestyle symptoms, (4) control symptoms, (5) behavioral symptoms, (6) and tips and complaints. Revenue-related fraud involves revenue-related accounts such as Revenue, Accounts Receivable, Bad Debt Expense, Cash, and Sales Returns. Generally, revenue-related fraud schemes result in the overstatement of revenues and thus the overstatement of net income.*

Inventory and Cost of Goods Sold Frauds

Besides revenue-related fraud schemes, the next most common financial statement fraud schemes involve the manipulation of inventory and cost of goods sold accounts. Several high-profile financial statement frauds have involved the overstatement of inventory. For example, Phar-Mor significantly overstated the value of its inventory and then moved inventory back and forth between stores so that it could be counted multiple times. A more recent example of inventory fraud was Rite Aid Corporation. Although Rite Aid committed several different types of fraud, one of the most prevalent was overstating net income by managing the value of its inventory. Specifically, senior management allegedly failed to record millions in shrinkage of its physical inventory due to loss or theft. The CFO also made topside journal entries to lower the cost of goods sold.

Historically, inventory frauds have been such a significant problem that a few years ago *The Wall Street Journal* featured a front-page article titled "Inventory Chicanery Tempts More Firms, Fools More Auditors."[5] To understand why inventory-related fraud schemes are so common, you should understand how inventory accounts affect the income statement. The calculations on a typical income statement are shown in Table 12.4.

From this analysis, you can see that if inventory is overstated, cost of goods sold is understated, and gross margin and net income are overstated by an equal amount (less the tax effect). To better understand the effect of cost of goods sold on inventory, consider how cost of goods sold is calculated as shown in Table 12.5.

This analysis shows that the overstatement of ending inventory in period 1 has an effect on cost of goods sold in both periods 1 and 2. Furthermore, cost of goods sold can be understated by either understating purchases or overstating inventory. It can also be understated by overstating purchase returns or purchase discounts. Of these alternatives, overstating the ending inventory tends to be the most common fraud because it increases net income *and* recorded assets, making the balance sheet look better.

The previous analysis also illustrates why overstating inventory is a fraud that is very difficult to maintain without getting caught. In the first period, when ending inventory is overstated, cost of goods sold is understated, making gross margin and net income overstated. However, that overstated ending inventory becomes the beginning inventory in period 2, meaning that further

TABLE 12.4 EFFECTS OF INVENTORY OVERSTATEMENT ON THE INCOME STATEMENT

INCOME STATEMENT	WHEN INVENTORY IS OVERSTATED, THEN
–Gross Revenues (Sales)	Are not affected
–Sales Returns	Are not affected
–Sales Discounts	Are not affected
Net Revenues (Sales)	Are not affected
–Cost of Goods Sold	Is understated
Gross Margin	Is overstated
–Expenses	Are not affected
Net Income	Is overstated

TABLE 12.5 COST OF GOODS SOLD CALCULATION

COST OF GOODS SOLD CALCULATION	PERIOD 1, OVERSTATEMENT OF ENDING INVENTORY	PERIOD 2
Beginning Inventory	Not affected	Overstated
+Purchases of Inventory	Not affected	Not affected
−Returns of Inventory to Vendor	Not affected	Not affected
−Purchase Discounts on *Inventory Purchases*	Not affected	Not affected
= Goods Available for Sale	Not affected	Overstated
−*Ending Inventory*	Overstated	Not affected
= Cost of Goods Sold	Understated	Overstated

overstatements of ending inventory must be made or cost of goods sold in period 2 will be overstated and gross margin and net income will be understated. This offsetting effect from one period to the next makes it necessary for perpetrators to overstate ending inventory in period 2 by an even larger amount in order to both offset the effect of having an overstated beginning inventory and to commit additional fraud. Perpetrators who are smart should commit other types of financial statement fraud other than overstating inventory because of this compounding effect from period to period.

Identifying Inventory-Related Fraud Exposures

To understand inventory-related financial statement frauds, we follow the same process we used to discuss revenue-related frauds. That is, we first identify financial statement fraud exposures. Then we discuss inventory-related fraud symptoms. Third, we consider ways to actively search for fraud symptoms. Last, we cover ways to follow up on symptoms to discover inventory-related frauds.

There are numerous potential inventory-related fraud schemes. Some of the most common schemes include the following:

- ***Double counting*** *occurs when specific inventory items are counted twice. This may result when a*

company moves inventory from one location where inventory counts have already been taken to another location where they have yet to be counted. Altering inventory counts may also result in double counting.
- ***Capitalizing costs that should be expensed*** *occurs when a company inflates the value of its inventory by adding costs such as sales expense or general and administrative expense to inventory rather than record the costs as an expense in the period incurred.*
- ***Cutoff problems*** *occur when a company delays the write-down of obsolete inventory, records returns from an earlier period, records purchases in a later period, and performs other such practices.*
- ***Overestimating inventory*** *can occur by applying incorrect sampling methods. When inventory is estimated using sampling or projection techniques, the company can apply incorrect methods to overstated ending inventory.*
- ***Bill-and-hold sales*** *were mentioned in the revenue-related fraud section and involve the seller holding goods for the buyer because the buyer may not be ready or able to accept shipment at the time of the order. If held goods are counted as inventory and as a sale, then sales, receivables, and inventory will all be overstated, while cost of goods sold is understated.*
- ***Consigned inventory*** *are goods that the company holds and sells for another company. Because the company holding the goods does not own them, it may inflate ending inventory by including the consigned inventory in its year-end physical count.*

As with revenue-related frauds, one of the best ways to identify financial statement fraud exposures is to diagram the various kinds of inventory-related transactions that can occur in an organization. For many companies, the inventory-related transactions might appear as shown in Figure 12.3.

As you can see from the flowchart in Figure 12.3, nine different transactions affect the accounting for inventories and cost of goods sold. Table 12.6 shows the accounts and the fraud schemes that could occur in each of these transactions.

As you can see, by focusing on the various transactions and inventory counts, we have identified 16 fraud schemes that can be used to overstate inventory or understate cost of goods sold. Obviously, some of these schemes are more common than others, but all can be used to misstate inventory and cost of goods sold.

FIGURE 12.3   EXPOSURE TO INVENTORY-RELATED FINANCIAL FRAUD

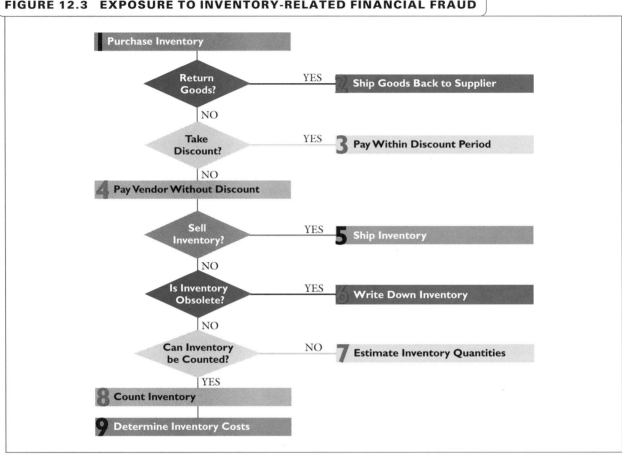

As with revenues, all of these fraud schemes can be used to increase net income. Additionally, it is possible to commit inventory fraud by understating inventory and net income. However, this is a rare situation that may arise in a privately owned company that wants to decrease the amount of income taxes paid to the government. Because it is so rare, we ignore this situation in our discussion.

As stated earlier, inventory overstatement frauds are much more difficult for perpetrators than revenue frauds. With revenue-related frauds, reported revenues are overstated in the current period, and accounts receivable are overstated on the balance sheet.

However, a reversing effect does not automatically occur in the subsequent period as it does with inventory. With inventory frauds, the "overstated ending inventory" of one period becomes the "overstated beginning inventory" of the next period and causes net income to be understated in the second period.

Thus, if a dishonest management wanted to continue the fraud and overstate net income in a second period (most frauds are multiple-period frauds), it would have to perpetrate a fraud of an equivalent magnitude just to offset the overstated beginning inventory and then commit an additional fraud if they again wanted to increase net income. The results are larger misstatements of inventory and a fraud that is much easier to detect. Fortunately, most financial statement frauds are perpetrated because of desperation. As such, a perpetrator generally worries only about how income can be overstated in the current period, with no thought of the problems it creates in subsequent periods.

Identifying Inventory-Related Fraud Symptoms

Once again, we use the six categories of fraud symptoms to discuss inventory and cost of goods sold frauds. Some of the most common symptoms with

TABLE 12.6 TYPES OF TRANSACTIONS SUBJECT TO INVENTORY FRAUD

TRANSACTION	ACCOUNTS INVOLVED	FRAUD SCHEMES
Purchase inventory	Inventory, Accounts Payable	• Understate purchases • Record purchases too late • Do not record purchases
Return merchandise to supplier	Accounts Payable, Inventory	• Overstate returns • Record returns in an earlier period (cutoff problem)
Pay vendor within discount period	Accounts Payable, Inventory, Cash	• Overstate discounts • Do not reduce inventory cost
Pay vendor, without discount	Account Payable, Cash	Considered in Chapter 13
Inventory is sold; cost of goods sold is recognized	Cost of Goods Sold, Inventory	• Record at too low an amount • Do not record cost of goods sold or reduce inventory
Inventory becomes obsolete and is written down	Loss on Write-Down of Inventory, Inventory	Do not write off or write down obsolete inventory
Inventory quantities are estimated	Inventory Shrinkage, Inventory	Overestimate inventory
Inventory quantities are counted	Inventory Shrinkage, Inventory	• Overcount inventory (double counting, etc.) • Capitalize amounts that should be expensed
Inventory cost is determined	Inventory, Cost of Goods Sold	• Use incorrect costs • Make incorrect extensions • Record fictitious inventory

these frauds are listed here. Rather than discuss them in detail as we did for revenue-related frauds, we will simply list them by category.

Analytical Symptoms
- *Reported inventory balances that appear too high or are increasing too fast.*
- *Reported cost of goods sold balances that appear too low or are decreasing too fast.*
- *Reported purchase returns that appear too high or are increasing too rapidly.*
- *Reported purchase discounts that appear too high or are increasing too rapidly.*
- *Reported purchases that appear too low for sales or inventory levels.*
- *Capitalized inventory that looks as if it should be expensed.*

Accounting or Documentary Symptoms
- *Inventory or cost of goods sold transactions that are not recorded in a complete or timely manner or improperly recorded as to amount, accounting period, classification, or entity.*
- *Unsupported or unauthorized inventory or cost of goods sold-related transactions.*

- *End-of-period inventory or cost of goods sold adjustments that significantly change the entity's financial results.*
- *Missing documents related to inventory and/or cost of goods sold.*
- *Unavailability of other than photocopied documents to support inventory or cost of goods sold transactions when original documents should exist.*
- *Cost of goods sold-related accounting records (purchases, sales, cash payments, etc.) that do not balance.*
- *Unusual discrepancies between the entity's inventory or cost of goods sold records and corroborating evidence (such as inventory counts).*
- *Systematic differences between inventory counts and inventory records.*
- *Differences between receiving reports and inventory actually received.*
- *Differences between purchase orders, purchase invoices, receiving records, and inventory records.*
- *Purchases from suppliers not approved on vendor lists.*
- *Missing inventory when performing inventory counts.*
- *Duplicate purchase orders or invoice numbers.*

- *Vendors not listed in Dun & Bradstreet or telephone directories.*
- *Nonstandard journal entries in terms of who, what, when, where, or why.*

Control Symptoms

- *Management override of significant internal control activities related to purchases, inventory, or cost of goods sold.*
- *New or unusual vendors that appear not to have gone through the regular vendor-approval process.*
- *Weaknesses in the inventory counting process.*

Behavioral or Verbal Symptoms

- *Inconsistent, vague, or implausible responses from management or employees arising from inventory, purchase, or cost of goods sold-related inquiries or analytical procedures.*
- *Denied access to facilities, employees, records, customers, vendors, or others from whom inventory or cost of goods sold-related evidence might be sought.*
- *Undue time pressures imposed by management to resolve contentious or complex inventory or cost of goods sold-related issues.*
- *Unusual delays by the entity in providing requested inventory or cost of goods sold-related information.*
- *Untrue, inconsistent, or questionable responses by management to inventory, cost of goods sold, or other queries made by auditors.*
- *Suspicious behavior or responses from members of management when asked about inventory or cost of goods sold-related transactions, vendors, obsolescence, or accounts.*

Lifestyle Symptoms

- *Similar symptoms to the revenue-related frauds (e.g., stock sales, bonuses, and stock ownership). However, remember that lifestyle symptoms are often not very effective for detecting financial statement frauds.*

Tips and Complaints

- *Tips or complaints generated through the whistleblowing system or through other means may suggest that inventory-related fraud schemes might be occurring.*

While these lists are not exhaustive, they represent some common inventory and cost of goods sold-related fraud symptoms that can be observed.

Proactively Looking for Inventory-Related Fraud Symptoms

Observing fraud symptoms is a key to detecting inventory-related financial statement frauds. Take the MiniScribe Corporation financial statement fraud, for example.

———

MiniScribe's management, with the assistance of other officers and employees, engaged in a series of fraudulent activities that overstated inventory and materially inflated reported net income. Since MiniScribe fraudulently inflated its inventory using schemes that reversed each period, there was a constant need to misstate larger and larger amounts, and the fraud grew rapidly. In the first year, the inventory overstatement was $4.5 million. In the second year, the overstatement was $22 million. In the third year (two quarters only), the overstatement was $31.8 million.

To understand the symptoms available, understanding how management perpetrated the fraud is necessary. In the first year, managers from MiniScribe broke into the auditors' files to find inventory lists that designated which items in inventory had been test-counted. With this information, the officers inflated the values of the inventory items that were not counted by the auditors. In the second year, with the need to misstate inventory by a much larger amount, management used the following three different approaches:

1. Created fictitious "inventory in transit" amounts.
2. Recorded a transfer of $9 million in nonexistent inventory from MiniScribe's U.S. books to the books of MiniScribe's Far East subsidiaries.
3. Received raw materials into inventory just prior to the fiscal-year end without recording the corresponding accounts payable liability.

In the third year, management resorted to even more egregious ways to overstate inventory. As an example of its desperate attempts to misstate inventory, it shipped boxes of bricks labeled as disk drives to two MiniScribe distributors and recorded the shipments as consigned inventory. Management even created a computer program called "Cook Book" to generate fictitious inventory numbers. It also accumulated scrap that had been written off the company's books, repackaged it, and added it to the accounting records as inventory. Employees of the company even prepared false inventory tickets to increase recorded inventory.

———

In the first year, the MiniScribe fraud would probably have been very difficult to detect. When management breaks into auditors' files, steals information, and forges computer records that are not test-counted by auditors, the fraud has little chance of being caught. Maybe management's behavior or responses to auditors' inquiries will change and possibly someone will provide a tip, but there are not many accounting, documentary, or control symptoms that can alert an auditor that fraud is occurring. Also, since the fraud in that first year was only $4.5 million, the analytical symptoms were not too significant.

In the second year, as the fraud grew to $22 million and took on different forms, more and more symptoms must have appeared. For example, the huge increase in the inventory balance was a glaring analytical symptom. Also, the large in-transit inventory amounts, especially at year-end, must have appeared unusual. Together with the $9 million transfer of inventory from the U.S. parent's books to an Asian subsidiary's books, these two transactions should have raised concerns. Certainly, inventory that is listed as an asset without a corresponding purchase creates an accounting symptom. With these kinds of suspicious year-end transactions, inquiries of management should increase, providing auditors and fraud examiners with an opportunity to observe the consistency of management's behavior and verbal responses. In the second year, some overriding of key controls and maybe even a tip or two were likely to appear as more and more people became aware of the fraud.

In the third year, when boxes of bricks were being shipped, consigned inventory increased, and a new fraudulent computer program was written, more and more symptoms had to surface. Returns of merchandise (bricks) and customer complaints were likely increasing. More and more employees were involved, leading to a higher probability of a tip, false inventory tickets, and the reclassification of obsolete inventory as good inventory had to be present.

Searching for Inventory and Cost of Goods Sold Analytical Symptoms

As with other types of fraud, inventory-related fraud symptoms can be found in one of the following two ways:

1. Wait until you "happen on to them by chance."
2. Proactively search for them.

The specific way you search for symptoms depends upon the kinds of symptoms for which you are looking. Remember that analytical symptoms relate to accounts or relationships being too high or too low or exhibiting unusual characteristics. Also, remember that to

determine whether accounts are unusual, you must have a point of reference—an expectation or some basis against which recorded amounts can be compared. As with revenue-related fraud symptoms, the most practical way to look for analytical symptoms is to focus on changes and comparisons within and from the financial statements. Table 12.7 summarizes the methods we previously discussed with a focus on inventory.

Focusing on Changes in Recorded Balances from Period to Period

Recall from our discussion of revenue-related frauds that there are three ways to focus on changes in recorded balances from period to period. The first and usually least effective method is to focus on the changes in the actual financial statement *numbers*. Because financial statement inventory and cost of goods sold numbers are often large, it is often difficult to assess the magnitude of changes or to distinguish significant from insignificant changes by examining the numbers alone. A second, similar method is to study the statement of cash flows. This statement identifies changes in account balances from one period to the next. The advantage of focusing on the statement of cash flows is that the "change" numbers have already been calculated.

Probably the best way to examine changes in account balances from period to period is to use horizontal analysis. As you will recall, horizontal analysis allows you to examine percentage changes in account balances from period to period. Generally, fraud is suggested when inventory increases are unrealistically high, there is a monotonic increase in inventory balances from period to period, or cost of goods sold increases do not mirror the increases in either sales or inventory. However, any change that appears unusual or unrealistic can be an analytical financial statement fraud symptom. Importantly, it isn't the change itself that signals that something may not be right but the pace of the change. The faster and more dramatic the pace of change in these accounts, the more likely it is that fraud is occurring.

Focusing on Changes in Relationships from Period to Period

As with revenue-related financial statement frauds, two primary methods can be used to focus on changes in relationships from period to period. The first is to examine ratio changes from one period to the next. The second is to convert the financial statements to common-size statements and use vertical analysis to examine the percentage changes from period to period.

TABLE 12.7 ANALYZING FINANCIAL STATEMENTS FOR INVENTORY FRAUD

Analyzing financial balances and relationships *within* financial statements	Look for unusual changes in inventory and cost of goods sold account *balances* from period to period.	Look for unusual changes in inventory and cost of goods sold *relationships* from period to period.
Comparing financial statement amounts or relationships with other information	Compare financial results and trends of the company with those of *similar firms* in the same industry.	Compare recorded amounts in the financial statements with nonfinancial statement amounts.

The most helpful ratios used to examine inventory and cost of goods sold relationships are as follows:

Gross profit (margin) ratio is calculated by dividing gross profit by sales. The reason this ratio is helpful for identifying inventory fraud is that when a company overstates its inventory balance, cost of goods sold is usually understated. The result is an increase in the gross profit ratio. Thus, a significant increase in the gross profit ratio can signal either a revenue- or an inventory-related fraud.

Inventory turnover is computed by dividing cost of goods sold by the average inventory and is useful for determining whether inventory is overstated or cost of goods sold is understated. Generally, overstating inventory has the effect of decreasing this ratio because the denominator is increased. Similarly, understating cost of goods sold will also decrease this ratio.

Number of days' sales in inventory measures the average time it takes to sell inventory and is computed by dividing the number of days in a period by the inventory turnover ratio. Thus, if cost of goods sold is $500, average inventory is $200, and there are 365 days in a year, the inventory turnover ratio is 2.5 ($500 / $200), and the number of days' sales in inventory is 146 (365 / 2.5). It means that the company "turns" or sells its inventory, on average, every 146 days. When a company overstates inventory or understates cost of goods sold, the number of days' sales in inventory increases.

Four other ratios can also help detect inventory-related frauds. Even though they are usually not as sensitive as the three ratios already discussed, asset turnover, working capital turnover, operating performance ratio, and earnings per share can sometimes help identify inventory-related financial statement frauds. The asset turnover ratio, calculated by dividing net sales by average total assets, provides a measure of how many times an organization "turned over" its assets. This ratio is most helpful in detecting fraud when inventory comprises a large percentage of an organization's assets.

The working capital turnover ratio is calculated by dividing net sales by average working capital (current assets – current liabilities) for a period. When inventory is overstated, the denominator of this ratio increases, causing the overall ratio to decrease. Again, this ratio is most helpful in detecting financial statement fraud when inventory comprises a major portion of current assets. The operating performance ratio is calculated by dividing net income by net sales. It provides a measure of the profit margin of a company. When inventory is overstated or cost of goods sold is understated, net income is artificially increased causing this ratio to increase. Finally, earnings per share, the most commonly used ratio, measures the profitability of an organization. When net income is overstated, earnings per share increase. When earnings increase dramatically, the cause should be investigated, with the result sometimes being overstated inventory or understated cost of goods sold. Remember that when using ratios to discover financial statement fraud symptoms, an absolutely large or small ratio does not mean much. Rather, the *change* in the ratios from period to period is what is of interest.

The second way to focus on financial statement relationships is to convert the financial statements to common-size statements and perform vertical analysis. If inventory as a percentage of total assets or as a percentage of sales keeps increasing, or if cost of goods sold as a percentage of net sales keeps decreasing, fraud may be occurring. Consider, for example, the financial statement fraud at Crazy Eddie, Inc.

———

At one point, Crazy Eddie was one of the hottest names in consumer electronics. What began in 1970 as a single store selling consumer electronics mushroomed into an empire with so many stores that The New Yorker magazine once ran a cartoon in which all roads led to Crazy Eddie. The piercing slogan "C-r-r-r-azy Eddie! His Prices are ins-a-a-a-ne!" blurted incessantly on radio and TV stations and attracted customers in droves. At one point, Crazy Eddie stock traded for $43.25 per share.

In the end, however, the company was under court-protected bankruptcy because of its much-publicized inventory problems. As much as $65 million in inventory was suddenly and inexplicably missing. When new management took over the company in a desperate rescue attempt, the $65 million inventory write-off more than erased all the earnings the company had reported. During inventory counts, company officers drafted phony inventory count sheets and improperly included merchandise so that the reported ending inventory and net income would be higher. The resulting artificially high profits and stock price allowed its founder, Eddie Antar, to rake in $68.4 million from stock sales.

Crazy Eddie's fraud schemes increased inventory balances from period to period, increased gross profit margin, decreased the inventory turnover ratio, increased the number of days' sales in inventory, and were quite obvious in the percentage changes using vertical and horizontal analysis. Indeed, Crazy Eddie, Inc. was rich in analytical symptoms for anyone who looked for them.

Comparing Financial Statement Information with Other Companies

Maintaining large amounts of inventory is quite expensive, especially if the inventory is large, bulky, heavy, or requires special handling. Because inventory handling and warehouse costs, as well as financing costs, are extremely expensive, most companies are taking major steps to decrease the inventory they have on hand. For example, Dell Computer keeps very little inventory on hand and purchases its inventory just in time to assemble computers already ordered by its customers. Investors often see large amounts of inventory as a sign of inefficiency in a company's operations. Therefore, in most cases, when a company's reported inventory balance increases, you should ask why.

Increasing amounts of inventory are especially questionable when other companies against which a company competes are not increasing their inventory balances. Increased inventories can represent poor management decisions, fraud, or increased sales expectations, which if not realized, can cause significant losses for the company. Economic and industry-wide factors usually affect similar firms in similar ways. Financial results that are inconsistent with those of other similar firms often signal a problem. The comparisons can be made using horizontal or vertical analysis, ratio analysis, changes reported in the statement of cash flows, or mere changes in the financial statement numbers themselves.

STOP & THINK   *What are some potentially legitimate reasons for a company to have high inventory balances?*

In comparing inventory balances and trends with similar companies, the type of inventory a company has should be considered. Increasing inventory balances in rapidly changing industries (such as the computer or software industries), in industries with high amounts of spoilage or obsolescence (such as groceries or pharmaceutical firms), or in industries that normally would not have high inventory balances should raise serious questions. When inventory balances are increasing, either by themselves or in relation to other numbers, you should always ask yourself why or what it is about this company that makes it different from other similar firms. If a ready answer is not forthcoming, you may have a fraud on your hands.

Comparing Financial Statement Amounts with the Assets They Represent

Comparing recorded amounts in the financial statements with the assets they are supposed to represent is an excellent way to detect inventory-related financial statement frauds. In a fraud perpetrated by Laribee Wire Manufacturing Co., the inventory represented by the financial statement amounts would have required three times the capacity of the buildings the company had in which to store it. In another case, auditors were suspicious of inventory amounts reported on the financial statements. Their observation of inventory had revealed no serious shortages, and yet it seemed dramatically overstated as it increased fivefold in one year. Suspecting that something was awry, the auditors decided to look at the physical attributes of the inventory that was supposed to be owned by their client. Their investigation revealed that management had falsified the inventory by preparing fictitious records. Management prepared inventory tags and delivered them to the auditors. The auditors had verified the amount of inventory shown on the tags and deposited them in a box in the room they used during the audit. At night, a manager added spurious tags to the box. The manager also substituted new inventory reconciliation lists to agree with the total of the valid and fictitious tags.

The magnitude of the fraud was discovered when the auditors performed volume tests on the inventory. First, they converted the purported $30 million of sheet metal stock into cubic feet. Then they determined the volume of the warehouse that was supposed to contain the inventory. At best, it could have contained one-half the reported amount. The auditors then examined the inventory tags and found that some rolls of sheet metal were supposed to weigh 50,000 pounds. However, none of the forklifts that were used to move the inventory could lift over 3,000 pounds. Finally, the auditors verified the reported inventory purchases and found purchase records supporting an inventory of about 30 million pounds. Yet, the reported amount was 60 million pounds. Faced with this evidence, management admitted to grossly overstating the value of the inventory to show increased profits to meet investors' earnings expectations.

Actively Searching for Accounting or Documentary Symptoms

As with revenue-related frauds, a common way for management to commit an inventory-related fraud is by posting topside journal entries to the accounting records. Software such as ACL© or IDEA© can be used to determine if any journal entries are unusual in terms of the five Ws: (1) *who* posted the entry, (2) *what* the entry was for, (3) *when* the entry was posted, (4) *where* the entry was posted in the accounting system, and (5) *why* the entry was posted.

Actively Searching for Inventory-Related Control Symptoms

Because inventory frauds, like revenue-related frauds, are so prevalent, a good control environment and control procedures should be in place. Recall that the COSO study of financial statement fraud found that most companies committing financial statement fraud were relatively small, had "inactive" audit committees, had boards of directors that were dominated by insiders and "grey" directors with significant equity ownership and little experience serving as directors of other companies, and had family relationships among directors or officers. The relatively small size of fraudulent companies suggests that the inability or even unwillingness to implement cost-effective controls is probably a factor affecting the likelihood of financial statement fraud. These environments foster management's ability to override controls.

Inventory controls must be examined closely. Remember that the lack of a key control provides a fraud opportunity that completes the fraud triangle. With respect to inventory, purchases, and cost of goods sold, we are primarily concerned with the controls over the purchasing process (purchase requisitions, purchase orders, etc.), receiving (receiving reports, physical control, etc.), recording of liabilities (vendor's invoice, debit memos, etc.), cash disbursements (checks, etc.), storage, processing, and shipping of inventory, transferring the cost of inventory sold, accurately tracking inventory costs (especially in manufacturing firms), and physically observing inventory. In each case, we want to make sure that recorded inventory represents goods actually received or manufactured, existing acquisition transactions are actually recorded, transaction amounts are accurate, transactions are properly classified, transactions are recorded in the proper periods, and transactions are included in the proper financial statement accounts. Where inventory controls are weak or easily overridden, a missing control or an observance of an override represents a fraud symptom, not just a control weakness. As such, it should be pursued with the same vigilance as any other fraud symptom.

Actively Searching for Behavioral or Verbal and Lifestyle Symptoms

As with other financial statement frauds, lifestyle symptoms are usually not very effective in helping you find inventory-related financial statement fraud because financial statement fraud usually does not benefit the perpetrators directly. However, searching for behavioral and verbal symptoms can be very fruitful. Often, recorded inventory amounts are subject to management's intent. For example, if management plans to, and believes it can, sell existing inventory, it will not write off inventory amounts as obsolete. Usually, the best evidence relating to management's intent is interviewing or inquiry. Where possible, inquiries should be corroborated, but such corroborations sometimes are not possible. With inventory, it is important that financial statement auditors and fraud examiners ask many questions relative to the nature, age, salability, and other characteristics of inventory as well as inventory levels (increases or decreases), significant changes in vendors, and so on. The best way to determine if management is lying is to identify inconsistencies between what you observe (e.g., analytical and documentary symptoms) and what management is telling you.

Actively Searching for Tips and Complaints

Tips and complaints are fruitful areas for detecting inventory-related frauds. In most cases, because of its physical characteristics, inventory must be brought into a firm, handled within the firm, and shipped when sold. All this movement means that people must be involved in managing and handling the physical flow of inventory. Usually, these individuals do not understand the nature of audits or forensic examinations, nor the kinds of fraud that could be occurring. As an example of the value of asking questions and getting tips, consider the case of a staff auditor for what was formerly a Big Six CPA firm that was auditing the inventory of a sprinkler pipe manufacturer. As he observed the inventory, some of it looked old and not salable. However, when he asked the CFO and CEO about the inventory, they stated that it was fine and would be sold in the normal course of business. Being curious, however, he brought a sack lunch the next day and ate in the inventory warehouse with the warehouse workers. After discussing his background with them, telling them he was a small town country boy, and talking about sports, he asked them to tell him how the various types of pipe were used. They were very forthright in telling him that most of the pipe on hand would never be sold because it was "useless." His firm ended up insisting that the client write down the pipe inventory by several million dollars. Talking to those who actually handle the inventory will often reveal information that is very helpful, especially when you ask the right questions.

In addition to individuals who handle the inventory, it is often helpful to communicate directly with vendors to determine their relationships with the company. Although you have to be careful not to intrude in the company's business and hurt its relationships with vendors, you can often learn valuable information about inventory costs, amounts of purchases, and other factors by speaking with those vendors. Similarly, talking with large customers and assessing inventory quality and product returns will often provide evidence about whether bricks are being shipped as disk drives or whether inventory is overvalued.

The important point to remember is that even though most companies today have a whistle-blower system, you must still actively look for tips. As we stated earlier, individuals often suspect that something wrong is going on, but are afraid to come forward or are just not asked. As with revenue-related fraud, if the company has a whistle-blower system, you should review the system's records to see if they have received complaints about inventory-related frauds and whether the complaints have been investigated. Most discoveries of frauds of all types result from a tip or complaint that is investigated.

> **Remember this …**
>
> *Revenue and inventory financial statement frauds are closely related, since revenues are generated by selling inventory. Inventory, by its nature, generally has unique physical characteristics. Identifying these physical characteristics and making sure the numbers reported on the financial statements match these characteristics (volume, weight, etc.) is a good way to make sure the reported amount of inventory is realistic. Again, when dealing with inventory-related frauds, it is important to identify related exposures and symptoms, actively search for those fraud symptoms, and follow up.*

Review of the Learning Objectives

- **Identify revenue-related financial statement fraud schemes.** Revenue-related financial statement fraud schemes are numerous and can involve various transactions. These can include the sale of goods or services, estimating uncollectible receivables, accepting returned goods from customers, writing off uncollectible receivables, and recording sales discounts when cash payments are received. Revenue-related financial statement fraud schemes mainly result in overstated revenues and thus overstated net income. Various revenue accounts can be used to accomplish this task, so it is important to understand the implications of various fraud schemes.

- **List ways to proactively search for revenue-related financial statement fraud symptoms.** To proactively search for revenue-related financial statement fraud schemes, one can look for analytical symptoms focusing on changes and comparisons within and from the financial statements. This can be done by analyzing financial balances and relationships within financial statements and also by comparing financial statement amounts or relationships with other things. Other symptoms can also be searched for, including accounting or documentary symptoms such as topside journal entries, control weaknesses (especially in the control environment), behavioral or verbal symptoms, and tips or complaints.

- **Understand the importance of, and ways to follow up on, revenue-related fraud symptoms.** If revenue-related fraud symptoms exist, it is important to follow up to determine if a fraud has been perpetrated. The specific investigative procedures used, and the order in which they are used, depends on the kind of fraud suspected and the ease of collecting evidence. Techniques learned in prior chapters should be employed in the follow-up process.

- **Discuss inventory-related financial statement fraud schemes.** Similar to revenue-related fraud schemes, inventory-related financial statement fraud schemes are numerous and involve various transactions. These often result in the overstatement of inventory and the understatement of cost of goods sold, thus inflating net income. Inventory-related financial statement fraud symptoms can be observed in the same six areas as that of revenue-related fraud and are as follows: analytical symptoms, accounting or documentary symptoms, control symptoms, behavioral or verbal symptoms, lifestyle symptoms, and tips and complaints.

- **Identify ways to search for inventory-related financial statement fraud symptoms.** Inventory-related financial statement fraud symptoms are generally present in the following accounts: Inventory, Accounts Payable, Cash, Cost of Goods Sold, and Inventory Shrinkage. Various analytical analyses can be used to search for inventory-related financial statement fraud. In addition, comparing the financial statement data with nonfinancial characteristics can help in searching for potential fraud in these areas.

- **Explain the importance of, and ways to follow up on, inventory-related fraud symptoms.** Like revenue-related fraud, following up on discovered symptoms of potential inventory-related fraud is very important. Questioning employees regarding inventory-related transactions or practices, inquiring of management in an attempt to corroborate findings, and physically inspecting inventory levels are only a few actions one can use to follow up.

KEY TERMS

revenue-recognition,
   p. 401
topside journal entries,
   p. 402
gross profit (margin)
   ratio, p. 408

cost of goods sold
   (COGS), p. 408
sales returns, p. 408
sales return percentage
   ratio, p. 408

sales discount
   percentage ratio,
   p. 409
accounts receivable
   turnover, p. 409
number of days in
   receivables ratio,
   p. 409
allowance for
   uncollectible
   accounts as a
   percentage of
   receivables, p. 409

asset turnover ratio,
   p. 409
working capital
   turnover ratio, p. 409
operating performance
   margin ratio, p. 409
earnings per share,
   p. 409
percentages, p. 410
bad debt expense, p. 414
inventory turnover,
   p. 420
number of days' sales in
   inventory, p. 420

QUESTIONS
Discussion Questions

1. What are some common revenue-related financial statement fraud schemes?
2. What are some possible ways to proactively search for revenue-related financial statement fraud schemes?
3. Why is it important to follow up on revenue-related fraud symptoms?
4. What are some of the most common inventory-related financial statement fraud schemes?
5. What are some of the ways to proactively search for inventory-related financial statement fraud schemes?
6. What are common-size financial statements?
7. Why do you suspect that revenue-related financial statement fraud schemes are most common and inventory-related fraud schemes are next most common?
8. What is the effect on net income of not recording sales returns?
9. What is the effect on net income of overstating ending inventory?
10. How can comparing statement amounts with actual assets help determine if fraud is present?

True/False

1. Understated revenues and understated net income are among the most common types of financial statement fraud.
2. Two reasons revenue-related financial statement fraud is so prevalent are because revenue

recognition can be highly subjective and because revenue is so easily manipulated.

3. Performing a horizontal analysis of the statement of cash flows is an excellent way to proactively search for revenue-related financial statement fraud.

4. The most common accounts manipulated when perpetrating financial statement fraud are revenues and accounts receivable.

5. An increase in gross margin and an increase in number of days' sales in inventory could be an indication of inflated inventory fraud.

6. A "sales discounts" amount that appears too low could be a fraud symptom.

7. Comparing financial results and trends of a company with those of similar firms is an ineffective way to look for fraud symptoms.

8. Focusing on changes in financial statements from period to period can help identify analytical fraud symptoms.

9. Controls over inventory should be closely examined when searching for fraud symptoms.

10. The gross profit (margin) ratio is calculated by dividing gross profit by cost of goods sold.

11. Working capital turnover ratio is calculated by dividing average working capital by sales.

12. Accounts receivable turnover is one of the most widely used ratios to analyze revenues and is a measure of the efficiency with which receivables are being collected.

13. One of the most practical ways to look for analytical symptoms of fraud is to focus on changes and comparisons within and from the financial statements.

Multiple Choice

1. The most common account(s) manipulated when perpetrating financial statement fraud are:
   a. Expenses.
   b. Inventory.
   c. Revenues.
   d. Accounts Payable.

2. Why might a company want to understate net income?
   a. To increase profits.
   b. To increase stock price.
   c. To gain consumer confidence.
   d. To pay less taxes.

3. Reported revenue and sales account balances that appear too high are examples of:
   a. Analytical symptoms.
   b. Documentary symptoms.
   c. Lifestyle symptoms.
   d. Verbal symptoms.

4. Horizontal analysis is a method that:
   a. Examines financial statement numbers from period to period.
   b. Examines percent changes in account balances from period to period.
   c. Examines transactions from period to period.
   d. None of the above.

5. Recording fictitious receivables will usually result in a(n):
   a. Sales return percentage that remains constant.
   b. Increased sales discount percentage.
   c. Increase in accounts receivable turnover.
   d. Increase in the number of days in receivables.

6. Comparing recorded amounts in the financial statements with the real-world assets they are supposed to represent would be most effective in detecting:
   a. Cash and inventory fraud.
   b. Accounts payable fraud.
   c. Revenue-related fraud.
   d. Accounts receivable fraud.

7. Lifestyle symptoms are most effective with:
   a. Revenue-related financial statement frauds.
   b. Inventory-related financial statement frauds.
   c. Employee frauds.
   d. Accounts payable financial statement frauds.

8. Which of the following is *not* an inventory-related documentary symptom?
   a. Duplicate purchase orders.
   b. Missing inventory during inventory counts.
   c. Unsupported inventory sales transactions.
   d. All of the above are inventory-related documentary symptoms.

9. When looking for inventory fraud, an important question to ask is:
   a. What is the nature of inventory?
   b. What is the age of inventory?

c. What is the salability of inventory?

d. All are important questions to ask.

10. Which of the following ratios would *not* generally be used to look for inventory- and cost of goods sold-related frauds?
    a. Accounts payable turnover.
    b. Gross profit margin.
    c. Inventory turnover.
    d. Number of days' sales in inventory.

11. In order to analyze financial statements for fraud, an auditor or fraud examiner should consider all of the following except:
    a. The types of accounts that should be included in the financial statements.
    b. The types of fraud to which the company is susceptible.
    c. The nature of the company's business and industry.
    d. The auditor should consider all of the above.

12. Last-minute revenue adjustments, unsupported balance sheet amounts, and improperly recorded revenues are examples of:
    a. Analytical symptoms.
    b. Documentary symptoms.
    c. Control symptoms.
    d. Perceptional symptoms.

13. Accounts that can be manipulated in revenue fraud include all of the following except:
    a. Accounts Receivable.
    b. Bad Debt Expense.
    c. Inventory.
    d. Sales Discounts.

14. Which financial ratio is *not* useful in detecting revenue-related fraud?
    a. Gross profit margin ratio.
    b. Account receivable turnover ratio.
    c. Asset turnover ratio.
    d. All of the above are useful revenue-related fraud detection ratios.

15. The asset turnover ratio measures:
    a. The average time an asset is used by the company.
    b. The average useful life of capital assets.
    c. Sales that are generated with each dollar of the assets.
    d. Assets that are purchased with each dollar of sales.

16. The most common way to overstate revenues is to:
    a. Record revenues prematurely.
    b. Abuse the cutoff line for recording revenues.
    c. Create fictitious revenues.

    d. None of the above.

17. Which of the following is a possible scheme for manipulating revenue when returned goods are accepted from customers?
    a. Understate allowance for doubtful accounts (thus overstating receivables).
    b. Record bank transfers when cash is received from customers.
    c. Write off uncollectible receivables in a later period.
    d. Avoid recording of returned goods from customers.

18. All of the following ratios are useful in detecting large revenue frauds except:
    a. Gross profit margin.
    b. Current ratio.
    c. Working capital turnover.
    d. Accounts receivable turnover.

19. Each of the following illicit revenue transactions is correctly linked with the financial statement accounts involved except:
    a. Recognizing revenues too early—Accounts Receivable, Revenue.
    b. Understate allowance for doubtful accounts— Bad Debt Expense, Allowance for Doubtful Accounts.
    c. Don't write off uncollectible receivables—Sales Returns, Sales Discounts.
    d. Don't record discounts given to customers—Cash, Sales Discounts, Accounts Receivable.
    e. Record returned goods after the end of the period—Sales Returns, Accounts Receivable.

20. Identify which ratio is correctly linked to the information it could reveal about the company's potential for revenue fraud.
    a. Gross profit margin—this ratio will increase if management overstates inventory.
    b. Sales return percentage—a sudden decrease in this ratio can mean that customer discounts are not being recorded in the accounting records.
    c. Allowance for uncollectible accounts as a percent of receivables—when a company records fictitious receivables, this ratio increases.
    d. Operating profit margin—a dramatic decrease in this ratio could indicate fraud.

21. Which of the following is a common way to perform financial-statement analysis while searching for revenue-related analytical symptoms?
    a. Look for unusual changes in revenue-related account balances from period to period (trends).
    b. Look for unusual changes in revenue-related relationships from period to period.
    c. Look for unusual changes in the cost of goods sold account from period to period.
    d. Both a and b are common ways to perform within-statement analysis while searching for revenue-related analytical symptoms.
    e. All of the above are common ways to perform financial-statement analysis while searching for revenue-related analytical symptoms.

22. Primarily occurring at the end of the year in an attempt to inflate sales, the practice of shipping more items to distributors than they can sell in a reasonable time period is known as:
    a. Lapping.
    b. Channel stuffing.
    c. Bill-and-hold transactions.
    d. Consignment sales.

SHORT CASES

Case 1
During the audit of a major client, you notice that revenues have increased dramatically from the third to the fourth quarter and especially over the previous periods of last year. You've received tips alleging that the company is overstating its revenues. What steps would you take to examine the legitimacy of management's assertions regarding its reported revenue?

Case 2
Thomas is the CEO of a business that just went public. He is feeling intense pressure for the business to succeed because all of his relatives have invested heavily in his company. Since going public, sales have been flat, and Thomas is worried about not meeting analysts' and even relatives' expectations. Which financial statement accounts might Thomas attempt to manipulate in order to meet analysts' projected earnings?

Case 3
The following information is provided for TechnoWorld, a company specializing in providing Internet technology assistance for clients:

CASE 3

	2007	2008	2009	2010
Cash	$1,000	$1,200	$1,400	$1,500
Accounts Receivable	250	375	600	900
Inventory	600	700	825	975
PP&E (net)	1,500	1,700	1,800	1,950
Notes Receivable	500	500	500	500
Total Assets	$3,850	$4,475	$5,125	$5,825
Accounts Payable	$700	$900	$1,000	$1,100
Other Current Liabilities	200	300	350	425
Notes Payable	1,200	1,400	$1,500	$1,750
Total Liabilities	$2,100	$2,600	$2,850	$3,275
Stock Outstanding	$1,000	$1,000	$1,000	$1,000
Retained Earnings	750	875	1,275	1,550
Total Shareholders' Equity	$1,750	$1,875	$2,275	$2,550
Total Liabilities and Shareholders' Equity	$3,850	$4,475	$5,125	$5,825

Perform a horizontal analysis of this balance sheet and identify any accounts that may be questionable. Take into account technology industry trends when performing the analysis.

For Cases 4 and 5, use the following information:

CASE 4 AND 5

	FIVE-YEAR FINANCIAL DATA FOR COMPANY A				
	YEAR 1	YEAR 2	YEAR 3	YEAR 4	YEAR 5
Sales	$100,000.00	$105,000.00	$110,250.00	$137,812.50	$206,718.75
COGS	75,000.00	78,750.00	82,687.50	66,150.00	59,535.00
Margin	25,000.00	26,250.00	27,562.50	71,662.50	147,183.75

Case 4

Perform horizontal analysis of the data in the previous table to indicate any potential red flags regarding possible overstatement of sales.

Case 5

Perform vertical analysis of the data in the previous table to indicate any potential red flags regarding possible understatement of the COGS.

Case 6

Fraud investigators found that 70 percent of the nearly $160 million in sales booked by an Asian subsidiary of a European company between September 2006 and June 2007 were fictitious. In an effort to earn rich bonuses tied to sales targets, the Asian subsidiary's managers used highly sophisticated schemes to fool auditors. One especially egregious method involved funneling bank loans through third parties to make it look as though customers had paid, when in fact they hadn't.

In a lawsuit filed by the company's auditors, it was alleged that former executives "deliberately" provided "false or incomplete information" to the auditors and conspired to obstruct the firm's audits. To fool the auditors, the subsidiary used two types of schemes. The first involved factoring unpaid receivables to banks to obtain cash up front. Side letters that were concealed from the auditors gave the banks the right to take the money back if they couldn't collect from the company's customers. Hence, the factoring agreements amounted to little more than loans.

The second, more creative, scheme was used after the auditors questioned why the company wasn't collecting more of its overdue bills from customers. It turns out that the subsidiary told many customers to transfer their contracts to third parties. The third parties then took out bank loans, for which the company provided collateral, and then "paid" the overdue bills to the company using the borrowed money. The result was that the company was paying itself. When the contracts were later canceled, the company paid "penalties" to the customers and the third parties to compensate them "for the inconvenience of dealing with the auditors."

The investigators also found that the bulk of the company's sales came from contracts signed at the end of quarters, so managers could meet ambitious quarterly sales targets and receive multimillion-dollar bonuses. For example, 90 percent of the revenue recorded by the subsidiary in the second quarter of 2007 was booked in several deals signed in the final nine days of the quarter. But the company was forced to subsequently cancel 70 percent of those contracts because the customers—most of them tiny start-ups—didn't have the means to pay.

List revenue-related fraud symptoms and schemes used in this case. Briefly discuss how actively searching and understanding revenue-related fraud symptoms could have led to discovering the fraud by the company's auditors.

Case 7

Tool Co. is a medium-sized company that buys copper rod and plastic materials to produce insulated copper wiring. Tool Co. operates out of a single building of about 500,000 square feet that includes office space (3%), production area (57%), shipping and receiving (15%), and finished goods and raw materials inventory warehousing (25%). You have gathered the following data about the company's inventories and performance, and now you are ready to conduct an analysis on these numbers to discover possible fraud symptoms.

CASE 7

	2010	2009
Finished goods inventory (Approx. 300 million ft.—2010)	$1,654,500	$1,175,500
Copper rod inventory (Approx. 5.9 million lbs.—2010)	$2,625,000	$1,650,000
Plastics inventory (Approx. 1.1 million lbs.—2010)	$224,500	$182,000
Accounts payable (for inv. purchases)	$450,000	$425,000
Days purchases in A/P	43.6 days	44.2 days
Days sales in receivables	56.3 days	48.4 days
Market price of insulated wire (per ft.)	$0.008	$0.009
Market price of copper rod (per lb.)	$0.480	$0.480
Market price of plastics (per lb.)	$0.120	$0.190

1. How would you go about looking for red flags?
2. Do you think red flags of possible fraud are present in 2010? By comparing these numbers to Sales you can do a vertical analysis. To do so, assume that Sales were $8,450,000 and 8,150,000 for 2010 and 2009, respectively. Also, Cost of Goods Sold were $6,242,500 and $6,080,000 for 2010 and 2009, respectively

Case 8

Decide whether each situation is or is not a symptom of revenue fraud. Then explain (1) why the situation is or is not a symptom and (2) if it is a symptom, how it would be found using computer queries or traditional methods.

Y/N Sales discounts appear too high.

Y/N Accounts receivable increases as a percentage of revenues.

Y/N Bad debt allowance increases by the same percentage as accounts receivable.

Y/N Increase in sales returns.

Y/N Large percent of revenues recorded in the fourth quarter.

Y/N Unexplained reconciling items on the bank statement.

Case 9

Your auditing firm has just landed a new client: a large software company managed by two brothers who together own 15 percent of the stock. You learn that the company fired its last auditor. You also notice that the company is involved in a lot of off-the-book business ventures. Identify the possible symptoms of fraud and to which aspect of the fraud exposure rectangle each symptom corresponds.

Case 10

After graduating from college with your MBA, you decide to take your grandma's secret cinnamon roll recipe and open up a bakery. You grew up devouring your grandma's rolls, and you have convinced her to give you the secret. You are confident that your bakery will be the next big hit in the fast-food business.

You take out a business loan for the maximum amount your bank will give you, hire several employees, and open a beautiful store that is designed to look like your grandma's home. After eight months of hard work and diligence, you are crushed when you realize that your store manager has been stealing from you. One of your recent hires tells you that during her last shift, the manager, Stephanie, voided a sale of two-dozen cinnamon rolls, stamped the receipt as a return, and pocketed the money. Stephanie warned the new hire not to say anything and told her she deserved the money because she didn't get paid enough. Encouraged by your open-door policy, the employee confides in you.

1. Identify what symptoms this fraud will generate. In addition, identify how this fraud will directly affect your revenue and inventory accounts.
2. Explain the steps you should take to search for each symptom you identified in part (1). In particular,

describe the computer queries and transactions that should be searched to find this fraud.
3. After you have identified several symptoms, do you have enough evidence to prove that she is guilty? What other evidence is required or useful in this case?
4. Besides searching for symptoms of the fraud, what other investigative steps can be taken to elicit a confession or otherwise prove the fraud?
5. What steps could have been taken to prevent this fraud from occurring in the first place?

Case 11

Sue is a customer account representative for ABC Company. She recently acquired several new accounts when a previous representative, Dan, took an early retirement. Sue reviewed each of Dan's accounts to help familiarize herself with his clients and understand how she can better serve each one's individual needs. As she was reviewing the client list, she found a major customer she had never heard of before. Surprised that she had not yet done business with the company, she called it to introduce herself as the new representative.

When Sue placed the call, she found that the reported number had been disconnected. Thinking that the customer may have done business with ABC in the past and have moved on, she reviewed the account transactions and found that the most recent transaction had taken place the week prior. During her review, she also noticed the latest transaction was for an unusually large amount for ABC.

As Sue pursued her curiosity, she went to other employees to find out more about the company. In her questioning, she found that none of the employees had ever heard of the customer. Once she had run out of other avenues, Sue decided to contact the controller to find out if he could provide any additional information. When Sue opened the company directory, she was amazed when she recognized his home address: it was the same address as the mystery customer!

1. What are some of the possible scenarios for why the addresses match?
2. What other symptoms would be present in each of the scenarios you identified in part (1)?
3. What are the implications of the address match if the company is private? If the company was publicly traded?
4. Assuming the company was preparing for an IPO, who should Sue contact, and what should she say?
5. If Sue believes these revenues are fictitious, what should her next course of action be?

Case 12

Pablo is studying financial statements to decide which companies would be wise investments. Pablo identifies Jawanna Corporation as having abnormally high financial ratios compared with other companies in its industry. Skeptical, he examines the footnotes of the financial statements further for indications that the company might be deceiving investors. Name and explain four common symptoms that fraudulent companies try to hide in the disclosures to their financial statements.

Case 13

Financial statements are the end product of the accounting cycle and are used by investors to make informed decisions. They can be analyzed to help determine if there are any fraudulent activities in the company. As you know, the balance sheet, income statement, and statement of cash flows are the three primary financial statements. List and briefly describe some of the ways these three financial statements can help detect fraud.

Case 14

Although financial statement fraud can be committed in many different ways and by people in different positions, history shows that the majority of financial statement fraud is committed by people in upper management who have added pressures as well as more opportunities to commit fraud. Using the Internet, research the following individuals related to Enron and match each individual with the position he or she held within each company.

CASE 14

PERSON	POSITION
1. Kenneth Lay	a. Audit firm attorney
2. David Duncan	b. CFO
3. Jeff Skilling	c. Audit partner
4. Andrew Fastow	d. Founder as well as last CEO
5. Michael Odom	e. CEO only six months
6. Michael Kopper	f. Assistant to Fastow
7. Nancy Temple	g. Risk management partner of audit firm

1. Write a short summary of the fraud each committed, focusing on how each person's position could have allowed him or her to perpetrate or participate in fraud.

Case 15

Introduction   Home Safety, Inc.'s management has been trying for months to acquire one of its largest competitors in the home security industry—Lock-It-Up Company. Before agreeing to the acquisition, Home Safety's board of directors wanted Lock-It-Up's books to be audited. They have asked your firm to perform the audit and due diligence, and they have asked that you specifically examine the owner's family and roles in the company.

Lock-It-Up Company   Lock-It-Up is a large, local home security business that has been in the area for a long time. It has held a large market share for several years and has received many referrals from present users of its home security systems. It owns five large properties in the area from which it performs business and is an optimal takeover target.

Internal Environment

- **Management style:** *The owner of the business, Jeff Johnson, has taken a hands-off approach to managing his business. He frequently takes extended vacations with his family and rarely examines the books of his business. He is happy with his level of income and is not concerned with the future, believing that his company will always be profitable.*
- **Executives:** *Several of the owner's relatives hold high positions in the company. The owner's brother, Chucky "Gambling Genius" Johnson, is the chief accountant and answers only to his brother, Jeff. He is majority owner of a local amateur sports team, which has struggled to sell tickets and is facing bankruptcy.*
- **Employees:** *The company takes advantage of the cheap labor at the large, local university. Each summer, it hires hundreds of students to sell its products door to door. Successful students from previous years train the new students, and expectations and motivations are high. The temporary labor force is paid sub-minimum wage but can earn significant commissions on sales. Last year, some of the students earned over $80,000 in commissions in just four months of summer sales, with some receiving quota rewards such as cruises and new cars.*
- **Internal controls.** *In order to facilitate quicker purchases and obtain deals from vendors, Jeff has left Chucky a stack of blank, presigned checks.*

Anyone in the purchasing department has access to these checks and can use them as needed.

1. As the auditor, list the concerns you have that *may* suggest fraud is occurring in the company.
2. What controls would you suggest that the company put in place to prevent potential fraud from occurring for each of the concerns you listed in part (1)?

3. Would you feel comfortable signing off on Home Safety's financial statements if it were to acquire Lock-It-Up this year? Why or why not?
4. What are some factors in the auditor–client relationship that can make it more difficult for the auditor to detect fraud?

Case 16

Several years ago, a medical device company was charged with improperly recognizing approximately $1.5 million in revenue from bill-and-hold transactions. One distributor placed orders with the medical device company for a total of approximately 15,000 units of a particular product in April and July. As part of the agreement with the distributor, the medical device company invoiced the distributor for the total 15,000 units for more than $500,000 in September, but held the product at its own refrigerated facility until the distributor requested the product, which did not occur until March the following year. Yet, the company still recorded the revenue in the previous year.

1. What accounts would this fraudulent transaction affect?
2. What could an auditor do to discover the nature of the relationship between the company and its distributor regarding these products?

CASE STUDIES

Case Study 1

The Enron Fraud   Enron Corporation began as a small natural gas distributor and over the course of 15 years grew to become the seventh largest company in the United States. Soon after the federal deregulation of natural gas pipelines in 1985, Enron was born by the merging of Houston Natural Gas and InterNorth, a Nebraska pipeline company. Initially, Enron was merely involved in the distribution of gas, but it later became a market maker in facilitating the buying and selling of futures of natural gas, electricity, broadband, and other products. However, Enron's continuous growth eventually came to an end as a complicated financial statement fraud and multiple scandals sent Enron on a downward spiral to bankruptcy.

During the 1980s, several major national energy corporations began lobbying Washington to deregulate the energy business. Their claim was that the extra competition resulting from a deregulated market would benefit both businesses and consumers. Consequently, the national government began to lift controls on who was allowed to produce energy and how it was marketed and sold. But, as competition in the energy market increased, gas and energy prices began to fluctuate greatly. Over time, Enron incurred massive debts and no longer had exclusive rights to its pipelines. It needed some new and innovative business strategies.

Kenneth Lay, chairman and CEO, hired the consulting firm McKinsey & Company to assist in developing a new plan to help Enron get back on its feet. Jeff Skilling, a young McKinsey consultant who had a background in banking and asset and liability management, was assigned to work with Enron. He recommended that Enron create a "gas bank" to buy and sell gas. Skilling, who later became chief executive at Enron, recognized that Enron could capitalize on the fluctuating gas prices by acting as a middleman and creating a futures market for buyers and sellers of gas; it would buy and sell gas to be used tomorrow at a stable price today.

Although brilliantly successful in theory, Skilling's gas bank idea faced a major problem. The natural gas producers who agreed to supply Enron's gas bank desperately needed cash and required cash as payment for their products. But Enron also had insufficient cash levels. Therefore, management decided to team up with banks and other financial institutions, establishing partnerships that would provide the cash needed to complete the transactions with Enron's suppliers. Under the direction of Andrew Fastow, a newly hired financial genius, Enron also created several special purpose entities (SPEs), which served as the vehicles through which money was funneled from the banks to the gas suppliers, thus keeping these transactions off Enron's books. As Enron's business became more and more complicated, its vulnerability to fraud and eventual disaster also grew. Initially, the newly formed partnerships and SPEs worked to Enron's advantage. But, in the end, it was the creation of these SPEs that culminated in Enron's death.

Within just a few years of instituting its gas bank and the complicated financing system, Enron grew rapidly, controlling a large part of the U.S. energy market. At one point, it controlled as much as a quarter of all of the nation's gas business. It also began expanding to create markets for other types of products, including electricity, crude oil, coal, plastics, weather derivatives, and broadband. In addition, Enron continued to expand its trading business and with the introduction of Enron Online in the late 1990s, it became one of the largest trading companies on Wall Street, at one time generating 90 percent of its income through trades. Enron soon had more contracts than any of its competitors and, with market dominance, could predict future prices with great accuracy, thereby guaranteeing superior profits.

To continue enhanced growth and dominance, Enron began hiring the "best and brightest" traders. But Enron was just as quick in firing its employees as it was in hiring new ones. Management created the Performance Review Committee (PRC), which became known as the harshest employee ranking system in the country. Its method of evaluating employee performance was nicknamed "rank and yank" by Enron employees. Every six months, employees were ranked on a scale of 1 to 5. Those ranked in the lowest category (1) were immediately "yanked" (fired) from their position and replaced by new recruits. Surprisingly, during each employee review, management required that at least 15 percent of all the employees ranked were given a 1 and therefore yanked from their position and income. The employees ranked with a 2 or 3 were also given notice that they were liable to be released in the near future. These ruthless performance reviews created fierce internal competition between fellow employees who faced a strict ultimatum—perform or be replaced. Furthermore, it created a work environment where employees were unable to express opinions or valid concerns for fear of a low-ranking score by their superiors.

With so much pressure to succeed and maintain its position as the global energy market leader, Enron began to jeopardize its integrity by committing fraud. The SPEs, which originally were used for good business purposes, were now used illegally to hide bad investments, poor-performing assets, and debt; to manipulate cash flows; and eventually, to report over $1 billion of false income. The following examples illustrate how specific SPEs were used fraudulently.

Chewco   In 1993, Enron and the California Public Employees Retirement System (CalPERS) formed a 50/50 partnership called Joint Energy Development Investments Limited (JEDI). In 1997, Enron's Andrew Fastow established the Chewco SPE, which was designed to repurchase CalPERS' share of equity in JEDI at a large profit. However, Chewco crossed the bounds of legality in two ways.

First, it broke the 3 percent equity rule, which allowed corporations such as Enron to "not consolidate" if outsiders contributed even 3 percent of the capital, but the other 97 percent could come from the company. When Chewco bought out JEDI, however, half

of the $11.4 million that bought the 3 percent equity involved cash collateral provided by Enron, meaning that only 1.5 percent was owned by outsiders. Therefore, the debts and losses incurred at Chewco were not listed where they belonged, on Enron's financial reports, but remained only on Chewco's separate financial records.

Secondly, since Fastow was an Enron officer, he was, therefore, unauthorized to personally run Chewco without direct approval from Enron's board of directors and public disclosure with the SEC. In an effort to secretly bypass these restrictions, Fastow appointed one of his subordinates, Michael Kopper, to run Chewco under Fastow's close supervision and influence. Fastow continually applied pressure to Kopper to prevent Enron from getting the best possible deals from Chewco and therefore giving Kopper huge profits.

Chewco was eventually forced to consolidate its financial statements with Enron. By doing so, however, it caused large losses on Enron's balance sheet and other financial statements. The Chewco SPE accounted for 80 percent (approximately $400 million) of all of Enron's SPE restatements. Moreover, Chewco set the stage for Fastow as he continued to expand his personal profiting SPE empire.

LJM 1 & 2   The LJM SPEs (LJM1 and LJM2) were two organizations sponsored by Enron that also participated heavily in fraudulent deal making. LJM1 and its successor, LJM2, were similar to the Chewco SPE in that they also broke the two important rules set forth by the SEC. First, although less than 3 percent of the SPE equity was owned by outside investors, LJM's books were kept separate from Enron's. An error in judgment by Arthur Andersen allowed LJM's financial statements to go unconsolidated. Furthermore, Fastow (now CFO at Enron) was appointed to personally oversee all operations at LJM. Without the governing controls in place, fraud became inevitable.

LJM1 was first created by Fastow as a result of a deal Enron had made with a high-speed Internet service provider called Rhythms NetConnections. In March 1998, Enron purchased $10 million worth of shares in Rhythms and agreed to hold the shares until the end of 1999, when it was authorized to sell those shares. Rhythms released its first IPO in April 1999, and Enron's share of Rhythms stock immediately jumped to a net worth of $300 million.

Fearing that the value of the stock might drop again before it could be sold, Enron searched for an investor from whom it would purchase a put option (i.e., insurance against a falling stock price). However, because Enron had such a large share and because Rhythms was such a risky company, Enron could not find an investor at the price Enron was seeking. So, with the approval of the board of directors and a waiver of Enron's code of conduct, Fastow created LJM1, which used Enron stock as its capital to sell the Rhythms stock put options to Enron. In effect, Enron was insuring itself against a plummeting Rhythms stock price. But, since Enron was basically insuring itself and paying Fastow and his subordinates millions of dollars to run the deal, Enron really had no insurance. With all of its actions independent of Enron's financial records, LJM1 was able to provide a hedge against a profitable investment.

LJM2 was the sequel to LJM1 and is infamous for its involvement in four major deals known as the Raptors. The Raptors were deals made between Enron and LJM2 that enabled Enron to hide losses from Enron's unprofitable investments. In total, LJM2 hid approximately $1.1 billion worth of losses from Enron's balance sheet.

LJM1 and LJM2 were used by Enron to alter its actual financial statements and by Fastow for personal profits. Enron's books took a hard hit when LJM finally consolidated its financial statements, a $100 million SPE restatement. In the end, Fastow pocketed millions of dollars from his involvement with the LJM SPEs.

Through complicated accounting schemes, Enron was able to fool the public for a time into thinking that its profits were continually growing. The energy giant cooked its books by hiding significant liabilities and losses from bad investments and poor assets, by not recognizing declines in the value of its aging assets, by reporting over $1 billion of false income, and by manipulating its cash flows, often during fourth quarters. However, as soon as the public became aware of Enron's fraudulent acts, both investors and the company suffered. As investor confidence in Enron dropped because of its fraudulent deal making, so did Enron's stock price. In just one year, Enron stock plummeted from a high of about $95 per share to below $1 per share. The decrease in equity made it impossible for Enron to cover its expenses and liabilities, and it was forced to declare bankruptcy on December 2, 2001. Enron had been reduced from a company claiming almost $62 billion worth of assets to nearly nothing.

Questions

1. What important internal controls were ignored when LJM1 was created?

2. How might Enron's harsh Performance Review Committee have aided company executives in committing the fraud?

3. The fraud at Enron is one of many major financial statement frauds that have occurred in recent years (Qwest, Global Crossing, WorldCom, etc.). What are some factors that could explain why the falsifying of financial statements is occurring so frequently? List four factors.

4. Suppose you are a certified fraud examiner but enjoy investing in the stock market as an additional source of income. Upon research of Enron's stock, you notice that although its stock has a history of strong growth and a seemingly promising future, Enron's financial reports are unclear and, frankly, confusing. In fact, you can't even explain how Enron is making money. Could this lack of clarity in its financial reporting serve as a red flag in alerting you to the possibility of fraud at Enron? Why or why not?

5. How could the auditor, Arthur Andersen in this case, have performed Enron's audits and not caught the fraud? Is it possible for a financial statement auditor to perform an audit in compliance with generally accepted auditing standards (GAAS) and not catch major financial statement fraud? How would GAAS auditing need to change to guarantee that all frauds are caught?

INTERNET ASSIGNMENTS

1. Horizontal and vertical analyses are effective ways to search for analytical fraud symptoms. Search the Internet for the annual report of a company of your choice. Perform both a horizontal and vertical analysis for the assets portion of the balance sheet. You may find it helpful to use Excel or similar spreadsheet software.

2. Go to the IBM company's Web site (www.ibm.com) and download the most recent financial statements. In the notes to the financial statements, read the significant accounting policies concerning revenue and inventory. Do the policies seem legitimate? What concerns might you have? Then, go to the financial statements and do a year-to-year comparison of the three accounts. Were the changes as expected? Is anything unusual? Does IBM explain any unusual fluctuations in the notes?

DEBATES

Mendoza is considering investing in IBM. However, he is captivated by IBM's growth. IBM had made a remarkable change from a struggling company to a leading company in the personal computer market. Mendoza has asked for your advice as to whether or not the growth is genuine. He suspects there might have been some fraudulent or unethical actions taken by IBM to increase its income.

After a brief look at the recent history and performance of IBM, you decide to look more closely at the financial statements. As you review the financial statements, you begin to have some concerns about the true nature of IBM's growth. Certain accounting procedures cause you to have doubt as to whether the growth came from IBM's core business operations or from carefully planned accounting adjustments that seem to be unethical. As you proceed in your investigations, you pay particular attention to the following areas.

Pensions IBM changed its pension plan to a cash balance plan. The returns of this plan exceeded the amount recognized as an expense. Accounting rules require the company to add the excess returns to earnings, but the gains cannot be spent on anything other than pension benefits. IBM increased its earnings per share by making this adjustment.

Stock Repurchases Since 1995, IBM has spent a lot of money making stock repurchases. A stock repurchase may be beneficial to a company by increasing earnings per share, since there will be fewer shareholders across which to spread the earnings.

You conclude that the financial statements were in accordance with generally accepted accounting principles (GAAP), and you are confident that all accounting rules were followed. However, you have to explain to Mendoza whether the behavior was ethical. What would you tell him?

END NOTES

1. Daniel Wise, "Cendant Lawyers Get Record $262 Million in Securities Fraud Case," *New York Law Journal* (August 22, 2000).

2. See Brazel, J. F., K. L. Jones, and M. F. Zimbelman, "Using Nonfinancial Measures to Assess Fraud Risk," in *Journal of Accounting Research*, Vol. 47, No. 5 December 2009, pp. 1135–1166.

3. www.yourlawyer.com/articles/read/5973, accessed May 12, 2010.

4. Converting financial statements to percentages is often referred to as using *common-size financial statements.* The percentages take away the effect of size of the dollar amounts and allow observers to see all financial statements as a percentage of revenues (on the income statement) and total assets (on the balance sheet).

5. "Inventory Chicanery Tempts More Firms, Fools More Auditors," *The Wall Street Journal* (December 14, 1992): 1.

Strategic Reasoning and Detecting Revenue- and Inventory-Related Fraud

Many standard audit procedures can be used to detect financial statement fraud. In this appendix, we list the common audit procedures that correspond to revenue- and inventory-related fraud schemes and show how these procedures may help detect the various schemes.

Revenue-Related Fraud Schemes

Table 12A.1 lists several common audit procedures and shows the revenue-related fraud schemes and transactions that each procedure may help detect.

As displayed in Table 12A.1, some audit procedures can be used for detecting multiple fraud schemes or transactions. For example, analytical procedures and interviewing can be used for all the schemes. Importantly, although analytical procedures give an indication that a fraud may be occurring, they are not conclusive of fraud. On the other hand, interviews may provide much stronger evidence of a particular scheme. Because each audit procedure is limited in its ability to confirm or disconfirm a particular fraud, a combination of audit procedures will increase the probability of discovering fraudulent behavior. Also important to note is that even though these audit procedures may help in discovering fraud, they do not ensure this discovery. Auditors are required to use professional skepticism while conducting an audit and should also employ strategic reasoning. Strategic reasoning is especially important given that smart fraud perpetrators know the common audit procedures and can design their scheme to be concealed from these procedures.

Strategic Reasoning Relating to Revenue-Related Fraud

As discussed in Chapter 11, strategic reasoning is important for discovering financial statement fraud. While an auditor hopes that performing typical audit procedures will assist in the discovery of financial statement fraud, he or she should be aware that fraud perpetrators may be consciously attempting to prevent the auditor from discovering their fraud. Because management may apply strategic reasoning in their attempts to conceal their fraud schemes, they have probably anticipated the standard audit procedures—especially if the auditor has historically performed these procedures.

Applying strategic reasoning to standard audit procedures can be as simple as making slight modifications to the procedures. For example, a standard audit procedure is to send out confirmations for accounts receivable. An auditor who suspects that the client may be recording fictitious accounts receivable could apply strategic reasoning to try to detect management's efforts to conceal this scheme. Management, knowing that confirmations are standard in an audit, may give the auditor the address of an executive to which the confirmation can be sent. The auditor should realize this as a possibility and confirm mailing addresses before sending confirmations. By confirming an address to find out if the correct business corresponds with the correct address, a fraud such as this can be detected.

TABLE 12A.1 COMMON AUDIT PROCEDURES FOR REVENUE-RELATED FRAUD SCHEMES

COMMON FRAUD SCHEMES AND TRANSACTIONS	COMMON AUDIT PROCEDURES
Record fictitious sales	• Perform analytical procedures on sales, sales returns, allowance for doubtful accounts, bad debts and the aging of receivables. • Review the AR ledger, cash receipts journal, and sales journal for large or unusual items. • Select A/R balances to confirm and send positive and negative confirmation requests. • Examine evidence of subsequent cash collection from the customer for the following: any positive confirmations not returned, negative confirmations returned with significant exceptions, and other account balances deemed appropriate. • For positive confirmations not returned and for negative confirmations returned with significant exceptions, examine supporting documentation such as billing and shipping documents. • Review the sales returns after year-end to determine the effect on the AR balance. • Test cutoff of sales, sales returns, and cash receipts at year-end by looking at supporting documents before and after year-end. • Review the reconciliation of the sub-ledger to the general ledger and investigate unusual items. • Test occurrence of sales by tracing details from the sales journal to supporting documents. • Ensure proper treatment of all related party sales and AR. • Conduct interviews of client personnel.
Recognize revenues too early	• Perform analytical procedures on sales, sales returns, allowance for doubtful accounts, bad debts and the aging of receivables. • Select A/R balances to confirm and send positive and negative confirmation requests. • Examine evidence of subsequent cash collection from the customer for the following: any positive confirmations not returned, negative confirmations returned with significant exceptions, and other account balances deemed appropriate. • Review the sales returns after year-end to determine the effect on the AR balance. • Test cutoff of sales, sales returns, and cash receipts at year-end by looking at supporting documents before and after year-end. • Conduct interviews of client personnel.
Understate allowance for doubtful accounts/don't write off uncollectables	• Perform analytical procedures on sales, sales returns, allowance for doubtful accounts, bad debts and the aging of receivables. • Examine evidence of subsequent cash collection from the customer for the following: any positive confirmations not returned, negative confirmations returned with significant exceptions, and other account balances deemed appropriate. • Conduct interviews of client personnel.
Not record returned goods/discounts from customer	• Perform analytical procedures on sales, sales returns, allowance for doubtful accounts, bad debts and the aging of receivables. • Select A/R balances to confirm and send positive and negative confirmation requests. • Examine evidence of subsequent cash collection from the customer for the following: any positive confirmations not returned, negative confirmations returned with significant exceptions, and other account balances deemed appropriate.

TABLE 12A.1 COMMON AUDIT PROCEDURES FOR REVENUE-RELATED FRAUD SCHEMES (CONTINUED)

COMMON FRAUD SCHEMES AND TRANSACTIONS	COMMON AUDIT PROCEDURES
Not record returned goods/discounts from customer, continued	• Review the sales returns after year-end to determine the effect on the AR balance. • Conduct interviews of client personnel.
Record returned goods/write off receivables after the end of the period	• Perform analytical procedures on sales, sales returns, allowance for doubtful accounts, bad debts and the aging of receivables. • Examine evidence of subsequent cash collection from the customer for the following: any positive confirmations not returned, negative confirmations returned with significant exceptions, and other account balances deemed appropriate. • Review the sales returns after year-end to determine the effect on the AR balance. • Test cutoff of sales, sales returns, and cash receipts at year-end by looking at supporting documents before and after year-end. • Conduct interviews of client personnel.
Manipulation of cash received	• Perform analytical procedures on sales, sales returns, allowance for doubtful accounts, bad debts and the aging of receivables. • Review the AR ledger, cash receipts journal, and sales journal for large or unusual items. • Select A/R balances to confirm and send positive and negative confirmation requests. • Examine evidence of subsequent cash collection from the customer for the following: any positive confirmations not returned, negative confirmations returned with significant exceptions, and other account balances deemed appropriate. • For positive confirmations not returned and for negative confirmations returned with significant exceptions, examine supporting documentation such as billing and shipping documents. • Test occurrence of sales by tracing details from the sales journal to supporting documents. • Conduct interviews of client personnel.
Related party transactions	• Perform analytical procedures on sales, sales returns, allowance for doubtful accounts, bad debts and the aging of receivables. • Examine evidence of subsequent cash collection from the customer for the following: any positive confirmations not returned, negative confirmations returned with significant exceptions, and other account balances deemed appropriate. • Test occurrence of sales by tracing details from the sales journal to supporting documents. • Ensure proper treatment of all related party sales and AR. • Conduct interviews of client personnel. • Compare prices and terms on sales invoices with that of the company's authorized list and terms. • Inquire of management and other client personnel about related-party receivables.
Sham sales	• Perform analytical procedures on sales, sales returns, allowance for doubtful accounts, bad debts and the aging of receivables. • Review the AR ledger, cash receipts journal, and sales journal for large or unusual items.

TABLE 12A.1 COMMON AUDIT PROCEDURES FOR REVENUE-RELATED FRAUD SCHEMES (CONTINUED)

COMMON FRAUD SCHEMES AND TRANSACTIONS	COMMON AUDIT PROCEDURES
Sham sales, continued	• Select A/R balances to confirm and send positive and negative confirmation requests. • Examine evidence of subsequent cash collection from the customer for the following: any positive confirmations not returned, negative confirmations returned with significant exceptions, and other account balances deemed appropriate. • For positive confirmations not returned and for negative confirmations returned with significant exceptions, examine supporting documentation such as billing and shipping documents. • Review the sales returns after year-end to determine the effect on the AR balance. • Test cutoff of sales, sales returns, and cash receipts at year-end by looking at supporting documents before and after year-end. • Review the reconciliation of the sub-ledger to the general ledger and investigate unusual items. • Test occurrence of sales by tracing details from the sales journal to supporting documents. • Conduct interviews of client personnel. • Inquire of management and other client personnel about related-party receivables.
Bill-and-hold sales	• Perform analytical procedures on sales, sales returns, allowance for doubtful accounts, bad debts and the aging of receivables. • Select A/R balances to confirm and send positive and negative confirmation requests. • Examine evidence of subsequent cash collection from the customer for the following: any positive confirmations not returned, negative confirmations returned with significant exceptions, and other account balances deemed appropriate. • For positive confirmations not returned and for negative confirmations returned with significant exceptions, examine supporting documentation such as billing and shipping documents. • Test occurrence of sales by tracing details from the sales journal to supporting documents. • Conduct interviews of client personnel.
Side agreements	• Perform analytical procedures on sales, sales returns, allowance for doubtful accounts, bad debts and the aging of receivables. • Examine evidence of subsequent cash collection from the customer for the following: any positive confirmations not returned, negative confirmations returned with significant exceptions, and other account balances deemed appropriate. • Ensure proper treatment of all related party sales and AR. • Conduct interviews of client personnel. • Compare prices and terms on sales invoices with that of the company's authorized list and terms.
Consignment sales	• Perform analytical procedures on sales, sales returns, allowance for doubtful accounts, bad debts and the aging of receivables. • Select A/R balances to confirm and send positive and negative confirmation requests. • Review the sales returns after year-end to determine the effect on the AR balance.

TABLE 12A.1 COMMON AUDIT PROCEDURES FOR REVENUE-RELATED FRAUD SCHEMES (CONTINUED)

COMMON FRAUD SCHEMES AND TRANSACTIONS	COMMON AUDIT PROCEDURES
Consignment sales, continued	• Test occurrence of sales by tracing details from the sales journal to supporting documents. • Conduct interviews of client personnel. • Compare prices and terms on sales invoices with that of the company's authorized list and terms.
Channel surfing	• Perform analytical procedures on sales, sales returns, allowance for doubtful accounts, bad debts and the aging of receivables. • Select A/R balances to confirm and send positive and negative confirmation requests. • Examine evidence of subsequent cash collection from the customer for the following: any positive confirmations not returned, negative confirmations returned with significant exceptions, and other account balances deemed appropriate. • Review the sales returns after year-end to determine the effect on the AR balance. • Test occurrence of sales by tracing details from the sales journal to supporting documents. • Conduct interviews of client personnel.
Lapping/kiting	• Perform analytical procedures on sales, sales returns, allowance for doubtful accounts, bad debts and the aging of receivables. • Select A/R balances to confirm and send positive and negative confirmation requests. • Examine evidence of subsequent cash collection from the customer for the following: any positive confirmations not returned, negative confirmations returned with significant exceptions, and other account balances deemed appropriate. • Test occurrence of sales by tracing details from the sales journal to supporting documents. • Conduct interviews of client personnel.
Redating	• Perform analytical procedures on sales, sales returns, allowance for doubtful accounts, bad debts and the aging of receivables. • Review the AR ledger, cash receipts journal, and sales journal for large or unusual items. • Select A/R balances to confirm and send positive and negative confirmation requests. • For positive confirmations not returned and for negative confirmations returned with significant exceptions, examine supporting documentation such as billing and shipping documents. • Test occurrence of sales by tracing details from the sales journal to supporting documents. • Conduct interviews of client personnel.
Liberal return policy	• Perform analytical procedures on sales, sales returns, allowance for doubtful accounts, bad debts and the aging of receivables. • Select A/R balances to confirm and send positive and negative confirmation requests. • Examine evidence of subsequent cash collection from the customer for the following: any positive confirmations not returned, negative confirmations returned with significant exceptions, and other account balances deemed appropriate.

TABLE 12A.1 COMMON AUDIT PROCEDURES FOR REVENUE-RELATED FRAUD SCHEMES (CONTINUED)

COMMON FRAUD SCHEMES AND TRANSACTIONS	COMMON AUDIT PROCEDURES
Liberal return policy, continued	• Review the sales returns after year-end to determine the effect on the AR balance. • Conduct interviews of client personnel.
Partial shipments	• Perform analytical procedures on sales, sales returns, allowance for doubtful accounts, bad debts and the aging of receivables. • Review the AR ledger, cash receipts journal, and sales journal for large or unusual items. • Select A/R balances to confirm and send positive and negative confirmation requests. • For positive confirmations not returned and for negative confirmations returned with significant exceptions, examine supporting documentation such as billing and shipping documents. • Conduct interviews of client personnel.
Improper cut-off	• Perform analytical procedures on sales, sales returns, allowance for doubtful accounts, bad debts and the aging of receivables. • Select A/R balances to confirm and send positive and negative confirmation requests. • For positive confirmations not returned and for negative confirmations returned with significant exceptions, examine supporting documentation such as billing and shipping documents. • Test cutoff of sales, sales returns, and cash receipts at year-end by looking at supporting documents before and after year-end. • Conduct interviews of client personnel.
Roundtripping	• Perform analytical procedures on sales, sales returns, allowance for doubtful accounts, bad debts and the aging of receivables. • Review the AR ledger, cash receipts journal, and sales journal for large or unusual items. • Ensure proper treatment of all related party sales and AR. • Conduct interviews of client personnel. • Compare prices and terms on sales invoices with that of the company's authorized list and terms.

TABLE 12A.2 COMMON AUDIT PROCEDURES FOR INVENTORY-RELATED FRAUD SCHEMES

COMMON FRAUD SCHEMES OR TRANSACTIONS	COMMON AUDIT PROCEDURES
Recording fictitious inventory	• Compare gross profit percentage for each product and compare with industry as well as previous years' figures. • Compare budgeted cost of goods sold with actual amounts. • Inquire of personnel about inventory that may be held on consignment or involve a bill-and-hold agreement. • Perform sample test counts and record in audit working papers. • Obtain cutoff information including the number of the last shipping and receiving documents on the date of the physical inventory count. • Observe the physical count of inventory. • Reconcile totals on the compiled total inventory counts to the general ledger.
Improper cutoff	• Compare days outstanding in inventory with industry as well as previous years' figures. • Perform sample test counts and record in audit working papers. • Obtain cutoff information including the number of the last shipping and receiving documents on the date of the physical inventory count. • Observe the physical count of inventory. • Examine a sample of receiving and shipping documents several days before and after year-end.
Failure to write off or write down obsolesce	• Compare days outstanding in inventory with industry as well as previous years' figures. • Perform sample test counts and record in audit working papers. • Observe the physical count of inventory. • Inquire regarding slow-moving or obsolete inventory.
Underrecorded purchases	• Compare gross profit percentage for each product and compare with industry as well as previous years' figures. • Obtain cutoff information including the number of the last shipping and receiving documents on the date of the physical inventory count. • Examine a sample of receiving and shipping documents several days before and after year-end.
Overstate returns/discounts	• Inquire of personnel about inventory that may be held on consignment or involve a bill-and-hold agreement. • Perform sample test counts and record in audit working papers. • Obtain cutoff information including the number of the last shipping and receiving documents on the date of the physical inventory count. • Observe the physical count of inventory. • Examine a sample of receiving and shipping documents several days before and after year-end.

TABLE 12A.2 COMMON AUDIT PROCEDURES FOR **INVENTORY-RELATED** FRAUD SCHEMES (CONTINUED)

COMMON FRAUD SCHEMES OR TRANSACTIONS	COMMON AUDIT PROCEDURES
Understate cost of goods sold	• Compare gross profit percentage for each product and compare with industry as well as previous years' figures. • Compare budgeted or standard manufacturing overhead costs with actual manufacturing overhead costs. • Compare budgeted cost of goods sold with actual amounts. • Inquire regarding slow-moving or obsolete inventory. • Audit standard costs used to price inventory.
Overestimate inventory	• Compare budgeted cost of goods sold with actual amounts. • Perform sample test counts and record in audit working papers. • Observe the physical count of inventory.
Overstating or double counting inventory	• Compare gross profit percentage for each product and compare with industry as well as previous years' figures. • Inquire of personnel about inventory that may be held on consignment or involve a bill-and-hold agreement. • Perform sample test counts and record in audit working papers. • Obtain cutoff information including the number of the last shipping and receiving documents on the date of the physical inventory count. • Observe the physical count of inventory. • Inquire regarding inventory that may be pledged or assigned. • Reconcile totals on the compiled total inventory counts to the general ledger.
Capitalize inventory costs	• Compare gross profit percentage for each product and compare with industry as well as previous years' figures. • Compare budgeted or standard manufacturing overhead costs with actual manufacturing overhead costs. • Compare budgeted cost of goods sold with actual amounts. • Audit standard costs used to price inventory.

Inventory-Related Fraud Schemes

Similar to revenue-related fraud, audit procedures can be used to detect inventory-related fraud. Table 12A.2 is similar to Table 12A.1 and lists common audit procedures related to inventory and indicates which procedures help in detecting inventory-related fraud schemes or transactions.

Again, no one procedure will detect all potential fraud schemes, but by combining these procedures, an auditor has a greater chance of detecting any fraud that is being perpetrated. Because management is likely to know the procedures that the auditor will perform, auditors should

apply strategic reasoning in an attempt to discover concealed fraud schemes involving inventory.

Strategic Reasoning Relating to Inventory-Related Fraud

As with revenue-related fraud, inventory-related financial statement fraud is likely to be concealed by management. Because management is aware that auditors perform specific audit procedures, they likely will attempt to conceal the fraud from standard audit procedures. For example, if management is attempting to overstate inventory and knows the dates and locations of the auditor's physical inventory counts, it may ship already counted inventory from one warehouse to another which has not yet been counted. With regard to this double-counting inventory scheme, an auditor can apply strategic reasoning and modify the standard procedure by doing one or more of the following:

- Perform surprise visits and counts to inventory locations.
- Ensure that the audit plan is confidential and not discussed with the client regarding the locations, times, and sampling amounts of the physical inventory counts.
- Perform nonfinancial analytics to determine unusual relationships (e.g., calculating the total volume required for holding reported inventory and comparing that to the actual space in the existing warehouse to discover an overstatement or double counting).
- Inquire of personnel in the shipping department of recent shipments between inventory warehouse locations close to the physical inventory count date.

Although these are only a few examples of how strategic reasoning could be used during an audit, they illustrate why and how auditors should consider management's efforts to conceal fraud schemes from standard procedures.

CHAPTER **13**

Liability, Asset, and Inadequate Disclosure Frauds

LEARNING OBJECTIVES

After studying this chapter, you should be able to:

- Identify fraudulent schemes that understate liabilities.
- Discuss the understatement of liabilities fraud.
- Describe fraudulent schemes that overstate assets.
- Understand overstatement of assets fraud.
- List fraudulent schemes that inadequately disclose financial statement information.
- Explain inadequate disclosure fraud.

TO THE STUDENT

This chapter concludes our discussion on financial statement fraud by covering several other types of financial statement frauds, including understating liabilities, overstating assets, and inadequate disclosures. In dealing with these frauds, we look at how to identify fraud exposures and to actively search for and detect fraud symptoms. While not as common as revenue- or inventory-related frauds, they can be just as significant, as is illustrated in the Waste Management, Inc., fraud.

Waste Management, Inc., is the leading provider of comprehensive waste and environmental services in North America. Headquartered in Houston, the company's network of operations includes hundreds of collection operations, transfer stations, landfill disposal sites, and recycling plants, among other things. Waste Management provides services to millions of residential, industrial, municipal, and commercial customers. A few years ago, Waste Management improperly inflated its operating income and other measures of performance by deferring current-period operating expenses into the future by netting one-time gains against current-and prior-period misstatements and current-period operating expenses. Senior management increased income by understating depreciation expense on its equipment, by improperly capitalizing interest on landfill development costs, and by failing to accrue properly for tax and self-insurance expenses. It also improperly used purchase accounting, charged operating expenses to environmental remediation reserves, and failed to write off costs on impaired or abandoned landfills. These schemes resulted in the company restating its 1992–1997 earnings by $1.7 billion, the largest restatement in corporate history up to that time.

Waste Management, Inc., used several financial statement fraud schemes to deceive investors. We will review some of the schemes used by Waste Management, Inc., in this chapter.

Understating Liabilities

We begin by reviewing an example that we referred to in a previous chapter. A number of years ago, one of the Big Five CPA firms was sued for not detecting a financial statement fraud in its audits. The company that committed the fraud was involved in a series of real estate partnerships organized under a state's Uniform Limited Partnership Act. The largest of the partnerships—and the one with the most fraud—had more than 5,000 limited partners and two general partners. The partnerships were engaged in the business of acquiring, owning, and operating commercial convenience retail businesses leased to and operated by national and regional retail chains under long-term leases. The retail business lessees consisted primarily of restaurants (fast-food, family-style, and casual theme, such as Wendy's, Hardee's, Peso's, Country Kitchen, Applebee's, Popeye's, Arby's, and Village Inns) but also included Blockbuster Video stores and childcare centers. Investments by limited partners were used to purchase or construct and fully pay for properties. None of the properties had mortgages.

The two general partners had significant real estate investments of their own and needed money to support their cash-strapped personal investments. They saw the equity in the partnership's fully paid commercial properties as a great source of cash. Accordingly, they approached a bank in another state (where they did not think the loans would be discovered) and borrowed millions of dollars against the equity in the limited partnership's assets, thus incurring significant amounts of debt for the partnership.

Fortunately, the auditors recognized that the partnership had significant risk in their leases because failing to pay local property taxes or utilities, for example, could encumber the properties with liens. As a result, to determine if all the lessees were current on their obligations, the auditors performed lien searches on the properties. Surprisingly, their lien searches revealed several liens against Arizona and Texas properties by a Kansas bank. Because the partnership had no business in Kansas, these liens raised the auditors' attention and they asked management about the liens. Management claimed that the liens were recorded as part of a lending arrangement with the bank that was never completed and should have been released. To corroborate the explanations of management, the auditors sent a confirmation to the Kansas bank. The confirmation letter read as follows:

In connection with the audit of the [named] partnership for the year ending December 31, 1995, our auditors became aware of several mortgage liens held by your bank on properties located in Arizona and Texas. These liens were recorded as part of a lending arrangement with your bank which was not completed. Because the liens have not been released, our auditors would like confirmation from you on the enclosed form as to the balance of loans or other liabilities outstanding to your bank from the [named] partnership at December 31, 1995. If such balance was zero at that date, please so state.

Your prompt response will be appreciated. Please fax a copy of your response to the attention of [named auditor] at [telephone number] and also return the enclosed form in the envelope provided. Thank you for your attention to this matter.

In response, the auditors received both a fax and an original letter dated April 12, 1996, from the executive vice president of the bank that read as follows:

In response to [name of signer] letter of January 24, 1996, regarding your audit of [named partnership], please be advised as follows: (1) [named partnership] has no debt or obligation outstanding to the bank and (2) the bank's attorneys are in the process of releasing the collateral liens, since it is the bank's understanding that the borrower does not intend to utilize its existing line of credit arrangements.

Like the real auditors in this case, at this point, you might have been content with your belief that this partnership had no unrecorded liabilities and that the line of credit had never really been used. Unfortunately, that assumption was wrong. You should read the letters one more time. While the first letter specifies December 31, 1995, as the date on which the auditors wanted to know if liabilities existed, the response letter from the bank does not specify any date, except that the letter was dated April 12. However, significant liabilities existed on December 31, 1995, that continued until April 11, 1996, at which time they were removed. On April 12, the bank could truthfully say it held no unrecorded liabilities; but on April 13, 1996, new liabilities were recorded. In other words, the liabilities were eliminated on one day only—April 12! The bank's president and executive vice president had been coerced by the partnership's general partners to remove the liabilities for one day and respond to the auditors. They were acting in collusion with the general partners to mislead the auditors. Although this incident was not the only financial statement fraud perpetrated by the general partners, it was the largest. These unrecorded liabilities, which could never be paid off, resulted in significant adverse consequences for the limited partnership.

Understatement of liability frauds, such as these, are difficult for auditors to detect. Financial statement auditors use predictable audit procedures that are required by generally accepted auditing standards (GAAS). Using predictable audit procedures allows fraud perpetrators to find ways to conceal their schemes from GAAS auditors. Financial statement frauds can be viewed as being on a continuum of "easy to detect and probably should have been detected by GAAS auditors" to "difficult to detect and probably could not have been detected by any auditor performing a GAAS audit." Perpetrators use several methods to conceal financial statement frauds from auditors, including the following:

- *Collusion by insiders or outsiders, as was the case with the bank executives in the fraud discussed previously*
- *Forgery, which financial statement auditors are not trained to detect*
- *A complex audit trail that is mainly revealed on internal reports that are not reviewed as part of a GAAS audit*
- *Lying by management and other key people*
- *A fraud that takes the form of normal transactions of the company—in other words, it is not unusual*
- *Silence by individuals who knew about the fraud*
- *Off-book nature of the fraud, meaning that the records on the company's books are not fraudulent, such as the fraud discussed previously*
- *The existence of misleading documentation*
- *Small frauds relative to financial statement balances, or large frauds that are broken up into small amounts and scattered throughout subsidiaries*
- *Fictitious transactions that use normal-looking amounts rather than rounded amounts*
- *Fictitious documents created by management to support the fraud*

Ways to Manipulate Liabilities

Before we discuss how to identify understatement of liability fraud, it is important to note that in some major frauds, the perpetrators have manipulated liabilities in more complicated ways than just understating or hiding them. One way to manipulate liabilities is to improperly use **restructuring** and other liability reserves. Recording a reserve on a company's books, whether for a merger, restructuring, environmental cleanup, litigation, or other reasons, usually involves recognizing an expense and a related liability or contra-asset. In establishing reserves, companies should comply with generally accepted accounting principles (GAAP) by recording reserves only if a liability exists. Once a reserve is established, payments made by the company properly related to the reserve are offset against the reserve and not reported as an expense in the current period.

Unfortunately, reserves have been fraudulently used by companies to manage earnings. These companies typically create excess reserves (by initially over-accruing a liability) in one accounting period and then reduce the excess reserve in later accounting periods. The reserve is commonly created during good times or when new management takes over to turn around a company that experienced poor performance under the previous management. After its creation in one period, the reserve is used in future periods to inflate profits and to make it appear that the company is turning around or to meet or exceed earnings expectations (i.e., to manage earnings). These overstated reserves are sometimes referred to as "cookie jar" reserves because, like money stored in a cookie jar, they represent a stash of accounting earnings that can be used to bolster the perceived performance of the company in the future.

Xerox Corporation, Sunbeam Corporation, and W. R. Grace & Co., all major corporations, were charged by the Securities and Exchange Commission (SEC) for using cookie jar reserves to manipulate income. These companies recorded extra liabilities (such as recording income as deferred income) when results were better than expected or when management decided to take what is known as a "big bath." Sometimes management will fictitiously increase and create reserves when they believe the consequences for incurring a large loss would not lead to a significant amount of additional negative consequences to them or the company. For example, a company that is expecting a significant loss may also expect the stock price to be severely impacted and conclude that writing off assets or accelerating expenses to increase the loss may not lead to much more of a decline in the stock price. This is known as "taking a big bath." The reserve is reversed to create accounting earnings when better results are needed in a future period. In some cases, the companies reported the creation of the reserves as nonoperating expenses and reversed the liability to income as operating income. Thus, they overstated liabilities in one period and understated them in subsequent periods.

Xerox allegedly manipulated its reserves in order to meet earnings expectations. Specifically, the SEC charged that Xerox had $396 million in cookie jar reserves, which the company periodically released into earnings to artificially improve its operating results from 1997 through 2000. Sunbeam and W. R. Grace & Co. were also charged with similar schemes.

Identifying Understatement of Liability Fraud Exposures

As with revenue and inventory frauds, the easiest way to identify understatement of liability fraud exposures is to identify the various transactions that involve liabilities and can be understated. In identifying these transactions, you should understand the type of organization you are dealing with, because different kinds of companies have different types of liabilities and liability-fraud exposures. Table 13.1 lists the six primary types of transactions that can create liabilities for a typical retail or wholesale company. By analyzing the accounts involved in these transactions, we can identify at least 19 different ways (some are similar) in which liabilities can be understated and the financial statements misstated.

Understating Accounts Payable

The first category of fraud schemes involves various kinds of cutoff problems related to inventory purchases. Even though minor cutoff problems probably occur in many companies, large financial statement misstatements can result from committing this type of fraud. In one case, for example, the auditors discovered a $28 million unrecorded liability for inventory purchased before year-end. It was not recorded as a liability or discovered because management altered purchasing records, bank statements, and correspondence with vendors to make it look like the company paid for the inventory before year-end.

Another example was Sirena Apparel Group, Inc. The SEC alleged that Sirena's CEO and CFO materially overstated their revenue and earnings by instructing personnel to hold open the March 1999 fiscal quarter until Sirena had reached its sales target for that period but not to record the costs incurred for these sales. Thus, not only did Sirena's management commit a revenue fraud, but by not recording the purchases that corresponded to future revenues, it had no corresponding cost of goods sold and purchase-related liabilities.

Understating liabilities related to the purchase of inventory involves the other side of the transactions considered in Chapter 12. Assuming a company's accounting records balance (i.e., debits equal credits), an income statement account, such as Cost of Goods Sold, is generally used to balance the ledger. If accounts payable liabilities are understated and inventory is not, then cost of goods sold will be understated, leading to

TABLE 13.1 LIABILITY TRANSACTIONS

TRANSACTION	ACCOUNTS INVOLVED	FRAUD SCHEMES
1. Purchase inventory	Inventory, Accounts Payable	1. Record payables in subsequent period. 2. Don't record purchases. 3. Overstate purchase returns and purchase discounts. 4. Record payments made in later periods as being paid in earlier periods. 5. Fraudulent recording of payments (e.g., kiting).
2. Incur payroll and other accrued liabilities	Payroll Tax Expense, Salary Expense, various expenses, Salaries Payable, Payroll Taxes Payable, various accrued liabilities	6. Not record accrued liabilities. 7. Record accruals in later period.
3. Sell products	Accounts Receivable, Sales Revenue, Unearned Revenue	8. Record unearned revenues as earned revenues (or vice versa when creating cookie jar reserves).
4. Sell services, repay deposits, or repurchase something in the future (future commitments)	Warranty (Service) Expense, Warranty or Service Liability	9. Not record warranty (service) liabilities. 10. Underrecord liabilities. 11. Record deposits as revenues. 12. Not record repurchase agreements and commitments.
5. Borrow money	Cash, Notes Payable, Mortgages Payable, etc.	13. Borrow from related parties at less than arm's-length transactions. 14. Don't record liabilities. 15. Borrow against equities in assets. 16. Write off liabilities as forgiven. 17. Claim liabilities as personal debt rather than as debt of the entity.
6. Incur contingent liabilities	Loss from Contingencies, Losses Payable	18. Don't record probable contingent liabilities. 19. Record contingent liabilities at too low an amount.

the inflation of net income. Accounts payable can be understated by a combination of (1) not recording purchases or recording the purchases after year-end, (2) overstating purchase returns or purchase discounts, or (3) making it appear as if liabilities have been paid off or forgiven when they have not. When purchases are understated, net income is normally overstated. This occurs because cost of goods sold for the period is calculated as beginning inventory plus purchases (which are understated) minus ending inventory. As a result, cost of goods sold is understated, and income before taxes is overstated by the amount of the understated purchases.

Understating Accrued Liabilities

Accrued liabilities that should be recorded at the end of an accounting period but are not can often add up to millions of dollars. Some common **accrued liabilities** are salaries payable, payroll taxes payable, rent payable,

utilities payable, interest payable, and so forth. When these liabilities are not recorded or are understated, net income is usually overstated because the other (debit) side of an accrual entry is usually to an expense account. These types of financial statement frauds tend to be rather small, and they are easy to perpetrate and can result in misstated financial statements. For example, one company experienced a $2.1 million understatement of payroll taxes payable and a $1 million understatement of accrued salaries. In another fraud, the CFO failed to pay or recognize as liabilities various property and payroll taxes. Instead, he deposited the money in his own bank accounts. This nearly $10 million fraud was discovered when a state complained to the company that it had not been making payroll tax deposits. Although this case involved employee fraud, it was large enough to constitute financial statement fraud as it resulted in materially misstated financial statements.

Recognizing Unearned Revenue (Liability) as Earned Revenue

The third category of liabilities that may be intentionally understated (or overstated in the case of cookie jar reserves) is **unearned revenues**. Sometimes, cash is received prior to the performance of a service or the shipment of goods. Also, some companies may require customers (e.g., tenants) to make deposits for future goods or services that can be intentionally recorded as revenue. When someone pays in advance of the performance of a service or the sale of a product, the entry recorded should recognize the cash received and a liability for the future service or product. Later, when the service is performed or the product is shipped, the liability should be eliminated and revenue should be recognized.

Companies that collect cash in advance and want to understate liabilities can merely record revenues at the time cash is received, rather than later when the service is performed or goods are delivered. Recognizing revenues instead of recording a liability has a positive effect on a company's financial statements because it understates the company's liabilities and overstates its revenues and net income. Similarly, if a company collects deposits that may have to be returned in the future and recognizes them as revenues, it is overstating revenues and understating liabilities. In one case, a company recorded $3 million of customer deposits as revenues, overstating net income by the full $3 million. The important point to remember about deferred revenue liabilities is that revenues should almost always be recorded as earned when the service is performed or the product is shipped.

By manipulating the timing of revenue recognition, a company can very easily either understate or overstate deferred revenue liabilities. To understand the motivation for these types of frauds, remember that stock prices are affected by both risk and return. A company that can report smoothly growing earnings may not have a higher cumulative return than a company whose earnings go up and down, but the former company's perceived risk will be much lower. As a result, the stock price of the company reporting smooth earnings will be considerably higher. This motivation to smooth earnings or meet Wall Street's earnings forecasts has been the motivation for many frauds.

Underrecording Future Obligations

The fourth category, underrecording future obligations such as warranty or service obligations, is also a type of fraud that is easy to perpetrate and results in overstated net income and understated liabilities. For example, every time a large automobile manufacturer sells a car, it provides some kind of warranty agreement, such as a three-year, 36,000-mile coverage. According to the matching principle, the expense and liability that is expected to be incurred to service these warranties must be recorded in the period in which revenue is recognized for the automobiles that are sold. A company can understate this liability by not recording any amount or by recording an amount that is too low.

Consider, for example, the case of a company, such as a fitness center, that offers a money-back guarantee if the customer is not satisfied after 30 days. If revenue is recorded at the time customers enroll, and an adequate expense is not estimated and recorded for customers who will demand their money back, liabilities can be significantly understated. In the Lincoln Savings and Loan case, revenue was recognized on land-sale transactions, even though hidden promises were made to buyers that Lincoln would buy the property back in two years at a higher price. According to *Statement of Financial Accounting Standards No. 66,* "Accounting for Sales of Real Estate," revenue should not have been recognized on these transactions. Similarly, in the ESM case, significant repurchase commitments were recorded, but were offset by fictitious receivables from an affiliated company that was not audited. In reality, the affiliated company had no assets, and the reported receivable was just a ruse to hide the fact that liabilities exceeded assets by approximately $400 million. ESM's financial statement footnote explained these liabilities as follows:

The Company entered into repurchase [liability] and resale [receivable] agreements with customers whereby specific securities are sold or purchased for short durations of time. These agreements cover securities, the rights to which are usually acquired through similar purchase/resale agreements. The company has agreements with an affiliated company for securities purchased under agreements to resell [receivables, meaning the company will get cash when it resells the securities] amounting to approximately $1,308,199,000 and securities sold under agreement to repurchase [liabilities] amounting to approximately $944,356,000 at December 31, 1983.

When the balance sheet numbers are combined with this footnote, it becomes apparent that a net receivable from an affiliate was $363,843,000 ($1,308,199,000–

$944,356,000), and a net liability to third parties was the same amount. This net obligation (liability) to repurchase securities was being camouflaged by a fictitious receivable from a related entity. Whether the obligation in the future is to service a warranty on a product, to repay a deposit, or to repurchase securities, the result is the same—understated liabilities.

Not Recording or Under-recording Various Types of Debt (Notes, Mortgages, etc.)

The limited partnership scenario discussed at the beginning of this chapter is one way to understate debt—unauthorized borrowing against the equity in a company's assets. Other ways to underrecord debt and similar liabilities include:

- *Either not reporting or underrecording debt to related parties*
- *Borrowing but not disclosing debt incurred on existing lines of credit*
- *Not recording loans incurred*
- *Claiming that existing debt has been forgiven by creditors*
- *Claiming that debt on the company's books is personal debt of the owners or principals, rather than debt of the business*

The following case illustrates how far fraud perpetrators may go in order to understate their debts:

Debt was understated in the case of General Electrodynamics Corporation (GEC), a manufacturer of hydraulic scales. In 1983, GEC was facing a loss of roughly $5,000. The company's management wrote off an outstanding loan and recognized the write-off as revenue. The company justified the revenue classification by claiming that the debt was forgiven. The transaction converted the loss to a profit of nearly $113,000. Even though the debt had neither been forgiven by the supplier nor paid by the company, the managers wrote it off anyway. Auditors were unable to confirm the transaction or support it through alternative audit procedures. GEC's financial statements did discuss the (fraudulent) entry in the footnotes, and the auditors issued an unqualified opinion. When the fraud was discovered, the managers involved in the write-off defended their actions, stating "the vendor could not demand payment," because it never pressured GEC for the balance, and it continued to do business with GEC.

Omission of Contingent Liabilities

Statement of Financial Accounting Standards No. 5, "Accounting for Contingencies," requires contingent liabilities to be recorded as liabilities on the balance sheet if the likelihood of loss or payment is "probable." If likelihood of loss is reasonably possible, the contingent liability should be disclosed in the footnotes to the financial statements. If the probability of loss is "remote," no mention of the liability needs to be made in the financial statements. Contingent liabilities can be used to fraudulently misstate financial statements by underestimating the probability of occurrence and not recording or disclosing contingent liabilities in the financial statements. As an example, consider the case of Pfizer, Inc., a pharmaceutical company:

In a civil case, plaintiffs alleged that Pfizer failed to disclose material information concerning the Shiley heart valve. This material information included the results of at least one product liability suit that Pfizer lost. Four years earlier, Pfizer reportedly knew that the Shiley heart valve was problematic, and it took the valve off the market. However, by that time, approximately 60,000 valves had been implanted. As of the date of the complaint, 389 fractures of the valve had been reported, and the FDA reported that 248 deaths had been attributed to failed Shiley valves. Moreover, Pfizer maintained that surgery to replace the implanted valves would be more risky than leaving them in. Pfizer did not record a contingent liability for this potential liability.

Detecting Understatement of Liability Fraud Symptoms

In discussing how liability-related frauds can be detected, we focus on accounting/documentary and analytical symptoms because they are some of the most effective methods to apply for detecting these frauds. As was the case with inventory and revenue frauds, we will not cover control symptoms in detail because they are adequately covered in other texts and standards. Lifestyle symptoms will also not be covered, except to note that in the case where management uses company assets to benefit themselves personally, their lifestyles can exhibit symptoms of fraud. Behavior and tip symptoms for understatement of liability frauds are similar to those of other types of financial statement fraud and so will not be discussed further. Remember, however, that inconsistent, vague, or implausible responses or behavior by or from management or employees can represent fraud symptoms.

Analytical Symptoms

Analytical symptoms related to accounts payable understatements usually relate to reported balances that appear too low. They also include purchase or cost of goods sold numbers that appear too low or purchase returns or discounts that appear too high. Analytical symptoms related to unearned revenues involve reported payroll, payroll tax, rent, interest, utility, or other accrued liabilities that appear too low. Sometimes, income that is too "smooth" can also signal a fraud. Whether these balances are "too low" is determined by comparing the balance to an independent expectation of the balance by analyzing balances in past periods, relationships with other accounts, and comparisons with balances in other companies within the same industry.

Analytical symptoms for premature recognition of unearned revenues involve unearned liability balances that appear too low and revenue accounts that appear too high. In most cases, significant judgment is needed to determine whether revenues are being recognized before they are earned, including examining terms of contracts, sales agreements, and other revenue-related documentation.

Analytical symptoms for the under- or nonrecording of service warranties or other future commitments include balances in such accounts as warranty, repurchases, or deposits that appear too low. In many cases, the assessment of whether they are too low can be made by comparing them with other accounts (e.g., comparing warranties with sales).

Analytical symptoms for unrecorded notes and mortgages payable include: unreasonable relationships between interest expense and recorded liabilities; significant decreases in recorded debt; significant purchases of assets with no recorded debt; and recorded amounts of notes payable, mortgages payable, lease liabilities, **pension** liabilities, and other debts that appear to be too low.

Finally, analytical symptoms are usually not particularly helpful in discovering unrecorded contingent liabilities. These accounts are hard to project because prior balances to compare with or ways to develop an expectation of a contingent liability balance normally do not exist.

Accounting or Documentary Symptoms

Documentary symptoms involve such things as: vendor invoices that have been received but no liability is recorded; large purchases recorded after the end of a period but the goods were received before the period ended; large payments made in subsequent periods, backdated to the current period; the presence of receiving reports with no recorded liability; amounts listed on vendor statements with no recorded liability; and errors in cutoff tests. Documentary symptoms that relate to all kinds of understatement of liability fraud include the following:

- *Photocopied purchase-related records where originals should exist*
- *Unusual discrepancies between the entity's records and confirmation replies*
- *Transactions not recorded in a complete or timely manner or improperly recorded as to amount*
- *Balances or transactions that lack supporting documents, including adjustments by the entity that significantly affect financial results*
- *Missing documents*
- *Unexplained items on reconciliations*
- *Denied access to records, facilities, certain employees, customers, vendors, or others from whom audit evidence might be sought*

Documentary symptoms can also relate to specific accounts. With payroll, for example, documentary symptoms might include employees with no withholdings, no accruals at year-end, payroll tax rates that are too low, fewer employees paid than are listed on the payroll records, and **capitalization** of employee wages as start-up or other deferred costs when they should be expensed.

Documentary symptoms for understatement of interest might include notes payable with no or too little interest expense, bank confirmations indicating the existence of notes not recorded by the company, and interest expense deducted on tax returns but not recorded on the financial statements. Documentary symptoms can include inconsistencies between revenue-recognition criteria and timing specified in contracts and sales agreements, large reclassification entries near the end of a period that result in increased revenues and lower liabilities, differences between confirmation amounts and the revenue recognized by the company, lack of shipping documentation for recorded revenues, revenues recognized before customers are

TABLE 13.2 TYPES OF FINANCIAL STATEMENT ANALYSIS

Analyzing financial balances and relationships *within* financial statements	Look for unusual changes in liability *balances* from period to period (trends) by (1) focusing on changes in the actual financial statement numbers, (2) studying the statement of cash flows, and (3) using horizontal analysis.	Look for unusual changes in *liability relationships* from period to period by (1) computing relevant ratios and examining changes in the ratios from period to period and (2) using vertical analysis.
Comparing financial statement amounts or relationships with related information	Compare financial results and trends of the company with those of similar firms in the same industry.	Compare recorded amounts in the financial statements with nonfinancial statement amounts.

billed, and inconsistencies in the timing or method of recording unearned revenues.

Documentary symptoms related to the underrecording of service or other future obligations take the form of differences between the amount expensed as warranty or service costs and the amount that should have been expensed, based on actual experience, sales contracts or sales agreements, differences between the way deposits are treated and the way they should be treated, differences in confirmations of **repurchase agreements**, deposit or other confirmed amounts and balances reported on the financial statements, and differences between what contracts imply should be recorded as a liability and what the company is doing.

Documentary symptoms for underrecording of liabilities include liabilities listed on bank confirmations but not recorded by the company, the presence of unrecorded liens, differences between contract amounts and loans recorded, interest expense with no recorded debt, writing off liabilities without payment of cash, significant purchases of assets without a comparable decrease in cash or increase in liabilities, and significant repayment of debt immediately prior to year-end, with new borrowing immediately after year-end.

Documentary symptoms provide the best opportunity to find contingent liabilities that should be recorded. Symptoms of possible underrecording include: identification of lawsuits by attorneys; payments to attorneys without acknowledged litigation; mention of litigation in corporate minutes; correspondence with governmental agencies such as the Environmental Protection Agency or the SEC; significant payments to plaintiffs and others; filing of an 8-K with the SEC; withdrawal or issuance of an other-than-clean audit opinion by predecessor auditors; or correspondence from previous auditors, banks, regulators, or others.

Proactively Searching for Symptoms Related to the Underreporting of Liabilities

In the limited partnership fraud discussed at the beginning of this chapter, the auditors found liens for loans on properties that were not supposed to have loans. Although dishonest bankers misled them, the auditors discovered the liens only because they were concerned that, under the client's lease arrangement, some lessees might be putting partnership properties at risk by not paying property taxes, utilities, and other expenses. In this case, a fraud symptom was discovered by accident. Rather than waiting for such accidents, proactively searching for fraud symptoms is much more effective.

Proactive searching for analytical symptoms means that we are searching for accounts that are unusual in some way (e.g., too high, too low, etc.). As discussed in Chapter 12, in determining whether accounts are unusual, changes and comparisons should be evaluated. Table 12.2 provided in Chapter 12 focused on revenue and receivable schemes; Table 13.2 is a similar table that focuses on liability schemes.

Focusing on Changes in Recorded Balances from Period to Period

Because of management's motivation to understate liabilities, you should look for fraud in both reported liabilities and liabilities that may not have been recorded. As noted in Table 13.2, you can focus on the changes in liability account balances by looking for changes in the actual numbers, by studying the statement of cash flows (which looks at actual change numbers but may not separately list every liability account), or by using horizontal analysis, which is our preferred method. In using these three methods to focus on changes in liability balances, you should compare balances over several years and focus on liabilities that have been eliminated. Also, be sure you investigate significant reductions in long-term liabilities and accruals. Furthermore, you should focus on service liabilities that have not been recorded or are recorded at significantly lower amounts than in previous periods and you should ensure that contingent liabilities that have been disclosed in the footnotes are not needed on the face of the financial statements.

Using horizontal analysis, you can quickly examine the percentage changes in the liability accounts and determine if they are unusual. For example, an expert who was retained as a witness in the ESM fraud case performed a horizontal analysis on ESM's balance sheets and income statements. What he found was liability (and other) account balances that were changing by 400 percent, 1,700 percent, 250 percent, and so forth, which are large changes, especially in accounts that had large balances. His conclusion was that someone was manipulating the financial statements because the changes were too large to be believable. As it turned out, management was manipulating the financial statements and plugging in numbers to make them balance.

When examining changes in account balances, remember that every liability account is a candidate for fraud. Therefore, in performing your horizontal analysis, you should look at each liability, consider the most common types of fraud exposures (those discussed in the first part of this chapter), and then look to see whether the kinds of changes are suggestive of that fraud. For example, if long-term notes payable changes from $2.1 million to $1.1 million and back to $2.1 million in three consecutive years, you might be concerned about year 2, especially considering the possibility that liabilities were paid off to be immediately restored after the end of the year. Similarly, if service or **warranty liabilities** decreased from $3.2 million to $2.2 million to $1.7 million at the same time total sales were increasing, you would probably be concerned that warranty liabilities were understated. Analytical symptoms are most diagnostic when you engage in the following process:

1. Ask what kind of fraud could be occurring.
2. Identify what symptoms those frauds would generate.
3. Determine whether those symptoms are being observed.
4. Determine whether what was observed is caused by fraud or by something else.

Focusing on Changes in Relationships from Period to Period

Focusing on changes in relationships to identify analytical fraud symptoms is one of the best ways to detect understatement of liability frauds. Some of the ratios that are most revealing in detecting liability fraud are listed in Table 13.3.

The second way to focus on financial statement relationships is to prepare common-size financial statements and perform vertical analysis. Using this approach, you compute each liability as a percent of total assets (or total liabilities and stockholders' equity) and then focus on the change in these percentages. In conducting this analysis, remember that large financial statement balances generally do not change much while small liability balances may change significantly and be normal. Ask yourself why every major change is occurring, and whether you think it is unusual, given other changes in the financial statements. Also, make sure you understand which balances should be changing due to economic factors or operating decisions and question balances that you would expect to change but that are staying constant. For example, purchasing significant amounts of **fixed assets** and not incurring additional long-term debt may be unusual, especially if the company does not have a large cash balance. Similarly, decrease in liabilities but increase in interest expense, or vice versa, would be rare.

Comparing Financial Statement Information with Other Companies

Generally, comparing a company's liability balances with those of other companies is not as useful as comparing revenues, accounts receivable, inventory, and other balances. A company can finance its operations in three different ways as follows:

- *Earnings*
- *Borrowing*
- *Owner (stockholder) investments*

The amount of each of these financing methods used is often a matter of management philosophy rather than industry norm. For example, in the computer industry, Hewlett-Packard (HP) has had very little debt and has financed its operations mostly from owner investments and earnings, while Texas Instruments has mostly financed its business through borrowing. However, the relationships between interest expense and debt, the amount of warranty expense as a percentage of sales, and other similar relationships

TABLE 13.3 SOME RATIOS USED IN DETECTING FRAUD

TYPE OF LIABILITY FRAUD	RATIOS TO EXAMINE
Underrecording accounts payable	1. Acid-test ratio (quick assets/current liabilities). 2. Current ratio (current assets/current liabilities). 3. Accounts payable/Purchases. 4. Accounts payable/Cost of goods sold. 5. Accounts payable/Total liabilities. 6. Accounts payable/Inventory. All these ratios should be examined over time and changes observed. The ratios focus on the reasonableness of the accounts payable balance relative to related account balances. Increases in the first two ratios and decreases in the last four ratios are most indicative of fraud.
Underrecording accrued liabilities including salaries, payroll taxes, interest, and rent	7. Various accruals/Number of days to accrue compared with same ratio in previous years. 8. Various accruals/Related expenses. The amount to be accrued depends on the length of time between the end of the accounting year and the last time expenses were recorded. You would probably be concerned about any lack of accruals or significant decreases in these ratios from previous years on a per-day basis. With certain accruals, you can examine the relationship between various expenses (e.g., payroll tax expense/salary expense) to see whether enough payroll taxes have been recorded.
Underrecording of unearned revenues (a liability)	9. Unearned revenue/Revenue. It is difficult to find good ratios to search for unrecorded, unearned revenues. Generally, to determine whether revenues have been recognized as earned when they are, in fact, unearned, you need to examine actual contracts and sales agreements to determine what services have to be performed or what products provided.
Underrecording of service (warranty) liabilities and other liabilities to perform something in the future (e.g., repurchase securities, repay deposits, etc.)	10. Warranty expense/Sales. The amount of warranty or service expense and liability should relate directly with sales volume. Ratios that reveal that deposits, repurchase agreements, or other similar liabilities are understated are more difficult to find.
Underrecording various liabilities (notes, mortgages, leases, pensions, etc.)	11. Interest expense/Notes payable. 12. Long-term debt/Stockholders' equity. 13. Various types of debt/Total assets. 14. Total liabilities/Total assets. 15. Pension expense/Salary expense. 16. Lease expense/Total fixed assets. In thinking about the kinds of ratios to examine, you need to focus on each individual liability on the balance sheet. The questions you should ask are: "What should this liability balance relate to, and has that relationship changed over time? If so, why?"
Not recording contingent liabilities	Ratios are not generally helpful for detecting un-recorded contingent liabilities. Generally, you will have to look for documentary symptoms to find unrecorded or undisclosed contingent liabilities.

can be compared across firms. For example, you would probably be very concerned if a company's warranty expense and liability were only 1 percent of sales, when all other companies in the same industry recorded warranty expense of 3 percent of sales.

Comparing Financial Statement Amounts with Assets They Are Supposed to Represent or with Nonfinancial Statement Factors

Because most liabilities do not represent specific assets, comparing liability balances with nonfinancial statement amounts is usually difficult. The notable exception, of course, is mortgage liabilities, which are loans that are secured with specific assets. You can examine assets on which mortgages are incurred. Eliminating a mortgage payable or finding no mortgages on new buildings (when the company practice is to mortgage all buildings) are fraud symptoms that should be investigated.

Actively Searching for "Accounting and Documentary" Symptoms

Documentary symptoms can be very helpful in detecting understatement of liability frauds. The specific documentary symptoms you search for vary according to the liability that is understated. Table 13.4 summarizes some of the most common kinds of documentary symptoms by type of liability. In most cases, queries can be designed using either commercial packages, such as ACL, or tailored queries to search for these symptoms.

Following up on symptoms observed is very important since there are so many different types of liabilities and ways in which they can be understated. Companies that are struggling financially have strong motivation to understate liabilities. Sometimes the understatements are small, but sometimes they are large (e.g., $350 million in the ESM case).

Because understated liabilities may involve only one or two omitted transactions, unusual information, such as surprise liens, surprise loan contracts, written-off debt, and surprise debt on bank confirmations, must be followed up carefully. In many cases, management will offer alternative explanations, such as the lien or contract is a mistake, it is personal debt, or it is a line of credit never activated. You should make sure that management's explanations are true and support the explanations with corroborating evidence to the extent deemed necessary under the circumstances.

Before leaving understatement of liability fraud, it is important to note that finding understated liabilities is one of the most difficult frauds to find. In some cases, the understated liabilities are with accounts, vendors, or lenders with whom the company has no other business or has a reported zero balance at the time. Searching for unrecorded liabilities by examining board minutes, bank and vendor confirmations, and letters from attorneys can be fruitful. Also, anytime evidence (such as a tip) emerges that indicates a liability might exist, it should be vigorously examined. In many ways, finding unrecorded liability frauds is the same as finding off-book frauds since no evidence of the fraud exists in the books of the company. Asset or revenue frauds, on the other hand, are often easier to detect because they involve reported assets that can be examined.

> **Remember this ...**
>
> *Understatement of liability frauds is often difficult to detect. A common way to commit understatement of liability fraud is to understate or hide liabilities; however, in some major frauds, the perpetrators can manipulate liabilities in more complicated ways. Abnormal analytical symptoms or documentary symptoms relating to liability accounts are helpful for detecting these fraud schemes. Financial statement analysis focusing on changes in recorded balances and relationships from period to period, comparing information with that of other companies, and comparing statement amounts with actual assets or with nonfinancial statement factors, is important for proactively searching for fraud symptoms.*

Overstatement of Asset Fraud

Overstatement of asset fraud can occur in many ways. Most physical assets are valued at historical cost, less accumulated depreciation. As such, assets could be improperly depreciated or amortized. The value of many assets should be written down, and a corresponding expense or loss recorded, if the asset is permanently impaired. GAAP includes different impairment standards for different types of assets. If the impaired asset values are not properly valued, the company's expenses or losses will be understated and net income overstated. In addition, expenditures may be improperly capitalized as assets or reported asset values may be too high for other reasons.

As an example of failure to record asset impairment, consider the case of New Jersey Resources Corporation (NJR):

NJR, an energy company, allegedly failed to recognize an impairment of the carrying value of its oil and gas properties, resulting in the overstatement of the company's net income by $6.3 million. Also, as already discussed, Waste Management used a non-GAAP method of capitalizing interest on landfill development costs (thus recognizing assets that should have been expenses) and made repeated fourth-quarter adjustments to improperly reduce depreciation expenses on its equipment cumulatively from the beginning of the year, thus overstating its landfills and other assets.

TABLE 13.4 DOCUMENTARY SYMPTOMS OF FRAUD

TYPES OF LIABILITY UNDERSTATEMENT	SYMPTOMS TO ACTIVELY SEARCH FOR
Accounts Payable	1. Payments made in subsequent period for liabilities that existed at the balance sheet date and were not recorded. 2. More inventory counted than identified through purchasing and inventory records. 3. Receiving reports near the end of a period, without corresponding purchase invoices. 4. Amounts listed on vendor statements not recorded as purchases. 5. Differences on confirmations not easily reconciled with purchase records. 6. Discrepancies in cutoff tests.
Accrued Liabilities	7. 1099s with no withholdings, where withholdings should exist. 8. Employees with no withholdings. 9. Vendor statements (utilities, etc.) where no liability is recorded. 10. Loans with no interest. 11. Leased buildings with no rent or lease expense.
Unearned Revenues	12. Reclassification entries near the end of the period that increase earned revenues and decrease unearned revenues. 13. Differences between customer confirmations and company records about how much revenue has been earned.
Service (Warranty) Liabilities, Deposits, Repurchase Agreements—Obligations to Perform Services, Deliver Products, or Return Money in the Future	14. Inconsistencies in customer agreements or contracts and recording of expenses. 15. Differences in customer confirmations regarding client obligations (e.g., repurchase agreements, etc.). 16. Warranty payments that exceed warranty liabilities. 17. Deposits recognized as revenues.
Liabilities to Pay Money (Notes Payable, Mortgage Payable, Pension Liabilities, Lease Liabilities, etc.)	18. Liens on properties that are supposed to be paid for. 19. Approval of loans by board of directors but not listed as liabilities. 20. Loans listed by banks on bank confirmations but not recorded by company. 21. Lack of pension accrual. 22. Lease payments with no lease liability. 23. Conservative assumptions used to calculate pension liability. 24. Unusually large credits on bank statements.
Contingent Liabilities	25. Discussion of contingent liabilities in board minutes. 26. Contingencies discussed in footnotes. 27. Significant payments to lawyers. 28. Lawsuits brought to your attention for the first time in attorney letters. 29. Letters from regulators, such as OSHA, EPA, SEC, etc.

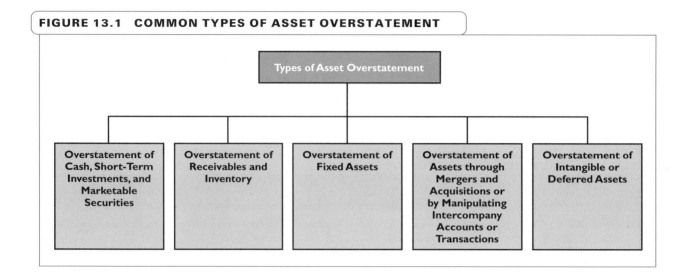

FIGURE 13.1 COMMON TYPES OF ASSET OVERSTATEMENT

Types of Asset Overstatement

- Overstatement of Cash, Short-Term Investments, and Marketable Securities
- Overstatement of Receivables and Inventory
- Overstatement of Fixed Assets
- Overstatement of Assets through Mergers and Acquisitions or by Manipulating Intercompany Accounts or Transactions
- Overstatement of Intangible or Deferred Assets

Identifying Asset Overstatement Fraud

Most organizations have several types of assets on their balance sheets. Waste Management was an alleged example of the overstatement of tangible assets. As with liabilities, different assets can be overstated in different ways. Figure 13.1 identifies the five most common assets that are overstated.

Improper Capitalization of Costs as Assets That Should Be Expensed in the Current Period

Most financial statement frauds occur in smaller, less-established companies. These companies are often not very old and, in many cases, are not very profitable. In trying to make their financial statements look better, a way to overstate assets is to capitalize as **intangible assets** such things as start-up costs, advertising costs, research and development, marketing costs, salaries, and other initial costs. Management often argues that it is in the start-up or development phase and therefore these costs should be capitalized as **deferred charges** and written off against profitable future operations. In some cases, capitalizing these charges is justified; in other cases, it is clearly fraudulent. Whether these costs should be capitalized usually depends on whether the costs are incurred to generate future revenues and whether sufficient future revenues are likely to be generated, against which the costs can be written off.

CAUTION *For costs to be capitalized, they must have been incurred for the purpose of generating future revenues and those revenues must be likely to be generated. If costs do not meet these requirements, they should be expensed in the period in which they are incurred.*

Consider the following cases where litigation or SEC action took place:[1]

Computer Science Corporation (CSC) developed and sold computer-related services including one service known as "Computicket" (CT). CSC's policy regarding capitalizing development costs stated that CSC would initially capitalize development costs rather than treat them as charges against current income. When a system (such as CT) became fully operational (defined as generating revenue in excess of expenses), CSC would begin to amortize the capitalized expenses over a specified period of time, presumably over the revenue-generating period. At one point, CSC had approximately $6.8 million in capitalized costs for CT. In a registration statement filed with the SEC, CSC stated that it expected to begin amortizing CT's capitalized expenses in the future.

From its inception, CT failed to meet internal projections for market share. CT supposedly experienced problems getting equipment installed, and it had been running deficits of $500,000 per month. In addition, CT lost a major contract. Moreover, CSC attempted, without success, to sell CT proprietary packages. Eventually, CSC had gone so far as to discuss the abandonment of CT. The inference was clear: the likelihood of CT's commercial success became progressively more doubtful with the passage of time.

An investor sued CSC for violations of SEC Rule 10b-5. The court stated that the failure to disclose facts indicating that CT was not successful was an omission "to state a material fact necessary, in order to make the statements not misleading."

Capitalizing costs that should be expensed has the effect of increasing net income by the same amount of the capitalized costs, because expenses that should be deducted from revenues are not deducted until future periods when they are amortized. In many cases, these illicit capitalized costs are not written off for many years into the future.

The Slippery Slope of Earnings Management

Like many financial statement frauds, the inappropriate capitalization of deferred charges does not occur overnight. Instead, it often starts out as a company capitalizes small amounts of deferred charges that are, at worst, questionable. With time, however, what started as a seemingly innocent case of "earnings management" progresses to the point where management capitalizes costs that are not even remotely proper under GAAP.

Financial statement fraud often begins when management adopts aggressive accounting methods or assumptions when a seemingly innocent change in accounting methods will give the organization the profits it needs to meet an earnings target. Soon, however—like starting down a slippery slope—the pressure to commit fraud gains speed and momentum. Before long, the company's operations are failing to provide the profits needed to satisfy investors or lenders, and manipulating the accounting is the organization's only hope of appearing profitable. At some point, the company must focus so much energy on managing the fraud that there is no way to manage the operations.

At this point, what began as a seemingly innocent tweaking of the numbers has grown to the point where it will soon consume the organization. The pressure to meet financial targets and the history of using accounting methods to meet such targets pushes management so far down the slope that it is nearly impossible to climb back up. In this situation, justifications for absurd capitalizations of inappropriate costs are considered rational as management engages in motivated reasoning to justify their behavior.

Unfortunately, organizations that start down this slippery slope often end up involving several other employees in the fraud. Many times, these include lower-level employees who go along with the fraud even though they believe it is wrong and, acting on their own, they would never lower their integrity to such levels. Their justification for going along often involves a belief that others above them are ultimately responsible for the decision. At this point, the organization's ethical values have essentially rotted away and the fraud grows so large that it can no longer be contained. Before long, many victims, including shareholders and lenders, suffer when the fraud comes to light for all to see.

The most prominent example of a company improperly capitalizing expenditures involved the World-Com fraud:

In its amended complaint against WorldCom, the SEC alleged that WorldCom overstated the income reported in its financial statements by approximately $9 billion. One way WorldCom allegedly accomplished this overstatement was to improperly reduce its operating expenses by capitalizing certain expenses as assets. As pressure built to meet earnings targets in an industry that was suffering from excess supply and dwindling demand, WorldCom turned to earnings management through fraud schemes to buoy its financial performance. Specifically, senior officials at the company directed accounting managers to transfer certain "line costs" and "computer costs" (which should have been reported as current operating expenses) to its asset accounts. This transfer caused the company to materially understate expenses and overstate net income and allowed the company to report earnings that were in line with analysts' estimates.

Inflated Assets through Mergers and Acquisitions (or Restructuring) or by Manipulating Intercompany Accounts and/or Transactions

In several financial statement fraud cases, companies involved in **mergers** or **acquisitions** overstated their assets (or overstated their liabilities by creating cookie jar reserves, as discussed earlier). Schemes involved inappropriately recording market values for assets, having the wrong entity act as the purchaser of the other entity, improperly allocating book values to assets (e.g., assigning higher book values to assets that will be amortized or depreciated over longer periods or not depreciated at all, and lower values to assets that will be amortized or depreciated over shorter periods), or other means. In fact, Warren Buffet, chairman of

Berkshire Hathaway and world-famous investor, included the following comments in his March 1999 letter to his company's shareholders[2]

Many managements purposefully work at manipulating numbers and deceiving investors when it comes to mergers and big restructurings. ... During mergers, major auditing firms sometimes point out the possibilities for a little accounting magic (or a lot).

As an example of financial statement fraud associated with a merger, consider the case of Malibu Capital Corporation:

For at least three and a half years, Lehman, Lucchesi & Walker (LLW) served as the auditors for Malibu Capital Corporation. Malibu subsequently merged with Colstar Petroleum Corporation. Prior to the merger with Colstar, Malibu supposedly had no business purpose other than to merge with or acquire one or a small number of private companies. LLW gave Malibu an unqualified opinion on the financial statements. These statements identified Colstar as the "acquired corporation." The combination was treated as a "purchase" of Colstar by Malibu, and Colstar's primary asset was adjusted up from $11,055 to $1,342,600.

Under generally accepted accounting principles, the combination should have been treated as a "reverse purchase" with Colstar as the "acquiring corporation" with no adjustment to Colstar's assets. As a result of the improper accounting treatment, Malibu allegedly overstated its assets 102 times. In this case, the asset was written up by having the wrong entity act as the purchaser.

In another case, Chester Holdings, Ltd., assets were overstated in a merger by overstating the fair value of the assets. The SEC alleged that officers and directors of Chester Holdings overstated the value of consideration paid for five acquisitions of assets and businesses and overstated the value of assets acquired in the company's financial statements. For example, the officers claimed that the company acquired a knitting company for $14 million in stock when the fair value of the assets was worth no more than $4.9 million. This case shows that in any instances of a revaluation of assets or a merger of two companies, the values used may not be appropriate, especially when the companies merging are related parties, when companies are struggling, or when they have a strong incentive to report profits. In addition to merger-related problems, fraud is sometimes perpetrated by manipulating intercompany accounts or transactions.

As an example of using intercompany transactions to commit fraud, consider the AFCO fraud:

AFCO started as a medical-dental equipment leasing business. The company was mildly successful during its first two years. Several new branches were formed, including a land development company. The land development company purchased 1,000 acres of undeveloped property and began to develop an "old English" family resort in northern Utah called Sherwood Hills. As the resort struggled financially, limited partnerships were sold, mostly to physicians and dentists, to raise money for additional development and marketing.

AFCO had several other projects including Glenmoor Village which was touted as Utah's biggest real estate development. As with Sherwood Hills, Glenmoor Village was extremely expensive and failed to create a positive cash flow. Because of severe cash shortages and an inability to obtain additional bank financing, AFCO turned to middle-class homeowners to fund the company. AFCO would promise to service homeowners' second mortgages and pay each homeowner an additional 10 percent on the money used. Since second mortgage rates were approximately 20 percent, AFCO was paying nearly 30 percent for the money borrowed from these homeowner. AFCO was very accommodating: if a homeowner did not want the return in cash, it offered to lease a BMW or a Mercedes for the homeowner and promised to service the lease.

Returns promised to homeowners were based on inflated financial statements and imaginary resources. The investment was nothing more than a Ponzi scheme. Early investors were paid returns from subsequent investments, and the second mortgage payments were never paid. When the scheme finally failed, the assistant U.S. attorney in the district of Utah called the president of AFCO "one of the most ruthless swindlers seen in these parts in years." In the end, he had sweet-talked about 650 people into investing about $70 million. He later declared bankruptcy, foreclosing his investors' chances of getting their money back.

In getting people to invest in AFCO, the company used fraudulent financial statements to make the company look better than it really was. By transferring funds within the organization, and by manipulating intercompany accounts, the company was able to create the appearance of success. The financial statements used by the company and restated as they should have been are shown in Figure 13.2. In this case, the outside CPA firm issued an adverse opinion because some of the assets on AFCO's financial statements had been stated at fair market value instead of at cost and because a large portion of AFCO's assets were comprised of a related party transaction. Because of the related-party nature of the sale, the CPA firm could not determine whether the transaction was arm's length.

In AFCO's case, the adverse opinion served as a significant warning to investors. As it turned out, the sale of land to the related company, the income from this sale, the receivable arising from that transaction, and the interest on the receivable were all misstatements generated by a fictitious sale. When the phantom sale and its impacts

were subtracted from AFCO's balance sheet, all that remained was $1,299 in cash and some real estate whose cost financial statement readers could not evaluate because it was recorded at market value. Total assets were far less than the approximate $21 million represented by the company.

FIGURE 13.2 AFCO FINANCIAL STATEMENTS

AFCO
Balance Sheet and Income Statement

	Originally Issued	Restated
BALANCE SHEET		
Assets		
Current assets:		
Cash	$ 1,299	$ 1,299
Current portion of contract receivable	276,084	0
Interest receivable	124,197	0
Total current assets	$ 401,580	1,299
Contact receivable long-term portion	8,373,916	0
Investment property:		
Real estate Jackson Village (at market)	$10,832,480	
Real estate Mountainland Hills	1,800,000	?
	$12,632,480	?
Total assets	$21,407,976	$ 1,299+?
Liabilities and stockholders' equity		
Current liabilities:		
Accounts payable to related parties	$ 27,000	$ 27,000
Accrued interest	176,965	176,965
Current portion of long-term debt	902,944	902,944
Total current liabilities	$ 1,106,909	$ 1,106,909
Long-term debt less current portion	$12,781,668	$12,781,688
Deferred income taxes	$ 3,041,729	$ 3,041,729
Contingencies		
Stockholders' equity:		
Common stock, par value $1.00, authorized 50,000 shares; issued and outstanding, 1,000 shares	$ 1,000	$ 1,000
Appraisal increase	1,672,626	0
Retained earnings	2,804,044	?
	$ 4,477,670	
	$21,398,976	
INCOME STATEMENT		
Gain on sales of Mountain Hills	$ 4,887,000	0
Interest income	324,197	0
Total income	$ 5,211,197	
Interest expense	$ 627,796	$ 627,796
General and administrative expenses	27,190	27,190
	$ 654,986	$ 654,986
Income before income taxes	$ 4,556,211	$ (654,986)
Provision for federal and state income taxes	2,258,855	0
Net income	$ 2,297,356	$ (654,986)

STOP & THINK *Why would so many people invest in a company like AFCO? What could investors have done to have prevented themselves from falling into investment schemes such as this?*

Overstatement of Fixed Assets (Property, Plant, and Equipment)

Fixed assets can be overstated in many ways. Some of the most common are leaving worthless or expired assets on the books (not writing them off), underreporting depreciation expense or overstating residual values (e.g., Waste Management), recording fixed assets at inflated values (sometimes through sham or related-party purchases), or just fabricating fixed assets to record on the financial statements. One company, for example, recorded assets on its balance sheet at their "estimated fair market value" when, in fact, the assets had been fully depreciated in prior years.

Sometimes these asset overstatements become quite significant. For example, *The Wall Street Journal* carried an article titled "Audit Showing Baby Bells Can't Locate $5 Billion in Gear Could Spur Rate Cuts." This article described how the Baby Bell companies (e.g., Bell Atlantic Corp., SBC Communications, Inc., Nynex Telephone Company, Southern Bell Telephone, and Bell South) could not locate $5 billion in telecommunications and other equipment that they were carrying on their balance sheets as assets. Whether these companies committed fraud is a question that would have to be investigated, but the article reported how a Federal Communications Commission (FCC) audit of these companies could not find nearly one-tenth of the equipment it surveyed and was recommending that the assets be written off.

As an example of overstatement of asset fraud, consider the following case:

One of the major fraud schemes perpetrated by Lincoln Savings and Loan involved purchasing property at inflated amounts and then reselling the property at even higher amounts to "straw buyers." This "land flipping" resulted in overstated assets on the balance sheet and unrealistically high profits when the land was "sold." Many of these transactions took place at Lincoln, and most of them happened on or near the end of quarters so as to inflate quarterly income. In one transaction involving property known as the "Continental Ranch," Lincoln purchased land at arguably inflated prices and recorded the asset on its financial statements. Then, on September 30, 1986, when Lincoln was desperate for profits, it sold 1,300 acres of the ranch to R. A. Homes (a straw buyer) for $25 million, including $5 million in cash and a $20 million note receivable. What was not easily detectable by the auditors and others was that a related entity loaned R. A. Homes $3 million on September 25, 1986, and another $2 million on November 12, 1986. In essence, Lincoln "paid the down payment to itself." This transaction, like many others in the company, resulted in inflated assets on the balance sheet and overstated income on the income statement.

A final way to overstate fixed assets is to underrecord depreciation expense. This can be done by using asset lives that are too long, allocating too much cost in a basket purchase of land and building to land that is not depreciated, using salvage values that are too high, failing to make the accrual entries for depreciation, or reversing the accrual entries as Waste Management did.

Cash and Short-Term Investment Fraud

In several famous cases, **marketable securities** were materially overstated, but it is generally considered quite hard to overstate cash because the balances can be easily confirmed with financial institutions. However, this is not always the case, as in the Parmalat fraud where the company overstated billions of dollars in cash by falsifying audit confirmations. Recently, a similar case came to light when Satyam Computer Services, an Indian company, was found to have recorded fictitious cash balances exceeding $1 billion.

Other fraud schemes involving cash include fraudulently reporting cash that is restricted (i.e., the company cannot spend it) as unrestricted on the balance sheet. However, what is more common with respect to cash is to have employees or vendors steal significant amounts of cash such that it results in misstated financial statements. For example, consider the following three cases: (1) a small thrift where a vice president embezzled several million dollars over a period of 16 years; (2) a small, five-branch bank where a proof operator embezzled $7 million over eight years; and (3) General Motors where one car dealer embezzled $436 million. These large cash thefts resulted in financial statement fraud of a different type than we have been discussing in this book—financial statement misstatement without upper-management's knowledge.

Compared to cash, management can usually overstate marketable securities more easily, especially securities that are not widely traded. What many people do not realize is that *publicly traded securities* involve more than just securities traded on the large stock exchanges such as the New York Stock Exchange, the

American Stock Exchange, and the NASDAQ. Many smaller, over-the-counter stocks are traded only rarely and are not actively listed even by over-the-counter stock exchanges. These stocks are marketed through "pink sheets," which list the price of these stocks. Pink sheets are distributed daily to brokers and listing dealers who might be willing to buy and sell them. Valuing these securities is often difficult, and sometimes dishonest management will materially overstate the security's value. For example, one company used sham transactions with related parties to inflate the value of securities listed as current assets on the balance sheet. Another case involved a minority investment in a separate company that was carried at several million dollars. However, the company invested in had negative stockholders' equity and losses of several million dollars in each of the preceding five years. The investment was worthless and should have been written off.

Another way assets and liabilities can be manipulated is to either keep liabilities off the balance sheet or transfer troubled assets off the balance sheet into another entity and record an investment or receivable from that entity. This scheme allowed Enron and others to commit massive fraud:

Similar to Enron, PNC Financial Services Group, Inc., also used special purpose entities (SPEs) to get poor-performing assets off the company's books. This case was the SEC's first enforcement action resulting from a company's accounting for and disclosure of off-balance-sheet arrangements involving SPEs. The SEC found that, in violation of GAAP, PNC transferred from its financial statements approximately $762 million of volatile, troubled, or underperforming loans (assets for a financial institution) and venture capital assets to three SPEs created by a third-party financial institution in 2001. These transactions resulted in material overstatements of PNC's earnings. The SEC's order stated that PNC should have included the SPEs in its financial statements because it retained the risks of ownership.

Another well-known case involving off-balance-sheet debt was Adelphia Corporation. The SEC alleged that Adelphia failed to record over $2.3 billion in bank debt by deliberately shifting those liabilities onto books of Adelphia's off-balance-sheet, unconsolidated affiliates. Adelphia's senior management disguised the liabilities by creating sham transactions backed by fictitious documents that gave the false impression that Adelphia had actually repaid the notes.

Finally, in September 2008, Lehman Brothers Holdings, Inc., filed the largest bankruptcy filing in U.S. history. In early 2010, a 2,200-page bankruptcy report was issued and called into question Lehman's accounting for fraudulently structuring transactions known as repo 105 and repo 108 sales in order to structure a loan as a sale of assets so that the company's financial statements could appear stronger. With repo 105, assets valued at $105 are used as collateral for a short-term loan of $100. Outcome of the case, including whether Lehman's accounting was fraudulent, is still pending.

Overstatement of Accounts Receivable (Not Related to Revenue Recognition) or Inventory (Not Related to Cost of Goods Sold)

In Chapter 12, we discussed the inflation of accounts receivable in conjunction with the recording of fictitious revenues and the overstatement of inventory in conjunction with the understatement of cost of goods sold. Sometimes, however, accounts receivable or inventory can be overstated in an attempt to overstate assets and cover thefts of cash rather than to overstate reported income. That was the case with ESM where management had stolen approximately $350 million and covered the theft by creating a fictitious receivable from a related entity. In the Phar-Mor case, one of the reasons inventory was overstated was to offset cash that Micky Monus had taken out of the business to support his now-defunct World Basketball League.

Summary of Overstatement of Asset Fraud Exposures

Table 13.5 summarizes some of the most common asset overstatement fraud schemes used.

Identifying and Actively Searching for Asset Overstatement Fraud Symptoms

In many ways, the methods used to overstate assets are quite similar to those used to detect understated liabilities. That is, often just one or two large fictitious accounting entries, rather than a series of smaller entries, result in asset overstatement. In some ways, however, asset overstatements are easier to detect than other types of financial statement fraud because the overstated assets are included on the balance sheet, whereas understated liabilities are not on the financial statements. Fraud investigators can start their detection

TABLE 13.5 FRAUDS INVOLVING OVERSTATEMENT OF ASSETS

KIND OF ASSET OVERSTATEMENT	ACCOUNTS INVOLVED	FRAUD SCHEMES
Improperly capitalize costs that should be expensed	Various deferred charges and intangible assets accounts	1. Inappropriately capitalize as assets various kinds of start-up costs, marketing costs, salaries, research and development costs, and other such expenditures.
Inflate assets through mergers, acquisitions, and restructuring or through manipulation of inter-company accounts and transactions	Can be any asset	2. Use market values rather than book values to record assets. 3. Have the wrong entity be the "purchaser." 4. Allocate costs among assets in inappropriate ways. 5. Record fictitious assets or inflate the value of assets in intercompany accounts or transactions.
Overstate fixed assets	Land, Buildings, Equipment, Leasehold Improvements, and so forth.	6. Sham purchases and sales of assets with "straw buyers." 7. Overstate asset costs with related parties. 8. Record too little depreciation. 9. Collude with outside parties to overstate assets (e.g., allocating inventory costs to fixed assets).
Misstate cash and marketable securities	Cash, Marketable Securities, and other short-term assets	10. Misstate marketable securities with the aid of related parties. 11. Misappropriate cash resulting in misstated financial statements without management's knowledge.
Overstate accounts receivable or inventory to hide thefts of cash by management	Accounts Receivable, Inventory	12. Cover thefts of cash or other assets by overstating receivables or inventory.

process by examining the assets that make up the reported amounts, determining whether they really exist and whether they are listed in the appropriate amounts and periods.

In the following paragraphs, we discuss asset overstatement fraud according to the five types of asset overstatement discussed earlier. Because the various types of asset overstatements are different, we will discuss what the relevant symptoms are and how to actively search for them. Although this approach is different from the method used in previous sections, it is more efficient, given the nature of the assets involved. Once again, we will not separately discuss control, lifestyle, behavioral, or tips and complaint symptoms for each category of asset overstatement because, for the most part, they are not unique to asset overstatement schemes. Rather, we will discuss analytical and documentary symptoms and then discuss other symptoms where appropriate. Remember, this emphasis does not mean that these other symptoms are not important. In fact, in some cases, they are the best type of fraud symptoms. However, they are more generic and can be symptomatic of many different types of fraud, not just asset overstatement.

Inappropriately Capitalizing Costs That Should Be Expensed

Before discussing specific analytical and documentary symptoms related to inappropriately capitalizing costs, we will discuss some general characteristics of these transactions. In identifying symptoms, the first thing you should ask is whether these types of deferred charges exist on the balance sheet. In many companies, they do not. When they do exist, you should always consider them candidates for fraud and then convince yourself that their capitalization is appropriate, rather than assuming that they are appropriate and then determining if they are fraudulent. This more skeptical approach is often justified because these assets are often intangible and can easily be abused. Questions you should ask include the following:

1. Do the deferred charges have future benefits that are specifically identifiable?
2. Is it likely that there will be sufficient future revenues and profits against which the costs can be specifically written off, and if so, when?
3. Are the deferred charges the types that could be acceptable under GAAP (in most cases, for

example, research and development costs are not) and are capitalized by other similar companies?

4. Are there strong incentives to manage earnings in this company?

5. How are the deferred charges or intangible assets valued? Are these methods proper?

Analytical Fraud Symptoms

In most cases, analytical symptoms relate to what the size of the deferred charges are on the balance sheet relative to prior periods and to other similar companies or whether the same types of assets exist at other companies. You should be concerned, for example, if deferred charges make up a major portion of a company's total assets. Other analytical symptoms might include the size of various deferred charges (e.g., advertising costs) relative to the related expenses (e.g., advertising) on the income statement. You would probably be less concerned with a company that capitalizes only a small part of its advertising costs than you would with a company that capitalizes a large portion of its advertising costs.

As stated earlier, the four kinds of analysis that can be used in searching for analytical fraud symptoms are as follows:

1. Comparing changes and trends in financial statement account balances
2. Comparing changes and trends in financial statement relationships
3. Comparing financial statement balances with nonfinancial information (see Chapter 11) or other information, such as the number or quality of the assets they represent
4. Comparing financial statement balances and policies with those used by other similar companies

Regarding nonfinancial information, if a company is making acquisitions of additional entities or entering new ventures, you might expect additional capitalization of deferred charges. In this case, you could determine whether any significant events have occurred for which it would make sense to capitalize these expenditures. When looking at trends, you would probably be quite concerned, for example, if the amount of deferred charges increased substantially without the occurrence of significant events that might trigger such capitalization. In addition, you would normally expect more capitalization in the early years of a business rather than in later years. Thus, it would be unusual for the deferred charge accounts to increase as the company became

more mature. If anything, you would expect these balances to decrease over time.

Examining changes in the deferred charge financial statement relationships from period to period is an important exercise. You would probably also want to compare the financial statement amounts and capitalization policies with those of other similar companies. Some of the most appropriate financial statement relationships on which to focus include the following:

- *Total deferred charges/Total assets*
- *Total deferred charges/Total intangible assets*
- *Deferred charge write-offs (amortization)/Deferred charge balance*

Through examining these and similar ratios over time, you could quickly determine whether deferred charges are increasing as a percentage of total assets or total intangible assets and what percentage of deferred charges are being written off or amortized each year.

If, when you compare your company with similar companies, you note that your client is the only firm capitalizing certain expenditures as deferred charges, you should probably be skeptical. If a company is capitalizing certain costs while other similar firms are expensing them in the current period, you should ask yourself: "What is unique about my client that makes capitalizing more appropriate for them than for these other companies?" If you cannot arrive at a clear, defensible answer to that question, you should probably recognize that your client's income is being inflated.

Accounting or Documentary Symptoms

As with other types of frauds, documentary symptoms are of two types: (1) general symptoms that could relate to most financial statement fraud schemes and (2) documentary symptoms that relate to improper capitalization of costs that should be expensed in the current period. Some of the general asset overstatement symptoms will be presented here and then not repeated for other asset overstatement schemes:

- *Asset-related transactions not recorded in a complete or timely manner or improperly recorded as to amount, accounting period, classification, or entity policy*
- *Unsupported or unauthorized asset-related balances or transactions*
- *Last-minute asset adjustments that significantly improve financial results*
- *Missing documents related to assets*

- *Unavailability of other than photocopied documents to support asset transactions when documents in original form are supposed to exist*
- *Asset-related ledgers that do not balance*
- *Unusual discrepancies between the entity's asset-related records and corroborating evidence or management explanations*

Documentary symptoms specifically related to capitalization of costs as assets that should be expensed include invoices from related parties that could misstate the nature of expenses, year-end reclassifications or journal entries that reduce recorded expenses and increase recorded deferred charges, and differences between the way costs are described on invoices and the way they are recorded in the accounting records.

In many cases, examining the exposures and motivations may reveal an incentive to overstate assets that may be more important than searching for specific documentary or analytical symptoms. For example, management is more likely to stretch what they consider to be appropriate accounting when strong incentives to show profits are present, when the organization is new or is in an industry where capitalization may or may not be appropriate, or where financial results and operating characteristics could motivate misstatement. In one case, for example, a firm capitalized significant costs while other firms in the same industry expensed similar expenditures. After lengthy litigation, it was determined that the capitalization was improper and that the company should have been using the same accounting methods as its competitors.

Overstating Assets through Mergers, Acquisitions, or Restructurings or Manipulating Intercompany Accounts or Transactions

As with improper capitalization, understanding the general context of a merger or an intercompany transaction may be more important in determining whether fraud exists than trying to identify specific analytical or documentary symptoms. For example, when concerned about overstatement of assets through a merger, you should ask the following five questions:

1. Are the accounts used by the merged companies appropriate?
2. Is the way the merger was recorded appropriate given the nature of the companies involved?
3. Are the after-merger book values higher or lower than the pre-merger amounts and, if so, why?

4. What motivated the merger?
5. Is the company treated as the purchaser appropriate?

Again, with mergers, acquisitions, and restructurings, understanding management, the motivations affecting management, the nature of the companies involved, whether the merged companies were related parties, and what financial results or operating characteristics could have motivated the merger are important. For example, several companies, including Cendant and Kimberly-Clark, have allegedly entered mergers so as to create large merger reserves that could be reversed into income to create better post-merger results. The SEC accused Kimberly-Clark of improperly accounting for merger-related reserves. The company took a $1.44 billion charge in relation to an acquisition. Periodic reevaluations of its reserve balance determined that the original estimate for certain of its merger-related reserves was too high. Instead of reducing the reserve, as required by GAAP, the company reallocated excess amounts to other merger-related programs or to new programs. The company also allegedly released into earnings certain amounts of its merger-related reserves without adequate support. Good fraud detection efforts require that examiners always look at how reserve accruals were subsequently used. Were they used in the way they were established to be used? If not, were excess reserves handled according to GAAP?

Analytical Fraud Symptoms

Analytical fraud symptoms are usually not very helpful in determining asset overstatements related to mergers or restructurings. With analytical symptoms, you are comparing trends and changes. When a merger or another change in the form of a business entity occurs, you have a new entity that has no history. As a result, you usually cannot look for either changes in account balances or financial statement relationships. The one exception that may be helpful is to compare asset ratios for the individual companies prior to the merger and the combined company after the merger. By looking at such ratios as total intangible assets divided by total assets, total fixed assets divided by total assets, and total current assets divided by total assets, you can quickly get an idea of how the structure of the companies has changed. You would probably be concerned, for example, if the total intangible assets as a percentage of total assets increased from an average of 10 percent in the two previous companies to 40 percent of total assets in the combined company.

Comparing the recorded post-merger assets with the actual assets they are supposed to represent is often helpful. If reported asset values have increased substantially, for example, you should check to see that the assets are not listed on the balance sheet at amounts that exceed their fair market values. Unfortunately, when mergers occur, finding similar companies against which the financial statement balances of your company can be compared is difficult.

Accounting or Documentary Symptoms

When a merger occurs, one of the first steps should be to make sure that the accounting methods are appropriate and consistent with accounting standards. After that, you can examine the specific merger or intercompany transactions to make sure that the transactions and amounts make sense. If, for example, a merger or intercompany transaction was between related parties, you should probably make sure that the amounts used (such as market values of assets) are appropriate. Finding inconsistencies between appraised and recorded amounts for assets is an excellent documentary fraud symptom. Similarly, if more of the post-merger assets have longer amortization or depreciation periods than the assets of previous companies, you should probably examine them closely. In one company, for example, the post-merger asset values were significantly inflated over the same assets in the pre-merger companies. Upon further analysis, examiners determined that the lesser-known merged company did not really exist. It was a fabricated company set up to inflate the financial results.

CAUTION *Anytime transactions take place between related companies, these transactions should be carefully scrutinized. These transactions are often subject to inappropriate accounting manipulations or fraud. Related-party transactions must be properly disclosed in the financial statements. Fraud perpetrators often use these transactions to inflate income and assets or remove debt from the balance sheet.*

Overstatement of Fixed Assets (e.g., Property, Plant, and Equipment)

Overstated fixed assets generally arise from one of the following three ways:

1. Inflated amounts are recorded in non-arm's-length purchases.
2. Assets are not written down to their appropriate values because insufficient depreciation is recorded,

they are obsolete, or their values are otherwise impaired.
3. Assets are fictitiously recorded in financial statement accounts.

In the Penn Central fraud case, railroad cars that had been abandoned in old mine shafts for many years were still being carried on the balance sheet at significant book values. These "assets" had been abandoned and could not have been recovered even if the company had wanted to, because in many cases, the railroad tracks that led to the mineshafts had been removed and the railroad ties had been sold to landscaping companies. Similarly, in another case, an oil company inflated the value of several fixed assets including a refinery that was no longer in use and oil reserves in the ground.

Analytical Symptoms

All four types of analysis can be performed to determine whether fixed assets are overstated. Horizontal analysis, analysis of the statement of cash flows, or comparisons of account balances from period to period can be used to determine how much the fixed asset accounts have changed. Unrealistically large changes in land, property, equipment, or other fixed asset balances could indicate that fraud is occurring. Fixed asset relationships can also be examined by computing ratios such as the following:

- *Total fixed assets/Total assets*
- *Individual fixed asset account balances/Total fixed assets*
- *Total fixed assets/Long-term debt*
- *Depreciation expense for various categories of assets/Assets being depreciated*
- *Accumulated depreciation/Depreciable assets (per asset category)*

The first two ratios provide evidence about whether fixed asset balances are reasonable relative to other asset balances. The third ratio identifies the relationship between debt and fixed assets, providing a measure of solvency. If fixed assets increase significantly while long-term debt does not, a fraud may exist, especially if evidence that cash, marketable securities, or other assets used to purchase the fixed assets is not present. The last two ratios examine whether fixed assets are being adequately depreciated.

Vertical analysis can also be used to determine the changes in financial statement balances and relationships over time. You might be concerned, for example, if fixed assets increased from 50 percent of total assets to 70 percent of total assets at a time when the revenues of the company were relatively stable. Because fixed assets are tangible, you can compare the financial statement balances with the actual assets to determine whether the recorded amounts represent assets that actually exist and are recorded at appropriate amounts. Even though you may not know how to value complicated or company-specific assets, many different analyses can help identify problems. For example, if you were concerned about a retail company like Sears or Wal-Mart, you could compute total assets on a per-store basis and see how that amount changed over time. You would not expect significant per-store changes unless the companies started building larger superstores, for example. You can also ask questions, such as: "Does it make sense that this company would have these types of assets in these locations?" Also, you should always consider whether the changes in the assets make sense given your understanding of the company's operations and the industry and economic conditions affecting the company.

Finally, comparing total fixed assets or fixed assets as a percentage of total assets with other similar companies helps to determine if a company's asset amounts are reasonable. For example, suppose that you compared two automobile manufacturing companies. If one had $50 of fixed assets for every $1 of sales while the other had $100 of fixed assets for every $1 of sales, you should ask why this is so. Perhaps the first company is that much more efficient, the second company has just spent millions renovating its manufacturing facilities, the second company's fixed assets are newer and less depreciated, or the second company is overstating its assets and committing fraud—all are alternatives that you should consider. Another analytical test that is often helpful is to determine the percentage of a class of asset costs that are being depreciated each year (a measure of depreciable life). If one company depreciates its assets over 10 years while another similar company used 20-year asset lives, you should probably ask why.

Accounting or Documentary Symptoms

Overstating fixed assets by recording inflated amounts usually occurs with transactions between related parties. Therefore, determining whether large purchases of fixed assets are arm's-length transactions or are purchases from related entities is important. If the vendor or provider of the assets is a related party, you need to determine why the company bought the assets from

that entity and whether the amounts recorded are reasonable. You should ask the following questions:

- *Were there appraisals of purchased fixed assets?*
- *Were the transactions recorded near the end of the year?*
- *Did the transactions involve exchanges of assets or a purchase of assets?*
- *Are the assets purchased the kinds of assets this company would normally purchase?*
- *Are there inconsistencies in the documentation for the transactions?*
- *Are the assets recorded on your client's books at the same or lower amounts than they were on the seller's books?*

Overstatement of Cash and Short-Term Investments (Including Marketable Securities)

As stated earlier, it is rare for a company to significantly overstate cash such that the financial statements are materially misstated. There are two reasons for this. First, verifying recorded amounts of cash is usually easily done with confirmations from financial institutions. If cash frauds are going to be concealed on bank confirmations, they usually require the collusive efforts of outsiders, which is quite rare. The Parmalat and Satyam cases are notable exceptions that should alert auditors to the fact that confirmations must be carefully controlled and scrutinized. We don't have details on how the Satyam fraud was concealed but in the Parmalat case, management falsified the signature of a Bank of America employee who had no authority to sign a confirmation. Because the confirmation represented billions of dollars of the company's assets, the auditors probably should have performed additional procedures to ensure the amount was valid. Second, the amount of cash that a company has is usually small relative to the amounts of receivables, inventory, or fixed assets. If the company reports large amounts of cash, an examiner should be skeptical and carefully verify that these amounts are correct. With regard to cash misstatements, it is more common for an employee, a customer, or someone else to embezzle enough cash from a company to materially and adversely affect the financial statements than it is for fictitious cash to be reported.

Analytical Symptoms

For both cash and marketable securities, it is usually helpful to perform all four types of analyses. Recorded amounts of individual categories of cash and marketable securities can be examined over time to detect unrealistic changes. For example, if marketable securities increase, then cash should usually decrease by a similar amount, since cash was probably used to purchase the securities. An exception is when the company incurred debt or traded an asset for the securities. Various relationships can be examined over time using the following ratios. These ratios help you understand whether the relationship between cash and marketable securities is reasonable in relation to current assets or total assets:

- *Current ratio: Current assets/Current liabilities*
- *Quick ratio: Current assets except inventory and prepaids/Current liabilities*
- *Current assets/Total assets*
- *Marketable securities/Current assets*
- *Cash/Current assets*

Because cash balances can be confirmed, banks provide an independent verification that the recorded amounts are appropriate. With marketable securities, you can confirm the market values and amounts by checking with brokers or by checking the financial pages of newspapers or the Internet. Comparing cash and marketable security balances with those of similar companies is usually not very helpful. Even similar companies often have significantly different amounts of cash and marketable securities because they have different strategies and spending patterns. In determining whether cash and marketable securities balances are reasonable, you should always ask questions such as: "Does it make sense for the company to have the amount of cash or marketable securities it has?" If the balances are high, the reason for the large balances should be plausible because, in many cases, having large amounts of cash on hand is not a wise use of resources. In cases when companies keep large amounts of cash on hand, they are often the targets for a hostile takeover as the buyer can use the cash to finance some of the purchase.

Accounting or Documentary Symptoms

The best accounting symptoms for discovering cash or marketable security misstatements are usually differences between recorded amounts and amounts confirmed with banks, brokers, and other independent parties. It is also common to obtain statements directly from financial institutions as of the date you are concerned about. You might be concerned if it makes sense for the company to have physical possession of marketable security certificates and they do not. Also, you

should consider it to be a red flag whenever a company doesn't have bank statements or bank reconciliations, or if they have bank statements but they are not reconciled. You would also be concerned if banks used by the company are offshore in other countries or have other specific characteristics that do not make business sense. For example, the fictitious cash and marketable securities on Parmalat's financial statements were supposed to be held by Bank of America in New York even though the company being audited was in Europe. These red flags, along with the generic documentary symptoms discussed earlier, can provide a signal that financial statement fraud is occurring.

Overstatement of Receivables and/or Inventory (Not Revenue- or Cost of Goods Sold-Related)

Almost always, when accounts receivable are overstated, revenues are overstated. Similarly, when inventory is overstated, cost of goods sold is usually understated. Once in a while, however, inventory or accounts receivable (or other assets) are overstated to conceal large thefts of cash or other assets. As stated earlier, much of the Phar-Mor inventory overstatement was used to conceal large thefts of cash by Micky Monus. Similarly, accounts receivable were overstated by about $350 million in the ESM case to hide the fact that the three principals had embezzled approximately $350 million from customers.

Remember this …

Overstatement of asset fraud can occur in many ways including the following: improperly capitalizing costs, inflating assets through mergers and acquisitions by manipulation of intercompany accounts and transactions, overstating fixed assets, misstating cash and marketable receivables, and overstating accounts receivable or inventory to hide thefts. As with other financial statement frauds, it is important to identify and actively search for fraud symptoms when looking for overstatement of asset fraud. One good way of doing this is by performing the four kinds of analysis discussed.

Inadequate Disclosure Fraud

The final type of financial statement fraud we will discuss is inadequate disclosure fraud. Financial statements consist of line items on the face of the statements themselves (e.g., cash is a balance sheet line item) and disclosures in the footnotes or other documents related to the financial statements (e.g., Management's Discussion and Analysis in the SEC Form 10-K or a press release).

Inadequate disclosure fraud involves the issuance of fraudulent or misleading statements in the disclosures. That is, somewhere in its annual report or through press releases or other media, management makes statements that are wrong but do not impact the numbers, or line items, on the financial statements. Disclosure fraud can also include statements that should have been, but were not, made by management (misleading because of what is not said—fraud by omission).

As an example, the SEC alleged that a private manager of elementary and secondary public schools, Edison Schools, Inc., failed to disclose significant information regarding its business operations. The SEC alleged that Edison failed to disclose that a substantial portion of its revenues consisted of payments that never reached Edison. These funds were instead expended by school districts (Edison's clients) to pay teacher salaries and other costs of operating schools that were managed by Edison. The SEC did not find that Edison's revenue-recognition practices violated GAAP or that earnings were misstated. However, the SEC found that Edison committed violations by failing to provide accurate disclosure in Management's Discussion and Analysis (MD&A). The MD&A section of an SEC filing is supposed to discuss the company's financial condition and results of operations to enhance investor understanding of financial statements.

Because no financial statement impact occurs with inadequate disclosure fraud, analytical symptoms will not be present. Documentary symptoms may be present, depending on the type of misstatement. Because of the unique nature of disclosure frauds, we first categorize these frauds and then introduce some frauds in each category. From these examples, we identify the symptoms that are available for detecting disclosure fraud. Because misleading disclosures can relate to anything, disclosure symptoms generally vary from case to case. As a result, drawing generalizations is difficult.

One thing you should remember is that fraud exposures are very relevant to disclosure-type frauds. Perpetrators will rarely make misstatements if they lack significant pressures or opportunities to do so. Therefore, when you observe management, the organizational structure, the relationships with other parties, or operating characteristic exposures, you should increase your skepticism, not only about the numbers in the financial statements, but also about the disclosures and representations that are being made by management throughout the annual report or in other information.

Kinds of Disclosure Fraud

Disclosure frauds can be categorized into the following three groups:

1. Misrepresentations about the nature of the company or its products, usually made through news reports, interviews, annual reports, and elsewhere.
2. Misrepresentations or omissions in the MD&A, such as Edison Schools, Inc., or in other nonfinancial statement sections of annual reports, 10-Ks, 10-Qs, and other reports.
3. Misrepresentations or omissions in the footnotes to the financial statements, such as the failure to disclose related-party transactions.

We discuss each of these three disclosure fraud schemes below.

Misrepresentations about the Nature of the Company or Its Products

Quite often, the business press reports on a company or an organization that has completely misrepresented what it is about or makes misleading claims about the nature of its products. The following two examples of frauds involve companies that misrepresented the nature of the company or its products:

They called it the "dog-and-pony" show. A "prospect" would be brought to Comparator Systems, a tiny company that, in June 1996, was accused of securities fraud by the SEC. On a table would be a small fingerprint identification device that Comparator says could help the world stop imposters and make investors who bought its penny-priced shares rich. The company claimed it had a technology that would let businesses and government entities quickly and affordably verify that people are who they claim to be. Comparator executives would demonstrate the technology, sometimes using a machine that the SEC says was stolen from Scottish inventors. These demonstrations were part of one of the largest stock market scandals of the 1990s. The SEC says Comparator was telling a convincing story about a phony product and turning that story into money through stock sales.

Comparator is a story of how a company with allegedly worthless assets, a product it did not own, a

29-person payroll it had not met for 11 of 13 years, and a stock market value of $40 million became worth $1 billion in three days of frenzied stock trading. The stock of this virtually unknown company was the most active ever on the NASDAQ, rising from 6¢ per share to $2 per share in three days. Comparator's stock accounted for one-fourth of the NASDAQ trading volume during those three days. In the end, Comparator was an imposter—exactly what its "technology" was supposed to detect.

Another case of disclosure fraud involved Bre-X Minerals, which we discussed in Chapter 11. The company claimed that it discovered as much as 71 million ounces of gold, worth $21 billion, in Indonesian Borneo. The hype surrounding Bre-X transformed the tiny Calgary, Alberta-based firm over three years into a company with a $4.5 billion market value. The stock's run-up transformed its executives into millionaires. The "gold discovery" now appears to have been faked by adding outside gold to samples taken from the site in Borneo. The stock's price plummeted 80 percent in one day when the fraud was discovered.

Comparator and Bre-X are examples of companies that misrepresented themselves or their products. Apparently, Comparator never had a state-of-the-art fingerprinting machine that could distinguish imposters from real people; similarly Bre-X did not have a mine in Borneo containing 71 million ounces of gold. Yet, combined, these companies cost investors billions of dollars and had an aggregate market value of nearly $6 billion.

Companies that misrepresent their products or operations are certainly not alone. Many have claimed to be something they were not. These misrepresentations are the worst type of disclosure fraud, because they are "imposters." They are no different from a person who enters a bank, claims to be a certain bank customer, and withdraws money from that customer's account using fictitious or stolen identification.

Misrepresentations in MD&A and Other Nonfinancial Information in Financial Reports

In recent years, a company's annual report has become as much a public relations document as it is a report of financial condition and operations. Most annual reports include various statements by management, including MD&A, historical performance charts, announcements of new products and strategic directions, and plans and goals for the future. Sometimes, management's statements included in the annual report contain false disclosures and outright lies. Other times, management

fails to make disclosures that are necessary to help investors and creditors understand what is really happening.

E. F. Hutton Group, Inc., allegedly developed a cash management system for moving customer funds received by branch offices through bank accounts maintained at regional offices and ultimately to Hutton's corporate bank accounts in New York City and Los Angeles. The system required the branch offices to calculate the daily net activity in their branch accounts and then to remove from the accounts all funds in excess of the required compensating balances.

On certain days, the branches were alleged to have overdrafted their bank accounts. If, on the day after a branch overdrafted its bank account, insufficient funds were collected from customers to cover the overdraft or if a delay occurred in the check clearing process, the branch was to deposit a "branch reimbursement check" in the branch bank account to make up the difference. Branch reimbursement checks were drawn on zero balance checking accounts that were funded at the end of each day. Certain members of senior management allegedly encouraged greater use of the draw-down procedures, which increased Hutton's interest income and reduced its interest expense. Net interest income was significant in Hutton's financial statements.

An investigation showed that Hutton failed to disclose in its MD&A that the increased use of the overdrafting practices was a material cause of the significant increase in net interest income. The complaint also alleged that Hutton's MD&A failed to disclose that the reduced use of the bank overdrafting practices the next year was a material cause of the significant decrease in Hutton's net interest income that year.

In Hutton's case, the company materially changed the nature of its operations, making as much money from using bank floats and kiting as from selling securities. In this case, the MD&A section of the annual report should have described these events. As you can see from this example, fraudulent financial reporting can occur as much from failure to disclose as it can from disclosing misleading information.

Misleading Footnote Disclosures

The third type of disclosure fraud involves misleading footnote disclosures or the omission of key or required disclosures. A company's footnotes should provide relevant disclosures necessary to help investors and creditors understand the financial statements and make investment and credit decisions. Sometimes, disclosures that should be made in the footnotes are missing, and other times the disclosures that are included are misleading. Many misleading disclosures affect financial statement balances, but some do not. In this section, we will focus only on those that have no financial statement impact.

Probably the most frequent type of footnote disclosure fraud is not disclosing transactions with related parties. Auditors and others are required by both GAAP and GAAS to look closely at related-party transactions, and management often believes it can avoid such scrutiny if it does not reveal that related parties exist. Intentionally failing to disclose all material related-party transactions in the footnotes constitutes fraud.

A recent example of failing to disclose related-party transactions was Adelphia Corporation:

———

The SEC alleged that Adelphia engaged in numerous undisclosed related-party transactions with board members, executive officers, and entities it controlled. The SEC alleged that Adelphia failed to disclose the existence of these transactions or misrepresented their terms in its financial statements. More than $300 million of company funds were diverted to senior management without adequate disclosure to investors. In 2002, Adelphia and certain of its subsidiaries filed for bankruptcy. The executive officers were also handcuffed and hauled off to jail. Former Adelphia CEO and founder, John Rigas, as well as his son and former CFO, Timothy Rigas, were both convicted of fraudulent activity. John received a 20-year sentence and Timothy received a 15-year sentence in federal prison, which began in August 2007:

———

In addition to disclosure fraud involving related-party transactions, other common types of disclosure fraud include the following:

- *Failing to disclose contingent liabilities that are reasonably possible or probable and that would create a loss for the company*
- *Failing to disclose contractual obligations, including restrictions on specific assets or liabilities*
- *Disclosing contingent gains that are unlikely to occur*
- *Failing to disclose information regarding loans to creditors*
- *Inadequately disclosing significant accounting policies*
- *Inadequately disclosing information about market value declines of assets, including marketable securities*

- *Inadequately disclosing information about pension or other long-term liabilities*
- *Lack of disclosure of significant events*

Of course, to be fraud, the lack of disclosure or misleading disclosures must be intentional. As another example of disclosure fraud, consider the case of Centennial Savings and Loan:

———

Centennial Savings and Loan began in the mid-1970s with about $18 million in assets. The company eventually increased those assets to a supposed $408 million before the fraud was discovered. In 1985, examiners began to discover discrepancies within the company's financial statements. In January 1986, the FBI began to investigate Centennial. Among other illegal acts and fraud, Centennial had conspired with executives of other savings and loans to create loans for former Centennial officials. These loans violated federal regulations that prevent thrifts from making more than $100,000 in unsecured loans to affiliated persons. Executives of Centennial also received and paid kickbacks to help these loans go through. In addition, the company was involved in suspicious joint ventures with other savings and loans that were highly speculative. It also engaged in various real estate deals that significantly overstated asset values. None of this information was ever disclosed in the footnotes to the financial statements. The related-party nature of the loans to former Centennial officers was never disclosed (probably because the loans were illegal). Also, the related-party transactions of the questionable joint ventures with other savings and loans were not disclosed.

In this case, the fraud involved failing to disclose related-party transactions, among other things. In other cases, disclosures about asset impairment, contingent liabilities, and significant events were either missing or misleading. Sometimes, as was the case with ESM discussed earlier, information about fraud that is occurring is actually provided in the footnotes, but is concealed in a way so that readers will not detect it.

———

Detecting Inadequate Disclosure Fraud

Detecting inadequate disclosure fraud is not as easy as detecting other types of fraud. In fact, without a tip or complaint, it is difficult to know that disclosure fraud is occurring. It is usually easier to detect inadequate disclosure fraud that involves misleading disclosures than it is to detect disclosure fraud that involves missing disclosures. Also, the symptoms you look for are different, depending on the kind of disclosure fraud you are concerned about. With overall misrepresentation of a company or its products, it is necessary to look for symptoms related to the nature of the company, its assets and organization, its management, and its operating characteristics. With disclosure fraud relating to the nonfinancial statement part of annual reports or in the footnotes to the financial statements, you look for different kinds of symptoms. In the two sections that follow, we discuss symptoms related first to overall misrepresentation and then to footnote and annual report disclosure-type fraud.

STOP & THINK   *How often do investors review the nonfinancial section of annual reports? Why is it important to read the nonfinancial sections of annual reports or the footnotes to the financial statements?*

Symptoms Related to Overall Misrepresentation about the Company or Its Assets

Taking a broad view, the kinds of symptoms you look for to find frauds such as those of Comparator and Bre-X are similar to the symptoms you search for when looking for investment scams and Ponzi schemes. For example, to discover whether a company like AFCO, Comparator, or Bre-X is fraudulent, you need to understand the client's financial situation, financial goals and objectives, and risk tolerance. You also need to look out for companies that have unrealistically large growth in assets, revenues, or profits and companies that have a short history, involve unknown management, or have other characteristics that make their performance or representations look suspicious. In addition, the following list of questions should prove useful in determining whether a company and its products are legitimate:

- *Does the company's performance make sense when compared with the performance of similar companies?*
- *Is the company cash poor and desperate for immediate investors?*
- *Does the success of the company depend on a tax loophole or tax avoidance scheme?*
- *Is there anything that cannot be disclosed because it is purported to be the company's unique success factor?*

- *Is the business new in town?*
- *What is the background of the principals? Where do they come from, and what were their operations in previous locations?*
- *Have any of the principals been involved in bankruptcy or scandals before?*
- *Are the appraisal figures and financial claims provided by the company's representatives true?*
- *Does the company's success depend on kickbacks, complicated marketing schemes, special concessions to those who have money, or unwritten deals that cannot be talked about because of domestic or foreign laws?*
- *Are the company's financial reports audited? If so, for how many years? What type of audit opinion did they receive?*
- *Does the company's success depend on someone's "unique expertise" (such as an uncanny ability to predict commodity prices or unusually good salesmanship) for financial success?*
- *What would happen if one person's special skills were removed from the company?*
- *Is the company making guaranteed promises? Can the promises be verified?*
- *Does the company's success depend on high financial leverage?*
- *Would investors be liable if the company's debts were not paid?*
- *Are the principals in the business living "high on the hog," even though the business is relatively new?*
- *Is the company's stock listed on a national exchange? If so, which one, and what has been its history on that exchange?*
- *What is the nature of the company and its board of directors? Does the company have an audit committee or internal auditors?*
- *Is the company's success based on the recent announcement of a major success or discovery? If so, have independent sources confirmed the truthfulness of the announcements?*

In the Comparator case, Comparator compiled bad debts in approximately 27 cases, owing over $478,000 in principal and accrued interest from final court judgments, according to the company's last 10-K report to the SEC. Another eight cases, worth $300,000, were in dispute. The company's bad debts included rent owed for three different offices. The company used stock to pay veterinarian, dental, and legal bills. The CEO, Robert Reed Rogers, distributed shares of stock like water. Rogers, himself, was past president of several companies that had previous brushes with the law. In one, his company claimed to have "exclusive right" to certain mining processes for producing jewelry. In another, a bench warrant was issued for his arrest for failure to appear in court in connection with a lawsuit filed by investors. As the general partner of a health care company, Rogers and his partners were sued and had judgments against them. Comparator was also late with, and did not make, some SEC filings. One investor who looked at the company called the company's balance sheet "puff" and "inflated," because it included worthless patents and other assets.

Another example of misrepresentation came to light when a professor received a call from a fellow professor at another university, who asked about a company in which his university was investing. The professor making the call was suspicious, because the company was making claims that if his university and other universities and not-for-profit groups invested their endowments in the company, they would double their endowments in a year or less. The company had a wealthy investor who would match the amount the university invested. The more this faculty member described the company, the more it sounded like a classic Ponzi scheme. After about 30 minutes, the professor who called concluded by stating, "I do not know whether this company is fraudulent. However, I have always believed if something crawled like a snake, looked like a snake, and acted like a snake, it was probably a snake." He told the caller that the company had all the characteristics of a "snake," or an investment scam. The calling professor investigated the company and discovered the now famous "New Era" fraud.

Disclosure Fraud Related to Financial Reports and Financial Statement Footnotes

Several fraud examination techniques can be used to detect inadequate disclosures. First, you should look for inconsistencies between disclosures and information in the financial statements and other information available. Second, you should make inquiries of management and other personnel concerning related-party transactions, contingent liabilities, and contractual obligations. These inquiries should be made at several levels of management and be done separately and judiciously. In fact, interviewing lower-level employees who may be aware of such transactions (e.g., a credit manager or clerk) can be more important than interviewing upper management who may be trying to conceal the fraud. Inquiries should also be made about different accounting policies of which management is aware. Even though some of these inquiries may be routine or involve basic questions, differences in responses could tip you off that management is engaging in disclosure fraud.

Another way to identify inadequate disclosures, especially concerning related parties, is to review the company's files and records with the SEC and other regulatory agencies concerning names of officers and directors who occupy management or directorship positions in other companies. It is possible, given the databases available today, to search for common ownership and directorship interests. If you suspect something may be awry, you can use databases such as LexisNexis to perform background searches on key individuals. Other good places to look for inadequate disclosures are in the board of directors' minutes, correspondence and invoices from attorneys, confirmations with banks and others, contracts, loan agreements, loan guarantees, leases, correspondence from taxing and regulatory authorities, pension plan documents, sales agreements, and other legal documents.

In many disclosure fraud cases, financial statement auditors have "had their hands on the fraud" but did not recognize it. To detect disclosure fraud, auditors and others need to realize that inconsistencies between financial statements and other information, for example, represent a fraud symptom and not just an unintentional error. When investigating a fraud symptom, you should not allow management to explain away the problem. Detecting fraud requires looking beyond transactions, documents, and other information and asking what possible reasons there are for this symptom. These days, key information, such as business relationships or management backgrounds, is often available and easily accessible from public sources. If something looks suspicious or questionable, look for ways to research the issue or gather independent evidence, rather than simply accepting management's explanation. If members of management will commit financial statement fraud, they will certainly lie to you!

Remember this ...

Inadequate disclosure fraud involves the issuance of fraudulent or misleading statements, press releases, or disclosures without affecting financial statement balances. Disclosure frauds can be categorized into three groups: (1) misrepresentations about the overall nature of the company or its products, (2) misrepresentations in MD&A and other nonfinancial information in financial reports, and (3) misleading footnote disclosures. Various techniques can be used to detect inadequate disclosures including looking for inconsistencies between disclosures and information in the financial statements; inquiring concerning related-party transactions, contingent liabilities, and contractual obligations; and reviewing a company's files and records with the SEC and other regulatory agencies.

Other Types of Financial Statement Fraud

Obviously, we have not covered all types of financial statement fraud. We have covered those types that are most common. Before we conclude this final chapter on financial statement fraud, we introduce you to some of the less common types of financial statement frauds.

Inappropriate Accounting for Nonmonetary Transactions

Most business transactions involve either the exchange of cash or other monetary assets or the incurrence of a liability for goods or services. The assets exchanged or liabilities incurred generally provide an objective basis for measuring the cost of nonmonetary assets or services received by an enterprise as well as for measuring gain or loss on nonmonetary assets transferred from an enterprise. Exchanges that involve little or no monetary assets or liabilities are referred to as nonmonetary transactions. In general, under GAAP, accounting for nonmonetary transactions should be based on the fair value of the assets (or services) involved, which is the same basis as that used in monetary transactions.

An example of inappropriately accounting for nonmonetary transactions was Critical Path, Inc:

———

The SEC found that Critical Path improperly reported as revenue several transactions, the largest of which was a barter transaction. In this transaction, a software company agreed to buy out a periodic royalty obligation for $2.8 million and buy another $240,000 of software, in exchange for Critical Path's agreement to buy approximately $4 million of software services from the software company. The SEC alleged that Critical Path recorded a $3.09 million sale to the software company improperly as revenue for the third quarter. The company failed to establish the fair value of either the software it received from, or the software it sent to, the software company. Furthermore, the SEC found that Critical Path did not ensure that the value ascribed to the software it received reasonably reflected its expected use of the software as required under GAAP.

———

Inappropriate Accounting for Roundtrip Transactions

During the past decade, the SEC has brought enforcement actions against companies that engaged in improper accounting for roundtrip transactions. Roundtrip transactions involve prearranged sales and repurchases of an item, often the same product, in order to create a false impression of business activity and revenue.

An example of inappropriate accounting for roundtrip transactions involved Homestore.com, Inc. (Homestore):

———

The SEC charged three former executives of Homestore with arranging fraudulent roundtrip transactions for the sole purpose of artificially inflating Homestore's revenues. The essence of these transactions was a circular flow of money by which Homestore recognized its own cash as revenue. Specifically, the SEC alleged that Homestore paid inflated sums to various vendors for services or products; in turn, the vendors used these funds to buy advertising from two media companies. The media companies then bought advertising from Homestore either on their own behalf or as agents for other advertisers. Homestore recorded the funds it received from the media companies as revenue in its financial statements, in violation of GAAP. Global Crossing and WorldCom also engaged in roundtrip transactions.

———

Improper Accounting for Foreign Payments in Violation of the Foreign Corrupt Practices Act (FCPA)

The FCPA was passed in 1977 to combat corrupt business practices such as bribery. Some FCPA cases also involve the improper accounting by companies for payments to foreign government officials. In these cases, the company is committing financial statement fraud due to its accounting while also violating the FCPA. BellSouth and IBM were two companies that had such transactions:

———

The SEC alleged that BellSouth violated the FCPA by authorizing payments to local officials through its subsidiaries in Venezuela and Nicaragua. Senior management at Bell-South's Venezuelan subsidiary allegedly authorized more than $10 million in payments to six offshore companies that were improperly recorded as bona fide services. In addition, the SEC alleged that management at the Nicaraguan subsidiary authorized payments, recorded as "consulting services," to the wife of a Nicaraguan legislator who presided over a hearing that allowed BellSouth to increase its ownership interest in its Nicaraguan subsidiary.

IBM had a $250 million contract to integrate and modernize the computer system of a commercial bank owned by the Argentine government. IBM-Argentina allegedly entered into a subcontract with an Argentine corporation for $22 million, which funneled approximately $4.5 million of these funds to several directors of the government-owned commercial bank. IBM recorded the expenses as third-party subcontractor expenses. IBM-Argentina's former senior management overrode IBM's procurement and contracting procedures and hid the details from financial personnel. Management provided the procurement department with fabricated documentation and stated inaccurate and incomplete reasons for hiring the Argentine corporation.

———

Improper Use of Non-GAAP Financial Measures

When improperly used, non-GAAP financial measures that include or exclude unusual expenses or gains may provide a misleading financial picture. These financial measures are generally referred to as "pro-forma earnings." In December 2001, the SEC issued a cautionary release on pro-forma earnings and subsequently issued antifraud enforcement actions in this area. The

first two enforcement actions involved Trump Hotels and Casino Resorts, Inc., and Ashford.com, Inc:

———

The SEC alleged that Trump Hotels issued a press release announcing positive results for its third-quarter earnings using a pro-forma net income figure that differed from net income calculated in conformity with GAAP. Although the release expressly stated that the results excluded a one-time charge, it failed to disclose the inclusion of a one-time gain of $17.2 million. The release created a misleading impression that the company had exceeded earnings expectations when actual net earnings were lower than the same quarter of the previous year and the company had in fact failed to meet analysts' expectations.

Ashford.com misstated its pro-forma results by improperly deferring $1.5 million in expenses under a contract with Amazon.com. The SEC also alleged that Ashford.com incorrectly classified certain marketing expenses as depreciation and amortization expenses that materially understated the company's true marketing expenses. In addition, because Ashford. com allegedly excluded depreciation and amortization from its non-GAAP financial results, Ashford.com's expense misclassification improved its non-GAAP financial results. In its year-end 10-K, the company reclassified the expenses in question.

———

Improper Use of Off-Balance-Sheet Arrangements

Off-balance-sheet arrangements are often used to provide financing, liquidity, market, or credit risk support or to engage in leasing, hedging, or research and development services. A common use of off-balance-sheet arrangements is to allocate risks among third parties. Off-balance-sheet arrangements may involve the use of complex structures, including structured finance or special purpose entities (now called *variable interest entities* by the Financial Accounting Standards Board), to facilitate a company's transfer of, or access to, assets.

In many cases, the company transferring assets to a variable interest entity (VIE) has some contingent liability or continuing involvement with the transferred assets. Depending on the nature of the obligations and the related accounting treatment under GAAP, the company's financial statements may not fully reflect the company's obligations with respect to the VIE or its arrangements. Transactions with VIEs are commonly structured so that the company that establishes or sponsors the VIE and engages in transactions with it is not required to consolidate the entity into its financial statements under GAAP. In the 1990s, several prominent companies, including Adelphia Communications Corporation, Dynegy Inc., and Enron, made improper use of these arrangements. Because Enron is such a famous case, we will discuss it in a little more detail than normal.

Enron's fraud was primarily conducted through what were then known as special purpose entities, which were formed solely to accomplish some specific tasks. SPEs were not illegal, and are not illegal today, but are subject to accounting requirements that designate which SPEs are considered part of the larger company and which are independent entities not controlled by a parent. The SEC's complaint alleged that certain of Enron's SPEs should have been consolidated onto Enron's balance sheet. Further, Andrew Fastow, Michael Kopper, and others used their simultaneous influence over Enron's business operations and the SPEs as a means to secretly and unlawfully generate millions of dollars for themselves and others.

Fastow's use of SPEs was widespread; the following are two examples. In 1997, Enron decided to sell its interest in a California windmill farm. However, Enron did not want to lose control of the profitable wind farm. As such, Fastow created an SPE (known as RADR) and recruited "Friends of Enron" (actually friends of Kopper) as outside investors. Because these investors lacked sufficient funds, Fastow made a personal loan of $419,000 to fund the purchase of the wind farm. RADR became immensely profitable. Fastow's loan was repaid with $62,000 interest, and Kopper arranged for yearly "gifts" of $10,000 each (keeping the gifts beneath the limit of taxable income) to members of Fastow's family. Because the RADR investment was funded by Fastow and because Fastow and Kopper controlled RADR's operations, the entity should have been consolidated with Enron's financial statements.

In 1993, Enron created an independent entity called JEDI. In 1997, a major independent investor wanted to sell its portion of JEDI. Rather than consider other independent investors, Fastow created Chewco, an SPE that would buy the investor's share of JEDI. As structured by Fastow, Chewco (and now JEDI) was not independent and, therefore, was no longer eligible for off-the-book status. In this transaction, Fastow substituted Kopper as the main investor; Kopper being an Enron executive who was essentially controlled by Fastow. Also, Chewco's investment in JEDI was not "genuinely at risk" since it was funded through two $190 million bank loans which were guaranteed by Enron. As with RADR, Fastow directed Kopper to continue funnel payments to his family, including a $54,000 payment to Fastow's wife for performing administrative duties for Chewco.

> **Remember this …**
>
> *A few additional financial statement frauds include inappropriate accounting for nonmonetary transactions, roundtrip transactions, inappropriate accounting for payments in violation of the Foreign Corrupt Practices Act, improper use of non-GAAP financial measures, and improper use of off-balance-sheet arrangements.*

As we end our discussion of financial statement fraud, we hope you realize that there are many ways to commit financial statement fraud. In addition, as business models evolve and new accounting standards are issued, perpetrators develop new schemes to deceive investors and creditors. As such, finding financial statement fraud is often very difficult. Clever perpetrators expend great efforts to conceal their frauds. To discover a concealed fraud, a person must look for analytical symptoms, accounting or documentary symptoms, behavioral and lifestyle symptoms, control symptoms, and tips and complaints. By searching for these fraud symptoms or tips and by using strategic reasoning to design unexpected procedures, auditors and others can discover many of these cleverly concealed frauds.

Review of the Learning Objectives

- **Identify fraudulent schemes that understate liabilities.** Schemes that understate liabilities include the following: understating accounts payable, understating accrued liabilities, recognizing unearned revenue as earned revenue, not recording or underrecording future obligations, among others.
- **Discuss the understatement of liabilities fraud.** Understatement of liability frauds is often difficult for auditors to detect. However, abnormal analytical symptoms or documentary symptoms relating to liability accounts are helpful in detecting this type of fraud.
- **Describe fraudulent schemes that overstate assets.** Common ways that assets are overstated include improperly capitalizing costs, inflating assets through mergers and acquisitions by manipulation of intercompany accounts and transactions, overstating fixed assets, misstating cash and marketable receivables, and overstating accounts receivable or inventory to hide thefts.

- **Understand the overstatement of assets fraud.** Many fraudulent companies will attempt to overstate assets to make their financial positions look better. As with other financial statement frauds, it is important to identify and actively search for fraud symptoms when looking for overstatement of asset fraud.
- **List fraudulent schemes that inadequately disclose financial statement information.** Disclosure fraud can be categorized into the following three groups: (1) misrepresentations about the overall nature of the company or its products, (2) misrepresentations in MD&A and other nonfinancial information in financial reports, and (3) misleading footnote disclosures.
- **Explain the inadequate disclosure fraud.** One can detect and better understand disclosure fraud by doing some of the following activities: looking for inconsistencies between disclosures and information in the financial statements; inquiring of management concerning related-party transactions, contingent liabilities, and contractual obligations; and reviewing a company's files and records with the SEC and other regulatory agencies.

KEY TERMS

leases, p. 446
mortgages, p. 446
understatement of liability frauds, p. 447
restructuring, p. 447
accrued liabilities, p. 449
unearned revenues, p. 450
footnotes, p. 451
contingent liability, p. 451
pension, p. 452
capitalization, p. 452
repurchase agreements, p. 453

warranty liabilities, p. 454
fixed assets, p. 454
overstatement of asset fraud, p. 456
intangible assets, p. 458
deferred charges, p. 458
mergers, p. 459
acquisitions, p. 459
marketable securities, p. 462
inadequate disclosure fraud, p. 470

QUESTIONS

Discussion Questions

1. Why is understatement of liability fraud difficult to discover?
2. List the four methods used to perform analytical analyses to search for financial statement fraud symptoms. Give an example of each method as it applies to searching for symptoms related to underreporting of liabilities.
3. Explain what is meant by "cutoff problems" as they relate to accounts payable.
4. Why might liabilities be understated if proper adjusting entries are not made at the end of an accounting period?
5. What is the difference between unearned revenue and earned revenue?
6. If a contingent liability is only a possible liability, why might not disclosing contingent liabilities constitute financial statement fraud?
7. What are some documentary symptoms of contingent liabilities that should be recorded?
8. Explain why improper capitalization of amounts spent could result in financial statement fraud and overstatement of assets.
9. Is cash an asset that is frequently overstated when committing financial statement fraud? Why or why not?
10. In what ways could financial statement fraud result from a merger?
11. If all financial statement amounts are presented appropriately, could financial statement fraud still be occurring?
12. What are the four kinds of analysis that can be used in searching for analytical fraud symptoms?
13. If you were to compare two companies in the same industry and found that one company had $100 of fixed assets for every $1 of sales while the other had $200 of fixed assets for every $1 of sales, what would be a possible explanation for the difference?
14. What are the three different categories into which disclosure frauds can be categorized?

True/False

1. Fraud auditors should be equally concerned with liabilities being overstated as well as understated.
2. Proactive searching for analytical symptoms means that we are looking for accounts that appear too high or too low or that are unusual in some other way.
3. Confirmations with vendors that the company owes money to are an effective way to discover unrecorded liabilities.
4. Accrued liabilities are important accounts to look at when searching for fraud because it is easy to understate liabilities in these accounts.
5. Symptoms of unrecorded contingent liabilities can be found by performing analytical procedures on certain financial statement ratios.

6. Some misleading footnotes have no effect on financial statement balances.

7. Understatement of liability fraud is usually more difficult to find than overstatement of asset fraud.

8. When searching for unrecorded liabilities, investigating vendors with zero balances would be just as important as investigating vendors with large balances.

9. Assets most often improperly capitalized are fixed assets such as property or equipment.

10. Financial statement fraud involving footnote disclosures can be either frauds of omission or frauds of commission.

11. A company that claims to be something it is not in a 10-K report is committing a kind of financial statement fraud.

12. Financial statement frauds most often occur in large, well-established companies.

13. Documentary symptoms provide the best opportunity to find contingent liabilities that should be recorded.

14. Comparing financial relationships such as interest expense and debt, or the amount of warranty expense as a percentage of sales, is not helpful in identifying fraud symptoms of understating liabilities.

15. One of the best ways to detect inappropriate capitalization of costs is by making comparisons with other similar companies.

16. Comparing cash and marketable securities balances with those of similar companies is usually very helpful when looking for analytical symptoms of fraud.

Multiple Choice

1. Which of the following is a primary type of transaction that can create liabilities for a company?
   a. Purchasing inventory.
   b. Borrowing money.
   c. Selling purchased goods.
   d. Leasing assets.
   e. All of the above.

2. When accounts payable-related liabilities are understated, purchases and inventory are often, or the financial statements don't balance.
   a. Overstated.
   b. Understated.
   c. Correctly stated.
   d. It is impossible to tell.

3. Recognizing something as a revenue instead of as a liability has a positive effect on the reported financial statements because:
   a. It understates liabilities.
   b. It overstates revenues.
   c. It overstates net income.
   d. It overstates assets.
   e. All of the above.
   f. a, b, and c are correct.

4. The most common fraud involving car companies and the warranties they offer would most likely be:
   a. Understating accrued liabilities.
   b. Recognizing unearned revenue.
   c. Not recording or underrecording future obligations.
   d. Not recording or underrecording various types of debt.

5. FAS 5 requires contingent liabilities to be recorded as liabilities on the balance sheet if the likelihood of loss or payment is:
   a. Remote.
   b. Reasonably possible.
   c. Probable.
   d. Not determinable.

6. Analytical symptoms of accounts payable fraud most often relate to reported "accounts payable" balances that appear:
   a. Too low.
   b. Too high.
   c. Too perfect.
   d. Unchanged.

7. Proactively searching for analytical symptoms related to financial statement fraud means that we are looking for accounts that appear:
   a. Too low.
   b. Too high.
   c. Unusual.
   d. All of the above.

8. When focusing on changes, you should consider changes from period to period in:
   a. Recorded balances.
   b. Relationships between balances.
   c. Balances of other nonsimilar companies.
   d. Both a and b.
   e. All of the above.

9. Overstating cash is usually difficult because:
   a. Cash balances can be easily confirmed with banks and other financial institutions.
   b. Cash is hard to steal.
   c. Cash is normally not a fraudulent account.
   d. Cash is usually a small asset.

10. Inadequate disclosure fraud usually involves:
    a. Statements in the footnotes that are wrong but do not impact the financial statement.
    b. Disclosures that should have been made in the footnotes but were not.
    c. Both a and b.
    d. Neither a nor b.

11. When examining whether a company has under-recorded accounts payable, each of the following ratios is helpful except:
    a. Acid-test ratio.
    b. Accounts payable/Purchases.
    c. Accounts payable/Cost of goods sold.
    d. Unearned revenue/Accounts payable.
    e. Current ratio.

12. Each of the following is a symptom relating to understatement of liability frauds except:
    a. Original purchase-related records where copies could exist.
    b. Denied access to records, facilities, certain employees, customers, vendors, or others from whom audit evidence might be sought.
    c. Last-minute adjustments by the entity that significantly affect financial results.
    d. Missing documents.
    e. All of the above are documentary symptoms of understatement of liability fraud.

13. Each of the following assets is correctly linked with how it can be overstated except:
    a. Inventory can be overstated by improperly capitalizing these assets.
    b. Marketable securities can be overstated because they are not widely traded, and it is difficult to assign an accurate value to the securities.
    c. Fixed assets can be overstated by leaving expired assets on the books.
    d. Assets can be inflated in mergers, acquisitions, and restructurings by having the wrong entity act as the acquirer.

14. Which of the following factors does *not* make fraud more difficult to detect?
    a. Collusion with outsiders.
    b. Forgery, which GAAS auditors are not routinely trained to detect.
    c. Off-book frauds in which no records on the company's books are fraudulent.
    d. All of the above make fraud more difficult to detect.

15. A form 1099 with missing withholdings (where they should be reported) may be a fraud symptom for which liability account?
    a. Accounts Payable.
    b. Unearned Revenues.
    c. Contingent Liabilities.
    d. Accrued Liabilities.

16. In liability fraud, liabilities are most often:
    a. Understated.
    b. Overstated.
    c. Recorded as assets.
    d. Recorded as expenses.

17. Which of the following is usually the hardest fraud to detect?
    a. Liability fraud.
    b. Revenue fraud.
    c. Asset fraud.
    d. Disclosure fraud.

18. You observe that a company's current ratio is dramatically increasing. This may indicate fraud in that:
    a. Probable contingent liabilities that will settle in the next year for an amount that can be estimated are not recorded.
    b. Accounts payable are understated.
    c. Expenses have been inappropriately capitalized as fixed assets.
    d. Fixed assets are overstated.
    e. Two of the above are true.

19. Of the following, the most difficult account for management to intentionally misstate is:
    a. Income Taxes Payable.
    b. Cash.
    c. Securities.
    d. Prepaid Expenses.

20. Which of the following is *not* a way to underrecord liabilities?
    a. Borrowing but not disclosing debt incurred on existing lines of credit.
    b. Claiming that existing debt has been forgiven by creditors.
    c. Not recording loans incurred.
    d. All of the above are ways to underrecord liabilities.

21. When looking for accounting or documentary symptoms of fraud when a merger occurs, one of the first steps should be to:
    a. Make sure that the purchasing company got a fair deal.
    b. Make sure that the selling company properly disclosed its financial troubles.
    c. Make sure that both the buyer and the seller were content with the deal.
    d. Make sure that the accounting methods used were appropriate and consistent with accounting standards.

22. Which of the following is a good place to look for inadequate disclosures?
    a. Board of directors' minutes.
    b. Correspondence and invoices from attorneys.
    c. Confirmations with banks and others.
    d. Loan agreements.
    e. All of the above are good places to look for inadequate disclosure.

SHORT CASES

Case 1

John is the manager of a small computer sales and support chain. He has stores located throughout the state of California and is in strong competition with all of the major computer providers within that state. John's company is known for providing quick support and friendly service. In the process of selling goods to customers, John's company will often offer deals that include free service or low-priced service for the products being purchased. John's competitors offer the same types of deals to their customers, but because of the small mobile size of John's company, he is better able to provide quick service to his customers. John is the president of his company and has raised funding through issuing stock. He has not used external loan funding much in the past. John has approximately 50 stores located in California and is in the process of obtaining business locations outside of the state. John's main goal is to be successful in the computer business because of the quick customer service his company provides. He believes his company will be able to charge higher prices because people will be willing to pay the initial higher price on computer components for the added customer service on the back end.

John has managers in all of the different stores who report directly to him. They do not communicate regularly with other store managers on inventory issues or customer service representative availabilities. John has found much success in the past because of the customer service he has been able to provide. In recent years, the competition has become more successful in duplicating his activities or in providing low-maintenance products. John's company has provided financial statements on a yearly basis, so investors can follow the company's success. With the growing success of competitors, John has found it more difficult to be successful. During the past year, John's company recorded significant revenues from sales that will require warranty service over the next few years. However, John's reported warranty expenses stayed the same. In addition, the reported inventory levels remained approximately the same as in previous years. No additional financing or loans were recorded on the financial statements, even though assets continued to grow. Revenue was the only financial statement amount that changed dramatically.

1. What are possible fraud symptoms in this case?
2. What could look like fraud but be explained by industry trends?

Case 2

Enron is a large energy trading company that allegedly committed massive fraud. Enron's primary method of committing fraud was to record liabilities in related partnerships, then known as special purpose entities, that were not consolidated, or combined, with Enron's financial statements. Company executives have maintained that they did not know about these massive off-balance-sheet liabilities, which have been estimated to be several billion dollars.

1. As a fraud investigator, how would you go about finding the existence of these liabilities and partnerships?

Case 3

Qwest is the dominant local telephone company in 14 states and the owner of an international fiber-optic network. In 2002, the company was investigated by the SEC for not including certain expense items related to its merger with U.S.

1. West, among other issues. Why would the SEC be concerned if Qwest had not included certain expense items in a merger?

Case 4

Until its involvement as Enron's auditor, Arthur Andersen was recognized as one of the most respected CPA firms in the world. Arthur Andersen, as did other large CPA firms, operated as a limited liability corporation, or LLC. At the time that its involvement as Enron's auditor was making news every day, an article in *The Wall Street Journal* stated that it wasn't clear whether the LLC form of organization was going to offer Andersen's partners protection from creditors' lawsuits or whether creditors would be able to take the personal assets of Andersen's partners. Assume that Andersen had 2,000 partners and that creditor claims in the Enron case totaled $50 billion.

1. If Arthur Andersen had been a corporation, how would you have expected creditor litigation to have been reported in the financial statements?
2. Would failure to report the litigation constitute financial statement fraud?

Case 5

In its 2001 annual report, investors of Adelphia Communications were startled to find a footnote in its financial statements that reported the company had guaranteed as much as $2.7 billion in loans to a private entity owned by CEO John Rigas and his family. As a result of the footnote, Adelphia lost more than 50 percent of its market value in little more than a week.

1. Explain why you think the market value of Adelphia fell so dramatically with the footnote disclosure that the company had guaranteed loans to an entity owned by the company's CEO and his family.

Case 6

The officers of an oil refiner, trader, and hedger based in New York were arrested by the FBI for committing massive financial statement fraud. The executives used many schemes to perpetuate the fraud, one of which was to hide a $30 million accounts payable from the auditors and show it as a payable arising in the following year. To conceal the fraud, they altered purchasing records, using correction fluid, and provided only photocopies of the records to the auditors. The Big 4 firm that audited this company was later sued for audit negligence in not finding this fraud.

1. In your opinion, were the auditors negligent for accepting photocopies of purchasing records and not detecting this accounts payable understatement?

Case 7

The following two comparative balance sheets and statements of income are for XYZ Company for the years 20x1–20x3:

CASE 7

CONSOLIDATED BALANCE SHEETS — XYZ COMPANY

	20X1	20X2	20X3
Assets:			
Current assets			
Cash and cash equivalents	$ 1,542	$ 851	$ 317
Receivables	5,602	4,115	3,329
Inventories	1,524	1,112	900
Deferred income taxes	851	302	456
Total current assets	$ 9,519	$ 6,380	$ 5,002
Land	22,547	15,239	12,045
Buildings	10,982	8,475	7,698
Machinery	6,233	5,008	3,511
Accumulated depreciation	(396)	(305)	(235)
Total assets	$48,885	$34,797	$28,021

Liabilities and Stockholders' Equity:			
Current liabilities			
Accounts payable	$ 5,603	$ 4,112	$ 4,758
Taxes payable	786	543	235
Total current liabilities	$ 6,389	$ 4,655	$ 4,993
Long-term debt	16,987	16,115	19,546
Deferred income taxes	845	562	354
Stockholders' Equity:			
Common stock	22,220	12,764	2,907
Retained earnings	2,444	701	221
Total liabilities and stockholders' equity	$48,885	$34,797	$28,021

CASE 7

CONSOLIDATED STATEMENTS OF INCOME— XYZ COMPANY

	20X3	20X2	20X1
Revenues	$26,534	$22,473	$18,739
Cost of goods sold	18,201	18,161	15,406
Gross margin	$ 8,333	$ 4,312	$ 3,333
Operating expenses	5,428	3,512	2,965
Operating income before taxes	$ 2,905	$ 800	$ 368
Income taxes	1,162	320	147
Net income	$ 1,743	$ 480	$ 221

Calculate all ratios needed to determine if XYZ is possibly underreporting accounts payable. If you detect possible fraud, explain why you think it might exist.

Case 8

During the audit of a manufacturing client, you are instructed to do vertical and horizontal financial statement analyses. In your analyses, you notice little increase in the client's overall long-term liabilities. However, you remember that a note was extended to the client by a bank in the region, and you cannot find where the note is reflected on the financial statements. When you ask the controller about the loan, he claims that the debt has been forgiven by the regional bank, but upon further investigation, he cannot provide you with corroborating evidence to support his claim.

Claiming that creditors have forgiven existing debt is one way to understate liabilities. Describe several other ways a company might try to understate liabilities.

Case 9

ABCDE Technologies, Inc., designs, manufactures, and markets an extensive line of PC cards. The company sells its PC cards primarily to original equipment manufacturers (OEMs) for industrial and commercial applications in a market with intense competition. In fact, many OEM companies ran into financial difficulty in 2008 because of fierce competition. The following tables are part of the company's financial statements for 20x1 and 20x2:

CASE 9

ABCDE TECHNOLOGIES, INC., CONSOLIDATED BALANCE SHEET (PARTIAL)—UNAUDITED		
	DECEMBER 31, 20X1	DECEMBER 31, 20X2
Assets:		
Current Assets:		
Cash and cash equivalents	$6,181,520	$ 970,446
Available-for-sales securities	4,932,763	
Accounts receivable, net of allowance for doubtful accounts of $148,300 and $139,200 at December 31, 20X1 and 20X1, respectively	12,592,231	3,932,170
Inventories	18,229,317	8,609,492
Other current assets	18,229,317	8,609,492
Total current assets	$60,165,148	$22,121,600

CASE 9

ABCDE TECHNOLOGIES, INC., CONSOLIDATED INCOME STATEMENT (PARTIAL) YEAR ENDED DECEMBER 31—UNAUDITED			
	20X1	20X2	20X3
Sales	$37,847,681	$12,445,015	$8,213,236
Cost of goods sold	15,895,741	6,832,927	4,523,186
Gross margin	$21,951,940	$5,612,088	$3,690,050

1. Determine the red flags that exist in these financial statements. Describe the scenarios that might contain these symptoms.
2. Based upon the red flags and scenarios you identified, determine what types of financial statement fraud the company may be involved in. (*Hint:* Pay careful attention to cost of goods sold, sales, and allowance for doubtful accounts.)

Case 10

On a beautiful spring morning in 2002, Stephen Lowber, chief financial officer of Cutter and Buck, Inc., slowly arose from his bed, walked across the bedroom floor, and gazed out the window. It was a surprisingly clear, sunny day in Seattle, Washington. Despite the beauty of the day, the expression on Mr. Lowber's face was not positive. Cutter and Buck, a company that designs and markets upscale sportswear and outerwear, had enjoyed financial success. It recently announced revenue of $54.6 million for the fourth quarter and $152.5 million for the entire fiscal year. Cutter and Buck also announced it was rated as the hottest golf apparel brand from 1997 to 2001 by *Gold World Business Magazine*, a leading golf trade publication. Despite the success and positive publicity of his company, Lowber was haunted because he knew the company had engaged in fraud.

Cutter and Buck, Inc., had been encountering declining sales as it approached the end of its fiscal year. In the final days of the fiscal year, the company negotiated deals with three distributors under which Cutter and Buck would ship them a total of $5.7 million in products. The distributors were assured they had no obligation to pay for any of the goods until customers located by Cutter and Buck paid the distributors.

Sometime later, Lowber learned that these three distributors were operating as Cutter and Buck's warehouses. Rather than restate and correct the company's financial statements, Lowber concealed the transactions from Cutter and Buck's independent auditors and board of directors by arranging for distributors to return $3.8 million in unsold inventory. The returns were accounted for as a reduction in sales during the following year. Additionally, Lowber instructed personnel to override the recorded business lines instead of the business line under which those sales were originally recorded to hide the magnitude of the returns.

As a result of these fraudulent transactions, Cutter and Buck's management overstated true fourth quarter and annual revenue of fiscal year 2000 by 12 percent and 4 percent, respectively[3]

1. What were the main types of financial statement fraud committed at Cutter and Buck? Do these types of fraud occur often?
2. What should have been the appropriate accounting treatments?
3. The three parts of the fraud triangle are pressure, opportunity, and rationalization. List some of the pressures that may have led to this fraud.

Case 11

In November 2011, Wehav Funds, a profitable engineering firm, signed a loan guarantee as a third party for No Certainty Company, a newly formed organization focused on pharmaceutical research and development. Because Wehav Funds was a reputed and successful company, the loan was processed and approved by National Bank at the end of November 2007.

Due to the nature of the pharmaceutical industry, No Certainty projects are considered inherently risky. The company is currently awaiting FDA approval of a miracle drug that, according to marketing research, has the potential to generate millions of dollars of revenue per year. If the drug is not approved, No Certainty will not have the financial resources to continue business. The loan guarantee by Wehav Funds will come into effect, and Wehav Funds will have to front the full amount of the loan.

The end of the fiscal year is approaching, and as the auditor, you must decide how Wehav Funds should account for this loan guarantee in its financial statements.

1. Under what circumstances must a contingent liability be recorded on the balance sheet?
2. When must it be disclosed in the notes?
3. What is the appropriate accounting treatment for the No Certainty transaction with Wehav Funds?
4. Would your "fraud radar" go off if the company refused to record this item in the financial statements?

Case 12

David Sutherland, a partner and fraud examiner in Rachin Cohen & Holtz LLP, was driving to a client when he heard a CNN announcement that LucidCom, a newly emerged provider of network infrastructure and connectivity products, reported strong fourth-quarter earnings and announced a 14 percent jump in the company's stock. David quickly picked up his cell phone and dialed the number of his friend who was recently laid off from Netledger, a company LucidCom acquired just a few months prior.

David made a few other calls, and in a matter of weeks, he learned that Netledger had assets that were practically worthless to LucidCom and that those assets were reported as goodwill instead of written down after acquisition. For David, this change in the allocation of the purchase price represented a big red flag. When a company acquires another company, it is common to assign part of the purchase price to assets and part to goodwill. The assets are recorded at fair market value, and the remainder of the cost is assigned to goodwill. David questions whether LucidCom was being honest about the disclosures and causes of growth.

1. Were the earnings impressive because of the company's productivity and sound business strategy or because LucidCom took advantage of an acquisition and toyed with financial reports?
2. What type of fraud is represented in this case?
3. Can you think of ways this type of fraud can be prevented?

Case 13

You keep looking over the financial statement to see where your analysis is going wrong, but you can't see any problems—it just looks like inventory is getting larger and larger, but you know that you haven't seen growth in the actual levels of inventory that the financials seems to be indicating. You just finished a comprehensive audit of all the physical controls of inventory, so you doubt that inventory is being stolen. Everything else in the financials seems to look fine. In fact, they seem to indicate that the company is improving in profitability.

1. What might be a valid reason for the increase in inventory cost?
2. Assuming that fraud is being committed, how could a fraud perpetrator commit this type of fraud?
3. What could be done to prevent this type of fraud?

Case 14

In 2005, the SEC filed a civil action suit against Samuel Israel III and Daniel E. Marino, managers of a group of hedge funds known as the Bayou Funds. The SEC alleged that Israel and Marino defrauded millions of dollars in investor funds for their personal use. In addition to the civil suit, criminal fraud charges against Israel and Marino were also made.

The SEC's complaint alleged that from 1996 through 2005, investors deposited more than $450 million into the Bayou Funds. During that time period, Israel and Marino defrauded current investors and attracted new investors by grossly exaggerating the Bayou Funds' performance to make it appear that the funds were profitable and attractive investments. In actuality, the funds had never posted a profit.

In addition, Israel and Marino fabricated and distributed periodic account statements and performance summaries to the funds' investors containing fictitious profit and loss figures. They also forged audited financial statements in order to hide millions of dollars of trading losses from investors.

In its complaint, the SEC also alleged the following:

- In 2003, the Bayou Funds' performance was overstated, claiming a $43 million profit in the four hedge funds, while trading records show that the Bayou Funds actually lost $49 million.
- In 1999, Marino created a sham accounting firm, "Richmond-Fairfield Associates," that he used to fabricate annual "independent" audits of the Bayou Funds. This sham firm attested to the fake results that he and Israel had assigned to the Bayou Funds.
- Israel and Marino stole investor funds by annually withdrawing "incentive fees" from the Bayou Funds that they were not entitled to receive because the Bayou Funds were never profitable.
- By mid-2004, Israel and Marino suspended trading securities on behalf of the Funds and transferred all remaining assets (about $150 million) to non-Bayou-related entities for investment in fraudulent prime bank note trading programs and venture capital investments in nonpublic startup companies.
- Bayou management continued to send to investors periodic account statements and financial statements that falsely showed profitable hedge trading activities through mid-2005 despite having abandoned their hedge trading in 2004. (www.sec.gov/news/press/2005-139.htm.)

Despite the fact that the Bayou Funds fraud consisted of many red flags, many people invested large amounts of money in the funds. What are a few ways that these investors could have prevented their monetary loss?

CASE STUDIES

Case Study 1

On March 26, 2002, the SEC charged six Waste Management executive officers for the perpetration of a five-year financial fraud. The following is an article summarizing the SEC's complaint against these officers:

The complaint names Waste Management's former most senior officers: Dean L. Buntrock, Waste Management's founder, chairman of the board of directors, and chief executive officer during most of the relevant period; Phillip B. Rooney, president and chief operating officer, director, and CEO for a portion of the relevant period; James E. Koenig, executive vice president and chief financial officer; Thomas C. Hau, vice president, corporate controller, and chief accounting officer; Herbert Getz, senior vice president, general counsel, and secretary; and Bruce D. Tobecksen, vice president of finance.

According to the complaint, the defendants violated, and aided and abetted violations of, anti-fraud, reporting, and record-keeping provisions of the federal securities laws. The Commission is seeking injunctions prohibiting future violations, disgorgement of defendants' ill-gotten gains, civil money penalties, and officer and director bars against all defendants.

The complaint alleges that defendants fraudulently manipulated the company's financial results to meet predetermined earnings targets. The company's revenues were not growing fast enough to meet these targets, so defendants instead resorted to improperly eliminating and deferring current period expenses to inflate earnings. They employed a multitude of improper accounting practices to achieve this objective. Among other things, the complaint charges that defendants:

- Avoided depreciation expenses on their garbage trucks by both assigning unsupported and inflated salvage values and extending their useful lives,
- Assigned arbitrary salvage values to other assets that previously had no salvage value,
- Failed to record expenses for decreases in the value of landfills as they were filled with waste,
- Refused to record expenses necessary to write off the costs of unsuccessful and abandoned landfill development projects,
- Established inflated environmental reserves (liabilities) in connection with acquisitions so that the

excess reserves could be used to avoid recording unrelated operating expenses,

- Improperly capitalized a variety of expenses, and
- Failed to establish sufficient reserves (liabilities) to pay for income taxes and other expenses.

Defendants' improper accounting practices were centralized at corporate headquarters, according to the complaint. Each year, Buntrock, Rooney, and others prepared an annual budget in which they set earnings targets for the upcoming year. During the year, they monitored the company's actual operating results and compared them to the quarterly targets set in the budget, the complaint says. To reduce expenses and inflate earnings artificially, defendants then primarily used "top-level adjustments" to conform the company's actual results to the predetermined earnings targets, according to the complaint. The inflated earnings of prior periods then became the floor for future manipulations. The consequences, however, created what Hau referred to as a "one-off" problem. To sustain the scheme, earnings fraudulently achieved in one period had to be replaced in the next.

Defendants allegedly concealed their scheme in a variety of ways. They are charged with making false and misleading statements about the company's accounting practices, financial condition, and future prospects in filings with the Commission, reports to shareholders, and press releases. They are also are charged with using accounting manipulations known as "netting" and "geography" to make reported results appear better than they actually were and avoid public scrutiny. Defendants allegedly used netting to eliminate approximately $490 million in current period operating expenses and accumulated prior period accounting misstatements by offsetting them against unrelated one-time gains on the sale or exchange of assets. They are charged with using geography entries to move tens of millions of dollars between various line items on the company's income statement to, in Koenig's words, "make the financials look the way we want to show them."

Defendants were allegedly aided in their fraud by the company's long-time auditor, Arthur Andersen LLP, which repeatedly issued unqualified audit reports on the company's materially false and misleading annual financial statements. At the outset of the fraud, management capped Andersen's audit fees and advised the Andersen engagement partner that the

firm could earn additional fees through "special work." Andersen nevertheless identified the company's improper accounting practices and quantified much of the impact of those practices on the company's financial statements. Andersen annually presented company management with what it called Proposed Adjusting Journal Entries (PAJEs) to correct errors that understated expenses and overstated earnings in the company's financial statements.

Management consistently refused to make the adjustments called for by the PAJEs, according to the complaint. Instead, defendants secretly entered into an agreement with Andersen fraudulently to write off the accumulated errors over periods of up to ten years and to change the underlying accounting practices, but to do so only in future periods, the complaint charges. The signed, four-page agreement, known as the Summary of Action Steps (attached to the Commission's complaint), identified improper accounting practices that went to the core of the company's operations and prescribed 32 "must do" steps for the company to follow to change those practices. The Action Steps thus constituted an agreement between the company and its outside auditor to cover up past frauds by committing additional frauds in the future, the complaint charges.

Defendants could not even comply with the Action Steps agreement, according to the complaint. Writing off the errors and changing the underlying accounting practices as prescribed in the agreement would have prevented the company from meeting earnings targets and defendants from enriching themselves, the complaint says.

Defendants' scheme eventually unraveled. In mid-July 1997, a new CEO ordered a review of the company's accounting practices. That review ultimately led to the restatement of the company's financial statements for 1992 through the third quarter of 1997. When the company filed its restated financial statements in February 1998, the company acknowledged that it had misstated its pre-tax earnings by approximately $1.7 billion. At the time, the restatement was the largest in corporate history.

As news of the company's overstatement of earnings became public, Waste Management's shareholders (other than the defendants who sold company stock and thus avoided losses) lost more than $6 billion in the market value of their investments when the stock price plummeted by more than 33 percent.

Questions

1. The SEC is often called the "watchdog" of corporate America. How does it assist in preventing fraud?
2. According to the summary, why did the Waste Management executives commit the fraud?
3. You are an ambitious manager in the sales department of a company and have just received the upcoming year's targeted earnings report. You are concerned that top management has set revenue targets for your division that are practically unreachable. However, anticipating a promotion to vice president of sales if your division maintains good performance, you are determined to reach management's goal. What actions would you take to satisfy management's expectations and still maintain your integrity?

Case Study 2

WorldCom Corporation began as a small company in the 1980s. Under the direction of CEO and cofounder Bernie Ebbers, it quickly grew to become one of the largest telecom companies in the world. Ebbers' success resulted in his theory that survival in the telecommunications industry would come only through company growth and expansion. Therefore, during the next two decades, WorldCom grew through acquisitions, purchasing more than 60 different firms in the latter half of the 1990s alone. In 1997, WorldCom acquired MCI in a transaction that cost the company roughly $37 billion, and it would have purchased Sprint if it had not been prevented by federal antitrust regulations.

In less than two decades, WorldCom had grown from a small telephone company to a corporate giant, controlling about half of the U.S. Internet traffic and handling at least half of the e-mail traffic throughout the world. The value of WorldCom stock followed the company's growth, eventually reaching more than $60 per share. However, corporate scandal and falsified financial statements soon led the company down the dreaded spiral until, in 2002, it filed for the largest Chapter 11 bankruptcy in U.S. history.

In 1998, WorldCom experienced a sudden and unexpected halt in its formerly increasing revenues. WorldCom's stock immediately took a hit. As its stock continued to drop, WorldCom became unable to reach Wall Street expectations, and in a desperate effort to maintain investor confidence, the company resorted to dishonesty.

WorldCom had established a large reserve account, which was initially maintained to cover the liabilities of companies it purchased. However, when revenues from operations continued to decrease, the company decided to use these reserve funds to boost its numbers. In total, WorldCom illegally converted $3.8 billion of reserve funds into revenues from operations.

However, these fictitious revenues were not enough to help WorldCom meet its expected level of revenue. So, in December 2000, CFO Scott Sullivan ordered accountants at the company's Texas division to reclassify many of the company's expenses. Members of the accounting staff were to reclassify operating expenses (an income statement account) as capital expenses (a long-term asset account). For example, lease expenses and computer expenses would become lease assets and computer assets.

This reclassification of expenses did two things. First, by greatly decreasing operating expenses on its income statement, WorldCom increased its net income. Secondly, by converting operating expenses into capital assets, the company increased its long-term asset account. The idea was that a huge increase in both retained earnings (from an increase in net income) and assets would inevitably lead to an increase in the value of WorldCom and its stock. Overall, nearly $3.85 billion of operating expenses were misclassified as capital assets.

Other fraudulent activity dug the company's fraud deeper and deeper until the schemes were eventually detected and investigated by the company's own internal audit department and the SEC. In the end, it was discovered that more than $11 billion had been defrauded from a company that was soon forced to file the largest Chapter 11 bankruptcy ever recorded. As a result of the fraud, thousands of employees lost not only their jobs, but also their entire retirement savings. The fraud cost investors billions of dollars as the company quickly went from a multibillion-dollar franchise to bankruptcy. Several company executives were indicted on counts of conspiracy and security fraud. The main perpetrator, Scott Sullivan (CFO), received a sentence requiring him to pay as much as $25 million in fines and serve up to 65 years in prison. Other executives received similar sentences. In essence, the WorldCom fraud left those involved in the company with nearly nothing. It proved a prominent example of the age-old adage "cheaters never prosper."

Questions

1. Suppose you are an accountant for pre-fraud WorldCom. You have just been instructed by the CFO to alter specific company accounts in order

to boost the company's numbers before fourth-quarter disclosures. You know the actions are unethical, but you fear that refusing to comply with executive orders may result in punishment and possible termination of your job. What would you do?

2. Although it usually doesn't involve physically stealing money, financial statement fraud is commonly considered the most expensive type of fraud. Why is this true?

3. The Sarbanes-Oxley Act of 2002 has, in many ways, changed the role of financial statement auditors. In addition to ensuring financial statement accuracy, independent auditors are now required to review a company's internal controls and report their assessments in the company's annual report. How might these new policies help prevent financial statement fraud from occurring?

INTERNET ASSIGNMENTS

1. Enron founder and former Chairman and CEO Kenneth Lay was indicted in July 2004 for his role in the Enron scandals. The SEC's complaint against Lay, ironically, seemed to corroborate Lay's protests that he had nothing to do with the manipulation of Enron's books. The complaint, however, did heavily accuse Lay, in concert with Jeff Skilling and Richard Causey, of disclosure fraud. Review the SEC's complaint at www.sec.gov/litigation/complaints/comp18776.pdf, beginning with paragraph 59, and answer the following questions:

a. The SEC complaint accuses the defendants of disseminating false and misleading statements through which seven forums?

b. How many separate incidents does the SEC complaint identify with Causey, Skilling, and Lay making false and misleading statements?

c. How many false or misleading reports does the SEC accuse the defendants of causing to be filed with the SEC?

d. Using the SEC's online EDGAR database, look up the last false and misleading form listed: Form 8-K dated November 9, 2001. As stated in Footnote 11 of Chapter 10, "Form 8-K is the SEC report filed at the end of any month in which significant events have occurred that are of interest to public investors." Summarize the significant events reported by this particular 8-K (reflected by the six bullet points at the beginning of the document).

DEBATES

The following discussion is found in the U.S. Bankruptcy Report on Lehman Bros. Holdings dated March 22, 2010:

Lehman employed off-balance sheet devices, known within Lehman as "Repo 105" and "Repo 108" transactions, to temporarily remove securities inventory from its balance sheet, usually for a period of seven to ten days ... in late 2007 and 2008. Repo 105 transactions were nearly identical to standard repurchase and resale ("repo") transactions that Lehman (and other investment banks) used to secure short-term financing, with a critical difference: Lehman accounted for Repo 105 transactions as "sales" as opposed to financing transactions ... By recharacterizing the Repo 105 transaction as a "sale," Lehman removed the inventory from its balance sheet.

Lehman regularly increased its use of Repo 105 transactions in the days prior to reporting periods to reduce its publicly reported net leverage and balance sheet. Lehman's periodic reports did not disclose the cash borrowing from the Repo 105 transaction ... Lehman used the cash from the Repo 105 transaction to pay down other liabilities, thereby reducing both the total liabilities and the total assets reported on its balance sheet and lowering its leverage ratios.... A few days after the new quarter began, Lehman would borrow the necessary funds to repay the cash borrowing plus interest, repurchase the securities, and restore the assets to its balance sheet.

Lehman never publicly disclosed its use of Repo 105 transactions, its accounting treatment for these transactions, the considerable escalation of its total Repo 105 usage in late 2007 and into 2008, or the material impact these transactions had on the firm's publicly reported net leverage ratio. According to former Global Financial Controller Martin Kelly, a careful review of Lehman's Forms 10-K and 10-Q would not reveal Lehman's use of Repo 105 transactions.

Lehman failed to disclose its Repo 105 practice even though Kelly believed "that the only purpose or motive for the transactions was reduction in balance sheet;" felt that "there was no substance to the transactions;" and expressed concerns with Lehman's Repo 105 program to two consecutive Lehman Chief Financial Officers … advising them that the lack of economic substance to Repo 105 transactions meant "reputational risk" to Lehman if the firm's use of the transactions became known to the public. In addition to its material omissions, Lehman affirmatively misrepresented in its financial statements that the firm treated all repo transactions as financing transactions—i.e., not sales—for financial reporting purposes.

Starting in mid-2007, Lehman faced a crisis: market observers began demanding that investment banks reduce their leverage. The inability to reduce leverage could lead to a ratings downgrade, which would have had an immediate, tangible monetary impact on Lehman.… In mid-to-late 2007, top Lehman executives from across the firm felt pressure to reduce the firm's leverage for quarterly and annual reports.…

By January 2008, Lehman CEO Fuld ordered a firm-wide deleveraging strategy, hoping to reduce the firm's positions in commercial and residential real estate and leveraged loans in particular by half. In the words of one internal Lehman presentation, "Reducing leverage is necessary to remove refinancing risk and win back the confidence of the market, lenders, and investors." Fuld recalled that Lehman had to improve its net leverage ratio by selling inventory …

Selling inventory, however, proved difficult in late 2007 and into 2008 because, starting in mid-2007, many of Lehman's inventory positions had grown increasingly "sticky"—i.e., difficult to sell without incurring substantial losses.… In light of these factors, Lehman relied at an increasing pace on Repo 105 transactions at each quarter-end in late 2007 and early 2008 …

Notably, during Lehman's 2008 earnings calls in which it touted its leverage reduction, analysts frequently inquired about the means by which Lehman was reducing its leverage.… CFO Callan told analysts that Lehman … was reducing its leverage through the sale of less liquid asset categories but said nothing about the firm's use of Repo 105 transactions.

Is it ethical to keep the types of liabilities discussed in this article off the balance sheet, or is this a type of financial statement fraud?

END NOTES

1. A triple-net lease means that the lessee is responsible for paying property taxes, maintenance, insurance, and utilities. Most of the leases were for periods of 14 years or more.

2. www.berkshirehathaway.com/1998ar/1998final.html

3. Securities and Exchange Commission, www.sec.gov/news/press/2003-93.htm and Cutter and Buck, www.cutterbuck.com

Strategic Reasoning and Detecting Liability, Asset, and Inadequate Disclosure Frauds

As a continuation of Appendix 12 from Chapter 12, this appendix lists the common audit procedures that correspond to many of the financial statement frauds discussed in this chapter. Specifically, it will address liability, asset, and inadequate disclosure frauds and show how these procedures may help detect the various schemes.

Liability-Related Fraud Schemes

Table 13A.1 lists several common audit procedures and shows the liability-related fraud schemes and transactions that each procedure may help detect. The primary concern is that liabilities are understated. Finding unrecorded liabilities is often difficult, but can be done by performing the proper audit procedures.

As displayed in Table 13A.1, some audit procedures can be used for detecting multiple fraud schemes or transactions. It is important to note that although analytical procedures may indicate fraud is occurring, they are not conclusive of fraud. Because each audit procedure is limited in its ability to confirm or disconfirm a particular fraud, a combination of audit procedures will increase the probability of discovering fraudulent behavior.

Auditors are required to use professional skepticism while conducting an audit and should also employ strategic reasoning. Strategic reasoning is especially important given that smart fraud perpetrators know the common audit procedures and can design their scheme to be concealed from these procedures.

Strategic Reasoning Relating to Liability-Related Fraud

As mentioned previously, strategic reasoning is important for discovering financial statement fraud. While an auditor hopes that performing typical audit procedures will assist in the discovery of financial statement fraud, he or she should be aware that fraud perpetrators may be consciously attempting to prevent the auditor from discovering their fraud. Because management may apply strategic reasoning in their attempts to conceal their fraud schemes, they have probably anticipated the standard audit procedures—especially if the auditor has historically performed these procedures.

Applying strategic reasoning to standard audit procedures can be as simple as making slight modifications to the procedures. For example, to look for unrecorded liabilities, an auditor may send out a positive confirmation to all vendors a company has dealt with in the past, whether they have a current payable balance owed to that vendor or not. An auditor who suspects that the client may not be recording all liabilities could apply strategic reasoning to try to detect management's efforts to conceal this scheme. Management, knowing that confirmations are standard in an audit, may not give the auditor a complete list of vendors it has dealt with in the past (especially those recorded as a zero liability balance when in fact they do owe money). The auditor should realize that obtaining an incomplete list from management is a possibility and should compare the current list with lists in prior years or with vendor invoices, purchasing department records, or other purchasing documents. By searching for other sources of vendor listings such as invoice sheets or prior years' lists, a fraud such as this may be detected more easily.

Asset-Related Fraud Schemes

Similar to liability-related fraud, audit procedures can be used to detect asset-related fraud. The primary concern is that assets are overstated. Table 13A.2 is similar to Table 13A.1 and lists common audit procedures related to assets and indicates which procedures help in detecting the asset-related fraud schemes or transactions.

While no one procedure will detect all potential fraud schemes, by combining these procedures, an auditor has a greater chance of detecting a fraud that is being perpetrated. Because management is likely to know the procedures that the auditor will perform, auditors should apply strategic reasoning in an attempt to discover concealed fraud schemes involving assets.

Strategic Reasoning Relating to Asset-Related Fraud

As with liability-related fraud, asset-related financial statement fraud is likely to be concealed by management. Because management is aware that auditors perform specific audit procedures, they will likely attempt to conceal the fraud from standard audit procedures. For example, if management is attempting to overstate fixed assets and knows that the auditor will be physically inspecting these assets, they may try to borrow or rent equipment or property that is not theirs to be included in the fixed assets counts. An auditor applying strategic reasoning would realize this possibility and not only count the fixed asset, but also examine public records databases that specify ownership of the assets.

Inadequate Disclosure Frauds

When companies issue fraudulent or misleading statements or press releases knowingly, they are trying to deceive the public and are committing disclosure fraud. Table 13A.3 is an example of audit procedures that will help identify various disclosure-fraud schemes.

As you can see, inadequate disclosure is often identified by observing or questioning management or reviewing announcements and press releases in comparison with financial statements. Again, auditors must apply strategic reasoning to better identify potential disclosure fraud.

Strategic Reasoning Relating to Disclosure Fraud

Typically, an auditor will review minutes from the board of directors' meetings. Management, attempting to conceal a fraud it hopes to avoid, may exclude discussions about the company's business operations from the minutes. An auditor applying strategic reasoning would be aware of this possibility and inquire of lower-level employees about the company's claims regarding its business operations.

Detecting inadequate disclosure fraud is not as easy as detecting other types of fraud. In fact, it is often difficult to detect inadequate disclosure fraud without a tip or complaint. Thus, auditors need to be observant and maintain a high level of professional skepticism when reviewing press releases and important announcements, when conversing with management, and when considering the current state of the company.

Although these are only a few examples of how strategic reasoning could be used during an audit to detect financial statement fraud, they illustrate why and how auditors should consider management's efforts to conceal fraud schemes from standard procedures.

TABLE 13A.1 COMMON AUDIT PROCEDURES FOR LIABILITY-RELATED FRAUD SCHEMES

COMMON FRAUD SCHEMES	COMMON AUDIT PROCEDURES
Record Payables in subsequent period	• Review notes paid or renewed after the balance sheet date to determine if unrecorded liabilities exist at year-end. • Compare dates on vouchers with the dates transactions were recorded in the purchases journal. • Review debt activity for a few days before and after year-end to determine if the transactions are included in the proper period. • Examine board of directors' minutes, company files, service agreements, and correspondence with others.
Don't record purchases	• Trace a sample of vouchers to the purchases journal. • Examine board of directors' minutes, company files, service agreements, and correspondence with others.
Overstate purchase returns and purchase discounts	• Examine board of directors' minutes, company files, service agreements, and correspondence with others.
Record payments made in later periods as being paid in earlier periods	• Obtain a standard bank confirmation that requests specific information on notes from banks. • Review notes paid or renewed after the balance sheet date to determine if unrecorded liabilities exist at year-end. • Recompute accrued interest payable. • Compare current year's interest expense with that of prior years. • Compare dates on vouchers with the dates transactions were recorded in the purchases journal. • Review debt activity for a few days before and after year-end to determine if the transactions are included in the proper period. • Examine board of directors' minutes, company files, service agreements, and correspondence with others.
Fraudulent recording of payments	• Obtain a standard bank confirmation that requests specific information on notes from banks. • Review interest expense for payments to debt-holders not listed on the debt analysis schedule.

TABLE 13A.1 COMMON AUDIT PROCEDURES FOR LIABILITY-RELATED FRAUD SCHEMES (CONTINUED)

COMMON FRAUD SCHEMES	COMMON AUDIT PROCEDURES
Fraudulent recording of payments, continued	• Review notes paid or renewed after the balance sheet date to determine if unrecorded liabilities exist at year-end. • Recompute accrued interest payable. • Compare current year's interest expense with that of prior years. • Examine board of directors' minutes, company files, service agreements, and correspondence with others.
Not recorded Liabilities	• Obtain a standard bank confirmation that requests specific information on notes from banks. • Review interest expense for payments to debt-holders not listed on the debt analysis schedule. • Review notes paid or renewed after the balance sheet date to determine if unrecorded liabilities exist at year-end. • Recompute accrued interest payable. • Compare current year's interest expense with that of prior years. • Trace a sample of vouchers to the purchases journal. • Examine board of directors' minutes, company files, service agreements, and correspondence with others.
Record accruals in later period	• Review notes paid or renewed after the balance sheet date to determine if unrecorded liabilities exist at year-end. • Recompute accrued interest payable. • Compare dates on vouchers with the dates transactions were recorded in the purchases journal. • Review debt activity for a few days before and after year-end to determine if the transactions are included in the proper period. • Examine board of directors' minutes, company files, service agreements, and correspondence with others.
Record unearned revenues as earned revenues (or vice versa)	• Trace a sample of vouchers to the purchases journal.

TABLE 13A.1 COMMON AUDIT PROCEDURES FOR LIABILITY-RELATED FRAUD SCHEMES (CONTINUED)

COMMON FRAUD SCHEMES	COMMON AUDIT PROCEDURES
Record unearned revenues as earned revenues (or vice versa), continued	• Review debt activity for a few days before and after year-end to determine if the transactions are included in the proper period. • Examine board of directors' minutes, company files, service agreements, and correspondence with others.
Not recorded warranty (service) liabilities	• Trace a sample of vouchers to the purchases journal.
Record deposits as revenues	• Trace a sample of vouchers to the purchases journal.
Not record repurchase agreements and commitments	• Review debt for related-party transactions or borrowing from major shareholders.
Borrow from related parties at less than arm's length transactions	• Review interest expense for payments to debt-holders not listed on the debt analysis schedule. • Review debt for related-party transactions or borrowing from major shareholders.
Borrow against equities in assets	• Obtain a standard bank confirmation that requests specific information on notes from banks.
Write off liabilities as forgiven	• Obtain a standard bank confirmation that requests specific information on notes from banks. • Review interest expense for payments to debt-holders not listed on the debt analysis schedule. • Review notes paid or renewed after the balance sheet date to determine if unrecorded liabilities exist at year-end. • Recompute accrued interest payable. • Compare current year's interest expense with that of prior years. • Review debt for related-party transactions or borrowing from major shareholders.
Claim liabilities as personal debt rather than as debt of the entity	• Obtain a standard bank confirmation that requests specific information on notes from banks. • Review interest expense for payments to debt-holders not listed on the debt analysis schedule.

TABLE 13A.1 COMMON AUDIT PROCEDURES FOR LIABILITY-RELATED FRAUD SCHEMES (CONTINUED)

COMMON FRAUD SCHEMES	COMMON AUDIT PROCEDURES
Claim liabilities as personal debt rather than as debt of the entity, continued	• Review notes paid or renewed after the balance sheet date to determine if unrecorded liabilities exist at year-end. • Recompute accrued interest payable. • Compare current year's interest expense with that of prior years. • Review debt for related-party transactions or borrowing from major shareholders.
Don't record contingent liabilities that are probable	• Review legal bills. • Discuss with in-house and outside legal counsel. • Inquire of management. • Examine board of directors' minutes, company files, service agreements, and correspondence with others.
Record contingent liabilities at amounts too low	• Review legal bills. • Discuss with in-house and outside legal counsel. • Inquire of management. • Examine board of directors' minutes, company files, service agreements, and correspondence with others.

TABLE 13A.2 COMMON AUDIT PROCEDURES FOR ASSET-RELATED FRAUD SCHEMES

COMMON FRAUD SCHEMES	COMMON AUDIT PROCEDURES
Inappropriately capitalizing as assets various kinds of costs	• Verify the existence of major additions by physically examining the capital asset. • Examine or confirm deeds or title documents for proof of ownership. • Vouch transactions included in repairs and maintenance for items that should be capitalized. • Examine asset valuation to determine appropriate research and development expense and other potentially capitalized expenses and compare to prior years. • Compare financial statement balances and policies with those used by other similar companies.
Using market values rather than book values to record assets	• Compare financial statements of companies in pre- and post-merger or acquisition. • Compare financial statement balances with nonfinancial statement information or things such as the assets they represent. • Compare financial statement balances and policies with those used by other similar companies.
Having the wrong entity be the 'purchaser'	• Examine board of directors' minutes, company files, and correspondence. • Compare financial statements of companies in pre- and post-merger or acquisition.
Allocating costs among assets in inappropriate ways	• Vouch transactions included in repairs and maintenance for items that should be capitalized. • Compare asset depreciation life to that of other comparable assets in comparable companies. • Examine board of directors' minutes, company files, and correspondence. • Compare financial statements of companies in pre- and post-merger or acquisition. • Examine asset valuation to determine appropriate research and development expense and other potentially capitalized expenses and compare to prior years. • Compare financial statement balances with nonfinancial statement information or things such as the assets they represent. • Compare financial statement balances and policies with those used by other similar companies.

TABLE 13A.2 COMMON AUDIT PROCEDURES FOR ASSET-RELATED FRAUD SCHEMES (CONTINUED)

COMMON FRAUD SCHEMES	COMMON AUDIT PROCEDURES
Recording fictitious assets or inflating the value of assets in intercompany amounts or transactions	• Verify the existence of major additions by physically examining the capital asset. • Examine or confirm deeds or title documents for proof of ownership. • Review lease agreements to ensure that lease transactions are accounted for properly. • Compare financial statements of companies in pre- and post-merger or acquisition. • Compare financial statement balances with nonfinancial statement information or things such as the assets they represent. • Compare financial statement balances and policies with those used by other similar companies.
Sham purchases and sales of assets with 'straw buyers'	• Verify the existence of major additions by physically examining the capital asset. • Examine or confirm deeds or title documents for proof of ownership. • Compare financial statement balances and policies with those used by other similar companies.
Overstating asset costs with related parties	• Verify the existence of major additions by physically examining the capital asset. • Examine board of directors' minutes, company files, and correspondence. • Examine asset valuation to determine appropriate research and development expense and other potentially capitalized expenses and compare to prior years. • Compare financial statement balances and policies with those used by other similar companies.
Not recording depreciation	• Compare asset depreciation life to that of other comparable assets in comparable companies. • Examine asset valuation to determine appropriate research and development expense and other potentially capitalized expenses and compare to prior years. • Compare financial statement balances and policies with those used by other similar companies.

TABLE 13A.2 COMMON AUDIT PROCEDURES FOR ASSET-RELATED FRAUD SCHEMES (CONTINUED)

COMMON FRAUD SCHEMES	COMMON AUDIT PROCEDURES
Collusion with outside parties to overstate assets (e.g., allocating inventory costs to fixed assets)	• Vouch transactions included in repairs and maintenance for items that should be capitalized. • Examine board of directors' minutes, company files, and correspondence. • Examine asset valuation to determine appropriate research and development expense and other potentially capitalized expenses and compare to prior years. • Compare financial statement balances and policies with those used by other similar companies.
Misstating marketable securities with the aid of related parties	• Examine board of directors' minutes, company files, and correspondence. • Compare financial statement balances with nonfinancial statement information or things such as the assets they represent. • Compare financial statement balances and policies with those used by other similar companies.
Misappropriation of cash resulting in misstated financial statements without management's knowledge	• Compare financial statement balances with nonfinancial statement information or things such as the assets they represent. • Compare financial statement balances and policies with those used by other similar companies.
Covering thefts of cash or other assets by overstating receivables or inventory	• Compare financial statement balances with nonfinancial statement information or things such as the assets they represent. • Compare financial statement balances and policies with those used by other similar companies.

TABLE 13A.3 COMMON AUDIT PROCEDURES FOR DISCLOSURE-RELATED FRAUD SCHEMES

COMMON FRAUD SCHEMES	COMMON AUDIT PROCEDURE
Misrepresentation about the overall nature of the company or its products	• Review company announcements and compare with disclosure in financial statements. • Review press releases mentioning the company. • Review board of directors' minutes, company files, etc. • Interview management regarding the company's financial situation, financial goals and objectives, risk tolerance, etc.
Misrepresentations in MD&A and Other Nonfinancial information in financial reports	• Review company announcements and compare with disclosure in financial statements. • Review press releases mentioning the company. • Review board of directors' minutes, company files, etc. • Interview management regarding the company's financial situation, financial goals and objectives, risk tolerance, etc.
Misleading footnote disclosure	• Examine note or bond agreements for any restrictions that should be disclosed in the footnotes. • Examine note or bond agreements to ascertain whether any capital assets are pledged as collateral and require disclosure in the footnotes. • Review company announcements and compare with disclosure in financial statements. • Review board of directors' minutes, company files, etc. • Interview management regarding the company's financial situation, financial goals and objectives, risk tolerance, etc.

PART **6**

Other Types of Fraud

CHAPTER 14

Fraud against Organizations

LEARNING OBJECTIVES

After studying this chapter, you should be able to:

- Understand the extent to which employees and others commit occupational fraud.
- Describe the nature and various types of asset misappropriations.
- Discuss the nature and various types of corruption.

TO THE STUDENT

This chapter, the first in Part 6 where we discuss various types of frauds, focuses on frauds against organizations, sometimes called *occupational fraud*. These types of fraud are by far the most common, and nearly every organization experiences occupational fraud. In this chapter, we cover embezzlement and theft, commonly referred to as *asset misappropriation*, and corruption, where employees use their influence in business transactions to obtain unauthorized benefits contrary to their duties to their employers.

Don Best (name changed) began work selling insurance in Wheeling, West Virginia. After 10 months, he was fired for stealing $200. After an assortment of odd jobs, he moved to Ohio and worked as an accountant for a local baker. Best was caught embezzling funds and paid back the $1,000 he had stolen. Subsequently, he was dismissed but not reported to authorities. Best then returned to West Virginia and went to work for Wheeling Bronze, Inc., a bronze-casting maker. A short time later, the president of Wheeling Bronze discovered that several returned checks were missing and that there was a $30,000 cash shortfall. After an extensive search, workers uncovered a number of canceled checks with forged signatures. Best was questioned, and he confessed to the scheme. He was given the choice of paying back the stolen amount or going to jail. Best's parents took out a mortgage on their home to pay back the stolen money. No charges were ever filed.

Several months later, Best found a job in Pennsylvania working for Smithfield Pipe Cleaning. When Best was caught embezzling funds, he again avoided prosecution by promising to repay the $20,000 he had stolen. Shortly thereafter, Lincoln Industries hired him as an accountant. Best proved to be the ideal employee and was quickly promoted to the position of office manager. He was very dedicated, worked long hours, and did outstanding work. Soon after his promotion, he purchased a new home, a new car, and a new wardrobe. Two years later, Best's world unraveled again when Lincoln's auditors discovered that $31,000 was missing. Once again, Best made a tearful confession and a promise to repay all money stolen. Best confessed that he had written several checks to himself and had

then recorded payments to vendors on the copies of the checks. To cover his tracks, he altered the company's monthly bank statements. He used the stolen money to finance his lifestyle and to repay Wheeling Bronze and Smithfield Pipe Cleaning.

Best claimed that he had never before embezzled funds. He showed a great deal of remorse—so much that Lincoln Industries even hired a lawyer for him. He gave Lincoln a lien on his house, and was quietly dismissed. Because the president of Lincoln did not want the publicity to harm Best's wife and three children, Lincoln never pressed charges against him.

Best next took a job as an accountant in Steubenville, Ohio, with Rustcraft Broadcasting Company, a chain of radio and TV stations. Associated Communications acquired Rustcraft, and Best moved to Pittsburgh to become Associated's new controller. Best immediately began dipping into Associated's accounts. Over a six-year period, he embezzled approximately $1.36 million, $445,000 of that in one year when he was promoted to CFO. Best used various methods to embezzle the money. One approach to circumvent the need for two signatures on every check was to ask another executive who was leaving on vacation to sign several checks "just in case" the company needed additional cash while he was gone. Best used most of these checks to siphon funds off to his personal accounts. While working at Associated, Best was able to lead a very comfortable lifestyle. He bought a new house and several expensive cars. He bought vacation property and a very expensive wardrobe.

Best's lifestyle came crashing down while he was on vacation. A bank officer called to inquire about a check written to

Mr. Best. An investigation ensued, and Best confessed to embezzling funds. As part of the out-of-court settlement with Best, Associated Communications received most of Best's personal property. After leaving Associated, Best was hired by a former colleague. Best underwent therapy and believed he had resolved his problem with compulsive embezzlement.

When interviewed about his past activities, Best said that he felt his problem with theft was an illness, just like alcoholism or compulsive gambling. The illness was driven by a subconscious need to be admired and liked by others. He thought that by spending money, others would like him. Best stated that once he got started, he couldn't stop.[1]

In Part 4 of this book, we focused on the investigation of fraud. In Part 5, we discussed financial statement frauds. Part 6 covers various other types of fraud. In this chapter, we describe occupational fraud, or fraud committed by employees, customers, and vendors against organizations. In Chapter 15, we discuss consumer fraud, including scams in which perpetrators deceive individuals into paying or investing their money (commonly called *investment scams* or *investment frauds*). In Chapter 16, we concentrate on frauds associated with bankruptcies, divorce, taxes, and money laundering. We conclude the section with Chapter 17, which defines e-commerce frauds, including fraud committed via the Internet and through other uses of technology. These chapters will help the student recognize that there are additional types of frauds. In thinking about various types of fraud, always remember that fraud perpetrators are creative, and new schemes are developed every day. Our approach in this section is to introduce you to some of the most common types of fraud so that you will want to study other types of fraud on your own.

STOP & THINK *Besides the frauds introduced in the above paragraphs, what other types of frauds can individuals perpetrate against organizations?*

Fraud Statistics

In this chapter, we draw heavily (with permission) from Joseph Wells's book *Occupational Fraud and Abuse*, as well as his other works and from two surveys: (1) the 2010 ACFE Report to the Nation on Occupational Fraud & Abuse and (2) KPMG's Integrity Survey for 2008–2009. Both of these surveys are redone on a periodic basis. Joseph Wells's book provides an excellent taxonomy of occupational fraud.[2]

The 2010 ACFE Report to the Nation on Occupational Fraud & Abuse covers three types of fraud against organizations: (1) **asset misappropriation**—any scheme that involves the theft or misuse of an organization's assets, (2) **corruption**—any scheme in which a person uses his or her influence in a business transaction to obtain an unauthorized benefit contrary to that person's duty to his or her employer, and (3) **fraudulent statements**—fabrication of an organization's financial statements to make the company appear more or less profitable. As financial statement frauds were covered in Chapters 11–13, this chapter will focus on misappropriation and corruption.

The following statistics about occupational fraud are based on 1,843 fraud cases reported in the ACFE's 2010 study by certified fraud examiners (CFE):

- *Occupational fraud and abuse impose enormous costs on an organization. The median loss caused by occupational frauds in the study was $160,000. Nearly one-quarter of the cases caused at least $1 million in losses.*
- *Participants in the study estimated that organizations lose 5 percent of their annual revenues to fraud. Applied to the 2009 Gross World Product, this 5 percent figure would translate to approximately $2.9 trillion in fraud losses.*
- *Occupational fraud schemes can be very difficult to detect. The median length of the schemes in the study was 18 months from the time the fraud began until it was detected.*
- *Occupational frauds are more likely to be detected by a tip than by other means such as internal audits, external audits, or internal controls.*
- *Certain antifraud controls have a significant impact on an organization's exposure to fraud. Antifraud controls include internal audit departments, surprise audits, and antifraud training for employees and managers. Victim organizations that had such antifraud controls in place had lower losses compared to organizations without antifraud controls in place.*

- *Small businesses continue to suffer disproportionate fraud losses. The most common occupational frauds in small businesses involve employees fraudulently writing company checks, skimming revenues, and processing fraudulent invoices.*
- *One reason small businesses suffer such high fraud loss is that they generally do a poor job of proactively detecting fraud. Only a small percentage of small businesses in the study had anonymous fraud reporting systems, internal audit departments, surprise audits, or fraud training for their employees and managers.*
- *The size of the loss caused by occupational fraud is strongly related to the position of the perpetrator. For example, frauds committed by owners/executives were more than three times as costly as frauds committed by managers.*
- *Most of the occupational fraud schemes in the study involved either the accounting department or upper management and more than 80 percent of the frauds involved in the study were committed by employees in accounting, sales, upper management, customer service, or purchasing departments.*
- *Less than 15 percent of the perpetrators had convictions prior to committing their frauds.*

The KPMG 2008–2009 Integrity Survey, which was based on responses from more than 5000 U.S. employees, found similar results. For example, it found that nearly three out of four employees reported that they had observed misconduct in the prior 12-month period, with nearly half of these employees reporting that they had observed serious misconduct that could cause "a significant loss of public trust if discovered." KPMG also found that fraud against organizations was significantly reduced when proactive antifraud measures, such as hotlines and ethics training, were implemented.

> **Remember this ...**
>
> *Both the ACFE Report to the Nation on Occupational Fraud & Abuse and KPMG's Integrity Survey reveal that occupational fraud is common and expensive. Both studies also report that occupational fraud can be significantly reduced by using proactive fraud prevention and detection measures such as hotlines, ethics training, and audits.*

Asset Misappropriations

Employees, vendors, and customers of organizations have three opportunities to steal assets: (1) they can steal *receipts* of cash and other assets as they are coming into an organization; (2) they can steal cash, inventory, and other assets that are *on hand*; or (3) they can commit *disbursement fraud* by having the organization pay for something it shouldn't pay for or pay too much for something it purchases. With each of these three types of fraud, the perpetrators can act alone or work in collusion with others. Figure 14.1 outlines the misappropriation possibilities.

The fraud taxonomy developed by Joseph Wells is more complicated and detailed than the one shown in Figure 14.1. He divides asset misappropriations into

FIGURE 14.1   TYPES OF ASSET MISAPPROPRIATIONS

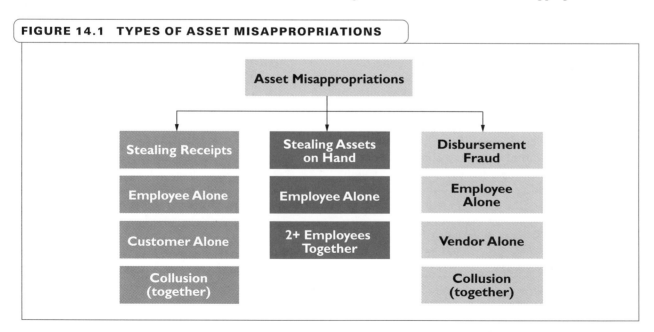

FIGURE 14.2   OCCUPATIONAL FRAUD CLASSIFICATION SCHEME

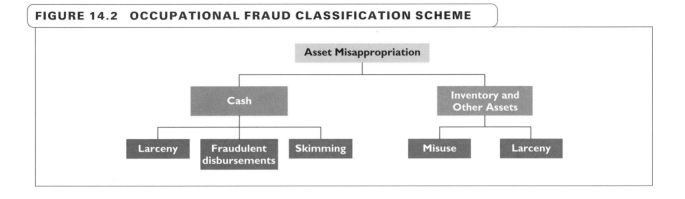

two major categories: (1) thefts of cash and (2) thefts of inventory and other assets. He subdivides thefts of cash into three subgroups: (1) larceny (intentionally taking away an employer's cash without the consent and against the will of the employer), (2) skimming (the removal of cash from a victim entity prior to its entry in an accounting system), and (3) fraudulent disbursements. Similarly, he divides the misappropriation of assets other than cash, including inventory, into two groups: (1) misuse and (2) larceny. Figure 14.2 illustrates the main elements of Wells's classification scheme. The ACFE study showed that asset misappropriations are by far the most common form of occupational fraud. We will now discuss the misappropriation of assets according to Wells's classification scheme.

Theft of Cash through Larceny

With **larceny**, cash is stolen by employees or others *after* it has already been recorded in the company's accounting system. As a result, larceny schemes are easier to detect than skimming schemes and are far less common.

Cash larcenies can take place in any circumstance in which an employee has access to cash. Common larceny schemes involve the theft of cash or currency on hand (in a cash register or petty cash box, for example) or from bank deposits. Cash larcenies are most successful when they involve relatively small amounts over extended periods of time. With such thefts, businesses often write the small missing amounts off as "shorts" or "miscounts," rather than as thefts. For example, in one bank, the annual cash shortages by tellers exceeded $3 million per year. Some of this teller shortage could have been caused by miscounting, and certainly customers are more likely to inform a teller when he or she gives them too little cash than when the teller gives them too much cash. However, a significant portion of the shortage is probably caused by larceny. As an example of a cash larceny fraud, consider the case of Jane Doe (name changed):

Jane Doe was a long-term accounting employee of a consumer electronics firm in Los Angeles. Although lacking a formal education, she was well-rounded; originally hired as an accounts receivables clerk, her most recent position required her to oversee the accounting department's petty cash funds. Jane was responsible for immediately depositing all cash in excess of $3,150, the maximum allowable "cash on hand," into her employer's bank account.

Jane's responsibilities entailed receiving cash, paying for miscellaneous expenses out of the petty cash fund, and documenting the cash coming in and going out. She also prepared a cash schedule at the end of each month for her supervisor, who posted cash entries into the company's computerized accounting system based on Jane's handwritten cash schedule.

The primary source of the cash handled by Jane came from the company's distribution center (DC). Customers, some of whom were employees, paid for merchandise, parts, and miscellaneous services inside the distribution center, and although only a small percentage of the company's sales were cash transactions, every week DC employees hand-delivered to Jane an average of $1,000 cash, inside envelopes.

Along with the cash, these DC employees handed Jane copies of a form indicating the amount being delivered to Jane. These forms were signed by the DC employees, but Jane was not required to give the DC employee any documentation (receipt) in return, nor was any other employee required to verify the cash exchange.

One day, Jane's supervisor reviewed an end-of-the-month cash report submitted by Jane. The report consisted of customers' names, invoice numbers, and method of payment. This indicated the cash paid by the customers. The total cash balance was then indicated, and all funds in excess of $3,150 were supposed to have been deposited to the bank.

Jane's supervisor discovered that Jane's reported total did not balance the sum of all the entries on her end-of-the-month cash report; there was an 8 cent discrepancy. Normally, this would have been sent back for Jane to correct. However, Jane was absent on that particular day and was, therefore, unable to correct the simple error.

Jane's supervisor totaled the cash listed on the report again, but it did not match the total Jane had shown on the report—it was not even close.

Since Jane was absent and Jane's supervisor wanted to be sure she posted the correct amount into the company's computerized accounting system, using the bank's online banking system, the supervisor then turned to the company's online banking records and looked for whether the deposits correlated with Jane's reports.

She discovered, much to her surprise, that cash deposits had not been made in several months. Was this a mistake? Jane's supervisor subsequently contacted a bank representative and checked to see whether the deposits were accidentally posted under any of the company's other numerous accounts.

There were no such deposits.

Sensing something was wrong, Jane's supervisor notified the controller, who launched an immediate investigation. After close review of the company's cash records, Jane's files, accounting entries, and Jane's computer, the company discovered Jane had embezzled over $150,000 in cash from the petty cash fund over the past four years.

Theft of Cash through Skimming

Skimming is any scheme in which cash is stolen from an organization before it is recorded on the organization's books and records. An example of skimming is the fraud perpetrated by Marvin Culpepper:

Marvin was the business manager at Muffler's Incorporated. Two of his responsibilities were to collect cash from customers and open all incoming mail. He was also responsible for making daily bank deposits. At Muffler's Incorporated, customers paid for their automobile repairs in one of three ways: (1) by check, (2) with cash, or (3) with a credit card. Over a period of six years, Marvin skimmed approximately half of the receipts from customers who paid by cash. He concealed his thefts by never recording the work as being done. Never once did he skim money from customers who paid by check or credit card because those types of thefts would have been much harder to conceal. In total, Marvin stole over $600,000 from Muffler's Incorporated.

Marvin's theft illustrates the most basic skimming scheme—taking money from the sale of goods or services but making no record of the sale. Another example of this type of skimming is the ice cream store cashier who sells two-scoop ice cream cones to customers and either does not enter the sales into the cash register or enters the sales as single-scoop sales.

More complicated skimming schemes occur when employees understate sales and collections by recording false or larger-than-reality sales discounts, misappropriate customer payments and write off the receivable as "uncollectible," embezzle a first customer's payment and then credit that customer's account when a second customer pays (a delayed recognition of payment, called **lapping**), or work together with customers to allow them to pay later than required or less than required.

As an example of collusive skimming, consider the $2.2-million fraud experienced by a Fortune 500 company:

This fraud was perpetrated when an employee who was responsible for making receivable collections from customers gave a high-volume customer extra time to pay receivables without reporting them as delinquent. As a result of this fraud, the dishonest customer was able to invest cash that should have been used to pay the accounts payable in short-term securities prior to payment, thus earning interest exceeding $2 million. The money was then split with the accounts receivable manager, who worked for the victim company. This fraud had elements of both skimming and corruption.

Cash Theft through Fraudulent Disbursements

The ACFE found that fraudulent disbursements comprised by far the highest percentage of asset misappropriations. It identified six cash schemes involving outgoing disbursements of cash. Table 14.1 summarizes these six disbursement schemes.

In the following paragraphs, we will discuss each of these disbursement schemes:

Check Tampering

Check tampering is a type of fraudulent disbursement scheme in which an employee either (1) prepares a fraudulent check for his or her own benefit or (2) intercepts a check intended for another person or entity and converts the check to his or her own benefit. Check tampering is unique among the disbursement frauds because it is the one group of schemes in which the perpetrator physically prepares the fraudulent check. In most fraudulent disbursement schemes, the culprit generates a payment to himself or herself by submitting some false document to the victim company, such as an invoice or a timecard. The false document represents a claim for payment and causes the victim company to

TABLE 14.1 DISBURSEMENT SCHEMES

TYPE OF DISBURSEMENT SCHEME	DESCRIPTION OF SCHEME	EXAMPLES
Billing	Any scheme in which a person causes his or her employer to issue a payment by submitting invoices for fictitious goods or services, inflated invoices, or invoices for personal purchases.	• *Employee creates a shell company and bills employer for nonexistent services.* • *Employee purchases personal items, submits invoice to employer for payment.*
Check tampering	Any scheme in which a person steals his or her employer's funds by forging or altering a check on one of the organization's bank accounts, or steals a check the organization has legitimately issued to another payee.	• *Employee steals blank company checks, makes them out to himself or herself or an accomplice.* • *Employee steals outgoing check to a vendor, deposits it into his or her own bank account.*
Expense Reimbursements	Any scheme in which an employee makes a claim for reimbursement of fictitious or inflated business expenses.	• *Employee files fraudulent expense report, claiming personal travel, nonexistent meals, etc.*
Payroll	Any scheme in which an employee causes his or her employer to issue payment by making false claims for compensation.	• *Employee claims overtime for hours not worked.* • *Employee adds ghost employees to the payroll.*
Wire Transfers	Any scheme in which a person steals his or her employer's funds by fraudulently wire transferring them out of the employer's bank accounts.	• *Employee fraudulently wires company money to a personal bank account.*
Cash Register Disbursements	Any scheme in which an employee makes false entries on a cash register to conceal the fraudulent removal of cash.	• *Employee fraudulently voids a sale on his or her cash register and steals the cash.*

issue a check, which the perpetrator then converts. These frauds essentially amount to trickery: the perpetrator fools the company into handing over its money. Check-tampering schemes are fundamentally different. With check tampering, the fraud perpetrator takes physical control of a check and makes it payable to himself or herself by forging the maker (signing the check), forging endorsements, or altering payees.

As an example of check tampering, consider the case of Barbara (name changed):[3]

The quiet, hard-working bookkeeper who came on board as a temp at a construction firm impressed her boss so much that within four months, she had been hired full time and given increasing responsibilities over the company's finances. But two months later, Barbara cut herself a $650 check from ABC Construction Supply Company—the first of many fraudulent checks in a massive embezzlement that she admits reached $9 million.

Over six years, Barbara used the stolen money to buy property in three states, dozens of cars and recreational vehicles, a stable of horses, and lavish gifts for her friends and family.

Before her deceit was discovered by her employer, the 40-ish mother of two owned a half-million-dollar house, 10 thoroughbred and quarter horses, a Vermont country estate, a property in Maine, a two-story home, and time-shares in Walt Disney World and the Bahamas.

The first company check Barbara made to herself paid the rent for the house where she and her husband lived. Her husband was unemployed, and they were about to be evicted.

Hired as a temp, Barbara quickly moved up the company ranks by earning her boss's trust. At her peak, Barbara was overseeing the finances of four of the companies in her boss's multimillion-dollar construction and masonry operation.

Barbara was known as a steady, consistent worker. She was quiet and kept to herself. She rarely worked with oversight.

"What I would do is in the beginning write checks out of one of the [company] accounts and just deposit them into my personal account," Barbara said in a court deposition. "I wrote them out of one account into another company's account, and then I would write myself a check." The stolen money never stayed in Barbara's three bank accounts very long, and when the company's lawyers seized her accounts, they found less than $5,000.

In addition to the real estate she bought, Barbara used the money to shower others with gifts and vacations, saving little for herself. She allowed her husband to indulge in firearms, power tools, and an assortment of vehicles. They also owned four snowmobiles; four all-terrain vehicles; and 26 cars, pickup trucks, and sport utility vehicles, including a 1923 Ford Model T, a 1986 Jaguar coupe, and a rare 1937 Chevy delivery truck. She purchased 10 horses for herself and her daughter.

When caught, she was planning on financing a $240,000-plus wedding for her brother.

Register Disbursement Schemes

Register disbursement schemes are among the least costly of all disbursement schemes. Two basic fraudulent schemes take place at the register: false refunds and false voids. With false refunds, a fraud perpetrator processes a transaction as if a customer were returning merchandise, even though there is no actual return. The fraud perpetrator then takes money from the cash register in the amount of the false return. Since the register tape shows that a merchandise return has been made, it appears that the disbursement is legitimate. The concealment problem for perpetrators is that, with false refunds, a debit is made to the inventory system showing that merchandise has been returned. Since no inventory was returned, the recorded inventory amount is overstated and an inventory count may reveal the "missing" inventory. A similar but more difficult fraud to detect is the overstating of refunds. In these cases, merchandise is actually returned, but the value of the return is overstated. For example, assume that a customer returned merchandise costing $10. The dishonest employee may record the return as $15, give the customer $10, and pocket $5.

Fictitious voids are similar to refund schemes in that they generate a disbursement from the cash register. When a sale is voided on a register, a copy of the customer's receipt is usually attached to a void slip, along with the signature or initials of a manager that indicates the transaction has been approved. To process a false void, the cashier usually keeps the customer's receipt at the time of sale and then rings in a voided sale after the customer has left. Whatever money the customer paid for the item is removed from the register as though it was being returned to the customer. The copy of the customer's receipt is attached to the voided slip to verify the authenticity of the transaction. Unfortunately for the perpetrator, voided sales create the same kind of concealment problem that false returns

do—that is, someone might discover that inventory that was supposed to have been returned is missing.

Consider the following example of a cash register fraud:

A hospital received an anonymous phone tip that a parking supervisor and others were stealing from its three "pay-as-you-go" lots. The tip was taken seriously because management had discovered that monthly cash receipts from those lots were on the decline. The hospital's security office and the police investigated but found it difficult to determine how the money was being stolen and how much was lost. Forensic accountants were called in to find those answers. They soon uncovered a pattern of employee theft that had gone on for several years, costing the hospital more than a quarter of a million dollars in lost revenue. To catch the culprits, the forensic accountants began by analyzing the cash register tapes. They discovered that the tape was removed or deactivated during certain times of the day, which coincided with shifts worked by the lot supervisor and his wife. The forensic accountants determined that if attendants wanted to pocket money, they would have to ring up the sale on the cash register to open the parking lot gate and determine the parking fee. Then they would have to void the sale.

No record of the void would appear on the cash register tape, but the forensic team learned that—unbeknownst to the employees—a record was kept on what's known as the cash register's "Z" total, which counts daily transactions. While the cash register tape showed few, if any voids, the "Z" total often recorded more than 100 voids a day during the hours worked by the couple.

When questioned, the couple admitted to pocketing cash sales. Because the cash register did not record the transactions, they thought the thefts could not be discovered.

The forensic accountants subsequently discovered five other ways the couple was stealing, ranging from punching in "no sale" to jamming parking meters and removing the coins. They estimated that the hospital lost approximately $300,000 over three years. The couple ultimately pled guilty to fraud and served time in prison, and their bonding company reached a settlement with the hospital.

Billing Schemes

Both check-tampering and register disbursement schemes require perpetrators to physically take cash or checks from their employers. With **billing schemes**, the perpetrator does not have to undergo the risk of taking company cash or merchandise. In a billing scheme, the perpetrator submits or alters an invoice that causes his or her employer to willingly issue a check or make other types of payments. Though the support for the payment is fraudulent, the disbursement itself is facially valid. Billing schemes are extremely common and quite expensive. The median cost of billing schemes in the ACFE study was $130,000, second only to wire transfers. Since the majority of most businesses' disbursements are made in the purchasing cycle, larger thefts can be hidden through false billing schemes than through other kinds of fraudulent disbursements. Employees who utilize billing schemes are just going where the money is.

The three most common types of billing schemes are (1) setting up dummy companies (shell companies) to submit invoices to the victim organization, (2) altering or double-paying a nonaccomplice vendor's statements, and (3) making personal purchases with company funds. **Dummy** or **shell companies** are fictitious entities created for the sole purpose of committing fraud. Many times, they are nothing more than a fabricated name and a post office box that an employee uses to collect disbursements from false billings. However, since the checks received will be made out in the name of the shell company, the perpetrator will normally also set up a bank account in the new company's name, listing himself or herself as an authorized signer on the account.

CAUTION *Any time you pay anyone for anything, you should make sure that the amount you actually pay is the amount you are supposed to pay. When shopping, paying bills, or using your credit card, you should always double-check the amounts. Sometimes, vendors and others think you won't notice the overcharges, and other times the mistakes are unintentional. In addition, you should be aware of the myriad fees you pay when banking, paying your telephone bill, paying your cable bill, etc. You should never accept the amount you are charged for anything without making sure it is reasonable or accurate.*

Rather than using shell companies as vessels for overbilling schemes, some employees generate fraudulent disbursements by using the invoice of nonaccomplice vendors. For example, perpetrators using this scheme may double-pay an invoice. By intentionally paying some bills twice and then requesting the recipients to return one of the checks, the perpetrator keeps the returned check. Another related scheme is to intentionally pay the wrong vendor and then ask for the payment to be returned. Or, a dishonest employee might intentionally overpay a legitimate vendor and ask for a return of the overpayment portion.

The final common billing scheme is making personal purchases with company funds. The purchases may be for perpetrators themselves, their businesses, their families, or others.

Here is an example of a billing scheme:[4]

———

A federal grand jury returned an indictment against four individuals for participating in self-dealing schemes that netted them more than $2 million while acting as executives and purchasing representatives of the archdiocese of New York.

According to a nine-count indictment filed in U.S. District Court in Manhattan, the individuals used their positions as employees and consultants at Institutional Commodity Services Inc. (ICS), the purchasing arm of the archdiocese, to receive more than $1.2 million from vendors supplying goods to the archdiocese. Those charged also diverted at least $1 million to shell companies they controlled.

The victims in this case included a not-for-profit corporation and a religious institution operating schools, hospitals, and convents.

According to the charges, the individuals unlawfully conspired to defraud the archdiocese of more than $2 million. They required numerous vendors to pay money—ostensibly as commissions—to them. Vendors paid the individuals more than $1.2 million, which the purchasing agent secretly shared with the others charged. The amount of the commissions paid was included in the prices charged to ICS, which resulted in the archdiocese paying artificially inflated prices for the goods and services purchased. In addition, the perpetrators embezzled more than $1 million from the archdiocese through a self-dealing scheme in which they diverted funds earmarked to buy food for the children enrolled in the archdiocese's schools to fictitious companies they owned and controlled.

———

Expense Schemes

Expense and **payroll schemes** are similar to billing schemes. The perpetrators of these frauds produce false documentation that causes the victim company to unknowingly make a fraudulent disbursement. With expense and payroll schemes, the false documentation includes items like timecards, sales orders, and expense reports. Expense schemes involve overbilling the company for travel and other related business expenses, such as business lunches, hotel bills, and air travel.

Four common types of expense disbursement schemes are (1) mischaracterizing expenses, (2) overstating expenses, (3) submitting fictitious expenses, and (4) submitting the same expenses multiple times. The first type of fraud involves mischaracterizing a personal expense to make it look like a business expense. For example, personal travel might be claimed as a business trip, a personal lunch as a business lunch, or a personal magazine subscription as a company subscription. Overstating expenses usually involves doctoring a receipt or other supporting documentation to reflect a higher cost than what was actually paid. The employee may use eradicating fluid, a ballpoint pen, or some other method to change the price reflected on the receipt. If the company does not require original documents as support, the perpetrator generally attaches a copy of the receipt to his or her expense report. In some cases, such as taxi receipts, the perpetrator actually completes the receipt, writing in an amount higher than what was actually spent.

Fictitious expense schemes usually involve creating bogus support documents, such as false receipts. The emergence of personal computers and graphics programs has made it possible to easily create realistic-looking counterfeit receipts. Alternatively, perpetrators committing this type of fraud sometimes obtain blank receipts from vendors or printers, fill them out, and submit them. The least common of the expense schemes is the submission of multiple reimbursements for the same expense.

Here is an example of travel reimbursement fraud:

Over a period of four years, an employee charged 338 airplane tickets for personal use to the company's travel office. The tickets were for the employee's wife and two sons, who traveled from the United States to Asia and Europe on several occasions. One trip to Asia was for the family's annual Thanksgiving vacation. The employee had used the company credit card he had been given to book the tickets and pay other personal expenses.

Payroll Disbursement Schemes

Payroll fraud schemes fall into four major categories: (1) ghost employees, (2) falsified hours and salary, (3) commission schemes, and (4) false worker compensation claims. Of all payroll fraud schemes, ghost employee schemes tend to generate the largest losses. According to the ACFE, the average loss per occurrence is very high and can be quite costly to organizations. Ghost employee frauds involve putting someone on the payroll (or keeping a former employee on the payroll) who does not actually work for the victim company. Through the falsification of personnel or payroll records, fraud perpetrators cause paychecks to be generated to a ghost. These paychecks are then cashed by the fraud perpetrators or their accomplices.

For ghost-employee fraud schemes to work, four things must happen: (1) the ghost must be added to the payroll, (2) timekeeping and wage rate information must be collected, (3) a paycheck must be issued to the ghost (unless direct deposits are used), and (4) the check must be delivered to the perpetrator or an accomplice. By far, the most common method of misappropriating funds from payroll is the overpayment of wages, accounting for 55.4 percent of all payroll frauds. For hourly employees, the size of a paycheck is based on two essential factors: the number of hours worked and the rate of pay. Therefore, for an hourly employee to fraudulently increase the size of a paycheck, he or she must either falsify the number of hours worked or change the wage rate. Since salaried employees do not receive compensation based on their time at work, in most cases these employees generate fraudulent wages by increasing their rates of pay.

Commissions are a form of compensation calculated as a percentage of the amount of transactions a salesperson or another employee generates. This unique form of compensation is not based on hours worked or a set yearly salary, but rather on an employee's revenue output. A commissioned employee's wages are based on the amount of sales he or she generates and the percentage of those sales he or she is paid. Thus, an employee on commission can fraudulently increase his or her pay by (1) falsifying the amount of sales made or (2) increasing the rate of commission. The most common method of committing commission-based payroll fraud is to falsify the amount of sales made in one of three ways: (1) creating fictitious sales, (2) falsifying the value of sales made by altering prices listed on sales documents, or (3) overstating sales by claiming sales made by another employee or in another period.

Some commission payment plans are structured in ways that almost encourage fraud. Take, for example, a graduated commission scheme, such as one that pays 5 percent if a salesperson generates revenue of less than $100,000, 7 percent if the salesperson generates revenues of between $100,000 and $200,000, and 10 percent if sales exceed $200,000. Working under this system, sales agents have a very strong incentive to generate revenues exceeding $200,000 so they can earn a 10 percent commission on all sales. Thus, if their total sales fall just short of $200,000, they have a strong incentive to create "additional revenues" that will help them qualify for the higher commission rate.

Workers' compensation is not a payroll account, but rather an insurance expense. Nevertheless, it is essentially an employee benefit, entitling persons injured on the job to compensation while they recuperate. By far, the most common way to commit workers' compensation fraud is to fake an injury and collect payments from the victim company's insurance carrier. In some cases, the employee colludes with a doctor, who processes bogus claims for unnecessary medical treatments and then splits the payments for those fictitious treatments with the "injured" employee.

The primary victim of a workers' compensation scheme is not the employer, but rather the insurance carrier for the employer. The insurance carrier pays for the fraudulent medical bills and the unnecessary absences of the perpetrator. Nevertheless, employers are also victims of these crimes because bogus claims can result in higher premiums for the company in the future.

An example of a payroll fraud is the following incident involving placing a ghost employee on the payroll:

———

Mark, a payroll specialist for a large nonprofit organization, was HIV-positive and needed expensive drugs to control the disease. Over the course of two years, he embezzled $112,000 to cover his medical costs. Although Mark needed the extra cash, there were alternatives to stealing. But he couldn't bring himself to ask for help. Mark's duties included posting time and attendance information to the computer system and preparing payroll disbursement summaries. Adding and deleting employee master records were separate tasks, performed by another staff member. As an additional safeguard, a supervisor approved all payroll disbursements, and the company deposited them directly into employees' personal bank accounts.

It took a bit of doing to circumvent the internal control system, but Mark was up to the task. First, when the coworker who added and deleted master records logged onto the system, Mark peeked over her shoulder and noted her user ID and password.

This enabled him to add fake master records—for "ghost" employees—to the system. Because tax deductions were programmed to fall within a given range of employee numbers, each time Mark added the name of a phony worker to the system, he assigned to it an employee number higher than the range. Thus, the payroll summary report—which was printed each week in ascending order by employee number—displayed fake workers at the end of the printout where they wouldn't be selected for deductions.

Next, Mark entered false wage information for the ghost workers. At the same time, he arranged for their paychecks to be direct-deposited into his own bank account. Based on past dealings with his own financial institution, Mark knew the bank did not match the employee name to the one on the depositor's account.

Finally, to get over the last internal control hurdle—approval of the payroll disbursements by a superior—Mark prepared his own fake payroll summary for the supervisor's signature. Because Mark was seen as an exemplary employee, the supervisor didn't check his work carefully and failed to notice that the fraudulent documentation was printed in a typeface different from the one used in the real reports.

———

STOP & THINK *The federal government gives huge rewards for taking action to expose fraud against itself. Under federal law, if you have personal knowledge that an individual, business, city, county, or town has provided false information to obtain money from the federal government or to avoid paying money to the federal government, you may file a claim to recover more than triple the amount of monies defrauded from the government. Federal law protects you against any retaliation. Why do you think the federal government offers rewards for whistle-blowing about government fraud?*

Executive Cash Frauds

Before we move on to theft of assets other than cash, it is important to know that in the past few years, executives of some corporations have allegedly looted their companies of huge amounts of cash, usually through disbursement frauds. The two most famous of these types of frauds, sometimes referred to as *corporate looting*, were Chief Executive Officer Dennis Kozlowski, Chief Corporate Counsel Mark Belnick, and Chief Financial Officer Mark H. Swartz of Tyco International Ltd. (Tyco) and John Rigas and his sons of Adelphia Corporation (Adelphia).

The case of Tyco is one of looting. It involved egregious, self-serving, and clandestine misconduct by the three most senior executives at Tyco. From at least 1996 until June 2002, Dennis Kozlowski and Mark Swartz took hundreds of millions of dollars in secret, unauthorized, and improper low-interest or interest-free loans and compensation from Tyco. Kozlowski and Swartz concealed these transactions from Tyco's shareholders. They later pocketed tens of millions of dollars by causing Tyco to forgive repayment of many of their improper loans. These actions were also hidden from Tyco's shareholders. In addition, Kozlowski and Swartz engaged in numerous highly profitable related-party transactions with Tyco and awarded themselves lavish perquisites—without disclosing either the transactions or perquisites to Tyco shareholders. At the same time that Kozlowski and Swartz engaged in their massive covert defalcation of corporate funds, Kozlowski regularly assured investors that at Tyco "nothing was hidden behind the scenes," that Tyco's disclosures were "exceptional," and that Tyco's management "prided itself on having sharp focus with creating shareholder value." Similarly, Swartz told investors that "Tyco's disclosure practice remains second to none." From 1998 into early 2002, Belnick received approximately $14 million in interest-free loans from Tyco to buy and renovate a $4 million apartment on Central Park West and to buy and renovate a $10 million ski chalet in Park City, Utah. The original loans and the forgiveness of these loans were hidden from the compensation committee of the board of directors.

Kozlowski, Swartz, and Belnick also spent lavishly on themselves. One of the most egregious expenditures involved Kozlowski throwing a party for his second wife, Karen, which he paid for with company funds. The party was held on the island of Sardinia in the Mediterranean Sea and cost approximately $2 million (or $70,000 per person), including paying travel costs for the guests. The planning memo for the party, with certain obscene parts deleted, was as follows:

Guests arrive at the club starting at 7:15 p.m. Two gladiators are standing next to the door—one opens the door, and the other helps the guests. We have a lion or horse with a chariot for the shock value. We have gladiators standing guard every couple feet. The guests come into the pool area, the band is playing, and they are dressed in elegant chic. There is a big ice sculpture of Dennis with lots of shellfish and caviar at his feet. The waiters are dressed in linen with fig wreathes on their heads. There is a full bar with fabulous linens. The pool has floating candles and flowers. We have rented fig trees with tiny lights everywhere. At 8:30 p.m., the waiters instruct that dinner is served. The tables have incredible linens with chalices as wineglasses. The band continues to play light music through dinner. After dinner, they kick it up a bit. We start the show of pictures on the screen, great background music in sync with the slides. At the end, Elvis is on the screen wishing Karen a happy birthday and apologizing that he

could not make it. It starts to fade, and Elvis is on stage and starts singing happy birthday with the Swingdogs. A huge cake is brought out. The cake explodes. Elvis kicks it in full throttle. At 11:30 p.m., the light show starts. People are displayed on the mountain, and fireworks are coming from both ends of the golf course in sync with the music. Swingdogs start up, and the night is young.

Like the situation at Tyco, the Adelphia fraud was also a case of corporate looting (as well as financial statement manipulation to cover the frauds). John Rigas, the founder of Adelphia Communications, was sentenced to 15 years in prison, and his son, Timothy, the company's former CFO, was sentenced to 20 years in prison.

At a five-month trial following the fraud, prosecutors accused the Rigases of conspiring to hide $2.3 billion in Adelphia debt, stealing $100 million in cash, and lying to investors about the company's financial condition. They claimed that the Rigases had effectively used Adelphia as their personal piggy bank to pay for luxury condos and a golf course and to cover personal investment losses.

Theft of Inventory and Other Assets

A person can misappropriate company assets other than cash in one of two ways. The asset can be misused (or "borrowed"), or it can be stolen. Simple misuse is obviously the less egregious of the two types of fraud. Assets that are misused but not stolen typically include company vehicles, company supplies, computers, securities, information, and office equipment. These assets are also used by some employees to conduct personal work on company time. In many instances, these side businesses are of the same nature as the employer's business, so the employee is essentially competing with the employer and using the employer's equipment to do it.

Table 14.2 describes the most common noncash types of frauds against organizations.

While the misuse of company property might be a problem, the theft of company property is a much greater concern. Losses from inventory theft, for example, can run into millions of dollars. The means employed to steal company property range from simple larceny—walking off with company property—to more complicated schemes involving the falsification of company documents and records. Larceny usually involves taking inventory or other assets from the company premises, without attempting to conceal it in the books and records or "justify" its absence. Most noncash larceny schemes are not very complicated. They are typically committed by employees (such as

TABLE 14.2 NONCASH FRAUDS AGAINST ORGANIZATIONS

TYPE OF FRAUD	DESCRIPTION OF SCHEME	EXAMPLES
Inventory	Any scheme involving the theft or misappropriation of physical, noncash assets such as inventory, equipment, or supplies.	• *Employee steals inventory from the warehouse.* • *Employee uses company equipment for personal businesses.*
Information	Any scheme in which an employee steals or otherwise misappropriates proprietary confidential information or trade secrets.	• *Employee sells research to competing organization.* • *Employee provides trade secrets to competing organization.*
Securities	Any scheme involving the theft or misappropriation of stocks, bonds, or other securities.	• *Employee fraudulently steals company bonds.* • *Employee fraudulently steals stocks options from the organization.*

warehouse personnel, inventory clerks, and shipping clerks) who have access to inventory and other assets.

Another common type of noncash asset theft is the use of asset requisitions and other forms that allow assets to be moved from one location in a company to another location. Often, fraud perpetrators use internal documents to gain access to merchandise that they otherwise might not be able to handle without raising suspicion. Transfer documents allow fraud perpetrators to move assets from one location to another and then take the merchandise for themselves. The most basic scheme occurs when an employee requisitions materials to complete a work-related project and then steals the materials. In more extreme cases, a fraud perpetrator might completely fabricate a project that necessitates the use of certain assets that he or she intends to steal.

A third type of noncash asset theft involves the use of the purchasing and receiving functions of a company. If assets are purchased by employees for personal use, it is considered to be a purchasing scheme fraud. On the other hand, if assets were intentionally purchased by the company but simply misappropriated by a fraud perpetrator, a noncash asset fraud has been committed. In this case, the perpetrator's company is deprived not only of the cash it paid for the merchandise, but also of the merchandise itself. In addition, because the organization doesn't have as much inventory on hand as it thinks it has, stockouts and unhappy customers often result.

Two examples of inventory theft are the following:

A New Jersey TRANSIT employee stole New Jersey TRANSIT inventory and replacement bus parts and then sold the stolen items via the Internet using an Internet auction site. When investigated, the employee attempted to conceal the thefts and obstruct the investigation by returning stolen parts to inventory and by eliminating the eBay Web page.

Two employees of a large paper manufacturing company that owned thousands of acres of forestland had their own entrepreneurial venture, which competed with their employer. While clocked in for their employer, they cut trees and had a friend sell them to a competitor. The company was being hurt in two ways: first, it was paying employees who were nonproductive while working for someone else and second, they were selling the trees to a competitor.

Stealing information can also be very costly to organizations. Consider the case of a DuPont scientist[5] who supposedly downloaded 22,000 sensitive documents and accessed 16,000 others as he got ready to take a job with a competitor. According to the U.S. attorney's office in Delaware, the trade secrets were worth $400 million. The perpetrator faces up to 10 years in prison, a fine of $250,000, and restitution.

Remember this …

Asset misappropriations are the most common type of fraud against organizations. Asset misappropriations fall into two categories: thefts of cash and thefts of other assets. The three ways to steal cash are through larceny, skimming, and fraudulent disbursements. Of these, the six different types of fraudulent disbursements comprise the most common types of misappropriations. Noncash assets can either be misused or stolen (larceny). Noncash assets that are stolen are most often physical assets, such as inventory, supplies, equipment, information, and securities.

Corruption

All the schemes we have discussed thus far in this chapter fall into the broad category called *asset misappropriation*. A second major type of occupational abuse or fraud committed against organizations is corruption. Corruption is one of the oldest white-collar crimes known to mankind. The tradition of "paying off" public officials or company insiders for preferential treatment is rooted in the crudest business systems developed.

Corruption can be broken down into the following four scheme types: (1) bribery schemes, (2) conflict of interest schemes, (3) economic extortion schemes, and (4) illegal gratuity schemes. Table 14.3 from the 2010 ACFE report summarizes these types of frauds.

Bribery

Bribery involves the offering, giving, receiving, or soliciting of anything of value to influence an official act. The term "official act" means that traditional bribery statutes only proscribe payments made to influence the decisions of government agents or employees. Certainly, one of the most infamous cases of bribery in early history was that of Judas Iscariot, the disciple who betrayed Jesus Christ. Judas was paid 30 pieces of silver by the chief priests and elders of Jerusalem to disclose the location of Christ so that he could be captured and executed. Another example of bribery

was the scandal that rocked Washington, D.C., in the early 1920s. The paper trail of corruption led back to the White House cabinet and nearly implicated then-President Warren G. Harding. Known as the Teapot Dome scandal, the incident surrounded several key members of Harding's staff who mishandled the leasing of naval oil reserve lands.

Many occupational fraud schemes involve **commercial bribery**, which is similar to the traditional definition of bribery, except that something of value is offered to influence a business decision rather than an official act of government. In a commercial bribery scheme, payment is received by an employee without the employer's consent. In other words, commercial bribery cases deal with the acceptance of under-the-table payments in return for the exercise of influence over a business transaction.

Bribery schemes generally fall into two broad categories: **kickbacks** and **bid-rigging schemes**. Kickbacks are undisclosed payments made by vendors to employees of purchasing companies. The purpose of a kickback is usually to enlist the corrupt employee in an overbilling scheme. Sometimes vendors pay kickbacks simply to get extra business from the purchasing company. Unfortunately, once kickbacks are paid by vendors, the control of purchasing transactions usually transfers from the buyer to the vendor. When the vendor is in control of the purchasing transactions, more

TABLE 14.3 TYPES OF CORRUPTION

TYPE OF CORRUPTION SCHEME	DESCRIPTION OF SCHEME	EXAMPLES
Conflict of interest	Any scheme in which an employee, a manager, or an executive has an undisclosed economic or personal interest in a transaction that adversely affects the company as a result.	• *Manager establishes a beneficial relationship with an organization in which he or she has a personal financial interest.*
Bribery	Any scheme in which a person offers, gives, receives, or solicits something of value for the purpose of influencing an official act or a business decision without the knowledge or consent of the principal.	• *Vendor provides a manager with a bribe to secure a sales contract.* • *Employee receives payment for securing a contract.*
Illegal gratuities	Any scheme in which a person offers, gives, receives, or solicits something of value for, or because of, an official act or business decision without the knowledge or consent of the principal.	• *Manager is influenced to make a financial decision based on undisclosed gifts or awards.*
Extortion	The coercion of another to enter into a transaction or deliver property based on wrongful use of actual or threatened force, fear, or economic duress.	• *Vendor threatens an executive into a specific course of action.*

goods are usually sold at higher prices, and the quality of goods purchased can deteriorate substantially.

Earlier in this book, we described the kickback scheme that resulted in a security firm buying approximately $11 million of unneeded guard uniforms at increased prices and lower quality. In a common type of kickback scheme, a vendor submits a fraudulent or inflated invoice to the victim company, and the employee of that company helps make sure that payment is made on the false invoice. For his or her assistance, the employee receives some form of payment from the vendor. That payment, or kickback, can take the form of cash, reduced prices for goods purchased, the hiring of a relative, the promise of subsequent employment, or some other form. Kickback schemes almost always attack the purchasing function of the victim company.

At the time this book was being revised, a congressman from Louisiana was being indicted for supposedly accepting bribes. A recent example of bribery is the following:[6]

Rep. William Jefferson (D-LA) was indicted on federal charges of racketeering, soliciting bribes, and money-laundering. The charges stem from a long-running bribery investigation into business deals Jefferson tried to broker in Africa. Federal prosecutors Monday outlined a case that has all the features of a potboiler, including clandestine meetings, code words, and a freezer full of cash.

"Mr. Jefferson traded on his good office to enrich himself and his family through a pervasive pattern of fraud, bribery, and corruption that spans many years and two continents," said U.S. Attorney Chuck Rosenberg.

Prosecutors allege that Jefferson collected more than $400,000 in bribes.

Jefferson's lawyer responded to the charges by saying that his client is innocent. He is due to be arraigned Friday in U.S. District Court in Alexandria.

In May 2006, the FBI raided Jefferson's congressional office, the first such raid on a sitting congressman's Capitol office. That move sparked a constitutional debate over whether the executive branch had stepped over the line.

Jefferson and some congressional legal experts say the raid on his office violated the "speech-or-debate" clause of the U.S. Constitution, which protects federal lawmakers in their legislative duties. The FBI maintains the raid was "necessary, appropriate, and constitutional." The debate over the raid has tied the case up for a year, and it is still working its way through the courts.

Federal prosecutors now suggest that they can make their case against Jefferson without relying on the documents seized during the contested raid of his congressional office.

The alleged violations include racketeering, soliciting bribes, wire fraud, money-laundering, obstruction of justice, conspiracy, and violations of the Foreign Corrupt Practices Act. Prosecutors allege that Jefferson had his hands in a number of corrupt dealings, including a sugar plant in Nigeria and a satellite transmission firm in Botswana.

Court records indicate that Jefferson was videotaped taking a $100,000 cash bribe from an FBI informant. Most of that money later turned up in a freezer in Jefferson's home. He had separated the money into $10,000 increments and wrapped the bundles in aluminum foil, federal investigators say.

Two of Jefferson's associates have already struck plea bargains with prosecutors and have been sentenced. Jefferson is accused of soliciting bribes for himself and his family, and also for bribing a Nigerian official.

Bid-rigging schemes occur when an employee fraudulently assists a vendor in winning a contract through the competitive bidding process. This process, in which several suppliers or contractors are vying for contracts in what can be a very cutthroat environment, can be tailor-made for bribery. Any advantage one vendor can gain over his or her competitors in this arena is extremely valuable. The benefits of "inside influence" can ensure that a vendor will win a sought-after contract. Many vendors are willing to pay for this influence. The way competitive bidding is rigged depends largely upon the level of influence of the corrupt employee. The more power a person has over the bidding process, the more likely the person can influence the selection of a supplier. Therefore, employees involved in bid-rigging schemes, like those in kickback schemes, tend to have a good measure of influence over or access to the bidding process. Potential targets for accepting bribes include buyers, contracting officials, engineers and technical representatives, quality or product assurance representatives, subcontractor liaison employees, or anyone else with authority over the awarding of contracts.

An example of bid rigging is the following:

Four Wisconsin construction executives were indicted by a federal grand jury for their alleged role in a bid-rigging scheme involving more than $100 million in state road projects. The four men worked for two different construction companies that were also indicted. According to the U.S. attorney's office, the indictment charges that between 1997 and 2004, the four men fixed low bids on road, highway, bridge, street, and airport construction projects.

Conflicts of Interest

A **conflict of interest** occurs when an employee, a manager, or an executive has an undisclosed economic or personal interest in a transaction that adversely affects the company. As with other corruption schemes, conflicts of interest involve the exertion of an employee's influence to the detriment of his or her company. Conflicts usually involve self-dealing by an employee. In some cases, the employee's act benefits a friend or relative, even though the employee receives no financial benefit from the transaction.

To be classified as a conflict of interest scheme, the employee's interest in a transaction must be undisclosed. The essential element in a conflict case is that the fraud perpetrator takes advantage of his or her employer: the victim company is unaware that its employee has divided loyalties. If an employer knows of the employee's interest in a business deal or negotiation, there can be no conflict of interest, no matter how favorable the arrangement is for the employee.

Most conflict schemes fall into one of two categories: (1) purchase schemes or (2) sales schemes. The most common type of purchasing scheme involves the employee (or a friend or relative of the employee) having some kind of ownership or employment interest in the vendor that submits the invoice. The bill must originate from a real company in which the fraud perpetrator has an economic or personal interest, and the perpetrator's interest in the company must be undisclosed to the victim company.

The most common sales scheme involves an employee with a hidden interest having the victim company sell its goods or services below fair market value. This type of fraud results in a lower profit margin or even a loss on the sale. As an example, a few years ago, one of the largest U.S. paper and pulp companies discovered a major fraud being perpetrated by some of its employees. To get wood for making paper, the company both owned its own forests and purchased lumber from others. One of the vendors providing lumber to the company turned out to be a group of its own employees who were cutting timber on the company's own forest reserves and then selling the timber back to the company. In this case, the company was losing twice—once by paying for lumber it already owned, and then by having less of its own lumber to process.

Some of the most egregious cases of conflict-of-interest frauds that have ever occurred were the mutual fund frauds that took place recently in the United States. Since the beginning of the mutual fund industry in the 1920s, mutual funds have been thought of as a relatively safe investment vehicle. Mutual funds were sold as a limited risk investment which were, in the words of the great poet Bob Dylan, "always safe" and, thus, represented as a "shelter from the storm."[7] However, recent revelations have shown that America's $7 trillion mutual fund industry was rife with self-dealing, conflicts of interest, illegality, and impropriety. Not only were funds preferentially allowing select investors to unlawfully trade in exchange for higher fees and other forms of profit, but fund insiders, including the most senior executives and founders of certain funds, also engaged in the same unlawful trading conduct for their own personal gain. Most of the mutual fund frauds involved basic schemes in which mutual fund companies allowed certain preferred clients to make illegal trades, including rapid in-and-out trades as well as trades based upon information not yet reflected in the price of the mutual fund's assets. The unlawful trading schemes engaged in by mutual funds involved two practices known as "market timing" and "late trading." These manipulative practices were possible because of the way in which mutual funds are valued. Specifically, mutual funds in the United States are valued once a day, at 4:00 p.m. Eastern Time (ET) following the close of the financial markets in New York. The price, known as the **net asset value (NAV)**, reflects the closing prices of the securities that comprise a particular fund's portfolio plus the value of any uninvested cash that the fund manager maintains for the fund. Thus, although the shares of a mutual fund are bought and sold all day long, the price at which the shares trade does not change during the course of the day. Orders placed any time up to 4:00 p.m. are priced at that day's NAV, and orders placed after 4:01 p.m. are priced at the next day's NAV. This practice, known as "forward pricing," has been required by law since 1968.

Illegal market timing is an investment technique that involves short-term "in-and-out" trading of mutual fund shares. According to a Stanford University study,[8] market timing may have caused losses to long-term mutual fund investors of approximately $5 billion each year. Rapid trading is antithetical to the premise that mutual funds are long-term investments meant for buy-and-hold investors. In-and-out trading capitalizes on the fact that a mutual fund's price does not reflect the fair value of the assets held by the fund. A typical example of market timing involves a U.S. mutual fund that holds Japanese shares. Because of the time zone difference, the Japanese market may close at 2:00 a.m. ET in the United States. If the U.S. mutual fund manager uses the closing prices of the Japanese shares in his or her fund to arrive at an NAV at 4:00 p.m. in New York, the manager is relying on market information that is 14 hours old. If there have been positive market moves during the New York trading day, which is a reliable indicator that the Japanese market will rise when it later opens, the fund's stale NAV will not reflect the expected price change and, thus, will be artificially low. The NAV does not reflect the time-current market value of the stocks held by the mutual fund. Thus, a trader who buys the Japanese fund at the "stale" price is virtually assured of a profit that can be realized the next day by selling at the higher NAV. Because the artificial difference between the NAV and fair value has long been recognized, mutual funds imposed policies to prevent investors from profiting from the stale pricing by rapidly trading in and out of the funds. Most mutual fund prospectuses represent to investors that the funds monitor, prohibit, and prevent rapid trading because it is detrimental to long-term investors. Despite their representations to the contrary, mutual funds as well as their investment advisers, permitted such trading for their own profit. The resulting harm caused by the transfer of wealth from long-term investors to market timers, known as "dilution," came dollar-for-dollar from long-term investor's profits.

Late trading was a fraudulent practice that was even worse than in and out trading. Late trading allowed selected investors to purchase mutual funds after 4:00 p.m., using that day's NAV, rather than the next day's NAV, as required under the law. It has been likened to betting today on yesterday's horse races. Because a fund's NAV is calculated after the markets close at 4:00 p.m. ET, orders to buy, sell, or exchange mutual fund shares placed before 4:00 p.m. ET on a given day receive that day's NAV. Orders placed after 4:00 p.m. ET are supposed to be priced at the following day's NAV. This pricing mechanism was legislated in order to place all investors on a level playing field whereby no investor can benefit from after-hours information in making investment decisions. Certain mutual funds, however, allowed select customers to capitalize on positive earnings news by agreeing to sell them mutual fund shares at the prior trading day's NAV. In essence, these select investors were allowed to immediately reap the benefit of the stock's upward movement the following day due to information learned after 4:00 p.m. ET. In contrast, all other investors who purchased after 4:00 p.m. ET were required to pay the next day's NAV. Again, any money made in this manner comes out of the value of the mutual fund and, therefore, on a dollar-for-dollar basis, the pockets of its investors. Mutual funds presumably allowed this to happen in exchange for the hedge funds' business in other areas. This egregious late trading was not limited to a few isolated cases but rather was rampant throughout the industry, which allowed certain investors to trade using that day's NAV after the 4:00 p.m. deadline.

Examples of mutual fund violators were Putnam Investments and Pilgrim, Baxter & Associates:

Putnam was the fifth largest fund firm in the United States with $263 billion in assets. In Putnam's case, four investment fund managers engaged in market time trades and personally made large windfalls. Two other fund managers made market timing trades in funds they didn't manage and also made huge windfalls. It turns out that Putnam discovered the problem as early as 2000, but took no disciplinary action. As a result, the SEC charged Putnam and the managers with civil securities fraud. An executive of Pilgrim supposedly gave nonpublic portfolio information to a friend, who in turn gave that information to clients who conducted rapid trades in Pilgrim's PBHG family of funds. Supposedly, executives of the mutual funds made millions in profits from short-term trading.

CAUTION *Assume you are a professor at a prestigious university. Because of your specialty and expertise, you have many opportunities to consult with business organizations. Is such consulting a conflict of interest, or are you gaining valuable experience in the business laboratory that will help you become a better teacher and researcher? Potential conflicts like these are rampant in every business setting. As an employee or a supervisor, you must constantly be aware of what you are doing as well as what those who work for you are doing. If you, the professor, use the university telephone, the computer, or secretarial support to facilitate your consulting, is that a conflict of interest?*

Economic Extortion and Illegal Gratuities

Compared to bribery and conflicts of interest, **economic extortion** and **illegal gratuities** occur relatively infrequently and are usually quite small. Economic extortion is basically the flip side of a bribery scheme. Instead of a vendor offering a payment to an employee to influence a decision, the employee demands a payment from a vendor in order to make a decision in that vendor's favor. In any situation where an employee might accept bribes to favor a particular company or person, the situation could be reversed to a point where the employee extorts money from a potential purchaser or supplier. Illegal gratuities are also similar to bribery schemes, except that there is not necessarily an intent to influence a particular business decision but rather to reward someone for making a favorable decision. Illegal gratuities are made after deals are approved.

Extortion is similar to illegal gratuities but always involves the use of actual or threatened force, fear, or economic duress. Extortion is a criminal offense, which occurs when a person either obtains money, property, or services from another through coercion or intimidation or threatens one with physical or reputational harm unless he or she is paid money or property. Extortion is commonly practiced by organized crime groups. The actual obtainment of money or property is not required to commit the offense. Making a threat of violence or a lawsuit which *refers* to a requirement of a payment of money or property to halt future violence or lawsuit is sufficient to commit the offense. The four simple words "pay up or else" are sufficient to constitute the crime of extortion. An extortionate threat made to another in jest is still extortion.

In the United States, extortion may also be committed as a federal crime across a computer system, by phone, by mail, or by using any instrument of "interstate commerce." Extortion requires that the individual sent the message "willingly" and "knowingly" as elements of the crime. The message only has to be sent (but does not have to reach the intended recipient) to commit the crime of extortion. There have been many famous cases of kidnapping and extortion including many children of the rich and famous.

> **Remember this …**
>
> *There are four types of corruption: (1) conflicts of interest, (2) bribery, (3) illegal gratuities, and (4) extortion. Conflicts of interest and bribery are by far the most common and are often very difficult to detect.*

Review of the Learning Objectives

- **Understand the extent to which employees and others commit occupational fraud.** Occupational fraud includes corruption, asset misappropriation, and fraudulent financial statements. Misappropriation of assets is by far the most

common type of occupational fraud. According to KPMG's Integrity Study, nearly three-fourths of all employees noted some form of asset misappropriation at their companies.

- **Describe the nature and various types of asset misappropriations.** Misappropriations of cash can be committed using larceny, skimming, or fraudulent disbursements. Misappropriations of assets other than cash involve the misuse of assets and larceny. Cash is embezzled significantly more than other assets, and fraudulent disbursement is the most common type of cash theft. Physical assets such as equipment, supplies, inventory, information, and securities are the most common types of noncash assets taken.

- **Discuss the nature and various types of corruption.** There are four types of corruption: (1) conflicts of interest, (2) bribery, (3) illegal gratuities, and (4) extortion. Conflicts of interest and bribery are by far the most common.

KEY TERMS

asset misappropriation, p. 505

corruption, p. 505

fraudulent statements, p. 505

larceny, p. 507

skimming, p. 508

lapping, p. 508

check tampering, p. 508

register disbursement schemes, p. 510

billing schemes, p. 510

dummy companies, p. 511

shell companies, p. 511

expense schemes, p. 511

payroll schemes, p. 511

bribery, p. 516

commercial bribery, p. 516

kickbacks, p. 516

bid-rigging schemes, p. 516

conflict of interest, p. 518

net asset value (NAV), p. 518

economic extortion, p. 519

illegal gratuities, p. 519

QUESTIONS

Discussion Questions

1. What are the three types of fraud against organizations that employees, vendors, and customers use to steal an organization's assets?
2. Describe what is meant by an organization's theft of cash through larceny.
3. Describe what is meant by theft of cash through skimming.

4. How does the ACFE categorize fraudulent disbursements?
5. What is meant by check tampering?
6. What is a register disbursement scheme?
7. What is meant by a billing scheme?
8. What are expense fraud schemes?
9. How do executives illegally loot their companies to receive large financial benefits?
10. What are payroll disbursement fraud schemes?
11. What is meant by the term "corruption"?
12. What is meant by the term "bribery"?
13. Briefly describe how the use of databases could help in detecting kickback fraud schemes.
14. When does a conflict of interest occur? Give an example.
15. What are the six kinds of fraudulent disbursements?
16. What are the four types of corruption?
17. Why are theft of cash through larceny schemes easier to detect than skimming schemes?

True/False

1. At the present time, approximately 25,000 members make up the Association of Certified Fraud Examiners.
2. Employee frauds constitute a greater percentage of all frauds and have greater median losses than do management and owner frauds combined.
3. Statistics show that fraud losses are directly proportional to age and inversely proportional to education.
4. Larceny, skimming, and misuse are all subdivisions of theft of cash.
5. Skimming schemes are far less common than larceny schemes.
6. Billing schemes have by far the highest median costs per incident of all frauds.
7. Kickback schemes always involve the purchasing function of the victim company.
8. Bribery is one of the four types of corruption.
9. Commercial bribery is different from traditional bribery in that the offer made in commercial bribery is to influence an official act of government and traditional briberies never involve government officials.
10. Failure to account for missing inventory that was supposed to have been returned is a problem found in voided sales frauds.
11. Asset misappropriations are divided into two categories: theft of cash and theft of inventory.
12. Larceny is the stealing of cash by employees before the cash has been recorded in the company's accounting system.

13. Understating sales and stealing cash are examples of skimming.
14. The two basic fraudulent register disbursement schemes are false refunds and false voids.
15. Ghost employee schemes usually generate the largest losses among the payroll disbursement fraud schemes.
16. Corruption is divided into four fraud scheme types: (1) bribery, (2) conflict of interest, (3) economic extortion, and (4) illegal services.
17. Kickbacks are undisclosed payments made by employees of purchasing companies to vendors.
18. Compared to bribery and conflicts of interest, economic extortion fraud schemes occur relatively infrequently.
19. Illegal gratuities are made before deals are approved but after payment has been accepted.
20. Of all the different kinds of corruption, bribery schemes have the greatest median loss of fraud schemes committed against an organization.
21. Bid rigging involves establishing a predetermined amount of money that bidders will have to exceed in order to win a bid.
22. The false refund fraud scheme involves any refund given in cash for an item that was originally stolen from the store.

Multiple Choice

1. Most frauds against organizations are perpetrated by:
   a. Employees.
   b. Owners.
   c. Vendors.
   d. A collusion of two of the above.
2. What are the three major classes of asset misappropriation?
   a. Stealing receipts, purchasing fraud, and disbursement fraud.
   b. Stealing receipts, stealing money as it comes into a company, and purchasing fraud.
   c. Stealing receipts, disbursement fraud, and stealing assets on hand.
   d. Stealing receipts, stealing inventory, and stealing information.
3. Out of all the types of frauds discussed in this chapter, which type is perpetrated least often?
   a. Skimming schemes.
   b. Larceny.
   c. Check schemes.
   d. Payroll.

4. Which of the following is *not* one of the most common billing schemes?
   a. Setting up dummy companies to submit invoices to the victim organization.
   b. Changing the quantity or price on an invoice to favor a customer.
   c. Altering or double-paying nonaccomplice vendor's statements.
   d. Making personal purchases with company funds.

5. The most affected party in a workers' compensation fraud case is which of the following?
   a. Employer.
   b. Employer's insurance carrier.
   c. Other employees.
   d. Government.

6. Which of the following is a major difference between larceny and skimming?
   a. Larceny is committed before the cash is entered into the accounting system, while skimming is committed after the cash is entered into the system.
   b. Larceny is committed after the cash is entered into the accounting system, while skimming is committed before the cash is entered into the system.
   c. Larceny involves fraudulent disbursements of cash, while skimming involves fraudulent receipts of cash.
   d. Larceny involves fraudulent receipts of cash, while skimming involves fraudulent disbursements of cash.

7. Which of the following types of disbursement fraud occurs least frequently?
   a. Expense tampering.
   b. Payroll schemes.
   c. Register disbursement schemes.
   d. Billing schemes.

8. Which of the following results in the highest loss per case?
   a. Expense tampering.
   b. Payroll schemes.
   c. Register disbursement schemes.
   d. Billing schemes.

9. Which of the following is *not* considered a misappropriation of assets?
   a. Payroll disbursement schemes.
   b. Kickbacks.
   c. Expense schemes.
   d. Skimming.

10. Which of the following is *not* true of billing schemes?
   a. The perpetrator takes physical possession of his or her employer's cash.
   b. The perpetrator often sets up a "dummy" company.
   c. It is one of the most commonly committed disbursement schemes.
   d. It usually involves dealing with the victim organization's purchasing department.

11. Which of the following is *not* one of the ACFE's types of fraudulent disbursement?
   a. Check-tampering schemes.
   b. Skimming disbursement schemes.
   c. Expense schemes.
   d. Register disbursement schemes.

12. "Putting someone on the payroll who does not actually work for the victim company" is an example of a(n):
   a. Expense scheme.
   b. Payroll scheme.
   c. Register disbursement scheme.
   d. Commission scheme.

13. One key element of skimming is that cash is taken:
   a. Directly from the cash register.
   b. When no one is watching.
   c. By someone who does not ordinarily have cash-handling responsibilities.
   d. Prior to its entry into an accounting system.

SHORT CASES

Case 1

Regina has finally landed her dream job at Abercroanie & Fetch. After just a couple of days on the job, we find out why. Often, when people return merchandise, Regina will ring up on the register that they returned something of more value than it was really worth. She then pockets the extra cash and gives the customer the amount due. Regina finds this method very effective because people really are returning something, so inventories and the register totals won't be out of balance at the end of the day.

1. What type of fraud is Regina committing?
2. How could her employer detect this kind of fraud?

Case 2

In a Las Vegas casino, an employee discovered a flaw in the accounting system. The accounts payable clerk discovered that he was able to change the names of vendors in the computer system to his name. He would create false invoices and create a check for the false invoice. The name on the check would be changed to the name of the employee. After the check was printed, the name in the system could then be changed back to the appropriate vendor. The check register would show only the name of the vendor. The fraudulent employee had authorization to sign checks under $1,000. By writing small checks, he was able to defraud the company of $10,000. This fraud was caught by accident. An employee of another department was looking through the vendor list on her computer after the fraudulent employee had changed the vendor name to his name. A few entries later, the vendor name changed again. She wondered how this could occur and asked her supervisor. Soon after, the fraudulent employee was caught.

1. What kind of fraud is being committed?
2. What percent of frauds are of this type?
3. How could this fraud have been prevented?

Case 3

You work as the assistant to the controller of a small, privately owned company. Part of your job is to create weekly reports of the company's inventories. For the past several months, you have been excluding from your report a room full of damaged and/or obsolete inventory. Although these assets would usually have little or no market value, one of the owners recently found an interested buyer who wants to purchase the goods for scrap material at a deep discount. Even with this discount, the sales price of these items will be approximately $50,000.

The company has been experiencing severe financial difficulties. Today, in fact, the owners filed for bankruptcy. The controller has asked you to create one last inventory report, reminding you to ignore the damaged/obsolete inventory like usual. When you ask him about the fact that there is now an interested buyer, he says that the owner found the buyer only by a stroke of luck, and that the goods really are worthless, so you should record them as such.

1. What should you do?
2. What issues are involved?

Case 4

Ed Neilson is the purchasing agent for Style, a nationwide high-fashion women's online store. He joined the company after graduating from college five years ago. Over the years, Ed developed a close relationship with one of the company's vendor's owners—Sarah Love. Sarah owns a small manufacturing line, designing exclusive French fashion clothes and accessories. After dating for seven months, Ed and Sarah became engaged

four months ago. Sarah's fashions have historically sold very well in the Style chain, but with the recent decline in the retail industry, high-fashion, high-cost item sales have decreased substantially. Ed believed that this was just a short-term trend and thus decided to help his fiancée by guaranteeing $50,000 worth of monthly purchases from Sarah's line.

1. Is Ed involved in a fraud scheme? Explain your answer.

Case 5

Conduct a survey of managers or owners of at least 10 local businesses. Ask whether or not, to the best of the manager or owner's knowledge, the organization has ever been a victim of fraud. In each case determine the following:

1. Whether the perpetrators were employees, management, owners, or customers.
2. The dollar amount of the fraud.
3. The gender, age, marital status, and education level of the perpetrator.
4. The size of the company by number of employees.

Case 6

Ken was the only accountant for a small-town land development company. He was terminated when the company fell on hard times. One year later, when the owner of the company was reviewing the payments received from a landowner for development cost, he discovered that the landowner was three payments behind for a total of $60,000. He contacted the landowner who showed him the check stubs and the canceled checks. After further research, he found that the account in which the checks were deposited belonged to Ken, his former accountant.

1. What type of fraud did Ken commit?
2. What actions should be taken against Ken?
3. How could this fraud have been prevented?

Case 7

Jill has recently begun working at a local florist. In addition to creating floral arrangements, Jill spends a good deal of her time talking to customers and ringing up sales. Over time, she identifies a weakness in the procedures for ringing up voids. No approval is necessary to void a sale, and the void slip collects very little information about the sale. After Jill has completed a sale and the customer has left, she voids the sale and pockets the cash that was just received. The floral shop doesn't miss the lost inventory because it has a high inventory turnover ratio and high losses due to flowers losing their bloom.

1. What type of fraud is Jill committing?
2. What could the florist do to prevent this type of fraud from occurring?

Case 8

Hospital administrator Jake Rosen[9] was recently convicted for fraud he committed against his employer, Cedar Hospital Systems. Over a period of six years, he allegedly made payments to a dummy company for maintenance charges while simultaneously running a scheme with maintenance contractors where he either paid them for work never performed or overpaid them for work. The skyscraper where Jake worked was only 10 years old. Maintenance charges rose from $5.2 million in 1994 to $16.4 million in 2000. It was worth noting that the judge on the case questioned whether Cedar Hospital Systems deserved less than full restitution for failing to notice the problem. However, it was determined that federal law on restitution does not allow such charges, so Jake Rosen will be making monthly payments towards the alleged $8 million he stole until he makes full restitution after leaving prison. He was able to quickly repay $3.2 million of the theft with assets recovered by the government, including two homes and a nice yacht. Not bad for a man who was supposed to be making $90,000 per year.

1. In what specific types of fraud was Jake Rosen engaged?
2. The judge questioned whether the hospital should be held partially responsible for not having detected the fraud. What could the hospital have done to prevent or detect the fraud earlier?

Case 9

Steve Stevenson had noticed that the contracts for custodial work for the schools in the district in which he worked had almost all been going to the same custodial company, Johnson Cleaning, and it seemed to just barely manage to be the lowest bidder on each of the bids it had won. He was especially concerned because now it was charging more than it had contracted for and the budget for custodial work was starting to be stretched. Something seemed fishy, but he didn't want to jump to any conclusions. John Johnson, who also works for the district, handles the bid process. Steve thought that he might go and ask if he knew anything about what was going on. He should have some ideas

since his cousin owns Johnson Cleaning. What might be an explanation for what Steve is seeing?

Case 10

Hank just loves his new job as a sales clerk at the local classy department store, Fashion's My Style®. It's a great way for him to earn a few dollars while attending high school. Not only does his job pay quite well, but it allows him to receive discounts on all his clothes. Because Fashion's My Style® is the coolest place to shop, Hank sees many of his friends while he is working. He has found that, in addition to enhancing his social standing with his friends, he can supplement his income by selling items to friends at a price far below market level. Hank does this by taking additional markdowns and discounts off at the register. For doing this, his friends pay him a portion of the savings as well as allow him to come to all their parties.

1. What type of fraud is Hank committing?
2. How could the company find out that this is occurring?

Case 11

Match the following terms with their corresponding definitions:

  Billing scheme

  Asset misappropriation

  Check tampering

  Disbursement fraud

  Expense scheme

  Investment scam

  Illegal gratuities

  Lapping

  Payroll fraud scheme

  Skimming

1. Scheme in which perpetrators produce false documents to claim false expenses.
2. Fraud that involves stealing one customer's payment and then crediting that customer's account when a subsequent customer pays.
3. Scheme in which employees prepare fraudulent checks on their own behalf or intercept checks intended for a third party and convert the checks for their own benefit.
4. Submission of a false or altered invoice that causes an employer to willingly issue a check.

5. Using the payroll function to commit fraud, such as creating ghost employees or overpaying wages.

6. A reward given to someone for making a favorable decision.

7. Theft that is committed by stealing receipts, stealing assets on hand, or committing some type of disbursement fraud.

8. Removal of cash from a victim organization prior to its entry in an accounting system.

9. Having an organization pay for something it shouldn't pay for or pay too much for something it purchases.

10. Scheme in which perpetrators deceive individuals into putting their money into a false investment.

Case 12

Every year, Transparency International makes public its "Corruption Perceptions Index," a measure of how corrupt different countries are in relation to each other. Go to www.transparency.org/policy_research/surveys_indices/cpi/2009 and learn about the index.

1. Which are some of the most corrupt countries?
2. Which are some of the least corrupt countries?
3. Do you notice anything in common between the countries in the less corrupt group?
4. How about the more corrupt group?

Case 13

John is a waiter at a local diner. The diner has a policy that tips are to be pooled between the waiters. Accordingly, each night the cash tips are collected, pooled, and divided up between the various waiters. Then, when employees are paid by the diner, their share of the tips is included in each waiter's biweekly check. John has determined that since he works harder than everyone else, it is not fair that he has to share his tips. To compensate himself for his hard work, each night he takes half of every tip he collects and puts it in the pot—the other half he keeps. What kind of fraud is John committing?

Case 14

For many large, international companies that do business in less developed countries, corruption is a part of everyday life. Without bribing public officials, their companies could never build a factory, hire employees, get permission to build infrastructure, or receive shipments from international vendors. Shipping merchandise out of these countries can be equally difficult, with customs agents demanding unofficial payments to allow the shipment to be made.

1. If you worked for one of these companies, how would you respond to being asked by your boss to pay a bribe?
2. Are such bribes a necessary part of doing business abroad?

CASE STUDIES

Case Study 1

In 1997, Bill Eaves worked in the purchasing department of Mavis County. In 2000, Eaves was promoted to assistant county administrative officer for personnel. Five years later, Eaves was promoted to county administrative officer—the county's top executive. At the time of this promotion, he hired James Hart from Billings County to replace him as the county's human resource administrator. In 2009, Eaves retired as county administrative officer. But he continued to manage the county as a contract employee while the county searched for a successor. At that time, Hart was selected to replace Eaves as county administrative officer.

Following his retirement, Eaves asked Bell Waste Systems Company (Bell) if he could buy the firm out of its contract to operate some of the county's landfills because he believed the landfills could turn a profit if operated privately. Bell turned down Eaves's offer, but hired him as a consultant to help it develop and pitch a proposal to take over the operation of all the county's landfills. Eaves asked Hart for help. Hart promised to help Bell win county business in exchange for thousands of dollars in cash or in-kind payments from Eaves. Eaves accepted this exchange.

Eaves signed a consulting agreement with Bell, which ultimately paid him $4.6 million. Under the agreement, Bell promised to pay Eaves $1 million if the county allows Bell to operate the county landfill system and $50,000 per month if the amount of garbage dumped at county landfills exceeds 850,000 tons a year, and the county issued municipal bonds to finance landfill closure and postclosure of maintenance.

Hart headed the county board of supervisors and approved a $20 million a year contract with Bell to operate all the county's landfills. Bell started work on the contract. Hart, his friends, and other county officials were given free lodging, meals, fishing, and golf in Cabo San Lucas, the costs of which were covered by Eaves. In addition, Hart signed a promissory note for $90,000, which he received from Eaves.

Hernandez Trucking started paying kickbacks to Robert Max, vice president of Bell, equaling about $2 per truckload of dirt delivered to county landfills to cover garbage. Max received approximately $256,000, which he shared with Eaves and Hart.

In January 2011, Eaves, Hart, and Max were under investigation by the FBI because of a tip from one county official. They were among numerous people to testify in front of a special grand jury convened to investigate a failed trash project and political corruption in the county.

Questions

1. Identify the type of fraud being committed and explain your reasons.

Case Study 2

Mikos Frederick, an immigrant from Ukraine, is a hotel owner in Las Vegas. Since his arrival in America during the 1960s, Frederick has built a very successful and popular hotel. Until recently, the hotel averaged $20 million in total revenue per year. Lately though, there have been rumors that Frederick's hotel, the Russian Roulette, may be suffering unusual losses.

Recently, several of Frederick's key staff have quit, complaining about low wages and nonexistent benefits. In fact, the hotel's main attraction, its popular restaurant chef Alec Klarinko, quit as well as the hotel's headlining performer.

While Frederick focused on coming up with a new compensation policy, he hired CPA Tony Slinko to look into the hotel's diminishing cash flows. The first thing Tony did was head for the kitchen to partake of the award-winning food. The new chef, Jim Smoot, wasn't what Tony expected. First of all, he wasn't Russian, as most of the employees seemed to be, and second he refused to talk about why he had come to the Russian Roulette when so many wanted to leave.

After his visit to the kitchen, Tony began sifting through the accounting documentation looking for possible fraud symptoms. Tony reasoned that if employees felt like they weren't being compensated accordingly, they may be apt to defraud the hotel.

Questions

1. Could Tony be right? Are employees defrauding the company, or has the Russian Roulette finally bit the bullet?
2. What possible fraud activities are associated with declining cash flows?

INTERNET ASSIGNMENTS

1. Visit the Association of Certified Fraud Examiners Web site and read a short introduction on Joseph T. Wells (www.acfe.com). (*Hint:* He was not only the founder but is listed as an instructor too.)
   a. What was Wells's background before becoming chairman of the Association of Certified Fraud Examiners? What major aspects of his background would be crucial to his success as a CFE?
   b. What books has Wells written? (*Hint:* You may want to look in the ACFE's bookstore section.)
   c. Of what organizations and/or groups is Wells currently a member?

DEBATES

Look at the various fraud statistics earlier in this chapter. Determine the characteristics of the person most likely to perpetrate a large fraud. Then, debate your decision over a person with these characteristics and give the reasons why such a person is more likely to be a fraud perpetrator than a person with different characteristics.

END NOTES

1. Bryan Burrough, "David L. Miller Stole from His Employer and Isn't in Prison," *The Wall Street Journal* (September 19, 1986): 1.

2. After working for the FBI, Joseph Wells started Wells & Associates, a group of consulting criminologists concentrating on white-collar crime prevention, detection, and education. That venture led to the formation of the Association of Certified Fraud Examiners (ACFE), a professional organization of fraud professionals that now has approximately 25,000 members. Since its inception, Joe Wells has been the chairman of the board of directors and the CEO. His book was published by the Obsidian Publishing Company, Inc., in 1997 (800 West Avenue, Austin, Texas 78701).

3. www.disboards.com/showthread.php?t=1233939, accessed June 22, 2007.

4. www.usdoj.gov/atr/public/press_releases/2006/214014.htm, accessed June 22, 2007.

5. www.informationweek.com/showArticle.jhtml?articleID=197006845, accessed June 22, 2007.

6. www.foxnews.com/story/0,2933,277774,00.html, accessed June 22, 2007.

7. Much of this discussion was taken from Berstein Litowitz Berger & Grossman LLP, *Institutional Investor Advocate*, Vol. 5 (Fourth Quarter 2003).

8. www.fool.com/News/mft/2003/mft03091208.htm, accessed May 1, 2004.

9. Ideas in the case were taken from a true case discussed in the article "Legal Issues; Former Blue Cross Official Sentenced to Prison for $14.1 Million Billing Scheme," *Health and Medicine Week* (December 1, 2003): 544.

CHAPTER **15**

Consumer Fraud

LEARNING OBJECTIVES

After studying this chapter, you should be able to:

- Define what consumer fraud is and understand its seriousness.
- Understand identity theft.
- Classify the various types of investment and consumer frauds.

TO THE STUDENT

So far, all the topics in the book have related to fraud in general and frauds where organizations and shareholders are victims. In this chapter, we turn our attention to frauds where consumers (people like you and us) are victims. These types of frauds are called consumer frauds, named after their victims. Consumer frauds include such fraudulent schemes as identity theft, investment scams, and other schemes where perpetrators try to earn your trust to get you to transfer money to them. The material in this chapter will be extremely useful to you as you navigate life, enter into financial transactions, and try to protect your identity.

Jacob,[1] an 18-year-old senior in high school, had the misfortune of being educated first-hand about identity theft. While attending an after-school club, his car was broken into in the school parking lot. His wallet and stereo were stolen, and his car was vandalized. At his parent's urging, Jacob called the local police and filed a report. After a few days, Jacob had fixed the car, been reissued a new driver's license, and returned to what he believed would be a normal life. However, the worst was yet to come. Three days later, he realized his bank account balance of $1,800 had been drained, and within a few months, Jacob was receiving bogus credit card bills. After a careful investigation, Jacob realized that not only had he been robbed of his wallet and money, but his identity had also been stolen—someone else was pretending to be Jacob. By the time Jacob reported his identity theft to the credit card companies, his credit rating had been ruined. As part of the investigation, Jacob asked his mother to call the FBI to report the fraud. When Jacob's mother notified the local FBI office of the fraud, she was told that claiming their identity had been stolen was a common excuse teenagers use to justify their spending habits and a way for teenagers to get their parents to give them more money for drugs, music, or other teenage "necessities." The FBI told Jacob's mother to get a report of the expenses from the credit card agency and then look around Jacob's room to find those items that had been purchased. Jacob's mother did as the FBI asked, but to her relief, found none of the items listed. After several more calls, the FBI finally decided to investigate and file a report. Upon investigation, it was determined that Jacob's identity truly had been stolen. However, it would take years to clean up his credit report, bills, and other problems created by the theft.

Consumer Fraud and Its Seriousness

With advances in technology, **consumer fraud** is on the increase. Consumer fraud is any fraud that targets individuals as victims. For example, consumer frauds can involve telephone fraud, magazine fraud, sweepstakes fraud, foreign money offers (such as Nigerian money scams), counterfeit drugs, Internet auctions, identity theft, and bogus multilevel marketing schemes.

Thus far in this book, we have discussed employee fraud, management fraud, vendor fraud, and customer fraud. We have also briefly discussed investment fraud, a form of consumer fraud. However, there are many other types of consumer frauds that we will discuss in this chapter. Our focus on consumer fraud will be how to protect you and your families from becoming victims. While the topics discussed earlier in this text are of use daily by those who pursue employment in government, accounting, corporations, law, universities, hospitals, or technology corporations, the contents of this chapter should affect and help every individual, regardless of future occupation or even whether they are employed or not. Because of its practical application, this chapter may be the most important material you study throughout your college career. The best defense against becoming a victim of consumer fraud is education.

CAUTION *As a consumer, you should never give your personal information, such as credit card or driver's license numbers, to someone who contacts you. It is probably okay to provide personal information when you initiate the call or transaction, but, even then, you should exercise extreme care. Armed with your personal information, fraudsters, pretending to be you, can ruin your credit, obligate you for large debts, and create tremendous headaches for you as you try to convince law enforcement and others that it really wasn't you who entered into the transactions.*

Consumer fraud is a very serious problem in the United States and elsewhere in the world. In October 2007, the United States Federal Trade Commission (FTC)[2] released its second survey of consumer fraud in the United States. The survey estimates that over 30 million adults—13.5 percent of the adult population—were victims of fraud during 2005. African Americans were the most likely to be victims with 20 percent experiencing one or more frauds in the preceding year. In addition, 18 percent of Hispanics were victims and 12 percent of non-Hispanic whites were victims.

The survey of over 3,800 randomly chosen consumers showed that younger consumers, those who did not complete college, and those with high levels of debt were more likely to be victims of fraud. The top 10 frauds identified in the report included the following:

1. Fraudulent weight-loss products (4.8 million victims)
2. Foreign lottery scams (3.2 million victims)
3. Unauthorized billing—buyers' clubs (3.2 million victims)
4. Prize promotions (2.7 million victims)
5. Work-at-home programs (2.4 million victims)
6. Credit card insurance (2.1 million victims)
7. Unauthorized billing—Internet services (1.8 million victims)
8. Advance-fee loan scams (1.7 million victims)
9. Credit repair scams (1.2 million victims)
10. Business opportunities (0.8 million victims)

The most frequently reported type of consumer fraud involved fraudulent weight-loss products that promised to allow one to lose weight without diet or exercise but didn't deliver on the promises; this fraud is estimated to have affected nearly 5 million Americans in 2005. Foreign lottery scams, where a consumer was told that he or she had won a foreign lottery and made payment to receive promised winnings, were the second most commonly reported category of consumer fraud. Third on the list were buyers' club memberships with an estimated 3.2 million estimated victims who were billed for memberships they did not authorize. A similar scam listed seventh on the report involved consumers who were billed for Internet services that were unauthorized.

Three of the top 10 most common scams involved services related to consumer loans or credit including credit card insurance (sixth), advance fee loans (eighth) and credit repair scams (ninth). While federal law limits consumers' credit card fraud liability to $50, fraudsters sell credit card insurance by falsely claiming that cardholders face significant financial risk if their credit cards are misused. Advance fee loans involved consumers who paid a fee to obtain a promised loan or credit card that was not received. In addition, some fraudsters falsely promise consumers that they can help them remove truthful, negative information from their credit report, or establish a new credit record; these credit repair schemes are illegal. An estimated 5 million Americans were affected by these three types of scams.

The remaining three scams on the list involved prize promotions, work-at-home programs, and business opportunities. Prize promotions involved consumers who paid something or attended a presentation to receive a promised prized that was not as promised. Work-at-home programs and business opportunities involved programs and opportunities that generally failed to deliver at least one-half of the promised level of earnings.

The survey revealed that 27 percent of fraud victims first learned about a fraudulent offer or product from print advertising (e.g., newspapers, magazines, direct mail, catalogs, posters, or flyers). Twenty-two percent of fraudulent offers were promoted using the Internet and e-mail. Television or radio advertising accounted for 21 percent of fraudulent offers and telemarketing was used for 9 percent.

In the last few years, law enforcement agencies across the world have started working together to target consumer fraud. Consumer Sentinel is a complaint database that was developed by the U.S. Federal Trade Commission. It tracks information about consumer fraud and identity theft from the FTC and over 150 other organizations and makes it available to law enforcement partners across the United States and Canada. Launched in 1997, the Sentinel database now includes over 5.4 million complaints. You can access Consumer Sentinel at www. sentinel.gov. You can use this site to lodge a complaint, examine fraud trends, and obtain other valuable information about consumer fraud.

> **Remember this ...**
>
> *Consumer fraud represents those frauds where consumers are the victims. Technology has made consumer fraud much more common than it used to be, with an estimated over one in eight Americans falling victim in a given year. Several governmental databases have been established to help you understand the kinds of consumer frauds that exist and to help you report consumer fraud if you become a victim.*

Identity Theft

According to the Federal Trade Commission, **identity theft** is the most common type of consumer fraud, affecting thousands of people every day. Approximately one-fourth of the complaints reported to the FTC over the last few years have involved some type of identity theft.[3] Identity theft is used to describe those circumstances when someone uses another person's name, address, Social Security number (SSN), bank or credit card account number, or other identifying information to commit fraud or other crimes. In one case that we are aware of, an individual (we'll call him Tom) returned from a vacation to find out that his sister (let's call her Jane) had stolen his credit card and stolen his identity. Jane ran up a large bill that Tom refused to pay and he reported her to the police. Jane was sent to jail as Tom decided to prosecute her. Then, to add insult to injury, Tom discovered that he was denied housing because Jane's actions had ruined his credit.[4]

Unfortunately, personal data such as bank account and credit card numbers, SSNs, telephone calling card numbers, and other valuable information can be used by others to profit at your expense. The most detrimental consequence of identity theft isn't the actual loss of money, but rather the loss of credit, reputation, and erroneous information that is extremely difficult to restore or fix. If a fraudster ensures that bills for the falsely obtained credit cards or bank statements showing the unauthorized withdrawals are sent to an address other than the victim's, the victim may not become aware of what is happening until the criminal has already inflicted substantial damage on the victim's assets, credit, and reputation. Indeed, as with most fraud, the most important way to fight identity theft is to prevent it from happening in the first place. Once identity theft has occurred, it is very difficult, expensive, and time-consuming to investigate and resolve.

STOP & THINK   *Do you think it is possible to completely eliminate identity fraud risks from your life?*

Identity fraud, like all fraud, can be explained by the fraud triangle of pressure, rationalization, and opportunity. Many times, those we trust are in the best position to defraud us. Some consumer fraud victims trusted their neighbors to get their mail while they were away. Other victims innocently trusted their dinner servers while they were out to eat to process their credit card payment. Other victims simply trusted a babysitter while they were out or left personal information where it could be accessed by a friend, a family member, or even a stranger.

Some identity thefts have completely ruined individuals' lives. For example, one criminal incurred more than $100,000 of credit card debt; bought homes, handguns, and motorcycles; and obtained a federal loan—all

in the victim's name. What's more, the perpetrator then called the victim and taunted him stating that he had stolen the individual's identity—and that there was nothing he could do about it. After the perpetrator was finally caught, the victim and his wife spent nearly four years and $15,000 of their own time and money to try to restore their ruined credit and reputation. The perpetrator served a brief sentence for making a false claim while buying a firearm, but never had to make restitution to the victim for the harm he had caused.

How Identity Theft Occurs

Perpetrators of identity theft follow a common pattern after they have stolen a victim's identity. To help you understand this process, we have created the "identity theft cycle." Although some fraudsters perpetrate their frauds in slightly different ways, most generally follow the stages in the cycle shown in Figure 15.1.

Stage 1. Discovery

1. Perpetrators gain information.

2. Perpetrators verify information.

Stage 2. Action

1. Perpetrators accumulate documentation.

2. Perpetrators conceive cover-up or concealment actions.

Stage 3. Trial

1. 1st dimensional actions—Small thefts to test the stolen information.

2. 2nd dimensional actions—Larger thefts, often involving personal interaction, without much chance of getting caught.

3. 3rd dimensional actions—Largest thefts committed after perpetrators have confidence that their schemes are working.

Stage 1: Discovery

The discovery stage involves two phases: information gathering and information verification. This is the first step in the identity theft cycle because all other actions the perpetrator takes depend upon the accuracy and effectiveness of the discovery stage. A powerful discovery stage constitutes a solid foundation for the perpetrator to commit identity theft. The smarter the perpetrator, the better the discovery foundation will be. If a perpetrator has a weak foundation, the evidence gathered will be less likely to support a high-quality

FIGURE 15.1   THE IDENTITY THEFT CYCLE

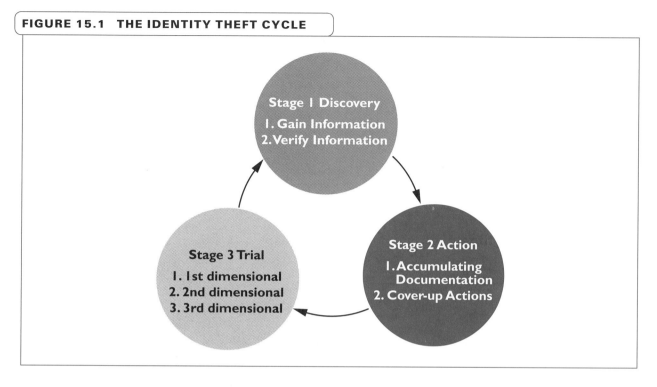

identity theft, which minimizes the victim's overall financial losses.

During the *gaining information phase*, fraudsters do all they can to gather a victim's information. Examples of discovery techniques include such information-gathering techniques as searching trash, searching someone's home or computer, stealing mail, **phishing**, breaking into cars or homes, scanning credit card information, or using other means whereby a perpetrator gathers information about a victim.

During the *information verification phase*, a fraudster uses various means to verify the information already gathered. Examples include telephone scams, where perpetrators call the victim and act as a representative of a business to verify the information gathered (this is known as *pretexting*), and trash searches (when another means was used to gather the original information). Although some fraudsters may not initially go through the information verification process, they will eventually use some information verification procedures at some point during the scam. The scams of perpetrators who don't verify stolen information are usually shorter and easier to catch than scams of perpetrators who verify stolen information.

Step 2: Action

The action stage is the second phase of the identity theft cycle. It involves two activities: accumulating

documentation and devising cover-up or concealment actions.

Accumulating documentation refers to the process perpetrators use to obtain needed tools to defraud the victim. For example, using the information already obtained, perpetrators may apply for a bogus credit card, fake check, or driver's license in the victim's name. Although the perpetrator has not actually stolen any funds from the perpetrator, he or she has now accumulated the necessary tools to do so. Any action taken by the perpetrator to acquire information or tools that will later be used to provide financial benefit using the victim's identity fall into this category.

Cover-up or *concealment actions* involve any steps that are taken to hide or cover the financial footprints that are left through the identity theft process. For example, in this stage, a fraudster might change the physical address or e-mail of the victim so that credit card statements are sent by the financial institution to the perpetrator rather than the victim. These concealment actions allow the perpetrator to continue the identity theft for a longer period of time without being noticed.

Stage 3: Trial

The trial stage involves those activities of the identity theft that provide perpetrators with financial benefits. There are three phases of the trial stage: first dimensional actions, second dimensional actions, and third dimensional actions. The trial stage is considered to be the most critical stage of the identity theft cycle because this is where the fraudster's work starts to pay off.

1st dimensional actions are the first frauds committed, mostly to test the effectiveness of fraud schemes and the stolen information. For example, a fraudster might go to a gas station and use a stolen credit card to actually determine if the card really works. If the card works, the fraudster gains confidence in the theft and moves on to bigger scams. However, if the card does not work, the fraudster faces no immediate threat of consequences and can quickly discard the card without facing anyone.

2nd dimensional actions are the actions taken by a fraudster once initial trials have been successful. These actions often involve face-to-face interactions with others. For example, if the card used at the gas station was successful, the fraudster may move on to bigger items. The perpetrator may go to a mall and buy shoes, stereo equipment, or other "large-ticket" items. Any actions used to benefit the perpetrator after the initial testing period are considered to be 2nd dimensional actions.

3rd dimensional actions are thefts committed after the perpetrator has considerable confidence in the identity theft. For example, a fraudster may establish telephone accounts, open new bank accounts, secure an auto loan, or perform other actions that provide significant benefits to the perpetrator. 3rd dimensional actions are the most risky for the identity thief. The likelihood of a fraudster being caught during 3rd dimensional actions is greater than at any other period in the identity theft.

Once a fraudster has committed 3rd dimensional actions, he or she often discards the information of one victim and starts over with the discovery stage using another victim's information.

The following actual identity theft represents a 3rd dimensional theft:[5]

George left the United States for several years but still owned a home in the states. Eventually, when he decided to sell the home, he discovered that it had been rented to strangers and someone who had stolen George's identity was collecting the rent. In addition, the thief was using George's identity to receive loans on his property and on a business venture!

How Fraudsters Convert Personal Information to Financial Gain

Once fraudsters have accessed personal information, they use that information to their financial benefit. Some of the common purchases made by identity theft perpetrators are as follows:

- *Buying large-ticket items, such as computers or televisions.* Using a fake credit/debit card, a fraudster will often buy items that are quite expensive and can easily be sold on the black market. Fraudsters then spend the stolen money very quickly, usually on drugs or other vices.

- *Taking out car, home, or other loans.* Once a fraudster has gained confidence that the identity theft (through other successful small purchases) is working, he or she often takes out a loan using the victim's identity. The most common type of fraudulent loan is for an automobile. Because automobiles can easily be traced [using the license plates or vehicle identification number (VIN)], the car is usually quickly sold so that it cannot be traced to the fraudster.

- *Establishing phone or wireless service in victim's name.* Fraudsters often set up a phone or wireless service in the victim's name. This is done so that the fraudster can more easily convince banks, businesses, and others that he or she really is the person he or she claims to be. Fraudsters also use telephones as a form of communication to buy or sell drugs, gain information to steal more identities, begin telemarketing schemes, and/or support other fraud schemes.

As an example of this type of identity theft and the grief it can cause, consider the following case:[6]

Drew found out that someone had stolen his identity when he received a phone call from his wireless provider. After some investigation, Drew discovered that the thief had racked up cell phone debts at other providers too and had incurred other debts that he was delinquent on. Drew contacted the numerous businesses that showed him delinquent and notified them of his situation. After he filed a police report he began the painful process of disputing the many problems that showed up on his credit report.

- *Using counterfeit checks or debit cards.* Using debit cards or counterfeit checks, fraudsters often drain victims' bank accounts. As will be discussed *later in the chapter, one of the biggest risks of debit cards is the lack of insurance to cover fraudulent transactions. This makes it extremely important that consumers only have a reasonable amount of cash in their checking and/or debit accounts. That way, if a fraudster drains a victim's checking account, the loss will be minimal.*

- ***Opening a new bank account.*** *Fraudsters often use victim's personal information to open new checking accounts under their name. Using the checks received from the new account, they then write checks that will not only cause problems such as NSF (bounced checks) transactions, but in the process, they destroy the person's name and credit.*

- ***Filing for bankruptcy under the victim's name.*** *Fraudsters sometimes file for bankruptcy under a victim's name. Such filings keep victims from knowing that their identity has been stolen. In the process, the victim's credit report and reputation are damaged, a problem that can take years to repair.*

- ***Reporting a victim's name to the police in lieu of their own.*** *Fraudsters have even been known to use the victim's name and identity to keep their own records from being blemished. Furthermore, if a fraudster has a criminal record, he or she might use a victim's name to purchase guns or other difficult-to-obtain items. If a fraudster does have an encounter with the police and uses a victim's identity, many times, the fraudster will be released because the victim has no previous criminal record. However, if the fraudster is summoned to court and does not appear, a warrant for the victim's arrest may be issued. Again, it may take years to clear a victim's name and reputation from federal, state, local, and business records.*

- ***Opening new credit card accounts.*** *Fraudsters often open new credit card accounts enabling them to spend money in a victim's name with no immediate consequences. This is one of the easiest ways for perpetrators to defraud a victim once his or her identity has been stolen.*

- ***Changing victim's mailing address.*** *Fraudsters often change the mailing address on a victim's credit card accounts. This prevents the victim from knowing that there is a problem and enables the fraudster to continue using the credit card and identity. Because the perpetrator, not the victim, receives the billing statements, the fraudster can continue the scheme for increased lengths of time.[7]*

Stealing a Victim's Identity

Stealing a victim's identity isn't as difficult as it may seem. Fraudsters can obtain the information required to commit identity theft in numerous ways. The U.S. Department of Justice Web site lists some of the following methods as common ways for one's identity to be stolen.

1. Fraudsters gain personal information by posing as a legitimate employee, government official, or representative of an organization with which the victim conducts business.

2. Fraudsters watch or listen to you enter a credit card number in what is known as **shoulder surfing**.

3. Fraudsters rummage through consumers' trash—an activity sometimes called **dumpster diving**. Once a garbage container is in the street it is considered public property and anyone can rummage through it. Preapproved credit card applications, tax information, receipts containing credit card numbers, Social Security receipts, or financial records are valuable sources of information for identity thieves.

4. Fraudsters *skim* victims' credit cards for information when they pay their bills. **Skimming** is a process where fraudsters will use an information storage device to gain access to valuable information when a credit card is processed. Skimming is a hi-tech method by which thieves capture personal or account information from a credit card, driver's license, or even a passport. An electronic device used to capture this information is called a "skimmer" and can be purchased online for under $50. A credit card is swiped through the skimmer, and the information contained in the magnetic strip on the card is then read into and stored on the device or an attached computer.[8]

Skimming is predominantly a tactic used to perpetuate credit card fraud but is also gaining in popularity among identity thieves. Skimming is a problem, not just in the United States, but globally. Some foreign countries are considered as high risk for travelers making credit card purchases. One traveler in France recently reported that his credit card had been used to purchase goods from Thailand, Kuala Lumpur, Hong Kong, and Malacca totaling thousands of dollars.

Skimmers are quite a creative bunch—and since the skimming devices are so small and easy to hide, it is not difficult for them to skim your card without you noticing. The following are some examples of how cards can be skimmed:

- ***Skimming at restaurants.*** *Many skimming rings have been known to employ restaurant serving staff* *to capture credit card information. An example of such an incident occurred in Charlotte, North Carolina, where two waiters of a well-known steak house were accused of skimming more than 650 credit card numbers from unsuspecting patrons and selling them for $25 each.*

- *Skimming at ATM machines or gas stations. It is not uncommon for a thief to be bold enough to tamper with an ATM machine. Typically, a "card trapping" device is inserted into the ATM card slot or a card reader is inserted into a gas station pump. ATM skimming has been a major problem in Britain with estimates that one in every 28 ATM machines has been equipped with skimmers from thieves. Gas station skimming is a growing problem in the United States.*

- *Skimming by store clerks. A very common form of skimming involves store clerks skimming a credit card when a consumer makes a purchase. The clerk scans the card twice, once for the expected transaction and another in a skimmer for later retrieval. There have also been reports of clerks skimming driver's licenses when customers that are writing checks supply the license for verification.*

Stealing a victim's identity isn't as difficult as it may seem. Fraudsters use numerous ways to get the information required to commit identity theft. Some of the more common types of information gathering techniques used by identity fraudsters are as follows:

1. Fraudsters gather information from businesses. They accomplish this by stealing information from their employer, hacking into organizations' computers, or bribing/conning an employee who has access to confidential records. As an example, thousands of Hotels.com customers could have been put at risk for identity theft after a laptop computer containing their credit card information was stolen from an auditor. The password-protected laptop belonging to an external auditor was taken from a locked car in Bellevue, Washington.[9]

2. Fraudsters steal wallets or purses to gain confidential information or identification. Valuable information is contained in almost every wallet.

3. Fraudsters sneak into victims' homes and steal their information.

4. Fraudsters steal mail, which can include bank information, checks, credit card information, tax information, or preapproved credit cards.

5. Fraudsters complete a "change of address form" at the local post office and have victims' mail

delivered to a PO box or another address of the fraudster's convenience.

6. Fraudsters engage in shoulder surfing where criminals will watch consumers from a nearby location as they give credit card or other valuable information over the phone.[10]

7. In recent years, fraudsters have begun to use the Internet to steal important information. They do this through phishing, a high-tech scam that uses spam or pop-up messages to deceive consumers into disclosing credit card numbers, bank account information, Social Security numbers, passwords, or other sensitive information. **Phishers** (fraudsters who engage in phishing) will send e-mail or pop-up messages claiming to be from legitimate businesses or organizations that consumers deal with—for example, Internet service providers, banks, online payment services, or even government agencies. The message will usually say that the victim needs to "update" or "validate" his or her account. The message then directs the victim to some Web site that looks like a legitimate organization site. The purpose of this site is to trick the victim into divulging personal information.[11]

Minimizing the Risk

There are many ways to minimize vulnerability to identity theft. The harder it is for a fraudster to access personal information, the less likely a fraudster is to try and defraud someone.

There are many proactive means to minimize the risk of identity theft. Some of the most effective ways are as follows:

1. **Guard your mail from theft.** When away from home, have the U.S. Postal Service hold your personal mail. Consumers can do this by calling 1-800-275-8777. It is also beneficial to deposit outgoing mail at post office collection boxes or at a local post office, rather than in an unsecured mailbox outside your home.

2. **Opt out of preapproved credit cards.** One of the most common and easiest ways for a fraudster to commit identity theft is to simply fill out the preapproved credit card applications consumers receive via the mail and send them in. While many individuals will destroy preapproved credit cards, this only protects consumers from having fraudsters go through their trash. Fraudsters still have the opportunity to open a victim's mail box and steal preapproved credit card applications even

before victims are aware that they have arrived. What most consumers don't know is that they have the opportunity to opt out of preapproved credit card offers. Consumers can do this by calling 1-888-5-OPTOUT (1-888-567-8688) to have their name removed from direct marketing lists.

3. **Check your personal credit information (credit report) at least annually.** The Fair Credit Reporting Act (FCRA) requires each of the nationwide consumer reporting companies—Equifax, Experian, and TransUnion—to provide you with a free copy of your credit report, at your request, once every 12 months. The FCRA promotes the accuracy and privacy of information in the files of the nation's consumer reporting companies. The Federal Trade Commission, the nation's consumer protection agency, enforces the FCRA with respect to consumer reporting companies. A credit report includes information on where you live; how you pay your bills; and whether you have been sued, have been arrested, or have filed for bankruptcy. Nationwide consumer reporting companies sell the information in your report to creditors, insurers, employers, and other businesses that use it to evaluate your applications for credit, insurance, employment, or renting a home. Instructions on how to access free credit reports can be found at the Federal Trade Commission's Web site or by typing key words such as "free credit report" into an Internet search engine. You can also access the credit rating agencies individually by going to their Web sites.

4. **Guard Social Security card and numbers.** An individual's Social Security number is valuable information for any fraudster. With knowledge of someone's Social Security number, fraudsters can open all kinds of new accounts in the victim's name. Therefore, consumers should always keep their Social Security card in a safe place. If individuals are living with roommates, it is even more important that they safeguard this information. Although a roommate may never steal an individual's information, a friend, brother, or sister of a roommate may. Remember, it is those we trust who have the greatest opportunity to commit fraud. Many organizations still use students' Social Security numbers as a form of recognition that must be used in order gain access to the organization's intranet. It is important to change this number as often as possible. Many computers automatically remember passwords so that users do not have to enter them again. It is wise to make sure these numbers are not easily

accessible. Many states give citizens the option to have their Social Security number printed on their driver's license; however, it is never required. If an individual's driver's license contains his or her Social Security number, that person should get a new driver's license as soon as possible. Never keep your Social Security card in your wallet or purse.

STOP & THINK *How could a fraudster use only a victim's Social Security number to perpetrate a fraud?*

---

5. **Safeguard all personal information.** Safeguarding personal information is very important for every individual. Consumers who have roommates, employ outside help to clean or perform other domestic services, or have outside people in their house for any reason need to be particularly careful. One certified fraud examiner recommends that individuals put their most important documents in an empty ice cream container in their freezer. It is his belief that if someone does come in an individual's house, this is probably the last place he or she will look. For the normal consumer, however, a locked safe may be sufficient.

6. **Guard trash from theft.** Consumers need to tear or shred receipts, insurance information, credit applications, doctor's bills, checks and bank statements, old credit cards, and any credit offers they receive in the mail, as well as any other source of personal information. Remember all consumers can opt out of prescreened credit card offers by calling 1-888-567-8688. (See previous section on opting out of preapproved credit cards.) Buying a shredder is one of the wisest purchases individuals can make.

CAUTION *Be sure not to set your garbage out too long before the garbage truck comes and, whenever possible, shred all documents before you discard them. Also, never leave your mail in your mailbox any longer than necessary.*

---

7. **Protect wallet and other valuables.** Consumers should carry their wallet in their front pocket and never leave it in their car or any other place where it can be stolen. It is important for consumers to always be aware of where their wallet is and what its contents are. Individuals should only carry identification information and credit and debit cards

that they regularly use in their wallet. Many individuals lose track of the number of credit cards they have. Consumers should limit themselves to only two or three credit cards and keep the 24-hour emergency telephone numbers of all credit cards they possess in their cell phone's address book. That way, if credit cards are ever stolen, the victim can quickly call the issuing credit card company and put a block on all transactions. Although debit cards help consumers stay out of debt, most do not have fraud protection insurance. On the other hand, nearly all credit cards now come with fraud protection insurance. Before getting debit or credit cards, consumers should realize the risks that are involved with each and try to minimize those risks to protect themselves. A good practice is to photocopy both sides of all your credit cards, travel cards, and other personal information you keep in your wallet or purse. This way, if your purse or wallet is stolen, you will have all the information about what was stolen and can quickly notify banks, credit bureaus, and other organizations.

8. **Protect passwords.** Individuals should use passwords on credit card, bank, and telephone accounts that are not easily determinable or available. Consumers should avoid using information that can be easily associated with them, such as their birthday, their mother's maiden name, their spouse's name, the last four digits of their telephone number, a series of consecutive numbers such as 1-2-3-4, or anything else that is predictable. Many organizations will use a default password when opening new accounts. Consumers need to make sure they change these default passwords as quickly as possible. Many individuals use the same password for all accounts. While this does prevent individuals from forgetting their passwords, it makes it extremely easy for a fraudster to gain access to all of the victim's accounts, once the fraudster has gained access to one account. For example, a fraudster who works for a bank may have access to your bank password. If the password is the same for all other transactions, the fraudster will now have unlimited access to all of a victim's information and financial accounts. Consumers should not use the same password for everything and should change their password periodically.

9. **Protecting the home.** Consumers should protect their house from fraudsters. Some fraudsters have been known to actually break into a home and not steal a single physical object. The victims may not

even know someone has been inside their home. The perpetrator will steal all information that is needed to easily commit identity theft and then leave. In order to prevent this from happening, it is important to lock all doors, preferably with deadbolts or double locks, and lock all windows. It is a good idea to have an alarm system. If an alarm system is considered too expensive, consumers can buy an alarm system sticker, sign, or box and set it outside their house to make thieves believe that the house has a security system when it does not. If consumers have an automatic garage door with a code box to open the garage door, they need to pay particular attention that others are not watching when they press the numbers on the code box. Fraudsters will wait for hours to watch someone enter the code box numbers so that they have easy access into the victim's home. It is important to periodically change the password to the code box. On a typical code box, it is easy to determine which numbers are used in the password by noticing that the three or four numbers used in the password contain more wear and tear than the numbers that are not used in the password. Finally, if consumers have baby monitors in the house, they should make sure that they are not being monitored by neighbors or anybody else. Much like in the movie *Signs*, starring Mel Gibson, baby monitors actually do pick up frequencies of other baby monitors. Fraudsters have been known to listen to phone calls and intercept valuable personal information because someone has been talking on the phone in a room with a baby monitor.

10. **Protect the computer.** Remember that legitimate companies rarely ask for confidential information via e-mail. If an individual has a question about his or her account, the person should call the company using a phone number he or she knows is legitimate. If consumers get an e-mail or pop-up message that asks for personal or financial information, they should not reply or click on the link in the message. Fraudsters are even using "cookie" type software to gather personal and confidential information from consumers' hard drives.

E-mail is not a secure way to send personal information. If a consumer needs to send information over the Internet, it should be encrypted and the Web site should be checked to verify that it is genuine. Many Web sites will have an icon on the browser's status bar that shows the site to be secure. If a Web site begins with "https:" it is more secure than a Web site that only starts with "http:" The "s" means that the site is secure. However, no matter what anyone says, no Web site is completely secure.

When using credit cards to do anything online, consumers need to make sure that they check their credit card and bank account statements as soon as possible. Remember that if a statement is late by even a couple days, consumers should contact their bank or credit card company and check the billing addresses and account balances. This could be a red flag that something isn't right.

While nearly all banks now use the Internet for automatic payments and other purposes, Internet transactions are still not completely secure. One of the authors of this book was recently talking to the CEO of a large regional bank. The CEO confessed that while his bank did not feel that it was completely safe to conduct online banking, it felt that it was necessary to keep up with all the other banks that were now using online banking. As a result, this bank also provides Internet banking despite the risk to its customers.

Customers should not open any attachment or download any files from e-mail unless they know who has sent them and their purposes for sending them. Everyone with Internet access should use anti-virus software and keep it up to date. Many phishing e-mails contain software that can harm computers and trace activities while consumers are on the Internet. Anti-virus software will watch incoming communications for bad files. A firewall is an effective way to block communications from unauthorized sources. Broadband connections are especially vulnerable, and caution should be used with them. If a consumer feels that he or she has received a fraudulent e-mail or a suspicious file, without opening the attachments, it should be forwarded to www.ftc.gov for the FTC's inspection.

11. **Take advantage of the Gramm-Leach-Bliley Act.** Everyone in America who has an account with a credit union, savings and loan, bank, insurance agency, investment account, or mortgage company will have their private information sold to marketing companies, company affiliates, or other third parties. Under the **Gramm-Leach-Bliley Act**, financial institutions have the *right* to share personal information for a profit. Have you ever wondered why you get more advertisements for clothing than your roommate? Or perhaps your roommate gets more preapproved credit card applications than

you do. Part of the reason is because banks, credit unions, and financial institutions actually sell your information to marketing groups. These groups know how much money consumers spend on clothes, food, gas, and travel for any given year. These marketing agencies then market to consumers in a way that is most effective. The Gramm-Leach-Bliley Act makes it possible, via the Internet, to determine how much someone's mortgage is, as well as other personal information.

The Gramm-Leach-Bliley Act also gives individuals the *right* to opt out of having their information sold. The problem is that many individuals are unaware that they have this option. The majority of individuals aren't even aware that their information is being sold, used, and circulated through various marketing and other agencies. To prevent identity theft and protect confidentiality, individuals should go to their financial institutions and opt out of having their information shared.[12]

Prosecution of Identity Theft

When people commit identity theft, they can now be prosecuted criminally and/or civilly. To succeed in criminal or civil prosecution, it is usually necessary to show that the perpetrator acted with **intent** to defraud the victim. This is best accomplished by gathering appropriate evidential matter. Appropriate **evidential matter** consists of the underlying data and all corroborating information available. With most identity thefts, once evidential matter is obtained, such as proof that a credit card, an auto loan, or any large-ticket item was purchased with a fake identity, it is relatively easy to prove intent.

In Chapter 1, we stated that criminal law is that branch of law that deals with offenses of a public nature. Criminal laws generally deal with offenses against society as a whole. They are prosecuted either federally or by a state for violating a statute that prohibits some type of activity. Every state as well as the federal government has statutes prohibiting identity theft in its various forms. Table 15.1 lists some of the more common identity fraud federal statues that every fraud examiner should know about.

These are some of the more common statutes covering identity thefts. Usually, when perpetrators are convicted, they serve jail sentences and/or pay fines. Before perpetrators are convicted, they must be proven guilty "beyond a reasonable doubt." Juries must rule unanimously on guilt for the perpetrator to be convicted.[13]

TABLE 15.1 COMMON IDENTITY FRAUD STATUTES

STATUTE	TITLE AND CODE	DESCRIPTION
Identity Theft and Assumption Deterrence Act	Title 18, U.S. Code § 1028	This act is one of the most direct and effective statutes against identity theft. This act was passed as a result of many identity thefts that resulted in little or no fines or forms of punishment.
Gramm-Leach-Bliley Act	Title 15 U.S. Code § 6801-6809	Passed in 1999, this law prohibits the use of false pretenses to access the personal information of others (before this time it was actually legal to call up the bank and act as someone else to gain his or her confidential personal information).
Health Information Portability and Accountability Act of 1996	Standards for Privacy of Individually Identifiable Health Information, Final Rule—45 CFT Parts 160 and 165	This law came into effect on April 14, 2001. It protects the privacy and confidentiality of patient information.
Drivers Privacy Protection Act of 1994	Title 18 U.S. Code § 2721	This act ensures that personal information contained by departments of motor vehicles is not disclosed.
Family Educational Rights and Privacy Act of 1974	Title 20 U.S. Code § 1232	This act makes it illegal for any agency that receives federal funding to disclose any educational or personal information of any individual.
Fair Credit Reporting Act	Title 15 U.S. Code § 1681	This act gives exact procedures for correcting mistakes on credit reports. It also requires that credit reports can only be obtained for legitimate business needs.
Electronic Fund Transfer Act	Title 15 U.S. Code § 1693	This act provides some consumer protection for all fraudulent transactions that involve using a credit card or other electronic means to debit or credit an account.
Fair Debt Collection Practices Act	Title 15 U.S. Code § 1692	This act protects consumers from unfair or deceptive practices used by debt collectors to collect overdue bills that a creditor has forwarded for collection.
Fair Credit Billing Act	Title 15 U.S. Code, Chapter 41	This act limits consumers' liability for fraudulent credit card charges.

Once Identity Theft Has Occurred

Chances are that at some time in the future, you or someone you know will become a victim of identity theft. If you are so unfortunate, it is important to act quickly to minimize the damages. A small amount of time, such as a couple of days, can make a big difference when identity theft has taken place.

Victims of identity theft should immediately contact the Federal Trade Commission. The FTC is available online at www.ftc.gov or by telephone at 1-877-ID THEFT (877-438-4338). The FTC has the responsibility to work with those people who believe they have been victims of identity theft. The FTC will not only provide victims with valuable materials, but will also help contact enforcement agencies and credit reporting agencies to minimize damages.

Although the FTC is the primary agency responsible for helping victims of identity theft, a few other agencies are helpful for identity theft victims as well. The local FBI and/or U.S. Secret Service agencies in a victim's area can help report and investigate different types of identity theft. If a victim believes that some or part of his or her mail has been redirected, the local Postal Inspection Service can help fix the mail as well as identify if the perpetrator has used mail as a tool to help commit the fraud. If a victim suspects that the perpetrator may have used improper identification information and caused tax violations, he or she should call the Internal Revenue Service at 1-800-829-0433. If a victim believes that his or her Social Security number has been used fraudulently, he or she should call the Social Security Administration at 1-800-269-0271.

Because a victim's reputation and credit report are directly affected by identity theft, the principal credit reporting agencies—TransUnion, Equifax, and Experian—should be contacted as well. Due to the gravity of

TABLE 15.2 CHECK VERIFICATION AGENCIES

AGENCY	HELP LINE
Equifax	1-800-437-5120
CheckRite	1-800-766-2748
National Processing Company	1-800-526-5380
Shared Check Authorization Network (SCAN)	1-800-262-7771
TeleCheck	1-800-927-0188
CrossCheck	1-800-552-1900
ChexSystems	1-800-428-9623

identity theft, all three principal credit reporting agencies have developed fraud units to help victims of identity theft. These fraud units can be called at the following numbers: 1-800-680-7289 (TransUnion), 1-800-525-6285 (Equifax), and 1-800-397-3742 (Experian).

Many identity thefts involve fraudulent checks. Therefore, victims of identity theft should contact all major check verification companies. If a victim has had checks stolen or has had bank accounts set up in his or her name, check verification companies can help restore credit as well as clear up financial debts. If a victim is aware of a particular merchant that has received a stolen check, the victim should identify the verification company that merchant uses and contact them. While there are many check verification companies, some of the more popular agencies are listed in Table 15.2.

In addition to the agencies listed in Table 15.2, identity theft victims should contact all creditors with whom their name or identifying data have been fraudulently used. Victims should also contact financial institutions that they believe may contain fraudulent accounts in their name. Victims will probably need to change personal identification numbers (PIN), bank account cards, checks, and any other personal identifying data.[14]

Identity Theft—Concluding Comments

As we finish our discussion of identity theft, we want you to understand just how expensive, troublesome, and time-consuming having your identity stolen can be. We thus conclude this topic with the real story of an identity theft victim, told by the victim herself.[15]

Regardless of how many times I have been told that I am not, I am a victim. Our police agencies need to realize that having one's identity stolen is emotionally painful, humiliating, and costly. I have spent an ungodly number of hours trying to correct the damage that has been done by the individual who stole my identity. Professionally, as a teacher and tutor, my hours are worth $35. I have been robbed of $5,250 in time. I have been humiliated in my local stores because my checks have been rejected at the check out, and I am emotionally drained. I am a victim, and Congress needs to recognize me as such.

My fanny pack was stolen at a coffee shop in Chicago on Labor Day. By the time I drove home to cancel my credit cards, they had already been used. The credit card companies were very helpful in canceling my cards; however, none of them told me that I needed to notify the three major credit reporting agencies. The police failed to give me this information as well.

My credit union told me to cancel my stolen checks. Unfortunately, they did not advise me to close my account and open a new one. Both stolen checks were written and forged on the same night as the theft; one at a gambling boat, and the other at a major grocery store. Both places required a picture ID. I learned of the forged checks when a clerk at the Target store rejected my personal check for merchandise. The clerk allowed me to use the courtesy phone to see why my check had been rejected. I was told that I had bounced a check at Harrah's Casino (a gambling boat). I tried to explain the situation and was told to call Equifax Check Services the next morning. I called and was told that I needed to address the issue in writing.

That same day, I received a letter of intent to collect from this same company. I called again trying to explain, and I was given the information that I needed to include in the letter to them. This included an affidavit of forgery (to be filled out after I requested and received copies of the forged check from my banking institution which took four days), my mother's maiden name, and proof of identity (which had been in the fanny pack). I was told that once they had received the information, it could take up to 30 days to clear my records.

In the meantime, I could not cash a personal check at any store. I then received a letter of intent to collect from Telecheck for the forged check to the grocery store. Again, I called to explain. Again, I had to send various pieces of information and would have to wait 30 days for my record to clear. Neither company advised me to contact the credit reporting agencies.

In October, thanks to an investigator for Target, I was made aware that someone was opening charge accounts in my name. An employee of Target was suspicious after opening a new account in my name. She realized that the woman opening the account was much younger than what the birth date on the application indicated. She followed the woman and her male companion out to the car and wrote down the license plate number. Of course, all of this happened after she had charged $989 of stereo equipment and electronics.

The investigator was calling to verify that I had not opened an account. The investigator told me that I should call the credit reporting agencies and request reports to see who else had inquired into my credit and to flag my reports with an identity theft alert. Unfortunately, I cannot say that this woman was then arrested, and my chaos ended. I called my friend in the Department of Motor Vehicles and had her run the license plate number. I then called the police to give them the woman's name, address, and phone number. The police detective in charge of my case refused to take any information. I tried to tell him about the witness at the Target store; again, he would not take any information. His exact words to me were "You are not a victim." He explained to me that I was not actually out any money; therefore, I was not the victim, the credit card companies were. Shocked, I asked him how he could say that. My identity had been stolen, checks were forged, new accounts had been opened, and my credit was ruined. He again stated that I was not actually out any cash. I hung up angry and frustrated.

I then followed through on the investigator's advice; I called the credit reporting bureaus. TransUnion was easy to contact and extremely helpful. Over the phone, I was able to get the names of all the credit companies who had inquired into my credit since the theft. The representative even went so far as to give me phone numbers for each of the companies. I started calling companies. Sears opened a new account even though I had just reported my card stolen and told them not to send me a new card. It was "maxed out" at $4,000. JCPenney's turned down the new application because I had just closed the other account (smart people there). And Sprint wireless had given the "new me" a phone and a service. I closed the accounts immediately, and page by page filled out all the required paperwork for each company.

Since I now had a cell phone number with a well-used service, I decided to call my detective once again. As a civilian, I figured that the police might call the numbers that had been called on the service and get some clues—even though I already had her name and address. Again, I was told that I was not a victim.

Discouraged, but with a lot of work yet to do, I called the Equifax credit reporting bureau. They were harder to reach, but very helpful. The "new me" went on a gift certificate buying spree at Montgomery Ward and at Ashley Stewart—a store I had never even heard of before. Ward told me that they couldn't void the gift certificates that were purchased on the fraudulent account. It wasn't their policy. They told me that they would close the account and that it was over the limit of $2,500. Of course, I would have to fill out all of their forms and return them with an affidavit of forgery. Ashley Stewart is a clothing store. The "new me" is now well dressed in over $1,000 worth of new clothes. They closed the account after two phone calls and sent me the forms. That left one credit reporting agency to contact.

Contacting Experian was an experience—a nightmarish experience. No human ever answered the phone at Experian. I called over 20 times at all times of the day. I tried every possible number option on that recording. I made up numbers to try. I sent a letter including the long list of information they requested and received nothing in 10 days—all the while still trying to call them. I sent a second letter. No answer after another 10 days. I sent a certified letter telling them that the FTC requires them to send me a copy of my credit report. They sent back a form requesting all the information that I had sent previously. I filled out the form and sent it back certified and registered.

I called the FTC to complain; they told me to send Experian a letter. In 15 days, I finally received my credit report. Again, I called the companies who had made inquiries into my credit. Ameritech told me that a phone had been installed in my name at an address in Chicago. The "new me" had installed a new phone at a "new address." Even better, Providian Financial didn't know why they had inquired into my credit history. The credit report had given me access to a new phone number for Experian so I called and was put on hold. It gave me time to look over my report.

I discovered that Experian had listed the address of the house with the newly installed phone as my address. My entire credit history had changed its address without my ever having to move. After 30 minutes on hold (no exaggeration), I finally heard a person's voice. I told the customer service representative about the erroneous address and asked her how they received that information. She said that Providian Financial had sent it to them. Confused, I asked her to explain. She said that Providian had inquired in order to send out preapproved credit card applications to me. Remember, Providian had no record of me, or so they said.

I boldly asked why Experian would change my address. Her response was that it was policy to add or change addresses whenever they received information from credit card companies. This means that Ameritech sold my "new fraudulent address" to a credit card company that was sending preapproved credit card applications to the person who stole my identity. How much easier for a thief could it get?

Well, it does get easier if the police won't do anything. Upset with my detective, I called his supervisor and complained. I was assured that something would be done and my case would be reassigned. I got a new detective all right. She even called me—to tell me that I hadn't gotten the other detective in trouble and she really didn't know what I expected her to be able to do. After over three months, I blew up. I told her that I didn't care whether he was in trouble or not. And that considering the Chicago Police Department had just put out a propaganda piece on the local news about how they were now going to go after identity thieves, that I expected them to do something or that I'd be happy to call the press and let them know that the piece was propaganda (the press loves that). She shut up. I continued with the fact that I gave them a name and address, that I had a witness, and that she had just installed a phone at a residence in Chicago. I asked her if she wanted me to drive over there and pick her up for them as well. She told me that I couldn't do that. She finally took the information I had collected and said that she'd get back to me. That was on December 20.

Trying to get a step ahead of this criminal, I realized that if she were receiving mail in my name at a fraudulent address that maybe it would fall under postal fraud. I called the postal inspector, got a voice mail, and left a message. An inspector called me back the next day. I was informed that it was indeed his job to investigate identity theft, and he took the information that I had on the individual and the number of the investigator from Target. In three days, I received a letter from him requesting copies of anything I had regarding opened accounts, fraudulent charges, and any correspondence with credit card companies. That was three weeks ago.

The irony of all this is that two weeks ago, Experian tried to send me additional information and left my PO box number off the envelope. The Federal Post Office sent them a corrected address notice. Experian sent me the notice with a letter saying because of the confidentiality of the information they provide, I needed to send a copy of my driver's license and two pieces of mail to verify my identity before they could change my address. They changed my address because a credit card company sent a credit card application to an unknown address, yet they won't fix their own error when the Federal Post Office sends them a corrected address notice.

Remember this …

Identity theft is fraud that targets consumers as victims. Identity thieves steal personal information, such as credit cards, Social Security numbers, and so on, from victims and then, pretending to be that victim, make purchases and incur other expenditures in that person's name. Identity thieves will go to great length and various means to steal your identity, including using skimmers, dumpster diving, accessing your mail box, phishing, and even breaking into your car or home. While it is never possible to completely eliminate all identity theft risks, you should take precautions that make you a much harder target than others.

Other Types of Consumer and Investment Scams

We have spent almost the entire chapter discussing identity theft. In the next section, we will briefly cover various other types of scams that target consumers as their victims.

Foreign Advance-Fee Scams

Foreign advance-fee scams have been around for years; however, with the advent of the Internet, they have recently become much more widespread and common. Unfortunately, many individuals have become victim to this form of consumer fraud. In the following paragraphs, we will discuss some of the more common types of foreign advance-fee scams.

Nigerian Money Offers

Nigerian money offers are a form of foreign advance-fee scams where individuals from Nigeria or another (usually underdeveloped) country contact victims through e-mail, fax, or telephone and offer the victim millions of dollars. The catch is that in order to transfer the victim these monies, it is necessary to provide name and bank account numbers, including routing numbers, and so on, so the money can be transferred. The fraudster then uses this information to drain the victim's account and commit other types of frauds. Figure 15.2 shows an actual Nigerian money offer received via e-mail. This e-mail was received by one of the authors who receives 5 to 10 such letters each week!

Notice that this letter contains several characteristics that are common to almost all fraudulent money offers. The first characteristic of this e-mail is the promise of money. The e-mail states that for your minimal help, you will receive "25 percent of $35,750,000" or about $8,937,500, plus "5 percent of $35,750,000" or about $1,787,500, for any expenses incurred. Receiving just over $11 million for helping someone sounds like a pretty good deal to most people. However, remember if something sounds too good to be true—it usually is.

The second characteristic of this fraudulent e-mail is that the letter asks for help. In order to obtain victims' personal information, the perpetrator will deceive (con) the victim into believing that he or she really is needed for one reason or another. Usually, the perpetrator will state that this is a "once-in-a-lifetime" opportunity. Third, the perpetrator will try to build a relationship of confidence with the victim. The perpetrator will use different means to make the victim feel sorry for

FIGURE 15.2   E-MAIL OF NIGERIAN MONEY OFFER FRAUD

Subject: PLS ASSIST A WIDOW
Date: Fri, 06 Aug 2004 14:38:44 +0200
From: maryam_abacha13@virgilio.it
To: xxxxxxxxxxxxxxxxxxxxxxxxxx

DEAR Sir, Madam.

I am Hajia Maryam Abacha, Widow of the Late Gen. Sani Abacha former Nigerian Military Head of State who died as a result of cardiac arrest. The name of your company appeared in one of our directories as one of the companies my Late Husband wanted to do business with before he died. I therefore decided to contact you in confidence so that I can be able to move out the sum of US $35,750,000.00 (Thirty Five Million Seven Hundred and Fifty Thousand U.S Dollars) which was secretly defaced and sealed in big metal box for security reasons in your account.

I personally therefore appeal to you for your urgent assistance to move this money into your country where I believe it will be safe since I cannot leave the country due to the restriction of movement imposed on me and members of my family by the Nigerian Government. You can contact me or my family lawyer.

Upon the receipt of your acceptance to assist me, my lawyer shall arrange with you for a face-to-face meeting outside Nigeria in order to liaise with him towards the effective completion of this transaction. However, arrangement has been put in place to move this money out of the country in batches in a secret vault through a diplomatic security company to any European Country as soon as you indicate your interest.

I also want you to be assured that all necessary arrangement for the hitch-free of this transaction has been concluded. Conclusively, I have decided to offer you 25% of the total sum 5% will be for whatever expenses that will be incurred, while 70% is to be used in buying shares in your company subsequent to our free movement by the Nigerian Government.

Please reply.
Best regards,
HAJIA M ABACHA

---

him or her. In the example below, the perpetrator relates the death of her husband so that the victim will further sympathize with the perpetrator. Fourth, as with most of these requests, this letter states the need for "urgent assistance." Nearly all fraudulent money offers ask that the victim respond immediately and confidentially. Fifth, this e-mail makes the victim feel like he or she is the only person to receive this "special" opportunity. However, literally thousands of people are getting this exact same e-mail daily. Sixth, this e-mail states that it is necessary to meet "for a face-to-face meeting outside Nigeria." This request is again to instill confidence. Meetings such as these never take place, or, if they do, victims never know the true identity of the perpetrator or the reason for the meeting. Victims who have tried to attend such meetings have been kidnapped, robbed, and even killed. It is almost always dangerous to meet anybody that someone has met online. Seventh, the perpetrator of this letter claims to be the "Widow of the Late Gen. Sani Abacha former

Nigerian Military Head of State who died as a result of cardiac arrest." Nearly all fraudulent money offers will claim to have strong ties to high-ranking foreign officials.

Many fraudulent money offers will also send official-looking documents. These documents are always forgeries; yet, to many victims they add credibility to the perpetrators' claims. Often, fraudulent money offers will also ask victims to send their bank account number to show that the victim is willing to accept the offer. Other offers will ask victims to pay large "fees" to process the transaction. Once a victim responds to the e-mail, or has been deceived one time, the perpetrator will continue to have the victim pay transaction fees—each time telling the victim that this is the last fee required.

Other Foreign-Advance Fee Scams

Although Nigerian money offers are the most common type of foreign advance-fee scams, several other foreign-advance fee scams are becoming more and more popular. The following are examples of some of these schemes. One of these scams is a **clearinghouse scam**. A clearinghouse scam involves a victim receiving a letter that falsely claims the writer represents a foreign bank. This foreign bank is supposedly acting as a clearinghouse for venture capital in a certain country. The fraudulent company will try to get victims to invest in foreign venture capital companies for high returns. To give the impression that they are legitimate, the perpetrators will set up bank accounts in the United States. When the victims transfer money into the domestic account, the perpetrators quickly transfer the money overseas where it will never be seen again. Some clearinghouse scams will actually give back a portion of the original investments in the form of dividends. However, such transfers are made only to give the victim more confidence in the scam so that the victim will invest additional money. Eventually, the money is transferred and lost.

Another type of foreign advance-fee scam is the **purchase of real estate scam**. This scam usually takes the form of someone trying to sell a piece of real estate or other property to the victim. Perpetrators will see advertisements for land (or other assets) being sold and send possible victims letters offering to purchase the property on behalf of a foreign concern. The victims are defrauded when they agree to pay "up-front fees" to a "special broker." Once paid, the victim will never hear from the perpetrator again.

Sale of crude oil at below market price is another type of foreign advance-fee scam. In this scam, the victim receives an offer to purchase crude oil at a price well below market price. However, in order to receive these "below market prices," it is necessary to pay special registration and licensing fees. Once the victim pays these fees, the seller disappears.

Finally, **disbursement of money from wills** is a foreign advance-fee scam that is becoming ever more popular. In this scam, perpetrators con charities, universities, nonprofit organizations, and religious groups. These organizations will receive a letter from a mysterious "benefactor" interested in contributing a large sum of money. However, to get the money, the charity is required to pay inheritance taxes or government fees. Once these taxes and fees are paid, the victims are unable to contact the benefactor.

All of these schemes have common elements. They all come from an unknown party who claims to have access to large sums of money or assets. The perpetrators are always willing to transfer that money or other assets to the victims, but only after money or information is extracted from the victims. The perpetrators are not well-known businesses (even though they sometimes represent that they are), and there is usually some urgency to participate. The best advice we can give to avoid being a victim to these types of schemes is that given above: if it sounds too good to be true, it probably is. Or, stated another way, "if it looks like a snake, crawls like a snake, and acts like a snake, it probably is a snake."[16]

Just a final point about these types of scams. An investigator friend of ours sent us a mailing that was sent to various perpetrators of foreign-advance fee scams. The letter was an advertisement for a conference, which was to be held at a five-star hotel in Africa. The topic of the conference—"Ways to Improve the Collectibility and Success of Foreign Advance-Fee Scams." Isn't it interesting that those who would deceive others would have a conference at an expensive hotel to trade secrets on how to be more successful at deception?

Work-at-Home Schemes

Nearly everyone has seen advertisements that read, "I work at home and love it—work part time and earn $1,000–$5,000 a week." While not all work-at-home schemes are illegal or fraudulent, many of them are.

You can find people marketing fraudulent work-at-home schemes on the telephone, in chat rooms, on the Internet, through telephone polls, as banners or advertisements on automobiles, through the use of fliers, on message boards, in classified ads, and through all other types of communications media. According to one report,[17] con artists pitching work-at-home schemes rake in approximately $427 billion a year. Here are some of the more common work-at-home schemes.

Multilevel Marketing

Just about everyone has been approached at some time or another to join a **multilevel (or network) marketing (MLM) company**. When structured correctly, with honest people, multilevel marketing is a legitimate form of business. In fact, it is really another marketing approach from which organizations may choose. In most multilevel marketing programs, company representatives act as sellers of real products such as facial creams, health aids, detergents, and foot supplements. These individuals are independent distributors of a legitimate business. In order to increase the distribution process, representatives of these organizations recruit friends, family members, and others to join them in selling the products. Generally, distributors make money both on what they sell personally and what those they have recruited sell.

However, one of the most common work-at-home schemes is the fraudulent manipulation of legitimate multilevel marketing organizations. While there are many variations of fraudulent MLMs, one kind of fraudulent multilevel marketing organization is also called a **pyramid** or **Ponzi scheme**. Instead of selling real, legitimate products, they have only illusionary products and profits. As stated previously in this book, one of the most famous frauds of all time was a pyramid scheme perpetrated by Carlo "Charles Ponzi." Because Charles Ponzi's scam was one of the first large-scale frauds of the twenty-first century, pyramid schemes and many fraudulent MLMs have been dubbed "Ponzi schemes." Ponzi MLMs can look just like nonfraudulent MLMs. However, Ponzi MLMs tend to focus their efforts on the recruiting of new members instead of the selling of legitimate products. In the beginning of a pyramid scheme, the investments

of subsequent investors are used to pay promised returns to earlier investors. These seemingly real returns excite early investors who then spread the "good news" about the "investment" to their friends and relations. Sooner or later, however, the scheme either becomes too big and too exposed and, as a result, subsequent investors dry up or the perpetrator disappears with the assets. With no new money to make the scheme look like it is working, the entire organization usually collapses, leaving only a few people at the top of the pyramid who have actually made money—those at the bottom always lose their investment (see Figure 15.3 for the structure of a pyramid scheme).

So how do consumers tell the difference between a legitimate MLM and a fraudulent MLM, including Ponzi schemes? Usually, investors can tell the difference by the focus of the marketing and by the company's compensation plan. If the focus is on recruitment, instead of products, the MLM may be fraudulent. As stated, fraudulent pyramid schemes make their money by getting new people to invest in the company, which

FIGURE 15.3   THE STRUCTURE OF A PYRAMID SCHEME

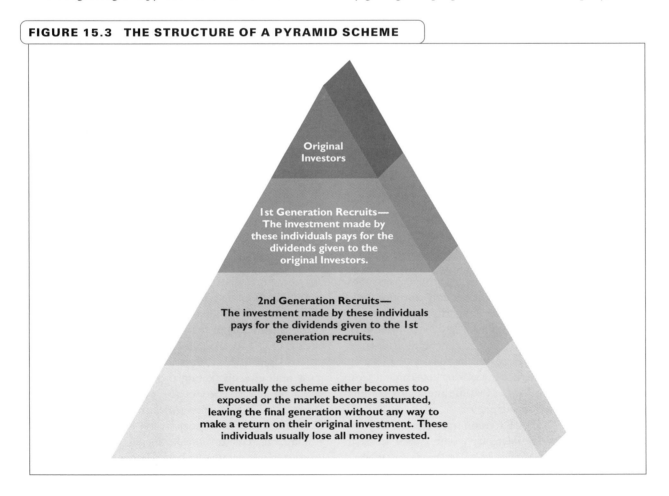

Original Investors

1st Generation Recruits— The investment made by these individuals pays for the dividends given to the original Investors.

2nd Generation Recruits— The investment made by these individuals pays for the dividends given to the 1st generation recruits.

Eventually the scheme either becomes too exposed or the market becomes saturated, leaving the final generation without any way to make a return on their original investment. These individuals usually lose all money invested.

in turns pays dividends to those who have already invested. **Headhunter fees**, which are fees paid for signing additional recruiters, signal one type of problem. It is illegal for MLM distributors to receive a commission simply for signing up new distributors—a product must be part of the distribution process. When investing in an MLM, investors should avoid MLMs that include headhunter fees. Some MLMs are organized much like a matrix, meaning representatives only get paid when the organization becomes "X number of distributors deep" or "Y number of distributors wide." This, too, can be a red flag that the organization's focus is on recruitment instead of marketing products.[18]

Front loading is a related, fraudulent process whereby even representatives of legitimate MLMs are required to buy large, expensive amounts of inventory. These types of companies often require distributors to buy the goods because there really isn't a legitimate demand from other people for the goods. It is only the promise of making large windfalls that motivate the purchase of unusually overpriced goods or services. In these cases, when the organization collapses, individuals are unable to sell their inventory and are left with substantial financial losses. The widespread use of front loading in the MLM industry has led critics to estimate that up to 99 percent of all MLM distributors lose money.

Investors should avoid paying money or signing contracts in any high-pressure situation. It is always wise as an investor to take sufficient time to contemplate the business opportunity so you can understand all aspects of the investment. Many fraudulent organizations will pressure individuals to pay money during special **opportunity meetings**. Perpetrators know that if they can't hook a possible victim during an opportunity meeting, they probably won't. A fraudster's success is determined by how well he or she can manipulate victims' emotions. Most consumer fraud perpetrators have great people skills. They understand people, and they understand how to get what they want. It is usually the honest, innocent, and gullible who are especially susceptible to consumer fraud. For this reason, the uneducated and elderly, as well as those who don't understand the language or who are dependent on others, are especially vulnerable.

Individuals should be skeptical of business opportunities that make any promises that seem too good to be true. For example, many businesses promise unusually high returns with little or no hard work. If these promises were really true, the perpetrators certainly wouldn't need another consumer's help or his or her money. Successful, legitimate MLMs require considerable amounts of

work. Any business that promises the contrary should raise a red flag. One of the biggest marketing campaigns of illegal MLMs is the promise that investors will always make money from their future downline (distributors under them) growth. However, this is not only a sign of the focus on recruitment—instead of the focus on product sales—but also a sign that the business is trying to use emotional excitement to lure investors. No one can guarantee that an investor's downlines will grow. It is the individual investor's hard work and effort that will determine downline growth.[19]

Snake oil plans are plans that promise enormous earnings or claim to sell miracle products. Just because a business promises that its product will do something special or unique does not necessarily mean that the product will actually deliver as promised. There is no such thing as a "miracle product" that fixes all ailments. Any business that promises its product will fix or heal every ailment should raise immediate red flags. Another warning signal is a business that promises a **ground floor opportunity**. This is a classic marketing scheme that makes people believe that they will make money simply because they are one of the earliest investors in this new venture. These consumers are guaranteed that they will make money as the business grows. However, what most investors don't realize is that any company that offers ground floor opportunities probably has no track record and history. Furthermore, it is difficult to determine if the new company is fraudulent. Businesses whose opportunities are greater for those who are the first to invest have a high possibility of being fraudulent. Legitimate MLMs provide the same opportunity for all investors to earn equal profits, regardless of placement in the organizational pyramid. Legitimate MLMs usually have many products, have been around for many years, and have proven track records. Of course, these MLMs don't have the attractiveness of high-risk, possibly fraudulent MLMs. Any investor who is seriously considering investing in a MLM should contact the Better Business Bureau and state attorney general to determine if complaints have been made against the company.[20]

International Multilevel Marketing Schemes

Some countries have outlawed all types of pyramid and MLM organizations, regardless of whether the company has valid products or not. The reason these countries have outlawed multilevel organizations is because they believe that all plans that pay a commission for recruiting new distributors will inevitably collapse when new distributors can no longer be recruited. When a pyramid collapses, it leaves thousands of people with no savings or income, which causes instability within a country. Such collapses have even caused economies to fail. In the early 1990s, Albania, a former communist state, had a free economy for the first time. Capitalism was developing anew and few people had property or contacts. Soon after, however, people began using politics as a means to financial gain. Those who were politicians could open or close doors and were the first to take advantage of new opportunities. Many individuals learned that through crime they could also improve their lives—or so it seemed. Criminals started to gain power and money. The politicians needed that money to stay in power. The people were not educated and had no experience with capitalism. Albania soon became an economic matrix, where anything was legal. Many individuals were kidnapped by gangsters. Thousands of people left the country. The only way the new "free" economy could survive was through crime. Most people within the country did not pay taxes. Countries, such as the United States, which applauded the country when it abandoned communism, watched the country turn from a free economy to a criminalistic economy. The economy soon became engulfed with fraudulent multilevel marketing schemes. Individuals began to put the little money they had into these fraudulent pyramid schemes. The recruiters for the schemes promised investors that they would get ahead financially and even become rich. Instead of working and investing, many citizens of Albania just waited for their money to come to them—after all, this is what had been promised. The Albanian government allowed the schemes to continue. The multilevel marketing schemes became so common that instigators of the schemes became celebrities. These owners were invited to political and social parties. They were accepted and legitimized. One fraudulent organization even sponsored an Italian race car team. MLMs became a fever, and even the most educated Albanian citizens were soon investing in them. Unfortunately, in 1997, these schemes collapsed, causing angry Albanians to ransack their own state. Albania was thrown into complete economic confusion. The Albanian economy was destroyed and the negative effects of the pyramid schemes and MLMs are expected to last for a long time.[21]

Chain Letters, Mail Stuffing, Product Testing, and Craft Assembly

There are numerous ways for fraudsters to con victims out of small amounts of money. Chain letters, mail stuffing, product testing, and craft assembly are all common ways for fraudsters to do this.

Chain letter scams usually begin when a gullible consumer sees an advertisement stating something like the following, "Make copies of this letter and send them to people whose names we will provide. All you have to do is send us $10 for our mailing list and labels. Look at the chart below and see how you will automatically receive thousands of dollars in return!!!" However, the only people who benefit from chain letters are the mysterious few at the top of the chain who constantly change names, addresses, and post office boxes. They sometimes attempt to intimidate consumers by threatening bad luck, trying to impress, or by describing themselves as successful professionals who know all about nonexistent sections of alleged legal codes. Any such chain letter program is illegal and a scam. In essence, it is an MLM without a product.

Mail stuffing is a scam where consumers respond to an advertisement that promises income simply for stuffing envelopes. When answering such ads, consumers don't receive envelopes for stuffing, but instead get promotional material asking for cash in exchange for details on money-making plans. The details usually turn out to be instructions on how to go into the business of placing the same kind of ad the advertiser ran in the first place. Pursuing the envelope ad plan may require spending several hundred dollars more for advertising, postage, envelopes, and printing. This system feeds on continuous recruitment of people to offer the same plan. There are several variations on this type of scheme, all of which require the customer to spend money on advertising and materials.

Product testing is a fraud that typically begins when consumers receive brochures featuring different products. The brochures usually request that consumers review the products presented and send their commentaries to the supplier for review. The brochure promises that participants, in addition to payments for services rendered, will be able to keep the products reviewed. There is usually some sort of enrollment fee ranging from $10 to $25. Usually, those who respond to these advertisements never receive any information after the fees are paid. On the other hand, those who are enrolled and request products for testing may end up paying hundreds of dollars in postage and handling for items worth far less than the fees.

Craft assembly is a scam where perpetrators promise high pay for working on different projects. These projects can include anything from wooden calendars, to paper towel holders, to hair clips, and even holiday decorations. Victims are usually required to purchase costly materials, equipment, and training. The victims are usually required to sign a contract that obligates the victim to purchase more material and equipment than is needed. Normally, the perpetrator will promise to pay the investor for the goods he or she produces. However, in the end, the perpetrators will almost always refuse to pay the investor for the work rendered, declaring that the work does "not meet standards." Unfortunately, no work is ever "up to standard," leaving consumers with overpriced equipment and supplies, and no income. In order for the consumers to sell their goods, they must find their own customers.

Bogus Mystery Shopping Scams

Fraudsters take advantage of many consumers through a scheme known as a **bogus mystery shopping scam.** During this bogus scam, perpetrators promise victims a job that involves strolling through stores, enjoying the displays, shopping for merchandise, and then filing reports on the experiences they have had. Fraudsters promise victims compensation ranging from $10–$40 an hour, plus the opportunity to keep all products evaluated. Although some mystery shoppers' advertisements are legitimate, the majority are not. Usually, victims are conned out of $19.95, $29.95, or $49.95. For this fee, or "application charge," consumers are promised supplies with a list of places and companies that may hire mystery shoppers. However, this list is a simple collection of department store addresses and contact information. Other scams require that consumers buy merchandise from a particular Web site. The employer promises, after the evaluation, to refund all costs including expenses. But after the item is purchased, the employer will always find a reason not to issue a refund. Because teenagers and college students are constantly looking for supplemental income, they are especially vulnerable to this type of fraud. Figure 15.4 provides an example of three mystery shopping letters. These letters were received by a college student. The second and third letters were received by this same student after inquiring about the initial proposal.

Notice that when the victim did not respond to the second e-mail, the perpetrator quickly sent out another e-mail offering an even lower price. This is typical of any type of consumer fraud. Perpetrators will ask for a certain amount of money and if the victim is unwilling to commit that much money, the price will quickly be lowered. The letter is also appealing to the perpetrator's target group—teenagers and college students. By offering a flexible schedule, great compensation, and the

opportunity to eat at the best restaurants, the perpetrator is appealing to just about every teenager and college student in the country. The truth, however, is that mystery shopping is not nearly as glamorous as it sounds. Normally, mystery shopping is done by merchandise managers who are familiar with suppliers, prices, products, and other trades of the industry. Furthermore, real mystery shoppers have years of experience in the industry. Therefore, whenever a teenager or college student receives this type of offer, he or she can almost be sure that it is some type of a scam.

Telemarketing Fraud

"Really it's the truth," replied the confident voice on the other end of the telephone. "Normally, I don't make these kinds of calls. I've got a whole staff to do that. I have 15 years of experience in the business. I'm currently in charge of a large staff. I have over 600 clients and manage over $60 million for those clients. I don't even need this account—but I want it—this is a great opportunity for you."

The script above is typical of the kind of messages used throughout the United States by **telemarketing fraud** artists. Fraudsters set up giant rooms (referred to as boiler rooms) in rented offices where they train salespeople to find and defraud victims. These professional fraudsters move from city to city using different names. Calling people in other cities and states in an effort to hinder law enforcement, these con artists swindle victims out of money. Gathering compiled lists from magazine subscriptions, they identify investors believed to be good targets. New recruits are given scripts like the one above and receive specialized training to counter every possible objection. These recruits hook victims through promises of no-risk investments, secrets tips, and incredible rates of returns.

The North American Securities Administrators Association, an association of state investment regulators, estimates that unwary investors lose about $1 million every hour to investment fraud promoted over the telephone. Throughout the last two decades, the telephone has become a major tool used to defraud innocent victims. The opportunity to speak with a person directly makes telemarketing fraud more effective than Internet or mail-based approaches. Furthermore, the lack of face-to-face contact gives fraudsters added schemes and opportunities to commit fraud. Offenders can act as corporate or government employees without the victims' knowledge. Younger perpetrators can impersonate middle-age authority figures in order to add credibility with older victims. Fraudsters can call anywhere anytime, making it possible to focus on more likely victims.

In August 2004, when Hurricane Charley swept through Florida and destroyed countless homes, thousands of people applied for government grants to help cover the cost of damage. One year later, Hurricane Katrina hit New Orleans, Louisiana, and again thousands of victims sought government assistance. Fraudsters used these disasters to their advantage and committed fraud in two ways: First, fraudsters began calling hurricane victims and telling them that in order to process their government grants, they would need their bank account number and other personal information. As if the victims of the hurricane had not been through enough, they quickly saw their bank accounts drained. Second, fraudsters would call hurricane victims and tell them that in order to process their government grant they needed to pay up-front fees. Fraudsters had the victims send these fees to PO boxes, where the fraudsters quietly took the money and vanished.

Hurricanes Charley and Katrina are just two examples of how fraud perpetrators use disasters and other events to identify susceptible victims and perpetrate fraud.[22] Another method is to solicit contributions under the guise of providing relief to victims only to use the money for fraudulent purposes. For example, in January 2010, a devastating earthquake in Haiti destroyed property and killed hundreds of thousands of individuals and severely affected millions of individuals

FIGURE 15.4 MYSTERY SHOPPING LETTERS

Dear Student,

I would like to bring to your attention a special part-time job opportunity. If you wish to increase your budget by spending only a few hours a week working as a mystery shopper, please consider this offer.

The mystery shoppers are people, who pretend to be regular customers, so they can secretly evaluate various companies' products and customer services. On average, most of the mystery shoppers earn from $150 to $400 per week. In addition, they shop at different stores, eat at the best restaurants, and see the newest movies for free.

All their expenses are covered by the company that hires them. The best part is that as a secret shopper you can get free goods and have all your transportation costs covered.

The job we offer you has a very flexible working time. You can easily combine your daily responsibilities with your work as a mystery shopper; because you can choose only the assignments you like and work at a convenient time for you!

If you are interested, please reply to this e-mail and I will send you more information on how you can start.

Best regards,
Mike Monroe

After initially inquiring about the offer, the following letter was received.

Hello (student's name),

Thank you for your reply and interest in being a Mystery Shopper! You will be working for the companies who need your evaluation services. We are an agent that brings you a database of information in which you can find all the companies that are looking to hire Mystery Shoppers. Our staff is contacting, testing, and researching such companies to bring you only the best of them—the serious ones. We give you only approved ones with direct links to their application forms and exclusive help if you have any questions. Today, we are running an exclusive special—$29.95 for a lifetime membership.

(Continued)

FIGURE 15.4 (CONTINUED)

You can obtain more information by visiting our Web site at:
http://www.(address of fraudulent Web site).com

Please look through the FAQs and if you still have questions I will be more than happy to answer you.

Looking forward to working with you.

Best regards,
Mike Monroe

After not responding to the second letter, the following letter was received two weeks later.

I would like to inform you of the special promotion we are running today. It is a limited offer and you can sign up for a lifetime account for only $14.99 (regular membership costs $30). You have shown interest in our program but maybe the sign-up fee was too much for you—this is your chance to get access to our database for a half price!

The Web address for the promotion is:
http://www.(address of fraudulent Web site).com

Simply click on the link or Copy & Paste in your browser. Sign up today! Do not miss this limited time offer of only $14.99 for a Permanent Membership.

—-

Best wishes,
Mike Monroe

on the island. A few days after the earthquake, the FBI released a fraud alert stating, "past tragedies and natural disasters have prompted individuals with criminal intent to solicit contributions purportedly for a charitable organization and/or a good cause."[23] Apparently, fraud perpetrators will always look for ways to get other people's money—even when it involves massive suffering.

Scams That Prey on the Elderly

As with all consumer frauds, those who are most susceptible are usually the uneducated and the elderly. However, the elderly are more susceptible to telemarketing fraud than almost any other type of fraud. Fraudsters target the elderly for several reasons: First, many older individuals are extremely lonely and fraudsters use this loneliness to build a relationship of trust. Second, when elderly people are conned out of money, they rarely tell family and friends or even report the incident. The elderly are usually extremely embarrassed that they have been a victim of fraud. They are also afraid if they report the fraud, family members may deem them unable to take care of themselves and take away their financial responsibility and independence. Third, the elderly are extremely trusting and many do not believe that someone would actually take advantage of them. Once defrauded, these gullible victims often go into a state of denial. Fourth, because fraudsters are able to build such strong ties between themselves and the victim, fraudsters will con elderly victims out of money seven or even eight times before the victim refuses to pay more money. Remember, these fraudsters are masters of manipulation. They focus on manipulating human traits such as greed, fear, excitement, and gullibility.

Because the elderly are susceptible and reluctant to report fraud, it is important that family and friends of the elderly exercise special caution. If you personally know someone in your family who appears to have been defrauded by a telemarketer, it is important to avoid confronting that person directly. Many parent–child relationships have been strained and even irreparably damaged because children have approached the issue in a confrontational and/or threatening manner. Fraudsters will even manipulate a victim's emotions to believe that they are more concerned about the victim's welfare than the victim's own family is, convincing the victim that his or her family is greedy and wants his or her money. When approaching a possible victim of telemarketing fraud, it is important to avoid words such as "defrauded," "victimized," "duped," "swindled," or any other word that the victim can possibly interpret as confrontational or judgmental. Family members should approach the matter indirectly and patiently. Usually, if the victim of fraud is approached in a sensitive and respectful way, the person's dignity will not be offended. As with all fraud, the most effective way to combat telemarketing fraud is through prevention. Education is the best form of prevention. Therefore, it is a good idea to educate parents, grandparents, or anyone else you believe might be susceptible to telemarketing fraud. Remember, because fraudsters need the voluntary participation of the victim, possible victims can defend against the fraud perpetrator by just saying "no" or hanging up the telephone.

Safeguards against Telemarketing Fraud

There is never a legitimate reason to give Social Security, credit card, or other information over the telephone unless you initiate the call. If anyone ever asks for Social Security numbers or personal information, it should send a red flag that something isn't right. Fraudsters sometimes even act as government officials or other representatives to get this vital information.

It is always risky to provide credit or bank account information over the telephone when making purchases. Consumers should only provide this information when they are actually purchasing something and have initiated the transaction. Even if the company is completely legitimate, the salesperson or representative who enters a consumer's information may capture the victim's credit card number, expiration date, and verification number and use the information later to commit fraud.

A telemarketer who won't take no for an answer should send a red flag that something isn't right. Legitimate companies will send detailed information about a product or service. They will give consumers time to make an informed decision. They don't pressure individuals into buying something now. Language such as, "this special offer will no longer be available after today," or "there are only a few products left— hurry and buy now" are also signals of a fraudulent transaction.

Magazine sweepstakes and prize-winning scams are often perpetrated via the telephone. Fraudulent companies usually require individuals to buy something or pay a fee in order to claim a prize. However, it is illegal for a company to require consumers to buy something or pay a fee in order to claim a prize. Therefore, if a proposal or contest requires up-front cost, it is probably fraudulent. Buying something should not improve chances of winning a sweepstakes or other contest. If so, the contest is illegal.

In the last decade, it has become extremely common for fraudsters to deceive individuals who have been victims of fraud, telling them that for an up-front fee, they can recover their lost money. This is just another way for perpetrators to get more money from a gullible victim. If an individual receives a telephone call from someone who claims to be from the FBI, Department of Justice, or any other government agency and insists that the individual send money, it is almost certain the call is coming from a fraudster. It is illegal for any federal law enforcement agent to ask for "fees" or "taxes." The FBI and Department of Justice receive funding from Congress through the appropriations process. They do not receive money from any other source. If someone calls representing a government organization, consumers should write down their name and telephone number and then call their local FBI office to verify validity.

Remember, telemarketers will use any language they can to deceive possible victims. They are professionals and make money through manipulating victims' emotions. Consumers should never believe any promise of easy money. If someone promises money with little or no work, loans or credit cards with bad credit, or any type of money-making investments with no risk, it should signal that something is not right.

When entering into transactions over the telephone, it is critical that individuals know who they are dealing with. If someone claims to be from a certain company or organization, consumers should verify that claim by calling a legitimate phone number of the organization they are dealing with before giving out any personal information. If the company or organization is unfamiliar, individuals should check it out with the Better Business Bureau or a state consumer protection agency group. However, even if the organization being dealt with is not identified as a fraudulent organization, it still could be. To avoid detection, fraudsters start up new companies every few months. As a result, the fact that no one has made a complaint with the Better Business Bureau doesn't mean that the organization is legitimate.

Avoid Sales Calls

To minimize their risk to telemarketing fraud, consumers can avoid getting on marketing or calling lists by choosing to register with the national "do not call" registry. This is a free service provided by the federal government. Consumers can register either by phone or via the Internet. The national do not call registry's phone number is 1-866-290-4326 or 1-888-322-1222. Individuals can also register online at the Web site www.donotcall.gov. Once consumers have registered on the do not call registry, companies can still call if a consumer has inquired about a product, submitted an application, or made payments on or purchased an item within the last 18 months. Registration expires every five years; therefore, consumers must re-register with the registry periodically. The registry does not track number changes or disconnections. Therefore, if a consumer has received a new number or been disconnected, it is necessary to re-register. When signing up for a service, buying a product, or communicating with an organization, individuals will often sign a contract that gives an organization permission to contact them or give their information to marketing agencies. Therefore, it is important to read all contracts, order forms, and other correspondence before signing any document. Marketing agencies update their own records with the do not call registry every three months. As a result, some agencies don't stop calling individuals for a while after they register with the do not call registry. If telemarketers ignore the fact that an individual's number is on the do not call registry, they can be liable for up to $16,000 in fines. Some agencies, such as nonprofit groups, charities, political organizations, and survey groups, are still allowed to call consumers. However, if these organizations use professional organizations to raise funds, they must honor requests not to call.

Telemarketing Fraud Involves Large and Small Transactions

Telemarketing frauds can involve large or small transactions. Large transactions usually involve some type of investment scam, while smaller transactions usually involve sweepstakes, bogus fees, or magazine subscriptions. Large transaction frauds provide much more benefit for the perpetrator; however, they require considerably more effort and are more risky for the perpetrator. We have seen investment scams as large as $50,000–$100,000 per victim. Smaller transactions usually involve amounts anywhere from $10, $15, or $20 to a few hundred dollars. The smaller the transaction, the easier it is for fraudsters to deceive victims. Once a perpetrator has had success with a victim, the perpetrator will continue to call that victim using other fraud schemes. Telemarketing fraudsters are innovative and come up with new ways and means to defraud consumers every day.

Investment Scams

Investment fraud is any fraud that is related to stocks, bonds, commodities, limited partnerships, real estate, or other types of investments. In investment fraud, perpetrators usually make fraudulent promises or misstatements of fact to induce people to make investments. Investment frauds are often set up as Ponzi schemes. Investments frauds can occur within or outside business organizations. An example of investment fraud in a business was the loans made by General Motors Acceptance Corporation (GMAC) to a Long Island, New York, automobile dealer:

John McNamara, a wealthy car dealer, conned $436 million from GMAC. He first set up a company, Kay Industries, to produce invoices showing he was buying vans. The vans didn't exist. Then he sent inventories to GMAC to get a 30-day loan, worth about $25,000, for each van. Over seven years, he got $6.3 billion in loans, and he used most of the money to pay off old loans. He paid back a total of $5.8 billion over the seven years. He pocketed $436 million—about 7 percent of the total loans—and invested it in real estate, gold mines, oil businesses, and commodities brokerages.

While GMAC thought it was loaning money to a legitimate car dealer, it was really investing in a classic Ponzi scheme (a scheme in which early investments are repaid with subsequent investments; see previous discussion). The only difference between this investment scam and one that is perpetrated outside an organization was that this investment scheme had only one investor, GMAC.

An example of an investment scam that took place outside a business organization and involved numerous investors was the AFCO fraud covered in Chapter 13. While the company sounded legitimate, returns to be paid to homeowners were based on inflated financial statements and empty promises. The investment was nothing more than a twist on a traditional Ponzi scheme. Early investors were paid the returns from subsequent investments, and later investors were never paid. The assistant U.S. attorney in the district of Utah called the president of AFCO "one of the most ruthless swindlers seen in these parts." The president of AFCO sweet-talked about 650 people, many of them business professionals, into investing some $70 million in his schemes. He later declared bankruptcy, foreclosing investors' chances of getting their money back.

More recently, what is believed to be the largest and longest running Ponzi scheme in history came to light in December 2008 when two of Bernard Madoff's sons reported to authorities that their father had been running a massive Ponzi scheme for decades.

———

Bernie Madoff was the former chairman of the NASDAQ stock market. In March 2009, Madoff plead guilty to 11 federal crimes involving defrauding investors of billions of dollars. He was sentenced to 150 years in prison, the maximum allowed, and is currently serving time. When Madoff's scheme unfolded, approximately $18 billion was missing. As of late 2010, the value of the assets collected are expected to total a small fraction of that amount—perhaps 10 cents on the dollar. However, the trustee in charge of collecting the assets has several lawsuits pending where he is attempting to obtain funds from individuals who took out more money than they invested or who he contends should have known the scheme was a fraud. Recoveries from the net winners in a Ponzi scheme are known as **clawbacks** but are subject to a complex litigation process. Numerous lawsuits have been filed in the Madoff case.

The Madoff fraud began decades earlier when Madoff offered guaranteed returns of around 10 to 12 percent. His initial clients were wealthy individuals in the Jewish community that Madoff associated with. As such, Madoff's scheme is an example of affinity fraud mentioned in Chapter 1. Later, his clients became hedge fund managers who took investors' money and gave it to Madoff, presumably with little or no due diligence on the part of the hedge fund manager. Some of these hedge fund managers (including J. Ezra Merkin, former Chairman of GMAC) collected hundreds of millions of dollars by simply being a conduit between wealthy investors and Madoff. One investor who lost more than $1 billion of his client's money, Thierry de la Villehuchet, reportedly committed suicide when he realized Madoff was a fraudster. While Madoff's investors included many wealthy and famous individuals such as Zsa Zsa Gabor and Steven Spielberg, other investors include charities and university endowment funds such as the endowments of the business school at Yeshiva University and the New York Law School.

Unlike many Ponzi schemes, Madoff did not offer outrageous rates of return but, rather, claimed he had a stock investment strategy that allowed him to return a steady rate in both good and bad times. Harry Markopolos first questioned Madoff's investment strategy when he sent an extensive report to the SEC in the late 1990s that detailed why he believed it was mathematically impossible to achieve the returns that Madoff was claiming, among other things. His report to the SEC listed numerous red flags that the SEC failed to effectively respond to.

One of the first individuals other than Madoff who plead guilty to his role in the Madoff fraud was David G. Friehling. Friehling was Madoff's public accountant who issued clean audit opinions on the Madoff fund under the name of Friehling and Horowitz, a three-person accounting firm that employed two accountants and a secretary. Friehling admitted later that he had never conducted the audits that formed the basis of his audit opinions. Apparently, Friehling was much like the hedge fund managers who were happy to take their fees and look the other way. A purported audit of this massive fund by a two-man accounting firm may have been the largest red flag of all and probably should have been identified by a competent hedge fund manager.

———

The ultimate reason for discovering the Madoff fraud is probably due to the severe economic recession that occurred during 2008. Because of the recession, many individuals were trying to liquidate their investments. As such, Madoff was unable to meet the large amount of redemptions. During this recession, numerous Ponzi schemes came to light—many of which were much smaller but many still amounting to hundreds of millions of dollars. However, another massive scheme that was revealed at this time was an operation run by Robert Allen Stanford. Stanford is alleged to have lost billions of dollars in a Ponzi scheme that was the basis of the Stanford Financial Group of companies. These companies had numerous business outlets that sold certificates of deposit that paid double-digit returns. The group's headquarters were on a small island in the West Indies known as Antigua. Stanford was knighted by the country of Antigua in 2006 and, as such, was known by Antiguans by the name of Sir Allen Stanford! In October 2009, the National Honors Committee of Antigua and Barbuda voted unanimously to strip Stanford of his knighthood!

Investment frauds such as Ponzi schemes can have devastating effects on the individuals and the economies involved in the schemes. There are numerous red flags or fraud symptoms that signal potential investment fraud. Anyone considering investing money or other assets in any organization, real or fictitious, should watch for the following symptoms, which have been associated with numerous investment scams:

- *Unreasonably high or guaranteed rates of return*
- *Investments that do not make sound business sense or that lack details of how the business operates*
- *Pressure to get in early on the investment*
- *Use of a special tax loophole or a tax avoidance scheme*
- *A business that is new in town and does not offer an adequate history of where its principals came from and what their operations were in previous locations*
- *A business with a history of bankruptcy or scandals*
- *Appraisal figures and/or financial claims that have not been soundly verified*
- *Project dependency on kickbacks, complicated marketing schemes, special concessions to people who have money, or unwritten deals that can't be talked about because of domestic or foreign laws*
- *Unaudited financial reports or adverse opinions given on financial reports*
- *Investments that assume continued inflation or appreciation in predicting attractive rates of return that are unrealistic over time*
- *Investment success that is dependent on someone's "unique expertise" (such as an uncanny ability to predict commodity prices or unusually good salesmanship) for financial success*
- *Representation of the emotional desirability of holding an investment as its principal attraction*
- *Insufficient verification or guarantee of an investment*
- *Dependency on high financial leverage for success*
- *Investor liability for debts that are not paid*
- *Luxurious lifestyles of principals, even though the business is relatively new*
- *An investment that is not suitable for your risk tolerance*
- *Pressure to put all your savings into a particular investment*
- *Inability to pull out or liquidate the investment*
- *Inducements that make investors feel sorry for the principals and/or put in additional money to help them overcome temporary problems*

Remember this ...

In addition to identity theft, there are many other types of consumer fraud, including telemarketing schemes, work-at-home schemes, foreign investment schemes, and others. They all have one characteristic in common that is different from other types of fraud—they all take advantage of individuals. Consumers lose billions of dollars every year to these types of consumer fraud. The uneducated, elderly, gullible, and trusting are the most susceptible to consumer fraud. Consumer fraud artists are excellent manipulators of emotion. They feed on the ability to successfully manipulate victims' emotions. The best way to prevent consumer fraud from happening is through education and taking proactive measures to protect one's self.

Review of the Learning Objectives

- **Define what consumer fraud is and understand its seriousness.** Consumer fraud is any type of fraud that targets consumers as its victims. The two primary types of consumer frauds are identity theft and other types of consumer scams. With identity theft, fraudsters steal a person's identity and then, pretending to be that person, enter into financial transactions. With other types of consumer scams, fraudsters use various schemes to earn a consumer's confidence and then use that confidence to get the consumer to pay or invest money or provide personal information. Advances in technology have made consumer frauds much easier to commit.
- **Understand identity theft.** Identity theft is a growing consumer problem where fraudsters steal a person's identity and then, using that person's credit cards or personal information, incur debts, make purchases, and enter into other financial transactions on behalf of the victim. Identity thieves steal personal information through various means, including skimming; dumpster diving; phishing; observing PIN numbers, garage codes, or passwords; or breaking into a person's car or home. Once the perpetrator has stolen personal information, he or she usually goes through a cycle of fraudulent

behaviors from simple transactions to more complex and expensive transactions. Victims of identity theft spend many hours trying to clear their names and restore their creditworthiness.

- **Classify the various types of investment and consumer fraud.** In addition to identity theft, there are many other types of consumer fraud, not all of which were covered in this chapter. Schemes such as foreign investment scams, work-at-home scams, multilevel marketing scams, investment scams, and others have the goal of earning a person's confidence and then using that confidence to defraud the consumer. Any offer that sounds too good to be true is probably a type of consumer fraud.

KEY TERMS

consumer fraud, p. 530
identity theft, p. 531
phishing, p. 533
shoulder surfing, p. 535
dumpster diving, p. 535
skimming, p. 535
phishers, p. 536
Gramm-Leach-Bliley
    act, p. 539
intent, p. 539
evidential matter, p. 539
foreign advance-fee
    scams, p. 543
Nigerian money offers,
    p. 543
clearinghouse scam,
    p. 545
purchase of real estate
    scam, p. 545
sale of crude oil at below
    market price, p. 545
disbursement of money
    from wills, p. 545

multilevel marketing
    (MLM) company,
    p. 545
pyramid scheme, p. 546
Ponzi scheme, p. 546
headhunter fees, p. 547
front loading, p. 547
opportunity meetings,
    p. 547
snake oil plans, p. 547
ground floor
    opportunity, p. 547
chain letter scams,
    p. 548
mail stuffing, p. 548
product testing, p. 548
craft assembly, p. 548
bogus mystery shopping
    scam, p. 549
telemarketing fraud,
    p. 549
investment fraud, p. 553
clawbacks, p. 554

QUESTIONS

Discussion Questions

1. Why is it important to study consumer fraud?
2. What is identity theft?
3. What are some methods perpetrators use to steal a person's identity?
4. What are some proactive steps that consumers can take to minimize their risk to identity theft?
5. What are some examples of foreign advance-fee scams?
6. What is a Nigerian money offer?
7. What is the difference between a fraudulent multilevel marketing organization and a legitimate multilevel marketing organization?
8. How does consumer fraud affect the economies of entire countries?
9. Why are the elderly and/or uneducated so susceptible to fraud?
10. What are investment scams?
11. How does the expression "If it sounds too good to be true, it probably is" relate to consumer fraud?
12. While consumer fraud often affects individual people directly, in what ways does consumer fraud affect everyone?
13. After working out at the gym, you notice that your car has been broken into and your wallet has been stolen. What should you do?

True/False

1. Identity theft is the largest type of consumer fraud.
2. Identity theft can result in an individual's loss of credit.
3. The best way to prevent a fraudster from establishing a preapproved credit card in your name is to destroy all credit card applications as soon as you receive them.
4. Keeping your wallet in your front pocket will help prevent it from being lost or stolen.
5. The Gramm-Leach-Bliley Act states that it is illegal for organizations to share your personal information with any other party or individual.
6. A fraud scam in which the perpetrator, falsely claiming to represent a foreign bank, tries to get victims to invest in nonexistent foreign venture capital companies for high returns is called a clearinghouse scam.
7. Illegal multilevel marketing companies almost always focus their efforts on the recruiting of new members rather than on the selling of legitimate products.
8. Elderly people are more susceptible to chain letter scams than any other type of fraud.
9. The larger the amount requested by a fraudulent telemarketer, the easier it is for him or her to deceive victims.

10. By federal law, no organization or company can sell individuals' personal information without their express written consent.
11. Once an identity theft victim has reported a fraud to the FTC, the FTC will help a victim contact the FBI, Secret Service, and local police to coordinate an investigation.
12. The National Processing Company was given authority by the FTC to pre-register consumers for the do not call registry.
13. Pyramid organizations eventually fail, causing all but a few investors to lose their investments.
14. Congress outlawed pyramid organizations in the United States in 1934.
15. Consumer fraud only affects those who often use credit cards online.
16. Only stupid people who are not careful are victims of consumer fraud.
17. Because it is impossible to "market" at an assortment of levels, every multilevel marketing scheme is fraudulent.
18. A discarded tax return has enough information to steal someone's identity.
19. Since a Social Security card does not contain your photo, it is impossible to have your identity stolen by merely losing your Social Security card.

Multiple Choice

1. Phishing is the method of:
   a. Using e-mail or other Internet applications to deceive people into disclosing valuable personal information.
   b. Convincing a person to divulge personal information over the telephone.
   c. Hacking into another's computer files to access personal information.
   d. Hiring a con artist to steal personal information from a person.
2. Multilevel marketing companies:
   a. Are illegal.
   b. Increase their distribution process by recruiting additional company sales representatives.
   c. Can legally pay commission to representatives for simply signing up new recruits.
   d. Require little time and effort to be successful.
3. In order to protect yourself from identity theft, you should:
   a. Only give out your when purchasing a product online or over the telephone.

   b. Always shred receipts, credit card offers, doctor's bills, insurance information, or any other documents that contain sensitive personal information.
   c. Leave your wallet at home or in the car.
   d. Maintain the same password for every personal account.
   e. Do all of the above.
4. The Gramm-Leach-Bliley Act gives you the right to:
   a. Periodically change your Social Security number to avoid identity theft.
   b. Receive a yearly stipend to cover the losses incurred as a victim of identity fraud.
   c. Claim your high credit report although an identity fraudster has damaged it severely.
   d. Sue the perpetrator for more money than he or she defrauded from you.
   e. Opt out of having your personal information sold to organizations.
5. If you become a victim of identity theft, you should first:
   a. Wait to see where the perpetrator is spending your money; then, using this information, plan an investigation with the local FBI organization.
   b. Contact friends and neighbors to inquire if they have any useful information about the perpetrator.
   c. Contact the Federal Trade Commission for assistance and advice.
   d. Do none of the above.
6. Which of the following is a common characteristic of fraudulent money offer letters?
   a. The letter will ask for help, convincing the victim that assistance is desperately needed.
   b. Through the letter, the perpetrator will try to build a relationship of trust with the victim.
   c. The letter promises the victim a large amount of money for little or no effort on the victim's part.
   d. The letter will make the victim feel that he or she is the only person receiving the "once in a lifetime" offer.
   e. All the above.
7. The major reason that elderly people are so susceptible to telemarketing fraud is that they:
   a. Are often financially in need.
   b. Have an excess amount of cash to invest.
   c. Are often lonely and enjoy talking to friendly callers.
   d. Are none of the above.

8. Consumers should provide credit card numbers or bank account information over the telephone only when:
   a. They initiated the call and are purchasing a legitimate product.
   b. They are asked to give the information.
   c. The entity receiving this information is a legitimate company.
   d. They feel confident that the receiving entity will protect such information.
   e. Doing so qualifies them to receive certain financial benefits.

9. What is the best defense against consumer fraud?
   a. Signing up with the national do not call registry.
   b. Purchasing credit card insurance.
   c. Educating yourself about credit card risks.
   d. Calling the Federal Trade Commission (FTC).

10. What does "https" stand for?
    a. Hypertext transfer protocol (secure).
    b. Hypertext transfer point (site).
    c. Hypertext transfer protocol (system).
    d. Hypertext transfer protocol (sign).

11. Which federal statute requires that credit reports can only be obtained for legitimate business needs?
    a. Title 15 U.S. Code § 1692.
    b. Final Rule—45 CFT Parts 160 and 165.
    c. Title 15 U.S. Code, Chapter 41.
    d. Title 15 U.S. Code § 1681.

12. Which of the following is *not* listed in the chapter as a common characteristic of Nigerian scam letters?
    a. The promise of money to lure victims.
    b. Urgency to invest quickly.
    c. Picture of perpetrator to assure victims.
    d. Strong ties to high-ranking foreign officials to lure victims.

13. Which of the following institutions would *not* be very helpful to call in the event of identity theft?
    a. IRS.
    b. Social Security Administration.
    c. Local chamber of commerce.
    d. A credit reporting agency.

14. What is one way to determine if a Web site is secure or not?
    a. Look for the official logo of the company you want to deal with.
    b. Look for an "s" after the "http" in the URL of the Web site.
    c. Click on a link to see if it works.
    d. Call the FTC and ask about the ISP address of the Web site.

15. Those most susceptible to consumer fraud are often:
    a. Uneducated or elderly.
    b. Wealthy and prominent.
    c. Troubled with credit card debt.
    d. Lonely and depressed.

SHORT CASES

Case 1

In 2003, the FTC conducted a survey on the frequency and types of identity thefts perpetrated in the United States. The survey's results are available online at www.ftc.gov/os/2003/09/synovatereport.pdf.

From each of the six main sections in the report, choose and report on two statistics of interest (12 total). Your report should list the statistic; the page number in the report where it was mentioned; and one or two paragraphs detailing why you find that statistic interesting, important, or applicable to what you have learned in this chapter.

Case 2

The following paragraph from the FTC's pamphlet "When Bad Things Happen to Your Good Name" describes the headaches for identity theft victims trying to restore their credit.

> *Unlike victims of other crimes, who generally are treated with respect and sympathy, identity theft victims often find themselves having to prove that they're victims, too—not deadbeats trying to get out of paying bad debts. So how do you go about proving something you didn't do? Getting the right documents and getting them to the right people is key.*

Throughout this course, you have learned the importance of fraud examiners keeping accurate, detailed records. In this respect, identity theft victims become detectives who need evidence to prove somebody beside themselves is responsible for the accounts, debts, and misdeeds committed in their name. Unfortunately, victims often don't have documents to prove their innocence.

To help victims begin the process of proving innocence, the FTC and others developed an ID theft affidavit. An affidavit is a document with some legal status when signed in the presence of a witness or notary. Look up the affidavit at www.ftc.gov/bcp/conline/pubs/credit/affidavit.pdf. Fill out the affidavit using the example of Jacob at the beginning of this chapter.

Be as detailed as possible [be creative when asked for pertinent information that wasn't provided as part of the example (dates, etc.)]. Turn in the completed affidavit, along with your answers to these questions:

1. T/F All companies are required to accept the affidavit as a valid legal document?
2. T/F This affidavit is designed for both existing accounts fraudulently used and new accounts fraudulently opened.
3. To what organizations might a victim send a completed affidavit?
4. To what organizations should victims *not* send an affidavit?

Case 3

Following the directions discussed in this chapter, write to the direct marketing association and the three credit bureaus and request to opt out of preapproved credit card mailings. Turn in a copy of the letter to your professor.

Case 4

On September 24, 2007, Miguel Carcamo was going through his mail. For some reason, Miguel had not yet received his bank statement, which he usually received at the beginning of each month. Although he was concerned, he took no action and decided not to worry about it. After all, was it his fault that the bank was a little behind? Two weeks later, Miguel got a mysterious call from a creditor claiming that he needed to pay an overdue balance on his Visa card. Miguel, frustrated to receive such a call in the middle of dinner with his family, told the person that he must be mistaken and that he had paid his bill already this month. Before the caller was able to ask any more questions, Miguel hung up the phone. On October 15, 2007, Miguel tried to use his credit card. Unfortunately, the card didn't work because of insufficient funds. Upset and embarrassed, Miguel called his bank to inquire about the card. The bank had already closed for the day; however, Miguel left a message explaining what had happened. On October 16, 2007, Miguel's bank called regarding the message he had left the night before. The caller stated that Miguel had not only maxed out the credit limit on his Visa card but had also maxed out on the increased credit limit for which he had recently applied. Miguel stated that he had not applied for an increased credit limit.

It took several days, but after an investigation, Miguel discovered that he had been a victim of identity theft. Fortunately, besides his bank account being drained for a few thousand dollars, two fraudulent credit cards had been issued in his name. Both his bank statement and the new credit card statements were sent to a PO box at the post office.

1. What were some of the obvious red flags of identity theft that Miguel should have noticed?
2. When Miguel noticed the red flags, how could he have minimized his losses?
3. Now that Miguel has been a victim of identity theft, what are some of the steps he should take to repair the damage to his reputation, credit, and finances?

Case 5

Jenny Lanstrom regularly visits her grandfather, Mike Lanstrom, every Thursday night. Jenny's grandfather has been a widower for the past six years. Jenny's grandfather is very intelligent. He is a decorated veteran of World War II, and over the years, he has been active in community service. Because Mike Lanstrom practiced as a family doctor for 46 years, he is a respected member of the community. For the last several months, Jenny has noticed something different about her grandfather. Lately, he has been agitated and upset.

One Thursday night, Mike told Jenny about products he had been buying over the phone. As Jenny investigated further, she realized that her grandfather had bought several products from a vendor by the name of Products for Life. Although the transactions were not large, the total amount had already added up to several hundred dollars. The next day, Jenny decided to research the company on the Internet. Surprisingly, she was unable to find any information about the company. She became extremely worried that someone was taking advantage of her grandfather.

1. What should Jenny do? Should she confront her grandfather about the possibility of fraud? If so, how should she approach him?
2. Jenny realizes that certain words and phrases should be avoided when talking to the elderly about fraud. What are these words and phrases?
3. Why are the elderly so susceptible to fraud?
4. In what ways do fraudsters manipulate elderly victims' emotions?

Case 6

Go to the Florida attorney general's consumer fraud Web site at myfloridalegal.com/pages.nsf/4492 d4797dc0bd92f85256cb80055fb97/81bf89afaf04dbeb85 256cc6006ff6bf!OpenDocument. Pick a transaction that you will likely be involved in from the list on the home page. Read about that transaction, including tips for consumers.

Write a one-page paper describing the potential fraud schemes that occur with your transaction. Include the red flags that show up, and detail the preventative measures one should take.

Case 7

You are trying to sell your car. You have been trying to sell it for a while and have it posted on an online classified ad. You receive the following e-mail:

Hello. My name is David Meganimus, and I am an assistant to the Greek ambassador to the United States. I will soon be moving to the United States as part of my job and have been seeking to purchase an automobile to use as I work in the United States. I saw your car on XXXXXX Web site and believe it is exactly what I am looking for. I would like to purchase your car and agree that your price of $8,500 is fair. However, I need the car shipped to New York and cannot send money directly to the shipper because of currency exchange problems. I would like to send you a certified cashier's check for $12,500, which you can cash at any bank. Then you can wire the $4,000 shipping charge to the shipping company's bank account using Western Union. The shipping company will then come and retrieve the car and ship it to me. Please let me know if this is agreeable so I can send the $12,500 as soon as possible. Thank you for your help.

1. How do you respond to David?
2. What might be going on? Do some research and determine what could happen if you agree, accept the $12,500 check, and wire the $4,000.

Case 8

You have been searching for a job for some time. One day, while searching through some online want ads, you see the following advertisement:

Wanted: Persons seeking high paying corporate jobs in the Cayman Islands. Live the life of your dreams as you work for Globular Corp. Serious inquiries only. Send your resume to Amy Rickson at XXXXXX.

Out of curiosity, you e-mail Amy your resume and get the following e-mail the next day:

Congratulations!! We have reviewed your resume and determined you are exactly the kind of employee we are looking for to fill the position at Globular Corp. in the Cayman Islands. We would like to interview you in the Cayman Islands. We would like to fly you here, put you up in a five-star hotel, and see if you are a good fit for our company. However, in the past, we have purchased tickets and had people not come for the interview. To prevent this, we have the policy of requiring interviewees to wire us $500 to cover the cost of the tickets. You will then be refunded this money in full when you show up for the interview. Please respond to this e-mail with a range of days in which you will be available to interview and wire the $500 to XXXXXX account as soon as possible so we can purchase the tickets. Thank you, and we looking forward to meeting with you.

1. How would you respond to this e-mail? What do you think might happen if you send the money?

Case 9

You are a certified fraud examiner, and a local community group, the Silver Years Senior Squad, has requested that you give a presentation about consumer fraud. They want to hear about examples of recent scams that have happened to people and how they can avoid being scammed. Use the Internet to research current scams, and determine the main points you would cover in your presentation. A good place to start would be snopes.com/fraud/fraud.asp.

CASES STUDIES

Case Study 1

The letter on the following page is example of a foreign advance-fee money scam. Read the letter and respond to the questions below.

Questions

1. Do you think Gardiah Mfana is an actual person?
2. Do you believe that his proposition is real? Why or why not?
3. List and explain at least three elements of fraud that are present in this letter.
4. What are some of the characteristics found in this fraud that are similar to the characteristics found in all types of Nigerian money offers?

(Continued on page 562)

——— **Original Message** ———

Subject: Fruitful Transaction
Date: Tue, 31 Jul 2007 17:12:55 -0700 (PDT)
From: Gardiah Mfana <u><inquiriesgm4@yahoo.com></u>
Reply-To: <u>inquiriesgm5@yahoo.com</u>
To: <u>steve_albrecht@byu.edu</u>

Gardiah Mfana
#45 Pine Way, 1 Close,
Sandton-Johannesburg,
South Africa.

Dear Sir,

In order to transfer from a Bank some amount of money, I have the courage to look for a reliable and honest person who will be capable for this important business believing that you will never let me down either now or in the future.

I am Gardiah Mfana, a consulting auditor of prime banks here in South Africa. On June 6, 2000 an American Mining Consultant/Contractor with the South African Mining Corporation, Mr. Gregory A. Williams made a numbered time (fixed) deposit for twelve calendar months, value US $50,200,000.00 an account. On maturity, the bank sent a routine notification to his forwarding address but got no reply.

After a month, the bank sent another reminder and finally his contract employers, the South African Mining Corporation, wrote to inform the bank that Mr. Gregory A. Williams died from an automobile accident, that he died without making a will, and all attempts by the American Embassy to trace his next of kin was fruitless.

I therefore, made further investigation and discovered that Mr. Gregory A. Williams in fact was an immigrant from Jamaica and only recently obtained American citizenship. He did not declare any kin or relations in all his official documents, including his Bank deposit paper work. This money, total U S $ 50,200,000.00, is still sitting in my bank as a dormant account. No one will ever come forward to claim it, and according to South African banking policy, after 5 years, the money will revert to the ownership of the South African Government if the account owner is certified dead. This is the situation, and my proposal is that I am looking for a foreigner who will stand in as the next of kin to Mr. Gregory A. Williams, and a Bank Account abroad will then facilitate the transfer of this money to the beneficiary/next of kin. This is simple, all you have to do is to immediately send me a bank account anywhere in the world for me to arrange the proper money transfer paperwork. This money (total USD $50.2M) will then be paid into this Account for us to share in the ratio of 70% for me, 25% for you and 5% for expenses that might come up during transfer process. There is no risk at all, and all the paper work for this transaction will be done by me using my position and connection in the banks in South Africa.

This business transaction is guaranteed. If you are interested, please reply immediately, sending the following details:

1. Your full name/Address
2. Your private telephone/Fax number
3. Your full bank account details, where these funds will be transferred into, a new/an empty account can serve

Please observe the utmost confidentiality, and rest assured that this transaction would be most profitable for both of us because I shall require your assistance to invest my share in your country. You have to note that you must send me a private fax number where I will be sending you documents in case I cannot e-mail it to you.

I look forward to your earliest reply.

Yours,

Gardiah Mfana.

5. Why do you think so many people become victims of this type of fraud?
6. What can you do to protect yourself from becoming a victim of consumer fraud?

Case Study 2

Is This a Ponzi Scheme?[24]   Recently, a student came into a faculty member's office and handed the faculty member a card he had found in the business school building advertising a company called 12 Daily Pro. He said someone had been distributing these cards around the building, encouraging students to invest in a "business opportunity." It suggested that you could invest $6 to $6,000 and earn a 44 percent return in 12 days. The card called this program a "new economic paradigm." The faculty member decided this had to be a Ponzi-type scheme and sent an e-mail to all students in the school reminding them that such schemes are illegal, unethical, and immoral. The next day a local TV channel carried the story, and the following day the electronic payment service for the scheme froze all the company's accounts and essentially shut them down. A few weeks later, the SEC filed a securities fraud charge against the head of the company and against the company itself, calling it a Ponzi scheme.

Questions

1. What do you think made the faculty member believe this was a Ponzi-type scheme?
2. What is the annual return the scheme operators were promising on investments in this scheme?
3. Why do you think this scheme, which had been operating for over a month, attracted so many investors?
4. Was the action taken by the faculty member appropriate?

INTERNET ASSIGNMENTS

1. Using an Internet browser such as Google, type in *telemarketing schemes* or similar words. Find an example of a telemarketing scheme and answer the following questions about that scheme:
   a. How was the scam perpetrated?
   b. What were some of the common characteristics of each of the scams?
   c. What was the dollar amount lost to the victim?
   d. What other interesting facts did you notice?

DEBATES

In this chapter, we have discussed the Gramm-Leach-Bliley Act, which gives credit unions, savings and loans, banks, insurance agencies, mortgage companies, and other financial institutions the right to sell customer information to marketing companies, affiliates, and others. Some individuals believe that doing this is ethical since customers have the right to opt out of having their information sold and because by law these organizations have the right to make additional income through selling customers' information. On the other hand, some individuals believe that these organizations do not educate customers and unfairly keep them ignorant to the use of their information.

Split the class into small groups. Have the groups discuss the following:

a. Is the Gramm-Leach-Bliley Act ethical? Why or why not?
b. Do organizations have a responsibility to educate customers about the Gramm-Leach-Bliley Act? Why or why not?
c. Just because something is legal, is it ethical? Why or why not?

END NOTES

1. This is a true story; however, the names have been changed to protect the individual.
2. www.ftc.gov/opa/2007/10/fraud.shtm, accessed August 11, 2010.
3. www.ftc.gov/sentinel/reports/sentinel-annual-reports/sentinel-cy2009.pdf, accessed August 11, 2010.
4. www.privacyrights.org/cases/victim25.htm, accessed August 12, 2010.
5. www.privacyrights.org/cases/victim30.htm, accessed August 12, 2010.
6. www.privacyrights.org/cases/victim24.htm, accessed August 12, 2010.
7. http://consumer.gov/ncpw/?s=ID+theft, accessed September 25, 2007.
8. http://idtheft.about.com/od/methodsoftheft/p/Skimming.htm, accessed September 26, 2007.

9. www.msnbc.msn.com/id/13123967, accessed August 12, 2010.

10. www.justice.gov/criminal/fraud/websites/idtheft.html, accessed August 12, 2010.

11. www.ftc.gov/bcp/edu/pubs/consumer/alerts/alt127.shtm, accessed August 12, 2010.

12. www.ftc.gov/bcp/conline/edcams/gettingcredit/optingout.html, accessed August 12, 2010.

13. www.ftc.gov/bcp/edu/microsites/idtheft/reference-desk/federal-privacy.html, accessed August 12, 2010.

14. www.privacyrights.org/fs/fs17a.htm, accessed August 12, 2010.

15. www.privacyrights.org/cases/victim6.htm, accessed August 12, 2010.

16. Foreign advance-fee scams: JosephWells, "There Are Many Variations of These Con Games," *Journal of Accountancy* (April 2004).

17. www.aarp.org/money/consumerprotection/scams/Articles/a2002-10-02-FraudsWorkatHome.html, accessed August 12, 2010.

18. www.quatloos.com/multi_level_marketing.htm, accessed August 12, 2010.

19. www.stopspam.org/faqs/mlm_vs_pyr.html, accessed August 16, 2004.

20. www.fraud.org/tips/telemarketing/pyramid.htm, accessed August 12, 2010.

21. Thomas L.Friedman, *The Lexus and the Olive Tree* (New York: Anchor Books, 2000): 156–157.

22. www.pueblo.gsa.gov/scams/sc5181.htm, accessed October 4, 2007.

23. www.fbi.gov/pressrel/pressrel10/earthquake011310.htm, accessed August 11, 2010.

24. This case comes from an article written by Ned C. Hill in the *Marriott Alumni Magazine* (Brigham Young University, Fall 2007): 8–13.

CHAPTER **16**

Bankruptcy, Divorce, and Tax Fraud

LEARNING OBJECTIVES

After studying this chapter, you should be able to:

- Explain why fraud is so prevalent in bankruptcy, tax, and divorce cases.
- Describe the nature of bankruptcy and be familiar with bankruptcy codes.
- Understand civil and criminal bankruptcy fraud statutes.
- Identify the participants involved in the bankruptcy process.
- Recognize different bankruptcy and divorce fraud schemes.
- Understand how perpetrators fraudulently conceal and transfer assets and income in bankruptcies and divorces.
- Define tax fraud and be familiar with common tax fraud schemes.
- Understand how money laundering is used to commit fraud.

TO THE STUDENT

This chapter is the third of four chapters that covers types of fraud other than financial statement fraud. This chapter discusses the various types of fraud not yet addressed in the text. We will primarily focus on two types of bankruptcy fraud (bankruptcy used to perpetrate fraud and bankruptcy used to conceal fraud), divorce fraud, tax fraud, and money laundering. However, various types of bankruptcy are also briefly discussed. You will also find an overview of the Bankruptcy Code, civil and criminal bankruptcy fraud statutes, and activities of key participants in the bankruptcy and divorce process. Two common bankruptcy and divorce fraud schemes will be addressed— bust-outs and the fraudulent concealment of assets or income. At the end of the chapter, we discuss what money laundering is, how it is used to commit fraud, and how it relates to other frauds.

Robert Brennan, a former penny-stock tycoon, was convicted in April 2001 of bankruptcy fraud. Jurors found Brennan guilty of hiding $4.5 million in assets from the federal government before he filed for bankruptcy in 1995. The legal proceedings spanned six weeks, including 19 days of testimony and arguments that exposed federal jurors to high-stakes action at the Mirage hotel-casino in Las Vegas and the complexities of international finance.

Brennan was well-known in Las Vegas because of his ties to the now-imploded El Rancho hotel-casino on the Strip. The case alleged that Brennan continued to live a lavish lifestyle, despite being millions of dollars in debt. Testimony came from or references were made to a soap-opera star whom Brennan dated, a Catholic cardinal whom Brennan knew, international arms traders, and former football coach Bill Parcells, who posted assets for Brennan's bond.

Brennan, 57, was convicted on 7 of 13 counts. The jury was convinced that he had hidden money offshore and cashed in casino chips without reporting them just three weeks after he filed for bankruptcy protection. Brennan was acquitted on charges that cash was delivered to him in a handoff in a London hotel. He was found guilty of spending $100,000 on private flights around the world but innocent of illegally spending $60,000 on a yacht cruise.

Brennan filed for bankruptcy protection just before he was due to pay millions to compensate investors whom U.S. District Judge Richard Owen in Manhattan determined had been cheated. That judgment, won by the Securities and Exchange Commission (SEC), was more than $78 million. That ruling led to a series of legal setbacks for Brennan, who is now barred from the securities industry after regulators found that he continued to use high-pressure "boiler room" tactics to sell stocks.[1]

Overview of Tax, Divorce, and Bankruptcy Frauds

The occurrence of bankruptcy—the legal process that allows a debtor to work out an orderly plan to either settle debts or liquidate assets and distribute them to creditors—is on the increase. Bankruptcy fraud, like the one just described, is a growing problem in the United States. Entering false financial information on bankruptcy petitions and schedules occurs in an estimated 70 percent of bankruptcy cases. The same is true of divorce and tax fraud cases. Although actual statistics aren't available, most divorces involving significant amounts of assets include allegations of fraud. The reason that fraud is so common in bankruptcies, divorces, and tax payments is because, in all three situations, assets are being taken away from someone or some organization and given to someone else. In bankruptcy cases, the assets taken are given to creditors. In divorces, assets taken are given to spouses and attorneys representing spouses. In tax cases, assets taken away are claimed by the government. To keep assets from being taken, individuals often attempt to fraudulently hide or transfer assets so that they are unknown or cannot be discovered. Transfers of assets to offshore bank accounts, relatives, friends, and other hiding places are all too common in bankruptcy, divorce, and tax fraud.

Both bankruptcy and divorce fraud can be criminal or civil matters. Criminal divorce and bankruptcy frauds are often investigated by the FBI or other law enforcement agencies. Civil bankruptcy and divorce frauds may be investigated by trustees, examiners, creditors, and creditors' committees appointed by the bankruptcy or divorce courts. Tax fraud cases are usually criminal matters.

Fraud Examiners' Roles in Bankruptcy and Divorce Cases

CPAs and other fraud examiners can play an important role in both investigating and testifying in bankruptcy and divorce fraud cases and in testifying in tax fraud cases. The arm of the IRS that investigates tax fraud is known as Criminal Investigation (CI).

Roles that fraud examiners can assume in divorce and bankruptcy cases include the following:

- *Serve as an examiner or a trustee in bankruptcy cases.*
- *Serve on creditors' committees or represent creditors' committees by investigating the debtor's financial affairs and preparing investigation reports in bankruptcy cases.*
- *Assist the U.S. Department of Justice, the Office of the United States Trustee, panel trustees, and others by preparing detailed reports of investigation findings in bankruptcy cases.*
- *Assist in recovering assets for creditors in both divorce and bankruptcy cases.*
- *Serve as private investigators to find hidden assets or examine lifestyles of divorce or bankruptcy participants.*

Several different types of bankruptcy and divorce frauds are noteworthy:

- ***Bankruptcy or divorce resulting from fraud.*** *When fraudulent activity results in too few assets remaining to pay creditor and investor claims, an entity will generally file bankruptcy. Similarly, when one marriage partner discovers that his or her spouse has committed fraud, he or she often seeks divorce to salvage a reputation or because of a lack of trust in the partner. The fraudulent activity can involve hiding assets from others, stealing money or other assets, or misrepresenting business dealings as in financial statement fraud.*
- ***Bankruptcy and divorce used to perpetrate fraud.*** *During bankruptcy and divorce, an automatic stay is often granted during which creditors or marital partners are prohibited from taking any action against the debtor or marriage partner. Some debtors and marital partners use this period to perpetrate fraud. For example, a divorcing spouse may fraudulently transfer assets to other (often related) individuals, or a debtor may fraudulently transfer assets to other organizations.*
- ***Bankruptcy and divorce used to conceal fraud.*** *This type of fraud generally results in the books and records of the debtor or marital partner being destroyed, inaccurate, or hard to locate.*

When a fraud examiner is engaged to investigate a bankruptcy or divorce resulting from fraud, the focus is on the fraudulent activity occurring before the bankruptcy filing or divorce. Such fraud may be any of the types of fraud already discussed in this book.

This chapter covers divorce fraud, tax fraud, and money laundering. We discuss tax fraud first followed by a discussion of divorce fraud. When we turn to bankruptcy fraud, we will focus on two types of bankruptcy fraud—bankruptcy used to perpetrate fraud and bankruptcy used to conceal fraud. Our coverage of bankruptcy fraud includes an overview of the Bankruptcy Code and the various types of bankruptcy. We also discuss civil and criminal bankruptcy and fraud statutes and provide an overview of the activities of the key participants in the bankruptcy and divorce process. Near the end of the chapter, we discuss bust-outs (a common type of bankruptcy fraud) as well as the concealment of assets or income and fraudulent transfers of assets, both of which are common in divorce and bankruptcy. Finally, we discuss money laundering, including how this fraud can be related to other frauds.

Tax Fraud

Tax fraud can be committed against any governmental or other organization that collects taxes, including the federal government, state governments, local governments, or other taxing authorities. The types of tax frauds committed against all of these organizations are similar. In this book, we will confine our discussions to tax fraud committed against the U.S. government and its tax-collecting agency, the Internal Revenue Service (IRS). The IRS, a branch of the Department of Treasury, deals directly with more Americans than any other institution, public or private. In 2009, the IRS collected more than $1.9 trillion in revenue and processed more than 236 million returns. It cost taxpayers 50 cents for each $100 collected by the IRS in 2009.

The tax system in the United States depends on voluntary compliance, which means that each citizen is responsible for filing a tax return when required and for determining and paying the correct amount of tax. Fortunately, most Americans recognize their legal responsibility and properly report and pay their tax obligations. Unfortunately, some Americans are not as honest and intentionally pay no tax at all or underpay their taxes. This intentional underpaying of taxes is tax fraud. You should recognize that tax fraud is different from trying to follow complex tax rules and underpaying taxes or even being aggressive in taking advantage of legal tax minimization strategies. Citizens of any country should pay the least amount of tax they legally owe. However, intentionally underreporting income that should be taxed or deliberately overstating (without basis) tax deductions and exemptions is illegal and constitutes tax fraud.

If the IRS suspects that an individual or entity is underpaying its taxes, the individual's or entity's tax return will be audited by an IRS tax compliance auditor. If the audit reveals that taxes were underpaid, the auditor can either assess civil fines and penalties or, worse, refer the case to the IRS's Criminal Investigation Division.

IRS auditors are trained to look for tax fraud—a willful act done with the intent to defraud the IRS. Using a false Social Security number (SSN), keeping two sets of financial records, hiding income, or claiming a blind spouse as a dependent when you are single are all examples of tax fraud. Even though IRS auditors are trained to look for fraud, they do not routinely suspect it. They know the tax law is complex and expect to find a few errors in every tax return. They will give the benefit of the doubt most of the time and not assume tax fraud has been committed.

Fraud and the Criminal Investigation Division

A careless mistake on your tax return might tack on a 20 percent penalty to your tax bill. While this is significant, this penalty is much less severe than the penalty for tax fraud, which is 75 percent. The line between negligence and fraud is not always clear, even to the IRS and the courts. CI is directed at the taxpayers who willfully and intentionally violate their known legal duty of voluntarily filing income tax returns or paying the correct amount of income, employment, or excise taxes. These individuals pose a significant threat to tax administration and the U.S. economy.

The Criminal Investigation's fraud work encompasses a wide variety of cases involving tax and money laundering crimes. CI investigations involve a broad spectrum of individuals and industries from all facets of the economy, including small business owners, self-employed individuals, and large corporations.

The mission of CI is to investigate potential criminal violations of the Internal Revenue Code and related financial crimes in a manner that fosters confidence in the tax system and compliance with the law. CI special agents combine accounting skills with law enforcement skills to investigate financial crimes. Special agents are trained to "follow the money." No matter what the source, all income earned, both legal and illegal, has the potential of becoming involved in crimes that fall within the investigative jurisdiction of the IRS Criminal Investigation. Because of the expertise required to conduct these, often complex,

investigations, these special agents are highly skilled fraud investigators.

The specific laws under which tax fraud perpetrators are charged can be found in Table 16.1. Table 16.2 summarizes the tax fraud investigation activity of CI over three recent years. As examples of the kinds of tax fraud investigated by CI, consider the following five cases:

Case 1: Former IRS Employee Sentenced on Fraud and Tax Evasion Charges

On June 3, 2004, in Minneapolis, Minnesota, Sandra Jean Valencia was sentenced to 33 months in prison, followed by three years' supervised release and ordered to pay $605,203 in restitution. Valencia pleaded guilty to mail fraud, wire fraud, and tax evasion. Appointed by her grandmother to take care of her financial affairs, Valencia admitted in court that she used her positions under the power of attorney and as trustee from 1997 through 2000 to transfer the vast majority of her grandmother's assets to herself. Valencia depleted her grandmother's stock holdings, sold 76 acres of her farmland and household belongings, and emptied her bank accounts. Valencia also deposited approximately $41,000 of her grandmother's life insurance proceeds into her own bank account. Valencia admitted to evading income taxes for calendar years 1997 through 2000.

Case 2: Three Employees Who Defrauded Pitney Bowes Sentenced to Federal Prison

On May 28, 2004, in New Haven, Connecticut, Raymond J. Wisnieski, Otto Guhl, Jr., and Robert J. Wilson were sentenced after previously pleading guilty to engaging in a scheme to commit mail fraud and with filing a false U.S. income tax return. Wisnieski was sentenced to 37 months in prison, Guhl was sentenced to 21 months in prison, and Wilson was sentenced to 18 months in prison. All were also sentenced to three years of supervised release and a fine of $5,000. Wisnieski, an assistant controller of a division of Pitney Bowes, arranged for false entries to be made to the accounting records at Pitney Bowes to the benefit of himself, Guhl, and Wilson. Guhl and Wilson worked under Wisnieski in the same department. The false entries suggested that Pitney Bowes had withheld from the defendants' income significantly more federal and state income taxes than, in fact, had been withheld. As part of the scheme, the defendants would tell Pitney Bowes that the withholding amounts were mistakenly overstated and have Pitney Bowes refund to them a portion of the monies that the company's accounting system suggested had been withheld.

TABLE 16.1 TAX LAWS FOR FRAUD PERPETRATORS

LAW	NATURE OF LAW	DESCRIPTION AND PUNISHMENT
Title 26 USC § 7201	Attempt to evade or defeat tax	Any person who willfully attempts to evade or defeat any tax imposed by this title or the payment thereof shall, in addition to other penalties provided by law, be guilty of a felony and, upon conviction thereof: • Shall be imprisoned not more than five years • Or fined not more than $250,000 for individuals ($500,000 for corporations) • Or both, together with the costs of prosecution
Title 26 USC § 7202	Willful failure to collect or pay over tax	Any person required under this title to collect, account for, and pay over any tax imposed by this title who willfully fails to collect or truthfully account for and pay over such tax shall, in addition to penalties provided by the law, be guilty of a felony: • Shall be imprisoned not more than five years • Or fined not more than $250,000 for individuals ($500,000 for corporations) • Or both, together with the costs of prosecution
Title 26 USC § 7203	Willful failure to file return, supply information, or pay tax	Any person required under this title to pay any estimated tax or tax, or required by this title or by regulations made under authority thereof to make a return, keep any records, or supply any information, who willfully fails to pay such estimated tax or tax, make such return, keep such records, or supply such information, at the time or times required by law or regulations, shall, in addition to other penalties provided by law, be guilty of a misdemeanor and, upon conviction thereof: • Shall be imprisoned not more than one year • Or fined not more than $100,000 for individuals ($200,000 for corporations) • Or both, together with the cost of prosecution
Title 26 USC § 7206(1)	Fraud and false statements	Any person who willfully makes and subscribes any return, statement, or other document, which contains or is verified by a written declaration that is made under the penalties of perjury, and which he does not believe to be true and correct as to every material matter; shall be guilty of a felony and, upon conviction thereof: • Shall be imprisoned not more than three years • Or fined not more than $250,000 for individuals ($500,000 for corporations) • Or both, together with cost of prosecution
Title 26 USC § 7206(2)	Fraud and false statements	Any person who willfully aids or assists in, or procures, counsels, or advises the preparation or presentation under, or in connection with any matter arising under, the Internal Revenue laws, of a return, affidavit, claim, or other document, which is fraudulent or is false as to any material matter, whether or not such falsity or fraud is with the knowledge or consent of the person authorized or required to present such return, affidavit, claim, or document; shall be guilty of a felony and, upon conviction thereof: • Shall be imprisoned not more than three years • Cr fined not more than $250,000 for individuals ($500,000 for corporations) • Or both, together with the cost of prosecution
Title 26 USC § 7212(A)	Attempts to interfere with administration of Internal Revenue laws	Whoever corruptly or by force endeavors to intimidate or impede any officer or employee of the United States acting in an official capacity under this title, or in any other way corruptly or by force obstructs or impedes, or endeavors to obstruct or impede, the due administration of this title, upon conviction: • Shall be imprisoned not more than three years • Or fined not more than $250,000 for individuals ($500,000 for corporations) • Or both
Title 18 USC § 371	Conspiracy to commit offense or to defraud the United States	If two or more persons conspire either to commit any offense against the United States, or to defraud the United States, or any agency thereof in any manner or for any purpose, and one or more of such persons do any act to effect the object of the conspiracy, each: • Shall be imprisoned not more than five years • Or fined not more than $250,000 for individuals ($500,000 for corporations) • Or both

TABLE 16.2 IRS CRIMINAL INVESTIGATIONS ACTIVITY, 2004–2006

	FY 2006	FY 2005	FY 2004
Investigations Initiated	1,863	1,873	1,736
Prosecution Recommendations	1,020	1,157	1,197
Indictments/Information	830	953	941
Sentenced	691	804	657
Incarceration Rate	75.1%	79.1%	83.6%
Average Months to Serve	26	28	27

Because the defendants would not typically seek payment from Pitney Bowes for the entire overstated withholding amount, Pitney Bowes would still forward to the IRS, at the required time, the taxes that allegedly had been withheld from each defendant's salary. Thereafter, the defendants would file their yearly federal personal income tax returns. Because the withholding payments made by Pitney Bowes to the IRS far exceeded the taxes due on the defendants' actual salary, the defendants would each year receive a substantial refund. During the scheme, the tax returns filed by the defendants were materially false because they did not include as income the money the defendants had stolen from Pitney Bowes as a result of their scheme.

During the scheme, Wisnieski illegally obtained over $492,000 from Pitney Bowes and failed to pay over $112,000 in federal income taxes. Guhl unlawfully obtained over $351,000 from Pitney Bowes and failed to pay over $78,000 in federal income taxes. Wilson unlawfully obtained over $177,000 from Pitney Bowes and failed to pay over $37,000 in federal income taxes.

Case 3: Sister and Brother Convicted in International Money Laundering Criminal Enterprise Case

On May 28, 2004, in Seattle, Washington, Nghiem Nu-Doan Truong and her brother, Tung Quoc Truong, were convicted of conspiracy to engage in money laundering and immediately sentenced to four years' and three years' imprisonment, respectively. After their imprisonment, both defendants were sentenced to serve three years of supervised release. Also, a preliminary order was entered into court authorizing the criminal forfeiture of more than $1 million in cash and real property seized from Nghiem Nu-Doan Truong and My-A, Inc. According to court documents, the Truongs operated a lucrative money transfer business under the name of My-A, Inc., which opened its doors in mid-2001 to the Vietnamese community in Seattle. My-A, Inc., expanded

to include more than 20 branch offices and subagents in at least 13 other states. During 2002 and 2003, the Truongs transferred more than $11 million derived from marijuana trafficking by using various bank accounts to conceal and disguise the nature, location, source, and ownership of the funds belonging to, or intended for, Cong Chinh Dinh and Andy Hoang. The Truongs were accused of violating various laws by engaging in activities that included intentionally failing to document currency transfers, falsifying business records, not paying taxes on money laundering profits, and transporting and smuggling currency from the United States into Canada, among other things.

Case 4: Doctor Sentenced to 41 Months in Prison for Tax Evasion

On May 30, 2003, in Athens, Georgia, Dr. Bradford G. Brown was sentenced to serve 41 months in federal prison for tax evasion. At trial, the government introduced evidence that Brown, during the 1994 and 1995 tax years, evaded income taxes on more than $1.2 million of income by failing to deposit all of his medical receipts into his business account. Instead, he deposited income into bank accounts that he never disclosed to his accountant, thus breaching their explicit agreement that all of his income would be deposited into his business bank account for purposes of computing his income. Brown's scheme included the 1996–2001 tax years when he delinquently filed tax returns for these years that included a total tax liability in excess of $1 million while only being credited by the IRS with paying $4,192 of his total tax liability for the 1994–2001 tax years. In addition to his prison sentence, Brown was ordered to pay a $40,000 fine and make restitution in excess of $3 million.

Case 5: Woman Sentenced for Tax Fraud Relating to Embezzling More Than $3 Million

On May 8, 2003, in Charleston, West Virginia, Patricia Griffith was sentenced to 27 months in prison and fined $6,000 for income tax evasion. Griffith, who pled guilty, admitted she embezzled in excess of $3 million from 1990 through 1999 from Kanawha Valley Radiologists, Inc. Griffith failed to report to the IRS the money she embezzled. In particular, in the 1997 tax year, Griffith failed to report over $400,000 that she embezzled resulting in a tax liability of $120,000 for that year alone. Griffith was ordered to work with the IRS with respect to restitution for the 1997 tax year. Some common tax fraud schemes include the following:

- *Deliberately underreporting or omitting income*
- *Overstating tax deductions*
- *Keeping two sets of books*
- *Making false entries in books and records*
- *Claiming personal expenses as business expenses*
- *Claiming false deductions*
- *Hiding or transferring assets or income*
- *Illegal money laundering schemes*

The most common of these tax fraud schemes is deliberately underreporting income. Among individuals, a government study found the bulk of underreporting of income was done by self-employed restaurateurs, clothing store owners, and car dealers. Telemarketers and salespeople came in next, followed by doctors, accountants, and hairdressers. Self-employed taxpayers who overdeducted business-related expenses, such as auto expenses, came in a far distant second among tax fraud criminals.

Just how much tax fraud is there in the United States? In 2009, 2,105 Americans were convicted of tax crimes, which is .00089 percent of all taxpayers.[2] This number is small, especially considering that the IRS estimates that 17 percent of all taxpayers are not complying with the tax laws in some way or another. According to the IRS, individual taxpayers commit 75 percent of the tax fraud—mostly middle-income earners. Corporations do most of the rest.

CI Investigative Careers

As with the FBI, working for IRS Criminal Investigation means you are a government employee and are part of the network of local, state, and federal law enforcement agencies. The IRS works closely with the Department of Justice, U.S. attorneys, the FBI, U.S. Customs, the Drug Enforcement Administration, the U.S. Postal Inspection Service, inspectors general of all federal agencies, and the U.S. Marshals Service. Many federal agencies rely on CI to unravel criminal activities by following the financial trail, which ultimately leads to violation of the tax laws and numerous

other related financial crimes or other federal offenses. It is not unusual for a tax fraud investigation to uncover motives for other serious crimes such as corruption, embezzlement, extortion, or even murder.

To work as an entry-level CI special agent, you must be a U.S. citizen and not be older than 37 years of age. You must have completed a four-year course of study or bachelor's degree in any field of study that included or was supplemented by at least 15 semester hours in accounting, plus an additional nine semester hours from among the following or closely related fields: finance, economics, business law, tax law, or money and banking. Or you must have a combination of education and experience that together meet the total qualification requirements, such as being a CPA. Individuals with more education or experience can be hired into more advanced positions in CI.

> ### Remember this ...
>
> *The U.S. tax system depends on voluntary compliance; most people properly report and pay tax obligations, but some people do not pay or underpay taxes they owe, which is considered tax fraud. The CI Division is an arm of the IRS that investigates tax fraud. IRS CI special agents combine accounting skills with law enforcement skills to investigate financial crimes.*

Divorce Fraud

More than one-million **divorce** cases are filed annually in the United States for the purpose of dissolving a marriage relationship. Having worked together to construct a marriage, with long-range plans and sincere effort, the decision to tear apart a marriage, to declare that the good intentions have failed, and to change to a distinctly different lifestyle evokes emotions of all kinds, and often at a fever pitch. If children are involved, the complexity and alternatives are magnified even more. As such, amicable breakups are rare and, instead, divorce wars take their place.

In some cases, what begins as an amicable breakup is soon all-out war when the legal process of divorce begins. Our legal system is adversarial—a battle by definition. Divorce attorneys can ethically serve only one party of a divorce, and their job is to advocate for that party. Pit two divorce attorneys against each other, each trying to achieve the best results for his or her client, and even amicable couples can quickly find themselves in a legal battle against each other. Add in the formality of court proceedings, and the original participants often find that their relationship and intentions are no longer recognizable. Either during or after a divorce, many individuals feel cheated by the divorce proceedings. In particular, the economically dependent spouse may begin to question whether the planned or actual settlement is fair and whether the other spouse may be withholding vital information about the existence or value of relevant assets.

It should not be surprising, therefore, that much of the debate in divorce proceedings and a great deal of post-judgment divorce motions are filed seeking to set aside or reopen the decree. The basis for these disagreements and motions are often fraud on the part of the other spouse. Several steps must be taken to prove fraud in a divorce. As in all frauds, the party attempting to prove divorce fraud must prove (1) that a false representation, usually one of fact, was made by the other party; (2) that the defendant had knowledge or belief that the representation was false or made the representation with reckless indifference to the truth; and (3) that the defendant had intent to induce the plaintiff to act or refrain from acting in a certain way. Most divorce fraud litigation results from two allegations: (1) the plaintiff spouse claims that the defendant hid assets so they would not have to be shared or taken away or (2) the values assigned to assets were unrealistically low, thus resulting in an unfair divorce settlement.

The predication, detection, and investigation approaches for divorce fraud are no different from those discussed in previous chapters. It is important to understand, however, that individuals sometimes go to great lengths to hide assets in a divorce case. We will discuss some ways that assets are concealed as we discuss bankruptcy in this chapter. As stated previously, divorce and bankruptcy frauds are both committed to hide and protect assets.

Participants in Divorce Cases

Divorce actions are usually initiated by a disgruntled spouse who believes he or she has been wronged or injured in some way. The parties involved are usually the husband and wife, attorneys for both sides, and a divorce court. When allegations of fraud, such as hiding or illegally transferring assets arise, the attorney for the party alleging fraud usually hires investigators to try to locate such hidden assets. Investigative techniques such as surveillance, public records searches, and even subpoenas of private records are often used. Any evidence that is discovered by the investigators will be presented by the attorney to the divorce court in order

to obtain the most favorable divorce settlement possible. Most divorce fraud cases are civil, but where evidence of egregious fraudulent acts by one marital partner has been shown, law enforcement officials are often involved and criminal charges can be filed.

> **Remember this ...**
>
> *More than 1 million divorces are filed in the United States every year. Often, divorces result in a division of assets between a husband and wife. Sometimes a husband or wife will hide assets from the divorce court to avoid losing them in a divorce settlement. An action such as hiding assets is considered divorce fraud.*

Bankruptcy Fraud

While most readers of this book are probably familiar with divorce, many are not familiar with how bankruptcy works. As such, we will explain important concepts related to bankruptcy. However, because the motivation for and schemes used to commit divorce and bankruptcy fraud are often similar, much of what we discuss in this section is applicable to divorce fraud.

Bankruptcy frauds, such as the one described at the beginning of the chapter, represent an ever-growing problem in the United States. The bankruptcy system, an arm of the U.S. District Court, is a critical component of the U.S. government because of the impact bankruptcy filings have on the national and local economies. Abuse of the system by an individual filing for bankruptcy (debtor) or a professional within the system undermines the integrity of the system as a whole. Through abuse and corruption of the system, the effectiveness of the rehabilitation process, the system's primary function for the debtor, is reduced.

Monies defrauded from a bankruptcy never reach the pockets of deserving creditors and investors. As bankruptcy frauds occur more frequently, creditors and investors lose faith that their interests will be protected. This loss of faith can have a ripple effect in the economy through the tightening of credit, the raising of interest rates, and subsequent economic reactions.

The number of bankruptcies and associated bankruptcy frauds has generally been increasing for many years. Recently, professionals involved in the bankruptcy system have seen a decrease in the stigma attached to an individual or a corporation filing for bankruptcy. Bankruptcy relief is perceived to be more acceptable than ever before. Along with this perception, the changing economic climate in the United States contributed to a significant rise in bankruptcy filings over the past decade.

As the number of petitions filed with the **bankruptcy court** increases, there is a corresponding increase in administrative activity and less available time and resources to enforce policy and procedures. Also, increasing bankruptcies have stressed the bankruptcy court infrastructure such that it has less ability to convict bankruptcy fraud perpetrators.

The majority of bankruptcies filed in the United States come in the form of complete liquidations. An analysis of current FBI bankruptcy fraud investigations reveals that the most common fraud scheme utilized in fraudulent bankruptcy filings, like divorce, involves the concealment of a debtor's assets. Concealment prevents these assets from being liquidated and transferred to creditors to extinguish debts.

STOP & THINK *Why do you think the hiding of assets is so common in bankruptcy and divorce fraud cases?*

Even though concealing assets from the bankruptcy court is a fairly self-explanatory fraud scheme, it can be accomplished in a variety of ways. For example, an individual in Chapter 7 bankruptcy listed his assets as being well below his liabilities. Although this situation should be typical in most bankruptcy filings, the eventual outcome was not. After the debtor's bankruptcy was dismissed, the debtor continued living an extravagant lifestyle. The debtors were reported by their neighbors, who claimed that the debtors concealed several assets from the bankruptcy court, including boats, Rolex watches, and country club memberships. An investigation determined the debtors did not list these assets on their bankruptcy schedules in hopes of avoiding total liquidation of their assets.

In the case of a business entity filing for bankruptcy protection, concealment of assets typically occurs on a larger scale. For example, a business owner placed his company in Chapter 11 bankruptcy because the company was facing a severe cash shortage. However, just prior to filing for bankruptcy, the business owner transferred large sums of cash and other assets to family members as well as outside business interests controlled by the owner. The debtor's objective was to protect these assets from sale or liquidation.

Bankruptcy fraud also involves schemes to include petition mills, multiple filings, false statements, trustee fraud, attorney fraud, forged filings, embezzlement, credit card fraud, and bust-outs. After the concealment-of-assets fraud schemes, petition mills and multiple filings are the most prominent bankruptcy fraud schemes.

Petition mill fraud schemes are becoming increasingly popular in large cities with poor or immigrant populations. The scheme revolves around keeping an individual from being evicted from his or her dwelling, usually a person who is renting versus owning. Typically, when an individual is experiencing financial troubles, the first "creditor" to contact the distressed individual is his or her landlord. In order to avoid eviction as well as the cost of a lawyer, the individual answers an advertisement in the newspaper or responds to a billboard or poster intentionally posted in targeted neighborhoods. The advertisement explains how a "typing service" will help them keep their homes or apartments if faced with eviction. Unbeknownst to the individual, the service files a bankruptcy on the individual's behalf. The service charges an exorbitant fee for this service and drags the process out for several months, leading the individual to believe that the company is providing them a great service. In reality, the service is stripping the individual of any savings he or she might have and prolonging the inevitable eviction.

CAUTION *Distressed tenants facing eviction are often victims of petition mill fraud schemes. Unlike many bankruptcy frauds, the one committing the fraud is not the individual facing bankruptcy; instead, the fraudulent individuals or organizations are those filing bankruptcy on behalf of the distressed tenants without their knowledge. Because these fraudulent individuals charge enormous amounts and file bankruptcy on behalf of the distressed tenants, these individuals are left in even greater economic despair.*

The following two methods of perpetrating the multiple filing fraud schemes are the most popular:

- *Filing for bankruptcy in different states by utilizing true personal identifiers.*
- *Using false names or SSN's to file in the same or different states.*

Typically, a debtor who files several bankruptcies in two or more states lists nearly identical assets and liabilities in each filing. The debtor becomes discharged from the debts and, in the process, makes off with several of the assets left off a particular petition. If the debtor fears being caught, then the debtor simply travels to another state and files for another bankruptcy.

The Bankruptcy Code

When people or organizations are unable to pay their debts and have more liabilities than assets, they can file for bankruptcy by filing a bankruptcy petition with the courts. The filing of a bankruptcy petition initiates a legal process under the jurisdiction of the U.S. District Court that automatically refers the petition to the bankruptcy court. Bankruptcies have several purposes, including giving a debtor relief from creditor collection and foreclosure actions and protecting creditors from unfair collection efforts by other creditors. A bankruptcy filing allows the debtor to work out an orderly plan to settle debts or liquidate assets and distribute the proceeds to creditors in a way that is intended to treat creditors fairly. The filing of a bankruptcy petition creates a separate entity, or an "estate," which consists of the property or income of the debtor that will be used to settle the debts and over which the bankruptcy court has control.

Title 11 of the U.S. Code is referred to as the **Bankruptcy Code**. Title 11 is a federal statute that governs the bankruptcy process. The code provides for several types of bankruptcy. Chapters 1, 3, and 5 contain general provisions that apply to all bankruptcies. Chapters 7, 11, and 13 apply to specific types of bankruptcy.

Chapters 7 and 11 may be used by corporations or individuals. Under Chapter 7, the bankruptcy involves a complete sale or liquidation of all assets and the proceeds are used to pay creditors, usually at some percentage of the debts owed. In contrast, under Chapter 11, the creditors are told to give the bankrupt entity some time until it can reorganize its operations and finances so as to settle its debts and continue to operate in a reorganized fashion. Chapter 13 bankruptcies are reorganizations (similar to Chapter 11) that can be used by individuals with regular income and debts of $1 million or less. Debtors make regular payments to creditors over a specified number of years under Chapter 13. If reorganization does not work in Chapter 11 or 13 bankruptcies, judges often order a Chapter 7 bankruptcy.

In Chapter 11, if the bankruptcy court confirms a plan for reorganization in corporate cases or a discharge in individual cases, it becomes legally binding on the debtor and creditors. Only obligations provided for in the reorganized plan remain, and these obligations are settled in the amount, time, and manner provided for in the plan. If assets are liquidated, the proceeds are distributed to creditors in the order of priority specified in the Bankruptcy Code. For example, secured creditors are usually paid before unsecured creditors.

Civil and Criminal Bankruptcy Fraud Statutes

Criminal bankruptcy fraud cases are generally prosecuted by the U.S. Attorney's office in the applicable U.S. District Court. In criminal cases, the government must prove its case beyond a reasonable doubt. Convictions may result in jail sentences or other criminal penalties. Some of the more relevant sections of the Bankruptcy Code relating to criminal fraud are as follows:

1. Concealment of Assets, False Oaths and Claims, and Bribery (18 USC 152). This section makes it a crime for a person to "knowingly and fraudulently" do any of the following:

    - *Conceal property of a debtor's estate from creditors or from the bankruptcy trustee, custodian, or other officer of the court charged with custody of the property.*
    - *Make a false oath or account in a bankruptcy case.*
    - *Make a false declaration, certification, verification, or statement under penalty of perjury, such as intentionally omitting property, debt, or income from an official form required in a bankruptcy case. The court may infer fraudulent intent from the existence of an unexplained false statement unless the debtor can prove that the false statement was an unintentional mistake.*
    - *Present a false proof of claim against the debtor's estate. A proof of claim is a document filed with the bankruptcy court by a creditor stating the nature and amount of the claim against the debtor. The debt settlement plan takes into account "allowed" claims, that is, claims that the bankruptcy court accepts as valid claims. A creditor would be the likely perpetrator of this crime.*
    - *Receive a "material amount of property" from a debtor after the filing of a bankruptcy petition, with the "intent to defeat the provisions" of the Bankruptcy Code.*
    - *Give, offer, receive, or attempt to obtain money or property, remuneration, compensation, reward, advantage or promise thereof for acting or forbearing to act in a bankruptcy case.*
    - *In a personal capacity or as an agent or officer of a person or corporation, transfer or conceal his or her or the other person's or corporation's property, in contemplation of a*

bankruptcy case involving himself or herself or the other person or corporation, or with the "intent to defeat the provisions" of the Bankruptcy Code.

- *In contemplation of a bankruptcy filing, or after such a filing, "conceal, destroy, mutilate, falsify, or make a false entry in any recorded information (including books, documents, records, and papers)" relating to the debtor's "property or financial affairs."*
- *After a bankruptcy filing, "withhold any recorded information (including books, documents, records, and papers)" relating to the debtor's "property or financial affairs" from a custodian, a trustee, or another officer of the court.*

Obviously, this statute is intended to target fraudulent acts by someone filing bankruptcy. You should also note that even though criminal statues related to divorce aren't as specific as those related to bankruptcy, these same kinds of offenses in divorce cases are often prosecutable in criminal court.

2. Embezzlement Against the Debtor's Estate (18 USC 153). This section applies to bankruptcy trustees, custodians, attorneys, or other court officers, and to anyone engaged by a court officer to perform a service for a debtor's estate. The statute makes it a crime for such persons to "knowingly and fraudulently appropriate to [their] own use, embezzle, spend, or transfer" any property, or to hide or destroy any document, belonging to the debtor's estate. This section of the code is intended to punish those who abuse their appointment to assist in the orderly transfer of assets in a bankruptcy. As an example of someone who was prosecuted under this section of the code, a court-appointed trustee was convicted of stealing $15 million from a debtor's assets before the remaining assets were distributed to creditors. Similarly, many divorce lawyers who were hired to assist in wealthy divorce cases have been prosecuted for misappropriating assets of the divorced couple.

3. Adverse Interest and Conduct of Officers (18 USC 154). This section prohibits a custodian, trustee, marshal, or other court officer from knowingly:

   - *Purchasing, directly or indirectly, any property of the debtor's estate of which the person is an officer in a bankruptcy case.*
   - *Refusing to permit a reasonable opportunity for the inspection by parties in interest of the*

documents and accounts relating to the affairs of the estate in the person's charge when directed by the court to do so.

- *Refusing to permit a reasonable opportunity for inspection by the U.S. Trustee of the documents and accounts relating to the affairs of the estate in the person's charge.*

This section of the code targets conflicts of interest by those appointed or hired to equitably dissolve assets in bankruptcy cases. For example, this section makes it an offense for court-appointed individuals to purchase property of a debtor for fear that an unreasonably low price will be paid.

4. Bankruptcy Fraud. This section makes it a crime to do any of the following to execute or conceal a fraud scheme:

   - *File a bankruptcy petition.*
   - *File a document in a bankruptcy proceeding.*
   - *Make a false or fraudulent representation, claim, or promise with respect to a bankruptcy proceeding, either before or after the bankruptcy petition is filed.*

This section is the "catch-all" section that prohibits every other type of fraud associated with bankruptcies.

Civil Bankruptcy Statutes

As discussed previously, the purpose of criminal laws is to "right a wrong," while the purpose of civil laws is to seek monetary remedies or recover stolen funds. Bankruptcy cases can involve civil proceedings conducted in the U.S. Bankruptcy Court. Plaintiffs may seek remedies when they are damaged by inappropriate conduct, for example, in a fraudulent transfer matter. The plaintiff (who is usually a trustee) need only demonstrate a preponderance of evidence (or sometimes clear and convincing evidence) that the defendant (normally the debtor or a related party) is liable for civil remedies. The specific remedies that may be sought depend on the charges involved.

CAUTION *It is important to distinguish between civil and criminal bankruptcy frauds. Criminal bankruptcy fraud cases are usually prosecuted by the U.S. Attorney's office in U.S. District Court and look to convict persons and sentence them to serve time in jail or to pay hefty fines. Civil bankruptcy fraud cases are conducted in the U.S. Bankruptcy Court and look to seek monetary remedies or recover stolen funds.*

The following are some of the most pertinent sections of the Bankruptcy Code that provide civil remedies for bankruptcy fraud:

1. Offenses Leading to Revocation of Debt Discharge in Chapter 11 and Chapter 13 Cases. Section 1144 of the Bankruptcy Code provides for the revocation of a Chapter 11 reorganization plan and for the revocation of debt forgiveness or discharge in a Chapter 11 bankruptcy if the plan's approval was obtained through fraudulent means. Similarly, Code Section 1328(e) provides for the revocation of debt forgiveness or discharge in a Chapter 13 case if the discharge was obtained through fraudulent actions. Sections 1144 and 1328(e) are not specific as to what constitutes fraud for their purposes, but include any intentional deceit or criminal action discussed previously in this text. As an example of the kind of fraud targeted by this section, if a debtor lied about (usually by understating) the amount of his or her assets in order to get debts forgiven, the forgiveness or discharge of the debts could be revoked.

2. Fraudulent Transfers. Section 548 of the Bankruptcy Code defines a fraudulent transfer as a transfer made, or obligation incurred, *within one year before the bankruptcy petition's filing date* that was:

   a. Made with the actual intent to hinder, delay, or defraud creditors, for example, by giving debtor property to relatives with the intent of placing it beyond the reach of creditors, or

   b. Made for less than reasonably equivalent value if:

      1. *The debtor was insolvent or became insolvent as a result of the transfer, or*

      2. *The debtor's capital remaining after the transfer was unreasonably small (for instance, the debtor was constantly behind in paying bills after the transfer), or*

      3. *The debtor intended to, or believed it would, incur debts it would be unable to repay when they matured.*

This statute is one of the real workhorses of the Bankruptcy Code because hiding assets or trading or selling them at amounts below market value to relatives or friends (often involving kickbacks) is probably the most common type of fraud committed in both bankruptcy and divorce cases.

Participants in the Bankruptcy Process

It is important for fraud examiners to understand the roles of key participants in the bankruptcy process. The parties discussed in this section are as follows:

- *Bankruptcy court*
- *U.S. Trustee*
- *Court-appointed or panel trustee*
- *Examiners*
- *Debtors*
- *Creditors*
- *Adjusters (operations or field agents)*

Bankruptcy Court

Bankruptcy petitions are filed with the U.S. Bankruptcy Clerk's Office. All bankruptcy petitions are subject to U.S. District Court jurisdiction, but are automatically referred to the U.S. Bankruptcy Court for supervision. Bankruptcy judges hear cases involving debtors' and creditors' rights, approve reorganization plans, award professional fees, and conduct hearings and trials to resolve disputes. A divorce court would play a similar role in divorce hearings.

U.S. Trustee

The Office of the U.S. Trustee is an agency in the Department of Justice that is responsible for the following functions:

- *Administering bankruptcy cases*
- *Appointing trustees, examiners, and Chapter 11 committees*
- *Overseeing and monitoring trustees*
- *Reviewing employees and fee applications*
- *Appearing in court on matters of interest to the debtor's estate and creditors*

A U.S. Trustee or Assistant Trustee heads each of 21 regions in the United States. Each regional branch of the Office of the U.S. Trustee may have the following staff:

- *Staff attorneys. Staff attorneys review fee applications, motions to appoint trustees and examiners, motions to convert or dismiss a case, and other pleadings. They also represent the U.S. Trustee as a party in interest.*
- *Bankruptcy analysts. These analysts review operating reports and other financial information and oversee the debtor's case to assure compliance with*

the Bankruptcy Code and to protect the estate's assets.

- ***Special investigative units (SIUs).*** *Some regions have SIUs that investigate criminal complaints in bankruptcy cases.*

Court-Appointed or Panel Trustee

Court-appointed or panel **trustees** are usually individuals or firms, such as accountants or lawyers, who identify and collect a debtor's assets and then allocate those assets to creditors in an orderly manner. The duties of a court-appointed or panel trustee in Chapter 7 cases, as set forth in 11 USC 704, include the following:

a. Collect and liquidate the property of the debtor's estate and close the estate as quickly as is compatible with the best interests of the involved parties.

b. Account for all property received.

c. Ensure that the debtor files the statement of intention to retain or surrender property as specified in the bankruptcy code.

d. Investigate the financial affairs of the debtor.

e. If necessary, examine proofs of claims and object to improper claims.

f. If appropriate, oppose the discharge of the debtor.

g. Furnish information about the estate and its administration when requested by a party in interest, unless the court orders otherwise.

h. If the business of the debtor is authorized to be operated, file with the court, the U.S. Trustee, and any applicable tax-collecting governmental unit periodic reports and summaries of the operation of the business, including a statement of receipts and disbursements and such other information as the U.S. Trustee or the court requires.

i. Make a final report and file a final account of the administration of the estate with the court and with the U.S. Trustee.

In Chapter 11 cases, the court-appointed or panel trustee's duties, as set forth in 11 USC 1106, are as follows:

a. Perform the duties of the trustee specified in items b, e, g, h, and i of the preceding paragraph.

b. If the debtor has not done so, file the list, schedule, and statement required under 11 USC 521 (1).

c. Except to the extent that the court orders otherwise, investigate the acts, conduct, assets, liabilities, and financial condition of the debtor, the operation of the debtor's business and the desirability

of the continuance of that business, and any other matter relevant to the case or to the formulation of a plan.

d. As soon as practical:

(1) File a statement of any investigation conducted under item c of this paragraph, including any fact ascertained pertaining to fraud, dishonesty, incompetence, misconduct, mismanagement, or irregularity in the management of the affairs of the debtor, or to a cause of action available to the estate.

(2) Transmit a copy or a summary of any such statement to any creditors' committee or equity security holders' committee, to any indenture trustee, and to such other entity as the court designates.

e. As soon as practical, file a reorganization plan under 11 USC 1121, file a report of why the trustee will not file a plan, or recommend conversion of the case to a case under Chapters 7, 12, or 13 or dismissal of the case.

f. For any year for which the debtor has not filed a tax return required by law, furnish, without personal liability, such information as may be required by the governmental unit with which such tax return was to be filed, in light of the condition of the debtor's books and records and the availability of such information.

g. After confirmation of a plan, file such reports as are necessary or as the court orders.

Bankruptcy trustees often hear allegations of fraud by the debtor or its principals. In Chapter 11 cases, alleged fraud is generally the reason the court appoints a trustee. The trustee's authority to investigate fraud involves investigating the affairs of the debtor in Chapter 7 bankruptcies and (a) investigating the acts, conduct, assets, liabilities, and financial condition of the debtor, the operation of the debtor's business and the desirability of the continuance of such business and (b) filing a statement of investigation conducted in the case of a Chapter 11 bankruptcy. If the trustee conducts an investigation and decides that sufficient evidence of bankruptcy fraud exists, a report on the results of the investigation should be filed with the U.S. Attorney.

The trustee has significant powers to gather information in an investigation. A trustee, in effect, assumes the role of the debtor with all the rights thereto. Thus, the trustee can obtain information from the debtor's attorneys and accountants. The trustee can even break the attorney–client privilege because the trustee becomes the client. The trustee can also obtain access to the debtor's records that are in the hands of the criminal authorities.

Examiners

An examiner (usually some type of fraud examiner or investigator) is generally appointed by a bankruptcy judge in a Chapter 11 proceeding to investigate allegations of fraud or misconduct by the debtor or its principals. The examiner's role is to investigate and report the results of the investigation to the court and other interested parties as soon as possible. Examiners can subpoena records and depose witnesses. Generally, they cannot operate businesses, make business decisions, or propose reorganization plans. However, the court may expand an examiner's role to perform some functions of trustees or debtors-in-possession.

Debtors

A **debtor** is the person or entity who is the subject of a Chapter 11 filing. A debtor in an involuntary, or forced, bankruptcy proceeding is called an *alleged debtor*. The debtor's primary goal in a bankruptcy proceeding is to settle its obligations as favorably as possible. Bankruptcy fraud by individual debtors often results from concealing assets or making false statements. Bankruptcy fraud by business debtors often results from inflating debt and underreporting assets.

Creditors

A **creditor** is defined as one who holds a valid claim against a debtor. The Bankruptcy Code allows committees to represent classes of creditors. In Chapter 11 cases, creditor committees have the power to investigate the acts, conduct, and financial condition of a debtor and any other matters relevant to the case.

Adjusters

Adjusters are also called *operations* or *field agents*. Adjusters assist the trustee by performing such duties as securing business facilities and assets, locating assets of the debtor's estate, locating business records, opening new bank accounts, investigating asset thefts, and arranging asset sales.

Fraud Investigator's Relationship to Participants in Bankruptcy Proceedings

Code Section 327(a) allows trustees to employ, with the court's approval, attorneys, accountants, or other professionals to represent or assist the trustee. Also, Code

Section 1103 allows a creditors' committee to employ, with the court's approval, attorneys, accountants, or their agents to perform services for the committee. Although the code does not specifically authorize it, bankruptcy courts have typically allowed examiners to employ CFEs, CPAs, and other professionals. Fraud examiners may be used to conduct fraud investigations as well as provide consulting and other financial services.

Before professionals can be compensated from estate funds, they must be employed under Code Section 327. The court must approve the employment of those professionals. Code Section 330 sets forth the conditions regarding compensation of professionals and lists specific requirements relating to retention.

A creditor may engage a CFE, a CPA, or another professional independently from the court to investigate allegations of bankruptcy fraud. In such cases, the creditor usually compensates the investigator directly without court approval. Under certain conditions, the creditor may apply to the court to have the costs of the investigation paid by the state if they result in criminal prosecution.

The bankruptcy judge must approve the retention of a fraud examiner or investigator in a bankruptcy proceeding. This approval is required whenever the investigator is paid by the debtor's estate, whether the investigator is engaged by the debtor, trustee, debtor-in-possession, creditors' committee, or stockholders. However, in the rare case when an investigator provides services to and is directly paid by an individual creditor or stockholder, these requirements do not apply.

When a fraud investigator is retained, an affidavit of a proposed investigator (see sample affidavit in Appendix A) is prepared. The affidavit is addressed to the court and is submitted by the attorney for the person who engaged the investigator (such as the trustee, examiner, or creditors' committee) as part of the application for retention. The affidavit is a legal document that is sworn under oath (under penalty of perjury) and must be notarized. The exact content and extent of detail required in an affidavit varies by jurisdiction.

A description of the proposed services is generally included and is particularly important. U.S. Trustees require the services of professionals to be categorized and have developed broad categories of service. One such category is litigation consulting, which includes fraud examination. Fraud investigation services would be included in this category. Another category is asset analysis and recovery, which would be relevant in hiring someone to search for possible fraudulent transfers.

The description of services should be reasonably detailed, but the extent of detail required depends on the preferences of the bankruptcy judge. In considering the request for compensation, the judge will compare actual services rendered to proposed services in the application and order for retention. Judges often disallow compensation for services that were not authorized.

Once the services of a fraud investigator are approved, an application for retention (see sample application in Appendix B) is usually prepared by the attorney for the person engaging the investigator, based primarily on information in the affidavit and discussions with the investigator. Once the application for retention is approved, the judge issues an order authorizing the services. The investigator generally should verify that the order is signed before beginning work.

> **Remember this ...**
>
> *The number of bankruptcies and associated bankruptcy frauds has been increasing over time. Bankruptcy fraud primarily refers to the concealment of assets while filing for bankruptcy. Concealment of assets encompasses about 70 percent of bankruptcy fraud and prevents assets from being liquidated and transferred to creditors to extinguish debts. The Bankruptcy Code, Title 11 of the United States Code, is the federal statute that governs the bankruptcy process. Various types of bankruptcies can be filed under the Bankruptcy Code. Bankruptcy cases can involve civil proceedings conducted in the U.S. Bankruptcy Court, and key participants in the bankruptcy process have different roles.*

Bankruptcy and Divorce Fraud Schemes—The Planned Bankruptcy (Bust-Out)

The two most common bankruptcy fraud schemes are the planned bankruptcy, or bust-out, and the fraudulent concealment of assets during, or in contemplation of, a bankruptcy. This latter scheme is also the most common type of fraud in divorce cases.

A **bust-out** may take several forms, but essentially involves intentionally obtaining loans or purchasing inventory on a credit basis and concealing, or absconding with, the proceeds from the loan or sale of the inventory or with the inventory itself before creditors are paid. Insolvency is declared and bankruptcy is

filed, but the creditors find no assets left from which they can be paid. If the scam works, the perpetrators retain the cash proceeds (from the loan or sales) or the inventory but escape liability for the unpaid debt. Government statistics estimate that losses to creditors from bust-outs amount to billions each year. For example, in 2007, it is estimated that creditors lost nearly $50 billion from bust-outs.[3]

A bust-out may involve setting up a new company or using an established company. In the first type of bust-out, the fraud perpetrators set up a new company and operate it legitimately for a while in order to establish credibility (a reputation for honesty) and credit with banks (that provide loans) or suppliers (who sell goods on credit). The new company may purposely take a name very similar to that of an existing, well-known, and reputable company in order to trick unwary lenders and suppliers into thinking they are dealing with the well-known company or with a subsidiary or an affiliate of a well-known company. The scam company may also submit intentionally misstated financial statements to suppliers or creditors to inflate its financial position and profitability.

In the second type of bust-out, the perpetrators quietly buy an established company that already has a good reputation and credit rating and take over its management. Credit-rating agencies are usually not aware of the ownership and management change. The perpetrators then rely on the established credit rating to get credit from suppliers and loans from banks.

In either type of bust-out, the perpetrators buy large amounts of inventory on credit from numerous suppliers. The perpetrators may also obtain bank loans on the basis of the credit rating. At first, the perpetrators pay the suppliers promptly in order to build up their credit rating, creating incentives for suppliers to extend higher amounts of credit. The cash with which to pay the suppliers is obtained from the loans or from the goods being sold at deep discounts through co-conspirators in other markets. (The merchandise usually is of a type that can be sold quickly at cost.) The perpetrators buy larger and larger amounts of inventory on credit and eventually stop paying the suppliers. They stockpile the inventory and either conceal it for later sale in another location or secretly liquidate it at bargain prices. If the perpetrators obtained bank loans, they siphon off some or all of the proceeds into accounts of hidden "shell" corporations. The perpetrators then either claim insolvency and file for bankruptcy or simply close up shop without filing bankruptcy and abscond with the sales and loan proceeds. The company will appear to be insolvent because the sales of inventory at bargain or liquidation prices reduced profits and cash flow, and the siphoning off of the sales proceeds reduced assets and cash, while the liabilities to lenders and suppliers remain. If the perpetrators flee without filing for bankruptcy, the unpaid lenders and suppliers may file an involuntary bankruptcy petition against the company. In either case, however, the lenders and suppliers find few or no assets left in the company with which to pay off the company debts.

In a bust-out, the typical intent is to make a company insolvent and to file bankruptcy in a scheme to defraud creditors. If the perpetrators do not file a bankruptcy petition, they cannot be charged with bankruptcy fraud. Almost all bust-out schemes involve concealing assets—such as the proceeds from sales or loans or the inventory itself.

A bust-out can be difficult to detect. If a company claims insolvency and files for bankruptcy, creditors may find it difficult to determine that the insolvency was deliberately taken for the purpose of perpetrating fraud. Indicators of a bust-out include the following:

a. A company's only listed address and phone number are a post office box and an answering service. (Investigators should be aware that post office boxes can appear as street addresses.)

b. A new company is owned and managed by persons from another state or is vague about its ownership or type of business.

c. A sudden change is made in a company's management, especially if the change is made without public notice.

d. Credit references either cannot be verified or seem too eager to provide favorable references. (These references may be phony or collusive.)

e. The size of orders placed on credit and the credit balances with suppliers suddenly and dramatically increase.

f. The inventory is suddenly deleted, without explanation.

g. "Customers" have a history of buying goods at unreasonable discounts.

Remember this ...

Bust-outs are planned bankruptcies where a person or business will intentionally obtain loans or purchase inventory on credit and conceal the proceeds or inventory before creditors are aid. When bankruptcy is filed, creditors often fail to collect the full amount due to them because of the intentional concealment of assets.

Fraudulent Concealment of Assets or Income in Bankruptcies or Divorces

Although bust-outs are unique to bankruptcy, fraudulent concealment of assets or income is a common type of fraud in both bankruptcy and divorce. This section discusses what constitutes the debtor's or divorcee's estate so as to understand what assets and income might be concealed. We also cover methods of concealing these assets or income and procedures to investigate possible concealments.

The Debtor's or Divorcee's Estate

When a company or an individual (including an individual who owns an unincorporated business) files for bankruptcy or an individual files or is involved in a divorce, an estate is created. This estate consists of the property (or income, in some cases) of the debtor or divorcee, that will be divided among claimants and over which the bankruptcy or divorce court has control. In a **Chapter 7 bankruptcy**, all the estate assets are liquidated and the proceeds are used to settle debts. In **Chapter 11 bankruptcies** or **Chapter 13 bankruptcies**, some of the estate's assets may be liquidated or turned over to creditors in settlement of debt, but most estate assets are not liquidated or turned over to creditors because the purpose of these two bankruptcy types is to allow the individual or organization to retain assets and to settle debts from future income. In a divorce case, the estate or assets of the married couple are usually divided between the two marital partners after the debts of the couple are paid.

Generally, the debtor's estate or divorce partner's assets consist of all property as of the date the bankruptcy or divorce petition was filed as well as the proceeds or earnings from such property after the petition was filed. For example, an estate would include a building owned as of the petition date and the rent earned from the building during the post-petition period.

Bankruptcy Statutes Concerning Concealment of Assets

Title 18, Section 152, of the U.S. Code makes it a crime to knowingly and fraudulently conceal property of a debtor's estate or falsify any documents, records, or statements during, or in contemplation of, a bankruptcy. As previously discussed, the Bankruptcy Code provides for revocation of debt forgiveness or discharge obtained through fraud, including concealment of assets or intentional misstatement of records or statements filed in the case. Even if the debtor is not convicted of criminal or civil fraud, any concealed assets or income that are located can be brought back into the estate to be used to settle debts.

Means of Concealing Assets or Income

The following are some ways in which assets or income may be fraudulently concealed:

a. Cash received in payment of receivables may be diverted to another entity, usually a related party.

b. Inventory may be shipped to an off-site location or sold to a related party or co-conspirator at a steeply discounted price.

c. Assets or income may be shifted to another entity controlled by the debtor or the divorced party. The transfer may be accomplished through means such as changing the title to assets, depositing amounts into accounts of other individuals or companies, and paying bogus or padded fees and expenses.

d. Sales may not be reported in the debtor company's books; instead, the sales proceeds are diverted.

e. Payments may be made to fictitious individuals or vendors and the amounts diverted to the debtor or to a divorced party. Also, payments to conspiring vendors or individuals may be padded, or purchase discounts may not be recorded, and the overpayment diverted to the debtor or a marriage partner.

f. Income from controlled organizations may be intentionally understated by overstating expenses. Also, a debtor company may pay excessive compensation to owners.

g. The debtor's personal expenses may be paid by the company and mischaracterized as business expenses.

h. The debtor's or divorced partner's books and records or other financial information may be damaged or hidden.

i. Interests in partnerships, corporations, lawsuit proceeds, or other assets may not be disclosed.

Indicators of Concealment

Some indicators of possible asset or income concealment include the following:

a. Transfers of property or large payments to related parties or individuals, such as insiders, shareholders, or relatives.

b. Frequent and unusual transfers between bank accounts, particularly between business and personal accounts.

c. Numerous transactions made in cash that normally are made on account (sales, purchases, etc.)

d. Unusually large and unexplainable payments to vendors.

e. Unusual or rapid reductions in assets.

f. Increases in operating losses that are not explained by economic factors.

g. Inconsistencies between financial statements or tax returns and the official forms filed for the bankruptcy or records filed in divorce cases.

h. Travel to offshore tax havens or locations that allow secret bank accounts.

i. Missing, inaccurate, or damaged records.

Fraudulent Transfers

Section 548 of the Bankruptcy Code defines a fraudulent transfer as a transfer made, or obligation incurred, within one year before the bankruptcy petition's filing date that was:

1. Made with the actual intent to hinder, delay, or defraud creditors, for example, by giving debtor property to relatives with the intent of placing it beyond the reach of creditors, *or*

2. Made for less than the reasonably equivalent value if:
   a. The debtor was insolvent or became insolvent as a result of the transfer (insolvency for this purpose is defined beginning in Paragraph 906.5), *or*
   b. The debtor's capital remaining after the transfer was unreasonably small (for instance, the debtor was constantly behind in paying bills after the transfer), *or*
   c. The debtor intended to, or believed it would, incur debts it would be unable to repay when they matured.

Part (1) of the definition constitutes actual fraud, for which fraudulent intent must be shown. Part (2) constitutes constructive fraud, for which intent to defraud need not be shown, as long as one of the conditions in part (2) is met. The one-year cutoff date applies to either type of fraudulent transfer. However, a longer cutoff period may apply if state statutes are applied in the bankruptcy case.

The preceding paragraph indicates that a fraudulent transfer may be made with or without actual intent to defraud creditors. The statutes discussed in Section 901 generally apply when actual intent to defraud creditors is proved. Also, the bankruptcy court can avoid (cancel) the transfer and bring the property back into the estate for use to settle debts.

The Bankruptcy Code also contains provisions that apply when a transfer meets the code's definition of constructive fraud, even if the transfer cannot be shown to involve actual intent to defraud creditors. The bankruptcy court can avoid constructively fraudulent transfers and bring the assets back into the estate for use to settle debts.

> ### Remember this …
>
> *Many ways exist to conceal assets or income; however, many indicators of possible asset or income concealment also exist. Divorce and bankruptcy statutes exist to help minimize fraudulent activity.*

Civil Liability for False Accusations

An important issue for fraud investigators in both bankruptcy and divorce cases is the risk of civil liability for false accusations. Debtors and divorced partners often have little to lose by challenging the investigator on every word of his or her report. In this situation, the investigator may be placed on the defensive by the debtor's or divorcee's aggressive attacks. The investigator should be careful to ensure that all findings and conclusions in any report provided are properly supported with evidence. Unsupported conclusions could expose the investigator to charges of false accusations, which could result in costly civil liability.

> ### Remember this …
>
> *Fraud investigators should always have evidence supporting claims of alleged fraud. Without supporting evidence, charges of false accusations could result in civil liability against a fraud investigator. This is especially true in cases involving bankruptcy and divorce fraud.*

Money Laundering

As mentioned earlier, **money laundering** is among the most common tax fraud schemes and often accompanies other fraud schemes as well. Money laundering involves engaging in financial transactions so as to conceal the source, identity, or destination of funds. The U.S. Department of Justice defines money laundering as "the process by which one conceals the existence, illegal source, or illegal application of income and then disguises that income to make it appear legitimate."[4] The phrase "money laundering" implies that money which is "dirty" because it was generated illegally is "laundered," or made to appear that it came from legitimate sources. Various transactions are used to take this money that originated illegally through a process in which the origin of the money and the details of the transactions become separated from the illegal activity.

The phrase *money laundering* has often been used in reference to attempts to legitimize apparent sources of funds that were generated through illegal activities such as drug trafficking, bringing illegal money into another country to fund terrorist activities, and organized crime. However, it is now used to refer to a broad spectrum of illegal activities such as tax evasion or fraudulent accounting. As such, businesses and individuals can launder money through complex transactions involving a network of "shell" companies or trusts that are often based offshore. Commonly, criminals who launder money are drug traffickers, embezzlers, corrupt politicians and public officials, mobsters, terrorists, and con artists. Thus, money laundering is not only associated with drug dealers and the mafia, but also with prominent and, often, respectable individuals and organizations that have been indicted for money laundering.

How could money laundering be related to bankruptcy, divorce, or tax fraud? The following case led to charges of tax fraud:

In the United States, some candidates running for political offices are not allowed to receive corporate campaign donations. In October 2005, a Texas grand jury brought charges of money laundering against U.S. Congressman Tom DeLay. Prosecutors alleged that DeLay hid funds originating from corporations that ended up in the hands of Republican candidates in Texas. This alleged money laundering scheme involved sending corporate donations from Texas to the Republican National Committee (RNC) headquarters in Washington, DC, and the RNC then sending money back to Texas for campaigning. While DeLay maintains his innocence related to these indictments, two of his aides and his top campaign contributor pleaded guilty to crimes including conspiracy; wire, tax, and mail fraud; and corruption of public officials.

The Money Laundering Process

The money laundering process involves the following three steps: placement, layering, and integration. In the placement stage, the launderer inserts "dirty money" into a legitimate financial institution. Usually, this involves making cash deposits to a bank. This is often the riskiest stage of the laundering process because large cash deposits raise red flags and banks are required to report details regarding large cash transactions to the government.

The layering stage is the most complex step in a laundering scheme. The purpose of this stage is to make the dirty money difficult to trace. Layering involves conducting various financial transactions to make it difficult to follow the flow of funds. Layering may consist of such activities as making wire transfers between accounts located in different countries attached to different names. It may also include making multiple bank-to-bank transfers, making deposits and withdrawals to continually vary the amount of money in the accounts, exchanging the money to a new currency, and purchasing high-value items (e.g., houses, cars, jewelry) to change the form of the assets.

In the final or integration stage, the money reenters the economy in a form that appears to come from a legal transaction. This transaction may involve the sale of other assets (e.g., real estate) bought during the layering stage or giving funds to a business in which the launderer is supposedly "investing." Once the money is reintroduced as "clean" into the economy, the launderer can use the funds for personal consumption. If a document trail of the previous stages does not exist, it is extremely difficult to unravel a laundering scheme in the integration stage. Figure 16.1 illustrates the money laundering process.

STOP & THINK *Most illegal transactions such as drug deals and terrorist activities are conducted in cash. Why is it important for criminals to get their cash deposited into financial institutions?*

Efforts to Combat Money Laundering

Because money laundering often takes place across many national borders, no one government entity has power to stop money laundering, and cooperative international efforts are necessary to combat money laundering. The Financial Action Task Force (FATF) is an intergovernmental body that strives to combat money laundering globally. In 1990, the FATF launched an initiative to combat the laundering of drug money. The recommendations from this initiative have been revised to reflect evolving money laundering schemes, and recommendations on fighting terrorist organizations that take part in money laundering schemes have been added. The FATF recommendations have been recognized by the International Monetary Fund (IMF) and the World Bank as the international standards for combating money laundering and the financing of terrorism.[5]

A detailed list of the FATF recommendations can be found at its Web site (http://www.fatf-gafi.org). The FATF encourages its members not to deal with countries that do not comply with these rules. The recommendations deal with the following categories:

- *Customer due diligence and record keeping*
- *Reporting of suspicious transactions and compliance*
- *Other measures to deter money laundering and terrorist financing*
- *Measures to be taken with respect to countries that insufficiently comply with the FATF rules*
- *Regulation and supervision*

As money laundering schemes change, the FATF will likely revise these recommendations to reflect new conditions. Although other international organizations such as the United Nations, the International Monetary Fund, the World Bank, and others are making efforts to combat money laundering, the FATF sets the international standards with its recommendations.

In the United States, Title 18, USC §§ 1956 and 1957, and Title 31, USC §§ 5316 and 5324 deal with money laundering. These statutes deal with money laundering instruments, the transportation or transferring of funds into or out of the United States, and transactions deriving from specified unlawful activity. Title 18 focuses primarily on laundering and racketeering, and Title 31 focuses on records and reporting. In addition to federal statutes, individual states, as well as local governments, have developed statutes prohibiting money laundering.

Detecting Money Laundering Schemes

Money laundering is much less likely to affect financial statements than financial statement fraud does. Thus, external auditing procedures are often unlikely to detect money laundering. Because money laundering is often related to other illegal activities, investigations of money laundering often uncover other fraud or illegal activities. As such, investigators are often able to discover numerous criminals involved in several illegal activities by uncovering a money laundering scheme.

FIGURE 16.1 MONEY LAUNDERING PROCESS

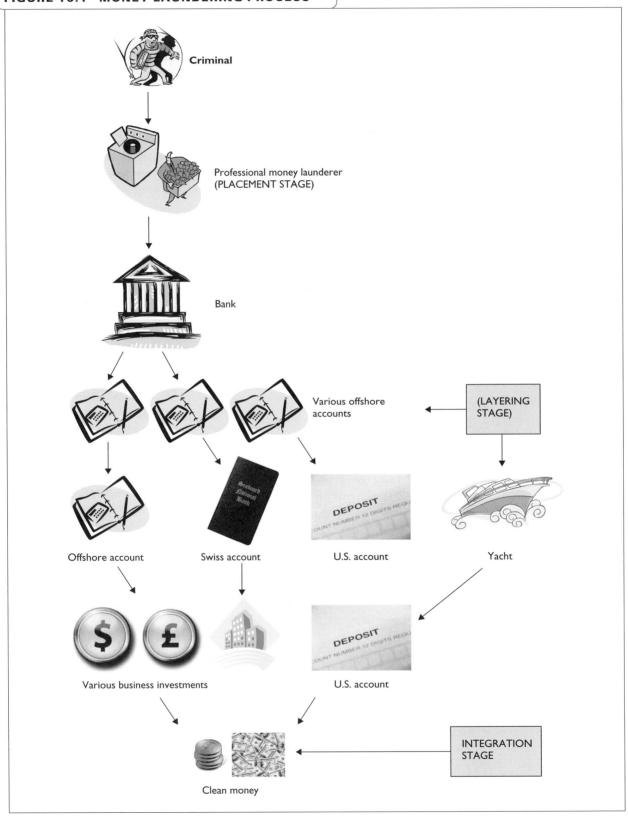

Criminal

Professional money launderer
(PLACEMENT STAGE)

Bank

Various offshore accounts

(LAYERING STAGE)

Offshore account

Swiss account

U.S. account

Yacht

Various business investments

U.S. account

INTEGRATION STAGE

Clean money

There are as many different money laundering schemes as there are people who participate in them. Therefore, no exact method of detection exists for uncovering every money laundering scheme. However, red flags exist that indicate the existence of money laundering. One single indicator does not prove that a suspicious transaction is money laundering. However, multiple red flags often exist, and a money launderer is typically identified from a combination of facts and events. The following list includes some red flags that may indicate money laundering:

- *Purchasing large assets or paying periodic expenses with cash.*
- *Purchasing property in the name of a nominee, such as an associate or a relative, or using different names on offers, closing documents, and deposit receipts.*
- *Purchasing personal use property under a corporate veil, whose ordinary business is inconsistent with this type of transaction.*
- *Using a post office box or general delivery address instead of a home address when dealing with contracts.*
- *Owning expensive assets without legitimate means of being able to afford them—exhibiting signs of unexplained wealth.*
- *Conducting suspicious banking activities such as excessive use of cashier's checks or money orders.*
- *A business that does not appear to produce a sustainable amount of legitimate income.*
- *A person who is secretive about his or her occupation yet seems to be living an extravagant lifestyle.*

As mentioned earlier, money laundering is often accompanied by other illegal behavior, so these red flags may correspond with those as well. Due to the many methods used to launder money, looking for specific red flags may not be successful in detecting laundering schemes. Thus, those attempting to detect money laundering must be aware of various schemes, red flags, and related illegal activities to be successful.

Review of the Learning Objectives

- **Explain why fraud is so prevalent in bankruptcy, tax, and divorce cases.** Many people hope to maintain assets while minimizing debts. Thus, they often conceal assets or income that could be taken from them in divorce or bankruptcy cases.

Tax frauds are prevalent because people are too aggressive in their attempts to minimize tax liabilities.

- **Describe the nature of bankruptcy and be familiar with bankruptcy codes.** Bankruptcy is the legal process that allows a debtor to work out an orderly plan to settle debts or liquidates a debtor's assets and distributes them to creditors. Title 11 of the U.S. Code is referred to as the Bankruptcy Code and is a federal statute that governs the bankruptcy process in the United States.

- **Understand civil and criminal bankruptcy fraud statutes.** These statutes determine exactly what constitutes fraudulent activity regarding bankruptcy. They also prohibit specific behaviors of certain people involved in the bankruptcy process.

- **Identify the participants involved in the bankruptcy process.** Key participants have varying roles in the bankruptcy process. These key participants include the following: the bankruptcy court, U.S. Trustee, court-appointed or panel trustee, examiners, debtors, creditors, adjusters, and others.

- **Recognize different bankruptcy and divorce fraud schemes.** Bankruptcy and divorce fraud schemes often involve the intentional concealment of assets or income. A bust-out, or planned bankruptcy, is also a fraud scheme. Many means exist for concealing assets and income.

- **Understand how perpetrators fraudulently conceal and transfer assets and income in bankruptcies and divorces.** Perpetrators often conceal assets and income by transferring funds to another entity (often a related party), shipping inventory to an off-site location, not reporting sales on company records, making payments to fictitious individuals, and many other methods.

- **Define tax fraud and be familiar with common tax fraud schemes.** Tax fraud is the intentional violation of the known legal duty of voluntarily filing income tax returns and paying the correct amount of tax. Some of the most common tax fraud schemes include underreporting or omitting income, overstating the amount of deductions, keeping two sets of books, making false entries in books and records, claiming personal expenses as business expenses, claiming false deductions, hiding or transferring assets or income, and illegal money laundering schemes.

- **Understand how money laundering is used to commit fraud.** Money laundering is often related to other illegal activities. People or businesses that obtain money via illegal means must "clean" or "launder" the "dirty" money so it can be used freely in the economy. Knowing signs of money laundering often leads to the discovery of other illegal activity, and uncovering other illegal activities such as fraud can often help in the discovery of money laundering activities.

KEY TERMS

bankruptcy, p. 566
tax fraud, p. 567
divorce, p. 571
bankruptcy court, p. 573
Bankruptcy Code, p. 574
trustees, p. 577
debtor, p. 578
creditor, p. 578

bust-out, p. 579
chapter 7 bankruptcy,
  p. 580
chapter 11 bankruptcies,
  p. 580
chapter 13 bankruptcies,
  p. 580
money laundering, p. 582

QUESTIONS

Discussion Questions

1. Why is fraud so prevalent in bankruptcy and divorce cases?
2. What is bankruptcy? What are the most common types of bankruptcy?
3. What are some of the more relevant sections of the Bankruptcy Code related to fraud?
4. What is tax fraud?
5. When a bankruptcy takes place, who are the major participants involved?
6. What are some of the most common bankruptcy fraud schemes?
7. What are some of the most common divorce fraud schemes?
8. What are some of the most common tax fraud schemes?
9. What are some of the most common ways that fraud perpetrators conceal and transfer assets or income during bankruptcy and divorces?
10. What is a court-appointed or panel trustee?
11. What is an affidavit of proposed investigator?
12. Who usually initiates the filing of an application for retention of an investigator?
13. Why should fraud investigators involved in bankruptcy or divorce cases be careful about what they put in their report?
14. What is the CI Division of the IRS?

15. Is it necessary to report illegal income (such as embezzled money) on income tax returns?
16. What is money laundering?
17. How is money laundering related to other illegal activities or fraud?

True/False

1. Civil bankruptcy cases are usually investigated by the FBI and other law enforcement agencies.
2. A person acting as an officer in a bankruptcy case is prohibited from purchasing any property of the debtor's estate.
3. Fraudulent transfers can occur up to two years before the debtor files for bankruptcy.
4. Bust-out schemes usually involve the concealment of assets, sales proceeds, and inventory.
5. Concealment of assets typically occurs on a larger scale for individuals filing for bankruptcy protection than it does for businesses filing for protection.
6. Debtors in bankruptcy cases have the power to sue investigators over false accusations.
7. Chapter 11 bankruptcies represent complete liquidation or shutting down of a business.
8. A debtor is the person or entity who is subject to a bankruptcy filing.
9. Most divorce-related fraud cases are civil rather than criminal.
10. The purpose of civil laws is to "right a wrong" or send someone to jail or have them pay fines, whereas the purpose of criminal laws is to seek monetary remedies or recover stolen funds.
11. The retention of a fraud investigator in a bankruptcy case must always be approved by the bankruptcy court's judge.
12. A "planned bankruptcy" is usually referred to as a bust-out.
13. The IRS can add a 20 percent penalty to your tax bill for a careless mistake and a 75 percent penalty for tax fraud.
14. The U.S. tax system is based on voluntary compliance.
15. Americans should pay the least amount of taxes they legally owe.
16. The U.S. Department of Treasury is a branch of the IRS.
17. Tax fraud can be committed against state, federal, or local governments.
18. To work as an entry-level CI special agent, you must be at least 29 years of age.

Multiple Choice

1. Which of the following is *not* a type of tax fraud?
   a. Using a false SSN.
   b. Overstating income.
   c. Keeping two sets of financial books.
   d. Claiming a dependent when you do not have one.

2. Which of the following describes a Chapter 13 bankruptcy?
   a. All assets are liquidated and used to pay creditors.
   b. Reorganizations can be used by individuals with debts less than $1 million.
   c. The entity is given time to reorganize its financial affairs, settle debts, and continue operations.
   d. Debtors receive all their payments up front from liquidated assets.

3. Bankruptcy courts do *not* have which of the following responsibilities?
   a. Appointing trustees, examiners, and committees.
   b. Supervising bankruptcy petitions.
   c. Approving reorganization plans.
   d. Conducting hearings and trials to resolve disputes.

4. Which of the following is *not* a characteristic of an affidavit of proposed investigator?
   a. Content and extent of detail required do not vary by jurisdiction.
   b. Is prepared when a fraud investigator is retained.
   c. Legal document is sworn under oath and must be notarized.
   d. Addressed to the court and is submitted by an attorney for the person who engaged the investigator.

5. Which of the following is the least likely symptom of a bust-out?
   a. Company's only listed address is a post office box.
   b. Dramatic increase in size of credit orders.
   c. Public notice of change in management.
   d. Sudden decrease in inventory.

6. Which of the following is the major reason why there is so much divorce fraud?
   a. Assets are being taken away from one divorce partner and given to another.
   b. Divorce proceedings usually take a long time.
   c. States make divorces very difficult.
   d. Children usually get most assets in divorce cases.

7. Which of the following investigative methods would most likely be used more in divorce cases than in bankruptcy cases?
   a. Surveillance.
   b. Public records searches.
   c. Subpoena of private records.
   d. Interviews.

8. The person appointed by a bankruptcy judge in a Chapter 11 proceeding who investigates allegations of fraud or misconduct by the debtor or its principals is a(n):
   a. Creditor.
   b. Adjuster.
   c. Auditor.
   d. Examiner.

9. The retention of a fraud investigator in a bankruptcy proceeding must be approved by the bankruptcy judge unless:
   a. The debtor's estate pays the investigator.
   b. The trustee pays the investigator.
   c. The creditors' committee pays the investigator.
   d. An individual creditor or shareholder pays the investigator.

10. Which of the following is *not* an indicator of a possible bust-out?
    a. An address that is a post office box.
    b. New ownership of a company.
    c. Slow buildup of inventory.
    d. Dramatic increase in the size of credit orders.

11. Which of the following is an indicator of possible hiding of assets in a divorce?
    a. Assets transferred to an off-site location.
    b. Changing the title to assets.
    c. Payments made to fictitious individuals.
    d. All of the above are indicators of possible hiding of assets.

12. Which of the following is *not* a way that individuals can commit tax fraud?
    a. Overstating the amount of deductions.
    b. Keeping two sets of books.
    c. Paying the least amount of taxes the individual owes.
    d. Making false entries in books and records.

13. The Criminal Investigation Division's chief responsibility is to:
    a. Detect taxpayers who willfully and intentionally violate their known legal duty of voluntarily filing an income tax return.
    b. Check the accuracy of tax returns.

   c.　Detect fraud in public corporations' tax filings.

   d.　Detect fraud in U.S. citizens' tax filings.

14. Which of the following is *not* an example of tax fraud?

   a.　Using a false SSN.

   b.　Keeping two sets of financial books.

   c.　Reporting information regarding passive income.

   d.　Claiming a blind spouse as a dependent when you are single.

15. If an audit reveals that an individual has underpaid his or her taxes, the auditor:

   a.　Can assess civil fines.

   b.　Can assess penalties.

   c.　Can refer the case to the CI Division.

   d.　An auditor can do all of the above.

16. To work as an entry-level CI special agent,

   a.　You must be a U.S. citizen.

   b.　You must not be older than 37 years of age.

   c.　You must have completed a four-year course of study or earned a bachelor's degree.

   d.　You must meet all of the above conditions.

SHORT CASES

Case 1

Willy and Buck Forsythe are brothers who often engage in shady business deals and regularly swindle honest people out of their money. Willy and Buck have decided to take their business to a new level. There is a small hardware store in town with a good reputation for honesty and friendly service. With the large amounts of money they have accumulated from other schemes, Willy and Buck decide to buy the hardware store. They make the owner an offer he can't refuse, and they are soon in the hardware business.

As new managers of the store, Willy and Buck make some changes. They begin to order bigger shipments from suppliers, paying them off promptly, using money acquired through loans. They sell off a lot of these shipments at cost to their unruly friend, Billy the Kid. As orders get larger and payments remain prompt, the suppliers are willing to extend more and more credit to the hardware store. Also, because it appears that business is good, the bank is willing to lend more money.

Things are going just as planned for our crooked friends, Willy and Buck. Just as they had planned to do all along, when they have a lot of money on loan from the bank and have just sold huge amounts of inventory to Billy that they had purchased on credit, they file for bankruptcy. The suppliers and the bank are perplexed. Upon investigation, they find that Willy and Buck have neither the money to pay them back nor the inventory to liquidate in order to pay them. Willy and Buck have successfully "sold" their inventory or hidden their cash in other bank accounts, so it appears they don't have the means to pay back their creditors. What kind of scheme are Willy and Buck involved in, and how could the bank and the suppliers have detected it sooner?

Case 2

You have been asked by a small credit union to help investigate an alleged fraud in a bankruptcy case in which it is involved. It wants you to start right away because it is worried that the debtor will destroy evidence vital to the case. The credit union has not received permission from the judge involved in the case to contract you, but it tells you that if you find fraud, there will be no problem with the judge. What should your response to this be?

Case 3

You have been hired as a fraud auditor to examine the assets of a company that recently filed for Chapter 11 bankruptcy. The company manufactures and sells circuit boards for children's computerized toys. You have access to its financial statements and warehouses. The company is a closely held corporation. The company is suspected of fraudulently concealing assets. Give three red flags that you would look for to indicate fraudulent asset concealment.

Case 4

Colleen Matthews had just turned 22 when her hard work finally started to pay off. Six months earlier, Colleen had graduated from a state university with a master's degree in accounting. Colleen graduated with honors and was one of the youngest in her class. Unlike most of the intellectuals she had studied with throughout her career, Colleen was extremely social and had great communication skills. After graduation, she took a job with a well-known regional accounting firm. The firm specialized in assisting companies with their technology problems. Colleen knew that the connections and knowledge she would gain working for the firm would be beneficial throughout her career. Now, six months after graduation, she has a full-time job offer with one of the firm's strongest clients.

Within a few days on her new job, Colleen had adapted to her new environment. Colleen and two other recent graduates were running the entire accounting department. However, it wasn't long until Colleen began to notice that something wasn't right. After a few weeks, Colleen realized that the firm's executives were participating in illegal transactions. The company executives were importing expensive technological products from China and selling them under the table to contacts unknown to Colleen. Once the firm received the products at the shipping dock, the executives' "personal employees" marked the products and took them to a separate location. The entire operation was done with little paperwork. The money received from the special products received special attention. Colleen was told to report this inflow of cash in an account called "Personal Executive Consulting Services." This allowed the executives to personally use the money at their convenience.

1. Does Colleen have a responsibility to report the apparent fraud?
2. If so, to whom should she report the fraud?
3. Assuming that the fraud has been continuing for several years, what would be the tax ramifications to the executives of not reporting earnings on their tax returns?
4. Even though the money is from illegal sources, are the executives required to report the income on their annual tax returns?
5. Earlier in the book, we discussed the net worth method. How do you think the net worth method can help prosecutors determine the extent of these executives' illegal income?

Case 5

Trek, Inc., has experienced two bad financial years, resulting in too few assets remaining to pay creditors in full. Trek, Inc., wants to file for bankruptcy. What are its options, and which one would be best for Trek, Inc.?

Case 6

Suppose you are working with the CI Division of the IRS. You have recently been assigned to a case that involves a $3 million tax evasion scandal. The IRS discovered the case when it was performing a routine audit. Because the IRS believed that the case involved fraud, the IRS agent referred the case to the CI Division, which has now assigned the case to you. After investigating the case, you determine that it involves significant fraud. Before prosecuting the case further, you want to review the specific laws under which fraud perpetrators are charged.

1. Identify the specific laws under which tax fraud perpetrators can be charged.

2. Explain how each of these laws relates to tax fraud.
3. In prosecuting fraud, are some laws more applicable than others? Are all of the laws you listed broken when tax fraud occurs? Why or why not?

Case 7

In the fall of 2001, Enron, the eighth largest corporation in the United States, declared bankruptcy unexpectedly, and investors lost approximately $60 billion. From your reading about this famous case, did Enron's bankruptcy involve fraud? If so, what type?

Case 8

Your best friend Sue has always wanted to be an FBI agent for the U.S. government. However, because of the recent restructured changes in the FBI (due to the increased terrorism threat), Sue is uncertain whether she wants to pursue an FBI career. She feels that the FBI does not provide as much career security as she once thought that it did. Sue is excellent with numbers, taxes, law, and communication. After reading about the CI Division of the IRS in this chapter, you are excited to tell Sue about it.

1. Explain the purpose and mission of the CI Division.
2. Explain what other governmental agencies the CI Division works with.
3. Explain the requirements for an entry-level CI special agent.

Case 9

John Dewey is the husband of Mary Dewey. He is also the CEO of a large public relations firm. Mary recently filed for divorce, alleging mental brutality, and is asking for half of John's and the couple's assets. In the six months prior to being served for divorce, John had taken business trips to the Cayman Islands, Switzerland, Hong Kong, and Barbados. These were the first business-related trips he had ever made to these locations. When John's and the couple's assets were identified during the divorce proceedings, Mary was surprised to learn that John's and his company's net worth totaled only $50,000 and that her half would only be $25,000. She was very disappointed because, up until the divorce, John had been giving her $200,000 per year to spend. What kind of fraud is most likely occurring in this case?

Case 10

As mentioned in the chapter, lawyers, creditors, and trustees can often be involved in bankruptcy fraud.

Read the letter at http://www.clr.org/Safford6c04.html. It was written by a debtor to the U.S. Attorney's office. List the individuals the debtor accuses, these individuals' roles in the bankruptcy proceedings, and the fraudulent behavior of which the debtor accuses them.

Case 11

Look up the U.S. Trustee Program's 2009 Annual Report at http://www.justice.gov/ust/eo/public_affairs/annualreport/docs/ar2009.pdf.

1. How is a trustee defined (p. 1)?
2. What are the functions of the trustee program (p. 1)?
3. The program routinely hires bankruptcy analysts of what two certifications (p. 3)?
4. What initiative did the program launch in 2001 (p. 7)? For what purpose?
5. What specific actions can the program take under this initiative?
6. According to the report, with what other crimes is bankruptcy fraud often connected (p. 21)?
7. The trustee program refers criminal cases to the district attorney's office. The report separates these referrals into six categories. List the categories and provide a one-sentence description of each type of scheme.
8. List the ten duties of a U.S. Trustee (p. 31)?

Case 12

Attorney Mark E. of Newport, Virginia, pleaded guilty to wire fraud in the Eastern District of Virginia, based on his actions of embezzling from a client in Chapter 13 bankruptcy. Mark embezzled more than $22,000 intended for payment to the client's mortgage holders under the Chapter 13 plan. Evidence of the embezzlement came to light when the debtor client complained to the Chapter 13 trustee, who notified the Newport office. After investigating, the U.S. Trustee filed a civil complaint against Mark seeking disgorgement of all fees paid by the debtor, an accounting of all monies received, a surcharge for all late fees and penalties levied against the debtor by his mortgage companies, and disbarment from practice before the bankruptcy court. During discovery, which included subpoenaing Mark's trust account records, further misconduct was discovered in unrelated cases. The allegations in the U.S. Trustee's civil complaint formed the basis of his criminal indictment. Before the criminal trial, Mark agreed to disbarment for at least five years. Which section of the Bankruptcy Code makes Mark's activities illegal?

Case 13

After a jury trial, Charles H. and his parents, Charles M. and Helen J. of White Plains, New York, were found guilty on charges of theft of public funds, wire fraud, bankruptcy fraud, and money laundering conspiracy. The charges arose from the family's schemes to defraud and their use of bankruptcy proceedings to further those schemes. Both father and son were convicted of concealing assets from the bankruptcy trustee and creditors and making false statements under penalty of perjury. The father was also found guilty of transferring approximately $489,000 from his brokerage account to an account in the Bahamas in contemplation of bankruptcy, and the mother was found to have engaged in bankruptcy fraud by receiving property in her name to defeat the bankruptcy laws. The White Plains office assisted in the investigation and preparation for the bankruptcy aspects of the trial. If the father was to be prosecuted criminally, what fact would have to hold regarding his transfer of money?

Case 14

BBB Company has been a successful manufacturer of quality electronics products for the past 20 years. It is a publicly traded company with 1 million shares outstanding. During the past three years, the company has fallen on hard times. Profit margins in the electronics manufacturing industry have been squeezed due to competition in Japan. For most of the company's history, research and development (R&D) costs have been a substantial portion of expenses. However, in the last three years, there have not been any R&D expenses. This may have led to the decline in perception of quality, for which customers have expressed concern.

Suppliers have also been complaining that BBB Company has bought increasing amounts of inventory on credit and has pressured them to loosen credit terms. However, the company shows a decreasing inventory over the last three years as sales have declined. Recently, the company CFO talked the local bank into increasing BBB's credit limit, and the company has used its entire line of credit. The CFO convinced the bankers that the current downturn in sales was temporary and that the company had a new product line that would be very lucrative.

With all its financial pressures, BBB recently decided to file for bankruptcy. It cannot cover the interest payments on loans, nor can it meet its growing accounts payable balance. As creditors begin to seek monetary recovery through assets, they discover that there seems to be very little inventory, and expenses seem extraordinarily high in the current year. Also, some cash (from loans) has disappeared without leaving a paper trail.

1. What evidence indicates that the company has been planning to declare bankruptcy? If so, for how many years?
2. If this bankruptcy was fraudulently planned and assets have disappeared, will BBB Company still be allowed to declare bankruptcy?

Case 15

Liz Clayton, supermodel and wife of Andrew Dyce, better known as Flash, lead guitarist and vocalist for the popular heavy metal band Flash Metal, is filing for divorce. Each cited that their careers kept them separated and that they have drifted apart over the 12 years of their marriage. The divorce settlement was quick, and both sides were pleased. Little did Liz know that Flash had been concealing assets from her over the past year. Liz didn't know much about Flash Metal, including who the current and past members were. Over the 20 years that Flash Metal has been a group, musicians have come and gone with only one original person still in the band, Flash.

When the marriage started to get rocky, Flash decided to hide some assets from Liz just in case of divorce. Over the past six months while Flash Metal was on its record-breaking world tour, Flash would take his concert profits and make a check out to a past band member to hide his income from Liz. After the divorce was settled, the checks were voided, and Flash had successfully hidden $1.2 million from his unsuspecting wife. What could Liz have done to avoid being swindled by her ex-husband?

Case 16

Bill and Sue were college students when they met each other in the library and began dating. After a few short months, they decided to get married. After a time of marital bliss, both Bill and Sue discovered the relationship was not what they had planned. Bill did not like Sue's candles and stuffed animals with which she insisted on filling the house, and Sue did not care for Bill's habit of spending all his money on the lottery. So, after a few failed attempts at reconciling the marriage, both concluded that divorce would be best. Each agreed to split their assets 50–50.

Due to Sue's displeasure in seeing lottery tickets cluttering the house, Bill kept most of the tickets inside his desk on campus. A few months before the divorce,

one of Bill's lottery tickets hit the jackpot, giving him a little under $1 million. Instead of depositing the money into the couple's joint account, he hid it by creating a different bank account. Bill never brought up the news to Sue, and the court did not find out about the money during the court proceedings.

1. What type of fraud did Bill commit?
2. What can Sue do about this situation?

Case 17

John and Sally have recently been experiencing serious marital problems. They are seeing a counselor in order to "save their marriage." During the past several months, John has been selling their recreational assets including an expensive boat, snowmobiles, four-wheelers, and a cabin in the beautiful Smoky Mountains. John has been selling all these toys to his friend Sam for extremely low prices. Sally believes his story that he is selling them because they are hard up for money and that he is putting the money into their savings account. However, she does not know who has been purchasing the assets. She is shocked during the divorce to find out that there is very little money in the savings account. Where had it all gone? She had never paid much attention to the finances and had trusted John completely.

1. In what kind of scheme are John and Sam involved?
2. How could Sally verify that the assets were actually sold?
3. What are some possible motivations for John to sell the recreational assets at extremely low prices?

Case 18

Go to the homepage for the U.S. Department of Justice Office of Justice Programs and find the July 2003 Bureau of Justice Statistics' Special Report on "Money Laundering Offenders, 1994–2001." It can be found at http://bjs.ojp.usdoj.gov/index.cfm?ty=pbdetail&iid=790. Read the report and answer the following questions:

1. Which federal judicial district had the "largest number of matters referred with money laundering as most serious charge" in 2001? How many money laundering matters were referred in that district?
2. Within the U.S. Department of Defense and the Department of Treasury, what are some of the investigative agencies that look into money laundering?

3. What are the main money laundering and related federal legislation acts in the United States?

4. What is the total number of cases adjudicated in U.S. district court with money laundering as the most serious offense in 2001? What percent of those cases led to a conviction? What was the average prison sentence imposed for defendants convicted of money laundering?

CASE STUDIES

Case Study 1

Hotel worker Danny Ruiz was living with his wife and four children in a cramped New York apartment when he saw a television ad promising the family a way out. "Why rent when you can own your own home?" Pennsylvania builder Gene Percudani asked. The company even offered to pay his rent for a year, while he saved for a down payment. So the Ruiz family fled the city for the Pocono Mountains, where they bought a three-bedroom Cape Cod home in 1999 for $171,000. However, when they tried to refinance less than two years later, the home was valued at just $125,000. "I just about flipped," said Mr. Ruiz. Later Mrs. Ruiz remarked about her husband, "He went nuts."

Percudani, a 51-year-old native of Queens, New York, built a thriving homebuilding business in this market, running folksy television ads offering New Yorkers new homes in Pennsylvania. If they joined Percudani's program, called "Why Rent," homeowners would find financing through another of his companies, Chapel Creek Mortgage, which brokered loans from J. P. Morgan Chase and the company's Chase Manhattan Mortgage unit.

For years, the "Why Rent" program appealed to workers with modest salaries, such as Eberht Rios, a truck driver for UPS. Rios bought a home in the Poconos for $140,000. This year, when he tried to refinance, he was told the home was valued at only $100,000. One local appraiser, Dominick Stranieri, signed off on most of the "Why Rent" deals that state officials now say were overpriced, including the Rios and Ruiz homes. Percudani's firm picked Stranieri as his appraiser because of his quick work and low fee of $250, instead of the typical $300 to $400. In exchange for a steady stream of work, Mr. Stranieri accepted without question valuations from Percudani's company.

Other common methods of creating revenues include investors and others buying distressed properties and then, using inflated appraisals, selling them for a big profit. In order to secure the efforts of a "dirty appraiser," those involved with the fraud would pay up to $1,500 under the table on top of the appraiser's standard fee of $400.

Another unique twist to the plot is that few of the people involved in making mortgage loans have a long-term interest in them. Traditionally, bankers made loans directly and held them, giving the lenders a strong incentive to find fair appraisals to protect their interest. Today, however, many appraisers are picked by independent mortgage brokers, who are paid per transaction and have little stake in the long-term health of the loans. Many lenders have also lost a long-term interest in their loans, because they sell them off to investors. Appraisers increasingly fear that if they don't go along with higher valuations sought by brokers, their business will dry up.

Do you think a county appraiser would do a lot better than a private practitioner? Joel Marcus, a New York-based attorney recently had his property valued at $2.2 million by a county appraiser, up from $2 million the previous year, which means a $7,200 jump in his property tax bill. Based on recent home sales in his neighborhood, Marcus believes his property is valued at between $1.7 million and $1.8 million. Based on this information, Marcus has appealed his appraisal.

Although a good appraisal requires doing hours of legwork, visiting a property to check its condition, and coming up with at least three comparable sales, Percudani says he isn't surprised that later appraisals, or even different appraisals made at the same time, could result in different values. "Appraisals are opinions," he says. "Value, like beauty, is in the eye of the beholder." Stranieri and Percudani deny any wrongdoing and say they operated independently and that any home that declined in value did so because of a weak economy. "It's like buying a stock," Percudani says in an interview. "The value goes up. The value goes down."

Questions

1. How is an opportunity created to commit appraisal fraud? Does the appraiser act alone, or is collusion routinely involved?

2. How is appraisal fraud detected? Is intent to deceive easy to prove in appraisal fraud?

3. What pressures or perceived pressures can motivate appraisers to make faulty valuations?

4. How do appraisers rationalize their fraudulent behavior?

5. Why would a county perceive pressure to fraudulently inflate property values?
6. What controls would help to prevent appraisal fraud?
7. What natural controls exist to prevent homeowners from the desire to "massage the value" of their homes? (*Hint:* Think about a homeowner's motivation.)

INTERNET ASSIGNMENTS

1. Visit the IRS's bankruptcy site at http://www.irs.gov/compliance/enforcement/article/0,,id=117520,00.html and answer the following questions:
   a. What percentage of bankruptcy petitions does the IRS estimate contain some kind of fraud?
   b. What are the major goals of the CI Division's bankruptcy fraud program?
   c. Read two or three examples of bankruptcy fraud and be prepared to discuss them in class.

END NOTES

1. Sun Staff and Wire Reports, "Vegas Casino Figure Jailed after Bankruptcy Fraud Conviction," *Las Vegas Sun* (April 17, 2001).

2. 2009 IRS Data Book Web site accessed August 28, 2010. http://www.irs.gov/pub/irs-soi/09databk.pdf

3. Tozzi, John. "Identity Theft: The Business Bust-Out," Bloomberg Businessweek (July 23, 2007).

4. *The Cash Connection: Organized Crime, Financial Institutions and Money Laundering* (Presidential Commission on Organized Crime, October 1984).

5. See http://www.fatf-gafi.org/document/28/0,3343,en_32250379_32236920_33658140_1_1_1_1,00.html, FATF Web site accessed September 25, 2010.

Affidavit of Proposed Investigator

UNITED STATES BANKRUPTCY COURT
WESTERN DISTRICT OF TEXAS

In the Matter

of

ARCHIBALD, WALL & CO.

Debtor.

No. X5-30870-BKC-RAM

AFFIDAVIT FOR RETENTION

AS INVESTIGATOR

FOR THE EXAMINER

STATE OF TEXAS   )
) **SS:**
COUNTY OF SAGE   )

MARY JONES, being duly sworn, deposes and says:

1. THAT I am a Certified Fraud Examiner (CFE) or Certified Public Accountant (CPA), licensed under the laws of the State of Texas and a member of the firm of Jones, Sally, & Doo, LLP with offices at 950 N. Beacon Street, Monroe, Texas 77034.

2. THAT neither deponent nor any member of deponent's firm is related to or has any business association with the debtor, the examiner, or the official Creditors' Committee except that our firm may have been retained in other matters in which some of the aforementioned persons may have been parties.

3. THAT deponent's firm maintains offices in Monroe, Texas. Total personnel numbers approximately 45 of whom nine are partners. Applicant has been known for many years for its expertise in accounting practice as related to the field of bankruptcy and fraud investigation, and has frequently been requested to serve in such matters by the legal, financial and business community.

4. THAT deponent has surveyed the books and records of the debtor and is familiar with the matter and is familiar with the work to be done. That work is contemplated to be the following:

   a. Review of incorporation documents and other documents of the Debtor related to the formation and operation of the Debtor and consideration of whether they indicate that two separate entities were one entity.

   b. Investigation of the circumstances of the Debtor's obtaining of bank loans, including review of bank loan applications and related documents and financial statements submitted in obtaining the loans, and interviews of bank officials about the loan applications.

c. Tracing of the disposition of loan proceeds and transfers of certain assets.

d. Investigation of the Debtor's accounts receivable collection effort, including analysis of accounts receivable history, write-offs, setoffs, and collections, and review of the collectibility of account balances.

e. Interviews of current or former principals of the Debtor with respect to the foregoing matters.

f. Provision of litigation consulting services and expert witness testimony if necessary and requested by examiner.

g. Performance of other services as requested by the examiner consistent with professional standards to aid the examiner in its investigation of the debtor.

5. THAT in addition to the foregoing, the firms of JONES, SALLY, & DOO, LLP may be required to attend before the Bankruptcy Court with respect to the acts and conduct of the Debtor.

6. THAT the cost of the foregoing services is based on the following current hourly rates:

Partner	$250 per hour
Senior	$100 per hour
Paraprofessional	$ 30 per hour

7. ACTUAL and necessary out-of-pocket expenses will be incurred in connection with the rendition of these services. These will be billed separately in addition to the above.

WHEREFORE, your deponent respectfully requests that an Order be entered authorizing the retention of JONES, SALLY, & DOO, LLP to perform the above mentioned services.

_____

MARY JONES

Sworn to before me this

10th day of May 2003

_____

NOTARY PUBLIC

APPENDIX **B**

Application for Retention
of Investigator

Phillip Gallagher, Esq.

GALLAGHER, JOHNSON & SMITH

P.O. Box 75609

Sage, Texas 76031

ATTORNEYS FOR GEORGE SMITH, EXAMINER

IN THE UNITED STATES BANKRUPTCY COURT

FOR THE WESTERN DISTRICT OF TEXAS

IN RE: §

                                           §

ARCHIBALD, WALL & CO., PA   §   CASE NO. X5-30870-BKC-RAM

                                           §

DEBTOR.   §

APPLICATION FOR AUTHORITY TO

EMPLOY INVESTIGATOR FOR THE EXAMINER

TO THE HONORABLE Linda Alright, U.S. BANKRUPTCY JUDGE:

COMES NOW, George Smith, the Court-appointed Examiner herein ("Examiner"), by and through his counsel, and files this his Application for Authority to Employ Investigator for the Examiner ("Application"), and in support thereof would respectfully show this Court as follows:

1. On March 15, 2003, Archibald, Wall & Co., PA ("Debtor") filed its voluntary petition under Chapter 11 of the Bankruptcy Code ("Code"), 11 U.S.C. §§ 101, et seq., thereby commencing the above-captioned bankruptcy case. Thereafter, on May 5, 2003, George Smith was appointed the Examiner of the Debtor's estate and continues to act in that capacity.

2. Your Examiner requests authority to employ the firm of Jones, Sally, & Doo, LLP (the "Firm").

3. Your Examiner has selected the Firm for the reason that it has had considerable experience in matters of this nature and he believes that the Firm is well qualified to provide him with investigation services in his capacity as Examiner.

4. The professional services, which the Firm is anticipated to render, include: (a) to provide the Examiner with litigation consulting and forensic accounting services in connection with allegations of bank fraud and bankruptcy fraud by current or former principals of the Debtor; (b) to provide financial analysis in connection with the write-

offs and collectibility of accounts receivable balances of the Debtor estate; (c) to investigate the disposition and transfers of certain loan proceeds and assets for possible fraudulent transfers; (d) to provide evidence for determining whether there is cause for the appointment of a trustee; and (e) to perform all other investigation services for your Examiner which may be, or become, necessary herein.

5.   As evidenced by the Affidavit of Proposed Investigator . . . and to the best of your Examiner's knowledge, the Firm has no relationship that would raise a possible disqualification or conflict of interest. Consequently, the employment of the Firm is in compliance with § 327 of the Code.

6.   Your Examiner believes that the employment of the Firm would be in the best interest of this estate by providing your Examiner with the necessary and beneficial services set forth in paragraph four (4) above.

WHEREFORE, PREMISES CONSIDERED, your Examiner respectfully requests that this Court enter an Order authorizing him to employ Jones, Sally, & Doo, LLP as Investigator of the Examiner in this bankruptcy proceeding; and for such other and further relief to which he may be justly entitled.

Respectfully submitted,

GALLAGHER, JOHNSON & SMITH

By:_____

Phillip Gallagher, Esq.

CHAPTER **17**

Fraud in E-Commerce

LEARNING OBJECTIVES

After studying this chapter, you should be able to:

- Understand e-commerce fraud risk.
- Take measures to prevent fraud in e-commerce.
- Detect e-business fraud.

TO THE STUDENT

E-commerce fraud is one of the most significant problems in business today. As you read this chapter, consider the skills required for e-commerce fraud detection and investigation. Many students find it an exciting field to specialize in because of its highly technical nature and its need for the modern application of fraud principles. It is one way you can specialize and differentiate from other fraud examiners. Use this chapter as a high-level overview of this type of work and as a starting point to more in-depth books.

James, Vijay, and Em became good friends through their group work in MBA school; after graduation, they decided to start an Internet business together. After careful research, they started an online store selling anti-spam software. Sales were slow for the first year, and the business was in danger of failing. Vijay, a marketing major, contacted Google, Bing, and several other search engines and purchased advertisements linked to specific search terms.

Initially, the advertising campaign went very well. During the first few weeks, Vijay's advertisement campaign generated a 1–2 percent click-through rate (CTR), meaning that 1–2 percent of users clicked on his advertisement link when it was presented in search results pages. Vijay knew he had to pay a few dollars or cents each time a potential customer clicked on his advertisement links, but felt this cost was more than offset in the resulting purchases of anti-spam software.

Imagine Vijay's surprise when he returned from an extended vacation and found that his campaign statistics had jumped from 1 to 2 percent to an abnormal 35–40 percent CTR! At first he was elated, but then he realized something must be amiss. Overall sales had not changed, and Web site traffic had remained relatively stable.

Vijay had been a victim of click-through fraud. Although names have been changed, this fraud occurred in a real firm with several large search engines. Click-through fraud occurs when a competitor or an adverse individual repetitively clicks advertisement links with no intention of purchasing products or services at the target site. Advanced implementations of this fraud use custom scripts and robots to quickly generate enormous numbers of clicks. These robots can impersonate different IP addresses through the use of anonymizers and different browsers through faked user agents. They fool search engines into thinking each click is a unique user. Click-through frauds can cost businesses tens or even hundreds of thousands of dollars if they are allowed to continue over time.[1]

Although its growth occurred only about 20 years ago, the Internet has become a foundation part of modern society. From business home pages to informational wikis to social networking sites, it has permeated almost every aspect of professional and individual life. Consider how its adoption compares with other technological advances. It took radio more than 35 years and television 15 years to reach 60 million people; it took just 3 years for the Internet to reach over 90 million people. The Internet is now available in most homes, businesses, and mobile devices. When Jack Welch (former CEO of General Electric) was asked where the Internet ranks in priority in his company, he responded that "it's numbers 1, 2, 3 and 4."[2]

This technology revolution has provided perpetrators with new ways to commit and conceal fraud and to convert their ill-gotten gains. It has challenged regulators, educators, and fraud examiners to keep up with both technological and cultural advances. New opportunities exist in the consumer Internet and in e-business networks. Essentially, **e-business**[3] uses information technology (IT) and electronic communication networks to exchange business information and conduct paperless transactions. While most consumers primarily use Web browsers to access the Internet, businesses routinely connect to one another over Internet lines through e-business connections, virtual private networks (VPNs), and other specialized connections. For example, even if you only purchase items at local stores and conduct transactions with your local bank in person, an Internet transaction occurs each time you purchase with a credit card or conduct a bank transaction. Even though you are not using the Internet, the businesses you interact with use it continually. Because most businesses rely on Internet-based transactions, many fraud examiners are consulted for fraud information related to e-commerce.

In this chapter, we discuss unique aspects of e-business fraud, risks specific to e-business, and ways to prevent electronic fraud. We discuss e-business fraud detection briefly, but do not discuss fraud investigation in detail because technology-based methods are beyond the scope of this book. However, remember that the processes used to investigate e-business fraud are the same as those for other frauds. The specific tasks used to detect e-business fraud may require more technical knowledge, but the overall process is the same. Once you understand the risks inherent in this new area of fraud, you will know where to target your detection efforts and how to involve advanced forensic specialists in the process.

STOP & THINK   *How has the Internet changed your day-to-day life? What security precautions do you take each time you use the Internet?*

Fraud Risks in E-Commerce

Although fraud can occur in any environment, several aspects of e-business environments present unique risks. These characteristics of the Internet-driven economy create pressures and opportunities specific to e-commerce fraud. Just like other frauds, these new frauds are perpetrated when pressures, opportunities, and rationalizations come together. E-commerce elements that create increased or unique risks are listed in Table 17.1.

E-Commerce Risks Inside Organizations

Many of the most serious e-commerce fraud risks are found within organizations. Once perpetrators are within firewalls and security checks, it is much easier to infiltrate systems, steal money and information, and cause damage. Perpetrators with inside access know the control environment, understand security mechanisms, and find ways to bypass security. One of the most serious problems is the abuse of power that has been granted to users. For example, programmers and technical support personnel usually have full, superuser access to the systems they create and administrate. Often, removal of programmer access is overlooked when systems go into production, allowing them free and unlimited access of corporate data years into the future. In one survey, more than a third of network administrators admitted to snooping into human resource records, layoff lists, and custom

databases[4] A related survey found that 88 percent of administrators would take sensitive data if they were fired, and 33 percent said they would take company password lists.[5]

The theft of money is usually the primary goal in traditional fraud. In the electronic environment, the **data theft** is normally the first concern because data have many useful attributes. First, they can be converted to cash fairly easy. For example, stolen personal information about customers can be sold or misused, and individuals can be blackmailed. Second, information is replicable, allowing the perpetrator to simply copy data rather than remove them as traditional fraud would require. Theft acts often leave very few tracks because the source data remain intact and usable. The easy replication of data is one reason that e-commerce frauds often go undetected for long periods of time—unless companies are carefully monitoring access logs, they will not notice the act of replication. Third, data can be transferred easily and quickly to any location in the world. If perpetrators use cell phones or other private connections to the Internet to transfer data, detection can be very difficult. Finally, many managers lack the technical expertise to prevent and detect data theft. IT managers and assurance providers need to be aware of the critical points in e-business infrastructures at which data can be stolen.

Even if a perpetrator does not have personal access to needed systems, he or she can hijack others' passwords to achieve access. **Passwords** can be the Achilles' heel of many systems because password selection is left to the end user and cannot be fully controlled. Mothers' maiden names, birthdays of children, favorite locations, and other personal information used to generate passwords can be guessed by perpetrators when fraud is internal and employees know each other personally. Hackers often use **social engineering** techniques to gain access to passwords. Instant messaging, blog entries, Facebook walls, and other social networking devices provide perpetrators with a new method of gathering information. When a hacker presents valid information to a user and asks for "just a little more," some users think the request is appropriate. For example, a hacker may call a targeted user and pose as technical support. Statements like the following place users in a position of urgency and unease, and they often lead users to take risks and provide information:

Hi. This is technical support in room 415. We have been monitoring your account all day, and it appears

TABLE 17.1 ELEMENTS OF FRAUD RISK IN E-COMMERCE

Pressures
- Dramatic growth, which has created tremendous cash flow needs.
- Merger or acquisition activity, which creates pressures to "improve the reported financial results."
- Borrowing or issuing stock; additional pressures to "cook the books."
- New products, which require intensive and expensive marketing and for which an existing market does not yet exist.
- Unproven or flawed business models, with tremendous cash flow pressures.

Opportunities
- New and innovative technologies for which security developments often lag transaction developments.
- Complex information systems that make installing controls difficult.
- The transfer of large amounts of information, a factor that poses theft and identity risks such as illegal monitoring and unauthorized access.
- Removal of personal contact, which allows for easier impersonation or falsified identity.
- Lack of "brick-and-mortar" and other physical facilities that facilitate falsifying Web sites and business transactions.
- Inability to distinguish large and/or established companies from new and/or smaller companies, making it easy to deceive customers by falsifying identity and/or business descriptions.
- Electronic transfer of funds, allowing large frauds to be committed more easily.
- Compromised privacy, which results in easier theft by using stolen or falsified information.

Increased Propensity to Rationalize
- The perceived distance that decreases the personal contact between customer and supplier.
- Transactions between anonymous or unknown buyers and sellers—you can't see who you are hurting.
- New economy thinking contends that traditional methods of accounting no longer apply.

that a hacker is trying to get into your account. If the hacker succeeds, it will start an investigation into your computer use, password selection, and use of company property. We need to stop this before it goes any further. Let's start by verifying your username and password. What is your exact username and password?

Even when corporate policies require periodic password changing, many users circumvent the intent by adding a sequential number or another character to the end of their old password. It is common to find a few employees who write their passwords down on sticky notes placed in their desk drawers or even on their computer monitors! In addition, in a world with increasing numbers of passwords, secret PINs, and account numbers to remember, many users reuse the same password from internal system to Internet site and from e-mail client to application login. If a perpetrator can discover a user's password to a relatively unprotected system, that password is likely useful in more secure systems.

Unencrypted communications between users often pose a threat that many employees do not appreciate. For example, although encrypted e-mail access has been available for decades, many users still check their mail using unencrypted Post Office Protocol 3 (POP3), Internet Message Access Protocol (IMAP), or other protocols. Since most e-mail clients log in and check for new mail every few minutes, perpetrators have significant opportunities to sniff passwords and infiltrate

systems. E-mail text is also not regularly encrypted, even if a user is using an encrypted connection to his or her server. Unless the e-mail text itself has been encrypted using Secure/Multipurpose Internet Mail Extensions (S/MIME) or another technology, the e-mail transfers in plain text from the sending server to the receiving server. **Sniffing** is the logging, filtering, and viewing of information that passes along a network line; it is a common method of gathering information from unencrypted communications. Sniffing is easily done on most networks by hackers that run freely available applications like Wireshark and tcpdump. Figure 17.1 shows a screen shot of the Wireshark software. Note that these applications have legitimate uses in activities like troubleshooting network problems, so the applications themselves are not the problem.

Even though firewalls, spam filters, and virus applications protect organizations from external attack, employee laptops and mobile devices present risks that are difficult to manage. For example, each time employees go on business trips, they connect their laptops to unprotected environments like hotel and other business networks. On these networks, computers can be exposed to viruses, spyware, and hackers that are often not as present in work networks. In addition, information on stolen laptops can provide significant opportunities for perpetrators. Finally, when employees return to the office from trips or home and plug their laptops back into the corporate network, they bypass firewalls and controls. Viruses, trojans, and worms are able

FIGURE 17.1   WIRESHARK SOFTWARE

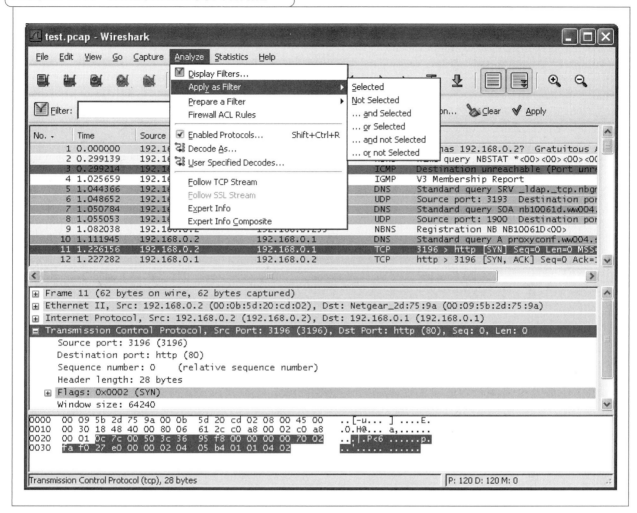

to enter protected areas because employees physically walk laptops from unprotected networks to protected networks.

One of the more recent scams for business travelers is called wartrapping. In this scam, hackers go to known business traveler locations like airports and set up access points through their laptops to the Internet. Their laptops look like regular wireless networks to which others can connect. When travelers open their laptops, their wireless cards connect automatically to these "free" Internet access points. Many travelers think they are connected to the airport's official wireless network, but they are actually passing network traffic through the hackers' computers. As the travelers browse the Internet, check e-mail, and use their corporate networks, the hackers sniff for passwords and other important information.

Recently, the advent of USB drives, increased memory on phones, and portable external hard drives poses security threats. Their large capacities allow them to quickly download significant amounts of information from internal networks. These devices, including camera phones and iPod-like music players, have been banned at many military installations because of the potential threat they pose. For example, when iPods first hit the market, a common tactic by customers at electronics stores was to connect iPods to a demonstration computer and quickly steal software like Microsoft Office. Because of the iPod's fast interface and ubiquitous appearance, stealing hundreds of megabytes of data could be done within just a few minutes.

Vandalism is always a risk with internal systems. From sophisticated denial-of-service attempts on local machines to deletion of files to physical damage, vandalism is an easy way for employees to harm internal systems. Vandalism can be obvious, or it can be very difficult to find—hiding for weeks or months before its effects are discovered.

E-Commerce Risks Outside Organizations

In 2009, hackers set a new high score for credit card theft by allegedly stealing 130 million credit cards at one location.[6] Albert Gonzalez, a 28-year-old, used SQL injections (described later in this chapter) to get around corporate firewalls and steal credit and debit card information. They attacked several companies, including convenience store chains, credit card processors, and supermarket chains. When federal agents raided his home, they found computers, firearms, expensive jewelry, and $1.1 million in cash buried in the backyard. While this case may be the largest in history, it is certainly not the only one; a web search for "hackers credit cards" yields many such stories of stolen credit cards.

The Internet provides a rich medium for external hackers to gain access to personal systems. Hackers are relatively protected because they cross international boundaries and are mostly anonymous—making tracking and prosecution difficult. When successful investigation and prosecution do occur, sentences are typically light and do little to deter would-be attackers. For example, Jeffrey Lee Parson, a 19-year-old who unleashed part of the MSBlast worm attack, received 18 to 37 months in prison. Jan de Wit, author of the Anna Kournikova virus, was required to complete 150 hours of community service in the Netherlands. These viruses infected millions of computers and caused significant damage, costs, and time loss worldwide.

Computer viruses must be taken seriously in today's e-commerce environment. Viruses come in three varieties. True viruses attach themselves to existing programs on a computer. Viruses were rampant during the 1980s and 1990s. They are still in existence today, but are used less by hackers. Today's largest threat is from Internet worms, self-contained programs that spread via direct transfer, e-mail, or another mechanism. Hackers use social engineering techniques more than technical prowess to get users to spread their malware. Compared with previous decades where viruses were written in the difficult assembly language, today's worms are extremely easy to write and distribute because they are usually written in relatively simple languages like Visual Basic or Javascript. Have you ever gotten an "urgent" e-mail telling you to click on an attachment? These attachments often take the form of operating system patches, tracking information for packages, or interesting graphics. Despite their appearance, the e-mail attachments are actually programs that infect your computer and spread to your contacts. Whereas viruses were written by sophisticated hackers

in previous years, today's worms can be written by intermediate programmers. Finally, a trojan horse is a program that claims to do something useful, but also contains hidden behavior. The ubiquitous nature of some programs, like Windows, Microsoft Outlook, and Internet Explorer, provides rich fields for viruses, worms, and trojans to spread through. In addition to their ubiquity, these programs are often used by less experienced users who are more susceptible to social tricks.

Spyware has become a difficult online problem in recent years. This type of malware—similar to a trojan horse—installs monitoring software in addition to the regular software that a user downloads or buys. For example, peer-to-peer music and video-sharing applications are some of the worst spyware offenders. Many of these programs install monitors that send online user behaviors to companies that turn a profit on the personal information they collect. More targeted spyware can lift financial or other sensitive information from internal directories and files and send it to external entities.

Phishing is a common method that hackers use to extract personal or corporate information from employees. Phishers send e-mail or pop-up messages to users asking for personal information in inventive ways. For example, a hacker might send an e-mail impersonating technical support to company employees. If even 1 percent of the employees respond with their password or other information, the hacker may be able to access a company's internal networks and open future back doors before preventative steps can be taken. False Web sites are another method of tricking users into providing personal information. A well-known scam on PayPal involves e-mail being sent to many customers with a link to a PayPal-like site. Users who click the link are presented with a login page that impersonates PayPal's regular login screen. Their attempt to log in with their usernames and passwords inadvertently sends their login information to the false site. Users are then redirected back to the regular PayPal login screen where they try to log in once again. Most users never realize they are at an imposter site on the first try.

Spoofing changes the information in e-mail headers or IP addresses. Perpetrators hide their identities by simply changing the information in the header, thus allowing unauthorized access. Since e-mail was one of the first network-based applications, very few security measures were placed into its protocols. E-mail headers are created by e-mail clients and, as such, are extremely easy to forge. Most users receive spam on a daily basis, much of which has forged headers.

Falsified identity is another significant risk in e-business. For an electronic transaction to take place, each party to the transaction needs to be confident that the claimed identity of the other party is authentic. These threats are less of a concern in traditional electronic data interchange (EDI) settings because traditional EDI uses relatively limited access points, dedicated lines, and established value-added network providers as intermediaries. But authenticity is a significant concern for transactions conducted through public electronic channels in e-business. In particular, identity theft (discussed in Chapter 15) is a significant problem today. Public and private key encryption technology is one of the best ways to prevent falsified identity, but advanced hackers can spoof this technology as well.

> **Remember this ...**
>
> *Fraud risks in e-commerce systems are significant. Due to the rapidly changing tactics of perpetrators and new opportunities offered, e-commerce fraud is likely to remain a major problem in the future.*

Database query (SQL) injections and cross-site scripting (XSS) present risks that many sites are not designed to handle. In an SQL injection, hackers send a database command after regular data in an online submission form. Since many back-end systems simply relay commands from forms to databases, the SQL injection is executed by the corporate database. This command might insert an unauthorized record giving a hacker access, or it might simply drop tables with common names (such as the users table, customers table). XSS is a method of injecting Javascript and other browser commands into Web site data. When these commands are interpreted by users' browsers, unauthorized behavior occurs. Common examples are redirection of users to a false Web site and hijacking of user cookie IDs for unauthorized access.

As noted in Chapter 16, one of the most common frauds in traditional business is the "bust-out"—the planned bankruptcy. In its simplest form, perpetrators set up a business, buy inventory on credit, sell it for low prices, and then disappear with the money before the bills are paid. Bust-outs are especially problematic in e-business. Instead of renting a brick-and-mortar store, the perpetrators merely establish a false Web site (at significantly less cost). The false Web site may grab confidential information or conduct fraudulent transactions. False Web sites look like the site of a real bank or an online broker or retailer and collect identification and credit card numbers from unsuspecting customers. Alternatively, perpetrators use false Web sites to conduct business transactions for which they never intend to pay.

E-mail messages and Web visits can be hijacked because subtle differences in Internet host names often go unnoticed by Internet users. For example, "computer.com" and "computer.org" are two completely different host names that can be easily confused. If the two names are owned by different entities, one site could mimic the other and trick users into thinking they are dealing with the original Web site or e-mail address. Many businesses purchase all the domain names for all forms of their company names, including misspellings, to prevent these types of Web sites from being set up and to help customers find the legitimate site.

Fraud risks in e-commerce systems are significant. While traditional methods of fraud, such as bribery and kickbacks, are understood by many people, many employees do not fully appreciate the risks and methodologies that online fraud perpetrators take. Fortunately, users are becoming increasingly educated on the types of online and e-commerce fraud. For example, most business users and students now know they should not click on e-mail attachments from unknown senders. However, due to the rapidly changing tactics of perpetrators and new opportunities presented by changing protocols and technology, e-commerce fraud is likely to remain a major problem in the future.

Preventing Fraud in E-Commerce

Preventing fraud in each business setting involves reducing or eliminating the elements that motivate fraud: pressure, opportunity, and rationalization. In e-business settings, reducing pressures and eliminating rationalizations has thus far proved difficult. The lack of personal contact makes it hard to know what pressures exist or what rationalizations perpetrators are using.

One of the greatest fallacies of e-commerce security is a prevention measure known as **security through obscurity**. Security through obscurity is the tactic of keeping security holes, encryption algorithms, and processes secret in an effort to confuse attackers. Many managers are lured into a false sense of security when they feel that entry into their system is convoluted enough to discourage attackers. Rather than employing robust, proven security measures, companies that employ security through obscurity play the odds by hoping that attackers will not figure out how their security works. Experience shows that obscurity only heightens the challenge to a hacker! The early computer industry of the 1970s and 1980s is littered with failed attempts at hidden algorithms and obscure security. For example, try searching the Internet for password crackers for programs like WordPerfect or Microsoft Excel. Because these programs didn't use robust encryption, password crackers abound.

CAUTION *Security through obscurity is an appealing, yet ineffective, type of security. Rather than take chances with security through obscurity, employ robust, time-tested security methods.*

In contrast to obscurity, true security is found when algorithms and processes are subjected to intense review and stand the test of time. For example, the triple-DES and AES encryption algorithms have been public for many years, and yet they are still generally considered secure because they seem to be mathematically sound. As far as we know, neither algorithm has been broken. Secure Web connections over HTTPS (the protocol you use when connecting to your bank or credit card site) are based in these robust algorithms, and they work very well. VPNs and other security measures based on public, tested algorithms are always more secure than algorithms based on private, untested methods. Of course, we are not suggesting that companies publish their security measures on their Web site home page! We are proposing that security measures be based on time-tested methods that have withstood public scrutiny.

The Control Environment

One of the best ways to prevent fraud in an e-business settings is to focus on reducing opportunities, usually through the implementation of appropriate internal controls. In traditional businesses, internal controls involve five different elements: (1) the control environment, (2) risk assessment, (3) control activities or procedures, (4) information and communication, and (5) monitoring. In e-businesses, the first three elements are often the most important. Therefore, we limit our discussion to the control environment, risk assessment, and control activities.

The essence of effectively controlled organizations lies in the attitude of their management. If top management believes that control is important, others in an organization will respond by conscientiously observing established controls. On the other hand, if it is clear

to employees that management is only giving lip service to the idea of controls, rather than meaningful support, the organization's control objectives will almost certainly not be achieved, and fraud is a more likely occurrence. Because controls are so important, firms endeavoring to prevent e-business fraud must do everything possible to establish and observe good controls. Another key strategy is understanding the controls in place in the companies with which the organization conducts its electronic business.

As noted in earlier chapters, the following are the most important components of the control environment:

Integrity and Ethical Values

An organization's culture of integrity and ethics is the product of what its standards are and how they are communicated and reinforced in the firm. This includes management's actions to remove or reduce incentives and temptations that might prompt personnel to engage in fraud. It also includes the communication of organizational values and behavioral standards to personnel through policy statements and codes of conduct and by example. A good question to ask about companies that engage in electronic business is whether they have a formal code of conduct and whether it is available to be examined.

Board of Directors and Audit Committee Participation

An effective board of directors is independent of management, and its members carefully scrutinize management's activities. The board delegates responsibility for internal control to management, but it undertakes regular, independent assessments of management-established internal controls. In addition, the presence of an active and objective board often discourages management from overriding existing controls. A study of financial statement frauds during the period 1987–1997 revealed that a weak or ineffective board was one of the most common elements in firms that issued fraudulent financial statements[7]

Management's Philosophy and Operating Style

Management provides clear signals to employees about the importance of internal controls. For example, does management take significant risks, or is it risk-averse? Are profit plans and budget data set as "best possible" plans or "most likely" targets? Can management be described as "fat and bureaucratic," "lean and mean," or dominated by one or a few individuals, or is it just right? Understanding these and similar aspects of management's philosophy and operating styles provides a sense of management's attitude about internal controls and fraud.

> **Remember this ...**
>
> *The "tone at the top" is the most important factor in control effectiveness.*

Human Resources Policies and Practices

The most important aspect of internal control is personnel. If employees are competent and trustworthy, other controls can be absent and reliable transactions will still result. Honest, efficient people are able to perform at a high level, even when there are few other controls to support them. However, dishonest people can reduce to shambles a system with numerous controls in place.

Risk Assessment

Risk assessment identifies the risks of doing business with e-business partners. A key part of the assessment focuses on the control environment of those organizations. Another part identifies key risks in the electronic exchange of information and money, so that control procedures tailored to the special challenges that these exchanges present can be installed—procedures that counter the risk of data theft, sniffing, unauthorized access to passwords, falsified identity, spoofing, customer impersonation, false Web sites, and e-mail or Web site hijacking.

A specialized branch of risk assessment is intrusion detection. Firms specializing in intrusion detection try to gain access to networks and secure information, and they report their findings directly to management. Normally, a security audit includes an investigation into technology, processes, controls, and other factors at a client. The Robert Redford movie *Hackers* highlighted a firm doing just this type of work.

Preventing Fraud through Control Activities

As you learned earlier in this textbook, control activities are the policies and procedures that ensure that necessary actions are taken to address risks and frauds. As you also learned, control activities generally fall into the following five types:

1. Adequate separation of duties.
2. Proper authorization of transactions and activities.
3. Adequate documents and records.
4. Physical control over assets and records.
5. Independent checks on performance.

Adequate Separation of Duties

In e-business, this control is useful for making sure that individuals who authorize transactions are different from those who actually execute them. Probably the most common frauds in purchasing and sales transactions are kickbacks and bribery. Kickbacks occur when one individual becomes too close to suppliers or customers. Adequate segregation of duties prevents bribery because employees don't have complete control of transactions.

Proper Authorization of Transactions and Activities

Proper authorization is another key control in e-business. The most common authorization controls are passwords, firewalls, digital signatures and certificates, and biometrics. Every transaction must be properly authorized.

Passwords Passwords are a vital part of the security of any electronic system, but they are also an Achilles' heel because they involve people. Compromised passwords allow unauthorized transactions to be made. To prevent fraud, organizations should have clearly communicated policies regarding selecting, changing, and disclosing passwords. In an electronic environment, no other control can better prevent fraud than the wise use of passwords and adequate training of users regarding them.

Digital Signatures and Certificates Just as signatures on paper documents serve as authorization or verification, digital signatures reassure users that transactions are valid. **Digital signatures and certificates** thus prevent falsified identity and impersonation and as such are increasingly important.

Biometrics One of the most promising areas of technology and systems security is **biometrics**—the use of unique features of the human body to create secure access controls. Because each person possesses unique biological characteristics (for example, iris and retina patterns, fingerprints, voice tones, facial structures, and writing styles), scientists and technology firms are developing specialized security devices that have the potential to be highly accurate in authenticating identity. Access and permission to execute a transaction is granted or denied based on how similar the subsequent reading is to the reference template.

Adequate Documents and Records

Documents and records (sales invoices, purchase orders, subsidiary records, sales journals, employee time cards, and even checks) are the physical objects by which transactions are entered and summarized.

In e-business, these documents are present in electronic form. This lack of hard-copy documentation, the very essence of e-business, creates new opportunities for fraud. Documents and records typically are detective controls, not preventive controls. They are the audit trail and enable auditors and fraud examiners to investigate suspected wrongdoing. Although most computer systems create records of transactions that can be accessed or reconstructed, smart perpetrators figure out how to remove evidence of transactions from servers and computers.

Because many of the traditional document controls aren't available in e-commerce, additional controls must be put in place. The primary electronic transaction and document control is encryption, which protects confidential and sensitive information (such as checks or purchase or sales transactions) from being "sniffed" or stolen. Public-key encryption allows information to be sent in encrypted format over unsecured networks like the Internet and is widely used to protect data and ensure privacy. In public-key arrangements, communicating parties have two keys, one that is made public and another that is held private. These keys are inversely related: If one key is used to "lock" a message, the other must be used to "unlock" it. Thus, a message locked by a public key can be read only by the party holding the private key. Similarly, a message that can be unlocked by a particular public key can have originated only from the party holding the corresponding private key. Public-key encryption is thus used for privacy (by locking a message with the intended recipient's public key) and for authenticity (by locking a message with the originator's private key).

Physical Control over Assets and Records

When records—electronic or paper—are not adequately protected, they can be stolen, damaged, or lost. Highly computerized companies need to go to special lengths to protect computer equipment, programs, and data files.

Three categories of controls protect IT equipment, programs, and data files from fraud. As with other types of assets, physical controls are used to protect computer facilities. Examples are locks on doors to the computer room and terminals and adequate and safe storage space for software and data files. In addition to software-based security, the software and hardware that comprise the IT infrastructure must be physically secure. Remember that authorized personnel who can access computers and servers can also execute unauthorized transactions or steal sensitive information. Sometimes physical infrastructure is so sensitive and critical to e-business operations that the system is placed in an isolated location with only high-level security access.

Many firms use third-party providers—often known as application service providers—to provide data storage and application services. Because their entire business is based on data security, these firms generally take security very seriously. They provide 24-hour monitoring and security and effective password and encryption management. They are normally located in geographic locations considered "safe" from power outages, political unrest, and natural disasters like hurricanes or earthquakes. For many companies, the additional security benefits these firms provide are well worth the additional cost. Regardless of a company's security precautions, physical controls must be a primary consideration. A recent twist on offsite location of services is cloud-based architectures like Google's App Engine or Amazon's S3. These services can co-locate data on multiple continents to provide speed and reliability. If your firm uses these services, be sure to understand the unique advantages and challenges they have in regard to fraud risks and protection.

> **Remember this ...**
>
> *One of the best ways to prevent e-commerce fraud is by focusing on reducing opportunities through sound security measures and a solid control system.*

Independent Checks on Performance

As with traditional business, a key component in e-business controls is the careful and continuous review of the other four components—the independent checks and internal verification. The need for independent checks arises because internal controls change over time. Personnel forget or fail to follow procedures, or become careless—*unless* someone observes and evaluates their performance. The likelihood of fraudulent transactions goes up when controls break down.

Independent checks are particularly important in preventing fraud in e-business. Organizations should always conduct checks on their e-business partners. These checks can range from simple Dun & Bradstreet reviews to full-fledged investigations of the firm and its officers. A quick search of LexisNexis and other financial databases on the Internet often reveals problems the organization should be aware of before it conducts electronic business.

Electronic fraud, especially that perpetrated by smaller companies, is often committed by individuals high in the organization, and quite often on behalf of the organization as opposed to against the organization. Because management is usually involved, management and the directors or business partners must be investigated to determine their exposure to, and motivation for, committing fraud. To prevent fraud, gaining an understanding of the management or the organization's business partners and what motivates them is important. In particular, three items— (1) backgrounds, (2) motivations, and (3) decision-making influence—must be examined. What organizations and situations have management and directors been associated with in the past? What really drives and motivates the organization's leaders? Is their personal worth tied up in the organization? Are they under pressure to deliver unrealistic results? Is their compensation primarily based on performance? Do any debt covenants or other financial pressures exist? Management's ability to influence decisions is important to understand because perpetrating fraud when only one or two individuals have primary decision-making power is much easier.

Detecting E-Business Fraud

In Chapter 6, we introduced data-driven fraud detection, in which the types of fraud that can occur are identified and then technology and other activities are used to look for fraud symptoms. That is, fraud examiners (1) endeavor to understand the business or operations of the organization, (2) identify what frauds can occur in the operation, (3) determine the symptoms that the most likely frauds would generate, (4) use databases and information systems to search for those symptoms, (5) analyze the results, and (6) investigate the symptoms to determine if they are being caused by actual fraud or by other factors.

STOP & THINK *How can the data-driven fraud detection approach be used to detect e-business fraud? What data sources can be used to discover potential frauds?*

This method of fraud detection works very well in detecting e-business fraud. One of the best techniques for implementing this type of fraud detection is to use

technology to catch technology fraud. Many of the hacker tools were actually written to troubleshoot networks and catch perpetrators rather than to hack into systems. It is extremely important for fraud investigators who specialize in e-commerce to understand the tools and methods that perpetrators use. Knowledge of Web servers, e-mail clients and servers, and intrusion programs like Nmap, Airsnort, and Wireshark is critical to catching perpetrators and securing systems. Fraud investigators who want to specialize in e-commerce fraud should take several information systems or computer science networking and security courses. Since many of today's corporate servers and the Internet infrastructure are Unix-based, knowledge of Unix/Linux is imperative. Because clients' applications are often Windows-based, knowledge of the security strengths and weaknesses in Windows is also important.

Computer scripts, written in languages like Perl, Python, Ruby, and Bash, can monitor logs and systems for potential break-ins. An assortment of different intrusion detection systems (IDS) is on the market today. Careful use and monitoring of these systems should be done by every organization.

STOP & THINK *What skills are required to detect and investigate e-business fraud? What other classes might help you learn these skills?*

The appendix to Chapter 6 provides an introduction to detecting fraud in e-commerce systems and corporate databases. Planting automated queries in electronic purchasing records that examine changes in the percentage of goods purchased from different vendors by individual buyer, price changes, the number of returns (indicating lower quality), and comparisons of these factors with other vendors is easy. These variables can even be analyzed on a combined basis; for example, the system will look for increased purchases from the vendor whose prices are increasing the fastest. Computer systems can be programmed to provide information when changes equal or exceed a certain amount. For example, price changes of a certain percentage within a certain period might be queried.

The advantage of e-business transactions is that information about the transactions is captured electronically in databases that can be analyzed in numerous ways. These data make fraud detection much faster than ever before, but the techniques require more computer expertise to run. The most difficult aspect of detecting e-business fraud is correctly specifying the types of frauds that can occur and the symptoms they will generate. Also, symptoms are only circumstantial evidence at best. There may be perfectly legitimate explanations for factors that appear to be symptoms. However, just as e-business transactions make fraud easier to commit, they also make it much easier to detect.

As discussed earlier in this chapter, a rigorous, time-tested process for security should be used. Security through obscurity should never be an option. Standards-based systems like VPNs, firewalls, public and private key infrastructure, strong encryption, and other means should be employed and monitored at all times.

> **Remember this ...**
>
> *The use of time-tested security principles will help prevent e-business fraud. The data-driven approach to fraud detection is an excellent way to discover and investigate e-business fraud.*

In addition to technical measures, social preventions and detections are important. Regular audits of user behavior on the system should be done by watching how users interact with their systems. Employees need to be trained on what e-commerce fraud looks like so they can spot problems. For example, in the autobiographical book *The Cuckoo's Egg*, Clifford Stoll discovered an international spy using his systems for entrance into U.S. military systems. Stoll's investigation started with a mere $0.75 discrepancy in system audit logs! Users need to be trained that while computer anomalies may not look significant, they can often highlight deeper problems. Just as employee tip lines can provide information in traditional fraud cases, tips can be useful in electronic fraud if employees understand what to look for.

Review of the Learning Objectives

- **Understand e-commerce fraud risk.** E-commerce presents new challenges and opportunities for fraud and its detection, but the risks can still be described in terms of pressures, opportunities, and rationalizations. Because the Internet-driven economy removes the need for physical access and interpersonal contact, e-commerce creates risks inside organizations, outside organizations, and to consumers.
- **Take measures to prevent fraud in e-commerce.** Preventing fraud in e-commerce involves reducing

or eliminating the elements that motivate fraud: pressure, opportunity, and rationalization. In particular, the use of time-tested, publicly available procedures for security is the best measure for security; security through obscurity is seen by most professionals as a false sense of security.

- **Detect e-business fraud.** E-business fraud occurs in electronic transactions from business to business—usually from one corporate system to another. The data-driven fraud detection approach works well in discovering this type of fraud because it focuses on the transactions and log files involved in the electronic process.

KEY TERMS

e-business, p. 602	phishing, p. 606
data theft, p. 603	spoofing, p. 606
passwords, p. 603	falsified identity, p. 607
social engineering, p. 603	security through obscurity, p. 607
sniffing, p. 604	digital signatures and certificates, p. 609
wartrapping, p. 605	biometrics, p. 609
spyware, p. 606	

QUESTIONS

Discussion Questions

1. In what ways do e-business transactions pose heightened fraud risks?
2. What are some common ways e-business fraud is perpetrated?
3. How can the authenticity of a party in an e-business transaction be verified?
4. What is sniffing?
5. Why is spoofing a significant risk in e-business?
6. What principles are important in password use and training?
7. Why does biometrics offer significant promises as a way to authenticate e-business transactions?
8. How is the data-driven, six-step detection approach relevant to e-business fraud detection?
9. Why can it be dangerous to provide credit card information over the Internet? Does it stop the risk if you only use credit cards at local businesses?
10. Can e-business fraud risks ever be completely eliminated?

11. What methods of security through obscurity does your school employ? How do these methods increase security? How do they decrease security?
12. What advantages do third-party providers like application service providers offer?

True/False

1. Fraud risks are higher when the entity with whom you are transacting business can't be seen.
2. Data theft is a bigger problem in e-business transactions than money theft.
3. Sniffing changes e-mail headers or IP addresses.
4. Falsified identity and customer impersonation are the same thing.
5. In many e-business sales, password protection is the only barrier to unauthorized access.
6. Customer impersonation is similar to a bust-out fraud.
7. Segregation of duties is an important control in preventing e-business fraud.
8. Digital signatures use human features to create secure access controls.
9. Biometrics is a form of authorization control.
10. It is often easier to analyze e-business transaction data than data from other types of transactions because information is captured in databases that can be manipulated.
11. Intrusion detection is the activity of trying to break into competitors' computer networks.
12. Using secret measures as the basis for a security system is generally seen as less effective than using public, time-tested procedures.

Multiple Choice

1. Which of the following is *not* a fraud risk unique to e-business transactions?
   a. Innovative technologies where security lags process development.
   b. Selling new products.
   c. Complex information systems.
   d. Removal of personal contact.
2. E-business transactions make it easier to commit which of the following types of frauds?
   a. Kickbacks.
   b. Customer impersonation.
   c. Setting up dummy companies.
   d. Stealing petty cash.
3. Which of the following is *not* an element of a company's control environment?
   a. Audit committee participation.
   b. Management's philosophy.
   c. Hiring policies.
   d. Independent checks.
4. Which of the following is *not* an internal control activity or procedure?
   a. Physical safeguards.
   b. Segregation of duties.
   c. Internal auditors.
   d. Documents and records.
5. Which of the following fraud risks involves changing IP addresses?
   a. Spoofing.
   b. Sniffing.
   c. False Web sites.
   d. Customer impersonation.
6. Which of the following fraud risks involves viewing information as it passes along network channels?
   a. Sniffing.
   b. Spoofing.
   c. False Web sites.
   d. Web hijacking.
7. Using a subtly different Internet host name to mimic another business is known as:
   a. Spoofing.
   b. Sniffing.
   c. Web-visit hijacking.
   d. Falsified identity.
8. Passwords and biometrics are both:
   a. Authorization controls.
   b. Independent check controls.
   c. Physical controls.
   d. Document controls.
9. Which of the following human features is generally *not* used in biometrics?
   a. Fingerprints.
   b. Voice tones.
   c. Retina patterns.
   d. Weight.
10. Which of the following types of controls is *least often* used to protect IT processing equipment?
    a. Physical controls.
    b. Authorization controls.
    c. Independent checks or reference.
    d. Documents and records.

11. What is the most important factor in control effectiveness?
    a. Clear policies regarding controls.
    b. An understanding of e-business networks.
    c. The use of random monitoring.
    d. The "tone at the top."
12. Secure Web connections are based in:
    a. DNS.
    b. FTP.
    c. HTTPS.
    d. FTPS.

SHORT CASES

Case 1

Your company, ImSecure Inc., is a security investigation firm. You have been contacted by Darling Company, a producer of cardstock for greeting card companies like Hallmike and Birthday Wishes Company. Darling currently requires orders to be placed several weeks in advance of the delivery date. Orders come in through traditional channels (account reps, paper forms, etc.). Hallmike, Darling's largest client, now requires Darling to use e-commerce for order transmission and payment. Because of this new change, Darling is considering moving all of its clients to EDI for orders and payments.

Detail the new opportunities e-commerce solutions like EDI present for internal and external perpetrators trying to defraud Darling Company.

Case 2

Search the Internet for a recent story on information being stolen from a company. Examples of this are stolen credit card numbers, personal information, and proprietary secrets. Summarize the article in two or three paragraphs. Detail several measures that could have prevented and/or detected this fraud.

Case 3

Dan Jones is the new CIO of Ricochet Systems, an Internet securities broker. After assessing the e-commerce risks in his company, he determines that passwords are a weak link that needs additional protection. However, he is unsure as to what the requirements for a robust password are. At your monthly golf outing, Dan asks you—knowing your background in computer forensics—what checks and policies should be in place on passwords in his company.

1. How often should passwords be changed?
2. What requirements should be enforced on passwords chosen by employees (length, dictionary words, etc.)?
3. Are there alternatives to passwords that Dan should investigate?

You tell Dan you'll send him a detailed e-mail message answering these questions when you get back to work. Write this message giving Dan advice on his password policies.

Case 4

1. What is a VPN?
2. How do VPNs provide security within organizations?
3. Search the Internet for the term "IPsec"? What is it? Is it considered secure?
4. Search for other VPN-related protocols and name two. Are the two protocols you identified considered secure?

Case 5

Your company, ABC Reading, writes unique OpenGL-based reading software for children in grade school. ABC employs about 30 sales representatives who interact with school districts around the nation to sell and support your software. ABC has given each sales representative a powerful laptop on which to demonstrate your 3D software to principals and district representatives. Because of the nature of their jobs, sales reps are constantly connecting their laptops to school and hotel networks during the day and to your corporate network via VPN. You are worried about viruses and worms entering your corporate network through one of their laptops. What protections and preventions would you take to guard against this?

Case 6

As the new intern for the summer, you have been asked to investigate two methods of e-mail encryption: S/MIME and Pretty Good Privacy (PGP). Compare and contrast the two systems.

1. Why do two standards exist?
2. Which do you think your employer should standardize on? Why?

Optional activity: Set up S/MIME or PGP-based plugins in student e-mail clients. Use the activity to learn how to get/create a public/private key pair and encrypt mail.

Case 7

A number of security/intrusion detection firms exist in the market. Research one of these firms and report on its services, costs, and benefits.

1. Would you hire a firm like this for a start-up company?
2. Would you hire one for an established, small company?
3. Would you hire one for a *Fortune* 1000 company? Why?

Case 8

(If allowed by your school's policy) Download and install a network sniffer application like Wireshark, tcpdump. Sniff the traffic on your local network for 10 minutes and report on your experience.

1. What did you find?
2. Why do these applications exist?
3. How does their existence and distribution affect worldwide hacking and detection of hackers?

Case 9

1. Where have you seen security through obscurity employed (other than a key under the doormat at home)?
2. Did it work?
3. How did it make the situation more or less secure?
4. Are there more robust methods that could have been used to provide security?

Case 10

eBay has become one of the most popular auction sites in the world. Each day, millions of products and services are bought and sold on the site. Because of its popularity, eBay is also a home for many different types of scams.

Your business wants to start buying and selling on eBay, and you have been asked to find one type of scam that is popular on eBay. Search the Web for common eBay scams and pick one to write about. Include a description of how the scam occurs, what types of products or services it is often found on, and how it can be prevented or detected by potential buyers.

Case 11

One of the riskiest parts of an e-commerce transaction is the payment process. Several different companies, such as Authorize.net, Google, and Yahoo! checkouts, and others provide robust solutions for this risky process. Pick a provider that services the payment process (or some part thereof, such as credit card validation) and write a short summary of what services are provided and why an e-commerce site owner may want to use the services. Include the risks that are mediated by the service.

CASES STUDIES

Case Study 1

E-Commerce Security Identify a local company that conducts e-commerce, preferably one with whom you have previously done business or are otherwise familiar. Research the company and become knowledgeable in its basic operations and services. Contact the company and inform it of your interest as a student, in learning more about its business. Inquire as to how the company guarantees the security of its site and consumers' personal information. Ask the company whether it has a formal code of conduct and, if so, whether it is available to be examined.

In essay format, describe your conversation with the company's representative, explain the security measures the company uses, and comment on the company's code of conduct. Conclude your essay by stating whether and why you would be comfortable engaging in online transactions with this company.

Case Study 2

E-Commerce Survey Conduct a random survey of at least 30 people. From the survey responses, draw several conclusions about attitudes of consumers toward e-commerce. Write a brief essay summarizing your conclusions.

Attach to it any spreadsheets or charts used in your analysis. The survey should include, but not necessarily be limited to, the following questions:

1. How often do you purchase products or services over the Internet?
   a. Never.
   b. Two or three times a year.
   c. At least once a month.
   d. Several times a month.
2. If "never," why?
3. Name two or three companies from whom you purchase products online.
4. What steps do you take to check the security of the sites and the legitimacy of the companies from whom you make purchases online?

5. How often do you pay your bills over the Internet?
   a. Never.
   b. Two or three times a year.
   c. At least once a month.
   d. Several times a month.
6. If "never," why?
7. Name two or three companies with whom you make online payments?
8. What steps do you take to check the security of the sites and the legitimacy of the companies with whom you pay bills online?
9. How often do you view and/or manipulate banking and credit card information over the Internet?
   a. Never.
   b. Two or three times a year.
   c. At least once a month.
   d. Several times a month.
10. If "never," why?
11. What is the name of your bank or credit card provider that provides your financial information online?
12. What steps do you take to check the security of the sites and the legitimacy of the companies with which you access online financial information?
13. How often do you double-check your bank and credit card statements for accuracy?
    a. Never.
    b. Sometimes.
    c. Every month.
14. How comfortable are you submitting your Social Security number over the Internet?
    a. Extremely uncomfortable.
    b. Uncomfortable.
    c. Neutral.
    d. Comfortable.
    e. Extremely comfortable.
15. How comfortable are you submitting your credit card number over the Internet?
    a. Extremely uncomfortable.
    b. Uncomfortable.
    c. Neutral.
    d. Comfortable.
    e. Extremely comfortable.
16. How regularly do you run spyware removal programs on your personal computers?
    a. Never.
    b. Once a year.
    c. Several times a year.
    d. At least monthly.
17. Your age?

Case Study 3

E-Commerce Fraud Prevention   Together with other students from your class, identify a small, local company that does e-business and whose owner or manager is willing to talk with you about its operations. With your professor's approval, meet with the company manager and explain to him or her that you are studying fraud examination and would like to discuss the company's vulnerability to fraud. Follow the following steps to proactive fraud examination:

1. Endeavor to understand the business or operation of the organization.
2. Identify what frauds can occur in the operation.
3. Determine the symptoms that the most likely frauds would generate.
4. Propose several queries that might identify those symptoms.
5. Propose methods to follow up on any revelations of those symptoms.

The interview with the owner or manager should only last 30–40 minutes and should cover Steps 1, 2, and 3. After the interview, brainstorm Steps 4 and 5 as a group. Write a 500-word essay that includes your responses to each step. Before the interview, offer to submit a copy of the completed essay to the owner or manager.

Case Study 4

Two years ago, your best friend Scott Adams started a home business selling custom-made chairs and tables. His original designs quickly became popular, and he began selling in large quantities. To take advantage of the upcoming holiday season, Scott decided to begin selling over the Internet. He contacted a Web page designer and is now ready to go live with the site. Although he is familiar with the gist of Internet retailing, Scott is concerned about the possibility of fraud involving false online purchases where perpetrators impersonate customers and place orders. Knowing about your background in fraud, he asks you how to prevent and detect fraud in his new venture.

Questions

1. List three fraud schemes that Scott should be concerned about.
2. Identify the steps Scott should take to prevent and/or detect each scheme.

END NOTES

1. www.vnunet.com/News/106245

2. Nanette Byrnes and Paul C. Judge (June 28, 1999). "Internet Anxiety," *Business Week.*

3. "Preventing and Detecting Fraud in Electronic Commerce Systems," 2002. *The E-Business Handbook* (Boca Raton, FL: St. Lucie Press): 315–338.

4. R. Paul, 2008. "The BOFH lives: 88% of IT workers would steal data if fired," *Ars Technica,* http://arstechnica.com/security/news/2008/09/the-bofh-lives-88-of-it-workers-would-steal-data-if-fired.ars

5. J. Cheng, 2009. "IT staff snooping HR and layoff lists, taking data with them," *Ars Technica,* http://arstechnica.com/security/news/2009/06/it-staff-snooping-hr-and-layoff-lists-taking-data-with-them.ars

6. S. Hiaasen, R. Barry, N. Shah, and M. Sallah (August 22, 2009). "From snitch to cyberthief of the century." *The Miami Herald.*

7. M. S. Beasley, J. V. Carcello, and D. R. Hermanson, 1999. *Fraudulent Financial Reporting: 1987–1997: An Analysis of U.S. Public Companies,* Committee of Sponsoring Organizations (COSO).

PART **7**

Resolution of Fraud

18   Legal Follow-Up   621

CHAPTER **18**

Legal Follow-Up

LEARNING OBJECTIVES

After studying this chapter, you should be able to:

- Identify important aspects of the court system.
- Understand the civil litigation process.
- Understand the criminal litigation process.
- Describe the nature of an expert witness.

TO THE STUDENT

After studying the previous chapters of this book, you should have a good understanding of various fraud topics, from the prevention and detection of fraud schemes to interviewing skills to consumer fraud. As our final discussion, we discuss the litigation process in the United States and legal remedies available when fraud has been uncovered. We discuss the U.S. court system, the litigation process, and the way fraud examiners play a role as expert witnesses. For those working outside the United States, this chapter should still provide an overview of the basic principles involved in legal follow-up.

The following appeared in the *Los Angeles Times* in 2001: "Federal regulators pounced on EarthLink cofounder, Reed. E. Slatkin, raiding his offices and persuading a federal judge to freeze his bank and brokerage accounts to prevent him from hiding investors' money or destroying documents. The actions turn what had been a civil matter—with investors accusing Slatkin of running a 16-year Ponzi scheme—into a criminal investigation. Moreover, documents filed Friday revealed several Hollywood names on Slatkin's list of investors. At 8 a.m., agents from the FBI and Internal Revenue Service began hauling boxes of documents from the converted garage of Slatkin's former home in the Santa Barbara suburb of Goleta, which since the early 1990s has housed his stock trading and money management businesses. Regulators also took documents from the Santa Fe, New Mexico, office of Slatkin's bookkeeper. At the same time, the Securities and Exchange Commission (SEC) asked a U.S. district judge for the Central District of California to freeze Slatkin's assets, claiming that he had been operating a fraudulent investment scheme since 1986. The request was granted.

Slatkin's attorney, Brian Sun, said his client was 'fully cooperating' with the investigations. Slatkin, through his attorneys, provided computer passwords and a computer hard drive to investigators at the scene, Sun said. The SEC said Slatkin provided investigators with investor account statements and year-end summaries showing he had invested in a wide variety of large- and small-company stocks. The SEC said its investigation of Slatkin's bank and brokerage records showed Slatkin used part of a $10 million deposit made by one investor to make payments to other investors."[1]

When a fraud occurs, investigators and victims must decide what actions to take against the perpetrators. Actions that can be pursued range from doing nothing to merely transferring or punishing the perpetrator to termination to pursuing various legal remedies. Obviously, such activities should not be pursued until an investigation has been completed and the identity of the perpetrator is known, along with some sense of the schemes used, the amounts taken, and other important facts of the case. The resolution decision should always involve legal counsel as well as other decision-makers involved. In this chapter, we discuss various legal remedies that are available. We begin by discussing the state and federal court systems in the United States. We then discuss civil and criminal fraud trials and the various elements of the trial with which fraud examiners should be familiar.

The Court System

To understand the legal outcomes possible in the United States, you need to know how the federal and state courts operate. The court organization in the U.S. justice system is the combination of separate, interlocking courts. The state courts throughout the United States can handle nearly every type of case. Only the U.S. Constitution, the state's constitution, and the state's laws govern state courts. The state and local courts handle most legal cases in the United States, including most fraud cases. **Federal courts** handle only those cases over which the U.S. Constitution or federal laws give them authority. The federal courts hear fraud cases that involve federal laws or include several states.

State Courts

Although state court organizations differ from state to state, Figure 18.1 shows how the state courts are generally organized.

The **lower-level trial courts** (often called trial courts of limited jurisdiction) try misdemeanors (small crimes) and preliminaries (pretrial issues) for felony and civil cases that are below some dollar amount, such as $10,000. The types of lower trial courts include housing courts that hear housing and landlord-tenant issues, small claims courts where individuals can inexpensively bring small actions against others, probate courts where the assets of deceased persons are distributed, and so forth. All actions are initially judged in lower trial courts.

FIGURE 18.1   ORGANIZATION OF STATE COURTS

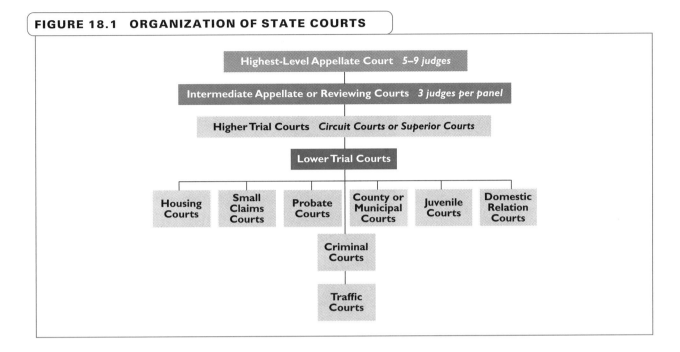

The **higher-level trial courts** (often called trial courts of general jurisdiction, circuit courts, or superior courts) also hear initial actions. These courts try felony and civil cases that are above the lower-level dollar amount. The distinguishing factors between the lower-level and higher-level trial courts are the amounts and the seriousness of the crimes. These courts usually sit in panels of two or three judges.

Plaintiffs or defendants who are not satisfied with the outcomes of trial courts can appeal court decisions to appellate or reviewing courts. Usually, the first level of review is conducted by the **appellate courts**. If these courts can satisfy plaintiffs and defendants, no further appeals are made. The last level of appeals at the state level is the highest-level appellate courts (usually called a state supreme court). These courts review decisions made by the lower appellate courts, and their decisions are final. They have discretionary power to decide whether to review appellate court decisions, and they usually sit in panels of three to nine judges.

Federal Courts

Figure 18.2 shows how the federal courts are organized. The federal courts are established to enforce federal laws and statutes. They include **bankruptcy courts** to adjudicate bankruptcy proceedings and **tax courts** to hear tax cases. For example, although bankruptcy fraud cases are usually tried in bankruptcy courts and tax fraud cases in tax courts,

FIGURE 18.2   ORGANIZATION OF FEDERAL COURTS

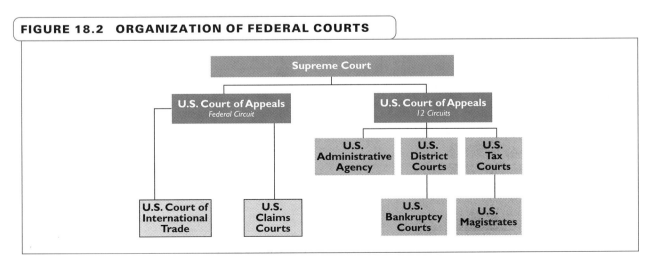

most fraud cases involving federal laws or statutes [such as mail fraud, violations of the Racketeer Influenced and Corrupt Organizations (RICO) Act, banking, and securities regulations] are tried in one of the U.S. district courts. These courts try criminal and civil cases under federal laws.

If defendants or plaintiffs are not satisfied with judgments rendered in district courts, they can appeal the findings in one of 12 circuit courts of appeal. The final court of appeal is the U.S. Supreme Court, which reviews decisions made by the appellate courts.

As an example of how an appeals court works, consider the following:

In 1994, a jury in Anchorage, Alaska, ordered Exxon Corporation to pay $5 billion to thousands of commercial fisherman and property owners for damages done in 1989 when the Exxon Valdez ship spilled 11 million gallons of oil in Alaska's Prince William Sound. Plaintiffs had alleged that the black "goo" that was spread across 1,500 miles of shoreline had reduced property value and damaged fishing and hunting grounds. When Exxon appealed the findings, the three-judge panel of the Ninth U.S. Circuit Court of Appeals said that some damages were justified, but that $5 billion was excessive. The appeals court ordered the lower court to determine a lesser amount of damages.[2]

Civil and Criminal Fraud Trials

When individuals commit fraud, they can be prosecuted criminally, civilly, or both. Once sufficient evidence is obtained—usually through a fraud investigation—the defrauded company must decide whether to pursue the case criminally, civilly, or both, or to take no action at all. Many times, a defrauded company will not pursue a case in criminal or civil court in order to avoid additional expenses and negative public exposure. Rather, it merely fires the perpetrator or files a claim with a fidelity bonding company. Sometimes it is the bonding company that pursues legal actions against the perpetrators.

When a defrauded company pursues civil remedies in court, the case is most often settled before it goes to trial. Even in criminal cases, plea bargains with perpetrators often avoid lengthy and costly trials.

As discussed in Chapter 1, **criminal law** involves laws that deal with offenses of a public nature and are generally considered to be offenses against society as a whole. Every state and the federal government have statutes prohibiting a wide variety of fraudulent and corrupt practices. Criminal offenses are prosecuted under either the federal or state system depending on the source of the statute prohibiting

a given activity. Criminal cases are prosecuted by the government rather than by an individual. Often, perpetrators who are convicted criminally serve jail sentences and pay fines. They are also required to make restitution to victims. Before a perpetrator is convicted criminally, he or she must be proven guilty "beyond a reasonable doubt." Juries must rule unanimously on guilt for the perpetrator to be convicted.

Civil law is the body of law that provides remedies for violations of private rights. Civil law deals with rights and duties between individuals or organizations. Civil claims begin when one party files a complaint against another, usually for the purpose of gaining financial restitution. The purpose of a civil lawsuit is to compensate for harm done to another individual or organization.

Just what is **fidelity bonding**? In a perfect world, employee fraud would never happen. Unfortunately, it does. To protect themselves, companies often purchase fidelity bonding coverage on their employees. Fidelity bonding is essentially an insurance contract that guarantees payment to an employer looking for protection in the event of unforeseen financial loss through the dishonest actions of an employee. Bonding is often an important strategy for businesses because it is estimated that one-third of all bankruptcies are caused by employee theft.

Companies can apply for three basic types of fidelity bonds. Of course, the more specialized the coverage is, the more the company pays.

1. *Name Schedule Fidelity Bond* The company designates a set amount of coverage for a list of employees that it provides to the insurance company. Each time the company hires a new employee, it contacts the insurance company to have that person added to the list if the company wants that person covered. Collection under this coverage hinges on absolute proof that an employee stole from the company.
2. *Blanket Position Bond* Under this contract, the employer specifies coverage for a position rather than the individual. Each employee of a business is covered, and new employees are added automatically. Coverage is offered for each employee up to the maximum established in the insurance policy. Blanket position bonds do not require proof of the individual's responsibility for the theft.
3. *Primary Commercial Blanket Bond* Like the blanket position bond, this bond covers each employee in the company. This type of coverage does not accommodate each employee, but rather treats the employees as one unit. In other words, it does not matter whether one or five people were involved in the crime; the company will be able to claim the same amount.

Unlike criminal cases, the jury in civil cases need not consist of 12 jurors, but may have as few as six jurors. The verdict of the jury need not be unanimous. Civil cases are often heard by judges instead of juries. To be successful, the plaintiff in a civil case must prove his or her case only by the "preponderance of the evidence." In other words, the evidence supporting the plaintiff must only be slightly more than any evidence supporting the defendant.

CAUTION *Criminal and civil law differ in that criminal law is established to right a public wrong or offense against society and civil law involves righting a private wrong. To convict a person in a criminal trial, the evidence must meet a standard to eliminate all reasonable doubt. However, the evidence in civil trials need only be viewed as slightly more in favor of the plaintiff to get a remedy from a defendant.*

In both civil and criminal proceedings, the parties may call expert witnesses to give their opinion on matters thought to be too technical for the jurors or judge to understand. Fraud examiners and accountants are often used as experts in fraud cases to compute and testify to the amount of damages, the nature of the fraud, and whether the parties were negligent in their actions and committed fraud.

Remember this ...

The United States has both state and federal court systems. State courts handle nearly every type of case in the United States, including most fraud cases, whereas federal courts handle only certain cases that deal with the U.S. Constitution, federal laws, bankruptcy, or taxes. Civil and criminal law differ, in that criminal law deals with offenses of a public nature and civil law deals with providing remedies for violations of private rights.

Overview of the Civil Litigation Process

During the civil litigation process, cases go through common stages. Certain courts, such as divorce or bankruptcy courts, may have different procedures that we do not discuss in this book. Every civil case involves the following four basic stages:

1. Investigation and pleadings
2. Discovery
3. Motion practice and negotiation
4. Trial and appeal

Most fraud cases follow these four stages, although in some cases, the stages may overlap. For example, investigation may occur during motion practice.

Investigation and Pleadings

Litigating a civil fraud case usually begins when a client in a case of alleged fraud approaches an attorney. Prior to this, a fraud investigator should have gathered important evidence about the facts of the case, such as how the fraud occurred, the amount of the fraud, the accused perpetrator.

For litigation to begin, it is necessary for the plaintiff to file an initial pleading. The **initial pleading**, or **complaint**, explains the alleged violation of the law and the monetary expenses or damages sought in the case. The response to the claim is called a motion or an answer. The **motion** is usually an objection to the plaintiff's complaint that points out defects of the case and asks for a specific remedy. The **remedy** may include dismissal of all or part of the original complaint. The **answer** is the response to the complaint that denies or admits various allegations.

Sometimes, a defendant in a civil case will file a counterclaim, such as sex, race, or age discrimination or invasion of privacy rights. For example, in fraud cases, defendants may claim sex or age discrimination in order to divert the jury's attention from the fraud. These may or may not be valid claims, depending on the case.

Discovery

Discovery is the legal process by which each party's attorneys try to gain information about the other side's case before the trial begins. Because discovery can be time-consuming and expensive, this stage is often the most challenging part of civil litigation. Attorneys obtain information about the other side's case by filing motions for the production of documents, interrogatories, and requests for admissions. They also obtain information through subpoenas and depositions taken of both parties and nonparties to the litigation. Fraud examiners acting as expert witnesses are often deposed during this phase.

Production Requests

A production request is a means of securing documents in the other party's possession that are relevant to the case. Examples of these documents include bank statements, property records, stock certificates, accounting records, or contracts. Attorneys may request documents to establish that the opposing party has no documents or to avoid the appearance of documents presented at trial that have not been previously reviewed. The production request should be specific, contain the facts of the case, and be defensible in court if necessary. Fraud investigators can provide significant assistance in preparing a production request because of their knowledge of the case. Fraud investigators can also assist in evaluating whether documents produced by the opposing side satisfy requests.

Document requests are typically made at the beginning of discovery to allow attorneys time to review all relevant documents before eliciting testimony of witnesses or consultants. After both parties have received responses and if the responses contain no objections, the counsels of both parties arrange to exchange documents at a convenient time and place.

Interrogatories

An **interrogatory** is a series of written questions that specifically identify information needed from the opposing party. Fraud investigators can often provide important interrogatory service by providing and suggesting relevant questions to ask the other side. Fraud investigators can draft responses to questions received and ensure that answers are consistent with the presentation to be made at trial. Normally, responses to interrogatories usually must be made within 30 days. If answers are not given in a timely fashion, the court may issue an order demanding that all questions be answered and may charge the noncomplying party with fees and costs incurred by the other party in obtaining the order. Interrogatories usually ask questions about personnel, documents, and the nature of the organization. Often, responses to interrogatories will include statements such as "the request is unduly burdensome" or "the infraction is unavailable."

Requests for Admission

A **request for admission** asks the opposing party to admit designated facts relevant to litigation. These facts may relate to the authenticity of documents or precise facts about certain issues. For example, a request for admission may ask the opposing party to admit that the company was incorporated in a particular state during a specific period. These requests must be answered within a certain time period. If answers are not given in a timely fashion, the court may issue an order

demanding that all questions be answered and may charge the noncomplying party with fees and costs incurred by the other party.

Subpoenas

A **subpoena** is a written order in the name of the court, requiring a witness to submit to a deposition, give testimony at trial, or report to an administrative body. A *subpoena duces tecum* requires the recipient to produce documents pertinent to the case. The court clerk or an attorney as an officer of the court may issue subpoenas. Subpoenas are often the only method of ensuring production of information or documents from witnesses who are not parties to a lawsuit. For example, a subpoena could be used to require a brokerage house to produce records pertaining to the opposing party's account. Subpoenas are sometimes used to obtain documents to compare with documents produced by the opposing party. If the witness believes that the defendant has altered a bank statement sent as part of a document request, a copy of the defendant's bank statement might be subpoenaed from the bank, and documents supporting the transactions may be vouched to the statement to establish the completeness of information.

Depositions

A **deposition** is testimony taken before trial begins. Judges usually are not present at depositions. The conditions are usually less formal than in a courtroom, but the rules and regulations of court apply. The opposing side's attorney takes fact and expert witness depositions.

A deposition is a powerful tool in the hands of a skilled attorney. He or she can see how the witness reacts to questioning. If the witness is not prepared for the deposition, the attorney may be able to obtain admissions or errors not possible at trial. The attorney may also get a witness to commit to a particular position at deposition that can prevent him or her from suddenly recalling a favorable matter at trial.

The individual being deposed is under oath, and a court reporter records the questions and answers and later transcribes the notes. The witness generally is given an opportunity to approve the written transcript and make any necessary corrections. Deposition transcripts may be read to the court at trial for a variety of reasons. One of these reasons is to impeach or question the accuracy of the trial testimony of the witness. For example, if the witness gives seemingly contradictory evidence at deposition and trial, the transcript may be read to convince the jury to give the witness's testimony little weight. In some cases, the deposition will be video-taped and the tape will be shown at trial.

Fraud investigators may assist the client's attorney by preparing questions to ask opposing witnesses during depositions. Fraud investigators can sometimes attend the depositions of other witnesses. Although only attorneys can ask questions during depositions, the fraud investigator can communicate with the client's attorney during breaks or by using written notes. Attending the depositions of opposing experts may be especially helpful for fraud investigators. The depositions may reveal information and opinions that are not accurately reflected in the expert's written report or work papers. A fraud investigator's technical knowledge of the areas of testimony can help ensure that the deposition reveals all of the opposing expert's opinions and the methodologies and supporting information used in reaching those opinions.

In many ways, being deposed is much more difficult than testifying in court. Expert witnesses, for example, are questioned by the other side's attorneys but not by their own. Good witnesses realize that it is best to take a "defensive" posture in depositions and answer with minimal elaboration. On the other hand, good witnesses are often "offensive" when testifying in court and may elaborate on the question asked.

STOP & THINK *Why is it good for a witness to be "defensive" in depositions and "offensive" in court?*

Motion Practice and Negotiation

At various stages during discovery, the opposing parties may seek rulings from the trial judge on a variety of questions. For example, a defendant may file a motion for summary judgment before a case even goes to trial. In a **motion for summary judgment**, counsel requests the court to rule that all or a part of the claim should be dismissed because no genuine issue of a material fact is present. At times during discovery, the witness may be requested to execute an affidavit on a relevant fact in support of a motion. An **affidavit** is a written declaration given under oath.

Settlement Negotiations

Either of the parties may negotiate a **settlement** at any time during the litigation. If a settlement is reached, the case is usually resolved. However, settlement discussions and negotiations cannot usually be introduced at trial. Fraud investigators can be useful during

settlement negotiations in resolving differences between the two parties. Most large civil cases are ultimately settled before going to trial.

> **Remember this ...**
>
> *Every civil case involves the following four basic stages: (1) investigation and pleadings, (2) discovery, (3) motion practice and negotiation, and (4) trial and appeal. In each of the stages, a variety of information may be obtained or different actions may be taken. Appeals typically involve allegations that the trial contained a legal defect.*

Trial and Appeal

If the case is not closed by motion practice or settlement, it goes to trial. Before the trial begins, attorneys for both sides generally will meet with the judge and agree to certain ground rules regarding the scope of the litigation, what documents will be admitted, and how long the trial will last. In most jurisdictions, the litigating parties have the right to demand a jury trial, and in most cases, a jury trial is held. Usually, when one side prefers a jury, the other side wants a judge, or vice versa. If either party wants a jury, a jury trial is usually held.

A fraud investigator's testimony is intended to aid the jury in understanding the technical issues involved. In addition to providing trial testimony, fraud investigators often assist in developing questions that will be asked of the opposing side's expert or fact witnesses during cross-examination by the client's attorney.

In jury trials, the judge determines issues of the law. At the conclusion of the trial, the judge will *charge the jury*. In this charge, the judge provides instructions to the jury on the law to be applied in reaching its verdict. After the jury returns a verdict, parties have a limited period in which they may file motions to have the verdict set aside in whole or in part or to have the judge grant a new trial. If these motions are overruled, a judgment will be entered, and both parties will have a specified time to appeal.

An appeal usually relates to matters of law and not to facts of the case. It is a request to a higher court to overturn the verdict or order a retrial due to some legal defect during the trial. For example, an appeal may be based on the contention that some inappropriate evidence was admitted during the trial or that the trial judge wrongfully instructed the jury on one or more legal issues.

Overview of the Criminal Litigation Process

The litigation process in criminal cases differs significantly from civil cases because the criminal justice system includes more protections for the rights of the defendant. These protections arise primarily from three amendments to the U.S. Constitution—the Fourth, Fifth, and Sixth Amendments. Each stage of criminal litigation is also governed by rules established by the jurisdiction in which the case is tried. The Federal Rules of Evidence and Federal Rules of Criminal Procedures are applicable in providing testimony in federal courts. Many state courts follow the federal rules with little modification.

Filing Criminal Charges

After investigators and attorneys believe they have obtained enough evidence to prosecute a defendant, the defrauded party determines whether to pursue criminal charges. If the decision is made to pursue criminal charges, the victim of the fraud contacts the district attorney for the county in which the fraud was perpetrated. The district attorney coordinates with the local police in the preparation of an arrest **warrant** or summons. If the case involves a federal crime, notice is also sent to the U.S. Attorney's Office.

Arresting and Charging the Defendant

Representatives of the government do not have unlimited power to search or arrest citizens. Instead, they must comply with the requirements of the U.S. Constitution, including the Fourth and Fifth Amendments. The **Fourth Amendment** protects defendants against unreasonable searches and seizures by the government. It requires that probable cause exist before a defendant is arrested or searched. Probable cause is the level of evidence required for a reasonable person to believe that a crime has been committed and the accused committed it.

The level of evidence necessary to show probable cause is less than certainty but more than suspicion. Evidence seized without meeting this requirement can be excluded from trial. Searches at the place of business by employers or investigators hired by those employers generally are not subject to this amendment, unless they were carried out in a prejudicial or careless manner.

In fraud trials, documents seized by the employer are frequently turned over to the government. The government generally can use these documents as evidence, even though a search warrant was not issued to obtain the evidence. However, if the defendant's attorney can show that the fraud investigator was really an agent of the district attorney when gathering the information, and therefore was subject to the rules against unreasonable searches and seizures, the government may not be able to use some of the evidence gathered by the fraud investigator.

The **Fifth Amendment** provides defendants the following protections:

- *Requires an indictment of a grand jury before a defendant is held for a capital crime (one where the death penalty or other certain punishments are possible).*
- *Precludes a person from being tried twice for the same crime.*
- *Gives the defendant the right to refuse to incriminate himself or herself—often referred to as "pleading the fifth."*
- *Requires the state to apply due process of law.*
- *Forbids the state from taking a private party's property without just compensation.*

As we stated earlier, agents of the government must have probable cause before they can arrest the accused. Arresting for a crime occurs in the following three ways:

1. Arrest without a warrant by a private citizen or police officer who observes a crime being committed.
2. Arrest after a warrant has been issued (obtaining a warrant requires a preliminary showing of probable cause).
3. Arrest after an indictment by the grand jury. The purpose of the grand jury is to determine whether probable cause exists; grand jury indictments are generally used in fraud cases.

Preliminary Hearings

If the accused is arrested based on a warrant, the arrest will be followed by either a preliminary hearing or a grand jury proceeding depending on whether the defendant's attorney or the prosecutor is first to reach a judge. The purpose of a **preliminary hearing** is to determine whether "probable cause" exists to charge the defendant with a crime—not to establish his or her guilt or innocence.

Although preliminary hearings are held before judges, hearsay and illegally obtained evidence can be heard. The defendant is represented by an attorney who can cross-examine the prosecution's witnesses. The defendant attempts to demonstrate that the prosecution does not have enough evidence to show probable cause. Without enough evidence to show probable cause, charges are dismissed and the defendant is released. A dismissal of charges does not preclude the government from instituting a later prosecution for the same offense when and if better evidence has been gathered.

Grand Jury

Because a preliminary hearing is an opportunity for the defendant to obtain discovery of the prosecution's case without disclosing its evidence, the prosecution generally prefers to obtain a grand jury indictment. Once the defendant is indicted by a grand jury, probable cause is satisfied and a preliminary hearing is not held. The defense, however, may file a motion to obtain most, if not all, of the factual information they could have obtained during a preliminary hearing.

A **grand jury** is a body of 16 to 23 people, selected from the community, who are sworn as jurors and deliberate in secret. Grand jurors listen to evidence presented by witnesses and prosecutors. A grand jury also has the right to subpoena witnesses and documents and can issue contempt orders, fines, or jail terms to enforce the subpoena. A grand jury can consider any evidence, even that which would not be admissible at trial.

Defendants do not have a right to be notified that a grand jury is considering evidence against them. Nor are they allowed to review the evidence, confront their accusers, or present evidence in their defense. Defendants who appear before a grand jury cannot be accompanied by their attorneys. However, a defendant can periodically leave the grand jury room to discuss his or her case with counsel. Defendants appearing before grand juries retain the right against self-incrimination. At least 12 grand jurors must agree for an indictment to be issued. An indictment is not a conviction. At trial, the defendant will have the Sixth Amendment protections denied during the grand jury process.

The **Sixth Amendment** protections relate only to trials. This amendment provides the defendant with the following rights:

- *Receive a speedy and public trial.*
- *Be heard by an impartial jury.*
- *Have a trial held in the state and district in which the crime was committed.*
- *Be informed of the accusation.*
- *Confront witnesses against him or her.*
- *Compel witnesses to attend the trial.*
- *Be represented by legal counsel.*

Arraignment

Generally, in a fraud trial, the grand jury will hear evidence of wrongdoing before the defendant is in custody. Once the defendant is indicted, he or she will receive a summons to attend an arraignment that includes the time and place to appear. Alternatively, the defendant may be arrested and brought to the arraignment. At the **arraignment**, the charges against the defendant are read. The defendant may plead guilty, not guilty, or **nolo contendere** (the defendant does not contest the charges but does not admit guilt). A trial is held and bail is set if the defendant pleads not guilty. Alternatively, sentencing follows when the defendant pleads guilty or nolo contendere.

Discovery

Pretrial discovery in criminal trials differs significantly from that in civil trials. Depositions are allowed only in exceptional circumstances (such as the illness or anticipated death of a witness). According to Rule 16 of the Federal Rules of Criminal Procedure, upon request, the defendant may obtain the following:

a. Copies of all relevant statements made by the defendant that are in the government's possession.
b. A copy of the defendant's prior criminal record.
c. All documents, items, test results, written reports of expert witnesses, or other evidence the government intends to introduce at trial or that are necessary to the defense.
d. Copies of all prior statements made by witnesses relevant to the information about which they have testified.

If the defendant requests the prosecution to produce any or all of the items listed in (c), the defendant must provide the same items to the prosecution. However, defendants are not required to disclose information that is self-incriminatory—only information expected to be introduced as evidence at trial.

STOP & THINK *During the discovery stage in the legal process, why would opposing sides be cooperative in providing information about evidence they intend to introduce during the trial?*

Pretrial Motions

Before a criminal trial, the defendant can file motions with the court. This process is similar to that in civil trials. Two motions that are frequently made include the following:

- *A request that the charges be dismissed as a matter of law.*
- *A request to suppress certain evidence because it was illegally obtained.*

Trial and Appeal

Civil fraud trials in state courts are sometimes held before criminal trials. The prosecutor may choose not to investigate until the defrauded company finds evidence of fraud. In these cases, the defrauded party's attorney notifies the district attorney of the investigation. The district attorney may wait to indict the defendant until enough evidence has been obtained in the defrauded party's investigation to show probable cause and might use that evidence in the criminal trial. Federal criminal trials are generally held first. Having a civil trial first can benefit the prosecution because the defendant may make admissions during the civil trial that can be used in the criminal trial. Also, in civil trials, the defrauded party may have greater access to the documents of the defendant during discovery. If the defendant does not present requested documents during a civil trial, he or she can be held in contempt of court and fined.

Remember this ...

The criminal litigation process differs significantly from that of civil cases because the criminal justice system includes more protections for the rights of the defendant. The process includes the following: (1) filing criminal charges, (2) arresting and charging the defendant, (3) preliminary hearings, (4) arraignment, (5) discovery, (6) pretrial motions, and (7) trial and appeal.

Burden of Proof

Defendants in criminal trials are considered innocent until proven guilty. A unanimous jury decision may not be required in a civil case, but in most jurisdictions, a jury's decision in a criminal trial must be unanimous. The burden of proof necessary to find a defendant guilty in a criminal trial is also significantly greater than the level needed to prove civil liability. Civil actions require that there is a "preponderance

of the evidence" (usually interpreted to mean more than 50 percent) supporting one side of the allegation. In a criminal case, the guilt of the accused must be established "beyond a reasonable doubt."

Appeal

After the jury has returned a verdict, the defendant may file motions to have the verdict set aside. If that is unsuccessful, the defendant may appeal the verdict. An appeal is a request to a higher court to overturn the verdict or order a retrial due to some legal defect in the trial proceedings.

For fraudulent behavior, it is obvious that a perpetrator can be held liable for his or her actions, but what about third parties to a fraud? Can third parties that assisted a fraud perpetrator be held liable for the fraud committed by another? This is an interesting legal issue that has potentially serious consequences for corporations and others who do business with companies involved in financial statement fraud.

Third-party involvement in a fraudulent activity is often referred to as aiding and abetting. Many believe that third parties should be held liable for aiding and abetting in a fraud case. The issue of a recent Supreme Court case revolves around whether shareholders can sue third parties for assisting in a company that is committing fraud. In 1994, the Supreme Court ruled that third parties working with public companies cannot be sued by that company's shareholders for aiding and abetting in a fraud. However, shareholders of Charter Communications Inc. sued Motorola Inc. and Scientific Atlanta, now part of Cisco Systems Inc., for allegedly helping Charter inflate its financial performance. This case is similar to the one being fought by Enron shareholders against Merrill Lynch & Co.

This legal issue has traveled extensively through the legal system. Originally, a Missouri district court dismissed the case, citing the 1994 Supreme Court case mentioned. Shareholders then appealed to the Eighth Circuit Court of Appeals and lost. Next, they appealed to the Supreme Court, which ruled in January, 2008. The Supreme Court ruled that third parties who assist a securities issuer in misleading investors cannot be held liable for damages. The decision upheld the earlier interpretation of the law, but it also effectively imposed stricter pleading requirements on plaintiffs and tightened the rules related to damages in securities cases. This case is an interesting one, in that it not only shows how a case can move through the legal system but also deals with an interesting legal issue regarding fraudulent activity.[3]

Being an Expert Witness

Because fraud examiners and accountants are often retained as **expert witnesses** in both civil and criminal fraud cases, we conclude this chapter by discussing the role of expert witnesses and provide some guidelines for being an effective expert witness. The process of qualifying an expert witness to testify is known as **voir dire**. The judge rules on whether an expert witness is qualified to provide evidence on a matter before the court.

Once qualified, an expert witness can testify about the nature of the fraud, the damages suffered in the fraud, the negligence of the victim in allowing the fraud to happen, standards (such as accounting standards) that were violated, and other aspects related to the fraud. Expert witnesses usually study the facts of the case during the discovery stage of the trial. To prepare, they usually read fact witness depositions, study relevant documents and other materials related to the case, and make sure they understand all the authoritative literature related to the issues of the case. Often, the expert is required or asked to prepare a report that sets out his or her opinions.

After the discovery period ends, experts are usually deposed by the attorneys on the other side of the case. The deposition is probably the most stressful part of the case because, except for a few clarifying questions at the end, the opposition's attorneys ask the questions. Those attorneys have several goals during the deposition of the expert: (1) to understand what the expert's opinions are, (2) to understand the credentials and experience of the expert, (3) to identify evidence that can either impeach the expert or be used against his or her testimony during the trial, and (4) to obtain an assessment of how difficult the expert will be in the case.

During the deposition, a good expert takes a defensive posture—answering only the questions that are asked in the most abbreviated way possible. Good experts never volunteer anything beyond what is asked, and they always listen carefully to the questions to make sure they hear exactly what is being asked. Before answering, experts should pause to give the attorneys for their side of the case an opportunity to object to the question. At times, experts are instructed by their attorneys to not answer specific questions. Expert witnesses should never forget that their opinions are only as good as their reputation and integrity. They should never sell their opinions to the highest bidder, but rather should give their honest opinions at all times.

> ### Remember this ...
>
> *Expert witnesses are often people who can offer opinions in court because of their unique experience, education, or training. Expert witnesses must be deemed as qualified through a process known as voir dire. Expert witnesses can testify of such things as the nature and circumstances of a crime or damages suffered. It is important for an expert witness to give adequate thought to answers and to answer only those questions that are asked.*

Following the deposition, experts work with the attorneys representing their side of the case to prepare for the trial. During this period, the experts will decide how to best present their opinions to the judge or jury. Usually, graphics and other visuals are helpful for simply conveying complex fraud issues.

During the trial, the expert witness first encounters direct examination by the attorneys representing his or her side of the case. At the beginning of direct examination, the attorney asking the questions usually covers the qualifications of the expert, so that the judge or jury hearing the case can establish in their minds how well-qualified the expert is. Once the expert's qualifications are established, the attorney then asks the expert questions that, when answered honestly, will support the case he or she is trying to make. Following direct examination, the expert is cross-examined by the attorneys representing the other side of the case.

Several tips have been identified for effectively testifying as an expert witness, but no practice can substitute for good preparation. No matter how well-qualified the witness is, an expert's credibility is weakened by being unprepared or not being familiar with the facts of the case. Most experts agree that, once prepared, the dos and don'ts listed for the various situations in Tables 18.1, 18.2, and 18.3 should be followed when testifying as an expert.

TABLE 18.1 DOS AND DON'TS AT DEPOSITION OR TRIAL

1. Do listen carefully and concentrate on each question.

2. Do think about the question and digest it before attempting to respond; don't give snap answers.

3. Don't try to guess or bluff your way through an answer. If you do not know the answer to a question or do not understand the question, say so.

4. Do restrict your answer to the question asked; don't editorialize your answer or volunteer information.

5. Don't respond to statements or observations, only to questions.

6. Do answer questions convincingly; don't repeatedly attempt to hedge your answers or be overcautious.

7. Don't memorize answers to questions you expect to be asked; do phrase your response in your own words.

8. Do answer questions honestly; don't attempt to figure out what the best answer to each question might be.

9. Do speak out the answer to each question. Body language, such as hand signals or nods, cannot be recorded by the stenographer.

10. Do be cautious before answering any hypothetical question and make sure you understand the assumptions, and then spell them out as part of your answer.

11. Do try to "read messages" intended by objections to questions by the lawyer with whom you are working. His or her objection may be designed to caution you about some risk or problem with the question.

12. Don't hesitate to take the time necessary to review exhibits presented to you before responding to questions based on them.

13. Do explain all assumptions on which your conclusions are based and do be prepared for opposing counsel to attack them.

TABLE 18.2 ADDITIONAL DOS AND DON'TS AT TRIAL

1. Do be mindful that your personal characteristics and professionalism may influence the jury as much as or even more than the substantive content of your testimony.

2. Do be yourself; jurors are apt to sense when you are not being natural.

3. Do your best to appear authoritative, credible, businesslike, serious, assertive, polite, assured, self-confident, sincere, candid, forthright, fair, and spontaneous.

4. Don't appear pompous, aggressive, insincere, or unfair.

5. Do remember that you are independent—avoid bias or unnecessary advocacy of the client's position.

6. Do focus on the lawyer asking the questions, but remember to look at and direct your answers to the jury as well. Don't overlook the reactions of the jurors to your answers; do try to be responsive to their nonverbal signals.

7. Do correct any errors you make as soon as you can.

8. Do tailor your answers to the jury's educational level and do your best to speak in plain English; don't use technical terms that lay-people will not understand.

9. Don't bore the jury; try to speak with clarity and feeling and avoid long, overly detailed answers.

10. Don't hesitate to raise your voice; pause or use some other natural gesture to emphasize an important point.

11. Do speak just loud enough and just fast enough to be comfortably understood by the jury.

12. Don't bring notes, work papers, or other material to the witness stand unless counsel for your side approves.

13. Don't try to play lawyer while on the stand. Your job is to answer the questions honestly and responsively; counsel for your side will take care of the legal matters.

14. Don't look to counsel for your side or the judge or anyone else to bail you out if a question stumps you or you otherwise get yourself into a hole.

TABLE 18.3 DOS AND DON'TS IN CROSS-EXAMINATION

1. Don't lose your temper or become angry or antagonistic; do recognize that it is opposing counsel's job to attempt to discredit you.

2. Don't be concerned if opposing counsel scores points, which is entirely to be expected when your side relinquishes the offensive to the other side; all you can do is try to keep the damage to a minimum.

3. Don't quibble unduly or become argumentative with opposing counsel.

4. Don't respond evasively or ambiguously to questions, no matter how difficult they may be.

5. Do be extra careful if opposing counsel takes on a friendly air, which may be a tactic designed solely to catch you off guard.

6. Don't become hostile if opposing counsel tries to bully you. Jurors are likely to respect you for not becoming unduly perturbed and to sympathize with you if you get "beat up."

7. Do resist responding with simple yes or no answers that may be misleading without some qualification or explanation. Either provide the qualification or explanation directly by responding "yes, but" or "no, but" or request the opportunity to do so.

8. Do your best to recognize signals, such as careless answers, that you may be getting tired or losing your competitive edge. It is advisable in such a situation to indicate the need for a break.

9. Don't allow opposing counsel to entice you into answering questions that concern matters outside your area of expertise.

10. Do maintain the position you took in your direct testimony.

11. Don't allow opposing counsel to con you into an advocacy role; unduly taking your client's side can cause you to lose your independence in the eyes of the jury.

Review of the Learning Objectives

- **Identify important aspects of the court system.** The United States has both state and federal court systems. State courts handle nearly every type of case in the United States, including most fraud cases. Federal courts handle only those cases over which the U.S. Constitution or federal laws give them authority. State courts are organized with lower-level trial courts, higher-level trial courts, and appellate courts. The federal court system includes bankruptcy courts, tax courts, district courts, appeals courts, and the Supreme Court.

- **Understand the civil litigation process.** Every civil case involves the following four basic stages: (1) investigation and pleadings, (2) discovery, (3) motion practice and negotiation, and (4) trial and appeal.

- **Understand the criminal litigation process.** The litigation process in criminal cases differs significantly from civil cases because the criminal justice system includes more protections for the rights of the defendant. The process includes the following: (1) filing criminal charges, (2) arresting and charging the defendant, (3) preliminary hearings, (4) arraignment, (5) discovery, (6) pretrial motions, and (7) trial and appeal.

- **Describe the nature of an expert witness.** An expert witness is an individual who has unique experience, education, or training regarding a subject and can offer opinions about it. In essence, this person has special qualifications to offer opinions regarding a particular subject matter.

KEY TERMS

federal courts, p. 622
lower-level trial courts, p. 622
higher-level trial courts, p. 623
appellate courts, p. 623
bankruptcy courts, p. 623
tax courts, p. 623
criminal law, p. 624
civil law, p. 624
fidelity bonding, p. 624
initial pleading, p. 625
complaint, p. 625
motion, p. 625
remedy, p. 625
answer, p. 625
discovery, p. 625
interrogatory, p. 626
request for admission, p. 626

subpoena, p. 626
deposition, p. 626
motion for summary judgment, p. 627
affidavit, p. 627
settlement, p. 627
warrant, p. 628
Fourth Amendment, p. 628
Fifth Amendment, p. 628
preliminary hearing, p. 628
grand jury, p. 629
Sixth Amendment, p. 629
arraignment, p. 629
nolo contendere, p. 629
expert witnesses, p. 631
voir dire, p. 631

QUESTIONS

Discussion Questions

1. How are state courts organized?
2. How are federal courts organized?
3. What is the difference between civil and criminal fraud trials?
4. What steps are involved in the civil litigation process?
5. What is an interrogatory?
6. What is a deposition?
7. Why are depositions a powerful tool in obtaining information?
8. How might a fraud investigator benefit by attending the deposition of opposing experts?
9. What steps are involved in the criminal litigation process?
10. What is discovery?
11. How are fraud examiners used as expert witnesses?
12. What is the purpose of having a fraud investigator or another expert witness provide testimony in a trial?
13. What are some of the dos and don'ts of being an expert witness?
14. What types of fraud-related things can an expert witness testify about?
15. During deposition, what posture should an expert witness display?

True/False

1. Most fraud cases are tried in federal courts.
2. State courts hear bankruptcy cases.
3. Civil cases must consist of a jury of at least six jurors.
4. The prosecution usually prefers to present evidence at a grand jury because the accused does not have the right to hear the evidence.
5. If, during a preliminary hearing, sufficient evidence is not available to show probable cause, the defendant can still be prosecuted at a later time when more evidence is available.
6. The burden of proof necessary to prove a defendant is guilty in a criminal trial is significantly greater than that in a civil trial.
7. To be successful, the plaintiff in a civil case must prove his or her case beyond a reasonable doubt.
8. Investigation is the legal process by which each party's attorneys try to find all information about the other side's case before the trial begins.

9. An initial pleading or complaint generally includes an explanation of the alleged violation and the monetary expenses or damages sought.
10. An interrogatory is a series of written questions that specifically identifies information needed from the opposing party.
11. A request for confession asks the opposing party to admit designated facts relevant to litigation.
12. The parties in a civil case may negotiate a settlement during any stage of litigation.
13. If responses to interrogatories are not given in a timely fashion, the court may charge fees and costs to a noncomplying party and issue an order demanding that all questions be answered.
14. The federal courts will only hear cases that involve federal law, more than one state, or a federal statute.
15. The defendant can choose to have his or her case tried in either a state lower court or a state higher court.
16. An individual committing fraud can be prosecuted either criminally or civilly, but not both.
17. A deposition is a testimony taken before the trial begins in a situation that is usually less formal than a courtroom, but in which the court rules and regulations still apply.

Multiple Choice

1. To be convicted in a criminal case, the standard of evidence is:
   a. Beyond a shadow of a doubt.
   b. Beyond a reasonable doubt.
   c. Preponderance of evidence.
   d. All of the above.
2. Most court cases are decided in state courts, except when:
   a. Federal laws are in question.
   b. The case involves several states.
   c. The amount exceeds $100,000.
   d. Both a and b are correct.
3. What is/are the distinguishing factor(s) between the lower and higher state trial courts?
   a. Amount of monetary damage.
   b. Seriousness of the crime.
   c. Availability of the court.
   d. Both a and b.
   e. All of the above.

4. Which of the following rights is *not* provided by the Fifth Amendment?
   a. Individuals are protected from double jeopardy (being tried twice for the same crime).
   b. States cannot seize private property without just compensation.
   c. Individuals have the right to refuse to incriminate themselves.
   d. Miranda rights must be read upon arrest.
5. During a trial or deposition, expert witnesses should:
   a. Respond aggressively.
   b. Bring notes and work papers to cite.
   c. Answer questions convincingly, without hedging their answers.
   d. Memorize well-crafted responses to say what they think sounds effective.
6. During cross-examination, expert witnesses should:
   a. Address areas outside of their areas of expertise.
   b. Appreciate opposing council when they act very friendly.
   c. Respond evasively and ambiguously to tough questions.
   d. Maintain the same positions taken during direct testimony.
7. Fraud investigators can assist in a case in which of the following ways?
   a. By preparing questions to ask opposing witnesses during depositions.
   b. By evaluating whether documents produced by the opposing side satisfy a production request.
   c. By assisting in the preparation of a production request because of their knowledge of a case.
   d. By a and b.
   e. By a, b, and c.
8. When deposing an expert witness, the opposing attorneys try to achieve all of the following goals except:
   a. Understanding the expert's opinion.
   b. Understanding the expert's credentials.
   c. Seeking admission of guilt.
   d. Obtaining an assessment of how difficult the expert will be in the case.
9. Having a civil trial before a criminal trial has which of the following benefits?
   a. Defendant may make admissions during civil trial that can be used in criminal trial.
   b. Greater access to documents of the defendant.
   c. Defendant is not guaranteed the right to an attorney.
   d. Both a and b.

10. Which of the following is *not* one of the common stages of a criminal case?
    a. Filing a criminal charge.
    b. Filing a complaint.
    c. Discovery.
    d. Trial and appeal.
11. In a civil trial, settlements may be negotiated:
    a. At any time during the litigation.
    b. After arraignment.
    c. At no time once negotiation begins.
    d. Only after the judge orders negotiation between parties.
12. Which of the following actions can fraud victims pursue after sufficient evidence is obtained?
    a. Prosecute in a criminal court.
    b. Pursue civil litigation.
    c. Take no action at all.
    d. Two of the above.
13. The Fourth Amendment requires that probable cause exist before a defendant is arrested or searched. Which of the following levels of evidence is necessary to show probable cause?
    a. Less than certainty, but more than speculation or suspicion.
    b. Speculation or suspicion.
    c. Beyond a reasonable doubt.
    d. Preponderance of the evidence.

SHORT CASES

Case 1

Mr. Bill is the sole proprietor of a small play-dough production company. Over the last few months, he noticed revenues dropping and started wondering what is going on. After giving it much thought, he realizes that his accountant, Mr. Pringles, has been cooking the books and stealing money from him—at least that seems to be the case. Mr. Bill is pretty upset and immediately runs down to the local courthouse and files a complaint against his accountant. Too anxious to wait for the legal process to continue, Mr. Bill decides to go to his accountant's personal residence and search for evidence of fraud. To his delight, he finds some papers that document his accountant's illegal activities.

Mr. Bill hurries to the office, where he confronts his accountant and shows him all of the papers he found at his house, informing him that a complaint has been filed. Mr. Pringles, calmly laughs and walks away, apparently not affected at all by what Mr. Bill has told him.

Explain why Mr. Pringles is not worried in the least about Mr. Bill's discovery.

Case 2

A Wall Street bond trader turned on the television one day and saw a news report accusing him of committing a large securities scam. This trader learned that his employer had accused him of creating $300 million of phony profits and, as a result, getting bogus bonuses of $8 million. He claimed he was innocent, and it took about three years for him to prove his innocence. In the months that followed the accusations, he was investigated by the SEC, the National Association of Securities Dealers, and the Justice Department. Three years later, the bond trader was cleared of all major charges brought against him.

1. Assume that you are the employer. What type of legal action would you seek against this bond trader? Why?
2. To what type of court would your case most likely be assigned? Why?

Case 3

In June 2000, the SEC brought civil charges against seven top executives of Cendant Company. The SEC alleged that these officials had, among other things, inflated income by more than $100 million through improper use of company reserves. These proceedings were a result of a long-standing investigation by the SEC of financial fraud that started back in the 1980s. In your opinion, in which stage of the criminal litigation process is this case? Why?

Case 4

Briefly research a recent publicized fraud to become familiar with the major facts involved. Identify ways that a fraud investigator could add value in the (1) investigation, (2) legal follow-up, and (3) implementation of controls to prevent similar problems from happening in the future.

Case 5

When O. J. Simpson was tried for the murder of his wife, Nicole Simpson, he was ruled not guilty in the criminal court hearings. However, when Nicole Simpson's family sued Simpson civilly, he was ordered to compensate Nicole's family several millions of dollars. How could that be?

Case 6

You are a manager for a large department store. It has recently come to light that a receiving clerk has been stealing merchandise. About $5,000 has been stolen. The clerk has stopped stealing, and the faulty internal control weaknesses that were determined to have allowed the fraud

have been fixed. No action has been taken yet to punish the perpetrator, who still works at his same job. The clerk happens to be the nephew of one of the other managers, who, while he understands that his nephew's behavior was unacceptable, would like to keep the theft relatively quiet.

1. What action, if any, should be taken against the receiving clerk in this situation? What consequences will probably result from that action?

Case 7

Answer the following two questions:

1. After being named as a defendant in a corporate fraud case, the XYZ accounting firm was found guilty of negligence and fined $25 billion. As a partner for the firm, what would you recommend as the next course of action?
2. As part of the preparations for a large financial statement fraud case, you issue a production request to see the other party's bank statements. When the statements are provided to you, some of them are only photocopies. The opposing party claims that the originals were accidentally destroyed. What could you do in this situation?

Case 8

You are involved as an expert witness in a case of alleged fraud by top management against the corporation. Supposedly, working in collusion, top management defrauded the company of $5 million over two years. The allegations suggest that the fraud involved stealing $5 million and then concealing the fraud by overstating expense accounts and manipulating balance sheet accounts.

Following the initial discovery of this alleged fraud, shareholders of the company brought a lawsuit against top management. The prosecuting attorney for the shareholders has retained you to assist as an expert witness in this case. The case has already moved into the discovery phase.

1. What will your role likely be as an expert witness? At what point in the process will you be most involved? What might you do to assist the prosecution as much as possible?

Case 9

Bobby Jones, an accountant for ABC Corporation, has been suspected of committing fraud. Some information already gathered about the fraud points to Bobby Jones as the most likely perpetrator. In his scheme, Bobby supposedly stole more than $5 million over the past three years. Due to the magnitude of the fraud and to set an example in the company, ABC decides to prosecute Bobby both civilly and criminally.

Describe what will happen to Bobby Jones during the civil litigation, including the stages of civil litigation that he and ABC will go through.

Case 10

John was recently convicted by a jury of committing fraud against his employer. After the trial, it was revealed that some key evidence against John used in trial was obtained through his employer's records and John's workstation computer. Before searching John's computer, the investigators did not have any evidence or idea that John was involved in the fraud. In fact, they stumbled on the fraud by accident. John is convinced that he has grounds for appeal. He believes the evidence found on his work computer is inadmissible because the investigators did not have probable cause to search his computer.

1. Is John right that he could appeal the guilty verdict?
2. Were his rights violated?

Case 11

The FBI is on the trail of a drug supplier in Pineville, USA. The Feds believe that the supplier works at OHS Manufacturing, the employer of 75 percent of Pineville's citizens. The FBI asks OHS Manufacturing to assist in the investigation of one of its employees. Specifically, the FBI asks one of OHS's managers to search the employee's locker and give the FBI any illegal drugs found. OHS does not have a written policy allowing these searches or a history of performing these searches. Do you believe this action could be a possible violation of the Fourth Amendment? Why or why not?

Case 12

Mr. Oaks has worked as the CEO of Turley Bank for the last three years. This past year, the outside auditor discovered some fraudulent loan activity in which Mr. Oaks was circumventing internal controls to lend money to friends and family. After a thorough investigation, the board of trustees concluded that Mr. Oaks had committed more than $10 million in loan fraud. Mr. Oaks denied any wrongdoing. Now, the board is contemplating pursuing a civil case against Mr. Oaks, seeking repayment of the $10 million.

1. What are some reasons why Turley Bank would not pursue a civil case against Mr. Oaks?
2. If Turley Bank decides to pursue a civil case against Mr. Oaks, what are some reasons why the bank would settle out of court before the actual trial?

3. If Turley Bank decides to pursue a civil case against Mr. Oaks, what are some reasons why Mr. Oaks would settle out of court before the actual trial?

Case 13

Your friend recently attended a local mail fraud trial. In your conversation about the case, she described the cross-examination of the expert witness as follows:

After his counsel's questioning was done, expert witness Matthew Little was composed and gave off a confident impression. However, when the defendant's counsel questioned him regarding a comment he made earlier, he began to argue with the questioning attorney. The attorney continued to reiterate that the testimony that he gave contradicted the events of the fraud; Matthew seemed to lose his temper. It was then that Matthew seemed exhausted and asked the judge for a quick recess.

After the quick break, Matthew regained his composure and did not seem affected by the opposing counsel's efforts to discredit his testimony. I was a little surprised that he refused to answer some questions, but he said something about it not being his area of expertise. I was impressed with his detailed explanations of the intricacies of mail fraud—he would never answer a question with a simple "yes" or "no". Other than the brief moment before the break, I thought he did a great job as an expert witness.

Having read this chapter's "dos and don'ts" of an expert witness and listening to your friend's description, answer the following questions:

1. What did the expert witness do well?
2. What did the expert witness not do so well?

Case 14

To help you understand the material discussed in the chapter, do the following:

1. Give at least three characteristics of a grand jury.
2. Without looking at the list in the chapter, list at least three dos and don'ts that an expert witness should keep in mind during cross-examination.
3. During the discovery stage of a civil litigation process, several methods of obtaining information may be used. One of these methods is by taking depositions.
   a. What are depositions?
   b. Why are depositions a powerful tool in obtaining evidence?
   c. What are the other three stages of civil litigation that cases usually go through in addition to discovery?

CASE STUDIES

Case Study 1

John Rigas (founder and CEO of Adelphia Communications Corporation) was an extraordinary man. Throughout his professional career, he was honored for his entrepreneurial achievements and his humanitarian service. Among other awards, he received three honorable doctorate degrees from distinguished universities, was named Entrepreneur of the Year by Rensselaer Polytechnic Institute (his college alma mater), and was inducted into the Cable Television Hall of Fame by *Broadcasting and Cable* magazine. He worked hard to acquire wealth and status. But a $2.3 billion financial fraud eventually cost Rigas everything.

Rigas and his company, Adelphia Communications, started out small. With $72,000 of borrowed money, he began his business career in 1950 by purchasing a movie theatre in Coudersport, Pennsylvania. Two years later, he overdrew his bank account to buy the town cable franchise with $300 of his own money. Through risky debt-financing, Rigas continued to acquire assets until, in 1972, he and his brother created Adelphia Communications Corporation. The company grew quickly, eventually becoming the sixth largest cable company in the world with over 5.6 million subscribers.

From its inception, Adelphia had always been a family business, owned and operated by the Rigas clan. During the 1990s, the company was run by John Rigas, his three sons, and his son-in-law. Altogether, members of the Rigas family occupied a majority five of the nine seats on Adelphia's board of directors and held the following positions:

John Rigas, CEO and chairman of the board (father); Tim Rigas, CFO and board member (son); Michael Rigas, executive vice president and board member (son); James Rigas, executive vice president and board member (son); Peter Venetis, board member (son-in-law).

This family dominance in the company was maintained through stock voting manipulation. The company issued two types of stock: Class A stock, which held one vote each, and Class B stock, which held 10 votes each. When shares of stock were issued, however, the Rigas family kept all Class B shares to themselves, giving them a majority ruling when company voting occurred.

With a majority presence on the board of directors and an effectual influence among voting shareholders, the Rigas family was able to control virtually every financial decision made by the company. However, exclusive power led to corruption and fraud. The family established a cash management system, an enormous account of commingled revenues from Adelphia, other Rigas entities, and loan proceeds. Although funds from this account were used throughout all the separate entities, none of their financial statements were ever consolidated.

The family members began to dip into the cash management account, using these funds to finance their extravagant lifestyle and to hide their crimes. The company paid $4 million to buy personal shares of Adelphia stock for the family. It paid for Tim Rigas's $700,000 membership at the Golf Club at Briar's Creek in South Carolina. With company funds, the family bought three private jets, maintained several vacation homes (in Cancun, Beaver Creek, Hilton Head, and Manhattan), and began construction of a private world-class golf course. In addition, Adelphia financed, with $3 million, the production of Ellen Rigas's (John Rigas's daughter) movie *Song Catcher*. John Rigas was honored for his large charitable contributions. But these contributions also likely came from company proceeds.

In the end, the family had racked up approximately $2.3 billion in fraudulent off-balance-sheet loans. The company manipulated its financial statements to conceal the amount of debt it was accumulating. False transactions and phony companies were created to inflate Adelphia's earnings and to hide its debt. When the family fraud was eventually caught, it resulted in an SEC investigation, a Chapter 11 bankruptcy filing, and multiple indictments and heavy sentences. The perpetrators (namely, John Rigas and his sons) were charged with the following counts:

Violation of the RICO Act

Breach of fiduciary duties

Waste of corporate assets

Abuse of control

Breach of contract

Unjust enrichment

Fraudulent conveyance

Conversion of corporate assets

Until he was convicted of serious fraud, everybody loved John Rigas. He was trusted and respected in the small town of Coudersport and famous for his charitable contributions and ability to make friends. He had become a role model for others to follow. With a movie theater and a $300 cable tower, he had built one of the biggest empires in the history of cable television. From small beginnings, he became a multimillion-dollar family man who stressed good American values. But his goodness only masked the real John Rigas, and in the end, it was his greed and deceit that ultimately cost him and his family everything.

Questions

1. The fraud triangle consists of perceived pressure, perceived opportunity, and rationalization. How do you think John Rigas rationalized his dishonest use of company assets?
2. What are other ways people rationalize fraudulent behavior?
3. How would owning and operating a family business create temptations and opportunities to commit fraud?
4. Based on the facts of the case, do you think this case has led to civil litigation, criminal prosecution, or both? Explain your answer.
5. Suppose you were an expert witness in this case. What would be some of the facts to which you would pay special attention?

INTERNET ASSIGNMENTS

Refer back to the beginning of this chapter to the excerpt from a *Los Angeles Times* article about Reed Slatkin's fraud. The article insinuates that the FBI and IRS's raiding of Slatkin's office marked the beginning of the government's investigation of Slatkin's financial activities. In fact, Slatkin was under investigation for at least four years prior to the raid, and nearly a year and half previous to it, the SEC had already conducted a series of depositions featuring, among others, Reed Slatkin as a witness. Transcripts of two of these frauds are available online: Open http://slatkinfraud.com/depo_jan.htm (Depo 1) and http://slatkinfraud.com/depo_feb.htm (Depo 2). All page numbers refer to Depo 1 except as individually noted.

1. *Page 1.* Where was this deposition conducted?
2. *Page 1.* Name the three individuals representing the SEC.
3. Based on the chapter's explanation of depositions, do you think these three are lawyers or SEC investigators (fraud examiners)?
4. *Page 1-11.* Using the explanation of *discovery* in the chapter, what is meant by "The above- entitled

matter came on for hearing at 10:12 a.m., *pursuant to notice*"? (italics added) (Also, see page 6-23 to page 7-7.)
5. *Page 2.* Another vital aspect of deposition is *subpoena duces tecum*, a written order that commands an individual or organization to produce case-related documents, which will often be used as evidence in the deposition or trial and are usually called *exhibits*. What two exhibits are presented in this deposition?
6. *Depo 2, Page 2.* Compare the number of exhibits used in Depo 1 to the number used in Depo 2. By the nature of the exhibits listed for Depo 2, why do you think the SEC employed so many more exhibits in the second part of the deposition than the first?
7. *Pages 7-9 to 10-13.* Quickly read over this discussion. Using the explanation of *subpoenas* in the chapter, why are the examiners so particular in their questions regarding the subpoenaed documents?
8. *Page 3.* According to Mr. Dunbar, what is the purpose of this deposition, or "investigation"?
9. *Depo 1, Pages 52-16 to 55-14; Depo 2, Pages 214-3 to 215-4.* Quickly read over these discussions. Referring also to the chapter, describe briefly the role of Mr. Boltz, Mr. Slatkin's attorney.
10. *Pages 134-14 to 137-17.* Quickly read over this discussion. Keeping in mind that Mr. Slatkin handled investments for hundreds of "friends" but was not a registered investment advisor, and paying particular attention to Mr. Boltz's "promptings" in this section, for what reason does Mr. Boltz apparently believe his client is under investigation?
11. *Page 142-2 to 144-25.* Throughout the deposition, both Mr. Slatkin and his interrogators reference NAA Financial, a Swiss institution housing most of Slatkin's "friends' money." On a scale of 1–10, how confident is Mr. Boltz concerning NAA Financial?
    a. When asked how he can be certain that NAA Financial is "good for the money," how does he respond?
    b. Is Mr. Boltz's method of verification legitimate?
    c. Has he personally made contact?
    d. Who is Mitchell Axiall?
12. Now go to www.sec.gov/litigation/litreleases/lr17796.htm. This SEC litigation release identifies Daniel Jacobs as a co-conspirator in Slatkin's effort to deceive the SEC. Pay close attention to the bulleted section.
    a. What do you learn about NAA Financial?
    b. Who is Michel (Mitchell) Axiall?

DEBATES

1. Sam's Electronics Universe has discovered and investigated a kickback fraud perpetrated by its purchasing agent. The fraud lasted eight months and cost the company $2 million in excess inventory purchases. The perpetrator personally benefited by receiving kickbacks of $780,000. Your boss wants to seek restitution of what the company has lost, but is worried about the ramifications of a trial and its effect on your company's image in the market. She is trying to decide if she should pursue remedies through a civil trial, or turn the case over to the district attorney to prosecute the perpetrator criminally. Pair up with somebody and choose sides. Discuss the pros and cons of each approach of legal follow-up to fraud.

2. Daren has been retained by the defendants, as an expert witness in a recent fraud case. He will be providing information concerning the defendant's activities, explaining why the defendant's activities are in accordance with generally accepted accounting principles (GAAP) and normal business practice. Throughout the litigation process, Daren has been completely honest with the attorneys in his deposition and any other correspondence. Daren believes that the activities of the defendant have been in accordance with GAAP. The case continues and is brought to trial. A few days before Daren is called to testify in the trial, he discovers some new documents and information, which could possibly represent fraudulent behavior by the defendant.

What ethical issues does Daren face in the light of this new information he has received? What concerns should Daren have? What are some possible actions Daren could take?

END NOTES

1. Liz Pulliam Weston, "Money Talk, FBI and IRS Raid Offices of Slatkin," *Los Angeles Times* (May 12, 2001).

2. Associated Press, "Alaskans Shocked by Exxon Valdez Ruling," *USA Today* (November 8, 2001): 6A.

3. For more information on this case, you can read the following articles: Kara Scannell, "Bush Sides with Business over Lawsuits," *The Wall Street Journal* (August 16, 2007): A4 and "Motorola-Cisco Case May Be Pivotal in Enron Suits," *Chicagotribune.com* (August 16, 2007).

Financial Statement Fraud Standards

This textbook contains three chapters on financial statement fraud. Because of the high costs associated with financial statement fraud, regulators have paid much attention over the years to this problem. Such scrutiny has resulted in both auditing standards as well as influential reports issued by organizations and parties interested in the fair presentation of financial statements. In this appendix, we review the professional standards and reports that have been issued related to financial statement fraud in order to provide you with the necessary historical background to understand issues related to fraudulent financial statements. Standards and reports are presented chronologically.

Auditors' Responsibility to Detect Financial Statement Fraud: A Brief History

During the early part of this century, there was universal agreement, even among auditors, that the detection of fraud was one of the primary purposes for conducting an audit of financial statements. Indeed, as noted in a best-selling auditing textbook by Carmichael and Willingham (1971), detecting fraud is deeply rooted in the historical role of auditors, dating back to the early sixteenth century. As late as the 1930s, most auditors emphasized that one of the primary purposes of an audit was detection of fraud. Mautz and Sharaf (1961) stated, "Until recently there was substantial acceptance of the idea that an independent audit had as one of its principal purposes the detection and prevention of fraud and other irregularities."[1] An early edition of Montgomery (the first auditing text) listed three objectives of the audit as follows:

1. The detection of fraud,
2. The detection of technical errors, and
3. The detection of errors in principle.

By the late 1930s, a visible change occurred in the auditing profession's willingness to accept responsibility for fraud detection as a purpose for auditing financial statements. This revolutionary change culminated in the issuance of Statement on Auditing Procedure (SAP) No. 1, *Extensions of Auditing Procedure*. SAP No. 1 contained the following statement:

> *The ordinary examination incident to the issuance of financial statements, accompanied by a report and opinion of an independent certified public accountant, is not designed to discover all defalcations, because that is not its primary objective, although discovery of defalcation frequently results.... To exhaust the possibility of all cases of dishonesty or fraud, the independent auditor would have to examine in detail all transactions. This would entail a prohibitive cost to the great majority of business enterprises—a cost which would pass all bounds of reasonable expectation of benefit or safeguard there from, and place an undue burden on industry.*

Since SAP No. 1 was issued, the profession has struggled to refine and articulate its position on detecting fraud and to establish standards capable of convincing users that auditors should have only a limited role in detecting fraud. During the late 1950s, SAP No. 1, as well as the profession, endured vigorous attacks, and pressure mounted for the AICPA to reconsider its official position as stated in SAP No. 1. The AICPA responded in 1960 by issuing a new standard, SAP No. 30, *Responsibilities and Functions of the Independent Auditor in the Examination of Financial Statements.* Many accounting professionals viewed SAP No. 30 as unresponsive to user concerns because it added no new responsibility to detect fraud. Specifically, SAP No. 30 stated an auditor's responsibility to detect irregularities as follows:

> *The ordinary examination incident to the expression of an opinion on financial statements is not primarily or specifically designed, and cannot be relied upon, to*

disclose defalcations and other similar irregularities, although their discovery may result. Similarly, although the discovery of deliberate misrepresentations by management is usually more closely associated with the objective of the ordinary examination, such examination cannot be relied upon to assure its discovery.

Although the standard did stress that an auditor was obliged to "be aware of the possibility that fraud may exist," it also clarified that an auditor held no responsibility beyond the minimum duty to design tests that would detect fraud.

Although the courts appeared to hold auditors responsible for failure to detect fraud, it took the Equity Funding case and its associated scrutiny of the profession to determine that SAP No. 30 was inadequate.

The Committee on Auditor's Responsibility (Cohen Commission), comprised largely of non-AICPA members, reached a different conclusion, however. The Cohen Commission issued a report in 1978 that highlighted the widening gap between auditor performance and financial statement user expectations. The Cohen report primarily targeted the development of conclusions and recommendations regarding appropriate responsibilities of independent auditors, including the auditor's responsibility for the detection of fraudulent financial reporting. According to the Cohen Commission, the auditor:

... has a duty to search for fraud, and should be expected to detect those frauds that the examination would normally uncover.

The commission went on to say that:

... users of financial statements should have a right to assume that audited financial information is not unreliable because of fraud.... An audit should be designed to provide reasonable assurance that the financial statements are not affected by material fraud.

SAS No. 16, *The Independent Auditor's Responsibility for the Detection of Errors or Irregularities*, was issued in 1977, admitting some obligation to search for fraud in the normal course of a GAAS audit. According to SAS No. 16:

The independent auditor's objective in making an examination of financial statements in accordance with (GAAS) is to form an opinion on whether the financial statements present fairly financial position, results of operations, and the changes in financial position in conformity with (GAAP).... Consequently, under

(GAAS), the independent auditor has the responsibility, within the inherent limitations of the auditing process ... to plan his examination to search for (material) errors and irregularities.

Although SAS No. 16 required auditors to "search for" fraud, it did not require them to "detect" fraud. Even after SAS No. 16 was issued, auditors remained unwilling to accept or acknowledge a substantial responsibility for detecting fraud. SAS No. 16 contained similar "defensive and qualifying" language that was included in SAP No. 1 and SAP No. 30: phrases such as "inherent limitations of the auditing process" and "unless the auditor's examination reveals evidentiary matter to the contrary, his reliance on the truthfulness of certain representations and the genuineness of records and documents obtained during the examination was reasonable" allowed auditors to justify the unwillingness to detect fraud.

Report of the National Commission on Fraudulent Financial Reporting

In October 1987, the National Commission on Fraudulent Financial Reporting (Treadway Commission) issued a landmark report in response to concerns about fraudulent financial reporting. This report helped refocus the business community on the problem of fraudulent financial reporting. Considered an update to the Cohen report, the Treadway study of incidents of financial statement fraud also focused on a broader range of parties playing a vital role in the financial reporting process. The report included 49 extensive recommendations embracing the roles of top management and boards of directors of public companies, independent public accountants and the public accounting profession, the SEC and other regulatory and law enforcement bodies, and the academic community. The Treadway Commission identified numerous causal factors that can lead to financial statement fraud.

Although the Treadway report is not covered in detail in this book, it is strongly recommended that you become familiar with its contents. The report highlights many of the problems that lead to financial statement fraud and provides a basis for activity by organizations such as the AICPA and others. Since the issuance of the Treadway report, there have been many efforts to build upon the commission's findings—that is, to minimize incidents of fraudulent financial reporting. These efforts have primarily focused on the roles that auditors, managers, boards of directors, and audit committees play in the financial statement process.

Efforts Related to the Role of Auditors— SAS No. 53

Soon after the issuance of the Treadway report, the AICPA's Auditing Standards Board (ASB) issued Statement on Auditing Standards No. 53, *The Auditor's Responsibility to Detect and Report Errors and Irregularities*. The ASB issued SAS No. 53 to strengthen the auditor's responsibility related to the detection of instances of material fraudulent financial reporting. SAS No. 53 modified the auditor's responsibility to require the auditor to "design the audit to provide reasonable assurance of detecting errors and irregularities." SAS No. 53 was designed to narrow the expectation gap between the assurances auditors provide and what financial statement users expect regarding the detection of fraudulent financial reporting. SAS No. 53 required the auditor to provide reasonable assurance that material irregularities would be detected, which extended the auditor's responsibility beyond what was required by SAS No. 16.

Public Oversight Board's 1993 Special Report

Subsequent to the issuance of SAS No. 53, the Public Oversight Board of the AICPA SEC Practice Section (the POB) issued a Special Report entitled *In the Public Interest: Issues Confronting the Accounting Profession*. The report was issued primarily in response to continuing signs of failing public confidence in public accountants and auditors, particularly the widespread belief that auditors have a responsibility for detecting management fraud, which many viewed auditors as not meeting. Based on the POB's belief that the integrity and reliability of audited financial statements are critical to the U.S. economy, the Special Report contained specific recommendations for improving and strengthening the accounting profession's performance by enhancing its capacity and willingness to detect fraud and improve the financial reporting process. It also called for improved guidance beyond that in SAS No. 53 to assist auditors in assessing the likelihood of fraud, a strengthening of the process to ensure auditor independence and professionalism, and changes in the corporate governance process. The POB was especially interested in enhancing the auditing profession's potential for detecting management fraud.

AICPA Board of Director's 1993 Report

Also in 1993, the AICPA's Board of Directors issued its report, *Meeting the Financial Reporting Needs of the Future: A Public Commitment for the Public Accounting Profession*. In that report, the AICPA Board of Directors expressed its determination to keep the U.S.

financial reporting system the best in the world, supporting the recommendations and initiatives of others to assist auditors in the detection of material misstatements in financial statements resulting from fraud, and encouraged every participant in the financial reporting process —management, their advisors, regulators, and independent auditors—to share in this responsibility.

AICPA SEC Practice Section Initiatives

Soon after the issuance of the POB's Special Report and the AICPA's Board of Directors' report, the AICPA undertook efforts related to improving the integrity of the financial reporting process, particularly through improved detection of fraudulent financial reporting. The AICPA's SEC Practice Section formed a Professional Issues Task Force that has published guidance about emerging or unresolved practice issues that surface through litigation analysis, peer review, or internal inspection. The SEC Practice Section also amended membership requirements to require that concurring partners provide assurance that those consulting on accounting and auditing matters are aware of all relevant facts and circumstances related to the consultation issue and to the auditee, to ensure that the conclusion reached is an appropriate one. The AICPA SEC Practice Section also created the Detection and Prevention of Fraud Task Force. That task force issued a document in 1994 entitled *Client Acceptance and Continuance Procedures for Audit Clients*. That document emphasized that understanding the components of engagement risk is critical to deciding whether to accept new clients, continue old ones, and in any event to manage the "audit risk" that accompanies those decisions.

Panel on Audit Effectiveness

At the request of the chairman of the SEC, the Public Oversight Board appointed a panel of eight members, charging it to thoroughly examine the current audit model. The panel made recommendations that it believed would result in more effective audits that would improve the reliability of financial statements, enhance their credibility, contribute to investors' confidence in the profession, and improve the efficiency of the capital markets. One of the panel's recommendations was because "audit firms may have reduced the scope of their audits and level of testing and because the auditing profession may not have kept pace with a rapidly changing environment, the profession needs to address vigorously the issue of fraudulent financial reporting, including fraud in the form of illegitimate earnings management." It recommended that the auditing standards should create a "forensic-type" fieldwork phase on all audits. The panel suggested that this work should be based on the possibility of dishonesty and collusion, overriding of controls, and falsification of documents. Auditors would be required during this phase, in some cases on a surprise basis, to perform substantive tests directed at the possibility of fraud. The panel's recommendations also call for auditors to examine nonstandard entries, and to analyze certain opening financial statement balances to assess, with the benefit of hindsight, how certain accounting estimates and judgments or other matters were resolved. The intent of the panel's recommendations was twofold: to enhance the likelihood that auditors will be able to detect material fraud, and to establish implicitly a deterrent to fraud by positing a greater threat to its successful concealment.

SAS No. 82

In 1997, the AICPA responded to various calls for improved auditing guidance related to the detection of material misstatements due to fraudulent financial reporting by issuing SAS No. 82, *Consideration of Fraud in a Financial Statement Audit*. SAS 82 was written to help reduce the "expectation gap" that exists between financial statement auditors and users of financial statements. It was determined that SAS 82 would only be successful in narrowing the expectation gap if, as a result of applying the standard, (1) auditors detect more fraud sooner (that is, the standard bolsters the actual fraud detection performance of auditors), or (2) the standard is successful in convincing financial statement users that auditors should not be held responsible for detecting all financial statement fraud. Although many people were optimistic about the standard accomplishing the first of these possibilities, few believe that the second result will ever happen.

Although SAS 82 was a giant step forward, it did not narrow the expectations gap as much as hoped, and it has now been replaced by SAS 99.

SAS 82 was an auditing standard that clarified the fraud detection responsibilities of certified public accountants (CPAs) and provided guidance to those who performed financial statement audits. Like all other standards, SAS 82 offered instructions on how the 10 generally accepted auditing standards (GAAS) should be interpreted and followed. SAS 82 primarily provided guidance on how financial statement auditors should consider the possibility of fraud when:

- Exercising due professional care (general auditing standard No. 3)

- Planning an audit (fieldwork standard No. 1)
- Evaluating internal controls (fieldwork standard No. 2), and
- Gathering sufficient, competent evidentiary matter to support the audit opinion (fieldwork standard No. 3)

SAS 82 was much more comprehensive than the preceding fraud-related auditing standards. Although it did not change the overall responsibilities of GAAS auditors to provide "reasonable assurance that material misstatement of the financial statement does not exist," it more explicitly identified what auditors must do to try to discover such fraud. The following are the key provisions of the standard that were intended to remove the "fuzziness" that existed with previous standards, and that attempted to help auditors better detect material financial statement misstatement caused by fraud.

1. SAS 82 was the first-ever auditing standard to solely address fraud. Previous standards addressed "errors" and irregularities" together.
2. SAS 82 was the first GAAS auditing standard to use the term *fraud*. Previous standards used the more nebulous term *irregularity* when referring to fraud.
3. SAS 82 made it clear that the auditor's responsibilities with respect to fraud extend throughout the entire audit and do not end when the planning phase is finished. Previous standards were not clear regarding post-planning responsibilities.
4. SAS 82 required GAAS auditors to document how they assessed the risk of fraud in their audits. Previous fraud standards did not require specific documentation. There was a general feeling among SAS 82 task force members that requiring documentation would, in many cases, drive behavior that is consistent with the standard.
5. SAS 82 required GAAS auditors to document how they responded to the risks of fraud they discovered when conducting their audits. Previous standards hardly mentioned how risks of fraud should be documented, evaluated, or addressed.
6. SAS 82 emphasized the need for "professional skepticism" in dealing with clients.
7. SAS 82 provided specific guidance to auditors about the kind of risks they must consider (more than 30 different examples of risk factors are presented), and how observed risk factors should be considered and addressed.

8. SAS 82 required GAAS auditors to ask management specifically about the risks of fraud, what they perceive to be the company's greatest fraud exposures, and whether they have knowledge of fraud that has been perpetrated on or within the company.

Statement on Auditing Standards No. 99: Considerations of Fraud in a Financial Statement Audit

Statement on Auditing Standards (SAS) 99 establishes standards and provides guidance to auditors in fulfilling their responsibility as it relates to fraud in an audit of financial statements conducted in accordance with generally accepted auditing standards. SAS 99 does not change the auditor's responsibility to plan and perform the audit to obtain reasonable assurance about whether the financial statements are free of material misstatement, whether caused by error or fraud. However, SAS 99 does establish standards and provide guidance to auditors in fulfilling that responsibility, as it relates to fraud. The following is an overview of the content of SAS 99:

Description and characteristics of fraud. This section of the statement describes fraud and its characteristics, including the aspects of fraud particularly relevant to an audit of financial statements.

Discussion among engagement personnel regarding the risks of material misstatement due to fraud. This section requires, as part of planning the audit, that there be a discussion among the audit team members to consider the susceptibility of the entity to material misstatement due to fraud and to reinforce the importance of adopting an appropriate mindset of professional skepticism.

Obtaining the information needed to identify the risks of material misstatement due to fraud. This section requires the auditor to gather the information necessary to identify the risks of material misstatement due to fraud, by the following:

1. Making inquiries of management and others within the entity.
2. Considering the results of the analytical procedures performed in planning the audit. (The statement also requires that the auditor perform analytical procedures relating to revenue.)
3. Considering fraud risk factors.
4. Considering certain other information.

Identifying risks that may result in a material misstatement due to fraud. This section requires the auditor to use the information gathered above to identify risks that may result in a material misstatement due to fraud.

Assessing the identified risks after taking into account an evaluation of the entity's programs and controls. This section requires the auditor to evaluate the entity's programs and controls that address the identified risks of material misstatement due to fraud, and to assess the risks taking into account this evaluation.

Responding to the results of the assessment. This section requires the auditor to respond to the results of the risk assessment. This response may include the following:

1. A response to identified risks that has an overall effect on how the audit is conducted; that is, a response involving more general considerations apart from the specific procedures otherwise planned.
2. A response to identified risk that involves the nature, timing, and extent of the auditing procedures to be performed.
3. A response involving the performance of certain procedures to further address the risk of material misstatement due to fraud involving management override of controls.

Evaluating audit test results. This section requires the auditor's assessment of the risk of material misstatement due to fraud to be ongoing throughout the audit and the auditor evaluate at the completion of the audit whether the accumulated results of auditing procedures and other observations affect the assessment. It also requires the auditor to consider whether identified misstatements may be indicative of fraud and, if so, directs the auditor to evaluate their implications.

Communicating about fraud to management, the audit committee, and others. This section provides guidance regarding the auditor's communications about fraud to management, the audit committee, and others.

Documenting the auditor's consideration of fraud. This section describes related documentation requirements.

The Roles of Management, Boards of Directors, and Audit Committees

Although auditors play a vital role in the detection of instances of material fraudulent financial reporting, the

Treadway Commission's 1987 report noted that the prevention and early detection of fraudulent financial reporting must start with the entity that prepares the financial statements. Every fraudulent financial statement for which the auditor has been held responsible was prepared by executives who intentionally misstated financial information to deceive not only shareholders, investors, and creditors, but the auditor as well. Thus, the Treadway report contains several recommendations for public companies, particularly addressing responsibilities of top management, the board of directors, and audit committees. The Treadway report calls for all public companies to maintain internal controls that provide reasonable assurance that fraudulent financial reporting will be prevented or subjected to early detection. The Treadway Commission specifically calls for the development of additional, integrated guidance on internal controls.

COSO's 1992 Report

In 1992, COSO issued *Internal Control—Integrated Framework* in response to calls for better internal control systems to help senior executives better control the enterprises they run. In addition to noting that internal controls can help an entity achieve its performance and profitability targets and prevent the loss of resources, COSO's report also notes that internal control can significantly help an entity ensure reliable financial reporting. Specifically, the COSO report:

- Provides a high-level overview of the internal control framework directed to the chief executive and other senior officers, board members, legislators, and regulators.
- Defines internal control, describes its components, and provides criteria against which managements, boards of directors, and others can assess their internal control systems.
- Provides guidance to those entities that report publicly on internal control over the preparation of their published statements.
- Contains materials that might be useful in conducting an evaluation of internal controls.

Audit Committee Requirements of Major U.S. Stock Exchanges

Often, boards of directors of companies assign responsibility for oversight of the financial reporting process to an audit committee, comprised of a subgroup of the board. In the United States, all three major securities markets—the New York Stock Exchange (NYSE),

American Stock Exchange (AMEX), and National Association of Securities Dealer's Automated Quotation System (NASDAQ)—have requirements addressing audit committee composition. The NYSE requires, and the AMEX recommends, that listed companies have audit committees made up entirely of outside directors.[2] NASDAQ requires only that a majority of the audit committee consist of outside directors for companies trading on the National Market System; however, companies trading as a NASDAQ Small-Cap Issue are not required to maintain a minimum number of outside directors on their audit committees. These audit committee requirements were generally in place by the time the Treadway report was issued. However, other regulatory actions were undertaken in the 1990s related to the corporate governance process. For example, the Federal Deposit Insurance Corporation implemented new audit committee composition requirements mandating the inclusion of independent directors who, for certain large depository institutions, must include individuals with banking experience.[3]

Public Oversight Board's Advisory Panel Report

In 1994, the POB issued a report entitled *Strengthening the Professionalism of the Independent Auditor*. This report encouraged boards of directors to play an active role in the financial reporting process and for the auditing profession to look to the board of directors—the shareholders' representative—as its client. The Advisory Panel urged the POB, the SEC, and others to encourage adoption of proposals such as increasing the representation of outsiders on the board and reducing board size to strengthen the independence of boards of directors and their accountability to shareholders. In addition to strengthening the role of the board of directors in the oversight of management, the Advisory Panel recommended that audit committees should expect auditors to be more forthcoming in communicating first with the audit committee and then with the full board to provide the auditor's perspective on the company's operations, as well as the company's financial reporting policies and practices.

Public Oversight Board's 1995 Report

The POB stated in its 1995 publication, *Directors, Management, and Auditors: Allies in Protecting Shareholder Interests*, that practices followed by well-governed corporations should foster an environment where the independent auditor, management, audit committee, and board of directors play interactive and timely roles in the financial reporting process.

After the Enron "debacle," there was significant controversy about the accounting profession and its regulation and oversight. Because of the criticism of the Public Oversight Board, it went out of business effective March 31, 2002.[4]

The Independence Standards Board

To strengthen the role of the auditor as an independent assurer of credible financial information and a major source of information for the audit committee and board, the accounting profession and the SEC agreed in 1997 to establish a new private sector body—the Independence Standards Board—to set independence rules and guidance for auditors of public companies. The Independence Standards Board did not make a significant difference in the profession.

Sarbanes-Oxley Act of 2002

All of the efforts described thus far have helped focus attention on and reduce the number of incidences of fraudulent financial reporting. However, none of them have had the impact that the Sarbanes-Oxley Act of 2002 had. SOX, as it is unofficially called, completely changed the corporate landscape with respect to fraud prevention, detection, and investigation. Sarbanes-

Oxley significantly increased the responsibility of auditors, boards of directors, audit committees, management, and others. It was the most significant securities legislation since the SEC acts of 1933 and 1934 that established the SEC and required SEC reporting.

Since we discussed Sarbanes-Oxley in detail in Appendix A in Chapter 11, we will not discuss it here. You should recognize its significance, however. Anyone interested in preventing, detecting, or investigating fraud or in working in a public company environment should be familiar with its contents.

END NOTES

1. R. K. Mautz and H. A. Sharaf, "The Philosophy of Auditing," American Accounting Association, 1961.

2. http://www.sec.gov/rules/sro/ny9939o.htm

3. This information can be accessed at the Federal Deposit Insurance Corporation Web site at http://www.fdic.gov/regulations/laws/rules/ 2000-8500.html. Section D: Audit Committees.

4. http://www.smartpros.com/x33441.xml.

Bibliography

Albrecht, Conan C., "Proactively Detecting Fraud," *Financial Post* (July 2001): 13–15.

———, "Root Out Financial Deception," *Journal of Accountancy* (April 2002): 30–36.

———, and J.G. Dunn, "Can Auditors Detect Fraud?" *Journal of Forensic Accounting* (January–June 2001): 1–12.

———, and ———, "Conducting a Pro-Active Fraud Audit: A Case Study," *Journal of Forensic Accounting* (December 2001): 203–219.

———, Chad Albrecht, and T. Williams, "Conducting Ethical Investigations," *Security Management*, (November 2004).

Albrecht, W. Steve, and J. J. Willingham, "An Evaluation of SAS No. 53: The Auditor's Responsibility to Detect and Report Errors and Irregularities," *The Expectation Gap Standards: Progress, Implementation Issues, Research Opportunities* (New York: AICPA, 1993).

———, and M. B. Romney, "Redflagging Management Fraud: A Validation," *Advances in Accounting* (1986): 323–333.

———, Conan C. Albrecht, and Chad Albrecht, "Fraud and Corporate Executives: Agency, Stewardship and Broken Trust," *Journal of Forensic Accounting* (January–June 2004): 109–130.

———, K. R. Howe, and M. B. Romney, *Detecting Fraud: The Internal Auditor's Perspective* (Maitland, FL: The Institute of Internal Auditors Research Foundation, 1982).

———, G. W. Wernz, and T. L. Williams, *Fraud: Bringing Light to the Dark Side of Business* (New York, NY: Irwin Professional Publishing, 1995): 56–59 and 118–119.

———, M. B. Romney, D. J. Cherrington, I. R. Payne, and A. J. Roe, *How to Detect and Prevent Business Fraud* (Englewood Cliffs, NJ: Prentice-Hall, 1982).

American Institute of Certified Public Accountants (AICPA), *Consideration of Fraud in a Financial Statement Audit*. Statement on Auditing Standards No 53. (New York: AICPA, 1988).

———, *Consideration of Fraud in a Financial Statement Audit*. Statement on Auditing Standards No. 81 (New York: AICPA, 1997).

———, *Consideration of Fraud in a Financial Statement Audit*. Statement on Auditing Standards No. 99 (New York: AICPA, 2002).

Apostolou, B., J. Hassell, S. Webber, and G. Sumners. "The Relative Importance of Management Fraud Risk Factors," *Behavioral Research in Accounting* (2001): 1–24.

Asare, S. K., and A. M. Wright. "The Effectiveness of Alternative Risk Assessment and Program Planning Tools in a Fraud Setting," *Contemporary Accounting Research* (Summer 2004): 325–352.

Ashton, R. E., and A. M. Wright, "Identifying Audit Adjustments with Attention-Directing Procedures," *The Accounting Review* (October 1989): 710–728.

Association of Certified Fraud Examiners, *Report to the Nation: Occupational Fraud and Abuse* (Austin, TX: 2006).

Beasley, M. S., "An Empirical Analysis of the Relation Between the Board of Director Composition and Financial Statement Fraud," *The Accounting Review* (October 1996): 443–465.

———, J. V. Carcello, and D. R. Hermanson, *Fraudulent Financial Reporting: 1987–1997: An Analysis of U.S. Public Companies*, Committee of Sponsoring Organizations (COSO) (1999).

———, ———, ———, and P. D. Lapides. "Fraudulent Financial Reporting: Consideration of Industry Traits and Corporate Governance Mechanisms," *Accounting Horizons* (2000): 441–454.

Bell, T. B., and J. V. Carcello, "A Decision Aid for Assessing the Likelihood of Fraudulent Financial Reporting," *Auditing: A Journal of Practice and Theory* (Spring 2000): 169–184.

Beneish, M. D. "Detecting GAAP Violation: Implications for Assessing Earnings Management Among Firms with Extreme Financial Performance," *Journal of Accounting and Public Policy* (1997): 271–309.

_____. "Incentives and Penalties Related to Earnings Overstatements that Violate GAAP," *The Accounting Review* (1999): 425–457.

_____. "The Detection of Earnings Manipulation," *Financial Analysts Journal* (1999): 24–36.

Bernardi, R. "Fraud Detection: The Effect of Client Integrity and Competence and Auditor Cognitive Style," *Auditing: A Journal of Practice & Theory* (Supplement 1994): 68–84.

Bloomfield, R. "Strategic Dependence and Inherent Risk Assessments," *The Accounting Review* (January 1995): 71–90.

Bonner, S. E., Z. V. Palmrose, and S. M. Young, "Fraud Type and Auditor Litigation: An Analysis of SEC Accounting and Auditing Enforcement Releases," *The Accounting Review* (October 1998): 503–532.

Braun, R. L. "The Effect of Time Pressure on Auditor Attention to Qualitative Aspects of Misstatements Indicative of Potential Fraudulent Financial Reporting," *Accounting, Organizations and Society* (2000): 243–259.

Brazel, J. F., K. L. Jones, and M. F. Zimbelman. "Using Nonfinancial Performance Measures to Assess Fraud Risk," *Journal of Accounting Research* (December 2009): 1135–1166.

_____, T. D. Carpenter, and J. G. Jenkins. "Auditors' Use of Brainstorming in the Consideration of Fraud: Reports from the Field," *The Accounting Review* (July 2010): 1273–1301.

Burton, F. G., T. J. Wilks, and M. F. Zimbelman. "The Impact of Audit Penalty Distributions on the Detection and Frequency of Fraudulent Reporting," *Review of Accounting Studies*, (Forthcoming).

Carcello, J., and A. Nagy. "Audit Firm Tenure and Fraudulent Financial Reporting," *Auditing: A Journal of Practice & Theory* (2004): 55–69.

Carpenter, T. D. "Audit Team Brainstorming, Fraud Scheme Identification, and Fraud Scheme Assessment: Implications of SAS No. 99," *The Accounting Review* (October 2007): 1119–1140.

Cleary, R., and J. C. Thibodeau. "Applying Digital Analysis Using Benford's Law to Detect Fraud," *Auditing: A Journal of Practice & Theory* (2005): 77–81.

Cressy, D. R., *Other People's Money: The Social Psychology of Embezzlement* (New York: Free Press, 1953).

Durtschi, C., W. Hillison, and C. Pacini. "The Effective Use of Benford's Law to Assist in Detecting Fraud in Accounting Data," *Journal of Forensic Accounting* (June 2004): 17–34.

Efendi, J., A. Srivastava, and E. Swanson. "Why Do Corporate Managers Misstate Financial Statements? The Role of Option Compensation and Other Factors," *Journal of Financial Economics* (2007): 667–708.

Deshmukh, A., K. E. Karim, and P. H. Siegel, "An Analysis of the Efficiency and Effectiveness of Auditing to Detect Management Fraud: A Signal Detection Theory Approach," *International Journal of Auditing* (1998): 127–138.

DeZoort, F. T., and T. A. Lee, "The Impact of SAS No. 82 on Perceptions of External Auditor Responsibility for Fraud Detection," *International Journal of Auditing* (1998): 167–182.

Eining, M. M., and P. B. Dorr, "The Impact of Expert System Usage on Experiential Learning in an Audit Setting," *Journal of Information Systems* (Spring 1991): 1–16.

Eining, M. M_____, D. R. Jones, and J.K. Loebbecke, "Reliance on Decision Aids: An Examination of Management Fraud," *Auditing: A Journal of Practice and Theory* (Fall 1997): 1–19.

Elliott, R. K., and J. J. Willingham, Jr., *Management Fraud: Detection and Deterrence* (New York: Petrocelli Books, Inc., 1980).

Erickson, M., B. W. Mayhew, and W. L. Felix, "Why Do Audits Fail? Evidence from Lincoln Savings and Loan," *Journal of Accounting Research* (Spring 2000): 165–194.

_____, M. Hanlon, and E. L. Maydew. "Is There a Link Between Executive Equity Incentives and Accounting Fraud?" *Journal of Accounting Research* (March 2006): 113–144.

Farber, D. "Restoring Trust After Fraud: Does Corporate Governance Matter?" *The Accounting Review* (2005): 539–561.

Geis, G., *On White-Collar Crime* (Lexington, MA: Lexington Books, 1982).

_____, and R. F. Meier, *White-Collar Crime: Offenses in Business, Politics, and the Professions*, Revised Edition (New York: The Free Press, 1977).

Gillett, P. R., and N. Uddin. "CFO Intentions of Fraudulent Financial Reporting," *Auditing: A Journal of Practice & Theory* (2005): 55–76.

Glover, S. M., D. F. Prawitt, J. J. Schultz, Jr., and M. F. Zimbelman, "A Comparison of Audit Planning Decisions in Response to Increased Fraud Risk: Before and After SAS No. 82," *Auditing: A Journal of Practice & Theory* (September 2003): 237–251.

Green, B. P., and J. H. Choi, "Assessing the Risk of Management Fraud Through Neural Network

Technology," *Auditing: A Journal of Practice and Theory*, (Spring 1997): 14–28.

Hackenbrack, K. "Implications of Seemingly Irrelevant Audit Evidence in Audit Judgment," *Journal of Accounting Research* (Spring 1992): 126–136.

———, "The Effects of Experience with Different Sized Clients on Auditor Evaluations of Fraudulent Financial Reporting Indicators," *Auditing: A Journal of Practice and Theory* (Spring 1993): 99–110.

Hoffman, V. B., and J. M. Patton. "Accountability, the Dilution Effect, and Conservatism in Auditors' Fraud Judgments," *Journal of Accounting Research* (Autumn 1997): 227–237.

———, and M. F. Zimbelman. "Do Strategic Reasoning and Brainstorming Help Auditors Change Their Standard Audit Procedures in Response to Fraud Risk?" *The Accounting Review* (May 2009): 811–837.

Hogan, C. E., Z. Rezaee, R. A. Riley, and U. Velury. "Financial Statement Fraud: Insights from the Academic Literature," *Auditing: A Journal of Practice and Theory* (November 2008): 231–252.

Hooks, K. L., S. E. Kaplan, and J. J. Schultz, Jr. "Enhancing Communication to Assist in Fraud Prevention and Detection," *Auditing: A Journal of Practice & Theory* (Fall 1994): 88–117.

Hunton, J. E. and A. Gold. "Comparing the Outcomes of Nominal Group, Round Robin and Open Discussion Fraud Brainstorming," *The Accounting Review* (May 2010): 911–935.

Hollinger, R. C., *Dishonesty in the Workplace: A Manager's Guide to Preventing Employee Theft* (Park Ridge, IL: London House Press,1989).

Kaminski, K. A., and T. S. Wetzel. "Financial Ratios and Fraud: An Exploratory Study Using Chaos Theory," *Journal of Forensic Accounting* (2004): 147–172.

———, ———, and L. Guan. "Can Financial Ratios Detect Fraudulent Financial Reporting?" *Managerial Auditing Journal* (2004): 15–28.

Kaplan, S., and P. M. J. Reckers. "Auditor's Reporting Decisions for Accounting Estimates: The Effect of Assessments of the Risk of Fraudulent Financial Reporting," *Managerial Auditing Journal* (1995): 27–36.

Knapp, C. Z., and M. C. Knapp, "The Effects of Experience and Explicit Fraud Risk Assessment in Detecting Fraud with Analytical Procedures," *Accounting, Organizations and Society* (January 2001): 25–37.

Lie, E. "On the Timing of CEO Stock Option Awards," *Management Science* (2005): 802–812.

Lin, J. W., M. I. Hwang, and J. D. Becker. "A Fuzzy Neural Network for Assessing the Risk of Fraudulent Financial Reporting," *Managerial Auditing Journal* (2003): 657–665.

Loebbecke, J. K., M. M. Eining, and J. J. Willingham, Jr., "Auditors' Experience with Material Irregularities: Frequency, Nature, and Detect-Ability," *Auditing: A Journal of Practice and Theory* (Fall 1989): 1–28.

Merchant, K. A., *Fraudulent and Questionable Financial Reporting: A Corporate Perspective* (Morristown, NJ: Financial Executives Research Foundation,1987).

Nelson, M. W., J. A. Elliott, and R. L. Tarpley. "Evidence from Auditors About Managers' and Auditors' Earnings Management Decisions," *The Accounting Review* (Supplement 2002): 175–202.

Nieschwietz, R. J., J. J. Schultz, Jr., and M. F. Zimbelman, "Empirical Research on External Auditors' Detection of Financial Statement Fraud," *Journal of Accounting Literature* (2000): 190–246.

Nigrini, M., and L. J. Mittermaier. "The Use of Benford's Law as an Aid in Analytical Procedures," *Auditing: A Journal of Practice & Theory* (Fall 1997): 52–67.

Palmrose, Z. V., "Litigation and Independent Auditors: The Role of Business Failures and Management Fraud," *Auditing: A Journal of Practice and Theory* (Spring 1987): 90–103.

Pincus, K. V., "The Efficacy of a Red Flags Questionnaire for Assessing the Possibility of Fraud," *Accounting, Organizations, and Society* (1989): 153–163.

Rezaee, Z. "Restoring Public Trust in the Accounting Profession by Developing Anti-Fraud Education, Programs, and Auditing," *Managerial Auditing Journal* (2004): 134.

———. "Causes, Consequences, and Deterrence of Financial Statement Fraud," *Critical Perspectives on Accounting* (April 2005): 277–298.

Romney, M. B., W. Steve Albrecht, and D. J. Cherrington, "Red-Flagging the White-Collar Criminal," *Management Accounting* (March 1980): 51–57.

Shelton, S. W., O. R. Whittington, and D. Landsittel. "Auditing Firms' Fraud Risk Assessment Practices," *Accounting Horizons* (2001): 19–33.

Summers, S. L., and J. T. Sweeney, "Fraudulently Misstated Financial Statements and Insider Trading: An Empirical Analysis," *The Accounting Review* (January 1998): 131–146.

Sutherland, E. H., *White-Collar Crime* (New York: Dryden Press, 1949).

Wilks, T. J., and M. F. Zimbelman, "Decomposition of Fraud Risk Assessments and Auditors' Sensitivity to Fraud Cues," *Contemporary Accounting Research* (Fall 2004): 719–745.

_____, and _____, "Using Game Theory and Strategic Reasoning Concepts to Prevent and Detect Fraud," *Accounting Horizons* (September 2004): 173–184.

Zimbelman, M. F., "The Effects of SAS No. 82 on Auditors' Attention to Fraud Risk Factors and Audit Planning," *Journal of Accounting Research* (Supplement 1997): 75–97.

_____, and W. S. Waller. "An Experimental Investigation of Auditor-Auditee Interaction under Ambiguity," *Journal of Accounting Research* (Supplement 1999): 135–155.

Glossary

A

Acid-test ratio (quick ratio) Measure of a firm's ability to meet current liabilities; computed by dividing net quick assets (all current assets, except inventories and prepaid expenses) by current liabilities.

Accounting anomalies Inaccuracies or unusual entries or balances in source documents, journal entries, ledgers, or financial statements. These anomalies can be a red flag that fraud is occurring.

Accounting cycle The process and procedures for analyzing, recording, classifying, summarizing, and reporting the transactions of a business.

Accounting system An organization of policies and procedures for recording economic transactions.

Accounts receivable turnover Sales divided by average accounts receivable; a measure of the efficiency and timing with which receivables are being collected.

Accrued liabilities Liabilities arising from end-of-period adjustments, not from specific transactions.

Acquisitions The purchase of something, such as the purchase of one company by another company.

Acute emotional crisis Psychological problems that are often experienced by persons committing fraud.

Admission-seeking questions Questions asked of interviewees (suspects) that are intended to result in a confession.

Affidavit A written statement or declaration given under oath.

Allowance for uncollectible accounts as a percentage of receivables Allowance for Doubtful Accounts divided by Accounts Receivable; a measure of the percentage of receivables estimated to be uncollectible.

Analytical anomalies Relationships, procedures, or events that are unusual or unexpected; these include events, transactions, or procedures that are too big or too small, that are done by the wrong person or at the wrong time, or that are unusual in some other way; analytical anomalies are one of the six categories of red flags.

Analytical procedures Procedures used by financial statement auditors to identify potential misstatements by comparing current financial information (including financial statement balances or ratios) with prior financial information, budgets, other companies, industry data, or other expected relationships.

Answer The response to a lawsuit written by the defendant in a legal proceeding; the answer is the response given to the initial complaint made by the plaintiff.

Appellate court A review court to which participants in lower court cases can have their cases reviewed or retried if they are unhappy with the outcome.

Arraignment A court hearing where the charges against the defendant are read. At the arraignment, the defendants may plead guilty, not guilty, or nolo contendere.

Assessment questions Preliminary questions asked in an interview to assess and better understand the situation.

Asset misappropriation Theft that is committed by stealing receipts, stealing assets on hand, or committing some type of disbursement fraud.

Asset turnover ratio Total sales divided by average total assets; a measure of the amount of sales revenue generated with each dollar of assets.

Association of Certified Fraud Examiners (ACFE) An international organization of approximately 50,000 members based in Austin, Texas, dedicated to fighting fraud and white-collar crime.

Audit trail Documents and records that can be used to trace transactions.

B

Backdating The practice of deliberately and improperly changing the effective dates on stock options for the purpose of securing extra compensation for the option holders.

Bad debt expense An expense representing receivables and/or revenues that are presumed not to be collectible.

Balance sheet The financial statement that reports a company's assets, liabilities, and owners' equity as of a specific date.

Bankruptcy A legal process that either allows a debtor to work out an orderly plan to settle debts or liquidates a debtor's assets and distributes them to creditors.

Bankruptcy Code Title 11 of the U.S. code—the federal statute that governs the bankruptcy process.

Bankruptcy courts Federal courts that hear only bankruptcy cases.

Bates numbers An identification scheme for marking evidence in criminal and civil trial cases; used by lawyers and others to track and refer to evidence; Bates numbers are used to sequentially number documents as they are scanned or processed in the discovery phase of an investigation.

Behavioral symptoms Unusual changes in behavior that are caused by stress (such as mood swings, sweating, rubbing the hands together, not looking straight in the eye) that accompany fraud perpetrators; behavioral symptoms are one of the six categories of red flags used in detecting fraud.

Benchmark admission An answer that implies guilt. This is an answer to a question that implies admission on the part of the interviewee.

Benford's Law Mathematical algorithm that accurately predicts that, for many data sets, the first digit of each group of numbers in a random sample will begin with a 1 more than a 2, a 2 more than a 3, a 3 more than a 4, and so on; predicts the percentage of time each digit will appear in a sequence of numbers.

Bid-rigging schemes Collusive fraud wherein an employee helps a vendor illegally obtain a contract that was supposed to involve competitive bidding.

Billing schemes Submission of a false or an altered invoice that causes an employer to willingly issue a check.

Biometrics Using unique features of the human body (for example, retinal scans) to create secure access controls.

Bogus mystery shopping scams Perpetrators falsely promise victims jobs that involve shopping for merchandise and filing reports on the experiences they have had for substantial compensation.

Bribery The offering, giving, receiving, or soliciting of anything of value to influence an official act.

Bust-out A planned bankruptcy.

C

Calibrating, calibration or norming That part of an interview that is intended to determine how an interviewee responds when answering questions about subjects he or she is comfortable with so as to be able to contrast the verbal and nonverbal cues from those questions with those exhibited when the interviewee is asked about a fraudulent or dishonest act.

Capitalization Recording expenditures as assets rather than as expenses. (For example, start-up costs of a company that are "capitalized" are recorded as assets and amortized.)

Catharsis The emotional reliving of painful past experiences.

Chain letter scams Fraudsters promise to pay victims to make copies of a letter and send them to consumers. In order to get the letter, the victims must pay an advance fee.

Chain of custody Maintaining detailed records about documents from the time they are received in the investigation process until the trial is completed. Helps to substantiate that documents have not been altered or manipulated since coming into the investigator's hands.

Chapter 7 bankruptcy Complete liquidation or "shutting down of a business" and distribution of any proceeds to creditors.

Chapter 11 bankruptcy Bankruptcy that allows the bankrupt entity time to reorganize its operational and financial affairs, settle its debts, and continue to operate in a reorganized fashion.

Chapter 13 bankruptcy Sometimes called the reorganization and repayment bankruptcy; a reorganization that generally allows debtors to repay all or some of their debts on an interest-free basis over a period of three to five years; these bankruptcies are similar to Chapter 11 bankruptcies but can be used by individuals with regular income and debts of $1 million or less.

Check tampering Scheme in which dishonest employees (1) prepare fraudulent checks for their own benefit or (2) intercept checks intended for a third party and convert the checks for their own benefit.

Chronemic communication The use of time in interpersonal relationships to convey meaning, attitudes, and desires.

Circular reaction The tendency of a person to repeat novel experiences.

Civil law The body of law that provides remedies for violation of private rights—deals with rights and duties between individuals.

Clawbacks The recovery of assets from Ponzi scheme participants who were net winners (i.e. they received more assets than they gave as participants in a Ponzi scheme) for the purpose of distributing the assets to those who were net losers in the scheme.

Clearinghouse scam Involves a victim receiving a letter that falsely claims the writer represents a foreign bank; the foreign bank falsely acts as a clearinghouse for venture capital in a certain country; used to defraud unsuspecting victims.

Codes of conduct Written statements that convey expectations about what is and is not appropriate in an organization.

Coercive power The ability that one person (person A) has to punish another person (person B) if he or she does not comply with that person's (person A's) wishes.

Comma separated values (CSV) A file format used by computers to store table and spreadsheet files; can be opened with Microsoft Excel and many other software packages.

Commercial bribery Giving gifts, promising favors, or otherwise bribing persons to gain a business advantage.

Committee of Sponsoring Organizations (COSO) An organization made up of representatives from major accounting organizations that is concerned about internal controls and financial statement fraud.

Complaint A request filed by a plaintiff to request civil proceedings against someone—usually to seek damages.

Computer forensics The use of sophisticated software to clone and investigate suspect hard drives, cell phones, and other digital devices.

Concealment Efforts taken to hide a fraud from being discovered.

Conflict of interest Fraud in which employees, managers, or executives put their personal interest above the company's interest, usually resulting in an adverse effect on the organization.

Consumer fraud Any fraud that targets a consumer or an individual as its victim.

Contingent liability A potential liability, often the result of contingent legal commitments or litigation. If the likelihood of payment is "probable," the contingent liability must be reported as a liability on the financial statements; if likelihood of payment is "reasonably possible," it must be disclosed in the footnotes to the financial statements; if likelihood of payment is "remote," no mention of the possible liability needs to be made.

Control environment A set of characteristics that defines good management control features other than accounting policies and control activities; one element of the control system of a corporation identified in the COSO framework.

Control activities (procedures) Specific error-checking routines performed by company personnel; the five types of control activities identified by COSO are (1) segregation of duties, (2) proper authorizations, (3) physical controls, (4) independent checks, and (5) documents and records.

Controlled-answer techniques A method of interview wherein the interviewer asks questions that will yield answers that are desirable.

Conversion The spending of stolen assets by perpetrators.

Corruption Dishonesty that involves the following schemes: (1) bribery, (2) conflicts of interest, (3) economic extortion, and (4) illegal gratuities.

Cost of goods sold (COGS) The cost of goods sold to customers; calculated by subtracting ending inventory from the sum of beginning inventory plus purchases.

Craft assembly Perpetrators falsely promise high pay for working on different projects. Victims are usually required to purchase costly materials, equipment, and training.

Creditor A person or an entity owed money by a debtor.

Criminal law The branch of law that deals with offenses of a public nature or against society.

Current ratio Measure of the liquidity of a business; equal to current assets divided by current liabilities.

Custom or habit An unconscious behavior exhibited during interviews.

Customer fraud Customers not paying for goods purchased, getting something for nothing, or deceiving organizations into giving them something they should not have.

Cyclic redundancy check (CRC) number A check performed on data to see if an error has occurred in transmitting, reading, or writing the data.

D

Data analysis software Software that allows the user to examine data, run analytical procedures, and determine if there is something wrong with the data.

Data theft Theft of data or personal information through such means as sniffing, spoofing, and customer impersonation.

Data warehouse Large storage areas for data, consisting of large databases able to store vast amounts of data.

Data-driven fraud detection A six-step method of analyzing large amounts of data for fraud schemes and indicators, usually with computer-based algorithms and searching techniques.

Debtor A person or an entity declaring bankruptcy.

Debt-to-equity ratio The number of dollars of borrowed funds for every dollar invested by owners; computed as total liabilities divided by total equity.

Deduction Reasoning from the general to the particular or from cause to effect.

Deferred charges An expenditure that has been capitalized to be expensed in the future.

Delimited text A file format with one record per line. Common examples of delimited text include comma separated values and tab separated values.

Deposition Sworn testimony taken before a trial begins. At depositions, the opposing side's attorneys ask questions of witnesses.

Descriptives Summary information that helps an investigator better understand a data set. Common descriptives include means, standard deviations, histograms, and ranges.

Digital analysis See Benford's Law.

Digital signatures and certificates A signature sent over the Internet.

Disbursement of money from wills Organizations receive letters from mysterious "benefactors" interested in contributing a large sum of money. However, to get the money, the charity is required to pay inheritance taxes or government fees.

Discovery The legal process by which each party's attorneys try to find all information about the facts of a case and of the other side's case before a trial begins.

Discovery sampling Sampling used in fraud detection that assumes a zero expected error rate. The methodology allows an auditor to determine confidence levels and make inferences from the sample to the population.

Divorce The legal separation of two married partners resulting in the dissolution of their marriage and, usually, their assets.

Document examination Analyzing and examining specific documents to search for forgery, alteration, or other problems associated with the documents.

Document experts People with supporting certifications and specialized training who make judgments about the authenticity of documents.

Documentary evidence Evidence gathered from paper; documents; computer records; and other written, printed, or electronic sources.

Documents and records Documentary evidence of all transactions that create an audit trail.

Dummy companies (shell companies) Fictitious entities created for the sole purpose of committing fraud; usually involve an employee making fraudulent payments to the dummy company.

Dumpster diving A form of identity theft where fraudsters go through a person's trash to secure personal identifying information.

E

Earnings per share Net income divided by the number of shares of stock outstanding; a measure of profitability.

E-business The use of information technology and electronic communication networks to exchange business information and conduct transactions in electronic, paperless form.

Economic extortion Demanding payment from a vendor in order to make a decision in the vendor's favor; opposite of bribery.

Elements of fraud The theft act, concealment, and conversion that are present in every fraud.

Employee assistance program (EAP) employee assistance program, or EAP, is a counseling service for employees and their eligible dependents who may be experiencing personal or workplace problems.

Employee embezzlement Employees deceiving their employers by taking company assets.

Ethical maturity model (EMM) The four stages in ethical developing with a general sense of right and wrong being the basic stage, the ability to translate that sense of right and wrong to professional and other settings being level two, having the courage to do what you know to be right even if there is a personal cost being level three, and ethical leadership being level four.

Evidential matter The underlying data and all corroborating information available about a fraud.

Expense schemes Fraud schemes that involve manipulating expenses and use the payroll function or the purchasing and reimbursement system to embezzle from a company.

Expert power The ability of one person to influence another person based on special knowledge or expertise.

Expert witness Trial witness who can offer opinions about a matter, based on unique experience, education, or training.

F

Facilitators of communication Sociopsychological forces that make conversations, including interviews, easier to accomplish.

Falsified identity Pretending to be someone you are not—a major problem in e-business transactions; sometimes called pretense.

Federal court A court established by the federal government to enforce federal laws and statutes.

Fidelity bonding Insurance coverage purchased on employees that provides reimbursement for amounts stolen by employees.

Fifth Amendment An amendment to the U.S. Constitution that provides defendants certain protections, including (1) an indictment by a grand jury before being held for a capital crime and (2) not being tried twice for the same crime.

Financial statement fraud The intentional misstatement of financial statements through omission of critical facts or disclosures, misstatement of amounts, or misapplication of accepted accounting principles.

Financial statements Reports such as the balance sheet, income statement, and statement of cash flows that summarize the financial status and results of operations of a business entity.

First-order reasoning The type of strategic reasoning that occurs when an individual (e.g., an auditor) considers conditions that directly affect his or her strategic opponent (e.g., management) while assuming that the opponent (i.e., the auditee) is engaging in zero-order reasoning.

Fixed assets Long-term assets of an organization including property, plant, and equipment.

Fixed-width format A file format used to transfer data from legacy applications to analysis applications. Most analysts prefer delimited text, but fixed-width is used when it is the only available export.

Footnotes Information that accompanies a company's financial statements so as to provide interpretive guidance to the financial statements or include related information that must be disclosed.

Foreign advance-fee scams Any scam where the perpetrator claims to be a foreigner, and the victim is required to pay "up-front" fees or taxes in order to receive a substantial amount of money.

Fourth Amendment An amendment to the U.S. Constitution that protects defendants against unreasonable searches and seizures by the government.

Fraud A generic term that embraces all the multifarious means that human ingenuity can devise, which are resorted to by one individual, to get an advantage over another by false representations. No definite and invariable rule can be laid down as a general proposition in defining fraud, as it includes surprise, trickery, cunning, and unfair ways by that another is cheated. The only boundaries defining it are those that limit human knavery.

Fraud detection The activity of searching for or finding indicators that suggest that fraud may be occurring; finding predication of fraud.

Fraud prevention All efforts and means extended to deter fraud from occurring; involves eliminating perceived pressures, perceived opportunities, and/or rationalizations; any action that discourages or diminishes the likelihood that fraud will occur.

Fraudulent statements Financial statements that have been altered, contain misleading or untrue amounts, or have omitted required information; fraudulent financial statements mislead users of the statements such as investors or debtors.

Free narrative In an interview, when the interviewer allows the interviewee to merely tell the story as it happened, without asking specific questions.

Front loading A fraudulent process whereby representatives of legitimate or fraudulent MLMs are required to buy large, expensive amounts of inventory.

Fuzzy matching A system of approximate matching of names, addresses, and other information.

G

Gramm-Leach-Bliley Act Passed in 1999, this law prohibits the use of false pretenses to access the personal information of others. It does allow banks and other financial institutions to share or sell customer information, unless customers proactively "opt out" and ask that their information not be shared.

Grand jury A body of 4 to 23 individuals who decide whether there is sufficient evidence to charge someone in a preliminary hearing (they deliberate in secret).

Graphology The study of handwriting to help identify fraud and other crimes; graphologists are often used to determine the legitimacy of written documents.

Gross profit (margin) ratio Gross profit (margin) divided by net sales; a measure of markup.

Ground floor opportunity A classic marketing scheme that makes people believe that they will make money simply because they are one of the early investors in a new venture.

H

Headhunter fees Fees paid to consultants to help fill executive and other positions in an organization; also the paying of commissions for signing additional recruiters of multilevel marketing organizations.

Higher-level trial court State courts that try felony (larger crimes) and civil cases above a predetermined amount.

Higher-order reasoning The type of strategic reasoning that occurs when an individual (e.g., an auditor) considers how his or her strategic opponent (e.g., management) is engaging in a level of strategic reasoning that is not zero-order reasoning.

Horizontal analysis Tool that determines the percentage change in balance sheet and income statement numbers from one period to the next.

I

Identity theft A term used to describe those circumstances when someone uses another person's name, address, Social Security number, bank or credit card account number, or other identifying information to commit fraud or other crimes.

Illegal gratuities Similar to bribery, except that there is no intent to influence a particular business decision, but rather to reward someone for making a favorable decision.

Inadequate disclosure fraud The issuance of fraudulent or misleading statements or press releases without financial statement line-item effect or the lack of appropriate disclosures that should have been but were not made by management.

Income statement Financial statement that reports the amount of net income earned by a company during a specified period.

Independent checks Periodically monitoring the work or activities of others.

Induction Reasoning from the specific to the general, or from effect to cause.

Inhibitor Any sociopsychological barrier that impedes the flow of relevant information by making respondents unable or unwilling to provide information.

Initial pleading complaint filed by a plaintiff to request legal proceedings against someone.

Intangible assets An asset that has no tangible existence (e.g., goodwill or patents).

Intent A required factor when prosecuting individuals for fraud. Not only must confessors have committed the act, they must also have intended to commit it.

Internal control weakness Weakness in the control environment, accounting system, or control activities or procedures.

Interrogatory A series of written questions that specifically identify information needed from the opposing party.

Interstate Identification Index (III) A measure database that contains criminal history records for almost 30 million offenders and can be queried using a name, birth date, and other data.

Interview A question and answer session designed to elicit information.

Interviewing The process of asking questions with the ultimate goal of obtaining predetermined information.

Inventory turnover ratio A ratio that measures the efficiency with which inventory is managed and the rate at which it is sold; the ratio is calculated as cost of goods sold divided by average inventory for the period.

Investigation The efforts made to identify the who, what, how, when, and how much of a fraud; an investigation is performed once there is predication that fraud is occurring; the process of inquiring into or examining questionable activities.

Investment fraud (scams) Any fraud that is related to stocks, bonds, commodities, limited partnerships, real estate, or other types of investments such as the selling of fraudulent and worthless investments to unsuspecting investors.

Invigilation Imposing strict temporary controls on an activity so that, during the observation period, fraud is virtually impossible. Involves keeping detailed records before, during, and after the invigilation period and comparing suspicious activity during the three periods to obtain evidence about whether fraud is occurring.

J

Jurisdiction The limit or territory over which an organization has authority.

K

Kickbacks Funds or gifts received secretly for performing some task or obtaining favorable treatment; for example, money received for purchasing from an uncompetitive bidder.

Kinetic communication Communication using body language, facial movements, and so forth; such communication represents a large part of the communication that takes place.

L

Labeling Teaching employees behaviors that are and are not appropriate within the organization.

Lapping Fraud that involves stealing one customer's payment and then crediting that customer's account when a subsequent customer pays.

Larceny Intentionally taking an employer's cash or other assets without the consent and against the will of the employer, after it has been recorded in the company's accounting system.

Leases Obligations to make payments over a specified period for use or "rent" of an asset; do not involve ownership of the asset.

Legitimate power The ability of one person to influence another person as the result of legitimate authority.

Lifestyle symptoms Spending patterns that suggest a potential fraud perpetrator may be using assets obtained through fraud to maintain a lifestyle that is not sustainable on the perpetrator's income; fraud perpetrators will often use their ill-gotten gains to purchase real estate, jewelry, fancy clothing or cars, and other things they could not afford without the fraudulent income; one of the six categories of red flags.

Link analysis The process of linking people, documents, and events in a case. Link analysis is often performed by automated software that helps coordinate large cases.

Lower-level trial court State courts that try misdemeanors (small crimes) and pretrial issues.

M

Mail stuffing A scam that promises income simply for stuffing envelopes. Victims are required to pay considerable up-front costs for information about the opportunity.

Management fraud Deception perpetrated by an organization's top management through the manipulation of financial statement amounts or disclosures.

Marketable securities Short-term stocks, bonds, and other noncash assets; sometimes called short-term investments.

Matosas matrix A two-dimensional display of red flag hits used in data-driven fraud detection. Columns usually represent red flags being searched for, and rows represent cases like individuals, bids, or other measures.

Mergers The combining of two organizations into one business entity.

Miscellaneous fraud Deception that doesn't fall into any of the other five categories of fraud.

Modeling Setting an example.

Money laundering The practice of engaging in economic transactions that are designed to conceal the identity, source, or destination of currency; such practice involves converting large amounts of money that were obtained illegally (e.g., drug sales or terrorist financing) into money that can be used to purchase goods and services without triggering currency transaction reports; often involves setting up a legitimate-looking business and depositing receipts on behalf of that business into the banking system.

Mortgage Long-term loan secured by property, such as a home mortgage.

Motion The response to a complaint or pleading by the defendant. Sometimes "motion" refers to any request made to the judge for a ruling in a case by either party.

Motion for summary judgment A request made to a judge to dismiss all or part of a claim prior to completion of a full trial because no genuine issue of a material fact is present.

Multilevel marketing (MLM) company A well-established, legitimate form of business. In most multilevel marketing programs, company representatives act as sellers of real products. These individuals are independent distributors of a legitimate business.

N

National Crime Information Center (NCIC) The major criminal database maintained by the FBI. This database contains information on stolen vehicles, securities, boats, missing persons, and other information helpful in fraud investigations.

Net asset value (NAV) The value of one unit of a mutual fund; changes as the assets that comprise the fund increase or decrease in value.

Net income An overall measure of the performance of a company; equal to revenues minus expenses for a period.

Net worth method Analytical method that estimates a suspect's unexplained income. Liabilities are subtracted from assets to give net worth, and then the previous year's net worth is subtracted to find the increase in net worth. Living expenses are then added to the change in net worth to determine a person's total income, and finally known income is subtracted from total income to determine the unknown income.

N-gram An advanced method of fuzzy matching that counts the number of matching runs of characters in two names, addresses, or other textual fields.

Nigerian money offers A form of foreign advance-fee scams where individuals from Nigeria or another underdeveloped country contact victims and offer millions of dollars.

Nolo contendere Plea by a defendant that does not contest the charges but does not admit guilt; means *no contest.*

Nonfinancial performance measures Statistics and data that are not financial in nature but can be used to assess an organization's performance such as the nonfinancial measures used in a balanced scorecard.

Nonsampling risk The risk that a sample will be examined and the true characteristics of the sample, including fraudulent or other elements of interest, will be misinterpreted or overlooked.

Norming or calibrating That part of an interview that is intended to determine how an interviewee responds when answering questions about subjects he or she is comfortable with so as to be able to contrast the verbal and nonverbal cues from those questions with those exhibited when the interviewee is asked about a fraudulent or dishonest act.

Number of days' sales in inventory Calculated by dividing the cost of goods sold by the average amount of inventory for the year, and divide that into 365. A measure of how long it takes a company to turn over its inventory.

Number of days in receivables ratio 365 (number of days in a year) divided by accounts receivable turnover; a measure of how long it takes to collect receivables.

O

Open Database Connectivity (ODBC) The standard method of connecting analysis applications to relational database management systems.

Operating performance margin ratio net income divided by total sales; a measure of the percentage of revenues that become profits.

Opportunity meeting A high-pressure meeting where fraudsters pressure individuals to invest money in fraudulent organizations.

Opting out Right of customers to give written notice to financial institutions that prohibits the institution from sharing or selling customer's personal information.

Overstatement of asset fraud Financial statement fraud involving recording assets at amounts higher than they should be.

P

Pacing Controlling the length of pauses and the rate of speech during an interview.

Paralinguistic communication Communicating not only by what you say, but how you say it.

Passwords Secret codes or names that allow users to access networks and other computer systems.

Payroll schemes Fraud schemes that involve manipulating the payroll function of the organization. These schemes may also involve manipulating the purchasing and/or reimbursement function as well.

Pencil-and-paper honesty tests Questionnaires or other written assessment tests that are intended to assess someone's honesty or propensity to be dishonest.

Pension Postretirement cash benefits paid to former employees.

Perceived opportunity A situation where someone believes he or she has a favorable or promising combination of circumstances to commit fraud and not be detected.

Perceived pressure situation where someone perceives he or she has a need to commit fraud; a constraining influence on the will or mind, as a moral force.

Percentages The fraction of a number; used in vertical analysis where financial statement numbers are converted to percentages to assess comparability.

Perpetrator A person who has committed a fraud.

Personal observation that is sensed (seen, heard, felt, etc.) by investigators.

Phishers Fraudsters who engage in phishing.

Phishing A high-tech scam that uses spam or pop-up messages to deceive consumers into disclosing credit card numbers, bank account information, Social Security number, passwords, or other sensitive information.

Physical evidence Evidence of a tangible nature—includes fingerprints, tire marks, weapons, stolen property, identification numbers or marks on stolen objects, and so on—that can be used in an investigations to provide information about a fraud or another crime.

Physical safeguards Vaults, fences, locks, etc., that physically protect assets from theft.

Pivot tables A data summarization tool found in data visualization programs such as spreadsheets. The primary use of pivot tables is to convert traditional "database-formatted" data to two- dimensional spreadsheet-structured data.

Polygraphs An electronic assessment of honesty that includes hooking a person up to a machine to assess the normalcy of breathing, pulse, and other physical abnormalities; used to assess stress to determine if people are telling the truth.

Ponzi schemes Fraudulent pyramid schemes where old investors are paid their gains out of new investors' funds so as to make the appearance that the scheme is generating an unusually large return; named after Charles Ponzi.

Postal inspectors Inspectors or investigators hired by the U.S. Postal Service to handle major fraud cases that are perpetrated through the U.S. mail system.

Power The probability that a person can carry out his or her own will despite resistance.

Predication Circumstances that, taken as a whole, would lead a reasonable, prudent professional to believe that a fraud has occurred, is occurring, or will occur.

Preliminary hearing A pretrial hearing to determine if there is "probable cause" to charge the defendant with a crime.

Product testing Perpetrators falsely promise consumers the opportunity to review products and send their commentaries to suppliers for substantial income. Victims are required to pay enrollment fees ranging from $10 to $25.

Profit margin Net income divided by total revenues; also known as return on sales, profit margin percentage, profit margin ratio, and operating performance ratio.

Proxemic communication Communicating with others by virtue of the relative position of the bodies.

Psychopath A person having a personality disorder, especially one manifested in aggressively antisocial behavior.

Purchase of real estate scam In this advance-fee scam, perpetrators will offer to purchase property on behalf of a foreign concern for an "up-front" payment.

Pyramid schemes Illegal fraud schemes where fraudsters— instead of selling real, legitimate products—sell only illusionary products and profits; the investments of subsequent investors are used to pay the promised returns of earlier investors.

Q

Quick ratio (acid-test ratio) Measure of a firm's ability to meet current liabilities; computed by dividing net quick assets (all current assets, except inventories and prepaid expenses) by current liabilities.

R

Rapport The feeling of trust and confidence an interviewer seeks to establish and maintain with interviewees.

Rationalization (rationalize) To devise self-satisfying but incorrect reasons for one's behavior.

Referent power The ability of one person to influence another person based upon a personal relationship with that person.

Register disbursement schemes Schemes that involve false refunds or false voids.

Remedy Judgments asked for in civil cases (what it would take to right a private wrong).

Repurchase agreements Agreements to buy back something previously sold.

Request for admission A request that the opposing party admit designated facts relevant to litigation.

Restructuring The reevaluation of a company's assets because of impairment of value or for other reasons. Restructured companies usually have lower amounts of assets and look quite different than before the restructuring.

Return on assets Net income divided by average total assets; an overall measure of profitability.

Return on equity Measure of the profit earned per dollar of investment; computed by dividing net income by equity.

Revenue Increases in a company's resources from the sale of goods or services.

Revenue-recognition Determining that revenues have been earned and are collectible and thus should be reported on the income statement.

Reward power The ability of someone to influence another person as the result of a promised reward or benefit.

Risk assessment The identification, analysis, and management of risk, such as the risk associated with the possibility of fraud.

S

Sale of crude oil at below market price Involves a victim receiving a letter that falsely offers the opportunity to purchase crude oil at prices well below market price.

Sales discount percentage ratio The percentage of the sales price waived for payment made within a predetermined discount period.

Sales Returns Sold merchandise that is returned by customers and/or damaged, or other sold merchandise for which credit is given.

Sales return percentage ratio Sales returns divided by total sales; a measure of the percentage of sales being returned by customers.

Sampling risk Risk that a sample is not representative of the population.

Sarbanes-Oxley Act of 2002 U.S. legislation passed in 2002 whose goal is to minimize the occurrence of fraud and increase the penalties for perpetrators when it occurs.

Scheme An elaborate and systematic plan of action usually involving illegal activity. Schemes usually have many indicators for which investigators search.

SEC enforcement release A public document released by the SEC when a company commits financial statement fraud or other perceived inappropriate activities.

Securities and Exchange Commission (SEC) Governmental organization with responsibility for regulating stock trading and the financial statements and reports of public companies.

Security through obscurity Reliance on secrecy of design, implementation, or holes to provide security rather than the use of time-tested methods that have withstood public scrutiny.

Segregation of duties Dividing a task into two parts, so one person does not have complete control of the task.

Settlement A negotiated pretrial agreement between the parties to resolve a legal dispute.

Shell companies (dummy companies) Fictitious entities created for the sole purpose of committing fraud; usually involve an employee making fraudulent payments to the dummy company.

Shoulder surfing A process where criminals watch consumers from a nearby location as they enter credit card pin numbers, garage codes, computer passwords, or other valuable information.

Silent probe An interviewing technique wherein an interviewer pauses and says nothing; usually used to elicit a more thorough response.

Sixth Amendment An amendment to the U.S. Constitution that provides trial-related protections to defendants, such as the right to a speedy trial and the right to be heard by an impartial jury.

Skimming A process where fraudsters use information storage devices to capture valuable information from victims' credit cards or other bar-encoded documents.

Snake oil plans Plans that promise enormous earnings or claim to sell miracle products.

Sniffing Illegal or unauthorized viewing of information as it passes along a network communication channel.

Social engineering Deceiving in order to breach security controls; often involves impersonating someone else, and can be done by e-mail, telephone, or face-to-face.

Soundex A phonetic algorithm for indexing names by their sound when pronounced.

Spoofing Changing the information in an e-mail header or an IP address to hide identities.

Spyware Rogue software installed on computers that collects and transmits personal information without the user's knowledge.

Statement of cash flows Financial statement that reports an entity's cash inflows (receipts) and outflows (payments) during an accounting period.

Statistical analysis The use of statistics and number patterns to discover relationships in certain data, such as Benford's Law.

Statute A law or regulation; a law enacted by the legislative branch of a government.

Strategic reasoning The reasoning process involved in the fraud setting where an investigator or auditor attempts to predict how a fraud perpetrator may be responding to likely behavior of the investigator (e.g., concealing the fraud from typical procedures).

Stratification Division of data into groups by employee, invoice, or other measure.

Structured query language (SQL) The standard programming language used to discover indicators in database management systems.

Subpoena (subpoena duces tecum) A written order in the name of the court, requiring a witness to submit to a deposition, give testimony at trial, or report to an administrative body.

Summarization A technique used in data-driven fraud detection that summarizes data using different functions or according to time period.

Surveillance Investigation technique that relies on the senses, especially hearing and seeing.

Symptoms Red flags or indicators of fraud; anything that provides some predications that fraud may be occurring.

System of authorizations system of limits on who can and cannot perform certain functions.

T

Tab separated values (TSV) A delimited text file format in which data are stored in a file where the items of data are separated by tab characters.

Tax court Federal courts that hear only tax cases.

Tax fraud Willfully and intentionally violating the known legal duty of voluntarily filing income tax returns and/or paying the correct amount of income, employment, or excise taxes.

Telemarketing fraud Any fraud where the perpetrator communicates with the victim via telephone.

10-K Annual report filed by publicly traded U.S. companies to the SEC.

10-Q Quarterly report filed by publicly traded U.S. companies to the SEC.

Testimonial evidence Evidence based on querying techniques, such as interviewing, interrogation, and honesty testing.

Theft act The commission of a fraud.

Theft act investigation Fraud investigation methods that focus on the fraudulent transfer of assets; includes surveillance, invigilation, seizing computers, and examining physical evidence.

Time trend analysis Examining and attempting to find patterns in financial information over time.

Times-interest-earned ratio The ratio calculated by dividing the net income of a company by the amount of interest expense; a measure of whether a company's profits are sufficient to pay the interest on its outstanding debt.

Topside journal entries Manual journal entries that can be used by management to commit fraud; these entries may involve overriding of internal controls.

Trashing Searching through a person's trash for possible evidence in an investigation.

Treadway Commission The National Commission on Fraudulent Financial Reporting that made recommendations related to financial statement fraud and other matters in 1987.

Trustee Individual or firm that collects a debtor's assets and distributes them to creditors.

U

Understatement of liability frauds Financial statement fraud that involves understating liabilities or amounts owed to others.

Unearned revenues Amounts that have been received from customers but for which performance of a service or sale of a product has not yet been made.

V

Vendor fraud An overcharge for purchased goods, the shipment of inferior goods, or the nonshipment of goods even though payment is made.

Vertical analysis Tool that converts financial statement numbers to percentages so that they are easy to understand and analyze.

Victim The person or organization deceived by the perpetrator.

Voice stress analysis An analysis that determines how much stress a person is experiencing through analyzing his or her voice; related to polygraph and lie detector tests.

Voir dire The legal process of qualifying an expert witness.

Volatile interviews Interviews in which there is a great deal of tension and possible contention; such interviews must be handled with great care.

Vulnerability chart Tool that coordinates the various elements of a fraud investigation to help identify possible suspects.

W

Warrant An order issued by a judge to arrest someone.

Warranty liabilities Obligations to perform service and repair items sold within a specific period of time or use after sale.

Wartrapping Rogue access points accrued at shifting user information on wireless networks.

Whistle-blowing systems Response mechanisms that make it easy for employees and others to report questionable activities (also called hotlines).

Working capital turnover ratio Sales divided by average working capital; a measure of the amount of working capital used to generate revenues.

Z

Z-score The number of standard deviations above or below the mean or average value in a standard normal distribution. This technique is useful to describe how far a data value is outside the norm for a given data set.

Zero-order reasoning The type of strategic reasoning that occurs when an individual who is interacting with another party (e.g., an auditor interacting with management) only considers the conditions that *directly* affect themselves but not the other party.

Index

Note: Page numbers followed by f or t refer to Figures or Tables

A

AAER. *See* Accounting and Auditing Enforcement Releases

ABFDE. *See* American Board of Forensic Document Examiners, Inc.

Abusing the cutoff, 401

Academic requirements, 17

Acceptance stage, 280

Accounting
    anomalies, 137–142, 168–169, 404, 406, 410–411, 417–418, 422, 452–453, 456, 457t, 465–469
    cycles, 183
    systems, 42, 114

Accounting and Auditing Enforcement Releases (AAERs), 364

Accounts payable, 448–449

Accounts receivable fraud. *See* Revenue-related fraud

Accounts receivable turnover, 184, 185t, 409

Accrued liabilities, 449

ACFE (Association of Certified Fraud Examiners), 5

Acid-test ratio, 184, 185t

ACL Audit Analytics, 172, 179, 238, 411, 422

Acquisitions and mergers, 459–461, 466–468

Acute emotional crisis, 284

Adelphia Communications Corp., 102, 359, 362, 463, 472, 477, 513–514, 638

Adjusters, 578

Admission-seeking questions, 299–300

Advance fee scams, 531, 543–545, 560

AFCO fraud case, 48, 460–461, 553–554

Affidavit of proposed investigation, 594–597

Affidavits, 627

AICPA. *See* American Institute of Certified Public Accountants

Albania, 548

Alibis, 303

Allowance for uncollectible accounts as a percentage of receivables, 409

Altruistic appeals, 284

American Board of Forensic Document Examiners, Inc. (ABFDE), 243, 245

American Institute of Certified Public Accountants (AICPA), 390, 401

American National, 376

Analytical anomalies, 137–138, 144–148, 171f, 404–410, 417, 419–422, 452, 453–456, 465–469

Analytical procedures, 147

Andersen, Arthur, 358, 362, 374

Anger stage, 279

Annual reports, 471

Answers, 625

Antar, Eddie, 149

Anti-Kickback Act of 1986, 14t

AOL Time Warner, 359

Appeals, 627, 630

Appellate courts, 623

Application for retention of investigator, 598–600

Arraignments, 629

Arrest warrants, 628

Ashford.com, 476

Assessment questions, 294, 296–298

Asset fraud
    accounting symptoms, 457t, 465–469
    analytical symptoms, 465–469
    audit procedures, 491, 496–498
    earnings management, 459–463
    identification of, 458–459
    symptoms of, 463–464
    types of, 458f, 464t

Asset misappropriations
    defined, 10
    disbursement schemes, 508–514
    larceny, 507–508
    noncash assets, 514–515
    overview, 505
    skimming, 508

Asset turnover ratio, 409

Association of Certified Fraud Examiners (ACFE), 5

Attribute sampling, 238

Audit departments, 41, 77, 120

Auditing Practices Board (APB), 365

Auditors
    fraud detection, 152
    relationship with company, 373–374
    Sarbanes-Oxley Act and, 390–391
    strategic reasoning and, 368–369, 435–443, 490–499

Audits, 237–241

Audit sampling, 169

Audit trails, 42, 48–49

Authorization control procedures, 43, 114–115

B

Backdating, 359–360, 382–383

Bad debt percentage, 185t, 414

Bakker, Jim, 49–50

Balance sheets, 184

Bank Fraud Statute, 14t

Bank records, 258

Bankruptcies by size, 359, 389

Bankruptcy court, 573, 576, 623–624

Bankruptcy fraud
    affidavit of proposed investigation, 594–597
    application for retention of investigator, 598–600
    bankruptcy code, 574
    bust-out, 579–580, 607
    concealment of assets, 580–581
    false accusations, 582
    fraud investigators and, 578–579
    fraudulent transfers, 576, 581–582
    overview, 566–567, 572–573
    process, 576–578
    statutes, 574–576

Baptiste, Linus, 229

Bargaining/rationalization stage, 280

Bartolo, Edward J. de, 366

Baskin-Robbins, 44

Bates numbers, 236

Behavior changes, 138, 148–151, 171f, 405–406, 412–413, 418, 422

BellSouth, 476

Belnick, Mark, 513–514

Benchmark admissions, 304

Benford's law, 173, 175–177

Berkshire Hathaway, 460

Bid-rigging schemes, 517

Bill-and-hold sales, 402, 415

Billing schemes, 510–511

Biometrics, 609

Blue, John, 12

Boards of Directors, 370–372, 608

Bogus mystery shopping scams, 549, 550t–551t

Bok, Derek, 88

Brennan, Robert, 566

Bre-X Minerals, 386, 471, 473

Bribery, 516–517

Bribery of Public Officials and Witnesses, 14t

Brown, Bradford G., 570

Brown-Forman Distillers, 129

Buckhoff, Thomas, 222